PLANNING THE USES AND MANAGEMENT OF LAND

AGRONOMY

A Series of Monographs

The American Society of Agronomy (ASA) and Academic Press published the first six books in this series. Subsequent books were published by ASA alone, but in 1978 the associated societies, ASA, Crop Science Society of America (CSSA), and Soil Science Society of America (SSSA), published Agronomy 19. The books numbered 1 to 6 on the list below are available from Academic Press, Inc., 111 Fifth Avenue, New York, NY 10003; those numbered 7 to 20 are available from ASA, 677 S. Segoe Road, Madison, WI 53711.

General Editor Monographs 1 to 6, A. G. NORMAN

1. C. EDMUND MARSHALL: The Colloid Chemistry of the Silicate Minerals, 1949
2. BYRON T. SHAW, *Editor:* Soil Physical Conditions and Plant Growth, 1952
3. K. D. JACOB: Fertilizer Technology and Resources in the United States, 1953
4. W. H. PIERRE and A. G. NORMAN, *Editor:* Soil and Fertilizer Phosphate in Crop Nutrition, 1953
5. GEORGE F. SPRAGUE, *Editor:* Corn and Corn Improvement, 1955
6. J. LEVITT: The Hardiness of Plants, 1956

7. JAMES N. LUTHIN, *Editor:* Drainage of Agricultural Lands, 1957

General Editor, D. E. Gregg
8. FRANKLIN A. COFFMAN, *Editor:* Oats and Oat Improvement

Managing Editor, H. L. Hamilton
9. C. A. BLACK, *Editor-in-Chief,* and D. D. EVANS, J. L. WHITE, L. E. ENSMINGER, and F. E. CLARK, *Associate Editors:* Methods of Soil Analysis, 1965.
  Part 1—Physical and Mineralogical Properties, Including Statistics of Measurement and Sampling
  Part 2—Chemical and Microbiological Properties

Managing Editor, R. C. Dinauer
10. W. V. BARTHOLOMEW and F. E. CLARK, *Editor:* Soil Nitrogen, 1965

Managing Editor, H. L. Hamilton
11. R. M. HAGAN, H. R. HAISE, and T. W. EDMINSTER, *Editors:* Irrigation of Agricultural Lands, 1967

Managing Editor, R. C. Dinauer
12. R. W. PEARSON and FRED ADAMS, *Editors:* Soil Acidity and Liming, 1967

Managing Editor, R. C. Dinauer
13. K. S. QUISENBERRY and L. P. REITZ, *Editors:* Wheat and Wheat Improvement, 1967

Managing Editor, H. L. Hamilton
14. A. A. HANSON and F. V. JUSKA, *Editors:* Turfgrass Science, 1969

Managing Editor, H. L. Hamilton
15. CLARENCE H. HANSON, *Editor:* Alfalfa Science and Technology, 1972

Managing Editor, H. L. Hamilton
16. B. E. CALDWELL, *Editor:* Soybeans: Improvement, Production, and Use, 1973

Managing Editor, H. L. Hamilton
17. JAN VAN SCHILFGAARDE, *Editor:* Drainage for Agriculture, 1974

Managing Editor, R. C. Dinauer
18. GEORGE F. SPRAGUE, *Editor:* Corn and Corn Improvement, 1977

Managing Editor, D. A. Fuccillo
19. JACK F. CARTER, *Editor:* Sunflower Science and Technology, 1978

Managing Editor, D. A. Fuccillo
20. ROBERT C. BUCKNER and L. P. BUSH, *Editors:* Tall Fescue, 1979

Managing Editor, D. A. Fuccillo
21. M. T. BEATTY, G. W. PETERSEN, and L. D. SWINDALE, *Editors:* Planning the Uses and Management of Land, 1979

Managing Editor, R. C. Dinauer

PLANNING THE USES AND MANAGEMENT OF LAND

Edited by

MARVIN T. BEATTY

GARY W. PETERSEN

LESTER D. SWINDALE

Managing Editor: RICHARD C. DINAUER

Assistant Editor: ELIZABETH L. SHEMA

Editor-in-Chief ASA Publications: MATTHIAS STELLY

Number 21 in the series

AGRONOMY

American Society of Agronomy,
Crop Science Society of America,
Soil Science Society of America, Inc., Publisher

1979

American Society of Agronomy, Inc.
Crop Science Society of America, Inc.
Soil Science Society of America, Inc.
677 South Segoe Road, Madison, Wisconsin 53711 USA

Library of Congress Cataloging in Publication Data

Beatty, Marvin T.
    Planning the uses and management of land.
    (Agronomy, a series of monographs; no. 21)
    Includes index.
    1. Land use—Planning. I. Swindale, Lester D.,
1928–   joint editor. II. Petersen, Gary W.,
1930–   joint editor. III. Title and series
HD111.B4   333.7   79-53845
ISBN 0-89118-058-3

Printed in the United States of America

CONTENTS

Page

GENERAL FOREWORD xvii
FOREWORD xix
PREFACE... xxi
CONTRIBUTORS xxiii
CONVERSION FACTORS FOR U.S. AND METRIC UNITS xxvii

SECTION I—PRESENT STATUS OF LAND USES AND LAND USE PLANNING

1 Soils, Plants, and Land Use in the United States

RALEIGH BARLOWE

   I. Introduction 3
  II. Overall Framework for Public Policy........................... 4
 III. Land Settlement Patterns..................................... 8
 IV. Recent Trends in Land Use Patterns 12
  V. Effects of Soils and Plants on Land Use Patterns................ 22
LITERATURE CITED 24

2 National and State Experiences with Land Use Planning

NORMAN WENGERT

  I. Introduction 27
 II. National and State Experiences............................... 27
LITERATURE CITED 43

3 Principles of Land Use Planning

JOHN C. ROBERTS

   I. Introduction 47
  II. Why Plan?.. 47
 III. A Definition of Planning 48
 IV. Some Recent Trends in Land Use Planning..................... 60
LITERATURE CITED 62

SECTION II—DATA BASES

4 Soils Data

F. TED MILLER AND JOE D. NICHOLS

    I. Introduction 67
   II. Soil Surveys and Related Maps and Manuscripts 67
  III. Kinds of Soil Surveys 71
  IV. Soil Surveys and Soil Variability.............................. 71
   V. Other Kinds of Soil Maps..................................... 76
  VI. Related Soil Data 83
 VII. Sources of Information 86
LITERATURE CITED 88

5   Interpreting Soil Data

LINDO J. BARTELLI

I. Introduction 91
II. Kinds of Soil Data.. 91
III. Soil Properties and Associated Land Features 97
IV. Predicting Performance of Soils 104
V. Soil Interpretation at the Soil Family Level 110
VI. Soil Information Systems.................................... 113
LITERATURE CITED 114

6   Hydrologic Data

H. B. PIONKE AND R. L. KLECKNER

I. Introduction 117
II. Determining and Fulfilling Hydrologic Data Needs for Land-Use
    Planning... 118
III. Identification and Description of Hydrologic Data Indexes and
    Data Bases for Obtaining Potentially Useful Hydrologic Data..... 121
IV. Summary 138
APPENDIX—ABBREVIATIONS AND DEFINITIONS 139
LITERATURE CITED 139

7   Plant Cover Data

RICHARD H. RUST

I. Introduction—Historical Development 143
II. Modes of Acquisition of Plant Cover Data 143
III. Plant Cover Data Systems 146
IV. Example of a System—Minnesota Land Management Information
    System 148
V. Quantitative Development in Plant Cover Analysis 148
VI. Modeling Plant Cover Data—Corn and Wheat Models 150
VII. Analysis of Factors in Plant Cover Models 153
VIII. Development and Use of Soil Productivity Indices................ 154
IX. Purposes and Uses of Plant Cover Data 154
X. Summary 155
LITERATURE CITED 156

8   Data Acquisition Through Remote Sensing

E. R. STONER AND M. F. BAUMGARDNER

I. Introduction—A New Look at an Old Scene 159
II. Data Acquisition... 160
III. Data Analysis 166
IV. Data Utilization... 167
V. Data Availability.. 179
VI. The Future of Remote Sensing for Land Use Planning 181
APPENDIX—ADDRESSES OF REMOTE SENSING DATA AND
COMPUTER PROGRAM SOURCES............................ 182
LITERATURE CITED 183

9   Spatial Data Analysis and Information Communication

      BERNARD J. NIEMANN, JR., AND MICHAEL M. MCCARTHY

        I. Introduction and Definitions.   187
       II. Evolution and Development of Analysis and Communication
           Techniques.   188
      III. Types of Communication and Analysis Users.   197
       IV. Examples and Studies.   198
        V. Conclusion.   220
      LITERATURE CITED   221

SECTION III—PLANNING CULTIVATED LAND USES

10   Planning Uses of Cultivated Cropland and Pastureland

                  MICHAEL J. SINGER, KENNETH K. TANJI, AND
                                           J. HERBERT SNYDER

        I. Introduction   225
       II. Agronomic Land Use in the United States.   228
      III. Data Requirements for Planning   231
       IV. Planning Agricultural Land Uses to Reduce Their Effect on the
           Environment   251
        V. Methods of Controlling Land Use for Agriculture.   262
       VI. Summary   267
      LITERATURE CITED   268

11   Planning Large-scale Agricultural Systems with Integrated Water
     Management

          W. A. HALL, G. H. HARGREAVES, AND G. H. CANNELL

        I. Introduction   273
       II. Water Resources Management   275
      III. Resource Data Use in Planning and Design.   278
       IV. Institutions for Integrated Management of Large-scale Systems . . .   287
      LITERATURE CITED   289

12   Defining, Delineating, and Designating Uses for Prime and Unique
     Agricultural Lands

                                           FRED P. MILLER

        I. Introduction   291
       II. The Concept of Prime and Unique Land.   294
      III. Criteria for Defining Prime and Unique Lands.   296
       IV. Prime Farmlands.   299
        V. Unique Farmlands   306
       VI. Other Lands.   307
      VII. Delineating Prime and Unique Lands   307
     VIII. Designating Prime and Unique Lands   310
       IX. Epilogue.   316
      LITERATURE CITED   316

SECTION IV—PLANNING RANGELAND USES

13   Planning the Use of Rangeland for Public and Private Lands

THADIS W. BOX AND DON D. DWYER

I. Introduction 321
II. Levels of Planning 322
III. Developing the Plan 324
IV. The Operational Plan....................................... 326
V. Planning Livestock Grazing on Rangelands 329
VI. Feedback Mechanisms and Evaluation of the Plan 333
VII. Summary 334
LITERATURE CITED 334

14   Planning Other Land Uses for Public Rangelands

G. H. ELSNER, A. W. MAGILL, C. F. SCHWARZ, AND
E. C. THOR

I. Introduction 335
II. Landscape Planning for Public Rangelands 336
III. Planning for Wildlife on Public Rangelands................... 342
IV. Planning for Recreation on Public Rangelands 346
V. Historical-Archeological Resources in Planning................ 351
VI. Tying it all Together—Land Use Planning on Public Rangelands .. 353
LITERATURE CITED 359

SECTION V—PLANNING FOREST AND WOODLAND USES

15   Timber Production on Extensive Holdings

S. P. GESSEL AND W. A. ATKINSON

I. Introduction 365
II. Forest Management Goals.................................... 365
III. Land Use Planning 366
IV. Information Needs for Timber Production..................... 367
V. Maintenance of Forest Productivity........................... 373
VI. Forest Regulation 376
VII. The Forest Management Plan 377
VIII. Planning for Operational Forest Management Activities 381
IX. Conclusion.. 384
LITERATURE CITED 385

16   Timber Production on Intensive Holdings

WILLIAM J. LLOYD AND WILLIAM M. CLARK

I. Introduction 387
II. Timber Production.. 388
III. Windbreaks and Shelterbelts................................ 415
LITERATURE CITED 423

17 Noncommodity Values of Forests and Woodlands

HERBERT E. ECHELBERGER AND J. ALAN WAGAR

I. Introduction 429
II. Planning for Scenic Amenities 429
III. Planning for Recreation Benefits 435
IV. Wildlife Resources 438
V. Multiple-Use Planning and Noncommodity Values 440
LITERATURE CITED 441

18 Low-Intensity Recreational Uses for Wildland Environments

BRUCE F. LEESON

I. Introduction 445
II. Wildland Ecosystems 447
III. Resource Planning Considerations 449
IV. Resource Data Considerations 450
V. The Nature of Environmental Impact 461
VI. Other Primitive Area Recreation Considerations 463
LITERATURE CITED 464

SECTION VI—PLANNING METROPOLITAN LAND USES

19 Planning Metropolitan Land Uses in Relation to Natural Landscape Features

KURT W. BAUER

I. Introduction 467
II. Importance of Soils in Metropolitan Land Use Planning 469
III. Detailed Soil Surveys 470
IV. Soils Data Interpretations 471
V. Graphic Data Reduction and Display 473
VI. Quantification of Mapped Data 477
VII. Use of Soils Data in Metropolitan Land Use Planning 477
VIII. Soils Data and Regional Land Use Plan Implementation 482
IX. Summary and Conclusion 483

20 Residential, Commercial, and Light Industrial Land Uses

CHRIS J. JOHANNSEN, TERRY W. BARNEY, AND
ALBERT A. KLINGEBIEL

I. Introduction 485
II. Important Soil Conditions 486
III. Site Selection 487
IV. Controlling Erosion 493
LITERATURE CITED 495

21 Vegetation Types, Functions, and Constraints in Metropolitan Environments

JAMES A. SCHMID

I. Introduction 499
II. Types of Urban Vegetation 500
III. Roles of Urban Vegetation 502
IV. Constraints that Affect Urban Vegetation.................... 516
V. Planning Urban Revegetation 522
LITERATURE CITED 525

SECTION VII—PLANNING FOR TRANSPORTATION
SYSTEMS AND UTILITY CORRIDORS

22 Soil Considerations in Siting Highways, Airports, and Utility Corridors

DONALD E. MC CORMACK AND DONALD G. FOHS

I. Introduction 531
II. Sources of Soils Data 533
III. Soil Properties Affecting Transportation Systems 538
IV. Use of Soil Surveys in Planning Transportation Systems....... 542
V. Uses of Soil Surveys in Planning Utility Corridors........... 552
VI. Cost and Other Savings Resulting from the Use of Soil Surveys.... 552
LITERATURE CITED 553

23 Soil Considerations in Highway Design and Construction

J. ALLAN TICE

I. Introduction 555
II. Role of Geotechnical Information in Site Evaluation 556
III. Engineering Characteristics of Soil Important to Transportation Facility Design... 557
IV. Obtaining Soil and Rock Information 571
V. Coping with Geotechnical Limitations........................ 574
LITERATURE CITED 579

24 Vegetation for Transportation Systems and Utility Corridors

ROBERT W. DUELL

I. Introduction 581
II. Roles of Vegetation.. 586
III. Fitting Vegetation to the Environment....................... 592
IV. Modification of Soils 599
V. Seedling Establishment 602
VI. Developing Final Plans..................................... 605
LITERATURE CITED 606

SECTION VIII—PLANNING FOR WASTE DISPOSAL AND UTILIZATION ON LAND

25 Principles and Processes Involved in Waste Disposal and Management

V. VAN VOLK AND EDWARD R. LANDA

   I. Introduction 611
  II. Waste Products and Current Disposal/Utilization Practices 612
 III. Land, Water, and Air Resource Information 614
  IV. Interactions Between Waste and Soil, Water and Air 616
   V. Transportation of Waste Products 627
  VI. Community Involvement in Planning for Waste Disposal......... 627
 VII. Local, State, Federal Agency Cooperation 628
VIII. Summary 628
LITERATURE CITED 629

26 Surface Application of Sewage Effluent and Sludge

WILLIAM E. SOPPER

   I. Introduction 633
  II. Historical Background 633
 III. Waste Water Treatment 634
  IV. Application Techniques 637
   V. Expected Treatment Performance 641
  VI. Crop Selection and Management 642
 VII. Applications in Forest Ecosystems 646
VIII. Land Application of Sludge................................. 657
  IX. Water Quality Monitoring.................................. 660
   X. Planning... 661
  XI. Summary 662
LITERATURE CITED 662

27 Subsurface Applications of Sewage Effluent

JOHANNES BOUMA

   I. Introduction 665
  II. Soil Limitations Using Current Criteria for the Conventional
      System 665
 III. Basic Principles of Soil Absorption and Purification of Sewage
      Effluents 668
  IV. Alternative Systems 682
   V. Use of Soil Survey to Extrapolate Experimental Data 696
LITERATURE CITED 700

28 Application of Thermal Effluent

LARRY L. BOERSMA

   I. Introduction 705
  II. Characterization of the Resource 705
 III. Plan for Use of Waste Heat................................. 714

    IV. Problems 718
     V. Soil Warming.. 719
    VI. Engineering Considerations................................. 723
   VII. The Soil as a Heat Sink.................................... 729
  VIII. Crop Growth 729
  LITERATURE CITED 732

29 **Locating Animal Feedlots and Managing Animal Wastes Applied to Land**

                              FRED A. NORSTADT

     I. Introduction 733
    II. Locating Animal Feedlots 736
   III. Managing Animal Wastes 746
    IV. Summary 757
  LITERATURE CITED 757

30 **Sanitary Landfill Site Selection and Management**

              F. GLADE LOUGHRY AND WILLIAM D. LACOUR

     I. Introduction 763
    II. Site Selection 766
   III. Sites for Municipal Wastes with Natural Renovation............. 770
    IV. Sites for Sanitary Landfill with Collection and Treatment of
        Leachate... 780
     V. Storage of Nondegradable Wastes 783
    VI. Demolition Wastes, Site Clearance Wastes, and Excavation Spoils
        —Range in Characteristics................................. 784
   VII. Emergency Sites for Quick Disaster Response 785
  VIII. Use of Soil in Containing and Renovating Waste............... 787
    IX. Future Land Use of Sanitary Landfill Sites..................... 788
  LITERATURE CITED 791

SECTION IX—PLANNING DIVERSE LAND USES AND MANAGEMENT PROGRAMS

31 **Watershed Planning and Management**

                              W. D. STRIFFLER

     I. Introduction 795
    II. Watershed Management Objectives 796
   III. Watershed Characteristics to be Considered in Planning and
        Management 799
    IV. Hydrologic Processes to be Considered in Planning and
        Management 804
     V. Hydrologic Models... 808
  LITERATURE CITED 810

32 Land Uses on Shorelands, Flood Plains, Wetlands, and Coastal Zones

VICTOR W. CARLISLE AND FRANK G. CALHOUN, JR.

I. Introduction 813
II. Definitions.. 814
III. Shorelands and Coastal Zones 815
IV. Floodplains 820
V. Wetlands 824
VI. Concluding Remarks 827
LITERATURE CITED 827

33 Nonpoint Pollution: Problem Assessment and Remedial Measures; Economic and Planning Considerations for Designing Control Methods

T. C. DANIEL AND ROBERT R. SCHNEIDER

I. Introduction 829
II. Nonpoint Pollutants of Major Environmental Concern 830
III. Major Source Areas of Nonpoint Pollution 833
IV. Planning Nonpoint Pollution Control 838
V. Summary and Conclusions 848
LITERATURE CITED 849

34 Reclamation Alternatives for Disturbed Lands and Their Application in Humid Regions

PAUL SUTTON

I. Introduction 853
II. Survey Classification and Characterization of Disturbed Lands ... 854
III. Effects on Water Table 860
IV. Purpose of Reclamation and Alternatives 862
V. Stabilization and Erosion Control 863
VI. Vegetation Adaptability and Revegetation Techniques 865
LITERATURE CITED 871

35 Reclaiming Disturbed Lands in Arid Regions

A. D. DAY AND K. L. LUDEKE

I. Introduction 875
II. Classification and Characterization 875
III. Reclamation Purposes and Alternatives........................ 876
IV. Spoil Replacement and Revegetation Techniques................ 877
V. Vegetation Adaptability...................................... 881
VI. Environmental Considerations 882
LITERATURE CITED 884

SECTION X—INTEGRATED LAND USE PLANNING AND PLAN IMPLEMENTATION

36 **Information Systems for Land Use Planning**

CHARLES R. MEYERS, MICHAEL KENNEDY, AND
R. NEIL SAMPSON

    I. Introduction 889
   II. Land Use Planning and the Need for Information 889
  III. The Primary Need: A System for the Organization of Data 893
  IV. Products of a Spatial Information System...................... 902
   V. Conclusion.. 904
LITERATURE CITED 906

37 **The Canadian Land Inventory System**

DONALD B. COOMBS AND J. THIE

    I. Introduction 909
   II. The Canada Land Inventory Program: A National System for
      Collecting Resource Data................................. 910
  III. The CLI Land Capability Classification Systems 914
  IV. Use of CLI Information................................... 925
   V. Impact of CLI on Resource Management in Canada 930
LITERATURE CITED 932

38 **A Case Study in Ecological Planning: The Woodlands, Texas**

ARTHUR H. JOHNSON, JONATHAN BERGER, AND
IAN L. MC HARG

    I. Introduction 935
   II. Outlines of the Methods................................... 936
  III. Application 943
LITERATURE CITED 955

39 **Incorporating Soils Information into Land Use Controls**

D. A. YANGGEN

    I. Introduction 957
   II. The Physical and Legal Basis for Use of Soils Information in
      Land Use Controls 958
  III. Examples of Soil-Based Land Use Regulations.................. 959
  IV. Summary and Conclusions 976
LITERATURE CITED 979

40   Institutional Mechanisms for Land Use Planning and Land Use Controls

RAYMOND D. VLASIN AND DANIEL A. BRONSTEIN

I. Introduction 981
II. Important Considerations and Relationships for Land Use
     Planning and Control....................................... 981
III. Institutional Setting of Land Use Planning Processes 987
IV. Means for Directing Land Use 993
V. Some Challenges for Action 1002
LITERATURE CITED 1009

GLOSSARY—Common and Scientific Names of Plants................... 1013

SUBJECT INDEX 1016

GENERAL FOREWORD

Planning the Uses and Management of Land is the twenty-first publication in the "Agronomy" series of monographs. This series, started in 1949, attempts to meet the need for comprehensive treatment of specific subjects in agronomy, crop science, and soil science.

Dr. A. G. Norman, an eminent member of the society, was editor of the first six monographs in the series. ASA, a nonprofit organization, was not initially able to finance the project, so Academic Press, Inc. of New York published the monographs edited by Dr. Norman.

As a result of the growth of ASA, by 1957 the responsibility of preparation, editing, financing, and publishing the monograph series was undertaken by the society. In recent years, this activity has flourished. These publications represent a significant and continuing activity of ASA, its officers, and approximately 11,000 of its members located in more than 100 countries.

The American Society of Agronomy is closely associated with the Crop Science Society of America and the Soil Science Society of America. While the three societies are autonomous, they share the same Headquarters Office, executive officer, and other staff members in Madison, Wisconsin. The members of these three educational and scientific societies work together to promote basic and applied research in the agronomic sciences, to make information available to the public, and to encourage improvement of all scientists in their professions. This close association of the societies makes it possible for ASA to publish material relating both to crop science and soil science in the "Agronomy" series.

The numerous authors in each section of *Planning the Uses and Management of Land* serve as an excellent example of the wealth of knowledge emanating from cooperative members of these societies in this joint effort as copublishers of this monograph. The publication provides recent, up-to-date scientific and practical information on this topic which is of worldwide concern.

In behalf of the societies and myself, sincere and profound thanks are offered to the officers, editorial committee, authors and reviewers, managing and assistant editors, keyliner, and typesetter, who together have made this project a success.

Madison, Wisconsin   MATTHIAS STELLY
September, 1979   *Editor-in-Chief*
           ASA Publications

FOREWORD

Land is virtually the sole source of our sustenance because it supports the plants and animals providing our food, fiber, and shelter. It is the watershed or reservoir for our water supply. Also, land provides the minerals we use, the space in which we build our homes, communication systems, and the other elements of our economic intrastructure as well as a source of pleasure and satisfaction which we derive from our environment—the things we see, hear, smell, and touch every day. In addition, land is the receptacle for our waste; it helps hide and correct some of our mistakes.

Land is in limited supply—a fact which Mark Twain pointed out to us so clearly. We are not making any more land so the *per capita* amount declines as our numbers increase. We feel this "loss of space" every day as we travel clogged streets and roads, attend crowded events, try to get space in an overused park, push our way through a crowded supermarket, or look for a parking place on campus or a street.

Our forebears used and misused land as though the supply were inexhaustible. However, the supply of land was soon shown not to be inexhaustible for economic crop production and the great move to the west started. By purchase, war and treaty we pushed across a continent and beyond, seldom stopping to consider differences in the capability of land to serve various personal and national purposes. If we had not learned this before in the humid regions, the lesson struck us full force when the Dust Bowl days of the 1930's arrived. Clearly, we overextended certain land uses under available management technology. This continues as we watch billions of tons of soil erode to foul our waters and spoil our landscape, and additional land is being lost to silt accumulation. The pressure of numbers, new technology, and poor management every day wrest land from food and fiber production and convert it permanently to other uses.

We do not have enough land to do with it as we wish. The crush shall intensify. Restrictions on land are being added by economic reality and by society through its power to make and enforce laws. As each restriction takes effect, land becomes less of a commodity to be traded freely on the market and used up, and more of a resource which must be preserved and maintained for the common good of all.

Members of the American Society of Agronomy, the Crop Science Society of America, and the Soil Science Society of America believe that the time is ripe for a monograph such as *Planning the Uses and Management of Land*. The organizers, editors, and authors of this publication have carefully considered all aspects of land and its use and management, and have tried fully to present all facets in carefully documented form. The monograph is written not only for ourselves and our students, but for other scientists in related disciplines and for those who would make and administer land use and land management plans.

xix

We hope that this publication will be used and will lead to wise land use decisions which will benefit our descendents.

July 1979

Leo M. Walsh, *president*   Roy G. Creech, *president*
Soil Science Society of America   *Crop Science Society of America*

John Pesek, *president*
American Society of Agronomy

PREFACE

The increasing human population and the accelerating scope of human activities impact all natural resources. Since humans are basically terrestrial their activities particularly affect the land resource. As land values and the diversity of land uses have increased, conflicts among the competing land uses have multiplied. The sustaining base of land resources which supports us all has been damaged, or in some cases destroyed, by land uses which are inappropriate, exploitive, or inadequately planned.

While human uses of the land have been increasing in scope, diversity, and intensity so have our bases of scientific knowledge of land, our inventories of the geographic distribution of land resources, and our institutional tools for achieving land use goals. One of the many challenges of land use planning is that of linking information from the physical and biological sciences with social values and political realities in a participatory process of establishing goals and making decisions. There are many publications which deal with the scientific, technical, and geographic information on land resources. Likewise, many others deal with planning principles, processes, and programs. Few publications link these two major topic areas. Interest in land use problems and issues among agronomists and other scientists has prompted development of this monograph. It brings under one cover information on several of the data bases for land resources and gives overviews of major land use planning principles, problems, and processes.

The book is organized into 10 sections and 40 chapters. In section I, the authors set the background on patterns of land use and their development in the United States, on the U.S. institutional framework for dealing with land use, and describe principles of land use planning. In section II, a series of chapters describe data bases which are useful for land use planning.

These fundamental sections of the monograph are followed by applications to the planning of the major kinds of land uses important in the world today. These include, first, land uses for cultivated crops, for rangelands, for forests and woodlands, and for recreation. Then the monograph deals with the planning of metropolitan land uses, land uses for transportation, and utility corridors. A series of chapters deals with planning for waste disposal on land, and with planning for a series of diverse but very important land uses including watersheds, shorelands, wetlands, and coastal zones. Planning considerations for control of nonpoint pollution and for reclamation of disturbed lands are discussed in separate chapters.

The final section of the book deals with integrated land uses planning and plan implementation. It includes important contributions on information and inventory systems, uses of soil surveys, a case study in comprehensive ecological planning and a survey of future needs for land use planning and plan implementation tools.

We feel that this book will be of significant value as a reference and source of background information for the many different professionals who deal with planning the uses and management of land—for whatever purpose or purposes. Many universities and colleges have a course or a series of courses on land use planning. We believe that this book will be a valuable reference for students and teachers of such courses, both those with a social science and a natural science orientation.

Readers will note differences in the approaches of authors to planning land use and land management. The state-of-the-art is such that planning for some land uses, cultivated land for example, deals primarily with management or operational planning. In other cases, such as metropolitan land uses, planning deals with decisions affecting the broad array and distribution of possible land uses. It is possible that a significant change in planning for cultivated lands, and other lands which are now planned mainly by individual owners or operators, will occur during the decades to come as the Nation strives to meet water quality goals and to apportion scarce land among competing uses.

The editors wish to acknowledge with sincere appreciation the contributions of the numerous authors and other colleagues who have cooperated in planning and developing this book.

Madison, Wisconsin
14 July 1979

MARVIN T. BEATTY, *editor*
University of Wisconsin, Madison, Wisconsin

GARY W. PETERSEN, *editor*
The Pennsylvania State University,
University Park, Pennsylvania

LESTER D. SWINDALE, *editor*
ICRISAT, Hyderabad, India

CONTRIBUTORS

William A. Atkinson   Associate Professor of Forest Resources, College of Forest Resources, University of Washington, Seattle, Washington

Raleigh Barlowe   Professor, Department of Resource Development, Michigan State University, East Lansing, Michigan

Terry W. Barney   Senior Research Specialist, Department of Agronomy, University of Missouri, Columbia, Missouri

Lindo J. Bartelli   Formerly Director of Soil Survey Interpretations, Soil Conservation Service, U.S. Department of Agriculture; presently Professor, School of Forestry and Wood Products, Michigan Technological University, Houghton, Michigan

Kurt W. Bauer   Executive Director, Southeastern Wisconsin Regional Planning Commission, Waukesha, Wisconsin

Marion F. Baumgardner   Professor of Agronomy, Laboratory for Application of Remote Sensing, Purdue University, West Lafayette, Indiana

Jonathan Berger   Assistant Professor, Department of Landscape Architecture and Regional Planning, University of Pennsylvania, Philadelphia, Pennsylvania

Larry L. Boersma   Professor, Department of Soil Science, Oregon State University, Corvallis, Oregon

Thadis W. Box   Professor and Dean, College of Natural Resources, Utah State University, Logan, Utah

Johannes Bouma   Soil Scientist, Department of Soil Physics, Soil Survey Institute, Wageningen, The Netherlands

D. A. Bronstein   Associate Professor of Environmental Law, Department of Resource Development, Michigan State University, East Lansing, Michigan

Frank G. Calhoun, Jr.   Professor of Tropical Crops and Soils, Department of Soil and Crop Sciences, Texas A&M University, College Station, Texas

Glen H. Cannell   Soil Physicist, Department of Soil and Environmental Sciences, University of California, Riverside, California

Victor W. Carlisle   Professor, Soil Science Department, University of Florida, Gainesville, Florida

William M. Clark   Forester, Soil Conservation Service, U.S. Department of Agriculture, Lincoln, Nebraska

Donald B. Coombs   Formerly Director, Land Evaluation and Mapping Branch, Lands Directorate, Environment Canada, Ottawa, Ontario, Canada (now retired, located in Manotick, Ontario, Canada)

T. C. Daniel   Assistant Professor, Department of Soil Science, University of Wisconsin, Madison, Wisconsin

Arden D. Day   Agronomist, Department of Plant Sciences, University of Arizona, Tucson, Arizona

Robert W. Duell   Associate Research Professor, Department of Soils and Crops, Cook College, Rutgers University, New Brunswick, New Jersey

Don D. Dwyer   Professor and Head, Range Science Department, Utah State University, Logan, Utah

Herbert E. Echelberger   Research Forester, Northeastern Forest Experiment Station, Forest Service, U.S. Department of Agriculture, Durham, New Hampshire (formerly located at Syracuse, New York)

Gary H. Elsner   Project Leader, Pacific Southwest Forest and Range Experiment Station, Forest Service, U.S. Department of Agriculture, Berkeley, California

Donald G. Fohs   Chief, Soils and Exploratory Techniques Group, Materials Division, Office of Research, Federal Highway Administration, Washington, D.C.

Stanley P. Gessel   Professor, College of Forest Resources, University of Washington, Seattle, Washington

Warren A. Hall   Elwood Mead Professor of Engineering, Department of Civil Engineering, Colorado State University, Fort Collins, Colorado

George H. Hargreaves   Research Engineer, Department of Agricultural and Irrigation Engineering, Utah State University, Logan, Utah

Chris J. Johannsen   Professor, Department of Agronomy, University of Missouri, Columbia, Missouri

Arthur H. Johnson   Assistant Professor, Department of Landscape Architecture and Regional Planning, University of Pennsylvania, Philadelphia, Pennsylvania.

Michael D. Kennedy   Professor, College of Agriculture, University of Kentucky, Lexington, Kentucky

Richard L. Kleckner   Geographer, Geography Program, U.S. Geological Survey, Department of the Interior, Reston, Virginia

Albert A. Klingebiel   Soils Consultant, Soils and Land Use Technology, Inc., Silver Spring, Maryland

William D. LaCour   Planning Analyst, MPH, Division of Solid Waste Management, Pennsylvania Department of Environmental Resources, Harrisburg, Pennsylvania

Edward R. Landa   Formerly Research Associate, Departments of Soil Science and Agricultural Chemistry, Oregon State University, Corvallis, Oregon; presently Hydrologist, U.S. Geological Survey, Department of the Interior, Lakewood, Colorado

Bruce F. Leeson   Head, Natural History Research Division, Parks Canada, Calgary, Alberta, Canada

William J. Lloyd   Chief Forester, Soil Conservation Service, U.S. Department of Agriculture, Washington, D.C.

F. Glade Loughry   Formerly Chief, Soil Science Section, Pennsylvania Department of Environmental Resources, Harrisburg, Pennsylvania (now retired, located in Lancaster, Pennsylvania)

CONTRIBUTORS xxv

Kenneth L. Ludeke	Formerly Agronomist, Cyprus Pima Mining Company, Tucson, Arizona; presently located in Poway, California
Arthur W. Magill	Principal Resource Analyst, Pacific Southwest Forest and Range Experiment Station, Forest Service, U.S. Department of Agriculture, Berkeley, California
Michael M. McCarthy	Assistant Professor, Department of Landscape Architecture, School of Renewable Natural Resources, University of Arizona, Tucson, Arizona
Donald E. McCormack	Director, Soil Survey Interpretations Division, Soil Conservation Service, U.S. Department of Agriculture, Washington, D.C.
Ian L. McHarg	Professor and Chairman, Department of Landscape Architecture and Regional Planning, University of Pennsylvania, Philadelphia, Pennsylvania
Charles R. Meyers, Jr.	Formerly Chief, Technical Programs, Office of Land Use and Water Planning, U.S. Department of the Interior, Washington, D.C.; presently Land Use Planner, Office of Surface Mining, U.S. Department of the Interior, Washington, D.C.
F. Ted Miller	Formerly Assistant Principal Soil Correlator, South Technical Service Center, Soil Conservation Service, U.S. Department of Agriculture, Fort Worth, Texas; presently Soil Specialist, Foreign Programs, Saudi Arabia
Fred P. Miller	Professor of Soil Science and Extension Soil and Water Resource Specialist, Department of Agronomy, University of Maryland, College Park, Maryland
Joe D. Nichols	Formerly Principal Soil Correlator, presently Head, Soils Staff, South Technical Service Center, Soil Conservation Service, U.S. Department of Agriculture, Fort Worth, Texas
Bernard J. Niemann, Jr.	Professor, Department of Landscape Architecture, School of Natural Resources, University of Wisconsin, Madison, Wisconsin
Fred A. Norstadt	Soil Scientist, Science and Education Administration, Agricultural Research, U.S. Department of Agriculture, Fort Collins, Colorado
Harry B. Pionke	Soil Scientist, Northeast Watershed Research Center, Science and Education Administration, U.S. Department of Agriculture, University Park, Pennsylvania
John C. Roberts	Formerly Associate Professor, Department of Urban and Regional Planning, University of Wisconsin-Extension, Madison, Wisconsin; presently Statewide Program Leader, Natural and Environmental Resources Programs, University of Wisconsin-Extension, Madison, Wisconsin
Richard H. Rust	Professor, Department of Soil Science, University of Minnesota, St. Paul, Minnesota
R. Neal Sampson	Soil Conservationist, Resource Development Division, Soil Conservation Service, U.S. Department of Agriculture, Washington, D.C.
James A. Schmid	Vice President, Jack McCormick and Associates, Inc., Berwyn, Pennsylvania

Robert Roy Schneider   Formerly Project Associate, Water Resources Center, University of Wisconsin, Madison, Wisconsin; presently Assistant Professor, Department of Economics, Williams College, Williamstown, Massachusetts

Charles F. Schwarz   Landscape Architect, Pacific Southwest Forest and Range Experiment Station, Forest Service, U.S. Department of Agriculture, Berkeley, California

Michael J. Singer   Assistant Professor of Soil Science, Department of Land, Air, and Water Resources, University of California, Davis, California

J. Herbert Snyder   Professor, Department of Agricultural Economics, University of California, Davis, California

William E. Sopper   Professor of Forest Hydrology, Institute for Research on Land and Water Resources, The Pennsylvania State University, University Park, Pennsylvania

Eric Royer Stoner   Graduate Research Agronomist, Laboratory for Applications of Remote Sensing, Purdue University, West Lafayette, Indiana

William D. Striffler   Professor of Watershed Sciences, Department of Earth Resources, Colorado State University, Fort Collins, Colorado

Paul Sutton   Professor, Department of Agronomy, Ohio Agricultural Research and Development Center, Wooster, Ohio

Kenneth K. Tanji   Professor of Water Science, Department of Land, Air, and Water Resources, University of California, Davis, California

Jean Thie   Chief, Ecological Land Classification Division, Lands Directorate, Environment Canada, Ottawa, Ontario, Canada

Edward C. Thor   Research Economist, Land Use and Landscape Planning, Pacific Southwest Forest and Range Experiment Station, Forest Service, U.S. Department of Agriculture, Berkeley, California

J. Allan Tice   Chief Soils Engineer, Raleigh Branch, Law Engineering Testing Company, Raleigh, North Carolina

Raymond D. Vlasin   Formerly Chairman, Department of Natural Resource Development, presently Dean of Lifelong Education Programs and Professor of Resource Development, Michigan State University, East Lansing, Michigan

V. Van Volk   Associate Professor, Department of Soil Science, Oregon State University, Corvallis, Oregon

J. Alan Wagar   Formerly Leader, Recreation Research Project, Northeastern Forest Experiment Station, Forest Service, U.S. Department of Agriculture, Syracuse, New York; presently Leader, Urban Forestry Research Project, Pacific Southwest Forest and Range Experiment Station, Forest Service, U.S. Department of Agriculture, Berkeley, California

Norman Wengert   Professor of Political Science, Department of Political Science, Colorado State University, Fort Collins, Colorado

Douglas A. Yanggen   Professor, Agricultural Economics Department, University of Wisconsin and University of Wisconsin-Extension, Madison, Wisconsin

CONVERSION FACTORS FOR U. S. AND METRIC UNITS

To convert column 1 into column 2, multiply by	Column 1	Column 2	To convert column 2 into column 1, multiply by
Length			
0.621	kilometer, km	mile, mi	1.609
1.094	meter, m	yard, yd	0.914
0.394	centimeter, cm	inch, in	2.54
Area			
0.386	kilometer², km²	mile², mi²	2.590
247.1	kilometer², km²	acre, acre	0.00405
2.471	hectare, ha	acre, acre	0.405
Volume			
0.00973	meter³, m³	acre-inch	102.8
3.532	hectoliter, hl	cubic foot, ft³	0.2832
2.838	hectoliter, hl	bushel, bu	0.352
0.0284	liter	bushel, bu	35.24
1.057	liter	quart (liquid), qt	0.946
Mass			
1.102	ton (metric)	ton (U.S.)	0.9072
2.205	quintal, q	hundredweight, cwt (short)	0.454
2.205	kilogram, kg	pound, lb	0.454
0.035	gram, g	ounce (avdp), oz	28.35
Pressure			
14.50	bar	lb/inch², psi	0.06895
0.9869	bar	atmosphere, atm	1.013
0.9678	kg(weight)/cm²	atmosphere, atm	1.033
14.22	kg(weight)/cm²	lb/inch², psi	0.07031
14.70	atmosphere, atm	lb/inch², psi	0.06805
Yield or Rate			
0.446	ton (metric)/hectare	ton (U.S.)/acre	2.24
0.892	kg/ha	lb/acre	1.12
0.892	quintal/hectare	hundredweight/acre	1.12
Temperature			
$\left(\dfrac{9}{5}\,°C\right) + 32$	Celsius −17.8C 0C 100C	Fahrenheit 0F 32F 212F	$\dfrac{5}{9}\,(°F - 32)$
Water Measurement			
8.108	hectare-meters, ha-m	acre-feet	0.1233
97.29	hectare-meters, ha-m	acre-inches	0.01028
0.08108	hectare-centimeters, ha-cm	acre-feet	12.33
0.973	hectare-centimeters, ha-cm	acre-inches	1.028
0.00973	meters³, m³	acre-inches	102.8
0.981	hectare-centimeters/hour, ha-cm/hour	feet³/sec	1.0194
440.3	hectare-centimeters/hour, ha-cm/hour	U.S. gallons/min	0.00227
0.00981	meters³/hour, m³/hour	feet³/sec	101.94
4.403	meters³/hour, m³/hour	U.S. gallons/min	0.227

Plant Nutrition Conversion—P and K

P (phosphorus) $\times$ 2.29 = P_2O_5

K (potassium) $\times$ 1.20 = K_2O

section I

Present Status of Land Uses and Land Use Planning

USDA Soil Conservation Service

1   Soils, Plants, and Land Use in the United States

RALEIGH BARLOWE

Michigan State University
East Lansing, Michigan

I. INTRODUCTION

Now, as never before, world attention is focused on the need for protecting and effectively using our life-sustaining earth resources. World population numbers increased from 2.5 to 4.0 billion people between 1950 and 1975. Medium-level projections suggest that these totals may rise to 6.4 billion in 2000 and 12.2 billion by 2075 (United Nations, 1974). Meanwhile, we can expect no expansion of our physical resource base for producing food and other raw materials.

Increasing population numbers provide only a partial measure of the growing pressure on our land resource base. Economic development, industrialization, and the opening of the gates of knowledge have brought major increases in average per capita demands for the products of land. Higher productivity has brought larger real incomes, increased purchasing power, added mobility, more emphasis on education and leisure time activities, expanding wants and tastes, and an upward surge in individual demands for a wide gamut of resources.

With significant increases in population numbers and rising levels of living, the world is experiencing steadily increasing demands for most natural resources. Annual production of the world's top 20 minerals, for example, rose 40.5% from 15.8 to 22.2 trillion tons in the 9 years between 1965 and 1974 (USDI, Bur. Mines, 1976). This exponential rate of increase cannot be continued indefinitely (Meadows et al., 1972). Rising demands or not, we must accept the fact that continuation of our current rates of use will bring the depletion of our known and expected reserves of many minerals within the next few decades.

Overall, we must accept the constraints of a finite earth. But this does not mean that the future is hopeless. People are not fruitflies impelled to breed to a Malthusian level of survival. Man is blessed with the ability to think and reason. If we have the will, we can adapt our resource uses to the necessary conditions of our world and devise plans and strategies that will permit us to provide the food and raw materials needed to supply a stable population with opportunities for high levels of life for centuries to come.

But this objective will not just happen. To attain it, we must expect to make plans and develop programs for our future on this planet.

Those who plan for the future well-being of mankind must obviously consider many issues. Thought must be given to policies that will affect population growth, economic development, urbanization, energy, and housing. Food production and the uses we make of our soil, plant, and animal resources must rank near the top of any list of policy issues. Land use policies dealing with the implications of land use both for production of necessary goods and for the quality of man's environment also have a necessary place on our agenda for the future.

Emphasis is given in this chapter and in the later chapters of this book to the paramount role soil and plants play as a part of our land and natural resource base. Four aspects of this larger picture are considered in this chapter. First attention is given to the framework within which plans and policies affecting land resources operate. Emphasis then is directed to a description of past land settlement patterns in the United States, to an examination of recent changes in land use patterns, and to some observations concerning the effects of soils and plants on land use patterns.

II. OVERALL FRAMEWORK FOR PUBLIC POLICY

Public plans and policies are ordinarily devised to facilitate the attainment of some rationally desirable goal. By their very nature, they are idealistic in that they point the way to where we should, rather than where we may actually be going. With the development of plans and policies affecting soils, plants, and other natural resources, planners and policy makers should be practical and realistic in their approaches. One can ask for the moon, but it is reasonable to plan only for that which is obtainable.

A. Threefold Framework

A practical real-world approach requires recognition of the fact that plans, policies, and programs affecting the conservation, development, management, and use of natural resources must operate within the context of the threefold framework pictured in Fig. 1. This framework requires the linkage of physical and biological, economic, and institutional considerations in the carrying out of any program (Barlowe, 1978, p. 5–7; Clawson, 1975, p. 28; Ely & Wehrwein, 1940).

One can separate these factors in the university classroom and deal with single disciplines to the exclusions of all others. But under real-world operating conditions plans and policies must be physically and biologically possible, economically feasible, and acceptable from the standpoint of man-made institutions if they are to have any chance of success.

The physical and biological framework focuses on the world's natural and physical resource base. On the physical side, it is concerned with in-

PHYSICAL AND BIOLOGICAL FRAMEWORK

Acceptable physical base—geology, soils, water, air, climate

People and groups of human beings

Plant, animal, and other biological resources

Sound ecological relationships

ECONOMIC FRAMEWORK

Productive input-output relationships

Effective marketing and transportation arrangements

Acceptable distribution of income and other benefits

INSTITUTIONAL FRAMEWORK

Legality—compliance with constitutions, laws, ordinances, and
    public regulations

Political acceptability—no conflicts with political practices and
    traditions

Social and cultural mores—acceptability in terms of accepted
    customs, attitudes, and beliefs

Administratively workable

Fig. 1—Threefold framework within which resource policies operate.

aminate resources—with geological features, soils, rocks, water, air, sunlight, and climate. Biologically, it involves living things—plants, animals, including human beings, birds, fish, and other living creatures.

This framework is concerned with the natural world with which and within which man operates. The resources of this framework can be viewed as our natural resource endowment, as God's gift to man. But gift or not, they must be used with discretion. Some resources come as a fixed fund which can be exhausted through use (mineral fuels) or dissipated and wasted (metals) if we fail to assemble used resources for recycling. Some such as sunlight, rain, or wind come in a predictable flow over time. Still others such as plants, animals, and, to some extent, soils, can be used up like fund resources but have the biological ability to replenish themselves if care is taken to safeguard the necessary seed stock for future regeneration (Barlowe, 1978).

A key feature of the physical and biological framework centers is the need for maintaining healthy ecological relationships. Our physical and biological endowment is bountiful and rich in its potential for supporting manifold human activities. But it has its limits. One must accept the ecological constraints set by these limits and recognize that fragile resources, once destroyed, cannot be replaced.

The economic framework points the way to those productive practices and enterprises that are economically feasible in our society. Emphasis must always be given to the costs associated with various alternative combinations of inputs that can be utilized in production, to the amounts of production that can be expected with each combination, to marketing and transportation costs and facilities, and to the question of whether operators can expect to receive acceptable returns for their labor and management. Without promise of sufficient returns to more than pay their costs of production, operators lack incentives for engaging in production.

Another feature of the economic framework relates to the distribution of the returns and incomes secured from production. It is not enough that there be an overall surplus of benefits or returns above costs. Surpluses must be realized by those who make the production decisions and by those who bear the production costs. Bargaining groups (labor unions, management, stockholders, and lenders of capital) insist that they receive equitable shares of the expected fruits of production. Governments, acting as the agents of society, also use production regulations, minimum wage laws, health and safety rules, tax measures, and the like to effect transfers of benefits from the more economically powerful to less-advantaged individuals.

With the institutional framework, the key question is whether proposed plans or programs are acceptable within the context of the working rules of society. Plans must be constitutional and legal in that they do not call for actions prohibited or not accepted by constitutions, laws, ordinances, agency rules, or court decisions. Unless one is willing to campaign for change, plans must be in accord with national traditions and political concepts of what is acceptable. They must not be greatly in conflict with social norms or widely held views concerning religious and moral responsibilities. They must also involve arrangements that are administratively workable.

The institutional framework involves several major factors that have intimate impacts on decisions concerning the use of soils and plants. Basic among these is our concept of rights in land—who owns what, who has the right to decide the use that will be made of a given tract of land, and who will share in the productivity of the land. Also important are the operations of governmental and legal systems and the role custom plays in influencing the use one makes of resources.

Unlike the physical and biological framework, with which man has no long-run alternative to accepting the laws of nature if he is to continue to enjoy nature's bounty, the economic and institutional frameworks can be modified by human action. Cost and price relationships can change over time and in so doing affect the economics of production decisions. A rise in food prices relative to costs, for example, will encourage operators to farm more intensively and also to extend cultivation to lands hitherto submarginal for this use.

Changes in human attitudes also can bring changes in the institutional framework. Our present institutions have emerged as the product of centuries of human interaction. This interaction process is still going on, and more modifications of this framework will come with changing events and attitudes in the future.

B. Significance of Soils and Plants in Planning

Soils and plants represent a significant component of the physical and biological framework. Without them, the framework would be meaningless because the earth's surface would be unusable for food production and the support of human life.

Much of every nation's agricultural productivity is geared to the quantity and quality of its soil resources and to the types and varieties of plants it can raise to advantage. The United States possesses unique advantages among the food producing nations of the world because of the productive capacity of its soils. Its soil resources, location in a temperate zone, and range of climatic conditions favor the commercial production of a wide assortment of plants.

Soil and plant conditions vary greatly throughout the United States. Some areas benefit from the presence of deep rich soils that are admirably suited for the production of cotton, corn, or wheat depending upon climatic conditions. Farmers in other areas have found that they can operate successfully with less productive soils. Areas covered with drifting sand, undrained marshes, rocky mountainsides, or arid deserts, however, are generally not fit for commercial agricultural use.

Overall, the settlers on this portion of the American continent and the farmers who followed them have usually had a clear perception of the importance of soil and plants for their expected operations. Most settlers sought what they considered as productive soils. Their choice of cash and secondary crops depended on their area of settlement. But with each crop they were attentive of the soil needs that could spell the difference between the success and failure of their production plans.

Much has been written about subsistence farmers on the American frontier. Some settlers did indeed operate on a subsistence basis for awhile. But the goal of nearly every farmer was that of operating on a commercial basis (Loehr, 1952). Settlers yearned for the day when they could sell cash crops that would provide them a surplus of income they could use to raise their living standards and increase their scale of operations.

Farm sites with fertile soils and high potentials for successful crop production were necessary parts of their settlement objective. With these features of their physical and biological resource framework in hand, operators could venture forth on development programs that demonstrated the economic feasibility of their plans. Once their settlements were made, they also were quick to supply themselves with public infrastructures of laws, public services, and social organizations that supported and legitimized their developmental efforts.

III. LAND SETTLEMENT PATTERNS

Agricultural historians have described and documented the settlement of our eastern seaboard and the western movement that filled the nation with thriving farms between the late 1700's and the early 1900's (Bidwell & Falconer, 1925; Gray, 1925; Edwards, 1940). What settlers wanted in land varied from one person to the next. In most cases they sought good soils and open lands that were ready for tilling or wooded lands that could easily be cleared. Timber was needed for fuel and building materials and reliable supplies of potable water were required for household uses. Locations near navigable streams or transportation routes were always in demand. With the early settlements, sites also were selected with an eye to defense against possible foreign invaders, pirates, and Indians.

A. Settler Preferences in Land

Some insight to settler and investor preferences can be secured by examining the land settlement and purchase decisions of selected individuals. An early example involves the choice of colonization sites in Massachusetts.

Religious and political freedom are often emphasized as reasons for the migration of the first Puritan settlers to Massachusetts. Historians report that most of these colonists were "well-to-do yeomanry and craftsmen; men of some estate and standing" (Hart, 1927, p. 54). Martin Pring visited the area in 1603 and wrote of "the goodness of the Climate and of the Soyle" (Bradford, 1912, p. 178 and 180). Thereafter, the qualities of the area for agricultural development were more or less assumed.

Governor William Bradford's letters of 1620–21 from the Plymouth colony make little mention of soil or plants (Bradford, 1912). The first settlements of the Massachusetts Bay colony came 10 years later. These settlements were located mostly on the black earth meadows ("champion" lands) along the bays and rivers north of Plymouth. Some time passed before much attempt was made to move into the higher, better drained, and harder-to-clear forests that stretched inland. Adequate supplies of good water were a problem with many coastal settlements. John Winthrop faced this problem at Cambridge and moved his house to Boston where he found a site that boasted both good soil and a "fine spring" (Adams, 1963, p. 238; Morgan, 1958, p. 61).

One hundred and forty years later in November 1770, George Washington sent instructions to William Crawford who was acting as his agent in the purchase of western lands. Washington insisted that Crawford buy "Lands that are really fine." Hilly lands would be acceptable only if they were "of the richest kind; the growth of which shall be Walnut, Cherry, and such other sorts of timber, as denote the most luxuriant Soil.'' With more level lands, ''I wou'd put up with a soil less fertile but in either case I shou'd expect the Tract to be well watered and well timbered with a sufficiency of meadow ground upon it. . . .If the Land is equally good I wou'd choose to have it laid off as convenient to the Fort on the river as possible'' (Fitzpatrick, 1932, p. 31).

Forty-seven years later and several hundred miles farther west, Morris Birkbeck, an English investor and developer, indicated his settlement choices in a description of a large tract he bought in southern Illinois in 1817. ''The land is rich natural meadow bounded by timbered lands, within reach of two navigable rivers, and may be rendered immediately productive at small expense'' (Birkbeck, 1918, p. 14). Birkbeck's report was typical of a school of promotional pamphlets and books that were published to glamorize and help sell lands along the frontier during the 1800's. The authors of these reports commonly used superlatives to praise the climate, soils, timber, water, and other merits of their favored locations.

Still another example of investment considerations is provided by the case James S. Easley and William W. Willingham, two partners who bought over 400,000 acres for speculative resale in the Midwest during the middle 1800's. Easley and Willingham were ready to buy land almost anywhere in Iowa. Where possible, however, their agents were instructed to buy land close to promising towns and proposed railroad routes. Where timber was scarce, they favored purchases of timber lands or the partially wooded wetlands that skirted rivers and streams in the state (Swierenga, 1968, p. 165).

B. Changing Emphasis on Use-Capacity Factors

While settlers often differed in the relative emphasis they gave to preference factors, most sought sites that were accessible to markets, that provided access to wood and water, and that had climates and soils suited to the uses they planned. These factors and the changing emphasis given to them over time provide an excellent example of the workings of the economic concept of land use-capacity.

Land use-capacity refers to the relative ability of a tract or grade of land to provide a surplus of returns or satisfactions above its cost of utilization (Barlowe, 1978, p. 13). The concept has two major dimensions: accessibility and resource quality. Tracts may be highly productive relative to their costs of utilization because of favorable location with respect to markets or transportation and communication facilities. They may also be productive primarily because of resource characteristics such as soil fertility, climatic conditions, or the presence of wood and water.

Commercial-minded investors and settlers wanted both accessibility and land quality or as good a combination of these factors as might be available. When choices had to be made, top priority was usually given to accessibility.

The first settlements along the eastern seaboard from Massachusetts to Virginia, the Carolinas, and Georgia were almost always made at sites along bays or rivers that provided ready accessibility to the occasional ships that crossed the Atlantic to and from England. Accessibility to sea-going vessels was emphasized even though this meant that many settlements were sited in low, swampy, and poorly drained locations. Large expenditures of time and effort for clearing forests and building roads together with some daring were needed before many settlers would move inland to higher and better drained sites.

Once the forests were cleared, settlements often moved from low locations such as at Jamestown to healthier sites such as at Williamsburg. But even though they were often willing to move inland, planters and settlers still tended to favor locations along navigable streams. Clear evidence of this is provided by the population density maps published by the Bureau of the Census for the decennial years between 1790 and 1860 (U.S. Census Off., 1883).

As the tide of settlement pushed westward, the frontier surged forward along the navigable rivers and their tributaries. Settlers pushed west along the Ohio, Kentucky, and Tennessee rivers to the Mississippi, then up and down the Mississippi and westward along the Red, Arkansas, Missouri, Des Moines, and Iowa Rivers. Considerable filling in took place in each decade in the older settled areas while the prodding fingers of new settlement were moving on along the navigable waterways.

Sound reasoning lay behind the emphasis the first settlers gave to accessibility. Transportation of goods and produce on the rude trails through the forests was a tedious and difficult task. Goods could be moved far more economically by water than by wagon. Bulky and heavy articles could be shipped across the Atlantic in the early 1800's for about the same cost as for 30 miles over land (MacGill et al., 1917, p. 78). The opening of the Erie Canal in 1825 reduced the cost of shipping grain from Buffalo to New York City from approximately $100 to $8.81 per ton (MacGill et al., 1917, p. 84).

Transportation cost problems fired a persistent demand for public internal improvements along the frontier. Programs for improving river navigation, and for building roads, canals, and, later, railroads were widely favored as means for making new areas more accessible to market.

While much emphasis was given to the paramount need for accessibility, settlers and investors also were greatly interested in land quality. With the opening of every new area for public land sales, there was usually a rush to buy the choice locations. Water power sites, potential sites for towns, and tracts with obvious soil and farming advantages were in great demand. Most public lands sold at the $2.00 an acre minimum until 1820 and $1.25 an acre thereafter until sales ceased in 1891. But choice tracts sometimes bought bids of $40 an acre or more (Hibbard, 1924, p. 79).

Millions of acres were available for purchase throughout most of the 1800's. Only 31.0 million of the 135.2 million acres that had been surveyed and offered for sale were sold by 1833. Ten years later the area offered for sale had increased to 272.6 million acres, of which 88.4 million had been sold and 34.6 million disposed of in various public grants. But even with 149.6 million acres on the market, frontiersmen still eagerly pressed for public surveys and sales that would give them access to choice new tracts.

Settlers and investors were able to pick and choose the best lands. The rougher, more swampy, and less desirable timbered lands were usually by-passed. Preference was given to prime locations that offered prospects of early value appreciation. Frequently these locations had transportation advantages. But high values also were associated with the "oak openings" in Ohio and the small prairies in southern Michigan.

Many settlers held back when they reached the rich prairies of Illinois. Some writers have asserted that they were suspicious of the prairies. Recent research shows that this thesis has been overworked (Jordan, 1964). Whatever avoidance there was of the prairies can be attributed mostly to their inland location away from navigable rivers and the fact that the prairies often needed drainage and lacked ready access to timber.

Impressive evidence concerning settler preferences is presented in an official government report of 1856 which indicates the areas by townships in the 11 midwestern and south central public land states which were still available for sale after being listed on the market for 10 years (U.S. House of Rep., 1856). Tabulations of these data show that most of the land had been sold in the townships among the navigable streams and along the rights-of-way of railroads.

Most of the land also was sold in northern and central Indiana, southern Michigan, southeastern Wisconsin, northern and central Illinois, southeastern Iowa, west central Mississippi, and in the black soil belt of Alabama and Mississippi. Less than half of the land had been sold in large blocks of townships in northern Michigan and Wisconsin, Missouri, Arkansas, northern and western Louisiana, southern Mississippi, northcentral and southern Alabama, and northern Florida.

Overall, the data show that buyers had high preference for lands in the more fertile soil areas as well as for lands with rail and water transportation advantages. Far less sales activity had taken place in the areas with heavy forest cover and with the lower quality soils.

Similar preference patterns applied as settlers moved west across the 100th meridian to the high plains, mountain states, and the west coast. Accessibility was still important, but land quality became a more significant choice criterion as transportation facilities were developed and extended. Settlers on the plains had to import most of their timber, and those in the arid regions had to adjust their operations for shortages of water supplies.

Frederick Jackson Turner and others talked of the end of the frontier in 1890 (Turner, 1920). But while the frontier was disappearing, the filling-up process continued. Homesteaders claimed more than 381 million acres in the 45 years between 1891 and 1935. Millions of acres of potential productive land awaited reclamation. Large tracts of public and private forest and grazing land were in need for management. Hundreds of sites with a potential for providing public recreation also were waiting for the public to discover their value.

IV. RECENT TRENDS IN LAND USE PATTERNS

Significant changes in land use patterns have occurred in the United States during the past century. In 1880, the nation had a total population of 50.2 million people and 4 million farmers who operated 536 million acres or 28.2% of the nation's land area. Large areas of new land in the western states and substantial areas of by-passed lands in the midwest and southern states were developed for farming in the decades that followed. By 1900 the nation's population had risen to 76.2 million and the number of farms to 5.7 million. A total of 841 million acres or 41.2% of the nation's land was then in farms (cf. Table 1).

As the nation's population continued to increase to 106.0 million in 1920, 151.3 million in 1950, and 213.1 million in 1975, the number of farms rose to a peak of 6.45 million in 1920 and thereafter declined. By 1950 the number had dropped to 5.4 million and by 1975 to 2.3 million. Meanwhile, the acreage included in farms rose to an all-time high of 1,158.6 million or 60.9% of the nation's land area in 1950. Total land in farms was down to 1,063.3 million in 1969 and 1,018.0 million acres in 1974 (USDA, 1975, p. 418; USDC, Bur. Census, 1974).

A. Trends with Cropland

Table 1 summarizes the major trends in utilization of the nation's land since 1880. The area used for cropland purposes increased steadily until 1950. With the decrease in farmland area after 1950, the area used for crops dropped from 387 million in 1950 to 335 million acres in 1969. Increasing demands for food production prompted an increase in this total to 363 million acres in 1974. With the large drop in farm numbers, the size of the average farm increased from 156.9 acres in 1930 to 174.0 acres in 1940, 215.5 acres in 1950, 302.8 acres in 1959, 398.9 acres in 1969, and 439.5 acres in 1974.

National averages such as those reported in Table 1 conceal wide variations in state and regional trends. New England and the Middle Atlantic, South Atlantic, and East South Central regions experienced considerable declines in their farm and harvested cropland acreages between 1950 and 1974, while minor increases occurred in the Mountain and Pacific regions (cf. Table 2).

An extreme example of decline occurred in Maine where the areas of farmland and cropland harvested dropped approximately 60% between 1950 and 1974. Meanwhile, the acreage of cropland harvested increased in Arkansas and Florida while the area of farmland dropped, and the acreage of both farms and harvested cropland increased in Idaho and Montana.

Another view of the shifts in cropland use that have taken place is provided by the dot maps presented in Fig. 2. These maps show significant decreases in cropland area between 1944 and 1964 in the eastern and south-

Table 1—Land utilization in the United States by census years: 1880–1974†.

Census year	Land in farms	Land used for crops‡	Other cropland§	Pasture and grazing¶	Forest and woodland#	Farmsteads and service areas††	Other uses#	Total land area
				millions of acres				
				Contiguous states				
1880	536	166	22	935	628	152		1,903
1890	623	220	28	892	604	159		1,902
1900	841	283	36	831	574	179		1,903
1910	879	326	23	1,084	293	57	122	1,903
1920	956	374	28	1,046	286	58	111	1,903
1930	987	379	34	1,053	267	45	125	1,903
1940	1,061	363	36	1,060	266	44	136	1,905
1950	1,159	387	22	1,020	281	45	149	1,904
1959	1,120	358	33	939	366	37	169	1,902
1969	1,060	333	51	886	406	27	194	1,897
				50 states area				
1950	1,162	387	22	1,023	401	46	394	2,273
1959	1,124	359	33	944	485	37	413	2,271
1969	1,064	335	51	840	525	28	435	2,264
1974	1,018	363	20	861	539	8	473	2,264

† Source: U.S. Census reports; USDA, 1975, p. 420; and H. Thomas Frey. 1977. Major uses of land in the United States, preliminary estimates for 1974. Working Pap. no. 34. Aug. 1977. Econ. Res. Serv., USDA.

‡ Includes area of cropland harvested, crop failure, and cultivated summer fallow.

§ Includes cropland used for cover crops and idle cropland.

¶ Classification includes acreage of grassland pasture, cropland planted to pasture, pastured farm woodland, and grazing land and pastured forest lands not in farms.

Includes nonpastured woodland in farms and nonpastured forests outside of farms.

†† Land in farmsteads, farm lanes and roads, and other farm service lands.

‡‡ All lands not includes in the other classifications; includes areas used for urban, industrial, nonfarm industrial uses, parks, and recreation areas, wildlife refuges, military lands, roads, railroad and airfield lands, ungrazed desert, mountain, wetland areas, etc.

Table 2—Land acreage in farms and acreage of cropland harvested, regions of the United States, 1950 and 1969.†

Region and selected states	Land in farms			Cropland harvested		
	1950	1969	1974	1950	1969	1974
	million acres					
Regions						
New England	12.6	5.6	4.8	2.8	1.5	1.45
Middle Atlantic	31.9	20.1	18.6	12.2	8.0	8.6
East North Central	112.1	94.6	90.0	59.6	51.2	58.1
West North Central	284.3	278.8	273.9	113.3	106.4	123.0
South Atlantic	102.2	68.0	60.9	25.0	15.9	17.6
East South Central	79.6	60.7	53.7	22.5	14.1	15.0
West South Central	211.5	204.1	191.0	49.1	38.3	38.3
Mountain	250.2	256.5	253.0	24.5	22.5	24.3
Pacific	74.3	75.0	72.0	15.4	15.1	16.5
United States	1,158.6	1,063.5	1,018.0	324.4	273.0	302.8
Selected states						
Connecticut	1.27	0.54	0.44	0.309	0.162	0.159
Georgia	25.75	15.81	13.88	7.098	3.651	4.161
Maine	4.18	1.76	1.52	0.932	0.458	0.450
Michigan	17.27	11.90	10.83	7.797	5.502	6.318
Arkansas	18.87	15.70	14.64	5.930	6.805	6.639
Florida	16.53	14.03	13.20	1.728	2.235	2.304
Oklahoma	36.007	36.008	33.08	11.896	8.265	8.990
Wyoming	34.42	35.48	34.27	1.901	1.686	1.680
Idaho	13.22	14.42	14.27	3.648	3.954	4.531
Montana	59.25	62.92	62.16	7.576	7.937	8.427

† Source: U.S. Census reports.

eastern states, in eastern Oklahoma and northeastern Texas, and in the metropolitan areas of northeastern Ohio, southeastern Michigan, northeastern Illinois, southeastern Wisconsin, east central Minnesota, and coastal California. Large increases occurred in southcentral Florida, the delta area of eastern Arkansas and Missouri, across the corn and northern wheat belts, in northern Montana, eastern Colorado and western Kansas, in westcentral and southern Texas, in central Washington, southeastern Idaho, southern Arizona, and the central valley of California.

Several factors contributed to these trends. Low prices associated with surpluses in agricultural production, government programs for reducing production, lost comparative advantage for growing traditional crops, proximity of expanding urban developments, and the attraction of urban-oriented jobs explains much of the decrease in both farm operators and acreages used for crop production. Mechanization, acceptance of new production techniques, and land reclamation programs in turn explain most of the increases in cropland usage.

Overall, the declines in farm and harvested crop acreage have not signalled a decrease in farm production. Crop yields and efficiency in livestock production have increased steadily. The U.S. Department of Agriculture indices of cropland productivity and of total farm output (which includes livestock as well as crop production) rose from 52 in 1930 (1967 = 100) to 112

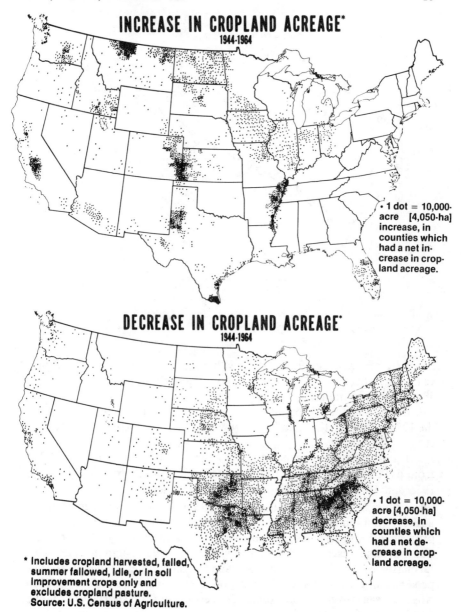

INCREASE IN CROPLAND ACREAGE*
1944-1964

• 1 dot = 10,000-
acre [4,050-ha]
increase, in
counties which
had a net in-
crease in crop-
land acreage.

DECREASE IN CROPLAND ACREAGE*
1944-1964

• 1 dot = 10,000-
acre [4,050-ha]
decrease, in
counties which
had a net de-
crease in crop-
land acreage.

* Includes cropland harvested, falled,
summer fallowed, idle, or in soil
improvement crops only and
excludes cropland pasture.
Source: U.S. Census of Agriculture.

Fig. 2—Cropland acreage changes, 1944–1964.

in 1975 (USDA, 1975, p. 443). Altogether, the nation's farms produced
121% more farm output from 21% less cropland in 1972 and 112% more
farm output from 9% less cropland in 1975 than in 1930 (Fig. 3).

Between the late 1940s and the early 1970s, farm production policy was
far more concerned with the problem of averting agricultural surpluses than
with that of encouraging more production. Acreage allotments were used

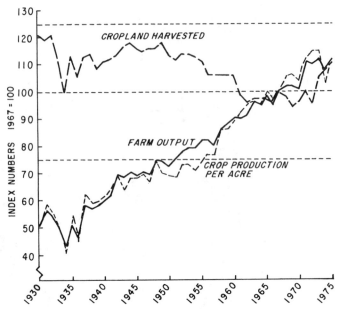

Fig. 3—Comparative trends in acreage cropland harvested, total farm output, and average crop production per acre, United States, 1930–1975 (1967 = 100 with all indices).

every year between 1949 and 1972 with peanuts and tobacco, in all but 3 years with wheat, all but 4 years with cotton and rice, and in 1950 and 1954–58 with corn to limit the acreages planted to these crops. It was only when world food shortages brought increased demands for U.S. grain supplies in the 1973–75 period that public policy was reoriented to encourage increased crop production.

Programs providing payments to farmers for withholding cropland from use or for diverting it to other uses were utilized extensively between 1956 and 1972 to relieve the farm surplus problem. As Table 3 indicates, totals ranging from 13.6 million acres in 1956 to 64.7 million acres in 1962 and 62.7 million acres in 1972 were withheld from production under these programs. Emphasis was given between 1956 and the early 1960's to a Soil Bank acreage reserve and a Conservation Reserve program under which farmers contracted to take farm acreage and sometimes whole farms out of production. Emphasis shifted during the 1960's to the use of feed grain and wheat acreage diversion programs. Concerns over food shortages brought a deemphasis of these programs in 1973.

At the same time that acreage allotment and cropland diversion programs were operating to hold down agricultural production, two opposing forces were influencing operator decisions. On one side, the lure of off-farm employment opportunities and the shifting of rural lands to urban-oriented uses favored a shift of farm operators and farmland out of farming. At the same time, new farmland and technological developments (machinery, pesticides, improved seed, etc.) upgraded the productive capacity

Table 3—Cropland acreage withheld from production under diversion programs, United States, 1956–75.†

Year	Soil bank acreage reserve	Conservation reserve contracts	Diversions			Other adjustment programs	Total acreage withheld
			Feed grain	Wheat acreage	Cotton acreage		
			million acres				
1956	12.2	1.4					13.6
1957	21.4	6.4					27.8
1958	17.2	9.9					27.1
1959		22.5					22.5
1960		28.7					28.7
1961		28.5	25.2				53.7
1962		25.8	28.2	10.7			64.7
1963		24.3	24.5	7.2		0.1	56.1
1964		17.4	32.4	5.1	0.5	0.1	55.5
1965		14.0	34.8	7.2	1.0	0.4	57.4
1966		13.3	34.7	8.3	4.6	2.4	63.3
1967		11.0	20.3		4.8	4.6	40.7
1968		9.2	32.4		3.3	4.5	49.4
1969		3.4	39.1	11.1		4.4	58.0
1970		0.1	37.4	15.7		3.9	57.1
1971		‡	18.2	13.5	2.1	3.8	37.6
1972		‡	36.6	20.1	2.0	3.3	62.1
1973			7.4	7.4		2.8	19.6
1974						2.4	2.4
1975						2.4	2.4

† Source: USDA, 1975, p. 518.
‡ Less than 50,000 acres.

of large areas already in farms. These developments encouraged those operators who stayed in farming to expand their scales of operation.

Total irrigated area in farms increased from 18.0 million acres in 1939 to 41.2 million acres in 1974 (cf. Table 4). As one might expect, the largest increases came in the semiarid and arid western half of the nation. Major increases occurred in Texas, California, Nebraska, and Kansas. Large increases also came in Florida, Arkansas, Louisiana, and some other eastern states. Some of this increase involved the bringing of nonfarm lands into agricultural use, while much of it entailed the irrigation of lands previously used for less intensive farming purposes.

Technological developments with farm irrigation—particularly the use of pumping equipment, light weight pipes, and improved spray techniques—also have favored the acceptance of supplemental irrigation practices on numerous humid area farms. The total acreage irrigated in the eastern states rose almost sixfold between 1939 and 1974. In Arkansas and Florida, two humid area states where the acreage used for crops increased between 1950 and 1974, the new area brought under irrigation greatly exceeded the increase in cropland.

Many of the recent shifts in areas used for agriculture are directly related to upward and downward adjustments in the acreages used to produce particular crops. Between 1930 and 1975 there were substantial reductions in the acreages planted to cotton, corn, oats, potatoes, tobacco, and fruits

Table 4—Trends in irrigated farm land acreage, United States and major geographic regions, 1939–1974.†

Geographic regions	1939	1949	1959	1969	1974
			thousand acres		
Northeast	20	87	206	225	241
Lake states	8	28	87	219	303
Corn Belt	9	16	87	290	149
Northern Plains	631	1,128	3,003	4,593	6,200
Appalachian	2	6	118	131	102
Southeast	127	375	490	1,470	1,695
Delta states	573	1,004	1,296	1,862	1,812
Southern Plains	899	3,166	5,854	7,412	7,109
Mountain	9,913	11,642	12,095	12,798	12,871
Pacific	5,800	8,334	9,787	9,984	10,619
Hawaii	n.a.	117	141	146	142
United States‡	17,983	25,905	33,164	39,129	41,243

† Source: USDA, 1972, p. 508; U.S. Dep. of Commerce, Bur. Census, 1974.
‡ Totals do not include Alaska where only 823 acres were irrigated in 1969.

and nuts (Fig. 4). Meanwhile, more land was planted to rice, soybeans, and sugar beets, while the acreages used for wheat, hay, sorghum, peanuts, and commercial vegetables fluctuated up and down.

Cotton provides a dramatic example of a crop traditionally raised mostly in one region which is being grown increasingly in a different region. Cotton was still king in the Old South in 1930 when 9.85 million acres in Alabama, Georgia, and North and South Carolina were planted to cotton. By 1974 only 1.3 million acres were used for cotton in these states, while the acreage planted to cotton in Arizona and California had risen from 408,000 to 1,543,000 acres. Improved cultural practices allowed farmers to raise considerably more cotton per acre than in 1930. These new practices, however, had major impacts in implementing a shift to the drier southwestern

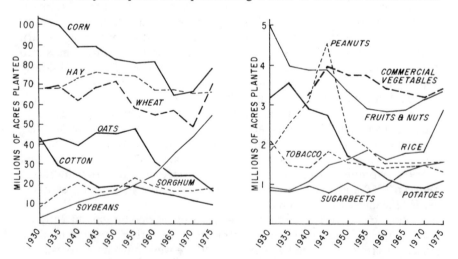

Fig. 4—Trends in acreage planted to 14 major crops.

states where irrigation and mechanical pickers are used to greater advantage.

Land use for corn production dropped from 110.6 million acres in 1932 to 60.4 million acres in 1969 before rising again to 77.9 million acres in 1975 (U.S. Dep. Commerce,Bur. Census, 1976, Series K-502). Thanks to the adoption of hybrid seed corn, larger applications of commercial fertilizer, and improved cultural practices, average corn yields have more than doubled since 1930. Most of the decrease in corn acreage came in the 13 southern states where the area planted to corn dropped from 29.6 million acres in 1930 to 7.9 million in 1969 and 10.1 million in 1975, as compared with a drop from 62.6 million acres in 1930 to 48.4 million in 1969 and a bounce back to 62.2 million acres in 1975 for the 12 north central states. The comparative advantage of the north central states for corn production was enhanced during this period by its greater production response to increased fertilization and improved cultural practices.

Increasing crop yields also affected the acreages needed for other crops such as wheat and potatoes. Fifty-four percent more wheat was produced from 36% less acreage in 1970 than in 1930. During this same period, potato production increased 58% from 56% less acreage. The acreage used for potatoes decreased in most states but increased substantially in Idaho, Oregon, and Washington. The acreage used for tobacco dropped from 2.1 million acres in 1930 to 899,330 acres in 1970 with only a slight decrease in total production. A general reduction in demand meanwhile prompted a decline in oats production.

Soybeans have been the miracle crop of the post-1930 period. The total area used for their production rose from 3.1 million acres in 1930 to 54.7 million acres in 1975, while average yields doubled. The largest acreages used for this crop are the midwestern and southern states. Rice production increased substantially, mostly in Arkansas, Louisiana, Texas, and California. The acreage planted to peanuts was expanded during the 1930s and 1940s but has dropped back to a lower level with the doubling and trebling of average yields. Sugarbeet acreage increased, particularly in California, Idaho, Minnesota, North Dakota, and Washington. Sorghum production increased, primarily in Kansas, Nebraska and Texas. Hay production in turn increased slightly in the western region while it was declining in most other parts of the country.

B. Trends with Grazing and Forest Lands

Pasture and grazing lands accounted for 1,053 million acres in the 48 contiguous states in 1930, rose to 1,060 million acres in 1940, and thereafter steadily declined to 857 million acres in 1974 (cf. Table 1). Meanwhile, the area of nongrazed forest and woodlands rose from around 267 million acres in 1930 and 1940 to 406 million acres in the 48 contiguous states in 1969. Addition of the forested areas of Alaska and Hawaii brings this total up to 401 million acres for 1950 and 539 million acres in 1974.

The totals reported for pasture and grazing and for forest and woodland are interrelated and vary from year to year depending upon the area of forest and woodland used for grazing purposes. Much of the decrease in grazing lands since 1940 is balanced by an increase in forest land acreage which was accomplished simply by changing the classification of no longer grazed forest lands.

Four additional observations concerning grazing and forest land use trends are highlighted by the following tabulation of acreages used for specific purposes in 1930, 1950, and 1969.

	1930	1950	1969
	(Millions of acres)		
Grazing land not in farms	589	400	288
Farm pasture	379	485	537
Total grazing land excluding grazed woodlots		968	885	825
Farm woodlands	150	220	112
Nongrazed nonfarm forests	202	196	356
Total forest lands		352	416	468
Total grazing and forest lands		1,320	1,301	1,293

First, it may be noted that much of the grazing land not in farms in 1930 shifted to the farm pasture classification in later years. This shift was prompted by the enactment of the Taylor Grazing Act of 1934 which provided a legal basis for establishing grazing districts in the western states and made 142 million acres of public range, which had been grazed without supervision, available for grazing on a lease basis. With the issuance of grazing permits, ranchers reported the leased acreages as parts of their farm and ranch operations.

Some of the increase in farm pasture since 1950 resulted from the diversion of a considerable acreage of farm cropland to pasture usage. An increase of cattle numbers on farms from 78 million in 1950 to 132 million in 1975 created need for the additional pasture. The decline in farm woodlot acreage in this same period resulted primarily from a decline in farming activities that prompted the reclassification of many forested areas from farm woodlots to nonfarm forest holdings.

Significant areas of grazing and forest lands were taken for urban-oriented uses, public parks and recreation areas, wildlife refuges, and national defense areas after 1930. These diversions were often balanced by a shifting of farmlands to the grazing and forest classifications. But considerable shifting took place. Around 45 million acres shifted from farm, grazing, and forest to other uses, of which only about 18 million acres were taken for urban or transportation purposes. The total land area in farms decreased by 145 million acres between 1950 and 1974 with very substantial decreases in farmland area occurring in many eastern states. Some of this farmland shifted to higher and better uses but the bulk of it shifted to less intensive forest and grazing classifications. Meanwhile, many grazed and wooded tracts were reclaimed and developed for cropland use.

C. Trends With Other Land Uses

Some of our more spectacular changes in land use in recent years involve the miscellaneous uses described in Table 1 as "other uses." A summary review of the trends with these uses (Table 5) shows that substantial areas have shifted to urban and transportation uses, state and national parks, and wildlife refuges since 1950. Altogether, 91.4 million acres were classified in these uses in 1950 and 159.1 million acres or 67.8 million additional acres in 1974.

Urbanization and suburbanization have created major demands for the shifting of farm and other rural lands for residential, commercial, industrial, and urban service uses since the end of World War II. U.S. Census reports show that 8.2 million acres were delineated as "urbanized" in 1950, 16.0 million acres in 1960, and 22.5 million acres in 1970. These totals provide only a partial picture of what has happened. Large additional areas around most cities are suburbanized and can properly be counted as urban even though they have not been formally incorporated as cities. Frey classified 34.7 million acres as "urban" in 1974 (Frey, 1977). Several million additional acres are urban-associated in that their management is affected by scattered nearby suburban developments and speculative pressures for future suburban developments.

Highway building programs have called for public acquisition of substantial acreages since 1956 but these incremental additions added only slightly more than 10% to the area already used for highways and roads. Abandonment of some railroad rights-of-way has brought a slight reduction in the acreages used by railroads. Airports in turn are continuing to take more land (2.0 million acres in 1974) as more airports are built or enlarged.

Substantial acreages have been acquired or designated in recent decades as parks, recreation areas, or wildlife refuges. The area of state and national parks almost trebled between 1930 and 1974, while the area of public wildlife refuges increased 36-fold. Meanwhile, the areas used for na-

Table 5—Approximate acreages of land in principal nonagricultural land uses, 1930–1974.†

	1930	1945	1950	1959	1964	1969	1974
	million acres						
Urban areas	12.0	15.0	18.3	27.2	29.3	31.0	24.7
Highways and roads	19.0	19.1	19.4	20.5	21.2	21.0	21.6
Railroad rights of way	4.0	3.4	3.4	3.4	3.3	3.2	3.1
Airports	n.a.	1.3	1.3	1.4	1.5	1.8	2.0
State and national parks	12.0	17.9	18.7	29.7	31.9	35.0	36.8
Wildlife areas	1.0	4.7	8.9	17.2	29.0	32.0	35.8
National defense areas	2.0	24.8	21.4	24.4	23.6	23.4	25.1

† Sources: Data for 1930 from Natl. Resour. Board, 1934; for 1945 from Ruess et al., 1948; for 1950 from Wooten, 1953; for 1959 from Wooten et al., 1962; for 1964 from Frey et al., 1968; for 1969 from Frey, 1973; and for 1974 from Frey, 1977.

tional defense sites were greatly expanded during World War II, cut back after the war, and have since expanded again.

Several important miscellaneous uses of land are not itemized in Table 5. Among these are the large acreage of wilderness areas that have been designated mostly in National Forest areas, some 10 million acres of reservoir and man-made lakes, and around 3 million acres associated with open pit and other mining operations.

V. EFFECTS OF SOILS AND PLANTS ON LAND USE PATTERNS

Incomplete as it is, the above discussion indicates an obvious relationship between soil quality and the nation's land use practices. Our first settlements often utilized low-grade soils because of the initial emphasis given to accessibility. As transportation facilities developed, soil quality became a prime determining factor that influenced both the location of varying types of production and choices as to whether land would or would not remain in agriculture.

Plants also have had important deterministic effects on land use. Our first settlers were largely dependent upon the native maize for food and on the forests of New England and tobacco of the southern colonies for cash crops. Large areas are still used for these crops. But wheat, cotton, soybeans, peanuts, rice, sugarcane, and other crops have been successfully introduced and now account for large areas of cropland.

The planting of wheat corresponds closely with the westward push of settlement in the northern states. Wheat became a leading cash crop in the Connecticut Valley in the 1600's and was widely grown in the middle colonies (Edwards, 1940, p. 182). When disease adversely affected production in these areas, the peak areas of production moved successively to western New York, Ohio, Wisconsin, and the High Plains states.

Cotton followed a similar course. With the rise of European demand for cotton for textiles in the 1700's and Eli Whitney's development of the cotton gin in 1793, cotton production suddenly became a promising enterprise for southern planters. Production centered first in the coastal states, but then moved west as fertile areas were opened up for cultivation in Alabama, Mississippi, Louisiana, Arkansas, and Texas. A century later, the traditional cotton belt lost much of its comparative advantage for cotton production as irrigation and the adoption of mechanical pickers favored production in Arizona and California.

A. Significance of Emerging Demands

Soil and climatic conditions and the introduction of new plants and new cultural practices have given many areas in the United States high comparative advantages for certain types of land use. With our present perspective, we can continue to look to the midwestern U.S. for the production of corn and soybeans, the Great Plains states for wheat, the Lake states for hay and dairy products, Florida and California for citrus products, south Georgia for peanuts, southern Louisiana for sugarcane, and southern Texas and California for market vegetables.

Past experience demonstrates, however, that we live in a changing world. No area can assume that it will always enjoy the comparative advantages that now favor production of certain crops. New developments can be expected with changes in consumer demands and production technology. To keep on top, farm operators must adjust to changing demands and conditions. Yet important as it may be for businessmen to keep their options open, this practice is not always desirable when considered from the standpoint of public land use policy.

America's farms face a tremendous challenge in providing the supplies of food and other materials needed to meet our emerging domestic and international export demands. It is important that plans and policies be devised to help farmers meet this challenge. Many factors must be considered in the drafting of these plans. They must operate within the constraints of the threefold framework. Allowances must be made for changes in population numbers and purchasing power, adjustments for new technology, probably more expensive energy resources, and other factors such as changing tastes that may cause variations in either the demand for or the expected supplies of farm products. Recognition also must be given to the probable need to provide additional sites for urban and other high-valued developments.

Much as we need good agricultural land use planning, however, it must be noted that sound plans for the future cannot be developed without basic assumptions as to the areas that will remain in agricultural use. Identification and reservation of these areas will necessarily foreclose the opportunities many present owners have for selling their lands for nonagricultural uses.

Continued suburbanization poses a major threat to a stable agriculture. True, urban and suburban uses account for only about one and one-half percent of the nation's land area. But the expansion of these uses onto prime agricultural lands can have an impact on farming operations greatly out of proportion to the areas actually taken for these purposes. Millions of acres of farmland located near cities have already been blighted for continued agricultural use because: (i) they have been acquired by speculators who are waiting for the expected market conditions that will warrant their development, (ii) sales of scattered homesites to urban workers have raised rural property values and tax costs, and (iii) farm owners are managing their land with the expectation that it will soon be sold for urban-oriented developments.

One can compare what is happening to the spread of gully erosion in a fertile field. The fact that some lands have shifted to commercially higher and better uses and brought handsome capital gains to their owners has stirred up false hopes among thousands of others who hope that their lands will follow the same succession process. Many now assume that just as the forests of eastern America and the grasslands of the Great Plains gave way to cultivated fields, so too will their lands shift to urban uses. This logic is obviously misled. Enough land has already been preempted in and around our cities to care for a considerably larger urban population than we have or expect to have for years to come.

B. Need for Positive Land Use Policies

Positive policies are needed to stop the suburban erosion of our agricultural base. Steps must be taken to classify and identify the areas that should be retained in agriculture. Programs should then be developed to direct future urban developments onto the less productive lands and to work out equitable taxation and capital gains-sharing arrangements that will protect, not penalize, farm operators for keeping productive lands in permanent agriculture. Comparable policies and programs are needed to deal positively with pertinent nonagricultural land problems.

Acceptance of land use planning as a tool of community policy, and development of programs to carry area land use plans to fruition, can do much to bring about effective, efficient, and orderly land resource use in the United States. It must be recognized, however, that acceptance of this approach can bring far-reaching impacts on the environment in which individual decisions are made concerning future land uses. For 370 years American landowners have given primary emphasis to personal economic and physical and biological considerations as they have decided how land should be used. We are now more aware of the spillover effects individual actions and decisions can have on one's neighbors, one's community, and society-at-large. Land use planning and policies offer a means for minimizing the adverse effects and negative externalities that can result from unguided private actions. But their adoption will make the land use decision-making process more rigid and complex than it has been. More attention will be given to the impact individual decisions have on society, and operators will almost certainly find themselves subject to more public constraints and regulations.

LITERATURE CITED

Adams, C. F. 1963. Three episodes of Massachusetts history. Vol. 1. Russell & Russell, New York.

Barlowe, R. 1978. Land resource economics. 3rd ed. Prentice-Hall, Inc., Englewood Cliffs, N.J.

Bidwell, P. W., and J. I. Falconer. 1925. History of the agriculture of the northern United States, 1620–1860. Carnegie Inst. Publ. 358. Washington, D.C.

Birkbeck, M. 1918. Notes on a journey from the coast of Virginia to the Territory of Illinois. p. 1–37. In M. M. Quaife. Pictures of Illinois one hundred years ago. R. R. Donnelley & Sons, Chicago.

Bradford, W. 1912. History of Plymouth Plantation, 1620–1647. Vol. 1. Massachusetts Hist. Soc., Boston.

Clawson, M. 1975. Forests for whom and for what. Johns Hopkins University Press, Baltimore, Md.

Edwards, E. E. 1940. American agriculture—the first 300 years. p. 171–276. *In* Farmers in a changing world: 1940 yearbook of agriculture. U.S. Government Printing Office, Washington, D.C.

Ely, R. T., and G. S. Wehrwein. 1940. Land economics. The Macmillan Co., New York.

Fitzpatrick, J. C. (ed.) p. 32. The writings of George Washington. Vol. 3. U.S. Government Printing Office, Washington, D.C.

Frey, H. T. 1973. Major land uses for the United States: summary for 1969. U.S. Dep. of Agric., Agric. Econ. Rep. no. 247.

Frey, H. T. 1977. Major uses of land in the United States: summary for 1974. U.S. Dep. of Agric., Agric. Econ. Rep. 34.

Frey, H. T., O. E. Krause, and C. Dickason. 1968. Major uses of land and water in the United States with special reference to agriculture. U.S. Dep. of Agric., Agric. Econ. Rep. 149.

Gray, L. C. 1925. History of agriculture in the southern United States to 1860. Carnegie Inst. Publ. 430. Washington, D.C.

Hart, A. B. (ed.). 1927. Commonwealth history of Massachusetts. Vol. I. The States History Co., New York.

Hibbard, B. H. 1924. A history of the public land policies. The Macmillan Co., New York.

Jordan, T. G. 1964. Between the forest and the prairie. Agricultural history. Vol. 38. p. 205–216.

Loehr, R. S. 1952. Self sufficiency on the farm. Agricultural history. Vol. 26. p. 37–41.

MacGill, C. E., et al. 1917. History of transportation in the United States before 1860. The Carnegie Inst., Washington, D.C.

Meadows, D. H., D. L. Meadows, et al. 1972. The limits to growth. Universe Books, New York.

Morgan, E. S. 1968. The Puritan dilemma: the story of John Winthrop. Little, Brown & Co., Boston.

National Resources Board. 1934. Land planning committee report. U.S. Government Printing Office, Washington, D.C.

Ruess, L. A., H. H. Wooten, and F. J. Marschner. 1948. Inventory of major land uses. U.S. Dep. of Agric. Misc. Publ. no. 663.

Swierenga, R. P. 1968. Pioneers and profits: land speculation on the Iowa frontier. Iowa State University Press, Ames.

Turner, F. J. 1920. The frontier in American history. Henry Holt and Co., New York.

United Nations. 1974. The world population situation in 1970–1975 and its long range implications. U.N. Dep. of Social and Econ. Studies Rep. no. 56. United Nations, New York.

U.S. Census Office. 1883. Statistics of the population of the United States at the tenth census, 1880. Vol. I. U.S. Government Printing Office, Washington, D.C. p. XII–XVIII.

U.S. Department of Agriculture. 1972. Agricultural statistics, 1972. U.S. Government Printing Office, Washington, D.C.

U.S. Department of Agriculture. 1975. Agricultural statistics, 1975. U.S. Government Printing Office, Washington, D.C.

U.S. Department of Commerce, Bureau of the Census. 1974. Census of agriculture. U.S. Government Printing Office, Washington, D.C.

U.S. Department of Commerce, Bureau of the Census. 1976. Historical statistics of the United States, colonial times to 1970. U.S. Government Printing Office, Washington, D.C.

U.S. Department of Interior, Bureau of Mines. 1976. Minerals in the U.S. economy: ten-year supply-demand profiles for mineral and fuel commodities (1965–74). U.S. Government Printing Office, Washington, D.C.

U.S. House of Representatives. 1856. House Executive Doc. no. 13, 34th Congress, 1st Session.

Wooten, H. H. 1953. Major uses of land in the United States. U.S. Dep. of Agric. Tech. Bull. no. 1082.

Wooten, H. H., K. Gertel, and W. Pendleton. 1962. Major uses of land and water in the United States: summary for 1959. U.S. Dep. of Agric., Agric. Econ. Rep. 13.

2 National and State Experiences with Land Use Planning

NORMAN WENGERT

Department of Political Science
Colorado State University
Fort Collins, Colorado

I. INTRODUCTION

At local, state, and federal levels planning, regulation, and control of land uses are among the more controversial issues on the current political agenda. At the beginning of this decade Fred Bosselman and David Callies, two eminent land use lawyers, optimistically titled a report they had prepared for The Council on Environmental Quality *The Quiet Revolution in Land Use Control* (Bosselman & Callies, 1971). But the subject has been all but quiet, and there is reason to wonder whether a revolution has in fact been occurring. Pressures for change are intense, but resistance to change is equally persistent. And the wave of reform anticipated by Bosselman and Callies has often been thwarted and confused by legislative and judicial actions. But certainly the situation is not static. Change is everywhere apparent.

II. NATIONAL AND STATE EXPERIENCES

A. The Role of Controversy

In the American democratic political system the extent and intensity of controversy and conflict provide a rough measure of the importance of particular issues or topics. At the same time, Americans are often uncomfortable with controversy and conflict, preferring conformity and stability. Rocking the boat or challenging established ways is frequently frowned upon. But if controversy and conflict did not develop around important, critical issues, we would either be dead or living under a totalitarian dictatorship! Argument, conflict, debate, and struggle are indispensable in the American political system.

Because many different and inconsistent values and beliefs may be involved, resolution of policy issues almost inevitably creates winners and losers. And the struggle to win may involve formation of group support and the building of alliances and alignments—in some cases the "bare knuckled" application of power. And the rightness or virtue of the cause neither guarantees victory nor limits the methods used to achieve the goals sought. There is no assurance that the winners are always right and the losers wrong. Democracy learns by mistakes as well as by successes (Lindblom, 1968; Thompson, 1972; Wengert, 1971, 1973a, 1975c). At the same time, when controversy rests on misinformation and ignorance, debate and conflict may result in developing better data and increasing understanding. These are the classic premises of John Stuart Mill in justifying freedom of speech and press (Mill, 1939).

B. Land Use Issues and Interests

Current disputes over land use control are evidences of social change—change in the economy, change in where people live and in life styles, and change in consumption and production. These issues also reflect growth—population growth, economic growth and prosperity, and growth in economic resources or spendable income. They also evidence attempts by various groups and interests to impose their views of what is good for the community, not infrequently cloaking personal interests in the mantle of the public good (Schubert, 1960; Wengert, 1961).

The literature on urban problems abounds with self-criticism and castigation of the flight of Americans from central cities to suburbs, implying that urban and especially suburban growth and development since World War II has been racially biased, immoral, and generally reprehensible. To be sure, racial and economic segregation has been a factor in urban and suburban growth and related land use regulations. But perhaps more significant has been the impact of the increase in the number of people living in the United States, and their location and relocation. United States population jumped from about 145 million in 1945 to approximately 215 million in 1976.

It has been no mean achievement (unequaled in any other nation in the world) that in the years since 1945 the U.S. economy provided new housing for 70 million (about 20 million families), to which must be added increases in housing stock necessitated by internal migrations and relocations, and by the fact that few houses were built from 1929 to 1945. In these data lie the root causes of our land use planning and regulation problems. Development occurred at a fantastic rate. Given the magnitude of the task, it is perhaps significant that mistakes and dislocations were not more serious. In many cases, only hindsight has permitted identification of land use problems and encouraged a resolve to learn from past mistakes (Cribbet, 1965).

A cautionary comment is in order! By definition planning deals with the future and rests on assumptions with respect to that future. Neither planners nor policy makers have access to an unclouded crystal ball. Even the most highly motivated public as well as private actions and programs may result in unanticipated or unanalyzed externality effects (Wengert, 1976). Often we just do not know enough to make wise decisions for the future; too many independent variables may intervene to distort the best laid plans of mice or men.

The most frequently referred to ills of land use development of the past 30 years include so-called urban sprawl, strip development, fragmented and scattered suburbanization, overdevelopment, destruction of farm lands, exclusionary and discriminating regulations, failure to provide adequate open spaces, and escalating costs with resulting property tax inflation (Listokin, 1974). At the same time, it is clear that not everyone agrees with the diagnosis of these ills nor with the assessment of their severity (Wengert, 1975b). It is even more apparent that little consensus exists as to what the public interest in better land use is and how it is to be achieved (Inst. for Contemp. Studies, 1975).

Involved in the controversy over land use planning and control are three broad categories of interests: One of these interests is that of landowners (often farmers) whose lands are threatened by urbanization or who anticipate profits from development. Another group is composed of land developers who in the American economy unquestionably provide a necessary service, even though some are primarily seeking speculative profits. And finally a third group, less clearly identifiable, is essentially oriented to values rooted in the urban situation and includes conservationists, environmentalists, planners, and others interested in preservation of attractive landscapes, open spaces, and rural countrysides, promoting what they consider to be desirable living conditions and life styles. Others are, of course, also involved including taxpayer groups, and business and commercial interests favoring growth for the economic benefits which result.

Implicit in the controversies over planning and land use control are deeply held and divergent values with respect to what constitutes a quality environment and a satisfying way of life. And basic to the definition of these interests are very practical questions:

1) To what extent can *private* land use be regulated to achieve *public* benefits and purposes;

2) Does the owner of open or rural undeveloped land have a *right to an unrestricted monetary profit,* resulting not simply from the productivity of his land and from his labor and managerial inputs, but from unearned increments due to such fortuitous factors as location and population growth; and

3) To what extent is government authority to manage, direct, control, or prevent development and land use limited by federal and state constitutions and laws (Wengert, 1972, 1973b).

In oversimplified terms, the issues involve tensions between and reconciliation of public interests and private interests. In legal terms, the issue is one of defining limitations on government police power action. But definition of the police power does not involve a static set of principles, but evolving concepts. The following authoritative definition is considerably broader than that which would have been stated 50 years ago, reflecting the fact that principles of law are instruments of society, articulating its values and aspirations, as well as serving as constraints on public action. "The police power of a State today embraces regulations designed to promote the public convenience or the general prosperity as well as those to promote public safety, health, and morals, and is not confined to the suppression of what is offensive, disorderly, or unsanitary, but extends to what is for the greatest welfare of the state" (U.S. Senate, 1973).

C. The Historic Context

Selective land use controls were found in some cities even in Colonial times. Philadelphia, for example, required planting of shade trees along public sidewalks, and use of brick and other protective steps to minimize fire hazards were required in some communities. Regulation of nuisances, such as slaughter houses, was not uncommon (Beuscher & Wright, 1969, p. 1-15) and the platting of early cities to accommodate growth and development was not infrequent (viz. the standard grid pattern of many American cities) (Reps, 1965). But New York City zoning in 1916 (to deal with intensive, competing land use pressures in Manhattan) is usually considered the first comprehensive attempt at regulation. And zoning as a general practice received major impetus from the model state zoning act promoted by the U.S. Department of Commerce in 1924, to be followed by a model planning act in 1928. Both remain important elements in the wording of authorizing statutes in many states (Hagman, 1971, Ch. 4).

Two factors contributed to the rapid adoption of these model acts. *First,* was the fact that the 1920's was an era of rapid urbanization and suburban growth (accompanied by significant changes in the mode of land development and housing construction from small-scale individual lots and homes to larger projects and subdivisions—a trend carried even farther after World War II). The *second* was the dominantly protective character of zoning directed to preserving neighborhood homogeneity and preventing introduction of inconsistent or incongruous uses. Zoning, thus conceived, was built firmly on Common Law nuisance doctrines—and this remains the emphasis in many communities.

Most state statutes provided that zoning was to be "in accordance with the master plan" (Haar, 1955), the tool by which the goals and objectives of the master plan were to be achieved. But as zoning law developed few courts insisted on a master plan as a precondition for zoning, being willing to accept the sum of zoning decisions as the equivalent of a plan. Only recently have some state courts required comprehensive data as the logical underpinning for zoning decisions. Since zoning was not usually based on a master plan, three results became apparent: i) zoning became an ad hoc process concerned with single tracts or small neighborhoods; ii) it was dominated by developers and real estate interests; and iii) the amount of land in any particular zone category usually bore little relationship to community needs or interests. It is generally conceded, for example, that most communities have zoned far too much land industrial or commercial. And decisions with respect to residential lands often were based on the developers' desires for profit or on attempts to exclude low income or minority residents, rather than on concepts of community needs, interests, and responsibilities.

D. Constitutional Hurdles

Land use planning, regulation, and control has encountered (and continues to encounter) frequent and far-reaching challenges under state and federal constitutions, giving lawyers a unique and pervasive (some would say subversive) influence in this field.

Contrary to some assertions, it has never been a principle of Anglo-American law that the owner of land in fee simple could do anything he chose with his property. As Jeremy Bentham emphasized: "Property and law are born together, and die together. Before laws were made there was no property; take away laws and property ceases" (Cribbett, 1965, p. 245). Nuisance doctrines, well established in the Common Law, require one to so use his property as not to damage another. While of limited importance in frontier society where neighbors were often distant, externality effects, the essence of Common Law nuisance doctrines, are more evident and more damaging as population density increases. And since a more sophisticated technology permits measurement of externalities, the need for regulation becomes more apparent and more justifiable. Nuisances committed by Robinson Crusoe before Friday came did damage only to Crusoe himself. But once Friday reached the island, Crusoe's "monarchy over all he surveyed" had to be qualified by the interests of the new arrival!

But property, especially property in land, has had a special status in the development of democratic institutions, especially in the 17th and 18th centuries. It was not just convenient wording that led Virginia in June of 1776 and Massachusetts 4 years later to link property with *life* and *liberty* in their respective Bills of Rights (Commager, 1934, p. 103 and 107). Two hundred years of English history had established the importance of property in resisting government tyranny and oppression. The "Glorious Revolution of 1688" and John Locke's justifications of it articulating the importance of property and property rights were well-known to American Revolutionary leaders. It was not surprising, therefore, that the U.S. Bill of Rights specified (Amendment V) that "No person shall be . . . deprived of life, liberty, or property, without due process of law; nor shall private property be taken for public use, without just compensation."

The history of the due process and "taking" clauses is long and involved and cannot be reviewed in this chapter. "The Taking Issue" as related to land use control has, however, been thoroughly explored in an excellent study by Fred Bosselman, David Callies, and John Banta published by The Council on Environmental Quality (Bosselman et al., 1973), although not all legal scholars accept the conclusions of that study.

Zoning was accepted by the U.S. Supreme Court as a proper exercise of the police power in *Village of Euclid v. Ambler Realty Co.,* (U.S. Supreme Court, 1926), but strict constitutional constraints on land use regulation had been spelled out 4 years earlier by Justice Holmes in *Pennsylvania Coal Co. v. Mahon* (U.S. Supreme Court, 1922). It is the latter opinion, in fact, which has provided the foundation for hundreds of cases challenging zoning and other types of land use regulation as a taking of property requiring compensation. Since most subsequent litigation involving "The Taking Issue" has been in state courts, a great variation in application and in interpretation of what constitutes a "taking" has resulted. And despite the persuasive analysis by Bosselman and associates that *Pennsylvania Coal Co. v. Mahon* was neither sound nor in accordance with previously established constitutional doctrines, "The Taking Issue" remains one of the most frequently used challenges to land use regulation.

A constitutional concept making it difficult to attack the substantive content of land use plans and regulations is the almost universal practice of courts to regard land use regulations as "legislative" in character. This classification brings into play hoary doctrines of separation of powers which (at least since 1937) has meant that courts will defer to declaratory and conclusory statements of legislative bodies (City Councils or County Commissions in cases of land use regulation) without examining the logical relationship between the action taken and supporting data concerning the problem to be solved, nor permitting challenges with respect to the reasonableness of the action taken, nor the motives of the regulating body. In short, standards of administrative due process, applied regularly and consistently to most regulations emanating from federal and state agencies (Davis, 1971), are not generally applied to land use regulations.

E. Zoning Assessed

Zoning and subdivision control remain major forms of land use regulation in most communities. Although one or the other or both of these types of land use regulation may have been authorized in many states for many years, being optional in character, they have often not been utilized by local governments (Marcus & Groves, 1972). The last decade has seen these techniques used more widely. In some states, some new approaches are being tried and others are being proposed, reflecting new and different perceptions of problems of land use planning and control.

As suggested, urban zoning, initially conceived of as a protective device to secure neighborhood homogeneity and preserve property values, was never intended as a dynamic technique for growth management. Yet, in many jurisdictions, zoning is the dominant device to influence growth and shape land use (Williams, 1975). Many criticisms of zoning therefore reflect the conclusion that it is a technique unsuited for dealing with present land use problems as these are presently perceived in many quarters (Healy, 1976). The more important criticisms have been:

1) *Parochial emphasis and responsibility; jurisdictional conflicts.*
   Those critical of zoning point out that its scope is too local, being limited to the boundaries of the zoning jurisdiction, usually the city.

While a few states extend extraterritorial zoning powers to cities, their exercise often conflicts with powers of adjacent communities or counties. Thus annexation is often a prelude to effective zoning. Such growth zones as lie immediately outside the boundaries of a city are usually inadequately controlled. And in most states, county zoning, often dominated by rural and development interests, is primitive and ineffective. Conversely, many land use problems transcend local boundaries, and affect regional or state interests.

2) *Negative.* Zoning tends to be negative or restrictive, spelling out what *cannot* be done, rather than indicating how growth or development should occur. Zoning, together with most subdivision controls, provides a kind of check list which when complied with permits development to proceed. It does not provide a means for determining whether a particular development is in the public interest. As a result, most zoning is ineffective in limiting strip development or urban sprawl.

3) *Not usually related to a specific growth plan.* Zoning tends to be based on a kind of land capability and suitability assessment and not on community need concepts. Hence the overzoning of commercial and industrial lands and a failure to determine housing mixes that meet human needs and are not discriminatory.

4) *"Wait and See" approaches.* In many communities, in the absence of tightly reasoned comprehensive planning, much zoning represents a "wait and see" stance with zoning authorities ready and willing to change zoning on application and ad hoc justification. As a result, zoning has become a political game played for the advantages of developers rather than as a device for achieving public land use goals (Makielski, 1966).

5) *"Windfalls and Wipeouts."* Zoning (as is true of many land use regulations) may bring windfall profits to particular landowners. But it may also result in substantial losses, particularly in expectations, to others. The latter may not involve a taking, since some courts accept rather drastic zoning restrictions as proper applications of police power authority, seeking to balance private vs. public costs and benefits, with compensation being required only in extreme situations.

6) *Zoning is permissive or passive.* While all states authorize local zoning, according to the Council of State Governments, as of 1975, zoning and subdivision control was required in less than 10 states. And these mandatory requirements have been enacted only in the past decade. Moreover, even where mandatory, there are often no sanctions or review from higher authority. And while a few of the mandatory statutes indicate that in the absence of local action the state will act, the record in this regard is weak (Siegan, 1972). It is a hard fact of local politics that zoning and other land use action occur most frequently when federal or state funds are made available for implementing state requirements. The carrot seems more effective than the stick!

7) *Review of zoning decisions is inadequate.* While most zoning laws provide for review on application to a local review board, such surveillance has tended to be procedural rather than substantive. In most cases, an aggrieved party may appeal to the courts where again procedure rather than the substantive wisdom of the land use decision is of primary concern.

8) *Zoning and discrimination.* In far too many jurisdictions, partly because zoning has not been required to be in accordance with a master plan, and partly because the number of zones and sub-zones have proliferated to 10 or even 20 categories, zoning has provided a means for excluding racial minorities and low-income housing (Babcock & Bosselman, 1973).

F. Master Planning Assessed

Although authorized, development of a comprehensive or master plan was also usually optional with local governments (Linowes & Allensworth, 1973). Middle-sized and larger cities tended to have planning commissions supported by technically trained planning staffs. Urbanizing counties and some regional governments were similarly manned. But many rural-agricultural counties, even when planning commissions had been established, often had no professional staffs and preparation of master plans was not pressed (Reps, 1967). But in the past decade, a growing number of state legislatures have been requiring preparation of master plans by both cities and counties, although as of 1975 the Council of State Governments found that less than 15 states mandated planning. In a few states, courts have begun to insist the zoning must be "in accordance with the comprehensive plan." Having planning staffs, or employees designated *planners,* does not warrant the quality or relevance of plans produced. In fact many comprehensive plans have been idle exercises in report writing and map making—providing no effective basis for government action, and ending up ignored. State surveillance, virtually nonexistant, would seem to be badly needed—provided state review is other than pro forma, and deals with real issues of land use development needs and goals.

G. Subdivision Controls Assessed

Subdivision controls represent a recent addition to the regulatory structure (Hagman, 1971, Ch. 9). In part an extension of zoning, subdivision controls are a means by which local governments specify the terms and conditions for large tract development. Subdivision controls may require construction of streets, provision of water and sewer facilities, dedication of school and park lands, and certification of the suitability of an area for development (e.g., geologic conditions such as drainage). To some extent subdivision controls provide a kind of consumer protection. But more importantly they give the growing community some control over the character of growth. In most cases, however, subdivision controls represent a kind of check list which, when complied with, tend to be regarded as giving the developer the right to proceed. Thus subdivision controls have not prevented urban sprawl or strip development—one reason being that most control agencies themselves have not had goals and objectives (a master plan) for their communities and thus have not been in a position to challenge the wisdom of a proposed development, contenting themselves with testing whether it meets the check list requirements.

H. Rural Zoning

Although the technique is similar (i.e., an ordinance usually enacted by the county), rural zoning has a history considerably different from urban zoning, posing a different set of administrative, legal, and constitutional problems (USDA, 1972). Rural zoning, authorized in all fifty states, originated in Wisconsin in the 1920's (Rowlands et al., 1948) where it was regarded as a device for rationalizing land uses in the northern cut-over areas of the state. As originally developed rural zoning was regarded as a technique for designating best uses of land and in some cases for restricting uses of hazard areas. There is an implication in rural zoning that land classification will bear some relationship to basic soil capability as determined by soil surveys, but jurisdictional confusion between county planning commissions and soil conservation districts (which may have unused ordinance making powers) has limited uses of soils data. Federal pressures through the Flood Insurance act has encouraged designation of flood plains, and restriction of flood plain development. But in general, where rural zoning has been utilized it has been descriptive of *existing land uses* rather than a tool for indicating *desired land uses* or for restricting land uses not desired. This descriptive status of most rural zoning explains why rural zones tend to be considered holding categories readily changed to accommodate development. Rural zoning has not shaped patterns of urbanization or constrained urban sprawl and strip development. It has not prevented unwanted recreation homes, or industrial and commercial establishments. Neither has rural zoning contributed significantly to preservation of agriculture or forestry, or to maintenance of open spaces.

There is serious question, in any case, whether rural zoning under the police power prescribing specified uses, where alternate uses do not damage others and do not involve natural hazard threats, can be constitutionally enforced. The assertion by a community of a desire to achieve "rational" land uses or even to save taxpayers money at the expense of particular landowners probably does not provide a sufficient basis for police power regulation. The issue has seldom been clearly drawn, however, because of the readiness of most rural zoning authorities to change zoning restrictions to accommodate landowners and development.

I. Growth Management and Newer Control Techniques

In looking at land use problems as well as solutions, it is probably useful to distinguish between those that are *urban related* or *urban instigated* and directly involve urbanization and urban growth and those that concern *preservation of agricultural land, open spaces, outdoor recreation.*

Land development for urban purposes, of course, has housing as its primary objective. While most surveys still indicate that the American dream is the detached single-family home surrounded by a substantial amount of land, present-day housing costs are said to be out of the reach of 80% of the population. Urban-related problems include subdivision and strip development where "leap frogging" and scatteration of subdivisions has been particularly apparent. The resulting urban sprawl, which includes both scatteration and low-density development, is often criticized because of social costs associated with it.

In nonurban areas increasing concern has been voiced regarding preservation of prime agricultural lands. This concern is based upon a desire to protect the base for food production, but often may include a desire to preserve agriculture as an attractive way of life, and to sustain job and other economic opportunities associated with farm enterprise.

Preservation of open space and attractive rural landscapes benefits people living in rural areas, but most interest in the subject tends to be urban based. Similarly, interest in development of second homes and of recreation areas usually has an urban base, but both positive and negative impacts of such developments are felt in rural or nonurban communities.

In any case, a major element in the demand for more effective planning and land use control is the desire to respond rationally to growth. Put another way, land use problems are most acute where growth rates are high, most growth representing expansion of urban populations requiring new housing and related public facilities, including shopping centers, utilities, roads, and schools.

"Growth Management" is thus becoming a popular term for designating a variety of approaches to urban-generated and urban-related land use problems (Burchell & Listokin, 1975; Carter, 1974; Hughes, 1974; Reilly, 1973; Scott et al., 1975; Brower et al., 1976).

Basically, proposals for growth management rest on an assumption that the rate, density, and location of residential growth in urban areas must be directed in accordance with specifically identified community interests. Typically, growth management is defined in terms of regulating the conversion of rural lands to urban needs, and tends to be introvertive in its concern for the growth problems of a particular community; as will be suggested later, herein lie difficult constitutional problems.

Among factors leading to a consideration of growth management are situations in which development of new lands (subdivisions) may exceed administrative or fiscal capacity of local government to provide adequate infrastructure facilities or necessary services. Another strong rationale for growth management is the desire among some communities to protect a way of life, often to remain small and rural. Sometimes a concern for environmental damage and for the relationship of growth to the natural environment may be reflected in growth management proposals. Related to this latter concern is that focusing on the loss of productive lands in agriculture, forestry, and perhaps in minerals. Growth management may also be motivated by a desire to adjust growth to available water and energy supplies. In summary, growth management deals with the management of change, seeking to direct forces of change to achieve community interests and objectives.

Still largely untried but arousing much discussion are growth-management systems which require government to identify growth zones in which, to the exclusion of all other areas, growth will be encouraged.

The establishment of greenbelts and open space areas (whether by purchase or by regulation) can shape growth patterns. Here, more research seems called for, the British experience suggesting that unanticipated externalities often result from the establishment of greenbelts and open space areas.

A great deal has been written on using utility extensions (water, sewerage, gas, electricity) as tools for shaping growth. In most cases, such controls tend to provide guidance rather than complete direction. In Ramapo, New York, the control system, which placed considerable emphasis upon planned and phased development of capital facilities including utilities, allowed developers, by themselves investing in certain facilities, to speed up their inclusion in the growth plan. In some cases, legal doctrines of a utility's obligation to serve have prevented the use of utility extensions as control mechanisms (Wengert & Held, 1975).

Control over school facilities, parks, roads, and services has been suggested as an additional means for controlling growth. But, in this respect also, obligations of governments to provide services, and the rights of citizens to live and work where they choose, may restrict this approach to growth management.

Implicit in questions of utility extensions and provision of schools and other services has been the question of who pays for what. It is often asserted that the suburban homeowner, living in a new development, is subsidized by those living in older sections of the city. Many of the discussions of this point are, unfortunately, not based upon good cost accounting.

Two factors tend to confuse the situation. *First,* many of the capital facilities are paid for over a time period far less than their actual physical life. Water supply mains, for example, have a physical life of as long as 75 years, and yet are most commonly paid for in from 20 to 40 years. Thus the question of "subsidy" from one generation to another may always be involved no matter where one lives in a city. *Second,* given high population mobility, it is rare for a particular resident to live in the same house for the full period during which the physical capital facilities are being paid for. Charges are assessed against particular pieces of property under the property tax system which dominates the local tax structure, and unless taxes are capitalized in the price of a property, it is difficult to determine the extent to which particular individuals subsidize other individuals because movement from one residence to another makes analysis of the burdens and benefits in personal terms difficult if not impossible.

Two major court cases have recently dealt with this subject of timing or phased zoning. The one case involves the City of Ramapo, New York, in which the highest court of New York State approved the phasing of growth (New York Court of Appeals, 1972). The other case is that of the City of Petaluma, California, in which, after the federal district court found phased development to be unconstitutional (U.S. Federal District Court for Northern California, 1974), the Circuit Court of Appeals sustained the Petaluma plan (U.S. Federal Court of Appeals, Ninth Circuit, 1975).

The Circuit Court of Appeals decided the Petaluma case on the basis of standing to sue, pointing out that the plantiff, Construction Industry Association, was not about to have its "right to travel" infringed by the Petaluma Plan, and "right to travel" was the sole basis for the lower court decision. Such comments as the Circuit Court made on the substantive issues, and they were very few, were in the nature of *obiter dicta* and thus of doubtful precedential value. From the point of view of growth management, however, a significant difference between the two situations would seem to have been that phased development in Ramapo was based on detailed study and voluminous reports, whereas the limit to new housing units in Petaluma reflected a more arbitrary determination, with much of the justification for the number of units permitted being developed in the attorneys' briefs.

A major problem of growth management to which far more analysis needs to be devoted concerns possible externality effects. There seems little doubt but that governmental actions to control growth may result in "windfalls" for some and "wipeouts" for others.

From the point of view of the larger community—the region, the state, or the nation, costs to provide education and many infrastructure facilities will occur no matter where the families may live or the growth occur, and so attempts to keep people out of a particular community on grounds of costs to present taxpayers may in fact reflect an unwillingness to absorb a "fair share" of national, state, or regional growth.

In developing "fair share" doctrines some courts have emphasized that local governmental units cannot make land use decisions out of context from the larger area of which they may be a part. This view was expressed by Chief Justice Hall of the New Jersey Supreme Court, in the recent case of Southern Burlington County NAACP vs. the Township of Mt. Laurel (New Jersey Supreme Court, 1975). The court found that there was no deliberate exclusionary policy, but stated that the township of Mt. Laurel could not make its land use decisions without relating them to the larger region of which it was a part. In this context, the court concluded that the *effect* of land use zoning by the township of Mt. Laurel was in fact exclusionary. The court stated: "However, it is fundamental and not to be forgotten that the zoning power is a police power of the state, and the local authority is acting only as a delegate to that power and is restricted in the same manner as is the state. So, when regulation does have a substantial external impact, the welfare of the state's citizens beyond the borders of the particular municipality cannot be disregarded and must be recognized and served.''

Thus the New Jersey Supreme Court and some other state courts have been firm in insisting that communities must absorb a ''fair share'' of low income and minority housing. But holdings have not been uniform. And a very recent U.S. Supreme Court decision (U.S. Supreme Court, 1977) has stated that there must be evidence of an actual intent to exclude, rather than simply an exclusionary effect. As a practical matter, in addition, unless a community is itself involved in housing construction, it may be difficult to develop inclusionary programs (Franklin et al., 1974; Babcock & Bosselman, 1973). Certainly the simple act of zoning certain tracts for low cost and/or multiple family units will not bring about their construction.

Another problem, clearly implied in the ''fair share'' decisions, concerns the level of government at which growth management should be undertaken. Given the tradition of local control of land use planning, it is often assumed that the local level should continue to handle these questions. There are, however, a number of reasons which suggest that reasonable and responsible growth manaement cannot occur at the local level, but must be at the regional or state level (Bosselman, 1973). Some wise comments on the over-emphasis on the very local level were expressed by Chief Justice Vanderbilt of the New Jersey Supreme Court: ''. . . the effective development of a region should not and cannot be made to depend upon the adventitious location of municipal boundaries, often prescribed decades or even centuries ago, and based in many instances on considerations of geography, commerce, or of politics, that are no longer significant. . .'' (New Jersey Supreme Court, 1949).

J. Moratoria on Development

In some situations where growth has clearly outrun the capacity of a community to manage it, a moratorium on housing starts or on new subdivisions has sometimes been declared. Most frequently this device is used where water, sewer, and sewage treatment facilities lag behind development (USDA, 1963). The moratorium tends to be an emergency device, subject to rather severe limitations as to the period of time for which it may be utilized. Since the development of a master plan may take several years, and since that plan may shape development in the future, courts in some states have allowed moratoria on development as an interim control while planning is proceeding.

K. Land Banking

In several Canadian provinces, in Australia, and in Sweden, ''land banking'' is an important adjunct of the planning and land use control process. In its simplest form, land banking means that government purchases land for later use in accordance with a long-range master plan. When the land is ready to be used it may be leased or sold to private owners. In the meantime, however, the government has control of the land by virtue of its title and may rent it out for temporary uses.

L. Development Rights

Two basic types of development rights are currently being discussed. The first type involves the purchase of development rights by a governmental unit, leaving the landowner with certain limited rights. Thus in Connecticut and Suffolk County, New York, the purchase of all rights to development of certain lands, leaving only agricultural use rights in the hands of owners, has been proposed. Similar approaches are being considered in New Jersey and Maryland. The major limitation of this approach to land use control is, of course, that of the fiscal capacity of the purchasing government. It is to be noted that the Connecticut proposal to preserve less than 16% of the area of the state involves an estimated cost of $500 million ($1,000 to $1,500/acre; $2,470 to $3,700/ha) and, in Suffolk County, the sponsors of the purchase program are talking in terms of $4,000 to $6,000/ acre ($9,900 to $15,000/ha) for a county total of as high as $120,000,000.

An imaginative proposal has been made to establish *transferrable* development rights systems, which, it is thought, would involve little or no public funding, although in some proposals a residual public land banking function is recognized. This approach has had little experimental development, and it is not at all clear that it will work as proposed (Rose, 1975; Wengert & Graham, 1974).

M. Preserving Agricultural Land

Preservation of open spaces can be secured by a variety of acquisition techniques ranging from eminent domain and fee simple purchases, through land banking, less than fee acquisition, leaseholds, and compensable regulations (Wengert, 1975a).

Among the consequences for agriculture resulting from recent patterns of urban growth have been:

1) Removing productive land from farming.
2) Fragmentation of farm units to the point where a viable agriculture was often impossible.
3) Increasing costs of land as agricultural land responded to the speculative opportunities of the development area.
4) Associated with the increased costs of land was the increase in property taxes applied to farm lands adjacent to cities. (Many states have provided a variety of tax relief systems which have had as their objective the preservation of farming, but the record of results from such efforts is not too favorable).
5) Difficulties for young farmers to begin farming operations in the shadow of cities.

6) Inflated land prices have complicated the inheritance of land because of high inheritance or estate taxes.

While few would today subscribe without reservation to the Jeffersonian declaration that those who toil in the earth are the sons of God, many Americans do have a romantic regard for family farming. One reason, of course, is that in terms of national geography a substantial portion of the 48 contiguous states is devoted to agricultural uses, even though the number of farms and farm families has declined substantially in the past 50 years.

In addition to a romantic regard for the agricultural way of life, there are those who wish to maintain farming because of its scenic or landscape attractiveness. A mixed pattern of land use, which includes pastures, meadows, cultivated fields, and forests, provides an attractive basis for recreational development.

For some, the preservation of agricultural lands and agricultural uses of those lands is directly related to America's capacity to provide food for at least some of the starving of the world. In this connection, it is often asserted with concern that we are giving up too much of our productive capacity for urban purposes. Here some statistics are useful.

It is estimated that at present approximately 3 to 4% of the area of the United States is devoted to cities, streets, roads, highways, and similar urban uses. It is also estimated that perhaps another 3% of the land area will be devoted to such purposes by the year 2000 (USDA, 1973, 1974a).

Gross data with respect to the impact of urbanization on agriculture can be misleading. About 70% of the U.S. population (1970) resides within standard metropolitan statistical areas (SMSA's). From 1960 to 1970 the density of SMSA's increased from 302 to 355 people/m² (117 to 137 people/km²). At the same time, a substantial amount of open land is found in the SMSA regions. Thus, about 13% of the land area of the 48 contiguous states lies within SMSA's, with 30% of the northeastern region being so situated. At the same time, *cropland harvested* in SMSA's is about proportional to the share of total U.S. land area, that is, 14%.

In 1969, SMSA's provided 21.5% of the total *value* of the farm products sold in the 48 contiguous states, a percentage about double that of the cropland in the SMSA's indicating generally high productivity (Otte, 1974). The challenge is to find ways and means to preserve agriculture in the shadow of the cities, not simply as a way to hold land until it can be urbanized. The inability to classify agricultural lands, and then to make the classification stick with legal force, contributes to the contrast between the situation in the United States and that found in Europe, in the Rhine Valley of Germany, for example, where farms and farming extend to the very boundaries of industrial facilities.

At the same time, aggregative data for the nation as a whole can be misleading since regional analysis may suggest relationships obscured in the national totals. A state like California, for example, produces the total crop for eight products, and 80% of the crop for nine other products. It ranks first, nationally, in the production of 40 crops. Thus neither California nor the nation can ignore consequences of urban development which take land out of production. While avacados may not be essential, oranges are (Snyder, 1966).

Within a regional context, moreover, certain land uses may have greater significance than others. With increasing transportation costs, it may become more significant to produce dairy products, especially fluid milk, as close as possible to the consuming markets. Transporting water by truck is costly!

In the western U.S., a particular problem arises in connection with the preservation of irrigated land in agricultural use. The land itself or the water rights, indispensible to continued agricultural uses, may be purchased. In either case, farming is ended. There is some reason for concern, moreover, that the loss of irrigated land has severe consequences for the region in which this loss occurs (Anderson et al., 1976). In this connection, the taking of irrigation water for urban uses has been slowed down in Colorado by a recently enacted statute requiring a thorough analysis of alternatives and impacts by the local government seeking such water, with ultimate court approval of its action. But urban demands for water continue to threaten irrigated agriculture (cp., the classic Owens Valley case involving Los Angeles).

Various approaches to preserving agricultural land have been proposed; some have been tried. Rural zoning and development rights have been discussed above. Another approach to preserve agricultural land and forest stands tried in a number of jurisdictions involves special taxation policies, primarily differential assessments or the taxing of the "use value" as against the "market value" of the land (U.S. Counc. on Environ. Qual., 1976; USDA, 1974b). Nine states have preferential assessment based on use value with no penalties if the uses are changed. Eighteen states have a kind of deferred taxation system with a kind of penalty or reachback tax assessed at the time use is changed from the favored use to some other use. And finally, several states have restrictive agreements whereby the landowner contracts to use his property in a particular way for a particular time (California and New York). Although touted as very significant, differential taxation systems seem to have been less than impressively successful in preserving land for desired uses.

A second approach to preserving agriculture is the designation of agricultural zones which often may include a contractual relationship between the landowner and the governmental unit. There is little evidence that this approach, if not supported by the purchase of development rights, goes very far in preserving agricultural land. In fact, devices and techniques short of purchase all seem inadequate.

N. Federal Programs

This chapter would not be complete if it did not recognize that some of the more drastic effects on land use may originate from a variety of federal programs—some only indirectly concerned with land use and others directly dealing with this subject. Even without a federal land use act, programs concerned with energy, water, air, and other major resources already deal with specific aspects of land use. Both the Air Quality Act of 1970 and the Water Pollution Control Act Amendments of 1972 recognize that these two major environmental problems have their origins in land use patterns. Various state air pollution programs focus on land use. Section 208 of the Water Pollution Control Act requires that area-wide waste treatment plans must be developed for the entire area of each state. Similarly, it has been charged that our inefficient use of land in the suburban areas of major cities accounts for the waste of substantial quantities of energy. Thus anyone considering trends in land use planning must take into account the way in which these federally dominated programs may influence state and local actions, which in turn may impinge on land use. This subject is crying for detailed analysis (Stevens, 1973; McAllister, 1973). In addition, the management of federal lands, especially in western states, can have important consequences for private land use.

LITERATURE CITED

Anderson, R. L., N. I. Wengert, and R. D. Heil. 1976. The physical and economic effects on the local agricultural economy of water transfer from irrigation companies to cities in the northern Denver metropolitan area. Completion Rep. no. 75. Environ. Resour. Center, Colorado State Univ., Fort Collins, Colo.

Babcock, R. F., and F. P. Bosselman. 1973. Exclusionary zoning: land use regulation and housing in the 1970's. Praeger Publ., New York.

Beuscher, J. H., and R. R. wright. 1969. Cases and materials on land use. West Publ. Co., St. Paul, Minn.

Bosselman, F. P. 1973. Can the town of Ramapo pass a law to bind the rights of the whole world? Fla. State Univ. Law Rev. 1:234–265.

Bosselman, F. P., and David Callies. 1971. The quiet revolution in land use control. Counc. on Environ. Qual., U.S. Government Printing Office, Washington, D.C.

Bosselman, F. P., David Callies, and John Banta. 1973. The taking issue. Counc. on Environ. Qual., U.S. Government Printing Office, Washington, D.C.

Brower, D. J., D. W. Owens, Ronald Rosenberg, Ira Botvinick, and Michael Mandel. 1976. Urban growth management through development timing. Praeger Publ., New York.

Burchell, R. W., and David Listokin (ed.). 1975. Future land use. Center for Urban Policy Res., Rutgers Univ., New Brunswick, N. J.

Carter, L. J. 1974. The Florida experience: land and water policy in a growth state. Johns Hopkins Univ. Press, Baltimore, Md.

Commager, H. S. (ed.). 1934. Documents of American history. F.S. Crofts & Co., New York.

Cribbet, J. E. 1965. Changing concepts in the law of land use. In Land Use Symp. Iowa Law Rev. 50:245–278.

Davis, K. C. 1971. Discretionary justice. Univ. of Illinois Press, Urbana.

Franklin, H. M., David Falk, and A. J. Levin. 1974. In-zoning, a guide for policy-makers on inclusionary land use programs. The Potomac Inst., Washington, D.C.

Haar, Charles. 1955. In accordance with a comprehensive plan. Harvard Law Rev. 68:1154–1175.

Hagman, D. G. 1971. Urban planning and land development control law. West Publ. Co., St. Paul, Minn.

Healy, R. G. 1976. Land use and the states. Johns Hopkins Univ. Press, Baltimore, Md.

Hughes, J. W. (ed.). 1974. New dimensions in urban planning: growth controls. Center for Urban Policy Res., Rutgers Univ., New Brunswick, N. J.

Institute for Contemporary Studies. 1975. No land is an island: individual rights and government control of land use. (A book of essays). Inst. for Contemp. Students, San Francisco, Calif.

Lindblom, C. E. 1968. The policy-making process. Prentice-Hall, Inc., Englewood Cliffs, N.J.

Linowes, R. R., and D. T. Allensworth. 1973. The politics of land use planning, zoning, and the private developer. Praeger Publ., New York.

Listokin, David (ed.). 1974. Land use controls: present problems and future reform. Center for Urban Policy Res., Rutgers Univ., New Brunswick, N.J.

McAllister, D. M. (ed.). 1973. Environment: a new focus for land-use planning. Natl. Sci. Found., U.S. Government Printing Office, Washington, D.C.

Makielski, Jr., S. F. 1966. The politics of zoning: the New York experience. Columbia Univ. Press, New York.

Marcus, Norman, and M. W. Groves (ed.). 1972. The new zoning: legal, administrative, and economic concepts and techniques. Praeger Publ., New York.

Mill, J. S. 1939. On liberty. p. 949–1039. *In* E. A. Burtt. The English philosophers from Bacon to Mill. The Modern Library, Random House, New York.

New Jersey Supreme Court. 1949. Duffcon Concrete Products Inc. v. Cresskill, 1 N.J. 509.

New Jersey Supreme Court. 1975. Southern Burlington County N.A.A.C.P. v. Twp. of Mt. Laurel, 67 N.J. 151:336 A. 2d 713.

New York Court of Appeals. 1972. Golden v. Planning Board of Ramapo, 30 NY 2d 359; 295 N.E. 2d 291; 334 N.Y.S. 2d 138.

Otte, R. C. Farming in the city's shadow. 1974. p. 101–171. *In* Agriculture, rural development, and the use of land. Pap. compiled by Subcomm. on Rural dev. of the Comm. on Agric. and For., U.S. Senate, 93rd Cong. 2d Sess.

Reilly, W. K. (ed.). 1973. The use of land: a citizens' policy guide to urban growth. Thomas Y. Crowell Co., New York.

Reps, J. W. 1965. The making of urban America: a history of city planning in the United States. Princeton Univ. Press, Princeton, N. J.

Reps, J. W. 1967. The future of American planning-requiem or renascence? Land Use Controls 1:1–16.

Rose, J. G. (ed.). 1975. The transfer of development rights: a new technique of land use regulation. Center for Urban Policy Research, Rutgers Univ., New Brunswick, N.J.

Rowlands, Walter, Fred Trenk, and Raymond Penn. 1948. Rural zoning in Wisconsin. Wisconsin Agric. Exp. Stn. Bull. 479. Univ. of Wisconsin, Madison.

Schubert, Glendon. 1960. The public interest. Bobbs-Merrill, Indianapolis, Ind.

Scott, R. W., D. J. Brower, and D. D. Miner. (ed.). 1975. Management and control of growth. 3 Vols. Urban Land Inst., Washington, D.C.

Siegan, B. H. 1972. Land use without zoning. Lexington Books, D.C. Heath and Co., Lexington, Mass.

Snyder, H. J. 1966. A new program for agricultural land use stabilization: the California land conservation act of 1965. Land Econ. 42:29–41.

Stevens, J. L. 1973. Impact of federal legislation and programs on private land in urban and metropolitan development. Praeger Publ., New York.

Thompson, D. L. (ed.). 1972. Politics, policy, and natural resources. The Free Press, New York.

U.S. Council on Environmental Quality. 1976. Untaxing open space: an evaluation of the effectiveness of differential assessment of farms and open space. U.S. Government Printing Office, Washington, D.C.

U.S. Court of Appeals, Ninth Circuit. 1975. Construction industry of Sonoma county v. the city of Petaluma, 522 F. 2d 897.

U.S. Department of Agriculture, Yearbook of Agriculture. 1962. Programming public facilities to shape community growth. p. 460–468.

U.S. Department of Agriculture, Economic Research Service. 1972. Rural zoning in the United States: analysis of enabling legislation. Misc. Pub. no. 1232, Washington, D.C.

U.S. Department of Agriculture, Economic Research Service. 1973. Major uses of land in the United States: summary for 1969. Agric. Econ. Rep. no. 247.

U.S. Department of Agriculture, Economic Research service. 1974a. Our land and water resources: current and prospective supplies and uses. Misc. Pub. no. 1290.

U.S. Department of Agriculture, Economic Research Service. 1974b. State programs for the differential assessment of farm and open space land. Agric. Econ. Rep. no. 256.

U.S. District Court for Northern California. 1974. Construction industry of Sonoma county v. the city of Petaluma, 375 F. Suppl. 574.

U.S. Senate. 1973. The constitution of the United States of America: analysis and interpretation. Document no. 92-82. U.S. Government Printing Office, Washington, D.C. p. 1317.

U.S. Supreme Court. 1922. Pensylvania Coal Co. v. Mahon. 260 U.S. 393; 43 S.Ct. 158; 67 L.Ed. 322; 28 A.L.R. 1321.

U.S. Supreme Court. 1926. Village of Euclid, Ohio, v. Ambler Realty Co. 272 U.S. 365; 47 S.Ct. 114; 71L.Ed. 303; 54 A.L.R. 1016.

U.S. Supreme Court. 1977. Village of Arilington Heights et al. v. Metropolitan Housing Development Corp. et al. Decided 11 Jan. 1977. Prepub. release.

Wengert, N. I. 1961. Resource development and the public interest. Nat. Resour. J. 1:207–223.

Wengert, N. I. 1971. Environmental policy and political decisions: the reconciliation of facts, values, and interests. p. 367–378. In E. J. Monke (ed.) Biological effects in the hydrological cycle. Purdue Univ., West Lafayette, Ind.

Wengert, N. I. 1972. Legal aspects of land use policies, plans, and implementation. p. 142–160. In National land use policy—objectives, components, implementation. Soil Conserv. Soc. of Am., Ankeny, Iowa.

Wengert, N. I. 1973a. Political and social accommodation: the political process and environmental preservation. p. 35–44. In A. E. Utton and D. H. Henning (ed.) Environmental policy concepts and international implications. Praeger Publ., New York.

Wengert, N. I. 1973b. Public rights in determining land use. p. 66–79. In Increasing understanding of public problems and policies. 1973. Farm Found., Chicago.

Wengert, N. I. 1975a. Urban containment and agricultural conservation. p. 79–95. In J. A. Quinn (ed.) Land resources—a rationale for policy, planning, and procedures. Univ. of Illinois, Bur. of Urban and Reg. Planning Res., Urbana-Champaign, Ill.

Wengert, N. I. 1975b. Public policy alternatives of federal, state and local governments in regulating land uses: political issues. p. 117–121. In Thomas Dickinson (ed.) Agriculture in the future and its implications for land-use planning. Div. of Environ. Studies, Univ. of California, Davis.

Wengert, N. I. 1975c. The evolvement process. p. 33–86. In D. W. Hendricks, E. C. Vlachos, L. S. Tucker, J. C. Kellogg (ed.) Environmental design for public projects. Water Resour. Pub., Fort Collins, Colo.

Wengert, N. I. 1976. The political allocation of benefits and burdens: economic externalities and due process in environmental protection. Inst. of Gov. Studies, Univ. of California, Berkeley, Calif.

Wengert, N. I., and Thomas Graham. 1974. Transferable development rights. J. Soil Water Conserv. 29:253–257.

Wengert, N. I., and Burnell Held. 1975. Fort Collins utility services and growth management. Environ. Resour. Center, Colorado State Univ., Fort Collins, Colo.

Williams, Norman, Jr. 1975. American planning law: land use and the police power. 5 Vols. Callaghan and Co., Chicago.

3   Principles of Land Use Planning

JOHN C. ROBERTS

University of Wisconsin-Extension
Madison, Wisconsin

I. INTRODUCTION

Some might consider an effort to lay out the principles of land use planning presumptuous or downright misleading on the ground that there is, currently, no general agreement in the profession as to what *planning* is. This may be true, in the sense that traditional ideas are being challenged. New definitions or descriptions of planning and the role of planning in today's society are constantly being proposed and debated. Thus, what one may call the principles—that is, the basic tenets or doctrines—of land use planning are never totally accepted by all. The last decade or so has been a particularly tumultuous time (Galloway & Makeyui, 1977). On the other hand, it is this author's belief that there is some measure of agreement—if only for operational purposes—among most practicing land use planners about the basic purposes and methods of land use planning. Thus, one can identify some rules of conduct or action that appear to guide land use planners as they go about their work. The purpose of this chapter is to present an overview of what those rules of action or conduct are.

II. WHY PLAN?

Why might one make a decision to plan for land use? Many conclude that man plans because he has an inherent need to shape his own destiny. This need, coupled with man's ability to visualize the future and his belief that he can effectively exercise control, is the fundamental reason he plans. Man's dependence upon natural forces, and his struggle to escape or at least manage these forces, through planning, was eloquently described by Renee Dubos:

> Man is as much influenced by natural forces as are other things; but he constantly tries to escape from his biological bondage. For this reason, his future is shaped not only by the . . . forces of nature . . . but even more by individual and collective decisions . . . The great moments of history . . . are determined by *purposeful responses,* which are guided by man's ability to visualize the future, and indeed by his propensity to plan for a future which transcends his own biological life (Dubos, 1977).

Other explanations have been offered. Galbraith, for example, sees planning not so much as inherent in man's nature, but as a necessary outcome of the complex industrial state that man has created (Galbraith, 1967). This view is echoed by Clawson and Hall:

> In the modern world, planning by the individual, the corporation, or any unit of government not only is essential but unavoidable. The making of an investment, whether in a manufacturing plant, public service facilities, or in one's own education makes sense, if at all, only in the context of some assumptions or some plans for the future. Denying an interest in planning or criticizing the planning efforts of others does not free one from dependence on the future (Clawson & Hall, 1973).

III. A DEFINITION OF PLANNING

Planning has been defined in a variety of ways. Dror (1963) has identified definitions that stress planning (i) as a means of making decisions concerning future action; (ii) as an effort that places a high value on rationality and the utilization of knowledge; (iii) as a means for achieving the "social good" or realizing the "public interest"; (iv) as a means for creating blueprints for the future; and (v) as a synonym for management. Others have defined planning as: ". . .a set of procedures" (Davidoff & Reiner, 1962); ". . .the thoughtful public guidance of change. . ." (Malone, 1973); and ". . .an effort to improve the making of decisions. . ." (Gaus, 1951).

As Dror has pointed out, many of these definitions have been subject to criticism on the grounds that they have limited validity (i.e., they don't reflect reality in enough cases to be useful definitions of planning), include irrelevant elements, or are unsatisfactory in some other respect.

More specifically, theorists and practitioners alike question, among other things, whether planning is necessarily more rational than some other means for deciding what society should do. Some point out the variety of values that exist in a pluralistic society and ask if it is not impossible to say, with any certainty, what is the "public interest" or the "social good." Still others ask: what distinguishes planning from other means, such as education, for improving the quality of decisions?

A. Attributes of Planning

These and other concerns and questions have led to the search for more valid definitions of planning—definitions that are truly descriptive of what those involved in planning really do, rather than prescriptions for what those involved in planning should be doing. The search is not ended and will, in all probability, continue on into the indefinite future. However, it is the opinion of this author that—for operational purposes at least—most planners today would agree that planning has at least these attributes (Dror, 1963; Woodbury, 1966):

1. It is a *process*, that is, a continuous, ongoing activity. In some quarters planning has been viewed as the preparation of static master plans or blueprints which, once prepared, need only to be carried out in order to achieve the community goals. The notion of process recognizes that planning occurs in a constantly changing

environment. Our values change, our knowledge expands, our understanding of how our environment functions changes. This requires continuous redefinition of goals, reassessment of resources, the taking into account of new knowledge. This in turn requires the reevaluation of information and modification of plans.

2. It involves the *preparation of alternative plans,* policies, or courses of action. These may be very general or quite specific or fall somewhere between those poles, but the development of plan/policies/courses of action are an essential part of planning.

3) It is *oriented toward the future.* While those involved in planning may be concerned about past trends and events, and the understanding of how various systems function, the purpose of that concern is to more effectively influence events in the future.

4) It is directed at achieving some defined *goals or objectives.* It is a purposeful activity.

5) It places a high value on *rational approaches* for arriving at plans/policies/courses of action. Objectivity, reason and logic, as opposed to emotion or self-interest, are highly valued. Information and knowledge—systematically gathered, analyzed, and integrated—is the preferred means for devising plans/policies/courses of action.

6) It seeks to recognize, insofar as is possible, that "everything is connected to everything else." In planning particular attention is given to the *spillover or side effects* of each alternative plan/policy/course of action under consideration. There is recognition and concern for the fact that proposed actions of one kind are inseparable from other proposals (e.g., proposed increases in recreational development in an area also requires consideration of the capacity and location of transportation systems, possible effects upon land and water quality, etc.).

B. Activities or Tasks in Planning

Planning is also often described in the form of diagrams which emphasize the tasks and general sequence of activities that occur in planning (Hall, 1975; Inst. of Traffic Eng., 1976):

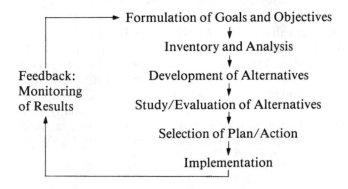

For clarity, the diagram shows a stepwise process. In reality, the discoveries or decisions made at each step in the process may lead to a reconsideration or modification of the result of previous steps. For example, one may discover that a certain plan or course of action which fulfills most of the goals and objectives earlier agreed upon simply costs too much to implement. This may lead to a rethinking and reformulation of goals and objectives. Thus, planning is viewed as an open, dynamic process, susceptible to new knowledge or forces.

Although not made explicit in the diagram, it may be implied that, when planning, one moves from an *understanding* of what it is he or his clients seek to change, and the environment in which that change may occur (the goals and objectives and/or inventory and analysis step), to the development of a *plan* of action for bringing about change (the development, study, and evaluation of alternatives step); to the *taking of actions* required to bring about change (the implementation step); to *monitoring and evaluating* the results of those actions; to any necessary *modification* of the plans of action.

1. GOALS AND OBJECTIVES

It has been suggested that there are a few very broad and fundamental goals toward which planning should be directed: (i) equity—a fair and just consideration and treatment for all those affected by a plan or course of action; (ii) efficiency; and (iii) choice—the creation or maintenance of the greatest number of possible options for the individual. Some suggest that the general objectives for land use planning include: livability, efficiency, amenity, flexibility and choice, minimum harm to natural communities of plants and animals, optimum use of resources, and public involvement in the planning process (Woodbury, 1966).

General goals such as these may be relatively easy to identify and agree upon. However, in a land use planning program, such general goals must usually be expressed in more specific terms in order to fashion effective plans and to eventually evaluate the extent to which the chosen goals are being achieved.

In many planning programs, generalized goals may be stepped down to more specific, measurable goals. Hall (1975), for example, identified three levels of goals: the very generalized which he calls "goals," the more specific which he calls "objectives," and the very detailed which he calls "targets." In planning for agricultural land use at the state level, an example might be: *Goal*—maintenance of the agricultural land base; *Objective*—preservation of prime agricultural land; *Target*—adoption of exclusive agricultural zoning for prime agricultural lands in 15 southern counties over the next 5 years. Others use different terminology. One prominent regional planning commission identifies "objectives": "a spatial distribution of various land uses which will result in protection, wise use, and development of the natural resources of the region"; "principles": "The proper relation of land use to soils can serve to avoid many environmental problems, aid in the establishment of better settlement patterns, and promote the wise use of an irreplaceable resource"; and "standards": "land developed or proposed to be developed without public sanitary sewer service should be located only on areas covered by soils rated in the regional soil survey as having very slight, slight or moderate limitations for such development" (Southeast. Wis. Reg. Plan. Comm., 1972).

In large scale planning programs where multiple land uses and public services are being planned, and where a premium is placed on the evaluation of plans, great effort may be expended on developing extensive statements of goals and objectives. In the planning program from which the above example was taken, there were identified 29 *objectives,* 45 *principles,* and 127 *standards.* For additional detail on these, see Chapter 20, "Planning Metropolitan Land Uses in Relation to Natural Landscape Features," in this book.

In a totalitarian society, goals and objectives may be specified by the rulers. In democratic societies, however, they are identified through a complex process of interaction involving elected and appointed officials (including planners), citizens, and interest groups. A wide variety of tools or methods may be utilized in determining what the goals and objectives should be. The U.S. Department of the Interior, Bureau of Land Management (BLM), for example, utilizes a wide array of sources in identifying goals and objectives for the use of the public lands for which they plan, including: major national policy documents (e.g., the national laws, administrative policies); the policies and plans of other agencies; assessments of local population and industry requirements, dependencies, trends, and problems; and consultation with public and private groups and government organizations having an interest in the land unit being planned for (U.S. Dep. of Interior, 1975a). Various methods are used: perusal of documents, public opinion surveys, hearings, meetings, consultation with government officials, etc.

Obviously, a wide variety of goals and conflicts between goals may come to the surface. Many, even most, may not be easily resolved or resolved at all. What one would hope to achieve—in addition to identifying generally agreed upon goals—is explicit recognition that multiple goals do exist, an identification of any conflicts between those goals, and resolution of the conflict where possible. Where conflicts cannot be resolved, decision-makers should be provided with enough information so they are cognizant of the unresolved conflicts.

2. STUDY, INVENTORY, ANALYSIS

Many of those involved in land use planning assume or believe that the future is built upon the past and the present. Therefore, they believe that an understanding of the physical, social, economic, and political environment is essential to developing realistic, achievable plans. Further, they believe or assume that the economic and demographic characteristics of the society are determinents (or, at least, useful indicators) of what future land needs or demands will be, and that the physical and natural characteristics of the land set limits on what land is capable of being used for. It is for these reasons that land use planning studies, inventories, and analyses are undertaken.

Demographic (population) and economic studies and analyses are common to most land use planning efforts. Population characteristics such as age, sex, locational distribution of the population, and birth, death, and migration rates, are linked to, and can therefore be used as, indicators of future land needs or demands (e.g., the amount, type, and location of outdoor recreation facilities needed in a metropolitan area are determined by the age, sex, geographic location, and size of the population in that area, as well as their recreation preferences).

Economic inventories and studies provide a basis for understanding the character of the area's economic base, strengths and weaknesses of the economy, and economic development obstacles and opportunities. Forecasts of economic activity (number of jobs, for example) also serve as a basis for deciding whether certain trends in population size and composition can continue (e.g., the nature of anticipated economic activity may limit the number of jobs available for people of certain ages or with certain types of training and experience and thus effect population size and composition).

But these forecasts are not statements of what must inevitably happen. They are simply estimates of what might happen given certain policies and values. Depending on the aspirations of the community, population and economic forecasts that indicate unwanted or undesirable trends (e.g., a very old or very young future population, or a relatively restricted economic base) may lead to modifications of the goals and objectives being pursued by the community.

Standard data sources and techniques for population and economic inventory and analysis have been developed and are widely utilized in land use planning: U.S. census data on population, housing, retail trade and wholesale trade, services, and agriculture are standard sources (Chapin, 1965; Inst. of Traffic Eng., 1976). Private sources such as the Sales Management reports, community directories, and telephone directories, are often utilized. In those cases where standard data sources are insufficient, surveys may be undertaken to obtain the necessary data.

Some of the more commonly used techniques (Chapin, 1965) for analyzing and projecting population and economic data are:

1) *Population*—population pyramids, cohort survival projection, straight line projections, rate of change projections;
2) *Economic*—economic base techniques (basic and nonbasic industries), i.e., income product or social product accounts, input-output studies, approximation analysis, industrial complex analysis, mathematical models.

In addition to these two common inventories/studies, a host of others may be undertaken depending on the type of land uses being planned. For example, the U.S. Department of the Interior, Bureau of Land Management (1975b), in its planning for the use of the public lands under its jurisdiction, attempts to inventory and analyze at least nine components of the natural and man-made environment: (i) air and climate; (ii) topography;

(iii) geology and soils; (iv) vegetation; (v) water resources; (vi) domestic and wild animals; (vii) fire; (viii) factors limiting resource use; and (ix) developments, facilities, and services. In addition, they inventory and analyze existing land uses, land controls, and land management practices; the location and status of mineral resources; watershed condition and use; location and condition of wildlife habitat; location, character, and quality of recreation resources; and more.

The information gathered and analyzed can become quite extensive. The Bureau of Land Management, for example, gathers and attempts to analyze the following specific information:

1) *Air and Climate*—precipitation, humidity, temperature, air movement, growing season, location of weather stations, and air quality;
2) *Topography*—general relief, mountain and valley structure/ orientation elevation, streams/canyons, slopes;
3) *Geology and Soils*—geological oddities, formations with recreation values, hydrology, parent material, drainage, pH, depth, structure, texture, nutrients, productivity, contaminants, soils moisture and management limitations;
4) *Vegetation*—vegetative types and subtypes, area and location;
5) *Water Resources*—drainage patterns, streams/springs/lakes, etc., water developments and control structures, water yield, underground reservoirs, groundwater, recharge areas, runoff areas;
6) *Domestic and Wild Animals*—distribution, concentration areas;
7) *Fire*—size/cause/location, behavior, resources threatened if fire should occur;
8) *Factors Limiting Resource Use*—vegetation, soils, erosion susceptability, faultlines, susceptability to flooding, swamps/marsh, susceptability to landslides/avalanches/snow cornices, unstable soils, blizzard areas, sandstorm areas, high wind areas, tidal wave areas, hazardous areas due to man's activity such as mining shafts or due to the existence of poisonous reptiles/insects/plants, areas of unpleasant sounds such as military test ranges;
9) *Developments, Facilities, and Services*—land treatment activities, access and transportation facilities, cadastral survey monumentation, aerial photo coverage.

While these are an unusually comprehensive set, they illustrate the wide range of inventories and analyses that may be undertaken in land use planning for natural resource lands. A splendid example of how planners analyze and draw meaningful conclusions from their data is contained in this book in Chapter 37 entitled, "Soil and Vegetation Considerations Important in Planning Spatial Relationships Among Land Uses" by Johnson and McHarg.

The specific inventories and analyses to be undertaken will vary depending upon the area being planned. Some of the same inventories and analyses utilized in planning for natural resource lands as well as others not mentioned above (e.g., origin-destination studies) would be part of a transportation planning process. Land use planning in an urban area might require inventory and analysis of pedestrian movement and the traffic, noise, dust, and glare generation characteristics of specific industrial or commercial land use, as well as other inventories and analyses.

As with population and economic inventories, many data sources may be utilized including data gathered by the agency responsible for planning or by other agencies (e.g., Bureau of Reclamation, U.S. Geological Survey, U.S. Soil Conservation Service, state natural resources agencies, state historical societies, industry associations, and universities). Obviously, if pertinent data is available it is not replicated. In those cases where it is not available, surveys may be undertaken to obtain it.

There may be large gaps between what one might consider *desireable* to inventory and analyze and what it is *practical* to do. Therefore, the nature of the planning to be done, professional judgements as to what it is necessary or feasible to do, the demands of those with an interest in the planning being done, and the availability of resources (time, money, skills) often play a large part in determining the specific inventories and analyses that will be undertaken.

A rather practical question that almost always arises is: for what geographic area should the inventory and analysis be done? Some national public lands, for example, are used by multi-state or even national populations (e.g., campers and backpackers). Some industrial activities (e.g., mining) are closely linked to national or even international economies. Thus, multi-state, national, or international demographic and economic characteristics may need to be inventoried and analyzed even though the land area being planned is relatively small (e.g., a county or other substate area).

In summary, (i) inventory and analysis in planning aims fundamentally at improving understanding of the amount and character of demand that will be placed on the land resource, and the capacity of the land to support various uses; (ii) inventories and analyses often extend beyond the relatively restricted geographic area for which a land use plan is being prepared; (iii) population and economic studies are common to most land use planning efforts; (iv) the character and depth of inventories and analyses undertaken in a particular land use planning effort will depend upon professional judgement, the resources available, the type of land use being planned (e.g., urban, rural, natural resource, transportation, public facility), and the demands of those with an interest in the planning effort; and (v) while standard data sources are available and normally are utilized, surveys to obtain information not available from standard sources are often necessary.

3. DEVELOPMENT AND EVALUATION OF ALTERNATIVES

A number of reasons can be cited for developing alternative rather than single courses of action (plans) (Boyce et al., 1970).

1) The consideration of alternatives to an existing plan may reveal that changes in values or conditions occurring since that plan was adopted require the development of a more viable plan. On the

other hand, if an existing plan proves to still be viable, its critics may be silenced or at least encouraged to devote their efforts to more productive actions.

2) Our information about and understanding of the complex social, physical, and natural systems which we attempt to guide or control is too limited to expect a single best course of action to automatically emerge from the studies, inventories, and analyses that are done. Each alternative has its costs and benefits, advantages and disadvantages. The comparison of alternatives provides an opportunity discover what particular advantages one plan may have over another.

3) Because the public generally is uninterested in goals and objectives in the abstract, it is often difficult to determine what goals and objectives are valued by the public. When presented with alternative plans of action, however, the public will often make known its values and views on key issues. The consideration of alternative plans can trigger the public debate that must precede the resolution of conflict and the agreement on the goals and objectives of the community.

4) The presentation of information and public debate on values and community goals and objectives that accompanies the consideration of alternatives can be an effective way of educating the public about the need for and value of land use planning.

5) The consideration of alternatives may reveal fundamental changes that are necessary in the community economic structure, financing, and government organization in order for the community to achieve its goals and objectives.

At one time, in some quarters, the development of land use alternatives, and the weighing and balancing among alternatives, was considered to be largely a matter for technicians (planners) and a few public officials. This may have been encouraged by a number of factors: public indifference to land use planning, a belief that the development and evaluation of alternatives was too complex and technical a process for nontechnicians to be involved in, and insufficient means for communicating with the public. Today, however, public demands, coupled with the development of more useful tools for involving more people, are bringing the development and evaluation of alternatives more into the open.

Ideally, evaluation should (i) be related to the objectives (ends, values) the decision-makers are attempting to achieve; (ii) cover all the systems being planned; (iii) cover all the affected sectors of the community; (iv) consider both producers and consumers; (v) take account of all costs and all benefits to all affected sectors of the community; (vi) show who benefits and who pays; and (vii) aim at determining the "best" alternative (Litchfield, 1970). This is a tall order. No single technique does all these things, but these are the general goals of evaluation.

Alternatives are evaluated in terms of how effective they are in achieving stated goals and objectives. They may be evaluated as to their economic (including fiscal), environmental, social, physical, and political effects. In practice much of evaluation of alternatives may be subjective and intuitive. There are however, some more objective and systematic techniques available. Three of these techniques, used with varying degrees of sophistication, are:

1) Cost-benefit analysis, which attempts to determine which alternative produces the greatest quantity of economic revenues in relation to economic costs. A limitation of this approach is that it is difficult to determine nonarbitrary economic values for certain costs and benefits such as savings in time, reductions of accidents, and preservation of historic structures and places. Some argue that psychological benefits and costs are at least as relevant as economic benefits and costs in evaluating alternative plans.

2) Planning balance sheets, which essentially evaluate economic costs and benefits for those items for which reasonable economic values can be determined, but also attempt to evaluate other noneconomic items (e.g., psychological, political, ecological), often through the use of point systems. Limitations of this technique are that it may be extremely complex, is not persuasive to those who place great faith in economic measures, and involves a certain amount of arbitrariness (hence, disagreement) in assigning weights to the noneconomic items.

3) Comparative cost analysis in which the costs of the alternatives are compared to each other. Since benefits are ignored, the results of this type of analysis may be biased in the direction of the least cost alternative.

Over the years, the trend has been toward expanding the use of qualitative measures and environmental considerations in evaluation. The evaluation of alternative transportation plans, for example, may now incorporate the consideration of impacts on nonusers as well as users of the transportation system. Factors such as noise, pollution, aesthetic intrusion, land consumption, social disruption, and relocation due to highway building are now considered along with the more traditional evaluations of capacity, accessability, quality of service, travel, and construction costs and financing considerations (Inst. of Traffic Eng., 1976). Recently, attention has also been focused on methods which permit significant participation in evaluating plans by nontechnicians or lay people. The most effective of these in terms of simplicity to use, simplicity in the data base, and ability to supply new insights and information are the qualitative evaluations (Runyon, 1977).

4. SELECTION OR ADOPTION OF A PLAN OR COURSE OF ACTION

In some cases, a preferred plan or course of action is formally adopted by the organization with the responsibility for implementing it. In other cases, formal adoption may not occur, but a concensus may develop as to which is the preferred plan of action, and the organization will implement it without formal adoption.

When several organizations will have responsibility for implementing a plan, implementation is more likely to occur if they all are involved in the development and evaluation of the alternatives and in the selection and formal adoption of the plan.

In many cases, land use planning at the local level has been assigned to independent planning commissions consisting primarily of appointed rather than elected officials. The principle behind this has been that nonelected officials could be more objective (meaning less political) about community goals and the means for achieving them. It was also argued that they would be less subject to interest group pressures. A premium was placed on the technical and objective aspects of land use planning. In recent years, however, considerable sentiment has developed for the idea of more directly involving elected officials in the development and implementation of land use plans, on the principle that elected officials may be more aware of certain goals and objectives of the general public and more likely to allocate resources toward the implementation of a plan which they have had a hand in preparing. Thus, proposals have been made and sometimes adopted for making the chief executive (mayor, county executive, governor) or the legislative body (city council, county council, state legislature) directly responsible for the planning function.

5. IMPLEMENTATION

A principal means of implementing land use plans—regulatory mechanisms such as zoning, subdivision controls, and official mapping—are discussed at length in Chapters 39 and 40 of this book, so they will not be discussed here.

A number of other nonregulatory means may be utilized in guiding land use or influencing land use decisions. These would include:

1) Control of the location of critical public services (roads, sewers, water, etc.) or the imposition of special charges attached to the development or use of such lands.
2) Tax incentives, such as differential assessment ratios that encourage the continuation of certain land uses, the transition to other uses, and land tax exemptions or write downs.
3) Direct or indirect aids or subsidies, such as grants in aid to encourage soil and water conservation facilities and practices, mortgage insurance, subsidies to support land price write downs such as the federal urban renewal program and loans.
4) Partial acquisition of property rights through easements or purchase of development rights.
5) Acquisition of fee simple title to land (Clarenbach et al., 1973).

In some cases, such as the federal or state agencies which manage large public land areas—state and national forests, parks, recreation areas, and national resource lands, for example—implementation is carried out by the agency which also is responsible for the planning. In these situations, administrative rules, formally adopted management procedures and practices, and internally adopted design standards are the principal means for guiding and controlling land use.

Where the responsibility for implementation is shared by a number of organizations, the working relationships between the organizations' staffs and leaders may be crucial in avoiding contradictions in implementation. This may be particularly important when organizations covering the same area are implementing independently prepared but interrelated land use plans (e.g., a sewer extension plan of a sewage service district and a transportation plan of a county transportation department) or where adjoining jurisdictions are planning independently for the same land uses (e.g., two rural counties independently planning for the preservation of agricultural lands).

6. FEEDBACK: MONITORING OF RESULTS

Planning is a purposeful activity. The principal reason for preparing plans is to more effectively move toward the achievement of some agreed upon goals and objectives. Since our knowledge of how the world works is imperfect, we are often uncertain that a given course of action will lead to our goals. Thus, there is a need to monitor the results of our actions. Monitoring may have several purposes:

1) To determine whether the actions being taken are, in fact, achieving the agreed upon goals and objectives.
2) To determine whether one is using the most efficient means for achieving the goals.
3) To determine whether the method of planning one is using, including the assumptions, information and knowledge that went into the planning, is valid.
4) To provide a basis for judgements and decisions about (i) whether one should devise new or modified strategies for achieving the goals, and (ii) whether one should modify the goals and objectives themselves.
5) To identify important unintended consequences of our actions.

In one recent report, a reevaluation of a regional plan, it was found, among other things, that: (i) environmental corridors and prime agricultural land were generally being satisfactorily protected from development by local action and by a slowing of population growth and, thus, it was decided that the courses of action proposed to protect these resources some years earlier were generally sufficient to protect them today; (ii) inthe light of consumer preference for low density development and actual development trends it would be desireable to reconsider proposed land use patterns set forth in an earlier land use plan; (iii) newly emerging uncertainties about motor fuel costs would make it prudent to reevaluate the regions transportation plan, giving consideration to possible changes in motor fuel price and availability; and (iv) declines in mass transit use were working against the development of a regional transportation system that could look to mass transit as a substitute for the auto. This, coupled with continuing decentralization of development and declines in population density, would require some reevaluation of the region's transportation plan (Southeast. Wis. Reg. Plan. Comm., 1975).

C. Another Dimension of Planning

Up to this point, we have described the principles of land use planning principally from the point of view of the planner-technician. The emphasis has been on the tasks he performs and the general sequence in which they occur. Many people today, planners included, feel uncomfortable with this definition because it implies that the planner-technician has a monopoly of skills and knowledge. It does not adequately provide for utilizing the skills and knowledge of other nonprofessionals which are, after all, necessary for the development of sensitive, realistic, and achievable plans. Consequently, other descriptions of planning which attempt to recognize the roles of both the planner-technician and those who use plans, that is, the nontechnician "client," are appearing. One of the most compelling of these, in this author's opinion, views planning as a process of "mutual learning" on the part of the planner-technician and his client (Friedmann, 1973). In this process, the technical expertise of the (land use) planner and the personal knowledge of the client are joined together to produce and carry out plans and courses of action. This process involves a dialogue or continual exchange of information and knowledge between planner and client, rather than the intermittent, one-way communication that some believe has characterized past efforts in land use planning.

To this dialogue the planner brings the fruits of his training and experience: for example, useful concepts (e.g., universal soil loss equation, the concept of carrying capacity of the land), theories (e.g., theory of traffic gravitation), an understanding of analytical techniques and skill in using those techniques (e.g., soils suitability analysis, landscape analysis), a knowledge of sources of useful data (e.g., census population and economic information, soils and crop surveys), and new ideas (e.g., new towns or cluster housing development as an alternative to continued urban sprawl). The client, on the other hand, brings to the dialogue the fruits of his experience: for example, a first hand knowledge of some physical attributes of a land use (e.g., location of areas of local archeological significance), useful judgements regarding which alternative land use proposals might be socially acceptable to his community, a sense of what the goals and high priority needs of the community are, a sense of how best to proceed politically to achieve those goals, and judgements about what land use proposals and strategies have worked or not worked in the past, and why they may have succeeded or failed.

Working together, the planner-technician and the client mutually devise courses of action—which may or may not be eventually expressed in formal documents called *plans*—based on the unique contributions of each.

Unlike some other definitions of planning, this view does not emphasize the production of formal, documented plans, nor does it separate the activities of the planner from the activities of those he is "planning for." Instead, it emphasizes that sensitive, realistic, and achievable plans require the close collaboration and unique knowledge of both the planner and client.

It seems to this author that each of these two views of the planning—planning as a sequence of activities, and planning as a process of mutual learning—capture the essential parts of what most professionals would agree are fundamental principles of land use planning.

IV. SOME RECENT TRENDS IN LAND USE PLANNING

While it is not possible to identify all, or perhaps even most, significant recent trends in land use planning, one can draw some general conclusions about where we seem to be heading with regard to public and institutional interest in land use planning, trends in the development of new land use planning tools, the role of environmental considerations, and the status of public participation in land use planning. Each of these trends affirm some principles of land use planning.

First, despite the public unhappiness and conflict that sometimes center on specific land use planning proposals, there appears to be growing public and institutional demand for the planning of land uses. The number of public planning aencies is growing. The number of people who can be categorized as professional planners (as measured by the numbers employed in public agencies and the numbers who are members of professional planning organizations) is also increasing. While some of this growth is due to expansion in some of the "newer" areas of planning interest such as health planning, social planning, and manpower planning, most professional planners are still primarily involved in those areas that we characterize as "land use" planning. One recent survey, for example, showed that nearly two-thirds of professional planners considered their major area of interest to be either physical land use, land use controls, zoning, environmental planning, urban design, transportation, housing, urban renewal, or resource development (Kaufman, 1974). Moreover, the adoption of planning as an essential part of the land use decision-making process appears to have both public and institutional support. Several more recent illustrations of this are: (i) the adoption of a land use planning system as a major component in the management of U.S. Bureau of Land Management lands, (ii) the requirement for water quality (including land use) plans as an integral part of the nation's effort to achieve fishable and swimmable waters by 1983, (iii) efforts to prepare land use plans for national wildlife refuges and national parks, (iv) the requirement for county-wide plans as a prerequisite to receiving federal sewer/water grants, (v) a renewed emphasis (by the federal department of Housing and Urban Development) on the land use and housing components of regional plans, and (vi) in some states, the adoption of tax incentives for farmland preservation that will lead to the development of agricultural land use plans.

Second, in recent years there seems to have been a renewed interest in the revival and application of some older but nontraditional concepts and tools. This includes new towns, transferable development rights, floating zones, moritoria on development, one-stop development permits, purchase of development rights, and land banks. This interest in nontraditional tools stems from the recognition of the limitations of the more traditional tools (Euclidean zoning, subdivision controls, and official maps) and the desire to develop more effective measures for guiding land use. Moreover, education to achieve voluntary cooperation in implementing plans seems to be more accepted as a method for achieving some land use goals.

Third, environmental and natural resource considerations, while never disregarded in reputable land use planning programs, are being given new prominence as a result of the nation's concern for a dwindling supply of some natural resources and the impacts of various pollutants on public health. For example, coastal zone management programs with a heavy orientation toward land use planning are underway in coastal states. Environmental considerations, often within the context of environmental impact analyses and statements, have become key considerations in approving or disapproving major urban and rural developments. The impact of land development patterns on energy consumption, as well as the relationship between land use patterns and practices and the quality of both surface and ground water, are being given greater attention in land use decisions. This, of course, has not come about simply because of a new awareness of the environment. At least as important has been the development of better basic data in the natural and physical sciences (e.g., soils, water chemistry, hydrology, ecology) and the interpretation of data into forms that are meaningful and therefore useful to land use planners (e.g., interpretations of soils limitations, evaluations of the effectiveness of various land management practices in limiting erosion).

Fourth, there has been a trend toward very substantial public participation or involvement in land use planning beginning with the requirement for participation attached to some of the Great Society programs of the 1960's, extending to the public participation requirements of various state and federal land use and environmental laws since then, and including the impact of such publications as the Sierra Club's *Ecotactics* (Mitchell & Stollings, 1970). While this may be disconcerting to the planner who sees his job as primarily technical in nature, it is difficult to imagine any decrease of citizen participation in land use decisions in the future. Largely because of the requirement that the land use planner communicate with citizens, but also because of a desire to make land use plans more relevant to peoples' needs as they—not the planners—see them, land use planners are having to learn and use new skills for communicating with the public and for managing and resolving conflict.

Fifth, there seems to be a growing public recognition that certain land use problems, or major parts of certain problems, can be most effectively dealt with at the metropolitan or rural regional (county and multi-county) level. These would include, but not be limited to, water and air quality, waste disposal and treatment, housing supply, particularly for lower income people and some racial minorities, transportation facilities, large scale residential-commercial-industrial development, public finance of regional communities, and critical resources such as wetlands, prime agricultural lands, and unique natural areas. Along with this recognition has come an expansion in the number of regional, substate planning agencies who devote a substantial part, if not all, of their energies to land use matters.

Sixth, while a recognition of the interdependency of social, physical, natural, economic, and political considerations has always been a basic tenent of land use planning, it appears that those involved in land use planning today are, by and large, more aware of the need to give great attention to the interrelationships of these aspects of life in the land use planning and decision making process. Thus, we see major regional transportation planning programs giving consideration to the transport needs of the handicapped. We see land use plans for large areas of the public lands being based on careful consideration of a large number of relevant factors and the "tradeoff" among them, such as: local and national economic needs, maintenance of the productive capacity of the land, the social impacts of types of intensive or nonintensive development, the need for preservation of unique natural areas, and the need for maintenance of air and water quality.

This, of course, is only a partial and personal list of major recent trends in land use planning. Other views, particularly those relating to trends that will affect the future of the planning profession and education for planners can be found in Godschalk (1974). This list, however, is illustrative of the general interest and vitality that exists in the field. It speaks favorably, in the opinion of this author, of the willingness and ability of those concerned with land use planning to respond creatively to the many challenges and opportunities that have arisen in years past. Given this experience there is good reason to be optimistic that the new challenges and opportunities confronting future land use planners will be responded to with the same enthusiasm and creativity.

LITERATURE CITED

Boyce, D., N. Day, and C. McDonald. 1970. Metropolitan plan making, Reg. Sci. Res. Inst., Philadelphia. p. 30.

Chapin, F. S., Jr. 1965. Urban land use planning. 2nd ed., Chap. 4 and 5. Univ. of Illinois Press, Urbana. p. 158–220.

Clarenbach, F., H. Jordahl, and C. Runge. 1973. Public rights in private lands. Univ. of Wisconsin, Madison, p. 1–2.

Clawson, M., and P. Hall. 1973. Planning and urban growth. Publ. for Resources for the Future, Inc., by Johns Hopkins Univ. Press, Baltimore, Md.

Davidoff, P., and T. Reiner. 1962. A choice theory of planning. J. Am. Inst. Planners. XXVII(2):103–115.

Dror, Y. 1963. The planning process: a facet design. Int. Rev. Admin. Sci. 29(1):46–58.

Dubos, R. 1977. A God within. Charles Schribner & Sons, New York. p. 250.

Friedmann, J. 1973. Retracking America: a theory of transactive planning. Anchor Press/ Doubleday, Garden City, N.Y.

Galbraith, J. K. 1967. The new industrial state. Houghton-Mifflin, Boston.

Galloway, T. D., and R. G. Makayui. 1977. Planning theory in retrospect: a process of paradigm change. J. Am. Inst. Planners. 43(1):62-71.

Gaus, J. 1951. Education for the emerging field of regional planning and development. Social Forces 29(3):230.

Godschalk, D. (ed.) 1974. Planning in America: learning from turbulence. Am. Inst. of Planners, Washington, D.C.

Hall, P. 1975. Urban and regional planning. Halsted Press/John Wiley and Sons, New York. p. 273.

Institute of Traffic Engineers. 1976. Transportation and traffic engineering handbook. Prentice Hall, Inc., Englewood Cliffs, N.J. p. 522.

Kaufman, J. 1974. Contemporary planning practice: state of the art. p. 124-125. *In* D. Godschalk (ed.) Planning in America: learning from turbulence. Am. Inst. of Planners, Washington, D.C.

Litchfield, N. 1970. Evaluation methodology of urban and regional plans: a review. J. Reg. Studies Assoc. 4(2):151-165.

Malone, W. 1973. Planning practice and technique. J. Soil Water Conserv. 28(1):17.

Mitchell, J., and C. Stollings. 1970. Ecotactics. Trident Press, New York, N.Y.

Runyon, D. 1977. Tools for community managed impact assessment. J. Am. Inst. of Planners. 43(2):125-135.

Southeastern Wisconsin Regional Planning Commission. 1972. The recommended comprehensive plan. Planning Rep. no. 14, Chap. III. *In* A comprehensive plan for the Racine urban planning district. Vol. 2. Waukesha, Wis.

Southeastern Wisconsin Regional Planning Commission. 1975. First volume of regional land use-transportation plan re-evaluation report published. Newsletter 15(5):52-55.

U.S. Department of the Interior, Bureau of Land Management. 1975a. Planning system procedures, Sec. 1601.

U.S. Department of the Interior, Bureau of Land Management. 1975b. Planning system procedures, Sections 1605 and 1607.

Woodbury, C. 1966. The role of the regional planner in preserving habitats and scenic environments. p. 571, 575, 576. *In* Future environments of North America. Natural History Press, Garden City, New York.

section II

Data Bases

II

4   Soils Data

F. TED MILLER AND JOE D. NICHOLS

Soil Conservation Service, USDA
Fort Worth, Texas

I. INTRODUCTION

Soils data in the United States include soil information for geographical areas and for selected points on the landscape. The soil information for areas is put on soil maps. There are two kinds of soil maps: those made from field methods, mainly large-scale detailed soil maps, and those compiled by generalizing data from the detailed maps, mainly small-scale generalized soil maps. The data gathered for selected points include laboratory and field measurements of soil characteristics, soil descriptions, measurements of vegetation, climatic data, and other observations.

II. SOIL SURVEYS AND RELATED MAPS AND MANUSCRIPTS

Soil surveys allow the measurement and observations of soil behavior and properties at one location to be used in making soil interpretations at other locations. A soil survey is an inventory of the soil resources of an area. It consists of (i) determining important characteristics of soil, (ii) classifying the soil into defined units, (ii) locating and plotting their boundaries on maps, and (iv) predicting their suitability for various uses (Simonson, 1952).

The soil scientist identifies the soils and plots their boundaries on maps by traversing the land at intervals. He observes the steepness, length, and shape of slopes; the size of streams and the general pattern of drainage; the kinds of native plants or crops; the kinds of underlying rock or softer material; and many facts about the soils. He makes numerous observations and recordings of the important soil characteristics needed to identify, classify, and plot the boundaries of the soils on maps. This process in itself does not comprise a soil survey. Additional research studies are needed as well to help define and characterize important facts and attributes of the soil. In addition, sound predictions concerning use or manipulation of the soil are made by the specialists in crops, native plants, planning, engineering, etc. A complete soil survey thus consists of soil mapping, associated research, soil descriptions, and multidisciplinary interpretations of soil use and behavior.

Soil surveys in the United States are made for practical purposes. They are used in planning alternative uses of the soil and alternative management practices for each use. The soil maps and supporting material—including narrative descriptions, diagrams, pictures, data, and interpretation—are made with several specific uses in mind. The soil survey is partly research, partly application of known concepts, and partly the art of designing soil map units, placing soil boundaries on a map, and explaining the soils to potential users. These users are interested in predictions about the results they can attain if they treat a specified soil with certain management practices. The scale and detail of a soil survey and the interpretations must meet the needs of the user. Several intensities of mapping are used in modern soil surveys. Soil survey information can be generalized further for broader evaluation.

The soil survey should begin only after consultations with as many of the potential users as possible. Too little detail on a soil survey can severely limit its usefulness; too much detail can cause extra difficulty in separating the needed level of information.

The soil survey program—the National Cooperative Soil Survey—is a cooperative effort between the Soil Conservation Service and other U.S. Department of Agriculture (USDA) agencies and state agencies, usually the agricultural experiment stations. In some surveys other federal and local agencies also participate.

During the course of the soil survey, the findings are summarized periodically and become a draft manuscript for the published soil survey. Before the soil survey is completed, and the soil names are correlated, both the maps and the related information can be used provisionally for land use planning.

Published soil surveys furnish information useful to farmers, ranchers, foresters, agronomists, community decisionmakers, hydrologists, engineers, teachers, students, and specialists in wildlife management, waste disposal, or pollution control.

A. Content of Published Soil Surveys in the United States

Soil surveys have been published since 1899. Each of these surveys is a record of the knowledge and concepts of the soils at the time of publication and the relationship of the soils to the landscape. Soil surveys with aerial photo base maps have been published since the early 1950's.

The table of contents is designed to assist users in finding the information they need. In the more recent publications, it is preceded by diagrams that show how to locate the area of interest on the index to map sheets and locate the area on the particular map sheet, as well as how to use the symbols on the map sheet as keys to finding the desired material in the text and tables. The published soil survey contains descriptions of the units on the detailed and general soil maps, descriptions of the soils, a section on the use and management of the soils, a section on soil properties, and a section on classification and formation of the soils.

B. Relationship of Soil Classification to Soil Surveys

The soil classification system contained in *Soil Taxonomy* (Soil Survey Staff, 1975; Smith, 1963) is used for classifying soils in the United States.

The taxa of the classification are conceptual. They represent the current knowledge of soils (Cline, 1961). The soil that we classify is a three-dimensional body of soil called a *pedon* (Johnson, 1963a; Soil Survey Staff, 1975). The pedon is the smallest body from which we describe and sample soils. In the usual situation, its area is about 1 m² and the pedon is thick enough to represent all soil horizons to a depth of about 2 m.

Many pedons collectively, called *polypedons,* are used to give a concept of a soil series, the lowest category in the classification system. The soil series is used to convey our concepts of what soils are and how they react to management. Further, it is used as a basis for our testing and research. The concept of each soil series is defined and issued as an "official" soil series description. This description includes the taxonomic classification, description of a typical pedon, a location for the typical pedon, the range in characteristics for the series, and a statement of how the series differs from closely similar series. In addition, the geographic setting is described; geographically associated soils are listed; drainage and permeability are given; and the vegetation, main use, and distribution and extent of the soil are described. The place and the time the series was established are listed along with other pertinent remarks and the laboratory data available for the series. Attached to the description of the soil are the coordinated soil interpretations. The interpretations are used to relate the soil characteristics and intrinsic behavior of the soil to the user (Kellogg, 1961). The interpretations represent our present understanding of the soil characteristics and how they react to management.

Soil series names are also used to name soil mapping units. They have a different meaning when so used. Alpha loam, 1 to 3% slopes, as a mapping unit name, is the concept of an area or areas on the landscape; this concept includes the taxonomic concept of Alpha as the dominant soil plus small areas of similar and dissimilar soils included in mapping. Often, soil series or other categories are subdivided. Such a subdivision is called a *phase.* The most common phases are those related to texture of the surface horizon, degree of erosion, slope gradient, and/or shape, flooding, and stoniness. The phase of the series is also used in most of the legends in large-scale soil surveys and in many of the legends in small-scale surveys. Soil categories higher than the series level are used if the intended use for the soils in an area does not warrant the detailed investigation required to classify them at the series level. Soils in higher categories can also be phased for use on small-scale maps.

A basic concept considered in classifying and interpretating soils is included in a statement from the *Soil Survey Manual* (Soil Survey Staff, 1951): "The influence on soil behavior of any one characteristic, or a variation in any one, depends upon the others in combination." The guides for making soil interpretations use combinations of classes of soil characteristics as criteria. Generally, the guides give ratings based on equal weight for all criteria and are first approximations only. The ratings are divided into about three classes and are supported by observations of soil behavior. Other kinds of interpretation such as yields of crops, grass, or trees are made mainly from observation and measurements.

The soil series is defined rather precisely for a naturally occurring body, but large areas of soil uniform enough to be classified within one series rarely occur in nature (Soil Survey Staff, 1975). Most large areas include more than one soil or soil and not-soil components, although one is usually dominant. The mapping unit is a device used to display on a map combinations of soil or soil and not-soil components.

Four kinds of mapping units provide for all the various combinations. The first kind is one in which three-fourths of the mapping unit consists of the soil furnishing the name or of similar soils. Similar soils are those soils that can be used like the named soil but that vary slightly in one or more characteristics. No one dissimilar soil may exceed one-tenth of the mapping unit, and the total area of all dissimilar soils may not exceed one-fourth of the mapping unit. Such single name mapping units are called *consociations.* Examples are Alpha loam, 1 to 3% slopes, and Udorthents, steep.

In some landscapes, two or more soils occur in such an intricate pattern that they cannot be separated on detailed soil surveys at a scale of about 1:24,000 or larger. These are called *complexes,* for example, Alpha-Beta complex, 1 to 3% slopes. The proportions and patterns of the component soils are relatively consistent in all mapped areas. Three-fourths of the complex must consist of the named soils or similar soils.

In other landscapes, two or more soils may be present with some regularity of pattern and are individually in large enough areas that they could be mapped separately at a scale of about 1:24,000. But they are not for reasons of the little need for intensive land management. These kinds of mapping units are called *soil associations.* An example is Alpha-Beta association, steep. Soil associations may be named for soil series or for higher categories in the classification system. The pattern of principal soils is relatively constant, but the relative proportion may vary from one area to another.

In a few places, two or more soils are mapped as one mapping unit even though they do not occur in a regular pattern. Either or both soils may occur in any given mapped area. These units are called undifferentiated groups. The soils are mapped together because some overriding factor, such as frequent flooding, dominates soil behavior. An example is Alpha and Beta soils, frequently flooded.

All areas on a soil map must be classified as soil or not-soil. The not-soil areas, called *miscellaneous areas*, are areas that support little or no vegetation. Examples are pits, beaches, or rock outcrops. These terms are used in naming mapping units, for example, *Rock outcrop,* or in combination with the name of a soil, for example, *Alpha-Rock outcrop complex.* Water is also considered a miscellaneous area.

III. KINDS OF SOIL SURVEYS

Although soil surveys help us increase our knowledge about soils, they are most commonly made for a more practical use. They permit the orderly transfer of knowledge gained through research and experience from one tract of land to another (Kellogg, 1959). Thus, they satisfy the need for soil information about specific geographic areas in preparing state or county land use plans, resource conservation plans for farms and ranches, plans for reclamation projects, plans for forestry management, preliminary plans for engineering projects and works, and plans for many other kinds of land use.

Soil surveys can be designed to meet the needs of users who need precise information about the soil resources of areas a few hectares or less in size, or for users who need a broad perspective of the soil resources of areas thousands of hectares in size. Soil surveys differ mainly in the kinds of mapping units, kinds of soil taxa used to identify components of mapping units, kinds and intensity of field procedures, and minimum size of delineated areas. Some of these factors determine the map scale. Adjustments in these attributes of soil surveys form the bases for differentiating the five orders of soil surveys listed in Table 1. These orders aid in the identification of the operational procedures used to make a soil survey and also indicate general levels of quality control.

The kind of survey to be made is decided jointly by those who are to use the survey and by representatives of the agencies making the soil survey. The survey can be as detailed as is needed, but the cost increases rapidly as the amount of detail is increased.

Soil landscapes vary widely in pattern and complexity. Some users want each different kind and area of soil shown on a map. This is not practical in most surveys because the size of some soil areas is too small for practical map scales. Therefore, mapping units must be designed to provide the degree of refinement required for the objective of the survey. Individual soils can be separated in mapping, or they can be mapped togehter in groups. Mapping units can be identified as consociations, an area dominated by a soil of a single taxon, or they can be identified as associations, complexes, or undifferentiated groups. A mixture of a group (multi-taxa) is more heterogeneous and less refined than a consociation (single taxon), even at the same categorical level. A soil series has a much more narrowly defined but larger, more comprehensive, set of soil properties than a suborder. If users need more information, a phase of a soil series can be used as a soil mapping unit. An association of suborders is used as a soil mapping unit if the users need a very broad perspective of the soil resources of very large areas.

IV. SOIL SURVEYS AND SOIL VARIABILITY

The purity of mapping units is important in the interpretation of soil surveys. Probably all delineations contain some soils outside the range of the kind of soil identified in the mapping unit name. Many of these soils

Table 1—Criteria for identifying kinds of soil surveys.†

Kinds of soils survey	Kinds of‡ map units	Kinds of components	Field procedures§	Appropriate scales for field mapping and published maps	Minimum size delineation¶
1st Order	Mainly consociations and some complexes	Phases of soil series	The soils in each delineation are identified by transecting and traversing. Soil boundaries are observed throughout their length. Air photo used to aid boundary delineation.	<1:12,000#	<0.6 ha (<1.5 acres)
2nd Order	Consociations, associations and complexes	Phases of soil series	The soils in each delineation are identified by transecting and traversing. Soil boundaries are plotted by observation and interpretation of remotely sensed data. Boundaries are verified at closely spaced intervals.	1:12,000 to 1:31,680	0.6–4 ha (1.5 acres to 10 acres)
3rd Order	Associations and some consociations and complexes	Phases of soil series and soil families	The soils in each delineation are identified by transecting, traversing and some observations. Boundaries are plotted by observation and interpretation by remotely sensed data and verified with some observations.	1:24,000 to 1:250,000	2.3–252 ha (6 acres to 640 acres)
4th Order	Associations with some consociations	Phases of soil families and subgroups	The soils of delineations representative of each map unit are identified and their patterns and composition determined by transecting. Subsequent delineations are mapped by some traversing, by some observation, and by interpretation of remotely sensed data verified by occasional observations. Boundaries are plotted by air photo interpretations.	1:100,000 to 1:300,000	40–370 ha (100 acres to 1,000 acres)
5th Order	Associations	Phases of subgroups, great groups, suborders and orders	The soils, their patterns, and their compositions for each map unit are identified through mapping selected areas (39 to 65 km²; 15 to 25 sq. miles) with 1st or 2nd order surveys, or alternatively, by transecting. Subsequently, mapping is by spaced observations, or by interpretation of remotely sensed data with occasional verification by observation or traversing.	1:250,000 to 1:1,000,000	252–4,000 ha (640 acres to 10,000 acres)

† Soil surveys of all Orders require maintenance of a soil handbook (legend, mapping unit descriptions, taxonomic unit descriptions, field notes, interpretations) and review by correlation procedures of the National Cooperative Soil Survey. Work plans for many survey areas list more than 1 order; the part to which each is applicable is delineated on a small scale map of the survey area.

‡ Undifferentiated groups may be used in any order with possible exception of 1st Order.

§ Field procedures used with meanings defined in preceding text.

¶ This is about the minimum size delineation for readable soil maps (i.e., 6 mm² or ¼ by ¼ inch area). In practice the minimum size delineations are generally larger than the minimum shown.

1st Order soil surveys are made for purposes that require appraisal of the soil resources of areas as small as experimental plots and building sites. Mapping scale could conceivably be as large as 1:1.

cannot be excluded from delineations by practical field mapping methods. Others are deliberately included to avoid excessive cartographic detail. The kind of inclusion is more important than the amount. Inclusions of soils having similar limitations and use potential do not detract from the usefulness of the survey. The kinds of inclusions that do detract most are those soils that have significantly different use and management needs.

The kinds of mapping units and their components are attained by adjusting the kind and intensity of field investigations. If, for example, the standards require that areas as small as 1 or 2 ha be delineated, the area must be traversed at intervals close enough to identify areas that small and the soil must be examined at enough places along each traverse to detect them. The map scale must then be large enough to delineate the small areas legibly on the map. It is important to remember the principle of cartographic generalization stated by Orvedal and Edwards (1941) in interpreting the five kinds of soil surveys: "As generalization of the map is made at successively higher levels, the assertions that can be made of any area become progressively fewer or less specific." Interpretations can be no more precise than the summation of the mapping unit refinement and the displayed mapping detail. Predictions of suitabilities of soils for use or management needs, for example, cannot be made for areas smaller than 256 ha (640 acres) if this is the minimum size delineation used in the survey area. In addition, if the mapping units consisted of soil associations, that is, mixtures of dissimilar soils, it would be equally in error to make precise interpretations. At this level of generalization, interpretations that determine suitability of areas for cropland are possible, but interpretations that determine specific suitability for growing corn are not.

Appropriate uses for different kinds of soil surveys are indicated in Table 2. This table shows the general relationship between orders of soil surveys and the use to be made of the soil map. The correlation between orders and use is not so sharp as indicated, since ranges in scales and minimum sized delineations overlap within orders. For example, 3rd Order soil surveys can be used for general planning for areas as large as a county or for more specialized planning of range resources on a single large ranch.

In the past, nonagricultural interpretations of soil surveys have been directed largely toward pointed out problems that should be avoided in soil use (Klingebiel, 1963). Indicating soil limitations has been beneficial, but if interpretations are geared solely to avoiding problems, highly productive areas such as the Corn Belt of the upper Midwest would never have been developed because of soil drainage problems. Farmers and ranchers were assisted in conservation planning in overcoming the limitations. In recent years considerable attention has been directed toward soil potential (Johnson and Bartelli, 1974; McCormack, 1974). This approach predicts the response of a soil to specific kinds of management or manipulation for nonagricultural as well as agricultural use. Limitations are still identified but, more important, practices commonly used to overcome those limitations and their cost are also identified. This procedure offers much more flexibility in that the planner can fit social objectives to soil use and suitability for maximum environmental enhancement.

Table 2—Kinds of soil surveys and their uses.

Kinds of soil survey	Examples of use	Type of planning
1st Order	Experimental plots, sites for houses	Detailed—very intesive planning
2nd Order	Farming, ranching, woodland management, urban development	Detailed planning
3rd Order	Extensive ranching or woodland management, watershed management	General—specialized planning
4th Order	Large watersheds Large resource conservation and development areas Large regional Council of Governments areas County or multicounty planning districts State planning districts	General planning
5th Order	Multistate or nations	General—very broad planning

Full appreciation of soil variability and map reliability first requires an understanding of the soil mapping process itself. The soil scientist maps through a process of predictions and verifications. His predictions are based on careful study of soil landscape features. He recognizes subtle differences in such features as configuration or gradient of slope, landforms, and vegetation as marks of potential soil boundaries. In mapping, the soil scientist plans his traverses across an area in such a way as to check his prediction of the soil boundaries and the kinds of soil within them. These predictions are verified as he crosses the areas and their boundaries. At all times he must keep in mind the definitions of the soils and the composition of the mapping units as stated in the map legend. A comprehensive descriptive legend is one of the standards needed for quality control, in making Order 1 and Order 2 surveys. For surveys in Orders 3 through 5, traverses are much farther apart and projected soil boundaries are not observed throughout their course.

During the mapping, the soil scientist is keenly aware of the kind of information the particular users need. He is constantly applying all his skills in basic principles of soil genesis, soil classification, and soil-landscape relationships in mapping soils. Usually, although he estimates proportions of different kinds of soils from scattered observations made during the course of the survey, he can improve these estimates by additional examinations that are statistically controlled.

Procedures commonly used by soil scientists are the transect methods described by Johnson (1961). The line-intercept method is used where the soil scientist can recognize each boundary between kinds of soil, and the point-intercept method is used where he cannot. Both methods use random selection of the direction of transects. The soil scientist then walks a straight line and records the number of steps taken between boundaries of each soil or, for the point-intercept method, the number of steps taken between observations at regular intervals. Bartelli and DeMent (1970) recommended these sampling techniques for determining the composition of low-intensity mapping units in the South Appalachians. They indicate that by using these methods, along with certain other controls on number of observations and spacing, they can approximate an error of ±5 with a 95% probability for the major components of a soil association.

Some investigators (White, 1966) have challenged the transect method because of the large number of transects needed for accurate estimates. It is true that a large number of randomly located transects are needed if stratification of soil on the basis of landscape features is ignored. However, stratification of the landscape is an integral part of the mapping process.

Another procedure occasionally used by a soil mapper to determine mapping unit composition is to use sample blocks. Highly detailed maps of selected small areas are made to determine the kinds and proportions of the principal constituent soils. Areas of kinds of soil are measured by planimeter or dot-counter. These measurements are summarized and extended to represent the composition of the mapping unit throughout the soil survey area. The number of blocks and their size are determined by statistical principles. Sampling by transects is usually a more efficient method than sampling by blocks.

It is important to remember that, during the mapping process, usually only qualitative appraisals of composition and variation of mapping units are made. Increasingly, the use of statistically controlled sampling procedures for making quantitative appraisals is being studied. Interest in the reliability of mapping units is indicated by the many papers reviewed by Beckett and Webster (1971) in their review of soil variability. A number of workers have examined the accuracy of soil surveys in the United States (McCormack and Wilding, 1969; Powell and Springer, 1965; Protz et al.; 1968; Wilding et al.; 1964 and 1965), but most of the techniques used do not readily lend themselves to an ongoing operational soil survey. Methods used require a large number of samples and are time consuming and expensive. Most methods use a random sampling technique, although some workers (Protz et al., 1968) have used a plot or grid design fitted to a specific geomorphic surface.

New and innovative techniques such as the Random Traverse Method developed by Steers and Hajek (Carter A. Steers and B. F. Hajek. Soil Conserv. Serv. and Alabama Agric. Exp. Stn., personal communications) are needed. This procedure provides for random sampling of mapping units and a statistical method for analyzing the field data. After the soil scientist has traversed the area and delineated soil areas on the field sheet, he locates available transects. These available transects are those that the soil scientist judges to be representative of specific delineations and which he believed would typify existent populations. These available transects are distributed evenly throughout the mapping unit as it exists in the survey area. A record of available transects is maintained, and from this record the transects to be sampled by field investigation are selected by use of a random numbers table. These random transects are then sampled by field investigation and the results are analyzed statistically. The analysis provides estimates of variance and compares the following parameters: (i) number of traverses needed to characterize soil at a specific confidence (n); (ii) arithmetic mean for a specific soil (x); and (iii) confidence interval ($c.i.$).

The random traverse method was developed primarily for use in heavily forested and highly dissected areas where, primarily, Order 3 soil surveys are made. It can also be used for quality control in Order 2 surveys. It has been used successfully in a number of Alabama counties and is an effective method of providing quality control and improving the usefulness of soil maps.

The random traverse method and other statistical methods of analyzing map reliability are not designed for use in locating soil boundaries. They are used to determine mapping unit composition and purity. They improve interpretation of soil maps by determining quantitative values for the soil components of the soil mapping unit, which increases the confidence of interpretations made for the individual mapping unit.

Although for scientific purposes it may be useful to know the variability of specific soil properties, for example, texture, horizon thickness, depth, etc., within soil mapping units, most studies should be designed to identify areas of soil that react differently to use and management or manipulation. Much of the work reported in the past has been through assessments of specific soil properties for defining taxonomic limits. Departures significant to use and management often have not been considered. If discussed at all, it has been done so in a relative way. For example, Beckett and Webster's (1971) summary of the work of seven different researchers indicates that three of the authors find that impurities do not appreciably affect management.

Obviously, the 85% purity assumed for so many years by the National Cooperative Soil Survey is not correct if mapping units are assessed strictly on the basis of the narrow class limits of Soil Taxonomy. But if the assessment is based on those properties that materially affect management or soil use, the 85% figure may have been realistic. It is possible to design mapping units in a way that keeps to a minimum included areas of soils whose behavior is different from that of the dominant soil or soils. One study in west-central Ohio (Wilding et al., 1965) indicates that "only a small percentage of the inclusions represent soils that would behave strikingly different than the dominant soil of the unit." Mapping units can also be designed for areas of complex soil patterns and areas where the intensity of land use is low. In using soil maps, it is important to remember that not all mapping units can be interpreted with the same degree of confidence. In properly designed soil surveys, the degree of reliability depends largely on mapping unit design. The description of the mapping unit should be read by the user wishing to make maximum use of the soil map.

V. OTHER KINDS OF SOIL MAPS

Soil maps are also made by other than field methods. Such maps are made at small scales, usually 1:63,560 to 1:1,000,000 or even smaller. They are made to give the user an overall picture of a large area. In the past such maps were colored line maps. Some later maps have used satellite photography as a base.

A. General Soil Maps

Generalized soil maps are constructed from more detailed soil maps. They reveal patterns of soil that are not apparent on more detailed soil maps. They are made for those who need information about an area larger than individual tracts or fields; many are used for planning. The scale of the soil maps should match the scale of the planning maps. More specifically, the minimum size of the decision-making units should match the minimum size of the delineations on the soil map (Nichols and Bartelli, 1974). Planning, especially urban planning, is often done at three scales. Maps for a broad look at about 1:250,000 are constructed for general planning. Maps at a scale of about 1:63,560 to 1:100,000 are used for an intermediate level. Detailed planning is usually done at a scale of 1:24,000 or larger. Soil maps are often constructed at all three scales in areas where there is a need.

Colored general soil maps at a scale of about 1:250,000 have been published in modern soil surveys. They are used to give an overall view of the area where photo atlas sheets are used for the detailed soil surveys. Intermediate scale maps of 1:63,560 to 1:100,000 of some areas are made in a few copies for local use but not for general distribution.

General soil maps overlap in scale with maps made by field methods. If the purpose for making the map is similar, there should be little difference in the map regardless of the method. If the map scale is smaller, some of the smaller delineations on the large-scale map must be combined. This reduction of scale and combination of soil areas has been called *cartographic generalization* (Orvedal and Edwards, 1941). Simonson (1971) pointed out that construction of a general soil map required a small enough number of map units for comprehension by the user. At the larger scale, general soil maps are usually named as combinations of two or three soil series. They were named *soil associations* in the past, but are now called *general soil map units* when they fail to meet the present definitions of soil associations. Maps at 1:1,000,000 or smaller scales are often named for higher categories in the soil taxonomy, such as subgroups or great groups. Examples of map generalization at various scales is shown in Fig. 1, 2, and 3.

B. Schematic Soil Maps

Schematic soil maps are compiled from existing data but not wholly from soil maps. Soil maps may be used in part, but maps of the vegetation, geology, topography, and climate are used if unavailable. Notes from travelers and other information are combined by skilled soil scientists to construct a relatively accurate small-scale map. Airphotos and other remote sensing maps for base maps can increase the reliability of such maps. Recently, remote-sensing data have furnished coverage that assist in prepar-

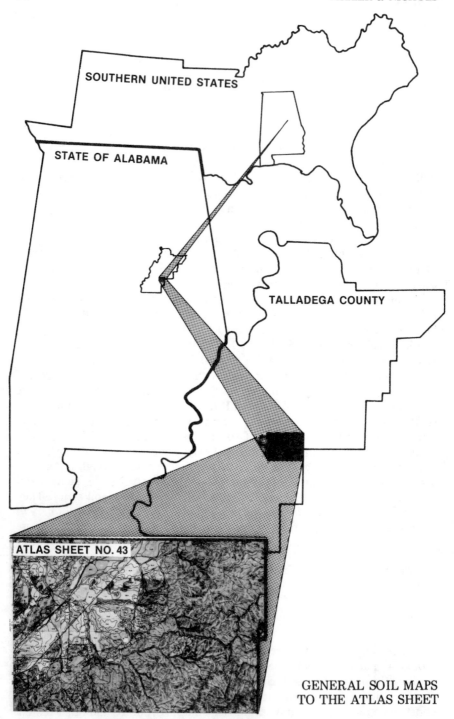

SOUTHERN UNITED STATES

STATE OF ALABAMA

TALLADEGA COUNTY

ATLAS SHEET NO. 43

GENERAL SOIL MAPS
TO THE ATLAS SHEET

Fig. 1—Sequence of soil maps shown in Fig. 2 and 3 showing the relation of atlas sheet no. 43
to the smaller scale maps.

Fig. 2—Part of the detailed soil survey of Talladega County, Ala., showing atlas sheet no. 43. Original scale—1:20,000. Note the enhanced soil line indicating major soil differences occurs on all four maps.

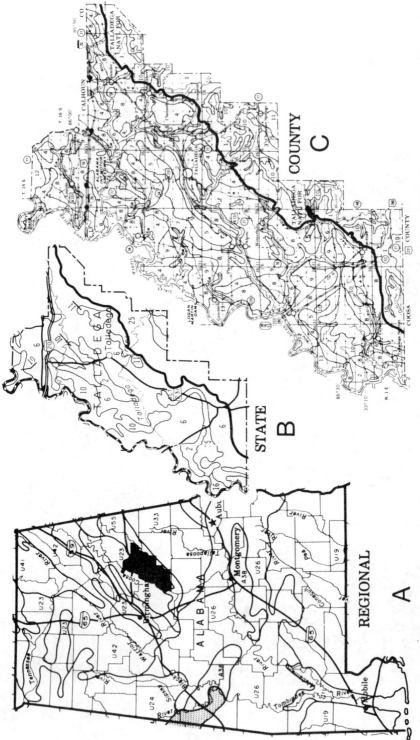

Fig. 3—Generalized soil maps showing: (A) Talladega County on the regional soil map. Original scale—1:5,000,000. (B) Talladega County on state soil map of Alabama. Original scale—1:1,000,000. (C) General soil map of Talladega County, Alabama. Original scale—1:316,000.

ing schematic soil maps. Such maps are usually made at small scales. They are made to give an identification of soil resources on a broad scale. The soil map of the United States on sheet 86 in the National Atlas (U.S. Geolog. Surv., 1970) at a scale of 1:17,000,000 is partly schematic, although much of it is generalized.

C. Interpretive Soil Maps

Interpretive soil maps are constructed from detailed soil maps. They give the viewer a quick visual pattern, usually in color. The advantage is that the 10 to as many as 100 or more mapping units can be interpreted for about three classes of use. An example is slight, moderate, and severe soil limitations for dwellings. Some of the delineations are also generalized, making the map much easier to read. Hunter et al. (1966), in their paper about the use of soil maps by city officials for planning, note that the greatest problem with the use of soil survey information has been the lack of interpretive maps.

Interpretive maps are not new. In the 1930's when the soil conservation movement was growing rapidly, farmers were furnished soil maps that showed land capability classes in colors. Interpretive maps were also made for corn yields and other uses. Interpretive maps can be made at any scale if soil maps are available. A page-size interpretive map *Soil Erosion of the United States* was issued in 1948 by the Soil Conservation Service. The map was compiled from a 1934 erosion survey. The map was colored to depict three degrees of erosion.

The recent rapid increase in the number of interpretive maps resulted from the increase in nonagricultural or urban planning. Many of the first interpretive maps were constructed from detailed soil maps, but the number of interpretive maps of general soil surveys increased rapidly. Bartelli (1962, 1966) and Wohletz (1966) describe the use of interpretive general soil maps in planning. The publication *Soil Surveys and Land Use Planning* (Bartelli et al., 1966) includes numerous examples of interpretive soil maps.

D. Interpretive Soils Maps from Computers

As the demand for interpretive maps increased, computers were used to speed and/or cut cost of the process. It is not surprising that this process was used to substitute for the slow hand construction of interpretive maps. In the early 1960's many computer-generated maps were prepared. Perhaps as many as 100 different cell-type computer programs were written. The cell-type maps are made by placing a grid over a soil map and coding either the dominant soil within a cell or the soil at a point within a cell and storing the code in the computer system. This code can be translated to a use and an interpretive map printed by the computer (Fig. 4). A later process allowed automatic drafting to replace the line printer map. If land use or other basic data are coded into the same cell, the computer can be programmed to make multiple rating interpretive maps from the different sources of data. An example is a map showing the location of Capability Class I land not now being farmed.

The Map Information and Display System (MIADS) computer program developed by personnel of the USDA Forest Service (Amidon, 1966) has been used by the Soil Conservation Service in making interpretive soil maps (Nichols and Bartelli, 1974) for many millions of acres of land. These type of maps have been used widely because of the lower cost and less time required compared with other methods.

The cell-type maps have been used mostly for the general planning for which they are best suited. There have been a few attempts at using cell-type maps with very small cells to reproduce detailed soil maps. The cost increases rapidly as the cell size decreases. Cell-type maps with 8- to 64-ha cells do offer advantages of faster and cheaper interpretive map construction. They also allow the user to store the larger number of mapping units from a detailed survey. This procedure allows more accurate interpretations than those made from a general soil map with only 10 or 15 mapping units.

A disadvantage of the cell type system is that the soil lines are moved from their original location to the squared format (Nichols, 1975), which in-

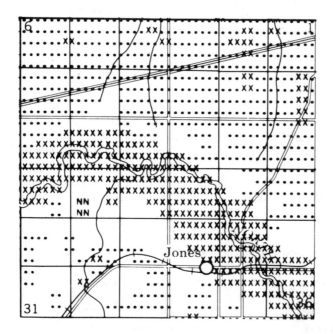

Severe limitations — X X
Moderate limitations — ..
Slight limitations — blank
Not surveyed — NN

Fig. 4—A 93.2-km² (36-mi²) segment of a computer-generated interpretive map. Limitations for dwellings without basements in Oklahoma County, Okla. Cells were 16.20 ha (40 acres).

creases the amount of dissimilar soils along the edges of soil delineations. For this reason cell type maps should be interpreted by those familar with the soil map. In most cases, interpretations of the soil map should be simple and somewhat generalized.

Computer systems that store line segments are under development. They will allow interpretive soil maps of greater precision and also interpretive maps of detailed soil maps.

VI. RELATED SOIL DATA

A. Point Data-Pedon Descriptions

The pedon is the smallest body of soil that we sample and describe. Descriptions of these individual sampling units form the basis for the soil series description. For most soils, it is not possible to determine all the properties important to soil use or manipulation by studying a sampling unit as small as a single pedon. A number of pedons must be examined before establishing class limits between one kind of soil and another. Basic to this understanding is the concept of the polypedon as defined in *Soil Taxonomy* (Soil Survey Staff, 1975): "The soil that we classify consists of contiguous similar pedons that are bounded on all sides by 'not-soil' or by pedons of unlike character." Johnson (1963b) likened the pedon to "building blocks" that provide a convenient method for "synthesizing descriptions of polypedons and soil-map entities."

Descriptions of pedons and polypedons are the fundamental bases for soil identification, classification, and interpretation. Through study of a number of pedons, the "central" or typical pedon along with its allowable ranges in characteristics is defined. The *Soil Survey Manual* (Soil Survey Staff, 1951) gives the procedures and nomenclature for describing soils.

In addition to describing the internal properties, soil descriptions also record those observed and inferred attributes that help identify the soil and distinguish it from all other soils. Geographical features such as landform, relief, nature of regolith, climate, and landscape features are included.

The many soil descriptions made during the course of a soil survey are recorded in the soil handbook for the area. The descriptions along with transect data characterize the mapping units.

B. Benchmark Soils

Benchmark soils have been described and studied in the National Cooperative Soil Survey for many years. *Benchmark soils* are those that, because of their large extent, their key position in the classification system, or their occurrence in critical areas, are important to our understanding of soils. It is impossible to make detailed studies of all soils because of their vast number. The practical approach is to obtain a thorough understanding of soil behavior through detailed studies on a few important soils. The information about these benchmark soils can then be extended to those soils that are closely related in classification and geography.

The Soil Conservation Service maintains lists of benchmark soils. Although the responsibility for maintaining this list rests with the Soil Conservation Service, all cooperating agencies who do research related to soils are consulted. Users interested in obtaining information on benchmark soils should contact the state office of the Soil Conservation Service.

C. Yield Data for Named Kinds of Soil

Soil productivity, expressed as estimates of average yields of specified plants under defined level of management, is indicated for each named kind of soil within a survey area. These yield estimates can be made for several levels of management if needed by users of individual soil surveys. Recently published soil surveys generally contain estimated yields for only one level of management. This is the level of management at which the latest soil and crop management practices are used. The management needed to achieve the indicated yields of the various crops depends, of course, on the kind of soil and the crop.

Yield estimates are based mainly on the experience and record of farmers, conservationists, and extension agents. Accurately measured yields are the most reliable sources, but these are not available for all kinds of soil within a survey area. Consequently, most estimates of yields are based on records for a few benchmark soils.

D. Laboratory Analytical Data

When classifying soils in the field, a soil scientist is limited in his ability to ascertain some soil properties important to soil classification and behavior. To establish certain distinctions between soils or to answer questions regarding soil morphology, genesis, classification, and behavior, detailed laboratory studies are needed. This is not meant to imply, however, that laboratory studies alone will produce the needed answers. More important is a combination of field and laboratory studies to get the most useful solution to specific problems.

Soil survey investigations combining field and laboratory work are conducted for four principal purposes: (i) To characterize soils so that they can be placed appropriately in the nationwide system of soil classification at the series or higher categorical level; (ii) To obtain quantitative data for interpretations; (iii) To increase our knowledge and understanding of soil genesis; and (iv) To provide field standards for specific soil characteristics such as soil texture and to check other field determinations.

In addition to the National Soil Survey Laboratory of the Soil Conservation Service, many state agricultural experiment stations, several state highway departments, the Bureau of Public Roads, and other federal and state agencies particpate in soil survey investigations and provide useful data.

E. Soil Mechanics Test Data

Increased use of soil survey information for other than agricultural uses has created the need for more data related to engineering uses of the soil. Modern soil surveys now contain interpretations important to constructing and maintaining buildings, roads, sanitary facilities, and many other engineering works. Engineering test data that help in making these interpretations are obtained during the course of the soil survey.

Most of the engineering test data available in support of soil surveys are obtained from cooperating state highway departments. Although kinds of test data from specific highway testing laboratories vary somewhat, they generally include mechanical analysis, liquid limit, plastic limit, maximum dry density, and optimum moisture. Some include volume change data, California bearing ratio, and other data useful in evaluating the soils for engineering purposes.

As in other detailed studies, the idea of benchmark soils is used. Test data are obtained on a few important soils, and the data are extended to other similar soils.

Although most engineering test data related directly to soil survey are obtained from state highway departments, additional data are available from the two soil mechanics testing facilities of the Soil Conservation Service.

VII. SOURCES OF INFORMATION

A. Soil Survey Coverage of the United States

Information on the availability of soil survey coverage of the United States can be obtained from Soil Conservation Service offices. A map of the United States is published periodically that shows counties or survey areas for which soil surveys have been published, areas in which the fieldwork has been completed and the survey is awaiting publication, and areas in which the fieldwork is underway. A list of published soil surveys by counties within states is issued annually. Copies of published soil surveys are available from field offices in the survey area. Copies of the soil surveys are available from U.S. Senators and Congressmen for a short time after the survey is published. They are sometimes available from cooperators in the survey.

Copies of the soil maps and soil handbooks are available for use in the local Soil Conservation Service field office for surveys in progress but not published.

Approximately 2,423 soil survey areas had been published by January 1975. About 1,150 of these surveys are out of print and not available for distribution. These surveys are available at many libraries. Most of the soil surveys published since 1957 contain soil maps printed in Atlas sheet format on a photo base. The usual scale is 1:24,000, 1:20,000, or 1:15,840.

Soil classification has improved as our knowledge about soils and their potential uses has increased. Because of this, soils bearing the same names are more narrowly defined in recent surveys than in older surveys. Some soil series have been divided into five or six series as improvement in classification has allowed the more narrow definition needed by users with more refined management inputs. Users may need the help of a soil scientist or person trained in the use of soil surveys to make maximum use of the older surveys.

B. Soil Survey Investigation Reports

The most common source of published laboratory data is the U.S. Department of Agriculture series *Soil Survey Investigation Reports.* This series was established to make available technical information from cooperative investigations of soils of the United States, Puerto Rico, and the Virgin Islands. To date, 30 reports have been published. *Soil Survey Investigations Report no. 1* (Soil Survey Staff, rev. 1972) describes in detail the methods and procedures now used or formerly used by the soil survey laboratories of the Soil Conservation Service. Most other reports in the series contain pedon descriptions and physical, chemical, and mineralogical data from the individual states. Some, such as *Soil Survey Investigations Report no. 21, A Toposequence of Soils in Tonalite Grus in the Southern California Peninsular Range,* report completed studies of soil genesis.

Before quoting from State Soil Survey Investigations Reports, users should contact the state soil scientist of the respective state. Many of the soil descriptions in these publications were originally prepared as working documents and not for publication. The information recorded, including concepts of soil series, relationships among pedons, and field estimates of properties, was compiled to meet a specific need of a soil survey. Editing of this material, therefore, is minimal. The emphasis is to preserve descriptive data. Users should also be aware of possible changes in series names. Refinements in soil classification have resulted in changes in the concepts of some series so that the series name may no longer be appropriate.

Other sources of published data include published soil surveys, technical journals, regional bulletins, and USDA technical bulletins.

It should be reemphasized that most soil survey investigations require both field and laboratory studies; few, if any, involve only the laboratory. As discussed by Kellogg (1962), the most effective use of the laboratory in soil survey investigations requires teamwork. Skilled field morphologists and laboratory scientists working together produce the best results.

C. Unpublished Laboratory Data

Not all laboratory data obtained during the course of a soil survey are published. Most of the data published in Soil Survey Investigation Reports, in published soil surveys, or in technical journals and articles are fairly complete. Data collected to confirm field observations, to solve minor classification and interpretation questions, or to aid in planning more comprehensive projects are often not published. Although not published, these data are available from both federal and state sources.

The most important sources of unpublished laboratory data in the Soil Conservation Service are the National Soil Survey Laboratory at Lincoln, Nebraska, the Soil Classification and Mapping Branch (SCAM) at Hyattsville, Maryland, and SCS state offices. The SCAM Branch maintains files of analytical data from both soil survey and engineering laboratories. This soil data bank also includes an index of soil laboratory data. The index contains only data that have been obtained by procedures that are widely used or that are widely accepted as reliable, and all pedons are classified as to soil series or soil family. Fairly complete sets of data as well as partial sets are stored. Many of the data originate in Soil Conservation Service, but data from cooperating agencies are also included if the agencies that produce the data agree to have it included. The soil data bank system became operational in 1976. Although all new data will be indexed, it will be some time before all the previously existing data can be stored. Therefore, users should refer to the National Soil Survey Laboratory for older data.

The department of soils or agronomy of land grant universities constitutes the major source of unpublished data in individual states. A wealth of data from ongoing research projects, special studies, and unpublished theses are available to help answer problems of immediate concern. Often these data are directly related to soil surveys as many of the studies are done cooperatively with participants of an active soil survey.

The Agricultural Research Service is another important source of unpublished laboratory data. Much of their research is cooperative with state agricultural experiment stations and other organizations. Often these data apply to soil surveys. The Agricultural Research Service has an information service in their Washington office on research projects. Through an ongoing computer program entitled Current Research Information Service (CRIS), information can be obtained on the nature and objective of ongoing research projects, as well as those that have been published.

LITERATURE CITED

Amidon, E. L. 1966. MIADS2 . . . an alphanumeric map information assembly and display system for a large computer. U.S. For. Serv. Res. Pap. PSW-38. Pacific Southwest For. and Range Exp. Stn., Berkeley, Calif. 12 p.

Bartelli, L. J. 1962. Use of soils information in urban-fringe areas. J. Soil Water Conserv. 17: 99–103.

Bartelli, L. J. 1966. General soils maps—a study of landscapes. J. Soil Water Conserv. 21:3–6.

Bartelli, L. J., J. V. Baird, M. R. Heddleson, and A. A. Klingebiel (ed.). 1966. Soil surveys and land use planning. Am. Soc. Agron., Madison, Wis.

Bartelli, L. J., and J. A. DeMent. 1970. Soil survey—a guide for forest management decisions in the Southern Appalachians. p. 427–434. In Proc. of the 3rd North Am. Forest Soils Conf. North Carolina State Univ. at Raleigh. Oregon State Univ. Press, Corvallis, Ore.

Beckett, P. H. T., and R. Webster. 1971. Soil variability: a review. Soils Fert 34(1):1–14.

Cline, M. G. 1961. The changing model of soil. Soil Sci. Soc. Am. Proc. 25:442–446.

Hunter, W. R., C. W. Tips, and J. R. Cover. 1966. Use of soil maps by city officials for operational planning. p. 31–36. In J. V. Baird, M. R. Heddleson, and A. A. Klingebiel (ed.) Soil surveys and land use planning. Am. Soc. Agron., Madison, Wis.

Johnson, W. M. 1961. Soil survey field letter, June. USDA Soil Conserv. Serv. p. 9–11.

Johnson, W. M. 1963a. The pedon and the polypedon. Soil Sci. Soc. Am. Proc. 27:212–215.

Johnson, W. M. 1963b. Relation of the new comprehensive soil classification system to soil mapping. Soil Sci. 96:31–34.

Johnson, W. J., and L. J. Bartelli. 1974. Rural development: a natural resource dimensions. J. Soil Water Conserv. 29:18–19.

Kellogg, C. E. 1959. Soil classification and correlation in the soil survey. Soil Conserv. Serv., USDA, Washington, D.C. 27 p.

Kellogg, C. E. 1961. Soil interpretation in the soil survey. Soil Conserv. Serv., USDA, Washington, D.C. 27 p.

Kellogg, C. E. 1962. The place of the laboratory in soil classification and interpretation. Soil Conserv. Serv., USDA, Washington, D.C. 21 p.

Klingebiel, A. A. 1963. Land classification for land use planning. p. 399–407. In USDA Agric. Yearbook, 1963. Washington, D.C.

McCormack, D. W. 1974. Soil potentials: a positive approach to urban planning. J. Soil Water Conserv. 29:258–262.

McCormack, D. E., and L. P. Wilding. 1969. Variation of soil properties within mapping units of soils with contrasting substrata in N.W. Ohio. Soil Sci. Soc. Am. Proc. 33:587–593.

Nichols, J. D. 1975. Characteristics of computerized soil maps. Soil Sci. Soc. Am. Proc. 39: 927–932.

Nichols, J. D., and L. J. Bartelli. 1974. Computer-generated interpretive soil maps. J. Soil Water Conserv. 29:232–235.

Orvedal, A. C., and M. J. Edwards. 1941. General principles of technical grouping of soil. Soil Sci. Soc. Am. Proc. 6:386–391.

Powell, J. C., and M. E. Springer. 1965. Composition and precision of several mapping units of the Appling, Cecil and Lloyd series in Walton Co., Georgia. Soil Sci. Soc. Am. Proc. 29:454–458.

Protz, R., E. W. Presant, and R. W. Arnold. 1968. Establishment of the modal profile and measurement of variability within a soil landform unit. Can. J. Soil Sci. 48:7–19.

Simonson, R. W. 1952. Lessons from the first half century of soil survey: II. Mapping of soils. Soil Sci. 74:323–330.

Simonson, R. W. 1971. Soil association maps and proposed nomenclature. Soil Sci. Soc. Am. Proc. 35:959–965.

Smith, G. D. 1963. Objections and basic assumptions of the new soil classification system. Soil Sci. 96:6–16.

Soil Survey Staff. 1951. Soil survey manual. USDA Handb. 18. U.S. Government Printing Office, Washington, D.C.

Soil Survey Staff. 1972. Soil survey laboratory methods and procedures for collecting soil samples. Soil Surv. Invest. Rep. no. 1, rev. USDA, Soil Conserv. Serv., Washington, D.C.

Soil Survey Staff. 1975. Soil taxonomy. USDA Handb. no. 436, U.S. Government Printing Office, Washington, D.C.

U.S. Geological Survey, U.S. Department of the Interior. 1970. The national atlas of the United States of America. Washington, D.C.

White, E. M. 1966. Validity of the transect method for estimating compositions of soil-map areas. Soil Sci. Soc. Am. Proc. 30:129-130.

Wilding, L. P., G. M. Schafer, and R. B. Jones. 1964. Morley and Blount soils: A statistical summary of certain physical and chemical properties of some selected profiles from Ohio. Soil Sci. Soc. Am. Proc. 28:674-679.

Wilding, L. P., R. B. Jones, and G. M. Schafer. 1965. Variation of soil morphological properties within Miami, Celina, and Crosby mapping units in West-Central Ohio. Soil Sci. Soc. Am. Proc. 29:711-717.

Wohletz, L. R. 1966. Soil maps in land planning. Soil Conserv. 32(1):8-9, 18-19.

5   Interpreting Soil Data

LINDO J. BARTELLI

Michigan Technological University
Houghton, Michigan

I. INTRODUCTION

A soil survey needs to be translated from a complex scientific language of the soil scientist to simple expressions of soil behavior that soil map users can understand. This is soil survey interpretation. Each user presents unique demands in that he is primarily concerned about his problems and usually each kind of user has an unique language. These demands vary. Some users are searching for the most suitable site for growing crops. Others are interested in the management and improvement inputs needed for most efficient land use. More recently, those concerned with broad land use problems common to a land use planning district have learned of the value of a properly interpreted soil survey. In contrast, there are soil map users who look to soil surveys for help in selecting and improving home sites, waste disposal sites, and roads and highway sites. A successful soil survey is designed to meet all of these needs.

The soil survey staff of the Soil Conservation Service is revising the *Soil Survey Manual, Agricultural Handbook 18.* A 1975 interim publication (fifth draft) is available for testing and review by the staffs of the National Cooperative Soil Survey. Several chapters deal with soil data. Chapter 11, in particular, concentrates on methods being used to interpret soil surveys. Much of the information is in the "how to" form and will supplement the material in this chapter.

II. KINDS OF SOIL DATA

Soil data are presented to the user in two forms. The unique spatial concept is produced through the soil map, and the other form is the more common narrative and tabular systems. The latter methods are related to a vertical scheme. In the vertical scheme data are presented for artificial classes of a soil classification system. These are the taxonomic units of *Soil Taxonomy* (Soil Survey Staff, 1975). The horizontal or spatial scheme is presented through the soil mapping unit.

A. The Soil Taxonomic Unit

Soil Taxonomy (Soil Survey Staff, 1975) is used to organize sets of soil properties and catalog them into taxonomic classes. It is based on man's concept of soil as a three-dimensional body that occupies space in the landscape (Simonson, 1968). The taxon includes soil pedons that are large enough to be described and sampled but a taxon, per se, is seldom mapped as a complete unit. *Soil Taxonomy* is a system of many categories (Fig. 1). Each category is a set of classes that subdivides the entire range of soils into compartments, each having the same degree of homogeneity. Field morphological descriptions and measured data from the laboratories are used to define the classes. Each step or subdivision creates classes of successively more limited ranges in a lower category. For example, all Alfisols, one of the orders, have distinct argillic horizons; at the suborder levels Alfisols are subdivided into Aqualfs—wet soils, Boralfs—the cold soils, Ustalfs—dry soils, Xeralfs—rainy winter and dry summer soils, and Udalfs—soils with humid moisture regimes. All have argillic horizons. Each taxa represents a defined set of soil properties.

The class of the lowest categoric rank is the soil series. Usually bodies of soils shown as delineations on soil maps are related to soil series. In this manner existing knowledge about nature, origin, and behavior of soils are brought to bear on specific tracts of land. The Mahaska series is an example

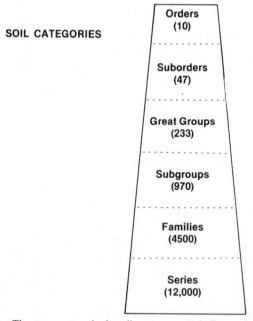

SOIL CATEGORIES

Orders (10)

Suborders (47)

Great Groups (233)

Subgroups (970)

Families (4500)

Series (12,000)

Fig. 1—The many categories in soil taxonomy. ( ) indicates the approximate number of classes in each category within the U.S.A.

Table 1—Engineering properties for the Mahaska series.†

Depth (in)	USDA texture	Unified	AASHTO	Fract. >3 in (PCT)	% of material < 3 in passing sieve	Liquid limit	Plasticity index	Permeability (in/hour)	Available water capacity (in/in)	Shrink-swell potential	Corrosivity Steel	Corrosivity Concrete
0-18	SICL	Cl,OL	A-7	0	100 100 100 95-100	41-50	15-25	0.6-2.0	0.21-0.23	Moderate	High	Moderate
18-51	SICL	CH	A-7	0	100 100 100 95-100	50-60	20-30	0.2-0.6	0.14-0.18	High	High	Moderate
51-73	SICL	CL	A-7	0	100 100 100 95-100	41-50	15-25	0.6-2.0	0.18-0.20	High	High	Moderate

† Classification and brief soil description: Fine, montmorillonitic, mesic, Aquic Argiudolls. The Mahaska series consists of nearly level to gently sloping, somewhat poorly drained soils. They have formed in loess under a native vegetation of tall prairie grasses. These soils are on moderately wide upland ridges, in coves to drainageways, and on high stream benches. Mahaska soils typically have a black silty clay loam surface layer 18 in thick. The subsoil, which extends to 60 in, is mottled dark grayish brown to olive brown, silty clay loam in the upper part and mottled light olive gray medium silty clay loam in the lower part. Substratum is gray silty clay loam. Slopes 1 to 5%.

of a class of the lowest category. These soils occur in central Iowa. Some of the data provided for the Mahaska series are shown in Table 1.

B. The Soil Mapping Unit

Veatch (1937) proposed the natural land type as a kind of natural division of the land surface which combines, or integrates, a number of separate features of topography and soil into units to which can be tied studies in human ecology, or economic studies pertaining to the use of land. Veatch referred to the natural land type as the *natural environmental unit.* These units, proposed by Veatch, occupy space in that he added the soil factor to the natural landscape divisions of the geologist and the physiographer. The soil mapping unit encompasses these ideas; it occupies space and is designed to be most useful to the agriculturist, the forester, the geographer, the land planner, and the civil and sanitary engineer. The soil mapping units are map delineations of landscape systems. The soil mapping unit is the result of the interaction among the various landscape components and is expressed as follows:

$$SMU = f(O_iS_il_ip_iy_i)$$

$$SMU = soil\ mapping\ unit$$

where
   f = function of interaction,
   O = organisms,
   S = soil factors as expressed by taxonomic units,
   l = landscape features,
   p = potential natural vegetation clusters, and
   y = potential yield.

The *Soil Survey Manual* (Soil Survey Staff, 1951) identifies the soil taxonomic unit, S in the equation, as the basic unit. All of the other components are recognized as subdivisions within the taxonomic unit or, more commonly, soil phases. In the equation all features are components of the soil mapping unit and are considered significant to the nature and functioning of the soil in the natural landscape. Thus, a significant change in any one of the landscape components may result in a different soil mapping unit.

Organisms reflect the actions of living beings. These actions may be beneficial or detrimental. The end result should influence the definition of the mapping unit. An example is a raw strip-mined area where man destroyed the original soil and left an unique soil area. Severe clearcutting of thickly stocked timber stands also may change the nature of the landscape unit to justify another mapping unit. Artificial drainage installed to change the vegetation from a natural swamp and marsh to a cultivated crop is another example.

Soil factors expressed as unique kinds of soil at the series level in *Soil*

Taxonomy (Soil Survey Staff, 1975) are considered. Some features, such as excessive wetness or shallowness to hard country rock, dominate the behavior pattern to the extent that other soil features become insignfiicant. Soil factors may be either morphological or compositional. They are those factors that affect either the soil-engineering behavior or the soil-plant root relations and are usually diagnostic at some level in *Soil Taxonomy*.

The landscape features are part of the soil environment. They are not considered in *Soil Taxonomy* (Soil Survey Staff, 1975), but are a part of the soilscape. Surface slope, erosion, aspect, soil pattern, rockiness, and geomorphic land forms are some features that have a strong influence in the definition of a soil mapping unit. The interactions between these features and soil series usually have dominating influence on the behavior pattern.

Kuchler (1964) defines potential natural vegetation clusters (PNVC) as the vegetation that would exist today if man were removed from the scene and if the resulting plant succession were telescoped into a single moment. The potential natural vegetation clusters (PNVC) is a sensitive item in the equation and is a good indicator of the kinds of interactions within the equation. In many cases it is theoretical in that the PNVC is predicted from expected interactions. In other cases it parallels Odum's (1971) and Eyre's (1968) concept of climax vegetation—a plant community that is in equilibrium with the physical habitat. In any case, each soil mapping unit will have its unique potential natural vegetation cluster, but some may be more difficult to ascertain than others. Some unique morphological or compositional feature of the soil usually provides the lead. An example is the Kalkaska soils of the upper Great Lakes area with their PNVC of hardwoods that have stronger developed spodic horizons (Typic Haplorthids) and higher calcium contents than the Rubican soils with PNVC of pines that have weaker spodic horizons (Entic Haplorthids) and lower calcium contents in the C horizons. Carleton et al. (1974) found striking correlations between potential natural vegetation and soil properties.

Potential yield is a measure of the plant growth either natural or cultivated. Plant yields should be collected for main kinds of soils for two levels—in the natural state and under good management—to enable the assessment of the response of the soil to management inputs. Response to management is an important input for determining the soil potential.

The soil mapping unit is analogous to the land treatment unit. It is the natural landscape unit that can be compared to the complete ecosystem. An association of soils, plants, and organisms demonstrates ecological kinship. The soil mapping unit is the key to a useful soil survey. It serves as the basic unit for inventorying and managing land.

C. Relations between the Soil Taxonomic Unit and the Soil Mapping Unit

The soil taxonomic unit is a vertical system. It occupies no space. The soil mapping unit is a horizontal system. It occupies space in the landscape. The class of any categorical level (any taxonomic unit) can be used to define and name soil mapping units. The soil mapping unit, however, may have many other soil taxa within its boundary, other than what appears in the name. Usually most soils within a mapping unit of a detail survey (field scale of 1:15,840) will have similar behavior. But unlike soils also may be included, for a natural soilscape that occupied space may not break into handy units that fit a vertical scheme such as *Soil Taxonomy*. The soil mapping unit is flexible. It can be designed to meet the needs of different intensities of soil surveys. In the more detailed soil survey, delineations are small and the components of the soil mapping units are precisely defined. Phases of soil taxonomic units are used at this level as the vehicle to carry the interpretations of soil mapping units. As the soil survey becomes less intensive, map scales are smaller, soil delineations are larger and soil mapping units are more broadly defined. The soil mapping unit may have two or more soil taxonomic units with each having distinctly different behavior patterns. An important factor that dominates the behavior is the manner in which they are associated with each other in addition to the relative total percentages of each soil. The behavior of the soil mapping unit may now be the result of the interaction between the two soil taxonomic units. An example would be a broad soil mapping unit of a pitted outwash sandy plain of the Great Lakes area. A well-drained, infertile, level sandy soil occupies a major part of the area, but is speckled with a random pattern of circular areas of organic soil 1 to 5 ha in size. Each soil acting alone would have different rating of suitability for a deer-hunting area. The sandy soil is rated poor because of a small number of low-yielding food plants. The organic soil has a good supply and growth of browse, but is excessively wet and makes poor bedding sites. However, when the pattern of the two soils is considered and the complementary nature of one soil to the other is noted, it is evident that this soil mapping unit has a high potential for deer hunting, whereas the individual soil taxonomic units would rate poor.

D. Land and Soil Classification

Land and soil classification are used so interchangeably that many soil map users are not aware of the distinction between the two. Land classification forms the starting point of land-use planning. Actually, there is no sharp distinction between land classification and land-use planning. Land classification groups soils according to their native characteristics, present use, yield capacity, crop potential, and behavior patterns; and classes are then assessed with reference to their suitability for the different uses contemplated in the plan. C. E. Kellogg (1940) defines general land classification as a classification of specific, defined, recognizable bodies of land according to their significant physical and cultural characteristics. A land classification may be made from a soil map. Soil classification then becomes a segment of land classification. Soil classification is based on soil characteristics; these properties are used to predict soil behavior. Soil classification does not consider social and economic factors, which are considered in most land classification schemes.

The Land Committee of the United States National Resources Planning Board (1941) distinguishes five types of land classification. The five types are:

Type I—Land classification in terms of inherent characteristics.

Type II—Land classification in terms of present use.

Type III—Land classification in terms of use capabilities.

Type IV—Land classification in terms of recommended use.

Type V—Land classification in terms of program effectuation.

Type I classification is a soil classification based on soil characteristics. It is the least dependent on the use to be made and is essential to the further development of any land classification. Its big advantage is that it provides a basis for drawing conclusions regarding more than one kind of land use. Type II classification is fundamental in the long-settled regions where use has reached an equilibrium with the physical, social, and political factors. Type III classification considers potentialities. The land is assessed according to its characteristics for a specified use. Type IV is a combination of types I, II, and III and serves as the initial stages of a land-use plan. Type V indicates on a map the different stages and methods whereby land-use recommendations are to be carried out. Both type IV and V encompass the economical, social, and political forces of an area. The five types represent a series of increasing complexities, starting in its simplest and most fundamental form as a soil classification and merging into land-use planning without any sharp distinction between them.

III. SOIL PROPERTIES AND ASSOCIATED LAND FEATURES

The data must identify the most important soil properties and associated land features that affect use and management for any selected use. In addition, one must know the limitation, if any, these parameters exert on the use in question. Such information is useful in determining what modifications and other management inputs are needed to develop the most efficient and effective use and management systems.

The Soil Conservation Service (SCS) maintains an up-to-date set of predictions of soil behavior for each kind of soil in a *Technical Guide* found in each Soil Conservation District field office. The *Technical Guide* has, in addition to instructions for planning and applying the principles of soil conservation, a description of the soils, soil limitations, and measures needed to overcome soil limitations. Standards and specifications for establishing engineering practices also are included. *Technical Guides* reflect the input of the various disciplines in the SCS and are used by technicians as a ready reference in their day-to-day work.

A. Soil Properties that Affect the Relationship between Soil and Plant Root Systems

Soil affects plants primarily through its effect on the root of the plant. The roots which are responsible for the water and nutrient absorption are easily injured by unfavorable environments such as poor aeration, lack of moisture, toxicity, and limited space for growth. Soil properties that affect plant root systems are grouped as follows: (i) Those that affect root ramification; (ii) Those that affect soil moisture supply; and (iii) Those that affect the supply of plant nutrients.

Roots only grow in soils in which there is space for the roots to penetrate (Black, 1960). Roots cannot ramify in hardpans, fragipans, or other subsoils where bulk density exceeds 1.8. Roots can penetrate these horizons only through preexisting channels or cracks. Also, roots ramify poorly throughout the bulk of a clay subsoil. They are restricted to the ped faces or to other channels. Roots grow vigorously in well-aerated soils where oxygen content in the soil air is adequate and toxic amounts of carbon-dioxide and byproducts of anaerobic decomposition have not accumulated (Stolzy, 1974). Roots do not live in water-logged conditions. On the other hand, roots do not do well in soils dried to its wilting-point moisture content. Soil temperature, also, affects root ramification. The temperature at which roots start to grow is 7°C but some workers have reported some growth at temperatures as cool as 2°C (Russell, 1961). Growth is also checked when temperature becomes too high. Soil temperature in the root zone has an important influence on the plant root development (Richards et al., 1952; Nielson, 1974).

The soil factors that affect both the storage capacity of available water and the rate of flow of moisture through the soil to the plant root-soil interface are related to the characteristics of the pore space in which water is stored or through which it moves. Number and size of pores and the continuity of pores within a soil horizon and between soil horizons control the amount and rate of movement. Water moves from a higher to a lower potential. Its rate of flow is dependent on the difference in hydrostatic pressure between the two ends of the system and the conductivity rate of the soil medium. Any change in conductivity caused by a change in soil horizons, such as from a porous A horizon to a compact B horizon will change the rate of flow, since the conductivity is changed. Soil water does not move through soil at a steady rate as the soil dries out. In dried soils the conductivity becomes increasingly influenced by the water-content gradient (Newman, 1974).

The available water is assumed to be the water held in tension by the soil between the field capacity and the permanent wilting point. The amount of water held by a soil depends on the amount held per unit volume of soil and on the depth of soil from which plants can extract their water. Studies have shown that silt and organic matter content of a soil layer have significant positive correlation with available water percentage (Bartelli &

Peters, 1959). Other factors, however, should be considered in estimating the soil moisture regime of a soil series. These are surface texture, root ramification zone, moisture conductivity, and depth to a free water zone. Associated land features such as slope and shape of soil surface affects the amount of rainfall that effectively recharges the soil moisture supply.

Roots do not do well in soils deficient in nutrients. Even if the root ramification zone is ample and moisture supply is adequate, root growth is stunted by a lack of nutrients (Russell, 1961). The root system tends to be more branched and more compact in fertile than in poor soils. There are three possible sources from which roots can extract their nutrients: the soil solution, the exchangeable ions, and the readily decomposable minerals. Plants also vary in their ability to extract nutrients. Each soil series, however, has an unique nutrient system. Some systems, such as the Ultisols and some of the Oxisols, are well weathered and devoid of important bases. Others, such as the Udalfs of the north central United States, still have an ample supply of both bases and weatherable minerals. The more fertile soils are able to continually supply from the solid phase bases lost due to uptake by plants.

Some systems have an unfavorable chemical environment with toxic amounts of minerals that inhibit root growth. Aqueous ammonia, copper, zinc, and lead are highly toxic to plant roots (Bennett, 1974). Absolute calcium deficiency inhibits root growth in very sandy, acid soils having low cation exchange capacities (Adams & Pearson, 1967). An accumulation of soluble salts in soils also inhibits growth of many plant roots. Soils with a saturation extract with electrical conductivities greater than 4 mmohs/cm at 25°C are classed as saline soils in the *Soil Survey Manual* (Soil Survey Staff, 1951). Aluminum toxicity is root-limiting in many acid Ultisols of southeastern U.S. and Puerto Rico. Aluminum toxicity does not occur in soils above pH 5.5 but becomes severe below pH 5.0. Aluminum toxicity is more prevalent in soils with colloids of low silica/sesquioxide ratio (Foy, 1974). The soils' behavior in fixing phosphate is very viable. Soils high in iron and aluminum are notorious fixers. Phosphate ions do not move very far in these soils. Fertilizer placement in relation to plant and time of placement in relation to plant growth are critical management measures.

Nitrogen is one of the most unique nutrients in soil. Most plants derive their supply of nitrogen from forms in the soil and nitrogen may occur in many forms, some readily available to plants, others not. Some forms are rather stable, other forms are very soluble in water and move out of the soil system readily. Nitrogen fertilizers applied in the nitrate form present a problem in that what is not used by a living plant leaves the plant-soil system by leaching. Nitrate is lost more rapidly from coarse- than from fine-textured soils. Loss also is greater in well-aerated, well-drained soils than from poorly drained and slowly permeable soils. Rate of movement is also greater when soil temperatures are high.

In summary, the measurable soil properties that are considered in assessing the soil-plant root environment are: effective depth of root ramification zone, size particle distribution, organic matter content, salt content, cation exchange capacity, base saturation, kind of clay mineral, permeability, saturated and unsaturated conductivity, soil wetness (drainage), depth to perched or apparent water table, and available moisture-holding capacity.

B. Soil Properties that Affect Soil Engineering Behavior

Engineers in recent years recognized the relation between soil engineering and the natural soil. Most soil classification systems used by engineers are based on removing the soil from its natural site and testing in the laboratory. Engineering soil behavior depends on pressure exerted by the structure over time and the environment. It brings the environmental features into the engineering judgement process. Spatial characteristics are added to the vertical soil classification system. The interpretations on engineering soil behavior are based on an understanding of the interaction between the properties of soil that can be measured in the laboratory and the soil environment as evaluated from soil morphology. Soil morphology permits an accurate evaluation of the soil moisture regime over time. Changes in soil moisture contents control the soil engineering behavior; great changes occur when a soil changes from the dry to the wet state. Expansive soils change volume only as soil moisture contents change.

The more important engineering soil properties reported by the Asphalt Institute (1969) are permeability, elasticity, plasticity, cohesion, shearing strength, compressibility, shrinkage and swell, and frost susceptibility. Clear definitions for these properties are given in this manual by the Asphalt Institute. Many of the soil properties that influence plant growth are also properties that affect the engineering use of soil. A slowly permeable subsoil not only restricts root growth but also limits the use of the soil for septic tanks (Morris et al., 1962) and makes a very poor subgrade for a highway. The presence of seasonal ground water, the mode of moisture flow through the soil system, and the soil moisture regime are soil environment factors that influence the soil engineering properties. Table 2 is a partial listing of the engineering properties and related natural soil properties that influence the soil engineering behavior (Bartelli, 1962).

The engineer has developed several empirical soil classification schemes

Table 2—Soil engineering properties and their soil characteristic determinants.

Soil engineering behavior	Soil characteristics and properties
Conduit corrosion	Texture, pH, drainage, conductivity
Road subgrades suitability	Drainage, texture, kind of clay, organic matter content
Susceptibility to frost action	Drainage, depth to water table, texture, soil temperature
Shrink-swell potential	Texture, kind of clay
Topsoil suitability	Texture, organic matter content
Behavior of above properties throughout the year	Soil temperature and soil moisture

to obtain soil data needed to better understand soil behavior. The Atterberg limits (Lamke & Whitman, 1969) have proved to be very useful for soil identification and classification. The plasticity index indicates the magnitude of water content range over which the soil remains plastic, and the liquidity index indicates the nearness a soil is to the liquid limit. These limits, however, are determined on soils that have been thoroughly worked into a uniform soil-water mixture. In 1952 the Bureau of Reclamation and the Corps of Engineers adopted a "unified system" intended for use in all engineering problems involving soils (Wagner, 1957). The "unified system" is based on gradation (particle size) and plasticity. The system groups together soils with similar behavior patterns for use in earth dams, canal sections, foundations, and runways. The American Association of State Highways and Transportation Officials (AASHTO) have also adopted a classification system for use in highway construction. It is based on highway performance (AASHTO, 1970). Soils in the same group are classified as A-1 for best soils for road subgrades and A-7 for poorest soils. This scheme also is based on particle size and plasticity. An important difference between the particle size classes recognized in the various engineering classification systems and those used by the soil scientist is in the definition of the clay size, which is <0.002 mm, compared to <0.005 mm in the AASHTO scheme. The AASHTO and unified systems also separate fines from sand at about 0.007 mm, whereas the soil scientist breaks at 0.005 mm.

C. Soil Properties that Affect Soil Erodibility

Van Doren and Bartelli (1956) reported that after standardizing soil loss data from the Flanagan soil at Urbana, Illinois, the Grantsburg soil at Dixon Spring, Illinois, and the Fayette soil at La Crosse, Wisconsin, for degree of slope, slope length, cropping systems, and rainfall patterns, the measured soil loss compared as follows: Flanagan silt loam = 1.0, Fayette silt loam = 1.3, and Grantsburg silt loam = 1.5. These differences were due to chemical and physical properties inherent in the natural soil. Wischmeier et al. (1971) reported soil texture, soil organic matter, soil structure, and permeability as the most influential. Soil erodibility increases with increase in the amount of silt and very fine sand and decreases with greater sand, clay, and organic matter content. The effect of the structure on permeability may be less correlative due to modification by antecedent moisture. Holzhey et al. (1976) suggests the soil taxonomic unit's soil erodibility be evaluated on the basis of modifying the K value solved with Wischmeier et al. (1971) with a synthesis of the water transmission and water retention characteristics, the soil moisture regime, and other features common to the soil taxonomic unit. This would result in a more accurate prediction of the actual soil behavior.

The Universal Soil Loss Equation (USLE) is designed to predict annual soil losses from sheet and rill erosion on specified field slopes. Stewart et al. (1975) presents the USLE as

$$A = RKLSCP$$

where:

A = estimated average annual soil loss,
R = rainfall and runoff erosivity index,
K = soil-erodibility factor,
LS = combined effects of slope length and steepness,
C = cover and management factor, and
P = supporting practices factor.

The USLE is a very useful tool for planning cropping systems. However, its most secure area of application is the midwestern U.S., for this is the area where most of the basic data were collected. Also, soil losses computed by the equation should be considered as estimates rather than as absolutes. Data used to arrive at some of the factors, notably LS, C, and K, are limited and insufficient to warrant complete variance analysis. The equation is most useful for comparing erosional control systems that match a tolerable soil loss rate (T). T value is substituted for A in the USLE equation and values for C and P are solved. The allowable soil loss rate is based on the acceptable level of erosion that the soil can sustain and with modern management can maintain soil productivity over a reasonable length of time. The most durable soils are assigned the highest T values. These soils have over 2 m of favorable subsoil. That is, the subsoil has no substances toxic to plants and with good management has the physical properties needed for abundant growth.

D. Soil Properties that Affect Waste Treatment

The natural soil has proved to be an effective treatment medium for agricultural, industrial, and municipal liquid wastes. The effectiveness of the treatment measure is governed by those soil properties that influence the rate at which liquid wastes will be taken into the soil and the mode of movement. Liquid waste treatment is most effective when the liquid moves through the soil as a moving front and comes in contact with every individual soil particle. The soil must adsorb the potential contaminants or destroy the harmful bacteria and viruses. Bartelli (1974) reported on the ability of the soil to remove cations and anions, decompose organic matter, and filter out and kill bacteria and viruses. The efficiency of the soil is conditioned by the amount of clay, the cation-exchange capacity, the pH, soil permeability or hydraulic conductivity, aluminum-sesquioxide ratio, soil moisture, soil temperature, C/N ratio, soil particle size, and aeration. Those soils best suited for growing cultivated crops are best suited for waste treatment. Soil temperature classes used at the family level in soil taxonomy (Soil Survey Staff, 1975) are useful for predicting the effectiveness of soil treatment in that thermic and hypothermic families have biological activity for 12 mo providing soil moisture is adequate. Water movement in unsaturated soil up to moisture content corresponding with moisture tensions of approximately 100 cm of water is considered marginal by Bouma et al. (1974) for soil disposal of liquid wastes. This rate approximates an unsaturated hydraulic conductivity of 1 cm/day. Bouma et al. (1974) characterized the flow rates of soil series common in Wisconsin. Their report showed that soil series can be grouped on the basis of the soil texture and pore space in selected soil horizons. Each group of soils has a characteristic K curve (See Fig. 1 in Chapt. 27 by Bouma). Olson (1964) presents an equation for a model to determine the retentive capacity of a soil for a pollutant as:

$$R = Cf + (X/M) B$$

where
  R = total retentive capacity of soil,
  X = weight of adsorbate,
  M = weight of adsorbent
  B = bulk density of the soil,
  C = concentration of the pollutant, and
  f = porosity.
Olsons' equation may overlook the antecedent storage of pollutants and also does not consider the possible interactions that may occur when more than one pollutant is involved.

A soil quality index has been proposed to measure the impact of spreading industrial and domestic wastes in addition to the application of fertilizers, weedicides, and pesticides on cropland. The equation includes factors for variations in crop, climate, soil, and potential pollutants. Soil factors are soil pH, organic mater content, and clay content. These workers also pointed out that those soils that can tolerate the highest residue are frequently most suitable for crop production. Peat soils could accommodate nearly 100 times as much residue as sandy soils without presenting a hazard.

E. Associated Land Features that Influence Soil Behavior

Associated land features include slope, flooding, wetness, rockiness, geomorphic position, or any other closely related soil features that are shown on soil maps. Slope is the incline of the surface of the soil and is usually expressed by a percentage (unit of elevation per 100 units of horizontal distance). In addition to gradient, shape, length, and pattern may be shown. Slope is important in that it influences soil erodibility and water runoff, equipment manipulation, street layout, underground conduits, harvesting of wood products, and land smoothing. Flooding and wetness presents problems to most developers of land. Most cultivated crops require drained soils. Excess wetness or flooding limits other uses such as roads, houses, and urban-related uses. Associated features are not incorporated in the concept of the soil taxonomic unit, however, they strongly influence the behavior of the soil taxonomic unit. They are a part of the soil map unit and add the horizontal or spatial characteristics. Many of the as-

sociated land features are discussed in the *Soil Survey Manual* (Soil Survey
Staff, 1951) as soil phases.

IV. PREDICTING PERFORMANCE OF SOILS

Soil data are not complete unless they include predictions of soil performance. Soil performanee data are being used increasingly to develop
plans for both urban and rural areas. The objectives of these plans are: (i)
efficient use of all resources; (ii) the protection of the environment; (iii)
stable production of adapted crops; and, (iv) efficient use of soils for grazing, forestry, wildlife habitat, and recreational areas (Kellogg, 1974). Soil
scientists working with one another, with their colleagues in other natural
and social sciences, and with people who have the skills for providing these
data, should provide the necessary soil predictions. Predictions, however,
should not be considered as recommendations for land use planning decisions. Prediction data provide alternatives from which planners and other
decision makers select the use that satisfies the need. Much of the data are
primarily edaphic. They reflect only the impact of the soil properties in the
natural soil. The Land-Capability Classification used by the SCS
(Klingebiel & Montgomery, 1961) is an example. The soil ratings in this system are based on the degree of hazard or limitation to cultivated crop use
that result from soil factors influencing soil erosion. More complex parametric methods have been introduced (J. Riquier, 1974). Here systems use
quantitative terms to express land evaluation. These systems also are edaphic in that soil properties are evaluated according to their importance within
and between each other. These relations are expressed in a mathematical
formula to calculate a final performance rating. Other systems such as soil
potentials (Bartelli, 1974) and land utilization types (Beek, 1974) are more
complex in that they evaluate, in addition to edaphic features, socio-economic factors such as skill of operators, costs of overcoming limitations,
environmental impacts, environmental demands of the people, and the level
of technical know-how. Following is a discussion of the more common
kinds of predictions being made of soil behavior.

A. Prediction Yields

Yields of plants can be given for soils in the natural condition which
measures the inherent quality of the soil. In addition, yields can be used to
measure the output of production systems that are based on inputs of soil
modification. Thus, it is necessary to define the management systems when
giving yield data. Listing yields under the two levels of management enables
an analysis of response to management. The *Soil Survey Manual* (Soil Survey Staff, 1951) outlines several procedures for collecting yield data. Data
can be collected by field obsrvations, experimental results, field samples,
farm experience, farm record books, and questionaires. It is very important, however to record the specific levels of management.

An example of presenting yield data in published soil surveys is presented in Table 3. Yields are given for two levels of management. Column A shows the yields that can be expected under management most commonly used by farmers. This level implies some soil treatment. Poorly drained soils are drained, but not perfectly, lime and fertilizers are used, and an economical crop production is maintained. Column B shows the predicted yields under the improved management used by some farmers. This is thought to be the level needed for maximum profit. Soil improvements are consistent with economic relationships, soil erosion is kept within tolerable limits, and suitable high yielding varieties of crops are planted. These managers maintain a flexibility that meets changes in the climatic and economic conditions.

Odell (1950) has described a technique for sampling yields of crops on different kinds of soil within the same field. A system proposed by the Food and Agricultural Organization (FAO) of the United Nations (Riquier et al., 1970) is based on the relations of costs of inputs to the productive capacity of the soil. It is an integral part of any land evaluating program. Predictions of yields are given for important crops in most published soil surveys. A more sophisticated system that includes yields of crops for soil types under specified levels of management and a discussion of major factors that causes differences in crop yield is presented for Illinois soils (Odell & Oschwald, 1970). The Bureau of Reclamation (McMartin, 1950) includes an analysis of productive capacity which connotes crop adaptability and crop yield in the analysis of the suitability of lands for irrigation. Yields used are judged to be what an average farmer can do. Usually, level of management for which yields are predicted are chosen to fit the needs of users of individual soil surveys.

Productivity of soils for trees is commonly expressed as "site index," an expression of forest site quality based on the height of dominant and codominant trees at an arbitrarily chosen age (Soc. of Am. For., 1958). Trees measured for site must have been free from suppression and damage throughout their lives. Such sites must have well-stocked, even-aged forest stands that have not suffered from past cutting, heavy grazing, repeated burning, or stagnation caused by overstocking. The site index is read from a harmonized site index curve developed for a region from a grouping of several sample sites. The harmonized index curve is based on the assumption that the pattern of height growth is the same for all site classes, localities, and soil conditions included in the regional site curve study (Carmean, 1970). Trees may follow entirely different patterns of height growth reflecting soil and topographic features. Carmean (1970) presents sound evidence that different height-growth patterns do exist on different sites and on different soils. Also, site curves do not reflect yield response from soil management, such as drainage or tree fertilization.

B. Edaphic Nonfarm Performance

Soil data that present performance for nonfarm uses are included in soil surveys published by the Soil Conservation Service. Guides that show how to rate engineering soil performance are included in various SCS memoranda, soil handbook notices, and SCS guides for engineering use of

Table 3—Portion of a table listing average yields of principal crops under two levels of management.†

| | Corn | | | | Soybeans | | | | Wheat | | | |
| | A | | B | | A | | B | | A | | B | |
Soil	bu/acre	hl/ha	bu/acre	hl/ha	bu/acre	hl/ha	bu/acre	hl/ha	bu/acre	hl/ha	bu/acre	hl/ha
Armstrong loam, 5 to 9% slopes	41	35.6	68	59.1	14	12.2	24	20.9	16	13.9	27	23.5
Gara loam, 9 to 14% slopes	44	38.2	74	64.3	16	13.9	27	23.5	19	16.5	31	26.9
Grundy silt loam, 1 to 5% slopes	74	64.3	98	85.2	28	24.3	37	32.2	31	26.9	41	35.6
Kennebec silt loam	89	77.4	118	102.6	34	29.6	45	39.1	37	32.2	49	42.6
Shelby loam, 9 to 14% slope	65	56.5	86	74.7	24	20.9	32	27.8	27	23.5	36	31.3

† Minor, P. E. 1977. Soil Survey of Dekalb County, Mo. USDA, SCS.

soils (USDA, 1971). Soil interpretations are based on degree of limitation to use. These guides reflect experience and judgment of many soil scientists working with engineers and others. An example of the data dealing with sanitary facilities is presented in Table 4. Degree of limitation and the major limiting soil property are listed for each soil on the soil map. The Western Regional Technical Work Planning Conference for Soil Survey prepared a guidebook to help users understand and use the interpretations resulting from the SCS guides (unpublished, limited copies available from the SCS Soil Correlators Office, Portland, Oreg.). This guidebook points out differences in terminology between soil scientists and engineers and also gives some of the reasons a soil property may be limiting. The San Diego County Planning Department (1975) published a supplement to the San Diego County soil survey publication to explain the limitations used in rating soil performance. For example, the section dealing with soil performance for homesites includes an explanation of the need for such evaluation, a discussion of each factor (soil drainage, erosion hazard, rockiness, slope, shrink-swell behavior, and alluvial soils), impact on rating, and a discussion on the use and application of such data in San Diego County. Similar discussions are presented for soil performance for urban uses, source of construction materials, land management, recreational uses, engineering uses, and for farming and ranching. The Ohio Department of Natural Resources (Marshall, 1975) supplements the soil survey with a land capability analysis for selected land uses. The ratings are based on soil properties and reflect the degree of limitation the combined soil properties exert on the land use. A rating of *slight* indicates no important restriction, *moderate* indicates soil

Table 4—Sanitary facilities.

Soil series and map symbol	Septic tank absorption fields	Sewage lagoons	Sanitary landfill	
			Trench	Area
Amy—Ae	Severe: percs slowly; wet	Slight	Severe: wet	Severe: wet
Af	Severe: floods; percs slowly; wet	Severe: floods	Severe: floods; wet	Severe: floods; wet
Ariel—Ar	Severe: floods; percs slowly; wet	Severe: floods	Severe: floods; wet	Severe: floods; wet
Arkabutla—At	Severe: floods; wet; percs slowly	Severe: percs rapidly floods	Severe: floods; wet	Severe: floods;
Cahaba—CaB, CaC	Slight	Severe: percs rapidly	Slight	Slight
CaD	Moderate: slope	Severe: percs rapidly; slope	Light	Moderate: slope

limitations that can be corrected, and *severe* indicates soil properties that are difficult to overcome. All of these systems define the highly suitable soils as having no significant limitation to the defined use. The best soils drift into uses that have the strongest economic clout.

C. Soil Potential

The soil potential is a system for evaluating the natural unit of soil as mapped in the soil survey.

Soil potential is defined as the ability of the soil using latest feasible technology to produce, yield, or support an activity at a cost expressed in economic, social, and environmental units of value (Bartelli, 1974). The soil potential rating considers the lasting effect on the environment. For example, soils with a high potential for farming must have a favorable cost input/output ratio, and, in addition, should not pollute the environment. The farming system should not accumulate toxic end products nor should it produce excessive sediment.

An editorial on preserving the land in a leading eastern paper (*Washington Post,* Washington, D.C., 6 Apr. 1976) quoted an English voyageur, John Sparke, who wrote on a visit to Florida in 1565, "the commodities of the land are more than one yet knowne to any man: for besides the land itselfe, where of there is more than any king is able to inhabit, it flourisheth with meadow, pasture ground, with woods of cedar and cypress, and other soils, etc." However, the land turned out to be neither endless nor inexhaustible. It is not reasonable to presume that society will utilize land areas according to natural dictates. Modification of soil is necessary and even desirable (McCormack & Bartelli, 1977). Soil data need to consider both the soil limitations and measures needed to modify these limitations.

The process of determining soil potential involves four basic steps: (i) Identify for each soil use those properties—soil and associated features— that influence the selection of crops, yields of plants, and performance of activities; (ii) Identify and evaluate the feasible practices that may be used to overcome or minimize the unfavorable effects of the limiting soil properties to achieve the performance that maintains quality in the natural resource base; (iii) Determine the relative cost or degree of difficulty of available practices or technologies; and (iv) Identify the continuing limitations that exist on specific soils after available practices are installed and evaluate and array the soils within an area in order from the best to those with the worst performance. This approach is most useful as an aid in making decisions about land use. It focuses on a positive expression of the quality of a soil relative to other soils that might be available.

The soil potential rating is developed within the context of the soil mapping unit. In addition to soil characteristics inherent in the soil taxonomic unit, the system weighs the associated landscape features of the map unit. The procedure for rating soil potential is expressed in the following model:

$$SPI = \sum_i W_i I_i + \sum_j W_j J_j$$

where

SPI = soil potential index,
W_i = index weight for factor i,
I_i = value of index for factor i,
W_j = index weight for factor j,
J_j = value of index for factor j,
i = soil properties influencing soil use, and
j = associated features influencing soil use.

The i and j factors are assigned values on the basis of controlled field studies and experience. These values reflect the sensitivity of that soil property on the use. The W values are based on judgment of the soil scientists working with others who have experience and research data to rely on. The values reflect the cost of treatment required to overcome the limitation and the cost of the continuing limitation if not removed. These values reflect the socio-economic demands and are based on the interactions among these demands (Kellogg, 1961). An example is in the New Orleans area where Hydraquents, soils of low strength and with severe limitations, are modified to make them suitable for urbanization. Slusher (D. F. Slusher. 1977. SCS, Washington, D.C. Office, personal communication) modified the W indexes to include a value for the cost of treatment required to overcome soil limitation and a value for continuing limitation if not removed. The equation after Slusher's modification reads:

$$SPI = \Sigma(W_{it}I_i + W_{ic}I_i)$$

where

I = soil and associated land factors,
W_{it} = treatment cost, and
W_{ic} = continuing limitation cost.

The Organic Soils Committee of the National Soil Survey Work Planning Conference (McKenzie. 1975. SCS, Lincoln, Neb., personal communication) evolved a scheme for rating organic soils that reflected the difficulty of overcoming the limitation. Ikawa (H. Ikawa. 1976. Univ. of Hawaii, Honolulu, personal communication) working with colleagues for the University and SCS, developed a model that was very successful in the assessment of the soil potential for the production of maize and soybeans in the North Central Wahiwa Plateau of Oahu, Hawaii.

A simple phase of Ikawa's model is as follows:

Soil factor	I	Degree of limitation	Treatment	Costs (W_{it})	Continuing limitation (W_{ic})	IW
P-fixation	3	Severe	None	$5 \times 3 =$	$15 + 0 \times 3 = 0$	15
			P added	$3 \times 3 =$	$9 + 8 \times 3 = 24$	33

The potential for maize production on an Hydric Dystrandepth is increased twofold by the application of phosphorus fertilizer. To be complete, however, the model will be expanded to consider the interaction among other fertilizer treatments. For example, phosphorus alone is good, nitrogen alone is good, but the two—phosphorus and nitrogen—may be even better, providing the additional cost does not offset the increase in yield. The completed model will include all of the soil and production factors that influence the prodution of maize and soybeans. Young (K. K. Young. 1976. SCS, Washington, D.C. Office, personal communication) prepared a soil potential analysis for private sewage disposal systems. An example is given in Table 5 where both modification costs and operating costs are listed for the various treatments for each kind of soil. The operating costs are similar to costs of continuing limitations.

Soil potential ratings can be used on large-or small-scale soil maps. A rating when applied to broad soil areas reflects interactions among soils. Less intensive soil maps where delineations are broad and more inclusive, such as cropland, pastureland, woodland, and urban land, are useful for general land use planning. They provide a basis for comparing the potential of large areas for general kinds of land use. (For an example of these kinds of soil map interpretations, see General Soil Map, Parishes of Louisiana, SCS, Alexandria, La.).

The supplement to the Seminole County, Florida, soil survey (USDA, SCS, and Seminole County Board of County Commissioners, 1975) updates the published soil survey by listing soil potential ratings for selected soil uses.

V. SOIL INTERPRETATION AT THE SOIL FAMILY LEVEL

One of the reasons for a multi-categoric system in *Soil Taxonomy* (Soil Survey Staff, 1975) was to satisfy the need to consider soils at different levels of generalization. The soil series is devised for the user who is concerned with soils of a field or a farm. The land planner may be interested in the soils of a state, a region, or a country. Soil series may be too detailed for such broad views. Other categories have been developed to enable us to think about soils at different levels of generalization. The soil family is the category above the series. It groups series together but is a subdivision of the subgroup. The principal differentiae of the family classes are particle size, mineralogy, and soil temperature. A few other properties, such as thickness of rooting zone, classes of cracks, coatings on sand, etc., are also used in unique groupings. The soil families do, however, recognize all of the class definitions used in the higher categories.

The criteria used in the soil family are indirectly related to soil behavior. Particle size and mineralogy are fundamental criteria for predicting soil engineering behavior. As defined in *Soil Taxonomy* (Soil Survey Staff, 1975) the new family textural class boundaries relate very closely to soil engineering classification. The break between coarse and fine (e.g., 18%

Table 5—Private sewage disposal systems

Soil	Limitations and restrictions	Treatment	Cost		Problems after treatment	Potential
			Initial, $	Operating, $		
Bruno sl, 0 to 1% slopes	Slight	Septic tank/leach field absorption bed	1,000-2,500	5/year	May require pumping every 8-10 years	Good
Bruno sl, 1 to 3% slopes	Slight	Septic tank/contour leach field absorption bed, serial distribution	1,500-3,000	5/year	May require pumping every 8-10 years	Good
Commerce sil	Severe: percs slowly; wetness	Septic tank/mound, tile drainage	3,000-7,500	20-40/year electric pump, pumping out every 5-10 years	May require pumping every 8-10 years	Good
Sharkey clay	Severe: percs slowly; wetness	(1) Underdrained sand filter/	3,000-6,000	50-100/year	May require pumping every 8-10 years, possible replacement of filter, wetness	Fair
		(2) Mechanical unit/chlorination	2,000-6,500	100-300/year	Possibility of mechanical failure, regular maintenance, wetness	
St. Lucy S	Severe: pollution hazard	Holding tank	2,000-4,000	70-100/mo	Requires frequent pumping out, cannot be used in inaccessible areas	Poor

clay) of the silty and loamy families separates the plastic from the non-plastic soils in many cases. Silty families are defined to approximate the silt size particle used in many engineering classification systems. The very fine sand particle-size is included in with the silty families. Another similarity to the engineering systems of soil classification is that particle size in *Soil Taxonomy* (Soil Survey Staff, 1975) refers to grain-size distribution of the whole soil. This differs from soil texture as used in soil survey, which refers to the fine-earth fraction. The fine-earth fraction is defined to include particles with diameters <2 mm. The control section for determining particle size in *Soil Taxonomy* is usually the layer below the variable surface. It is the zone where most of the roads and small engineering structures are placed and where much of the plant root activity is. The subsoil rather than the topsoil is emphasized.

The mineralogical characteristics of the control section is also recognized as a definitive feature in the soil family. The plasticity behavior of the soil is closely related to the amount and *kind* of clay. Since the AASHTO and Unified Classification systems of the engineers use both particle size and plasticity in the definition of classes, the soil family classes in *Soil Taxonomy* very closely approaches the engineering system. Resultantly, soil series within a family should have similar engineering classification in the control section. Families with clayey mixed or montmorillionitic families are usually A-7, A-6, and CH or CL. Data on soil properties is presented for the Mahaska series in Table 1. Note that in the control section (18–51 in depth) the family texture is clayey, mineralogy is montmorillionitic, USDA texture is silty clay loam, Unified classification is CH, and the AASHTO classification is A-7. All properties listed are related to the criteria that defined the soil family and engineering behavior would be similar for all series in this family.

Soil temperature is an important soil property that influences both engineering and plant growth behavior. Soil temperature is expressed as the mean annual temperature at a depth of 50 cm (20 in). Soil temperature classes also reflect amplitude of change from summer to winter. Those classes with changes of less than 5°C (9°F) are referred to as *iso*. Except for small areas where the climate is greatly modified by the oceans, these iso areas are confined to the tropical zones. The family temperature classes do correspond to the geographic range of key plants. For example, the hyper-thermic soils are essentially those where it is possible to successfully grow citrus. The thermic soils encompass the cotton-growing areas, or where bluegrass does not do well, or white pine does not reproduce. The mesic soils freeze, have frost problems, and the boundary between the mesic and frigid approximates the northern limits of corn for grain in the United States. Frigid soils are still colder. Root crops, such as rutabaga and potatoes, and small grains, such as oats and rye, are more at home in these areas. Pergelic soils have permafrost.

Soil moisture is recognized and used to define classes in categories above the family level. Soil families reflect these classes in that each family has a unique soil moisture regime that influences its performance. Soil moisture classes are based on the regimes of a control section that approximates the depth of wetting of 2.5-cm (1-in) and 7.5-cm (3-in) rains. The control section also approximates the rooting depth of many cultivated crops. Duration and seasonality of soil saturation and plant growth restricting soil dryness also are used. Soil moisture classes also have geographic distribution. Udic moisture regimes occur east of the 95° longitude in the United States. Soil moisture usually does not limit plant growth. Soils with Ustic soil moisture regimes are drier than soils with udic regimes and are transitional between the udic and the drier aridic or torric soils. The ustic soils occur in the western part of the Great Plains in the United States and are used mostly for grazing and wheat and sorghum production. The Xeric moisture regimes are unique in that they define those soil areas that receive moisture during the winter months. Soils with aquic regimes are saturated a great period of the time when soil temperatures are warm enough for plant growth. Water management is required for use of these soils for most crop production or human occupation. Soil moisture has a dominating influence on bearing strength. Soils with a high bearing strength when dry change abruptly to very low when wet. The silty soils are good examples. Expansive soils become active only with changes in soil moisture regimes. The Vertisols are most common in areas with ustic soil moisture regimes, where the soil experiences saturation and intensive drying.

Other criteria used to define family classes have some bearing on soil performance. The coatings of sands are used to identify a sand with some moisture-holding capacity. Soil slope or shape is used to identify peculiar water runoff behavior. The presence or absence of carbonates, soil reaction, depth of soil, and consistence may be used to reflect differences in soil behavior.

A monograph of the soils of the Southern Mississippi River Valley is a good example of the use of soil families to identify soil associations and to study the soil geography of the area (Brown et al., 1970).

VI. SOIL INFORMATION SYSTEMS

The natural soil is part of the ecosystem or biotic complex, and is related to the fauna, the vegetation, and the climate. The ecosystem is a complex interacting phenomena. Any change affecting any single element will have repercussions throughout the entire system. Man, through his manipulation of soil and vegetation, has made drastic changes, some good, others not so good. Water management has been introduced in the central states of the United States and a swamp has been converted into the breadbasket of the world. In some areas the vegetation has been completely eliminated and the soil has disappeared under a veneer of asphalt, concrete, brick, and tile, never to grow plants again. But still we find the same biotic complex, only the natural vegetation has been replaced, and the natural soil has been modified to suit man's needs. The landscape is now the product of human communities. Soil interpretation data are an integral part of human activities; and such data should be made available to all users as soon as possible. Automatic data processing systems have created immense opportunities for storing and disseminating soil data. Tables and text are being generated by computer. These tables and text provide interpretations that rank soils according to limitations or potential for given uses, include values of soil properties, practices needed for good use, productivity, etc. Programs are prepared so that the computer can print from the stored data maps that show the areal distribution of soils of different limitations, potentials, suitabilities, management needs, etc.

No interpretation of a soil survey is complete without due consideration of the principles of interaction. The most efficient soil behavior results from the interaction among practices when all necessary practices are applied. Fertilization, alone, may show no response on an infertile soil where the cultivator continues to grow the same plant, for the old crop cannot adapt to the changed plant-root environment. New plants that have been bred to take advantage of the fertile medium must be introduced with fertilization on these kinds of soil. Drainage, alone, may give some increase in timber growth on Aqualts, but drainage and fertilization may give greater yields on these wet, depleted soils. Each practice may have a small effect or none, but an interaction among the practices gives enormous responses. The soil scientist must acquaint himself with all of the soil properties that limit use. He must recognize the muted effect of a single management measure, and he must learn that maximum efficiency of soil behavior is not due to the cumulative effects of introduced practices.

LITERATURE CITED

Adams, F., and R. W. Pearson. 1967. Crop response to lime in the Southern United States and Puerto Rico. *In* R. W. Pearson and Fred Adams (ed.). Soil acidity and liming. Agronomy 12:161–206. Am. Soc. of Agron., Madison, Wis.

American Association of State Highway (and Transportation) Officials. 1970. Standard specifications for highway materials and methods of sampling and testing. 10th ed. 2 vol., Washington, D.C.

Asphalt Institute. 1969. Soils manual for design of asphalt pavement structures. 2nd ed. Manual Ser. no. 10. College Park, Md.

Bartelli, L. J. 1962. Use of soils information in urban-fringe areas. J. Soil Water Conserv. 17(3):99–103.

Bartelli, L. J. 1974. Soil surveys and environmental planning. Int. Congr. Soil Sci. Trans. 10th (Moscow, USSR) V:67–73.

Bartelli, L. J., and D. B. Peters. 1959. Integrating soil moisture characteristics with classification units of some Illinois soils. Soil Sci. Soc. Am. Proc. 23:149–151.

Beek, Klaas. 1974. The concept of land use types. p. 103–120. *In* Approaches to land classification. Soils Bull. 22. FAO, Rome.

Bennett, A. C. 1974. Toxic effects of aqueous ammonia, copper, zinc, lead, boron, and manganese on root growth. p. 669–680. *In* E. W.Carson (ed.) The plant root and its environment. Univ. Press of Virginia, Charlottesville.

Black, C. A. 1960. Soil-plant relationships. John Wiley & Sons, Inc., New York. 553 p.

Bouma, J., F. G. Baker, P. L. M. Verreman. 1974. Measurement of water movement in soil pedons above the water table. Univ. of Wisconsin, Dep. of Soil Sci., Inf. Circ. no. 27.

Brown, D. A., V. E. Nash, A. G. Caldwell, L. J. Bartelli, R. C. Carter, and O. R. Carter. 1970. A monograph of the soils of the southern Mississippi river valley alluvium. Arkansas Agric. Exp. Stn., Southern Coop Ser. Bull. 178.

Carleton, Owen, Lewis Young, and Carl Taylor. 1974. Climosequence studies of the mountain soils adjacent to Sante Fe, New Mexico. USDA For. Serv., Southwest. Reg., Albuquerque, N. Mex. 24 p.

Carmean, W. H. 1970. Tree height-growth patterns in relation to soil and site. p. 499–512. *In* C. T. Youngberg and C. B. Davey (ed.) Tree growth and forest soils. Oregon State Univ. Press, Corvallis, Oreg.

Eyre, S. R. 1968. Vegetation and soils: a world picture. The Aldine Publ. Co., Chicago. 328 p.

Foy, C. D. 1974. Effects of aluminum on plant growth. p. 601–642. *In* E. W. Carson (ed.) The plant root and the environment. Univ. Press of Virginia. Charlottsville, Va.

Holzhey, C. S., and M. J. Mausbach. 1976. Using soil taxonomy for estimating the K value of the USLE. p. 115–126. *In* Proc. Natl. Conf. on Soil Erosion, Purdue Univ., West Lafayette, Ind. Soil Conserv. Soc. of Am., Dukeny, Iowa.

Kellogg, C. E. 1940. The theory of land classification. I. The contribution of soil science and agronomy to rural land classification. p. 164–173. *In* Proc. 1st Natl. Conf. on Land Classification, Univ. of Missouri, Columbia, Mo., 10–12 Oct. 1940. Missouri Agric. Exp. Stn. Bull. 421, Columbia, Mo.

Kellogg, C. E. 1961. Soil interpretation in the soil survey. Soil Conserv. Serv., USDA, Washington, D.C.

Kellogg, C. E. 1974. Soil genesis, classification and cartography: 1924–1974. Geoderma 12: 347–362.

Klingebiel, A. A., and P. H. Montgomery. 1961. Land-capability classification. USDA, SCS Handb. 210.

Kuchler, A. W. 1964. Potential natural vegetation of the conterminous United States. Geograph. Soc.: Spec. Publ. no. 36:1–2.

Lamke, W. T., and R. V. Whitman. 1968. Soil mechanics. John Wiley & Sons, Inc., New York. 553 p.

Marshall, II, D. C. 1975. A manual land capability evaluation and scoring system for five development-related uses. Tech. Rep. 6. Off. of Planning and Res. and Div. of Land and Soil, Ohio Dep. of Natl. Resour., Columbus, Ohio.

McCormack, D. E., and L. J. Bartelli. 1977. Soils and land use—urban and suburban development. Trans. ASAE 20(2):266–270.

McMartin, Wallace. 1950. The economics of land classification for irrigation. Am. Farm Econ. Assoc. 22(4):553–570.

Morris, J. G., R. L. Newbury, and L. J. Bartelli. 1962. For septic tank design, soil maps can substitute for percolation tests. Public Works, Feb.

National Resources Planning Board. 1941. Land classification in the United States. Report of the Land Committee. U.S. Government Printing Office, Washington, D.C.

Newman, E. I. 1974. Root and soil water relations. p. 363–440. *In* E. W. Carson (ed.) The plant root and the environment. Univ. Press of Virginia, Charlottsville, Va.

Nielson, K. F. 1974. Roots and root temperatures. p. 293–333. *In* E. W. Carson (ed.) The plant root and its environment. Univ. Press of Virginia, Charlottsville, Va.

Odell, R. T. 1950. A study of sampling methods used in determining the productivity of Illinois soils. Agron. J. 42:328–335.

Odell, R. T., and W. R. Oschwald. 1970. Productivity of Illinois soils. College of Agric. Circ. 1016. Univ. of Illinois, Urbana.

Odum, E. P. 1971. Fundamentals of ecology, W. B. Saunders Co.

Olson, G. W. 1964. Application of soil survey to problems of health, sanitation and engineering. Cornell Univ., Agric. Exp. Stn. Memoir 387.

Richards, S. J., R. M. Hagan, and T. M. McCalla. 1952. Soil temperature and plant growth. p. 303–480. *In* B. T. Shaw (ed.) Soil physical conditions and plant growth. Agron. Vol. 2. Academic Press, New York.

Riquier, J. 1974. A summary of parametric methods of soil and land evaluation. p. 47–53. *In* Approaches to land classification. Soils Bull. 22. FAO, Rome.

Riquier, J., D. Luis Bramao, and J. P. Cornet. 1970. A new system of soil appraisal in terms of actual and potential productivity. FAO, AGL:TESR/7/6. 38 p.

Russell, E. W. 1961. Soil conditions and plant growth. Longmans, Green and Co., New York. 635 p.

San Diego County Planning Department. 1975. Soil survey, Part III (Soil interpretation manual). San Diego County Planning Dep. and Comprehensive Planning Organ., San Diego, Calif.

Simonson, R. W. 1968. Concept of soil. Adv. Agron. 20:1–47.

Soiety of American Foresters. 1958. Forest terminology. 3rd ed. Soc. Am. For., Washington, D.C.

Soil Survey Staff. 1951. Soil survey manual. Agric. Handb. no. 18, U.S. Government Printing Office, Washington, D.C.

Soil Survey Staff, U.S. Department of Agriculture, SCS. 1975. Soil taxonomy: a basic system of soil classification for making and interpreting soil surveys. Agric. Handbk. no. 436, U.S. Government Printing Office, Washington, D.C.

Stewart, B. A., D. A. Woolhiser, W. H. Wischmeier, J. H. Caro, and M. H. Frere. 1975. Control of water pollution from cropland. Vol. I. A manual for guideline development. SEA, USDA, and Off. of Res. and Dev., USEPA. U.S. Government Printing Office, Washington, D.C.

Stolzy, L. H. 1974. Soil atmosphere. p. 335–355. *In* E. W. Carson (ed.) The plant root and the environment. Univ. Press of Virginia, Charlottsville, Va.

U.S. Department of Agriculture, SCS. 1971. Guide for interpreting engineering uses of soils. U.S. Government Printing Office, Washington, D.C.

U.S. Department of Agriculture, SCS, and Seminole County Board of County Commissioners. 1975. Soil potentials and limitations, a supplement to the soil survey Seminole County, Florida. Soil Conservation Service, Gainesville, Fla.

Van Doren, C. A., and L. J. Bartelli. 1956. A method of forecasting soil loss. J. Am. Soc. Agric. Eng. 37(5):335–341.

Veatch, J. O. 1937. The idea of the natural land type. Proc. Soil Sci. Soc. Am. 2:499–503.

Wagner, A. A. 1957. The use of unified soil classification system by the Bureau of reclamation. p. 125–134. *In* Proc. of the 4th Int. Conf. on Soil Mechanics and Foundation, Aug. 1957.

Wischmeier, W. H., C. B. Johnson, and B. V. Cross. 1971. A soil erodibility monograph for farmland and construction sites. J. Soil Water Conserv. 26(5):189–193.

6   Hydrologic Data[1]

H. B. PIONKE

Science and Education Administration, USDA
Northeast Watershed Research Center
University Park, Pennsylvania

R. L. KLECKNER

U. S. Geological Survey
Reston, Virginia

I. INTRODUCTION

The effect of hydrology on land use has long been recognized. Flood control dams and levee systems designed to protect lives and flood-plain properties have existed in the United States and Canada for generations. In addition, flood plain and septic tank zoning or regulations have been in force in various North American locales for many years.

Conversely, the effect of land use on hydrology has been more recently emphasized. The impact of man's upstream activities on the quality and quantity of outflow waters is of particular public concern. This concern has been formalized in recent legislation and actions that set or promote target dates for point and nonpoint-source pollution control, water quality standards and regulations, cost sharing formulas for instituting pollution control plans and devices, funding for research and development into pollution control, and environmental impact statements. The expenditures of money, resources, and effort at all governmental levels indicate a general growing recognition of land use impact on downstream water quality and quantity and of the need for land use planning.

This concept of land-use planning assumes that the planner can reasonably estimate the major hydrologic consequences of adopting a proposed plan, or choose among several alternative plans. Numerous methods of varying complexity and accuracy are available for estimating the impacts of land use on the downstream water quality and quantity. However, specific methodologies will not be discussed here, because they represent the current product of a rapidly changing state-of-the-art. Instead, the methodology

[1] Contribution from the Northeast Watershed Research Center, Science & Education Administration, U.S. Department of Agriculture, and the U.S. Geological Survey, U.S. Department of the Interior, Reston, Va. In cooperation with the Pennsylvania Agricultural Experiment Station, The Pennsylvania State University, University Park, Pa.

will be discussed categorically and then generally as related to hydrologic data requirements.

In the context of land-use planning, the methodology chosen for evaluating downstream hydrologic impact of alternative land-use plans should be reasonably accurate, documentable, and objectively (rather than subjectively) based. If these three criteria are not adequately met, the hydrologically based land use decisions may be indefensible or publicly unacceptable. The terms *accuracy, documentation,* and *objectivity* all imply the need for data. Long-term extensive records may be required where data are exclusively used to derive the relationship between land use and hydrologic conditions. Short-term data records may suffice when data are used to calibrate and/or validate existing hydrology-land use models for a particular site. Regardless of which method is chosen, hydrologic data will be needed for making land-use planning decisions.

Before progressing further, a working definition of *hydrology* is needed. Hydrology is both broadly and specifically defined in this chapter. In the title and subsequent general discussions, hydrology is broadly defined according to the definition recommended by the Ad Hoc Panel on Hydrology of the Federal Council for Science and Technology, that is, "Hydrology is the science that treats of the waters of the Earth, their occurrence, circulation and distribution, their chemical and physical properties, and their reaction with their environment, including their relation to living things" (Chow, 1964). However, when a particular data base or index is discussed, *hydrology* is specifically defined in the context of that data base or index. In one case, hydrologic data may refer to surface runoff, in another, to a variety of meteorological, water quantity, and water quality data. In either case, the definition will be apparent.

The objective of this paper is to identify hydrologic data bases presently or potentially useful for making land-use planning decisions and provide a directory of the major hydrologic data bases in the U.S. and Canada. To achieve this, the paper is organized into two parts: (i) a discussion of how hydrologic data needs are determined and fulfilled for a specific land use plan, followed by (ii) identification and description of hydrologic data indexes and data bases potentially useful to the U.S. and Canadian land use planners.

II. DETERMINING AND FULFILLING HYDROLOGIC DATA NEEDS FOR LAND-USE PLANNING

Hydrologic data needs cannot be logically considered unless the acceptable alternative land use plans have been identified and the most appropriate methodology to estimate the hydrologic impact of these alternative plans has been chosen. This very important point is often not recognized and made a part of the planning procedure.

Consider how a land use planner might approach the land use-hydrology question and fulfill hydrologic needs.

First, the planner must determine the major criteria for plan selection, the land-use objectives. The objectives must be directed toward known or projected major land use problems of the area, and must be achievable using state-of-the-art methodology or remedies. The objectives must also be clearly stated and concise. Establishing workable, meaningful, and well-defined objectives is the most critical, but perhaps the least considered, step. For example, the objective "select one of several politically and economically feasible land-use plans proposed for Marsh Creek Watershed that produces the smallest annual phosphorus discharge," is much more achievable than is "minimizing downstream impact for all or many possible unconstrained land-use alternatives." The land-use plan objectives must be achieved within financial, social, political, and the site limitations. These limitations can eliminate many or most options.

The next step is to consider the individual component parts of the land-use plan. The overall land-use objectives and the objectives of the component parts are often not coincident. Instead, the land-use planning objectives are often constrained by the hydrology of the system. However, at the component level the hydrologic constraint on the land-use plan can be considered a hydrologic objective. Similar to the land use plan objectives, the hydrologic objective must be defined in terms of specifically stated hydrologic problems of the area. After establishing the appropriate hydrologic objective, hydrologic data evaluation or simulation techniques must be selected that can analyze the watershed relative to achieving the stated objectives. If the land-use planner is so fortunate as to have several equivalent techniques at his disposal, then it may be an added convenience to choose the one that makes best use of the available hydrologic data. Once a single data evaluation or simulation technique is chosen, the types and characteristics of the needed hydrologic input and/or output data are well specified and can be searched out and assembled. This allows the planner to identify what hydrologic data are not available, and then decide how to fill the data gap.

A. Determining Hydrologic Data Needs

Because the land use planning objectives and the hydrologic problems of the area dictate the choice of data evaluation or simulation approach, which in turn sets the specific data needs, several points need to be made regarding the basic characteristics of the hydrologic simulation models relative to their utility for land use planning and data requirements.

Hydrologic models can be generally classified as either stochastic, parametric, or deterministic. At one extreme, totally stochastic models describe statistical properties of an output data set and do not require that the underlying cause-effect relationship be included explicitly in the model. At the other extreme, totally deterministic models describe only the underlying cause-effect relationships and require only input data and not output data to provide an answer. The parametric models contain both stochastic and deterministic components. Most presently available hydrologic models use-ful in land use planning fall into the broad parametric category as defined here, that is, they contain conceptually based and defined relationships but also must be calibrated and fitted some way to the study area to provide realistic results. The most commonly used, conceptually based hydrologic models range from the relatively elementary regression-derived relation-ships between observed input and output data, for example, relate an out-flow parameter to the percentage of the watershed in a selected land use (Haith, 1976; Muir et al., 1973; Shannon & Brezonik, 1972), to the relative-ly complex and much more highly deterministic models, for example, Hy-drocomp (Crawford & Donigian, 1973) and ACTMO (Frere et al., 1975). The conceptually based models seem to have greater applicability to land use planning than do the stochastic models. The stochastic models do not describe relationships sufficiently well such that the effect of different land management practices can be directly imposed on the model to simulate the effect of alternative land uses on some hydrologic output. Also, a data-based analysis of historical hydrologic data related to land use may have little meaning if the hydrologic response was substantially altered during the period of record or is rapidly changing in response to recent land use changes. This should always be of concern because use of primarily data-based approaches for deriving relationships or calibrating models assumes steady or linearly changing state over the record period. Often where land use is an issue, changes are dramatic so that steady-state parameters do not apply. Thus, the outflow quantity and quality data record may be a mixed response to historic and present land uses, in addition to being time-buffered, if slowly moving ground water is a principal component. In these cases, the most recent segment of the data may be useful for calibrating and validating conceptual models, but use of the whole data set uniformly may provide misleading conclusions.

The data requirements of these models generally depend on where the model lies within the stochastic-parametric-deterministic classification. The need for long-term records progressively decreases from the stochastic to the deterministic. Stochastic models usually require a long data record de-scribing relatively few parameters. For the deterministic model, a much shorter data record may suffice, but a much greater variety of input hydro-logic data may be needed. Although selected flow, rainfall, and water quality data are available over the United States and Canada, most origi-nate from low-density instrument networks. In this case, the spatial resolu-tion of the stochastic models can be quite coarse, relative to the needs of the land-use planner. However, when the data exist and spatial resolution is sufficient relative to planning purposes, these models are useful for describ-ing hydrologic behavior over time at some monitored point.

Historically and presently, the models in the stochastic-parametric end of this classification are useful for estimating the effect of hydrology on land use, for example, establishing flood or water table stage records to de-lineate flood plain zones or setting septic tank placement guidelines. From the land-use planner's viewpoint, the stochastic techniques may be most useful for extending short-term data records or providing estimates of missing data for use in calibrating or testing the more conceptually based models. For a description of selected stochatic techniques see Session II, *Proceedings of the Second International Symposium in Hydrology* (Woolhiser, 1973).

Once the analysis method has been decided and the hydrologic data requirements are determined, all of the available pertinent hydrologic data should be identified and acquired.

B. Fulfilling Hydrologic Data Needs

Hydrologic data needs may be fulfilled in diverse ways. The use of available data is cheapest and quickest. The initiation of a basic data collection network is not only costly but often impossible under deadlines set for land use planning decisions. Rarely is sufficient data, both in type and record length, available to meet all the land use planner's needs.

After the available data sets are acquired, the needed missing data can be obtained in several ways. The data may be collected under a newly initiated short-term data collection program, synthesized from other data sets, or estimated. If a new short-term collection program is established, a followup short-term data collection program should be established to subsequently test or validate hydrologic predictions based on the initially collected data set.

Obviously, any of these considerations first requires an assessment of what hydrologic data are available. This assessment can be a tremendous job considering that in the United States alone about 19 Federal and 300 nonfederal agencies collect hydrologic data to meet a variety of standards and objectives. The remainder of this paper identifies and describes the major United States and Canadian hydrologic data indexes, bases, and sources.

III. IDENTIFICATION AND DESCRIPTION OF HYDROLOGIC DATA INDEXES AND DATA BASES FOR OBTAINING POTENTIALLY USEFUL HYDROLOGIC DATA

Much of the U.S. and Canadian hydrologic data are being organized into major data bases or referenced in data indexing systems. The data index serves as a directory and guide to hydrologic data sets available from the local to national level. The data bases provide the data per se.

Some hydrologic data are neither described in a major federal index nor included in a major federal data base. These data are predominantly from small watersheds, short-term, or local environmental research studies. In this last case, the agency conducting the research should be contacted to determine the availability of specific data. Eventually, many of these unlisted or unshared data will be transferred to a major data base or referenced in a data index. However, some of these data sets represent specialized research studies designed to achieve specific or short-term objectives. From an economics or general utility viewpoint, these data may never be justifiably included in a data base or index.

In selecting an index or data base for presentation, our philosophy was to prevent overlapping. Thus, if most or all of the hydrologic data base from a particular agency was described in an index or included in a major data base, the agency source was not identified and described specifically. This automatically excluded those U.S. agencies for which most or all hydrologic data are indexed in NAWDEX or ENDEX, or are stored in either STORET, WATSTORE, or the meteorological data base of the National Climatic Center. Those regional or national data bases not referenced or included are categorically treated under the headings of *Regional Data Bases* or *Agency Sources for Hydrologic Data from Representative and Experimental Watersheds.*

The major data bases and source agencies discussed in the text are keyed into simplified components of the hydrologic cycle in Fig. 1. To prevent duplication, this summary figure does not individually list source agencies for which most data are already included in the NCC, AES, WATSTORE, STORET, and NAQUADAT data bases. The addresses of contact points for each data index and base, and the definitions for abbreviations used on Fig. 1, are listed in Table 1 and the Appendix, respectively.

A. Major U.S. and Canadian Data Indexes

Two U.S. data indexes and one Canadian data index provide information on hydrologic data held by various Federal and nonfederal organizations. These are the National Water Data Exchange (NAWDEX), the Environmental Data Index (ENDEX), and the Water Resources Document Reference Center (WATDOC). NAWDEX and ENDEX are operated by the U.S. Geological Survey (USGS) and the National Oceanic and Atmospheric Administration (NOAA), respectively. WATDOC is operated by the Canada Department of Fisheries and the Environment. These indexes were established to assist the data user in identifying, locating, and acquiring hydrologic and other similar data. Although literature search and bibliographic information are part of ENDEX and WATDOC, they are not presented here.

1. THE NATIONAL WATER DATA EXCHANGE

The objective of NAWDEX is to assist the hydrologic data user and supplier by identifying or supplying hydrologic data from member organizations. The hydrologic data includes water quality and water quantity parameters. The member organizations include several federal and state agencies, river basin commissions, and private organizations. New agencies are continually being added.

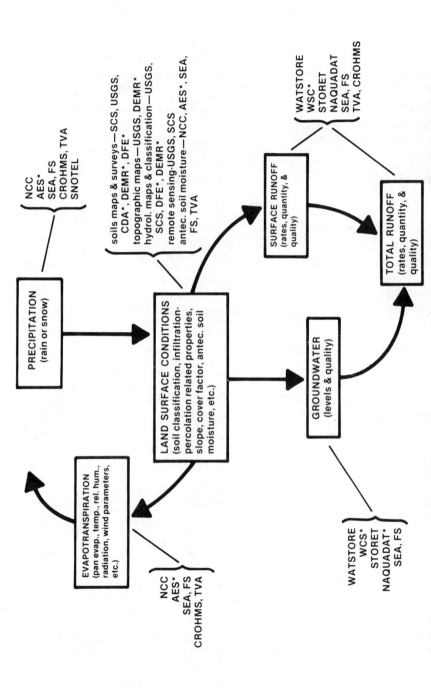

Fig. 1—U.S. and Canadian (*) sources of hydrologic data for nonurban areas keyed to components of a hydrologic cycle. ENDEX, NAWDEX, and WATDOC are not listed by components because they index a variety of hydrologic data sources and bases. Abbreviations are defined in the Appendix.

Table 1—Contacts for data indexes and data bases.

Data indexes and bases	Contact
Canadian climatic data bases (AES)	Atmospheric Environment Service Department of Fisheries and the Environment 4905 Dufferin Street Downsview, Ontario, CANADA M3H 5T4
Canadian hydrometric and sediment data bases (WSC)	Director, Water Resources Branch Inland Waters Directorate Department of Fisheries and the Environment Ottawa, Ontario, CANADA K1A 0E7
Columbia River Operational Hydromet Management System (CROHMS)	North Pacific Division Corps of Engineers P. O. Box 2870 Portland, OR 97208
Environmental Data Index (ENDEX)	National Oceanographic Data Center Data Index Branch D782, EDS/NOAA 2001 Wisconsin Avenue, N.W. Washington, D.C. 20235
Forest Service (FS)	Director for Watershed Management Forest Service, USDA P.O. Box 2417 Washington, D.C. 20013
National Water Data Exchange (NAWDEX)	Chief Hydrologist U.S. Geological Survey 421 National Center Reston, VA 22092
National Water Quality Data System (NAQUADAT)	Head, Data and Instrumentation Section Water Quality Branch Inland Waters Directorate Department of Fisheries and the Environment Ottawa, Ontario, CANADA K1A 0E7
National Water Data Storage and Retrieval System (WATSTORE)	Chief Hydrologist U.S. Geological Survey 421 National Center Reston, VA 22092
Quebec hydrometric data bases	Director of Hydrometric Services, Water Branch Department of Natural Resources Quebec City, P.Q., CANADA G1S 4N6
Science and Education Administration (SEA)	Chief, Hydrologic Data Laboratory USDA, SEA Building 007, Room 236 Beltsville Agricultural Research Center-West Beltsville, MD 20705
Snow Telemetry (SNOTEL)	Head, Waters Supply Unit SCS Regional Technical Center 511 N. W. Broadway, Room 510 Portland, OR 97209
Storage and Retrieval System (STORET)	U.S. Environmental Protection Agency Office of Water and Hazardous Materials STORET User Assistance Waterside Mall, 4th and M Street, S.W. Washington, D.C. 20460

continued on next page

Table 1—Continued.

Data indexes and bases	Contact
Tennessee Valley Authority (TVA)	Chief of the Data Services Branch 750 Evans Building Tennessee Valley Authority Knoxville, TN 37902
U.S. climatic data base (NCC)	The National Climatic Center National Oceanic and Atmospheric Administration Federal Building Asheville, NC 28801
Water Resources Document Reference Center (WATDOC)—Data Reference (D-REF)	WATDOC, Inland Waters Directorate Department of Fisheries and the Environment Ottawa, Ontario, CANADA K1A 0E7.

A variety of specific services are available through NAWDEX: (i) the identification of water data sources (ii) nationwide indexing of water data, and (iii) data search assistance.

The identification of water data sources is the objective of the Water Data Sources Directory. The Directory identifies organizations that collect water data, locations within these organizations from which water data may be obtained, the geographic areas in which water data are collected by these organizations, the types of water data collected and made available, alternate sources for acquiring the organization's data, and the media in which the collected data are available.

Nationwide indexing of water data is the objective of the Master Water Data Index. This index is oriented to individual sites rather than organizations. It identifies sites and site locations for which water data are available, and collecting organizations. The index also hydrologically classifies available data and provides record length, data characteristics, a list and measurement frequency of available parameters, and information on available data media. More than 61,000 water-data sites are being indexed from information contributed by 19 federal agencies and more than 300 nonfederal agencies to the *Catalog of Information on Water Data* (U.S. Geolog. Surv., 1974) maintained by the USGS Office of Water Data Coordination. The catalog consists of 21 sections which provide station listings for streamflow, stage, and ground and surface water quality for the 21 Water Resource Regions.

NAWDEX provides data search assistance by serving as a central contact point for locating water data that may be held by several different organizations. Selected types of data can be located in the Water Data Sources Directory, or the Master Water Data Index discussed earlier, and other indexes and reference sources made available by participating members. Included are data in computerized, published, and unpublished forms. Once the data are located, the user is referred to the member agency having the needed data. Service is provided through nationwide retrieval and Local Assistance Centers located in 45 states and Puerto Rico.

The NAWDEX Program Office and Local Assistance Centers provide services free to the greatest extent possible. However, users are charged for search assistance that requires extensive computer usage or is unusually costly, but these charges will not exceed the actual cost. Users requesting data or services through NAWDEX also may be assessed charges at the option of the member organization supplying the data or service. Again, the charge will, generally, not exceed the cost of supplying the data or service.

Further information, services, and publications are available from the listed contact (Table 1).

2. THE ENVIRONMENTAL DATA INDEX

The ENDEX system is an automated, documented, and comprehensive index describing environmental data collections including hydrologic data. The Environmental Data Service (EDS) in NOAA established the system and is responsible for its maintenance. Similar to NAWDEX, selective data acquisitions may be processed through EDS.

A wide variety of environmental data are included in ENDEX. Because the emphasis is on data files, only those projects that incorporate the measurement of environmental variables are indexed. Most of the indexed environmental data emphasize the more classical physical, chemical, and biological measurements of air, land, water, flora, and fauna samples. The system also locates and describes scope and content of permanent sample and photograph collections.

The following information is included: institution, sampling date(s), sampling location(s), parameter(s), measurement method(s), number of observations, file size, data output form, contact person, publications resulting from data, abstracts, project affiliations, and funding agency.

A user's guide to ENDEX is available from the listed contact and at many major libraries (Environ. Data Serv. 1976).

ENDEX is available to all individuals and organizations. Users can search ENDEX data bases interactively with their own terminals by special arrangement with the Data Index Branch in EDS. The cost for these services depends on whether the search is interactive or retrospective, and on the diversity or size of the search provided. Services, data publications, and additional information are available from the listed contact (Table 1).

3. THE WATER RESOURCES DOCUMENT REFERENCE CENTRE

WATDOC is a computer-based water resources information service operated by the Inland Waters Directorate of the Canada Department of Fisheries and the Environment. WATDOC contains D-REF (Data Reference) which references Canadian hydrologic data bases. The objective of D-REF is to provide the water data user with a mechanism to identify and locate pertinent data files. Each reference has information on 26 data descriptors, including parameter names, methods and times of data collection, availability, funding agency, name and address of data holder, and geographical area.

D-REF was initiated in 1976 and has more than 600 data file references, mostly federal. This index is being expanded and will eventually include references to most hydrologic data collected by public and private agencies in Canada. The objectives of D-REF and NAWDEX are similar. D-REF is a voluntary system in which the participating organization contributes or updates references.

D-REF and the other systems that comprise WATDOC are generally accessible, with approximately 150 Canadian computer terminals providing direct access. If a terminal is not available, searches can be requested from the WATDOC office on an interim basis until the user acquires access to a terminal. The cost to access D-REF from a computer terminal is nominal; users pay their own line charges except in the Vancouver, Edmonton, Calgary, Toronto, Ottawa, and Halifax Centers.

Costs, general information, staff assistance, and publications are available through the listed contact (Table 1).

B. Major U.S. and Canadian Data Bases

The major data bases presented are the U.S. and Canadian climatic data bases, National Water Data Storage and Retrieval System (U.S.), the Canadian hydrometric and sediment data bases, the Storage and Retrieval System (U.S.), and the National Water Quality Data System (Canada).

1. UNITED STATES CLIMATIC DATA BASE

The National Climatic Center (NCC) of NOAA is the primary supplier of U.S. climatological data. The NCC's primary functions include: i) collecting the observational records of the National Weather Service, the military weather services, and cooperative observers, ii) summarizing these data into useful statistical parameters, iii) maintaining a data repository, and iv) publishing and distributing these data.

The NCC data bank contains trillions of meteorological measurements grouped under the general categories of radar observations, surface observations, upper air observations, autographic records, and satellite films. Most of the meteorological data are on nearly 76,000 reels of magnetic tape. This data bank is generally described in Technical Report NCAR-TN/1A-111 (Jenne, 1975).

Presently, no dictionary or directory file exists for the NCC data bank. However, a rudimentary file is maintained in ENDEX that provides location, years of records, and identifies meteorological parameters for the meteorological files most requested and used. Site, data collection program, and data characteristics of the primary contributor, the National Weather Service, can be obtained from numerous publications held in the documents section of most large libraries. A good starting point is the reference entitled Selective Guide to Climatic Data Sources (Environ. Data Serv., 1969), supplemented by a periodically updated reference to both published and unpublished climatologic summaries (U.S. Navy, 1975). Precise and complete information on what data are available for a particular station or geographic area and the formats for the data can be requested from the NCC. Data output forms include microfilm, magnetic tape, punch cards, films of radar and multispectral satellite imagery, and computer printouts.

Special tabulations or summaries are prepared on request at cost to the user. When the tabulations already exist, costs can be limited to reproduction of data output. When new tabulations are necessary, the compilation costs will be added.

Services, publications, and further information are available through the listed contact (Table 1).

2. CANADIAN CLIMATIC DATA BASE

The primary Canadian climatic data base is assembled and maintained by the Meteorological Applications Branch of the Atmospheric Environment Service (AES), Canada Department of Fisheries and the Environment. The objective of this data base is to better and more effectively service the needs of climatic data users.

These climatic data are stored on tape files as historical weather information assembled on an hourly and daily basis, dependent on the frequency of data collection or observation. Data from most current and discontinued meteorological sites are on tape. Most files of hourly weather data start with the 1953 data year and are updated annually. Approximately 30 million of the possible 35 million hourly weather records are on magnetic tape.

Nearly all climatic stations provide data on total precipitation and the maximum and minimum air temperature for each 24-hour period. Substantially fewer stations provide either weather information on an hourly basis, accumulated wind distance, rainfall rates, and sunshine duration. Relatively few stations provide radiation, evaporation, other wind, relative humidity, snow course, soil temperatures, air pollution, radar, and atmospheric pressure data. This information, including the station location, type of data collected, and collection frequency is available from the Climatological Station Data Catalogue. The catalog is divided into six geographic units, for example, the Atlantic Provinces (Environ. Canada, 1976).

The AES data base includes nearly all Canadian climatic data collected at the federal and provincial level. This includes data from permanent, temporary, and seasonally operated stations. When provinces are actively engaged in standardized climatic measurements, their data are included in the AES archive. However, it may be also available from provincial sources. Quebec maintains a provincial data base.

The AES provides a number of computer services in addition to supplying the basic climatic data in card or tape form. The basic data file can be processed by approximately 40 utility programs maintained by the AES. Basically, these provide processing options whereby the daily or hourly observation frequency file can be processed individually by month, collectively by month, or by total file. The specific computation may be statistical, probabilistic, or provide a frequency distribution or duration analysis, etc., for the data record of choice.

The AES charges for providing or processing the data. A fee schedule is available upon request. Quebec does not charge for providing data as photocopies or on magnetic tape. However, the user must supply the magnetic tape.

In addition to the Climatological Station Data Catalogue, other AES publications may be useful for directly examining the available data or obtaining long-term summarized climatic data. These are documents which index publications containing summarized climatic data (Parker & Anderson, 1969) and climatic maps (Thomas & Anderson, 1967) with update supplements (Thomas & Parker, 1969; Parker, 1972).

The Canadian meteorological data, information, publications, and provincial contacts are available from the listed contact (Table 1).

3. NATIONAL WATER DATA STORAGE AND RETRIEVAL SYSTEM

This nationwide U.S. data base (WATSTORE) is operated by the Water Resources Division (WRD) of the U.S. Geological Survey (USGS). The purpose of WATSTORE is to make basic hydrologic data available for assessing the occurrence, quantity, quality, distribution, and movement of surface and ground water in the United States.

The WATSTORE consists of one informational and four data files. The one informational file is the Station Header File, an automated index to data stored in the system. The four data files are: i) Daily Values, which contains surface water, water quality, and ground water data measured daily or continuously; ii) Peak Flow, which contains annual peak values for streamflow stations; iii) Water Quality, which contains chemical and biological data for surface and ground water sites; and iv) Ground Water Site Inventory, which contains hydrologic, geologic, and well inventory data for ground water sites.

Hydrologic data from approximately 10,000 stream gaging stations, 1,300 lakes and reservoirs, 4,300 surface water quality stations, 4,100 water temperature stations, 880 sediment stations, 2,500 water level observation wells, and 1,500 ground water quality wells are contributed to WATSTORE. While these approximate numbers remain the same, many stations are dropped and added periodically. They provide both current and historical data diversification.

The wide diversity and large size of WATSTORE make it impractical to list all the hydrologic parameters included in the system. The reader is referred to the *WATSTORE User's Guide* (Hutchison, 1975), and a publication describing the ground water data base (Baker & Foulk, 1975) or the listed contacts (Table 1).

Hydrologic data in WATSTORE can be retrieved from WRD offices, which are a part of the nationwide telecommunications network. In addition, data may be retrieved via computer terminals in other federal and state agencies. The water quality data also may be retrieved from the Environmental Protection Agency's STORET system discussed later.

Data stored in WATSTORE are available in machine-readable form for use on other computers or for use as input to user-written computer programs. These data are available in the standard storage format of the WATSTORE system or as punch cards or punch card images on magnetic tape.

The data output is available at various levels of data processing depending on the users' needs. Output can be provided in computer-printed tables or graphs, digital plots, machine-readable form, or some statistically analyzed form. The computer-printed tables contain lists of actual data or condensed indexes that indicate the availability of stored data on file. Computer programs are available to produce bar graphs, line graphs, frequency distribution curves, point plots, site location map plots, and other similar graphics by means of line printers. By using USGS computer programs, regression analysis, the analysis of variance, transformation, and correlation can be provided at additional cost. Software systems are available to prepare data for digital plotting on peripheral, offline plotters. Plots include hydrographs, frequency distribution curves, X-Y point plots, contour plots, and three-dimensional plots. User costs include a minimal fee plus the actual computer cost for producing the requested data output. Further information regarding WATSTORE is available from the listed contact (Table 1).

The National Stream Quality Accounting Network (NASQAN) program operated by USGS deserves special mention even though the collected hydrologic data are available through either WATSTORE, STORET, or USGS state level data reports. NASQAN presently includes 345 stations at which systematic and continuing hydrologic measurements are made to determine the quality of U.S. streams. A total of 525 stations are planned. The stations are located so that the amount and quality of surface water leaving an accounting unit can be measured. The accounting unit geographically subdivides the United States into water planning regions and subregions.

A broad range of water quality parameters has been selected to fulfill the primary objectives of: i) accounting for quantity and quality of water moving within and from the United States, ii) depicting areal variability, iii) detecting changes in stream quality, and iv) laying the groundwork for future assessments of changes in stream quality. These water parameters include the common dissolved constituents, major nutrients, trace elements, organic and biological parameters, suspended sediment, water temperature, specific conductance, pH, discharge, fecal coliforms, and fecal streptococci. See Ficke and Hawkinson (1975) or the WATSTORE listed contact for further information.

4. CANADIAN HYDROMETRIC AND SEDIMENT DATA BASES

The hydrometric and sediment data bases are assembled and maintained by the Water Survey of Canada (WSC) with active provincial cooperation. These data bases provide ready and direct publication of hydrometric and sediment records as well as providing the user with better and more convenient access to the records.

These data bases are subdivided into the HYDEX, FLOW, PEAKS, LEVELS, SEDEX, SUSCON, and PARTSIZE files. The HYDEX file is descriptive and includes station number, name, drainage area, location, etc., for 2,700 active and 2,300 discontinued stations. The FLOW file contains daily, monthly, and annual discharges for 37,000 station years. The PEAKS file contains the annual maximum instantaneous discharge and water levels for all hydrometric stations. The LEVELS file contains daily water levels for 7,000 station years for 1969–1975. This file is in the process of being made available. The SEDEX file contains descriptive information similar to HYDEX except it applies to 240 sediment-measuring stations. The SUSCON file provides daily suspended sediment concentrations for 400 station years. The PARTSIZE file contains 13,000 sediment particle size analyses.

These data bases are combined in various ways to create data publications: the HYDEX file becomes the Surface Water Data Reference Index (Inland Waters Directorate, 1975c); SEDEX becomes Sediment Data Reference Index (Inland Waters Directorate, 1976d); the combined current HYDEX, FLOW, LEVELS, and PEAKS becomes a Surface Water Data Publication, for example, Surface Water Data, Alberta 1975 (Inland Waters Directorate, 1976c) and the combined current FLOW, SEDEX, PARTSIZE, and SUSCON becomes Sediment Data (Inland Waters Directorate, 1976a). The historic summaries of HYDEX, FLOW, and PEAKS files are combined into a Historic Streamflow Summary, for example, Historic Streamflow Summary, Saskatchewan to 1973 (Inland Waters Directorate, 1974). The historic summaries of FLOW, SEDEX, and SUSCON are combined into the Historical Sediment Data Summary (Inland Waters Directorate, 1976b).Thus, these documents can help define the characteristics of the data sets and sites for potential users.

These WSC data bases include data from federal, provincial, municipal, and private sources. The private sources are primarily irrigation districts and utilities. (One major exception is the Province of Quebec, which has created a similar but separate hydrometric data bank under the direction of the Quebec Department of Natural Resources). There is some minor duplication among data bases. Some of these data are shared between NAQUADAT and the Water Survey data base if water quality data are collected at the same site.Specifically, this duplication is between the (i) FLOW file and the NAQUADAT Data File, and the (ii) HYDEX and the NAQUADAT Station File. The data from International Gauging stations as defined by the Water Survey of Canada and the U.S. Geological Survey appear in both WATSTORE and the Water Survey data base.

Most of the data are available on cards or magnetic tape. The various card and tape formats available to the user when requesting daily, monthly, and annual discharges, annual maximum instantaneous discharges, and daily suspended sediment concentrations are published (Inland Waters Directorate, 1975a). Other publications useful for describing the system are available (Inland Waters Directorate, 1975b; Ozga, 1974). Data requests have been filled free by both the Water Survey of Canada and the Province of Quebec. The user must provide the magnetic tape for copying the data.

These publications, the WSC data bases, the list of contacts for provincial data banks, and the Quebec data base and information are available from the appropriate listed contacts (Table 1).

5. STORAGE AND RETRIEVAL SYSTEM

The objective of the Storage and Retrieval System (STORET) is to store and retrieve water-quality data collected or contributed from sources across the United States. STORET is operated by the U.S. Environmental Protection Agency (USEPA), with the water-quality data being supplied by numerous federal, state, local, and private agencies. Some of these data are listed in several data bases. For example, the USGS-contributed water-quality data also appears in WATSTORE.

STORET presently contains approximately 40 million individual observations of which about 12% are in WATSTORE. Approximately 20% of the data are contributed by USEPA directly; 80% originates elsewhere, usually from the individual states.

The general categories of water quality and other parameters available within the STORET system are radiologic, phosphorus, pesticides, biologic, bacteriologic, solids, nitrogen, oxygen demand, general organics, general inorganics, dissolved oxygen, metals, physical, and flow. There are 1,800 unique water-quality parameters defined within the STORET system. However, nearly 32 of the 40 million individual data observations are classified within 200 of these categories. There is no publication available from USEPA that could be considered a data directory to STORET. Instead, all the information on STORET data, for example, site location, parameters collected, and frequency of collection, is referenced and available from NAWDEX.

The STORET system is directly accessible to all users. More than 200 users are tied directly into the system by computer terminal. USEPA trains users on computer operations for entering and receiving information. Analytical routines are available to statistically process, transform, or change data output form. The data output form is optional, for example, tabular, graphic, machine readable, or digital plots on maps. If computer terminal linkage to STORET is unavailable, data may be obtained through a Freedom of Information request. The costs for written requests are based on the actual cost of the computer job plus a fixed cost for job submission. State agencies are provided with a fixed allowance to cover computer time, data storage, and processing. Federal and interstate agencies pay for their STORET usage through interagency agreements.

A STORET user's manual does exist and is available from USEPA. An overview of the system describing its capabilities may also be requested. Information and publications regarding STORET may be obtained from the listed contact (Table 1).

6. NATIONAL WATER QUALITY DATA SYSTEM

The National Water Quality Data System (NAQUADAT) is the Canadian water-quality data base. NAQUADAT was set up in 1969 to speed up and improve the flexibility in retrieving water-quality information for Canada. It is assembled and maintained by the Water Quality Branch of the Department of Fisheries and the Environment with active provincial cooperation.

The stated purposes of NAQUADAT are: i) to store chemical, physical, bacteriologic, biologic, and hydrometric data relevant to water quality for surface waters, ground waters, precipitation, waste water, and sediments; ii) to provide information for planning water use and setting water-quality objectives; iii) to monitor and identify water-quality trends and anomalies; and iv) to produce retrievals, summaries, plots, and published reports including statistics, calculations, and loadings.

The NAQUADAT system contains three interrelated files: the Station File, the Dictionary File, and the Data File. The Station File (6,000 stations) contains descriptions of sampling locations and includes geographical coordinates. Each station is assigned a code number, which reflects the type of water and its location in the Canadian Hydrometric basin subbasin scheme. The Dictionary File contains descriptions of the approximately 750 analytical procedures used. Each method is assigned a parameter code based on atomic number as well as other subdivisions, including a place-of-analysis code. The actual analytical results (2.4 million analyses) are stored in the Data File. This consists of the station number, the date and time of sampling, and a sequence of the appropriate parameter codes with the reported values. The encoded parameters include pesticides, hydrocarbons, dissolved metals, nutrients, bacteriologic, inorganic and organic classifications, instantaneous mean daily flows, and mean monthly flows. The stored water quality data are supplied by the Canadian Federal and Provincial Agencies.

NAQUADAT is interfaced with several other systems. The water quantity and flow data, particularly the FLOW and HYDEX files, are provided by the Water Survey of Canada. The NAQUADAT system has chiefly the Federal Regional Water Quality Branch laboratories as data sources. Although some provinces maintain separate data banks, much of the routinely collected water quality data are supplied to NAQUADAT. The Water Quality Branch will provide the provincial contacts or information upon request, so the user can decide if the provincial data bases must be searched as well.

The NAQUADAT system provides the capability to copy selective results from STAR (the data storage system operated by the Canada Centre for Inland Waters), to copy discharge data from the Water Survey of Canada, and to read and incorporate data from STORET.

NAQUADAT can be readily accessed in a variety of modes. The Data and Station Files are on magnetic tape. The Dictionary File is on tape and disc. Although information retrieval requests are normally provided on computer printout, the requestor has the option of receiving the detailed, summarized, or periodically summarized data on plot, map, or magnetic tape.

The key reference is the *NAQUADAT User's Manual* (Demayo & Hunt, 1975). An important additional reference is the *Dictionary of the National Water Quality Data Bank* (NAQUADAT) (Inland Waters Directorate, 1973). Also, the potential user can request a recent listing of the Dictionary File. Presently, no charge is made for supplying data to recognized organizations or members of the public. These publications, NAQUADAT user information, the list of contacts for provincial data bases, and NAQUADAT data are available from the listed contact (Table 1).

C. Regional Data Bases

Three data bases are discussed. One is the Tennessee Valley Authority (TVA) from which hydrologic data are presently available. The other two are newly initiated automated hydrologic data bases that presently contain nominal amounts of data. These are expected to be fully operational by about 1980. One data base (CROHMS) will contain a variety of hydrologic data collected from the Columbia River Basin; the other (SNOTEL) will contain snow and other related hydrometeorlogical data from mountain areas of the western United States.

1. TENNESSEE VALLEY AUTHORITY DATA BASE

The TVA collects hydrologic data within the Tennessee River Watershed, which includes most of Tennessee and small parts of Alabama, Georgia, North Carolina, Virginia, Mississippi, and Kentucky. These hydrologic data are used for the design and operation of TVA projects, including the operation of the TVA multipurpose reservoir system, and for the support of a wide variety of programs related to the water and land resources of the valley. Most of the data are collected as part of a continuing monitoring program, with a minor portion collected for design or research purposes.

Many of the water quality data collected in recent years are stored in STORET. Flow, climatic, and other hydrologic data collected at TVA-owned stations are held by TVA in computer storage, tabular, or other form. Substantial amounts of the data on reservoir levels, stored and suspended sediment, and water temperature are available only from TVA.

There are some publications for acquainting the reader with selected hydrologic data that are available (TVA, 1970, 1972, and 1975). Substantial amounts of other TVA data useful for land-use planning or relating hydrologic data to the effect of land use are available. These include fish and animal surveys; forest inventories; and soil, land-use, and mineral-resource maps.

Some TVA data are available on magnetic tape but most are in tabular or report form. Usually there is no charge unless large amounts of data are requested. The aforementioned publications, data, and information on the data base are available from the listed contact (Table 1).

2. COLUMBIA RIVER OPERATIONAL HYDROMET MANAGEMENT SYSTEMS

The Columbia River Operational Hydromet Management System (CROHMS) is a real time system that proposes a centralized data base for storing approximately 1,000 streamflow, reservoir stage, snow course, and meteorological data for the U.S. portion of the Columbia River Basin. Data from the Canadian part of the Columbia River Basin will also be available through this bank. The primary purpose of this system is to forecast the operation of water resource projects in the basin. Most of the data collection, storage, and monitoring is done by the Columbia River Water Management Group, which is composed of the federal and state water data and water user agencies in the region. Eventually, most of the CROHMS data will probably be indexed in NAWDEX or ENDEX with selected portions becoming part of WATSTORE. However, the CROHMS data base will be the most up-to-date because of its forecast emphasis. Other hydrologically related data, such as land use and soils information, are available for the basin in map overlay form.

Generally, CROHMS data will be available to the cooperators in the region at no charge. For large orders, other users will be charged the actual cost for furnishing tapes, cards, or hard copy printouts. These data and other information will be available from the listed contact (Table 1).

3. SNOW TELEMETRY

This program (SNOTEL) being initiated by the Soil Conservation Service (SCS) will include measurements of snow water equivalent, precipitation, and ambient air temperature for mountain areas in the western U.S. (Barton, 1975). The data from these stations (~ 500), including historic and continuing data from snow course sites ($\sim 1,700$), will be computerized, centralized, and available from the USDA computer at Fort Collins, Colorado. The objective of this data base is to forecast water supply from snowmelt. Most of the data collected by SCS will not be available from other sources. The SNOTEL system will contain snow data collected by many other federal, state, and local agencies. Two notable exceptions are California and British Columbia, Canada. The output medium for the data will be magnetic tape. The SCS has not established final policy on the cost of this service. General information, data, and appropriate publications are available from the listed contact (Table 1).

D. Agency Sources for Hydrologic Data from Representative and Experimental Watersheds

Most of the agencies not discussed previously that collect hydrologic data either contribute it to a major data base, collect only nominal amounts, or are primarily committed to the so-called *Representative and*

Experimental Watershed Programs. The primary objective of most Representative and Experimental Watershed Programs is not monitoring, but instead data interpretation for research or developmental purposes in which data becomes a means to an end rather than the end product. Consequently, much supplementary data are often available for making better hydrologic interpretations. This can include data on land use, geology, topography, cover complex, soil moisture, remote sensing measurements, etc., not normally part of a monitoring program. Furthermore, research watersheds may be characterized by small size with few land uses and continually collected data from spatially dense data collection networks according to the objectives of the particular study. Thus, hydrologic data from these watersheds may be particularly useful to the land-use planner. The primary disadvantage is that the hydrologic data collected from research watershed studies, particularly the older discontinued studies, may not be readily available in a usable form, or may no longer exist.

The U.S. agencies with major past and/or present efforts into Representative and Experimental Watersheds are USGS, USEPA, TVA, SEA, and Forest Service. The primary Canadian agencies are the Federal Department of Fisheries and the Environment and the Ontario Ministry of the Environment. The directory to the Canadian Watersheds is entitled *Canadian Participation in the International Hydrological Decade* (Canadian Natl. Comm. for the Int. Hydrolog. Decade, 1975). An outdated but still useful U.S. directory is entitled *Inventory of Representative and Experimental Watershed Studies Conducted in the United States* (Am. Geophys. Union, 1965).

The USGS watershed system is described by Cobb and Biesecker (1971) and Biesecker and Leifeste (1975) with most of the data going into WATSTORE and other major data bases. The USEPA watershed-oriented research programs are usually contractual rather than in-house. Many of these contracts require contribution of the collected data to STORET. The Tennessee Valley Authority program is described in a publication entitled *A Brief History of Watershed Research in TVA* (TVA, 1968) available from the listed TVA contact. Some of the states, notably Illinois, California, and Texas, have and continue to operate experimental or representative watersheds. Unfortunately, with the exception of the USGS and USEPA, many of these data or watersheds are not yet indexed within the NAWDEX or ENDEX systems. The two major sole sources of this type of watershed data are the Science and Education Administration (SEA) and the Forest Service (FS). Both agencies conduct numerous small watershed studies over the United States.

SEA has a national watershed research program that includes 11 watershed research centers, each containing anywhere from 1 to 40 watershed units. Most of the major watersheds are well described (Hershfield, 1971). The research objectives of these watershed studies are to better understand and estimate erosion, and the hydrologic and sediment transport from rural, predominately agricultural lands. The purposes were to evaluate and improve the effectiveness and design of presently used onsite water and sediment control practices and devices. In early years, water quality data were collected as part of specific short-term research studies. Since about 1970, some long-term water quality studies have been initiated on these watersheds. The water quality parameters under study are mostly nutrients, selected pesticides, and dissolved salts. Streamflow and meteorological data for discontinued and a few ongoing watersheds data back into the early 1930's. Most of the major watershed research centers still operating today were created between 1958 and 1967 and, thus, have a 10- to 19-year hydrologic record.

The Hydrologic Data Laboratory (HDL) is proceeding with the development of a standardized consolidated bank of SEA hydrologic data; however, only a small part of the data is now contained in the data bank. Substantial amounts of data at some Centers are still in chart and tabular form, with the degree of processing variable among Centers. Generally the meteorological and streamflow data are most highly processed, with much of it on magnetic tape or cards. The watershed centers (past and present) are identified and selected data are published (USDA, SEA, 1976). The most recent issue in this continuing series, which encompasses the period 1956–1968 in 12 publications, is USDA Miscellaneous Publication 1330. The continued preparation of the series is the responsibility of HDL. The HDL can: i) provide available flow and meteorological data sets in tabular, card, or magnetic tape form; ii) serve as a user information center to locate potential ARS data sources upon request; and iii) serve as a clearinghouse for facilitating transfer of available ARS research data from research source to user.

Costs for obtaining data in storage at HDL are nominal or none. Costs for data still at research watershed locations in some unprocessed form will vary depending on the processing required or the quantity requested. The publications, information, and data are available from the listed contact (Table 1).

The Forest Service has numerous "barometer" and research watersheds on forested and rangeland throughout the United States. The objective of the barometer watershed program is to develop water resource management methods and then provide a site for testing the accuracy of the method (Dortignac & Beattie, 1965). These 20,250- to 81,000-ha (50,000- to 200,000-acre) watersheds are at various locations in the United States and represent broad climatic and landscape complexes. In contrast, the Forest Service's research watersheds are generally one to two orders of magnitude smaller. The research watersheds are used to test the effect of different forestry management practices on water quality and quantity. Publications describing the location and characteristics of each watershed are available from the field offices that administer the individual watersheds.

The data collected on barometer and research watersheds are primarily meteorological and flow data with some water quality data. The flow and meteorological data are not contained in any major data base. However, most of the water quality data have been put into the STORET system. The degree to which the data are processed, for example, tabular, cards, or magnetic tape, varies among watersheds.

Inquiries related to acquiring information on the barometer and research watersheds or available data can be directed to the listed contact (Table 1).

IV. SUMMARY

Land-use planning is increasing in popularity and acceptability. One key component of any land-use planning system or technique is the hydrologic component. Occasionally, the primary land-use planning objective will be hydrologic. However, hydrology is usually not an objective of land use planning, but instead exists as a set of constraints placed on selecting among land-use plans. In either case, the hydrologic impact of alternative land-use plans must be predicted reasonably well if the hydrologically compatible or beneficial land use plan(s) is to be chosen objectively.

This hydrologic prediction can be accomplished by numerous methods. The land-use planner should seek professional advice regarding selection of a hydrologic simulation technique to meet the particular planning objectives and site requirements. Regardless of which technique is chosen, hydrologic data will be needed. It may serve as input data to sophisticated mathematical models, thus providing a simulated impact. It may serve as output data either to directly derive land use-hydrologic relationships, or to calibrate the model, or to validate the simulated impact. Once the simulation technique is chosen, the specific hydrologic data needs usually become well defined.

Both the United States and Canada have large amounts of hydrologic data potentially useful for land-use planning. Once the site location and data requirements are known, the planner should research these data sources. Many of these data are either indexed and are free or available at nominal cost. Furthermore, the data are often available in computer-compatible output and in some processed form. The land-use planner responsible for considering the hydrologic component should become familiar with and learn to use the indexes, major data bases, and agency sources.

ACKNOWLEDGMENTS

The authors gratefully acknowledge the assistance provided by staff members of the U.S. and Canadian agencies referenced in the text who supplied both publications and information needed to describe their data index or data base and reviewed the resultant writeup. These people according to data index or base are: NAWDEX—M. D. Edwards, USGS; ENDEX—E. W. McElroy, NOAA; WATDOC—L. Boychuk, Inland Waters Directorate; NCC data base—R. Davis, NOAA; Canadian climatic data base—G. A. McKay and F. B. Manning, AES; WATSTORE—C. R. Showen, USGS; Canadian hydrometric and sediment data base—W. J. Ozga, Inland Waters Directorate, and C. Pesant, Hydrol. Services (Quebec); STORET—C. F. Conger, USEPA; NAQUADAT—S. H. Whitlow, Inland Waters Directorate; TVA—C. H. Smith and W. Nicholas, TVA; CROHMS—F. A. Limpert, Bonneville, Power Authority; SNOTEL—M. Barton, SCS; SEA data base—J. B. BURFORD, SEA; and FS data base—E. Johnson, FS. Appreciation for general assistance is also expressed to W. Chin, Inland Waters Directorate, and W. J. Gburek, SEA.

APPENDIX—ABBREVIATIONS AND DEFINITIONS

Abbreviation	*Organization*
AES	Atmospheric Environment Service, Canada Department of Fisheries and the Environment
CDA	Canada Department of Agriculture
CROHMS	Columbia River Operational Hydromet Management System
DEMR	Canada Department of Energy, Mines and Resources
DFE	Canada Department of Fisheries and the Environment
DNR	Quebec Department of Natural Resources, Canada
D-REF	Data Reference, WATDOC, Canada Department of Fisheries and the Environment
EDS	Environmental Data Service, NOAA
ENDEX	Environmental Data Index, EDS
FS	Forest Service, USDA
NAQUADAT	National Water Quality Data System, Canada Department of Fisheries and the Environment
NAWDEX	National Water Data Exchange, USGS
NASQAN	National Stream Quality Accounting Network, USGS
NCC	National Climatic Center, NOAA
NOAA	National Oceanic and Atmospheric Administration, U.S. Department of Commerce
SCS	Soil Conservation Service, USDA
SEA	Science and Education Administration, USDA
SNOTEL	Snow Telemetry, SCS
STORET	Storage and Retrieval System, USEPA
TVA	Tennessee Valley Authority
USDA	U.S. Department of Agriculture
USEPA	U.S. Environmental Protection Agency
USGS	U.S. Geological Survey, U.S. Department of the Interior
WATDOC	Water Resources Document Reference Center, Canada Department of Fisheries and the Environment
WATSTORE	National Water Data Storage and Retrieval System, USGS
WRD	Water Resource Division, USGS
WSC·	Water Survey of Canada, Canada Department of Fisheries and the Environment

LITERATURE CITED

American Geophysical Union. 1965. Inventory of representative and experimental watershed studies conducted in the United States. Sponsored by AGU, Int. Assoc. Sci. Hydrol., and UNESCO.

Baker, C. H., Jr., and D. G. Foulk. 1975. Instruction for preparation and submission of ground-water data. U.S. Geol. Surv. Open-file Rep. 75-589.

Barton, Manes. 1975. Automatic snow surveys. p. 6–9. *In* Proc. 43rd Western Snow Conf., 23–25 Apr. 1975, San Diego, Calif. U.S. Courthouse, Spoke, Wash.

Biesecker, J. E., and D. K. Leifeste. 1975. Water quality of hydrologic bench marks—An indicator of water quality in the natural environment. Geolog. Surv. Circ. 460-E. U.S. Dep. of Interior.

Canadian National Committee for the International Hydrologic Decade. 1975. Canadian participation in the international hydrologic decade. Res. Basins Final Rep. Vol. 3.

Chow, Ven Te. 1964. Hydrology and its development. p. 1–21. *In* Ven Te Chow (ed.) Handbook of applied hydrology. McGraw-Hill Book Co., New York.

Cobb, E. D., and J. E. Biesecker. 1971. The national hydrologic bench-mark network. Geolog. Surv. Circ. 460-D. U.S. Dep. of Interior.

Crawford, N. H., and A. S. Donigian, Jr. 1973. Pesticide transport and runoff model for agricultural lands. Environ. Prot. Technol. Ser. EPA-660/2-74-013.

Demayo, Adrian, and Emelie Hunt. 1975. NAQUADAT users manual. Inland Waters Directorate, Water Qual. Branch, Environment Canada.

Dortignac, E. J., and B. Beattie. 1965. Using representative watersheds to manage forest and rangelands for improved water yield. p. 480–488. *In* Publ. no. 66 of the Int. Assoc.Sci. Hydrol. Symp. of Budapest, Budapest, Hungary, 28 Sept.–5 Oct. 1965.

Environmental Data Service. 1969. Selective guide to climatic data sources. Key to meteorological records documentation no. 4.11. Natl. Oceanic and Atmos. Admin. U.S. Dep. of Commerce.

Environmental Data Service. 1976. Users guide to ENDEX/OASIS. Key to oceanic and atmospheric information sources no. 1. Natl. Oceanic and Atmos. Admin. U.S. Dep. of Commerce.

Environment Canada. 1976. Climatological station data catalogue. Atlantic Provinces. UDC: 551. 5:06 (715/719).

Ficke, J. F., and R. O. Hawkinson. 1975. The national stream quality accounting network (NASQAN), some questions and answers. Geolog. Surv. Circ. 719. U.S. Dep. of Interior.

Frere, M. H., C. A. Onstad, and H. N. Holton. 1975. ACTMO an agricultural chemical transport model. USDA-ARS-H-3.

Haith, D. A. 1976. Land use and water quality in New York rivers. J. Environ. Eng. Div., Am. Soc. Civil Eng. Proc. 102(1):1–15.

Hershfield, D. M. 1971. Agricultural Research Service precipitation facilities and related studies. SEA, USDA, ARS-41-176.

Hutchison, N. E., Compiler. 1975. WATSTORE user's guide. U.S. Geolog. Surv. Open-file Rep. 75-476.

Inland Waters Directorate. 1973. Dictionary of the national water quality data bank (NAQUADAT). Water Qual. Branch. Environ. Canada.

Inland Waters Directorate. 1974. Historical streamflow summary Saskatchewan to 1973. Water Resour. Branch, Environ. Canada.

Inland Waters Directorate. 1975a. Description of card and tape formats for supplying data to users. Water Resour. Branch, Environ. Canada.

Inland Waters Directorate. 1975b. Manual of hydrometric data computation and publication procedures. Water Resour. Branch, Environ. Canada.

Inland Waters Directorate. 1975c. Surface water data reference index Canada 1975. Water Resour. Branch, Environ. Canada.

Inland Waters Directorate. 1976a. Sediment data Canadian rivers 1974. Water Resour. Branch, Water Surv. of Canada, Environ. Canada.

Inland Waters Directorate. 1976b. Historical sediment data summary Canadian Rivers to 1974. Water Resour. Branch, Water Surv. of Canada, Environ. Canada.

Inland Waters Directorate. 1976c. Surface water data Alberta. Water Resour. Branch, Water Surv. of Canada, Environ. Canada.

Inland Waters Directorate. 1976d. Sediment data reference index Canada 1974. Water Resour. Branch, Water Surv. of Canada, Environ. Canada.

Jenne, R. L. 1975. Data sets for meteorological research. Technical Note Report No. NCAR-TN/1A-111. Natl. Center for Atmos. Res., Boulder, Colo.

Muir, J., E. C. Seim, and R. A. Olson. 1973. A study of factors influencing the nitrogen and phosphorus contents of Nebraska waters. J. Environ. Qual. 2:466–470.

Ozga, W. J. 1974. Automated data processing techniques in the Water Survey of Canada. Inland Waters Directorate, Water Resour. Branch, Environ. Canada. Tech. Bull. no. 84.

Parker, J. E. 1972. Guide to Canadian climatic data. Supplement no. 1. Rep. no. CL1-1-72. Atmos. Environ. Serv., Environ. Canada.

Parker, J. E., and S. R. Anderson. 1969. Guide to Canadian climatic data. Rep. no. CL1-6-69. Dep. of Transport, Canada.

Shannon, E. E., and P. L. Brezonik. 1972. Eutrophication analysis: a multivariate approach. J. Sanit. Eng. Div., Am. Soc. Civil Eng. Proc. 98(1):37–57.

Tennessee Valley Authority. 1968. A brief history of watershed research in TVA. Muscle Shoals, Ala.

Tennessee Valley Authority. 1970. Stream gages in the Tennessee River Basin. Rep. no. 0-5898-R-1. Muscle Shoals, Ala.

Tennessee Valley Authority. 1972. Mineral quality of surface waters in the Tennessee River basin. Muscle Shoals, Ala.

Tennessee Valley Authority. 1975. Precipitation in Tennessee River basin. Rep. no. 0-243-A75. Muscle Shoals, Ala.

Thomas, M. K., and S. R. Anderson. 1967. Guide to the climatic maps of Canada. Rep. no. CL1-1-67. Dep. of Transport, Canada.

Thomas, M. K., and J. E. Parker. 1969. Guide to the climatic maps of Canada. Suppl. no. 1. Rep. no. CL1-4-69. Dep. of Transport, Canada.

U.S. Department of Agriculture, Science and Education Administration. 1976. Hydrologic data for experimental agricultural watersheds in the United States, 1968. USDA Misc. Pub. no. 1330.

U.S. Geological Survey. 1974. Catalog of information on water data. Station listings for Part A. Sreamflow and stage, Part B. Quality of surface water, Part C. Quality of ground water. Vol. 1–21. U.S. Dep. of Interior.

U.S. Navy. 1975. Guide to standard weather summaries and climatic services. NAVAIR 50-1C-534 with update NAVAIR 50-1C-534 CH-2. Nav. Weather Serv. Detachment, U.S. Navy, Asheville, N.C.

Woolhiser, D. A. (ed.). 1973. Decisions with inadequate hydrologic data. Proc. 2nd Int. Symp. in Hydrology, Sept. 1972, Fort Collins, Colo. Water Resour. Pub., Fort Collins, Colo. Lithocrafters, Ann Arbor, Mich.

7   Plant Cover Data

RICHARD H. RUST

University of Minnesota
Saint Paul, Minnesota

I. INTRODUCTION—HISTORICAL DEVELOPMENT

A primary concern, a first order of business, in any land use planning is an inventory of the existing land cover—its type and the characteristics relating to the type. Many states and agencies have initiated efforts to acquire this information and to develop data banks (Table 1). The demand for standardized land use and land cover data will increase as we seek to assess and manage areas of critical concern (Anderson et al., 1976).

One of the first efforts of national scope in this regard was the Conservation Need Inventory carried out by USDA in 1956 and again in 1966 (USDA, 1971). In this inventory, nonirrigated and irrigated cropland and pastureland, rangeland, commercial and noncommercial forestland, and other privately owned land in farms and not in farms were tabulated. This was, for the most part, a 2% sample, randomly drawn within township strata. The statistical approach to assessment of land cover, until recently, has presented the only economic method for large area analysis. Since the results can be stated with a prescribed reliability, the method has been employed by a number of agencies for a variety of purposes, for example, the Forest Service in their *Forest Survey* (1972). A limitation in this approach is that, while the amount of a given land cover type may be known with some certainty, its location will not be. Partly to overcome this deficiency, the random sampling procedure may be stratified according to geography, or location (USDA, 1971).

II. MODES OF ACQUISITION OF PLANT COVER DATA

Historically most plant cover data has been developed from aerial photography supplemented by field observations. The use of aerial photography has been a principal tool in land cover analysis since the mid-1930's. It has been employed particularly by the USDA in assessing crop and acreage compliance for certain commodity programs. The photography can be

Table 1 — Examples of database systems for land use and land cover, geographic resolution and representation, and suggested applications.

Source	Descriptor	Geographic resolution	Geographic representation	Applications	Reference
California	Land Use Mapping Programs (LUMP)	Variable	Grid cell, polygon	Land capability and land habitability rating; inventory & evaluation maps	Johnston et al., 1975
Canada	Geographic Information System (CGIS)	1:250,000, variable	Polygon, UTM	Express land capability in seven categories	McCormack, 1971
Illinois	Natural Resource Information System	Variable	Polygon, grid	Land capability	Tschanz & Kennedy, 1975
Iowa	Land Classification Method for Land Use Planning	Variable	Grid cell	Alternative land use decisions	Land Use Analysis Lab., 1973
Maryland	Automated Geographic Information System (MAGI)	1:63,360	Grid cell	Natural soil groupings; cropland, urban, recreational, wildlife & woodland displays	Shields, 1976
Minnesota	Land Management Information System (MLMIS)	1:500,000, qvariable	Grid cell	Depict level I land use; alternate land use decisions	Hsu et al., 1973
New Jersey	Land Oriented Information System (LOIS)	Variable	Grid cell, STC	Depict land use	New Jersey Dep. Community Affiars, 1973
New York	Land Use and Natural Resource Inventory (LUNR)	1:24,000, variable	Grid cell, polygon, UTM	Categories (51) of land use	Office of Planning Services, 1974
N. Carolina	Planning and Land Use Management Information System (PLUM)	Variable	Grid cell, UTM	Identification of critical areas	Skinner, 1974
Oklahoma	Land Use Information System	1:24,000 (level II) 1:250,000 (level I) 1:1,000,000	Grid cell, UTM	Alternative decisions in land use	Watson et al., 1973
Ohio	Statewide Land Use Inventory	1:62,500	Grid cell	Factors influencing water quality; level I land use categories	Baldridge et al., 1975
Tennessee	Natural Resource Planning Aid System (NRPAS)	1:24,000 1:250,000	Grid cell, UTM	Categories (6) of land use	Stevens, 1973
Wisconsin	Land Resource Analysis Program (LRAP)	1:250,000	Grid cell, UTM	Define critical resources; soil suitability for	Kiefer et al., 1975
USDA	Map Information Assembly and Display System (MIADS)	Variable	Grid cell	Display soil attributes	Nichols, 1975
USGS	Land Use and Data Analysis Program (LUDA)	1:250,000	Grid cell, UTM	Depict land use and land cover	Fegeas, 1975
USDI	Resource and Lands Investigations Program (RALI)	1:100,000–1:250,000		Wetlands evaluation, wild & scenic rivers, coastal zone management, critical areas.	

taken at a time and with film conditions that will maximize identification of specific crop, forest, or other land use (Colwell, 1973). Both panchromatic and color infrared film have been used, the latter more commonly for forest identification. Johnson and Johannsen (1975) reported successful discrimination of nine classes of rural land use cover types at level III category using an airborne multispectral scanner. The accuracy, ranging from 58 to 99%, was considered comparable to Census of Agriculture.

With the availability of satellite imagery, the possibility of obtaining synoptic coverage on a repeating basis has encouraged a number of workers (Anderson, 1976; Kiefer et al., 1975; Zirkle & Pile, 1973; Frazier et al., 1975) to develop an on-going land cover inventory. Additionally, precision-processing of LANDSAT imagery (Bernstein & Stierhoff, 1976) can provide multitemporal analysis so that land use and land cover changes may be updated with some facility and efficiency. A limitation is resolution attainable which, with present utilization of computer compatible tapes, would limit presentation to parcels larger than about 10 ha. But this is adequate for many aspects of plant cover analysis.

By comparative use of multispectral bands 5 (0.6–0.7 μm, red) and 7 (0.8–1.1 μm, near infra-red) of LANDSAT imagery Westin and Frazee (1976) reported ability to distinguish main uses of agricultural land in central South Dakota (scale 1:200,000). Lewis et al. (1975) made analysis of vegetative patterns in the Nebraska landscape using band 5 of LANDSAT. Cool-season grasses were distinguished from later grasses. This separation in turn was useful in distinguishing soil associations.

Lewis et al. (1975) estimated vegetative biomass by measurement of optical density of band 5 LANDSAT imagery for the Sand Hills region of Nebraska. This estimate of land cover condition provided an estimate of wind erosion or erosiveness of different soil landscapes. Peterson (1975) suggests that radar, particularly side looking radar, has considerable potential for identifying vegetative patterns as well as landform features.

It is possible, and often practical, to derive a rather detailed analysis of the plant cover. Lindgren and Simpson (1973) indicated that 14 to 18 classes of land use might be identified. Odenyo and Pettry (1977) utilized machine processing of LANDSAT-1 imagery to produce land use/land cover maps with about 24 subdivisions in an urban and rural setting.

While the possibility of regional, or statewide, land cover mapping is present with satellite imagery, most inventories have been accomplished with variously scaled aerial photography.

The nature of plant cover is defined depending on the discipline involved. Geographers have developed categories (Hsu et al., 1973) which tend to have somewhat broader definitions, nevertheless encompassing a wide range of cover, including the "urban asphalt." Foresters and agronomists will more narrowly consider land cover in relation to specific plant and tree species, or communities of plants. The input of botanists, hydrologists, and other disciplines is apparent in other instances (Frazier et al., 1975). See Table 2 for possible schemes for plant cover tabulations.

Table 2—Examples of land cover and land use classifications.

Land cover (resource)	Land use (activity)
Resource	
Urban and built-up land	Residential—urban
Cropland	Residential—low density
Pasture	Commercial & industrial
Forest	Governmental & institutional
Shrub and herbaceous wetland	Agriculture & related
Water	Park and recreation
Barren land	Forestry—forest crop
	Low-intensity uses
Botanic	Mineral extractive

A. Noncrop
  1) Name descriptors
    a) Major life forms (forest, grassland)
    b) Number of communities present (types)
    c) Species (vegetative)
      (1) No. native species/community
      (2) No. species/community/5 acres (2.02 ha)
      (3) % exotic plant species
      (4) % cover exotics
      (5) No. of different crops present
  2) Size of community
  3) Size of forest
  4) Scarcity
    a) in region (in relation to vegetation type)
    b) in state (in relation to vegetation type)
  5) Percent of township in openings
  6) Field division (vegetative, fence rows, hedgerows)
  7) Predominate wildlife habitat
  8) Number of wetlands present/mi^2
B. Crop
  1) Name descriptors
    a) Major lifeforms (forest, cropland, orchard, pasture)
    b) Vegetation type
    c) Species composition
  2) Forest variables
    a) age
    b) site index
    c) density
    d) tract size

III. PLANT COVER DATA SYSTEMS

An example of a hierarchial system of delineating land cover is that proposed by Anderson et al. (1972, 1976) and noted in Table 3. A hierarchial system has the flexibility which may be necessary to accommodate various scales of information.

A system under development by the U.S. Geological Survey (1975) is termed *Land Use Data and Analysis Program* (LUDA) which is also intended to provide physical resource data on a total land area basis (Fegeas, 1975). While geologic and hydrologic parameters would be the primary emphasis, land cover data will also be recorded. The approach to land use classification being proposed by the U.S. Geological Survey is resource oriented, that is to say, a "cover" rather than an "activity" approach. (Ex-

Table 3—Land use and land cover classification system for use with remote sensor data (partially abbreviated) (from Anderson et al., 1976).

Level I	Level II
1. Urban or built-up land	11. Residential
	12. Commercial and service
	13. Industrial
	14. Transportation
	15. Industrial
	16. Mixed urban
	17. Other urban
2. Agricultural land	21. Cropland and pasture
	22. Orchards, etc.
	23. Confined feeding operations
	24. Other agricultural
3. Rangeland	31. Herbaceous rangeland
	32. Shrub and brush
	33. Mixed
4. Forest land	41. Deciduous forest
	42. Evergreen forest
	43. Mixed
5. Water	51. Streams
	52. Lakes
	53. Reservoirs
	54. Bays
6. Wetland	61. Forested wetland
	62. Nonforested wetlands
7. Barren land	71. Dry salt flats
	72. Beaches
	73. Sandy areas
	74. Bare exposures
	75. Strip mines, etc.
	76. Transitional areas
	77. Mixed barren land
8. Tundra	81. Shrubs and brush
	82. Herbaceous
	83. Bare ground
	84. Wet
	85. Mixed
9. Perennial snow or ice	91. Snowfields
	92. Glaciers

amples of "cover" would be cropland, rangeland, forestland. Examples of "activity" would be farming, grazing, forestry).

The definition and delineation of so-called critical areas as derived by the American Law Institute has been shown to be a feasible operation from the Resource and Land Inventory (RALI) (USDI, 1975).

A recent proposal for a level II equivalent land cover inventory is the *Land Inventory and Monitoring System* (LIM) as proposed by USDA. In this system all land areas would be observed and a determination made of land cover in a categorical system. The scale of this inventory would correspond to about the scale of third-order soil mapping of the National Cooperative Soil Survey (1:100,000). Computer storage and retrieval on a grid-cell basis is envisaged, probably in the format of 40-acre (16.2-h) cells (Amidon, 1970). The relevance of the LIM inventory is indicated in the effort to identify prime and unique lands for agriculture as requested by the President's Council on Environmental Quality (1976).

A system used by the Housing and Urban Development department has emphasized land cover as it related to the urban and urbanizing landscapes (U.S. Urban Renewal Admin., 1965).

IV. EXAMPLE OF A SYSTEM—MINNESOTA LAND MANAGEMENT INFORMATION SYSTEM

An example of a system in operation is that employed by the state of Minnesota, termed the *Minnesota Land Management Information System* (MLMIS) (Hsu et al., 1973; Salmen, 1975). This is an inventory of land resource information (soils, land use, physiography) and demographic data (land value, ownership). Information on land use/cover was obtained by photo-interpretation of high altitude panchromatic photography (scale 1:90,000). Other sources of data are USGS topographic sheets, public records on land ownership, and property values. A 40-acre (16.2-ha) grid cell was chosen for recording land use in eight categories (Fig. 1). Computer storage and retrieval permits simulated overlay (or multi-factor) analysis by geographic coordinates.

A long-range goal of the MLMIS inventory is that it might serve as a custodian of information on the environmental effects of land use and production systems (Hanson, 1975). A more immediate goal is to translate the technical data on soils and landscape properties into relationships that can be used by economists and planners. Accordingly, suitability ratings for crop production, forest production, and residential development have been developed. Ratings for individual 40-acre parcels can be tabulated and summarized and also displayed in computer graphic format. This scale of mapping is not applicable to detailed, site-specific land use decisions but does provide a statewide and regional perspective of the relative suitability of land for specific uses (Hanson, 1975).

V. QUANTITATIVE DEVELOPMENT IN PLANT COVER ANALYSIS

The interest in plant cover analysis arises not only from a desire to know *what* is present and *where,* or how, it is distributed, but equally a need to estimate the *yield of biomass,* whether in board feet, bushels, or tons. Sharp et al. (1976) developed net primary productivity rates for some 18 land use cover categories of agriculture and silviculture. The results are displayed in computer graphics format and can be shown to reflect differences in the impact of technology on plant growth.

Research has continually been striving to sharpen the assessment of plant production. Various state crop reporting services attempt, on a voluntary basis, to gather sufficient annual data so as to project and confirm annual, or seasonal, production figures of principal economic species.

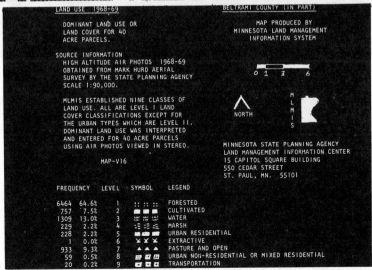

Fig. 1—Land cover map of Beltrami county, Minn., developed from airphoto interpretation and represented by 40-acre cells in the Minnesota Land Management Information System (MLMIS). Reproduction is by DICOMED image recorder.

The Large Area Crop Inventory Experiment (LACIE) project, a joint effort of USDA, NASA, and NOAA, has, as one objective, the determination of the potential and actual production of winter and spring wheat on the High Plains of the western U.S. (McDonald et al., 1975). Combining LANDSAT identification of wheat growing areas and a climatic model for yield production, a total crop evaluation can be made as the growing season progresses. With sufficient ground truth correlation, the goal of 90% accuracy on 90% of the area may be achieved (Johannsen, 1976).

A goal of agronomists, foresters, or any other discipline related to crop and forest growth is to predict the harvestable yield subject to the variety of soil management and climatic variables. Recent emphasis has been on modeling the growth of particular crops given the conditions of the total growing season.

The approaches to plant production estimation have been generally of two kinds. In the first, and older, models, a regression analysis has been followed. Fisher (1924), perhaps, was the first to explore the potentiality of a regression model. In some respects his polynomial model was an attempt to simulate growth. Subsequent workers, in the decades of the 1940's, 1950's, and 1960's have attempted to establish the salient parameters of climate, soil, and plant characteristics that would predict an ultimate yield. Regression models require much data, and the validity of data, or the variability of data, has been the source of considerable errors in estimate of yield, or biomass production.

This frustration has led a number of workers to approach the yield estimate from a simulation model, or a process model. In this approach the experimenter attempts to simulate, mathematically, the growth character of the particular plant using assumptions about functional relationships between leaf area, dry matter production, and assimilation of nutrients, on the one hand, and parameters of the micro-climate, light intensity, soil moisture, soil temperature, and others on the other hand—as well as some genetic factors of the particular species under consideration. In the latter case real data are not ignored but can be used as a test of the simulation model.

One of the benefits of the process model is that it frequently identifies principal areas of data deficiency. A weakness is that processes are not always properly "tied together." That is to say, the process rates or transitions from one process to another, for example, grain filling to maturation or leaf area development to grain filling, may be poorly bridged. Nevertheless, the latter models offer promise, particularly because they are well fitted to computer processing of incremental events.

VI. MODELING PLANT COVER DATA—CORN AND WHEAT MODELS

Probably more effort has been directed at forecasting corn yields than other crops. This may relate to its large economic value in this nation's agriculture and also to the variation in management response. Efforts in recent years have concentrated on finding the most suitable relationships with climatic variables (Thompson, 1969; Gross & Rust, 1972; Leeper et al., 1974; Runge & Benci, 1975). This effort has derived from the realization that the climatic variables presently are associated with the greatest yield variability. The development of these yield models and their subsequent reliability depends on availability of complete, adequate data.

Runge and Benci (1975) developed a corn yield model based on water supply and demand as related to the physiological response centered around pollenation date. This model was tested in six states of the Corn Belt over a 60-year period of climatic records. The model predicted 11 drought, 6 bumper, and 55 average years (Fig. 2). Drought and bumper years were defined as yields of one standard deviation below or above the long-term mean. Runge (1968) had earlier demonstrated the importance of evaluating the temperature and moisture balance of corn prior to and following pollenation.

Nix (1975) developed a wheat model for Australia which used climatic

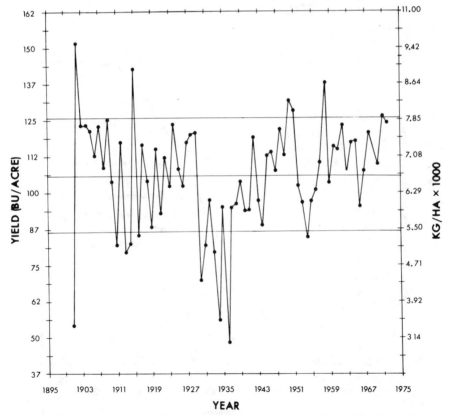

Fig. 2—Weighted mean corn yields for five cornbelt locations (Urbana, Ill.; Ames, Iowa; Manhattan, Kans.; Columbis, Mo.; and Lincoln, Nebr.). Yields adjusted for average 1968-72 technology of 80% and pollination date of 18 July. [Adapted from Runge & Benci (1975). Used by permission.]

conditions during specified development stages of the crop cycle rather than climatic conditions of an arbitrary calendar time unit. Using methods of numerical taxonomy the Australian wheat growing areas were separated into regions of similar climatic regimes related to rainfall and temperature.

Using simulation models of Splinter (1974) and Duncan (1975) Fritton et al. (1977) attempted evaluation of maize dry matter and yield. Solar radiation, precipitation, maximum and minimum temperatures, pan evaporation, soil water potential, silking date, leaf area index, and black layer date were all input parameters. Failure of the simulation models to predict silking and maturity dates (under Pennsylvania conditions) resulted in failure to agree with actual field measurements of dry matter. Nevertheless, as may be observed in Fig. 3, by modification of the Duncan model, relatively good agreement was obtained with 1975 maize data.

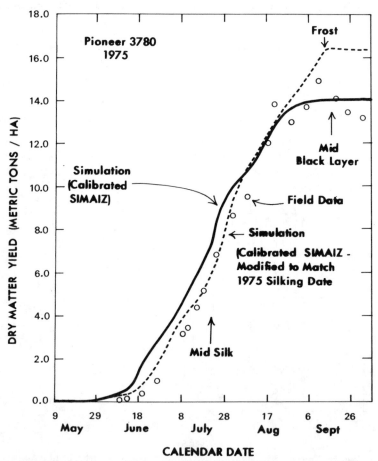

Fig. 3—Simulated and observed dry matter yield for maize (Pennsylvania conditions) using a Duncan (1975) model and a modification by Fritton et al. (1977). (Used by permission.)

VII. ANALYSIS OF FACTORS IN PLANT COVER MODELS

Soil scientists pursue the estimation of yield functions from a some-what different perspective from crop scientists, with emphasis on physical, chemical, and biological factors that relate, directly or indirectly, to yield. Henao (1976) categorizes variables affecting corn yield as soil, weather, and management-related. In an analysis of some 2,800 corn yields over 14 years some 72 variables with an R^2 value of 0.67 were selected. Soil variables included were slope, erosion class, plant-available water capacity, drainage class, subsoil permeability, percent carbon and clay in the plow layer, and clay in the subsoil. Moisture stress indexes were developed which related transpiration ratios to variations in soil moisture in the rooting zone. Management variables included planting date, stand level, weed growth, corn borer infestation, distance to tile, N, P, and K from manure and fertilizers.

In respect to soil factors, perhaps the principal item is the estimate of plant-available water in the rooting zone between wilting point and field capacity. The latter term is not easily established except by in situ observation. Gross and Rust (1972) found that estimates of soil moisture calculated on the basis of preseason recharge, water retention characteristics of the particular soil, and precipitation increments provided the most explanation of yield variance of some 12 variables used. Nix (1975) used a measure termed *potential water stress* ($P - E_t$) for the critical development stages of wheat where P = rainfall and E_t = potential evapotranspiration. This measure of rainfall deficit, plotted geographically, outlined areas of significantly different wheat growing potential.

Other soil properties, such as bulk density, relate to rooting development and therefore to yield. Stoniness is a feature of many soils which not only inhibits cultural practices but reduces the effective volume for root development.

Most yield relationships developed by soil or crop scientists endeavor to evaluate the available nutrient-supplying power of the soil. Nutrients have been classed as macro- and micro- based on plant consumption and have been estimated by a variety of chemical procedures, though a considerable effort has been made to standardize tests nationwide, or at least regionally. Response curves have been developed between crop and forest yields and available (or added) nutrients. These functions have taken a variety of forms but in general have been nonlinear and with some observable maxima. Since many soils are lacking, or are deficient, in some necessary plant nutrients, soil amendments are in order in most yield goals.

Many crops but particularly corn have a high nitrogen response. The response can be rather quantitatively estimated for a specific soil and crop but since the N response is highly dependent on the moisture regime and particularly at the growth stage of high demand, an N response must be evaluated in concurrence with the moisture regime of the rooting zone. A quadratic response curve is commonly useful for N-yield characterization.

In respect to biological factors, most crop yield studies relate to nitrogen evaluation—to measures of its availability and to responses to added increments of N. However, since organic matter bears a direct relationship to N supply, many studies have related production to organic matter content, both native and added.

VIII. DEVELOPMENT AND USE OF SOIL PRODUCTIVITY INDICES

Soil productivity indices have been developed on the basis of physical and/or economic analysis. On the physical basis various indices have been developed—some which relate almost entirely to measurable attributes of the soil and its landscape setting (Rudeforth, 1975). Others have been derived from consideration of gross production of principal crops or tree species weighted by cropping distribution. In a number of situations, single crops (corn in Iowa, wheat in North Dakota) have been used as a basis. Current and average management has usually been sought as the basis for estimating productivity.

It is, however, the synthesis of many factors—pedologic, climatic, cultural—which ultimately produces the crop and forest yield. In addition to the pedologic factors noted previously, perhaps cultural practices seem most amenable to manipulation. Over the relatively brief history of American agriculture and silviculture, cultural practices have undergone many changes and this effect on production is increasingly difficult to evaluate. Many practices are used only for a few years.

Because of the increasing cost of energy in crop production, a trend to minimum, or at least, minimizing, tillage operations is clearly underway. The trend is aided by the availability of improved weed and insect control. It is not necessarily related to a reduced energy cost (Pimentel et al., 1973). Pimentel et al. (1973) suggest, as a means of reducing energy costs, the use of rotations and green manure practices. These adoptions would be reflected by land cover analysis. Likewise, changes in harvesting procedures have had, as a goal, reducing losses and preserving quality.

IX. PURPOSES AND USES OF PLANT COVER DATA

The purpose of collecting land cover data and evaluating land productivity may, perhaps, be summarized by saying that such data form an integral part of any land use planning and decision making, however small in scope. In the earlier noted *Conservation Needs Inventory* (USDA, 1971), a primary purpose was to establish the percentage of privately owned land in need of conservation treatment. It was established that from 50 to 75% of the land suitable for cultivation was in need of some phase of conservation practices.

One of the increasing uses of the productivity indices together with the soil survey data is in the assessment of rural lands (Foth, 1971). Changing technology has sharply advanced the productivity and subsequent market value of many agricultural lands; this coupled with the relatively low turnover, in bona fide sales, has led many county assessors to view a productivity rating as well correlated with fair market value (Fenton, 1975b). Frazee et al. (1974) developed a unique application of LANDSAT imagery. By analysis of land cover and land condition, an assessment basis was established for a (mostly) rangeland county of western South Dakota.

If, indeed, the productivity ratings, whether for cultivated field, range, or forest crops, do objectively scale relative values of lands, then they can become useful in defining "prime" land for specific purposes. This is demonstrated in the current North Central Region (comprising 12 states) map (scale 1:5,000,000) depicting prime agricultural land in the region (Fenton et al., 1979).

Another use of land cover data is in the designation of potential use conflict areas. Frazier et al. (1975) indicated that a number of considerations underlie their (Wisconsin) resource analysis program: (i) the adequacy of land surrounding growth centers; (ii) presence of inherent land characteristics which may increase development costs; and (iii) distribution of public lands and resources relative to demand and use for transportation facilities. Areas that may have high potential for agriculture, as judged by present kind and quality of cover, may have equal potential (or nearly so) for low-density residential development. This has been a common conflict in many urbanizing areas. A somewhat related use of this kind of data is in the identification of open space (or sometimes termed *green belt*) areas, also in the urban growth areas. Not all the criteria for open space will relate to land cover and its quality but, to the extent that they do, selection can be aided.

Wetlands have been a land cover condition under considerable investigation. A number of states and agencies have sought to establish criteria for wetland identification and partially detailed analysis (Cowardin et al., 1976). The geographic areas of emphasis have been the east coast, the south, and the Great Lakes region.

X. SUMMARY

Acquisition of plant cover data is an integral part of any systematic land use analysis and decision making process. In addition to knowledge of spatial location there is need to recognize quality and quantity. In the first instance aerial photography and other means of remote sensing have been applied to the task. The evaluation of quality and quantity may be done by the same means but most often requires supplementary evaluation. Agroclimatic models have been developed to assist in this aspect.

As regards presently identified uses of plant cover data these would seem to be principally of two kinds: (i) identifying the existing patterns of land use and (ii) identifying the areas of conflict and changing land use. The present effort by USDA to identify prime and unique agricultural land (Fenton, 1975a) and efforts by other agencies to generally classify kinds of land use in varying degrees of detail is of the first type; one the other hand efforts by metropolitan governments to monitor changing land use and by the agricultural and urban sectors to identify erosion and effects of soil modification are examples of the second type.

Land cover analysis has been, and will continue to be, a preoperational environmental assay of the large-scale strip mining operations as well as a post-operational survey policy.

Quantifying biomass has been a major use of land cover analysis by agencies such as the Forest Service. Currently there is interest in quantifying other biomass types (grain and forage, for example) for possible energy production.

Thus, there is the aspect of monitoring change not only in *kind* of cover but also its quality and quantity, changes brought about by the action of man and/or nature, such as the present apparent desertification in tropical and subtropical areas.

LITERATURE CITED

Amidon, D. W. 1970. MIADS, An Alpha-Numberic Map Information Assembly and Display System for a Large Computer. U.S. For. Serv. Res. Pap. PSW-38. Berkeley, Calif.

Anderson, J. R. 1976. Applications to land use mapping and planning. Chapter 4 in ERTS-1-A New Window in our Planet. U.S. Geol. Survey Prof. Paper 929, U.S. Government Printing Office, Washington, D.C.

Anderson, J. R., E. E. Hardy, and J. T. Roach. 1972. A land-use classification system for use with remote sensor data. U.S. Geol. Survey Circ. 671. 16 p.

Anderson, J. R., E. E. Hardy, J. T. Roach, and R. E. Witmer. 1976. A land use and land cover classification system for use with remote sensor data. U.S. Geol. Survey Prof. Pap. 964. U.S. Government Printing Office, Washington, D.C.

Baldridge, P. E., P. H. Goesling, F. Leone, C. Minshall, R. H. Rodgers, and C. L. Wilhelm. 1975. Ohio's Statewide Land Use Inventory. Proc. of NASA Earth Resour. Surv. Symp., June 1975. Lyndon B. Johnson Space Center, Houston, Tex. NASA Tech. Manual X-58168, Wasington, D.C.

Bernstein, R., and G. C. Stierhoff. 1976. Precision processing of earth image data. Am. Sci. 64(6):500–508.

Colwell, R. N. 1973. Remote sensing as an aid to the management of earth resources. Am. Sci. 61:175–183.

President's Council on Environmental Quality. 1976. Analysis of impacts on prime and unique farmland in environmental impact statements. Memorandum for Heads of Agencies. Exec. Off. of the President, Washington, D.C.

Cowardin, L. M., V. Carter, F. C. Golet, and E. T. LaRoe. 1976. Interim classification of wetlands and aquatic habitats of the United States. *In* Proc. of Natl. Wetland Classification and Inventory Workshop, 1975, St. Petersburg, Fla. Fish and Wildl. Serv., U.S. Dep. of Interior, Washington, D.C.

New Jersey Department of Community Affairs. 1973. Land oriented information system. A data resource for planning. Trenton, N.J.

Duncan, W. G. 1975. SIMAIZ: A model simulating growth and yield in corn. *In* D. N. Baker, R. G. Creech, and F. G. Maxwell (ed.) An application of system methods to crop production. Mississippi Agric. and For. Exp. Stn., Mississippi State Univ. State College, Miss.

Fegeas, R. B. 1975. Graphic input procedure documentation. Geography Progr. U.S. Geological Surv., Reston, Va.

Fenton, T. E. 1975a. Definition and criteria for identifying prime and unique lands. p. 133–150. *In* Perspectives on prime lands. USDA.

Fenton, T. E. 1975b. Soil productivity ratings and their use in agricultural land evaluation. J. Soil Water Conserv. 30(5):237–240.

Fenton, T. E. (ed.). 1979. Essential agricultural lands of the North Central States. North Central Region Pub. Iowa Agric. Exp. Stn., Ames.

Fisher, R. A. 1924. The influence of rainfall on the yield of wheat at Rothamsted. Phil. Trans. Roy. Soc. London. Series B. 213:89–142.

Foth, H. D. 1971. Using soil survey information for tax equalization. Coop. Ext. Serv., Michigan State Univ., East Lansing.

Frazee, C. J., R. H. Rann, F. C. Westin, and V. I. Meyers. 1974. Use of ERTS-1 imagery for land evaluation in Pennington County, South Dakota. South Dakota Agric. Exp. Stn. J. Ser. no. 1276, Brookings, S.D.

Frazier, B. E., R. W. Kiefer, and T. M. Krauskopf. 1975. Statewide wetland mapping using LANDSAT imagery. p. 267–280. In F. Shahrokhl (ed.) Remote sensing of earth resources, IV. Univ. of Tennessee, Knoxville.

Fritton, D. D., D. P. Knievel, G. W. McKee, and J. D. Martsolf. 1977. Growth, yield, and simulation of maize. In World Meteorol. Organ. Maize Symp. 5–7 July 1976, Ames, Iowa.

Gròss, E. R., and R. H. Rust. 1972. Estimation of corn and soybean yields utilizing multiple curvilinear regression methods. Proc. Soil Sci. Soc. Am. 36(2):316–320.

Hanson, L. D. 1976. Land use interpretations of land resource information. p. 177–200. In State land use criteria. Center for Urban and Regional Affairs, Univ. of Minnesota, Minneapolis.

Henao, J. 1976. Soil variables for regressing Iowa corn yields on soil, management, and climatic variables. Ph.D. thesis. Iowa State Univ., Ames (Diss. Abstr. 77-10,317).

Hsu, M., K. Kozar, G. Orning, and P. G. Stread. 1973. Computer applications in land use mapping and the Minnesota land management information system. NATO Advanced Study Inst. on Display and Analysis of Spatial Data, Northingham, England.

Johannsen, C. 1976. The large area crop inventory evaluation (LACIE). NASA Rep., 1976. Houston, Tex.

Johnson, G. E., and C. J. Johannsen. 1975. Land use discrimination employing remote multispectral sensing techniques. p. 233–242. In F. Shahrokhl (ed.) Remote sensing of the earth's resources, IV. Univ. of Tennessee, Knoxville.

Johnston, R. A., L. J. Thorpe, and T. H. Long. 1975. Land use mapping programs. Div. of Environ. Studies, Univ. of California, Davis.

Kiefer, R. W., B. E. Frazier, and A. H. Miller. 1975. Statewide land cover mapping using ERTS imagery. Wisconsin Pap. Annu. Meet Am. Soc. Photogram. 41:141–145.

Land Use Analysis Laboratory Staff. 1973. A land use classification method for land use planning. Iowa State Univ., Ames.

Leeper, R. A., E. C. A. Runge, and W. M. Walker. 1974. Effect of plant available stored soil moisture on corn yields. I. Constant climatic conditions. II. Variable climatic conditions. Agron. J. 66:723–733.

Lewis, D. T., P. M. Seevers, and J. V. Drew. 1975. Use of satellite imagery to delineate soil associations in the Sand Hills region of Nebraska. Soil Sci. Soc. Am. Proc. 39:330–335.

Lindgren, D. T., and R. B. Simpson. 1973. Land use of northern megalopolis. In Symp. on Significant Results Obtained from Earth Resour. Technol. Satellite 1. Goddard Space Flight Center, Md. NASA Spec. Pub. 327.

McCormack, R. J. 1971. The Canada Land Use Inventory: a basis for land use planning. J. Soil Water Conserv. 26(4):141–146.

McDonald, R. B., F. G. Hall, R. B. Erb, P. J. Waite, J. D. Murphy, and R. I. Dideriksen. 1975. The Large Area Crop Inventory Experiment. p. 43–74. In Proc. of the NASA Earth Resour. Symp., June 1975, Lyndon B. Johnson Space Center, Houston, Tex. NASA Tech. Manual X-58168, Washington, D.C.

Nichols, J. 1975. Characteristics of computerized soil maps. Proc. Soil Sci. Soc. Am. 39:927–932.

Nix, H. A. 1975. The Australian climate and its effects on grain yield and quality. p. 183–226. In A. Lazenby and E. M. Matheson (ed.) Australian field crops. Angus and Robertson, Sydney.

Odenyo, V. A. O., and D. E. Pettry. 1977. Land use mapping by machine processing of LANDSAT-1 data. Photogramm. Eng. 43(3):515–523.

Office of Planning Services. 1974. Land use and natural resource (LUNR) inventory of New York State. What it is and how it is used. Albany, N.Y.

Peterson, J. B. 1975. Quantitative inventorying of soil and land use differences by remote sensing. Proc. Soil Conserv. Soc. Am. 39:202–208.

Pimentel, D., L. E. Hurd, A. C. Bellotti, M. J. Forster, I. N. Oka, O. D. Sholes, and R. J. Whitman. 1973. Food production and the energy crisis. Science 182:443–449.

Rudeforth, C. C. 1975. Storing and processing data for soil and land use capability surveys. J. Soil Sci. 26(2):155–168.

Runge, E. C. A. 1968. Effects of rainfall and temperature interactions during the growing season on corn yield. Agron. J. 60:503–507.

Runge, E. C. A., and J. F. Benci. 1975. Modeling corn production—Estimating production under variable soil and climatic conditions. Proc. 30th Annual Corn and Sorghum Res. Conf., Chicago, 9–11 Dec. 1975. Am. Seed Trade Assoc., Washington, D.C.

Salmen, L. J. 1975. Proposed MLMIS Systems Development Plan. Center for Urban and Regional Affairs. Univ. of Minnesota, Minneapolis.

Sharp, D. D., H. Lieth, G. R. Noggle, and H. D. Gross. 1976. Agricultural and forest primary productivity in North Carolina, 1972–73. Tech. Bull. 241. North Carolina Agric. Exp. Stn., Raleigh.

Shields, R. L. 1976. New generalized soil maps guide land use planning in Maryland. J. Soil Water Conserv. 31:276–280.

Skinner, C. W. 1974. Design concepts for the North Carolina Planning and Land Use Management Information System. North Carolina State Univ., Raleigh.

Splinter, W. E. 1974. Modeling of plant growth for yield prediction. Agric. Meteorol. 14:243–253.

Stevens, A. R. 1973. Land cover delineation methods and presentation alternatives applicable to the Tennessee River watershed. p. 1269–1285. In F. Shahrokhl (ed.) Remote sensing of earth resources, II. Univ. of Tennessee, Knoxville.

Thompson, L. M. 1969. Weather and technology in the production of corn in the U.S. Corn Belt. Agron. J. 61:453–456.

Tschanz, J. F., and A. S. Kennedy. 1975. Natural Resource Manaement Information Systems: A guide to design. Argonne Natl. Lab., Argonne, Ill.

U.S. Department of Agriculture. 1971. Basic statistics—national inventory of soil and water conservation needs, 1967. Stat. Bull. 461. USDA, Washington, D.C.

U.S. Department of Interior, Office of Land Use and Water Planning. 1975. Information—data handling requirements for selected state resource management programs. Technical Rep. C. Washington, D.C.

U.S. Forest Service. 1972. Forest surveys. Handbook 4813.1. Washington, D.C.

U.S. Geological Survey. 1975. Land Use Data and Analysis Program. Geography Progr. U.S. Geolog. Surv., Reston, Va.

U.S. Urban Renewal Administration, Housing and Home Finance Agency, and Bureau of Public Roads. 1965. Standard land use coding manual; a standard system for identifying and coding land use activities. Washington, D.C.

Watson, R. A., P. Hagle, S. W. Tweedie, and E. Bahm. 1973. Analysis of alternatives for an Oklahoma Land Use Information System. Dep. of Geography, Oklahoma State Univ., Normal.

Westin, F. C., and C. J. Frazee. 1976. Landsat data, its use in a soil survey program. Soil Sci. Soc. Am. J. 40:81–89.

Zirkle, R. E., and D. R. Pile. 1973. Determination of land use in Minnesota by automatic interpretation of ERTS MSS data. In Symp. on Significant Results Obtained from ERTS-1. Proc. 1(B):1635–39. Goddard Space Flight Center, Md. NASA Spec. Pub. 327.

8 Data Acquisition Through Remote Sensing

E. R. STONER AND M. F. BAUMGARDNER

Laboratory for Applications of Remote Sensing
Purdue University
Lafayette, Indiana

I. INTRODUCTION—A NEW LOOK AT AN OLD SCENE

Man is a curious creature, and he has been examining and describing the surrounding landscape for thousands of years. His early descriptions and views of the environment were simple. Even today many features of the landscape seem at first glance to be changeless. However, important events and trends since 1800 and especially during the twentieth century focus attention on the many significant and accelerating changes which are occurring in the old scene. These trends strongly suggest that new ways must be found to inventory the natural resources of our planet and to monitor regularly significant changes which occur in the quantity of these resources and in the quality of our environment (Handler, 1976; Pimentel et al., 1976).

Thoughtful consideration of some of the major dilemmas facing mankind—exploding human population, global hunger, a deterioration of the environment, and wasteful consumption of a finite supply of resources—suggests that new approaches are required for developing, managing, and conserving our resources. The need becomes increasingly critical for any information system which can provide useful, accurate, timely, and inexpensive information to decision makers.

Although there are many other important facets to resource management and land use planning, a key factor is information. Since the objective of this chapter is to discuss the application of remote sensing to land use planning, primary attention will be given to the acquisition and delivery of useful information through remote sensing methods.

Information is a valuable commodity, and many existing information systems, large and small, provide some decision makers with some information which contributes toward reaching rational decisions. However, evidence abounds that absence of or limitations in current information systems may contribute substantially to environmental deterioration, land degradation, food deficits, and mismanagement of land and water resources.

Remote sensing, in a broad sense, may be defined as the measurement or acquisition of information of some property of an object or phenomenon, by a recording device that is not in physical or intimate contact with the object or phenomenon under study (Reeves, 1975). The general concept of remote sensing has evolved over the past decade to include both data acquisition and data analysis to the extent that usable information is made available to the user.

Even before land use planning was recognized and practiced as a tool for the allocation and management of resources, the common remote sensor, aerial photography, came into general use as a tool in resources surveys. Since the mid 1930's the U.S. Soil Conservation Service has used black and white aerial photography as a base for mapping soils. For four decades the Agricultural Stabilization and Conservation Service of the U.S. Department of Agriculture used aerial photography for estimating areas of specific crops to check on farmer compliance with government allotments for individual producers. For many years the Forest Service has used aerial photography to estimate potential timber yield, evaluate forest conditions, and assess forest fire damage. It has been only during the past two decades that land use planners have begun to make substantial use of aerial photography for planning purposes.

During the past two decades technological advances have provided new methods and opportunities to inventory and monitor land use patterns and changes (Krumpe, 1976). New data acquisition methods in the laboratory, field, air, and space provide vistas of the earth never before available to man, from the sub-atomic structure to thousands of square kilometers in a single synoptic view of the earth's surface. The computer revolution since 1950 has provided man with a previously undreamed of capacity to store, retrieve, analyze, and interpret masses of data. Revolutionary changes in communications technology provide man with the means to transmit information and reach a multitude of different information users or decision makers with more accurate, timely, useful information than was ever possible before. There can be little doubt that present and future remote sensing technology will play a significant role in land use planning activities.

II. DATA ACQUISITION

A. The Electromagnetic Spectrum

One of the more basic systems for acquisition of remotely sensed data is that of conventional photography. In conventional photography the energy being sensed is the sum of all radiation reflected from the field of view and for the specific wavelength band to which the photographic emulsion is sensitive. The radiation source as with other so-called *passive* remote sensing systems is the sun. Photographic systems can measure or record energy from wavelengths of about 0.3 to 0.9 μm (Fig. 1). Reflective measurements, a phenomenon of energy up to 3 μm in wavelength, are important in land use research because of the range of response exhibited by different materials in that portion of the spectrum. Solar reflectant power decreases with increasing wavelengths until the radiation emitted by the object is dominant, the crossover point being at approximately 3 μm (Suits, 1960).

Energy recorded in the 3- to 15-μm portion of the spectrum is due pri-

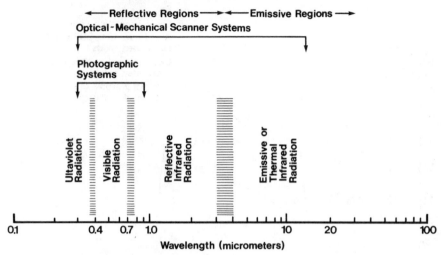

Fig. 1—A portion of the electromagnetic spectrum.

marily to emission from an object, which is a function of the true tempera-ture and the emissivity of the object. Atmospheric absorption by CO_2, O_2, and H_2O prevents the transmission of significant amounts of energy in re-maining portions of the spectrum making sensing systems such as passive microwave imagery impractical for present needs. Radar imaging utilizes a so-called *active* system which depends on reradiation of energy supplied by the sensor system in the long wavelength range, commonly between 0.86 and 3.3 cm (Holter et al., 1970). Side-looking airborne radar (SLAR), which produces a continuous strip image on photographic film, is the radar form most likely to be useful for land use surveys. Although direct photo-graphic techniques cannot be used effectively to record wavelengths of energy greater than 0.9 μm, instruments such as electro-optical multi-spectral scanners may be used to measure energy response in this region. The multispectral scanner systems may have a range from approximately 0.3 to 15 μm (Fig. 1). A scanner obtains energy responses of selected wave-length bands in a series of contiguous scan lines recorded on magnetic tape in either continuous or discrete format.

B. Radiation Characteristics of Earth Surface Features

Radiation characteristics of earth surface features involve variations in reflectance and emittance of the incident solar energy. It is these variations in reflectance and emittance that multispectral scanners are capable of re-cording.

Much of the current understanding of radiation characteristics of earth surface features is limited to the reflective portion of the spectrum. The amount of energy reflected by a material is a function of three factors: the

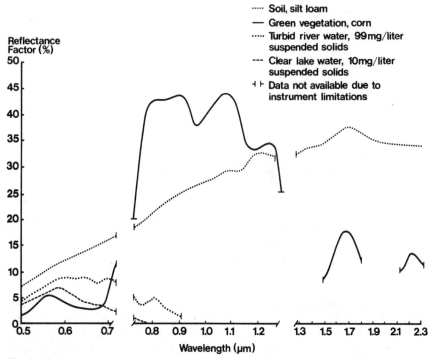

Fig. 2—Field-measured spectral characteristics of clear lake water, turbid river water, soils, and vegetation (after Bartolucci et al., 1977).

incident solar energy, the amount of energy absorbed, and the amount of energy transmitted through it. This relationship can be expressed as

$$R_\lambda = I_\lambda - (A_\lambda + T_\lambda)$$

or the reflectance (R) at a specific wavelength (λ) is equal to the incident energy at that wavelength (I_λ) minus the sum of the energy absorbed (A_λ) and transmitted (T_λ) at that wavelength.

Reflectance patterns for familiar earth surface materials vary with wavelength (Fig. 2). Spectral characteristics of clear lake water, turbid river water, soils, and healthy green vegetation follow these general patterns (Bartolucci et al., 1977).

A plant leaf reflects and transmits incident radiation in a manner that is representative of pigmented cells containing water (Knipling, 1970; Myers & Allen, 1968; Gates, 1962; Hoffer & Johannsen, 1969). Relatively low reflectance occurs in the visible wavelengths where the effects of the pigmentation in the leaf determine the shape of the curve. Chlorophyll absorbs energy in the blue and red wavelengths but reflects it in the green band (0.50–0.55 μm), making it appear green to our eyes. The abrupt increase in reflectance near 0.7 μm and the fairly abrupt decrease near 1.3 μm exist for all mature, healthy green leaves. The dips in the reflectance curve at infrared wavelengths of 0.9, 1.1, 1.4, and 1.9 μm are liquid-water absorption bands, so called because water absorbs greater amounts of energy at those wavelengths.

Soils cannot be said to have a unique characteristic reflectance curve, but in general it can be said that soil reflectance increases as wavelength increases from 0.3 to 2.5 μm (Bowers & Hanks, 1965; Myers & Allen, 1968). Condit (1970, 1972) found that soils could be identified as belonging to one of three general shapes of soil reflectance curves from 0.3 to 1.0 μm.

A variety of soil parameters and conditions individually and in association with one another contribute to the spectral reflectance of soils. Soil physical-chemical parameters which affect the reflectance patterns of air dry soils include organic matter content, texture (especially clay and silt content), iron oxide content, and cation exchange capacity (CEC) (Baumgardner et al., 1970; Cipra et al., 1971; Al-Abbas et al., 1972; Montgomery et al., 1976). Soil color also affects the reflectance properties of soils although the subjective determination of color is limited to the individual's perception in the visible wavelength region and is not a precise measure. Strong water absorption bands are evident at 1.4 and 1.9 μm for moist soils (Bowers & Hanks, 1965), but the overall shape of the curve is also affected by soil moisture levels to such an extent that generalized statements regarding a particular soil's spectral characteristics are difficult (Fig. 3). It can be said, however, that moist soils generally have a lower reflectance throughout the spectrum than dry soils and show the effects of the water absorption bands (Johannsen & Baumgardner, 1968).

Soils derived from different parent materials exhibit contrasting spectral curves (Fig. 4) (Mathews et al., 1973). Differing amounts of clay, organic matter, and iron oxide content are apparently responsible for the major differences observed in these three soils. Discrimination among these three soils based on spectral properties is evidence of the potential ability to discriminate among soils from a remote position. Additional conditions affecting the radiation characteristics of soils in their natural state are green vegetation, shadows, surface roughness, and nonsoil residue which vary according to tillage operations, cropping systems, or naturally occurring plant communities (Hoffer & Johannsen, 1969).

A significant reflectance characteristic of water is its distinct decrease in reflectance moving from the visible to the near-infrared wavelengths (Fig. 2) (Bartolucci et al., 1977). Both clear water and turbid water behave in this way, although turbid water has a spectral response of approximately 5% in the near-infrared portion of the spectrum whereas clear lake water is essentially black. In the visible wavelengths, turbid river water generally reflects more energy than clear lake water because of its higher level of suspended solids. Variations in reflectance can be used to determine water depth and condition.

An understanding of the physical and biological basis for variations in reflectance and emittance is essential for eventual analysis of data acquired by remote sensors.

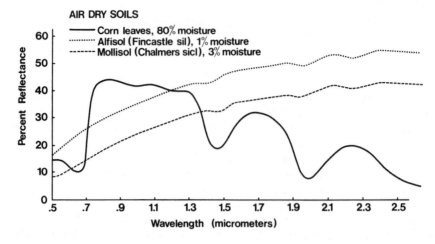

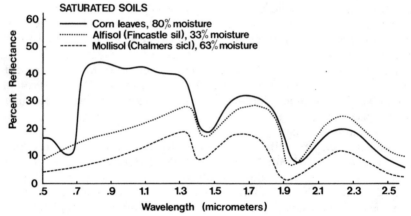

Fig. 3—Laboratory-measured spectral characteristics of corn leaves and of air-dry and saturated soils.

C. Measurement of Spatial Variations

Identification of earth surface features from a remote position,
especially in conventional aerial photography, also utilizes the measurement
of spatial variation as a key element leading to data interpretation. The size,
shape, pattern, and association of objects with their surroundings are
spatial characteristics which provide clues for positive identification of
targets. Both visual and numerical analysis methods make use of spatial
variation in interpretation procedures (Kettig & Landgrebe, 1976).

In general, photographic systems of data acquisition provide high
spatial resolution of ground features while electro-optical systems such as
multispectral scanners have poorer spatial resolution. Variables such as
film/filter combination, camera system, and film processing affect photographic resolution. Altitude of the data collection platform also influences
the spatial resolution, with resolution generally being degraded with in-

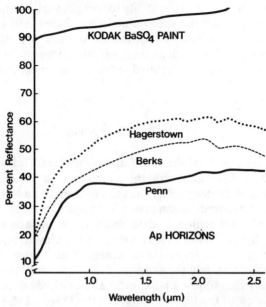

Fig. 4—Spectral characteristics of surface horizons of Hagerstown, Berks, and Penn silt loams; soils developed from limestone, shale, and sandstone, respectively (after Mathews et al., 1973).

creasing altitude. Spatial resolution is an important factor in determining the suitability of remotely sensed data to the land use planner. More detailed surveys require larger scale imagery with increased spatial resolution.

D. Measurement of Spectral Variations

Various film/filter combinations allow for measurement of spectral variation with photographic systems, but are by their nature limited to an upper wavelength limit of 0.9 μm. Perhaps the most significant contribution of remote sensing technology to earth resource survey is the development of sensors which are capable of measuring spectral variations of earth surface features from the ultraviolet to the emissive infrared regions of the spectrum. This capability to obtain a complete spectral characterization of objects in either a continuous wavelength plot or in the discrete bands over such a wide spectral range increases the utility of remotely acquired data for land use mapping (Landgrebe, 1976).

E. Measurement of Temporal Variations

Temporal variations become particularly important to the land use planner when his goal is monitoring land use changes. Repetitive passage of a sensor system over the same area on the ground provides a record over time which may contribute to the ability to identify earth surface features by use of variations in both the spectral and time dimensions (Anuta, 1970). This same record is a source of information on land use change. Orbital, sun-synchronous satellites such as the Landsat series provide an 18-day repetitive cycle which is quite well suited to the measurement of temporal variations.

F. The Landsat System

Since the launching of the first Earth Resources Technology Satellite (ERTS-1) in July 1972 and with the subsequent launching of a second identical satellite in January 1975, the then renamed Landsat satellites constitute the most advanced system presently in use for routine acquisition of spatial, spectral, and temporal data from earth surface features (Natl. Aeronaut. and Space Admin., 1972). Of special interest to land use planners is the Landsat system of repetitive coverage on an 18-day cycle with data collection at approximately the same local time each day in every location. The Landsat satellites follow a polar orbit at an altitude of 920 km, providing a synoptic view of the Earth's surface in the 185- by 185-km data collection frames.

The remote sensors on Landsat include a four-wavelength band multispectral scanner (MSS) and a three-wavelength band return beam vidicon (RBV) system. Of most interest to land use planners, the multispectral scanner system is the one always referred to in this chapter. The scanner gathers spectral reflectance in four spectral bands, two in the visible portion of the spectrum (0.5–0.6 μm and 0.6–0.7 μm) and two in the near infrared (0.7–0.8 μm and 0.8–1.1 μm). The spatial resolution of the MSS system is on the order of 0.5 ha, meaning that this is the minimum area commonly detectable on the ground.

Landsat data are available in both image and digital formats for data analysis by visual and numerical means, respectively. Black and white or simulated color infrared imagery is available for enlargement from master reproducibles at an image scale of 1:3,369,000. Computer-compatible tapes containing Landsat MSS data are especially well suited for performing analyses based on numerical techniques and for creating digitally enhanced and enlarged images.

III. DATA ANALYSIS

Land use planning is becoming an increasingly important approach for managing and allocating land resources. With the increasing demand for more information about specific parcels of land, land use planning agencies are faced with the growing problems of accumulation, storage, retrieval, analysis, and utilization of data. Data from a wide array of sources are now being used by these agencies. These data may include physical parameters,

economic statistics, social and cultural indicators, and political and ownership boundaries.

In this section attention will be given to the analysis of data which may
be obtained by remote sensing devices. From the preceding section it is apparent that remote sensing of use to the land use planner has had two major
thrusts, a result of development along two different types of technology.
Landgrebe (1976) refers to these two types as *image orientation* and *numerical orientation.* Analysis of data obtained through these two systems may be
referred to as *visual analysis* (more commonly as *photo-interpretation*) and
machine processing, often referred to as *pattern recognition.*

A. Visual Analysis

The technology of photographic systems is relatively well developed. A
wide variety of cameras and film-filter combinations have been in use for
many decades. Many instruments and image enhancement devices have
been developed to extend the capabilities of the photo-interpreter in extracting useful information from images. This system has the distinct advantage
over numerical analysis of being easily acceptable to the layman, an advantage important in land use planning.

Also, visual analysis is appropriate for producing subjective information and is especially adapted to situations in which the classes to be identified in analysis cannot be adequately defined in advance. Image-oriented
systems also offer the advantage of being relatively simple and inexpensive.

B. Numerical Analysis

Numerical, or *digital,* analysis relies heavily on the computer. The technology of numerically oriented systems is much newer and not nearly as well
developed as is the technology of image systems. Since the various steps in
digital analysis of numerical systems tend to be more abstract, these systems
are less readily understandable by the layman. Numerical analysis is better
suited than visual analysis for extracting information objectively. Digital
analysis also lends itself well to the production of extensive land use surveys
covering large areas. However, numerically oriented systems are generally
more complex than visual analysis systems.

IV. DATA UTILIZATION

A. Data Needs for Land Use Planning

Land use planning has been defined as planning for the allocation of
activities to land areas in order to benefit humans (Panel on Land Use
Plann., 1975). Data needs which may be supplied by remote sensing vary

Table 1—Generalized remote sensing data needs for land use planning
(Adapted from Panel on Land Use Planning, 1975).

User	Area	Map scale	Frequency	Resolution (grid size in m)
National Land Use agency	U.S. and continental shelf	1:1,000,000	One satellite orbit series	100
State and multi-state regional planners	State areas to entire U.S.	1:250,000	3 to 6 mo	100
Regional and urban private entrepreneurs	10% of total U.S. in 5,000-km² regional sites	1:24,000	1 year	10
Central business district, urban area, and transporation planners	1% of total U.S. in 500-km² regional sites	1:10,000	As required, about 1 year	1

depending on the specific task involved in this definition as follows:

1) Forecasting requirements or demands for goods and services. Remotely sensed data is potentially useful in this area to calibrate models which forecast growth patterns by extrapolation.

2) Evaluating, implementing, and monitoring alternative management and control strategies. The spatial implications of this task area require standardized data of a repetitive nature, such as Landsat is able to provide.

3) Estimating the supply of land available to produce goods and services (in terms of amount, location, quality, suitability, or capability). The most significant potential contribution of remote sensing may be in evaluation of the available land resources by augmentation of more conventional methods.

The type, complexity, quantity, and resolution (grid size) of data which the user requires from the remote sensing and data analysis system varies depending on whether the results are to be applied to local, regional, state, federal, or international problems. In general, as one proceeds from local to international user levels, the quantity of data needed increases, the aerial coverage increases, the scale decreases, the number of classes tends to decrease, and the classes tend to be homogeneous over large areas.

Rate of change of land use phenomena may determine the timeliness of data collection needed at any user level. Some regional users of remote sensing data may require very short delivery schedules of processed data for enforcement purposes. The general situation regarding data needs for land use planners is summarized in Table 1.

B. Resolution Requirements

The geometric characteristics of remotely sensed data are of prime importance for many land use applications. Ground resolution, which can be considered equivalent to ground instantaneous field of view (IFOV), is one

Table 2—Sensor data sources and scale requirements for four classification levels
(Adapted from Anderson et al., 1976).

Classification level	Sensor data source	Scale of original imagery
I	Landsat type (orbital data) at 920 km	1:3,369,000—original scale 1:250,000—largest standard enlargement
II	High altitude data at 12,400 m (40,000 ft) or above	Smaller than 1:80,000
III	Medium altitude data taken between 3,100 and 12,400 m (10,000 and 40,000 ft)	1:20,000 to 1:80,000
IV	Low altitude data taken below 3,100 m (10,000 ft)	Larger than 1:20,000

of the most critical sensor parameters determining the detail and accuracy of classification of patterns produced by human activity. The ground resolution required for discriminating a particular land use category is dependent on the physical size and geometry involved. Classes of land use categories have been identified which, in general, may be related to the resolution required. The classification system most often used in connection with remotely sensed land use information was devised by Anderson et al. (1972) and modified on the basis of testing (Anderson et al., 1976). Two levels of categories are distinguished hierarchically: Level I, consisting of broad, general classes, and Level II, which subdivides the Level I classes into more detailed categories.

While the 80-m ground resolution of Landsat 1 and 2 seems adequate for Level I mapping, Level II mapping requires a ground resolution of about 10–20 m, as was available with photographic data taken by the Skylab Earth Terrain Camera. For this reason, most state and local programs using satellite data also employ high altitude aircraft for high resolution data in an integrated approach to land use mapping.

Level III and IV categories require substantial amounts of supplemental information in addition to some remotely sensed information at scales of 1:40,000 to 1:15,000 or larger. These levels of categorization are intended to be developed by the users themselves so that their specific needs can be satisfied. Table 2 summarizes the sensor data sources and scale requirements for four classification levels.

C. Basic Cover Type Mapping and Classification Systems Based on Remote Sensing

The notion as to what consistutes land use is open to a diversity of opinions. Perhaps a good definition would be "man's activities on land which are directly related to the land" (Clawson & Stewart, 1965). Basic land cover differs in concept and can be considered "the vegetational and artificial constructions covering the land surface" (Burley, 1961). Land cover and land use activity are closely related, but it is important to remember that remote sensing systems do not record activity directly. Characteristics of the land surface, whether natural or artificial, determine the radiation responses which the remote sensor is capable of detecting. Information about land use activities is inferred from what is basically visually or numerically derived information about land cover.

Land use planners are faced with three general problems when collecting and using land use data: (i) definition of terms and description of categories, (ii) compatibility of systems used by different investigators, and (iii) establishment of hierarchical classification systems. The manner in which these problems are resolved varies among land use investigators. An inductive approach to land use classification is favored by some (Clawson & Stewart, 1965; Nunnally & Witmer, 1970) in which the interpreter analyzes the data in as much detail as scale and resolution limitations allow, and then groups the interpreted uses into the categories most appropriate to his own purposes. These categories may be hierarchical, but are not intended to be used with all scales or types of imagery. The classes would, however, be of use to other investigators if classes were defined according to the specifications of the original imagery.

A general-purpose approach to land use and land cover classification which can effectively employ orbital and high altitude remote sensor data should meet the following criteria (Anderson et al., 1972, 1976): (i) be applicable over extensive areas, (ii) be usable on imagery obtained at different times of the year, (iii) be at least 85% accurate, with equal accuracy for the several categories, (iv) be independent of interpreter bias for repeatable results, (v) permit effective use of subcategories obtainable from ground surveys or larger scale remote sensor data, (vi) allow aggregation of categories, (vii) permit comparison with future land use data, (viii) recognize possible multiple uses of land, and (xi) allow vegetation and other types of land cover to be used as substitutes for activity. Development of the U.S. Geological Survey classification system along these lines proceeded with much effort toward making this system compatible with other classification systems being used by the various federal agencies involved in land use inventory and mapping. The resulting classification system for land use and land cover is shown in Table 3 in the more generalized first and second levels (Anderson et al., 1976). Numerical data analysis advances may necessitate modification of this classification system in the future, but its strength continues to be the emphasis placed on remote sensing as the primary data source.

Level II categories are most appropriate for statewide and interstate regional land use and land cover compilation and mapping. In the case where sufficient information exists for local land use planners to devise a Level III classification of particular land uses, this information can be compiled into Level II categories for use by state or regional planning groups. A national inventory can use this same information as part of its data base. Land use mapping at the more detailed levels may provide flexibility for different users, but the cost of remote sensor data collection along with ancil-

Table 3—Land use and land cover classification system for use with remote sensor data (after Anderson et al., 1976).

Level I	Level II
1 Urban or built-up land	11 Residential
	12 Commercial and services
	13 Industrial
	14 Transportation, communications, and utilities
	15 Industrial and commercial complexes
	16 Mixed urban or built-up land
	17 Other urban or built-up land
2 Agricultural land	21 Cropland and pasture
	22 Orchards, groves, vineyards, nurseries, and ornamental horticultural areas
	23 Confined feeding operations
	24 Other agricultural land
3 Rangeland	31 Herbaceous rangeland
	32 Shrub and brush rangeland
	33 Mixed rangeland
4 Forest land	41 Deciduous forest land
	42 Evergreen forest land
	43 Mixed forest land
5 Water	51 Streams and canals
	52 Lakes
	53 Reservoirs
	54 Bays and estuaries
6 Wetland	61 Forested wetland
	62 Nonforested wetland
7 Barren land	71 Dry salt flats
	72 Beaches
	73 Sandy areas other than beaches
	74 Bare exposed rock
	75 Strip mines, quarries, and gravel pits
	76 Transitional areas
	77 Mixed barren land
8 Tundra	81 Shrub and brush tundra
	82 Herbaceous tundra
	83 Bare ground tundra
	84 Wet tundra
	85 Mixed tundra
9 Perennial snow or ice	91 Perennial snowfields
	92 Glaciers

lary data acquired at larger scales increases greatly as does the cost of data interpretation.

D. Development of Land Use Mapping Based on Remote Sensing Data

Early efforts at land use inventory using remote sensing techniques involved basic cover type mapping at a generalized level. Kristof (1971) used data from an airborne multispectral scanner to separate basic cover types of green vegetation, water, and six soil surface conditions (Fig. 5). The potential of small scale land use mapping was demonstrated by Rudd (1971) using 1:400,000 photo mosaics of the Pacific Northwest. Infrared color photographs taken during the Apollo 9 mission were used in an inventory of forest and nonforest land uses in one of the first applications of orbital remote sensing data to land use planning (Aldrich, 1971). Through simulation of satellite photography, Belcher et al. (1971) estimated that 90% of the data required for periodic land use reports of the U.S. Department of Agriculture could be obtained from satellite photography. Radar imagery was found to be a useful tool for the creation of small-scale land use maps (1:250,000 and smaller) depicting what Henderson (1975) refers to as rural landscape regions.

Land use classification of a metropolitan area using Landsat digital data indicated that a 95% accuracy of recognition could be achieved for six land use classes by applying prior separation of urban and rural land uses (Todd & Baumgardner, 1973). Urban land use mapping using aircraft and Landsat data pointed to the fact that these two data sources tend to complement one another when applied to land use classification with the USGS System (Joyce, 1973). Figures 6 and 7 compare a portion of a standard 1: 24,000 USGS Quadrangle map with a computer-assisted interpretation of the corresponding area from Landsat data.

Computer-assisted analysis facilitates the inclusion of ancillary data such as physical characteristics of the land and socio-economic data in the remote sensing data base. Spectral, spatial, and temporal remote sensing information can be supplemented with such information as soil characteristics, geology, topography, land ownership, political boundaries, etc., where available. Land cover information as classified from ground-registered Landsat data was used in an overlay analysis with soils, cover, topography, and ownership information to enhance greatly the value of both data sets for land management decisions (Hitchcock et al., 1975). Land Use Mapping Programs (LUMP) was developed to digitize data from maps according to X, Y geographic coordinates and Z variables consisting of soil types, present land use, geologic information, and social and political data as well as aerial data (Singer et al., 1975). Other computer programs have been designed to store, manipulate, and retrieve information as to the dominant soil within a grid or cell to furnish place-oriented soil interpretation for the land use planner (Nichols & Bartelli, 1974).

Although Landsat was not designed to identify land use at large scales, results of analyses of digital data from Landsat indicate that processing techniques and a data base broadened to include repeated observations allow land cover classes to be mapped down to pixel size (0.5 ha) at a level between II and III on the USGS land use classification system (Fischer et al., 1976; Ellefsen et al., 1973).

E. Monitoring Land Use Change

The repetitive nature of remote sensing data acquired by such systems as the Landsat satellite makes possible the detection of change for monitoring land use over time. Different change detection techniques based on

Fig. 5—Aerial photograph and gray tone computer printout of soil (light tone), vegetation (medium tone), and water (dark tone).

Water   Industrial   Woods   Residential 1

Grass   Commercial & Services   Parkland   Residential 2

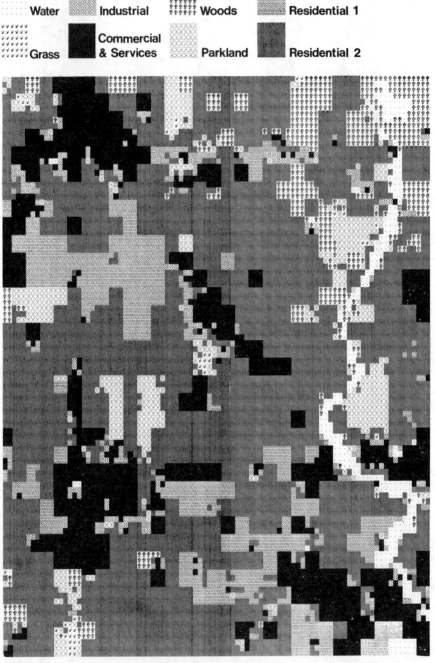

Fig. 6—Computer-assisted classification of urban land use from Landsat data at the scale of 1:24,000: Indianapolis West area.

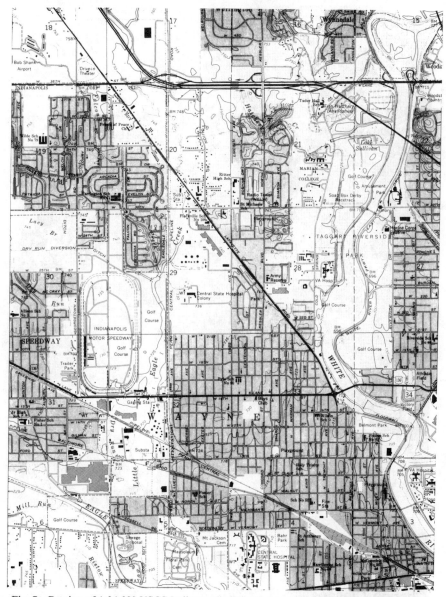

Fig. 7—Portion of 1:24,000 USGS Indianapolis West Quadrangle Map corresponding to area in Fig. 6.

computer-aided analysis of Landsat data have been studied with the goal of establishing operational monitoring procedures (Weismiller et al., 1977). Results of one of these change detection techniques are shown in Fig. 8 in which two standard classifications using LARSYS (Phillips, 1973) computer-implemented statistical procedures were compared by the data

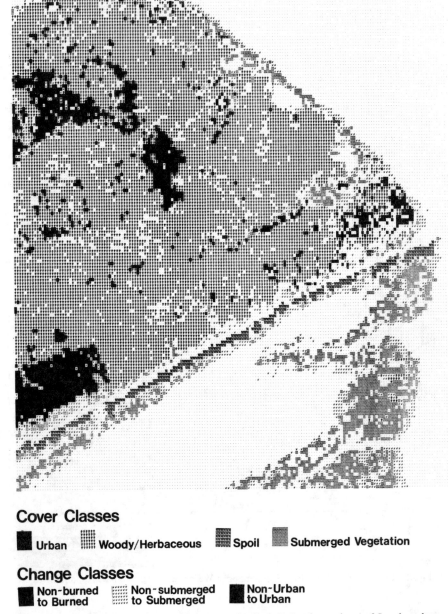

Cover Classes

■ Urban   ▦ Woody/Herbaceous   ▦ Spoil   ▨ Submerged Vegetation

Change Classes

■ Non-burned   ▦ Non-submerged   ■ Non-Urban
  to Burned   to Submerged   to Urban

Fig. 8—Land change detection by computer-assisted analysis of two dates of Landsat data
  from the Port O'Connor region, Texas (after Weismiller et al., 1977).

analyst for definition of change classes. Resultant informational categories
included residential areas, rangeland, wooded areas, marshes, burned
areas, spoil, and open water classes.

F. Statewide and Regional Land Use Planning Using Remote Sensing

Various state and regional agencies have developed comprehensive statewide land use inventories based on remote sensing data. Landsat data seems especially well suited to the requirements of operational inventory and monitoring programs.

Three departments in the state of Ohio have developed a cooperative inventory of statewide land use through the processing of Landsat data (Baldridge et al., 1975). Landsat data are subjected to geometrical and categorical processing to produce map files for each of the 200 fifteen-minute quad sheets covering Ohio. Digital Landsat data tapes are used to produce inventory tapes which identify eight Level I land use categories and a variety of Level II categories. Processing is done with a series of 10 software programs developed by the state of Ohio. A computerized inventory results which can be displayed in map or tabular form for various geographic units, scales, and for selected use categories. Results will be used in state, regional, and local planning programs. Estimated total costs for the Landsat-based land use inventory are lower than previous statewide inventories which were not based on remote sensing data.

Research applications of Landsat imagery to land use in the state of Minnesota has concentrated on evaluating the use of Landsat data to update and refine the detail of land use information in the Minnesota Land Management Information System (Sizer, 1973). The ability to extract surface cover information from Landsat imagery of Minnesota is highly variable among the range of surface cover types found in the state. Each broad class of land cover has an optimal season for interpretation while for individual classes this season varies according to location or local site conditions. Demonstration projects show that the Landsat-based land use system may be used to produce land cover information for all townships in the state for comparison with a variety of environmental information stored for the same area. Data can be manipulated to map change, nonconforming use, and use by type of ownership. Transfer of Landsat information capabilities to governmental agency users is being accomplished through local units of government and regional development commissions encompassing the entire state of Minnesota.

The New York state land use and natural resource inventory which was done from 1968–70 was the first statewide inventory of its kind. Estimates are that a satellite-based information system costing between \$4.50 and \$6.00 per square kilometer would have the attributes necessary for making a similar statewide inventory (Hardy, 1975).

Statewide land use/land cover information is being generated from Landsat digital data and high altitude photography by the South Dakota State Planning Bureau and the EROS Data Center in an ongoing Land Use and Natural Resource Inventory and Information System Program (Tessar et al., 1975). A statewide Level I inventory was visually interpreted from Landsat imagery. Level II and partial Level III information was numerically interpreted from Landsat computer-compatible tapes for selected priority areas at display scales ranging from 1:24,000 to 1:500,000. High and low altitude photography will be used in a future phase of the program to supplement Landsat data for Level III land use interpretations.

A comprehensive regional survey of land use and its associated environmental impact was carried out using Landsat, Skylab, and high altitude photographic data in the Central Atlantic Regional Ecological Test Site (CARETS). An archival collection of imagery, maps, data summaries, and technical reports has been assembled, constituting an environmental profile of the central Atlantic region (Alexander et al., 1975). Complete map coverages were produced for land use derived from high altitude aircraft photography at a scale of 1:100,000, whereas Landsat imagery was used for mapping selected portions at a scale of 1:250,000. Landsat-derived land use maps included 19 Level II and 4 Level III categories as well as the primary Level I categories.

The potential for the application of remote sensing technology to land use is quite evident in the state of Alaska where conventional means of data acquisition are difficult and costly because of difficulty of access. The Joint Federal-State Land Use Planning Commission and the Soil Conservation Service have published a statewide set of Landsat mosaics at 1:1,000,000 scale (Panel on Land Use Plann., 1975). The University of Alaska has mosaics from key areas at 1:500,000 scale.

Landsat scanner data were used as the primary data source for a current land use inventory of the 34 million ha included within the U.S. portion of the Great Lakes Basin. The Laboratory for Applications of Remote Sensing (LARS) at Purdue University analyzed the Landsat data by computer-implemented pattern recognition techniques to produce spectrally separable classes which were then related to certain Level I and Level II land use categories (Weismiller, 1977). Results of the land use inventory were reported in two forms: geometrically correct color-coded county maps of Level I land use and statistical tables of both levels. Adequate results were obtained when good quality, cloud-free satellite data were available for the appropriate season, and when ground observation data were collected for training the computer.

G. User Education

Programs which include training and assistance in the transfer of technology of remote sensing data utilization for land use planning have been developed in recent years. Educational centers often provide access to simplified interpretation systems which are within the reach of smaller agencies such as county planning groups. One such center with wide-ranging user training programs is the Earth Resources Observation Systems (EROS) Program of the Department of the Interior. Courses at the EROS Data Center are designed primarily to train resource personnel, including land use planners, in the use of Landsat and other remote sensing data through practical exercises stressing the hands-on use of data of specific interest to the participants (Reeves, 1974).

Remote sensing courses are an integral part of many college and university programs. In 1975, 38 universities in the United States and Canada offered 534 courses that emphasized remote sensing (Nealey, 1977). At least 63 books have been adopted as textbooks and reference books. A comprehensive listing of the courses and texts available is given by Nealey (1977).

Individualized small group training programs tailored to the specific needs of the user are available as week-long short courses in the fundamentals of remote sensing (Lube & Russell, 1977). At Purdue's Laboratory for Applications of Remote Sensing a multimedia approach is used, featuring case studies, optional hands-on activities, and personal interaction with an interdisciplinary research staff.

V. DATA AVAILABILITY

A. Sources of Remotely Sensed Data

Conventional photography has been obtained at various times for all parts of the United States at the request of certain government agencies. The Agricultural Stabilization and Conservation Service (ASCS), the Soil Conservation Service (SCS), the Forest Service (FS), and the U.S. Geological Survey (USGS) are examples of agencies with extensive photographic coverage of the country, some dating back to the 1930's. The major part of the photography is vertical black and white coverage of fairly large scale (1:20,000) although more recent photography is available in various scales.

Access to remotely sensed data of the earth's surface is provided by the Earth Resources Observation Systems (EROS) Data Center in Sioux Falls, South Dakota administered by the Geological Survey. Data reproductions of domestic and some foreign coverage for the following categories are available: NASA aircraft photography, USGS, Army and Air Force aerial mapping photography, Landsat products, and Skylab products. Landsat imagery can be ordered in a variety of formats—microfilm, black and white negatives of single bands, color composites as positive transparencies, and black and white and color prints—and at various scales. Computer-compatible tapes (CCT's) are available for computer-assisted analysis of Landsat data. In addition to the EROS Data Center, more than 20 local user centers have been established with the purpose of providing the following services: assistance in prepurchase evaluation of imagery, assistance in ordering data, the use of equipment for remote sensor data manipulation, and user access to reference collections of the EROS library.

Another important data bank for aerial and space imagery is the National Cartographic Information Center, formerly the U.S. Geological Survey's Map Information Office. The NCIC collects, classifies, catalogs, and disseminates information about cartographic data available for the United

States. Users are able to find out what cartographic information and materials are available from NCIC for an area of interest and can order copies. Information on imagery collected by ASCS, SCS, FS, USGS, Bureau of Reclamation, Bureau of Land Management, and space imagery can be provided by NCIC. In addition, NCIC is indexing private sources of aerial photography.

The USDA provides imagery from the Landsat and Skylab programs and has assigned responsibility to the ASCS Western Laboratory in Salt Lake City, Utah for image collection and distribution. In addition to the standard products such as prints and transparencies, the Laboratory provides index mosaics of each 18-day cycle of coverage and through the Cartographic Division of the SCS makes available mosaics covering the entire United States at scales ranging from 1:500,000 to 1:5,000,000.

Imagery collected by a series of environmental weather satellites beginning with TIROS 1 in 1960 is made available through the National Oceanic and Atmospheric Administration's (NOAA) National Climatic Center in Asheville, North Carolina. Generally low in resolution, this imagery provides a more synoptic view which may be of value in many situations.

The compilation of a statewide index to aerial and space photographic coverage was advanced by Barney and Johannsen (1976) for the state of Missouri. Complete lists of public and private photographic data sources are presented.

B. Analysis and Interpretation Services

In addition to the orientation provided by agencies such as the EROS Data Center related to analysis and interpretation of remotely sensed data, many university programs and private organizations are involved in the actual analysis and interpretation of imagery. Much recent effort has involved the development of educational programs such as short courses which are aimed at providing the user with the essential skills necessary for image analysis.

Clearly, the approach to image analysis differs greatly depending on whether visual or numerical analysis is desired. Many federal agencies have long utilized photointerpretive methods to analyze photographic images. With the advent of numerically oriented sensing systems, new analysis methods have developed which lend themselves to computer-oriented processing of digital image data. At least six major hardware/software systems are available commercially for use in the correction, analysis, and display of digital image data, each differing slightly in concept or operation (Carter et al., 1977). Many software systems which are primarily research oriented have been developed and adapted to university computer facilities. Landsat image processing software is available through the Computer Software Management and Information Center (COSMIC) at the University of Georgia. A number of computer programs designed for numerical analysis of remotely sensed data are available for distribution through this Center.

VI. THE FUTURE OF REMOTE SENSING
FOR LAND USE PLANNING

Societal demands for a more rational approach to the allocation and management of land resources places a high value on accurate and timely information about these resources and the changing conditions of these resources. Remote sensing techniques promise to play a prominent role in the decades ahead as a tool for land use inventories and for regular monitoring of land use changes.

Plans call for the launch of Landsat-D in the early 1980's. Equipped with a five-band multispectral scanner having a resolution of 70 m and a 6- or 7-band thematic mapper with a resolution of 30 m, this polar-orbiting satellite will provide coverage of the entire earth surface every 7 to 9 days (Comm. on Remote Sensing Progr. for Earth Resour. Surv., 1976). Advanced planning specified that multispectral data obtained by Landsat-D be preprocessed and available for distribution to the user within 5 to 7 days after data acquisition.

Just as advances are expected to continue in the design and development in data acquisition capabilities, the rapid improvement in machine processing hardware and software are expected to continue.

Whereas there were fewer than 1,000 computers in the United States in the mid 1950's, mostly owned by the federal government, there were some 220,000 computers by the end of 1976, with increasing access to business, industry, and the public in general (Davis, 1977). Withington (1972) reported his projections of the future size and cost of computers (Fig. 9) and the cost of computational services. He predicted that the cost of computational services will drop two to three orders of magnitude during the period 1970 to 1980.

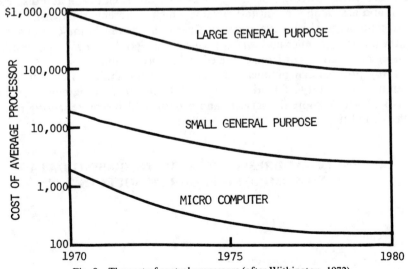

Fig. 9—The cost of central processors (after Withington, 1972).

Computer programming capabilities (or software) will continue to grow, making it possible to mix and overlay data of different kinds and sources and to extract useful information which has never been available to the land use planner before. Through a computer terminal the land use planner may have access to an information network which can provide a broad array of physical, ecological, cultural, social, economic, demographic, political, and other data related to a particular land area. With dynamic information systems which have been designed to respond to user needs, the land use planner will have access to data or information which is periodically being updated and corrected. For general scanning of the land areas of the world by satellite scanners it is not anticipated that a resolution greater than 30 m will be available during the next decade.

For those tasks of land use inventory and monitoring which require a resolution of 0.01 ha (10 by 10 m) or of areas smaller than the 0.1 ha (30 by 30 m) resolution of the Thematic Mapper of Landsat-D, the land use planner in the foreseeable future must rely on aircraft sensor data.

As photographic and multispectral scanner technology has improved in recent years, the trend has been toward high resolution, high altitude systems. The high altitude provides a more stable environment for the sensor platform, but the cost and maintenance of the high altitude is much greater than for a low altitude aircraft.

During the past decade emphasis in the analysis of image-oriented sensor systems has been placed on enhancement techniques based primarily on film-filter combinations and in the generation of a broad array of false colors which may emphasize or enhance specific features in the scene under study. This emphasis is expected to continue in the years ahead.

Since land use planners are in critical need of quantitative data bases, a considerable amount of attention is being given to the digitization of photography. This consists of the scanning of image line by line by laser beams or other devices, measuring the density of the emulsion at a discrete point and assigning a quantitative value which represents the density. For those data bases which have grid cells finer than the resolution of Landsat-D, the land use planner may wish to consider digital data from high resolution aircraft scanners or from digitized aerial photography.

Any professional planner who has the responsibility to examine the quantity and quality of land resources and the surrounding environment can ill afford to ignore the services and benefits which remote sensing technology can bring to the planning profession.

APPENDIX—ADDRESSES OF REMOTE SENSING DATA AND COMPUTER PROGRAM SOURCES

Data sources

U.S. Department of the Interior
Geological Survey
EROS Data Center
Sioux Falls, South Dakota 57198
Phone: (605) 594-6511

National Cartographic Information Center
USGS National Center
Reston, Virginia 22092
Phone: (703) 860-6052

Western Aerial Photography Laboratory
Administrative Services Division
ASCS-USDA
2505 Parley's Way
Salt Lake City, Utah 84109
Phone: (801) 524-5856

The National Climatic Center
National Oceanic and Atmospheric Administration
Federal Building
Asheville, North Carolina 28801
Phone: (704)258-2850

Computer program source for numerical analysis of remotely sensed data
COSMIC Information Services
112 Barrow Hall
University of Georgia
Athens, Georgia 30602
Phone: (404) 542-3265

LITERATURE CITED

Al-Abbas, A. H., P. H. Swain, and M. F. Baumgardner. 1972. Relating organic matter and clay content to the multispectral radiance of soils. Soil Sci. 114:477–485.

Aldrich, R. C. 1971. Space photos for land use and forestry. Photogram. Eng. Remote Sensing 37:389–401.

Alexander, R. H., K. Fitzpatrick, H. F. Lins, Jr., and H. K. McGinty, III. 1975. Land use and environmental assessment in the central Atlantic region. Proc. of NASA Earth Resour. Surv. Symp., Houston, Tex. I-C:1683–1727.

Anderson, J. R., E. E. Hardy, and J. T. Roach. 1972. A land use classification system for use with remote sensor data. U.S. Geol. Surv. Circ. 671. 16 p.

Anderson, J. R., E. E. Hardy, J. T. Roach, and R. E. Witmer. 1976. A land use and land cover classification system for use with remote sensor data. U.S. Geol. Surv. Prof. Pap. 964. 28 p.

Anuta, P. E. 1970. Spatial registration of multispectral and multitemporal imagery using fast fourier transform techniques. IEEE Trans. Geosci. Electron. GE-8:353–368.

Baldridge, P. E., P. H. Goesling, F. Leone, C. Minshall, R. H. Rodgers, and C. L. Wilhelm. 1975. Ohio's statewide land use inventory: an operational approach for applying Landsat data to state, regional, and local planning problems. Proc. of NASA Earth Resour. Surv. Symp., Houston, Tex. I-C:1541–1552.

Barney, T., and C. J. Johannsen. 1976. Index to aerial and space photographic coverage of Missouri. Univ. of Missouri, Columbia. 114 p.

Bartolucci, L. A., B. F. Robinson, and L. F. Silva. 1977. Field measurements of the spectral response of natural waters. Photogramm. Eng. Remote Sensing 43:595–598.

Baumgardner, M. F., S. J. Kristof, C. J. Johannsen, and A. L. Zachary. 1970. Effects of organic matter on the multispectral properties of soils. Proc. Ind. Acad. Sci. 79:413–422.

Belcher, D. J., E. E. Hardy, and E. S. Phillips. 1971. Land use classification with simulated satellite photography. USDA Agric. Inf. Bull. 352. 27 p.

Bowers, S. A., and R. J. Hanks. 1965. Reflection of radiant energy from soils. Soil Sci. 100: 130–138.

Burley, T. M. 1961. Land use or land utilization? Prof. Geographer 13:6:18–20.

Carter, V., F. Billingsley, and J. Lamar. 1977.Summary tables for selected digital image processing systems. USGS Open-File Rep. no. 77-414. 45 p.

Cipra, J. E., M. F. Baumgardner, E. R. Stoner, and R. B. MacDonald. 1971. Measuring radiance characteristics of soil with a field spectroradiometer. Soil Sci. Soc. Am. Proc. 35: 1014–1017.

Clawson, M., and C. L. Stewart. 1965. Land use information. A critical survey of U.S. statistics including possibilities for greater uniformity. The Johns Hopkins Press for Resources for the Future, Inc., Baltimore, Md.

Committee on Remote Sensing Programs for Earth Resource Surveys. 1976. Resource and environmental surveys from space with the thematic mapper in the 1980's. Comm. on Nat. Resour., Natl. Res. Counc. Nath Acad. of Sci., Washington, D.C.

Condit, H. R. 1970. The spectral reflectance of American soils. Photogramm. Eng. 36:955–966.

Condit, H. R. 1972. Application of characteristic vector analysis to the spectral energy distribution of daylight and the spectral reflectance of American soils. Appl. Opt. 11:74–86.

Davis, R. M. 1977. Evolution of computers and computing. Science 195:1096–1102.

Ellefsen, R., P. H. Swain, and J. R. Wray. 1973. Urban land use mapping by machine processing of ERTS-1 multispectral data: a San Francisco Bay area example. LARS Inf. Note 032973. Purdue Univ., West Lafayette, Ind.

Fischer, W. A., W. R. Hemphill, and A. Kover. 1976. Progress in remote sensing (1972–1976). Photogrammetria 21:33–72.

Gates, D. M. 1962. Energy exchange in the biosphere. Harper & Row Biological Monograph, New York.

Handler, P. 1976. On the state of man. Interdiscip. Sci. Rev. 1:189–201.

Hardy, E. E. 1975. The design, implementation, and use of a statewide land use inventory: the New York experience. Proc. of the NASA Earth Resour. Surv. Symp., Houston, Tex. I-C:1573–1601.

Henderson, F. M. 1975. Radar for small scale land use mapping. Photogramm. Eng. Remote Sensing 41:307–320.

Hitchcock, H. C., T. L. Cox, F. P. Baxter, and C. W. Smart. 1975. Soil and land cover overlay analyses. Photogramm. Eng. Remote Sensing 41:1519–1524.

Hoffer, R. M., and C. J. Johannsen. 1969. Ecological potentials in spectral signature analysis. p. 1–16. In P. Johnson (ed.) Remote sensing in ecology. Univ. of Georgia Press, Athens, Ga.

Holter, M. R., M. Bair, J. L. Beard, T. Limperis, and R. K. Moore. 1970. Imaging with non-photographic sensors. p. 73–163. In J. R. Shay (ed.) Remote sensing with special reference to agriculture and forestry. Natl. Acad. of Sci., Washington, D.C.

Johannsen, C. J., and M. F. Baumgardner. 1968. Remote sensing for planning resource conservation. Proc. of 93rd Annu. Meet. of Soil Conserv. Soc. of Am., Aug. 1968, Athens, Ga. 1:199–255.

Joyce, A. T. 1973. Land use and mapping. p. 138–146. In 3rd Earth Resour. Technol. Satellite Symp. Vol. II—Summary of Results. NASA Goddard Space Flight Center Rep., NASA SP-357.

Kettig, R. L., and D. A. Landgrebe. 1976. Classification of multispectral image data by extraction and classification of homogeneous objects. IEEE Trans. Geosci. Electron. GE-14: 19–26.

Knipling, E. P. 1970. Physical and physiological basis for the reflectance of visible and near infrared radiation from vegetation. Remote Sensing Environ. 1:155–160.

Kristof, S. J. 1971. Preliminary multispectral studies of soils. J. Soil Water Conserv. 26:15–18.

Krumpe, P. F. 1976. The world remote sensing bibliographic index. Sensor Industries, Inc., Fairfax, Va.

Landgrebe, D. A. 1976. Computer-based remote sensing technology—a look to the future. Remote Sensing Environ. 5:229–246.

Lube, B. M., and J. D. Russell. 1977. A short course on remote sensing. Photogramm. Eng. Remote Sensing 43:299–301.

Mathews, H. L., R. L. Cunningham, and G. W. Petersen. 1973. Spectral reflectance of selected Pennsylvania soils. Soil Sci. Soc. Am. Proc. 37:421–424.

Montgomery, O. L., M. F. Baumgardner, and R. A. Weismiller. 1976. An investigation of the relationship between spectral reflectance and the chemical, physical and genetic characteristics of soils. LARS Inf. Note 082776. Purdue Univ., W. Lafayette, Ind.

Myers, V. I., and W. A. Allen. 1968. Electro-optical remote sensing methods as nondestructive testing and measuring techniques in agriculture. Appl. Opt. 7:1819–1838.

National Aeronautics and Space Administration. 1972. Earth resources technology satellite. Data user's handbook. Goddard Space Flight Center, Greenbelt, Md.

Nealey, L. D. 1977. Remote sensing/photogrammetry education in the United States and Canada. Photogramm. Eng. Remote Sensing 43:259–284.

Nichols, J. D., and L. J. Bartelli. 1974. Computer-generated interpretive soil maps. J. Soil Water Conserv. 29:232–235.

Nunnally, N. R., and R. E. Witmer. 1970. Remote sensing for land-use studies. Photogramm. Eng. Remote Sensing. 36:449–453.

Panel on Land Use Planning. 1975. Practical applications of space systems. Supporting Pap. 3: Land use planning. Rep. to the Space Applications Board, Natl. Res. Counc., Natl. Acad. of Sci., Washington, D.C.

Phillips, T. L. (ed.). 1973. LARSYS user's manual. Vol. 1, 2. LARS, Purdue Univ., West Lafayette, Ind.

Pimentel, D., E. C. Terhune, R. Dyson-Hudson, S. Rochereau, R. Samis, E. A. Smith, D. Denman, D. Reifschneider, and M. Shepard. 1976. Land degradation: effects on food and energy resources. Science 194:149–155.

Reeves, R. G. 1974. Education and training in remote sensing. Photogramm. Eng. 40:691–696.

Reeves, R. G. (ed.). 1975. Manual of remote sensing. Am. Soc. of Photogramm., Falls Church, Va.

Rudd, R. D., and R. Hughsmith, Jr. 1971. Macro land use mapping with simulated space photos. Photogram. Eng. Remote Sensing 37:365–372.

Rudd, R. D. 1974. Remote sensing: a better view. Duxbury Press, Belmont, Calif.

Singer, M., R. Johnston, and L. Thorpe. 1975. Land use mapping programs (LUMP). . .a computer help for land use decision making. Calif. Agric. 29:12–14.

Sizer, J. E. 1973. ERTS-1 role in land management and planning in Minnesota. Third ERTS-1 Symp., Washington, D.C. I-A:341–350.

Suits, G. H. 1960. The nature of infrared radiation and ways to photograph it. Photogramm. Eng. 16:763–772.

Tessar, P. A., D. R. Hood, and W. J. Todd. 1975. The South Dakota cooperative land use effort: a state level remote sensing demonstration project. Proc. of the NASA Earth Resour. Surv. Symp., Houston, Tex. I-C:1499–1523.

Todd, W. J., and M. F. Baumgardner. 1973. Land use classification of Marion County, Indiana by spectral analysis of digitized satellite data. Lab. for Applications of Remote Sensing Inf. Note 101673. Purdue Univ., W. Lafayette, Ind.

Weismiller, R. A. 1977. Land use information of the Great Lakes Basin using computer analysis of satellite data. LARS Inf. Note 011077. Purdue Univ., W. Lafayette, Ind.

Weismiller, R. A., S. J. Kristof, D. K. Scholz, P. E. Anuta, and S. M. Momin. 1977. Evaluation of change detection techniques for monitoring coastal zone environments. LARS Inf. Note 062277. Purdue Univ., W. Lafayette, Ind.

Withington, F. G. 1972. The next (and last?) generation. Datamation. 18:71–74.

9 Spatial Data Analysis and Information Communication

BERNARD J. NIEMANN, JR., AND
MICHAEL M. MC CARTHY

University of Wisconsin, Madison, Wisconsin, and
University of Arizona, Tucson, Arizona, respectively

I. INTRODUCTION AND DEFINITIONS

Data about the land, having spatial characteristics, is used for the purpose of: assessing, evaluating, designing, planning, managing, regulating, and communicating. A premise of this chapter is that these activities are part of one continuous and ongoing process exemplified by the phrase "spatial data analysis and information communication." To explain this continuous process it is necessary to examine (i) the evolution and development of analysis and communication techniques; (ii) the types of communication analysis users; and (iii) examples and studies of analysis and communication techniques.

There is a fundamental difference between data lists and data with spatial descriptions. This difference has resulted in a variety of methods for dealing with spatial data. In addition to two-dimensional data formats (e.g., maps) many other techniques exist by which to record, use, and analyze spatial data. The use and application of any of these forms tends to be determined by need, knowledge, cost, and available technology. The costs associated with land data gathering and producing have been shown not to be trivial. For example, Wisconsin residents spent $17.00 each or 86 million dollars in 1976 for obtaining land and related data (Larsen, 1978). Effective use and communication of land data, therefore, seems quite warranted. This chapter of the monograph presents an array of examples from traditional to contemporary techniques. Definitions of terms utilized in this chapter follow.

Spatial	Relating to, or occupying, or having the character of, space.
Data	Factual information used as a basis for reasoning, discussion, or calculating.
Analysis	Separation of the whole into its component parts: an examination of a complex, its elements, and their relations.
Information	The communication or reception of knowledge obtained from investigation study, or instruction.

Communication   An act or instance of transmitting; information com-
                    municated; a process by which information is ex-
                    changed between individuals through a common system
                    of symbols, signs, or behavior; or the technology or the
                    transmission of information (as by the printed word,
                    telecommunication, or the computer).

II. EVOLUTION AND DEVELOPMENT OF ANALYSIS AND COMMUNICATION TECHNIQUES

A. Past and Present

The analysis procedures used for data with spatial characteristics have
evolved from both the arts and the sciences. Many of these procedures depend upon the use of the visual senses as an integral part of the data analysis
as well as for the communication of information. For example, the use of
color and symbols with soil maps assist in conveying the soil type location,
its overall distributional characteristics, and the relationship to other soil
types. When the soil map is combined with other spatial data, such as land
ownership boundaries, an additional set of potential analyses and comparisons results. Using the human integrative abilities the addition of data reflecting ownership now allows the analyst to determine, for example, which
person owns land having soil Type A, how much additional land is owned
by that person, who owns land adjacent to that individual, and also how
much land might support certain uses of the land in terms of soil capability.
Given that the soil patterns are not overly complex and that ownership is
known, the combination or overlay of the soils data with the ownership
data is an easy task both from the aspect of map making and from the
aspect of understanding the resultant relationships between soil and ownership.

The more additional spatial data required for the analysis process (e.g.,
zoning, levels of taxation, land value, vegetation types, water run-off patterns, etc.), the more difficult the task of understanding the relationships
between the data. This need to reduce large amounts of spatial data into information about various land units through analysis is the primary reason
for the evolution of a series of techniques which are unique to land and resource planning and management. This set of techniques has evolved not
solely for the purpose of documentation and communication, but also for
the purpose of manipulation, analysis, and understanding.

The concept for a common technique that assists in determining spatial
interrelationships and that provides for manipulation and analysis of physical data can be traced back to John Venn, a logician. The development and
employment of overlaying areas (polygons) and searching for common
interrelationships (Venn Diagrams) as a tool or procedure is the conceptual
basis for many of the contemporary physical data analysis and planning

procedures that are presently being used (Lewis, 1964, 1969; McHarg, 1966, 1969).

Many of these Venn logic/overlay analysis and communication techniques emerged in the 1960's. The overlay procedures have been applied to various land use allocation issues such as highways (McHarg, 1966), recreation assessment and planning (Lewis, 1969), and housing location in developing countries (Tishler & Niemann, 1971). Such applications portray the versatility of overlay procedures.

The analytical, integrative, and communicative power of a data overlay can often be used quite effectively. Lewis and Murray (1964) during this early period were developing procedures for determining appropriate areas for park and open space acquisition for the State of Wisconsin. The procedure consisted of utilizing a set of symbols which depicted 220 intrinsic and extrinsic recreational resources (Fig. 1). These resource symbols were plotted on state maps and were utilized with other maps (topography, water patterns, and certain cultural features, etc.). Prime areas for consideration in the Wisconsin State Park system were areas where a concentration of symbols resulted (Fig. 2). The popularity and application of the procedure resulted, in part, because for the first time: (i) the recreation resources of Wisconsin were comprehensively collected; (ii) the procedures showed for analysis what recreational resources were clustered with other resources; (iii) the procedure provided analysis as to where resources were located; and (iv) with the use of symbols the results were easily communicated to legislators, citizens, and fellow professionals. This ability to simultaneously reference, analyze, and communicate is a characteristic of overlaying procedures.

As the techniques evolved, there were numerous other applications of overlay and spatial data integration. For the University of Ife, Nigeria, Africa, Tishler and Niemann (1971) merged soil, slope, and windward slope data with a resulting pattern called *Optimum Housing Location Areas* (Fig. 3, 4, 5, and 6). Figure 3, soils suitable for development, depicts the portion of the University of Ife campus area set aside for faculty and staff housing. Within the heavy black boundary are soils which best support roads and residential development as determined by the University of Ife Soils Department. The light black lines depict already existing development at the time of consultation. Figure 4, flat topography, depicts the area which consists of slopes between 0 to 6%; Fig. 5, windward slopes, depicts the areas which lie perpendicular to the path of the cooling winds. Figure 6, optimum site potential composite, is the result of overlaying Fig. 3, 4, and 5. The figure illustrates zones where the three factors of good soils, flat topography, and windward slopes overlap or overlay. Also, from this illustration, it can be seen that some of the initial housing units were not constructed in the optimum areas. The resultant analysis provided Nigerian planners with information in addition to the traditional considerations such as building setback, etc. The eventual location was both reflective of traditional housing location considerations and sensitive to soil and climate factors (Fig. 7).

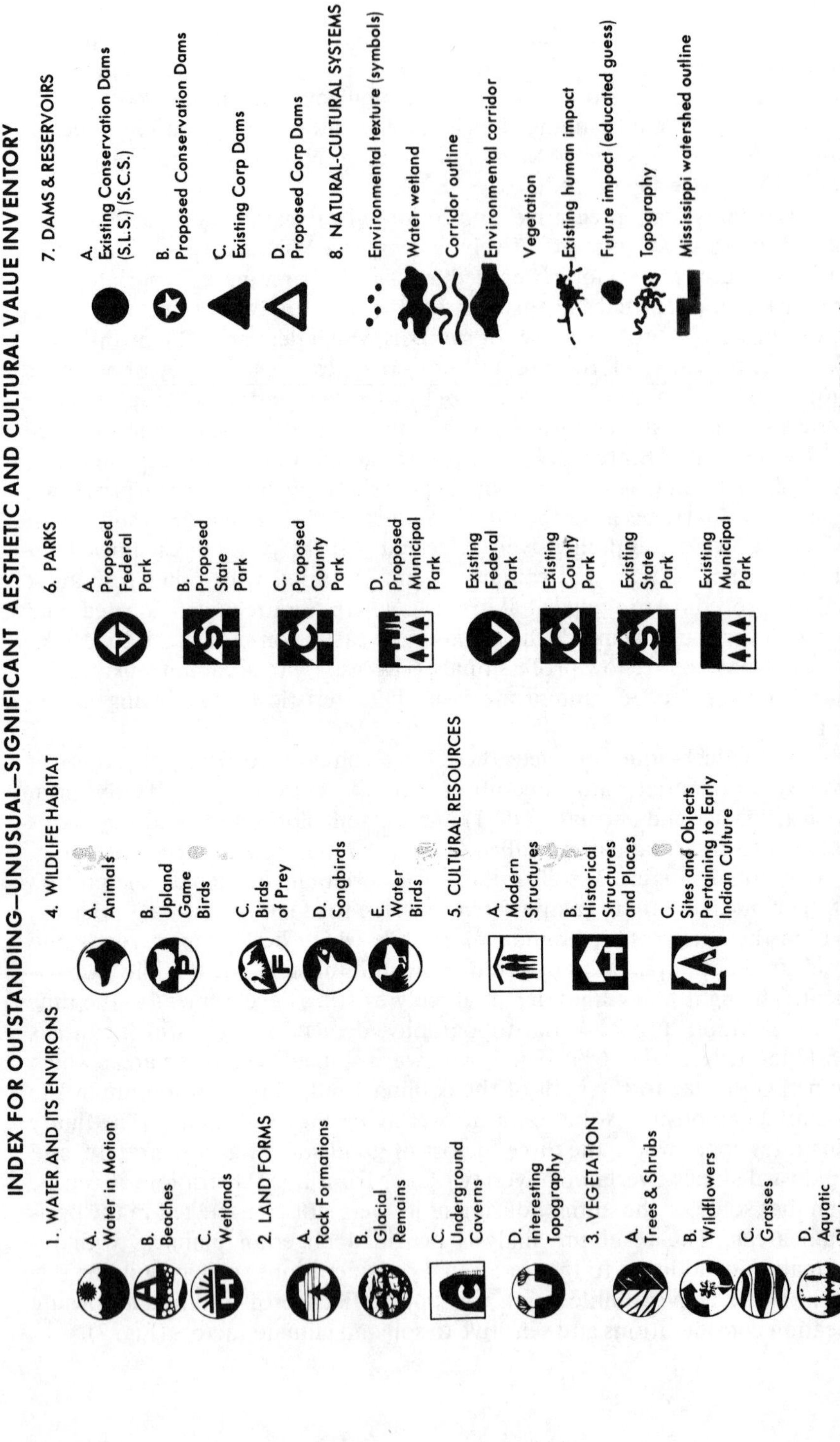

INDEX FOR OUTSTANDING–UNUSUAL–SIGNIFICANT AESTHETIC AND CULTURAL VALUE INVENTORY

1. WATER AND ITS ENVIRONS

A. Water in Motion

B. Beaches

C. Wetlands

2. LAND FORMS

A. Rock Formations

B. Glacial Remains

C. Underground Caverns

D. Interesting Topography

3. VEGETATION

A. Trees & Shrubs

B. Wildflowers

C. Grasses

D. Aquatic Plants

4. WILDLIFE HABITAT

A. Animals

B. Upland Game Birds

C. Birds of Prey

D. Songbirds

E. Water Birds

5. CULTURAL RESOURCES

A. Modern Structures

B. Historical Structures and Places

C. Sites and Objects Pertaining to Early Indian Culture

6. PARKS

A. Proposed Federal Park

B. Proposed State Park

C. Proposed County Park

D. Proposed Municipal Park

Existing Federal Park

Existing County Park

Existing State Park

Existing Municipal Park

7. DAMS & RESERVOIRS

A. Existing Conservation Dams (S.L.S.) (S.C.S.)

B. Proposed Conservation Dams

C. Existing Corp Dams

D. Proposed Corp Dams

8. NATURAL-CULTURAL SYSTEMS

Environmental texture (symbols)

Water wetland

Corridor outline

Environmental corridor

Vegetation

Existing human impact

Future impact (educated guess)

Topography

Mississippi watershed outline

Fig. 1—Symbols representing intrinsic and extrinsic recreation resources in Wisconsin.

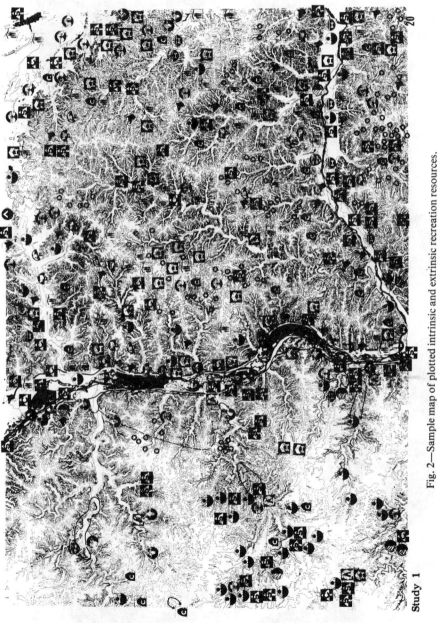

Fig. 2—Sample map of plotted intrinsic and extrinsic recreation resources.

Study 1

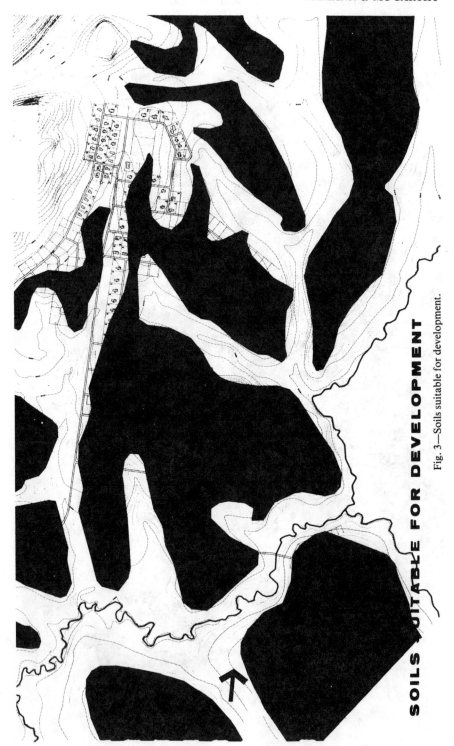

SOILS SUITABLE FOR DEVELOPMENT

Fig. 3.—Soils suitable for development.

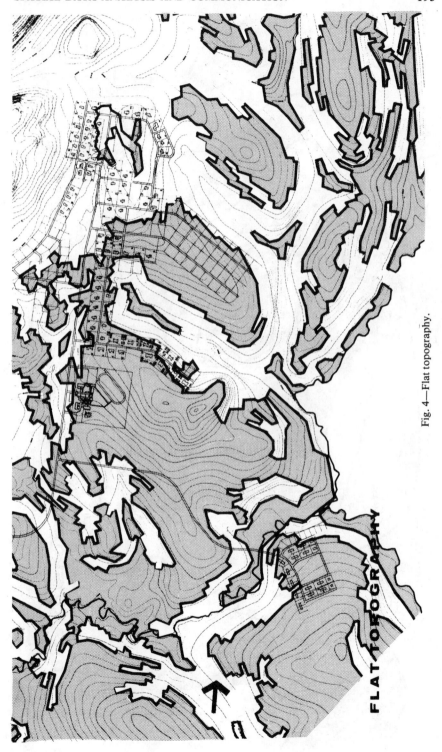

Fig. 4—Flat topography.

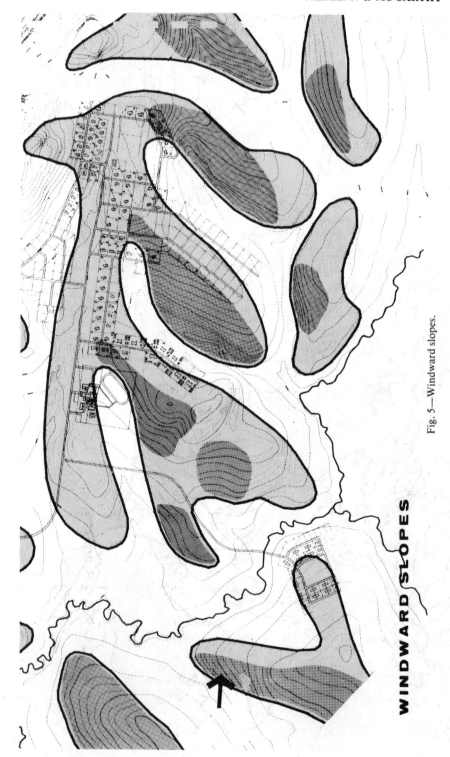

Fig. 5—Windward slopes.

WINDWARD SLOPES

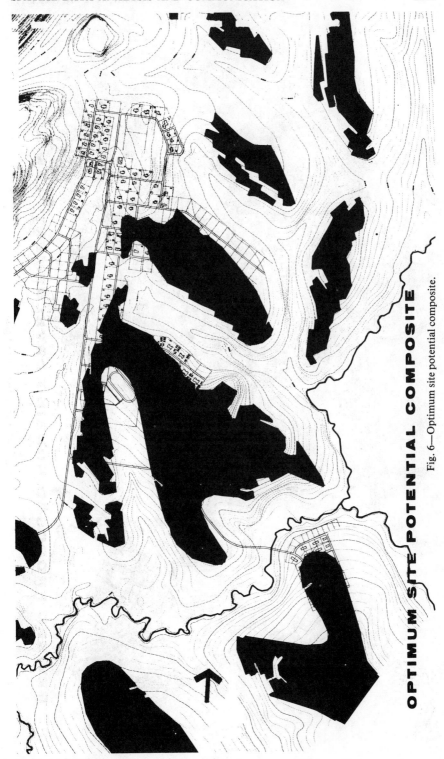

OPTIMUM SITE POTENTIAL COMPOSITE

Fig. 6—Optimum site potential composite.

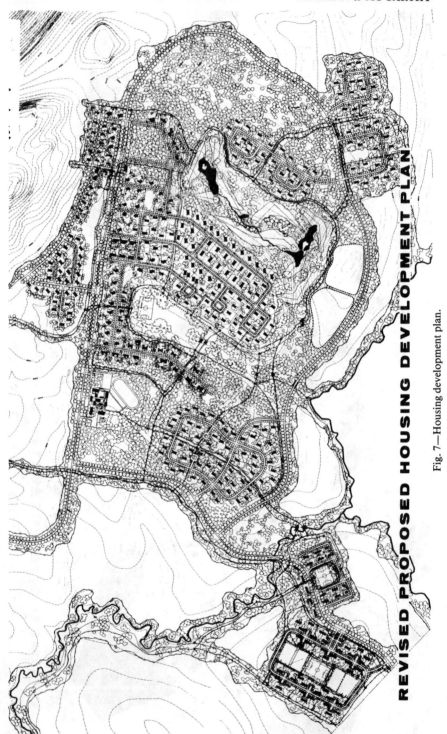

REVISED PROPOSED HOUSING DEVELOPMENT PLAN

Fig. 7.—Housing development plan.

PLANNING THE USES AND MANAGEMENT OF LAND

Chapter 9—Spatial Data Analysis and Information Communication

B. J. NIEMANN, JR., and M. M. MC CARTHY

Figures 8, 9, 10, 11, 14, and 15

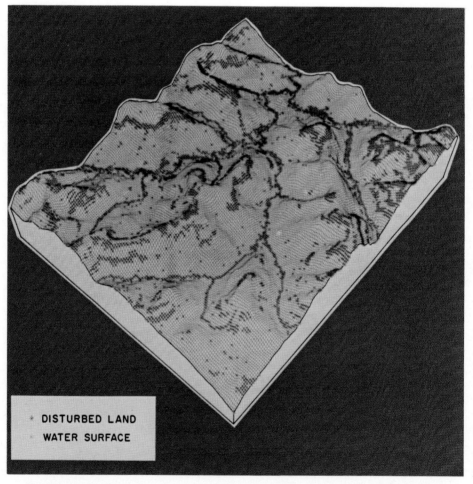

DISTURBED LAND
WATER SURFACE

Fig. 14—Disturbed lands and strip mines with water surfaces superimposed upon topography.

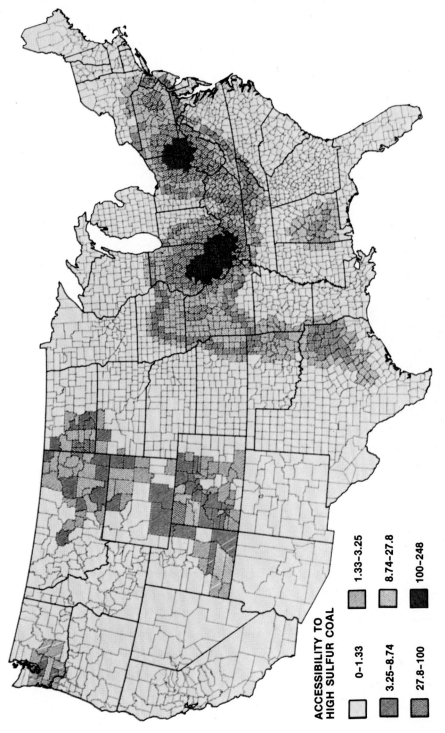

ACCESSIBILITY TO
HIGH SULFUR COAL

0–1.33		1.33–3.25
3.25–8.74		8.74–27.8
27.8–100		100–248

Fig. 15—The most likely areas of high S coal utilization in the eastern and western U.S.

B. Towards the Future: Some Reasons for Change

As the basic overlay concepts and procedures were being developed, tested, and applied, limitations were also being identified. For example, there were demands from resource planners and managers for: (i) the ability to handle larger geographical areas in greater detail; (ii) the inclusion of varying attributes for various land measures (e.g., soil erosion measures in addition to soil type); (iii) the necessity of integrating many data sets; and (iv) the need for flexibility in weighing various data sets in order to utilize the data sets for changing uses.

Other forces have also contributed towards a movement of increasingly more sophisticated procedures. The reasons include:

1) the introduction, continual improvement, and acceptance of information system technology;
2) the evolution of land planning from a procedure based upon principles of art and design to repeatable scientific methods;
3) the introduction and application of space-age, remote sensing data-gathering technology such as satellites and aircraft mounted with digital and analog scanning devices, etc.;
4) the demands from portions of our society that the quality and distributions of land resources become included in the land use planning process;
5) legislation, such as the National Environmental Policy Act of 1969, (NEPA) that established the beginnings of resource planning procedures requiring analytical, quantitative, and predictive techniques.

These factors are requiring decision makers, planners, designers, and managers to use more technically sophisticated procedures.

III. TYPES OF COMMUNICATION AND ANALYSIS USERS

Various techniques have evolved depending upon the user group, the group being communicated to, and what types of land data are involved. For example, it is improbable that a decision maker such as the chairman of a county board would use a satellite-derived image as the only information source to determine prime agricultural land. There are some very basic reasons for this. The definition of prime agricultural land needs to include more than what a remote sensing device such as satellite images can presently detect. In the state of Wisconsin, as an example, an array of factors must be considered before a farmer can be eligible for tax benefits from the Wisconsin Farmland Preservation Act (Wisconsin Statutes, 1977). Such an evaluation includes: soil types, contiguous ownership, profits gleaned from the land, proximity to markets, urban growth pressures, and zoning—all on a parcel-by-parcel basis. The above factors are simply not efficiently captured from remote sensing systems such as satellite imagery. However, to merge all of the above criteria which must be considered in determining eligibility of agricultural lands for protection and then portray the resultant areas in a map form on a TV-type screen would be understandable and useful. In this example, the hardware and display/communication medium is the same, to both the analyzer of the satellite image and the viewer of the results, but there has been considerable merger of the data types. *The result has been the reduction of data into information.*

This requires the reduction and simplification of the amounts of data that can be conveyed, utilized, and understood. At every level, however, there exists the need to reduce data into information. The data producer who must create a map is forced to reduce the field data into a map form. This need to reduce or simplify for the purpose of communicating information has a marked effect on the techniques utilized. The use of two overlays, one which depicts prime agricultural lands and one that depicts nonresident or alien land ownership to a county board chairman, represents a reduction and reorganization of the data since its original collection form as soil and ownership data. The important point is that communication requires that data be reduced into information. This is to say there is a continuum or sequence of users in the system beginning with the data producers and ending with the citizen.

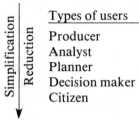

IV. EXAMPLES AND STUDIES

A. Distributions

The simplest format of both information for the research and communication to the decision maker is the distribution of a given type of data. Distributions of data which are without any prior form of interpretation represent the most basic information.

As an example, satellite-obtained data presently represents the reflectance characteristic of the land surface from 0.5 μm in the green wave lengths to 1.1 μm in the near infrared wave lengths, as measured and recorded by the Landsat satellite (Fig. 8). This 11 June 1973 Landsat satellite image of northeast Wisconsin provides an excellent overview of the Green Bay lobe of Wisconsin's glaciation period. The scale is 1:1,000,000 (185 by 185 km). On the east side of the image (right side) is Lake Michigan. Paralleling Lake Michigan is a bright red tone which is the Kettle Interlobate Moraine. The tone is created by deciduous forest vegetation in contrast to the light and dark tones which are mostly the effects of various agricultural patterns. In the center of the image, drumlin trends are visible. Madison, Wisconsin, with its four lakes, is visible in the lower left portion of the image and Milwaukee, Wisconsin, is visible in the lower middle right portion of the image.

This is considered raw data because no analysis or meaning has been applied to the resultant digital values. A similar, but different medium to obtain data about the land is through the use of photography with the use of film as a recording device. The high-altitude color infrared photograph at the scale of 1:120,000 of a portion of northwestern Wisconsin (Fig. 9) contains many varying color values. These values, when interpreted, indicate various land-related phenomena. For example, different resource parameters were detected when the photography was analyzed as a basis for rural land assessment for recreation (Niemann et al., 1975). These parameters included various types of vegetation, primarily Norway and Jack pine (see center of photograph), river patterns, areas managed for intensive forestry and sharptail grouse and various transportation features. The two rivers that are most prominent are the St. Croix (upper left portion of the photo) and the Namekagon (lower left portion of the photo). Both of these rivers are part of the National Wild and Scenic Rivers System.

The automation of information from "raw" data has and continues to receive considerable attention by the scientific community and by those federal and state agencies responsible for collection of large amounts of land resource data. For example, comprehensive statewide nonpoint source water quality detection is an important problem for the Wisconsin Department of Natural Resources. Various techniques for collection and analysis have been applied. Figure 10 illustrates various soil types in relation to water runoff characteristics. The picture of soil types is created by scanning a color infrared transparency with a microdensotometer. The digital imagery is radiometrically corrected and then classified. The classified file is then made into three separate black and white separations. The color composite was made by combining the three separate black and white separations.

Another example of the automation from "raw" data is shown in Fig. 11. This is an example of an edge-enhanced land cover/use map derived from Landsat data (James R. Irons. 1979. An analysis of digital image texture using Landsat multispectral scanner data. M.S. Thesis. Pennsylvania State Univ., University Park, Pa.). The digitally created image was made by photographing a color TV-type monitor. The image consists of approximately 350 elements by 250 scan lines in size and is presented at a nominal scale of 1:175,000. It is an area in Clearfield County, Pennsylvania, where considerable amounts of unreclaimed mined land exists. The colors represent the following:

Green—Forest
Yellow—Agricultural fields
White—Bare mine spoil
Purple—Vegetated mine spoil

Black—Unclassified
Red—Edges (those picture elements associated with large changes in reflectance such as water-land interfaces)

36°15' 0"

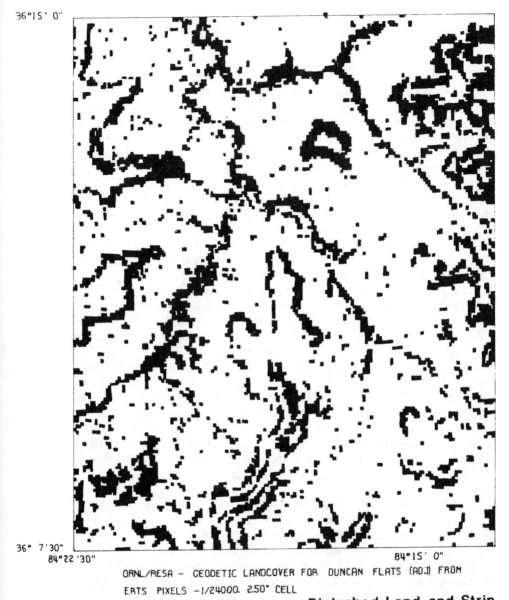

36° 7'30"
84°22'30"   84°15' 0"

ORNL/RESA – GEODETIC LANDCOVER FOR DUNCAN FLATS (ADJ) FROM
ERTS PIXELS –1/24000. 2.50" CELL

Disturbed Land and Strip Mines

Fig. 12—Disturbed lands and strip mines.

This type of display and use of digital-derived data is becoming more and more sophisticated (Lillesand & Kiefer, 1979). Figure 12 is an example of computerized output that depicts the extent of disturbed land and strip mines in an area of Tennessee. From such spatial distribution graphics, quantities can be determined, measurements can be made, and the informa-

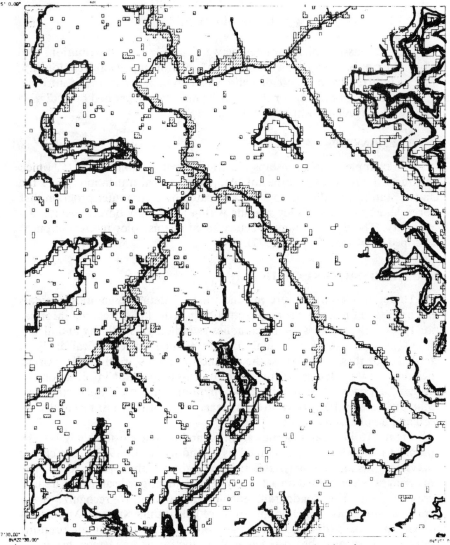

Fig. 13—Disturbed lands and strip mines with associated geology.

tion can serve as variables to be combined with other data. This distribution was also created by automated extraction of the data tapes from the Landsat satellite with correction to the tapes for geometric and radiometric errors (Durfee, 1977). Figure 13 shows the geodetic overlay of Landsat data of disturbed land onto a geological map for reference. Figure 14 illustrates, three dimensionally, the overlay of the disturbed land information and water surfaces superimposed on a data base generated from the Defense Department Topocon digital tapes of U.S. topography. The color illustration was created by assigning each color pen of the digital plotter to a different variable.

B. Relationships

This discussion differentiates between simple data distributions and those illustrations that depict a degree of relationship. Data relationships may be inferred from simple depictions of two or more forms of information shown simultaneously or they may be new data generated by analyzing statistically the relationships between factors.

1. RELATIONSHIPS/DEPICTIONS

An example of relationships illustrated by depiction is Fig. 15, which illustrates the most likely areas of high-sulphur coal utilization across the United States. This illustration was generated by a computer program that stores data by county. Color shading within the county border denotes accessibility. The programming which resulted in this color plotter output is described elsewhere (Durfee, 1977).

2. RELATIONSHIPS/STATISTICAL

Under this nomenclature are included all data presentation formats that are based on some means of statistically reducing or relating information types. This includes such techniques as indices of similarity and differences, principal component analysis, cluster analysis, canonical analysis, etc. In all of these techniques, the common elements are the degree of association between data types, or lack of it. This association information can result in a powerful analytical and communication tool. Such statistical techniques are well described in many texts. [One of the most recent is Clifford and Stephenson (1975)].

Figure 16 illustrates output from sampling and cluster analysis. The complete methodology is described by Frondorf et al. (1978). The cluster analysis results are summarized in the dendogram at the top of Fig. 16. The clustering was performed on a 10% systematic unaligned sample of natural resource data. The dendogram enables the analyst to recognize many groups of similarity, which in this study of Chiricahua National Monument in Arizona was a distinct advantage. In-depth analysis of all resulting dendograms revealed the existence of nine functional/manaement groups or functional landscapes. Two of the groups (Groups numbered 2 and 8) are the modal characteristics of plants and animals. They are also illustrated in Fig. 16. Some resources such as microclimate, topography, soils, and bedrock are not shown. As these groups represent combinations of natural resource properties, they could be thought of as one indication of the operative natural resource properties in that area.

The cluster analysis, through interpretation of the dendogram output, allows for the selective reduction of data types which need be actually entered into the computer and stored as files. Analysis of such dendograms reveals certain "indicator" data that carry other information with them. The explicit input of the "indicator" data leads to the implicit input of much of the remaining data. In the study mentioned above it was revealed that elevation, slope, vegetation type, and vegetation density were such "indicator" information. Figure 17 illustrates the relationship between that indicator data and all remaining information. An auxiliary importance of statistical techniques is that through a reduction of data types future studies are considerably reduced in size. Such statistical techniques lead to more advanced manipulations of data in optimizing and weighting.

C. Optimizations

1. OVERLAYS

There has already been considerable discussion of the use and importance in land planning of data overlays and the resultant effects that the use of Venn logic has had upon more advanced techniques. Figure 18 illustrates and provides the opportunity to compare the results which were used to delineate the most beautiful areas along the Lower St. Croix River by on-site users and by riparian owners. Users were asked to delineate on a map included in a questionnaire their perception of what areas along the river they considered to be most beautiful. The graph illustrates that river users perceived that three areas along the 52-mile segment of the St. Croix were very beautiful. This computer graphic was produced by assimilating (overlaying) approximately 1,000 responses (Becker et al., 1979). This type of data analysis was requested by the riverway managers to determine which areas require sensitive management. The technique of having each individual user provide one overlay representing his/her perception is an effective procedure for representing and assimilating data, particularly when the assumption is valid that every overlay is equal to every other overlay.

2. WEIGHTED OVERLAYS

The logical evolution from equally weighted overlays was the development of techniques which provide for applying different weights in varying combinations.Figure 19 represents a technique of weighted overlays using lithographic procedures which have recently been developed and applied to transmission line location issues (Murray, 1976; Steinitz, 1977).

3. WEIGHTED COMPOSITES

With the introduction of digital computing, considerable changes have occurred as related to the development and communication of land use alternatives. The use of digital computing provided for the first time the comparably "unlimited" introduction of data and "unlimited" abilities to weigh various resource data elements.

As an example of such weighted composites, Fig. 20 is a computer-generated map reflecting the relative cost to purchase a right-of-way for Interstate 43 in the State of Wisconsin. The map is the result of applying a series of numerical weights to various kinds of data. A data value reflecting

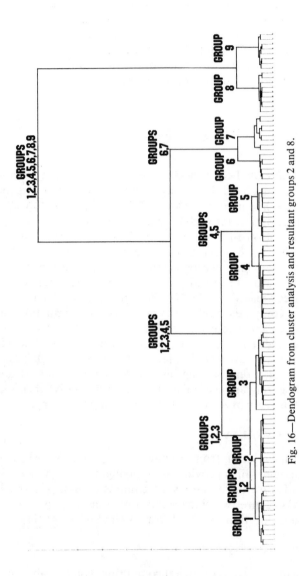

Fig. 16—Dendogram from cluster analysis and resultant groups 2 and 8.

CLUSTER   ANALYSIS   107–21   INDIVIDUALS
RHYOLITE CANYON WATERSHED
CHIRICAHUA NATIONAL MONUMENT, ARIZONA
SCHOOL OF RENEWABLE NATURAL RESOURCES
UNIVERSITY OF ARIZONA

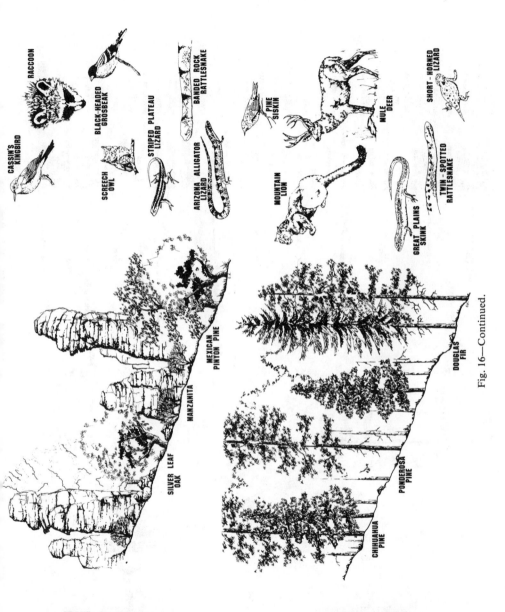

Fig. 16—Continued.

GROUP 2, 107-21
RHYOLITE CANYON WATERSHED
CHIRICAHUA NATIONAL MONUMENT, ARIZONA
SCHOOL OF RENEWABLE NATURAL RESOURCES
UNIVERSITY OF ARIZONA

GROUP 8, 107-21
RHYOLITE CANYON WATERSHED
CHIRICAHUA NATIONAL MONUMENT, ARIZONA
SCHOOL OF RENEWABLE NATURAL RESOURCES
UNIVERSITY OF ARIZONA

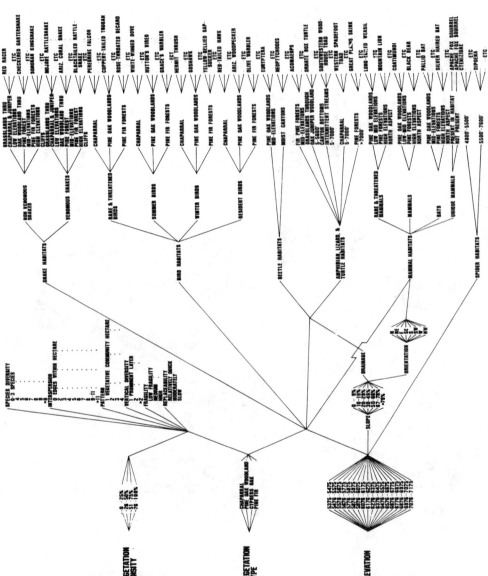

Fig. 17. Relationship between "indicator" data and other information.

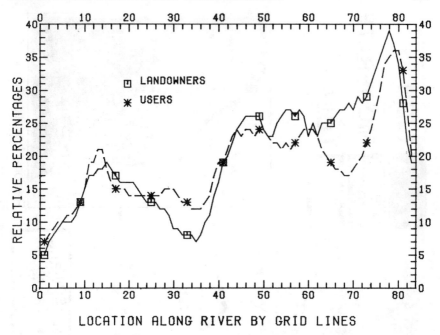

Fig. 18—The lower St. Croix: most beautiful areas.

land acquisition costs has been converted into each of the approximately 10,000 1-km² cells. (The darker the pattern, the more appropriate the location for the interstate.)

In contrast, Fig. 21 represents the most appropriate location for the interstate emphasizing agricultural concerns but still using the same overall data base. In this application of a weighted composite procedure, an appropriate location for the interstate is being identified using data weighted towards the protection of the most productive agricultural lands (Miller & Niemann, 1972).

Figures 22 and 23 are additional examples of weighted composite techniques. Figure 22 represents a computer map surface that indicates the most appropriate location for a 345-kVA electric transmission facility considering the likely impact created by transmission facilities upon farming practices. The line printer map consists of various symbols that create a continuum of grey values (light to dark). In this example, the lighter the symbols the less likely there will be impact from the transmission facility upon agricultural activities. For example, the dark area on the printout (Fig. 22) is the highly productive Wisconsin Arlington Prairie area in Dane and Columbia counties. Figure 23 represents and illustrates the results of a linear optimization algorithm. The algorithm uses numerical values associated with each of the cells. The optimization algorithm searches all numerical values and finds the route of lowest composite numerical value. In this particular example, the line plotter output is both an analysis tool as well as

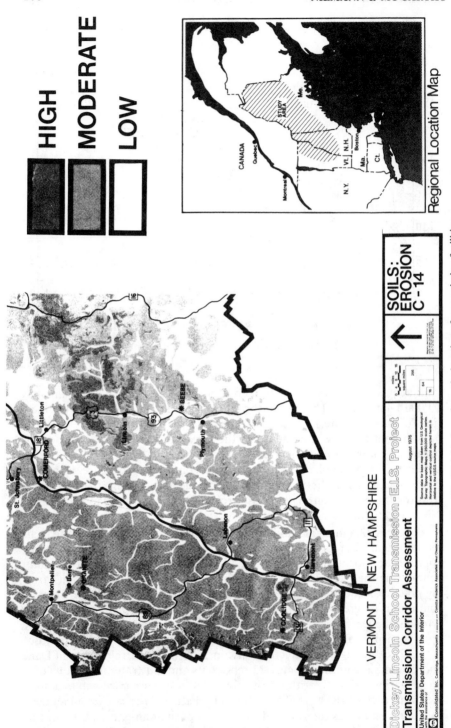

Fig. 19—Weighted overlays: the location of transmission facilities.

Table 1—Sensitivity index-comparison of alternative transmission routes.

Route analyzed	Mean value	Difference
901—Equal importance	24.88	−5.96
904—Naturalist's viewpoint	20.93	−2.01
906—Naturalist's viewpoint with all others	24.98	−6.06
907—Farmer's viewpoint	17.84	+1.88
910—Politician's viewpoint	23.92	−5.00
915—Tourist viewpoint with all others	26.02	−7.10
Mean surface value = 18.92		

a communication mechanism. The line printer and other associated output provides: (i) location information (where the route should be, given a particular policy or viewpoint); (ii) the extent other viewpoints or policies will be affected by the optimized route (see Table 1); and (iii) what resources will potentially be affected by the introduction of a transmission facility (Table 2) (Niemann, 1973).

For example, Table 1 provides a basis from which to compare various alternative transmission routes. The results indicate that Route 904, which reflects concern for the natural environment, is the most sensitive to the farmers' viewpoint and Route 915, which reflects the tourist viewpoint, is the most insensitive to the farmers' concern. This table, therefore, conveys important information to those persons and groups that are concerned with minimizing impact to agricultural lands. The table shows which route location policies will be the most insensitive to agricultural issues.

Another analysis technique is also quite easily given the digital form of the data. Table 2 illustrates a comparison between two potential optimized routes for a transmission facility. For example, Table 2 shows that one route will potentially affect more agricultural row crops (122.35 vs. 116.74 acres or 49.5 vs. 47.28 ha) and less oak-hickory vegetation (13.93 vs. 21.90 acres or 5.64 vs. 8.87) than an alternate route. This simply shows the transmission route planner which and how many resources and land uses will probably be affected by a given transmission route location.

Table 2—Area affected by a proposed 345-kV transmission line (200-foot right-of-way), Columbia to Wyocena, Wis., segment.

		Types of potential area affected			
		Route 1		Route 2	
		acres	ha	acres	ha
120	Agricultural—row crops	122.35	49.5	116.74	47.28
122	Agricultural—specialized crops	24.48	9.91	24.48	9.91
123	Agricultural—livestock	15.04	6.09	15.04	6.09
203	Communication—federal highway	0.29	0.18	0.29	0.18
206	Communication—local roadway	0.59	0.24	0.73	0.30
434	Popple with white birch—closed	3.24	1.31	3.24	1.31
437	Oak-hickory—closed	13.93	5.64	21.90	8.87
438	Oak-hickory—closed	1.77	0.72	1.77	0.72
	Total	181.71	73.60	184.22	74.61

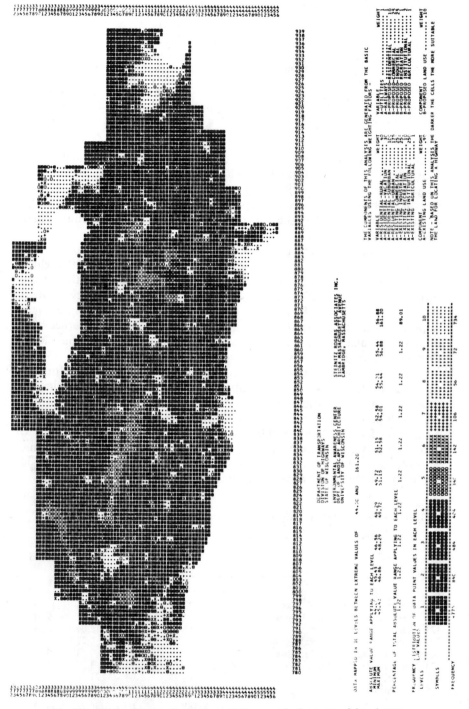

Fig. 20—Weighted composite: least acquisition cost for interstate right-of-ways.

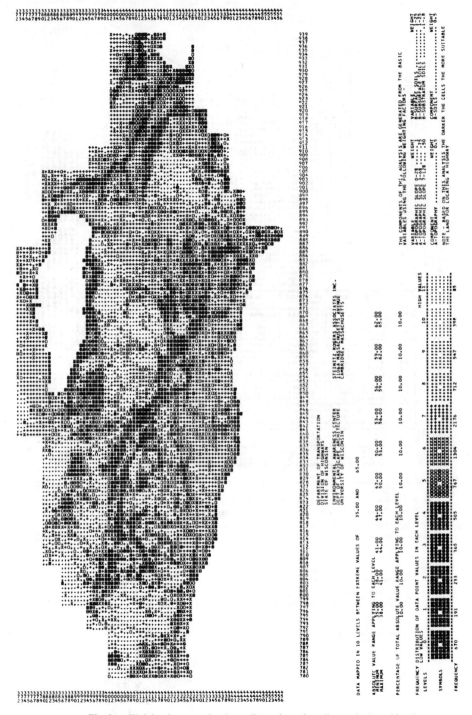

Fig. 21—Weighted composite: least disruption of quality agricultural land.

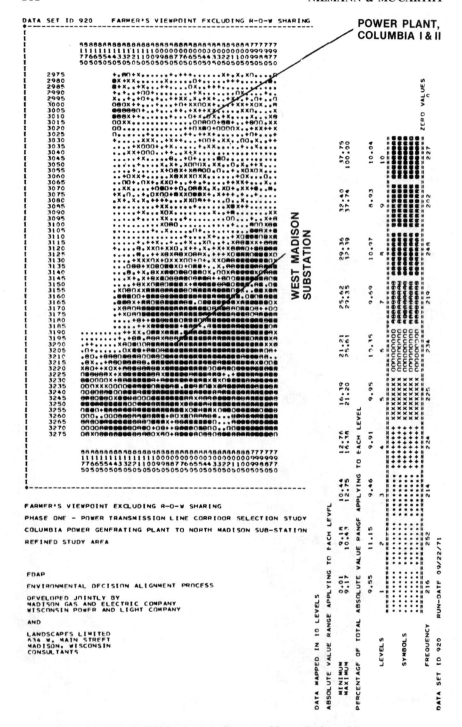

Fig. 22—Weighted composite: map of farmer's viewpoint.

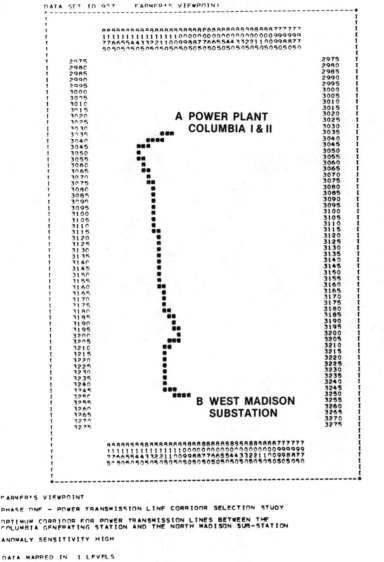

DATA SET ID 907   FARMER'S VIEWPOINT

A POWER PLANT
COLUMBIA I & II

B WEST MADISON
SUBSTATION

FARMER'S VIEWPOINT

PHASE ONE - POWER TRANSMISSION LINE CORRIDOR SELECTION STUDY

OPTIMUM CORRIDOR FOR POWER TRANSMISSION LINES BETWEEN THE
COLUMBIA GENERATING STATION AND THE NORTH MADISON SUB-STATION

ANOMALY SENSITIVITY HIGH

DATA MAPPED IN   1 LEVELS

ABSOLUTE VALUE RANGE APPLYING TO EACH LEVEL

```
        MINIMUM                    0.10
        MAXIMUM                    0.10
```

PERCENTAGE OF TOTAL ABSOLUTE VALUE RANGE APPLYING TO EACH LEVEL

```
                    100.00                 EDAP

        LEVELS          1               ENVIRONMENTAL DECISION ALIGNMENT PROCESS
                    =========
                    ■■■■■■■■■          DEVELOPED JOINTLY BY
                    ■■■■■■■■■          MADISON GAS AND ELECTRIC COMPANY
        SYMBOLS     ■■■■■■■■■          WISCONSIN POWER AND LIGHT COMPANY
                    ■■■■■■■■■
                    ■■■■■■■■■          AND
                    =========  ZERO VALUES
        FREQUENCY       67         2495    LANDSCAPES LIMITED
                                            634 W. MAIN STREET
DATA SET ID 907    RUN-DATE 01/11/72        MADISON, WISCONSIN
                                            CONSULTANTS
```

Fig. 23—Optimized corridor of farmer's viewpoint.

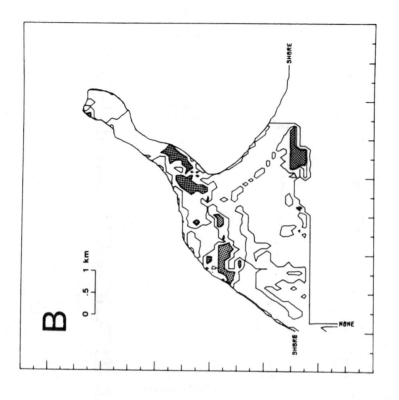

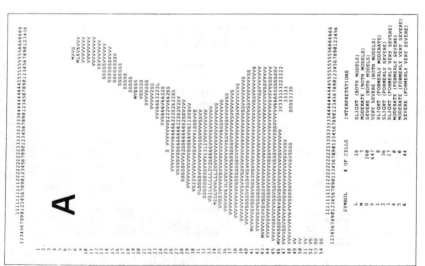

Fig. 24—Siting limitations at septic vs. mound disposal system: *(A)* A computer-generated character map showing changes in limitations for onsite waste disposal when siting criteria for conventional systems are revised to accommodate both mound and conventional systems: map was produced at a portable terminal; *(B)* A computer-generated plotter map showing siting limitations for both mound and conventional septic absorption systems: shading (manually applied) indicates suitable regions for onsite disposal.

The preceding examples show that the illustrations created by computer output techniques are essential in understanding the geographical areas most appropriate for various land uses and for communicating the results to analysts and planners. In addition, most recently the use of interactive graphic techniques have been applied to many resource problems. For example, an interactive resource data management system has been applied to evaluate on-site waste disposal alternatives (Butler et al., 1977). Figure 24 depicts the results as they would be viewed using a portable terminal (A) and a cathode ray tube (B) for analysis. Figure 25 illustrates the adaptation of the linear optimization technique discussed previously (see Fig. 23) from a batch line printer procedure to a graphic interactive procedure. The illustration depicts what would be viewed interactively. The importance of interactive techniques for this type of "optimization" procedure cannot be overstated. It allows the user to experiment with various value relationships and visualize the geographic location consequences immediately (Gregory Mills. 1978. The addition of corridor selection capability to an existing user oriented geographical information system. Senior Thesis. Dep. of Landscape Archit., Univ. of Wisconsin, Madison. 100 p.).

D. Predictions

For the purpose of analysis, predictions serve as methods of organizing and depicting complex concepts that deal with "what if" questions. Common to most predictions are the ideas of replicating given phenomena and then testing alternatives or variable futures.

Because problems are complex, predictive approaches have continual appeal. The land use analyst/planner, however, is faced with a certain enigma. Predictive methods definitely can be an asset to problem solving, yet land use problems tend to be so complex that replicating events accurately is extremely difficult. Nevertheless, continued attempts with predictive techniques can be expected. Probably most important is the understanding that predictive approaches represent a significant learning tool.

In an attempt to present examples of the output from different types of prediction techniques, a classificational breakdown that represents one means of simplifying the variety of simulation techniques is presented. There are many different ways of classifying prediction methods; this one is used principally for its simplicity. In the examples that follow, it is important to recognize that most modeling efforts are composites of a variety of different and separate data manipulations that are ultimately combined into a final solution. In all modeling approaches which attempt to replicate and thereby predict certain events, there are a range of options in methods of data manipulations. As an example, most predictive approaches would use some combination of: (i) statistical/trend representations, (ii) stocastic/probalistic, and (iii) deterministic/parametric.

```
              MAP OF MIN ROUTE
                         1
                1234567890

           1     ..+.......
           2     ..+.......
           3     .+........
           4     .+........
           5     .+........
           6     ..+.......
           7     .+........
           8     .+........
           9     .+........
          10     .+........
          11     +.........
          12     .+........
          13     ..+.......
          14     ..+.......
          15     ..+.......
          16     ...++.....
          17     .....+....
          18     ......+...
          19     .......+..
          20     .......+..
                         1
                1234567890
```

Fig. 25—Interactive corridor analysis and selection.

1. STATISTICAL/TREND REPRESENTATIONS

Trend or statistical prediction models are defined as those representations that are typically linear and whose results are based on that linearity. Such techniques are usually used where system understanding is incomplete. Statistical models range from historical air photo/trend projections to various averaging techniques.

An example of such trend predictions can be seen in Fig. 26 taken from Miller's work (Curtis A. Miller. 1975. Evaluation designated candidate areas for electrical generating station location utilizing projected far field impacts on atmospheric quality: A case study for the State of Maryland. M.S. Thesis. Dep. of Landscape Archit., Univ. of Michigan, Ann Arbor. 108 p.). This illustration depicts the sulphur dioxide emissions from a two-unit proposed power plant that intended to utilize scrubber technology. As a learning and communication device the predictive output reveals no significant impact of ambient SO_2 based on this new power plant.

In this illustration existing air quality for sulphur dioxide was obtained from Maryland's Bureau of Air Quality Control. This bureau has a number of monitoring stations throughout the state. Using an interpolation program the annual monitored records could be approximated for the entire region. A dispersion program for the emissions of the projected plant was also utilized (Stephenson, 1974). The resulting "trend" differences between the existing and the proposed air quality provides an initial understanding of the impact of the proposed plant.

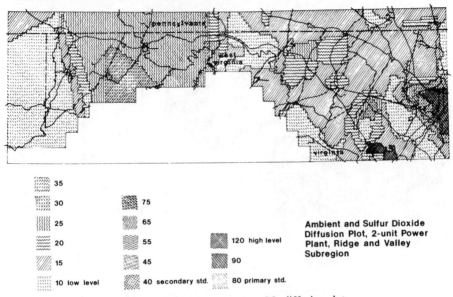

35

30   75

25   65   **Ambient and Sulfur Dioxide
                                                   Diffusion Plot, 2-unit Power
20   55   120 high level   Plant, Ridge and Valley
                                                   Subregion**

15   45   90

10 low level   40 secondary std.   80 primary std.

Fig. 26—Simulation of ambient + SO₂ diffusion plot.

2. STOCASTIC/PROBALISTIC

Models that use artificially generated data as either input or response itself are examples of this category. This synthetic data may be in the format of a rainfall generator for a hydrologic/arroyo-erosion model or simply a series of random numbers to assist in locating certain growth allocations in land use models. The illustrations in Fig. 27, 28, 29, and 30, depicting a simulation of changes in land cover from 1940 to 1987, are principally based on stocastic techniques. The specific model has been described elsewhere (Voelker et al., 1974). This model combined both natural and cultural changes over time. The natural successional changes of various vegetation communities were simulated by considering those land categories as states in finite markov chains. As the simulation moves into the future, man-induced changes often override the natural successional states. These land use changes are also determined stocastically. Figure 27 illustrates the actual 1940 land cover, while Fig. 28 depicts the simulated 1987 land cover. Figure 29 and 30 pick one variable unit "old field vegetation" and illustrate three dimensionally the changes between 1940 (Fig. 29) and 1987 (Fig. 30).

3. DETERMINISTIC/PARAMETRIC

In actual practice the difference between deterministic and parametric simulations is one of gradation. As knowledge of the system to be simulated increases and required input data is better known, representations become actual data. Generally speaking, deterministic simulations are based on very well-known relationships of model components, while parametric ap-

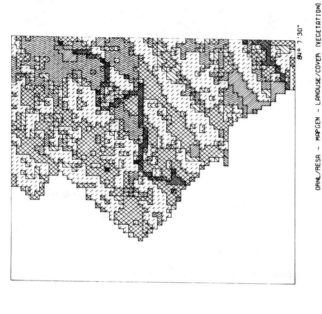

ORNL/RESA - MAPGEN - LANDUSE/COVER (VEGETATION)

1940 CLINTON SUBREGION ONLY - GROUPS 1-10

**Computer Map Showing 1940
Land Cover**

water

urban

residential

open & other

agricultural

old field

cedar hardwood

pine hardwood

pine

hardwood

Fig. 27—Computer map showing 1940 land cover.

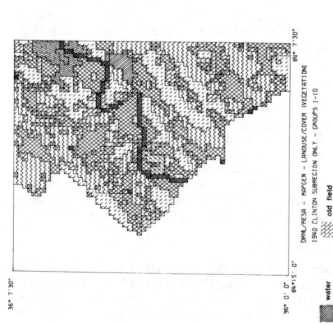

ORNL/RESA - MAPGEN - LANDUSE/COVER (VEGETATION)

- 1987 CLINTON SUBREGION ONL

**Computer Map Showing
Predicted 1987 Land Cover**

water

urban

residential

open & other

agricultural

old field

cedar hardwood

pine hardwood

pine

hardwood

Fig. 28—Computer map showing predicted 1987 land cover.

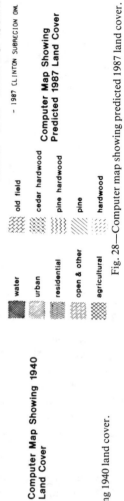

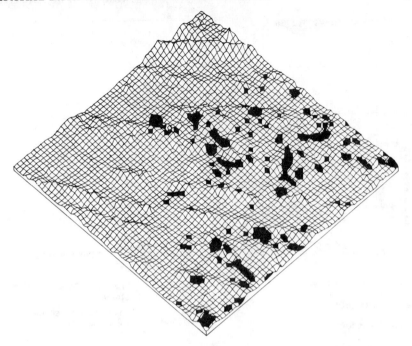

Fig. 29—Land cover (old fields, 1940).

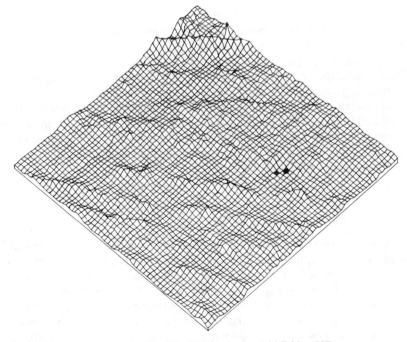

Fig. 30—1987 land cover (old fields, 1987).

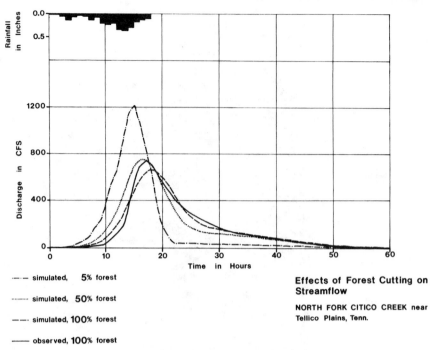

Fig. 31—Effects of forest cutting on streamflow.

proaches involve more empirical approximation from control or test sites. An example of parametric modeling is the non-point source mineral water quality model developed by Betson and McMasters (1974) in which relationships are described between stream flow and 15 water quality constituents. The resulting equation is based on data from over 50 control watersheds, yet is applicable to a much larger area. Since constituents and water quality are related to increases in water flow, parametric/deterministic simulations of changes to water flow discharge are important. Figure 31 shows the effects of different forest cutting intensities on streamflow. This model is described in Betson (1972) and McCarthy et al. (1974).

V. CONCLUSION

Spatial data analysis and information communication are inseparably linked as one continuous process. This is a major concept of this chapter. In attempting to explain this process, many of the ideas presented in this chapter have been, by necessity, subdivided. This division into abstract terms exists only as a fabrication to increase the reader's understanding. In contrast, the real process of analysis and communication not only exists as a continuum but *must be perceived and planned* as such to be successful. The perception of analysis and communication as one continuous ongoing process suggests that future applications will be increasingly "human interactive." Continued development of equipment such as video-cassette recorders, interactive plasma screen terminals, electronic disc typewriters, video tape zoom cameras, etc., only begin to identify the possible. Software development will also move towards increased human interface. It is not unreasonable to envision entire processes of spatial data analysis and communication becoming one continuous learning and analyzing interactive situation. It's an exciting thought.

ACKNOWLEDGMENTS

For the use of various illustrations and tables we wish to acknowledge the following: the Environmental Awareness Center of the University of Wisconsin-Madison for Fig. 1 and 2; the Department of Landscape Architecture at the University of Wisconsin-Madison for Fig. 3 through 7, 9, 18, 20, and 28; the Environmental Monitoring the Data Acquisition Group of the Institute for Environmental Studies at the University of Wisconsin-Madison for Fig. 8 and 10; the Center for Geographical Analysis, also with the Institute, for Fig. 24; Office for Remote Sensing of Earth Resources, Pennsylvania State University, for Fig. 11; the Oak Ridge Geographic Data Systems Group-Computer Sciences Division and the Energy Division of Oak Ridge National Laboratory for use of Fig. 12 through 15 and 26 through 30; the School of Renewable Natural Resources at the University of Arizona for Fig. 16 and 17; the Wisconsin Power and Light Company for Fig. 21 through 23 and Tables 1 and 2; the Bonneville Power Administration for Fig. 19; and the Tennessee Valley Authority for Fig. 31.

LITERATURE CITED

Becker, R. H., W. A. Gates, and B. J. Niemann, Jr. 1979. The Lower St. Croix; User and resource conditions. School of Nat. Resour., College of Agric. and Life Sci., Univ. of Wisconsin, Madison. 300 p.

Betson, R. P. 1972. Upper Bear Creek Project: A continuous daily streamflow model. Hydraulic Data Branch Res. Pap. no. 8. TVA, Knoxville, Tenn.

Betson, R. P., and W. M. McMaster. 1974. A first-generation nonpoint source mineral water quality model. Proc. 47th Annu. Conf. of Water Pollut. Control Fed., Denver, Colo.

Butler, K. S., B. H. McCown, and W. A. Gates. 1977. Use of a computer-based resource data system to evaluate on-site waste disposal alternatives. J. Soil Water Conserv. 32(5):214–219.

Clifford, H. T., and W. Stephenson. 1975. An introduction to numerical classification. Academic Press, New York. 229 p.

Durfee, R. C. 1977. ORRMIS—Oak Ridge Regional Modeling Information System. ORNL-NSF-EP 73. Oak Ridge Natl. Lab., Oak Ridge, Tenn. 103 p.

Frondorf, A. F., M. M. McCarthy, and W. O. Rasmussen. 1978. Data-intensive spatial sampling and multiple hierarchical clustering: Methodological approaches toward cost/time efficiency in natural resource assessment. Landscape Plan. 5:1–25.

Larsen, B., J. L. Clapp, A. H. Miller, B. J. Niemann, Jr., and A. L. Ziegler. 1978. Land records: The cost to the citizen to maintain the present land information base—a Wisconsin case study. Dep. of Admin., State of Wisconsin, Madison. p. 23.

Lewis, P. H., Jr., and B. H. Murray. 1964. Quality corridors for Wisconsin. Landscape Archit., 54:100–107.

Lewis, P. H., Jr., B. H. Murray, and B. J. Niemann, Jr. 1969. Regional design for human impact. Thomas Publ. Ltd., Kaukauna, Wis. 157 p.

Lillesand, T. M., and R. W. Kiefer. 1979. Remote sensing and image interpretation. John Wiley and Sons, New York.

McCarthy, M. M., R. C. Durfee, M. L. Newman, S. L. Yaffee, R. Betson, C. W. Craven, Jr., T. L. Cox, J. Holbrook, D. D. Huff, and R. Strand. 1974. Regional environmental systems analysis: An approach for management. p. 130–136. *In* Proc. 1st Int. Congr. of Ecology, TIE, The Hague, Netherlands. Center for Agric., Publ., and Document., Wageningen, The Netherlands.

McHarg, Ian. 1966. A comprehensive highway route selection method. Delaware-Raritan Committee on I-95. 100 p.

McHarg, Ian. 1969. Design with nature. The Natural History Press, Garden City, N.Y. 200 p.

Miller, A. H., and B. J. Niemann, Jr. 1972. An interstate corridor selection process: The application of computer technology to highway location dynamics. Phase I. Dep. of Landscape Archit./Environ. Awareness Center, School of Nat. Resour., College of Agric. and Life Sci., Univ. of Wisconsin, Madison.

Murray, T. J. 1976. Alternative power transmission corridors: Dickey/Lincoln School Hydroelectric Project. U.S. Dep. Interior, Bonneville Power Admin., Portland, Maine. 173 p.

Niemann, B. J., Jr. 1973. Environmental decision alignment process: The application of computer-assisted techniques in energy transmission corridor planning. Landscapes Limited, Madison, Wis. 264 p.

Niemann, B. J., Jr., X. A. Bonilla, and S. R. Bruno. 1975. Rural landscape assessment: A comparative evaluation of high platform remote sensors. Res. Bull. R2752. Dep. of Landscape Archit., School of Nat. Resour., College of Agric. and Life Sci., Univ. of Wisconsin, Madison. 243 p.

Steinitz, Carl. 1977. Hand-drawn overlays: Their history and prospective use. Landscape Archit. 67:444–455.

Stephenson, R. L. 1974. A program for computing the dispersion of airborne contaminants. ORNL TM-4674. Oak Ridge Nat. Lab., Oak Ridge, Tenn.

Tishler, W. H., and B. J. Niemann, Jr. 1971. Cool planning for a hot-humid campus in Ife, Nigeria. Landscape Archit. 61:216–227.

Voelker, A. H., M. M. McCarthy, M. L. Newman, R. C. Durfee, S. L. Yaffee, and C. W. Craven, Jr. 1974. Spatial disaggregation: Prerequisite to regional simulation. p. 525–532. *In* Proc. of Summer Computer Simulation Conf., Simulations Council Inc., La Jolla, Calif.

Wisconsin Statutes. 1977. Farmland Preservation Act, Chapt. 91.

section III

Planning Cultivated
Land Uses

USDA Soil Conservation Service

III

10 Planning Uses of Cultivated Cropland and Pastureland

MICHAEL J. SINGER, KENNETH K. TANJI, AND
J. HERBERT SNYDER

University of California
Davis, California

I. INTRODUCTION

Arable land, that land which is capable of cultivation and the production of food and fiber, is one of the major cornerstones of human society. Without a supply of arable land sufficient to support our population, society as we know it today would change dramatically. This chapter discusses the need for planning cultivated land. In so doing, we have assumed that no miracle technology or esoteric industrial solution to plant production will be readily available during this century. Thus, our discussion is based on conventional agricultural technology within current social, political, ecological, and economic restraints. Other chapters deal with range, timber, urban, and recreational land use planning. We intend to restrict this discussion to cultivated cropland and pastureland.

In this chapter we attempt to answer the question "why plan agricultural lands?". We discuss current agronomic land uses in the United States, and then detail the general data requirements needed for planning cultivated lands. We divide the discussion of cultivated lands into irrigated and non-irrigated lands. This chapter does not include a comprehensive list of all soil properties which need to be understood before planning or cultivation can begin. If the reader requires further detailed information, references to it can be found in the literature cited section.

Agricultural uses affect the land where their operations occur and may affect adjacent or distant land through movement of air and water across contiguous boundaries. We briefly discuss these before outlining two major methods of controlling land use. Each of these methods (agricultural zoning and environmental control laws) has been attempted in California. We have drawn upon examples with which we are familiar, to illustrate success and failure in agricultural land use planning. Other chapters will deal in greater depth with the whole question of land use regulation, and the reader is encouraged to go to those chapters for more in-depth coverage of the subject.

A. Why Plan Agricultural Land?

Planning is a word which arouses deep and sometimes violent emotions in many individuals and communities. Often one envisions lengthy court proceedings involving decisions on what crop to plant, date of planting, or other cultural practices. Yet, planning is the essence of successful agriculture. Agriculturists use the word *timing* or *rotation* to describe major planning operations. We are not discussing planning at this level. Planning, as we see it, involves the preservation and protection of agricultural land for agriculture. Regulation is the proscribing of agricultural practices. Rather, we need to discuss, and set our philosophical frame of reference for the kind of planning which involves choices such as: Should a piece of land be left in agriculture or should it be converted to nonagricultural use? Should land be brought into agricultural production which now is not in production? These questions are more complex because they often involve individual land owners and society in general.

There are three answers to the question about preserving agricultural land; yes, no, and maybe. Those who favor the yes answer cite the now familiar litany of limited resources and growing population as major reasons for resource conservation and planning. A smaller group answers no. Production technology, increasing efficiency of operations, marketplace allocation of resources, a surplus of potentially arable land, and future technology are cited as reasons for their lack of concern. Between these two divergent opinions are those who suggest that at times there is good reason to plan and at other times or places planning is not necessary. We are taking the advocacy position that proper planning of and for agricultural lands is necessary. Indeed, agricultural planning is occuring, and one purpose of this chapter is to provide planners and managers with information with which to make informed planning decisions.

Having taken an advocacy position, we shall defend it in more detail. Population is the driving force and raison d'etra of conservation and planning needs. This has been well documented (Comm. on Population Growth and the Am. Future, 1972; Counc. on Environ. Qual., 1974; Brooks & Andrews, 1974; Brown, 1975). Although the U.S. population growth rate is declining, we still add over 1 million people a year to the population (USHEW, 1976). The situation in other countries is far more serious. We must assume that export of American farm products will continue to be a major source of income towards the balance of payments, and that world demand, which is associated in part to population size, will put increasing pressure on our land resources. Thus, world population growth is not a side issue in the land use planning question.

Population alone would not be a problem were it not for the fact that resources are finite. Agricultural land resources in the United States have been estimated to be 56.7% of the total land area in the U.S. (Econ. Res. Serv., 1974). There are approximately 155.2 million ha (384 million acres) in production and as much as 40.5 million ha (100 million acres) of potential cropland. In the world, there is an estimated 3,190 million ha of arable land, of which 46% (1970) was being utilized (Anon., 1967). These are large but finite amounts. Bringing these lands into production will involve major economic and institutional changes in countries other than the United States. In the United States, it will require some changes in technology and economics. Much of the arable land in the United States is not the best land for agriculture and returning it to production will increase the likelihood of environmental problems such as soil erosion (Carter et al., 1975).

Agricultural expansion onto lands less suited for cultivation will require larger management and resource inputs. These resource inputs may be more limiting than the amount of land. Energy in the form of fertilizer, pesticides, or petroleum for fuel will be needed in larger quantities on the new land. Water also may be limiting. Pimentel et al. (1975) discuss these contraints on food production.

A corollary to the fact that agricultural land is limited is that it is also being removed from agriculture. Various estimates of the transfer of agricultural land to nonagricultural uses have been made. Clawson (1972) estimated that 0.61 million ha of agricultural land is converted to nonagricultural uses annually. Krause and Hair (1974) estimate that less than 2 million ha of cropland had been urbanized in the 20-year period 1950–1970. This is less than 1% of the 1950 cropland base. The Economic Research Service (1974) estimated that the total annual shift of rural land to other uses averaged 0.89 million ha/year over the 10-year period 1959–1969. Almost 0.40 million ha was converted to recreation, wilderness areas, parks, and wildlife refuges.

These megascale figures obscure the effects of changing land uses because they are small compared to the vast area of cropland in the United States. However, if 0.89 million ha/year are removed from cropland over the next 24 years, by the year 2000 more than half of the reserve of 40 million ha of arable land not now in agriculture will be gone. William Johnson[1] estimated that over 2 million ha/year was being lost from agriculture and that by the year 2000 all of the arable land in reserve plus some of the current cropland will be lost from production.

In the latter case the loss is not small. Even so, a more startling picture of the problem can be seen on a finer level of resolution. California's Santa Clara Valley was a prime orchard area prior to 1950. Between 1940 and 1970 over 56,700 ha (140,000 acres) was taken out of agriculture (Harley, 1971). California originally had over 3.5 million ha of prime agricultural land. By 1972 over 0.8 million ha had been urbanized (Heller, 1972). Such studies as these point out that major localized changes are occurring which affect local (regional) economies.

The conservative approach is to hedge ones' bet on the future by planning agricultural land. If world population ceases to be a problem, or if a super technology develops which relieves the pressure on agricultural land,

---

[1] William Johnson. Address before the Western Sec. American and Canadian Soc. of Animal Sci., Washington State univ., Pullman, Wash. 20 July 1976.

we are so much the better. If on the other hand, the most pessimistic predictions of population growth and resource dimunition continue, we would have made the only rational choice.

B. Preservation of Agricultural Land

Agricultural land use planning and preservation of land for agriculture are parallel but not identical goals. Preservation of agricultural land and preservation of the quality of agricultural land are both essential parts of a conservation land ethic which is badly needed. Agricultural land serves as open space in urban fringe areas. There are many problems for urban and agricultural participants who occupy the urban fringe. Noise, dust, and odors from agricultural practices are annoying to the urbanite. Thievery, malicious mischief, and vandalism are a problem the agriculturalist lives with. Yet, open space is a need felt by most urban dwellers. Preservation of agricultural land through land use planning can help to satisfy the need.

Preservation also means preservation of land quality. This is difficult to legislate and requires a land ethic—a land ethic which makes each of us realize that ownership of property does not give us the right to destroy it. In essence, each generation has a short tenure on earth where its actions can insure that the next generation will have the same or better quality land as we had, or where by thoughtlessness or carelessness it can insure that the next generation's survival will be more of a struggle. Perhaps the concept that Stone (1973) expressed is the one which we need to follow. That is, non-person natural objects have legal rights, and should be treated with respect just as we treat each other.

II. AGRONOMIC LAND USE IN THE UNITED STATES

Of the 0.92 billion ha (2,271,343,000 acres) of land in the 50 United States, the U.S. Census of Agriculture in 1969 identified some 372 million ha (918,312,000 acres) as land in farms, privately owned. Of this amount, about 105 million ha (261,138,000 acres) is actually harvested. Thus, the intensively cultivated land in crops comprises no more than about 12% of the total land area in the United States. Even here, there is some slippage in agronomic use of land as the degree of intensity varies by different types of farm.

Table 1 presents a broad summary of type of crop for the harvested cropland of the United States, giving both a total picture for the United States and a regional subdivision. Crops generally considered to represent intensively cultivated agricultural activity are the cash grains, field crops, tobacco, cotton, fruit, nut, and vegetable crops. Both the major acreage of land in farms and acres harvested for the cash grains and field crops dominate the scene in the central states. Livestock enterprises occupy great-

Table 1—Harvested cropland in the United States.†

	Total		Cash grains and field crops		Tobacco and cotton		Fruit, nut and vegetable		Poultry, dairy and livestock		General farms		Miscellaneous	
	Farm acres	Acres harvested	Farm acres	Acres harvested	Farm acres	Acres harvested	Farm acres	Acres harvested	Farm acres	Acres harvested	Farm acres	Acres harvested	Farm acres	Acres harvested
							1,000 acres							
The United States	918,313	261,138	198,906	106,703	30,390	13,076	12,408	6,666	609,033	109,440	56,822	24,379	10,756	874
New England	4,434	1,316	544	220	25	9	314	89	3,125	902	253	71	175	26
Middle Atlantic	15,979	7,171	1,114	663	6	4	973	553	12,401	5,351	1,093	522	392	79
East North Central	82,865	48,439	33,093	23,052	225	37	1,533	833	43,760	22,434	3,607	1,949	646	135
West North Central	257,893	103,975	82,874	43,752	340	277	205	124	157,547	51,312	16,323	7,609	603	72
South Atlantic	53,371	14,412	7,623	3,757	8,247	2,442	3,674	1,588	24,865	4,002	6,565	2,344	2,398	228
East South Central	43,324	12,427	5,900	3,604	8,171	2,861	260	96	21,727	3,837	5,926	1,945	1,339	84
West South Central	183,126	36,775	28,534	16,528	11,355	6,447	778	349	130,343	7,850	10,496	4,522	1,621	61
Mountain	208,716	21,899	25,642	9,462	1,121	450	595	276	172,329	7,122	7,176	2,437	1,853	50
Pacific	68,606	14,724	13,581	5,666	901	552	4,077	2,758	42,934	2,095	5,383	2,980	1,730	141

† Source: USDC. 1969. Bureau of the Census, 1969 Census of Agriculture, C. 8. Type of Farm/Vol. II.

er acreages in the mountain states and the specialized fruit, nut, and vegetable crops are more concentrated in the Pacific states.

Another way of viewing intensity of production is to examine the distribution of irrigated acreage in the United States, as presented for broad type of farming categories in Table 2. Starting with the same 372 million ha (918,312,000 acres) in farms in the United States, a subdivision by general type of land use and broad geographic area is presented. As is to be expected, intenstiy of cultivation, as reflected by irrigation, shows a dominance in the western states. Twenty million out of nearly 23 million irrigated harvested cropland acres—about 88%—is to be found in the 17 western states and Louisiana. Nearly 91% of all irrigated acreage—38,196,000 acres in the United States—is found in this same geographic region.

From this data, certain inferences are permitted concerning type of farming and land quality distribution in the United States. High quality agricultural land is being intensively cultivated throughout the country—it is used for the production of a wide variety of agronomic crops under both irrigated and nonirrigated production technology. From a pragmatic standpoint, we may consider that the best quality agricultural land is already under intensive cultivation. Although some untilled high quality land may undoubtedly be found in each of the 50 states, undeveloped agronomic crop land resources are at a premium.

Irrigation alone is not a unique indicator of intensity of agricultural production. Irrigated agriculture is characteristic of those parts of the United States with hot, dry summers where plant water requirements must be supplied by man. The western states have long dominated the irrigation picture, but increasingly irrigation is being introduced in the central and

Table 2—Distribution of irrigated acreage in the U.S.†

	All land		Farms irrigating harvested cropland only		Farms irrigating pasture and unharvested land only		Farms irrigating harvested cropland pasture and other unharvested land	
	Farm acres	Acres irrigated	Acres	Acres irrigated	Acres	Acres irrigated	Acres	Acres irrigated
				1,000 acres				
				United States				
Total	918,312	38,196	134,321	22,886	12,823	963	61,789	14,347
Non-irrigated	709,378		111,435		11,860			
Irrigated		38,196		22,886		963	47,442	14,347
			17 western states and Louisiana					
Total	615,976	34,642	119,834	20,169	11,874	779	58,715	13,694
Non-irrigated	425,552		99,665		11,095		45,021	
			30 eastern states, Hawaii, Alaska					
Total	302,337	3,554	14,487	2,717	949	184	3,075	653
Non-irrigated	283,826		11,770		766		2,423	

† Source: USDC. 1969. Bureau of the Census, 1969 Census of Agriculture, Irrigation/Vol. IV.

eastern states either as a production supplement to improve overall crop productivity or as an insurance program against the potentially damaging intra-seasonal drought. Thus, irrigation does not of itself indicate greater intensity of land use or higher quality of the land being farmed.

No attempt has been made to try and develop general statistical information on *prime* and *nonprime* agricultural land in the United States. The terms are in general popular use and are intended to identify the agricultural land of greatest actual and potential productivity. However, as will be shown later, use of the terms *prime* and *nonprime* are quite arbitrary and there is no general agreement as yet as to the use and application of the terms.

III. DATA REQUIREMENTS FOR PLANNING

Plans are made on many different temporal and areal scales, for example, daily, yearly, hectares, square kilometers. In addition, modern cultivated agriculture encompasses hundreds of crop types and agronomic practices. It is therefore impossible to set down a rigid, complete check list of data requirements. One can list some major critical data needs, with the implicit understanding that specific crop or specific area planning requires examination at a finer resolution than is being attempted here. We have divided the following discussion into three sections; one on general data needs, one on data needs for irrigated lands, and one for nonirrigated lands. We know full well that there will be some overlap in the discussion, but the divisions should enable the reader to find his/her area of interest more easily.

A. General Data Needs

Perhaps the most vital data needed in the land use planning process for agriculture is that which answers the two related questions: "What are the soils on the land, and what are the capacities of the soils to grow crops?". The former may be far easier to answer than the latter question.

Soils do not occur randomly across the landscape. Each soil individual is the result of a unique combination of the five soil-forming factors; parent material, climate, biotic potential, topography, and time (Jenny, 1941; Simonson, 1968). Because of the infinite number of combinations and permutations of these five parameters, it is necessary to develop a framework within which soils can be discussed, classified, and used. A number of methods have been suggested for dealing with soils as functions of their environment. Cline (1949) writes about the model soil individual and the variability around it. The concept that there is an average or central individual and a considerable variation to each soil is critical to understanding the need and usefulness of a data base that answers "What soils exist on a landscape?". Arnold (1965) has attempted to answer the question by suggesting that there are many paths that soil genesis can take. Each results in a recognizable product. Several paths may lead to the same product but may be temporally different. Other models of soils have been presented in the literature. Most recently, the idea of modeling the process of soil formation has been given more attention (Dijkerman, 1974; Yaalon, 1975). All of these authors present soils within a frame of reference that can be discussed.

In all cases, the soil individual is surrounded by a qualitative and quantitative range of properties and characteristics. It is important to recognize that this variability exists within what is known as the soil individual. The variability extends from morphological features to chemical and physical properties of the individual (Drees & Wilding, 1973; Wilding et al., 1964; Cassel & Bauer, 1975). In addition to the existence of variability within the individual, there is variation of soils as they exist on the landscape. This variation has been examined by numerous authors (e.g., Campbell, 1973; Ike & Clutter, 1968; McCormack & Wilding, 1969; Beckett & Webster, 1971).

1. SOURCES OF SOIL INFORMATION

The recognition of the inherent complexity of soils does not preclude their being mapped. It is up to the user of the maps to have a full understanding of what a soil individual is, and what a soil mapping unit is. Soil mapping in the United States is primarily the responsibility of the Soil Conservation Service (SCS), an agency of the United States Department of Agriculture (USDA). The SCS makes soil maps of private lands in the agricultural regions of the United States.

Three major publications document the methods of the SCS and the details of the mapping and classification of the soils. These are the *National Soils Handbook,* (SCS, 1975), the *Soil Survey Manual,* (Soil Survey Staff, 1951), and *Soil taxonomy* (Soil Survey Staff, 1975). Soil maps are generally published as part of county or area soil survey reports. They are the best source of soils information for most agricultural areas in the U.S. Numerous examples of the utility of soil survey reports and soil maps exist (e.g., Bartelli et al., 1966). Most are qualitative, although some attempts have been made to assess the value of soil surveys in quantitative terms (Bie et al., 1973; Beckett & Burrough, 1971; Bie & Ulph, 1972). The true value will be very difficult to calculate because of the lack of an accurate knowledge of who uses the soil survey and for what it is used. Regardless of this, the survey is a highly useful tool for locating soils on the landscape.

Other agencies make soil surveys, but they are generally restricted to noncultivated areas. The other major federal agency responsible for soil surveys comparable to the SCS effort is the Forest Service.

In California, much of the soil mapping in privately owned forest land and upland range is the responsibility of the California Soil Vegetation Survey. This is a cooperative survey funded by the State of California, run by the Pacific Southwest Forest and Range Experiment Station, aided by the University of California (Anon., 1969). These surveys do include areas of cultivated agriculture and irrigated pasture. Other states have similar cooperative agreements to speed the acquisition of soils information.

A final source of soils information is the Agricultural Experiment Station in State Universities. State agriculture schools have made special purpose soil maps as part of the cooperative extension program, or as M.S. and Ph.D. thesis problems. The scales and quality of the maps vary considerably, but are often excellent sources of detailed planning information. A more detailed discussion of sources of soil information may be found in Chapter 4, "Soils Data."

2. DETERMINING LAND CAPABILITY

In planning, an implicit question is "Planning for what?". The same question applies to the problem of determining land capability; capability for what? This discussion is restricted to methods for determining the capability of land for cultivated agriculture. Land evaluation is a technique which integrates the collection of basic inventory information with social and economic parameters (Vink, 1976). The process of land evaluation produces results which may be either qualitative or quantitative. In the latter, land suitability is measured by input/output ratios or by benefit/cost analyses. Qualitative land evaluation results in the ranking of land areas for specific uses. The kind of land evaluation technique used will depend on the level of planning (detailed or general) and the kinds of base information available.

Each system has a set of assumptions upon which the analysis is based. In all land capability evaluation systems, land suitability is a broader concept than soil suitability. Land suitability generally is a function of soil suitability as well as other parameters. Quantitative systems tend to be used in nations with large areas of developable land, while qualitative systems seem to be more prevalent in nations where much of the suitable land has been developed for agriculture. One quantitative system of land capability classification used in the United States is the U.S. Bureau of Reclamation Irrigation Suitability Classification. A review of the system is given by Maletic and Hutchings (1967) and Olson (1974). Details of the method are described in the Bureau of Reclamation Manual (Bur. of Reclam., 1953).

The bureau's system is used for the specific purpose of determining the extent and degree of suitability of lands for irrigation. Their definition of suitability includes the expectation that there will be profitable production on a permanent basis under irrigation. Thus, the land must have a favorable "payment capacity", which is defined as the residual funds available to pay the cost of irrigation water after all other costs have been paid by the farm (Bur. of Reclam., 1953). This can be written as Eq. [1] where Y = payment capacity, X_1 = productivity rating (%), X_2 = land development cost ($), and X_3 = farm drainage cost ($). Budget analyses are used to derive the constants $a, b, c,$ and d.

$$Y = -a + bX_1 - cX_2 - dX_3 \qquad [1]$$

In addition to the payment capacity, an overall economic evaluation of the land is made which considers soil (S), drainage (D), and topographic (T) characteristics of the land within a climatic setting. The individual factors within S, T, and D which are considered in an analysis vary from land area to land area depending on their relevance for making the economic evaluation.

Land classes are developed which represent specified ranges in the economic evaluation. Six classes of land are used. Four are arable lands and two are nonarable. The arable land is land which, in adequate sized units, and if properly provided with essential improvements such as leveling, drainage, and irrigation, would have sustained production capacity to meet all production expenses and pay a cost of the irrigation project cost.

Classes 1 to 3 represent lands with progressively less capacity to repay project costs. Thus, Class 1 lands are highly suitable for irrigation farming while Class 3 lands are suitable for irrigation farming, but are approaching marginality because of deficiencies in soil, topographic, and drainage characteristics. Class 4 is a limited arable or special use class. Lands are included in this class only after special economic and engineering studies have shown them to be arable. They may include lands suitable for high value crops such as fruits and truck crops, where high production costs can be justified on the basis of high returns.

Class 5 is a special study class. Lands in it are nonarable under existing conditions but have sufficient potential that they are segregated for special study prior to the completion of classification on a project. The designation of lands as Class 5 is tentative and must be changed to arable or Class 6 by the end of a project. They may be placed in Class 5 because of specific agronomic deficiencies which require additional observation. A second cause for placing land in Class 5 is when the deficiency is known and understood, but the lands are not allowed into an arable class until the deficiencies are corrected.

Class 6 lands are nonarable and nonirrigable. They are generally steep, rough, broken, or badly eroded lands, or lands with special subsoil problems such as shallowness to bedrock or pans, or excessively coarse- or fine-textured soils.

In the Bureaus' system, subclasses are established within classes to more specifically delineate the intended use or limitation of a land area.

The Storie index is one land capability system used in California and in other parts of the world which is semiquantitative. Soil and land properties are given values based on productivity indices. These are multiplied together to give an index rating (Storie, 1964). Storie has actually developed rating systems for agricultural, timber, and irrigated lands. The rating is semiquantitative because the actual productivity figures and economic returns are not directly included as part of the index, rather, they make up the basis for the system.

There are four factors in the Storie Index which are multiplied together to give the Storie Index rating for a soil. The Storie Index for a parcel of land is calculated by multiplying the rating of each soil by the acres of that soil, adding this to the other products of acres × soils rating, and dividing by the total acres in the parcel (Eq. [2]).

$$\sum_{i=1}^{N} (\text{soil N Storie index} \times \text{acres of soil N})/\text{acres in parcel} \qquad [2]$$

The four factors used in calculating the Storie Index are A—the soil profile factor, B—the surface texture factor, C—the slope factor, and the X factor—which includes drainage, salinity, alkali, nutrients, acidity, erosion, and topography.

Factor A rates the physical quality of the soil profile. It evaluates all of the combined morphological properties except surface texture which might influence plant growth. Storie places all soils into 12 soil profile groups (Table 3). A major separation is made between primary and secondary soils. Primary soils are those that have weathered in place from bedrock (nontransported) parent material. The primary soils have been further divided into three broad rock types which cover most of the rock parent materials found in California where the system was developed. Metamorphic rocks are placed in groups VII or VIII depending on whether they are metavolcanic, or metasedimentary rocks.

The secondary soils are formed from transported parent materials. These include soils formed from glacial till, river alluvium, alluvial fan deposits, and marine terrace deposits. These are divided into five profile groups based on the degree of profile development. Profile development is defined as the presence and thickness of an argillic horizon or hard pan. Profile group I soils are young soils without an argillic horizon. Profile

Table 3—Rating of soils on the basis of profile characteristics.†

Soil profile-group	Group number	Development of soil	Topography	Profile factor A
Unweathered or undeveloped profiles	I	Secondary soils, no argillic horizon	Flat or very gently sloping	100
Slightly developed profiles	II	Slightly developed secondary soils	Very gently to gently sloping	95–100
Moderately developed profiles	III	Moderately developed argillic horizon	Terraces, valley floors	80–95
Strongly weathered secondary soils	IV	Clay pan soils	Older plains or terraces	40–80
Maturely weathered hardpan soils	V	Hardpan soils	Older plains or terraces	5–80
Primary soils on hard igneous bedrock	VII—{ I ¦ IV	Formed in place on igneous bedrock	Hilly, rolling, steep, upland	10–90
Primary soils on hard sedimentary bedrock	VIII—{ I ¦ IV	Formed in place on hard sedimentary rocks	Hilly, rolling, steep, upland	10–100
Primary soils on soft sedimentary material	IX—{ I ¦ IV	Formed in place on soft sedimentary material	Hilly, rolling to steep upland	20–90

† Adapted from Storie (1964).

groups II, III, and IV have increasingly more pronounced expression of the argillic horizon. Profile group V is reserved for soils having hard pans. Profile Group VI was originally reserved for soils with clay pans resting on bedrock. This group has been incorporated into profile groups VII through IX. We have found it convenient to use designations of VII-I, VII-II through VII-IV to describe the profile development in primary soils. In Stories' system (Storie, 1964) he uses a subscript "C" to indicate soils formed on bedrock with clay pans. The I to IV system adds considerable flexibility to the system.

Numerical values for the A factor are assigned based on the profile group and depth to the argillic horizon, hard pan, or bedrock. Thus, a profile group V soil with a hard pan at 12 inches (30.5 cm) would receive an A value of 20, while a similar soil with a hard pan at 36 inches (91.5 cm) would receive an A value of 50. These ratings reflect resistance to root penetration in the soil, rooting, and water-holding volume of the soil, and ease of soil tillage.

Factor B rates the surface soil texture. Texture is used as an index of consistence, porosity, permeability, and tilth. The medium-textured soils rate the highest because they have the highest available water-holding capacity and are physically the easiest textures to manage. These are the loam, silt loam, and fine sandy loam textures. Clays (50–70), coarse sands, (30–60), and stony or gravelly sands (10–40) are rated lowest. There is a considerable range in the value of Factor B for any one texture because of the allowable range of percent sand, silt, and clay in each texture.

Factor C rates the slope on which the soil is found. Slope clearly influences the use of the land. Steep slopes are difficult to till, are subject to erosion, and require special planting and harvesting techniques. Two considerations are given to slope; the actual slope percent and slope complexity. A nearly level (0–2%) site received 100% while a very steep (>45%) slope receives 5–30%. A gently sloping (3–8%) area is rated from 95–100% while the same slope percent if undulating, is rated at 85–100%.

Factor X includes properties of the soil exclusive of those considered in factors $A, B,$ and C. They may be considered the changeable factors. Unlike profile group, surface texture, or slope, routine management can influence the X factor. The X factor includes drainage, alkali or salt content, general nutrient level, acidity, erosion, and microrelief. Well-drained soils get a rating of 100. Less well-drained soils, and those subject to frequent overflow, get ratings between 10 and 90% depending on the degree of problem. Salinity, alkalinity, and toxic conditions such as boron toxicity or Ca/Mg ratios of serpentine soils are rated in much the same way. Those soils with no problems are rated at 100%. A soil with a strong salinity, alkalinity, or toxicity problem may be rated as low as 5%.

Nutrient level is derived from plot tests, farmers' experience, and yield records. It is the ability of the soil to supply N, P, K, and micronutrients to plants. It is a somewhat subjective index and the X factor is only decreased slightly even when a soil is judged to have poor fertility (80–90%). In cases where soils are so acid that injury to field crops is likely, additional reduction is made in the X factor. One example of a location where acidity is a problem is the reclaimed tidal marshes of San Francisco Bay.

Soil erosion, as viewed in the field, is used to reduce the X factor. Both wind and water erosion are considered, and detrimental deposition from wind causes a reduction in the X Factor.

The final component of the X Factor is microrelief. Irregularities in the ground surface such as channels, hogwallows, hummocks, and dunes reduce the X value.

Tables 4 and 5 are profile descriptions of two California soils. The Storie Index can be calculated from these descriptions as examples of how the system works in determining land capability. The Yolo series is a young soil formed on alluvium from sedimentary and metasedimentary rocks. It has no argillic horizon and has no rooting limitation within 150 cm. The soil is therefore a Profile Group I, A factor rating = 100%. It has a silt loam surface texture which earns a rating of 100% for Factor B. This profile oc-

Table 4—Profile description of the Yolo soil series.†

Ap1—   0–5 cm—Grayish brown (2.5Y 5/2) silt loam, very dark grayish brown (10YR 3/2) moist; moderate thick platy structure; hard, friable, slightly sticky, plastic; many very fine roots; many very fine interstitial and tubular pores; neutral (pH 6.7); abrupt wavy boundary (5 to 25 cm thick).

Ap2— 5–20 cm—Grayish brown (2.5Y 5/2) silt loam, dark brown (10YR 3/3) moist; massive; hard, friable, sticky, plastic; many very fine roots; common very fine tubular pores; neutral (pH 7.1); clear wavy boundary (7.5 to 25 cm thick).

A13— 20–48 cm—Grayish brown (2.5Y 5/2) silt loam, dark brown (10YR 3/3) rubbed, very dark grayish brown (10YR 3/2) coatings moist; weak coarse subangular blocky structure; hard, friable, slightly sticky, plastic; common very fine roots; many very fine tubular and clusters of interstitial pores associated with worm casts; few thin clay films on peds and continuous thin clay films in pores; neutral (pH 7.2); clear, wavy boundary (15 to 30 cm thick).

A14— 48–66 cm—Grayish brown (2.5Y 5/2) silt loam, very dark grayish brown (10YR 3/2) moist, massive; slightly hard, friable, slightly sticky, plastic; many very fine and few fine roots; many very fine tubular pores; neutral (pH 7.3); clear irregular boundary (15 to 33 cm thick).

C1— 66–84 cm—Brown (10YR 5/3) silt loam, olive brown (2.5Y 4/4) moist; massive; slightly hard, friable, slightly sticky, plastic; common very fine roots; common very fine tubular and clusters of interstitial pores associated with worm casts; mildly alkaline (pH 7.4); clear irregular boundary (18 to 61 cm thick).

C2— 84–104 cm—Pale brown (10YR 6/3) silt loam, olive brown (2.5Y 4/4) moist; dark grayish brown (2.5Y 4/2) stains in root channels moist; massive; soft, very friable, slightly sticky, slightly plastic; few very fine roots; common very fine tubular and many very fine interstitial pores; mildly alkaline (pH 7.4); abrupt wavy boundary (20 to 76 cm thick).

A1b—104–147 cm—Grayish brown (2.5Y 5/2) silty clay loam, very dark grayish brown (2.5Y 3/2) moist; massive; slightly hard, friable, very sticky, plastic; few very fine roots; common very fine tubular pores; mildly alkaline (pH 7.4); clear wavy boundary (0 to 20 cm thick).

C3—147–165 cm—Pale brown (10YR 6/3) silt loam, mottled olive brown (2.5Y 4/4) and olive (5Y 4/3) moist; massive; slightly hard, very friable, slightly sticky, slightly plastic; few very fine roots; many very fine tubular and interstitial pores; mildly alkaline (pH 7.5).

† Adapted from the Yolo County Soil Survey Report. Soil Conserv. Serv., USDA. 1972.

Table 5—Profile description of the Hotaw soil series.

O1 and O2—2–0 cm—Litter and duff.
    A1—0–30 cm—Grayish-brown (10YR 5/2) coarse sandy loam, dark brown (10YR 3/3)
            when moist; moderate, fine, granular structure; soft, very friable, non-
            sticky, and nonplastic; many very fine, fine, and medium roots; many
            very fine and fine tubular and interstitial pores; slightly acid; clear,
            wavy boundary.
    B1t—30–56 cm—Pale-brown (10YR 6/3) heavy coarse sandy loam, brown (10YR 4/3)
            when moist; moderate, medium, subangular blocky structure; hard, fri-
            able, nonsticky and nonplastic; many very fine, fine, and medium
            roots; many very fine and fine tubular and interstitial pores; few thin
            clay films in pores; medium acid; clear, smooth boundary.
    B2t—56–88 cm—Light-brown (7.5YR 6/4) sandy clay loam, brown (7.5YR 4/4) when
            moist; moderate, medium and coarse, subangular blocky structure; very
            hard, firm, sticky and slightly plastic; many fine and medium roots;
            common very fine and fine tubular pores; many moderately thick clay
            films on ped faces, in pores, and as bridges; strongly acid; clear, wavy
            boundary.
    C > 88 cm—Weathered granodiorite.

curs on a level 0–1% slope, thus getting 100% for Factor C and it has no drainage, salinity, nutrient, pH, erosion, or microrelief problems. It gets 100% for X. The Storie rating for the Yolo silt loam is (1.0 × 1.0 × 1.0 × 1.0) × 100 = 100%.

The second soil is formed from hard igneous rock in the Sierra Nevada. It is classified as a Profile Group VII and because it is moderately well developed, it is given the modifier III. Thus, it is Profile Group VII-III. The Profile Factor A for Profile Group VII soils with 2–3 ft to bedrock ranges from 50–70. Since the soil is barely 3 ft deep it is given the lowest rating (50). The surface texture of coarse sandy loam earns a rating of 90 for the B factor. The soil is found in a range of slopes up to 50%. At this site it is found on a 45% slope. This gets a C factor rating of 30%. This soil is well drained, nonsaline and nonalkali, has fair nutrient level (95%), is moderately eroded (90%), and is not affected by microrelief. The Storie Index rating for this soil is (0.50 × 0.90 × 0.30 × 0.95 × 0.90) × 100 = 12%. It is obviously not an agricultural soil and, in fact, one would normally use the Storie Timber Rating for this site rather than an agricultural rating.

The different percentages have been grouped by Storie to give Storie Grades. Grade I is excellent agricultural soil (80–100%). Grade II (60–79%) soils are good for agriculture, but yields are less than for grade I under the same management, and fewer kinds of crops can be grown. Grade III soils (40–59%) are fair for agriculture and may be excellent for specialized crops (i.e., rice) but generally have restrictions which need major inputs. Grade 4 (20–40%) and Grade 5 (10–19%) are poor and very poor for agriculture, and Grade 6 < 10% is nonagricultural.

This system has been given major use in California and several Latin American countries. Its major advantage is that it is semiquantitative and it provides a numerical classification which can be coded and used in advanced land classification data handling systems. A major disadvantage is the user must be thoroughly familiar with soil morphology and geology.

Most other commonly used systems for determining land capability are qualitative. No attempt is made to quantify the variables. Three that are used are the USDA system of land capability classification (Klingebiel & Montgomery, 1973), the Canadian system of Soil Capability for agriculture (Anon., 1972a), and the new International System (Vink, 1976; Brinkman & Smyth, 1973; Beek & Bennema, 1972a).

The USDA system is based on a number of important assumptions which need to be understood before it can be used effectively. First, it is a capability classification based on climate and permanent soil characteristics. It is an interpretive grouping of soils, and as such it has biases. One of these biases is the major assumption of a moderately high level of management and a favorable input/output ratio on the land being classified. It does not assume that the land is classified according to its most profitable use. "Permanent" soil characteritics are not excess water or limitation of water, stones, soluble salts, alkali, or overflow, provided that it is economically feasible to alter these conditions. Thus, capability class may change with major reclamation projects.

Soil properties are the major considerations in the system. Soils are divided into two broad categories; arable soils are grouped according to the potentialities and limitations for sustained production of the common cultivated crops that do not require specialized site conditioning treatment. Nonarable soils are grouped for production of permanent vegetation according to the risks of soil damage if mismanaged (Klingebiel & Montgomery, 1973).

The system consists of three major categories; class, subclass, and units. There are eight classes (I–VIII) which are groups of capability subclasses or units that have the same relative degree of hazard or limitation. Class I soils have the least degree of hazard or limitation and VIII has the most. Classes I through IV are arable soils while V through VIII are nonarable. In special circumstances classes V and VI may be capable of producing crops.

Four subclasses exist in the system. These are groups of capability units which have the same major conservation problem. The four subclasses are *e*—erosion and runoff, *W*—excess water, *s*—root zone limitations, and *c*—climatic limitations. Soils are placed into the *e* class when their susceptibility to erosion is the major problem or where past erosion damage is a major limitation. The *w* subclass is used for soils where excess water due to poor soil drainage, wetness, high water table, and overflow is the major limitation. Soils that have limitations such as stones, low moisture-holding capacity, low fertility which is difficult to correct, salinity or alkalinity, or shallow root zone are placed in subclass *s*. In cases where the only major limitation is temperature or lack of moisture, the *c* subclass is used.

Capability units specify major management problems or limitations. Thus, soils of capability unit 1 in California all have erosion as the major limiting factor. Data needed to place soils into the system can be determined at the site (Table 6). A thorough understanding of soil morphology is needed to use the system correctly. One major limitation to the system is

Table 6—Guide for placing soils in land capability classes in California.†

Capability class	Effective soil depth (inches)	Surface layer texture Irrigated	Surface layer texture Dryland	Permeability	Drainage class	Available water capacity	Slope, % Irrigated	Slope, % Dry	Erosion hazard	Flooding hazard	Salinity EC×10³ at 25°C (mmhos).	Alkali	Toxic substances	Frost-free season (days)
I	>40	Moderately coarse, medium moderate slow	Moderately coarse, medium moderate slow	Moderately slow to moderately rapid	Well or moderately well >60 inch	>7.5 inch Average AWC >0.13 inch/inch Surface foot AWC >0.13 inch/inch	0–2	0–5	None or slight	None or rare	<4 (none)	None	None	>140
II	>40	Coarse (loamy sand) or loamy fine sand to fine (<60% clay) may be gravelly	Moderately coarse, medium, moderately fine and fine (<60% clay)	Rapid through slow	Somewhat poorly through somewhat excessive >36 inch	>5 inch Average AWC >0.08 inch/inch	0–5	0–9	None through moderate	None through occasional	<8 (none or slight)	None to slight	None to slight	>100
III	>20	Any, may be gravelly or cobbly	Moderately coarse, medium, moderately fine & fine may be gravelly or cobbly	Rapid through very slow	Poorly through excessive >20 inch	>3.75 inch Average AWC >0.06 inch/inch	0–9	0–15	None through high	None through occasional	<16	None to moderate	None to moderate	> 80
IV	>10	Any, may be very gravelly or cobbly or stony.	Coarse (loamy sand) or loamy fine sand to fine may be gravelly, cobbly or stony	Any	Poorly through excessive >20 inch	>2.5 inch Average AWC >0.04 inch/inch	0–15	0–30	None through very high	None through occasional	<16	None to moderate	None to strong	> 50
V	>20	Any and very stony or very cobbly	Any and very stony or very cobbly	Any	Somewhat excessive through very poorly	>2.5 inch Average AWC >0.06 inch/inch Irrigated: Root zone >5.0 inch average AWC >0.08 inch/inch Nonirrigated	0–15	0–15	None to slight	None through frequent	<8	None or slight	None to strong	> 80
VI	>10	Any and very stony or very cobbly	Any and very stony or very cobbly	Any	Any	>2.5 inch Average AWC >0.06 inch/inch	0–30	0–50	None to high	None through frequent	All— Irrigated <8 none or slight dry-land	All— Irrigated or slight dry-land	None to strong	> 50
VII	Any	Any	Any	Any	Any	>1 inch	<75		None to very high	Any	Any	Any	Any	Any
VIII	Any	Any	Any	Any	Any	Any	Any	Any	Any	Any	Any	Any	Any	Any

† Adapted from the Soil Conservation Service guide.

that many of the ratings are devised for commonly grown crops that require well-drained level soils. There are areas (notably California) and crops (e.g., rice) which do not fit neatly into the system. For this reason, caution should be used when employing this or any other system for rating land. One must know the reason the rating is being made and the assumptions of the rating system.

The Yolo and Hotaw soils can be placed into capability classes using Table 6. Table 6 is read from left to right and top to bottom. Like the Storie Index, a single property can drop the soil out of Class I. However, the Class II soil can have one or many limitations and remain in Class II. Starting at the top left, and reading across, the Yolo soil has an effective rooting depth greater than 40 inches (101.5 cm), under irrigation it has a moderately fine surface texture, rapid permeability, and it is well drained. The available water-holding capacity (determined on the basis of texture) is greater than 7.5 inches (19 cm) and the slope is less than 2%. There is no erosion hazard, flooding hazard, salinity, alkalinity, or toxicity. The frost-free season is over 140 days. Thus, Yolo silt loam is a Class I soil.

The Hotaw series has an effective rooting depth of >20 but <40 inches (>51 but <101.5 cm) and drops to Class III. It meets the criteria for Class III soil until the slope column is reached. For nonirrigated use the slope of 45% drops the soil into Capability Class VI. It meets all other requirements for Class VI.

These two examples illustrate that the Storie Index and USDA systems are not entirely parallel. The criteria used to rate the soils are both qualitatively and quantitatively different. In the Storie Index, the soils pedologic character is rated, whereas in the USDA system, it does not enter into the evaluation. An example of a quantitative difference between the two systems can be seen in the treatment of effective soil depth. In the USDA system, a soil with a 40-inch (101.5-cm) depth may be a Class I soil. However, in the Storie system, depending on the profile group, a rating of as low as 40% is possible with a depth of only 40 inches (101.5 cm). This point is being made to warn the reader that the two systems do not weight parameters the same and, thus, one system can not be substituted for the other with the same expected results.

The Canadian system (Anon., 1972a) is patterned after the USDA system with a few exceptions. The interpretive grouping is developed from soil mapping units. There are 7 classes and 13 subclasses. Capability Units are not part of the Canadian system. Organic soils are classified separately. The assumptions used in the Canadian system are essentially the same as those of the USDA.

Classes 1, 2, and 3 are soils capable of sustained production of common cultivated crops. Class 1 soils are the best. They have no significant limitations in use for crops. Class 2 soils have moderate limitations that restrict the range of crops or require moderate conservation practices. The limitations of soils in the class include climate, moderate effects of erosion, poor soil structure or slow permeability, gentle to moderate slopes, poor fertility which is easily correctable, and wetness correctable by drainage.

Class 3 soils have moderately severe limitations to cropping including those mentioned for Class 2 plus problems of stoniness, poor drainage, frequent overflow, restricted rooting zone, and moderate salinity.

Soils in Class 4 are marginal for crops due to severe limitations. Either the range in crops is restricted or special conservation practices are needed to farm the land. Class 5 soils have such severe limitations that they are not capable of sustained cultivation, but are capable of use for sustained production of native or tame species of forage plants. Some special crops may be grown on Class 5 soils, provided they have unusually intensive management. Permanent pasture and range are the most suitable uses for Class 5 soils.

Class 6 soils have severe limitations which restrict their use to wild (unimproved) pasture, and Class 7 soils have no capability for arable culture or permanent pasture. Forestry uses of these soils is not excluded from any of these classes. Neither are recreation or other uses. Soils for these uses are evaluated under different systems within the overall Canadian Land Classification program (Anon., 1972b; McCormack, 1971).

The 13 subclasses within classes group soils according to the kind of limitation for agriculture (Table 7). Guidelines for placing soils into classes and subclasses are made on the National and Regional levels in order to account for the large diversity of Canadian conditions. The Yolo soil (Table 4) should be a Class 1 soil. The Hotaw soil (Table 5) would not be classified by this system because it is a forest soil.

Vink (1976) describes a qualitative system being developed for international use by Brinkman and Smyth (1973) and Beek and Bennema (1972b). This system has three orders and an undefined (unlimited) number of classes, subclasses, and units. Unlike the Storie, USDA, and Canadian

Table 7—Capability subclasses within the Canadian soil capability classification for agriculture.

Subclass identification	Meaning
C	Adverse climate: low growing season temperatures, short growing season, inadequate precipitation.
D	Undesirable soil structure and/or low permeability—soils difficult to till, shallow root zone due to factors other than high water table (W) or bedrock (R).
E	Erosion—actual damage limits land's usefulness.
F	Low fertility—due to lack of plant nutrients, acidity, alkalinity, low exchange capacity, carbonates, toxic compounds.
I	Inundation by streams or lakes.
M	Moisture limitation due to drouthiness.
N	Salinity—class 3 soils or lower.
P	Stoniness—hinders tillage.
R	Consolidated bedrock at depths <3 ft.
S	Adverse soil characteristics—used in place of D, F, M, N on 1:250,000 maps or as a combination of more than one factor.
T	Topography—percent slope and complexity.
W	Excess water—inadequate soil drainage, high water table, seepage.
X	Cumulative minor adverse conditions. Two or more moderate limitations.

systems, the International system considers more variables than soil. The primary decision and the one of highest significance is the placement of a land parcel into an order. Order 1 contains land which is suitable for use for sustained production which will justify recurrent inputs without unacceptable risks to land resources on site or in adjacent areas. In the definition of suitable land given by Vink (1976), the words "Use for the defined purpose in the defined manner" is used rather than production. He makes the point that the classification is highly dependent on what use is being made of the land. In a sense, this classification scheme might best be discussed under the quantitative systems section because the primary determinent for placing land in Order 1 is its economic return to the land owner. This involves detailed political, social, economic, and physical resource information.

Order 2 lands are those which are "conditionally suitable." These are lands which normally would be unsuitable for use, but under special management, which might include special systems of tillage and cropping, the land might be suitable. Another example would be small parcels of land where high value crops, under very intensive production management, could be grown.

Lands placed in Order 3 are those which are unsuitable for sustained use. Land may be placed into Class 3 if they do not produce a net positive gain for the farmer. They may also be placed into Class 3 if their use would produce upkeep and/or conservation problems.

The classes, subclasses, and units within an order are unlimited in number and are left open for each project. The classes serve to distinguish degrees of suitability for a land utilization type. Decimal notation is suggested to separate classes. As an example, Order 1 could have the classes: 1.1, highly suitable; 1.2, moderately suitable; and 1.3, marginally suitable (Brinkman & Smyth, 1973). Other classes can be added if they are appropriate, and if sufficient data are available.

Land suitability subclasses are divisions within classes which distinguish the nature of the limitation(s). Letters are used to represent the major limitation. The number and choice of limiting critria are left open to the individual interpreters. Examples of subclasses are w—wetness, t—topography, s—soil limitation.

These are examples of systems currently in use for appraising the suitability of land for agriculture. Internationally there are other systems (FAO, 1974), but those described here serve to illustrate the major types and how they are used. It is quite obvious that they differ in philosophy, data requirements, and use. The differences reflect different needs and differences in available data. The USBR and International systems require significantly more social and economic data then the Storie, USDA, or Canadian systems. These last three are primarily soil-based systems, they assume availability of inputs and ability of the land manager to use them correctly.

Once the location of soils on the landscape has been determined, and the capability of the land has been evaluated, specific data are needed to plan the use of the agricultural land. These data needs are the subject of the next section. The section has been divided into irrigated and nonirrigated land use for convenience. In many cases the data needs will be the same, but the degree of detail may be different.

B. Data Needs for Irrigated Agriculture

This section does not serve as a checklist for the planning of land for irrigated agriculture. Rather, several major areas of data needs are discussed relative to irrigated agriculture with California used as the major example. The four general kinds of data needs are (i) water-source, availability, and quality (ii) climate, (iii) topography, and (iv) soils.

1. WATER

Surface water and ground water are the sources for irrigation water. Surface water is discussed in detail by Riesbol et al. (1967). Surface water is obtained from natural precipitation which has been stored in reservoirs or lakes, or which is in perennial flowing waterways. Considerable data are needed for planning an irrigation project based on surface water. Data needs include precipitation, snow accumulation, temperature, humidity, evaporation, streamflow, and the storage capacity of lakes and reservoirs in order to predict supply.

In addition to supply quantity, supply quality data are needed. This includes suspended load and dissolved salt load. High sediment load of streams reduces the storage capacity behind dams and can be detrimental to the soil. Perhaps the most important quality consideration is the total concentration of cations and anions in the water. This includes Ca, Mg, Na, K, B, CO_3, HCO_3, SO_4, Cl, and NO_3. Boron is toxic to plants and the presence of over 4 ppm B in water supplies makes growing of most plants difficult. The total concentration of salts is vital in determining what effect the irrigation water will have on soil salinity and alkalinity. Electrical conductivity (EC) is used most often as a measure of total salt concentration.

· Sodium (Na) is particularly important because of its effect upon soil. When Na is present in solution and on the exchange complex of soils, it causes adverse chemical and physical properties to develop. The U.S. Salinity Lab. Staff (1954) developed a sodium-adsorption-ratio (SAR) as an index of sodium hazard.

$$SAR = Na^+/(Ca^{2+} + Mg^{2+}/2)^{1/2} \qquad [3]$$

SAR is used as one measure of irrigation water quality. The concentration of Na, Ca, and Mg in meq/liter is used in Eq. [3].

Thus, there are many facets to irrigation water quality. These apply equally to water from surface and subsurface sources. In most cases, the standard water quality indices are adequate to evaluate a water supply. However, in areas where irrigation has never been attempted, a rigorous and complete analysis of the water is necessary to insure that the irrigation scheme will be successful over a long term.

Subsurface water is obtained from wells which tap ground water (aquifer) supplies. Development of ground water supplies requires a knowledge of the extent of the supply and rates of recharge. Recharge, or refilling during wet periods, is necessary to maintain a water supply. Depletion of ground water supplies is inevitable in areas where use exceeds natural and artificial recharge. In some areas of California, depletion of the ground water supply has led to as much as 3.6 m of surface subsidance.

Artificial recharge is practiced in many arid and semiarid areas to supplement natural supplies of ground water. The quality of this recharge water is as important as the quality of the water used for irrigation. Thus, the source, availability, and quality of recharge water must be as much a part of an irrigation plan as the irrigation water which is applied directly to crops.

2. CLIMATE

Climate is an important factor in irrigated agriculture because it directly influences the kinds and quality of soils as well as the kinds of crops which can be grown in an area. Climate is particularly important in influencing the kinds of crops which can be grown and therefore the economics of irrigation. As an example, citrus and avocados in California can be irrigated using expensive drip and sprinkler irrigation systems because they are high value crops. Similar or better soils in a climate which can only support alfalfa or sugar beets could not be irrigated profitably using these systems.

In addition, the likelihood of frost, the occurrence of intense storms, and high winds all affect the kinds of crops which can be grown and the economics of irrigation in an area. Data on precipitation amounts, and likelihood of droughts is also required in planning for irrigated agriculture, because of the need to refill reservoirs and recharge ground water supplies. The needed data may be for areas far from the site where the irrigation is to take place, but it is still very necessary.

3. TOPOGRAPHY

Degree of slope and slope complexity affect the irrigability of land. They affect costs and design of irrigation systems, erosion hazards, and drainage requirements. They influence the kinds of crops which can be grown and the irrigation method to be used. These interact to determine the economic feasibility of an irrigation project. There is no single set slope percent above which irrigation is not attempted. Recently, with the advent of drip irrigation, slopes as high as 70–80% are being used to grow citrus and avocados in Southern California. Maletic and Hutchings (1967) give a range of slopes from 35% as an upper limit for irrigation in the Pacific Northwest, to 3% as an upper limit in the Gulf Coastal Plain. Complexity affects the size and shape of fields and the type and number of irrigation structures required. Sprinkler and drip irrigation systems are especially useful for complex slopes.

4. SOILS

Soil data needs are much the same for irrigated and nonirrigated agriculture (see Section III. C. 3). The most important properties are those which relate to soil water relations. These include water-holding capacity, infiltration and percolation rates, water release curve, and drainability. Many of these properties can be inferred from other soils data when they can not be measured directly. Maletic and Hutchings (1967) refer to these as *performance characteristics*. Indeed, they do describe the performance of soils in taking in, holding, and releasing water.

Other soil data needs of importance include the clay mineralogy, exchange capacity, and cation content. These data relate to the soils salinity and alkalinity. From these data inferrences can be made on the likelihood of problems arising from irrigation and/or the need for or difficulty of soil rehabilitation because of salts. There is a wide range of soil characteristics and combinations of characteristics which influence its irrigability and productivity. These characteristics interact with climate and topography to determine the economic return and feasibility of irrigation.

The capacity of the soil to be drained, either naturally or through improved drainage works, is a major characteristic in determining its irrigation potential. This includes material below the solum. This is a major difference between soil data needs for irrigated and nonirrigated agriculture. Surface drainage is the removal of excess water from the land surface regardless of source. Subsurface drainage is the removal of excess water from within the soil profile. This is accomplished through downward or lateral movement of water and the control of the ground water table.

Soil drainage involves the recognition of drainage problems through examination of the soil and crops growing on the soil and the development of plans for surface and subsurface removal of excess water. These topics are dealt with at length by Luthin (1957).

C. Data Needs for Nonirrigated Agriculture

In humid areas or dry-land agriculture the availability of water and its quality is more a function of climate than in irrigated agriculture. Thus, climate, topography, and soils, which all play an important role, will be discussed.

1. CLIMATE

Temperature, precipitation, potential evapotranspiration, and likelihood of damaging winds are four major climatic variables needed for planning cultivated land. Microclimate, except for special cases where protection from frost is particularly important, is not as important as overall climate. Mean annual temperature as well as seasonal norms and variations around the mean are the major temperature variables needed. These are less critical for pasture and grain crops than for frost-sensitive crops. Growing season length for 0 and −3°C periods are needed. Because of the tremendous variety of crops grown in the United States, no single guideline for "best" temperature regime can be given.

Both winter and growing season precipitation data are needed. Winter season precipitation by monthly means and range are useful in forcasting soil water recharge and snow cover. Snow cover is important in areas for frost protection for winter grains as well as for potential soil water recharge. Growing season precipitation amount, intensity, and distribution are needed. Amount is important for both dryland crops and humid area crops. Under either cropping system, the likelihood of drought will determine the number of successful and unsuccessful crop years. Distribution of precipitation throughout the growing season is as important as the actual quantity of precipitation. An even distribution throughout the growing season is most useful, provided that heavy rains do not damage the crop near or during harvest or do not delay harvest due to wet soils. An uneven distribution requires that more be known about soil water holding capacity. It also limits the kinds of crops that can be grown.

Along with temperature and precipitation, potential evapotranspiration (PET) is a useful variable for which to have some data. Although it is not as critical as precipitation and temperature, it can give a useful measure of crop water needs.

Data of this kind are available from the National Oceanic and Atmospheric Administration (NOAA), State Weather Bureaus, County offices, University experiment stations, and Federal parks and forests. The United States is fortunate in having many years of accurate weather records with which to make forcasts and plans.

Last, the liklihood of occurrence of damaging winds and other weather phenomenon that may be damaging to crops needs to be known. Although all weather is stochastic in nature, and there is no absolute certainty of predicting problems, every effort needs to be made to determine if high winds that could damage or desiccate crops, or damaging rain or hail, frequently occur.

2. TOPOGRAPHY

Topographic data needs include slope percent and complexity of slope. These two factors affect the ease with which machinery can be used, the need for special cultivation practices such as contour plowing and strip cropping, the potential erosion, and soil drainage.

Steep slopes reduce the ease of cultivation and make special cultivation practices necessary to reduce soil erosion. What are "steep" slopes? To a certain extent, this depends on the use. Cultivation becomes difficult at 9% slope and hazardous over 15% under most irrigation practices. This is reflected in the USDA capability system where a 15% slope causes a soil to be placed into capability Class IV (Klingebiel & Montgomery, 1973). In Britain, a similar land gradient scheme is used. Slopes of 16–34% restrict the use of harvestors such as combines and increase the difficulty of loading trailers (Bibby & Mackney, 1969). They exclude mechanized operations above 54% slope. The USDA system has 30% slope under nonirrigated agriculture as the maximum that can be cultivated. Storie (1964) rates both slope and slope complexity, but only reduces the C Factor to 70% for a 30% slope. This would still be a Grade 2 soil if it had no other problems. He severely penalizes soils over 30%. The Canadian system of land classification considers slope and pattern (complexity). Slopes greater than 15% are placed in Class 5, 6, or 7T.

Thus, it appears that 15% slope or more is considered "steep". There are instances where much steeper slopes can be cultivated. One example frequently cited is the use of hand-built terraces in South East Asia. Another example is the growing of high-value citrus and avocado orchards on 50–70% slopes in Southern California. In these instances, special precautions are needed to reduce the erosion hazard.

Steeper land can be used for pasture because no cultivation is required. Above 30% slope, soil improvement such as liming and fertilization become very difficult and animal use greatly increases the chance of excessive erosion.

Slope complexity further complicates management of cultivated land. A steep straight slope can be managed more easily than an undulating complex slope. Complex land forms such as those one finds in glaciated terrain with concave and convex slopes require special cultivation procedures which restrict the use of large-scale (and generally more economical) equipment. Storie (1964) recognized this and included microrelief in the X factor. An increasing reduction in rating was given from smooth (100%) to dunes (10%).

Topography also affects soil drainage. Soils in basin positions or in pot holes are likely to be poorly drained in all but the driest climates. These are positions which require artificial drainage to remove excess water. The source of excess water is surface and subsurface runoff from the surrounding slopes.

3. SOILS

The number of soil variables one could consider in planning agricultural land is very large. The kinds of data which are collected in soil laboratories range from simple morphologic descriptions such as Table 4 to very detailed chemical and mineralogical data sets for one or more horizons. It is neither practical nor necessary to expect to have all possible data on soils of an area before making planning decisions. Those characteristics that are most important for planning purposes depends, to some extent, on what use will be made of the land. For this discussion on nonirrigated crop and pasture, some soil data are less important than others. This discussion is meant to be a guide because in some areas, special analyses will be needed. As an example of this, exchangeable sodium data may be important in semiarid and arid areas. However, they will not be useful in the humid areas, while exchangeable aluminum data might be.

The approach taken by Beek and Bennema (1972b) is useful to consider before elaborating on specific soil data needs. They discuss data needs with respect to major land qualities. A major land quality is "a complex attribute of the land which acts largely as a separate factor on the performance of a certain use. The expression of a land quality is determined by a set of interacting single or compound land characteristics. . ..." Each characteristic is given a weighted importance as in the Storie System. In the Beek and Bennema (1972b) system soil texture is a characteristic rather than a land quality while availability of water and nutrients, and the possibility of mechanization and resistance to erosion, are major land qualities. These qualities can not be measured directly, but are determined by measureable land characteristics. These characteristics are the data needs one must have for effective land use planning.

The soil data (other than climate and slope) used in various capability classification schemes is a useful guide in selecting specific variables of interest. Soil characteristics from six land classification systems are outlined in Table 8. The major data needs include soil drainage, presence of salts or alkali, erosion, soil depth, and available water-holding capacity.

Soil drainage status is important because it reflects both the availability of water and/or the need for special drainage schemes to make land cultivatable. Natural soil drainage data must be combined with climate for a full picture of the soil. Excessive drainage in soils of humid areas may not be detrimental if sufficient well-spaced precipitation occurs. In dry areas, where winter precipitation must be stored for summer crops, excessively drained soils would be poor ones for nonirrigated agriculture. At the other extreme, poorly drained soils in both humid and dry climates need artificial drainage to be useful for most crops. Drainage implies added costs which must be considered in the planning process.

Sodicity and salinity are major problems in arid and semiarid climates

Table 8—Comparison of data types from six capability classification systems.

Data†	Storie (1964)	Klingebiel and Montgomery (1973)	Canada (Anon., 1972a)	Beek and Bennema (1972a)	Obeng (1968)	Bartelli (1968)
Texture	✓	✓			✓	
Drainage	✓	✓	✓	✓	✓	✓
Alkali	✓	✓	✓	✓		
Salts	✓	✓	✓	✓		
Nutrients	✓		✓	✓	✓	✓
Acidity	✓		✓			
Erosion	✓	✓	✓	✓	✓	
Soil depth	✓	✓	✓		✓	✓
Permeability		✓	✓	✓	✓	
Available water		✓	✓	✓	✓	✓
Flooding		✓	✓			
Toxic substances		✓	✓			
Stoniness		✓	✓			

† Major soil qualities.

and, along with toxicities, need to be considered in land use planning for cultivated agriculture. Two considerations are needed. The first is the current status of the soils and the second is the potential salt problem which could occur after use of the soil has begun.

In the first instance, reclamation needs to be considered for saline and/or alkali soils. Salinity (excess salts dominated by Ca and Mg) is the easier (but not simple) problem to solve. Drainage and sufficient high quality leaching water are all that are required for reclamation. Reclamation of alkali soils, where Na^+ is the dominant cation, requires drainage, leaching, addition of Ca and Mg salts, and reduction of soil pH. Thus, it is the more complex and more expensive reclamation procedure.

Actual or potential soil erosion are major agricultural problems which must be considered prior to planning. Erosion reduces soil fertility through removal of nutrients. In addition, the capacity of the soil to retain nutrients is diminished through loss of organic matter and clay. The materials lost from a soil through erosion become pollutants when they reach streams and lakes. The creation of gullies due to severe erosion reduces the size of fields and makes cultivation difficult or impractical.

Actual erosion may be determined through on-site inspection or aerial photo interpretation if erosion is in advanced stages. Determining potential erosion is more of a problem and has been the subject of serious research for over 50 years in the United States. The most widely used tool for predicting erosion potential of an area is the Wischmeier and Smith (1965) soil loss equation

$$A = RKLSCP \qquad [4]$$

where A = soil loss in tons per acre, R is a rainfall erosivity factor, K is a soil erodibility factor, L is a slope length factor, S is a slope percent factor, C is a crop cover factor, and P is an erosion control practice factor. The equation was derived for areas east of the Rocky Mountains, and it has been very useful for those conditions.

The relative erodibility of soils is often of interest. Wischmeier et al. (1971) developed a nomograph for determining relative soil erodibility from several major soil characteristics which were found to be strongly correlated to soil erodibility (Wischmeier & Smith, 1958).

Some caution should be exercised in applying either of these tools to local planning problems. Wischmeier (1976) has pointed out the problems of expecting too much from the soil loss equation. In situations that do not meet the criteria for which Eq. [4] was developed, its predictive capacity will not be quantitatively accurate. It can be useful in determining the relative erosion potential for a soil: such information is useful and important in land use planning.

Soil depth is a variable of major importance in planning. It directly affects the volume of soil available to hold water and nutrients. It influences soil stability and the erosion hazard. Soil depth is considered to be the thickness of soil over an impermeable layer or layer which is very slowly permeable to water and roots. This layer may be bedrock, or pedogenic pans such as clay pans, silica cemented duripans, or calcium cemented petrocalcic (Caliche) horizons. Data on soil depth must be obtained through on-site inspection of the land being planned. Thus, if no soil maps and soil survey reports of the area are available, the planner needs to acquire this information through special studies.

The other data types in Table 8 will not be discussed in detail. There are a large number of variables which are needed to describe a soil. The soil's potential or limitations are dependent on what kind and level of use (i.e., what level of economic return is expected) will be made of the soil. These are major and perhaps minimum data needs for planning cultivated land. One must know what soil resources there are, and how they are distributed on the landscape. One must have some knowledge of what the lands potential for cropping or capability is, and one must have data on climate, topography, and soils to successfully plan an area.

As the world situation with respect to population, energy, and water changes, our frames of reference may change, and some variables not discussed may become of prime importance. Some of the variables will always be significant because they describe the basic resource. Our ideas of "capability" may and perhaps should change as external conditions change.

IV. PLANNING AGRICULTURAL LAND USES TO REDUCE THEIR EFFECT ON THE ENVIRONMENT

A. Kinds of Environmental Effects

Production agriculture may be broadly categorized into rain-fed (non-irrigated) crop production, irrigated crop production, and unconfined to confined animal production. The last category, animal production, will not be addressed and only cultivated agricultural systems shall herein be considered.

Agriculture, like any land use, has two effects on the land. First, its direct effects on the land and second its effect on the land adjacent and/or many miles from the site of use. It is the responsibility of the land user to minimize both effects and the responsibility of the planner to have some idea of what these effects are and how to account for them in the planning process. Many environmental effects of agriculture are discussed by Brady (1967).

Many agricultural uses of land produce minor changes in the land. Well-managed dry-land grazing of native plant species, as an example, may cause some soil compaction and change in species composition. Poorly managed grazing can cause destruction of plant communities, and increase soil loss due to erosion.

High-intensity agriculture, on the other hand, may have profound effects on the land. It is not unusual in California to invert soil profiles, rip hard pans, change the soil chemistry (pH, cation composition), and leave toxic residues in order to grow high value crops such as table and wine grapes, fruits, and nuts. These agronomic practices have long-term implications for the land. This is not to say that these are good or bad practices. From a crop production standpoint they are good. However, it is important to realize that the practices do have profound effects before committing the land to them. This realization must be held by both the farmer or land manager and the planner if the best use is to be made from the land.

Agriculture affects surrounding land as well. Dust raised in farming practices, spraying for insect or weed control, and soil erosion by wind and water may affect air, water, and land quality for great distances. The effects may be felt by city dwellers on the rural-urban fringe and by other agriculturalists. This section of the chapter deals with some of these kinds of effects.

The pollutants/contaminants emitted from rain-fed and irrigated agriculture (a component of the biosphere as well as the geosphere) to the atmosphere and hydrosphere may be due to natural as well as man-made/man-induced causes, or combination thereof. On a national or regional level, the two major pollution problems generated by this industry are the discharges of sediments and salinity to receiving waters. To a lesser degree, but not in terms of significance, are emissions of nutrients into receiving waters and of pesticide residues into water and the atmosphere. Other environmental effects may be caused by site-specific conditions and cultural practices such as emission of toxic metals and nonmetals, dust, and agricultural burning.

1. EFFECTS ON WATER QUALITY

The quality of water may be characterized in many ways. Water quality may be described without a specific usage in mind. It may include such physical parameters as temperature, turbidity, and color, chemical parameters as pH, salinity, and alkalinity, and biological parameters as bacteria, pathogens, and biochemical oxygen demand. This is referred to as nonspecific characterization because it does not identify how these parameters may affect the various beneficial uses of water.

A second more useful method (Water Qual. Crit., 1973) is to characterize water as related to its intended use. This approach is explicit and identifies the parameters of importance for each specific use. For instance, the use-related parameters for domestic water may include turbidity, toxicants, taste, and odor; for irrigation water, electrical conductivity, sodium adsorption ratio, and boron; for freshwater aquatic life and wildlife, oxygen demand and dissolved gasses, water temperature, and toxicants; for food canning industry, nitrate, bacterial count, taste, and odor; and for recreation and aesthetics, turbidity, vectors of diseases, and nuisance organisms. Some of these parameters are common to different characterization schemes and water uses, but the levels desired or required may be different.

Another method (Mancy, 1971) involves identification of those parameters used to detect water pollution in general, such as nutrient demand

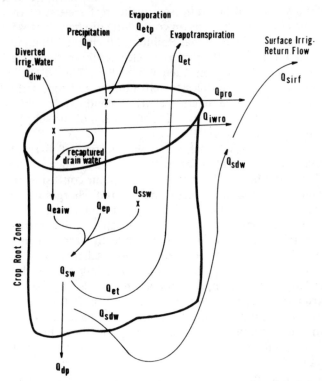

Fig. 1—A conceptual view of water flow in the crop root zone portion of the irrigated agriculture system.

(biochemical oxygen demand, dissolved oxygen, etc), specific nutrients (nitrate, orthophosphate, etc.), nuisances (sulfide, oil, and grease, etc.), and toxicity (pesticides, heavy metals, etc.).

Figure 1 gives a simplified view of various components of water and their flow pathways in the crop root zone in an irrigated agriculture system. This diagram is also applicable to rain-fed agriculture if the irrigation water components are deleted. Associated with these components and flow pathways are the quality parameters such as dissolved mineral salts and nitrogen.

On the one hand, water pollution may be generated by crop production-oriented problems, such as excessive soil salinity which requires leaching and drainage, or poor soil fertility which requires comparatively high fertilizer applications, some of which may be lost through leaching, runoff, and/or volatilization. On the other hand, supply waters degraded by these and other constituents may affect crop production. Furthermore, water as well as air pollution may arise due to natural sources and causes in addition to the man-made/man-induced ones. Because of these interrelationships and complexities it is often difficult to separate man-induced from natural causes, and rain-fed from applied sources of water.

The Federal Water Pollution Control Act Amendments of 1972 (Public

Law 92-500), which will be addressed in the next section of this chapter, gives the policies and regulations on controlling discharges of waste waters. A program known as the National Pollutant Discharge Elimination System (NPDES) was initiated in 1975 by the delegated enforcement agency, the U.S. Environmental Protection Agency (USEPA). The NPDES permit for irrigators requires the permittees to self-moniter and report the flow and certain water quality parameters (electrical conductivity and suspended solids, and other required site-specific parameters) of the supply and point-source surface irrigation return flows.

Irrigation return flow is defined as that portion of diverted water not consumptively lost to the atmosphere which returns back to either surface or subsurface water bodies. Presently, there is some confusion on what constitutes point and nonpoint sources of pollutant discharges for nonirrigated and irrigated agriculture. It appears that point-source return flow for rain-fed agriculture includes discharges of collected and controlled surface runoffs. For irrigated agriculture, point-source discharges are more broadly defined to include any collected return flows discharged as a discrete and discernible outfall (conduit, drain, canal, etc.) into a water body. Point-source discharges may comprise operational spills (bypass water) from water distribution systems, irrigation surface runoff (tailwater), and collected subsurface drainage water from under-drainage (tile-drainage, etc.), open drains, and drainage wells. Apparently the above interpretations on point and nonpoint discharges are related more to "collected or uncollected" return flows and not to "point or nonpoint origins" of pollutants. Some of the components of point-source irrigation return flow may have been initially diffuse (nonpoint) in origin, for instance, tile drainage effluents, but when collected and discharged are considered point-source irrigation return flow. Presumably this categorization was made because point-sources of return flows are more amendable to control than nonpoint.

Comprehensive reviews on the characteristics of irrigation supply water and irrigation return flows, and potential pollution problems are available (for instance, Utah State Univ. Found., 1969; Rhoades & Bernstein, 1971). In addition, reviews on water management in irrigated agriculture are also available (for example, USEPA and Colorado State Univ., 1972; Van Schilfgaarde et al., 1974; Hagan, 1976; Biggar & Tanji, 1977).

From the above literature and other sources, the quality characteristics of point-source surface irrigation return flows as related to supply water are summarized in Table 9. In general, tail water quality may not be significantly impaired with regard to the dissolved constituents but usually is with regard to the suspended constituents. Pesticide residues, phosphorus, and metals are often associated with sediments. In contrast, subsurface drainage waters usually contain substantial increases in dissolved constituents rather than suspended matter.

For illustrative purposes, two case studies (Tanji et al., 1976) will be examined. Figure 2 gives a location map of the 66,298-ha Glenn-Colusa Irrigation District (GCID) in the Sacramento Valley and the 17,724-ha Panoche Drainage District (PDD) in the San Joaquin Valley of California. GCID ob-

Table 9—Point-source irrigation return flow components and quality characteristics as related to applied waters.

Quality parameters	Operational spills	Irrigation tailwater	Subsurface drainage
General quality	†	‡	§
Salinity	†	†,‡	§
Nitrogen	†	†,‡,§	‡,§
Oxygen demanding organics	†	†,‡	†,‡,¶
Sediments	†,‡	§	¶
Pesticide residues	†	§	†,‡
Phosphorus	†	§	†,‡

† Not expected to be much different from supply water.
‡ Some slight increase/pickup or decrease/deposition may occur.
§ Usually expected to be significantly higher due to concentrating effects, application of agricultural chemicals, erosional losses, pickup of natural geochemical sources, etc.
¶ Usually expected to be significantly lower due to filtration, fixation, microbial degradation, etc.

tains its supply water by diverting water from the Sacramento River and Stony Creek, a tributary to the Sacramento River system. About two-third's of the irrigated acreage in GCID is devoted to flooded rice culture. GCID discharges its surface irrigation return flows into the Colusa Basin Drain which has an outfall in the Sacramento River about 113 km downstream.

Fig. 2—Location map of two case study areas in California for the evaluation of irrigation return flows.

Table 10—Flow and quality of supply and surface irrigation return flows from the 1975 irrigation season in Glenn-Colusa Irrigation District and Panoche Drainage District, California (Tanji et al., 1976).

Parameter	Supply water	Surface irrigation return flow
Glenn-Colusa Irrigation District (66,298 ha):		
Water flow, ha-m	103,005	30,024
Electrical conductivity, μmhos/cm	180	391
Total dissolved solids, mg/liter	116	244
Turbidity, Jackson Turbidity Units	15	22
Suspended solids, mg/liter	24	36
Panoche Drainage District (17,724 ha):		
Water flow, ha-m	15,875	4,035
Electrical conductivity, μmhos/cm	363	3,070
Total dissolved solids, mg/liter	215	2,053
Turbidity, Jackson Turbidity Units	33	126
Suspended solids, mg/liter	90	348
Boron, mg/liter	0.2	4.8

PDD is comprised of four irrigation districts and is served with imported water from the Sacramento Valley through the Delta-Mendota Canal and the California Aquaduct. The major crops grown are furrow-irrigated tomatoes, cotton, and melons. The irrigation return flow from PDD is discharged into the Grassland Water District, an entity devoted to irrigated pasture and waterfowl habitat, for reuse before eventual discharge into the middle reaches of the San Joaquin River.

Table 10 gives the seasonal water flows of supply and surface discharge waters, and their flow-weighted average qualities for the 1975 irrigation season in GCID (April–October) and PDD (May–November). The irrigation water for GCID is of exceedingly good quality and its discharge water is similar to that of PDD's supply water. In contrast, the surface irrigation return flow from PDD is substantially degraded. The soils in GCID are very low in salts, whereas the soils in PDD contain soluble salts, gypsum, and boron. The return flows from GCID are mainly comprised of surface run-off from flooded rice fields while the return flow from PDD is primarily a mixture of tile drainage effluent and some surface runoff.

The question before us is how does one evaluate the environmental effects of these two case-study cultivated systems? It is suggested, in some quarters, that such developed systems be compared with natural, virgin systems. In both locations, we do not have adequate baseline data as a frame of reference, and, in addition, the hydrologic flow regimes have been drastically modified by the construction of multipurpose reservoirs in the watersheds of both Sacramento and San Joaquin Valleys, including the export of water in the former and the import of water in the latter.

A better alternative would be to compare the concentration (mass/volume) and mass (concentration × volume) of selected quality parameters for the supply and discharge waters. On a concentration basis, Table 10 points out that in GCID suspended solids (SS) increased slightly and total dissolved solids (TDS) increased slightly in the return flows due to evapotranspiration, and volume-concentration of soil water by crop plants. In contrast, TDS in the return flow in PDD has increased nearly tenfold, due primarily to the dissolution of natural soil gypsum (Tanji, 1976) and SS has increased nearly fourfold, mainly due to the erosive nature of the soils in that area.

Although quality parameters in concentration units is an important criterion for appraising the impact(s) on beneficial uses of receiving waters, mass emission should be considered with regards to management and pollution control. Figures 3 and 4 are flow diagrams of the mass inputs and mass outputs for the two case studies under consideration. Let us compare the unit mass input and unit mass emission for water (ha-m/ha) and TDS and SS (metric tons/ha). Figure 3 for GCID shows that the surface irrigation return flow into the Colusa Basin Drain (CBD) is 29, 61, and 43%, respectively, of the water, TDS, and SS of the supply water, while Fig. 4 for PPD shows return flow into the Grasslands Water District (GWD) is 26, 239, and 118%, respectively, of the same. Thus, on a mass basis, there is a deposition of TDS and SS in GCID and a pickup of TDS and SS from PDD, as evaluated over the irrigation season.

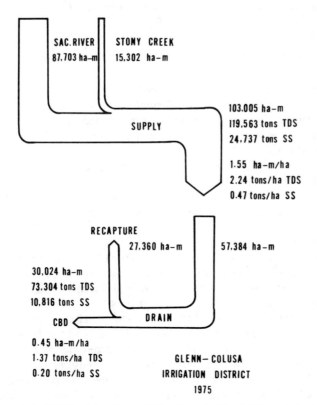

Fig. 3—Water, salt (TDS), and sediment (SS), flows in Glenn-Colusa Irrigation District, Calif., for the 1975 irrigation season (Tanji et al., 1976).

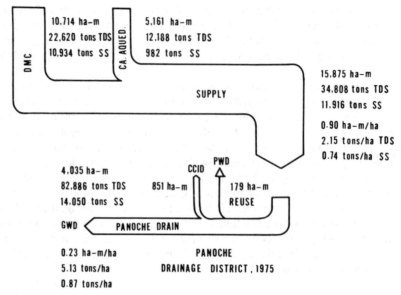

Fig. 4—Water, salt (TDS), and sediment (SS) flows in Panoche Drainage District, Calif., for the 1975 irrigation season (Tanji et al., 1976).

From the above two case studies it is concluded (Tanji et al., 1976) that:

1) Irrigation return flow is produced under a variety of conditions. It is exceedingly difficult to eliminate runoff from surface irrigation methods. Tail water is prominent in flooded rice culture and in certain other cultural practices, such as during seed germination in furrow beds.

2) In areas where water is scarce or costly, tail water is seldom produced or is nearly all reused at the site of production. It is not, however, unusual to find from 10 to 30% of the diverted water being reused, even in the areas where the supply of water is plentiful and inexpensive.

3) Tail water is seldom collected and/or disposed of in a drain separate from other surface irrigation return flow components.

4) Runoff discharged from irrigated fields may not always reach the receiving water body due to capture and reuse, either at the site of production or at downstream locations.

5) The quantity and quality of surface irrigation return flows are highly variable, reflecting local differences in the hydrologic and geologic conditions, soil properties, cropping patterns, cultural practices, supply water, and the extent of reuse.

6) In many instances, it is difficult to differentiate the sources of pollutants between natural and man-induced processes. In addition, it is often difficult to differentiate the source of discharge waters between rain-fed and applied irrigation waters.

7) In many sites, it is difficult to monitor water flow due to the lack of suitable structures and the prohibitive costs of setting up water flow measuring stations. Furthermore, in some sites, it is difficult to estimate water flow because the flow of water may reverse its direction for a variety of reasons.

8) Although the reuse of irrigation return flows is a desireable goal, the quality of irrigation return flow may at times be a major constraint. For instance, the boron and salinity levels may be exceedingly high. In spite of these hazards, such degraded waters are being utilized after blending with waters of higher quality.

9) Tail water control may be viewed as promoting greater water-use efficiency. This usually results in a higher concentration, but a smaller mass emission of pollutants. However, such a practice may lead to other potential problems, such as a diminished summer flow in streams, a diminished supply of water for subsequent or downstream water users, and perhaps an inadequate stream flow to repel sea water intrusion in the Sacramento-San Joaquin Delta.

10) Alternative tail water management practices have been identified. A few of them may be applicable, while others are not. Due to the site variability of receiving waters, and of tail water production and quality, it is difficult to recommend any single universally applicable tail water control technology. The effect(s) of tail water discharge into surface waters may be either beneficial or detrimental, or both, depending on the quality constituents of interest, and flow regime. A practice that is effective in one location may not be as effective in another.

A second major environmental problem is soil erosion. Soil erosion is a natural (geologic) process about which little can be done. Accelerated erosion due to man's use of the land is a major management problem that can be controlled through careful use of the soil resource. The consequences of soil erosion are of two types. First, the quality of the land which is being eroded is decreased and second, the quality of the receiving water is impaired.

When soil is eroded from the land it selectively removes nutrients and nutrient-holding capacity of soil (Massey & Jackson, 1952; Stottenberg & White, 1953; Barrows & Kilmer, 1963). It does this because organic matter and clays which are the major reservoirs of nutrients are selectively removed by the erosion process. A useful method for expressing the selective removal of nutrients and organic matter is the enrichment ration (ER) (Barrows & Kilmer, 1963). The enrichment ratio is calculated from Eq. [5].

$$ER = \frac{\text{Concentration of element in soil in runoff}}{\text{Concentration of element in soil from which runoff originated}} \quad [5]$$

Barrows and Kilmer (1963) reported a range of ER for O.M. (1.15–4.7), N (1.08–5.0), P (1.3–3.3), and available K (4.7–12.6). These serve to illustrate the effect of erosion on soils.

The consequences of soil erosion off-site may be equally severe as those on the site where erosion has occurred. Glymph and Storey (1967) list the impacts as including those on fish, recreation, increased cost of water purification, deposition on land, channels and reservoirs, siltation of estuaries, harbors, and coastal areas. In addition, sediment may carry nutrients, pesticides, and toxic chemicals. A good review of off-site sediment effects is given by Gunterman et al. (1975). Numerous papers have documented the characteristics of sediment and the effects on watersheds (e.g., Singer & Rust, 1975; Olness et al., 1975; Burwell et al., 1975; McColl et al., 1975).

The role of the planner is to recognize that soils do erode at different rates under different uses and to predict, as well as he can, the effect of any given use on accelerating the soil erosion process. The planner then needs to develop plans which will minimize soil erosion.

2. EFFECTS ON AIR QUALITY

The quality of our atmosphere may be characterized in several ways, such as classes of air pollutants present and their concentrations, impacts on human health, or degree of visibility and aesthetics (odor, for example). Our atmosphere contains certain gases which are essentially "permanent" or unvarying on a volume basis, for instance N_2 (78.08%), O_2 (20.95%), Ar (0.93%), and other gases in trace amounts. There are other gases that may vary temporally and spatially but in "clean" atmosphere may have certain background levels (Williamson, 1973), for instance H_2O vapor (0–7%), CO_2 (0.032%), CH_4 (15 ppm), CO (0.1 ppm), O_3 (0.02 ppm), NH_3 (0.01 ppm), NO_2 (0.001 ppm), SO_2 (0.0002 ppm), and H_2S (0.0002 ppm). Many of these "variable" gases are pollutants and may occur in high concentrations in urban areas. In addition to gases, our atmosphere may contain solid and liquid trace elements (aerosols) including those produced by man, referred to as *anthropogenic* sources (trace gases and aerosols), from the burning of fossil fuels, industrial exhaust stacks, and combustion engines.

The prevention and control of air pollution is legislated by the 1974 Amendments to the Clean Air Act. Similar to water pollution control, local and state regulations in addition to the federal are available.

Air quality may be affected by cultivated lands from the burning of crop residues, drift of aerial application of pesticides and other agricultural chemicals, dust, burning of fossil fuels for frost protection, and other gaseous losses (CH_4, NH_3, N_2, N_2O, etc.) from the land surface. It appears that burning of crop residue is probably the most prevalent and most significant while other sources may be significant under site-specific conditions. In general, pesticide and fertilizer residues are monitored and controlled as they occur in waters (PL 92-500) and/or the harvested products (for instance, California's Health and Safety Code).

To illustrate the problem we site examples from California. Knutson et al. (1976) reports that over 9 million metric tons of "collectable" crop residue is produced by cultivated lands in California. Of this total 73, 21, and 6% comes, respectively, from field crop residues (cotton, rice, barley, corn) fruit and nut crop residues (grapes, almonds, oranges, walnuts, peaches, etc.), and vegetable crop residues (tomatoes, asparagus, melons, etc.). More than 83% of this total is produced in the Sacramento and San Joaquin Valleys. This crop residue must be burned, incorporated into the soil, or disposed of by other means.

In California some 5 million metric tons of crop residue are burned annually. In 1970 the problems with poor visibility due to particulate emissions from open field burning resulted in legislation to regulate all open field burning in California. Burning of rice field residue, the largest single crop residue (120,000 to 200,000 ha) burned in the state, has been extensively studied. Unfortunately this residue is available for burning in the fall when meteorological dispersion is poorest in the Sacramento and San Joaquin Valleys. The major factors affecting particulate emissions are moisture content of the rice straw and stubble, and direction in which an open field is lit, i.e., headfire or backfire.[2] Headfire is the lighting of open fields from the upwind side while backfire is from the downwind side, against the direction of the prevailing wind. For larger fields an into-the-wind strip lighting is practiced by lighting downwind edges of the field first.

The 1972 and 1973 rice field burn studies by Miller[2] indicate that when the moisture content of the residue is 20%, headfire produced 16 kg of particulates/metric ton of residue while backfire produced about 5 kg/metric ton. At moisture content of 10%, 6 and 2 kg/metric ton of particulates were measured from headfire and backfire, respectively. A simple test known as the "crackle test" is used to determine when the moisture content of the straw is about 10–12% or less. Rice straw at these moisture contents would crackle when a handful of straw is bent.

Based upon the above findings and others, a rice residue burning program has been initiated as follows:

1) Burning would be permitted only on days declared "permissive-burn days" by the California Air resources Board.
2) Maximum permissive daily burn acreage is set at 5% of the planted acreage in each county.
3) All rice fields must be ignited by into-the-wind strip lighting or backfiring techniques.
4) Fields cannot be burned until they meet minimum drying time requirements: After harvest, spread straw must dry for 3 days and windrowed straw must dry for 10 days. It may be burned before these times if the straw passes the "crackle test." After a rain, straw must dry until it will pass the "crackle test" (10–12% moisture content or less).
5) Burning hours are from 1000 to 1700 hours.

This control program is an improvement on rice stubble burning and is quite successful. Monitoring of the occurrence of smoky days, when visibili-

[2]G. E. Miller, Jr., J. F. Thompson, J. R. Goss, S. Duckworth, J. F. Williams, and E. F. Darley. 1976. A program to minimize the effects of agricultural burning in California. Presented at the 69th Annu. Meet. of the Air Pollut. Control Assoc., Portland, Oreg., 27 June–1 July 1976. Pap. 76-3.2.

ty is less than 11 km, during permissive burn days at Sacramento in October reveals that the number of smoky October days has been reduced from 15 days in the 1963–70 period to 6 days in 1975.

B. Who Plans Farm Land?

Data needs for planning and reasons for planning agricultural land have been given in previous sections of this chapter. Most of these prior remarks relate to selecting large areas for agricultural use and do not deal with farm planning. It is our feeling that farm planning is up to the individual farmer with help from federal, state, local, and private agencies when he requests such help. The only proviso to this statement is that the farmer's land use does not destroy the resource or damage surrounding lands. There are examples of both excellent and horrible uses of agricultural lands, but, in general, today's growers and ranchers know the value of the resource and work to produce from it while protecting it as best they can.

There are sources of information and help available to the land owner. These range from the county extension agent and Soil Conservation Service to the private soil testing laboratory. Information is available in the form of extension bulletins, soil survey reports, and local field crop trials. The quality and kind of data available depends on the location (state and county) of the farm.

V. METHODS OF CONTROLLING LAND USE FOR AGRICULTURE

Two major methods of controlling land use exist in the United States. The first is direct control through zoning. The second, environmental quality laws, is less direct, but has major implications for land use. California has had an agricultural land use law for 13 years. Although many states have land use programs (see Jackson, 1974), California's will serve as an example.

A. Agricultural Zoning—The California Experience

The California Land Conservation Act (CLCA) of 1965—also known as the Williamson Act (California Government Code Sections 51200–51295) —was an attempt to cope with some of the land-use problems created for California agriculture by the pressure of population growth and urbanization. As originally conceived, it recognized an absolute limit on the physical amount of high quality agricultural land in California, the importance of agricultural production to the economy of the state and nation, the economic costs associated with loss of established agricultural production and the development of new agricultural production areas, the economic and social costs of premature land conversion, and the economic and social costs of disorderly land conversions.

In its present form, in addition to providing for scenic highway corridors, the CLCA has three major objectives: (i) To preserve a "maximum amount of the limited supply of agricultural land... (for) the maintenance of the agricultural economy of the state...", (ii) To discourage "...premature and unnecessary conversion of agricultural land to urban uses... and discourage discontinuous urban development patterns which unnecessarily increase the costs of community services to community residents" and (iii) To preserve open space and the "...preservation of agricultural production of such lands."

Earlier attempts to develop land-control devices such as preferential tax treatment and various types of agricultural zoning had not been effective in coping with the problems. They had also been subject to various criticisms such as lack of equity, difficulty of implementation, and ineffectiveness. The CLCA developed a new type of instrument—a voluntary contract between the land owner and local government to encourage stability in agricultural land use—and called for coordinated local land use planning and zoning that would identify areas in which the contracts would be used. Compensation features were developed that encouraged participation in the program but were relatively neutral regarding potential escalation of either land values or land taxes.

The voluntary contracts regulating nonagricultural development rights were the heart of the legislation. A contract calls for a minimum 10-year period during which time the property owner surrenders his nonagricultural development rights and the local government acquires those rights in the nature of a trusteeship. The contract includes automatic annual renewal. The 10-year status is thus maintained unless a termination notice is initiated by either party. After such notice, the contract continues for 9 more years, with restrictions on land use, but may be renewed again during that time if both parties agree.

Originally, the legislation emphasized the protection of prime land and defined it as Soil Conservation Service Land-Use Capability Classes I and II, (Klingebiel & Montgomery, 1973), or alternatively, land that provided a gross income of $200/acre per year for any 3 of the previous 5 years. Under the CLCA, assessment of covered land for property tax purposes is based on agricultural use value (i.e., capitalized rental incomes) rather than on market values. To minimize disrupting impacts on local governments from significantly reduced tax-based revenues, a scheme of subvention payments is provided for. Originally, the above definition of "prime" land was applied to qualify the subvention payment to local government. The present legislation has generally avoided using the word *prime* in discussing objectives of the legislation, but has expanded the basis for subvention payments to include the following categories: Land which qualified for rating of 80–100 in the Storie Index Rating, land which supports livestock and has an annual carrying capacity equivalent to at least one animal unit per acre as defined by the USDA, or land planted to fruit- or nut-bearing trees, vines, bushes, or crops which have a nonbearing period of less than 5 years and which will normally return $200/acre per year during the commercial bearing period. Thus, the productivity of the land—in cash—becomes a pragmatic basis for qualification for subvention.

The initial purposes of the CLCA stressed preservation of prime agricultural land and prevention of urban sprawl. There is disagreement as to whether the concept of prime land has completely disappeared. It is implied in the stated bases for subvention payments, but perhaps the emphasis has shifted enough to include environmentally significant lands so that those most concerned with prime agricultural land may have to seek other legislative approaches. The recent amendments to the CLCA have expanded the protective features to permit restrictive use contracts on scenic highway corridors, wildlife habitats, salt ponds, managed wetland areas, and land with open space values.

Table 11 indicates that the total impact of the CLCA program in California is quite significant, although the prime land preservation objective may not be as important as it was originally. Of the approximately 20.2 million ha (50 million acres) of privately owned land in California, over 5.7 million ha (14 million acres)—nearly 30%—is now covered by a restrictive use agreement. Of the estimated 4.5 million ha (11 million acres) that would fit one of the eligible prime land definitions, approximately 45% is covered by contract and about 30% of all land covered is in one of the prime land categories. Thus, after 13 years, the CLCA appears to have made significant gains in protecting land from undesired conversions in use.

Because some proponents of prime land perservation believe that more gains need to be made in this area, legislation has been introduced by Assemblyman Charles Warren to establish an Agricultural Resources Council for the state, delineate prime agricultural lands in accordance with the existing CLCA definition, and prescribe specific use limits that would be allowed on such lands. Introduced as AB 15 in the 1975–76 biennial session

Table 11—California Conservation Act selected enrollment data.

Year	Total land	Total prime land	Nonurban prime land	Urban prime land	Nonprime land
			1,000 acres		
1968–69†	2,062	131	NA‡	NA	1,931
1969–70§	4,252	573	NA	NA	3,679
1970–71¶	6,273	1,654	NA	NA	4,619
1971–72#	9,563	2,620	NA	NA	6,943
1972–73#	11,440	3,428	2,917	709	8,012
1973–74#	12,719	3,915	3,114	801	8,804
1974–75#	13,742	4,140	3,287	852	9,602
1975–76#	14,427	4,371	3,464	907	10,056

† Source: California Legislature. 1969. Joint Comm. on Open Space Preliminary Rep.
‡ NA—Not applicable.
§ Source: California Legislature. 1970. Joint Comm. on Open Space Final Rep.
¶ Source: California State Board of Equalization Memo. 1971.
# Source: California Resources Agency, Department of Conservation. 1976. Open Space Entitlements Program Data. Mimeo.

of the California State Legislature, the program was defeated and will not become law for at least 2 years. Similar legislation introduced into the 1977–78 biennial session of the California State Legislature was also defeated.

B. Environmental Quality Legislation

With the advent of public concern over environmental quality, legislation at the federal, state, and local levels has been enacted to protect our land, water, and air resources. The previous section dealt with an illustrative case on land use legislation while this section deals with water and air pollution control laws as they affect land use planning.

1. WATER POLLUTION CONTROL LEGISLATION WHICH AFFECTS AGRICULTURE

The Federal Water Pollution Control Act was amended by Public Law 92-500 in October 1972. The objective of the Act is "to restore and maintain the chemical, physical, and biological integrity of the Nation's waters." The ultimate goal of PL 92-500 is to eliminate the discharge of pollutants into navigable water by 1985, with an interim goal of achieving, wherever possible, water quality that is "fishable and swimmable" by 1 July 1983. The administrator of the U.S. Environmental Protection Agency (USEPA) has been given the responsibility to implement and enforce the Act.

To control discharge of pollutants into navigable waters, USEPA has a mandate under PL 92-500 to require the application of:

1) "Best practicable control technology currently available" (BPT or (BPTCA) by July 1977;
2) "Best available control technology economically achievable" (BAT or BATEA) by July 1983; and
3) "Elimination of discharge of pollutants" (EOD) by 1985.

The ultimate goal of EOD was later interpreted by the Staff of the National Commission on Water Quality as "the elimination of the discharge of pollutants shall apply to removal of those constituents which are added during use of the water. The resultant discharge must be of equal or lower concentration than that of the original supply." Moreover, EOD applied only to point-source discharge of pollutants and not to the nonpoint sources.

It should be pointed out that PL 92-500 does not explicitly identify the control technology desired, but only the goals to be achieved. However, in the implementation of the Act, uniform waste discharge requirements are being promulgated for municipal sewage effluents and most classes of industrial waste water discharges. For example, secondary treatment of municipal sewage effluents meets the 1977 BPT goal. Similar waste discharge requirement/control technology has not been spelled out for irrigation return flows. But, what is now being enforced is the National Pollutant Discharge Elimination System (NPDES) permit program, which does apply to surface irrigation return flows discharged from an identifiable point source. For example, the NPDES permit system as administered in the State of California for irrigated agriculture involves a self-monitoring program in which permittees are required, among other things, to report the flow, electrical conductivity, and suspended solids of supply and surface discharge waters. Permittees, in general, represent aggregates of large spatial entities having common hydrologic, institutional, or political boundaries.

Hagan (1976) points out a large array of alternative water management and related practices that may be considered for possible implementation by irrigated agriculture, specificallly for only salinity control. This listing of 20 possible alternative measures is difficult to appraise in terms of probable effects on salt concentration and salt load in irrigation return flows. Hagan also addresses other complex and interactive problems such as waste water reuse and/or disposal and energy requirements.

Former Vice-President Rockefeller, when Chairman of the National Commission on Water Quality in 1976, submitted a report on recommendations for mid-course corrections regarding PL 92-500 to the U.S. Congress. In essence, the Commission Report sustains and enforces most of the major goals and objectives of PL 92-500. However, they suggest some changes in the implementing strategy to give this water pollution control program stability, continuity, and flexibility. With regard to irrigated agriculture, the Commission recommends "flexibility in applying control or treatment measures to irrigated agriculture after an inventory of the problem, and support salinity alleviation projects to reduce salt loads from sources other than man's activities."

In addition to PL 92-500, additional federal legislation has been passed. Public Law 93-320, the Colorado River Basin Salinity Control Act of 1974, is addressed to a specific regional salinity problem designed to alleviate, among others, an international problem of water quality with Mexico. Public Law 93-523, the Safe Drinking Water Act of 1974, appears to supplement PL 92-500 by encompassing protection of ground water quality from nonpoint return flows, i.e., percolating waters from various sources including irrigated agriculture. State water quality and pollution control laws have also been enacted, and one of them predates federal legislation; namely the Porter-Cologne Water Quality Act of 1970 in California.

To date, it appears that the above-mentioned legislation has not caused any significant changes in land use, but is promoting better water management practices. It is believed that significant improvements are being made on water quality in some areas (Natl. Comm. on Water Qual., 1976).

2. AIR POLLUTION CONTROL LEGISLATION WHICH AFFECTS AGRICULTURE

The Clean Air Act was amended in June 1974 to "protect and enhance the quality of the Nation's air resources so as to promote the public health and welfare and the productive capacity of its population and to encourage and assist the development and operation of regional air pollution control programs." The Administrator of the USEPA is empowered to issue air quality criteria for an air pollutant within 12 mo after he has identified such pollutant as having an adverse effect on public health and welfare.

The air quality criteria are determined on the basis of known or suspected adverse effects on humans or animals, damage to vegetation, or impairment of aesthetic aspects. It indicates the level above which the presence of a pollutant is considered to have an adverse effect and may specify a threshold concentration, dosage, and exposure time for each pollutant or combination of pollutants which act synergistically.

In addition to air quality criteria (as in water quality criteria), air quality standards (as in water quality standards) are prescribed as a legal standard of enforcement for air quality. Those standards for protection of health are referred to as primary standards and those for protection of public welfare, secondary standards (Williamson, 1973). Emission standards are also used to control the amount or conditions of release of a pollutant from stationary sources (for instance, industrial exhaust stacks) or mobile sources (for instance, automobiles and aircraft).

In California the Air Resources Board, as delegated by the California Health and Safety Code, controls agricultural burning. It declares whether a day is a "permissive-burn day" or a "no-burn day" each morning at 0745 hours for each of the 11 air basins in the state. Burning permits are issued by the local air pollution districts or designated agencies which must follow the burning guidelines developed for agriculture by the State Air Resources Board.

Various meteorological criteria (Calif. Air Resour. Board, 1975) have been set up for regulation of agricultural burning. For example, in the southwest section (Colusa, Yolo, and Solano Counties) of the Sacramento Valley Air Basin, a permissive-burn day will be declared when at least three of the following criteria are met:

1) Near the time of day when the surface temperature is at a minimum, the temperature at 914 m (3,000 ft) above the surface is not warmer than the surface temperature by more than 10.6°C (13°F).

2) The expected temperature at 914 m above the surface is colder than the expected surface temperature by at least 11.7°C (11°F) for 4 hours.

3) The expected daytime wind speed at 914 m above the surface is at least 2.24 m/sec (5 mph).

4) The expected daytime wind direction in the mixing layer has a component from the south or from the east.

Air pollution control laws, as in water pollution control, have not affected land use per se but have resulted in better management and disposal practices. It is envisioned that considerations of potential water and air pollution problems will play a greater role in future comprehensive regional planning, in particular land use planning and zoning.

VI. SUMMARY

Agricultural land is one of America's greatest resources. Technology, climate, and hard work have made the land produce in abundance beyond the wildest dreams of anyone. In many ways we have become callous to these riches. Although the land is large, it is finite. As population growth and increasing per capita demand for food merge with a decreasing abundance of resources, the need for careful use of our agricultural land resource increases. Careful use takes several forms, particularly proper planning of land to maximize productivity, and conservation to minimize loss.

Planning requires detailed knowledge of resources and the willingness to use the resources to the greatest benefit of society. No single discipline can or should attempt to plan agricultural land use. The job is too big and too important. It is a multidisciplinary task which requires the expertise of physical and social scientists. We have outlined our philosophy about land use planning and briefly discussed the data needed to begin the planning process.

LITERATURE CITED

Anonymous. 1967. The world food problem. Rep. of the President's Science Advisory Comm. 2:405–569.

Anonymous. 1969. Soil vegetation surveys in California. State of California, Resour. Agency, Dep. of Conserv., Dep. of For., Sacramento, Calif.

Anonymous. 1972a. Soil capability classification for agriculture. The Canada Land Inventory. Rep. no. 2. Dep. of Environ., Ottawa, Canada. 16 p.

Anonymous. 1972b. Land capability classification for forestry. The Canada Land Inventory Rep. no. 4. Dep. of Environ., Ottawa, Canada.

Arnold, R. W. 1965. Multiple working hypothesis in soil genesis. Soil Sci. Soc. Am. Proc. 29: 717–724.

Barrows, H. L., and V. J. Kilmer. 1963. Plant nutrient losses from soils by water erosion. Adv. Agron. 15:303–316.

Bartelli, L. J. 1968. Potential farming lands in the coastal plain of southeast United States. Trans. 9th Int. Congr. Soil Sci. 8:243–251.

Bartelli, L. J., A. A. Klingebiel, J. V. Baird, and M. R. Heddleson (ed.). 1966. Soil surveys and land use planning. Soil Sci. Soc. Am. and Am. Soc. Agron., Madison, Wis.

Beckett, P. H. T., and P. A. Burrough. 1971. The relation between cost and utility in soil survey. V. The cost effectiveness of different soil survey procedures. J. Soil Sci. 22:481–489.

Beckett, P. H. T., and R. Webster. 1971. Soil variability: a review. Soils Fert. 34:1–15.

Beek, K. J., and J. Bennema. 1972a. Land evaluation for agricultural land use planning. Agric. Univ., Dep. of Soil Sci. and Geol., Wageningen, The Netherlands. 70 p. Mimeo.

Beek, K. J., and J. Bennema. 1972b. Land evaluation for agricultural land use planning, an ecological methodology. Agric. Univ., Dep. Soil Sci. and Geo., Wageningen, The Netherlands. 72 p. Mimeo.

Bibby, J. S., and D. Mackney. 1969. Land use capability classification. Tech. Monograph no. 1. Soil survey of England and Wales. Rothamsted Exp. Stn., Harpenden, Herts, England.

Bie, S. W., and A. Ulph. 1972. The economic value of soil survey information. J. Agric. Econ. 23:285–297.

Bie, S. W., A. Ulph, and P. H. T. Beckett. 1973. Calculating the economic benefits of the soil survey. J. Soil Sci. 24:429–436.

Biggar, J. W., and K. K. Tanji. 1977. Soil-salt interactions in relation to salt control. Trans. Am. Soc. Agric. Eng. 20(1):68–75.

Brinkman, R., and A. J. Smyth (ed.). 1973. Land evaluation for rural purposes. Int. Inst. Land Rec. and Improv./ILRI, Wageningen, The Netherlands. 116 p.

Brady, N. C. (ed.). 1967. Agriculture and the quality of the environment. Am. Assoc. for Adv. Sci. Pub. 85, Washington, D.C.

Brooks, D. B., and P. W. Andrews. 1974. Mineral resources, economic growth, and world population. Science 185:13–19.

Brown, L. R. 1975. The world food prospect. Science 190:1053–1059.

Bureau of Reclamation. 1953. Bureau of Reclamation manual V. Irrigated land use. Part 2. Land classification. USDI, Denver, Colo. 130 p.

Burwell, R. E., D. R. Timmons, and R. F. Holt. 1975. Nutrient transport in surface runoff as influenced by soil cover and seasonal periods. Soil Sci. Soc. Am. Proc. 39:523–528.

California Air Resources Board. 1975. Meteorological criteria for regulating agricultural burning. Revised Rep. 20, 1975. 9 p.

Campbell, I. B. 1973. Pattern of variation in steepland soils: variation on a single slope. N.Z. J. Sci. 16:413–435.

Carter, H. O., J. G. Youde, and M. L. Peterson. 1975. Future land requirement to produce food for an expanding world population. p. 37–61. *In* Perspectives on prime lands. USDA-Background Pap. for Sem. on Retetion of Prime Lands, 16–17 July 1975. USDA, Washington, D.C.

Cassel, D. K., and armand Bauer. 1975. Spatial variability in soils below depth of tillage: bulk density and fifteen-atmosphere percentage. Soil Sci. Soc. Am. Proc. 39:247–250.

Clawson, Marion. 1972. America's land and its uses. Johns Hopkins Press, Baltimore, Md.

Cline, M. G. 1949. Basic principles of soil classification. Soil Sci. 67:81–91.

Commission on Population Growth and the American Future. 1972. Population and the American future. Signet Books, New York. p. 362

Council on Environmental Quality. 1974. Environment quality. The 5th Annu. Rep. of the Counc. on Environ. Qual. U.S. Government Printing Office, Washington, D.C. 597 p.

Dijkerman, J. C. 1974. Pedology as a science: the role of data, models and theories in the study of natural soil systems. Geoderma 11:73–93.

Drees, L. R., and L. P. Wilding. 1973. Elemental variability within a sampling unit. Soil Sci. Soc. Am. Proc. 37:82–87.

Economic Research Service. 1974. Our land and water resources, current and prospective supplies and uses. USDA-ERS. Misc. Pub. no. 1290. 54 p.

Food and Agriculture Organization of the United Nations. 1974. Approaches to land classification. Soils Bull. 22. FAO, Rome. 120 p.

Glymph, L. M., and H. C. Storey. 1967. Sediment-its consequences and control. p. 205–220. *In* N. C. Brady (ed.) Agriculture and the quality of our environment. Am. Assoc. Adv. Sci. Pub. 85. Washington, D.C.

Gunterman, K. L., M. T. Lee, and E. R. Swanson. 1975. The off-site sediment damage function in selected Illinois watersheds. J. Soil Water Conserv. 30:219–224.

Hagan, R. M. 1976. Water management: some effects of new sociatal attitudes. p. 31–83. *In* F. L. Patterson (ed.) Agronomic research for food. ASA Spec. Pub. no. 26, Am. Soc. of Agron., Madison, Wis.

Harley, Ron. 1971. A valley weeps. Farm Q. (May–June):10.

Heller, Alfred. 1972. The California Tomorrow Plan. William Kaufmann, Inc., Los Altos, Calif. p. 120.

Ike, A. F., and J. L. Clutter. 1968. The variability of forest soils of the Georgia Blue Ridge Mountains. Soil Sci. Soc. Am. Proc. 32:284–288.

Jackson, H. M. 1974. State land use programs. Comm. Print. 93rd Congress, 2d Sess., Comm. on Interior and Insular Affairs. U.S. Government Printing Office, Washington, D.C. p. 95.

Jenny, H. 1941. Factors of soil formation—a system of quantitative pedology. McGraw-Hill, New York. p. 281.

Klingebiel, A. A., and P. H. Montgomery. 1973. Land capability classification. Agric. Handbk. 210. SCS, USDA.

Knutson, J., G. E. Miller, and V. P. Osterli. 1976. Crop residues in California. Univ. of Calif., Div. of Agric. Sci. Leafl. 2872. p. 23.

Krause, Orville and Dwight Hair. 1975. Trends in land use and competition for land to produce food and fiber. p. 1–26. *In* Perspectives on prime lands. USDA. Background Pap. for Sem. on Retention of Prime Lands, 16–17 July 1975. USDA, Washington, D.C.

Luthin, J. N. (ed.). 1957. Drainage of agricultural land. ASA Monograph 7. Am. Soc. of Agron., Madison, Wis. 620 p.

Maletic, J. T., and T. B. Hutchings. 1967. Selection and classification of irrigable lands. *In* R. M. Hagen, H. R. Haise, and T. W. Edminster (ed.) Irrigation of agricultural lands. Agronomy 11:125–173. Am. Soc. of Agron., Madison, Wis.

Mancy, K. H. (ed.). 1971. Instrumental analysis for water pollution control. Ann Arbor Sci. Publ., Inc., Ann Arbor, Mich. p. 331.

Massey, H. F., and M. L. Jackson. 1952. Selective erosion of soil fertility constituents. Soil Sci. Soc. Am. Proc. 16:353–356.

McColl, R. H. S., E. White, and J. R. Waugh. 1975. Chemical runoff in catchments converted to agricultural use. N.Z. J. Sci. 18:67–85.

McCormack, D. E., and L. P. Wilding. 1969. Variation of soil properties within mapping units of soils with contrasting substrata in northwestern Ohio. Soil Sci. Soc. Am. Proc. 33: 587–593.

McCormack, R. J. 1971. The Canada land use inventory: a basis for land use planning. J. Soil Water Conserv. 26:141–146.

National Commission on Water Quality. 1976. Rep. to the Congress by the Natl. Comm. on Water Qual., 18 Mar. 1976. U.S. Government Printing Office, Washington, D.C. p. 90.

Obeng, H. B. 1968. Land capability classification of the soils of Ghana under practices of mechanised and hand cultivation for crop and livestock production. Trans. 9th Int. Congr. Soil Sci. 4:215–223.

Olness, Alan, S. J. Smith, E. D. Rhoades, and R. G. Menzel. 1975. Nutrient and sediment discharge from agricultural watersheds in Oklahoma. J. Environ. Qual. 4:331–337.

Olson, G. W. 1974. Interpretive land classification in English-speaking countries. p. 1–26. In Approaches to land classification. Soil Bull. 22. FAO, Rome.

Pimentel, David, William Dritschilo, John Krummel, and John Kutzman. 1975. Energy and land constraints in food production. Science 190:754–761.

Rhoades, J. D., and L. Bernstein. 1971. Chemical, physical, and biological characteristics of irrigation and soil water. Ch. 3, p. 141–222. In L. L. Ciaccio (ed.) Water and water pollution handbook, Vol. 1. Marcel Dekker, Inc., New York.

Riesbol, H. S., C. H. Milligan, A. L. Sharp, and L. L. Kelly. 1967. Surface water supply and development. In R. M. Hagen, H. R. Haise, and T. W. Edminster (ed.) Irrigation of agricultural lands. Agronomy 11:53–69. Am. Soc. of Agron., Madison, Wis.

Simonson, R. W. 1968. Concept of soil. Adv. Agron. 20:1–47.

Singer, M. J., and R. H. Rust. 1975. Phosphorus in surface runoff from a deciduous forest. J. Environ. Qual. 4:307–311.

Soil Conservation Service. 1975. National soils handbook.

Soil Survey Staff. 1951. Soil survey manual. USDA Handbk 18.

Soil Survey Staff. 1975. Soil taxonomy—a basic system of soil classification for making and interpreting soil surveys. Agric. Handbk. 436, SCS, USDA, Washington, D.C. p. 754.

Stone, C. D. 1973. Should trees have standing? William Kaufmann, Inc., Los Altos, Calif. p. 102.

Storie, R. E. 194. Handbook of soil evaluation. University of California, Berkeley, Calif. p. 225.

Stottenberg, N. L., and J. L. White. 1953. Selective loss of plant nutrients by erosion. Soil Sci. Soc. Am. Proc. 17:406–440.

Tanji, K. K. 1976. A conceptual hydrosalinity model for predicting salt load in irrigation return flows. p. 49–67. In H. E. Dregne (ed.) Proc. Int. Conf. on Managing Saline Water for Irrigation: Planning for the Future, 16–20 Aug. 1976, Texas Tech. Univ., USEPA, and UNESCO. Texas Tech. Univ., Lubbock.

Tanji, K. K., J. W. Biggar, G. L. Horner, R. J. Miller, and W. O. Pruitt. 1976. Irrigation tailwater management. 1975–76 Annu. Rep. to USEPA, EPA Grant no. R 803603-01-1. Univ. of Calif. Water Sci. and Eng. Pap. 4011. p. 200.

U.S. Department of Health, Education and Welfare. 1976. Annual summary for the United States, 1975. Monthly Vital Stat. Rep. HRA 76;1120 Vol. 24, no. 13.

U.S. Environmental Protection Agency and Colorado State University. 1972. Proc. Natl. Conf. on Managing Irrigated Agriculture to Improve Water Quality, 16–18 May 1972, USEPA and Colorado State Univ., Fort Collins. Graphics Manage. Corp., Washington, D.C. p. 306.

U.S. Salinity Laboratory Staff. 1954. Diagnosis and improvement of saline and alkali soils. USDA Agric. Handbk. 60. p. 160.

Utah Stae University Foundation. 1969. Characteristics and pollution problems of irrigation return flow. Rep. to Fed. Water Pollut. Control Admin., Robert S. Kerr Water Res. Center, Ada, Okla. p. 237.

Van Schilfgaarde, J., L. Bernstein, J. D. Rhoades, and S. L. Rawlins. 1974. Irrigation management for salt control. J. Irrig. Drainage Div., ASCE 100(IR3):321–338.

Vink, A. P. A. 1976. Land use in advancing agriculture. Adv. Ser. in Agric. Sci. 1. Springer-Verlog, New York. esp. Chap. 6.

Water Quality Criteria. 1973. A report prepared by the National Academy of Sciences—the National Academy of Engineering Committee on Water Quality Criteria to EPA. Ecol. Res. Ser., USEPA. R3. 73.033. March 1973. U.S. Government Printing Office, Washington, D.C. p. 594.

Wilding, L. P., G. M. Schafer, and R. B. Jones. 1964. Morley and Blount soils: a statistical summary of certain physical and chemical properties of selected profiles from Ohio. Soil Sci. Soc. Am. Proc. 28:674–679.

Williamson, S. J. 1973. Fundamentals of air pollution. Addison-Wesley Publ. Co., Reading, Mass. p. 472.

Wischmeier, W. H. 1976. Use and misuse of the Universal Soil Loss Equation. J. Soil Water Conserv. 31:5–9.

Wischmeier, W. H., and D. D. Smith. 1958. Rainfall energy and its relationship to soil loss. Trans. Am. geophys. Union 39:285–291.

Wischmeier, W. H., and D. D. Smith. 1965. Predicting rainfall erosion losses from cropland east of the Rocky Mountains. Agric. Handbk. no. 282. ARS, USDA.

Wischmeier, W. H., C. B. Johnson, and B. V. Cross. 1971. A soil erodibility nomograph for farmland and construction sites. J. Soil Water Conserv. 26:189–193.

Yaalon, D. H. 1975. Conceptual models in pedogenesis: can soil forming functions be solved? Geoderma 14:189–205.

11 Planning Large-scale Agricultural Systems with Integrated Water Management

W. A. HALL, G. H. HARGREAVES, AND G. H. CANNELL

Colorado State University, Fort Collins, Colorado;
Utah State University, Logan, Utah; and
University of California, Riverside, California, respectively

I. INTRODUCTION

Large-scale development and operation has produced spectacular results in the modern world, so much so that it is often taken for granted that "big" produces more, and more efficiently, than "small." In reality, not all large-scale systems are more effective than small scale. It has been argued convincingly that our largest cities have long since passed the point of maximum efficiency of services to their citizens. On occasion, well-intentioned, integrated management systems have produced more bureaucratic tyranny than services intended when they were created.

As a result of these problem situations, there has developed a serious level of mistrust of the concepts of integrated management, thereby actually preventing the resolution of important problems.

There are certain characteristics of resources, particularly land and water, which favor the use of integrated systems management on a relatively large-scale basis. In some instances, these characteristics are so pronounced that the resource cannot be successfully managed and conserved without integrated management.

The most common characteristic is that of the existence of important *economics of scale.* If the decisions and actions available to individuals to accomplish their objectives are replaced by a single group decision and action, the objectives of all concerned can often be met at a higher level at far less cost. The car pool is one simple example. A water supply aqueduct is another. Coordinated marketing (and purchasing) is another. Transport systems also possess this characteristic. The entire modern system of industrial production is based on this principle and its corollary, "specialization of effort."

The second most common characteristic is exemplified by conditions equivalent to those described by Hardin in "Tragedy of the Commons" (Hardin, 1968). This term describes those situations where the optimal decision of each individual is antagonistic to the welfare of all individuals.

Often it results in the virtual destruction of the common resource. The basic resource involved in the original description of the Tragedy of the Commons was the common pasture or open range. The optimal decision of each stockman was to put as many animals on the open range as possible, since if he did not someone else would. At Signal Hill, California, it was an oil resource that was destroyed. Water quality in the United States and elsewhere is another resource that is adversely affected by this characteristic and by the failure to provide the necessary institutions for large-scale management of these systems.

There are two other interrelated characteristics which create a requirement for large-scale system management. These are the twin necessities for improving assurance of resources and/or security (economic, social, physical, etc.) in time and in place. The concepts of life and hazard insurance are obvious examples of these two characteristics, as are fire departments, police departments, national defense forces, mutual security treaties, etc. Not so obvious are water resource systems, marketing systems, transport systems, and utility systems. However, all these share the common characteristic of requiring large-scale systems management in order to provide a minimum assured level of a service.

Agricultural systems displaying these characteristics are many and varied, among these are marketing and storage systems, harvesting and processing (preservation) systems, agricultural supply systems, education systems, and water resource systems. In addition, the on-farm agricultural system itself may be highly responsive to large-scale management under certain circumstances.

Because of limitation of space, only the water resource systems will be discussed in this chapter. This will be supported with resource data in planning, design, and institutions required for integrated management.

As an example for which large-scale farming management is particularly suited, consider the large, uniform, almost flat areas in the Central and Imperial Valleys of California. On the other hand, land which is extensively cut into small pieces of farmable land by the erosion and stream structure is less suitable. Except for technical services and the power of mass purchasing, the size of the individual plot under such conditions will usually limit the scale of operations to small machinery units and, hence, will seriously limit economics of scale.

Many developing agricultural areas have encountered serious difficulties because inadequate attention was given to the development of large-scale management systems for marketing products, providing necessary agricultural inputs and services when and where needed, and shipping the products and supplies in a timely manner where they are needed. In a classical analysis, Haissman (1970) also demonstrated the necessity for large-scale management of educational systems to assure availability of balanced supplies of the right kinds of expertise at the right time and the right place. Serious mismatches in the timing of availability of expertise has doomed some development projects to almost permanent failure.

As an illustration of a distinctive large-scale agricultural system which requires integrated management, the water resource system is described in greater (but by no means exhaustive) detail in the following section. In addition, data requirements for soil and climate factors which are essential for integrated agricultural systems management are treated in Section III. The final section treats the problem, all too often neglected, of essential institutions required for integrated management of large-scale systems, particularly where substantial numbers of people are involved directly or indirectly in the various levels of decision making.

II. WATER RESOURCES MANAGEMENT

Water resources management is an excellent example of integrated management of large-scale systems since it possesses all of the characteristics which require community action. This necessity has not always been understood. There still exists major international, national, regional, and local examples where lack of recognition of the absolute necessity for integrated management has prevented the resolution of the associated problems, and has resulted in far more conflict and controversy (Hall, 1963).

No water project has ever been undertaken simply to provide more water per se. In fact, most projects result in less liquid fresh water than existed prior to the project. Rather, the puspose in virtually every case has been to increase by an order of magnitude the *assurance* with which a given level of water supply will be available for useful purposes *when* and *where* needed, or, alternatively, to assure it will *not* occur when and/or where it would be highly undesirable. A million cubic meters of water per se is quite worthless. A million cubic meters of water for a long series of time periods assured to a major industrial city in both time and place is extremely valuable (Wollman, 1962). Thus, it is obvious that the true value of water resource development is to be found in the degree of assurance of a given volume and not in the volume itself. Integrated management is the essential requirement for that assurance.

In addition, water resources structural systems often show major economics of scale. Doubling the size of the tunnels of the Colorado River Aqueduct resulted in only an 18 to 20% increase in total cost (MWDSC, 1939). For open-channel aqueducts, in general, doubling capacity will increase costs by only 25 to 30%. Reservoirs usually show economics of scale over some portion of the capacity range.

From these economic considerations it is obvious that pooling the water supply problems of many farmers through an irrigation district (or its equivalent) can allow a much more economical solution for everyone and also allow many more farmers to participate. Indeed, the original development of civilization (civil government) in the arid regions may well have been the result of this necessity for an institution-to accomplish large-scale integrated management of the flood waters of the Nile, Tigris-Euphrates, Indus, Ganges, and other major arid zone rivers.

The "Tragedy of the Commons" characteristic also pervades water resources management, but perhaps no example is more dramatic than the destruction of water quality throughout the world. This problem is still in the dark ages in terms of developing the integrated management systems absolutely necessary for resolving the problem (Hall, 1976).

Ground water is a second major water resource system where all the elements of "Tragedy of the Commons" generally exist. The necessary large-scale management systems have not yet been satisfactorily developed. Management of watershed areas is another problem where the fact that no one's problems becomes everyone's problem requires integrated management of the common, multiple-purpose resource. Development of the necessary institutional structure, again, is far behind the problem, and the productivity of major areas of the world has been and is currently being destroyed by this failure. Drainage and salt balance are also problems for which small-scale, individual efforts, however well intentioned, are useless if not actually counter-productive. These problems destroyed civilizations in the past and, if not corrected, will do so again and again in the future.

There are five major subsystems involved in water and related land use systems which must be recognized and provided with integrated management.

1. WATERSHED SUBSYSTEMS

Beginning with the precipitation, this subsystem serves as a resource collection device. Depending on the management practices on the watershed, it may result in increases or decreases in peak flow rates, low flow rates, and total discharge. These are not insignificant effects. An analysis of a number of arid zone western rivers by Christianson (1964) strongly suggests that improved watershed management from the standpoint of vegetative cover actually reduced mean annual runoff by as much as 30 to 50%. The Colorado River displays the same apparent correlations between streamflow and grazing management practices over a 90-year period. With about 95% of the precipitation lost by evapotranspiration on these watersheds, a 1% increase in this vegetative use represents a 20% decrease in annual streamflow.

Sediment production rates are also determined by management practices. The practices that apparently reduced runoff as cited above also appear to have drastically reduced erosion and sediment transport.

Snowpack can be managed to some extent to help increase runoff production and to delay spring runoff.

Perhaps the most important aspect for urban hydrology and flood potential is the urbanization process itself. Improperly managed, it can produce more sediment in 1 year than would occur naturally in centuries. The decreased permeability which comes with present practices usually increases both flood volumes and flood peaks. However, the individual developer of a few hundred hectares is in no position to provide anything like an optimal storm drain system or erosion control system for the property he is developing, both because of economics of scale and because of the effects of "Tragedy of the Commons."

In some tropical regions, modifications of the land use practices on the watershed, particularly the deforestation of slopes for conversion to farmland, has increased landslides and mass wasting with resultant sedimentation of reservoirs and destruction of fertile valley agricultural lands, as well as ultimate loss of the "new land" presumed to be developed.

2. RIVER REGULATION SUBSYSTEM

This important subsystem involves integrated water management. Few rivers (or other sources of supply) have a distribution of streamflow through the year which is compatible with the many demands placed upon it. The river regulation subsystem serves (by means of storage capacity) to convert an existing time sequence of flows into a more desirable sequence for all concerned. It reduces the probability of excess amounts of water at some times (e.g., floods) and increases the assurance of water availability at other times as may be desired, including low-flow augmentation for in-channel uses such as aquatic life, recreation, etc.

It would appear obvious that, from the point of view of economics of scale and of available reservoir sites, the river regulation subsystem must be a regionally managed large-scale system for all but trivial cases. Further (but less apparent), its management is greatly affected by the decisions of those concerned in the watershed management subsystem. At present these two systems are seldom adequately coupled for integrated management, except on an informal and voluntary basis.

3. WATER DISTRIBUTION SUBSYSTEM

In concept this system includes all means of transporting water to locations of use whether through natural channels or aqueducts. Its function is related to producing assurance of *where* water will be made available for whatever uses may be desired (including in-stream uses). These subsystems normally show major economics of scale. In fact, it would be economically infeasible to transport water much over a mile by pipeline for use by a single individual, unless that individual is in fact a manager of an aggregated use system involving many people or products for many people. Yet water has been transported at almost insignificant cost for distances of nearly 800 km (500 mi) to serve the aggregated needs of millions of people and millions of hectares of land.

Water use subsystems constitute a possible exception to the absolute necessity for integrated water management. Even so, where the management of use can be integrated, improvements of management and productivity will result. To a large extent this occurs because of the impact of the requirements (when-where) placed on other subsystems. One of the major causes of the derailment of the "green revolution" in India and other hungry nations was the lack of integration of water supply-distribution system management with water use management.

One important aspect of both urban and agricultural water use that requires integrated management is found in the fact that waste water from any one user is seldom actually lost but rather becomes a source of supply for other users. For all practical purposes the only water lost from the system is that which is evaporated or flows directly to the ocean or to a saline sink. In many instances the ground water and surface water channels through which the "waste" flows are simply parts of a very low-cost storage and redistribution system serving other users. Unilateral decisions by individual users to increase their nominal water use efficiency can have severe effects on these secondary natural channels and reservoirs requiring more, not fewer, dams and aqueducts to service the same area.

Other problems can also be traced to lack of integrated systems management. Water use can be modified from random demand to integrated or scheduled demand, with substantial savings. However, it is important to keep in mind that the water use (whatever and whenever it may be) is the primary reason for all the subsystems.

4. WASTE WATER DISPOSAL, RECLAMATION, AND REUSE SUBSYSTEMS

These last two subsystems require large-scale, integrated water management if the fruits of productivity are not to be destroyed. Many ancient civilizations destroyed themselves because the need for integrated, large-scale management of this subsystem was not recognized until an irreversible adverse salinity and water-logging situation destroyed the land resource on which those civilizations depended. Even in modern society, we have very poor recognition of this problem and many highly productive areas are moving along the exact path of ancient Mesopotamia.

III. RESOURCE DATA USE IN PLANNING AND DESIGN

The resource data base for planning and design consists primarily of a summary and inventory of soils, water, climate, and related resources. The development of large-scale agricultural systems dependent upon water management requires more precise and complete information and investigation than is typical for many local projects. Careful planning is necessary if large-scale systems are to produce at the anticipated level.

Geologic maps and geologic studies provide valuable information on possible faulting, sinks, or other engineering problems. A knowledge of the soil age, geology of the parent material, and mode of formation provides useful information related to fertility, structure, and general potential for agricultural development.

Topography is required for nearly all design features. The scale and contour intervals are dependent upon the detail of the studies required.

Large-scale agricultural systems with integrated water management include considerations relative to irrigation, drainage, flood control, and, to a lesser degree, management of dry-farmed, semiarid lands. In this section primary emphasis is given to hydrology, climate, and soils.

A. Hydrology

Surface water hydrology and ground water hydrology or geology are so interactive that they generally need to be investigated as part of a general process. Precipitation, which supplies the source for both surface flow and ground water, seldom exhibits definite trends but is characterized by a high degree of variability. Periods of 5 or more years significantly above or below normal are quite common. Occasionally, a period of 10 or more years may be significantly above normal. The effect of abnormal rainfall on streamflow and upon ground water is cumulative. A single high rainfall year may increase streamflow and ground water levels for several years thereafter.

Planning and design for the use of surface water or of ground water should be based upon reasonably adequate streamflow measurements and of water table and specific yield data. There is no easy answer to the question as to how many years of record should be required for minimum accuracy. However, many costly past mistakes could have been avoided by a study of long-term precipitation records and determinations as to how normal the rainfall was during the period of record.

A study of a number of long precipitation records indicates that a 5-year period of record has about a 32% probability of being 25% or more above or below a long-term normal. For a 10-year period there is about the same probability that the mean will be 15% above or below the long-term mean. Usually a 20-year precipitation record results in a statistically adequate sample for most planning purposes. Short records of surface water flow, say 5 years, are usually considered to be too short for good planning and design. However, interpretation of longer periods of precipitation records and use of correlations of streamflow with precipitation, giving adequate allowance for the lag between precipitation and runoff and for evapotranspiration losses on the watershed, can significantly improve the usefulness of short periods of streamflow measurements.

B. Climatic Data

The most important weather measurements or climatic values to be used in planning and design are listed in their approximate order of importance as follows:

1) Rainfall or precipitation—daily, monthly, probabilities, intensities;
2) Temperature—maximum and minimum, daily and monthly;
3) Solar radiation—Langleys per day;
4) Sunshine hours or percentage of possible;
5) Relative humidity—mean values and maximum and minimum;
6) Wind—extreme values or damaging velocities; and
7) Dew—prevalence of dew formation.

Temperature data relate to optimal ranges for production of various crops. These ranges are given in biological data handbooks. Within a definable range of temperatures, production increases with temperature. Radiation is more effective in producing photosynthesis and growth at higher temperatures. Within the optimum range potential yield increases as a straight-line function of temperature in degrees Celsius × incident solar radiation.

Radiation frequently correlates well with temperature. In other climates, such as in the tropics, temperature may be fairly constant with much greater variations in radiation. Various studies have shown yields as straight-line functions of radiation. However, the true relationship is best represented by a product of temperature and radiation.

Humidity, temperature, and dew formation interact to produce conditions that influence prevalence of plant diseases. These relationships are discussed in considerable detail in plant pathology texts.

1. ESTIMATING AGRICULTURAL WATER REQUIREMENTS

Potential evapotranspiration (ETP) measures the climatic potential influencing the use of water by crops and vegetation. Usually evapotranspiration (ET) by grass with use rates similar to perennial ryegrass is used for reference. Potential evapotranspiration can be estimated from mean temperature in degrees Celsius (TMC) and mean incident solar radiation in Langleys per day (RS). Potential evapotranspiration in mm per mo can be approximated from the equation:

$$ETP = 0.004 \times TMC \times RS. \qquad [1]$$

For areas where there is a fairly high percentage of possible sunshine, as in most arid climates, ETP in mm per mo can be approximated from the monthly percentage of daytime hours of the year (P) and TMC. The equation can be written:

$$ETP = 0.91 \times TMC \times P. \qquad [2]$$

Crop water requirements are estimated by multiplying ETP × a crop coefficient (KC). Values of KC to be used with the principal agricultural crops are given in Table 1. Table 1 presents an average KC for full crop cover to be used in designing the system capacity and an average seasonal KC to be used in estimating seasonal requirements and for economic analysis.

Water requirements for irrigated crops and rainfed agriculture are further discussed in a manual prepared by Hargreaves (1975).

2. MOISTURE ADEQUACY AND YIELD

Most crops have critical periods during which the effects of water stress on yield are more important than for average conditions. If moisture stress is not concentrated in a critical period then much moisture adequacy and

Table 1—Generalized crop coefficients (KC).

Crop	Average KC for full crop cover†	Average seasonal KC‡
Field and oil crops (including beans, castor beans, corn, cotton, flax, peanuts, potatoes, safflower, soybeans, sorghum, sugar beets, tomatoes, and wheat)	1.15	0.90
Fruits, nuts, and grapes		
Citrus fruits (oranges, lemons, and grapefruits)	0.75	0.75
Deciduous fruits (peaches, plums, and walnuts)	0.90	0.70
Deciduous fruits with cover crop	1.25	1.00
Grapes	0.75	0.60
Hay, forage, and cover crops		
Alfalfa	1.35	1.00
Short grass	1.00	1.00
Clover pasture	1.15	
Green manure	1.10	0.95
Sugar cane	1.25	1.00
Summer vegetables	1.15	0.85

† Recommended for designing system capacity.
‡ To be used in estimating seasonal requirements and for economic analysis. Provides satisfactory results for irrigation scheduling for most soils with good capacity to store readily available moisture.

yield data fit well into a definite pattern. Hargreaves and Christianson (1974) used Y to express a ratio of yield to maximum yield under the prevailing fertility and cultural conditions and X as the ratio of the actual moisture available to the amount for which the yield is a maximum. Plotting of data for a number of forage and field crops resulted in the equation:

$$Y = 0.8X + 1.3X^2 - 1.1X^3. \qquad [3]$$

Good data coverage was available for the range of $X - 0.40$ to $X - 1.00$.

The first derivative gives the incremental change in yield with change in moisture availability. The equation is:

$$dY/dX = 0.8 + 2.6X - 3.3X^2. \qquad [4]$$

From Eq. [4], when X exceeds 0.701, the rate of increase in yield with respect to the rate of increase in moisture adequacy is < 1.00.

3. MOISTURE AVAILABILITY INDEX

The concepts of dependable precipitation (PD) and a Moisture Availability Index (MAI) are useful in estimating possible increases in production and in evaluating climate. Dependable precipitation is the 75% probability of precipitation occurrence (the amount of rainfall that can expected to be equaled or exceeded during three-fourths of the years). Moisture Availability Index is a measure of the degree to which potential requirements (ETP) are met at the 75% probability of occurrence. Moisture Availability Index is given by the equation:

$$MAI = PD/ETP. \qquad [5]$$

The values of MAI have been found to correlate very well with crop yields under dry farming conditions. The concept is also useful when combined with Eq. [3] in projecting possible future crop yields after conversion to irrigated agriculture.

4. A CLASSIFICATION OF CLIMATE

A climatic classification that is related to water requirements and excesses and deficits of precipitation has considerable use for large-scale agricultural planning. The significance of temperature, radiation, and relative humidity have been briefly described above. In general, several rules are applicable to the planning process. Some of these rules are:

1) Potential gross crop income from irrigated lands increases with decreasing precipitation;
2) Potential income from agricultural lands increases with temperature up to an upper limit that varies with the crops produced;
3) Potential income from agriculture increases with length of growing season; and
4) Potential crop income decreases with increasing excesses of precipitation over plant water requirements unless the excess moisture is removed from the plant root zone. There are some notable exceptions, such as rice.

Based on the above considerations and practical application to the planning process, it would seem desirable to develop some form of standard classification for measuring moisture adequacies or deficits from the climatic conditions as the necessity arises. Hargreaves (1972) proposed that MAI be adopted as a standard index for measuring water deficiencies and excesses, and that the following classification be used:

MAI — 0.00 to 0.33	very deficient
MAI — 0.34 to 0.67	moderately deficient
MAI — 0.68 to 1.00	somewhat deficient
MAI — 1.01 to 1.33	adequate
MAI — 1.34 and above	excessive

This classification seems applicable for the more favorable soil conditions and is proposed for general usage. Where the soil moisture storage capacity is adequate for less than 1 week, the correlation between MAI and crop production probably will be lowered. The minimum values for economic production can then be expected to be correspondingly higher.

In a study of precipitation as related to agricultural production in northeast Brazil, Hargreaves (1974) used the following classification of climate:

Criteria	Climate classification	Productivity classification
All months with MAI in the range of 0.00 to 0.33	Very arid	Not suited for rainfed agriculture
1 or 2 mo with MAI of 0.34 or above	Arid	Limited suitability for rainfed agriculture
3 or 4 mo with MAI of 0.34 or above	Semiarid	Production possible for crops requiring a 3- to 4-mo growing season
5 or more consecutive months with MAI of 0.34 or above	Wet-dry	Production possible for crops requiring a good level of moisture adequacy during 5 or more mo

In the last three classifications, drainage may be the first development to be considered. With excessive precipitation during 1 or more months of the growing season, surface drainage needs to be considered for soils lacking adequate internal drainage and having slopes less than 2 or 3% depending upon surface irregularities.

C. Soils

A compilation of soil resources in large-scale, irrigated systems is essential in integrated water management. Soils to be irrigated should be carefully evaluated. Laboratory analysis should include texture, salinity, alkalinity, hydraulic conductivity, acidity, water quality, soil structure, and moisture retention. In some areas investigation of excesses or deficiencies of metals and other elements has been found necessary.

1. SOIL SURVEY CLASSIFICATION SYSTEMS

Various soil classification systems have been used for evaluating lands for irrigation and no single classification can fit all conditions. The results of soil surveys often are considered the essential part of soil resources development. However, in irrigation projects other important characteristics have to be taken into account and data developed on a quantitative basis, which is not often done in soil survey work (Hagan, 1967).

The scale of soil maps must be correlated with the detail intended for the large-scale field project to be conducted. For irrigation projects, maps on large scales, 1:25,000 or larger, are often required. The contents of the legend for any soil map for land use planning, which would include large irrigation projects, should contain aspects of the following (Vink, 1975):

1) Soil taxonomy, preferably in an internationally recognized system;
2) Soil materials, including not only their texture but also their chemistry and mineralogy;

3) Soil depth (either to the bottom of the pedological column or to rooting depth, whichever is deepest) and soil hydrology;

4) Soil topography (slopes, complex relief forms, microrelief) and surface characteristics.

The way in which these characteristics are used depends on the purpose of the soil map and the area which the map will cover.

Soil Taxonomy (Soil Survey Staff, 1975) is a precise tool for describing, classifying, and comparing soils around the world. Although it is not used on a worldwide basis, other classification systems, to some extent, can be adapted. For example, West African semiarid tropic soils (French classification system) are adapted to *Soil Taxonomy* (Charreau, 1974, 1977). The use of soil taxonomy in irrigation projects is often critical to their success. Comparison of soils already under irrigation is often used to predict changes in soil processes which may include secondary precipitates of calcium carbonates, iron and manganese oxides, and other processes, depending on worldwide geographical location and local conditions.

In order to embrace to the fullest extent the soil map legend needs as previously mentioned, a generalized land classification system should be used in conjunction with soil survey types. Specifications need to be modified to fit local practices and possible economic factors related to development. Various land classification systems are available to use in large-scale irrigation systems. The *New International Land Suitability Classification,* FAO Consultation on Land Evaluation for Rural Purposes (Brinkman & Smyth, 1973) is a product of several countries and brings into its format the experience of many experts, thus broadening its base to fit many regions of the world. Two major systems are used in the United States, the U.S. Soil Conservation Service (cited by Hudson, 1971; and Vink, 1975) and the Bureau of Reclamation (1953; and cited by Vink, 1975).

These systems and others have found wide use in many countries but only with suitable modifications that fit local conditions for the project. The following Bureau of Reclamation Standard System (1953) has been modified and used successfully in large irrigation projects (see Table 2).

2. GENERALIZED LAND CLASSIFICATION SYSTEM

a. Basic Classes of Land—Four basic classes are used to identify the arable lands according to their suitability for irrigated agriculture, and one class to eventually identify the nonarable lands. The first three classes represent lands with progressively lower potential for irrigated agriculture. The number of classes mapped in a particular investigation depends upon the diversity of the land conditions encountered and other requirements as dictated by the objectives of the particular investigation.

Class 1—Highly arable: lands in this class are highly suitable for irrigation farming, being capable of producing sustained and relatively high yields of a wide range of climatically adapted crops at reasonable cost. They are smooth lying with gentle slopes. The soils are deep and of medium to moderately fine texture. Roots, air, and water penetrate the soil readily. It is

Table 2—General land classification specifications.

Soil characteristics	Class 1—arable	Class 2-arable	Class 3—arable
	Soil		
Texture	Sandy loam to friable clay loam	Loamy sand to very permeable clay	Loamy sand to permeable clay
Depth			
To sand, gravel or cobble	90 cm plus of fsl or finer or 105 cm of sl	60 cm plus fsl or finer 75 cm sl to ls	45 cm plus fsl or finer or 60 cm of coarser soil
To shale or similar material 15 cm less to rock	150 cm plus 04 135 cm with minimum of 15 cm gravel overlying impervious material or sandy loam throughout	120 cm plus or 105 cm with minimum of 15 cm gravel	105 cm plus or 90 cm with minimum of 15 cm of gravel overlying impervious material or loamy sand throughout
To penetrable lime horizon	45 cm with 150 cm penetrable pH is <9.0	35 cm with 120 cm penetrable	25 cm with 90 cm penetrable
Alkalinity	Unless soil is calcareous, total salts are low and evidence of black alkali is absent	pH 9.0 or less unless soil is calcareous, salts are low and evidence of black alkali is absent	pH 9.0 or less unless soil is calcareous, total salts are low and evidence of black alkali is absent
Salinity	Total salts not to exceed 0.2%	Total salts not to exceed 0.5%	Total salts not to exceed 0.5%
	Topography		
Slopes	Smooth slopes up to 4% in reasonably large size areas	Smooth slopes up to 8% in general gradient	Smooth slopes up to 12% in general gradient
Surface	Even enough to require only small amount of leveling no heavy grading	Moderate grading required but feasible at reasonable cost	Heavy and expensive grading in spots but in amount found feasible
Cover (loose rocks)	Clearing cost small	Sufficient to reduce productivity and interfere with cultural practices. Clearing required but at moderate cost	Present in amounts to require expensive but feasible clearing
	Drainage		
Soil and topography	Soil and topographic conditions such that no specific farm drainage requirement is anticipated	Some farm drainage will probably be required. Reclamation by artificial means feasible at reasonable cost	Significant farm drainage required. Reclamation by artificial means expensive but feasible

moderately permeable, is well drained, and has good available moisture capacity. These soils are free from harmful accumulations of soluble salts and can be readily reclaimed. Both soil and topographic conditions are such that no specific farm drainage requirements are anticipated, minimum erosion will result from irrigation, and land development can be accomplished at relatively low cost.

Class 2—Arable: this class comprises lands of moderate suitability for irrigation farming, being measurably lower than Class 1 in productive capacity, adapted to a somewhat narrower range of crops, more expensive to prepare for irrigation, and more costly to farm. They are not so desirable nor of such high value as lands of Class 1 because of certain correctable or noncorrectable limitations. They may have a lower available moisture capacity, as indicated by coarse texture or limited soil depth; they may be only slowly permeable to water because of clay layers or compaction in the subsoil, or they may be moderately saline which may limit productivity or involve moderate costs for leaching. Topographic limitations include uneven surface requiring moderate costs for leveling, short slopes requiring shorter lengths of runs, or steeper slopes necessitating special care and greater costs to irrigate and prevent erosion. Farm drainage may be required at moderate cost, or loose rocks may have to be removed from the surface. Any of these limitations may be sufficient to reduce the land from Class 1 to Class 2 but frequently a combination of two or more of them is operating.

Class 3—Arable: this class comprises lands that are suitable for irrigation development but are approaching marginality for irrigation and are of distinctly restricted suitability because of more extreme deficiencies in the soil, topographic, or drainage characteristics than described for Class 2 lands. They may have good topography, but because of inferior soils have restricted crop adaptability, require larger amounts of irrigation water or special irrigation practices, and demand greater fertilization or more intense soil improvement practices. They may have uneven topography, moderate to high concentration of salts, or restricted drainage, susceptible to correction but only at relatively high cost. Generally, greater risk may be involved in farming Class 3 lands than the better classes of land.

Class 4—Limited arable or special use: lands are included in this class only after special economic and engineering studies have shown them to be arable.

Class 5—Nonarable: lands in this class are nonarable under existing conditions, but have potential value sufficient to warrant tentative segregation for special study prior to completion of the classification, or they are lands in existing projects whose arability is dependent upon additional scheduled project construction or land improvements. They may have a specific soil deficiency such as excessive salinity, very uneven topography, inadequate drainage, or excessive rock or tree cover. Special agronomic, economic, or engineering studies are required to provide adequate information, such as extent and location of farm and project drains, or probable payment capacity under the anticipated land use, in order to complete the classification of the lands. The designation of Class 5 is tentative and must be changed to the proper arable class or Class 6 prior to completion of the land classification.

Class 6—Nonarable: lands in this class include those considered non-arable because of failure to meet the minimum requirements for the other classes of land. Generally, Class 6 comprises steep, rough, broken, or badly eroded lands; lands with soils of very coarse or fine texture, or shallow soils over gravel, shale, sandstone, or hardpan; and lands that have inadequate drainage and high concentrations of soluble salts or sodium.

b. Basic Subclasses—The reasons for placing a class lower than Class 1 are indicated by appending the letters "s," "t," and "d" to the class number to show whether the deficiency is in "soils," "topography," or "drainage." The interaction of accumulative effects of deficiencies may justify placing the land in question in a lower class. Any combination involving a Class 3 deficiency with another deficiency of either Class 2 or 3 level will generally result in placing the land in Class 4, 5, or 6. The basic subclasses of the land classes are s, t, d, st, sd, td, and std.

IV. INSTITUTIONS FOR INTEGRATED MANAGEMENT OF LARGE-SCALE SYSTEMS

It is not sufficient to identify where large-scale integrated systems management can significantly improve the achievement of the objectives of all concerned. To be able to achieve that improvement, adequate mechanisms for executing integrated management on an appropriate scale must be provided. The usual mechanism is the creation of public or private institutions for this purpose. However structured, it must meet certain key requirements.

First of all there must be that "agreement to agree" sometimes known as a *charge, constitution, by-laws,* etc., which establishes a priori what shall constitute agreement (e.g., a majority vote) before any specific decisions are made. Second, those who agree to create the institution must grant it sufficient authority to carry out any assigned responsibility. Authority is like mass or energy, it must be conserved. If granted it cannot be retained. If retained by the creators, no authority is in fact granted.

It is by no means a simple task to accomplish this second step, even though there are good intentions on the part of all concerned. How much authority is enough? How much is too much? History contains far too many examples of abuse of grants of excessive authority for this to be a trivial question. As a result, the beneficiaries have often solidly elected to forego the benefits of integrated management in order to retain authority. However, serious adverse consequences have followed, as with the current desertification of the Sahel and the lack of military security in the Balkans after World War I, to cite two very different examples. A clear-cut definition and limitation of authority to be granted is always difficult to create but it may be the difference between well being and disaster.

Third, the grant of authority cannot be rescinded at will by any party (although the definition of an agreement to terminate or modify can be specified). The U.S. Constitution was an agreement to agree executed by the several states. The Civil War was not really fought over slavery, but rather the issue of the right of any state to withdraw from that agreement at will.

Although it would appear that the hazards and uncertainties involved would preclude any large-scale, integrated management of land use systems, this has not proved to be the case where the alternatives could be clearly presented and understood. Irrigation districts were formed rather easily, even from groups of former bitter competitors, when it became clear that the water supply objectives of all concerned could be met by cooperation. The infeasibility of accomplishing the same objectives by individual decision and action was all too apparent.

Potential benefits from other opportunities for integrated management of land, water, and other resources are not always as striking. Furthermore, problems of equity of decisions on beneficiaries may be much more serious. In some instances the authority of government has been exercised for the benefit of the (voting) majority but with major social and economic cost burdens unceremoniously dumped on the opposing minority. This has led to suspicion, mistrust, and outright rejection of integrated management. Thus, the final important requirement for integrated management of large-scale land (and other) resource use systems is an active recognition of the absolute necessity for the majority to seek the equitable compromise which minimizes the adverse impacts on the minority. "One man-one vote" is an excellent slogan, but in every instance where it has been used without a diligent search for equity, it has failed to accomplish the purposes for which the institution was created.

When these basic requirements are met, the results have been spectacular. The Metropolitan Water District of Southern California is one notable example where a number of cities granted authority to a single institution to resolve the water supply problems of all concerned. It has remained strong primarily because it has always searched for equity. Without it the Southern California Coastal Plain simply could not have developed much beyond its status prior to World War II. Individual effort was beyond the capability of all except Los Angeles.

The self-development of irrigation districts in the western U.S. is a second excellent example of success. Here the key was legislation at the state level authorizing voluntary self-governing associations of individual land owners under guideline laws, specifying the required authorities for management (including mandatory allocation of cost by a limited power of taxation and assessment) as well as the required responsibilities. With the necessary provisions for authority and equity in the guidelines for authorization, these associations were readily formed where desirable but were not imposed where they would serve no useful purpose.

These successes are all the more spectacular when contrasted with the almost universal failure of attempts to create private ditch companies for irrigation purposes. The latter did not have the authority to compel beneficiaries to pay their fair share of the capital costs of the system. Some mutual companies were able to resolve this problem where the beneficiary lands either provided the capital funding or were specifically liable for a specified share of the indebtedness (regardless of current ownership), but more often these funding arrangements were beyond the immediate financial capacity of the mutual owners.

LITERATURE CITED

Brinkman, R., and A. J. Smyth. (ed.). 1973. Land evaluation for rural purposes. Publ. 17. Int. Inst. Land Reclamation and Improvement (ILRI), Wageningen, Netherlands.

Bureau of Reclamation. 1953. Irrigated land use. U.S. Dep. of Interior, Bur. of Reclamation Manual. Vol. V, Part 2, Land classification. USDI, Denver, Colo.

Charreau, C. 1974. Soils of tropical dry and dry-wet climatic areas of West Africa and their use and management. Agron. Mimeo 74-26. Dep. of agron., Cornell Univ., Ithaca, N.Y.

Charreau, C. 1977. Some controversial technical aspects of farming systems in semi-arid West Africa. p. 313–360. *In* Proc. Int. Symp. on Rainfed Agriculture in Semi-Arid Regions, 17–22 Apr. 1977, Univ. Calif., Riverside.

Christianson, J. E. 1964. Precipitation and runoff trends, upper Sevier Basin, Utah. Utah State Univ., Logan, Utah.

Hagan, R. M., H. R. Haise, and T. W. Edminster. (ed.). 1967. Irrigation of agricultural lands. Agron. Ser. II, Am. Soc. Agron., Madison, Wis.

Haissman, I. 1970. Skilled-manpower planning for irrigation projects in developing countries. Univ. California, Berkeley (dissertation).

Hall, W. A. 1963. Los Angeles: Growing pains of a metropolis: Case History 5. p. 517–528. *In* Carle Hodge (ed.) Aridity and man. Pub. no. 74. Am. Assoc. Advance. Sci., Washington, D.C.

Hall, W. A. 1976. Regional integration for effective water resource management. *In* Environmental modeling and decision making: the U.S. experience. Proc. Planning Alternatives for Municipal Water Systems, Oct. 1976, Holcomb Res. Inst., Butler Univ., Indiana. Praeger Publ.

Hardin, G. 1968. Tragedy of the commons. Science 162:1243–1248.

Hargreaves, G. H. 1972. The evaluation of water deficiencies. p. 273–290. *In* Irrig. and Drain. Conf., Am. Soc. Agric. Eng., Spokane, Wash.

Hargreaves, G. H. 1974. Precipitation dependability and potential for agricultural production in Northeast Brazil (74-D155). Empresa Brasileira de Pesquisa Agropedquaria and Utah State Univ., Logan, Utah. 123 p.

Hargreaves, G. H. 1975. Water requirements manual for irrigated crops and rainfed agriculture (75-D158). Utah State Univ., Logan, Utah. 40 p.

Hargreaves, G. H., and J. E. Christianson. 1974. Production as a function of moisture availability. Int. Tech. Coop. Centre ITCC Rev. 3(1[9]):179–189.

Hudson, N. 1971. Soil conservation. Cornell Univ. Press, Ithaca, N.Y.

Metropolitan Water District of Southern California. 1939. History and first annual report. MWDSC, Los Angeles.

Soil Survey Staff. 1975. Soil taxonomy. USDA Handbook 436. Soil conserv. Serv., U.S. Department of Agriculture.

Vink, A. P. A. 1975. Land use in advancing agriculture. Springer-Verlag, New York.

Wollman, N. 1962. The value of water in alternative uses. Univ. of New Mexico Press, Albuquerque, N.M.

12   Defining, Delineating, and Designating Uses for Prime and Unique Agricultural Lands

FRED P. MILLER

University of Maryland
College Park, Maryland

I. INTRODUCTION

A. The Problem

In the first 200 years of U.S. history, about 236 million acres of farmland have been lost from production, an area half as large as that now under cultivation. Most of this loss has been due to erosion, the rest to development (Barney, 1977).

During the last few decades, millions of acres of U.S. cropland have gone out of production due to either economic obsolecence or competition from more intensive land uses. Concurrently, millions of acres of other lands were cleared, drained, graded, and/or irrigated and brought into crop production. While the result of these cropland shifts has been a net loss of the U.S. cropland base, the intensification of production per land unit has more than kept pace with demand. Where the nonagricultural competition for land is absent, the intrinsic quality of the land to produce and its capacity to accomodate agricultural production technology within the given economic framework have been the criteria governing the decisions to shift land in and out of agricultural production.

In the case of more intensive land uses competing with agricultural land at the urban fringe, agriculture has simply not been in the race against the land prices these more intensive urban-oriented land uses generate. Within the last decade, this nonagricultural and urban-oriented competition for prime agricultural land has become an increasing national concern among those who view the problem in a long-range perspective, and especially to those in regions and localities immediately impacted.

The tenor of this nonagricultural competition for agricultural land and the repercussions from excesses in the intensity of the land's use has reached such a peak in some areas that many local and state governments have considered alternatives to the free market in the allocation of land to other uses. These governments have questioned the sacred boundary between the rights to private property and the rights of society at large.

Until recently the loss of the agricultural land resource at the rural-urban fringe was viewed as a by-product of the growth syndrome. There was no national or general alarm because the land use decisions and development policies were (and still are) local. This provincial framework masked the regional and national impact of the erosion of the agricultural land resource in urbanizing areas. The ad hoc, discrete, piecemeal increments in which land changed ownership and use made it difficult to establish the aggregate character of the resulting "land product" (Smith & Barrows, 1975).

What is the perspective on this "resulting land product"? It would appear that the conversion of farmland to urban uses poses no immediate or foreseeable threat to the nation's capacity to provide agricultural products, aside from local shortages or specific (unique) crop losses (Miner, 1975; Peterson & Yampolsky, 1975; Krause & Hair, 1975). But as these authors and others (USDA, 1975) point out, there are other reasons which might justify a stronger farmland protection policy. The U.S. farmland resource base is used not only to provide food and fiber to our own population, but these land-derived commodities are also becoming an increasingly important economic factor in our foreign balance of payments. These farmlands also provide diversification to local and regional economies, as well as a local food source in times of transportation shutdowns and other temporary interferences with the food supply. Diversifying the nation's agricultural production in all geographic regions provides a hedge against catastrophic events such as floods, frosts, and other severe climatic factors, as well as disease and pestilance epidemics. The aesthetic pleasures of a rural environment and the open space concept are important factors in many state efforts to preserve farmland. And it is these best farmlands that can accomodate the necessary resource inputs with a minimal environmental impact and a maximum return for the energy expended.

However, as Peterson and Yampolsky (1975) have indicated, the adverse effects of urban encroachment on adjacent farmlands requires a viable and effective farmland protection policy, that is, one which results in a continuation of productive farming in metropolitan areas. This policy must do more than simply prohibit the conversion of randomly scattered agricultural land. It must provide for the preservation of entire districts which can be devoted to long-term agricultural use (Peterson & Yampolsky, 1975).

But the continued reliance of local land use control has made it difficult to develop such policies. Local land use control has resulted in many local governments developing land use policies which take the form of increasing the tax base and letting their neighboring jurisdictions worry about their own necks. There are about 3,100 counties and thousands of local jurisidctions in the United States forging the nation's "land product" every day through small-scale, local decisions made with little or no understanding or concern about the aggregate character of the resulting "land product." These local governments have struggled to maintain their power, and they have developed neither the will nor the mechanism to act collectively

(ECOP Task Force on Land Use, 1974). There is a lack of target goals and local planning attempts are not comprehensive. And there is a tendency for short-term benefits to receive undue weight while long-run costs of land use decisions are ignored (Smith & Barrows, 1975).

The suburban American lifestyle in the 1970's is an awesome consumer of land, contrasting sharply with an earlier lifestyle where the city center was the focus of life with the land use around the city characterized by concentric rings of declining intensity of use (Raup, 1975). The roots of this change are many, defying any simplistic analysis. But Raup (1975) has suggested the problem of the urban threat to rural lands can be characterized by three root causes—the automobile, affluence, and advertising.

As a result of these land use conflicts, soil scientists and agronomists are being pressed by legislative bodies and planners to help define, delineate, and designate uses for prime and unique lands. This process was deemed necessary thousands of years ago in ancient civilizations (Simonson, 1968). Contemporary society deems it necessary again today with a degree of sophistication which taxes our current capabilities. As Raup (1975) has indicated, these efforts to preserve certain lands as open space have suddenly acquired the sanctity heretofore accorded the buffalo and the golden eagle.

B. Land vs. Soil

In discussing and defining the concept of land, the soil scientist has been traditionally biased towards the physical or edaphic component of land. But the concept of land is much broader than soil, embracing all the attributes of the earth's solid surface.

Eren (as cited by Brinkman & Smyth, 1973) defines land as embracing the atmosphere, the soil and underlying geology, the hydrology, and the plants on, above, and below a specific area of the earth's surface. Land is also defined to include the results of past and present human activities as well as the animals within this area, insofar as they exert a significant influence on the present and future uses of land by man. Other concepts of land (Brinkman & Smyth, 1973) include land as space, nature, a gene resource, a production unit, a consumer good or commodity, a source of pleasure and recreation, property, and capital in the economic connotation.

These broad concepts of land present an immediate difficulty in defining prime land, for a tract of land may be used for a variety of purposes at any particular time. The value of the land, therefore, does not necessarily depend on its physical characteristics alone but is greatly influenced by social requirements and economic considerations. Furthermore, the most appropriate use of land should not be judged in a purely local context, but account should be taken of the influence of each possible use on other tracts of land (Brinkman & Smyth, 1973). Thus, there are numerous criteria which can be used to define various degrees of land quality.

II. THE CONCEPT OF PRIME AND UNIQUE LAND

To develop and define a concept of prime land, therefore, requires a carefully selected set of criteria and units to measure quality. Without such criteria, attempts to define prime land, especially in physical or edaphic terms, are doomed to failure as a result of the judgmental nature of the prime concept.

Raup (1975) addresses this point in suggesting that the concept of prime land is useful, but it cannot be defined in terms of a system of cardinal measurement. Raup maintains that the concept of prime land is merely an ordering device. While the chemical, physical, and geodetic properties of a tract of land can be expressed in quantitative terms that reflect cardinal measurements, the weights that must be attached to these properties (soil series, landscape position, spatial distribution and configuration, location, etc.) are always relative weights (Raup, 1975). Wood (1975) also makes this point.

As a guide to land classification, and a criterion for the protection of farmland, Raup (1975) states that the designation "prime land" has both a time frame and a space frame. If both of these frameworks must be specified for a prime land classification to have meaning, as Raup maintains, then the concept of prime land is both time-bound and space-bound and cannot be defined solely in physical or biological terms. It is Raup's contention that the concept of prime land is basically an economic concept and can only be adequately defined in terms of economic variables. For this reason, therefore, Raup holds the conviction that attempts to define prime land in physical terms are doomed to failure.

Regardless of the frameworks that may be necessary to define prime land and the complexity of doing so, the fact remains that legislative bodies and others requiring a definition of prime land will continue to press for a more simplistic definition. And there is evidence to suggest that defining prime land outside Raup's time and space frameworks can still reflect the economic concept in such a definition.

Asking farmers to define what they would choose in the way of prime farmland inevitably results in responses such as land having deep, well-drained, permeable, nearly level, medium-textured, salt-free soils in units large enough to work with modern machinery and having a suitable climate for growing a wide spectrum of crops. Farmers and others also recognize unique lands, that is, those lands that are prime for a relatively narrow spectrum of commercial crop species. Lands having a 35% slope with a given aspect and air drainage may be prime from the standpoint of several orchard crops, but unsuited to a wide variety of other crops. Thus, the concept of unique lands is one where the productive capability of a narrow range of crops is very high but the options for alternative uses are restricted.

To be sure, these farmers would also want to be near marketing and transportation centers—an acknowledgement of Raup's space frame concept. But farmers do recognize the economic value of such a physical and biological definition. This recognition takes the form of the prices and taxes they are willing to pay for such land as well as an appreciation among farmers of the energy, time, and resources necessary for given units of production from lands of varying quality.

Numerous states now rank their farmlands for tax purposes (Hady & Sibold, 1974), using primarily soil-related criteria. Recent (Tabor et al., 1974) efforts to refine this procedure have included the spatial arrangement and shape of the land units as criteria in the definition and ranking of land quality.

The impact of climatic variation on land value has also been investigated. Dirks (1974) cites studies in the Great Plains which indicate that agricultural land values change by $20 to $67 per ha ($8 to $27 per acre) for each 2.54 cm (1 inch) change in annual precipitation. A similar study in western North Dakota showed that an additional 2.54 cm (1 inch) of growing season rainfall produced more than $25 million in return to dryland agriculture for this local region alone (Dirks, 1974).

Westin (1974), Westin et al. (1973), and Fenton (1975b) have investigated the relationship of land quality based on edaphic and climatic criteria as reflected in the marketplace. Figures 1 and 2 illustrate the relationship of land quality to value in terms of prices paid for land. These studies illustrate the point that, despite the lack of a sophisticated definition of what constitutes prime or high quality land, the general public recognizes the criteria necessary for such a definition and reflects their understanding of land quality variations via the amount of money they are willing to pay for such land.

To be sure, as speculative value for other uses of this land increases, the

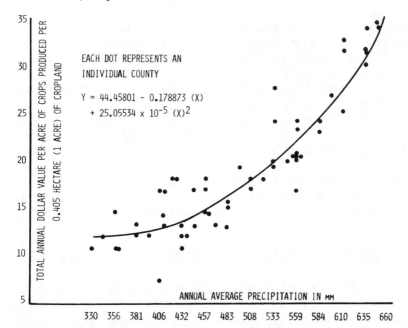

EACH DOT REPRESENTS AN INDIVIDUAL COUNTY

$$Y = 44.45801 - 0.178873 \ (X) + 25.05534 \times 10^{-5} \ (X)^2$$

Fig. 1—Relationship between total annual dollar value of crops produced per 0.405 ha (1 acre) of cropland and annual precipitation (after Westin et al., 1973).

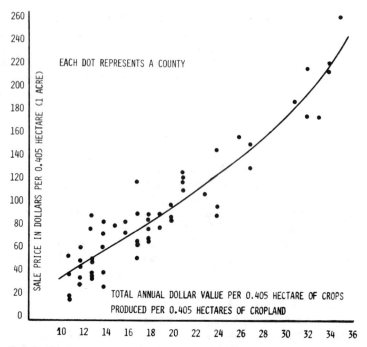

Fig. 2—Relationship between total annual dollar value of crops produced per 0.405 ha (1 acre) of cropland and sale price of land in dollars per 0.405 ha (after Westin et al., 1973).

marketplace will fail to distinguish between land quality criteria in terms of agricultural potential. At this point the value of the land is for a different use and the agricultural criteria no longer apply. The location of the land in proximity to a more intensive use potential becomes the dominant criterion on which the marketplace reflects its value. Thus, prime industrial land is defined by criteria heavily weighted to location, regardless of many physical land qualities. Prime agricultural land, however, must have criteria weighted toward soil and climatic properties, for these are the essentially unchanging criteria that determine the intrinsic value of the land for potential crop production. This is the point Brinkman and Smyth (1973) were addressing when they stated that a tract of land may be suited for a variety of uses at any given time. The potential of this suitability for other uses must be measured by differing sets of criteria specific to the proposed use.

III. CRITERIA FOR DEFINING PRIME AND UNIQUE LANDS

Table 1 lists some of the criteria that may be employed to establish a definition of prime agricultural land. The criteria in this table are not intended to be all-inclusive or complete, but provide a starting point for discussing how a definition of prime farmland might be synthesized.

Table 1—A listing of properties or criteria applicable to defining prime agricultural land and subsequent classes of agricultural land quality.

Soil properties

1. Texture—particle size distribution, coarse fragment make-up
2. Organic matter—cation exchange capacity (CEC), water-holding capacity, biology
3. Structure—tilth
4. Consistency—degree of firmness, friability
5. Pore space—total size, shape, water-holding capacity, bulk density
6. Permeability—air, moisture movement
7. Depth—rooting volume, moisture storage capacity
8. Drainage—behavior of soil in ridding itself of excess water
9. Chemical properties—CEC, pH, Eh, ESP, conductivity, base saturation
10. Mineralogy—nature of clay fraction
11. Topography—slope gradient, complexity, length and aspect
12. Erodibility—degree of erosion potential and actual erosion loss

Geographic-cultural properties

1. Climate—
   a. precipitation—amount, duration, intensity, and sequence of distribution
   b. temperature—solar energy flux and distribution during frost-free period
   c. air quality—wind velocity, duration, humidity, inversion potential
2. Spatial—size, shape, extent, aspect, accessibility (location)
3. Water availability—ground water, transported water
4. Ownership-use pattern—number, size, distribution, use

Economic factors

1. Production costs—
   a. land cost
   b. capital improvements (drainage, irrigation, clearing, grading, etc.)
   c. maintenance
   d. energy requirements
2. Payback capacity—production potential, market availability

Environmental factors

1. Aesthetics—type and accessibility of view
2. Open space—buffer between land use types, magnitude, quality
3. Aquifer recharge—potential for agricultural use to be compatible
   a. quantity of recharge
   b. quality of recharge—nutrients, salts, pathogens, chemicals
4. Flood plain—frequency, extent of flooding
5. Watershed—runoff characteristics, sediment delivery ratio

Productivity index

1. Productivity potential
2. Number of crops adapted to area

While many of the properties in Table 1 are self-explanatory, others have a more subtle impact. A tract of land may have excellent soil and climatic characteristics for a wide variety of crops. But shifting these lands to another crop which may have been displaced by urbanization might result in slight enzyme changes in the introduced species which may preclude its use for the canning industry. Only slight differences in the solar energy input between two landscapes can make the difference between the success and failure of marketing a crop. This difference may not be reflected in crop yield but show up in processing or marketing. Without knowing the production and processing requirement of specific crops, it is difficult to define prime land for each species.

It becomes obvious that all agricultural land in the United States could theoretically be ranked via a numerical index with weighted criteria for different species. This ranking could encompass all the factors listed in Table 1, thereby providing an assessment of the land's productive quality in relation to its environmental compatibility and economic and social desirability or feasibility. Such a numerical indexing of lands is not practically attainable today. But many simpler attempts at ranking the agricultural productivity or quality of soils and lands have been made and are being used, for example, the Land Capability Classification System, the Storie-Index System, and other productivity index systems such as the corn suitability rating in Iowa (Fenton, 1975b).

Now, if agreement on a suite of selected and measurable criteria can be made for assessing the quality of agricultural land, then an ordinal ranking of land units could be devised. A tract of land or a farm could then be expressed as a numerical value or index, reflecting its land quality, similar to index values calculated for land tracts by the various productivity index systems. Once the numerical values were assigned to each land unit and the ordinal ranking of all units was completed, a decision as to what point or value in the ordinal ranking constituted the boundary between prime and nonprime would have to be made. Selecting the criteria and ranking the land units are the domain of the scientist. Selecting the boundary between prime and nonprime land is the domain of the land use policy-maker, including society at large.

While it is not terribly difficult to compile a list of criteria to be considered in defining and delineating prime agricultural land, it is quite another matter to narrow the list to a workable number and determine the relative weights and ranges each criterion should receive. Even if a consensus on these two efforts could be obtained, the definition might still be so complex as to preclude any practical use of the definition. This brings us to the issue of providing a definition that is both categorical in design and utilitarian in purpose in the sense of accommodating current technologies and resources.

A legislative body charging a task force or commission with the job of defining and delineating the state's prime farmlands provides little time or resources for those responsible to conduct a detailed land survey using criteria heretofore unmapped. Unless the definition can accommodate itself to existing information and resources (e.g., soil surveys, climatic data, land use and zoning data), the practical value of an all-inclusive and complex definition is limited. Therefore, a compromise appears necessary between those of Raup's persuasion, concerned with the judgemental concept of what is prime, and those who opt for a more simplistic definition based on fewer and more stable and measurable criteria, such as those used in designating soil capability classes and productivity indexes.

In weighting the criteria for defining prime farmland toward the physical properties of land, one can rationalize that the most stable and readily measurable criteria have been selected. Furthermore, these criteria can be said to accurately reflect the land's responsiveness to modern management technology for crop production. Factors such as nearness to market and transportation facilities, as well as other economic and subjective factors, are certainly important in determining the value of land for agriculture. These factors and other data are indeed useful in making land use decisions. But these factors are also subject to change and are difficult to measure readily. It can be argued, therefore, that the physical parameters of the land provide a stable and reliable basis for interpreting the suitability of the land for a proposed use. These criteria and the land inventory derived from them can again be reinterpreted if social, economic, or technological changes necessitate new assumptions. Regardless of these changes, however, they do not affect the intrinsic quality of the land for agricultural use.

Therefore, prime farmland is subject to definition if we reject Raup's concept that the word *prime* is judgmental. Prime farmland is subject to definition if the word is used as a categorical term, with some outer boundaries identified and established. Once the requisite criteria are formulated, farmland meeting the criteria can be defined as *prime.*

IV. PRIME FARMLANDS

A. The Word *Prime*

Prime can be defined as that which is first in quality; the best part. It is not too difficult to identify the best part of the nation's farmlands. While one locality's prime land may be another's mediocre, the intrinsic qualities of the land parcels in both locations have been judged on their level of quality in comparison to the total farmland base.

B. Approaches for Defining Prime Farmland

The U.S. Council on Environmental Quality defines prime farmlands as those lands "whose value derives from their general advantage as cropland due to soil and water conditions".[1] While such a definition uses only two physical criteria and encompasses the quality sense of the term *prime,* it does not provide a working definition based on measureable and bounded criteria.

In approaching a working definition of prime farmland, various states and local jurisdictions have relied upon information and data already available. For the most part, soil surveys and the associated land capability classification systems, as well as various productivity indexes, have been used as a basis for defining and delineating prime farmlands. Some states

---

[1] R. W. Peterson. 30 Aug. 1976 memo to agency heads on analysis of impacts on prime and unique farmland in environmental impact statements. Counc. on Environ. Qual., Washington, D.C.

have considered Classes I and II as prime, whereas others have used Classes I–III or parts of Class III (e.g., IIIw-drained) as a prime farmland definition (USDA, 1975).

California has defined prime agricultural land in its governmental code as land in Capability Class I and II with a Storie Index above 60 and a gross value of crop product per 0.405 ha (acre) of at least $200 for 3 out of 5 years (Wood, 1975). The problem with attaching a monetary criteria to the definition is that each year additional land qualifies simply due to inflation with no relationship to land productivity. Several bills introduced in the 1976 California legislative session proposed to change this prime agricultural land definition to lands with over 8 undeveloped ha (20 acres) in capability Classes I and II having a Storie index of 80 and above. Several bills retained the $200 annual gross value per 0.405 ha (acre) while other bills proposed to omit any monetary criterion. Other criteria proposed in these bills included minimal depth (50 cm), minimal available water-holding capacity (6.4 cm), and minimal rainfall, frost-free days, slope, and salinity and alkalinity.[2]

Now that over 30 states have some type of farmland assessment law, various farmland classification systems have been devised for these states based on soil survey, land capability classes, or productivity indexes such as the Storie Index or the corn suitability index used in Iowa (Fenton, 1975b) and modified in other corn-belt states (Fenton, 1975a). These systems, designed originally for land appraisal, valuation, and assessment, have been employed or modified to define and delineate prime farmlands.

Several Iowa counties have defined prime farmland on the basis of the average corn suitability rating (CSR) for each 14–16 ha (35–40 acre) tract. This rating system is adapted to the modern detailed soil survey where each mapping unit is assigned a quantitative productivity index based upon soil properties as well as the quantity and distribution of rainfall. Where soil surveys are available, the CSR system will most likely be the tool used to define and delineate prime farmland if the Iowa legislature passes enabling legislation to preserve prime agricultural land (G. A. Miller, Iowa State Univ., Ames, personal communication).

Another example is Maryland's Natural Soil Group (Maryland Dep. of State Planning, 1973) approach. The State's 2,100 mapping units from the completed soil survey were recombined into 32 Natural Soil Groups based on the following criteria: permeability, texture, drainage, depth, flooding, slope-erosion, and stoniness-rockiness. Using the corn-producing potential of the mapping units comprising the 32 groups, a decision was made as to where the cutoff point would be for separating prime farmlands from productive and other farmlands. To be sure, someone else may select the prime boundary higher or lower on the scale. But experience with tax assessment classes provided a basis for obtaining a consensus as to what were the top quality farmlands in the state. Those soil groups that qualified, containing the appropriate mapping units, were then defined as prime and could be in-

---

[2] Memorandum (26 Aug. 1976) from Greg Dowds to members of the Urban Agric. Resour. Manage. Task Force, City of Visalia, Calif.

dicated on maps for each county. These prime groups corresponded mostly to Class I and II soils with some inclusion of Class III soils.

The extent of the land is also considered as a parameter for defining and delineating the better farmlands. The New Jersey effort to preserve prime farmland (Blueprint Comm., 1973) speaks of the "critical mass" necessary for a viable agriculture capable of maintaining the necessary support industries. The New York Agricultural Districts have a minimum size (202 ha) to qualify as a productive unit of farmland. Scrivner (1975) proposes a definition of prime agricultural land based upon two features: i) topography and landscape position and ii) size of the area where the smallest horizontal width is at least 0.4 km (¼ mile). Bauer (1974) suggests even larger land parcels (13 km²) as a criterion for prime farmlands.

Bauer (1974) defines prime agricultural areas for the southeastern Wisconsin Planning Commission as those areas containing soils rated in the soil survey as having only slight limitations for agricultural uses. In addition to the soil criteria, the definition incorporates a spatial criteria which requires prime agricultural areas to occur in concentrated areas over 13 km² (5 mi²) in extent that have been designated as exceptionally good for agricultural production by agricultural specialists.

Weighted soil criteria are now beginning to appear[3] that will help refine the definition and precision of prime farmland criteria. Despite these efforts, however, the challenge to compose a national definition of prime farmland has not waned.

The real challenge is to create a classification system that does more than simply identify the better lands. Political jurisdictions require some type of information that will be relevant to their needs and perspectives for decision-making.

Maintaining productive agricultural units is not the sole reason for public concern about farmland. There are environmental and other concerns as well. Therefore, the term *farmland* should combine the qualities of high productivity and relative environmental stability when utilized for modern agricultural production. While the measurement of this combined set of qualities becomes more complex, comparisons can still be made. And if these qualities could be measured accurately, an ordinal ranking could be devised that would give each piece of farmland a numerical value or index reflecting quality.

Soil survey data identify edaphic characteristics which have a strong bias toward both productivity and environmental stability. When combined, these characteristics provide a scientifically valid estimation of the qualities that make one parcel of land better suited for long-term productive farming than another. Once a division of the combined criteria is established, it is possible to identify the size of the parcel in the prime or higher category.

The reasons one parcel of land is better suited than another are the

---

[3] Definitions, Justifications and Weighting of Factors, Rural Valley Land Plan. 1975. Amendment to the Tulare County Area, California General Plan-Land Use Element, GPA 75-1D.

physical and environmental qualities that permit a wide spectrum of use alternatives with minimal environmental impacts and minimal inputs of energy and capital. Once these attributes of land quality are identified, a definition of prime land is within grasp. To be sure, these qualities receive less weight as more intense nonagricultural land uses exert pressure on farmland. But, for rural purposes, land quality is closely tied to physical and climatic criteria which influence a wide variety of plant growth. Again, we have returned to the physical and more stable criteria which reflect the intrinsic quality of the land for crop production. Varro in 35 B.C. also recognized the importance of these intrinsic physical land qualities which allowed a wide spectrum of crops to be produced (Simonson, 1968).

C. A Definition of Prime Farmland

Prime farmland can be defined, therefore, as land having the potential for the production of food, feed, forage, fiber, and oilseed crops and possessing soil qualities, growing season, and moisture supply needed to produce sustained high yields of a variety of crops economically when treated and managed (including water management) according to modern farming methods utilizing minimal amounts of energy and resource inputs (relative to output) and having minimal environmental impact.

This definition is a modified version of the Land Inventory and Monitoring definition (USDA, SCS) published in October 1975 and revised in August 1977.[4] This definition is based predominantly on the more stable and measurable physical criteria influencing the intrinsic value of land for potential crop production. The soil quality, growing season, and moisture supply characteristics as defined by USDA, SCS which are required for this definition are as follows:

  1) The soils have one of the following:
    a) Aquic, udic, ustic, or xeric moisture regimes and sufficient available water capacity within a depth of 1 m (40 in), or in the root zone if the root zone is less than 1 m deep to produce the commonly grown crops in 7 or more years out of 10; or
    b) Xeric or ustic moisture regimes in which the available water capacity is limited, but the area has a developed irrigation water supply that is dependable (a dependable water supply is one in which enough water is available for irrigation in 8 out of 10 years for the crops commonly grown) and of adequate quality; or,
    c) Aridic or torric moisture regimes and the area has a developed irrigation water supply that is dependable and of adequate quality; and,
  2) The soils have a soil temperature regime that is frigid, mesic, thermic, or hyperthermic (pergelic and cryic regimes are excluded).

---

[4] USDA, SCS Advisory LIM-12, LIM Task Force Rep., Nov. 1974 and revision, Apr. 1975. USDA, SCS LIM Memor. no. 3, Prime and unique lands, 15 Oct. 1975. USDA-SCS LIM Memo. no. 3 (Rev. 1), Important farmland inventory, 16 Aug. 1977.

These are soils that, at a depth of 50 cm (20 in), have a mean annual temperature higher than 0°C (32°F). In addition, the mean summer temperature at this depth in soils with an O horizon is higher than 8°C (47°F); in soils that have no O horizon the mean summer temperature is higher than 15°C (59°F); and,

3) The soils have a pH between 4.5 and 8.4 in all horizons within a depth of 1 m (40 in) or in the root zone if the root zone is less than 1 m (40 in) deep. This range of pH is favorable for growing a wide variety of crops without adding large amounts of amendments; and,

4) The soils either have no water table or have a water table that is maintained at a sufficient depth during the cropping season to allow food, feed, fiber, forage, and oilseed crops common to the area to be grown; and,

5) The soils can be managed so that in all horizons within a depth of 1 m (40 in), or in the root zone if the root zone is less than 1 m (40 in) deep, during part of each year the conductivity of saturation extract is less than 4 mmhos/cm and the exchangeable sodium percentage (ESP) is less than 15; and,

6) The soils are not flooded frequently during the growing season (less often than once in 2 years); and,

7) The soils have a product of K (erodibility factor) × percent slope which is less than 2.0 and a wind erosion product of I (soil erodibility) × C (climate factor) not exceeding 60. That is, prime farmland does not include soils having a serious erosion hazard; and,

8) The soils have a permeability rate of at least 0.15 cm (0.06 in) per hour in the upper 50 cm (20 in) and the mean annual soil temperature at a depth of 50 cm (20 in) is less than 15°C (59°F); the permeability rate is not a limiting factor if the mean annual soil temperature is 15°C (50°F) or higher; and,

9) Less than 10% of the surface layer (upper 15 cm) in these soils consists of rock fragments coarser than 7.6 cm (3 in). These soils present no particular difficulty in cultivating with large equipment.

In general, this prime farmalnd definition embraces all land in capability Class I, most of Class II, and Subclass IIIw that has an adequate water management system. These criteria for prime farmland exclude land in Subclass IIw if the water table is not maintained at a sufficient depth to allow growing crops common to the area, those soils where there is not enough moisture to permit annual cropping (summer fallow areas), and those soils that have a serious wind erosion hazard.[5] Based on estimated projections using these LIM criteria, about 156 million ha (386 million acres) qualify as prime farmland in the U.S., 101 million ha (250 million acres) of which are presently cropped.[6]

While it might be tempting to simply list the capability classes and subclasses that qualify as prime farmland, these classes do not necessarily

[5] USDA, SCS. 1975. Prime, unique and other important farmalnds. LIM Background Pap.
[6] USDA, SCS. unpublished data, personal communication.

reflect the productive capacity of soils. As these criteria are utilized by each state, however, limited experience to date suggests that a high correlation will be obtained between the lands qualifying as prime by these criteria and those lands qualifying as prime by the criteria used in formulating productivity indexes in various states.[6]

But there remain reservations about these USDA, SCS criteria. Nationally designed criteria produce a generalized approach to a problem often requiring additional criteria and more detailed information as may be deemed necessary by local or state jurisdictions. The USDA, SCS criteria still do not consider the economics or specific energy and resource requirements of crop production. Furthermore, the actual production potential of the land qualifying as prime by these criteria is not known or expressed. Applying these criteria rigidly will eliminate numerous productive lands having production potentials greater than many soils qualifying as prime. Field boundaries, extent, and homogenity with other soil mapping units within a field are likewise not considered. These and other more subjective criteria will have to be incorporated and weighted by each jurisdiction as they utilize these USDA, SCS criteria as the base or minimum requisite for prime farmland.

While energy relationships are not specifically addressed in these USDA, SCS criteria, one could argue that an indirect measure of energy requirements is possible. Land meeting these requisites as prime in southern California, but requiring irrigation, may have a much higher energy input per unit of produce yield as compared to rainfed prime soils elsewhere. Figure 3 is a hypothetical graph illustrating the energy (or other resource inputs) relationship to yield for lands of different quality under different management (irrigation vs. no irrigation). The point is that the aforementioned criteria have ranges wide enough to accommodate a broad spectrum of ecosystems without considering or weighting their input/output production factors.

Another problem with defining specific ranges and boundaries is that such ranges may overlap or cut through information or data units currently available. Specifying the erodibility product for prime farmland may yield an upper slope gradient of 7% for a particular soil. But if the soil mapping units in a soil survey for this soil range from 5 to 10%, then a decision on the amount of flexibility must be made—again, judgement will still be required regardless of the precision of the definition. Definitions must be able to accommodate the information base to which they apply.

The data base must also be expanded beyond the soil survey to accommodate these prime farmland criteria as well. Flooding frequency, potential irrigation, water quantity and quality, and laboratory data are necessary to use these criteria.

Nevertheless, these criteria provide a base and range of characteristics that knowledgeable people have perceived as necessary requisites for identifying the "best part" of the nation's farmland or those lands "which are first in quality" for sustained agricultural crop production. It would be desirable to be able to assign these criteria, as well as other more subjective criteria affecting land use, weighted values and rank these lands according

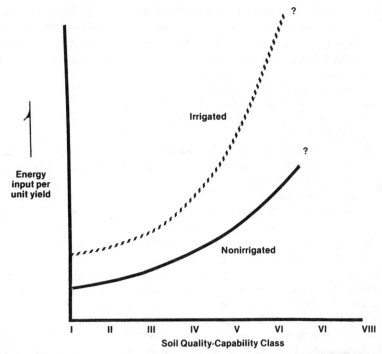

Fig. 3—Hypothetical energy requirements per unit of production for lands of differing quality.

to their totals on an ordinal scale of 0 to 100. The prime lands could then be defined on the basis of policy decisions as to how far down the scale one wishes to go before drawing the line between prime and nonprime. Planners (McHarg, 1969) have used a similar matrix approach for years in attempting to determine land quality, special uses, or areas susceptible to maximum or minimum impacts of proposed uses. While this alternative is possible, it is not among our options at this time, due to the lack of an adequate data base and provisions for large-scale application.

Using these physical criteria, prime farmlands can be identified. Using other available data such as zoning maps, land use maps, population projection data, and other more subjective information, areas of high quality farmland can be defined as well as delineated for the purposes of each locality. Even the physical criteria or their boundary limits can be altered to accommodate local conditions; a point that many localities have insisted upon. Chumney (1975), in commenting on these LIM criteria if applied in New Jersey, stated: "It appears that, in the unique situation of the most densely populated state in the nation, a single scientific definition with precise technical criteria adopted on a nationwide basis, may not be adequate, desirable or practical. Admittedly, this is not an academic or scientific approach, but a rationalization to reality."

But the fact remains that, regardless of the difficulties of weighting the criteria and determining their ranges, the intrinsic properties of land for crop production are measurable and identifiable in physical terms. In general, therefore, prime farmlands can be said to have the following qualities:

1) Soil qualities such as depth, drainage, permeability, slope gradient, and chemical properties that provide the potential for producing a variety of crops economically with minimal expenditures of energy for altering these properties.
2) A growing season suitable for a variety of crops.
3) An adequate moisture supply either through natural rainfall or irrigation.
4) Size, shape, and extent of the land units large enough to accommodate modern equipment and management practices with minimal environmental impacts.
5) Land units either currently under cultivation or with an immediate potential for relatively easy conversion to farmland in proximity to accessible markets and support industries.

In summary, these criteria are relatively simple, easily measured, and not difficult to understand by the layman as well as authorities requesting them. These authorities want simple and flexible criteria (USDA, 1975). As Chumney (1975) has stated, unless these criteria are capable of being understood and accepted by land owners who are afraid of government regulations and the loss of their property rights, these people will not vote upon themselves laws that will regulate their prime and unique lands. Chumney (1975) continues by saying that to pay no heed to this necessity will result in simply a paper exercise. Experience has shown this to be the case (USDA, 1975; NE Reg. Center for Rural Dev., 1974).

V. UNIQUE FARMLANDS

A. The Word *Unique*

Unique can be defined as the sole example; rare; having no equal; possessing qualities impossible to duplicate; limited in occurrence. Many special and highly valuable crops are produced on lands or ecosystems that would never qualify as prime farmland under the accepted prime criteria. But these lands are important, perhaps even more important to a region than prime farmland. The fruit orchards on steep slopes, cranberry bogs in poorly drained areas, and numerous other fruits and produce requiring a unique suite of ecosystem qualities, exemplify the variety of crops where special conditions are requisite for production.

B. Criteria and a Definition

Johnson (1975) states that one set of criteria will not serve to identify all kinds of unique farmland, although several general characteristics can be specified.

The USDA LIM Task Force[4] defines unique farmlands as follows:

Unique farmland is land other than prime farmland that is used for the production of specific high-value food and fiber crops. It has the special combination of soil quality, location, growing season, and moisture supply needed to produce sustained high quality and/or high yields of a specific crop when treated and managed according to modern farming methods. Examples of such crops are citrus, olives, cranberries, fruit, and vegetables.

Unique farmland has the following characteristics:

1) It is used for a specific high-value food or fiber crop.
2) It has a moisture supply that is adequate for the specific crop. The supply is from stored moisture, precipitation, or a developed irrigation system.
3) It combines favorable factors of soil quality, growing season, temperature, humidity, air drainage, elevation, aspect, or other conditions, such as nearness to market, that favor the growth of a specific food or fiber crop.

VI. OTHER LANDS

It has also been recognized that there is considerable farmland acreage in production that does not qualify as prime or unique. Many states (NE Reg. Center for Rural Dev., 1974; USDA, 1975) are interested in protecting some of these lands as well as their prime and unique farmlands. Criteria for defining these lands on a state and local basis will have to be developed by state and local agencies. Often the prime and/or unique farmlands are surrounded by or randomly scattered among other productive farmland that does not meet the prime or unique criteria. And yet the ownership and land use pattern in an area may not lend itself to segregating these unique and prime farmlands. For these reasons, the USDA, SCS Land Inventory and Monitoring System[4] recognizes the additional farmlands of statewide and local importance without specifying any national criteria.

VII. DELINEATING PRIME AND UNIQUE LANDS

A. USDA Inventory of Prime Farmlands

There is little to be gained if the criteria for defining prime and unique farmlands cannot be measured and applied to inventory techniques. If the criteria are too cumbersome, then the definition is not practical or useful in delineating the location of these land quality categories. This concern for facilitating the identification and inventory of the nation's best farmlands in a reasonable time using an existing data base (e.g., soil surveys) prompted the USDA adoption of physical criteria for identifying these lands.

Land units comprising the 156 million ha (386 million acres) delineated as prime farmland in the United States by these physical criteria vary in size and homogeneity, as well as in their proximity to markets, transportation facilities, and other physical and cultural amenities influencing the land's value. The size, shape, and homogeneity of the land unit are as important to its measure of quality or value as the physical properties are in determining the intrinsic value of the individual pedons that compose the soil. It remains for local, regional, or state governmental jurisdictions to determine the minimum size or "critical mass" they are willing to accept as a prime farmland unit.

The urgency of inventorying the nation's prime farmlands is such that long-range testing of various criteria and procedures for developing the inventory cannot be delayed. In addition to the interest and pressures from states and local governments to initiate an inventory, Sec. 302 of the Rural Development Act of 1972 directs the Secretary of Agriculture to carry out a program ". . . for the identification of prime agriculture producing areas. . .."[5] Recommendations from several committees established for the Prime Land Seminar (USDA, 1975) strongly urged USDA to complete soil survey mapping so that the base data could be used for the inventory. More recently, the Public Advisory Committee on Soil and Water Conservation expressed the view that an inventory to identify, locate, and determine the availability of prime farmland should be carried out without delay.[5] Others urging inventory and protection of the nation's prime farmlands include the National Research Council's Committee on Agriculture and the Environment (1974) acting in behalf of the National Academy of Sciences and the Council on Environmental Quality[1] which has interpreted the National Environmental Policy Act to include "highly productive farmland."

Approximately 120 counties in 46 states have been selected by the USDA to inventory prime, unique, and other important lands by the end of 1977 with a goal of inventorying 1,200–1,300 of the more rapidly developing counties by 1981. Peach County, Georgia, was the first county completed in 1976 using the USDA, SCS, LIM[7] criteria for delineating these lands of differing agricultural quality.

Complementary to this effort, USDA has nearly completed a potential cropland inventory designed to provide statistically reliable data on the potential and safety of converting noncropland to cropland. Since the 1958 Conservation Needs Inventory was updated in 1967 (USDA, 1971), the figure of 107 million ha (264 million acres) has been used (U.S. Senate Comm. on Agric. and For., 1975) as the potential cropland resource which could be converted to cropland from its current use of primarily forest and grassland within the next decade if needed. As a result of the preliminary estimates from the most recent study (Davis, 1976), 45 million ha (111 million acres) of noncropland could safely be switched to cropland if needed. About 22% of this land is prime farmland that can be converted easily. With 162 million ha (400 million acres) planted to crops (including hay for cutting) in 1976, nearly 80% of our nation's available cropland is already committed to crops. An increasing population, foreign commodity demands, nonagricultural land use demands, and other requirements continue

---

[7] USDA, SCS. 23 June 1976. Important farmlands of Peach County, Ga.

to pressure a currently adequate cropland base. The need to inventory and monitor this land resource base for agricultural production is obvious.

B. State and Local Efforts to Delineate Prime Farmland

State, regional, and local attempts to delineate agricultural lands of varying quality have commonly used soil survey data as a major input to the effort. Embellishments of this data base with other information sources and techniques have provided a variety of definitions and criteria in delineating prime farmlands.

Bauer's (1974) definition and delineation of prime farmlands in southeast Wisconsin utilized soil survey ratings and minimal spatial criteria. Using these criteria, the prime agricultural areas of southeast Wisconsin have been delineated with the policy statement that they should be preserved.

In delineating its prime farmlands, Maryland, in addition to its natural soil group criteria (Maryland Dep. of State Planning, 1974), used land use overlay maps and zoning (10-year sewer and water plans) maps to locate the prime and productive lands currently in agriculture and beyond the bounds of immediate development threats. These data were then entered into a computer data bank by cells. Automatic data processing equipment could then generate state, regional, or county maps delineating prime and other qualities of agricultural lands (productive, other, special, or unique) by use and proposed zoning.

McHarg (1969) has applied an ecological planning method to determine and delineate the most compatible land uses in the Potomac River Basin. The nature of this multiple land use comparison with natural or physical criteria means that multiple, not single, land uses are evaluated to determine which land use can best be accommodated by the environmental criteria with optimum compatibility with other land uses.

For example, in McHarg's (1969) study, a matrix of proposed land use categories is developed against the natural (physical) determinants and intercompatibility of other land uses. The consequences of the proposed land uses on such environmental factors as air pollution, stream pollution, flooding, and soil erosion can also be ranked in the matrix. In applying the results of the matrix to an area, the most compatible land uses are revealed with respect to both other land uses and the natural or environmental determinants. The prime agricultural areas will be identified and delineated, therefore, on the basis of having the best fit to the natural resources and other prospective land uses.

McHarg's (1969) technique adds other dimensions to the physical criteria for delineating prime agricultural ecosystems. The spatial arrangement, environmental impact, and alternative land use categories are considered.

C. The Delineation Process

Delineating prime agricultural land is a process resulting in a prediction of the type of agricultural endeavor that can be accommodated on specific kinds of land. This process also involves the determination of the types of improvements required for accommodating certain cropping systems and their management inputs. While this process may not give much weight to current land use, ownership, field patterns, and institutional supports for proposed land use changes (Vink, 1975), the situation in the United States today is such that delineating prime agricultural lands does require these factors to be weighed.

State and local legislative bodies often ask three basic questions: i) where are the best agricultural lands (physical resources), ii) what is the status of their current use, and iii) what is the relationship of this use to proposed planning policies? In delineating prime and unique agricultural lands, it is often the farmland most vulnerable to development pressure that prompts action to be initiated for delineating and preserving these lands (NE Reg. Center for Rural Dev., 1974; USDA, 1975). But those responsible for establishing land use policy in many states and localities have maintained an interest in delineating the best farmland currently in production both in proximity to urban pressures and beyond. Therefore, the land evaluation for prime farmland in the United States is heavily weighted toward both physical criteria and current use criteria (NE Reg. Center for Rural Dev., 1974).

In delineating prime and unique farmlands, one must end up with a map. These maps should identify: i) the classes of physical soil-land resources using established criteria, ii) current land use, and iii) current and proposed zoning or planning overlays. These three resource maps will provide at least an elementary picture of where the best farmlands are in a region, what they are currently used for, and what local decision-makers perceive as the best or desired land use. At this point, decisions can be made on alternative plans and policies for implementing these plans.

VIII. DESIGNATING PRIME AND UNIQUE LANDS

At the outset of this chapter, one of the concepts of land was described as property—a resource commodity or capital. For over a century after the United States gained its independence, the process of land disposal was a major social and political force. This policy of placing land in private ownership resulted in two-thirds of the land in the 48 conterminous states being removed from the public domain. Land was the capital given to citizens by their government (Madden, 1974).

Property ownership in the United States has dominated, and will continue to dominate, decisions affecting the use of land. Property ownership has been interpreted by some as implying absolute rights in how the land is used—a concept which is changing as pressure on the land increases (Bosselman & Callies, 1972; Engle, 1975).

A. Designation: Special Uses and Protections

The nation's forest resources are largely protected in national and state forests. Our unique and beautiful landscapes are preserved in our national and state parks. Much of our cultural heritage is protected in our national and state monuments and historical sites. The common method by which these resources are protected is that they are part of the public domain. The government has ownership rights and full control over the use and management of these resources.

But our nation's farmland resources are in private ownership. The decisions governing the use and management of this privately owned resource are determined by millions of individual owners with different motives and goals than society at large. And most people agree that it should remain so, for the agricultural production from these lands is in no small way tied to the management incentive of the individual owner-operators to maximize production and profit. Thus, while everyone is in agreement that our privately owned prime and unique farmland resources are an important and valuable asset to the United States strength as a country, there is no general agreement as to what policy should be followed to preserve these lands from being committed to irreversible uses.

Although our farmland resource will remain privately owned, the government does have extensive powers derived from both the federal and state constitutions as well as litigation results to control the use of private land. Madden (1974) reviews these powers. One power is that of eminant domain, the taking of private land for public purposes. Another is taxation, providing one of the largest costs of land ownership. A third is the police power from which zoning ordinances and other control mechanisms are derived. Madden (1974) also lists a fourth power—the power of the public purse to subsidize capital improvements as well as other service or control programs.

In protecting our unique and best farmlands through the actions of society (government), these powers provide the only arsenal from which weapons can be chosen to guide land use decisions. The various mechanisms by which these powers have been incorporated to guide, protect, and influence land use have been reviewed by Whyte (1968), Delafons (1969), Sargent (1973), Hagman (1974), Norman and Derr (1974), Wengert and Graham (1974), Bryant (1975), Engel (1975), Miner (1975), Healy (1976), and Moss (1977).

The intensity of the efforts to preserve farmlands has been directly related to the pressure to convert farmlands to other uses. Therefore, many of the more populous and urbanizing states have felt the pressures to do something to stem the tide of leap-frog development onto prime and unique agricultural land. While the motive of some of these attempts may be to preserve open space rather than farmland, the point is that governments are looking at alternatives to use their powers to control land use. These powers are being utilized to short circuit the marketplace in the allocation of land to various uses. While many of the rights accorded the private land owner are universally distributed (rights to sell, transfer, and use the land in many ways), the physical resources of the land are not always commensurate with the potential uses accorded the owner. It is for this reason that there is a growing sentiment that the ownership of property without development rights may become as common as the ownership of property without mineral rights (Bosselman & Callies, 1972; Reilly, 1973).

But in today's climate, there are several requisites to any effort to preserve farmland: the program must be politically and publicly acceptable and financially feasible. Any restriction of rights of the fee-simple landowner must be either within the legal powers of the government or the landowner must be compensated.

B. The Mechanisms to Preserve Agricultural Land

1. EXCLUSIVE AGRICULTURAL ZONING

Zoning is a police power which has been used in the United States for half a century to control certain uses of land in urban areas. Although zoning has its basis in the constitution and in specific legislation, it has, in fact, been shaped in litigation (Bryant, 1975). The courts have held that land use can be controlled through zoning to a certain point. Beyond this undefined point, the land use regulations have been considered to be a taking of the land requiring compensation since the use of the land is so severly restricted that the Fifth and Fourteenth Amendments of the U.S. Constitution have been violated.

It is this problem of defining the point of compensation that self-destructs any attempt to zone agricultural land in proximity to urban uses. As development encroaches on the farmland, the speculative value of the land increases until the low-density zoning regulation is ruled unconstitutional—the "point" has been crossed. Nearly 30 states have granted local jurisdictions the authority to zone rural land for farm uses. But farming in most semisuburban areas has in reality been treated as residential land use (Solber & Pfister as cited by Bryant, 1975).

As a means of preserving farmland, exclusive agricultural zoning provides for the creation of districts in which farming is the only permitted use. Applying this technique to rural areas experiencing development pressures (with attendant high land prices) would be declared an unfair taking under the Fifth Amendment (Bryant, 1975).

California used this technique to preserve farmland. As development pressures increased, however, the zones were not effective. New Jersey has considered the use of exclusive agricultural zoning (Norman & Derr, 1974). Hawaii's agricultural districts approximate exclusive agricultural zones.

But, as Bryant (1975) points out, Hawaii's experience is unique and probably will not be adapted to other areas.

Exclusive agricultural zoning suffers the same limitations as most other zoning efforts. The "taking issue" comes into play especially as development pressures increase land values.

The ease with which variances have been granted to previous zoning efforts and the vulnerability of zoning to political influence have not endeared zoning's acceptability to the public. The exclusive agricultural districts now used in New York and proposed in Maryland have attempted to avoid these limitations through voluntary acceptance and other incentives. But the fact remains that setting aside prime and unique agricultural lands through exclusive agricultural zoning is a concept that has constitutional limitations and is not likely to be effectively used wherever urban pressures are present.

2. DIFFERENTIAL ASSESSMENT

Since Maryland's enactment of its differential assessment law in 1956, about two-thirds of the 50 states have adopted varying forms of this law, making it the most commonly used farmland preservation tool in use today (Bryant, 1975).

The basis for the differential assessment technique is that farmers are relieved of high land assessments caused primarily by development pressures. It is assumed that rising property tax levies are one of the threats to continued farming. Providing tax relief, while not necessarily preserving farmland, does allow farmers to hold out longer against development pressures. Therefore, the main thrust of the various differential tax assessment programs has been to slow farmland conversion to other more intensive uses. In and of itself, differential assessment is ineffective in holding or preserving farmland over long periods whenever urban pressures are expressed in potential land prices higher than farm value.

3. AGRICULTURAL DISTRICTS

The New York legislature enacted the Agricultural District Law in 1971 in an effort to preserve agricultural land. This law combined both taxes and nontax incentives to encourage farming within specified areas, known as *agricultural districts* (Bryant, 1975). The initiative to form a district is voluntary, thereby circumventing any exercise of the police power and increasing public acceptance. The district must be a minimum of 203 ha (500 acres) and there is a time-obligation of 8 years where nonfarmland use change cannot occur. While other states have been discussing modifications of this concept, neither they nor New York has had enough experience to evaluate the efficacy of this technique. Nevertheless, the voluntary nature of the program, combined with other incentives, including differential land taxation, is believed to be more effective in the long run than either agricultural zoning or differential assessment programs alone. But the fact remains that the district concept still does not provide the owners of farmland in semirural areas, whose opportunity for capital gains is high, with adequate compensation or incentives, to cover the loss in control and any losses in land value that results from placing land in a district (Bryant, 1975).

4. TRANSFER OF DEVELOPMENT RIGHTS

Schnidman (1976) has reviewed this concept, which is based on the underlying principle that the development potential of privately held land is in part a community asset that government may allocate to enhance the general welfare. The transferable development right (TDR) severs the development potential from the land and treats it as a marketable entity. This technique, therefore, attempts to mesh the economic forces of the marketplace with the police power authority of government to protect the general welfare (Schnidman, 1976).

A farmer in proximity to urban pressures may sell his development right to a private buyer who could then increase his development density wherever permitted by society. Therefore, once an area is planned, there must be conservation zones (e.g., areas where prime and unique farmlands have been designated) and transfer zones (i.e., those areas receiving the transferred density). There are precedents for this mechanism in the form of planned unit developments, cluster zoning, airspace transfer, water rights allocation, mineral extraction and others (Schnidman, 1976).

Several localities have included the TDR option in their zoning ordinances. Buckingham Township, Pennsylvania, and Collier County, Florida, are examples. The interest in the TDR concept is great because it uses the free marketplace to determine the value of the rights, thereby relieving the government of picking up the cost of compensating the landowner for lost rights. But the problems in establishing the mechanisms are complex, often beyond the level of sophistication of most jurisdictions.

Bryant (1975) points out that, in addition to the establishment problem, there are other difficulties. The problem of adequate compensation, supposedly circumvented by the use of TDR's is not solved because the farmland owner's bundle of rights is altered without receipt of immediate compensation. And the problem of taxation is complicated by a TDR approach. Bryant (1975) concludes that implementing a TDR program in the real world with an active market for buying and selling of development rights may be extremely difficult. Nevertheless, the concept is very attractive because the compensation mechanism remains in the private marketplace.

5. FEE SIMPLE PURCHASE AND LEASEBACK

Governments have, over many years, bought land areas through park acquisition and open space programs. This land was then leased back to farmers until the park or other proposed use was ready for development. Because of the area and cost involved, however, this mechanism has not been extensively used to preserve agricultural land. The several proposed attempts to use this mechanism (New Jersey; Suffolk County, New York) have not proved successful due to public treasury costs and low farmer acceptance (Bryant, 1975). Pride of farmland ownership and limited restrictions are strong incentives for good agricultural land stewardship. Short-term leaseback arrangements do not foster such stewardship, thus resulting in low farmer acceptance. Long-term arrangements may solve some of this problem but the change from owner to tenant remains as a powerful disincentive for farmer acceptance of the program. No doubt prime and unique farmland could be preserved through this technique, but the cost to the taxpayer is such that public acceptance of this technique is generally low.

6. DEVELOPMENT RIGHTS PURCHASE

The complexity of the TDR concept and the low acceptability of the tenate relationship to the land in the purchase-leaseback program have prompted governmental units to consider purchasing only the development rights from the agricultural landowner. This option keeps the land in private ownership while the owner is compensated for the taking of his development rights. Although this concept still requires the expenditure of large sums of public funds, its simplicity and political feasibility make this concept more acceptable to the public.

Suffolk County, New York, has received nationwide attention in its effort as the first, large, urban-pressured political jurisdiction to institute a development rights purchase program (Bryant, 1975). In August 1976, the county authorized the sale of $21 million in bonds to purchase the development rights on the farmlands deemed most vulnerable to development pressure. While this amount represents only a fifth of the original goal, it is a start for a county development rights purchase program.

Furthermore, the Suffolk County program initiative included more than just an interest in preserving farmland. The interest in maintaining open space and using this mechanism to limit growth were companion incentives for the acceptance of this program. New Jersey, in 1976, adopted a development rights purchase program to preserve prime agricultural land. Connecticut and Maryland have considered state-wide programs for preserving prime and unique agricultural lands using the development rights purchase concept. This concept, coupled with other mechanisms, such as agricultural districts, differential assessments, covenants, easements, and other tools, may prove to be effective in designating and preserving prime and unique farmland. Governments are looking for more stable long-term land use control mechanisms. The constitutional limitations on governmental control over regulating the use of privately owned land result in only transitory controls. To be more effective in controlling land use, governments must step over the Constitutional taking line imposed by the Fifth Amendment. This step requires the consideration of compensable regulations of which the TDR and development rights purchase programs are examples. These regulations may also incorporate a windfall recapture provision (Hagman, 1974) whereby a landowner who had been compensated for a land use regulation would be taxed for any windfalls accruing to the land whenever the regulations were changed to permit the land to develop.

IX. EPILOGUE

The importance of the nation's prime and unique farmland resources cannot be overemphasized. These landscapes are a prized species in the spectrum of this planet's resources. In a local and regional context, these resources are an endangered species in some areas.

These prime and unique ecosystems are our nation's most productive agricultural lands. They are the most responsive to management and can accommodate resource inputs (fertilizer, pesticides, organic materials, etc.) with minimal energy requirements and environmental impacts. As Dubos (1976) has indicated, ecosystems altered by human intervention can remain fertile and attractive for immense periods of time. Ever since Neolithic times, human life has taken place, and will continue to take place, in managed environments. Dubos (1976) also states that "the earth is to be seen neither as an ecosystem to be preserved unchanged nor as a quarry to be exploited for selfish and short-range economic reasons, but as a garden to be cultivated for the development of its own potentialities of the human adventure." The prime and unique agricultural lands of the world are man's best chance for a stable and environmentally compatible food and fiber resource base.

The basic question, then, is: Should this prime and unique land resource be allocated to uses through the economic market structure or should there be an attempt to guide the use of these lands through mechanisms designed to accommodate future population increases in an orderly fashion based on careful planning and designation of these lands? While we are a long way from answering this question, numerous attempts are now under way in various states and local units of government to address the problem. These attempts are too new to evaluate under the test of time. But at least many parties and disciplines concerned with the use of land resources are sitting down at the same table to discuss the issues.

Do the current land use patterns and policies reflect what people would choose if they were provided with the facts and costs of the alternatives? Regardless of the answer, an effort must be made to promote this debate. The agronomist and soil scientist must be present at this debate. For the future of agriculture will not necessarily be measured by how farmland was defined, delineated, and designated, but whether we asked the right questions in an effort to determine the real costs of the alternatives.

LITERATURE CITED

Barney, G. O. (ed.). 1977. The unfinished agenda. The citizen's policy guide to environmental issues. Task Force Rep. sponsored by the Rockefeller Brothers Fund. T. Y. Crowell Co., New York.

Bauer, K. W. 1974. The use of soil data in regional planning. p. 1–26. In R. W. Simonson (ed.). Non-agricultural applications of soil surveys. Elsevier Co., NEW York.

Blueprint Commission. 1973. Report of the Blueprint Commission on the future of New Jersey agriculture. Dep. of Agric., Trenton, N. J.

Bosselman, F., and D. Callies. 1972. The quite revolution in land use control. Prepared for the Counc. on Environ. Qual., U.S. Government Printing Office, Washington, D.C.

Brinkman, R., and A. J. Smyth. 1973. Land evaluation for rural purposes. Int. Inst. for land reclamation and improvement, Wageningen, Netherlands.

Bryant, W. R. 1975. Farmland preservation alternatives in semisuburban areas. A. E. Ext. 75-5, Dep. of Agric. Econ., Cornell Univ., Ithaca, N.Y.

Chumney, R. D. 1975. Review of Definitions and criteria for identifying prime and unique lands. p. 159–162. *In* Perspectives on prime lands. USDA, Inf. Div., Soil Conserv. Serv., Washington, D.C.

Davis, R. M. 1976. What's left of our cropland frontier? Soil Conserv. USDA, August 1976. p. 1.

Delafons, J. 1969. Land use controls in the United States. MIT Press, Cambridge, Mass.

Dirks, R. A. 1974. Energy development in the West: is it the prelude to an agricultural disaster? J. Soil Water Conserv. 29(6):250–252.

Dubos, R. 1976. Symbiosis between the earth and humankind. Science 193:459–462.

Engle, N. E. 1975. Political and economic forces behind state and local approaches to retain prime lands. p. 211–227. *In* Perspectives on prime lands. USDA, Inf. Div., Soil Conserv. Serv., Washington, D.C.

Extension Committee on Organization and Policy Task Force on Land Use. 1975. Land resources today. Ext. Serv., USDA, Washington, D.C.

Fenton, T. E. 1975a. Definitions and criteria for identifying prime and unique lands. p. 133–150. *In* Perspectives on prime lands. USDA, Inf. Div., Soil Conserv. Serv., Washington, D.C.

Fenton, T. E. 1975b. Use of soil productivity ratings in evaluating Iowa agricultural land. J. Soil Water Conserv. 30(5):237–240.

Hady, T. F., and A. G. Sibold. 1974. State programs for the differential assessment of farm and open space land. Agric. Econ. Rep. no. 256. Econ. Res. Serv., USDA. U.S. Government Printing Office, Washington, D.C.

Hagman, D. G. 1974. Windfalls for wipeouts. p. 105–133. *In* C. L. Harriss (ed.) The good earth of America—planning our land use. The Am. Assembly, Columbia Univ., New York.

Healy, R. G. 1976. Land use and the states. The Johns Hopkins Univ. Press, Baltimore, Md. p. 233.

Johnson, W. M. 1975. Classification and mapping of prime and unique farmlands. p. 189–198. *In* Perspectives on prime lands. USDA, Inf. Div., Soil Conserv. Serv., Washington, D.C.

Krause, O., and D. Hair. 1975. Trends in land use and competition for land to produce food and fiber. p. 1–26. *In* Perspectives on prime lands. USDA, Inf. Div., Soil Conserv. Serv., Washington, D.C.

McHarg, I. L. 1969. Design with nature. Natural History Press, Garden City, N.Y.

Madden, C. H. 1974. Land as a national resource. p. 6–30. *In* C. L. Harriss (ed.) The good earth of America—planning our land use. The Am. Assembly, Columbia Univ., New York.

Maryland Department of State Planning. 1973. Natural soil groups. Tech. Rep., Baltimore, Md. p. 153.

Miner, D. 1975. Agricultural retention: an emerging issue. Environ. Comment. The Urban Land Inst., Washington, D.C. p. 1.

Moss, E. (ed.). 1977. Land use controls in the United States. Natl. Resour. Defense Counc., Inc., New York.

National Research Council, Committee on Agriculture and the Environment. 1974. Productive agriculture and a quality environment. Natl. Acad. of Sci., Washington, D.C. p. 189.

Norman, T., Esq., and D. A. Derr. 1974. The legal aspects of an agricultural open space preserve through exclusive agricultural zoning in New Jersey. Environ. Comment. The Urban Land Inst., Washington, D.C. p. 11–14.

Northeast Regional Center for Rural Development. 1974. Proc. of Conf. on Rural Land-Use Policy in the Northeast, 2–4 Oct. 1974, Atlantic City, N.J. Pub. no. 5. Northeast Reg. Center for Rural Dev., Cornell Univ., Ithaca, N.Y.

Peterson, G. E., and H. Yampolsky. 1975. Urban development and the protection of metropolitan farmland. The Urban Inst., Washington, D.C. p. 15.

Raup, P. M. 1975. Urban threats to rural lands: backgrounds and beginnings. Am. Inst. of Planners J. 41(6):371–378.

Sargent, F. O. 1973. Alternative methods for keeping land in agriculture. J. Northeast Agric. Econ. Counc. 2(2):198–208.

Schnidman, F. 1976. Transferable development rights: an idea in search of implementation. Land Water Law Rev. Univ. of Wyoming XI(2):339–382.

Scrivner, C. L. 1975. A proposed definition of "prime agricultural land." Crops Soils 27(8): 5–7.

Simonson, R. W. 1968. Concept of soil. Adv. Agron. 20:1–47.

Smith, S. C., and R. L. Barrows. 1975. Definitions and criteria for identifying "prime" lands that serve other than food and fiber production purposes. p. 163–178. *In* Perspectives on prime lands. USDA, Inf. Div., Soil Conserv. Serv., Washington, D.C.

Tabor, R. L., F. F. Bell, G. J. Buntley, H. A. Fribourg, and M. E. Springer. 1974. Agronomic productivity of the landscapes of three soil associations in Maury County, Tenn.: an analysis. J. Soil Water Conserv. 29(6):272–275.

U.S. Department of Agriculture. 1971. Basic statistics—national inventory of soil and water conservation needs, 1967. Stat. Bull. no. 461. U.S. Government Printing Office, Washington, D.C.

U.S. Department of Agriculture. 1975. Perspectives on prime lands, background papers for Semin. on Retention of Prime Lands. 16–17 July 1975. USDA, Inf. Div., Soil Conserv. Serv., Washington, D.C. p. 257.

U.S. Senate Committee on Agriculture and Forestry. 1975. Conservation of the land and the use of waste materials for man's benefit. Committee Print. U.S. Government Printing Office, Washington, D.C.

Vink, A. P. A. 1975. Land use in advancing agriculture. Springer-Verlag, N.Y.

Wengert, N., and T. Graham. 1974. Transferable development rights and land use control. J. Soil Water Conserv. 29(6):253–257.

Westin, F. C. 1974. Soil classification and land sale prices. Soil Sci. Soc. Am. Proc. 38:804–807.

Westin, F. C., M. Stout, Jr., D. L. Bannister, and C. J. Frazee. 1973. Land sale prices in South Dakota and their relationship to some soil, climatic, and productivity factors. Soil Sci. Soc. Am. Proc. 37:606–611.

Whyte, W. H. 1968. The last landscape. Doubleday, Garden City, N.Y.

Wood, W. W., Jr. 1975. Review of definitions and criteria for identifying prime and unique lands. p. 151–153. *In* Perspectives on prime lands. USDA, Inf. Div., Soil Conserv. Serv. Washington, D.C.

section IV

Planning Rangeland Uses

USDA Soil Conservation Service

IV

13 Planning the Use of Rangeland for Public and Private Lands

THADIS W. BOX AND DON D. DWYER

Utah State University
Logan, Utah

I. INTRODUCTION

Rangelands are a particular kind of land, although not always distinct from forests or croplands. They are those areas of the world in which such physical limitations as low and erratic precipitation, rough topography, poor soil drainage, and extreme temperatures prevent cultivation or intensive forestry. The popular image of rangelands is that of broad, open, unfenced areas over which domestic animals roam and graze. Often, however, rangelands are intensively managed with fences controlling the livestock, and with the vegetation manipulated for specific forage yields. They produce forage for free-ranging native and domestic animals as well as wood products, water, and wildlife (Stoddart et al., 1975).

Range management is the profession associated with the use and development of rangelands. Broadly defined, it is the science and art of optimizing the yields from rangeland in those combinations most desired by and suitable to society through the manipulations of range ecosystems (Stoddart et al., 1975). The products required by any given society will vary with the dominating cultures and the evolutionary stage of that society. In the few remaining hunter-gatherer groups of the world, rangelands are important as the origin of food from wild plants and animals. Many developing countries have pastoral economies where the major contribution of rangelands is forage for livestock. In developed countries rangelands produce goods and services associated with all phases of agricultural, industrial, and recreational enterprises. On certain national forest lands in the western U.S., the water yield alone may be more valuable than forage, timber, or wildlife produced. In other areas, recreation or mining may be more important than the traditional grazing use.

Regardless of its location, rangeland has the inherent capacity of being managed for multiple uses. Grazing is still the dominant economic use of rangeland. Unique ecological characteristics dictate that the grazing animal is the most efficient way to convert vegetation without economic value into products desired by society. Therefore, much of the planning for rangeland use is centered around grazing, although it is now common to consider grazing as only one of several possible multiple uses, rather than the single dominant use. We will consider in this chapter the value of rangelands for producing a variety of goods and services, but we will discuss grazing use in more detail and relate it to other land uses. Uses of rangeland other than for grazing are covered in this book in Chapter 14, "Other Uses for Public Rangelands," by Elsner, Magill, Schwarz, and Thor.

As the human population has grown and society become more affluent, demands for many and varied uses have been placed on rangelands. To satisfy these demands, uses of rangelands must be carefully planned. Where only a couple of decades ago it was the goal of range management to maximize production of animal products (Stoddart and Smith, 1955), the current goal is to optimize the returns from combinations of many products (Stoddart et al., 1975). Optimization of a mix of goods and services from land requires much more sophisticated planning than that needed for the maximization of a single product.

II. LEVELS OF PLANNING

Good land use depends at least in part on three factors: (i) the ecological potential of the land itself to sustain certain kinds of uses, (ii) the wants and needs of society, and (iii) the economic and political realities under which the land use must be implemented. The purpose of the land planner, then, is to interpret for society the capabilities and limitations of the land to sustain the uses desired and needed by society. A plan is simply a predetermined course of action (LeBrerton and Henning, 1961). Any plan must consider the inherent ecological characteristics of land, the products and services society desires from that land, and the logical and practical steps for producing those goods and services. Plans can be developed that are strategic in nature and technical or operational (Miller, 1971). Most plans for rangelands should consider both strategic and operational components.

A. Strategic Component

Strategic plans deal with establishing policies for rangeland use, including setting goals and objectives and defining broad guidelines under which ranges may be used. These policies vary with land ownership and may be influenced by public wants and needs.

1. PRIVATE LANDS

The private landowner operates a business of great complexity. His concerns are mostly those of maximizing income, minimizing losses, and attaining status in his community and profession (Boykin & Hildreth, 1958). Operating through the market place, he seeks to provide what the public wants from his land and to produce what people are willing to buy. This may be red meat, sport hunting, recreation, or other marketable products; items such as the aesthetic and historical values of rangeland are not readily reflected in the market place, and may not be of great concern to the private landowner.

Unlike the public land manager, the private landowner may be more concerned in his strategic planning with whether to raise cattle to produce calves for market or sheep for lambs and wool. In some private land areas, such as the Edwards Plateau of Texas, the production of wildlife may be balanced against the production of livestock. In all cases, decisions of the private landowner will be strongly biased toward producing products that have value in the market place.

2. PUBLIC LANDS

On public lands all goods and services valuable to society must be considered whether they have a market value or not. As a representative of society, the public land manager is required to manage rangelands for the many different products and services deemed valuable by various segments of the public. The strategy for planning the use of public rangelands, then, must include not only the economic but the social aspects as well. Instead of relying on the market place to determine how land will be used, the public land manager usually relies on the various interested publics which involve themselves in the decisionmaking process.

Certain units of public land may relegate the production of market value goods to a relatively low priority. Many prime watersheds exist on rangelands. Their product, water, is essential for culinary use, agriculture, and industry, yet the lands yielding that water are seldom credited with the monetary gain that comes as a result of the water produced. So, in planning the use of public rangelands the production of water has high priority, despite the low recognition of its economic worth.

B. Technical or Operational Component

Regardless of whether the land is in public or private ownership, each unit must have a technical or operational plan that prescribes how to reach the goals and objectives set in strategic planning. The kind of land unit to be planned varies. On private land the most common planning unit is that of the ranch (Dwyer, 1975).

Planning for public land use is usually done at three or more levels: national, regional, and local. For instance, the USDA Forest Service has a national program for rangelands as required by the Resources Planning Act of 1974. This plan is largely strategic in that it sets quantities of outputs for the nation to achieve. Each of the regions of the Forest Service likewise has its own area guides which are also primarily strategic in nature. The area on which local specific land uses are planned is usually a national forest, or sometimes even a district or grazing allotment within a national forest. At this level the plans are both strategic and operational but, in most cases, more operational than strategic.

Presently the Forest Service develops as many as 80 different technical plans for each national forest. Obviously only a few of the 80 dominate, but all must be integrated into a logical framework plan. Examples of the more important are plans for grazing management, timber sales, water yields, and recreation use. The Forest Service's proposed planning process insures that one single technical plan at the area or national forest level incorporates all the needed planning for the many land uses. Regulations for the planning required in the National Forest Management Act of 1976 will be promulgated in 1979.

The Bureau of Land Management (BLM), the agency responsible for managing over 170 million acres of arid rangeland in the contiguous states, approaches rangeland planning in a slightly different way. It, too, has national goals which are strategic in nature. However, the goals are not as well defined as those required of the Forest Service by the Resources Planning Act. Each BLM state office develops the strategic goals or plans that it wishes to achieve for the state. Management framework plans, the second level of planning, are developed for districts within each state. These are broadly based plans which consider the characteristics of the resource base and the trade-offs necessary among the various uses. They have both strategic and technical components. The third level of planning use for rangeland of the BLM is called the *allotment management plan.* It is here that specific management plans are developed for the grazing allotment and the livestock. This plan is more technical than strategic.

All agencies responsible for management of public lands must meet the requirements of the National Environmental Policy Act (NEPA) of 1969. This act requires the agency to seek public participation in determining which of the many alternative uses will be emphasized and where any significant management changes are contemplated for public lands. The NEPA also requires that an environmental impact statement be written by any federal agency planning a management action which will have a significant impact on the human environment. The development of the environmental statement can provide valuable information for the management plan since it sets out alternatives and obtains public reaction to them before direct action may be taken. The extent to which the land planning process for rangeland is integrated with the environmental impact statements varies with agencies, but all must conform to NEPA, and the NEPA provisions must be addressed at some stage of the planning process.

III. DEVELOPING THE PLAN

The degree of formality given the planning process for rangelands varies. Many successful ranchers operate with plans that have evolved through time and experience. No formal planning process appears to have occurred. Other ranch plans are the result of a careful examination and thorough evaluation of a ranching enterprise (Dwyer, 1975) or a study of the many demands placed on the rangeland resource (Anderson, 1977a, 1977b). Formal or not, all successful plans follow an iterative process. Goals are formed and plans are made using the data available. As information is collected and concepts validated, feedback systems serve to alter the original plan, deriving new goals, new operational techniques, and new evaluations. These new evaluations, in turn, feed back to alter the plan further. This iterative process must be encouraged and a system for continuing evaluation and revision included in the plan itself.

There are several strategic planning steps that should be included in all land use plans. The first of these is the identification of the issues and concerns associated with the subject land that the planner must face. On private land these issues may be rather straightforward, dealing almost entirely with maximizing returns on investments. On public lands they are much less clearly evident. Sometimes the issues and concerns are verbalized at a national policy level and then assigned to the planning units to develop and implement. For instance, the Resources Planning Act of 1974 requires that a national program be developed which includes stated output goals, such as the amount of timber, range forage, water, wildlife, and recreation. These are then broken down to regions and assigned to specific planning units to be incorporated in local plans. The production of these goods or services is taken as given by the planners at the local level in developing their management plans.

If output goals are not assigned by higher authority, someone in a line management position on public rangelands usually makes a subjective decision relative to which goods and services should be emphasized. These decisions are generally based on the individual's experience with the land itself and his or her perception of what land users want from the land. Once the important issues and concerns have been identified, at least in the mind of the manager, they must be taken to the public for verification and evaluation. This point marks the beginning of the iterative process in planning. If the issues perceived by the manager are not those perceived as important by society, then they must be reevaluated before management goals can be properly defined.

Once the issues and concerns are agreed upon by the land managers and the public, the next step is to define management goals and objectives to implement them. Selection of goals is only possible with a rather complete understanding of the capability of land resource. For instance, the planner must know whether it is feasible to set a goal for production of milk-fed lambs from the particular kind of rangeland even though he does not know at this stage the exact carrying capacity of the range for grazing sheep.

The third step in strategic planning is to develop evaluation criteria against which the plan's effectiveness will ultimately be judged. The private landowner may select as his main criterion a given return on investment, such as, for instance, a 6% return on total investment while maintaining or increasing the productive potential of the rangeland. Evaluation criteria for public rangelands are much more complex; the plan must meet the intent of the various laws, executive orders, and regulations that govern the use of public rangelands. A second criterion is that the public land should produce the goods and services set by national level plans as, for example, a certain unit of rangeland should produce a given number of animal unit months of grazing to meet the national goals for grazing. This is also the time for developing additional criteria associated with economic efficiency and meeting the expectations of local people. These evaluation criteria should rule out considerations that are not feasible. However, they should not be so restrictive as to eliminate realistic alternatives. Instead, they should specify the yardstick against which the possible alternatives will be evaluated.

Once broad goals and objectives of the plan have been set, the technical or operational plan is developed for implementing the strategies that have been selected. Normally, a technical plan will consist of an inventory of resources, a list of alternatives, and the method to be used for selecting the "best" alternative. In addition, it will have a detailed recipe for implementation of the plan.

The first step in the evaluation process is a careful documentation of results. This is followed by a detailed evaluation of the plan and, finally, such revisions as are indicated by the additional data brought in through the iterative process.

IV. THE OPERATIONAL PLAN

A technical or operational plan requires a rather detailed inventory of the resources available to determine the ecological potential and the basic carrying capacity of the land itself. Far too often this step is overlooked by planning agencies. Colbert (1977) observed:

> Next I find it interesting, but not too surprising, that amidst all the present clamor about land use planning one has difficulty in finding anything regarding the proper basis for land use planning. Maybe it's implied in all that's being said, but I'm more inclined to think that it's a case of not knowing what's involved. Nevertheless, the Public Land Law Review Commission report, the two annual reports of the Council on Environmental Quality, the pending legislation, and all the thousands of words on the subject all seem to lack a recognition of, or at least an acknowledgement of, *the fact that the primary basis for sound land use must lie in the determination of the land's capabilities and suitabilities as limited by climate, soil, and topography.*

We believe certain elements are essential in any physical inventory to determine the land's capability and suitability for uses. There must be a general understanding of the climate of the area. Of primary importance is the amount of effective moisture available for plant growth, as determined by the amount and distribution of precipitation, temperature, and evaporation rates.

The major soils of the planning unit must be identified. The detail required of the soil survey will depend upon the intensity of management intended for the unit. However, the soil should be surveyed and mapped in sufficient detail to allow the delineation of range sites. Range sites, those areas ecologically similar, actually become the basic land management units once they are delineated. A range site has a relatively uniform ability to produce a given kind and amount of vegetation. The basic capability of the rangeland to produce forage for grazing animals, as well as provide a basis for other uses, is determined from an identification and analysis of all the range sites that exist on the land for which a management plan is to be developed. Since each range site has its own potential for productivity based on its unique soils and vegetation, the collective productivity of all the sites sets the potential of the entire management unit for use. During the soil survey and range site delineation, any special hazards for given uses should be recorded. For instance, note should be made of soils with extreme erodibility on steep slopes or soils that puddle easily when wet. Knowledge of these soil characteristics is necessary for planning grazing use and for other uses, such as recreational and off-road vehicle use, which can cause severe damage if these soil hazards are not known.

It is well recognized that vegetation patterns are altered adversely on range sites that have been improperly managed. Overgrazing, if continued long enough, causes both kinds and amounts of plant species to change. It is therefore, essential that the manager know both the present and the potential vegetation for each important range site of the area on which he works. Present vegetation can be mapped using standard range survey techniques. The determination of potential vegetation is much more difficult. In the absence of a good local map showing potential vegetation, such broad-scale national maps as Kuchler's (1964) can be used, but as information is gained it must be refined and updated.

The inventory map should show the natural waters on the area as a part of the physical inventory. This will include all springs, flowing streams, and surface stored waters. It is also desirable to know if underground waters are available and can be developed at a reasonable cost.

A detailed accounting of the present use is another important requirement for the physical inventory. This will include the current use-patterns for all activities taking place on the rangeland, the number and kinds of livestock, the seasons they graze, and other items discussed in the ranch plan by Dwyer (1975). In addition, recreational use-patterns, timber sales, and other uses not related to grazing should be documented. The map should include the physical improvements on the property such as roads, fences, water developments, corrals, houses, and barns.

When requirements of the physical inventory are met, the range management planner has a basis for understanding the productive potential of the land. However, this is true only if proper interpretation of the vegetation data is made. We cannot emphasize too strongly that the vegetation survey is of special importance in planning the use of rangelands. It is the difference between the present vegetation that exists on the range site and the potential vegetation that could exist that determines the condition of the range itself. That difference is the amount of vegetation improvement the manager can expect if all things go right in the plan. Therefore, special care should be taken in developing the maps of present and potential vegetation.

As stated earlier, actual vegetation can be measured using standard techniques (Brown, 1954; Cook, 1962; Stoddart et al., 1975). The determination of potential vegetation involves a much more sophisticated application of the science of ecology. Integrating information on climate, soils, and historical data, the manager must infer the kind and amount of potential vegetation that could grow on each individual range site. Most commonly, this is done by mapping soils that are alike in texture, structure, elevation, and topography in given precipitation and temperature zones. Within each range site the vegetation is examined and those areas with the lightest use historically are taken as a guide to potential vegetation. Often relict areas, such as ungrazed exclosures, old cemeteries, and ungrazed mesas, are used. However, in all cases the determination of potential vegetation is an estimate at best. The map showing potential vegetation must be continuously revised as additional studies are made and more data become available.

We do not mean to suggest that the potential vegetation is necessarily the most productive for all the various goods and services to be derived from rangelands. For instance, the strategic goal for a given area of foothill rangeland in the Intermountain Region may be to maximize deer winter range while also producing livestock forage, water, and recreation. The potential vegetation for the site in the absence of fire could be a pinyon-juniper woodland. To manage grazing use so that the site produces the potential vegetation would gradually reduce the amount of deer forage available in the winter. Periodic burning or other means to remove the pinyon and juniper trees would cause the site to produce a mixture of shrubs and grasses desirable for deer feeding during critical periods of the year.

In other situations managing the site for its potential vegetation may also correspond with the strategic goal set by the planner. A ranch on the Southern Great Plains, for example, may have as its potential blue grama-dominated rangeland. If the goal of the rancher is maximum red meat production from this rangeland, his objective may be to manage for the potential vegetation rather than for some less productive seral stage.

After the range site inventory is complete, the next step is to form alternatives for using the resource to meet the goals selected in the strategic planning process. The strategic goals, evaluation criteria, and range site inventory must all be considered to delimit the bounds within which the alternatives can be selected. Any use that is not permitted because of limitations set by the physical environment or the strategic goals is automatically removed from consideration. The problem then becomes that of listing the various feasible alternate uses of the rangeland, given the restrictions listed above, and selecting the best alternatives to apply.

There are a number of tools available to evaluate the best alternatives. Linear programming techniques are often employed to determine the best economic alternative. Goal programming may be more appropriate when criteria other than economics are used. Regardless of the quantitative technique applied to determine the suitable uses of rangelands, the final decision is made on private land by the landowner and on public land it is made using input from the public.

A carefully developed plan on private land using the latest linear programming techniques might indicate that the landowner could maximize income by raising sheep for wool and lamb. The next best use might be a cow-calf operation, and the least economical use as a horse-breeding ranch combined with a dude-ranch operation and a hunting guide service. The landowner might still opt for the dude-ranch operation simply because that lifestyle is preferred. However, when the strategic goal of maximizing income is rejected, the plan must be revised to set the primary strategic goal as the maintainence of a more pleasing lifestyle.

On public land a well-designed plan may show that the alternative which uses livestock grazing to manipulate watershed vegetation is the most productive use of an area. In the public involvement process, however, the general public may decide the area under consideration should be designed for wilderness-recreation and that livestock be removed. Again, lifestyle, this time that of the public, serves to revise the plan all the way back to the strategic goals. Regardless of the alternative uses selected, the planning process should involve a logical sequence of goal setting, data collection, analysis of alternatives, and revision of the plan.

V. PLANNING LIVESTOCK GRAZING ON RANGELANDS

Using rangelands for grazing livestock is only one of several possibilities, although it is often mistakenly thought to be the only use of rangelands. Often the word *range* is misconstrued and misused, taken to be synonymous with grazing of the land. Colbert (1977) stated:

> I want to emphasize in the strongest possible way that range-or rangeland or range ecosystem—is a kind of land. It is *not* a land use. I must admit that the word "range" has always been associated with livestock grazing (a specific use) on uncultivated lands, and this is the connotation that is still prevalent, especially to the general public (if, in fact, the general public thinks of it as anything else than the kitchen stove!). Nevertheless, rangeland comprises at least 40 percent of the total land area, not only in this country but in the entire world, so I believe it's time that we made a serious effort to recognize range for what it really is: a kind of land—a major land resource—from which there is, and can be, obtained a wide variety of products and values, of goods and services.

The very nature of rangeland—its ecological characteristics and natural plant cover—makes it very suitable for grazing by wild and domestic animals. It is not surprising that grazing management has received a major emphasis. Although we will discuss the grazing plan separately, we emphasize again that grazing as a use of rangeland must be integrated with other land use plans for the range areas (*See* Chapter 14).

Ranch plans usually consider goals set in strategic planning as constraints or directives for the development of the technical or operational plan. The technical ranch plan will include (i) a detailed inventory of the physical facilities of the ranch along with economic evaluations of them, (ii) an inventory of the resource base (livestock and range), (iii) an analysis of the entire ranch operation, (iv) activity plans for necessary change, and (v) a timetable for implementing the various components of the plan (Dwyer, 1975). The steps for developing such a plan are outlined in Stoddart et al. (1975).

The first consideration in planning grazing on rangelands is to insure that the basic plant and soil resources are used in such a way that they will continue to be productive for all other outputs from that particular land unit.

Many times the difference between actual vegetation present on the range site and potential vegetation for that site is so great that it is desirable to move quickly from the vegetation producing little or no forage to one with higher forage production capabilities. It may, therefore, be to the advantage of the landowner or public land manager to rehabilitate or improve the area for grazing as well as other uses. Many techniques are available in range management for vegetation type conversion, reseeding, or other broad-scale vegetation manipulations.

Usually the most costly items necessary to increase long-term ranch productivity are those related to range improvements, especially artificial seeding and control of undesirable plants. It must be emphasized that arid ecosystems are delicately balanced and, once disturbed, are slow to improve naturally through natural plant succession. Often artificial improvements are not economically feasible due to the inherently low productivity of such lands. Almost without exception people have historically overestimated the capacity of arid rangelands to support livestock. Our cultural or market conditions have encouraged increasing livestock numbers at the expense of range condition and productivity. This usually means that future generations must pay the cost of past extravagances.

To restore range condition to its original productivity usually requires changing the plant species composition from its present status to a combination of plants considered more productive in terms of ranch goals. There are numerous tools and practices available to do this. Three of the major ones follow.

1. CONTROL OF UNDESIRABLE PLANTS

A serious problem of arid rangelands of the world is the past and continuing encroachment of undesirable plants on once productive rangeland. Each region of the world has its own set of particular problem species but the ecological relationships are much the same. The combination of overgrazing, control of fire, and recurring drought has served to favor undesirable species over desirable plants.

Costs of reducing the populations of undesirable plants and the benefits expected should be determined for each range site. The productive potential for each site to produce adequate quantities of desirable plants must be assessed. Usually the greatest and quickest response can be obtained from the better condition, high-potential sites with lower populations of undesirable shrubs. This generally goes against intuition which includes work on the "worst first." The worst should be saved for last because it generally will not continue to decline in productivity nearly as rapidly as sites in better condition on which shrub numbers are increasing.

Various methods and techniques of brush control practice available must be appraised to choose the ones best suited to the problem species, soil characteristics, topography, and weather conditions. Plans are then made to determine where, when, and how brush control is to be implemented within the economic constraints of the ranch operation.

2. RANGE SEEDING

Seeding range sites with adapted species is a rapid means of improving the quantity and quality of range forage (Cook et al., 1967). Often arid ranges have deteriorated beyond the point where natural improvement would justify the wait. All the range sites on the ranch that can benefit from reseeding should be treated. If a site is dominated by undesirable plants, with little or no forage species present, brush control and reseeding measures should be planned together.

Methods for artificially seeding arid rangelands will not be successful every time, especially where precipitation is less than 300 mm in hot desert areas. Therefore, contigency measures must go into the planning to handle failures in seeding.

Research indicates that, for treatment to be successful, the seeded areas must be free from grazing for a time adequate to assure plant establishment. Provisions must be made to leave the area ungrazed from one to three growing seasons. Plans must be made for the animals which normally would graze on the treated land.

Two tests appear to be necessary for range improvements or range rehabilitation through control of undesirable plants and reseeding. First, each activity should be justified economically. On public rangelands cost-benefit ratios are generally calculated and a ratio greater than one must be achieved before the improvement project is authorized. The test on private rangelands is usually whether the money expended on the improvement project will increase the net yield from the ranching unit over the long term.

The second test for range improvement projects should be whether it contributes to the overall strategic goals and objectives set in the plan. Failure to pass either test is normally reason to not proceed with the improvement plan. Range improvement projects should not be done simply to increase livestock production. The effects of a range improvement project on all goods and services should be considered.

3. GRAZING SYSTEMS

Most data indicate that under a system of grazing which allows vegetation periodic rest from grazing during the growing season, range condition will improve (Heady, 1961; Herbel, 1971; Hickey, 1966). There are many different grazing systems but most all have in them some method of rotating animals sequentially throughout a series of pastures. The decision to install a grazing system on a ranch is a broad commitment to more fences, water development, and, in general, more intensive management.

It is possible to correlate a rotation grazing system with brush control and reseeding, so that pastures not being grazed, or portions of them, can have treatments applied. Care must be taken in planning so that pastures treated can be left ungrazed for two consecutive growing seasons.

The selection of a particular grazing scheme or system will depend in part upon the kind of vegetation, the physiography of the range, the kind of animals to be grazed, and the management objectives set in the strategic plan.

Several systems of livestock grazing are available for the planner to consider. The first and most obvious is to graze the area continuously throughout a season or year with a given quantity of livestock. This system has the advantage that its use remains the same each year. The cattle or other livestock will always be present and other uses can be coordinated with them. Stocking rates and even species of animals may be varied but the land is grazed continuously.

The system of rotation grazing involves alternate grazing of various subunits of the range. First one unit is grazed, then another, followed by a third, usually in regular sequence. This type of grazing has several advantages. Since one unit is grazed at a time, animals from the other units are concentrated in the unit being grazed, thus resulting in a more uniform use of the plant resource. The subunits not being grazed have an opportunity to recover from past grazing, permitting the vegetation to improve so that it more nearly approaches its potential. Rotation schemes also have an advantage when other uses are a part of the plan. For instance, rotation grazing schemes can be used to separate livestock from campers or other recreationists during the season of most intensive recreation use. If the objectives of the plan require that some areas be free of livestock for certain periods of time, a rotation scheme may help to do so.

Deferred-grazing schemes delay spring grazing initiation to give the opportunity for new plants to become established or for old plants to gain vigor. Any delay in grazing constitutes deferemnt but deferred grazing most often means delaying grazing until after seed-set in the most important range plants (Sampson, 1952).

Deferred-rotation and rest-rotation systems involve combinations of the systems discussed above. The term *rest-rotation* has recently gained particular acceptance with land management agencies of the western U.S. It refers to grazing systems in which the rangeland is given a complete rest for an entire year. It differs from *deferred rotation* mainly by providing a longer rest period of ungrazed units and heavier uses of the grazed portion. Other specialized grazing schemes have been developed involving the principles of deferment and rotation. These include such systems as the short-duration, high-intensity grazing used in Africa (Goodloe, 1969) and the Merrill four-pasture, deferred-rotation systems in Texas (Merrill and Young, 1952; Merrill, 1954).

Each of these special grazing schemes has a particular set of advantages and should be considered in planning the use of the range. Generally, rotation and deferred-rotation schemes allow for plants to recover more quickly after prolonged grazing use. Systems involving frequent rotation may cause a loss in yield of animal products. Any system that employs high-intensity use for a short period of time will result in significant plant defoliation during that time. Although the long-term benefit may be more stable watersheds and greater plant cover, the short-term results may be increased runoff and erosion on the heavily used pastures. Rotation schemes also cause wildlife to move from the heavier grazed areas to the deferred areas and may result in a changing pattern of wildlife use. No specialized system of grazing offers a panacea for management, but they are useful tools in achieving the objectives of the grazing plan.

VI. FEEDBACK MECHANISMS AND EVALUATION OF THE PLAN

The kind of records required are listed in some detail in the documentation section of a good rangeland use plan. The details and kinds of records will vary according to the objective of the plan; however, each management plan should include a portion on monitoring the results of the management activities called for by the plan as well as an evaluation of the plan.

Quantity and quality of outputs from each rangeland use should be evaluated with a monitoring system that describes the parameters to be measured, the frequency of measurement, the predicted precision and reliability of the measurements, the time between reporting intervals, the efficacy of sampling and detecting significant levels of change in the biological and/or physical environment, and the rationale for selecting the particular sampling method for monitoring and evaluation of the system. After sufficient time has passed an evaluation of the plan should be made to detect changes in the parameters measured. This time period will vary with the activity and goals being evaluated. As each output is evaluated, if change is indicated, the plan should be revised; the revision may be a simple one involving only the change of a few technical details which will permit achievement of the original goals and objectives.

If evaluation of the plan indicates the strategic goals are no longer suitable, either for the resource or for what society wants from it, then a major revision of the plan may be necessary. If the plan is properly developed, each evaluation will serve as a feedback mechanism triggering a complete updating of the management plan. A change in range condition on a particular planning unit requires (i) the planner to reevaluate the strategic goals, looking at any new issues and concerns raised by the change, (ii) a new definition of goals, and (iii) the development of new evaluation criteria. An alteration of these may cause a readjustment of the technical and operational plans.

VII. SUMMARY

Rangeland is a particular kind of land capable of producing many goods and services. It is important that the range manager carefully plan so that he may satisfy society's wants and needs while working within the basic capability and carrying capacity of the land. A planning process involving both strategic and operational goals can best meet these needs. A feedback system in the plan that will allow a constant reiteration of goals, data gathering, implementation, evaluation, and reestablishment of new goals is essential to a good plan.

LITERATURE CITED

Anderson, W. E. 1977a. Planning the use and management of renewable resources. Range. J. 4(4):99–102.

Anderson, W. E. 1977b. Planning the use and management of renewable resources. Part II. Range. J. 4(5):144–147.

Boykin, Cal, and R. J. Hildreth. 1958. Management aspects of range management. J. Range Manage. 11:173–176.

Brown, Dorthy. 1954. Methods of surveying and measuring vegetation. Commonwealth Agric. Bur. Commonwealth Bur. of Pastures and Field Crops Bull. 42. Hurley Burks, England.

Colbert, F. T. 1977. Land use planning—a summary from the rangeman's point of view. Range. J. 3(3):74–77.

Cook, C. W. (ed.). 1962. Basic problems and techniques in range research. Natl. Acad. Sci. Pub. no. 890, Washington, D.C.

Cook, C. Wayne, L. A. Stoddart, and P. L. Sims. 1967. Effects of season, spacing, and intensity of seeding on the development of foothill range grass stands. Utah Agric. Exp. Stn. Bull. 467. 73 p.

Dwyer, D. D. 1975. The ranch plan: its development and application. Proc. U.S.-Australia Science Exchange, Alice Springs, Australia.

Goodloe, Sid. 1969. Short-duration grazing in Rhodesia. J. Range Manage. 22:369–373.

Heady, H. F. 1961. Continuous vs. specialized grazing systems: A review and application to the California annual type. J. Range Manage. 14:182–193.

Herbel, C. W. 1971. A review of research related to development of grazing systems on native ranges of the western U.S. Jornada Exp. Range Rep. no. 3. 32 p.

Hickey, W. C. 1966. A discussion of grazing management systems and some pertinent literature. U.S. Forest Service, Denver, Colo.

Kuchler, A. W. 1964. Potential natural vegetation of the conterminous United States. Am. Geogr. Soc. 116 p., plus vegetation map.

Lebrerton, P. P., and D. A. Henning. 1961. Planning theory. Prentice-Hall, Englewood Cliffs, N.J.

Merrill, L. B. 1954. A variation of deferred-rotation grazing for use under southwest range conditions. J. Range Manage. 7(4):152–154.

Merrill, L. B., and V. A. Young. 1952. Range management studies on the Ranch Experiment Station. Texas Agric. Exp. Stn. Prog. Rep. 1449.

Miller, E. C. 1971. Advanced techniques for strategic planning. Am. Manage. Assoc. Res. Study. 104.

Sampson, A. W. 1952. Range management principles and practices. John Wiley and Sons, Inc., New York.

Stoddart, L. A., and Arthur D. Smith. 1955. Range management. 2nd ed. McGraw-Hill Book Co., New York.

Stoddart, L. A., A. D. Smith, and T. W. Box. 1975. Range management. 3rd ed., McGraw-Hill Book Co., New York.

14 Planning Other Land Uses for Public Rangelands

G. H. ELSNER, A. W. MAGILL, C. F. SCHWARZ, AND E. C. THOR

Pacific Southwest Forest & Range Experiment Station
Berkeley, California

I. INTRODUCTION

This chapter covers planning on public rangelands. The account that follows is divided into four parts: management planning for visual resources, for wildlife, for recreation, and for historical or archeological resources. The chapter also covers the effects of the National Environmental Policy Act on rangeland planning. A case study illustrates the sequence of planning and how the various aspects are related to each other.

Emphasis is placed on the application of management planning to public rangelands. But some aspects of planning for visual resources and for historical or archeological resources can be applied to planning for other ecosystems. Some topics that might properly have been included have been omitted because they receive full treatment elsewhere in this volume. Watershed planning is covered in chapter 31 and surface mining in chapter 34 and 35. The rangeland planner should read Chapter 14 as well because the grazing uses and the uses discussed in this chapter are inextricably related and because public and private rangeland uses have many mutual effects.

There is a long history of planning for grazing on public rangelands and many sound methods and proven planning approaches now exist. The planning for visual, wildlife, recreation, and archeological values have, in most cases, a shorter history and, consequently, planning methods for these values are still being formulated. It is a real challenge to develop planning methods which provide a mechanism for all of these values to be fully considered. As this chapter will document, this challenge is being actively pursued by both managers and researchers in numerous agencies and universities. The literature in this area is dynamic. We have provided key references which we hope will prove practically useful for both the planning in each of these four areas and also in its task of total interdisciplinary range planning. The chapter is process oriented and aimed at planning for the variety of rangelands. Detailed technical information and discussions of problems specific to one type of rangeland can be found elsewhere; for example, the seven USDA Forest Service Research Papers RM-155 through RM-161 summarized in Paulsen (1975).

II. LANDSCAPE PLANNING FOR PUBLIC RANGELANDS

A. Aesthetic Values of Rangelands

Rangelands often have aesthetic values that contrast highly with those of other ecosystems. In many ways, rangelands are more subtle. The land may be gentle and rolling, the vegetation short and even, and the streams and lakes relatively scarce. Thus many rangelands lack the features which provide visual variety and excitement to other areas—for example, seashore or high mountain areas. But in their own subtle way, they are highly scenic to people who enjoy their openness, or their vastness, or even their sameness. And their very subtlety makes nearly any man-caused change noticeable—thus emphasizing the need for careful landscape planning and design.

One of the results of intensified range management is changes to the natural landscape. These include: vegetation manipulation; landform manipulation, such as surface mining or plowing; new or modified structures; water developments; and other supportive developments, such as access roads, fences, pipelines, and powerlines (USDI Bur. Land Manage., 1974). These modifications are important to increased range productivity, but may still provide a greater level of landscape variety (USDA Forest Serv., 1977).

People's sensitivity to the landscape and recreation value of rangelands has increased dramatically (McGuire, 1973). This growth may be part of an increased sensitivity to *all* kinds of natural environments—in that each is perceived as having its own ecological and aesthetic integrity. Or it may be part of an increased interest in deserts and semiarid areas as suitable environments for outdoor recreation (Schreyer & Royer, 1975). Consequently, landscape planning will become increasingly important.

A major part of range landscape planning will be to find alternative ways of achieving specific objectives and then to evaluate the *visual* consequences of each. To develop these alternatives, managers will look to landscape architects for specifying *design* alternatives, both for structures and vegetation patterns and landform, and to other specialists for their knowledge of methods of implementation.

When judging the visual effects of a planned action, the planner should note that, although the action itself may have a negative visual effect, it may provide other, offsetting visual advantages. For example, a new road may provide access to an important scenic area; vegetation control work may increase forage for wildlife which can be viewed by the general public; and the reservoir resulting from dam construction may add to the aesthetic appeal of an entire area (USDI Bur. Land Manage., 1974).

This opportunity for enhancing landscape values in rangelands should be accompanied by this caution: people desire unity (Litton, 1972) and variety in the landscape—but not too much complexity. As Schreyer and Royer (1975) have said, "Environments, either natural or man-made, will be perceived as desirable to the extent that they exhibit some coherence, unity, or stability which makes the scene understandable to the individual.

Confusing environments tend to be perceived more negatively than ones that can be interpreted."

B. Landscape Planning Processes

Only recently have landscape architects been included on most inter-disciplinary land planning teams; so procedures for incorporating landscape values into the planning process are, in some cases, still being developed. Key procedural questions include: Can landscape values be analyzed separately from other concerns? What is the best procedure for assessing the visual effects of alternative management actions? What is the most effective way of combining information on existing landscape quality with a visual analysis of management alternatives to reach the best conclusion concerning landscape values? And at what stage of the planning process should landscape values be incorporated with other values?

These questions and others have been answered by several land management agencies in the United States. For example both the USDI Bureau of Land Management (USDI-BLM) and the USDA Forest Service (USDA-FS) have produced useful and carefully thought-out directions for landscape planning for lands under their jurisdiction (USDI Bur. Land Manage., 1975b; USDA Forest Serv., 1974b). For planners and managers desiring more detailed information on landscape planning, the references cited are very valuable. The Visual Resource Management directives developed by USDI-BLM are designed to be used at the lowest level of the BLM's Management Framework Planning process. More specifically stated—the results of the directives are designed to be the resource inputs of the Unit Resource Analysis, which in turn provides information necessary for developing the Management Framework Plan (Fulcher, 1973). In addition, the Visual Resource Management directions can be used for analyzing the visual effect of specific project proposals. The directions cover all tasks from delineating scenic quality, determining visual sensitivity, and delineating visual zones, to determining a minimum visual resource management class, and finally providing a means to determine if a proposed management action will meet the assigned classification (USDI Bur. Land Manage., 1975b).

The USDA-FS has developed a well-illustrated procedure which is referred to as the *Visual Management System* (USDA Forest Serv., 1974b). Its procedures are useful at several planning levels but are probably implemented most frequently at the Forest and District levels. The information obtained has proved quite useful to Forest Service land management planning from the Unit Planning level to the Forest and Area Guide levels. The procedure is also useful for analyzing specific project plans. In addition to the general Visual Management System guidelines, the Forest Service is producing a series of handbooks dealing with the specifics of visual planning for utilities, timber harvesting, road design, range management, and other special concerns.

The BLM and FS landscape planning procedures are outstanding accomplishments—but they are not the only successful procedures. Others can now be found which were developed by states, other federal agencies, or planning organizations (USEPA, 1973). In Europe, landscape values are often of critical importance and many excellent references can be found describing their procedures (Crowe, 1966; Land Use Consult., 1971; Lovejoy, 1973).

Whatever the exact procedure the key ingredients seem to be (i) inventorying the existing landscape quality, (ii) identifying the sensitivity of people to possible landscape modifications in the area, (iii) assessing the visual effects of proposed manipulations, (iv) specifying limitations and development guidelines, and (v) establishing landscape monitoring and control procedures.

How people value specific landscapes is of considerable importance to successful land use and landscape planning process. But determining people's sensitivities to a specific landscape is a difficult and challenging task since these values vary considerably from person to person. Several approaches have been suggested (Arthur & Boster, 1976; Smardon, 1975) but whichever is used it is essential that a carefully designed public involvement process be implemented which (i) allows for public input, (ii) describes in detail the management objectives and the intermediate steps, (iii) explains the time period required by the plan, and (iv) illustrates how the finished project will appear (Williamson & Currier, 1971).

In addition to these five essentials, research is underway to assist in anticipating or predicting which landscapes are visually vulnerable or resistant to change (Litton, 1974). A procedure to predict visual vulnerability would be useful in specifying a feasible set of management alternatives.

C. Analyzing Landscape Quality

In both the USDI-BLM and USDA-FS landscape planning processes, an important element is the analysis of physical resources landscape quality. One important result of any landscape quality inventorying procedure should be to adequately describe the character of a particular landscape. When a planning area is small, a narrative description may be entirely adequate; but for larger or more complex areas the narrative description should be augmented with maps and photographs or sketches.

As noted inthe USDI-BLM directives, the landscape character is largely determined by the *relationship* between the four basic landscape dimensions of form, line, color, and texture. Since there are also the basic dimensions affected by landscape or landform manipulation, it may frequently be useful to prepare a separate description and map for each dimension. As an integral part of inventorying existing landscape quality the USDI-BLM approach suggests that land form, color, water, vegetation, landscape uniqueness, and man-made intrusions all be rated separately.

It is important to distinguish between the job of mapping separate landscape dimensions and that of producing a final analysis of landscape quality. Inventorying landscape quality is an appropriate job for well-trained landscape architects for it requires judgments about the *interrelationships* among the basic dimensions and decisions as to the visual attractiveness of each land area. These interrelationships describe the degree of variety, harmony, and unity which exists in the landscape and, consequently, the degree of visual attractiveness.

D. Analyzing Visual Vulnerability

As noted earlier the important considerations for determining the relative visual vulnerability of landscapes are currently being studied by both researchers and managers. Although it is difficult to arrive at valid generalizations about visual vulnerability for rangelands, it is fairly obvious that the following principles make some range landscapes more visually vulnerable than others:

1) *Edges* or lines in the natural landscape—distant and intermediate ridgelines, shorelines, and borders between different types of vegetation are partially vulnerable.
2) Areas of rangeland at *higher elevation* than the viewer are usually more noticeable than areas at the same elevation as the viewer.
3) Areas of *high uniformity* in either vegetation or landform are highly vulnerable to landscape modifications (Schreyer & Royer, 1975).

Litton's (1974) paper on visual vulnerability provides a more detailed listing of factors to be examined with regard to landscape compositional types, edges, location of alterations, outside influences, (climate, lighting, seasonal effects), and inherent effects (slope, topographic orientation, soil color).

The *time* required to revegetate an area or to return disturbed soil to its previously existing color is another important planning consideration. Generally the drier an area the longer this will take and the more visually vulnerable the area will be. Thus, sections of the desert are at the extreme end of the continuum for both revegetation and restoration of soil colors.

E. Determining the Visual Effect of Alternative Management Plans

It is important to know the relative effects of proposed management actions on landscape quality. Any proposed landscape manipulation will change either form, line, color, or texture, or a combination of these dimensions and will alter the degree of contrast (USDI Bur. Land Manage., 1975b). These dimensions may be used to record the visual effect of the proposal. Several research papers are available which describe precise measurements for each of these dimensions (Elsner, 1976; Zube et al., 1975).

It may also be important to describe the scale of the modification with respect to the existing landscape. This is particularly important in rangelands since there nearly any visible vertical structure will become a significant focal point (USDI Bur. Land Manage., 1974).

Exactly where the modification is located and how it is oriented with respect to viewers is of key importance. Whether the modification can be seen at all or how frequently is a first consideration (Travis et al., 1975). The distance to the modification and whether viewers see it with a level line of sight or with an upward or downward orientation partly determines the extent of the visual effect (Litton, 1968).

In addition to detailed narrative and map descriptions of each alternative, it may be helpful to use a contrast-rating procedure (USDI Bur. Land Manage., 1975b) to judge the overall effect of each alternative. Since the nature of the subject is visual it is always helpful to supplement narrative descriptions and maps with photographs and sketches of the existing landscape as well as accurate portrayals of how the area would appear after each alternative.

When planned modifications will affect large areas, it is helpful to tabulate the acreage which is natural in appearance, partially modified, or highly modified for each stage of development. Such a table will be useful to the manager in judging the relative change from the current level of naturalness for each defined management alternative. It should be noted, of course, that a change away from current naturalness to man-modified characteristics in rangelands need not imply a decrease in landscape quality. An increase in vegetation variety or a change toward a savannah appearance may indeed enhance landscape quality. And for that matter a change from shrub to grass or grass and shrubs is often only a return to an earlier natural condition.

Rangelands are subject to many demands beyond those of intensified management for livestock and recreation activities. For example, many range areas contain valuable coal, oil shale, and phosphate deposits. The extraction of these materials poses a serious visual challenge. The visual effect of coal or phosphate strip-mining operations may be a severe contrast to the natural landscape and can be long-lasting unless adequate rehabilitation is carried out. Many recent rehabilitation projects have produced satisfactory results. New portrayal techniques have been developed to illustrate accurately how a planned mining operation will appear at various stages and seasons (Entzminger, 1976).

F. Landscape Monitoring and Control Stations

Litton (1973) described a practical five-step procedure for establishing a network of landscape control points (LCP's) for forest landscape control. The same procedure can be used for rangelands with outstanding landscape values and for rangelands under intensive management. The procedure consists of five steps:

1) Establishing a network of LCPs to give a reasonably continuous view of an extended large area.
2) Plotting either by manual or computer techniques the limits of visibility for each LCP on a topographic map.

3) Photographing a panoramic view from each LCP.
4) Drawing field sketches of specific parts for more precise studies of possible changes or alternatives.
5) Utilizing the LCP's and the supporting graphic information to project the appearance of alternative land use plans and the appearance of selected plans in their intermediate and final stages.

G. Guidelines

Following a sound and systematic procedure for rangeland landscape planning is probably more important than attempting to create and use a complete checklist of landscape development guidelines. But the following are principles that ought to govern either the creation of such a checklist or the implementation of any thorough landscape planning procedure:

1) Where soils are highly variable, adhering to soil information will often produce ideal landscape patterns (Williamson & Currier, 1971).
2) Visual diversity and stability reinforce ecological values (Caldwell, 1971).
3) Coordination of new management proposals with previous manipulations is essential.
4) Designs for clearing areas and reestablishing grass should follow irregular lines and fit comfortably with the land form, although in practice the feathering of edges and the overall transferral of designs from paper to reality is a difficult task. When near farming country, use transistions from straight to curvilinear lines.
5) Vegetation control methods that disturb the soil create more color contrast than other methods, but in many cases they may be the most cost-effective.
6) Keeping the public informed about management objectives and the appearance of both intermediate stages and final results are extremely important.
7) Utilizing irregular layout lines is usually consistent with creating additional vegetation edges for wildlife cover.
8) Leaving selected groupings of trees in clearing operations can create a savannah-like appearance and, in the case of pinyon-juniper vegetation types, it can provide for the production of pine nuts.
9) Planning for views from the air will become more important with time, but utilizing conventional landscape principles will usually assure a pleasing view from the air (Williamson & Currier, 1971).
10) Landscape planning, like other functional planning, cannot be done effectively in a vacuum. It should be closely coordinated with other aspects of planning and in many cases they should utilize a common data base.
11) Landscape modifications, including either structures or vegetation

changes, have the potential of creating more visually acceptable variety in range landscapes. But people desire a significant degree of legibility or unity in the landscape, and, beyond a certain degree of complexity, scenes may be difficult to understand and appreciate.

12) Some areas of the rangelands are more important for their landscape qualities than other areas. It is often important to evaluate the sensitivity of the people toward landscape values before proceeding with modification plans.

13) Long- and short-term landscape planning objectives should always be distinguished.

14) Effective mitigation will always involve careful planning, design, and implementation of range resource activities in a manner which will minimize adverse effects on the visual resource and, when appropriate, increase visual variety.

III. PLANNING FOR WILDLIFE ON PUBLIC RANGELANDS

A. Importance of Planning for Wildlife

The inclusion of wildlife in plans for the management of public rangelands is dictated by the complex ecological relationships of wildlife with domestic range animals and with the range ecosystem of which they are a vital part. Past grazing practices, which have not always taken wildlife into account, have sometimes had serious detrimental effects not only upon wildlife but upon the rangeland itself. The Bureau of Land Management's *Range Condition Report* (USDI Bur. Land Manage., 1975a) indicates that the allocation of forage for domestic animals and not for wildlife is one of the more serious problems on the public range. That report also indicates that some grazing practices may have an effect upon fish populations by contributing to the deterioration of streams.

1. ROLE IN THE ECOSYSTEM

Indigenous species are important in maintaining the stability of natural ecosystems and may represent critical links in natural food chains (USDA Forest Serv., 1976a). Thus their loss could pose serious problems for management of the ecosystem. While domestic livestock grazing is known to interrupt the balance of native ecosystems (Stoddart et al., 1975), it has also proved beneficial in promoting native plants and thereby enhancing wildlife habitats (USDA, 1970; USDA Forest Serv., 1976a). Early summer cattle grazing, for example, helps to reduce grass competition and to increase browse on winter wildlife ranges (USDA Forest Serv., 1976a).

Small animals, especially rodents, often cause serious damage to range plants by girdling shrub stems, and eating seeds, forage, or stems and roots of perennial plants (Stoddart et al., 1975). Insects also attack foliage, flowers, and seeds, and they may serve as vectors for plant diseases. Yet rodents and insects are important parts of the food chain and perform other roles in the ecosystem which preclude their treatment as vermin unless justified by careful study.

2. VALUE TO MAN

Fish and wildlife are an important renewable resource despite the greater suitability of cattle, sheep, and goats as food sources. The importance of wildlife is not easily defined or readily comparable to the values associated with the livestock industry. Wildlife may be said to have that worth which is perceived by society—and that is partially economic and partially intrinsic (Stoddart et al., 1975).

Fish and wildlife are most obviously of economic value to hunters and fishermen. In 1970, there were 14.3 million hunters and 29 million freshwater fishermen in the United States (USDA Forest Serv., 1976a). A large proportion can be expected to have pursued their sport on rangelands or forest-range lands and associated waters. Nonconsumptive uses such as photography, wildlife study, drawing and painting, aesthetic enjoyment, and literary or musical inspiration are more difficult to evaluate economically. The significance of nonconsumptive values may be inferred from the estimated 4.5 million wildlife photographers and the 7 million birdwatchers pursuing their unique interests in 1970. It may also be judged from the rise in circulation of *National Wildlife* magazine from 60,000 in 1963 to 350,000 in 1975 (USDA Forest Serv., 1976a).

Our society places a high value on big game and fish, consequently, they tend to be the most intensively studied and managed forms of wildlife (Stoddart et al., 1975). Rodents, other small animals, insects, and predators which do not seem to contribute obvious value tend to be ignored by a majority of society. Yet rabbits are the number one game animal in the United States and predator hunting is rapidly increasing. Scientists should direct more effort toward understanding such species, and their economic value and roles in various ecosystems should also receive more attention (Stoddart et al., 1975).

B. Size and Diversity of Populations

For the most part, changes in wildlife populations can be related to man's activities—to fencing, hunting and fishing, range improvements, human contacts, timber harvesting and type conversion, interrupted migratory routes, and competition with livestock (USDA Forest Serv., 1976a). Hunting and fishing have provided the economic incentives for research on the more than five million big-game animals estimated to live on forage-producing forest range. Less is known about the countless populations of smaller game and nongame animals including songbirds, fish, reptiles, waterfowl, and insects (USDA Forest Serv., 1972), though some tentative evidence has indicated that nongame bird populations have been relatively stable over the past 10 years (USDA Forest Serv., 1976a). What is certain, as the Public Land Law Review Commission (1967) has indicated, is that public lands are not meeting their potential for producing wildlife—that wildlife production is a byproduct of other uses and occurs largely by chance. Planning for stimulation or control of wildlife populations must therefore consider not only the diversity and complex interrelationships of various species, but the public consensus about which species and which of man's activities ought to be favored at the expense of others.

C. Significant Planning Issues

Planning for the management of fish and wildlife resources, as with other resources, requires that planners not only have adequate survey information and methodological alternatives at their disposal, but that they evaluate all relevant issues and their possible effects. Thus, a spectrum of land use alternatives can be developed from which resource managers can make effective decisions in response to public needs.

1. POPULATION DYNAMICS AND HABITAT REQUIREMENTS

Outdoor recreation, including hunting, fishing, birdwatching, and nature photography, has been increasing, and thereby accelerating demands for larger populations and greater diversity of species. Therefore, fish and wildlife population levels and habitat requirements need to be identified and management strategies must be planned in accord with defined capabilities of range resources to support game and nongame species. Consumptive and nonconsumptive uses of wildlife are expected to continue to grow (USDA Forest Serv., 1972). As a consequence of heightened public concern for the environment, pressure can be expected to increase for more efficient maintenance and more diverse use of high quality forest range ecosystems.

2. COMPETITION WITH LIVESTOCK

Forage for wildlife should be planned for when forage for livestock is planned for, as the Public Land Law Review Commission (1970) has recommended. And, it seems clear from BLM's Nevada Study (Counc. Environ. Qual., 1975) that the water, cover, and forage requirements of all forms of wildlife need more complete attention. Planning to avoid forage competition should consider similarity of diets, quantity and quality of available forage, populations, nutritional requirements, species utilization for forage, and long-term influences on ecologic succession (Stoddart et al., 1975). But planners will be faced with limited and conflicting information: for example, some studies have shown that diversity of diets may allow cattle and big game to share grazing areas (Skovlin et al., 1969; Teer, 1972), while other research has demonstrated that deer and cattle compete for certain plants (Lesperance et al., 1970). Moreover, populations, forage needs, and cover requirements of many nongame species need to be more clearly defined.

3. HARASSMENT AND PREDATION

Urbanization, summer home and resort development, highway construction, recreational vehicles, and other intrusions by man have led to the harassment of all forms of wildlife (Neil et al., 1975; Baldwin, 1970; Howe, 1973; Ward et al., 1973). Off-road vehicles and aircraft produce undesirable noise and fumes, and snowmobiles in particular are known to be used to chase wildlife, sometimes to exhaustion and death (Baldwin, 1970). Excessive running at any time may lead to the development of emphysema in animals and finally death (Geist, 1971). Urbanization, recreation developments, summer homes, and new roads are known to destroy nesting and feeding areas and to disrupt migration routes of wildlife (Howe, 1973; Ward et al., 1973). On the other hand, such developments tend to benefit wildlife by increasing the edge effect—that is, the tendency of some species to thrive along the edges of vegetation types, so some species may actually flourish as a consequence of man's developments.

Along with human habitation come "predator" pets—dogs and cats that harass or kill wildlife. Songbirds, game birds, rabbits, and other small animals are the targets of free-roaming cats (Doucet, 1973). Packs of dogs are extremely destructive to cattle, deer, and elk (Caras, 1973; Colo. Div. Wildl., 1973). Thus pets must be included when planning for the well-being of wildlife on public range lands which are adjacent to developed residential areas.

Predation of domestic livestock by wildlife, especially coyotes, wolves, bears, and eagles, is of considerable concern to ranchers, whereas conservationists tend to regard such predation as insignificant. It seems unlikely that eagles and wolves are present in sufficient numbers to pose a significant threat. However, bears do destroy sheep and, in some areas, may be a more serious problem then coyotes. Yet, coyotes pose a more controversial problem. On the one hand, the sheep industry insists on control of coyotes, because any losses in sheep mean losses in profits. On the other hand, some conservationists insist that economic factors—not the coyote—are responsible for the industry's decline (Counc. Environ. Qual., 1975). Research in Nevada, which is in agreement with other studies, indicates that only 4% of all losses of sheep are attributable to coyotes (Klebenow & McAdoo, 1976).

Predation and harassment are certainly problems the planner must solve. Various control techniques can be used to reduce predation by coyotes, free-roaming dogs, and other predators, but stopping wildlife harassment necessitates more complex planning which involves zoning, law enforcement, design applications, and public education.

4. THREATENED AND ENDANGERED SPECIES

Planning to protect threatened and endangered species and their habitats is now required under the Endangered Species Act of 1973 (USDA Forest Serv., 1976a). Despite its apparent simplicity, such protection requires the coordinated planning of resource managers from widely different backgrounds to avoid any act that might upset the precarious balance of any of the endangered game animals, birds, lizards, insects, fish, or plants with their environment.

5. LEGISLATIVE CONTROLS AND PUBLIC ACTIONS

Planning can proceed only after the most thorough review of relevant federal and state legislation. Laws designed to protect or control wildlife, the environment, or the various commercial enterprises which affect public rangeland (timber cutting, tourism, ranching, mining) have often come into being through public controversy or are themselves the objects of current controversies. Such laws are closely watched by competing special interest groups. Chief among these, perhaps, is the National Environmental Policy Act of 1969, which requires preparation of environmental impact statements for management actions that might significantly influence the environment and its inhabitants (Fulcher, 1973). Two recent laws controlling planning on most public lands are the National Forest Management Act of 1976 and The Federal Land Policy and Management Act of 1976. Others of importance include the Wildlife Restoration Act of 1973 and similar acts authorizing the federal government to cooperate with the states in their traditional field of game management, the Endangered Species Act of 1973, agency organic acts, refuge establishment acts, and funding bills (Shepard's Cit. Inc., 1968; Udell, 1971; U.S. Congr., 1971; USDA Forest Serv., 1974c, 1976b; U.S. Libr. Congr., 1973).

Historically, man's use of public rangelands has reduced the quantity and quality of available forage, altered the species diversity, eliminated many valuable plants, and has been generally disruptive to the natural habitats of wildlife (USDA, 1936). Over the years, range management and fish and game harvesting techniques have not been ideal, the range situation has remained essentially static, and wildlife populations have continued to be adversely influenced. Yet as more evidence of the effect of grazing practices upon the range ecosystem becomes available, the planner, aided by wildlife and management experts, should be able to propose alternative arrangements for the accommodation of wildlife side by side with domestic animals.

IV. PLANNING FOR RECREATION ON PUBLIC RANGELANDS

Except for a few range ecosystems, recreational use of public rangelands is largely a matter of opportunity because ranges have few features that are inherently attractive for most recreation activities. Recreation on public ranges takes place almost exclusively where there are centers of attraction—spectacular scenery, points of historic or scientific interest, developed recreational facilities, interesting minerals or fossils—or where off-road vehicles are not prohibited or controls are lax, or where vacationers can pull off the road with their campers or camping gear. Recreation on public rangelands occurs most frequently when these attractions happen to be close to urban areas. And there are few recreational activities, notably hunting and ORV use, which can be pursued on public rangelands wherever they are found. Even these activities will occur first and most heavily on those public rangelands which are closest to urban centers.

The observation that rangeland typically "offers little opportunity for water-related activities" (USDA Forest Serv., 1972) is certainly the key difference between the opportunities, capabilities, and attractions that range environments possess and those of most other settings for recreation. The availability of streams or lakes is the single most important attraction for most recreationists (Mattyasovsky, 1967). Another important distinction is the dominance of grass, shrubs, or, at most, small, scattered trees over other more attractive forms of vegetation. But, tall tree cover is not nearly as important as the presence of water in attracting people for recreation.

The term *rangelands* includes a very diverse group of ecosystems which in the United States ranges from desert shrublands to alpine tundra. While many different classification systems for rangelands have been proposed, 14 types are generally recognized as occurring in the United States (McKell & Goodin, 1973). But for planning, it is useful to subdivide rangelands into two broad classes according to the commonly available presence of significant amounts of perennial surface waters.

The Alpine and Mountain Meadow range ecosystems consist of 10.3 million acres of the U.S. federal public rangelands. These rangelands commonly have significant perennial surface water, occur in the spectacular scenic settings of mountainous topography, offer panoramic views, and even have tree masses as a prominent part of the biotic diversity in subalpine areas. Thus they are inherently attractive recreational environments for hiking, backpacking, picnicking, camping, fishing, hunting, trail biking, and other activities.

The other federal public rangelands—the arid, semiarid, and desert grass and shrublands—consist of 231.1 million acres possessing few perennial water bodies. These rangelands are likely to be open, rolling, frequently visually monotonous landscapes dominated as far as can be seen by shrubs, grass, or small tree clumps, and generally one will not be able to see very far except in the infrequent instances where travel routes are lifted above the surrounding landscape. Unless there are specific attractive features present, these environments offer few reasons for lingering, besides hunting, ORV use, or rock collecting.

A. Recreation Carrying Capacity as a Supply Criterion

Recreation-carrying capacity can be defined as the intensity of use that can be supported by an area without causing excessive damage either to the experience of the visitor or to those aspects of the environment that originally made it desirable (Lime & Stankey, 1971; Sudia & Simpson, 1973). The intensity of recreation uses cannot be described adequately as a simple "consumption" function of various measures of natural productivity or other inherent biophysical capabilities. As Dooling has pointed out,

"People don't eat grass and shrubbery, they step on it" (R. J. Dooling. 1969. Soils, carrying capacity and resource based recreation systems. Paper given at 4th British Columbia Soil Sci. Workshop, Abbotsford, 15–17 Oct. 1969.). The benefits derived by recreationists are mostly psychological and are determined by many things besides land productivity (Wagar, 1974). While a relationship does exist between resource productivity and use, this productivity is measured by the rate and mix of satisfactions provided recreationists. "Recreational carrying capacity is largely a matter of judgment rather than bio-physical determinism" (Stankey, 1974). "Each site has a whole range of potential [carrying] capacities, each providing different consequences. Therefore, even if it can be shown how areas and experiences will change with various levels of use and various management practices, some one must still decide what changes are acceptable. Defining what is acceptable is a value choice rather than a technical issue" (Wagar, 1974).

1. PSYCHOLOGICAL CARRYING CAPACITY

Recreation carrying capacity becomes a more usable concept if divided into categories which may be titled "psychological" and "ecological." Stankey (1974) lists some guidelines for defining psychological carrying capacity. He divides the various types of recreation into five groups of motivationally distinct, activity-preference categories which satisfy certain social-interaction expectations and make generally similar impacts upon and requirements of the natural environment. These five categories are activities emphasizing:

1) Preservation and appreciation of natural environmental qualities (e.g., wilderness backpacking).
2) The extraction of "trophies" from the environment (e.g., mountain climbing, hunting).
3) Social interactions as the primary source of satisfaction (e.g., auto-access camping).
4) The instruments of the activity rather than the setting in which it takes place (e.g., trail biking, water skiing).
5) Activities typically requiring little physical effort and generally not requiring a wildland environmental setting (e.g., sunbathing).

Each of these categories can be related to such overall recreational carrying capacity factors as the intensity of use likely to occur, the degree to which change in the natural environment is acceptable, the level of site manipulation that can be undertaken without significantly altering the type of opportunity provided, and the principle expectations of participants in an activity concerning their contact with nature, other individuals, or groups of people.

The relationship of activity-preference categories to carrying capacity factors helps describe the implications of alternative decisions regarding recreational allocation and management. Relationships of the use and demand characteristics to the carrying capacity factors can provide criteria for allocating available recreation resources by helping define the trade-offs between the relative number of persons served by one alternative as opposed to another and also suggesting guidelines for alternative management actions.

Techniques are being developed for expressing some aspects of psychological carrying capacity as quantitative measurements. For example, Harrison (1975) presents data on the distances at which the noise from ORV's is no longer detectable in forest environments. Mikkelsen (1975) and Litton (1974) establish the distance at which objects are no longer visible when viewed through a number of different types and densities of vegetation. Travis et al. (1975) present a widely used computational technique based on topographic map data for delineating visible areas.

While many researchers are concentrating on the psycho-sociological aspects of recreation behavior and expectations, what has been produced so far is still too vague to provide much direction for land use planners.

2. ECOLOGICAL CARRYING CAPACITY

Much documentation exists on the cause-and-effect relationships between recreation use and site deterioration, and this information can be used as site selection criteria for land use planning. While little of this research has been specifically oriented toward recreational uses on grazing lands, much of the guidance which comes out of other ecosystem situations ought to be readily transfereable to range environments.

Establishment of ecological carrying capacities for recreational uses should involve evaluation of the potential for:

1) Site degradation—e.g., compaction of soil (Meineckie, 1929; Lull, 1959; A. W. Magill. 1963. Soil compaction in relation to forest recreation. M.S. Thesis. Univ. of California, Berkeley. On file at Pacific Southwest Forest and Range Exp. Stn., Berkeley), trampling of vegetation (Gibbons & Heady, 1964; La Page, 1967), pollution of water (Barton, 1969), and disturbance of wildlife (Jarvinen & Schmid, 1971).

2) Environmental hazards to recreationists—e.g., landsliding (Bailey, 1971; Crandell & Mullineaux, 1967), wildfires (Deeming et al., 1974), and tree fall hazards (Paine, 1971).

3) Maintenance or enhancement of site qualities—e.g., soil fertility, depth, and moisture-holding capacity, plant species hardiness (Magill, 1970; Magill & Leiser, 1972).

4) Characteristics favorable for different recreational uses—e.g., sun exposure (Cordell & James, 1972), favorable ground pitch and site drainage relationships (Cordell & James, 1972; Montgomery & Edminster, 1966), and stoniness of ground surface (Montgomery & Edminster, 1966).

B. Significant Recreation Planning Issues

Ideally, land use planning should seek to anticipate potential resource allocation conflicts and provide alternative resolutions to those conflicts. Unfortunately, only occasionally do public land management and planning agencies have the lead time and funding levels to do truly anticipatory planning. Because social values, and hence the nature of demands on wildland resources, seem to be rapidly changing, there is legitimate doubt about the possibility of successfully planning to avoid conflicts very far in advance of their emergence (Rittel & Webber, 1973). Moreover, because of the militant and uncompromising stances taken by many competitors for public resources, many resource allocation conflicts that do arise will have to be resolved at political decision-making levels—not by the planning efforts of most land management agencies. Thus, probably more out of necessity than conscious choice, the overall character of the planning being done by public land agencies can be described more accurately as reactive rather than anticipatory. Their planning efforts are, and perhaps must be, largely issue-oriented or even issue-initiated. Resources will be allocated to land use planning only when forced by political or legal pressures.

The most prominent range recreation issues are public access, off-road vehicle use, and vandalism of property or harassment of livestock by recreationists. These are complex problems whose remedies lie partly beyond the reach of the planner in questions of law enforcement, education, and even sociology. But by becoming thoroughly familiar with all aspects of these problems, the planner can take a step toward helping solve them.

In 1967 about 2.2 million ha (5.4 million acres) of land administered by the Bureau of Land Management were classified as blocked because of intervening private lands (USDA Econ. Res. Serv., 1968). Landowners holding grazing privileges on public lands are not required to grant access across their own lands to those who want to use public lands. But grazing permit holders have no legal right to deny public access directly onto public lands. The rights of the general public to use public grazing lands for recreation specifically extends to lands used by private persons under the terms of the Taylor Grazing Act (USDA Econ. Res. Serv., 1968). Loss of access also occurs because of poorly marked distinctions between public and private lands.

The availability of access routes through private land to public land is obviously a problem which will require careful planning. In fact the USDA Economic Research Service's 1968 publication *Public Access to Public Domain Lands,* which is the most authoritative work on this question, says:

> The question of what constitutes adequate public access to [public]. . .lands can only be answered within a comprehensive framework for planning and decision-making. [Such a framework must]. . .include operational criteria for selecting among uses and among intensity of uses. Until such plans and programs are developed, the controversy is likely to continue and expand.

The land use planner's role with respect to ORV use, in addition to the initial allocation of available land resources among competing and incompatible uses and juxtaposing incompatible uses to minimize conflicts (Bury & Fillmore, 1974; Calif. State Dep. Parks & Recreat., 1975), is one of choosing for ORV use those sites and trail locations which are most able to withstand impact and be managed for recovery. For this latter role planners will need data on soils, vegetation, acoustical properties, snow depth, and site visibility to be able to make their decisions. For example, to minimize adverse environmental impacts, snowmobile areas should be located where the snow is deepest and where nonwoody vegetation is predominant, where sound will not carry for great distances, and where wildlife or livestock are not likely to be sheltering (Wanek, 1973). Trail bikes and 4-wheel-drive vehicles should be restricted to areas where soils are resistant to compaction (Wilshire & Nakata, 1976) and dry rapidly, where there are no live streams or drainage swales, where site visibility and sound propagation is low (Harrison, 1975), where little surface runoff occurs, where ground fire hazards are low, and where there are few livestock or wildlife that would be sensitive to ORV use.

Vandalism and animal harassment are problems which can be reduced by control of access and by placement of use sites. Land use plans should attempt to place access routes and use areas so that they are away from private residences, private property or improvements located on public rangelands, places where livestock are likely to be concentrated (such as waterholes), unprotected archeological sites, and areas where there are wildlife species particularly sensitive to people, their pets, or certain recreational activities. It may also be necessity to regulate recreation seasons on the basis of sensitivity to injury that varies with time. A land use plan may also produce policy statements to guide, later, more detailed planning. For example, policies might recommend that: (i) certain vandal-prone facilities should not even be built or certain areas opened to use unless adequate protective measures can be provided; (ii) local property owners be reimbursed for vandalism or harassment losses; (iii) intensive use sites, especially group camping, be placed where they can be readily watched by supervisory personnel.

Planners must recognize that vandalism and harassment is going to be a major objection to opening up public rangelands to increased recreational use—especially on lands close enough to urban areas to be readily accessible by teenage and young adult populations. But vandalistic behavior is not an issue particularly associated with specific forms of recreational use—though certain activities lend themselves to misuse more than others. Thus viable planning solutions will seldom lie in absolute prohibition of specific recreational activities.

V. HISTORICAL-ARCHEOLOGICAL RESOURCES IN PLANNING

Land use planners have routinely inventoried such basic resources as the soil, geology, vegetation, and wildlife, and evaluated their importance for the planning decisions. But the historical, archeological, and paleontological resources of the planning area have been seldom thought of as important resource assets that can affect decision making. However, because these resources are nonrenewable and because numerous federal and state laws require their protection (McGimsey, 1972; Moratto, 1976), they should receive the planner's careful attention.

Historical, archeological, or paleontological resources usually cannot be readily moved on short notice without destroying much of their valuable information. Much of the information they contain is not transportable and, hence, each action which may deleteriously affect a site causes an irreversible loss.

On-site excavation work consumes only about 25% of the time needed to complete the study of each excavated site (McGimsey, 1973); and it has been estimated that 45,000 undisturbed sites exist in California alone (Moratto, 1973), and for a 9,712-km^2 (3,750-mi^2) area of southwestern Arizona considered as being habitable during prehistoric periods, Lipe (1974) estimates that about 65 sites occur per square kilometer (25 sites per square mile). While their protection is strongly mandated by numerous laws, adequate funding and trained personnel typically have not been available to thoroughly inventory and protect these valuable resources that may fact imminent destruction. Federal land management agencies are responding to these tasks as quickly as funding becomes available to establish real technical expertise in archeological and cultural resource planning. Thus, land use planners, as allocators of resources for land based uses, have a particularly important role to play in seeing that these resources are adequately inventoried, evaluated, and, when found to be significant, protected on their sites. All of these steps should be considered in the planning process.

Planning areas can typically be subdivided into zones on the basis of the relative likelihood that sites will be found. The distribution of archeological sites often correlates well with environmental features, such as physiogrphy, water supply, or vegetation zones (Lipe, 1974; Soc. Calif. Archaeol., 1970; Davis, 1972; McGimsey, 1973). Typically, sites should be expected to occur where fresh water and food supplies are now, where they were abundant during the last 10,000 to 20,000 years, where raw material deposits are found (such as obsidian, flint, or soapstone), where community defense could be easily provided, or along or at the confluence of trading routes (Soc. Calif. Archaeol., 1970).

Establishing the potential distribution of a population of sites should be approached with the principles guiding the layout of an explicit sampling design problem. "A sampling-based inventory, plus a search of existing literature, would provide valuable information to planners about environmental and geographic correlations of site distributions at a fraction of the cost of a 100% inventory" (Lipe, 1974).

A. Obtaining Expert Assistance

Planners can consult a number of agencies to find qualified archeological assistance or to determine evaluations or studies already performed on areas of concern; for example, the State Historical Preservation Officers, the National Register of Historic Places, the Historic American Building Survey, and the Inter-Agency Archeological Salvage Program. McGimsey (1973) and King et al. (1973) list criteria that can be used to evaluate the qualifications of potential consultant archeologists; and the Society of Professional Archaeologists has more recently developed new standards. Archeological evaluation and preservation are highly technical matters which must not be attempted without such expert assistance. The evaluation of site significance is a job for qualified professional archeologists and requires *detailed* studies.

B. Mitigating Impacts Upon Archeological Resources

In many cases, if archeological studies are begun in early planning stages, it will be possible to present alternatives which will preserve significant archeological resources at minimum expense and inconvenience. If preservation of archeological resources in place is not possible, the only other feasible protective measure is to excavate them before their destruction; but, this should be considered a last resort (King et al., 1973; Lipe, 1974; Matheny & Berge, 1976; Davis, 1972). Unless a site's integrity is threatened, it should be regarded as a data bank for future study (McKinney, 1976). King et al. (1973) suggest some measures to protect archeological resources from vandalism if sites cannot be avoided all together. These include obscuring sites in landscaping, inclusion of sites in limited-use or high-visibility areas where it would be difficult for looters to dig undetected, or use of sites for nondestructive, interpretive public displays.

C. Site Disclosure Problems

The problem of the potential exposure of sites to increased vandalism and looting is a complicating factor in the planning process (McGimsey, 1972, 1973; Verner, 1976; King et al., 1973). Public disclosure of site locations greatly increases the chance of illicit digging. Individuals with knowledge about the detailed information of sites may be reluctant to make this information available in their zeal to protect sites from increased vandalism. Satisfactory resolution of this complication will require understanding and cooperation among all concerned. In addition, it will require a degree of security and control over access to planning information. Such control would be unusual for a public decision-making process typified by the ready public accessibility to the decision-affecting data base.

VI. TYING IT ALL TOGETHER—LAND USE PLANNING ON PUBLIC RANGELANDS

A. Planning and Management Requirements

Throughout this chapter attention has been focused on aspects of public rangeland planning, one at a time. But the land, the plants, the wild and domesticated animals, and the various human activities on public rangeland are too interrelated to be examined in isolation. Neither the over-all land use nor any single factor can be adequately managed without con-sideration of all the factors together. On federally controlled rangelands this interdisciplinary planning, tying all the factors together, is mandated by law.

One key instrument is the National Environmental Policy Act of 1969 (NEPA). NEPA is best known for its subsection requiring environmental impact statements (EIS) for "major Federal actions significantly affecting the quality of the human environment." Most planning and day-to-day management of public rangelands do not qualify as "major Federal actions" (although court decisions have leaned toward requiring an EIS when in doubt), but other, less-publicized parts of NEPA require careful, interdisciplinary consideration of all federal actions or decisions, even when an EIS is not required. In short, NEPA required all federal decision-makers to use systematic, interdisciplinary approaches, to give appropriate con-sideration to environmental amenities, to find and use ecological information, and to study and develop alternatives whenever they plan for rangelands where there *may* be an impact on the environment or unresolved conflicts concerning alternative uses. Of course, all these requirements are very general. More specific requirements can be found in other acts, both state and federal, and the governing regulations of the different agencies in-volved with public rangelands. For the Bureau of Land Management and the Forest Service these requirements are developed in detail in the Federal Land Policy and Management Act of 1976 and the National Forest Manage-ment Act, respectively.

Instead of charging ahead in the single-minded pursuit of one goal, the planner is encouraged to examine possible consequences and then settle on that combination of actions which will best satisfy the whole range of uses without destroying the basic resource itself.

B. A Planning Framework

But tying it all together, incorporating all the different factors into planning and management, is not easy. Much of the information which ideally should be included is simply unknown. The manager has no choice but to depend on professional judgment where the facts are unknown. For a small project this process may be fairly direct. The manager can call to-gether experts on both the natural sciences and the different types of uses, and then together they can decide on the best way to complete the project. As the area of responsibility increases, so does the complexity of the prob-lem; the possible consequences are much greater, and the range of alterna-tives is much larger. It becomes necessary to adapt what has been variously called a hierarchical, a stratified, a multilevel, or a unified planning process.

In this process, different plans are developed for increasingly inclusive land bases. The plan for each successively larger land unit becomes more general, and is both built upon the plans below it and provides the unifying framework and direction for these plans. [See Carder and Oglesby (1973) for a detailed discussion of one way this could be implemented]. Several government agencies are currently using or moving toward this approach. Within the Forest Service's land use planning system a national program is prepared. Then very large areas are designated and a regional plan is prepared, setting out policy and direction for all the National Forests and Grasslands within the region. A more specific Forest Plan is developed for the overall management of each National Forest or Grassland. Each Forest Plan provides the specific management direction for that Forest. Of course, all of these plans are developed somewhat in parallel, with the higher level plans requiring information on resource and use capabilities from the lower level plans, and these in turn requiring direction from the higher level plans. For day-to-day management of the Forests or Grasslands, specific functional or project plans are then developed to implement the use decisions contained in the Forest Plans. Of course, any similar planning scheme is sufficient, provided it meets two key criteria: first, the higher planning levels must establish overall allocations and consider multiple project and cumulative effects; and, secondly, especially at the higher levels, the planning must be the result of an interdisciplinary team who work together throughout the process, particularly during the development of alternatives.

The need for the first of these criteria should be obvious, but the second deserves some discussion. There are three basic approaches to professional and specialist involvement in planning. The first, where the manager depends on his own knowledge and judgment, with occasional specialist input, can be discarded out of hand. The second approach is to involve a variety of different resource and functional specialists, but to have each functional group independently prepare an alternative indicating how the land could best be managed for their particular use. At the end these alternatives are presented and one is chosen, or portions of each are chosen to allow some tradeoffs among alternative uses. With this approach, concerns from different specialties and disciplines are at least aired, but by operating independently neither the conflicts nor the compatibilities among uses can be adequately explored. To adequately conduct public rangeland planning, an interdisciplinary team should, from the outset, consider alternatives involving different combinations of uses to avoid conflicts and to take advantage of compatibilities among uses.

C. Type Conversion—A Case Study

To pull the different parts of this chapter together, a case study will illustrate the application of those principles which until now have been presented in the abstract. A pinyon-juniper (P-J) type conversion project has been chosen because it involves a major modification of the land base with possibilities for impact on different values and resources, and because it is both a very common action, and one often surrounded by controversy. Additionally, since it is a common action, this discussion may have immediate, practical applications rather than remaining merely an illustration. And finally, up-to-date reviews of scientific research already exist (Gifford, 1976; USDA Forest Serv., 1974a; Clary et al., 1974; Nielsen & Hinckley, 1975), and so this discussion can focus on methodology rather than individual impacts.

Type conversion from P-J to grasslands falls within the planning framework presented earlier as a program or project plan. Before this manipulation is even considered, higher level plans should be established giving management direction and goals for the immediate area (the unit). We will assume that as a result of this planning, the unit is to be managed primarily for grazing, although other uses and resources are still considered important. To improve the grazing situation, P-J type conversion is proposed.

The first step is to define the planning job. Higher level planning sets the objective of improving grazing without destroying other uses or resources. It is important to note that the objective is not to decide the best way to do type conversion, but whether it is to be done. After identifying some of the key issues that may arise, the manager organizes the planning job and determines the major skills that will be needed. It is immediately obvious that these will include a detailed knowledge of grazing alternatives, wildlife biology, soils, hydrology, recreation, landscape management, and history or archeology. As the planning progresses other skills may be required. Through the higher level planning, much of the inventory and management information which the team will need has already been collected.

At this point, all the different skills are brought together. Through proper involvement of outside groups as well as internal specialists it should be possible to establish a broad range of well-defined alternatives for meeting the goal. Both good management and NEPA (for federal agencies) require that the alternatives truly cover the range of options. Once the alternatives are defined, each is examined in detail until either it is shown to be infeasible or it can be seriously considered. In this situation the alternatives might include decreasing total grazing, continuing present management, altering grazing patterns, and various methods of type conversion. Although each would be examined in detail, from this point on we will focus on type conversion alternatives.

There are two parts to P-J type conversion. First the P-J must be removed and then grass established. The approaches to be considered are chaining (where a heavy chain is dragged across the ground to break the stems), burning, herbicide treatment, bulldozing and root plowing, and dragging other devices besides chains. As part of some alternatives, the vegetation removal could be coupled with reseeding and temporary livestock removal. Once the P-J is removed, grasses must be established. This can be started by seeding the area, or depending on natural reseeding. Once the land is seeded it may be necessary to remove livestock until the plants are established (USDA Forest Serv., 1974a).

The first step in choosing an alternative is to determine how well each contributes toward the primary goal; that is, how much will grazing be improved. Once the ability of each alternative to meet this goal is evaluated for each site, the effects and costs associated with those alternatives are examined. Of course, at this point any alternative which both causes environmental damage and will not meet the goal can be discarded. Then the actual out-of-pocket costs of implementing each alternative are calculated to determine whether the project is feasible within the agency budget. A comparison of these costs with the anticipated levels of increased grazing will give some indication of the relative cost effectiveness of different alternatives. Depending on the magnitude of the contemplated program the manager may want to obtain economic expertise and conduct a full benefit-cost analysis. Several studies to date have indicated that benefit-cost ratios will vary greatly from site to site, and that very often mechanical methods of P-J type conversion may not be justified on economic grounds. (O'Connell, 1972; Richardson & Badger, 1974; Brown et al., 1974; Kearl, 1973; Workman & Kienast, 1975; Clary et al., 1974).

Before a decision can be made on choosing or rejecting alternatives much additional information must be collected. Workman and Kienast (1975) found market-priced, nonmarket-priced, and nonquantifiable benefits and costs associated with P-J conversion. Benefit-cost analyses are generally limited to the first category, and sometimes include the second. There are undoubtedly situations where alternatives which are not economically justified should be chosen because of their nonmarket and nonquantifiable benefits. Similarly, economically viable projects may be rejected because their costs in these two categories are too high.

At this point it is absolutely essential that specialists become involved in predicting impacts and in modifying the alternatives to reduce the adverse impacts and the costs and to increase the benefits. Not all of these specialists need to be from within the land management agency. This is another ideal opportunity to take advantage of the considerable expertise available on all sides of issues through public involvement. Even those groups opposed to P-J conversion have persons with considerable knowledge about the subject, and it is good management, good politics, and on major federal actions a legal requirement that their information be considered before, rather than after, any decision is made. Improving this communication is particularly important in view of the blocking effect that a strong opposition can have in the courts, and because of the generally bad communication that often exists between land managers and environmentalist groups.

Specialists should be consulted wherever alternatives involve technical problems—a hydrologist when major vegetative and soil disturbance is contemplated, a wildlife expert when changes in habitat are likely.

With any major modification there is the potential for major aesthetic impact. Major improvements in visual impacts can sometimes be achieved with relatively minor modifications of the alternatives. In place of square corners and straight lines, clearings can be made with uneven edges following the landscape. Islands and isolated trees can be left to break the barrenness. Unsightly rows or piles of debris can be avoided, and debris large enough to be used as fuelwood can be removed. However, eventually a point is reached where aesthetic improvements can only be attained by drastically changing the alternatives. At this point it is necessary to judge the aesthetic quality of the area and to identify the changes that would be associated with each alternative. This information must then be weighed by the manager at the moment of decision.

Where type conversion is proposed the manager will usually be concerned with dispersed recreation, such as hunting and ORV use. To be able to choose among the alternatives the manager will need to know what types of use are already occurring, and working with recreation and small game specialists he will have to estimate how this may change with each alternative. In many cases it will be possible to attack special recreation problems by slightly changing the alternatives. Where ORV wildlife harrassment is a problem, unlimited P-J conversion with resulting open space may only increase the problem. But a well-developed plan of cleared routes combined with vegetative barriers and patch clearings in other locations may funnel the ORV users to those routes, while protecting wildlife and livestock in other areas. Similarly, open routes on public lands combined with unbroken vegetative barriers at private land boundaries may reduce some conflicts over public access in areas of mixed ownership. These changes in alternatives are easy to make and have little effect on the overall amount of improved grazing, but they cannot be developed unless all the different specialists and interests are involved together in developing and assessing the alternatives.

Archeology is another area that should be considered in planning P-J conversion. Schreyer and Royer (1975) have asserted that many P-J areas are rich in archeological sites. Where these sites have been identified in higher level planning, they can be investigated and avoided if necessary. Additionally, there will be areas which are suspected of having archeological sites and other completely unknown sites. P-J conversion may have some special impacts on these sites. Burning should not damage the sites by itself, and may uncover unknown sites by removing the vegetation. This can be either good or bad. If responsible individuals make the discoveries, both scientific knowledge and public recreational benefits can increase. However, if the discoveries are made by vandals, pothunters, or thieves who steal the artifacts for sale, then valuable sites can be destroyed. Some of this danger can be avoided by including a quick archeological survey after the burning as well as before.

Once all the minor modifications to the alternatives have been made and the potential effects of each alternative identified, then the whole range of mánagement alternatives must be evaluated against each other and the best alternative chosen. The choice of this alternative is so dependent on site characteristics and management judgment and values that no generalizations can be made. However, if the manager follows this process, truly tries to cover the entire range of alternatives and effects, conducts the process openly and obtains public involvement, bases the decision on these results, and then documents his decision and the reasons for that decision, he can be assured of the quality and legality of both the process and the decision.

LITERATURE CITED

Arthur, L. M., and R. S. Boster. 1976. Measuring scenic beauty: a selected annotated bibliography. USDA For. Serv., Gen. Tech. Rep. RM-25.

Bailey, R. G. 1971. Landslide hazards related to landuse planning, Teton National Forest, northwest Wyoming. USDA For. Serv., Intermt. Reg., Odgen, Utah.

Baldwin, M. F. 1970. The off-road vehicle and environmental quality. The Conserv. Found., Washington, D.C.

Barton, M. A. 1969. Water pollution in remote recreation areas. J. Soil Water Conserv. 24(4): 132–134.

Brown, T. C., P. F. O'Connell, and A. R. Hibbert. 1974. Chaparral conversion potential in Arizona, Part II: an economic analysis. USDA Forest Serv. Res. Pap. RM-127.

Bury, R. L., and E. Fillmore. 1974. Design of motorcycle areas near campgrounds: effects on riders and nonriders. Texas Agric. Exp. Stn., Dep. Tech. Rep. 6.

Caldwell, L. K. 1971. Environment—a challenge to modern society. Doubleday and Co., Garden City, N.Y.

California State Department of Parks and Recreation. 1975. The off-road vehicle: a study report. Sacramento, Calif.

Caras, R. 1973. Meet wildlife enemy no. 2. Natl. Wildl. 11(2):30–31.

Carder, D. R., and C. H. Oglesby. 1973. Unified planning and decisionmaking: a conceptual framework for Forest Service management. Prog. in Eng. Econ. Plann., Stanford Univ. Rep. EEP-4.

Clary, W. P., M. B. Baker, Jr., P. F. O'Connell, T. N. Johnson, Jr., and R. E. Campbell. 1974. Effects of pinyon-juniper removal on natural resource products and uses in Arizona. USDA For. Serv. Res. Pap. RM-128.

Colorado Division of Wildlife. 1973. Dogs killing deer problem grows. Outdoor News, 22 Apr. 1973, p. 2.

Cordell, H. K., and G. A. James. 1972. Visitors' preferences for certain physical characteristics of developed campsites. USDA For. Serv. Res. Pap. SE-100.

Council on Environmental Quality. 1975. The sixth annual report of the Council on Environmental Quality. Washington, D.C.

Crandell, D. R., and D. R. Mullineaux. 1967. Volcanic hazards at Mount Ranier, Washington. U.S. Geol. Surv. Bull. 1238.

Crowe, S. 1966. Forestry in the landscape. For. Comm. Bookl. 18, London.

Davis, H. A. 1972. The crisis in American archeology. Science 175:267–272.

Deeming, J. E., J. W. Lancaster, M. A. Fosberg, R. W. Furman, and M. J. Schroeder. 1974. National fire-danger rating system (rev. Ed.). USDA For. Serv. Res. Pap. RM-84.

Doucet, G. T. 1973. House cat as predator of snowshoe hare. J. Wildl. Manage. 37(4):591.

Elsner, G. H. 1976. Quantifying landscape dimensions for land-use planning. Int. Union of For. Res. Organ. World Congr. Proc. (Div. 6) Oslo, 1976:28–38.

Entzminger, R. A. 1976. MOSAIC/photomontage: a new concept to help reclamation planning. Coal Min. Process. 13(6):76–78.

Fulcher, G. D. 1973. Political and social constraints on the use of arid lands for recreation, wildlife, water, and livestock grazing in the United States. p. 144–148. In D. N. Hyder (ed.) Arid shrublands—Proc. 3rd Workshop of the United States/Australia Rangelands Panel, 26 Mar.–5 Apr. 1973, Tucson, Ariz. Soc. of Range Manage., Denver, Colo.

Geist, V. 1971. Is big game harassment harmful? Oil Wkly. 22(17):12–13.

Gibbons, R. P., and H. F. Heady. 1964. The influence of modern man on the vegetation of Yosemite Valley. Univ. Calif. Agric. Exp. Stn. Manual 36.

Gifford, G. F. 1976. Vegetation manipulation—a case study of the pinyon-juniper type. p. 141–147. In Watershed management on range and forest land—Proc. 5th Workshop of the United States/Australia Rangelands Panel. 15–22 June 1975, Boise, Idaho. Utah State Univ., Logan.

Harrison, R. T. 1975. Impact of off-road vehicle noise on a national forest. USDA For. Serv. San Dimas Equip. Dev. Center Proj. Rec. ED & T 2428.

Howe, C. 1973. Environmental impacts of residential mountain developments in Colorado. Ecol. Today 2(2):6–11; 29–31.

Jarvinen, J. A., and W. D. Schmid. 1971. Snowmobile use and winter mortality of small mammals. p. 130–141. *In* M. Chubb (ed.) Proc. 1971 Snowmobile Off-the-Road Vehicle Res. Symp., 14–15 June 1971, Mich. State Univ., East Lansing, Mich.

Kearl, W. G. 1973. Economic and management constraints for livestock production from arid shrublands. p. 116–124. *In* D. N. Hyder (ed.) Arid shrublands—Proc. 3rd Workshop of the United States/Australia Rangelands Panel, 26 Mar.–5 Apr. 1973, Tucson, Ariz. Soc. for Range Manage., Denver, Colo.

King, T. F., M. J. Moratto, and N. N. Leonard, compilers. 1973. Recommended procedures for archaeological impact evaluation. Soc. Calif. Archaeol., Northridge, Calif.

Klebenow, D. A., and K. McAdoo. 1976. Predation on domestic sheep in northeastern Nevada. J. Range Manage. 29(2):96–100.

Land Use Consultants. 1971. A planning classification of Scottish landscape resources. Countryside Comm. for Scotland, Battleby, Redgorton Perth, CCS Occas. Pap. 1.

LaPage, W. F. 1967. Some observations on campground trampling and ground cover response. USDA For. Serv. Res. Pap. NE-68.

Lesperance, A. L., P. T. Tueller, and V. R. Bohman. 1970. Symposium on pasture methods for maximum production in beef cattle: competitive use of the range forage resource. J. Animal Sci. 30(1):115–121.

Lime, D. E., and G. H. Stankey. 1971. Carrying capacity: maintaining outdoor recreation quality. p. 174–184. *In* Forest Recreat. Symp., 12–14 Oct. 1971, Syracuse, New York. Northeast. For. Serv. Exp. Stn., Upper Darby, Pa.

Lipe, W. D. 1974. A conservation model for American archaeology, Kiva 39(3–4):213–245.

Litton, R. B., Jr. 1968. Forest landscape description and inventories—a basis for land planning and design. USDA For. Serv. Res. Pap. PSW-49.

Litton, R. B., Jr. 1972. Aesthetic dimensions of the landscape. p. 262–291. *In* John Krutilla (ed.) Natural environments. John Hopkins Press, Baltimore.

Litton, R. B., Jr. 1973. Landscape control points: a procedure for predicting and monitoring visual impacts. USDA For. Serv. Res. Pap. PSW-91.

Litton, R. B., Jr. 1974. Visual vulnerability of forest landscapes. J. For. 72(7):392–397.

Lovejoy, D., ed. 1973. Land-use and landscape planning. Leonard Hill Books, Alylesbury, Bucks, Great Britain.

Lull, H. W. 1959. Soil compaction of forest and range lands. USDA For. Serv. Misc. Pub. 768.

McGimsey, C. R. 1972. Public archeology. Seminar Press, New York.

McGimsey, C. R. 1973. Archeology and archeological resources: a guide for those planning to use, affect, or alter the land's surface. Soc. Am. Archeol., Washington, D.C.

McGuire, J. R. 1973. Status and outlook for range in the new politics. J. Range Manage. 26(5):312–316.

McKell, C. M., and J. R. Goodin. 1973. United States arid shrublands in perspective. p. 12–18. *In* D. N. Hyder (ed.) Arid shrublands—Proc. 3rd Workshop of the United States/Australia Rangelands Panel. Soc. for Range Manage., Denver, Colo.

McKinney, C. M. 1976. Cultural resource planning in federal project and land management activities. p. 24–32. *In* R. T. Matheny and D. L. Berge (ed.) Proc. Symp. Dynamics Cult. Resour. Manage. USDA For. Serv., Southwestern Reg. Archeol. Rep. 10, Albuquerque, N.M.

Magill, A. W. 1970. Five California campgrounds. . .conditions improve over 5 years' recreational use. USDA For. Serv. Res. Pap. PSW-62.

Magill, A. W., and A. T. Leiser. 1972. Growing plants on view landscapes and recreation areas. Guideline 2(5):57–61.

Matheny, R. T., and D. L. Berge. 1976. Some problems pertaining to cultural resources. p. 1–8. *In* R. T. Matheny and D. L. Berge (ed) Proc. Symp. Dynamics Cult. Resour. Manage. USDA For. Serv., Southwest. Reg. Archeol. Rep. 10, Albuquerque, N.M.

Mattyasovsky, E. 1967. Recreation area planning: some physical and ecological requirements. p. 221–236. *In* D. W. Fischer, J. E. Lewis, and G. B. Priddle (ed.) Land and leisure: concepts and methods in outdoor recreation. Maaroufa Press, Chicago.

Meineckie, E. P. 1929. The effect of excessive tourist travel on the California redwood parks. State Print. Off., Sacramento.

Mikkelsen, T. H. 1975. Visual absorption in selected vegetation types of the Lake Tahoe Basin. Pacific Southwest For. and Range Exp. Stn., Berkeley, Calif.

Montgomery, P. H., and F. C. Edminster. 1966. Use of soil surveys in planning for recreation. p. 104–112. *In* L. J. Bartelli et al. (ed.) Soil Survey and Land Use Planning, Soil Sci. Soc. Am., Madison, Wis.

Moratto, M. J. 1973. The status of California archaeology. Soc. Calif. Archaeol., San Francisco, Calif.

Moratto, M. J. 1976. A consideration of law in archaeology. *In* C. R. McGimsey and H. A. Davis (ed.) Guidelines for the profession. Soc. Am. Archaeol., Washington, D.C.

Neil, P. H., R. W. Hoffman, and R. B. Gill. 1975. Effects of harassment on wild animals—an annotated bibliography of selected references. Colo. Div. of Wildl., Spec. Rep. 37.

Nielsen, D. B., and S. D. Hinckley. 1975. Economic and environmental impacts of sagebrush control on Utah's rangelands—a review and analysis. Utah Agric. Exp. Stn. Res. Rep. no. 25.

O'Connell, P. F. 1972. Economics of chaparral management in the Southwest. p. 260–266. *In*Proc. Natl. Symp. on Watersheds in Transition, 19–22 June 1972, Am. Water Res. Admin., and Colorado State Univ., Fort Collins, Colo.

Paine, L. A. 1971. Accident hazard, evaluation and control decisions on forested recreation sites. USDA For. Serv. Res. Pap. PSW-68.

Paulsen, H. A., Jr. 1975. Range management in the central and southern Rocky Mountains: a summary of the status of our knowledge by range ecosystems. USDA For. Serv. Res. Pap. RM-154.

Public Land Law Review Commission. 1967. Fish and wildlife resources on the public lands. Vol. II, Colorado State Univ., Fort Collins.

Public Land Law Review Commission. 1970. One third of the nation's land—a report to the President and to the Congress by the Public Land Law Review Commission. Washington, D.C.

Richardson, J. W., and D. D. Badger. 1974. Environmental and economic impacts of methods of brush control on western Oklahoma rangeland. Proc. Okla. Acad. Sci. 54:36–39.

Rittel, H. W. J., and M. M. Webber. 1973. Dilemmas in a general theory of planning. Policy Sci. 4(2):155–169.

Schreyer, R., and L. E. Royer. 1975. Impacts of pinyon-juniper manipulation on recreation and aesthetics. p. 143–150. *In* The Pinyon-Juniper Ecosystem: A Symp. Utah State Univ., Logan.

Shepard's Citations, Inc. 1968. Digest of public land laws. Public Land Law Rev. Comm., Washington, D.C.

Skovlin, J. M., P. J. Edgerton, and R. W. Harris. 1969. The influence of cattle management on deer and elk. p. 169–181. *In* J. B. Treffethen (ed.) Trans. 33rd North Am. Wildl. and Natl. Resour. Conf., 11–13 Mar. 1968, Houston, Tex. Wildl. Manage. Inst., Washington, D.C.

Smardon, R. C. 1975. Assessing visual-cultural values of inland wetlands in Massachusetts. p. 289–318. *In* E. H. Zube, R. O. Brush, and J. G. Fabos (ed.) Landscape assessment—values, perceptions, and resources. Dowden, Hutchinson & Ross, Inc., Stroudsburg, Pa.

Society for California Archaeology. 1970. Archeological site identification in highway planning. Soc. Calif. Archaeol. Daly City, Calif.

Stankey, G. H. 1974. Criteria for the determination of recreational carrying capacity in the Colorado River Basin. p. 82–101. *In* A. B. Crawford and D. F. Peterson (ed.) Environ. Manage. Co. River Basin. Utah State Univ. Press, Logan.

Stoddart, L. A., A. D. Smith, and T. W. Box. 1975. Range manaement. 3rd ed. McGraw-Hill Book Co., N.Y.

Sudia, T. W., and J. M. Simpson. 1973. Recreation carrying capacity of the National Parks. Guideline 3(3):25–34.

Teer, J. G. 1972. Future of rangeland uses: wildlife. p. 41–44. *In* Symp. Commemorating 25 Years, 20–21 Mar. 1972, Texas A & M Univ., College Station, Tex.

Travis, M. R., G. H. Elsner, W. D. Iverson, and C. G. Johnson. 1974. VIEWIT: computation of seen areas, slope, and aspect for land-use planning. USDA For. Serv. Gen. Tech. Rep. PSW-11.

Udell, G. G., compiler. 1971. Laws relating to forestry, game conservation, flood control and related subjects. U.S. Congr., House of Represent., Washington, D.C.

U.S. Congress. 1971. United States Code (Title 7: Agriculture; Title 16: Conservation; Title 43: Public Lands.) U.S. Congr., House of Represent., Washington, D.C.

U.S. Department of Agriculture. 1936. The western range: a report on the western range—a great but neglected natural resource. U.S. Congr. 74th Congr., 2nd session, Doc. no. 199.

U.S. Department of Agriculture. 1970. Range ecosystem research: the challenge of change. U.S. Dep. Agric. Inf. Bull. 346.

U.S. Department of Agriculture, Economic Research Service. 1968. Public access to public domain lands: two case studies of land-owner-sportsman conflict. USDA Econ. Res. Serv., Washington, D.C.

U.S. Department of Agriculture, Forest Service. 1972. The nation's range resource—a forest-range environmental study. For. Resour. Rep. 19, For. Range Task Force, Washington, D.C.

U.S. Department of Agriculture, Forest Service. 1974a. Environmental statement, rangeland enhancement: plant control and revegetation on sagebrush and deteriorated grassland sites on National Forest land in California. USDA Forest Serv. Reg. 4 (Ogden, Utah) and Reg. 5 (San Francisco).

U.S. Department of Agriculture, Forest Service. 1974b. The visual management system. USDA Agric. Handb. 462. To be published as Chap. 1. *In* National forest landscape management, Vol. 2. USDA, Washington, D.C.

U.S. Department of Agriculture, Forest Service. 1974c. The principal laws relating to Forest Service activities. USDA Agric. Handb. 453.

U.S. Department of Agriculture, Forest Service. 1976a. RPA: the nation's renewable resources: an assessment, 1975. USDA For. Serv., Washington, D.C.

U.S. Department of Agriculture, Forest Service. 1976b. Supplement to the principal laws relating to Forest Service activities. USDA Agric. Handb. 453.

U.S. Department of Agriculture, Forest Service. 1977. Range. USDA Agric. Handbk. no. 484. To be published as Chap. 3. *In* National forest landscape management, Vol. 2. USDA, Washington, D.C.

U.S. Department of the Interior, Bureau of Land Management. 1974. Forest environmental impact statement—livestock grazing management on natural resource lands, December 31, 1974. USDI, Bur. Land Manage., Washington, D.C.

U.S. Department of the Interior, Bureau of Land Management. 1975a. Range condition report. USDI, Bur. Land Manage., Washington, D.C.

U.S. Department of the Interior, Bureau of Land Management. 1975b. Visual resource management, Manual section 6300. USDI, Bur. Land Manage., Washington, D.C.

U.S. Environmental Protection Agency. 1973. Aesthetics in environmental planning. USEPA, EPA-600/5-73-009, Washington, D.C.

U.S. Library of Congress. 1973. A compilation of Federal laws relating to conservation and development of our nation's fish and wildlife resources, environmental quality, and oceanography. U.S. Libr. Congr., Washington, D.C.

Verner, R. S. 1976. Problems in resource management. p. 33–37. *In* R. T. Matheny and D. L. Berge (ed.) Proc. Symp. Dynamics Cult. Resour. Manage. USDA For. Serv., South-western Reg. Archeol. Rep. 10, Albuquerque, N.M.

Wagar, J. A. 1974. Recreational carrying capacity reconsidered. J. For. 72(5):274–278.

Wanek, W. J. 1973. The ecological impact of snowmobiling in northern Minnesota. p. 57–76. *In* D. F. Holecek (ed.) Proc. 1973 Snowmobile and Off-the-Road Vehicle Res. Symp., Mich. State Univ., East Lansing, Mich.

Ward, A. L., J. J. Cupal, A. L. Lea, C. A. Oakley, and R. W. Weeks. 1973. Elk behavior in relation to cattle grazing, forest recreation, and traffic. Trans. North Am. Wildl. and Natl. Res. Conf. 38:327–337.

Williamson, R. M., and W. F. Currier. 1971. Applied landscape management in plant control. J. Range Manage. 24(1):2–6.

Wilshire, H. G., and J. K. Nakata. 1976. Off-road vehicle effects on California's Mojave Desert. Calif. Geol. 29(6):123–132.

Workman, J. P., and C. R. Kienast. 1975. Pinyon-juniper manipulation—some socio-economic considerations. p. 163–177. *In* The Pinyon-Juniper Ecosystem: A Symp., May 1975, Utah State Univ., Logan, Utah.

Zube, E. H., R. O. Brush, and J. G. Fabos, eds. 1975. Landscape assessment—value, perceptions, and resources. Dowden, Hutchinson & Ross, Inc., Stroudsburg, Pa.

section V

Planning Forest and Woodland Uses

USDA Soil Conservation Service

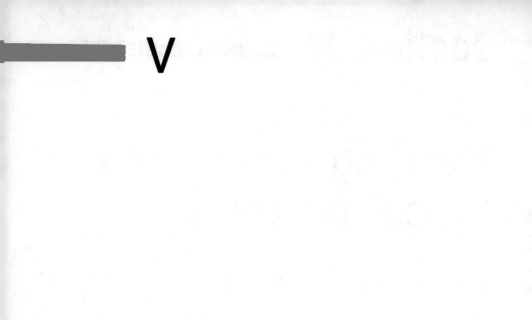

V

15

Timber Production on Extensive Holdings

S. P. GESSEL AND W. A. ATKINSON

University of Washington
Seattle, Washington

I. INTRODUCTION

For purposes of this discussion, extensive timberland holdings are defined as those owned by public forestry organizations or by private companies or individuals operating wood-using plants. In 1970 such properties totaled 82.3 million ha (203.4 million acres) of commercial forest land in the United States, which although only 41% of the total commercial forest land in the country, contained 80% of conifer sawtimber volume, 56% of conifer growth, and 70% of conifer sawtimber cut (President's Adv. Panel, 1973). Federally owned national forests constitute almost one-half (45%) of large land area holdings, with other public (federal, state, and counties) controlling 22%, and forest industry 33% (President's Adv. Panel, 1973). Because of the high proportion of growth capacity represented by extensive land holdings, their management occupies a prominent place in future wood supply projections. It is safe to say that decisions made in the next decade by owners of extensive forest land holdings will vitally affect wood supply in the next century.

This chapter focuses on forest management planning for extensive properties. A general discussion of management goals within a land use planning framework is followed by sections on forest soils, land productivity, tree nutrition, climate, timber inventory, accessibility, harvest regulation, management plans, and silvicultural systems. Final portions of the chapter discuss forestry cultural activities.

II. FOREST MANAGEMENT GOALS

Differences in product emphasis exist between public and private owners of extensive properties. All are concerned with production of an array of products and services (known as *multiple use*). Private owners, however, generally concentrate their attention on timber production, with recreation, water, and wildlife of lesser importance. Public owners, too, are frequently interested in timber production, but also give major emphasis to these other values. Multiple use is practiced by allowing several uses to coexist on the same area, as when hunting and camping are permitted in new plantations, or by zoning the property so that uses are separated, as with wilderness areas. Both of these approaches are used to satisfy the multiplicity of demands placed on forest properties.

III. LAND USE PLANNING

Before developing the subject of planning for timber production, it is useful to gain perspective by examining the general framework for land use planning. Land use planning is both product oriented and investment oriented. In addition to classifying land as to the use that it will support, planning also details the specific management regimes to be followed on the land. This includes timing of management activities as well as their levels of investment. Thus, the land use plan is the basis for determining not only the proper level of funding for forest management, but also the desired allocation of funds among management activities and the specific mix of activities to be undertaken on each land unit.

One might consider the planning process to be made up of three distinct stages. The first stage is a classification of land as to its investment and use potential—a general broad breakdown based on land suitability. For example, at this stage it would suffice to set aside high site forest land for wood production and lakeside areas for recreation.

The second stage defines management units within each primary land classification. Management units should be defined by management regime. A number of these regimes are likely depending on the variation in land conditions. For example, a large tract of land that is suitable for intensive wood prodution might contain well-drained upland soils where conifers thrive, and wetter areas where hardwoods only will grow; or it might have areas with steep slopes and special harvest and thinning problems as well as flat ground. Each broad land classification is a mosaic of small management units. It is here, in stage two, that the details of management are developed. When you get to the level of defining on-the-ground management activities, land use planning becomes important. Until then it is just an idle exercise.

The third stage can be called 'Revision and Feedback.' Knowledge generated in the first two stages could well change the primary land use classification, and hence the planning system must include evaluation and feedback. Fragile soil areas identified in stage two might have to be removed from the wood-producing base. Reassessment of the public interest can change management goals. The planning process obviously must include a mechanism for change.

The point in developing this line of argument is that effective planning as to land use cannot be divorced from detailed management decisions. The former depends upon the latter. In order to plan for land use you must know its capacity to produce products that are recognized as important. Hence, a great deal of detailed data are needed for land use planning. The timber inventory provides data on the present condition of the forest. Topographic maps, soils maps, and aerial photographs are other valuable sources of information. Estimates of the results of management activities are provided by forest research. Specifically, planners must know for each potential management activity the relationship that exists between inputs and outputs, both in physical and in economic terms.

A difference exists between land use planning as practiced in public and in private forestry organizations. Private companies, being oriented toward timber production, are most interested in classifying their lands as to timber investment opportunities. Public forestry organizations, on the other hand, are not only interested in timber management opportunities, but also must consider land use in a more general sense. Many demands must be satisfied, and within each type of demand are gradations of use requiring different management practices. For example, recreation use can range from complete preservation with practically no construction impacts to intensive development of campgrounds, boat launch ramps, and playing fields. Forest land can be set aside for each category of use, and management prescriptions assigned accordingly. Public agencies often employ multidisciplinary planning teams to study alternatives and recommend use-zone boundaries. Open hearings allow for inclusion of public input to management decisions, and requirements for environmental impact statements assure a thorough review of land use proposals.

IV. INFORMATION NEEDS FOR TIMBER PRODUCTION

A. Soils Information

1. GENERAL

Efficient production of timber on extensive land holdings within the restrictions imposed by forest practice regulations relating to environmental protection requires detailed knowledge of the environment, especially the soil. Soil is now recognized as the basic resource in forestry and as such determines the ultimate local productivity of the forest as well as many responses to environmental changes. The nature of forest soil must also come into decisions about which management and harvesting regimes to employ. Lloyd and Clark, in the accompanying chapter on timber production on small holdings (Chapter 17), have thoroughly reviewed the principles of soils as applied to forest growth, including soil/site relationships. The reader should refer to this chapter for details.

Much of the larger forest land ownerships in the western U.S. are in mountainous terrain where environmental parameters, especially soils, change rapidly. These changes are caused by differences in topography and land form, and are best expressed in terms of steepness of slope, position on slope, and exposure or aspect. Exposure affects both temperature and moisture content of forest soils because of its relationship to incoming radiation.

Table 1—Areas in which soil information input is needed for forest management
on extensive holdings.

A. General policy
   1. Long-range land use planning
   2. Environmental questions and problems

B. Technical problems
   1. Productivity of forest land
     a. Short-term
     b. Long-term
   2. Harvest methods
   3. Site preparation methods
   4. Regeneration
   5. Windfirmness
   6. Soil stability
   7. Transportation system planning and construction
   8. Water quality
   9. Silvicultural practices
  10. Municipal sewage and waste water disposal

Position on slope is generally correlated with soil depth, soil moisture, and soil productivity. Degree of slope affects soil stability, soil depth, and moisture status, among other parameters, and therefore many other soil properties. Slope also must be considered in economic and operational decisions. For instance, slope may make the difference between economically thinnable land and nonthinnable land, and will influence the economic decision as to number of stems for initial regeneration of the next crop. Degree of slope, therefore, has a major effect on land value. Stone content is also an important factor frequently changing over short distances in many forest soils and affecting productivity and operations on forest soils. Large forest land ownerships in other part of the United States may have a less diverse pattern of topography, but the need for soil information in management and operational decisions still exists. Soil mapping units must have clearly defined boundaries based on slope, land form, and stone content if they are to be most useful to the practicing forest land manager.

These considerations all add up to the fact that a modern forest manager dealing with substantial acreages should have basic soil survey information in each management unit and also considerable interpretive data. Table 1 summarizes areas in which soil information can be used in forest land management.

2. SOIL AND FOREST SITE

Foresters use the term *site* or *site quality* as an indication of productivity and have developed site indices based on the relationship between height and age for a given tree species. Factors which determine forest productivity are climate, species, forest management practices, forest age, biological factors such as disease and insects, and, most importantly, the soil. In any one local area where productivity factors other than soil are constant, soil becomes the important variable in site quality. A great deal of

research effort has gone into the determination of site based on soil parameters and many studies now exist relating soil to site. Chapter 16 by Lloyd
and Clark reviews some of this work and explains how it can be used.

One of the most important informational needs for any forest area is
productivity, which may be expressed in a number of ways and is related to
whatever the forest land is being managed for. In this chapter the emphasis
is on wood production, and productivity is expressed in units of wood produced such as cubic feet per acre or cubic meters per hectare. The potential
productivity of a forest area is a parameter upon which many management
decisions are based. The range of productivity in large forest areas is great,
varying from about 0.35 m³/ha (5 ft³/acre) per year to as much as 28 m³/ha
(400 ft³/acre) per year on better soils and under intensive management. Productivity has been used as a basis for distinguishing between what may be
called *commercial* and *noncommercial* forest land. Noncommercial forest
land is generally regarded as that with less than 1.4 m³/ha (20 ft³/acre) per
year of wood production. There is debate in forestry circles as to the growth
rate to be used to define the boundary between commercial and noncommercial land. Lakes, streams, meadows, roads, and rock outcrops are obviously nonproductive. However, the definition of productive forest land
can change with end product, utilization standards, and economics. What
was considered a scrub forest with useless wood volume a number of years
ago may now have value as small, tight-grained, high-quality saw logs, as
raw material for wood chips, or even for firewood. Therefore, the growth-
rate line between so-called commercial and noncommercial forest land is
flexible. In a current forest land grading project covering the state of Washington, this boundary line is 0.7 m³/ha (10 ft³/acre) per year.

The importance of productivity in forest management and the use of
soils to acquire the basic information is exemplified by two rather recent developments. A number of forest land companies have undertaken detailed
soil mapping of their lands. This mapping is being done in order to improve
management of the forest resource, with principal emphasis on deriving
better information on site quality. For example, Weyerhaeuser Company
has established its own soil survey staff and developed specific mapping
procedures. All of Weyerhaeuser's tree farm lands in the western U.S. are
now covered by soil surveys and these are being rapidly extended to company ownership throughout the United States. The program has been so
successful that contracts to conduct soil surveys on other ownerships are
now being undertaken.

Since the primary objective of the Weyerhaeuser soil survey is productivity information, each soil mapping unit has specific site quality information developed for it. This information is based on an extensive research
program relating soil properties to site quality. A different soil/site expression has been developed for Douglas-fir in northwestern Washington than
for slash pine in the southeastern U.S. or even for Douglas-fir in southern
Oregon. Soil/site relationships are expressed as regression equations using
soil properties easily identified in the field, such as soil depth, organic con-

tent, or stone content. When properly developed and used they have proven to be very accurate.

A similar program, but with a somewhat different objective, has been initiated in the state of Washington. All private forest land is being soil mapped to provide a basis for forest land taxation. Soil mapping units have site class and productivity rating assigned with respect to the tree species best suited. Productivity ratings are then incorporated into more general site classes for ultimate taxation purposes.

In addition to productivity, a great deal of information useful in forest land management can be taken from soil maps. Obvious applications are in road location and construction, and in harvesting operations, especially susceptibility of soils to damage during harvest. Soil maps also provide guidelines for site preparation and regeneration.

3. NUTRITIONAL STATUS OF FOREST SOILS

The nutritional status of forest soils and forest plants was considered a relatively unimportant factor in forest productivity and growth until recent years. Beginning about 1930 in the United States and with increasing emphasis after 1950, researchers clearly demonstrated that the early philosophy of water and light as the only environmental factors affecting tree growth was erroneous. In many forest areas of the world, nutrition deficiencies have now been shown to occur and to substantially reduce forest growth. Field experiments following basic nutritional research have demonstrated very marked response to a range of elements applied to the forest system. For instance, in the Pacific Northwest, Douglas-fir forests produce about 25% more volume growth after nitrogen application of 170–225 kg/ha (150–200 lbs/acre). The result is that over 500,000 ha (1.2 million acres) of forest land have now had nitrogen applied by helicopter, principally in the form of urea. Similar forest fertilizer practices have developed in most major forest areas of the world, with variation in elements applied and forest ages treated. For instance, phosphorus is commonly applied in Australia at the time new forests of radiata pine are established.

If such increases in production are possible, and application of essential elements over a wide area is a sound economic investment, then the forest landowner needs to know what growth response can be expected for each mapping unit. The process of evaluating the elemental supply for a forest soil and the expected response to additional elements is complicated and beyond the intent of this chapter. References are included for additional reading on the subject.

4. SOIL INFORMATION AND ENVIRONMENTAL PROBLEMS

Large forest land holdings are being increasingly subjected to public scrutiny on a wide range of environmental issues and problems. Perhaps the most important of these relate to water quality, as much of the nation's water originates on forest land. In addition, the land is used for public recreation and for wildlife habitats of all kinds. Many states now have forest practice acts which regulate what the landowner may or may not do in the use of the resource. These laws usually focus on soil and water.

Regulations relating to better management of the land are most likely going to increase and become more complex in the future. Therefore, the large forest landowner finds that soils information relating to potential problems of erosion, sediment, water quality, road construction, harvesting impacts, and a host of other environmental aspects is very important. Soil information supplied to the landowner must cover the entire range of forest land use and not be focused only on wood production.

5. OTHER SOIL-RELATED PROBLEMS

This category includes the area of regeneration and rehabilitation of forest land, along with some aspects of forest harvesting. Many large holdings include extensive areas of land that for a number of reasons may contain unmerchantable tree species at the present time and may actually be carrying a brush cover with little prospect of producing a wood supply. In order to become productive, the cover must be changed and a new species introduced. This requires rather substantial investments in forest type conversion. Before such investments are undertaken the landowner should know the nature of soils on the property, as it may be relatively easy to rehabilitate one particular kind of soil while attempts on another soil may lead to an immense array of problems. Soil mapping unit information must indicate expected problems. Conversion practices may include drainage or modification of hardpans that affect rooting of forest trees. Substantial areas of the southeastern coastal plains must be drained or mounded to ensure successful regeneration. Similar drainage problems exist throughout Pacific coastal forests. They may result from low elevation and natural water tables close to the surface, or from water permeability restrictions within the soil profile. In the latter case excess water may be a seasonal problem corresponding to high rainfall, as during the winter in the Pacific Northwest. Actual or potential drainage problems should be identified on soil maps for the landowner.

Other regeneration problems originate from animal damage of all kinds and especially burrowing animals such as mountain beaver and gophers. Observations in Washington and Oregon have indicated that these animals prefer certain soil types and, therefore, the problem may be identified with soils so that control practices can be planned.

B. Climate Information

The need for the forest landowner to have as much information on climatic parameters as possible should be self-evident. The form and amount of precipitation, along with temperature, determines in a broad sense the species to be grown and the general productivity of the area. In fact, this information determines whether the area is going to be forested at all or in some other form of wildland vegetation. After these broad generalities are resolved, information on the seasonable distribution of rainfall, snow cover, and temperature becomes very important. Length of the growing season is also a major factor. The temperature distribution and particularly frost-free periods are more important when new species are being introduced into the area. As an example, German foresters find that, although Douglas-fir grows very well and outproduces many of the native species in Germany, it occasionally has freezing problems. Douglas-fir buds break early in the spring in Germany, and the budbreaking is frequently followed by a late spring frost, severe enough to damage all new foliage. If this occurs in successive years the growth of the tree is reduced and eventually the species may be eliminated.

Wind is a factor which may often be overlooked in forestry, especially if one only observed the forest on mild summer days. The fact that trees project from the soil surface to varying heights makes them particularly susceptible to forces generated by wind movement. Therefore, tree trunks and branches must have stability to withstand great stresses and roots must have the ability to anchor the whole tree in the soil. The effects of disastrous wind storms such as hurricanes or typhoons on forests are well known. Less well known are the yearly losses due to pockets of windblown trees, particularly on soils that may be susceptible to windthrow. The landowner must know what to expect in potential wind damage as he reviews his forest productivity potential. Modern soil surveys provide information on windfirmness for the different mapping units.

C. Timber Cover Information

Previous sections have dealt primarily with information needs which describe the potential management possibilities and problems, and the potential productivity of forest areas. This section will deal with information required to describe the present forest vegetation and the possibility of its use and management.

The existing timber stand on a forest is not only a major component of current land and timber value, but also plays an important role in allowable cut calculations. Information is needed on current species composition, stocking, age, tree size distribution, and stand health. The planning tool used by foresters to record timber cover information is the timber type map, in which homogeneous stand units are delineated (usually on aerial photographs).

Species compositions can range from relatively pure single-species forests, such as pine, spruce or fir, to tropical forest conditions with several hundred species present on a small area. Individual species may vary from extremely valuable to unmerchantable.

Tree size determines the volume of wood in each stem and, therefore, influences costs of harvesting and manufacturing. Two forest acres with identical volumes but with trees of different sizes could command quite different prices. Stand age, especially, is important to know because of its relationship to tree size, growth rate, and general stand condition. Trees, like all living organisms, go through a cycle of youth to old age, and this is reflected in the forest characteristics. Trees generally start growing slowly, accelerate through a rapid period of growth, and then decline as they mature and begin to die.

D. Location Information

Distance to timber markets is perhaps less critical in its impact on value for large forest holdings than for small holdings because the large volume of wood involved makes it possible to bring mills close to large stands of timber. However, information on market location is essential in the management of extensive forest properties as it determines the cost of marketing the products, and therefore the eventual return. Short log hauls generally result in high values for standing timber. It is possible for land of low forest productivity to have a high economic value if it is adjacent to a good transportation system with a short-haul distance. Land so located may be more worthy of investment to increase forest profitability than land much farther removed from markets.

In this period of increased public interest in land management it is important that the large landholder recognize potential impacts of existing and potential recreation areas on his land. The same consideration applies to public transportation access across his holdings. The landholder must view management activities from the point of view of the public traveling a road transecting his property. In this case, all management and mismanagement is immediately opened to public scrutiny, and this definitely can have an effect on harvest scheduling, regeneration option, and eventual land value.

V. MAINTENANCE OF FOREST PRODUCTIVITY

Because forests often grow on poorer soils, as contrasted with agricultural soils, the large landholder must be concerned with nutrient drain and maintenance of forest productivity. At the present time there is little concrete evidence to suggest that when forests are properly managed, soil nutrient depletion is a serious factor affecting continuous yield on forest land. However, emerging concepts of total tree harvest, energy plantation culture, and very short pulpwood rotations may cause serious soil depletion. Historically, we know of many European forest areas that were degraded by litter-raking practices of the forest-dwelling

Table 2—Effect of clearcut harvesting on N loss for various rotation ages of Douglas-fir.†

Stand harvest age	Total N in ecosystem	Bole		Total tree	
		Removed	Annual loss‡	Removed	Annual loss‡
			kg/ha		
22	3,371	144	6.5	216	9.8
30	3,422	128	4.3	206	6.9
42	3,310	148	3.5	286	6.8
49	3,743	144	2.9	309	6.3
73	4,041	139	1.9	313	4.3

† Source: J. Turner. 1975. Nutrient cycling in a Douglas-fir ecosystem with respect to age and nutrient status. Unpublished Ph.D. Thesis, Univ. of Washington, College of Forest Resour., Seattle, Wash.

‡ Assumes an annual input of 1.1 kg/ha from the atmosphere and a leaching loss of 0.6 kg/ha for a net annual addition of 0.5 kg/ha.

peasants and by continuous charcoaling during the industrial revolution. Such degradation is more pronounced on poor soil systems. Those forests in which there is some evidence of successive rotation yield decline are on poor sandy soils in South Australia or in the southeastern U.S.

The recently concluded International Biological Program, expressed in the United States by Biome ecosystem studies, has completed detailed mineral cycling research in both coniferous and deciduous forests. These studies show that removal of stemwood on a 25- to 70-year harvest cycle constitutes a minor drain on the forest soil resource and that the amount of nitrogen removed in bole wood is almost balanced from atmospheric inputs (Table 2). Tables 3 and 4, and Fig. 1 depict the location of nutrient pools and pathways of movement in a second-growth Douglas-fir forest. Harvest removal of the total tree on an extremely short rotation will substantially change nutrient drain (Table 2) and may result in shortages of some elements in the more nutrient-poor forest soils. The large forest landowner must be aware of the possibilities of nutrient drain and concomitant productivity decline for specific soils. Many ways exist to ameliorate or correct nutrient drain problems, ranging from direct application of essential elements to changing

Table 3—Distribution of N, P, K, and Ca within the major components of a 36-year-old Douglas-fir plantation on a glacial outwash (modified from Cole et al., 1968).

Ecosystem components	N		P		K			Ca		
	kg/ha	% of total	kg/ha	% of total	kg/ha	% of total	% of exchange	kg/ha	% of total	% of exchange
Forest	320	9.7	66	1.7	220	0.3	44.6	333	0.3	27.3
Subvegetation	6	0.2	1	0.1	7	trace	1.4	9	trace	0.7
Forest floor	175	5.3	26	0.6	32	trace	6.5	137	0.1	11.2
Soil exchange†	--	--	--	--	234	0.3	47.5	741	0.7	60.8
Soil total	2,809	84.8	3,878	97.6	71,520	99.4	--	98,820	98.9	--
Total	3,310		3,971		71,793			100,040		

† Exchangeable with pH 7 ammonium acetate.

Table 4—Annual transfer of N, P, K, and Ca between components of the ecosystem—
36-year-old Douglas-fir stand.†

	N	P	K	Ca
		kg/ha		
Input (Precipitation)	1.1	T‡	0.8	2.8
Uptake by forest	38.8	7.23	29.4	24.4
Total return to forest floor	16.4	0.60	15.8	18.5
Leached from forest floor	4.8	0.95	10.5	17.4
Leached beyond rooting zone	0.6	0.02	1.0	4.5

† Source: Cole et al., 1968.
‡ Trace.

species composition and modification of management practices. The potential to utilize municipal sewage effluents on some forest lands should not be overlooked, and a great deal of research on use of sewage effluents on forest land is now in progress.

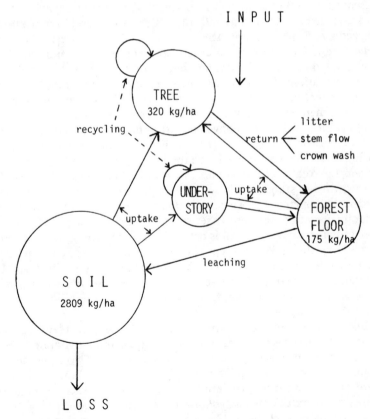

Fig. 1—Distribution and cycling of N in a second-growth Douglas-fir ecosystem (Cole et al., 1968).

VI. FOREST REGULATION

Turning specifically to timber production objectives, large public and private landowners most often direct management planning to a continuous annual production of wood, known as *sustained yield*. For public agencies such a production goal is generally based on legal mandates, while private owners of large forest parcels have sawmills, plywood plants, pulp mills, or other production facilities that require annual wood deliveries in order to maintain production. Whatever the reason, large forest properties are operated not for a wide fluctuation of annual cut, but for a reasonably steady cut.

The process of organizing a forest property for production of a continuous and reasonably steady supply of wood is known as forest regulation. These procedures have their roots in European forestry many centuries ago. The basic idea is simple: control harvesting and regeneration activities in the forest so that eventually a situation is attained in which each age class represents an equal proportion of the forest's productive capacity. Thus, if trees are to be harvested at age 50, then 10% of the land area would be in trees aged 1 to 5, 10% in trees aged 6 to 10, etc. Such a forest is known as a *normal forest*. Even though an exact representation of a normal forest is rarely attained because of natural (windstorm, fires) and man-made (wars, market fluctuations) interferences, such a model remains at the heart of forest management plans aimed at sustained yield. The age at which timber is cut and regenerated is known as *rotation age*, and its determination is a critical decision in forest management. Rotation age can be based on biological criteria or on economic criteria. From a biological standpoint, forests can be grown so as to maximize total production of wood on the area, known as the rotation of *maximum mean annual increment*. It is also feasible to grow forest stands until such age that the trees achieve a size objective (volume or diameter) known as a *technical rotation*. From an economic standpoint, rotation age can be set so as to maximize net profit from the timber-growing venture. Profit is determined by searching for that rotation age providing the highest present net worth, with interest cost on invested money included in the calculation. An approach first described by Martin Faustmann, an Austrian forest economist, known as *soil rent,* is generally used to compare rotation ages on the basis of profitability (Linnard & Gane, 1968; Davis, 1966).

Once rotation age is decided upon, the next step in forest regulation planning is to construct a plan for controlling the annual volume to be harvested from the property (called the *allowable cut*). Two approaches are available: area control and volume control. As the names imply, *area control* means controlling the area of timber cutover each year (and also the area regenerated), while *volume control* means controlling the volume of wood cut each year. Under an area control approach, A/R hectares (acres) are harvested and regenerated annually, with A representing the total area of commercial forest land on the property, and R being rotation age. Such an approach will bring about a fully regulated, normal forest in R years with each age class of trees equally represented. Volume control, on the other hand, will generally not achieve the normal forest condition in one rotation length but will allow for a steady volume production over this period. An example of a volume control formula is the Austrian formula:

$$A = (V_n - V_r)/R + I$$

where A = allowable cut, V_n = present timber volume, V_r = timber volume needed in the regulated normal forest, R = rotation age (either economically or biologically determined), and I = net annual forest growth for a short period, usually the next 5 years. A is generally recomputed every few years. Under the Austrian formula volume harvested will remain relatively stable over the rotation length, and the normal forest will be reasonably (but not exactly) represented at the end of one rotation.

With the advent of computer technology, allowable cuts are more often calculated today using sophisticated forest-growth simulators or optimizing techniques such as linear programming. Forest simulators can be used to project the forest over time, given a specific cutting plan. Many such plans can be tried out within the computer and the results compared using whatever criteria are desired. Optimizing models are designed to choose the best cutting plan from among the alternatives. *Best* can be defined in economic, physical, or biological terms. Even though computers are called on to determine allowable cuts today, behind these sophisticated techniques lie the basic principles of forest regulation planning which are many centuries old.

VII. THE FOREST MANAGEMENT PLAN

Forest management requires long-term investments of funds and effort, and thus should be based on long-term (and visionary) planning. Most large timberland organizations operate under a special document called the *forest management plan*. In this plan are compiled virtually all data needed for management. The plan can be thought of as made up of five parts: (i) management objectives, (ii) resource base, (iii) regulatory framework, (iv) action plan, and (v) provisions for updating and revision.

A. Statement of Management Objectives

Management objectives may be viewed as a hierarchy with perhaps one objective paramount (such as maximize timber volume production or maximize profit), several objectives that are in supporting roles to the paramount objective (such as "keep production facilities supplied with logs" or "maintain a community employment base"), and other objectives that, if carried to extreme, may be contradictory to the paramount objective (such as "start working toward a normal forest", "protect the productive capacity of the land", "practice multiple use", or "minimize stream sedimentation"). In practice the supporting and subordinate objectives operate as constraints on the paramount objective. Forest management planning often consists of juggling a number of contradictory and frequently incompatible goals. The search is for a reasonable combination of objectives that does a good job of meeting management goals. Forest managers must reexamine their objectives and priorities as conditions change.

B. The Resource Base

Fundamental to any forest management plan is a description of the resource being managed. An adequate resource description contains data on property location, timber inventory, and the forest land itself.

1. PROPERTY LOCATION

Before any forest property can be managed, it must be defined on the ground. A legal description is the starting point. Property corners must be found and boundary lines surveyed and marked. Records are kept on the condition of corners and lines. Points where property lines and roads intersect are especially important to monument. The forest management plan contains all known line and corner information. At an early point in the development of the management plan timber "working circles" are often laid out. Each working circle is a homogeneous portion of the property and is regarded as an individual planning unit, frequently defined along topographic and ownership boundaries. A separate management plan is then prepared for each working circle. Such organization of a large property allows for a delineation of job responsibilities so that individual foresters look after relatively small areas.

2. TIMBER INVENTORY

Since large forest operations are run according to business principles, an accurate timber inventory is essential. Current standing timber volumes are estimated using sampling methods (*timber cruising*). The forest manager is interested in current volume estimates by species, size, and quality. Current annual growth is also an important piece of information for the management plan, as it becomes an input to allowable cut calculations. Growth is preferably estimated from a series of permanent growth plots which are measured periodically. If plots are not available, other techniques for estimating growth utilize stand projection methods (based on increment cores) and yield tables. The timber inventory also provides information on stand condition (disease, insects, storm damage), on plant competition to favored tree species, and on survival and stocking of young plantations.

3. FOREST LAND CLASSIFICATION

Since land is the most basic of all forest resources, it plays a particularly important role in forest management planning. Soil is first classified as to productivity (site) class since all future growth calculations are based on productivity ratings. Soil types and their implications for logging, silvicultural techniques, site preparation, species selection, reforestation, and road construction are also fundamental as a base for planning. Eventually, the management plan should classify acres by site class, soil type, and slope class. The latter classification influences thinning, harvesting, and road building techniques. It is also important to establish at the beginning of a management plan exactly what the forest land base really is. Many acres within a large forest property are, for one reason or another, not available for wood production. Perhaps they are permanently devoted to another use such as campgrounds, sawmill sites, offices, buffer strips along streams and roads; or perhaps they are lakes, ponds, rock outcrops, meadows, or other noncommercial forest areas. Roads themselves, with associated rights-of-way, remove many acres from production, as do landings, skid trails, and rock pits. These areas cannot be included in future growth calculations.

C. Regulatory Framework in the Forest Management Plan

The framework for forest regulation consists of the allowable cut as determined by methods previously discussed, along with a description of the *target forest*. The target forest is the current conception of the forest which is to be eventually attained. It should be considered as a goal toward which forest management is moving. It also offers a standard against which to measure the cost of compromises in fitting plans together. Description of the target forest includes its species composition and stocking throughout the managed stand rotation. Hence, the forester knows exactly what he or she is trying to attain. The target forest is based on the very best managed stand yield information that is available along with economic and biological criteria. Since large forest holdings generally contain many combinations of site, soil, and steepness of slope, it is generally necessary to define more than one target forest. Ultimately, the management plan should relate each hectare (acre) in the forest growing base to a target forest and a plan for achieving that target forest.

The smallest level of resolution for forest planning units can be called *treatment classes*, which are areas receiving the same set of treatments throughout the rotation. Treatment classes are the basic unit of forest management. They are generally defined by harvest unit boundaries and, hence, depend primarily on topographic conditions and logging machinery capabilities.

D. The Action Plan

The forest *action plan* is the culmination of all prior planning activities. It documents all jobs scheduled to take place on the forest property over the next few years. Basically, the action plan describes how the target forest will be attained. It consists of two parts, activities in the existing forest and activities directed at establishing new plantations.

1. ACTIVITIES IN THE EXISTING FOREST

Management practices to be scheduled in the existing forest consist of spacing control (either precommercial or commercial thinning), salvage logging (removal of dead and dying trees), fertilization, road construction and maintenance, and the final harvest. The action plan describes exactly where and when these activities are to take place. A 5-year planning period is commonly used in order to give time for harvest unit layout, timber sale preparation, and road location.

2. ACTIVITIES IN NEW PLANTATIONS

When new plantations are to be established, a lead period is needed in order to produce planting stock of the desired size class. Seed must be collected from an acceptable source and sown in the forest nursery. Often the forester must plan at least several years ahead for planting stock delivery. The action plan contains details of where new stands will be established, types of site preparation to be done, number and types of seedlings needed, and areas to be sprayed with herbicides for control of competition.

The detailed planning necessary to put together the action plan is based not only on the regulation framework and the resulting jobs to be done, but also on the available budget. Since forestry activities required large investments, cash outflows must be coordinated with income and kept within budgeted limits.

E. Provisions for Updating and Revision

Management plans should be regarded as living documents so that they are continuously updated and revised. The forest resource base changes frequently with land acquisitions and disposal, unexpected fire and disease losses, more-accurate inventory data, new legal requirements, and policy decisions affecting land use. Forest management objectives can change as well. As new markets come to the fore, prodution technologies make possible new utilization standards, or the legal and political environment reacts to new social values. Flexibility in the forest management system, the ability to change not only year-to-year procedures but the entire allowable cut framework as well, is extremely important in this changing world. Foresters are learning to roll with the punches, to react to changing conditions, to take advantage of cyclical market opportunities, and still to maintain the basic structure of the regulatory framework. Since biological, social, and economic systems are all involved in forest management planning and since all of these systems are extremely variable, it is no wonder that forest management must be prepared for deviations from expected events. Such is the nature of long-term planning.

VIII. PLANNING FOR OPERATIONAL FOREST MANAGEMENT ACTIVITIES

This section is devoted to a discussion of the alternatives available for timber production. Modern-day foresters must decide among a multitude of options, each with specialized purpose and place in the job of timber production.

The forest management regime is a specification of the nature and timing of activities that are to occur in the forest. Included, along with selection of the silvicultural system to be followed, are details of site preparation, reforestation, stocking control, fertilization, commercial thinning, and final harvest.

1. SILVICULTURAL SYSTEMS

Silvicultural systems can be divided into two types: those aimed at growing trees in even-aged groups and those that allow a variety of ages within a small area. Even-aged management offers many advantages of efficiency since a large area can be treated as a single unit and, hence, is generally chosen by property owners seriously interested in fast timber volume production and low unit cost. Instances frequently arise, however, in which a continuous cover of forest trees must be maintained, and in these circumstances an all-aged silvicultural system is desirable.

By far the most frequently aplied even-aged silvicultural system is clearcutting. Here, all trees on the area are harvested at the same time for the purpose of creating a new, even-aged forest. The trend is toward smaller clearcut units than in the past (sometimes as low as 6 ha [15 acres]); however, most clearcuts are at least 16 ha (40 acres) in size. Large clearcut units result in treatment classes that can be managed efficiently. Clearcut areas are either planted or allowed to regenerate from seed produced by surrounding forest areas. A very old silvicultural system known as the *shelterwood system* is having a resurgence in application because of the necessity to provide shade to new seedlings in areas of high temperatures and low soil-moisture-holding capacity. Under the shelterwood system an overstory of mature trees is left at the time of harvest in order to provide an adequate seed source and shade for the new crop. Once new seedlings are established, the shelterwood overstory is removed either in one cut or in a series of cuts. This method is also useful in scenic areas if complete tree removal is not desired.

The seed-tree system differs from the shelterwood system in that only enough mature trees to provide an adequate seed source are left under the seed-tree system. No thought is given to providing shade to the new crop. Seed trees are removed as soon as the new stand is established.

Either single tree selection or group selection silvicultural systems will result in forests of many age classes all mixed together in the same stand. In the former approach individual trees are removed, while in the latter system small groups of trees are removed at the same time. These systems call for only a small percentage of the number of trees in the forest being harvested at one time. Small openings are created by the harvest of single trees or small groups of trees, and these soon are seeded in by surrounding trees. All-aged silvicultural systems are desirable in areas of high scenic value because the stand of mature trees always dominates the vegetative cover. They also are used in sites of extreme temperature and wind exposure. If such areas are cut heavily, resulting drought conditions cause high mortality among newly established seedlings.

2. SITE PREPARATION

Newly harvested forest land is not often in a condition to receive the new crop of trees. Logging debris must be treated to reduce fire hazard and eliminate obstacles to regeneration. Two techniques are most frequently used for this purpose; burning and tractor scarification. Slash burning is quite effective as a forestry tool, but resulting smoke can cause air pollution problems. Burning on some sites can also destroy valuable nutrients and organic matter and could eventually reduce forest productivity. Tractor scarification is carried out by a tractor equipped with a toothed blade. Logging residue is pushed into windrows or piles which may be burned. Heavy tractor equipment can cause soil compaction on certain types of soils, especially when wet, and this reduces productivity. Foresters must have a good knowledge of their soils so that they can prescribe the appropriate site preparation technique.

3. REFORESTATION

Prompt reforestation of harvested areas is of major concern to owners of large forest properties, especially those desiring continuous production of wood. The techniques available for reforestation are planting, artificial seeding, and natural seeding.

Trees may be planted either in a "bare-root" condition or with the roots still encased in the growing medium. This latter type of seedling is termed *container stock* or *plug seedlings*. Bare-root trees are grown in the forest nursery and are shipped to the forest planting site with soil removed from the roots. They can be grown to almost any size desired. Container trees are grown under controlled environmental conditions in a greenhouse and can be brought to plantable condition in just a few months. These trees are either grown in small containers or in styrofoam molds. When ready for planting the roots are taken out of the container or mold with the growing medium intact, thus lessening planting shock. One of the most important tasks facing the forester is determination of the size and number of planting stock needed. Large bare-root stock are preferred in situations of expected animal damage (deer, elk, and rodents) while container trees may perform best where soil-moisture problems are encountered. Another question to be answered before an area is planted concerns the number of trees per acre to plant. Experience with the performance of a certain type of planting stock in a given situation guides the forester is his estimate of the number of trees needed. He must examine the survival of previous plantations in order to make planting prescriptions.

The artificial application of forest tree seed to harvested areas has been an extremely important regeneration technique. Approximately 1 kg seed/ha (1 lb. seed/acre) is spread using a helicopter or small fixed-wind airplane. Results vary from excellent to complete failure, depending on seed quality, rodent population, and seedbed condition. Perhaps the biggest drawback in artificial seeding (and natural seeding as well) is lack of spacing control. Seed falls randomly so that overdense clumps of trees as well as understocked areas result. This is in contrast to planted seedlings where a mechanical spacing is relatively easy to obtain. As discussed below, overstocking and understocking have large negative impacts on wood production. Another problem with artificial seeding is that the large quantity of seed required rules out use of seed from selected desirable parent trees. Thus, seed quality tends to be inferior to that used for bare-root or container stock.

Since nature provides periodic heavy seed crops, foresters have also developed regeneration techniques that take advantage of natural seedfall. To be useful in a system of natural regeneration, a tree species must have frequent seed crops, heavy seed crops, and preferably lightweight seed that will travel far in the wind. A seed source must be left after harvest, either in the form of seed trees scattered throughout the harvested area or as leave strips of trees bordering the area. Seed from these sources should be cast into bare mineral soil for maximum germination and growth.

One of the most important applications of forestry technology is in the area of reforestation. The forester must "size up" each prospective reforestation opportunity and determine the species to regenerate and the technique to follow. Correct decisions at this stage of stand development will eliminate many problems in the future.

4. STOCKING CONTROL

A basic forestry maxim is that managed forest trees should have enough water, nutrients, and sunlight so that they can maintain a high growth rate, but not an excessive amount of these factors. Too few trees mean that portions of the soil and air space are not utilized, while too many trees leads to crowding and eventual death for many. The highest form of the art of forestry is in knowing how to capture all of the growth capacity of the site. This growth capacity is channeled onto a relatively small number of trees (fewer as the stand ages). As a result, individual trees become large in dimension and thus have high value for wood products. Stocking control consists of a number of forestry activities, including competition control (killing undesirable "weed species" that compete with valuable trees), pre-commercial thinning (selecting the best trees at an early age—10 to 15 years—and removing competing trees), and commercial thinning (logging selected trees in order to release those trees not cut and deriving a profit from the logging operation). If properly carried out, stocking control can greatly increase the production of usable wood.

5. FERTILIZATION

A relatively new forestry activity is fertilization. Research in several areas of the country has demonstrated that application of nitrogen, phosphorus, and occasionally other elements can greatly increase forest growth. When fertilized, trees develop larger and greener crowns and, hence, increase the size of the wood production "factory." Application of fertilizer on a large scale requires the use of helicopters as well as a sophisticated logistical system that ensures a continuing supply of fertilizer when it is needed. Forest fertilization is generally carried out on large blocks of land at one time, but increasingly flexible delivery systems allow treatment of areas 4 to 6 ha (10–15 acres) in size. Fertilizer effects on growth have been shown to depend on several site and stand factors (Gessel et al., 1969). The forester must be familiar with research results and must be able to apply them to his own property. To do this, he must be familiar with the various soil and stand conditions that exist on the area.

IX. CONCLUSION

This chapter provides an overview of planning for timber prodution on extensive landholdings. Planning efforts on these large properties differ from those carried out on small holdings in several important ways. First of all, because owners of large tracts must be sensitive to public needs, they consciously seek ways to make their properties satisfy a multiplicity of uses, rather than a single dominant owner-dictated use. Consideration of trade-offs between a variety of competing uses greatly enlarges the scope of forest planning and adds considerably to its complexity.

Large properties too, by virtue of their sheer size, contain a diversity of environmental conditions which must be evaluated in the planning process. Data requirements are considerably greater than for small properties and a large effort must be expended in collection and interpretation of resource inventory information. The types of data needed along with their subsequent use in timber production planning are discussed in this chapter.

LITERATURE CITED

Cole, D. W., S. P. Gessel, and S. F. Dice. 1968. Distribution and cycling of nitrogen, phosphorus, potassium, and calcium in a second-growth Douglas-fir ecosystem. *In* Primary Productivity and Mineral Cycling in Natural Ecosystems. Symp. of 13th Annu. Meet. of Am. Assoc. for Adv. of Sci, 27 Dec. 1967, New York. Univ. of Maine, Orono.

Davis, K. P. 1966. Forest management: regulation and valuation. 2nd Ed. McGraw-Hill, New York. 519 p.

Gessel, S. P., T. N. Stoate, and K. J. Turnbull. 1969. The growth behavior of Douglas-fir with nitrogenous fertilizer in western Washington—The 2nd Rep. Inst. For. Prod., College of For. Resour., Univ. of Washington, Seattle. 119 p.

Linnard, W., and M. Gane. 1968. Martin Faustmann and the evolution of discounted cash flow. Commonw. For. Inst., Univ. of Oxford, Oxford, England. 55 p.

President's Advisory Panel. 1973. Report of the President's advisory panel on timber and the environment. Supt. of Documents, Washington, D.C. 541 p.

ADDITIONAL REFERENCES

Edmonds, R. L. (ed.). 1974. Synthesis of results in the coniferous forest biome—1970–73. Conf. For. Biome Bull. no. 7. College of For. Resour., Univ. of Washington, Seattle. 245 p.

Regional Forest Nutrition Research Project—Biennial Report 1974–76. Univ. of Wash. Inst. of Forest Products Contrib. no. 25. College of For. Resour., Univ. of Washington, Seattle. 67 p.

Sharpe, G. W., C. W. Hendee, and S. W. Allen. 1976. Introduction to forestry. McGraw-Hill, New York. 544 p.

Steinbrenner, E. C. 1976. Mapping Forest Soils on Weyerhaeuser lands in the Pacific Northwest. p. 513–526. *In* Forest Soils and Forest Land Management—Proc. 4th North Am. For. Soils Conf., 1973, Quebec, Canada. Univ. of Laval Press, Quebec, Canada.

Stone, E. 1973. The impact of timber harvest on soils and water. Appendix M. p. 427–467. *In* Rep. of the President's Advisory Panel on Timber and the Environ. Supt. of Documents, Washington, D.C. 541 p.

16 Timber Production on Intensive Holdings

WILLIAM J. LLOYD AND WILLIAM M. CLARK

Soil Conservation Service
Washington, D. C., and Lincoln,
Nebraska, respectively

I. INTRODUCTION

Professional foresters tend to view the owner of a small forest holding as a problem. In forestry literature he is analyzed, categorized, epitomized, and criticized. Vardaman (1970) put it so well: "A small landowner at a forestry meeting must feel like a lady of ill repute at a Sunday school picnic. Everyone there thinks he is a problem and complains about his conduct, or at least why he doesn't do what they want him to do. Many, with little knowledge of his business, propose schemes for changing his ways and then complain because they don't work. Others have decided his case is hopeless and say so at every opportunity."

For one trained in forestry, the actions of a landholder may not seem entirely rational. But if the forester could crawl into the owner's skin, assume his debts and responsibilities, and operate his farming business or take over whatever occupation he has, that forester would then be able to accept and understand the set of priorities the owner has developed either voluntarily or in self defense. The owner's actions might then seem quite sensible.

The owner of a small holding may accept as a high priority the production of timber. More often he will not. This is not to say that he is not interested in growing trees but such may not be his first interest. Similarly the planter of windbreaks may not be interested in the trees, per se, but in the benefits he hopes to derive from them—soil protection, personal comfort for himself and his family, green surroundings which make for aesthetic improvement, wild animals and birds to be seen and enjoyed, protection for his livestock, reduced heating bills, perhaps a happier wife.

Landowners have long used soils information of one sort or another. Theophrastus, about 300 B.C., wrote: ". . . the soil also makes much difference, according as it is fat or light, well watered or parched, and it also makes quite as much difference what sort of air and winds prevail in that region; for some soils, though light and poor, produce a good crop because the land has a fair aspect in regard to sea breezes" (Kormondy, 1965).

With a diminishing land base, it becomes essential that Americans look to the use of the land and develop a concern for its protection in use. Although multiple use is the watchword of the day, there is a tendency for each special interest group to want to carve out some piece of the resource pie for its own use. This they would call "conservation." Others interested in the same resource seek to build legal fences to secure their own exclusive rights, again in the name of conservation.

In forestry, the multitude of landowners who hold small ownerships can be a balancing force since they are less subject to legal pressure and public opinion than are industrial owners and public land managers. With a proper economic and political climate, their lands can produce the needed wood and related amenities.

Forest landowners have not taken advantage of soils information as they could do. Bingham (1976) reflected on the need for soils information: "We cannot achieve our potential unless the Nation's most productive forest soils are available for timber growing. Obviously, the greatest investment in timber growth should flow to those acres where it can have the greatest effect. The most productive acres must be identified, on both public and private ownerships. Thus, whenever productive forest land is identified for conversion to other uses—housing, commercial development, recreation, dams, highways, wilderness, or whatever—we must study the capacity of the soil and assess economic impact and the implications of that conversion upon future timber supply. That simply isn't being done today." There are benefits to be gained by an understanding of soils and the management needs of trees growing on them. This chapter will touch on those benefits.

II. TIMBER PRODUCTION

A. Ownership Patterns, Sizes, and Distribution

Commercial forest land is usually defined as land capable of producing 1.4 m³/ha (20 ft³/acre of wood per year. Total commercial forest land for the nation is 202.2 million ha (499.6 million acres). Small holdings for most statistical purposes are those less than 202.4 ha (5,000 acres). These small holdings account for 119.9 million ha (296.2 million acres), which is 59.3% of the commercial forest land (U.S. For. Serv., 1974).

The ownership of small holdings is in constant change. Some actions create more ownerships as in the case of large estates being broken up to satisfy the demands of heirs. The consolidation of farm units to increase efficiency reduces the number of ownerships as does the purchase of small holdings by forest industry.

From 1952 to 1970, the total area of commercial forest land increased about 1%. In the same period, the forest land in farm ownerships dropped by 17.2 million ha (42.5 million acres), while the area in miscellaneous ownership increased about the same amount. In 1970, farm ownerships totaled 53.1 million ha (131.1 million acres) and the miscellaneous ownerships totaled 66.8 million ha (165 million acres) (U.S. For. Serv., 1974). The

1952 statistics showed almost 4.5 million small ownerships. Of these nearly one-half, 2.2 million, were less than 12.1 ha (30 acres) (U.S. For. Serv., 1958).

Small ownerships are held by people of many occupations as shown by ownerships studies made in several states. The one thing the studies reveal in common is variability. Very often such owners are absentee. They may live near or at some distance from the land they own. A West Virginia study (Basu, 1973) showed that 48% of the owners lived off the property. It is not unusual for an absentee owner never to have seen the land owned.

In a Georgia study (Holemo & Brown, 1975), forest landowner occupations were found to be: farmers—40.1%, retired—19%, business—16.1%, housewives—5.1%, laborers—3.7%, professional—2.9%, others—9.5%, and "no response"—3.6%. A Pennsylvania study (Larsen & Gansner, 1972) showed a change in ownership occupation pattern by size of ownership. For holdings under 202.4 ha (500 acres), the pattern was: white collar workers—32%, blue collar workers—19.5%, farmers—22%, retired—15.5%, others—11%. For holdings over 202.4 ha (500 acres) the pattern changed to: white collar workers—68%, blue collar workers—4%, farmers—4%, retired—20%, and others—4%. Muench (no date) listed small holdings in North Carolina by these classes of owners: farmers—36.2%, wage-earners—24.5%, business—7.4%, professional—3.5%, housewives/widows—8.2%, retired—10.9%, undivided estates—7.7%, institutions—0.2%, nonforest industry—0.4%, and miscellaneous—1.1%.

There is a lesson to be learned from these studies and similar ones made elsewhere. There is no such thing as an average forest land holder. When three-fifths of an important national resource is held by over 4 million pairs of hands, there is a measure of safety and an equal measure of difficulty. Four million persons of diverse ages, occupations, and backgrounds cannot easily be stampeded or coerced. Neither can those 4 million easily be led, nor influenced, toward management practices considered by professionals to be in the public interest.

B. Productivity Potential and Regional Patterns

1. ESTIMATION OF PRODUCTIVITY POTENTIAL

Potential productivity of forest soils can be estimated through the use of normal yield tables combined with measurements of site index taken on key or benchmark soils during the course of the National Cooperative Soil Survey. Site index is a measure of productivity based on the heights reached by certain species of trees at an arbitrary age. For trees growing west of the Great Plains, the base age is usually 100 years and for trees growing east of the Great Plains, the base age is commonly 50 years. When land is said to have a site index of 140 for Douglas-fir, it means that the dominant and co-dominant trees growing in a normally stocked stand can be expected to reach a height of 42.7 m (140 ft) at an age of 100 years. The index number is an indicator of potential productivity—the higher the number, the greater the potential. Normal yield tables show the growth potential by several measures of volume per unit of area. Yield predictions from normal yield tables cannot be expected to be accurate for a small area of land. For areas of some size, the predictions should be fairly reliable considering the assumptions upon which the tables are based. Normal yield tables assume full stocking and natural (normal) conditions. Many forests do not have full stocking nor have they developed under conditions which could be described as normal. Such forests may not reach the potential described by the yield tables. On the other hand, planted forests may produce yields much larger than those predicted by yield tables. The increase is generally attributed to better initial spacing and reduced competition.

2. THE PACIFIC COAST STATES

These states (California, Oregon, and Washington) contain some of the most productive forest lands in the nation. The most highly productive soils occur west of the Coast Range but very productive lands occur throughout the area west of the Cascade Mountains. The average potential productivity of the private nonindustrial holdings in the Pacific Coast states is estimated at 6.6 m^3/ha (94 ft^3/acre) (Seaton et al., 1973).

Productivity is very variable as can be shown. Schlots and Quam (1962) reported site index measurements (100-year basis) from 451 plots representing 16 groups of soils in southwest Washington. They found a low site index for Douglas-fir of 94, a high of 186, and a weighted average site index of 159. The potential mean annual increment for a site index of 159 according to Douglas-fir normal yield tables (McArdle et al., 1961) would be 11.8 m^3/ha (169 ft^3/acre). The potential is somewhat lower in the Puget Sound Trough with a weighted average site index of 133 for Douglas-fir (Schlots & Quam, 1966). Site index 133 indicates a potential of 9.4 m^3/ha (134 ft^3/ acre). Western Oregon and northern California are probably fairly close to southwestern Washington in average productivity potential.

Where the precipitation is limited, as in eastern Washington, eastern Oregon, and eastern California, the potential is very much lower. Meyer (1938), in developing the ponderosa pine yield tables, measured 66 plots in eastern Washington and Oregon with an average site of 78 which would translate to growth potential of 4.6 m^3/ha (66 ft^3/acre). Meyer's work was not intended as a sampling for average potential. It is quite likely that the true average potential is lower.

3. THE SOUTH (TEXAS AND OKLAHOMA EAST THROUGH VIRGINIA)

The states of the South have highly productive forest land. Although the potential may not be as high as for certain areas of the Pacific Coast, there are several other factors which favor the South. Topography in the Coastal Plain and Piedmont is generally conducive to intensive management. The coniferous species of the South have a rapid early growth rate and reach a point of maximum yield per acre at an early age. This alone makes the opportunities for practicing forest management attractive to the landowner. The potential productivity of the private nonindustrial holdings is estimated at 5.6 m³/ha (80 ft³/acre) (Seaton et al., 1973).

There are four principal southern pines—loblolly, slash, shortleaf, and longleaf—and a great number of hardwoods. Loblolly is the most important of the pines. Boyce et al. (1975) estimated the average biological potential for the loblolly pine ecosystem east of the Mississippi River at 7.3 m³/ha (104 ft³/acre). That estimate is reinforced by a review of studies to relate site index of loblolly pine to soil series. An average site index of 85 was calculated from 2,309 individual plot measurements (Author's summarization of SCS in-service reports). A site index of 85 translates to a growth potential of 8.4 m³/ha (120 ft³/acre) using loblolly pine yield tables (U.S. For. Serv., 1929). The much lower overall average potential given by Seaton can be attributed to the larger areas of hardwoods which have much lower potential and drag down the average.

4. THE NORTH (EAST OF THE GREAT PLAINS AND NORTH OF OKLAHOMA, ARKANSAS, TENNESSEE, AND VIRGINIA)

In general, the productivity declines from South to North, being higher in the southern Appalachians and the central states and lower toward the Canadian Border. There is less total range in productivity on contrasting soils in the North as compared to the South. The growth potential of the private nonindustrial holdings in the northern states is estimated at 4.8 m³/ha (69 ft³/acre) (Seaton et al., 1973).

Much of the forest land in the New England States is occupied by hardwoods although the land has a good potential for growing eastern white pine. Quite often, the more productive soils are the ones in hardwoods. Site index (50-year basis) will average about 60 for both hardwoods and pine with white pine being slightly higher and the upland oaks slightly lower (SCS, 1968). In terms of white pine (Leak et al., 1970), the growth potential for site index 60 is 9.8 m³/ha (140 ft³/acre). In terms of upland oaks, the potential is 3.0 m³/ha (43 ft³/acre) as interpreted from Schnur (1937). Thus, the potential with oak as the crop is about 30% of what it might be with pine.

Barrett et al. (1976) suggests consideration of opportunities for managing white pine on a broad scale because of its high level of sustained growth. There are problems with blister rust and white pine weevil. More serious may be the competition from hardwoods.

In the Lake States, where many of the soils are suited to either hardwoods or conifers, the disparity in yields is about as described for New England. A summary of existing site index data for Minnesota (SCS in-service reports for Land Resource Areas 88 and 90, St. Paul, Minn.) indicates the average potential for eastern white pine to be just slightly less than in New England, while aspen (quaking and bigtooth) had an average site index of 75. Gevorkiantz and Duerr (1938) were less optimistic showing an aspen site index of 70 to be "typical of hardwood land." Their yield tables indicate an aspen potential at site index 70 to be about 3.1 m³/ha (45 ft³/ acre).

The central states and the Appalachian area have relatively high potential but are limited by the predominance of hardwoods. The average potential is less than for the southern states but more than for the New England or Lake States.

5. THE ROCKY MOUNTAIN STATES (INCLUDES THE BLACK HILLS AND EVERYTHING WEST OF THE GREAT PLAINS EXCEPT CALIFORNIA, OREGON, AND WASHINGTON)

The small private forest land holdings in these states are often adjacent to and sometimes within national forest boundaries. The growth potential is very variable because of the mountainous terrain. Douglas-fir (inland form) and ponderosa pine are the two species of most importance. In northern Idaho, western white pine is a productive and valuable species. Western larch occurs in the northern Rockies, lodgepole pine is extensive north of New Mexico; quaking aspen occurs throughout the Rockies. The growth potential of the private nonindustrial holdings in the Rocky Mountain states is estimated at 3.5 m³/ha (50 ft³/acre) (Seaton et al., 1973). Reliable yield tables are available for ponderosa pine (Meyer, 1938), but yield information for the other species is somewhat sketchy. An SCS in-service report (M. R. Carlson. 1974. Soil-woodland interpretations for the northern Idaho panhandle of the northern Rocky Mountains and Valleys, unpublished) shows an average site index of 90 on 89 plot measurements in ponderosa pine. These measurements were made to document the productivity of the Panhandle soils. The estimates of growth potential which follow are based on that report and the average site index shown by Meyer for sections of the Rocky Mountains. They are the author's estimates. Idaho Panhandle and adjacent Montana counties—site index 90, 5.8 m³/ha (83 ft³/acre); northern Idaho, below the Panhandle, and western Montana—site index 75, 4.3 m³/ha (62 ft³/acre); eastern Montana and central Idaho—site index 60, 3.2 m³/ha (46 ft³/acre); Black Hills and southern Rockies—site index 50, 2.6 m³/ha (37 ft³/acre).

C. Soil-Site Relationships

1. APPROACHES TO SITE QUALITY EVALUATION

Two general approaches have been used in assessing the productivity of land for growing trees. Jones (1969) describes these as "factorial" and "holistic." In a factorial study, site index is related to one or more soil, climatic, or physiographic factors. In a holistic approach, the environment is defined by classifying the landscape as a whole.

Coile (1952), Jones (1969), and Carmean (1970, 1975) have made exhaustive reviews of the literature on site quality evaluation. Carmean lists nearly 200 references, most of which were factorial in nature. About one-quarter of the references related productivity to soil survey classification units, though many of these were factorial as well. Most of the later researchers developed regression equations to enable the calculation of site index for a particular species from various soil, climatic, and physiographic factors.

The National Cooperative Soil Survey is a holistic approach. The landscape is divided into taxonomic units, each of which has a characteristic soil profile, occurs in a characteristic position, supports a unique combination of plants in its natural condition, and has potentials and limitations that can be defined. Some soils mapping has included series with a broad range of potential. Coile (1960) and Carmean (1961) have noted that ranges within series in some surveys were so broad as to make the soil survey of little value in appraising potential productivity. Retzer (1958) defined soil surveys as a basis for management. Soils mapping is needed in order that soils interpretations can be related to areas which are delineated on a map.

There is room and need for both approaches. In keeping with modern concepts of soil taxonomy (SCS, 1975), the range in characteristics for individual soil series is being narrowed, thus recognizing the justified criticism of Coile and Carmean. But with the increase in number of soil series, the factorial approach is needed to determine productivity for individual series for which data are lacking.

In theory, with soils properly mapped and with soil series and phase properly delineated, it should not be necessary to consider particular soil, climatic, or physiographic factors to narrow the range of productivity to that which comes with the inescapable error in measuring site index. In practice, the science is not that well developed, and many workers have found it necessary to use such factors to sharpen productivity estimates.

In preparing soil-woodland interpretations when firm data are missing, it is customary to make ratings relying on information available from closely related soils in a similar climatic province. Ratings may be arrived at by inference drawn from soil characteristics. For each suspected limitation, or potential, rating guides are developed using individual characteristics such as depth, texture, stoniness, drainage, slope gradient, or aspect. As Carmean (1975) notes: "Ideally, factual data for interpretations should precede the survey so that mapping units can be designed that have the specific information required by land use planners."

2. REVIEW OF LITERATURE ON SOIL-SITE RELATIONSHIPS

One of the earlier researchers in this field was Haig (1929) who estimated the site index for red pine in Connecticut on the basis of the "silt plus clay" content of the soil. Coile (1935), in publishing his work on shortleaf pine, seemed to open the door on an untapped field for investigation. The review following is not intended to be complete.

a. **Douglas-Fir**—An early study in western Washington (Hill et al., 1948) showed a correlation between site quality for Douglas-fir and soil mapping units being used by the Soil Conservation Service. Site index appeared to be correlated with soil depth and total annual precipitation. A study in the north Puget Sound Area (Gessel & Lloyd, 1950) identified depth to a restricting layer and total annual precipitation as important factors.

Carmean (1954) related productivity of Douglas-fir in southwestern Washington to five factors. Site index increased with depth to substratum with the product of moisture equivalent and gravel content, and with total annual precipitation. Site index decreased with elevation and with gravel content of the soil.

Lemmon (1955) found effective total depth to be the most important soil factor affecting Douglas-fir site index in the Willamette Valley.

Effective soil depth was also an important factor identified by Steinbrenner (1963) in a western Washington study. Other findings were: a positive correlation with the depth of the A horizon and with the clay content of the B horizon; a negative correlation with microscopic pore space in the B horizon, and with elevation.

With very variable conditions in the Oregon Cascades—elevations 244 to 1,280 m (800 to 4,200 ft); slopes from 0 to 80%; annual precipitation from 168 to 368 cm (66 to 145 inches), annual snowpack of none to a few meters, and wide range in site index—Stephens (1965) concluded: "Despite this wide range of physiography and Douglas-fir productivity, the soil taxonomic unit, at the series level, provides an accurate prediction of site index on these soils."

b. Ponderosa Pine—For the Black Hills regions of South Dakota and Wyoming, Myers and Van Deusen (1960) made a distinction between the "crystalline" soils which had been developed from metamorphic and igneous rocks and the "limestone" soils formed wholly or mostly from limestone. Site index for "crystalline" soils could be estimated from four variables: soil depth to the top of the C horizon; position on slope; gradient or percent of slope; and aspect. In the limestone areas, site index could be estimated from two variables: soil depth to the top of the C horizon, and position on slope.

The growth of ponderosa pine in the Zuni Mountains of New Mexico was related to fertility, permeability, and available moisture of the surface horizons; and the effective depth of the permeable soil. In the same study, greenhouse productivity was related to soil parent material. Mixed alluvium was most productive followed by soils derived from limestone, sandstone, and granite, in descending order (Williams et al., 1963).

c. Lodgepole Pine—On pumice soils in central Oregon, Youngberg and Dahms (1970) found only a weak relationship between site index and soil factors. One soil series, Lapine, had a significant range in productivity related to the total thickness of the pumice mantle and the combined thickness of the A and AC horizons.

d. European and Japanese Larch—Growth of these two introduced species in New York State is positively correlated with degree of drainage and to depth of soil above a layer restricting root development (Aird & Stone, 1955).

e. **Oaks**—In the Northern Appalachians, Trimble and Weitzman (1956) found four variables which had a major influence on oak site index. These were: (i) aspect, or compass direction faced by the sloping land, (ii) position of the plot on the slope, (iii) gradient or slope percent, and (iv) total soil depth to rock.

Carmean (1961) studied black oak site index relationships in southeastern Ohio. He concluded that soil series and type were not defined properly for accurate productivity predictions. He found site index to be correlated with depth of surface soil, subsoil texture, subsoil stone content, aspect, slope position, and slope steepness. He suggested those factors be used to modify the existing soil series and type descriptions.

Yawney (1964) reported higher oak site index on West Virginia soils derived from limestone than on those from shale and sandstone. In unfavorable situations the effect was more pronounced than with more favorable.

Hannah (1968) found site index for oaks in Indiana to be correlated with A horizon thickness; slope position; silt content of the B_1 horizon; clay content of the B_2 horizon and material below this zone; and stone content of the B_2 horizon.

In a Dent County, Missouri study, Hartung and Lloyd (1969) found that more accurate productivity estimates of upland oak site index could be made for soils of the Clarksville series by recognizing aspect phases.

f. **Aspen**—Site index of aspen in Minnesota (Stoeckeler, 1948) is affected by the texture of the soil in the A and B horizons. Optimum texture for quaking aspen is about 50% of silt-plus-clay. Very sandy and sandy soils were inimical to best growth. Bigtooth aspen appeared to be less exacting. In a later paper, Stoeckeler (1960) identified calcareous drift as being more productive than noncalcareous drift. A shallow water table was conducive to better growth.

Stoeckeler's conclusions were confirmed and strengthened by Fralish (1972). He found a strong relationship between site index and available water-holding capacity and he showed that water tables within 0.9 and 2.5 m (3 and 8 ft) would increase growth. Below that depth there was little advantage to a water table. Water table within 0.6 m (2 ft) will decrease growth rate.

g. **Black Walnut and Black Locust**—Several factors have been identified with site index for these species. Auten (1945a) named the important ones as soil drainage, soil texture, plasticity and compactness of the subsoil, thickness of the A horizon, depth to the subsoil, and topographic position.

h. **Yellow-Poplar**—Auten (1945b) in a central states study showed site index of yellow-poplar to be correlated with depth to tight subsoil, thickness of the A horizon, aspect, exposure, position on slope, and drainage.

In a Virginia study, Van Lear and Hosner (1967) concluded that soil mapping units would need to be refined before they could be used with confidence to predict site index for yellow-poplar.

i. Southern Pines—Coile (1952), Gaiser (1950), Barnes and Ralston (1955), Zahner (1958), and Della-Bianca and Olson (1961) identified several factors affecting productivity: thickness of the surface soil; texture and consistency of the subsoil; available soil moisture; drainage, depth to mottling; and slope and slope position.

Ellerbee and Smith (1963), in relating site index of loblolly pine to soil series, suggested phasing to identify much higher site index for soils rich in phosphatic materials in South Carolina. In addition to factors identified by other researchers, Covell and McClurkin (1967) related the site index of loblolly pine to the amount of April-September rainfall.

Soil and topographic features significantly related to site index of pines in eastern Louisiana were identified by Linnartz (1963): "Depth to the least permeable layer in the soil profile, percent sand in the subsoil, and pH of the subsoil were related to the site index of loblolly pine. Site index of slash pine was related to depth to the least permeable layer, percent sand in the topsoil and in the subsoil, and degree of internal drainage. Longleaf pine site index was related to the sand content of the subsoil, the slope, and the degree of surface drainage."

The importance of depth in sandy soils is stressed by Hebb and Burns (1975): "For sandhills work, soil should be examined to depths of at least 13 or 14 feet (4 to 4.3 m) to insure that changes in soil texture that influence tree growth are not overlooked. Site productivity for planted slash pine is influenced most by depth of soil to a horizon impeding rapid percolation of moisture. . ."

j. Jack Pine—Glacial drift with a higher proportion of basic minerals gave a higher jack pine site index in Ontario (Chrosciewicz, 1963). From a Saskatchewan study, Jameson (1963) concluded that three interrelated factors have the major influence on height growth. These he identified as soil moisture regime, soil nutrient regime, and soil texture. He described six sites by texture, topography, soil derivation, soil profile types, and ground water conditions, and assigned four adjectival levels of productivity.

Shetron (1972) related site index of jack pine in Michigan to soil series. He found significant differences among five of eight soils. The Rubicon series had a very wide range in site index.

k. Northern Hardwoods—Sugar maple, American beech, and yellow birch were grouped together by Farrington and Howard (1958) in relating site index to soil series and type in a Vermont study. For some soil units, variation in site index appeared to be too great for acceptability.

Sugar maple site index as measured on four soil series in New York (Farnsworth & Leaf, 1963) did not show significant differences between the series—Mardin, Lordstown, Volusia, and Bath. The authors recognized a part of the problem as being the highly tolerant-to-shade nature of sugar maple combined with its tendency to develop all-aged stand conditions.

For the Green Mountains of Vermont, Post and Curtis (1970) isolated several variables as affecting the growth of four northern hardwoods—

sugar maple, white ash, yellow birch, and white birch. The factors of most importance were: drainage class, with highest site index on moderately drained soils; elevation, a negative correlation; and depth of solum, a positive correlation. Aspect had a minor effect.

l. Norway Spruce—This European spruce is widely used in the United States as an ornamental. Enough plantations are present in Vermont to stir interest in productivity as related to soil. Hannah (1972) identified these variables as influencing site index at 30 years age: site index is positively correlated with the depth of A plus all B horizons; it is negatively correlated with the depth of A horizon; and negatively correlated with the percent clay in the lower B horizon. The equations developed were considered weak.

m. Eastern White Pine—Working in Maine, Young (1954) found that white pine site index decreased as the thickness of the A horizon increased. Gaiser and Merz (1953) found the reverse to be true with white pine trees planted on old fields in Ohio and central Indiana.

Husch and Lyford (1956) recorded better height growth of white pine as soil drainage became increasingly poorer in New Hampshire.

A positive correlation exists between the site index of white pine and that of red maple according to Foster (1959).

n. Mixed Pine Hardwoods—The effect of soil and physiographic factors on the site index of five species—yellow-poplar, white oak, scarlet oak, black oak, shortleaf pine—was studied in upland Piedmont forests by Della-Bianca and Olson (1961). Their conclusions: "Surface soil conditions and slope position proved to be important gauges of productivity for all five species. Thickness and organic matter content of the A_1 horizon, thickness of the total A horizon, and percent sand in the A_2 horizon were correlated with yellow-poplar height growth. Percent organic matter in the A_1 horizon was negatively related to site index of oak and pine. Other findings include a positive effect of increase in slope percent on site index of black and scarlet oak, a positive effect of increasing latitude on site index of yellow-poplar, and higher site index for all species when yellow-poplar is present in the overstory."

o. Sweetgum—Soil series and type were used by Phillips and Markley (1963) to predict site index for sweetgum with reasonable accuracy. They developed a regression equation as well. The important factors determining productivity: the proportions of clay, fine sand, and silt in the B_2 and A horizons; and the thickness of the B_2 horizon.

3. ON-GOING ACTIVITIES IN SOIL-SITE RELATIONSHIPS

In addition to research being conducted by research institutions, there is a continuing program of relating site index for the principal species to soils as a part of the National Cooperative Soil Survey. Usually the work is done in survey areas prior to completion of the soil mapping to provide a reliable base for estimating potential productivity. In many areas, these studies are a cooperative effort between the Soil Conservation Service and the state forestry agency. Automatic data processing systems are being developed to store, process, array, and display the stored data using soil series or soil families as the basic organizational units. Data from approximately 17,000 plots from throughout the United States should be in storage by the end of 1978. Obviously, there will never be enough data to spply to all soil series, but by combining these data with factorial studies, accurate estimates of productivity are not an unattainable goal.

D. Soils Information as a Guide to Planning

In general, foresters have not made full use of soils information in management planning. Partly this is because their training has been focused on trees rather than soil on which trees grow. Partly it is because soil scientists were oriented toward agricultural use of their science and did not provide soils maps of value to the forester. A new breed of soil scientists is evolving. They are concerned with developing soils maps and interpretations tailored to the needs of forest managers. Similarly, foresters are becoming more aware of the need to include soils information as a planning base.

1. PRODUCTIVITY

The most universally recognized soil-woodland interpretation is that of productivity, usually stated in terms of site index. The utility of this interpretation is easily recognized and it is accepted most readily when presented in relative terms. The history of forestry in the United States is that there is always more work needed to be done than available funds and time can accomplish. In making cost-return analyses, certain assumptions must be made as to costs for planting, crop-tending, and harvesting; the time frame; the compound interest rate; predicted yields during the life of the forest and at final harvest; and probable stumpage prices. Detractors of cost-return analyses point out that the results of such an analysis can be altered appreciably by changing one or more of the assumptions. One fact will emerge despite the changes: land of high productivity offers much greater economic opportunity than does land of low productivity, other things being equal. Compound interest has a devastating effect on returns from long-term enterprises. A landowner with forest land of several levels ofproductivity will do well to concentrate his effort on his most productive land. Intensive management may be justified on his best land and very extensive (protection only) may be all that can be justified on his poorest. There has been a tendency to prescribe high levels of management intensity without regard to productivity. To do so is not sound management planning.

The same reasoning needs to be applied in national land use planning. The growth potential of forest land varies from less than 0.5 m^3/ha (7 ft^3/acre) on juniper-pinyon lands in the Rocky Mountains states to over 20 m^3/

ha (285 ft³/acre) on some of the Sitka spruce-western hemlock or redwood lands on the Pacific Coast. Incentive programs and cost-sharing programs need to be geared to the recognition of the growth potential differentials. Human uses, such as camping, hiking, and hunting, might be shifted to lands with lower wood-producing potential.

2. SPECIES TO PLANT

In some areas, planting is confined to a single species. When such is the case, soils information plays little part in species selection. In general, however, there is choice to be made among several species and soils information can be helpful in arriving at the best choice. Land planted to an unsuited species can be an expensive lesson. An example of such mismatch is reported by Stone et al. (1954). Red pine planted in New York on soils with restricted drainage flourished for many years, then sickened and sometimes died. Eight soil series—Lordstown, Oquaga, Manlius, Bath, Cattaraugus, Chenango, Tunkhannock, and Tioga—were identified as well suited for red pine. Five soil series—Mardin, Culvers, Braceville, Middlebury, and Landford—were indicated as "uncertain." Ten soil series were labeled as "hazardous" for red pine growth and survival. These were Volusia, Morris, Allis, Red Hook, Erie, Holly, Chippewa, Norwich, Chippwa, and Atherton.

Stevens and Wertz (1971) in a study of matching soils to tree species in northern Wisconsin concluded that proper matching could result in a "60 percent increase in sawtimber yield." Most states have developed planting guides to help landholders in the selection of tree species suited to the soil and related factors. Such guides are usually developed by interagency teams and are empirical in nature (Robbins et al., 1960). The basis for species selected may be soil series, woodland suitability groups, or generalized descriptions around such characteristics as soil texture, drainage, aspect, and topographical position.

Limstrom (1963) in his planting guide for the central states, listed by soil series the preferred species for planting. He gave consideration as well to aspect, latitude, and soil drainage. Parmenter and Beaumont (1952) listed for each of the principal trees planted in Massachusetts a general description of the soil requirements mentioning soil series by name as examples. For soils in Illinois, Losche et al. (no date), prepared a guide for suitability to black walnut. Criteria were first developed based on drainage class, effective depth, subsoil pH, slope, and percent volume of coarse fragments. Then each soil series (and phase) was rated as "suited," "questionable," or "unsuited." The importance of suitable soil for black walnut plantings is stressed by the U.S. Forest Service (1976): The soil should have 1.2 m (4 ft) of depth uninterrupted by a fragipan, a heavy clay layer, or a stratum of rock or gravel; a soil with evidence of poor drainage should not be planted to walnut.

The forest landholder need not guess which species is most suitable to plant for his land and his purposes. In most cases the state forestry agency, the Soil Conservation Service, and other concerned groups will have worked together to produce a planting guide specific to that area.

3. SPECIES TO FAVOR

In the central hardwoods region and throughout the southeast, there is an abundance of species, some more desirable than others for particular uses or purposes. Simple lists of priorities can be developed and applied to all forest conditions but to do so ignores the fact that priorities change with change in soil conditions. It is possible to build preference lists tied to groups of like soils and thus take advantage of the best information possible in improvement cuttings. This interpretation is of less importance in the western states where there are few species from which to choose. Roach and Gingrich (1968), for the upland hardwoods of the central states, developed preference lists for low, medium, and high levels of productivity. Their listing was by three categories: "preferred species," "satisfactory species," and "species undesirable as crop trees." Species composition is closely related to site quality as shown by Wiant et al. (1975).

4. EQUIPMENT LIMITATIONS

Next to productivity, foresters and forest managers recognize the utility of soils information bearing on the use of equipment. Many forestry jobs once done by manual labor are now accomplished with power-driven, sometimes highly specialized, equipment. Soil and physiographic factors affecting equipment use are wetness, stoniness, clayeyness, sandiness, and steepness.

a. Wetness—Soils may be seasonally wet or may be wet yearlong. The limitation may be avoided sometimes in the case of seasonal wetness by waiting for the dry season. In northern states, harvesting activities may be scheduled after freezing weather provides solid footing. Special equipment may be necessary to handle cultural operations in wet areas.

Equipment limitations are usually weighed in terms of the inconvenience or extra costs brought to the landowner. Another side of the issue is possible damage to the land. Moehring and Rawls (1970) in a study on Grenada and Calloway silt loams in Arkansas found significant reduction in growth of 40-year-old loblolly pine trees if, during wet weather, traffic passed along three or four sides of the trees. Dry weather logging did not affect growth. These two soil series are imperfectly drained loess soils underlain by a fragipan at a depth of 46 to 61 cm (18 to 24 inches). The pan restricts internal soil drainage and may cause a perched water table during the wet season.

Hatchell et al. (1970) observed that the greatest damage to the establishment and growth of loblolly pine appears to occur when severe compaction is coupled with excessive moisture on medium- to fine-textured soils. The soil survey report for the Millicoma Tree Farm in Oregon alerts the reader to the importance of refraining from tractor logging on certain soil series when the soil is wet. Several series are mentioned, all of which are fine textured. Some soil series so described are Bessee, Callahan, Doerner, Flournoy, Umpcoos, Yoakum, and Yonkers (Duncan & Steinbrenner, 1972).

b. Stoniness or Rockiness—Where stones or rock ledges occur, some kinds of equipment may not be usable. Planting machines cannot operate in extremely stony soils and operate with severe handicaps in soils with relatively minor stoniness. Keeping tree breakage to a minimum during harvesting operations may require special techniques and care in felling and yarding operations. Crop-tending practices may need to be kept to the bare minimum in stony soils because of the problems in efficient use of equipment.

c. Clayeyness—Excessive amount of clay may call for specialized equipment. Most often the limitations imposed by the clay show up only during wet conditions and the limitations can be avoided by waiting for dry weather. In addition to the problems of operating equipment on clay soils when they are wet, it must be recognized that serious damage is done to those soils when heavy equipment is used on them during wet periods.

d. Sandiness—The loose, coarse, sands of the South impose moderate to severe limitations on the use of cars, trucks, and other wheel-mounted equipment. Sandiness is rarely a limiting factor in equipment use except in the southern U.S.

e. Steepness—Silvicultural operations occur regularly on much steeper slopes in the western than would be deemed feasible in the southern U.S. Presumably this is because, with experience, workers have learned to perform in an efficient and safe manner on steep slopes while managers have designed or purchased equipment appropriate to the situation. For most cultural work, slopes less than 10% are not limiting. At about 25%, wheel tractors cannot be used efficiently and over about 40% track-laying equipment can be used only with great care. Cable systems are needed for work on steeper land.

5. EROSION HAZARD

Protected forests are essentially erosion proof except for what occurs in stream channels. Soil losses are very low and only a fraction of that per acre considered allowable under agricultural usage (Patric & Brink, 1976). Most erosion in forested land occurs along roads, logging trails, landings, and other areas of intensive use. Protection from erosion can be covered with four relatively simple rules—maintain a healthy growing forest, control fire, harvest the grazing resource with consideration for other values, and treat all roads, trails, and landings, and disturbed areas for erosion control. For the eastern U.S., erosion control measures for roads are well covered by Kochenderfer (1970) and Haussman and Pruett (1973). The principal measures are: (i) plan the road system so as to minimize the amount of land in roads—good planning can reduce skidroad areas as much as 40%; (ii) in steep terrain, use cable sytems to winch tree-length logs uphill to the roads—pulling uphill reduces the gouging of the forest floor; (iii) keep filter strips between roads and streams and winch logs away from streams; (iv) keep road grades gentle, 3 to 10% is about the right steepness; (v) to avoid land slippage, stay away from hillsides which are very steep; (iv) use bridges and culverts of sufficient capacity when crossing waterways; (vii) outslope road surfaces to prevent water from collecting; (viii) install open-top culverts or broad-based dips to dispose of water collecting on the road; (ix) seed roadbeds with grasses and legumes to protect them when not in use.

The hazard of slippage (land sliding) can be predicted in part from soils information. Two notorious examples of soils subject to slipping are soils of the Ontonagon series in northern Minnesota and Wisconsin, and the Kitsap series in the Puget Sound Area of the state of Washington.

6. WINDTHROW HAZARD

Windthrow, or tipover, is a soil-related hazard. Some soils have a restricting layer or a high water table that prevents the development of deep anchor roots. Windthrow on such soils may occur after heavy rains and during high winds. Windthrow should not be confused with wind breakage which may occur on windfirm soils during high gales. Soils subject to windthrow damage can usually be identified by the mounds formed by the root pads of trees tipped over in years past (Lyford & MacLean, 1966).

The landholder with forest land susceptible to windthrow should be conservative in his management. Thinnings should be fairly light. Access road development and maintenance becomes important in order that windthrown trees may be salvaged.

Sauerwein (1963) described the windthrow hazard on Donaca silt loam in the Willamette Valley of Oregon as "severe" and suggested that "cutting boundaries and roads must be laid out to minimize the windthrow potential as much as possible. When the soil body is small enough to be logged in one setting, this is thought to be the best way to minimize losses due to windthrow. Where this cannot be done, the area can be logged by settings in successive years until the entire soil body is logged clean. In this way, salvage of windthrow timber near cutting borders can be done before deterioration of the fallen tree takes place."

The soil survey report for the Millicoma Tree Farm in Oregon rates soils by four degrees of hazard for windthrow. The highly susceptible are those on precipitous slopes with shallow, stony soils. The Jolson, Oldham, and Oldland series are mentioned as being particularly susceptible (Duncan & Steinbrenner, 1972).

7. SEEDLING MORTALITY

Some soils are harder to regenerate after harvest than are others. Clark and Losche (1969) confirmed the beneficial effects of the natural surface soil (A horizon) upon the seedling growth of yellow-poplar and white ash. Apparently, loss of the surface soil through erosion is a cause of the poor survival of hardwood plantings in upland areas of the central states. An earlier study, Hansen and McComb (1958) had found early height and diameter growth of green ash to be inversely correlated with the degree of erosion of the A horizon.

Wherever the hazard of seedling mortality is believed to be moderate or severe, the planting operation needs to be given special attention and care. Containerized seedlings offer hope for successful planting on adverse sites. The seedlings cost more but may save money over the long run (Miller & Budy, 1974). Factors which may be involved in seedling mortality are sandiness, clayeyness, aspect (direction of slope), and wetness.

a. Sandiness—The deep sandy soils may give a high rate of seedling mortality. These are a problem in the southern U.S. primarily. The hazard may be overcome by careful planting, elimination of competition, and use of top grade, fairly large planting stock (Shipman, 1958). Planting in furrows substantially improved the survival of longleaf pine on Sandhills old fields. The furrows were about 20 cm (8 in) deep and 60 cm (24 in) wide (Shipman, 1956). Similar treatment gave best survival with jack pine and red pine on Plainfield sand in Wisconsin (Wilde & Albert, 1942). Harms (1969) reported that survival of slash pine on droughty sandhill soils could be improved by deep planting, to the terminal bud. At age 10, there were no detrimental effects in either tree height or diameter.

b. Clayeyness—Soils with a high clay content are difficult to plant and obtain satisfactory survival and growth. Wilde and Voigt (1967) described the problem of planting on the lacustrine soils along the southern shore of Lake Michigan: "The clay, either water-logged and sticky, or dry and stone-hard, makes tree planting a laborious task." The problem was overcome quite successfully by planting white pine on ridges formed by two furrow slices turned inward. In addition to good survival, the ridged plantings 14 years later showed remarkably increased height growth over other treatments. The trial was repeated with red pine and produced similar results. The soil in the trial was Ontonagon silty clay loam.

H. P. Garritt (personal interview with author) made successful plantings of white pine, red pine, and pitch pine on fine-textured soils in the Muskingum Conservancy District of Ohio by plowing double furrows on the contour and planting on the mound the following spring. Lemmien et al. (1969) was successful in planting on a furrow slice with Sebewa loam which has a poorly drained, mottled, clay loam subsoil. Six conifer species—black spruce, white spruce, Norway spruce, Scotch pine, European larch, and tamarack—were planted with good survival. Limstrom (1963) also recommended planting on top of a furrow slice to lessen frost heaving.

c. Aspect—The direction of slope is well recognized as bearing on seedling survival. Minckler (1941) studied survival rates of planted trees in the Great Appalachian Valley. He found survival to be significantly lower on south slopes as compared to north slopes. The southwest exposures tend to be more droughty and the soil surface reaches higher temperatures than on northeast aspects. Some planting guides recognize the problem and take care of it in part by recommending species more tolerant to drought. Other measures are the use of larger, higher grade planting stock, providing shade, and giving supplemental water during the establishment period. Planting on southwest aspects should not be delayed until the end of the planting season. The newly planted trees need opportunity to become established before the dry season begins.

   d. Wetness—Excessive moisture can be fatal to young trees. The problem cannot be sidestepped by waiting for the dry season. In the southern U.S., it is a common practice on sandy flatwoods sites where the water table is high to use heavy disks to form raised beds. The disks throw the soil to the middle forming a mound or bed which is about 5 inches above the normal ground surface. Competing vegetation is removed in the same operation. Mann and Derr (1970) did not find a statistically significant difference in survival of loblolly or slash pine planted on beds as compared to without beds. This lack of statistical significance they attributed to well distributed rainfall during the summer of establishment. They did measure a statistically significant increase in height growth on the bedded plantings 8 years after planting.

   Terry and Hughes (1975) report on comparison of bedding vs. flat-planting on a poorly drained Bladen soil. Although unreplicated, the trial after 13 years showed definite height gain for the bedded stands. Mean height growth of loblolly pines were 9.7 and 7.9 m (32 and 26 ft), respectively. They list these conclusions with respect to the value of bedding on poorly drained Coastal Plain soils:

   1) Bedding on the finer textured soils in the Lower Coastal Plain appears to give long-lasting growth benefits on soils where summer droughts are not prevalent. Fine-textured soils that have been badly puddled or compacted during logging and slash disposal are very responsive.

   2) Incorporation of phosphate during bedding can significantly improve bedding response, especially on certain poorly drained fine-textured mineral soils and on organic soils of the Atlantic Coastal Plain.

   3) Sandy soils that have excess water in the dormant season, but are droughty during the growing season, appear to benefit only marginally. Early response may be only temporary.

   4) Bedding generally improves seedling survival on poorly drained sites if the beds have enough mineral soil in them to prevent seedlings from going into drought stress following planting.

   Malac and Brightwell (1973) also stressed the importance of well-formed beds in poorly to very poorly drained soils; the seedlings must be elevated out of the water for planting success.

8. HARDWOOD COMPETITION

   That the competition of hardwoods with conifers is more severe on some soils than on others is accepted as a fact by some observers, but not all. In the New England States, hardwood competition is so severe on most soils as to make it very difficult to grow white pine. The soils with good internal drainage seem to be less affected than those with restricted internal drainage. The experience at Harvard Forest (Lutz & Cline, 1947) gives an indication of the fierce fight to be expected from hardwood competition. Following a clearcut of a nearly pure white pine stand, a full regeneration of white pine was established. To prevent the white pine from being overtopped by hardwoods, three hand weedings and an improvement cutting were made in the first 24 years in the life of the new stand. In spite of such intensive treatment, at the age of 30 years only 30 suppressed pine remained per hectare (12 per acre) on a well-drained area and *none* on a moist area.

In the Puget Sound Area, soils of the Alderwood and Everett series occur in close proximity. After harvest, natural regeneration of Douglas-fir may occur on either series but on the Alderwood series competition from red alder is so severe that few Douglas-fir trees can survive. On the Everett series, red alder may give some competition but the Douglas-fir has much better prospects. The two series have similar surface textures. The Alderwood is underlain with a cemented glacial till that is nearly impervious to moisture (author's observation).

In the Willamette Valley, plant competition is expected to be "severe" on Kinney silt loam and Donaca silt loam after removal of the overstory. Special considerations in harvesting are needed to insure rapid regeneration. Late summer logging during the dry season appears to give better natural regeneration and less brush competition for the seedlings as compared to late winter or early spring logging (Sauerwein, 1963).

In general, the competition to conifers from hardwoods appears to be more severe on poorly drained soils, on fine-textured soils, and on soils of higher productivity.

E. Packaging Soil-Tree Information

1. RECOGNIZING THE USER'S LEVEL OF APPRECIATION

Foresters, soil scientists, and soil conservationists who compile soil-tree information need to recognize that the potential user may be quite unaware of the existence and/or the utility of that information. Forestry for most holders of small forest tracts is a relatively new venture. Because forest management concepts are so new, at least to those landowners, professionals are inclined to despair when *their* ideas of management are not accepted with enthusiasm. Now we are suggesting that our unsophisticated landowner not only practice forestry, but that he utilize soil-tree information in his practice.

We must recognize a basic difference in knowledge and appreciation of soils information on cropland as compared to woodland. Consider, for instance, a landowner who has both cultivated and forest land in his ownership. Each year he plows, prepares, seeds, cultivates, tends, and harvests crops on his cropland. He has accumulated a great deal of empirical knowledge in the process. Through his repeated cultural operations, he knows which soils he can plow first, which can be worked in almost any kind of weather, and which must be handled literally with kid gloves. He knows something about the relative fertility of each individual piece and he has learned what problems he must overcome in management. But what does he know about the soils on which the trees grow? Very little! Even if he is an active and intensive forest manager, the long-term nature of a tree crop precludes the accumulation through experience of the response of his land to management. It is an unusual owner who has planted, tended the tree crop, made a harvest of the trees, and is ready to plant again on the same area.

If an understanding of soil-tree response-management techniques is to be had, it must be accumulated by professionals who know soils, and are keen observers. The packaging of soil-tree information must be done with a full recognition of the low level of understanding and appreciation on the part of the user.

2. WOODLAND SUITABILITY GROUPS

There may be from 50 to 100 or more soil series recognized in a county-wide soil survey. For simplification, these series are grouped by the Soil Conservation Service into what are called woodland suitability groups. A woodland suitability group is defined as a group of soils that for purposes of management are essentially alike. They have about the same productivity potential; are suited to the same species; have the same hazards, limitations, problems, and potentials in use.

It follows that the soils within a group have similar characteristics and occur in an homogeneous physiographic and climatic province. These groupings are useful in broad land use planning as well as planning with owners of small holdings.

3. ORDINATION SYSTEM

A woodland suitability group is identified by symbols which are connotative in nature. The leading symbol is an Arabic number, 1 to 5 (sometimes 1 to 7). This number denotes potential productivity level, 1 being the most productive and 5 being the lowest productivity level within the area of consideration.

The second symbol is a letter which alerts the user to the presence of soil or physiographic factors which would impose a moderate or severe limitation in operations such as the establishment, tending, or harvesting of a wood crop. The letters denoting the factors have a hierarchy which controls their use when more than one factor is present. The symbols arranged by hierarchy and their meanings are: x—the presence of stones or rocks; w—wetness; t—toxic materials; d—depth of rooting is restricted; c—clayeyness; s—sandiness; f—fragmental or skeletal soils; r—relief, meaning steepness or aspect; o—meaning no soil factor imposes a significant limitation.

A third symbol, an Arabic numeral, is used to make finer separations where necessary. In the southern states, this symbol signifies the severity of the hazard and indicates whether the soil is suitable for conifers, hardwoods, or both. Other sections of the country do not give special meaning to the third symbol.

The ordination symbols give the user a quick picture of the potential and problems of the group of soils in question. Some examples:

1*w*—Means that the land is in the top level of potential productivity for the area but there are limitations in use because of wetness;

3*c*—The land is in the third level of potential productivity—there are limitations because of the amount of clay in the soil;

5*f*—Denotes a low level of productivity and problems because of excessive gravels or stone fragments in the soil profile.

The ordination system makes it easier to categorize soils and get a feel for the characteristics which make each group unique.

4. PUBLISHED SOIL SURVEYS

In a modern published soil survey, each soil is carefully described. If woodland is a significant resource in the survey area, the description shows the ordination symbols for the woodland suitability group in which the soil is placed. The woodland section of the modern soil survey is in tabular form. Older reports may include either the table or narrative sections. Soils are listed by mapping unit (series, type, and phase), potential productivity is shown by site index for an indicator species, ratings of slight, moderate, or severe are given for soil-related hazards and limitations, species to favor are listed for existing stands and for planting, and the woodland suitability group symbols for the soil mapping units are shown. Knowledgeable professionals in forestry, conservation, or broad resource planning would find the woodland tables of soil reports very valuable because quick comparisons can be made. It is unlikely that a landowner by himself could make much use of the information because of the lack of narrative.

5. LOCAL TECHNICAL GUIDES

Each field office of the Soil Conservation Service has a document known as a *technical guide* which is the official repository of practice standards and specifications and soils interpretive information. If the working area has a woodland resource of significance, the technical guide will deal with soil-woodland relationships. To prevent needless repetition soils are placed in woodland suitability groups as described earlier in Sections E-3 "Ordination System" and E-4 "Published Soil Surveys."

Ordinarily, the technical guide will contain more narrative and there would be a fuller explanation of each limitation or hazard, including the cause of the problem and the steps which could be taken to overcome the problem. Most technical guides are fairly specific as to potential productivity and include tables showing expected wood yields in common units of measure for the area. These are derived from normal yield tables. Species to favor in existing stands and species recommended for planting are standard inclusions.

The technical guide is prepared for the guidance of Soil Conservation Service employees and other professional people who may work with them. As a rule, foresters from the state forestry agency and from the Forest Service or educational institutions have an input into the development of the technical guide. The guide is not intended for the use of the landowner, but for the guidance of a professional who may be working with him.

6. SPECIAL REPORTS

For many geographical areas—states, major land use areas, or sections of states—special reports have been prepared giving soil-woodland interpretations for the important soils. Most areas of the southern and eastern states and of the Pacific Coast west of the Cascades have been covered by such reports. Generally, the interpretations are prepared in tabular form as in published soil surveys. These special reports are available through Soil Conservation Service offices.

7. CONSERVATION PLANS

A landowner in a conservation district may request assistance in developing a conservation plan for his land. If available, a soils map is used as a base for the planning. Appropriate soil-woodland interpretations are given as part of the plan and explained in the planning discussions between the professional and the landowner.

F. Considerations in Planning Management Intensity

1. LOCATION AND ACCESSIBILITY

The first consideration pertains to the location of the land and how it may be reached. Accessibility is the key to management. Planning should include developing and maintaining a road and trail system. USGS quad maps, other line maps, and aerial photographs may be used to supplement the landowner's personal knowledge of his property.

A common mistake is to plan an improvement cutting including the marking of trees to be removed and then plan the road and trail system. A better approach is to plan the road and trail system before the selection of the trees to be removed. A more usable system will result and damage to the residual trees can be reduced.

2. MARKET SITUATION

Practical management will allow no more intensity of management than the market situation will support. If markets for some products are poor, at a considerable distance, or nonexistent, the landowner cannot be expected to get enthusiastic about practicing forestry to produce those products. The mere presence of markets does not insure good forestry either. Market demand may result in very poor management, at least temporarily.

In a free enterprise system, any enterprise which gives promise of a certain and profitable return will soon have takers. With a long-term crop such as trees, the time-lag may be a serious matter.

The owner of a small forest holding cannot be expected to be an expert on market conditions, nor need he be. Help is available from experienced persons working as consultants or in public employ. The owner should make a point of enlisting the help of others more knowledgeable. Too often in sales of stumpage, it is a case of a poorly informed seller dealing with a well-informed buyer—hardly an even match.

3. POTENTIAL PRODUCTIVITY

Another need is knowledge of the potential productivity. This may be obtained by interpretation from soils data, from general knowledge of relative productivity gained from experience in the area, or by determinations of site index through the measurement of tree heights and ages and the use of appropriate site index curves or tables.

4. TREE CROP INVENTORY

Inventory of the tree crop will be concerned with four principal items which the landowner or his agent must recognize to arrive at sensible planning decisions. These four items are: (i) kind or kinds of trees, (ii) size class and/or age of the trees, (iii) stocking of the trees, and (iv) condition of the trees as growing stock.

In planning, the owner will need to divide his holding into units (fields, blocks, or compartments), each of which is reasonably homogeneous with respect to the four inventory items. A small ownership may be made up entirely of trees of the same mixture of species at the same size and age and of uniform stocking and condition. For a larger holding, several divisions may be needed to achieve homogeneity of the management units.

a. Kinds of Trees—The landowner should know what kinds of trees he has. Also, he should recognize that *for his particular purposes,* some species are more desirable than others. Each crop-tending operation should be so planned as to favor the more desirable species by removing or disposing of the less desirable species.

b. Size Class and/or Age—The size (diameter) of the trees is a major consideration in what can be done with them. Small trees may be harvested as Christmas trees; larger ones as posts or pulpwood; larger still as poles or pilings; and the largest as sawlogs or peelers. There is overlap of course. New milling equipment makes it possible to make lumber and plywood as well as pulp chips out of fairly small trees. Where trees grow in even-aged stands, or where they have been planted, age is usually considered along with size in planning. Few owners realize that in most forests the trees which make up the main, or upper, canopy are essentially even aged, at least in groups of trees if not over broad areas.

c. Stocking—Stocking may be expressed by average spacing, by numbers of trees per unit of area, or by basal area per unit of area. To be meaningful, any of these three measures must be related to the size (diameter) of the trees. In fact, the three are interchangeable. If average tree diameter and one of the three stocking measures is known, the other two may be calculated. As a tree grows in size it develops a bigger crown which requires more room. Competition between trees soon sets in with a fight to the death. Each year some smaller and less thrifty trees lose out to their larger, more vigorous neighbors until at maturity only a few large trees remain out of thousands that began the race. With intensive management, the process is speeded up by the removal of trees. Competition is reduced; wood is harvested; and the larger, more desirable trees are given needed growing space.

d. Condition of Trees—Many of the trees in a forest stand are poor growing stock. A tree may be crooked, limby, forked, damaged, diseased. It may have a broken top, a poorly formed crown, or another undesirable characteristic. The object of an improvement cutting should be to eliminate or harvest trees in poor condition in order to favor trees which show good promise of future values. Too often through indiscriminate cutting the trees with most potential as growing stock are removed, leaving culls and low value species to claim the area. It is important that the forest owner recognize that it is to his benefit to develop growing stock made up of trees in the best possible condition and composed of desirable species.

5. PERSONAL OBJECTIVES

The intensity of management applied by a landowner will be determined primarily by his management objectives. Most landowner studies show that ownership of forest land is not primarily for the purpose of growing timber when the size of the holding is small. This does not preclude intensive management on a small holding but it does make it much less likely. The holder of a small ownership may choose less intensive management for these or other reasons:

1) As a farmer his livelihood comes from his cleared lands and livestock. These require his full attention.
2) He does not have the skills or the equipment to do his own work.
3) Vendor service is not readily available to install practices eligible for cost sharing.
4) He enjoys the area as a place to hike and recreate and prefers to keep it in a near-wild condition.
5) His woodland is the watershed for his water supply which he does not want to jeopardize.

Another holder of a small forest ownership may move toward fairly intensive management for reasons of his own:

1) The wooded parts of the farm offer a place to invest time otherwise wasted.
2) For many planting and crop-tending activities, inexpensive equip-

ment may suffice and the skills required are not beyond easy mastery for one used to working with his hands.

3) His woodland can be made more aesthetically pleasing as it is made more productive.

4) Using regular farm equipment, he can develop his access system during the off season and thus make it possible to manage more intensively while enjoying the area all the more.

5) Land values appreciate but they appreciate more rapidly when the land is occupied by a healthy, growing stand of trees.

The time span for planning may be a deterrent to some landowners. It is not to others. Many older persons pursue active planting programs even though the probability is slight that they will be alive to reap the benefits of their work.

G. Planning Decisions

The owner of forest land is the only person who can make planning decisions. To cut or not to cut, to graze or not to graze, to burn or not to burn, are decisions he alone can make. Some owners abdicate their management responsibility and others are so poorly informed that the decisions border on being irrational. With over four million owners in control of nearly 60% of the nation's commercial forest land, it is clearly in the public interest to provide guidance.

The holder of a small forest ownership may want a mix of multiple uses. Those whose task it is to assess the nation's potential for wood growth must take into account that full potential will never be realized on many small ownerships. Muench (no date) found that participation by landowners in technical assistance programs was significantly related to the size of the forest owned. Larsen and Gansner (1972) came to a similar conclusion: owners of larger holdings "are more interested in the income producing potential of their forest tracts." In a West Virginia study, Christensen and Grafton (1966) found that three-fourths of the privately owned woodland tracts in the state were in holdings of less than 40.5 ha (100 acres). Most of the West Virginia owners listed a number of reasons for owning the land. In descending order the reasons were: wildlife—62% of respondents, timber products for own use—48%, protection against soil erosion—45%, pasture for livestock—44%, recreation—36%, watershed—28%, timber products for sale—28%, secondary products for own use—18%. These objectives are not incompatible with each other and one could say that all the owners would eventually have timber products for sale even though the objective ranks seventh among those listed. Usable timber is often harvested even though the land seems to be dedicated to an incompatible use. Land within the boundaries of a city would not be considered as available for wood production. But that is not always the case. Just beyond the city limits of Philadelphia in a satellite city, there is a sawmill that appears to do quite well making lumber out of trees removed from streets and building lots.

Some owners do see incompatibility with timber harvesting and the enjoyment of the amenities. Marrama (1972) found that 63% of the nonresident owners in Berkshire County, Massachusetts, and 93% of the nonresident owners in Franklin County had never cut any timber products from their woodlands. There were many reasons given but 20% of the landowners emphasized that they were "fearful that harvesting operations would destroy the forest beauty and wildlife."

Most land managers would agree to at least some degree of compatibility between timber production and the other goods and services derived from forest land. Holemo and Brown (1975) in their owner survey in Georgia found that owners controlling 81% of the land stated their management intentions as "let grow and harvest." While that is hardly in the category of intensive management, it is evidence that those owners saw no incompatibility between timber harvest and their other objectives.

Landowners do respond to incentives as shown by the response of the southern U.S. to the Conservation Reserve Soil-Bank Program. In the few years of the operation of that program 777,985 ha (1,922,400 acres) of cropland were planted to trees. Georgia led the states in planting 280,655 ha (693,499 acres). Also in the 5-year period 1962–1966, 256,621 ha (634,110 acres) were planted to trees in the southern states under the Agricultural Conservation Program incentives (Squires et al., 1969).

H. Meeting the Nation's Needs for Wood

1. THE NEED FOR WOOD

The nation will need more wood, as expressed in the foreword of the *Outlook for Timber in the United States*: "The implications of comparisons of prospective timber supplies and demands presented in this report are clear—demands for lumber plywood, woodpulp, and other products are increasing more rapidly than available timber supplies" (U.S. For. Serv., 1974).

2. FORESTRY IN A FREE ENTERPRISE SYSTEM

The small ownerships can be expected to do their share, recognizing of course that each landowner will pursue a course best suited to his interests. Within the framework of a free enterprise society, his interests will not be inimical to those of the society as a whole although a time lag may be expected. As demand for wood increases, price will follow and owners will take steps to make their lands productive so as to benefit from what can be produced.

3. STEPS TO ACHIEVE GROWTH POTENTIAL

The President's Advisory Panel (Seaton et al., 1973) estimated average growth of small private ownerships at 2.7 m^3/ha (38 ft^3/acre), which is 49% of the productive capacity. Presuming that the wood will be needed, we need to address the opportunity to double the growth. Boyce (1975) wrote on how to double the harvest of loblolly and slash pine timber. The suggestions he makes can be applied to most small ownerships in the nation even though the species and physiographic conditions are not the same.

a. Reforest every Harvested Stand—When some stands are harvested the land is not returned to productivity. The removal of the larger, more saleable, trees often leaves the land occupied with cull trees, stunted understory hardwoods, and species that are less desirable than those removed. Such areas become more difficult to return to productivity as time passes. Consulting foresters and those in public or private employ who work with owners of small forest holdings need to place more emphasis on planning for reforestation at the time harvesting is being done.

b. Delay Harvest until the Culmination of Mean Annual Increment— The curve of mean annual increment over age rises to a flat, dome-shaped plateau which extends for many years. Forest stands cut before the plateau is reached do not yield wood at the full potential of the land. Foresters and conservationists giving technical assistance to owners of small forest holdings are aware of this fact and do all they can to extend the length of the rotation. One enticement is to help the landowner work out an improvement cut—an intermediate harvest—that will give him some return on his investment and encourage him to put off final harvest until some years later. Some conservation organizations interpret this type of a cutting as being part of a selection system of management which could eventually result in all-aged stand. Almost all of the more valuable forest trees require full sunlight for regeneration which means that the process of intermediate cuttings can be extended only so long. Eventually, for the purpose of regenerating the forest, a harvest cutting must be made.

Certain owners, most likely those with small holdings, will prefer to maintain their forest indefinitely. A forester might feel that the stand is already past the age for culmination of growth and should be harvested. The owner would sooner settle for a lower level of production in order to maintain the amenities.

c. Concentrate Efforts on Soils with Highest Potential—National planning, regional planning, and individual management planning must recognize the importance of intensifying management efforts in proportion to the biological potential of the land. It is not sound policy to urge a landowner to carry out intensive forest management when the benefits cannot justify the expenditures. Neither is it sound policy to allow land of high productive potential to lie idle, or nearly so, because it is occupied with brush or cull trees.

d. Work toward Sustained Yield—It is not feasible to place every small woodland ownership on a sustained yield basis in the same manner as might be done for an industrial holding or a national forest. But it is possible for every landowner to consider the benefits to himself and his land in having an annual or periodic return from it.

Consider the owner with a 40-ha (100-acre) holding of merchantable timber. If he cuts it all at one time, he has a glut of income with disproportionate taxes. And he has 40 ha of cutover land in which he may quickly lose interest because of the long time before another harvest. It is too big an area for one person to plant and return to productivity within a short period. A better approach is to divide the area into a number of fields with harvest cuttings to take place at perhaps 5-year intervals over his lifetime. Each cutover area is small enough that the owner can do the necessary site preparation and planting or seeding to put the land back into production. The gains are several: a more even flow of income; the development of a stairstep arrangement of age classes; a continued interest on the part of the landowner; a better income tax situation; and maintenance of a backlog of merchantable timber to meet the costs of that unforeseen emergency.

In the southern U.S., many landowners have developed their forest holdings into a stairstep arrangement of age and size classes by following the $D + X$ system for making regular stand improvement cuttings coupled with the planned harvest at each cutting cycle of groups of crop trees (H. C. Mitchell. 1962. A guide to stocking southern pine stands. In-service report of Soil Conserv. Serv., USDA, Washington, D.C.). Mitchell's system has several unique features:

1) The land manager is given a guide to the optimum spacing of "leave" trees. The spacing is derived from the average diameter of the dominant and co-cominant trees and stresses the principle of spacing trees "with room to grow but none to waste."

2) A cutting cycle is established based on the productivity of the land. Land of low productivity is managed on a longer cutting cycle than high productivity land. The differential in growth rate between sites of low and high productivity is thus recognized.

3) Adequate growing space is provided to the superior trees.

4) Regular harvest of trees in groups or blocks is advocated to provide periodic income and to provide for regeneration which with the passage of time will give the owner a stairstep arrangement of age and size classes and thus give a close approximation of area regulation. Minor openings are enlarged in making harvest cuttings so that areas can become stocked which would otherwise remain unstocked indefinitely.

5) Scheduling a time for woods work is stressed. Farmers are accustomed to scheduling activities according to the season of the year. This system encourages forest landowners to employ a similar approach, fitting the scheduling of woods work in with other things to be done.

Other advantages can accrue under this philosophy of management. As a succession of age classes develops, it is more likely that needed stand improvement work will be recognized and done at the time it is needed. Spare time can be put to better use because the amount of weeding, thinning, or pruning needed will not be beyond the capacities of the owner. The diversity in age classes and sizes means better wildlife habitat and more opportunity for aesthetic enjoyment. The result can be a favorable mix of high-yield forestry along with the other amenities a small holding can provide.

There is another "school of thought" for a less exacting planned system. Termed *harvest and let grow* or *let grow and harvest*, this system is put into practice by cutting timber only when a product can be economically sold. It too can result in a favorable mix of good forestry and compatible amenities and is a logical approach for those woodland owners with land of lower production potential and for those unable to practice high yield forestry. Improvement cuttings are done only when the wood has utility and regeneration cuttings rely on natural seeding, not planting. This system may not be high yield forestry but, when properly applied, is sustained yield forestry (Hartung, 1975).

III. WINDBREAKS AND SHELTERBELTS

A. History and Scope

The need for trees has been recognized since early pioneering days. Early settlers of the Great Plains found the lack of trees to be a serious handicap, and the Kansas Horticultural Society in its annual report for 1880 said, "Those settlers who planted shelterbelts and groves are fixtures on their land, while those who never planted trees have pulled up stakes and gone elsewhere" (U.S. For. Serv., 1938).

Windbreaks, among the earliest conservation practices in the Great Plains, have been supported by various federal programs over the past 100 years. Influenced, no doubt, by the recommendations of the then Secretary of Interior that if the Plains were to be opened to general settlement, a certain proportion of the area should be forested as a measure of protection to the soil, Congress in 1873 passed the Timber Culture Act. This act offered homesteaders 160 acres (65 ha) of land, solely on the provision that they plant trees on 40 acres (16 ha) of it. Plantings were made until the act was repealed in 1891.

But a massive effort wasn't launched until the 1930's when great clouds of dust began to darken midwestern skies. In 1934, the 73rd Congress approved Public Law no. 412, known as the Emergency Appropriation Act, and made appropriations to meet the emergency and necessity for relief in stricken agricultural areas. Part of this appropriation was allocated to the Secretary of Agriculture for the planting of forest protective strips (shelterbelts) in the Plains Region as a means of ameliorating drought conditions. This shelterbelt project became the Prairie States Forestry Project and was administered by the U.S. Forest Service. Plantings were made until the project was terminated in 1942. Since 1942, the Soil Conservation Service has used soil and moisture conservation appropriations to direct and effectuate shelterbelt plantings as an integral phase of a complete conservation program.

A very high percentage of windbreaks are planted on privately owned land. In 1975, 11,723 ha (28,946 acres) of windbreaks were established on private holdings. This was 96% of all windbreaks established. That year, eight states (South Dakota, Nebraska, Minnesota, Oklahoma, Colorado, Indiana, Montana, and Texas) reported landowners had planted more than 405 ha (1,000 acres) of windbreaks.

While the greatest need for windbreaks exists in the Great Plains states, many areas outside the Plains benefit from windbreaks. Through 1975, landowners in 36 states established windbreaks on 613,293 ha (1,514,304 acres). This represents 96% of all windbreaks established. The remaining 4% was on federal or other publically owned land (U.S. For. Serv., 1975).

B. Purposes of Windbreak Plantings

People in many areas include windbreaks as part of conservation planning. Although windbreaks are found more often in the nothern and western U.S. than in the southern and eastern U.S. they are proving useful in almost every state, even in the deep South. Windbreaks help people to live more comfortably, work more easily, and improve their quality of living.

1. EROSION CONTROL

Wind erosion seriously threatens any area of low, variable precipitation, where drought is frequent, and temperatures, evaporation, and wind speeds are high. It is the dominant problem on about 28 million ha (70 million acres) of land in the United States—an area that includes 22 million ha (55 million acres) of cropland, 3.5 million ha (9 million acres) of rangeland, and 2.5 million ha (6 million acres) of "other" land (Woodruff et al., no date).

Erosion may be expected wherever the surface is smooth and bare, and fields are unsheltered, wide, and improperly oriented to prevailing wind direction (Lyles, 1976).

Planning for wind erosion control involves one or more of four basic principles—establish and maintain land cover; produce stable nonerodible surface aggregates; maintain rough surfaces; and reduce field width. An empirical wind equation that considers these principles plus climate has been developed (Woodruff & Siddoway, 1965): $E = f(I, K, C, L, V)$, where E is the annual soil-loss rate, I is the soil erodibility index, K is the soil-ridge roughness factor, C is the climate factor, L is the unsheltered distance across a field along the prevailing wind direction, and V is the equivalent quantity of vegetative cover.

Principles of wind erosion control can be applied by planning for a combination of practices, some permanent, some temporary. Permanent or continuing practices include stubble mulching, cover crops, strip cropping, crop rotations, shelterbelts, and buffer strips. Temporary methods include emergency tillage, placement of artificial and earthen barriers, hauled-in mulches, and irrigation (Woodruff et al., no date). Usually a combination of permanent practices will be most effective and dependable on cultivated lands.

A planned windbreak system helps to control erosion by reducing the unsheltered distance across a field. A windbreak will provide full protection to an area 10 times the height of the trees measured in the direction the wind is blowing. Thus, a windbreak 9.14 m (30 feet) high gives protection to a strip about 91.4 m (300 feet) wide when the wind direction is at right angles to it. Some protection is provided for a distance of 20 to 25 times the height of the trees.

Field windbreaks have been used for many years in the muck, peat, and sandy soils of the Corn Belt and the northeastern U.S., the valleys of the Pacific Coast States, the southern U.S., and other parts of the country to control wind erosion and protect crops (Ferber, 1969).

2. FARMSTEAD PROTECTION

Windbreaks planted around homes and farmsteads moderate the influence that wind has on man and his activities. These windbreaks have proven to be most beneficial. They have cut fuel costs as much as 30% during the winter months. They also reduce dust, protect flowers and ornamental plants, protect home gardens, and control snow (Davis, 1976).

Evergreens, such as spruce, pine, and juniper, are excellent for windbreaks. They give year-round protection and are usually long lived. Where they grow fairly fast and survival is good, the entire windbreak may be made up of evergreens. Where evergreens grow more slowly or are hard to get started, broadleafs, such as elm, ash, and honeysuckle may be used along with evergreens to get protection as early as possible.

3. LIVESTOCK PROTECTION

Where winters are severe, livestock protected by windbreaks have gained weight more consistently and lost fewer pounds during blizzard conditions than cattle exposed to prolonged periods of extremely cold and windy weather conditions (Davis, 1976). Another important function of feedlot windbreaks is to prevent snow blocking the many lanes, roadways, feed bunks, and sorting and working areas where equipment and machinery must be able to operate 7 days a week (Robbins, 1976).

In areas where winters are relatively mild, research related to influence of windbreaks on feedlot environment is very limited. However, Johnson (1974) suggests four possible benefits that could be derived from barriers of trees and shrubs: reduction in feed lost from exposed feed bunkers, less drying out of feed, reduced possibility of snow drifts in travel areas and cattle yards, and reduction in odors and dust blowing from the feedlot.

4. WILDLIFE HABITAT

Windbreaks make valuable cover and nesting areas for upland game and song birds. The chances of wildlife survival are enhanced by every windbreak that is planted. Species composition has much to do with the ultimate wildlife value. For maximum wildlife benefits, shelterbelts should contain adapted conifers, hardwoods, and shrub species that provide winter food (Popowski, 1976).

Regardless of the basic purpose for establishing a windbreak, most windbreaks today provide multi-benefits for man, livestock, or wildlife. Too much wind is probably the biggest deterrent to outdoor recreation in the Great Plains. Wind blows tents down, fouls fishing lines, gets dust in picnic baskets, scatters campfires, and is even blamed for missing dead shots at pheasants. Windbreaks and shelterbelts provide opportunities for improved recreational experiences in the Great Plains (Naughton, 1976).

Old multi-row windbreaks make excellent outdoor classrooms. Subject matter that can be taught includes: Science, English, History, Mathematics, Music, Social Studies, Art, and Vocational classes. Windbreaks do not take the place of a natural wooded area, but in locations where natural woods do not occur, they make acceptable substitutes (Heintz, 1976).

Not to be overlooked in planning are the esthetic and community benefits windbreaks provide. The color, shape, texture, and size contrasts of the many species used in windbreaks has eye appeal that can be enjoyed by all. Windbreaks add an attractive profile to an otherwise flat and treeless landscape and bring beauty, permanence, and home-like settings to homes and communities alike.

C. Planning Design in Relation to Use

1. FIELD WINDBREAKS

Field windbreaks should be laid out at right angles to prevailing or damaging winds. These usually consist of one or more rows of trees placed along the windward side of a field with additional parallel windbreaks through the field. The distance between them should be about 10 times the height of mature trees (Ferber, 1969). In localities where damaging winds come from several directions, a pattern of windbreaks forming squares or two-direction combinations should be used.

2. FARMSTEAD

Windbreak designs vary from one section of the country to another. To afford the most protection, they should be located perpendicular to the prevailing winds so that two or three sides of the farmstead are protected.

Hintz (1976) suggests that in the nothern Great Plains, to provide adequate protection, a windbreak must be 6–10 rows wide with dense tree and shrub species in the first three rows on the windward side. There should be approximately 61 m (200 feet) from the area in need of primary protection to the windward row of the windbreak to prevent serious snow distribution problems.

Where winters are less severe and snow drifting does not create a problem, three rows of conifers perpendicular to the prevailing winds on two sides placed 30 m (100 feet) from the building will give adequate protection.

3. LIVESTOCK SHELTERS

Historically, landowners on the Great Plains have sought protection for livestock. In early years, this protection was in the form of topographic features, the limited native stands of trees, and, in some cases, crude structures. With advancements in technology, and the increased awareness of protection values, landowners have gone to great lengths to increase this protection. Supporting evidence can be seen in some rather ingenious approaches to the problem. Abandoned cars are chained together and dragged out on winter wheat pastures to furnish livestock protection. Farm machinery is located to furnish snow protection. Irrigation pipe is stacked to form fences. In some cases, earth is pushed into wind "dams" by bulldozers (Atchison, 1976). Trends in the livestock industry indicate a continued and increasing need for livestock protection. Presently, there is an increase in planted tree windbreaks for livestock protection.

Ferber (1969) suggests that 15 to 20 rows of trees, preferably evergreens, are needed in the north range country to protect cattle, trap snow, and reduce the chilling effects of winter winds. Fewer rows are ample further south. Plantings are made in the shape of an L, U, or E design.

In the Northern Plains, cattle confined to feedlots and dairy operations need winter protection. Charles Robbins, a cattle feeder of Florence, South Dakota, put it very aptly at the Shelterbelts on the Great Plains Symposium when he stated, "There is no substitute for a well-planned feedlot shelterbelt or even better, a well-planned combination of shelterbelts. With a modern dairy operation, it is equally important to use a well-planned shelterbelt to protect the entire area" (Robbins, 1976).

D. Soils and Windbreak Growth

All species of trees and shrubs do not grow at the same rate nor do they grow to the same mature height. Likewise, adapted species vary in their growth on different soils within a geographical area. The amount of available moisture during the growing season and soil aeration are two important factors affecting tree growth. These are largely determined by soil texture and depth.

Foresters have long known that soils have a significant influence on the growth, longevity, and overall performance of trees and shrubs. Conifers generally do better on droughty soils than hardwoods; water-tolerant willows and poplars are best for high watertable soils; some species are better than others on saline sites, and some can tolerate carbonates (Ferber, 1969). The soil conditions that are most conducive to good tree growth are found in the sandy and loamy soils. These soils are coarse to moderately fine textured.

Soils that are extremely sandy easily take in water but store little moisture. Sandy loams have moisture that is more evenly distributed to greater depths. Trees on these soils develop deeper and more extensive root systems and aeration is better. Clay soils, fine-textured, are less desirable for tree growth. Water infiltrates these soils slowly and the runoff is higher during high intensity storms. They can hold more water but a higher percentage of the water is not available for plant use. During dry periods, the topsoil moisture evaporates, the clay shrinks and cracks, and they become extremely droughty. Root systems on these soils are shallower and aeration is poorer.

George et al. (1957) states that the soil-held water which is not available for plant use may vary from 10 to 15% in clays to 2 to 4% in sandy soils.

Since 1951, soil scientists and foresters of the Soil Conservation Service have been studying soils and windbreaks to determine windbreak growth on different soils. They describe the soil, take measurements of tree height and age, and observe general vigor and conditions of the trees. This information is included in published soil surveys.

Table 1, abstracted from the published soil survey for Reno County, Kansas, displays the kind of information that is available in published soil surveys where windbreaks are commonly planted. A knowledge of the soils and the growth that can be expected for different trees on these soils is a great help in determining the kinds of trees to plant. To facilitate planning, the soils are grouped in windbreak suitability groups according to their physical characteristics. For example, Group 1 includes clayey soils that are poorly aerated and have poor soil-moisture relationships. In contrast, Group 4 includes soils that have a surface layer and subsoil of loamy fine sand to clay loam and that generally are well drained or moderately well drained.

E. Establishment and Management

Many kinds of trees and shrubs are suitable for windbreaks. Choose the species that are best suited to the particular soil, have proved hardy for the area, and will provide the kind of windbreak desired.

Bagley (1976) states that tree survival during the establishment years depends upon: (i) site preparation methods which conserve moisture and minimize erosion; (ii) proper planting of viable adapted stock; (iii) vegetation management after planting to conserve water and minimize erosion; and (iv) protection from mammals.

1. SITE PREPARATION

Dryland sites may require summer fallow for one or more seasons to insure enough available soil water to supply the tree seedling for the first summer. Cultivated sites should be fallowed by implements designed to retain crop residue on the surface. A good mulch reduces evaporation and

Table 1—Suitability of some adapted trees for windbreaks and their estimated height at 20 years of age on soils of five different soil groups (Abstracted from Table 3, Soil Survey, Reno County, Kans., 1966).

Windbreak suitability group	Eastern redcedar	Ponderosa pine	Green ash	Cottonwood	Siberian elm (Chinese)	Hackberry	Russian-olive
Group 1: Clayey soils that are poorly aerated and have poor soil-moisture relationships. (Examples are Smolan silty clay loam, 1 to 3% slopes, and Tabler clay loam.)	Excellent (22 ft)	Fair to good (17 ft)	Poor†	Poor	Fair (25 ft)	Poor	Poor
Group 2: Loamy soils that are fairly well aerated and have fair soil-moisture relationships. (Examples are Bethany silt loam, 0 to 1% slopes, and Farnum fine sandy loam, 0 to 1% slopes.)	Excellent (25 ft)	Fair to good (19 ft)	Poor	Poor	Good (44 ft)	Good (22 ft)	Poor
Group 3: Fine sandy loams that have a clayey subsoil. (Examples are Carwile fine sandy loam and Pratt-Carwile complex [Carwile soil only].)	Excellent (25 ft)	Fair to good (25 ft)	Good (28 ft)	Good (53 ft)	Excellent (46 ft)	Good (25 ft)	Poor
Group 4: Soils that have a surface layer and subsoil of loamy fine sand to clay loam and that generally are well drained or moderately well drained. (Examples are Clark fine sandy loam and Naron fine sandy loam, 0 to 1% slopes.)	Excellent (24 ft)	Good (25 ft)	Fair (26 ft)	Fair (40 ft)	Good (44 ft)	Good (27 ft)	Fair (18 ft)
Group 5: deep sandy loams and loamy fine sands that are mainly well drained or somewhat excessively drained. (Examples are Pratt loamy fine sand, undulating, and Pratt loamy fine sand, hummocky.)	Excellent (19 ft)	Good (26 ft)	Fair (22 ft)	Poor to good (45 ft)	Fair (36 ft)	Fair (18 ft)	Fair (15 ft)

† Measurements of height are not generally shown for soils rated poor.

erosion while increasing infiltration. Properly executed chemical fallow will accomplish the same results and can be used on sites not adapted to machine cultivation. Chemical fallow in strips 1 m (3 ft) wide is successful on grasslands and is especially useful on sandy or steep sites (Bagley, 1966). Protection of the site after fallow during winter and the following spring can be accomplished by planting a cover crop of annual plants such as sudan, sorghum, or oats in late summer of the fallow year (Bagley, 1976).

Where rainfall is adequate and in irrigated areas plow in the fall and fallow through the winter. Prior to planting in the spring, disk and harrow thoroughly. Where plowing is undesirable and a sod condition exists, post-emergent chemical control of the grass may be applied in strips during the early fall prior to spring planting (Slusher et al., no date).

2. SPACING

Where moisture is plentiful, 3.5 to 5 m (12 to 16 ft) between rows is best; in drier areas, as much as 9 m (30 ft) may be needed for best growth.

At wide spacings, a longer period of time is required for trees to form an effective wind barrier. This delay is more than offset by the increased growth and vigor of the trees, which will live longer, retain their lower limbs better, and produce more foliage.

Spacings within the row vary from as much as 1 m (3 ft) for shrubs to 6 m (20 ft) for trees, depending on the species and geographic location. Ferber (1969) suggests that regardless of the spacing between rows for farmstead, livestock, or wildlife plantings, space plants closer together within the row. Check planting of multiple rows accomplishes the same result as closer spacing. For the proper spacing within rows in any geographical area, consult a local authority.

3. PLANTING

Trees and shrubs should be planted with the roots positioned as naturally as possible and at the same depth they grew in the nursery. The soil must be firmly and uniformly packed around the roots. Any trees and shrubs that fail to survive should be replaced the following planting season.

4. CULTURE AFTER PLANTING

After planting control weeds and grass. Even where there is plenty of moisture, trees and shrubs do better when weeds and grass are controlled (Ferber, 1969).

Proper and timely cultivation will promote water infiltration and minimize evaporation and transpiration (Bagley, 1976). Sweep type cultivators, spring tooth harrows, or tamden disks can be used. Shallow cultivations 10 to 12 cm (4 to 5 inches) deep are best, as deeper cultivations may damage roots (Ferber, 1969). In dry areas or on unfavorable soils, cultivate for the life of the windbreak, otherwise, cultivate until tree branches close in and prohibit cultivation.

Herbicides are valuable tools for controlling competing vegetation, especially in the tree row where specialized cultivation equipment or hand labor is otherwise needed.

Mulching in place of cultivation is unsatisfactory in areas of dry land farming. Where rainfall is good and in irrigated areas, mulching with seed-free straw stalks, corncobs, polyethylene film, or wood chips may be satisfactory after the windbreak is at least 5 years old (Ferber, 1969). Cultivation and herbicides are still the best methods of controlling grasses and weeds.

5. PROTECTION

Windbreaks must be protected from poultry and livestock. Unless such protection is provided the survival and growth will never be satisfactory (Slusher et al., no date). Animals can seriously deform and kill trees and heavily grazed windbreaks lose their effectiveness rapidly.

Trees are susceptible to rodent damage. Individual wire mesh enclosures will protect trees from rabbits. Aluminum foil around the trunks of small decidous trees will prevent girdling (Bagley, 1976). Keeping the windbreak cultivated or closely mowed reduces rodent cover and allows predators such as owls and hawks to help protect the trees.

Periodic insepections should be made to discover insect buildup. Dix (1976) states that the major pests species are divided into two categories: borers and defoliaters. Pesticides can provide immediate relief. Long-term solutions involve integrating both direct or immediate silvicultural, biological, and chemical control methods with indirect control methods.

6. RENOVATION

Shelterbelt renovation means restoring or creating proper spacing, density, structure, and species composition to provide the desired protection (Van Duesen, 1976). Shelterbelts commonly need renovation because of combinations of six major silvicultural problems: need for thinning to relieve extreme crowding and loss of vigor; need for releasing conifers from competition; need for planting supplemental rows of conifers; need for modifying the level density of foliage; need for reducing the width of most multi-row shelterbelts; and a need for managing advance natural reproduction (Read, 1968).

LITERATURE CITED

Aird, P. L., and E. L. Stone. 1955. Soil characteristics and the growth of European and Japanese larch in New York. J. For. 53(6):425–429.

Atchison, F. D. 1976. Windbreaks for livestock protection in the central Great Plains. p. 101–103. In Great Plains Agric. Counc. Publ. no. 78, Shelterbelts on the Great Plains, Proc. of the Symp., 20–22 Apr. 1976, Denver, Colo.

Auten, J. T. 1945a. Some soil factors associated with site quality for planted black locust and black walnut. J. For. 43(8):592–598.

Auten, J. T. 1945b. Prediction of site index for yellow poplar from soil and topography. J. For. 43(9):662–668.

Bagley, W. T. 1966. Chemical weed control—reduce tree failure; increase growth. Farm Ranch Home Q. spring, p. 18–20.

Bagley, W. T. 1976. Techniques for tree establishment. p. 163–164. *In* Great Plains Agric. Counc. Publ. no. 78, Shelterbelts on the Great Plains, Proc. of the Symp., 20–22 Apr. 1976, Denver, Colo.

Barnes, R. L., and C. W. Ralston. 1955. Soil factors related to growth and yield of slash pine plantations. Fla. Agric. Exp. Stn. Bull. 559.

Barrett, J. P., R. J. Alimi, and K. T. McCarthy. 1976. Growth of white pine in New Hampshire. J. For. 74(7):450–452.

Basu, A. C. 1973. Forest management practices, problems and possibilities in the Little Kanawha region of West Virginia. West Virginia Univ., Morgantown, West Va.

Bingham, C. W. 1976. North America's role in future wood supply. J. For. 74(8):512–514.

Boyce, S. G., J. P. McClure, and H. S. Sternitzke. 1975. Biological potential for the loblolly pine ecosystem east of the Mississippi River. USDA, FS Res. Pap. SE-142, Southeast. For. Exp. Stn., Asheville, N.C.

Boyce, S. G. 1975. How to double the harvest of loblolly and slash pine timber. J. For. 73(12):761–766.

Carmean, W. H. 1954. Site quality for Douglas-fir in southwestern Washington and its relation to precipitation, elevation, and physical soil properties. Soil Sci. Soc. Am. Proc. 18(3):330–334.

Carmean, W. H. 1961. Soil survey refinements needed for accurate classification of black oak site quality in southeastern Ohio. Soil Sci. Soc. Am. Proc. 25(5):394–397.

Carmean, W. H. 1970. Site quality for eastern hardwoods. *In* The silviculture of oaks and associated species. USDA, FS Res. Pap. NE-144, Northeast For. Exp. Stn., Upper Darby, Pa.

Carmean, W. H. 1975. Forest site quality evaluation in the U.S. Adv. Agron. 27:209–269.

Christensen, W. W., and A. E. Grafton. 1966. Characteristics, objectives and motivations of woodland owners in West Virginia. West Virginis Univ. Agric. Exp. Stn. Bull. 538, Morgantown, West Va.

Chrosciewicz, Z. 1963. The effects of site on jack pine growth in northern Ontario. Can. Dep. For. Publ. 1015.

Clark, F. B., and C. K. Losche. 1969. Importance of the A horizon in hardwood seedling establishment. J. For. 67(7):504–505.

Coile, T. S. 1935. Relation of site index for shortleaf pine to certain physical properties of the soil. J. For. 33(8):726–730.

Coile, T. S. 1952. Soil and the growth of forests. Adv. Agron. 4:329–398.

Coile, T. S. 1960. Summary of soil-site evaluation. p. 77–85. *In* P. V. Burns (ed.) Southern forest soils. 8th Annu. For. Symp., Louisiana State Univ. School of For., Louisiana State Univ. Press, Baton Rouge, La.

Covell, R. R., and D. C. McClurkin. 1967. Site index of loblolly pine on Ruston soils in the southern Coastal Plain. J. For. 65(4):263–264.

Davis, R. M. 1976. Great Plains windbreak history: an overview. p. 8–10. *In* Great Plains Agric. Counc. Publ. no. 78, Shelterbelts on the Great Plains, Proc. of the Symp., 20–22 Apr. 1976, Denver, Colo.

Della-Bianca, Lino, and D. F. Olson. 1961. Soil-site studies in Piedmont hardwoods and pine-hardwood upland forests. For. Sci. 7(4):320–329.

Dix, M. E. 1976. Protection of Great Plains shelterbelts from insects. p. 169–171. *In* Great Plains Agric. Council Publ. no. 78, Shelterbelts on the Great Plains, Proc. of the Symp., 20–21 Apr. 1976, Denver, Colo.

Duncan, S. H., and E. C. Steinbrenner. 1973. Soil survey of the Millicoma Tree Farm. Weyerhaeuser Co. For. Res. Center, Weyerhaeuser Co., Tacoma, Wash.

Ellerbee, C. M., and G. E. Smith, Jr. 1963. Apparent influence of phosphate marl on site index of loblolly pine in the lower Coastal Plain of S.C. J. For. 61(4):284–286.

Farnsworth, C. E., and A. L. Leaf. 1965. An approach to soil-site problems in New York. p. 279–298. *In* C. T. Youngberg (ed.) Forest-Soil Relationships in North America. 2nd North Am. For. Soils Conf., 26–31 Aug. 1963. Corvallis, Oreg. Oregon State Univ. Press, Corvallis.

Farrington, R. A., and Montague Howard, Jr. 1958. Soil productivity for hardwood forests of Vermont. p. 102–109. *In* Proc. 1st North Am. For. Soils Conf., 8–11 Sept. 1958. Agric. Exp. Stn., Mich. State Univ., East Lansing, Mich.

Ferber, A. E. 1969. Windbreaks for conservation. USDA Inf. Bull. 339.

Foster, R. W. 1959. Relation between site indexes of eastern white pine and red maple. For. Sci. 5(3):279–291.

Fralish, J. S. 1972. Youth, maturity, and age. p. 52–58. *In* Aspen Symp. Proc. North Central For. Exp. Stn., St. Paul, Minn.

Gaiser, R. N. 1950. Relation between soil characteristics and site index of loblolly pine in the Coastal Plain region of Virginia and the Carolinas. J. For. 48(4):271–275.

Gaiser, R. N., and R. W. Merz. 1953. Growth of planted red and white pine in Ohio and Indiana. Central States For. Exp. Stn. Tech. Pap. 138.

George, E. J., R. A. Read, E. W. Johnson, and A. E. Ferber. 1957. Shelterbelts and windbreaks. USDA Yearbook. p. 715–721.

Gessell, S. P., and William J. Lloyd. 1950. Effect of some physical soil properties on Douglas-fir site quality. J. For. 48(6):405–410.

Gevorkiantz, S. R., and W. A. Duerr. 1938. Methods of predicting growth of forest stands in the forest survey of the Lake States. USDA, FS Lake States For. Exp. Stn. Econ. Notes no. 9.

Haig, I. T. 1929. Colloidal content and related soil factors as indicators of site quality. Yale Univ., Sch. of For. Bull. 24.

Hannah, P. R. 1968. Estimating site index for white and black oaks in Indiana from soil and topographical factors. J. For. 66(5):412–417.

Hannah, P. R. 1972. Soil-site relationships for Norway spruce plantations in Vermont. Bull. 673. Agric. Exp. Stn., Univ. of Vermont, Burlington, Vt.

Hansen, N. J., and A. L. McComb. 1958. Growth of planted green ash, black walnut and other species in relation to observable soil-site characteristics in southeastern Iowa. J. For. 56(7):473–480.

Harms, W. R. 1969. Deep planting of slash pine in the Carolina Sandhills. J. For. 67(3):160.

Hartung, R. E. 1975. Harvest and let grow. J. For. 73(7):413 and 434.

Hartung, R. E., and W. J. Lloyd. 1969. Influence of aspect on forests of the Clarksville soils in Dent County, Missouri. J. For. 67(3):178–182.

Hatchell, G. E., C. W. Ralston, and R. R. Foil. 1970. Soil disturbances in logging. J. For. 68(12):772–775.

Haussman, R. F., and E. W. Pruett. 1973. Permanent logging roads for better woodlot management. USDA, FS, State and Private Forestry, Upper Darby, Pa.

Hebb, E. A., and R. M. Burns. 1975. Slash pine productivity and site preparation on Florida Sandhill sites. USDA, FS Res. Pap. SE-1355, Southeast For. Exp. Stn., Asheville, N.C.

Heintz, R. H. 1976. Using old windbreaks for outdoor classrooms. p. 120–123. *In* Great Plains Agric. Counc. Publ. no. 78. Shelterbelts on the Great Plains, Proc. of the Symp., 20–22 Apr. 1976, Denver, Colo.

Hill, W. W., Albert Arnst, and R. M. Bond. 1948. Method of correlating soils with Douglas-fir site quality. J. For. 46(11):835–841.

Hintz, D. L. 1976. Farmstead windbreaks. p. 95–97. *In* Great Plains Agric. Counc. Publ. no. 78. Shelterbelts on the Great Plains, Proc. of the Symp., 20–22 Apr. 1976. Denver, Colo.

Holemo, F. J., and E. E. Brown. 1975. A profile of the private, non-industrial forest landowner in Georgia's Coastal Plain. Georgia For. Res. Pap. 82, Georgia For. Res. Counc., Macon, Ga.

Husch, B., and W. H. Lyford. 1956. White pine growth and soil relationship in southern New Hampshire. New Hampshire Agric. Exp. Stn. Tech. Bull. 95.

Jameson, J. S. 1963. Relation of jack pine height-growth to site in the mixed wood forest section of Saskatchewan. p. 299–316. *In* C. T. Youngberg (ed.) Forest-Soil Relationships in North America. 2nd North Am. For. Soils Conf., 26–31 Aug. 1963, Corvallis, Oreg. Oregon State Univ. Press, Corvallis.

Johnson, Dexter. 1974. Windbreak fences—Great Plains beef cattle feeding handbook. Great Plains Ext. 5200. 4 p.

Jones, J. R. 1969. Review and comparison of site evaluation methods. USDA, FS Res. Pap. RM-51. Rocky Mountain For. and Range Exp. Stn., Fort Collins, Colo.

Kochenderfer, J. N. 1970. Erosion control on logging roads in the Appalachians. USDA, FS Res. Pap. NE-158. Northeast. For. Exp. Stn., Upper Darby, Pa.

Kormondy, E. J. 1965. Enquiry into plants. p. 4. *In* Readings in ecology. Prentice-Hall, Inc., Englewood Cliffs, N. J.

Larsen, D. N., and D. A. Gansner. 1972. Pennsylvania's private woodland owners—a study of the characteristics, attitudes, and actions of an important group of decision-makers. USDA, FS Res. Pap. NE-219. Northeast. For. Exp. Stn., Upper darby, Pa.

Leak, W. B., P. H. Allen, J. P. Barrett, F. K. Beyer, D. L. Mader, J. C. Mawson, and R. K. Wilson. 1970. Yields of eastern white pine in New England related to age, site, and stocking. USDA, FS Res. Pap. NE-176. Northeast. For. Exp. Stn., Upper Darby, Pa.

Lemmien, W. A., V. J. Rudolph, and J. F. Marzec. 1969. Forest plantings on a wet site in Michigan. J. For. 67(3):186–189.

Lemmon, P. E. 1955. Factors affecting productivity of some lands in the Willamette Basin of Oregon for Douglas-fir timber. J. For. 53(5):323–330.

Limstrom, G. A. 1963. Forest planting practice in the Central states. USDA, FS Central States For. Exp. Stn. Agric. Handb. no. 247.

Linnartz, N. E. 1963. Relation of soil and topographic characteristics to site quality for southern pines in the Florida parishes of Louisiana. J. For. 61(6):434–438.

Losche, C. K., W. M. Clark, E. E. Voss, and B. S. Ashley (no date). Guide to the selection of soil suitable for growing black walnuts in Illinois. North Central For. Exp. Stn., FS and SCS, USDA.

Lutz, R. J., and A. C. Cline. 1947. Results of the first thirty years of experimentation in silviculture in the Harvard Forest, 1908–1938. Harvard For. Bull. no. 23, Petersham. Mass.

Lyford, W. H., and D. W. MacLean. 1966. Mound and pit microrelief in relation to soil disturbance and tree distribution in New Brunswick, Canada. Harvard For. Pap. no. 15, Harvard Univ., Petersham, Mass.

Lyles, Leon. 1976. Wind pattern and soil erosion on the Great Plains. p. 22–30. In Great Plains Agric. Counc. Publ. no. 78, Shelterbelts on the Great Plains, Proc. of the Symp., 20–22 Apr. 1976, Denver, Colo.

McArdle, R. E., W. H. Meyer, and Donald Bruce. 1961. The yield of Douglas-fir in the Pacific Northwest. USDA Tech. Bull. no. 201.

Malac, B. F., and C. S. Brightwell. 1973. Effect of site preparation on growth of planted southern pines. Union Camp Woodland Res. Note no. 29.

Mann, W. F., Jr., and H. J. Derr. 1970. Response of planted loblolly and slash pine to disking on a poorly drained site. USDA, FS Southern For. Exp. Stn., Res. Note SO-110, New Orleans, La.

Marrama, P. M. 1972. Private woodland owner characteristics and attitudes in Berkshire and Franklin Counties, Mass. Mass. Agric. Exp. Stn., Univ. of Mass., Amherst.

Meyer, W. H. 1938. Yield of even-aged stands of ponderosa pine. USDA Tech. Bull. no. 630.

Miller, E. L., and J. D. Budy. 1974. Field survival of container-grown Jeffrey pine seedlings outplanted on adverse sites. p. 377–383. In Proc. of the North Am. Containerized Forest Tree Seedling Symp., 26–29 Aug. 1974. Great Plains Agric. Counc. Publ. no. 68, Denver, Colo.

Minckler, L. S. 1941. Plantation survival as related to soil type, aspect, and growing season. J. For. 39(1):26–29.

Moehrng, D. M., and I. W. Rawls. 1970. Detrimental effects of wet weather logging. J. For. 68(3):166–167.

Muench, John, Jr. (No date). Private forests and public programs in North Carolina. The Am. For. Assoc., Washington, D.C.

Myers, C. A., and J. L. Van Deusen. 1960. Site index of ponderosa pine in the Black Hills from soil and topography. J. For. 58(7):548–555.

Naughton, G. L. 1976. Windbreaks for recreational uses. p. 117–119. In Great Plains Agric. Counc. Publ. no. 78, Shelterbelts on the Great Plains, Proc. of the Symp., 20–22 Apr. 1976. Denver, Colo.

Parmenter, R. B., and A. B. Beaumont. 1952. Forest planting in Massachusetts. Extension Service. Univ. of Mass. Ext. Leaf no. 213, Amherst, Mass.

Patric, J. H., and L. K. Brink. 1977. Soil erosion and its control in the eastern forest. p. 362–368. In G. R. Foster (ed.) Soil erosion: prediction and control. Proc. of Natl. Conf. of Soil Erosion, 24–26 May 1976, Purdue Univ., W. Lafayette, Ind. Spec. Pub. no. 21. Soil Conserv. Soc. of Am., Ankeny, Iowa.

Phillips, J. J., and M. L. Markley. 1963. Site index of New Jersey sweetgum stands related to soil and water-table characteristics. USFS Res. Pap. NE-6, Northeast. For. Exp. Stn., Upper Darby, Pa.

Popowski, John. 1976. Role of windbreaks for wildlife. p. 110–111. In Great Plains Agric. Counc. Publ. no. 78, Shelterbelts on the Great Plains, Proc. of the Symp., 20–22 Apr. 1976, Denver, Colo.

Post, B. W., and R. O. Curtis. 1970. Estimation of northern hardwood site index from soils and topography in the Green Mountains of Vermont. Agric. Exp. Stn. Bull. 664, Univ. of Vermont, Burlington, Vt.

Read, R. R. 1968. Silvicultural systems for rural populations: shelterbelts. Proc. 6th World For. Cong., Madrid, Spain, 6-18 June 1966, FAO of UN 3:3763-3768. Comercial y Artes Graficas, S.A., Barcelona, Spain.

Retzer, J. L. 1958. Soil—a factor affecting the distribution and growth of native and exotic forest vegetation. p. 110-115. *In* Proc. of 1st North Am. For. Soils Conf., 8-11 Sept. 1958. Agric. Exp. Stn., Mich. State Univ., East Lansing, Mich.

Roach, B. A., and S. F. Gingrich. 1968. Even-aged silviculture for upland central hardwoods. USDA, FS Agric. Hdbk. 355.

Robbins, Charles. 1976. Economics of windbreaks and our cattle industry. p. 107-108. *In* Great Plains Agric. Counc. Publ. no. 78, Shelterbelts on the Great Plains, Proc. of the Symp., 20-22 Apr. 1976, Denver, Colo.

Robbins, P. W. 1960. Coniferous tree planting practices for Lower Michigan. Lower Mich. Chap., Soc. of Am. For., The For. Tree Planting Practices Comm., East Lansing, Mich.

Sauerwein, W. J. 1965. Developing soil survey interpretations with a large forest landowner. p. 441-455. *In* C. T. Youngberg (ed.) Forest-Soil Relationships in North America. Proc. of 2nd North Am. For. Soils Conf., 26-31 Aug. 1963, Oregon state Univ. Press, Corvallis, Oreg.

Schlots, F. E., and A. N. Quam. 1962. Soil survey interpretations for woodland conservation. Progr. Rep., Southwest Washington. SCS, Spokane, Wash.

Schlots, F. E., and A. N. Quam. 1966. Soil survey interpretations for woodland conservation. Progr. Rep., Puget Sound Trough Area, Washington. USDA, SCS, Spokane, Wash.

Schnur, G. L. 1937. Yield, stand, and volume tables for even-aged upland oak forests. USDA Tech. Bull. 560.

Seaton, F. A., Marion Clawson, Ralph Hadges, Jr., Stephen Spurr, and Donald Zinn. 1973. Report of the President's advisory panel on timber and the environment. U.S. Government Printing Office, Washington, D.C.

Shetron, S. G. 1972. Forest site productivity among soil taxonomic units in northern Lower Michigan. Soil Sci. Soc. Am. Proc. 36(2):358-363.

Shipman, R. D. 1956. Furrow old fields to plant longleaf in the Sandhills. USDA, FS Southeastern For. Exp. Stn. Res. Notes no. 98, Asheville, N.C.

Shipman, R. D. 1958. Planting pine in the Carolina Sandhills. USDA, FS Southeastern For. Exp. Stn. Pap. no. 96, Asheville, N.C.

Slusher, J. P., Gary Nordstrom, and J. E. Wylie. (No date). Farmstead windbreaks. Univ. of Missouri, Columbia. Guide 5900.

Soil Conservation Service. 1966. Soil survey, Reno County, Kansas. USDA, SCS. p. 34-35.

Soil Conservation Service. 1968. Woodland interpretations for land resource areas 141-148. Prog. Rep., Upper Darby, Pa.

Soil Conservation Service. 1975. Soil taxonomy, a basic system of soil classification for making and interpreting soil surveys. USDA Agric. Handb. no. 436.

Squires, J. W. 1969. The South's third forest, how it can meet future demands. A report of the Southern Forest Resource Analysis Committee.

Steinbrenner, E. C. 1965. The influence of individual soil and physiographic factors on the site index of Douglas-fir in western Washington. p. 261-277. *In* C. T. Youngberg (ed.) Forest-Soil Relationships in North America. 2nd North Am. Soils Conf., 26-31 Aug. 1963, Corvallis, Oreg. Oregon State Univ. Press.

Stephens, F. R. 1965. Relation of Douglas-fir productivity to some zonal soils in the northwestern Cascades in Oregon. p. 245-260. *In* C. T. Youngberg (ed.) Forest-Soil Relationships in North America, Proc. 2nd North Am. Forest Soils Conf., Aug. 1963, Oregon State Univ. Press, Corvallis, Oreg.

Stevens, M. E., and W. A. Wertz. 1971. Soil-timber species mix. J. For. 69(3):161-164.

Stoeckeler, J. H. 1948. The growth of quaking aspen as affected by soil properties and fire. J. For. (10):727-737.

Stoeckeler, J. H. 1960. Soil factors affecting the growth of quaking aspen forest in the Lake States. Minn. Agric. Exp. Stn. Tech. Bull. 233. 48 p., illus.

Stone, E. L., R. R. Morrow, and D. S. Welch. 1954. A malady of red pine on poorly drained sites. J. For. 52(2):104-114.

Terry, T. A., and J. H. Hughes. 1975. The effects of intensive management on planted loblolly pine growth on poorly drained soils of the Atlantic Coastal Plain. p. 351-377. *In* B. Bernier and C. H. Winget (ed.) Proc. of 4th North Am. Forest Soils Conf., Quebec, Canada, Aug. 1973. Les Presses de L'Universite Laval, Quebec.

Trimble, G. R., and Sidney Weitzman. 1956. Site index studies of upland oaks in the northern Appalachians. For. Sci. 2(2):162-173.

U.S. Forest Service. 1929. Volume, yield, and stand tables for second-growth southern pines. USDA Misc. Publ. no. 50.

U.S. Forest Service. 1938. Trees that temper the western winds.

U.S. Forest Service. 1958. Timber resources for America's future. USDA For. Res. Rep. no. 14.

U.S. Forest Service. 1974. The outlook for timber in the United States. USDA For. Res. Rep. no. 20.

U.S. Forest Service. 1975. Forest planting, seeding and silvical treatments in the United States.

U.S. Forest Service. 1976. Hidden soil characteristics are important. Black Walnut Advisory Sheet no. 39. State and Private Forestry, Upper Darby, Pa.

Van Duesen, J. L. 1976. Shelterbelt renovation in the Great Plains. p. 181–186. *In* Great Plains Agric. Counc. Publ. no. 78. Shelterbelts on the Great Plains, Proc. of the Symp., 20–22 Apr. 1976, Denver, Colo.

Van Lear, D. H., and J. F. Hosner. 1967. Correlation of site index and soil mapping units. J. For. 65(1):22–24.

Vardaman, J. M. 1970. The smartest fellow around. Am. For. Vol. 76, Nov. p. 8 and 61–63.

Wiant, H. V., Jr., M. A. Ramirez, and J. E. Barnard. 1975. Predicting oak site index by species composition in West Virginia. J. For. 73(10):666–667.

Wilde, S. A., and A. R. Albert. 1942. Effect of planting methods on survival and growth of plantations on well-drained sandy soils of central Wisconsin. J. For. 40(7):560–562.

Wilde, S. A., and G. K. Voigt. 1967. The effect of different methods of tree planting on the survival and growth of pine plantations on clay soils. J. For. 65(2):99–101.

Williams, J. A., A. A. Leven, and H. E. Dregne. 1963. Relation of soil properties to ponderosa pine production in the Zuni Mountains, New Mexico. p. 381–398. *In* C. T. Youngberg (ed.) Forest Soil Relationships in North America, 26–31 Aug. 1963, Proc. of 2nd North Am. For. Soils Conf., Oregon State Univ. Press, Corvallis, Oreg.

Woodruff, N. P., and F. S. Siddoway. 1965. A wind erosion equation. Soil Sci. Soc. Am. Proc. 29(5):602–608.

Woodruff, N. P., Leon Lyles, F. H. Siddoway, and D. W. Fryrear. (No date). How to control wind erosion. USDA Agric. Inf. Bull. no. 354.

Yawney, H. W. 1964. Oak site index on Belmont limestone soils in the Allegheny Mountains of West Virginia. USFS Res. Pap. NE-30. Northeastern For. Exp. Stn., Upper Darby, Pa. 16 p., illus.

Young, H. E. 1954. Forest soils-site index studies in Maine. Proc. Soil Sci. Soc. Am. 18(1):85–87.

Youngberg, C. T., and w. G. Dahms. 1970. Productivity indices for lodgepole pine on pumice soils. J. For. 68(2):90–94.

Zahner, Robert. 1958. Site quality relationships of pine forests in southern Arkansas and northern Louisiana. For. Sci. 56(2):162–176.

17 Noncommodity Values of Forests and Woodlands

HERBERT E. ECHELBERGER

Forest Service, USDA
Durham, New Hampshire

J. ALAN WAGAR

Pacific Southwest Forest & Range Experiment Station
Forest Service, USDA
Berkeley, California

I. INTRODUCTION

In addition to timber, forests and woodlands provide a variety of "noncommodity" values that normally are not bought and sold. They include, but are not restricted to, scenic amenities, recreation benefits, and wildlife resources. Their relative worth is difficult to define because users are not forced or even accustomed to decide what they will give up to obtain such benefits. Planners should be aware of noncommodity values and include them in land use planning efforts.

The importance of noncommodity values has grown tremendously during the past 20 years. This growth can be attributed largely to an affluent society in which the quality of life is increasingly important to many people. Part of that quality of life comes from the noncommodity values of forests and woodlands found during leisure hours.

This chapter examines some of these values. Emphasis is on the scenic, recreation, and wildlife resources and how they conflict with or complement timber production. Current research that addresses these questions is described and some land use planning problems that involve commodity and noncommodity values are explored.

Readers who are interested in recreation and landscape management on range lands and in metropolitan areas will find this discussed in Chapters 15 and 21.

II. PLANNING FOR SCENIC AMENITIES

Scenic amenities in forests and woodlands have provided cherished noncommodity values for many years. For example, the scenic beauty of Yosemite National Park was recognized over 100 years ago. But only in recent years have such values gained sufficient recognition to be included as part of the planning process for forest areas in general. National prominence is no longer required for scenic resources to receive the same planning consideration as the more tangible goods produced by an area.

Getting scenic amenities recognized in the planning process took considerable effort by individuals and organizations within and outside land management agencies. The National Forest Management Act of 1976 and the Bureau of Land Management Organic Act are results of this continuing evolution. These acts recognize the importance of scenic resources as well as the continued production of commodities.

In forest management planning, scenic amenities should be considered from two viewpoints—the near view and the distant view.

A. The Near View

In the near view, one of the scenic factors that planners consider is the visual impact of timber harvests. Public concern with the appearance of a forest immediately after harvesting has become acute, especially as more people with more leisure time, mobility, and environmental awareness visit forested areas.

Until World War II, public concern about forest management was quite limited; foresters often operated with little or no guidance from the public at large. During the 1950s and 1960s, private citizens in increasing numbers expressed concern about forest management. For example, clearcutting is, for many species of trees, an economically and silviculturally sound practice. But by 1970 it had become controversial.

Viewer reaction to the on-site effects of logging operations had concerned some foresters for a long time. In his problem analysis for forest recreation research, Dana (1957) called for study of citizen reaction to timber harvesting. Olmsted (1967) told New York foresters they could only guess how people would react to timber management; and in calling for research to relate forest esthetics to timber management, Shafer (1967) said "now more than ever, many resource managers will be expected to manage wildlands for aesthetics as well as timber."

Since then, several research studies have investigated the relationship of timber management and forest esthetics. Shafer and Rutherford (1969) found no differences in viewer preferences between selectively cut and uncut Adirondack forest stands 10 to 12 years after logging. Hamilton et al. (1973) concluded that logging would be condoned by suburban forest owners if it did not violate the owner's preferences. In fact, orderly piles of slash as well as cordwood and logs gave an impression of "neatness and industrious endeavor despite the intensive logging that was being done at the time." Willhite and Sise (1974) described how two groups, one unfamiliar with forestry and the other a group of foresters, rated slides of West Coast timber harvest scenes. If the slides conveyed an impression of only slight vegetative disturbance, their ratings were similar. Heavily disturbed scenes, however, were rated quite differently by the two groups. Daniel and Boster (1976) made similar observations, and Echelberger (1976) concluded that knowledge of a group's affiliation would be helpful in anticipating its reaction to recently harvested northern hardwood sites (Fig. 1).

A brief overview of these studies suggests that (i) most people are not violently opposed to the on-site results of all timber-harvesting procedures; (ii) reactions to the on-site results of timber harvests differ among groups of viewers; and (iii) some postlogging practices may improve the esthetic im-

Fig. 1—Although group affiliation influences how people react to timber harvests, most viewers are strongly influenced by the amount and distribution of logging debris.

pact of some timber harvests. However, considerable study on how to improve the visual impact of timber harvests remains to be done. Should foresters make more effort to educate the layman? Or should they develop less disruptive harvesting procedures? Is the answer whole tree utilization so that no slash remains? Or is the answer to be found in zoning forest use? A better understanding of how viewers perceive harvested timber, coupled with improved harvesting technology and a more informed public, seems a reasonable approach for resolving the on-site issue.

B. The Distant View

Forest management planning must also consider the distant view. In viewing forests from a distance, visitors generally prefer naturalness first (Yarrow, 1966; Twiss & Litton, 1966; Lime & Cushwa, 1969; Peterson & Neumann, 1969). If that is not possible, they prefer orderliness, showing that someone is taking care of things (Wagar, 1974). Rabinowitz and Coughlin (1970) found that dislike of landscapes "seems to focus on individual elements, and primarily manmade ones." This emphasis on the individual elements is consistent with Alexander's (1964) analysis that, "while harmony requires a balance among many variables, only one variable need be wrong to create a 'misfit.' ". In discussing the classification of scenery, Sargent (1967) found the term "eyesore" useful.

People's perception of the distant scene depends greatly upon its visual texture. We normally perceive a shape or "figure" in contrast to its surroundings of "ground" (Bouman, 1968). In uniformly textured forests, any clearing tends to be perceived as figure and as a blight upon nature, especially if the clearing involves straight lines "cutting across contoured ground" (Crowe, 1966). However, if the texture is already coarse, with many small openings, additional clearings are not readily distinguished from the existing pattern and tend to be perceived as ground. Many of the European landscapes that are both highly cultivated and noted for their scenic quality have coarse textures in which fields, forests, meadows, and even villages become ground rather than figure (Wagar, 1975).

C. Management to Protect Scenic Landscapes

Three different levels of management can be applied to protect scenic landscapes. The first and broadest is to zone the whole region so that the most productive areas are left for production and the most scenic (and generally less productive) areas are left for scenery. Parks, wildernesses, roadside or streamside corridors, etc. are, in fact, zones. However, many additional area divisions seem possible. For example, timber harvests increasingly involve steep and highly visible slopes that are valued for scenery. Yet equivalent production at lower cost might be achieved by intensified management of the better quality sites at lower elevations. Such zoning might raise production while freeing scenic areas that are now contested by competing interest groups.

A second and more local level of landscape management protects single views. For these, legibility is important. Lynch (1960) defined legibility as "the ease with which . . . parts can be recognized and can be organized into a coherent pattern." If timber is harvested so that all stages of the process—from bare land to mature trees—are readily visible in one view, then the dynamics of sustained production will be self-evident even to the casual viewer. However, a view dominated by only a few stages is not legible and may lead to public outrage.

A third level of landscape management seems to soften or reduce the impact of management activities on individual sites. In Switzerland, for example, electric transmission lines are suspended above the trees on tall towers so that forests can remain unbroken. In the United States, landscape architects and foresters have provided an increasing number of guidelines for fitting timber harvesting into the landscape with minimal esthetic damage (Neff, 1966; U.S. For. Serv., 1973, 1974a). These guidelines generally require that the "characteristic landscape" of an area, and the landforms and vegetative patterns it comprises, be identified.

> The term "characteristic landscape" refers to the naturally established landscape being viewed. It provides that visual frame of reference within which the land manager must work. It establishes the visual constraints as well as the visual opportunities under which management activities can be manipulated (Bacon, 1971).

To reduce their visual impact, management activities can borrow form, line, color, and texture from the characteristic landscape. Thus, freeform clearcuts can be arranged to repeat or simulate natural openings, to follow the pattern of existing landforms, or to avoid abrupt discontinuities in the skyline. Partial cutting can soften the edges of clearcut areas, and "islands" of trees can be left within the larger clearings. For the forests surrounding Mount Baker in Washington state, Barnes[1] proposed freeform "planned pattern harvest" that would simulate natural clearings and would "turn inside out" in time, with islands of timber becoming clearings and clearings growing up into timber.

Application of these guidelines has been hindered by difficulties in visualizing how something on a map might look on the ground, and vice versa. Many of these difficulties are now being solved by computer graphics techniques that show areas as they might be seen by viewers or draw perspective views of landscapes. By generating maps depicting land and forests, the VIEWIT program (Travis et al., 1975) greatly facilitates identification of areas that are sensitive to scenic alteration. Twito and Warner have developed a perspective plot program for a desk-top computer connected to a digitizer and plotter that draws perspective views of ridge lines, roads, and

---

[1] Barnes, R. L. 1969. Planned pattern harvest: a proposal for visual and psychological improvement. Proc. Intermt. Sec. Soc. Am. For., Jackson Hole, Wyo. 5 p. mimeo.

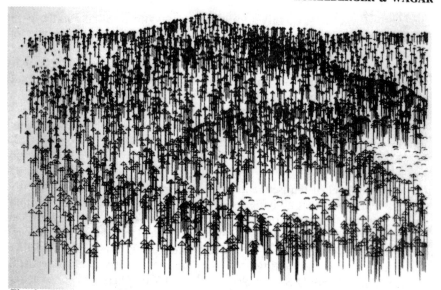

Fig. 2—Computer graphics techniques, such as PREVIEW, help to solve the problem of visualizing changes in landscapes over a period of time.

cutting boundaries; this program is interactive and permits trial-and-error adjustment of proposed changes.[2]

The PREVIEW program was developed specifically to examine the esthetic consequences of proposed timber harvesting throughout an entire rotation (Myklestad & Wagar, 1976). This permits designers to avoid visual problems that otherwise might not be recognized until the second or third timber harvesting entry. Effects of clearcutting and partial cutting can be shown, along with regrowth, water surfaces, rock outcrops, roads, and other features (Fig. 2).

Closely related is the MOSAIC program (Carey et al., 1976). This generates overlays for photographs to show how specific landscape changes would look. MOSAIC is designed to identify the point from which a photo was taken so that overlays can be precisely matched to the photo.

An orthographic projector has also been developed to show cutting boundaries as they would appear from different angles between line-of-sight and the area to be cut (U.S. For. Serv., 1976).

If a decision has been made to favor scenic amenities in a forest, the planning team—be it one person or a group—should include esthetic considerations early in the planning process. Depending upon the type of recreational use the planner anticipates for an area, near or distant views—or both—should be considered at the earliest possible time to avoid conflicts later in the planning or management process. The plan should include estimated costs as well as benefits.

[2] Roger Twito and John Warner. [n.d.]. Perspective plot program for evaluating visual impact of proposed timber harvest units with desk-top calculator, plotter, and digitizer. USDA-FS, Portland, Oreg. Copies available from Logging Systems Work Unit, USDA-FS, Pac. Northwest For. Range Exp. Stn., 4507 University Way, NE, Seattle, WA 98105.

On a planning team, esthetic considerations are usually developed by a landscape architect. If a landscape architect is not available, then the planner, forest manager, or other responsible individual should make sure that scenic amenities are not neglected. This requires familiarity with the forest and surrounding countryside so that the planner can identify areas of visual vulnerability (Litton, 1974), sites that should not be disturbed, and/or trails that may need to be rerouted.

Favoring scenic amenities does not preclude any timber management effort, but it may partially restrict the more drastic stand regeneration methods in areas that are used for recreation. Regardless of the silvicultural prescriptions, the decision to favor scenic amenities dictates a more gentle hand in the management of the forest. And this may entail a change in the philosophy of some forest planners and managers.

III. PLANNING FOR RECREATION BENEFITS

A second important noncommodity value provided by forests and woodlands is recreation. The increasing demand for forest recreation has accompanied the growing demand for other forest resources such as water, range, timber, and other commodities. Consequently, plans for the efficient and equitable allocation of forest resources must also include the intangible benefits derived from recreation experiences.

A pleasant forest setting enhances most forest recreation experiences. Clawson and Knetsch (1966) describe the trip to a recreation area as an important part of a person's recreation experience. If a trip from a city includes traveling through small towns, cultivated farmland, meadows, and forest stands of various ages, the total experience should be improved.

In some cases recreation demands have resulted in a loss of forest land for the production of commodities. In other cases recreation demands are compatible with those of production. Management decisions that will accomodate these increased demands will require planners to provide data on the possible trade-offs among them.

There have been a number of attempts to quantify recreation values. Beardsley (1970) compared three methods of estimating the economic value of recreation benefits—consumer's surplus, monopoly revenue, and a survey of visitors. Although all three methods yielded similar values per visitor-day, the total value figures differed significantly because each method used a different definition of total relevant use. More recently, O'Connell (1977) stated that monopoly revenue gives the most realistic value. He cautioned, however, that it is not determined in an actual market and does not address itself sufficiently to the problem of incremental value in determining the value of an additional site.

Krutilla and Fisher (1975) also have devoted considerable study to the problem of allocating forest resources. They express concern about the uncertainty of the decision-making process in view of the long spans of time required for resource management. They feel that in many allocation decisions there is an assumption that the resource has value only when extracted, or held in store for future extraction. The authors contend that the "resource may have another value, realized only if it is not extracted." It is this value they would like to see included in allocation decisions of the future.

Other problems associated with allocating recreation resources include forecasting recreation use (Johnson & Tharpe, 1963; ITTE, 1971; Moeller & Echelberger, 1974) and assessing the extent to which nonforest recreation activities can be substituted for forest recreation activities (Hendee & Burdge, 1974; Becker, 1976; Christenson & Yoesting, 1977).

A. Level of Development

Forest recreation may take place in areas that are highly or slightly developed, or in areas with no development. Highly developed recreation areas are characterized by small acreages with intensive use, such as campgrounds that have electricity, flush toilets, and showers, or ski areas with snowmaking equipment, groomed trails, and apres ski facilities. Capital investments for such areas are typically in excess of $100,000 plus the value of the land (Wayt et al., 1968) and maintenance costs usually are quite high. Because of the large financial commitment, other forest uses generally are not tolerated.

Such highly developed areas may be found on public land, but usually they are developed and managed by private interests. Facilities and services provided at the site are designed to enhance the visitor's enjoyment and increase the entrepreneur's profit. Clientele usually seeks an outdoor experience not available in an urban setting. However, the highly developed site may be a means to other ends. For instance, the camper may use the developed campground as a base of operation for backcountry or wilderness visits; the downhill skier may visit the ski area for social reasons; the vacation homeowner may be more interested in investments than vacations.

In contrast, the less developed recreation areas can accomodate other uses; they have a lower cost per acre, require fewer facilities, and have lower maintenance expenses. Large acreages are usually required and use intensity is quite low.

Undeveloped forest recreation areas are usually on public lands or on large industrial properties. There generally is little opportunity for a return on an investment in this type of enterprise. Visitors usually seek solitude and escape from man-made controls.

Problems, opportunities, clientele, and management usually differ between developed and dispersed recreation areas, but seldom are they completely unrelated. Furthermore, different people may perceive the problems differently. For instance, the downhill skier may think the biggest problem at an area is the long lift lines he waits in every weekend. The ski area operator, however, may perceive the biggest problem as the empty chairlift seats on Monday through Thursday. The hiker may perceive the biggest problem in the backcountry as too many other hikers, while the resource area manager worries about hikers' reactions to a clearcut that has become visible because of an insect infestation. Finally, visitors to a wilderness area who expect a "woodsy" experience complete with hot showers and flush toilets may not appreciate the quiet serene solitude of the area.

B. Conflicting Demands

The increased demand for forest recreation has spawned numerous conflicts. These conflicts are not only between groups who seek forest commodities and recreationists who seek noncommodity values, but also among the latter. Public involvement in forest management has emerged as a means to integrate the interests of the various groups of users and the land management agencies (U.S. For. Serv., 1974b; Clark et al., 1974; Clark & Stankey, 1976).

Conflicts between those who use developed recreation areas and those interested in forest commodities seldom extend beyond economics and profit-centered issues. However, conflicts between recreation area developers and people interested in preserving undeveloped forest resources can be intense and extended. An example is Mineral King, a quarter-mile-wide valley nearly surrounded by Sequoia National Park and currently managed as a game refuge within the Sequoia National Forest. Developers want to make the area a ski resort, while preservationists want to keep the area as it is. This has been a controversial issue since the first proposal for development over 10 years ago.

Conflicts between commercial interests and users of dispersed recreation areas are common. The number of such recreationists has increased dramatically in the past decade. They are usually well-educated people who are not afraid to express their opinions. Their interpretation of the law is often opposite to that of commercial interests. Both sides perceive their resource base as shrinking. Wilderness purists, especially, feel this way and their representatives work diligently to forestall encroachments. A good example of their lobbying strength is the passage of Public Law 93-622 on 3 Jan. 1975. This legislation added 207 thousand acres (84 thousand ha) in eastern national forests to the National Wilderness Preservation System. It also set aside an additional 125 thousand acres (50 thousand ha) of eastern national forests to be studied for future inclusion in the system.

Recreation is now recognized as a legitimate use of forests and woodlands, despite the problems this creates in public land planning. The benefits of recreation may not be fully understood or quantified, but there is growing support for the concept that it is more important in some forest areas than timber production or mineral extraction.

The planner who includes recreational use in his forest management plans may encounter extra work initially, but in the long run he will save time, money, and frustration. He should be familiar with the resource as well as the kinds and amounts of recreation activities it can support (see Chapt. 14 for a discussion of carrying capacity); he should also be aware of the possible conflicts among users, and attempt to prevent or resolve them. Jubenville (1976) describes five basic steps in the planning process, from the establishment of objectives and data gathering to coordination of planning, projection of needs, implementation of plans, and finally an evaluation.

One of the most important parts of the first step is including the public in decision making. Jubenville states that, "Involvement of public opinion in the planning process has become mandatory in our society." Bannon (1976) agrees, and emphasizes its importance in the opening chapter of his book on the comprehensive planning of leisure resources.

IV. WILDLIFE RESOURCES

The third important noncommodity value provided by forests and woodlands is habitat for wildlife. Enhancement of wildlife resources is often a major goal of private woodland owners, and game management plans have been in existence for many years. Interest in nongame wildlife has grown dramatically in recent years, but habitat management for nongame wildlife is still in the developmental stages.

Traditionally, wildlife habitat management has been for the production of game. The benefits that individuals derive from game production and the subsequent hunting and fishing have been categorized by Lewis (1951) as personal pleasure and a heightened ability to understand and appreciate the environment.

The importance of maintaining healthy game populations in forests and woodlands can be seen by the number of people who participate in hunting and fishing each year. The 1970 national survey of hunting and fishing showed that almost 55 million Americans spent 779 million days in hunting, fishing, or both (U.S. Bur. Sport Fish. Wildl., 1972). Even though license fees seem high, some researchers have concluded that the benefits derived from wildlife may be underpriced. For instance, Crutchfield (1962) argued that the use of differential fees in the Pacific Northwest would help alleviate the "grossly underpriced" sport of fishing. Colorado Outdoors stated that the most important game and fish legislation in 20 years called for increases in license fees (Schubert, 1967). And Sherwood (1970) found a substantial number of goose hunters in North Dakota who supported increased duck stamp fees.

A. Habitat Management

Habitat management has long been recognized as a critical element in game management, and at recent wildlife conferences the relationship of forestry to game management has received increased attention. For example, in their wildlife habitat problem analysis for Montana, Willard and Edleman (1974) found that the allocation of forest habitats primarily for wildlife use was generally by default; that is, wildlife generally received whatever was left after all other allocation interests had been satisfied. They also found that "wildlife are not viewed as an economic commodity by land management agencies" and that wildlife biologists seldom have "meaningful objectives." General statements such as "our objective is to protect wildlife habitat" were commonly made, but actual concern for elk habitat, beaver habitat, etc., was not found. Research projects, case studies, extension efforts, and other continuing education programs to solve these problems are now underway in Montana, but the authors recognize that the long-term solution should be the development of a "major program in habitat management" at the university level.

Nelson (1975) explained how wildlife considerations have become an important element in Pennsylvania's forest management planning. The Pennsylvania plan "calls for 2 to 5 percent of the forests to be in permanent, herbaceous openings." Although a 100-acre (40-ha) maximum size is imposed on individual clearcuts, wildlife considerations keep most cuts between 30 and 60 acres (12 and 24 ha). Furthermore, all natural openings up to 40 acres (16 ha) in size will be kept open for wildlife purposes. On state forests, the plan also calls for 200-ft (61-m) no-cut buffers on both sides of designated Wilderness Trout Streams and a 100-foot-wide (30-m-wide) uneven-age management buffer for all other trout streams. Small game also is provided for in the plan. In some management units, selected stands of good mast-producing trees will be allowed to exceed the 100-year rotation age.

Shaw and Gansner (1975) addressed the problems of timber and wildlife management on private woodlands. They recommended monetary incentives to (i) encourage long-term retention of woodland, (ii) encourage continuous maintenance of the woodland, and (iii) provide for continued public access. And Binger (1975) discussed the relationship of timber and wildlife management from the large corporate landowner's point of view. Binger contends that both society and corporate owners must differentiate between "needs" and "wants." Society must recognize "that a viable, dynamic, productive economy is a precondition to any program," and industry must accept that laissez-faire management is obsolete because the public is demanding new land use policies.

B. Nonconsumptive Use

Since the mid-1960s, interest in the nonconsumptive uses of wildlife has mushroomed (Fig. 3). Payne and DeGraaf (1975) estimated that total direct expenditures for the enjoyment of nongame birds in 1974 amounted to $500 million. Birdseed, binoculars, and camera equipment accounted for 95% of this. They estimated that in that same year expenditures by waterfowl hunters amounted to about $300 million, or only about 60% of birding expenditures.

Widespread interest in urban wildlife is an even more recent phenomenon. Based on their recent studies, Payne and DeGraaf estimated "with considerable confidence that approximately 20% of U.S. households purchase an average of 60 pounds of birdseed per year." A research program has been started to select management techniques that will enhance urban wildlife populations (DeGraaf & Thomas, 1973; Thomas et al., 1973). The

Fig. 3—Nonconsumptive uses of wildlife have become very popular in recent years.

program will emphasize three areas of study felt to be important in the man-wildlife-habitat matrix: first, to determine the species preferred by city residents; second, to identify habitat requirements for the species selected for research; and third, to develop techniques to optimize interaction between human and wildlife populations.

V. MULTIPLE-USE PLANNING AND NONCOMMODITY VALUES

One of the most difficult challenges that resource planners and managers face is to identify and incorporate noncommodity values into a defensible forest management plan. If the costs and benefits of noncommodity values are unknown, how can they be compared with cubic feet of timber, kilowatts of energy, or pounds of beef?

The problem of calculating values for recreation, scenic amenities, and similar benefits has been recognized for many years. It received considerable attention shortly after publication of the Outdoor Recreation Resources Review Commission reports of 1962. Since then, hundreds of papers and numerous books have addressed the issue without resolving it.

Because decisions must be made, whether monetary values can be computed or not, it is worth noting that monetary values are not absolute but are simply negotiated compromises among a number of buyers and sellers who often have widely differing opinions concerning whatever is being marketed (Wagar, 1976). By necessity, the action on resource allocations has shifted to the legislative and judicial branches of the political system. Special interest groups lobby, draft legislation, and go to court to further their causes; public hearings are held before decisions are made, and opinions from all sides of an issue are aired. Special interest groups can often provide information that a management organization is not staffed to obtain.

Although many public agencies were once reluctant to open their decision-making to citizen participation, they now seek it as a means to establish defensible rankings among conflicting values. And decisions are often better accepted by interest groups that have participated enough to understand the issues more fully. Legislation such as the National Environmental Protection Act of 1969 and the National Forest Management Act of 1976 mandates citizen participation in many decisions.

Increasingly, the role of public resource managers is to identify management alternatives and define as fully as possible the consequences of each. If these alternatives and consequences are adequately communicated to the public, we can expect an informed choice among them. Executing the choice is a managerial responsibility. Managers of private lands are less governed by public pressure but are not totally immune, especially if they manage large acreages. In a democratic society, an aroused public can exert substantial power through legislative regulation.

Recent trends may diminish the need for monetary evaluation of noncommodity values by establishing alternative ways of negotiating relative values. Once such values have been tested by repeated conflict among competing groups, it is likely that considerable discretion will again be delegated to managers.

LITERATURE CITED

Alexander, Christopher. 1964. Notes on the synthesis of form. Harvard Univ. Press, Cambridge, Mass. 216 p.

Bacon, W. R. 1971. Visual resource management guide. U.S. Dep. Agric. For. Serv. Reg. 6, Portland, Oreg. (unnumbered pages).

Bannon, J. J. 1976. Leisure resources: its comprehensive planning. Prentice-Hall, Inc., Englewood Cliffs, N. J. 454 p.

Beardsley, Wendell. 1970. Economic value of recreation benefits determined by three methods. U.S. Dep. Agric. For. Serv. Res. Note RM-176. Rocky Mt. For. Range Exp. Stn., Fort Collins, Colo. 4 p.

Becker, B. W. 1976. Perceived similarities among recreational activities. J. Leisure Res. 8(2): 112-122.

Binger, C. R. 1975. Corporate views and responsibilities for public values and profits. Trans. 40th North Am. Wildl. Nat. Resour. Conf. 40:405-413.

Bouman, J. C. 1968. The figure-ground phenomenon in experimental and phenomenological psychology. Fallmarks Boktrycker, Stockholm. 269 p.

Carey, J. B., G. W. Harju, and A. E. Stevenson. 1976. User's manual MOSAIC/PHOTO-MONTAGE. Prepared for U.S. Dep. Agric. For. Serv. Recreat. and Landscape Manage. Res. Proj., Berkeley, Calif. by The Aerospace Corp. Energy and Transp. Div., El Segundo, Calif.

Christenson, J. E., and D. R. Yoesting. 1977. The substitutability concept: a need for further development. J. Leisure Res. 9(3):188-207.

Clark, R. N., and G. H. Stankey. 1976. Analyzing public input to resource decisions: criteria, principles, and case examples of the CODINVOLVE system. Natl. Res. J. 16(1):214-236.

Clark, R. N., G. H. Stankey, and J. C. Hendee. 1974. An introduction to CODINVOLVE: a system for analyzing, storing, and retrieving public input to resource decisions. USDA-FS Res. Note PNW-233. Pac. Northwest For. Range Exp. Stn., Portland, Oreg. 16 p.

Clawson, Marion, and J. L. Knetsch. 1966. Economics of outdoor recreation. Johns Hopkins Press, Baltimore. 328 p.

Crowe, Sylvia. 1966. Forestry in the landscape. For. Comm. Bookl. 18. H. M. Stationery Off., London. 31 p.

Crutchfield, J. A. 1962. Valuation of fishery resources. Land Econ. 38:145-154.

Dana, S. T. 1957. Problem analysis—research in forest recreation. USDA-FS, Washington, D.C. 36 p.

Daniel, T. C., and R. S. Boster. 1976. Measuring landscape esthetics: The scenic beauty estimation method. USDA-FS Res. Pap. RM-167. Rocky Mt. For. Range Exp. Stn., Fort Collins, Colo. 66 p.

DeGraaf, R. M., and J. W. Thomas. 1974. A strategy for wildlife research in urban areas. p. 53-56. *In* Wildlife in an urbanizing environment. Holdsworth Natl. Res. Center Planning and Dev. Ser. 28. Univ. of Massachusetts, Amherst.

Echelberger, H. E. 1976. The visual impact of timber harvests on forest aesthetics. Ph.D. Thesis. SUNY College of Environ. Sci. and For., Syracuse, N.Y. (Diss. Abstr. 37/03P1050-B). 231 p.

Hamilton, L., T. Rader, and D. Smith. 1973. Aesthetics and owner attitudes toward suburban forest practices. North. Logger 22(3):18-19, 38-39.

Hendee, J. C., and R. J. Burdge. 1974. The substitutability concept: implications for recreation research and management. J. Leisure Res. 6(2):157-162.

Institute for Transportation and Traffic Engineering. 1971. Transportation analysis procedures for national forest planning. Proj. Rep. Univ. of California, Berkeley. 192 p.

Johnson, H. A., and M. M. Tharpe. 1963. Meeting the demand for outdoor recreation. p. 309-321. *In* A place to live: the yearbook of agriculture. USDA

Jubenville, Alan. 1976. Outdoor recreation planning. W. B. Saunders Co., Philadelphia. 399 p.

Krutilla, J. V., and A. C. Fisher. 1975. The economics of natural environments: studies in the valuation of commodity and amenity resources. Johns Hopkins Press, Baltimore. 292 p.

Lewis, H. F. 1951. Wildlife in today's economy: Aesthetic and recreational values of wildlife. Trans. 16th Conf. North Am. Wildl. 16:13-16.

Lime, D. W., and C. T. Cushwa. 1969. Wildlife esthetics and auto campers in the Superior National Forest. USDA-FS Res. Pap. NC-32, North Cent. For. Exp. Stn., St. Paul, Minn. 8 p.

Litton, R. B., Jr. 1974. Visual vulnerability of forest landscapes. J. For. 72(7):392-397.

Lynch, Kevin. 1960. The image of the city. Harvard Univ. Press, Cambridge, Mass. 194 p.

Moeller, G. H., and H. E. Echelberger. 1974. Approaches to forecasting recreation consumption. p. 43-55. *In* Outdoor recreation research: applying the results. USDA-FS Gen. Tech. Rep. NC-9. North Cent. For. Exp. Stn., St. Paul, Minn.

Myklestad, Erik, and J. A. Wagar. 1976. PREVIEW: computer assistance for visual management of forested landscapes. U.S. Dep. Agric. For. Serv. Res. Pap. NE-355, Northeast. For. Exp. Stn., Upper Darby, Pa. 12 p.

Neff, P. E. 1966. Applied silviculture in managing outdoor recreation sites. p. 34-35. *In* Proc. Annu. Meet. Soc. Am. For. 24-28 Oct. 1965. Detroit, Mich.

Nelson, J. C. 1975. Blending wildlife needs in forest management systems. Trans. 40th North Am. Wildl. and Nat. Resour. Conf. 40:185–192.

O'Connell, P. F. 1977. Economic evaluation of non-market goods and services. p. 82–90. *In* Proc. Symp. Outdoor Recreat. Adv. in Application of Econ. U.S. Dep. Agric. For. Serv. Gen. Tech. Rep. WO-2. Washington, D.C.

Olmsted, N. W. 1967. Recreation in the multiple-use complex. N.Y. For. 24(2):10–14.

Payne, B. R., and R. M. DeGraaf. 1975. Economic values and recreational trends associated with human enjoyment of nongame birds. p. 6–10. *In* Proc. Symp. Manage. For. and Range Habitats Nongame Birds. U.S. Dep. Agric. For. Serv. Gen. Tech. Rep. WO-1. Washington, D.C.

Peterson, G. L., and E. S. Neumann. 1969. Modeling and predicting human response to the visual recreation environment. J. Leisure Res. 1(3):219–237.

Rabinowitz, C. B., and R. E. Coughlin. 1970. Analysis of landscape characteristics relevant to preference. Discuss. Pap. Ser. 38. Reg. Sci. Res. Inst., Philadelphia. 89 p.

Sargent, F. O. 1967. Scenery classification. Vermont Agric. Exp. Stn. Rep. 18. Univ. of Vermont, Burlington. 28 p.

Schubert, Ted. 1967. Hunting, fishing, and license fees. Colo. Outdoors 16(4):1–4.

Shafer, E. L., Jr. 1967. Forest aesthetics: a focal point in multiple-use management and research. p. 47–71. *In* Proc. 14th Int. Union of For. Res. Organ. Cong. Pap. 7, Sect. 26. 4–9 Sept. 1967. Munich, Germany.

Shafer, E. L., Jr., and W. Rutherford, Jr. 1969. Selection cuts increased natural beauty in two Adirondack forest stands. J. For. 67(6):415–419.

Shaw, S. P., and D. A. Gansner. 1975. Incentives to enhance timber and wildlife management on private forest lands. Trans. 40th North Am. Wildl. and Nat. Resour. Conf. 40:177–185.

Sherwood, G. A. 1970. Characteristics of North Dakota goose hunters. N. D. Outdoors 33(3):8–11.

Thomas, J. W., R. O. Brush, and R. M. DeGraaf. 1973. Invite wildlife to your backyard. Natl. Wildl. 11(3):5–16.

Travis, M. R., G. H. Elsner, W. D. Iverson, and C. G. Johnson. 1975. VIEWIT: computation of seen areas, slope, and aspect for land use planning. FS Gen. Tech. Rep. PSW-11. Pac. Southwest For. Range Exp. Stn., Berkeley, Calif. 70 p.

Twiss, R. H., and R. B. Litton. 1966. Resource use in the regional landscape. Natl. Resour. J. 6(1):76–81.

U.S. Bureau of Sport Fisheries and Wildlife. 1972. 1970 national survey of fishing and hunting. Resour. Pub. 95. 108 p.

U.S. Forest Service. 1973. National forest landscape management, Vol. 1. USDA-FS Agric. Handbk. 434, Washington, D.C. 76 p.

U.S. Forest Service. 1974a. National forest landscape management, Vol. 2. USDA-FS Agric. Handbk. 462, Washington, D.C. 47 p.

U.S. Forest Service. 1974b. Guide to public involvement in decision making. 732-283/404. Washington, D.C. 22 p.

U.S. Forest Service. 1976. Orthographic projector. *In* Equip tips. USDA-FS Equip. Dev. Cent., Fort Missoula, Mont. 2 p.

Wagar, J. A. 1974. Recreational and esthetic considerations. p. H1–H15. *In* Owen P. Cramer (ed.) Environmental effects of forest residues management in the Pacific Northwest. A state-of-knowledge compendium. USDA-FS Gen. Tech. Rep. PNW-24. Pac. Northwest For. Range Exp. Stn., Portland, Oreg.

Wagar, J. A. 1975. Recreation insights from Europe. J. For. 73(6):353–357.

Wagar, J. A. 1976. Land use planning: a view from Holland. J. For. 74(1):13–17.

Wayt, W. A., R. W. Acton, and J. C. Whittaker. 1968. A look at commercial recreation on small woodlands in Ohio. USDA-FS Res. Pap. NE-101. Northeast. For. Exp. Stn., Upper Darby, Pa. 11 p.

Willard, E. E., and L. E. Edleman. 1974. Considerations for wildlife in the allocation of Montana's forested habitats. Trans. 39th North Am. Wildl. and Nat. Resour. Conf. 39:354–359.

Willhite, R. G., and W. R. Sise. 1974. Measurement of reaction to forest practices: a case in the Redwood Region. J. For. 72(9):567–571.

Yarrow, Chris. 1966. A preliminary survey of the public's concepts of amenity in British forestry. Forestry 39(1):59–67.

18   Low-Intensity Recreational Uses for Wildland Environments

BRUCE F. LEESON

Natural History Research Division
Parks Canada
Calgary, Alberta

I. INTRODUCTION

Contemporary history can demonstrate the recent development of widespread societal interest in pursuing simple recreational activities in natural surroundings. Since 1960, massive public support has been organized to promote the values of wilderness prophets such as Henry David Thoreau, Bob Marshall, John Muir, and Aldo Leopold. The establishment of Yellowstone National Park in 1872 represented a revolutionary idea; to preserve natural landscapes unimpaired for appreciation by future generations. However, it was not until nearly a century later that the ultimate inadequacy of the National Park System to meet future low intensity recreational demands was officially acted upon in a similarly serious manner. In 1964 the United States Congress undertook to secure the benefits of an enlarged enduring resource of wilderness for American people of present and future generations. The opportunity for primitive recreation is a major criteria in defining wilderness areas. The National Wild and Scenic Rivers legislation has similar objectives.

Much has been said about the physical and psychological values to be obtained from pursuing recreational activities in a primitive setting. Whether these benefits are received in fantasy or reality is apparently immaterial to the fervence of dedication by those who advocate low intensity recreational land uses. Many who do not anticipate actual realization of physically using a wilderness area are no less enthusiastic in their support of the idea than are frequent visitors. Undoubtedly, the anxiety produced by an inexorably complex life style and the ubiquitous perception of deteriorating natural environments enforces a passionate desire to preserve or create something which is simple. The very rapid transition from pioneer life style to a complicated technological society which has been experienced by all citizenry of North America is unprecedented in the world history of man. North American's fascination with the perpetuation of their frontier skills and individual outdoor abilities is akin to religious commitment. The utilization of technological amenities such as magnesium pack frames and nylon tents in the pursuit of solitude challenges does not diminish the devotion; on the contrary, it greatly expands the opportunity and range of almost any individual. In fact, industrial technology has responded so effectively to the imaginations of existing and potential recreationists with a bewildering array of cross-country skis, snowshoes, backpacking gear, bicycles, canoes, kayaks, and dozens of related gadgets that a sense of urgency to participate has developed throughout society. Extolation of the healthful benefits of being involved, however, were shortly followed by the anguish of overcrowding, overuse, and a quick realization that the burgeoning populations of outdoor afficionados posed the potential of literally loving their wilderness into oblivion.

To the planners and managers of primitive recreation areas fell the formidable task of accommodating annually increasing numbers of visitors while at the same time preserving an unimpaired natural environment. It has always been accepted that the mere presence of man would have some disruptive affect on the wilderness environment; the impending challenge is to understand the degree of influence and identify acceptable and unacceptable activities. Low-intensity recreation in primitive settings where the objectives of least disturbance are paramount involves a minimum of built facilities and extensive constraints in modern construction and maintenance techniques. Rudimentary facilities and comparatively unsophisticated implementation methodologies belie the high financial costs and elusiveness of success which frequently characterize management of wildland areas. The obvious implication is that the success of performance and degree of associated environment impact will be directly related to the sensitive implementation of good plans based on a sound knowledge of the resource components. It is imperative that basic ecological relationships, particularly those involving soils, plants, hydrology, climate, land form, and wildlife habitats be understood and considered in plans for recreational use of primitive areas.

The actual facilities or physical changes required are dictated by the activities intended for the area. Studies of recreation potential can ascertain the attractiveness and feasibility of any terrain for a variety of possible activities, such as; hiking, backpack camping, horse riding, horsepack camping, bicycling, cross-country skiing, snowshoeing, river tripping, hunting, fishing, and snowmobiling. These activities will require some or all of trails, primitive campsites, trailheads, destination facilities, and possible consumptive resources such as potable water, packstock forage, and firewood. Notwithstanding the attractiveness of an evaluated area for specific activities, an examination of the physical capability of the indigenous resources to sustain the activity within acceptable limits of environmental impact must be assessed before proceeding with the development of a plan which provides for any particular land use. Information within the purview of the various disciplines of biological, earth, and engineering sciences constitutes the basic data base upon which further analysis is undertaken. Interpretation of resource facts in terms of physical suitability to support possible land uses at various levels of intensity can be used to postulate corresponding environmental impact implications. Tradeoffs, forfeitures, merits, and demerits of various courses of action can thence be debated by decision makers and all others who participate in plan preparation.

An overwhelming volume of basic and interpreted data can be produced by unrestrained scientific research. Whether an exhaustive revelation of all interrelationships of any or all identifiable ecosystems contained in the planning area is possible or not is debatable. The important point is that most agencies have finite means available to gather information pertinent to making land use decisions. Some which are particularly affluent in time, expertise, and finances will be able to conduct more comprehensive investigations than will other agencies whose means may restrict data collection, analysis, interpretation, and recommendation formulation to one or two individuals. Regardless of the ultimate degree to which the resource inspection can be carried, there are certain basic information needs which are imperative to making good land use decisions in primitive areas. These basic pieces of information are small in comparison to all the possible descriptors which could be marshalled (Plantenberg et al., 1974). Nevertheless, they account for a major portion of decision-making regarding land use and resource disposition.

An ecosystem, regardless of how large or small, is an outstanding example of a holistic entity. Those recreational managers whose mandate includes preservation of unimpaired natural environments must possess an appreciation of the complexity and intricacy of their resource if major mistakes resulting in long-term environmental impacts are to be avoided.

II. WILDLAND ECOSYSTEMS

Ecology is the science of the interrelationship of living organisms with the other biotic and abiotic components of their environment. An ecosystem is the community of organisms and their nonliving environment contained within defined boundaries, for example, a marsh. All ecosystems, aquatic or terrestrial, have two functional components: the autotrophic components which fix energy from the sun and manufacture food from simple inorganic substances; and the heterotrophic components which utilize, rearrange, and ultimately decompose the materials produced by the autotroph. An aspen tree would be an autotrophic organism in the aspen parkland ecosystem and a moose which browsed on aspen seedlings would be a heterotroph. Structure is also an important subdivision of the following four constituents of an ecosystem: (i) *Abiotic substances* are nonliving organic and inorganic materials such as soil and water; (ii) The *producers* are the autotrophs, chiefly green plants, which, through the process of photosynthesis, manufacture food; (iii) *Consumers* are heterotrophic organisms, mainly animals which ingest plants or each other; and (iv) *Decomposers* are small heterotrophic organisms such as bacteria which break down dead organic protoplasm and release abiotic substances back to the ecosystem.

The cylic nature of materials disposition within an ecosystem becomes apparent when the food chain and food webs of the organisms which live there are revealed. Energy flows through the structure of the ecosystem and losses of energy between trophic levels, largely through heat dissipation, are replaced by the sun. As ecosystems mature through a process called *succession,* they become more complex. Increasing complexity and maturity provides an enlarged number of functional niches and habitats which can be occupied by a greater diversity of appropriately adapted organisms. The amount of energy fixation in any given ecosystem is limited, frequently below its absolute biomass potential by external factors such as climate or human interference. Homeostasis is the self-regulatory ability of biotic communities to adjust themselves in response to changing conditions of their environment. When a population reaches the limit imposed by ecosystem resources it will stabilize by starvation, reduced reproduction, or other means. Changes imposed on the environment constitute stress which a population's homeostatic defenses will respond to. The change may be so traumatic that the organism simply cannot survive in that ecosystem any longer; changes such as forest cover annihilation from smelter fumes at Sudbury, Ontario, and Anaconda, Montana.

Primitive ecosystems will vary from being comparatively simple to exceedingly complex. A simple ecosystem does not imply that it is hardier or less subject to change in response to an environmental stress. On the contrary, a simple ecosystem such as an alpine tundra or a sand dune may exhibit a rapid and dramatic reaction to a seemingly simple act. Disturbance of surface vegetation by concentrated trampling on alpine areas exposes dense but shallow root turf to wind dessication and probable death. Subsequent exposure of mineral soil changes the albedo and encourages needle ice, both of which greatly retard reinvasion by native species. Sand dune vegetation, particularly on the primary or seaward dune, develops tenuously in the face of high winds and pounding wave action. A break in the dune grass for a facility as simple as a beach access trail weakens the established stability and renders the dune vulnerable to extensive wind erosion or breaching by wind-driven storm waves. Complex ecosystems, because they often develop in response to less rigorous climatic conditions, are frequently more resistant to drastic reaction resulting from minor imposed changes. A parkland grass layer, for example, has a greater ability to recover from trampling than would an alpine heath. The important point is that whenever an environmental stress is introduced to a natural environment a series of direct and indirect changes may occur, ripple-like, throughout the whole ecosystem. One piece cannot be manipulated in isolation from all others that interact with it. It is imperative to accord knowledgeable consideration to at least the major resource components in order to avoid actions which may forfeit future options and/or create irreversible environmental impacts.

Man has demonstrated among all organisms which inhabit earth, his singular, superior ability to cause substantial changes to all habitats and ecosystems. There are no areas which have not been affected by man's activities, such as airborne materials. However, some areas, due to remoteness, rugged terrain, or lack of harvestable resources that are economically marketable, have remained comparatively unimpaired. Other areas such as National Parks have been legislatively protected. Many of these areas, however, present natural resource assemblages which are particularly susceptible to manipulation by man. Very often they are characterized by steep lands, poorly drained or flooded soils, and severe climatic phenomenon, and contain special wildlife habitats. The potential for disruption of delicate natural equilibriums is particularly high. A majority of the areas which are designated for low-intensity recreation in a primitive setting will be regions which display a comparatively mature state of ecological succession and many factors will contribute to the complex homeostatic equilibrium. The state of the wildland environments will appear to be affected mainly by natural processes and the results of man's activities will remain essentially imperceptible.

III. RESOURCE PLANNING CONSIDERATIONS

Planners require two types of resource data before proceeding with land use or facility placement deliberations. The first type of information requirements are virtually universally applicable considerations in planning primitive environments. Biophysical data including soils, vegetative cover, surface and ground water hydrology, active geomorphic processes, climate, land form, and present or potential wildlife resources and habitats are the critical information needs. Basic resource information can be used to determine where facilities can be constructed and where activities should occur. The indigenous characteristics of each will affect the installation and performance of facilities, as well as the degree of short- and long-term environmental impact. The best way of presenting such information is, of course, on large-scale maps, preferably orthophoto mosaics. Each basic resource would be interpreted as to use suitability, performance expectations, fragility, potential for rehabilitation, and opportunity for mitigation of potential impact. Many agencies will not have the financial or time capability to undertake such a comprehensive approach. Furthermore, low-intensity recreational facilities involve discreet or point source impact for many of the resources such as soils and vegetation. In such cases it is not absolutely essential to have a complete soil or forest cover map to identify a good location for a trail or campsite. An observant individual trained in practical aspects of field biology can do an adequate job of facility location analysis with airphotos, a stereoscope, soil auger, and strong hiking legs. This, in essence, is going directly to the site specific stage of environmental planning, which is mandatory, regardless of the extent of less precise information previously obtained.

Wildlife resources are an important exception to this shortcut approach, however. Territorial transience and critical but temporally and spatially diverse habitat requirements generally cannot be perceived without seasonal observations. Historic game management records and knowledgeable local people may provide useful information but it is unlikely to be adequate if a serious objective of preserving or enhancing wildlife habitats is to be realized. Most primitive areas will have some existing facilities, whether designed or impromptu. Wildlife will have adjusted to these situations; an important guideline in the initial stages of planning low-intensity recreation areas in the absence of good wildlife information is not to change the status quo in any way that would increase or concentrate human visitation. Such actions should be undertaken only after comprehensive investigations reveal the merits and demerits of potential land use changes for wildlife populations.

The second type of resource data required is that which describes the unique or special values which highlight the region and make it an attractive candidate for primitive area recreation. Areas chosen for primitive recreational land uses will fulfill predefined criteria with regard to minimum evidence of disturbance by man. Therefore, there should not be extensive impacts or facilities which must be rectified or removed. There may be instances where exploratory roads will be eliminated or downgraded to trail status. However, primitive areas will, for the most part, present a substantially unimpaired natural resource base to the ecological planner. In addition to protecting the basic natural resources in providing facilities, the unique ecological assets must be preserved, and interpreted to the visitors. This requires identifying those attributes which are expressive of the particular ecosystem and which identify this area as being different from others. The natural history of a wild river located on the Pre-Cambrian shield will be different from one which flows out of the Rocky Mountains to the prairies. Bighorn sheep range would receive protective efforts in Alberta whereas salmon spawning beds would receive priority in New Brunswick. This type of information will be of both general and site specific importance, for example, grizzly bear range in Glacier National Park vs. specific denning sites. Such information is critical to the placement of facilities where the intent is to provide an informative and pleasing aesthetic experience for the visitor without sacrificing the primitive attraction.

IV. RESOURCE DATA CONSIDERATIONS

Misplaced or improperly constructed facilities in primitive areas probably have more serious consequences with regard to environmental impact and rehabilitation opportunities than would a similar situation in a high-intensity recreation area. Access will be limited and it may not be possible, physically or financially, to use machinery more sophisticated than a garden tractor or chainsaw at remote sites. Procedures such as sodding, irrigation, transplantation, and seeding may not be possible or desirable. It is imperative, therefore, to locate facilities in ecosystems with high resistance to impact. If fragile areas are unavoidable, mitigative and rehabilitation schemes must be incorporated in initial construction design and subsequent management operations. Factors to be considered in the allocation of land uses in wildland settings and the location and design of facilities include: soil, vege-tation, surface and ground water hydrology, active geomorphic processes, faunal habitats, climate and microclimate, topographic characteristics, and natural attractiveness.

A. Soil

The quantity and quality of soil, water, and air, at the simplest level of abstraction, determines the form and productivity of all naturally occurring biotic processes. Man's ultimate dependance on soil as a food-producing and physical foundation medium has caused the science of soil to be one of the world's oldest. A large amount of pedological and edaphological in-formation can be produced about any soil. While any or all of the possible pieces of information may be important in making certain comparative or management statements, a relatively small amount is critical to the wildland planner who is designing low-intensity recreational facilities. The soil prop-erties of texture, structure, organic matter content, depth, stoniness, and drainage conditions are the most important soil facts in making decisions about trails, campgrounds, disposal sites, and activity areas.

Texture refers to the relative proportion of various-sized groups of mineral particles in a given soil. Clay is the smallest size and sand is the larg-est, with silt particles being intermediate in size. Clay particles are platelike in shape and have a high adsorptive capacity for water. When clay is wetted, it adsorbs comparatively large amounts of water and swells. When moist, clay soils are highly plastic and usually sticky. Under such circumstances, a clay soil has poor trafficability because muddy, slippery trail and campsite conditions will develop. Although clay soil has high pore volume, the spaces are small due to the close packing of small particles. Infiltration and perme-ability is therefore low and puddling with slow drainage results in mud holes which may persist in trails long after coarser textured soils would have dried out. The large capacity to absorb water gives most clay soils a high plasticity index, a condition under which clay soils perform poorly for pedestrian and equestrian traffic. The load-bearing capacity and internal friction decreases very rapidly as the moisture content is increased above the plastic limit. Upon drying, clay soils become hard and cloddy, and although they provide stable traffic surfaces at such times, any rough microtopography created by disturbance under wet conditions may present a very uneven walking sur-face. Cement-like surfaces of dried clays also present inhospitable environ-ments for seed sprouting. Heavy soil textures such as sandy clay, silty clay, and clay will present severe constraints to trail, campsite, and sewage dis-posal location. When present in smaller proportions, the same binder quali-ties of clay particles are desirable in that they impart structural stability and erosion resistance to mineral soils.

Silt particles are irregular in size and shape in contrast to the smooth platelike clay particles. Silt displays characteristics similar to clay with re-gards to water adsorption, plasticity, and stickiness, although to a much less extreme degree of expression. Exposed soils containing high silt fractions are slippery when wet. Silty soils are also somewhat more subject to sheet and rill erosion in that the particles are smaller than sand and have less cohesive attraction for each other than do clay particles. Silt-rich soils have rapid capillary rise and thus facilitate the formation of needle ice which greatly complicates rehabilitation of denuded sites that are subjected to alternate freezing and thawing. Silty soils tend to be dusty when dry. High silt content soils such as silt loam and silty clay loam present moderate limitations to low intensity recreational facilities.

Sand grains may be rounded or irregular shaped particles of predominantly quartz. Sandy soils have large pore spaces and consequently display rapid infiltration and permeability. The water-holding capacity is low, causing sandy soils to present droughty conditions which complicate rehabilitation processes. Similarly, sandy soils have serious constraints for underground sewage disposal. Sandy soils have little or no plasticity, stickiness, or slippery characteristics. Sandy soils which are completely deficient in fines and coarser materials lack stability under load except when damp. Dry beach, dune, and fine desert-blow sand present severe constraints for trails or campsites.

A loam soil is one which contains a mixture of sand, silt, and clay particles in roughly similar proportions, and displays the favourable characteristics of light and heavy soils. Consequently, the undesirable properties of clay and sand, such as slow drainage, stickiness, and compactness at one extreme, and lack of cohesive structure and difficult rehabilitation opportunities at the other, are suppressed. Therefore, sandy loams, fine sandy loams, very fine sandy loams, and loam generally present only very slight constraints to manipulation for primitive area recreational facilities.

A soil's structure is the arrangement or aggregation of the soil particles into units called *peds*. The actual structure, be it spheroidal, blocklike, prism-like, or platelike is probably of less significance than being aware of structural change implications resulting from manipulation. The presence of organic matter in a mineral soil is a major factor in maintaining the desirable conditions of aggregate stability and soil porosity. Soil manipulation under low organic matter content promotes a state of nonstructure, either single-grained or massive. Coarse-textured soils will tend towards becoming single-grained with attendant use and rehabilitation problems of extreme looseness, low moisture content, and reduced productivity. Fine-textured soils, on the other hand, will tend towards massive structure with compacted, impervious layers which puddle, restrict vertical drainage, induce surface erosion, and form cement-like clods when dry. Specific management strategies will be required in order to avoid environmental impact or useability problems which can occur from undesirable soil structure conditions which may develop. The complexity of manipulating even small pieces of the wildland ecosystem now starts to be revealed in the influential interrelationships which texture, organic matter, and use have on the state of soil structure.

Organic matter, when present in appropriate amounts, is critical to creating many of the desirable properties of mineral soils. It commonly accounts for at least half the cation exchange capacity of soils and is responsible perhaps more than any other single factor for the stability of soil aggregates (Buckman & Brady, 1975). While increasing organic matter, up to a point, promotes productivity and stability, it intensely complicates the use of soils for recreational amenities such as trails, campsites, and septic disposal fields. Trails in organic-rich mineral soils quickly become entrenched and often function more as ditches than as paths. Organic soil presents a severe, if not impossible, medium for the location of recreational facilities. Organic soils have low load-bearing capacity for a concentrated application of pressure such as a hoof. Organic material is highly compressible and is easily broken and disintegrated by foot traffic. Trails which cross organic areas become churned quagmires of perpetually wet, slippery ooze. Extreme widening occurs as hikers and horses attempt to skirt the boggy areas. Concerted attempts to avoid organic soil areas must be exercised in trail location. If avoidance is impossible, innovative designs such as boardwalks or northern road stabilization techniques must be employed. Campsites cannot be located directly on organic soils because of either the damp uncomfortable conditions or fire hazards which would exist. Drainage would not be considered acceptable in most primitive settings.

With the exception of the construction of trails on sidehill slopes, disturbance of more than the upper 15 cm (6 inches) of the soil profile in creating low-intensity recreation facilities will likely be uncommon. However, it is desirable to have at least 30 cm of soil material over bedrock wherever activities may occur. Such a practice ensures an adequate rooting medium for rehabilitation undertakings and less possibility of scouring to bedrock in the event of severe erosion. If bedrock could be exposed in any potential construction projects or other land uses it should be well considered that downslope erosion may be intensified and rehabilitation options are virtually forfeited in primitive settings. Septic tank disposal fields should not be installed where bedrock is less than 120 cm from the surface and preferably where the soil mantle is 180 cm deep over lithic contact.

Stoniness, both coarse fragments on the surface and rocks within the soil matrix will affect the ease of facility construction and the comfortableness of recreational activities. While high rock content within the soil profile will reduce overall rooting medium and water-holding potential, this is not a concern where denudation will be required for permanent trails, campsites, and corrals. On the contrary, some rock content in the subgrade of such facilities would lend stability to the site, provided it did not unduly restrict installation of tent pegs. Trails and campsites can be located with minimal difficulties if coarse fragments occupy no more than 20% of the soil surface, stones are more than 7.5 m apart, and bedrock outcrops cover less than 10% of the area and occur no closer than 30 m apart. Severe limitations for trails and camps are posed by coarse fragments covering more than 50% of the exposed surface, stones less than 1.5 m apart, and rock outcrops less than 9 m apart and covering greater than 25% of the surface (Knapik & Coen, 1974).

Drainage, as used here, refers to the position of the water table as well as the defined soil drainage classes (Canada Soil Surv. Comm., 1974). Internal drainage is the ability of a soil to permit downward flow of water, and is affected by texture, structure, or other soil layer features which may influence permeability, for example, hardpan. Most medium- and fine-grained soils experience decreasing load-bearing capacity as soil moisture increases. Compaction, disaggregation, and muddy conditions frequently result from use under such circumstances. Slow infiltration and permeability will also constitute poor drying conditions for camp and corral areas. Severe constraints for trails, campsites, and corrals are posed by imperfectly, poorly, and very poorly drained soils where the water table may occur closer than 50 cm to the soil surface during the season of use. No or slight limitations for the same uses occur on rapidly, well-, and moderately well-drained soils where the water table is more than 75 cm below the soil surface during the season of use. Water table limitations for septic tank filter fields are the same as for bedrock. In addition, percolation and permeability tests should be conducted and gauged against local health regulations in order to ascertain potential for acceptable effluent absorption.

B. Vegetation

The effects of human trampling on natural vegetation are variable, depending on the time and amount of trampling, and the vegetation involved (Douglas et al., 1975). The principles of vegetation management and prediction of performance under low-intensity recreation pressures are significantly less well developed than for soil science. Most of the soil science principles which evolved from agricultural research and engineering practices are applicable to land use decisions involving soil manipulation in wildland areas. In contrast, however, only small amounts of the botanical information produced in agricultural and landscape horticultural sciences are applicable to wildland vegetation management. Primitive area management has an objective of preserving natural community species composition and diversity, whether the preservation objective be era or evolutionary (i.e., artificially perpetuating the state of a particular natural ecosystem or permitting succession). The purposeful introduction of exotic plant species is therefore undesirable. On the other hand, seed or plant materials of many native species are generally not commercially available. Furthermore, the physiology and reproductive processes of many native plants which have occurred in primitive settings and not had any historic commercial value are largely unknown.

Sites which experience facilities construction or very intensive use will be purposefully denuded and hardened to an appropriate trafficability level. The kind and fragility of indigenous vegetation surrounding these sites is important, in that it can be destroyed. On the other hand, some very hardy and persistent vegetation species require intensive management in order to prevent reinvasion of trails and campsites, for example, salal and salmonberry encroach on Vancouver Island trails at the rate of roughly 50 cm/year. Activities associated with hiking, riding, camping, and sight-seeing, however, create a concern for unintended vegetation impact. While picking, digging, cutting, collecting, and littering will all affect vegetation, trampling has the most serious potential for obvious widespread impact. Trampling is likely to occur in the vicinity of scenic or interesting natural attractions, around camp areas, lakeshores, or other nodes of destination concentration. While it is presumed that traffic surfaces will be provided, unpredictable use patterns frequently develop with substantial vegetative impact occurring to delicate plant communities.

Although interest in recreational impact problems was reported as early as 1929 by Meinecke, it has been comparatively recent that intensive research was undertaken to determine relative hardiness of various plant species. Techniques range from comparing the differences of utilized sites to control areas, to actually performing trampling experiments to demonstrate impact and tolerance (Cieslinski & Wagar, 1970; Willard & Marr, 1970; Beardsley & Herrington, 1971; Harvey et al., 1972; Bell & Bliss, 1973; Dale & Weaver, 1974; Landals & Scotter, 1974; Campbell & Scotter, 1975; Knapik & Coen, 1974; Helgath, 1975; Merriam & Smith, 1974). All of these documents describe the relative degree of impact to the plants existing in the ecosystems studied. Many factors, including phenology; time, duration, intensity, and repetitiveness of impact force; wetness or dryness of plant material; light or shaded conditions; and numerous other possible circumstances affect both individual species and community vulnerability to stress. At this time, the diversity of the quantitative data is such as to preclude prudent, confident statements about specific botanical physiological principles relating to universal vegetative fragility. Phenotypic variability is simply too great to permit responsible recommendations which could be applicable to the complete spectrum of possible circumstances. The research results do, however, encourage speculation which, in the context of future research, will undoubtedly form hypotheses to be proven or disproven. While a great many factors can affect site-specific vegetative fragility, it appears likely that plant fragility to trampling, from least to most fragile, will be trees, grasses, sedges, shrubs, tree seedlings, forbs, mosses, and dry lichens.

Principles of managing fragile vegetation will likely never become precise because of the ecological amplitude of phenotypic resilience. The practice of managing fragile botanical resources will be no less intense however and managers of primitive natural environments will, therefore, be required to undertake investigations of comparative plant fragilities as they occur in the ecosystems of concern. Most fragility-rating schemes are landscape sensitivity evaluations and will reflect the impact susceptibility of both vegetation and soils. Scotter and several co-authors (see Knapik & Coen, 1974; Landals & Scotter, 1974; Campbell & Scotter, 1975; Douglas et al., 1975) have conducted extensive trampling research and presented various environmental fragility ratings. An *environmental fragility* is defined as a classification of plant communities and soils according to their predicted response to anthropogenic use. Response is evaluated by the estimated amount of potential change in the natural ecosystem. The relative suscepti-bility of vegetation types to damage is gauged by considering the loss of plant cover when subjected to trampling, the expected rate of regeneration provided there is no soil erosion, and the likelihood of changes in species composition. For the alpine and subalpine communities examined, eight classes of plant community fragility were presented. Extremely fragile classes would have about 90% of vegetation cover destroyed by moderate trampling (100 walks), little chance for recovery of dominant vegetation from season to season, and the likelihood of a major change in species com-position. At the other end, slightly susceptible vegetation would have less than 25% loss of vegetative cover by moderate trampling, and would ex-perience high recovery of vegetation with little species change from season to season. The practice of managing fragile vegetative resources for mini-mum impairment under the influence of low-intensity recreation would benefit greatly with expanded research on the biological carrying capacity of wildland floral resources.

C. Surface and Ground Water Hydrology

Most wildland areas represent a source of fresh water for man through-out the world. Land use planning must incorporate considerations for pro-tecting and maintaining the quality and quantity of water yield. Facility construction which has not accounted for water resources frequently leads to erosion, public hazards, and unnecessary environmental impact. While low-intensity recreation has considerably less potential for major watershed impact than urban, agricultural, or timber harvest industries, there are special considerations for sewage disposal, stream, crossings and lakesides.

Pit privies and septic tank disposal fields must be located in areas where the water table is adequately deep to preclude possible ground water contamination. A seasonal water table no closer than 75 cm to the bottom of the drainfield is desirable. Although local regulations will vary, it is good practice to locate septic absorption systems at least 30 m away from any water bodies. Subterranean leaching through porous soil layers could create a public health hazard if water which might be used for consumption be-came contaminated. Aquifer recharge areas should be avoided and special designs may be required for locations with ground slope exceeding 10%. Percolation tests using local health codes can provide good indications as to expected performance of septic systems.

Stream crossings frequently become the sites of serious trail deteriora-tion and undesirable environmental impact. Without approach modifications, streambanks are broken down, mudholes are created, and general widening of the trail occurs. Erosion and downstream sedimenta-tion, particularly in fine-grained soil areas, causes undesirable impacts on aquatic life. At times of flood conditions, high water will back up along the trail, and serious erosion can occur if the trail should actually capture and become the flow channel. This situation occurs most often where the trail crosses a stream at an angle on sloping ground. It is important to ensure that unbridged stream crossings are approached at an angle pointing downstream, or at least perpendicular. Bridge structures must have adequate span and height so as not to obstruct the channel under normal peak runoff conditions.

Waterbodies are frequently the destinations of many wildland users. The impacts of human concentration around lakeshores is often visible in extensive littering, vegetation trampling, mucky trails, multiple fire-circles, and near-shore water pollution. It is desirable to keep campsites several hundred meters back from the shore of any lake. Horses must not be allowed to approach the water except on specifically designed trails. It is important to provide convenient and effective trails which allow for frequent direct views and access to the water in order to prevent widespread trampling.

D. Active Geomorphic Processes

Many wildland areas, because they are comprised of steep lands and water bodies, will have mass wasting and erosional forces, either active or latent. Lack of consideration of such processes can lead to expensive maintenance liabilities, or loss of facilities in the event of extreme failure.

Most landscapes will reveal indicators or potential slope instability in stabilized slump topography, deflected tree stems, and truncated soil profiles. Mass wasting may occur as surface soil erosion or as mass movement of soil which may be either dry or wet. Surface erosion will develop whereever water moves over an exposed mineral soil. The retention of ground vegetation and litter is critical to preventing surface soil erosion. High soil moisture content and steep slopes are typical of most mass soil movement. This process may occur quickly in a landslide or slump, or may be slow as a creep or mudflow. Dry flow will occur mainly as downslope creep of cohesionless particles. In all circumstances of potential mass wasting it is critical not to disturb the toe slopes of stabilized slide features. Vegetation removal or slope cuts must be done carefully in order to avoid concentration of either surface or subterranean water flow. Cut banks which are steepened beyond the natural angle of repose are subject to slumping and are particularly difficult to rehabilitate.

Both wind and water erosional forces can create dramatic changes, either by natural processes or by man-induced accidents. Vegetative cover resists erosion by wind and water. Any activities or land uses which could change wind patterns or reduce vegetative cover in high wind areas must be carefully considered. Similarly, rivers are constantly changing their fluvial morphology by downcutting or lateral meandering. Vegetation and soil is swept away as banks are undercut. Deposition of such materials downstream creates point bars, and silts in channels which are abandoned to ultimately revert to terrestrial environments. The location of any river-related facilities must be evaluated in terms of low and high flow characteristics in order to avoid damaged facilities or hydraulically induced environmental impacts.

E. Present or Potential Wildlife Resources

Habitat which is adequate in quality and quantity is critical to healthy wildlife productivity. Cover and nutritional requirements are basic to all animals, but, in order to survive and reproduce, each wildlife species requires specific conditions for feeding, breeding, rearing, resting, and refuge. The primary goal in preserving or expanding wildlife resources is the provision of adequate habitat. An understanding of each species' habitat requirements is therefore imperative to making management decisions. The kind, amount, and dispersion of plant cover and water are the main features which can be manipulated by man in order to influence wildlife populations. Changes in these critical elements will induce dramatic responses in the kinds and numbers of faunal species which can survive in the conditions created.

The opportunity to view or see signs of indigenous wildlife is an important motivation of many visitors to wildland areas. The actual sighting of a conspicuous wild animal is frequently the highlight of a back-country trip. It is likely, therefore, that most primitive areas which encourage low-intensity recreation will actively manage to preserve or enlarge wildlife resources. All areas which exist in a primitive natural state will contain some wildlife species which occupy a favourable niche, for example, pronghorn antelope on shrubby prairies and pine marten in dense, subalpine forests. Knowledge of the plant, water, and predator circumstances that act to maintain the existing population levels is required before any decisions regarding changed land use is contemplated. The pattern of use of its habitat by wildlife is very important information in deciding upon the location of facilities or sites of concentrated human activity.

Seemingly minor intrusions may be seriously upsetting to wildlife at certain times, particularly during the period of reproduction and rearing. Some species will abandon nests or young if human disturbance occurs. In other instances, defense reactions may provoke attack with serious consequences for the human intruder, such as sow grizzly or cow moose protective responses. Winter habitats are also places of critical importance to individual animals. Disturbances which create flight stress can have deleterious results for animals which may be experiencing a net negative energy balance. The location and time of use of migration routes, display areas, mineral licks, stop-over and rest locations, or other locations which support site specific wildlife activities must be identified and avoided in the location or timing of human presence which might be disturbing.

Many species of animals utilize the ecotone or transitional edge between two different plant communities, particularly the interface between forest and open lands. The location of facilities such as trails or campsites in such environments therefore poses the potential of alienation of preferred habitat. It is much more desirable to locate human activity in areas which permit the possibility of viewing animals from a distance without actually disturbing them.

F. Climate and Microclimate

For many people, the success or failure of a primitive area expedition is determined by the climatic conditions. While there is essentially nothing the primitive area managers can do to change climate, there are many considerations in accounting for it. Sun and shade patterns are important to the comfortability of campgrounds, and their location will depend on whether warming or cooling is desired. As a general guideline, it is desirable to locate campgrounds to be exposed to early morning sun but to be shaded during midday. Campgrounds or trails which may have restricted drainage problems should have maximum exposure to hasten drying. Campgrounds should not be located in depressions where cold air sinks will exist at night. Wind exposure will involve considerations of smoke and insect dispersal vs. its convective nuisance.

Snowmobile and cross-country ski trails must be located to avoid areas which bare prematurely due to wind or sun exposure. The snow pack must be of adequate depth to prevent undesirable damage to ground cover or equipment. Areas of frequent but light snowfall are best. Exposure to high winds and shaded locations where prolonged cold temperatures are encountered are undesirable.

G. Landscape Characteristics

Topographic variability includes the considerations of slope, aspect, and landscape position. These landscape characteristics are of significant concern to the difficulty of constructing and maintaining facilities, as well as predicting the potential success or failure in performance. The extent of environmental impact is also intricately related to topographic form.

Steepness of slope is a major factor in determining human accessibility and ease of movement in any primitive area. As a general rule, the slope of the trail tread should not exceed 10%, as prolonged steeper sections are excessively fatiguing for both humans and horses. Erosion control also becomes difficult. Trails which are contoured on steep sideslopes will require cutting and filling in order to obtain a level tread. Only slight difficulty will be encountered on sideslopes up to 15% but serious difficulties are encountered on sideslopes which exceed 30% (Knapik & Coen, 1974). Campsites and picnic sites can be located on slopes up to 9% with only slight limitations, but serious constraints are posed by slopes in excess of 15%. Horse corrals and holding areas should be located on level ground or severe soil displacement will occur from the higher to the lower side of the site. Sewage systems, either pit privies or septic disposal fields, must not be located on grades which exceed 15%, as downslope surfacing of effluents may occur. Only slight limitations are presented by inclined landscape measuring less than 9%.

Aspect has substantial influence on the microclimate of any site. In the northern hemisphere, southerly exposed sites will generally be warmer and drier than north-aspect locations at similar altitude and latitude. The practical implications of this situation are important to snow retention and drying conditions in campsites or on trails. Because northern exposures receive less direct solar radiation, they will be cooler and damper. This difference is dramatically expessed in ecological variability. North-facing slopes develop markedly different plant communities, both in species composition and stand density. Soils on south-facing slopes frequently have shallower litter layers in partial reflection of more rapid decomposition processes. The microclimate and edaphic responses to aspect are of considerable consequence to rehabilitation undertakings.

Landscape position refers to the locational vulnerability to other natural forces such as overflow flooding, tidal flooding, high wind, lightning, snow avalanching, rockfall, or other locally unique phenomena, such as tree windthrow. In addition to posing possible visitor safety hazards, facilities located in the path of infrequent but predictable natural events will be rendered temporarily unuseable, if not damaged. There will be few primitive areas which are not characterized by some sort of powerful and potentially dangerous natural phenomenon. It is incumbent on the planners and managers to identify the nature of such events and undertake only those activities which do not unduly expose facilities or imperil visitors.

H. Natural Attractions

Scenic beauty and unique spectacular assets are some of the outstanding reasons for preserving primitive areas, for example, Yellowstone National Park and Old Faithful geyser. The location of facilities such as trails should include the provision of scenic vistas and viewing points. Impromptu trails with undesirable environmental impact often develop where built facilities do not lead people to where they desire to go. Similarly, concentration at interest sites causes widespread trampling and deterioration of the landscape immediately surrounding the highlight. Frequently the feature is very fragile, such as Rabbit Kettle Hot Spring in Nahanni National Park, or potentially dangerous such as Geyser Basin in Yellowstone National Park. Special efforts to protect the natural asset and visitors from each other are mandatory. Managers and planners are required to be particularly imaginative and perceptive of human behavior in order to design successful self-controlling facilities.

The viewing of pleasing aesthetic natural scenes unimpaired by evidence of man-made artifacts is an important objective of both visitors to and managers of wildland areas. Poorly located trails, campsites, and viewpoints will present discordant impressions when seen from other locations. It is required, therefore, to evaluate not only the visual resource potential from a proposed facility but also the visual effect the facility itself constitutes when seen from other positions. In all primitive area undertakings, the hand of man must appear to lie lightly on the land.

V. THE NATURE OF ENVIRONMENTAL IMPACT

Research dating back to 1929 (Meinecke) demonstrates that recreational activity can and does cause significant ecological change. The spatial extent and degree to which change occurs is dependent on the relative fragility of the environment, and the intensity and timing of the impact. Human actions which are responsible for the changes include trampling of soils and vegetation by feet and machines, using tents, collecting specimens, interacting with animals, polluting, and starting fires. A visitor returning to a favorite outdoor spot after an absence of several years is frequently dismayed at the degrading changes which have taken place. Popular literature might state that the area has reached or perhaps exceeded its carrying capacity. In an attempt to quantify physical recreational carrying capacity, research has produced a substantial amount of documentation of the process of environmental impact.

The impacts on vegetation are the first occurring and perhaps most striking to both the recreationist and researcher. The initial effects are seen in the physical bruising and crushing of ground cover plants, with moist, herbaceous species being affected first. Continued trampling leads to reduced species diversity and increased exposure of bare ground. Grass and hardy invaders such as dandelion often assume a larger percentage of plant cover. The effects on large trees are variable, but the most serious damage, which in some cases results in mortality, appears to occur as a result of actual vandalism to the tree. Vegetation impact resulting from trampling occurs quickly (Bell & Bliss, 1973) and can be expected to take a long time to recover without extensive management intervention (Herrington & Beardsley, 1970; Scotter, 1976).

Trampling compacts soils and increases the bulk density (Dotzenko et al., 1967). Compacted soils have decreased infiltration, and therefore the increased runoff poses potential erosion problems. Decreased pore space and lowered soil moisture content in surface soils constitutes an inhospitable growing medium for successful establishment of germinating seedlings. Soil structure is broken down in the surface layers with attendant creation of dust problems under dry conditions and puddling under wet circumstances.

Some research reveals that site-specific impact occurs quickly in the first several years of use, and then tends to level off (Merriam & Smith, 1974). In view of the comparatively long period required for natural recovery, campground rotation practices are only marginally beneficial and perhaps serve only to introduce impact to previously undisturbed locations. Sites with an open understory are highly subject to expansion.

Research has shown that numerous combinations of management intervention can be beneficial in combating environmental impacts at campsites (Beardsley & Herrington, 1971; Beardsley & Wagar, 1971). Cultural treatments such as seeding, fertilizing, and watering are effective in reclaiming and maintaining vegetative cover in trampled areas. However, the remoteness of most primitive area campsites usually precludes the practical or financial feasibility of such undertakings. The most productive technique in minimizing environmental impact in wildland campsites undoubtedly lies in careful facility location and good site design which incorporates hardened routes and activity areas.

Each campfire which burns on the soil surface creates dramatic local chemical and biological impacts which often have long-lasting effects. In campgrounds where unregulated fire use is permitted, damaging and unsightly proliferation of fire circles inevitably occurs. It is imperative, therefore, to designate fire sites, and ensure that any fireboxes provided are effective for the intended purposes.

Trail conditions are often the most obvious of deteriorated facilities in backcountry areas. Trails can become entrenched and eroded, muddy and potholed, or rocky and obstructed by exposed roots or fallen trees. Under such conditions, hikers, horses, and other travellers will commonly seek an easier route with the ultimate result being a corridor of multiple, parallel trails. Helgath (1975) concluded that vegetative habitat, landform, and trail slope were importantly related to trail erosion. Aspect, elevation, use, and parent material had variable relationships. All trail impact research concludes that serious trail problems can be expected where poor drainage conditions are encountered.

The effects of human presence on wildlife in primitive areas have been less intensively studied than have soils and vegetation. The presence of humans and particularly noisy machines induces behavioural changes in nearly all animals. Some animals such as black bears, racoons, and deer can become addicted to human garbage and handouts. While amusing to visitors, managers must contend with the public safety hazards and the ultimate unhealthy consequences to the animals involved. Other species such as wolves and grizzly bears display extraordinary stress to the presence of man in their territory and population dynamics are likely negatively affected. The potential for most serious human influences on wildlife populations occurs during breeding and rearing activities or when animals are occupying winter habitats.

Much of the concern for the obvious deterioration of natural environments as the result of recreational activity has caused vigorous research towards identifying the carrying capacity of wildland environments. Practical utility of the concept has proven to be much more elusive and complex than the comparative application of carrying capacity techniques in agricultural management. The great difficulty in formulating a carrying capacity lies in identifying the limits of acceptable environmental change. Furthermore, a disparity may exist between what a manager considers tolerable and what a visitor considers unacceptable (Hendee & Pyle, 1971). As Frissel and Stankey (1972) point out, "the soil compaction and dying vegetation that accompanies excessive use of a site is of significance not only to the ecologist, but also to the social scientist, for the perception of declining aesthetic quality might well be a more important constraint than reduced soil pore space."

VI. OTHER PRIMITIVE AREA RECREATION CONSIDERATIONS

Primitive area management mandates will range from the maximum environmental protection objectives of wilderness preserves to encouragement of recreation in backcountry settings. Regardless, planners and managers are faced with the often mutually exclusive objectives of resource preservation vs. providing for human use. Recreational use of any natural setting will constitute a force of modification. It is imperative, however, that these influences are to be minimized and the practical guidelines are to encourage only those activities which will leave man's imprint substantially unnoticeable. In attempting to determine the tolerable limits of environmental change, the psychological perception of desirable and acceptable natural environment conditions is as important as biological carrying capacity considerations.

Social carrying capacity may be more difficult to describe or incorporate into management strategies than biological concerns. Visitor satisfaction and behaviour patterns are greatly influenced by attitudes, values, and motivations. The response to the environment encountered is formulated by the unavoidable mental process of comparing perceptions to expectations. A complete range of possible visitor reactions is therefore likely. In general, however, visitors to primitive areas are seeking solitude, and over crowding at campsites is a source of particular dissatisfaction (Lucas & Stankey, 1973). Most primitive area recreationists prefer a minimum of facilities. The major user conflicts are directed towards large group camps, large horse parties, and especially mechanized recreationists. Canoeists' resent motorboats and snowmobiles displease cross-country skiers. It is crucial therefore to ensure that land use plans do not create recreational use conflicts or preclude satisfying experiences for a majority of the area's visitors.

Currently, there is considerable variability in the techniques used by various management agencies in controlling the numbers and activities of primitive area visitors (Merriam & Knopp, 1976). Furthermore, intensive debate as to acceptable and democratic means to achieve desirable and equitable results prevails (Hendee & Lucas, 1973; Behan, 1974). In view of the variability of geography, and financial and manpower resources, there is not likely any rationing system which is universally superior. It is incumbent, therefore, on each agency to formulate a program which best achieves the intent of their responsibilities and the visitors' legitimate objectives.

LITERATURE CITED

Beardsley, W. G., and R. B. Herrington. 1971. Economics and management implications of campground irrigation—a case study. Intermt For. and Range Exp. Stn., Ogden, Utah. USDA For Ser. Res. Note INT-129. 8 p.

Beardsley, W. G., and J. A. Wagar. 1971. Vegetation management on a forested recreation site. J. For. 69:728–731.

Behan, R. W. 1974. Police State Wilderness: A comment on mandatory wilderness permits. J. For. 72:98–99.

Bell, K. L., and L. C. Bliss. 1973. Alpine disturbance studies: Olympic National Park, U.S.A. Biol. Conserv. 5:25–32.

Buckman, H. O., and N. C. Brady. 1975. The nature and properties of soils. 8th Ed. The Macmillan Co., New York.

Campbell, S. E., and G. W. Scotter. 1975. Subalpine revegetation and disturbance studies, Mount Revelstoke National Park. Canadian Wildl. Serv. Rep., Edmonton. 99 p.

Canada Soil Survey Committee. 1974. The system of soil classification for Canada. Queen's Printer for Canada, Ottawa.

Cieslinski, T. J., and J. A. Wagar. 1970. Predicting the durability of forest recreation sites in northern Utah—preliminary results. Intermt. For. and Range Exp. Stn., Ogden, Utah. USDA For. Serv. Res. Note INT-117. 7 p.

Dale, D., and T. Weaver. 1974. Trampling effects on vegetation of the trail corridors of north Rocky Mountain Forests. J. Appl. Ecol. 11:767–772.

Dotzenko, A. D., N. T. Papamichos, and D. S. Romine. 1967. Effect of recreational use on soil and moisture conditions in Rocky Mountain National Park. J. Soil Water Conserv. 22(5):196–197.

Douglas, G. W., J. A. S. Nagy, and G. W. Scotter. 1975. Effects of human and horse trampling on natural vegetation, Waterton Lakes National Park. Canadian Wildl. Serv. Rep., Edmonton. 129 p.

Frissel, S. S., Jr., and G. H. Stankey. 1972. Wilderness environmental quality: search for social and ecological harmony. For. Sci. Lab., Missoula, Mont.

Harvey, H. T., R. J. Hartesveldt, and J. T. Stanley. 1972. Wilderness impact study report. California State Univ., San Jose.

Helgath, S. F. 1975. Trail deterioration in the Selway—Bitterroot Wilderness. Intermt. For. and Range Exp. Stn., Ogden, Utah. USDA For. Serv. Res. Note INT-193. 15 p.

Hendee, J. C., and R. M. Pyle. 1971. Wilderness managers, wilderness users: a problem of perception. Naturalist 22(3):22–26.

Hendee, J. C., and R. C. Lucas. 1973. Mandatory wilderness permits: a necessary management tool. J. For. 71:206–209.

Herrington, R. B., and W. G. Beardsley. 1970. Improvement and maintenance of campground vegetation in central Idaho. Intermt. For. and Range Exp. Stn., Ogden, Utah. USDA For. Ser. Res. Pap. INT-87. 9 p.

Knapik, L., and G. M. Coen. 1974. Detailed soil survey of the Mount Revelstoke Summit area. Alberta Inst. of Pedology no. M-74-3, Edmonton.

Landals, M., and G. W. Scotter. 1974. An ecological assessment of the Summit area, Mount Revelstoke National Park, Canadian Wildl. Serv. Rep., Edmonton. 197 p.

Lucas, R. C., and G. H. Stankey. 1973. Social carrying capacity for backcountry recreation. Outdoor recreation research: applying the results. USDA For. Serv. Tech. Rep. NC-9:14–23.

Meinecke, D. P. 1929. A report upon the effect of excessive tourist travel on the California Redwood Parks. California State Print. Off., Sacramento. 20 p.

Merriam, L. C., Jr., and C. K. Smith. 1974. Visitor impact on newly developed campsites in the Boundary Water Canoe Area. J. For. 72:627–630.

Merriam, L. C., and T. B. Knopp. 1976. Meeting the wilderness needs of the many. West. Wildlands 3(2):17–22.

Plantenberg, P. L., C. Montagne, and G. A. Nielsen. 1974. Natural resource inventory checklist. Capsule Inf. Ser. no. 2. Montana Agric. Exp. Stn., Bozeman, Mont.

Scotter, G. W. 1976. Recovery of subalpine meadows under protection after damage by human activities, Yoho National Park. Canadian Wildl. Serv. Rep., Edmonton. 22 p.

Willard, B. E., and J. W. Marr. 1970. Effects of human activities on alpine tundra ecosystems in Rocky Mountain National Park, Colorado. Biol. Conserv. 5:257–265.

section VI

Planning Metropolitan Land Uses

USDA Soil Conservation Service

VI

19 Planning Metropolitan Land Uses in Relation to Natural Landscape Features

KURT W. BAUER

Southeastern Wisconsin Regional Planning Commission
Waukesha, Wisconsin

I. INTRODUCTION

Historically, metropolitan development patterns in the United States have been determined largely by the operation of the urban land market and such minimal constraints as may have been placed on the operation of that market by the planning decisions of the individual local units of government comprising the metropolitan area. Growing dissatisfaction with the environmental and developmental problems created by the results of this historic approach to metropolitan development has led to a growing awareness of the need to shape metropolitan development patterns in the public interest through comprehensive, areawide planning. Such planning has accordingly become increasingly accepted as a necessary governmental function in most of the large urban regions of the United States. This acceptance has come about, in part, through federal insistence and, in part, through recognition at the local level that certain pressing problems of physical and economic development and of environmental deterioration do, in fact, transcend municipal corporate limit lines and require for sound resolution the cooperative efforts of all of the levels, units, and agencies of government concerned.

Such planning must recognize the existence of a limited natural resource base to which both rural and urban development must be properly adjusted in order to ensure a pleasant and habitable environment for life. Land and water resources are limited and subject to grave misuse through improper land use and supporting public works development, misuse which may not only needlessly increase the cost of such development but which may have severe adverse environmental impacts. In such a metropolitan planning effort, then, the selection of desirable areawide development plans from among the practical alternatives available must be based, in part, upon a careful assessment of the effects of each particular alternative plan on the underlying and supporting natural resource base. Such emphasis on the natural resource base is essential if better metropolitan development patterns are to be evolved and irreparable damage to limited and increasingly precious land and water resources avoided.

Although metropolitan planning should be comprehensive, addressing many functional areas, including transportation, sewerage, and water supply, its most basic concern must be with land use. The amount and spatial distribution of the land devoted to the various physical, social, and economic activities of man are among the most important determinants of the overall quality of life. Land use affects the levels of noise, air, and water pollution; determines the nature of drainage, flood control, and water supply problems; affects the level of traffic congestion and the time and distances involved in commuting between home and work, and the need for, and cost of, goods movement; determines the convenience of shopping and the accessibility of educational and recreational opportunities; affects the cost of providing essential public facilities and services and determines whether some services, such as mass transit and sanitary sewerage, can be provided at all; determines the cost and feasibility of the production of food and fiber; and establishes the degree of protection which is afforded the underlying and sustaining natural resource base.

The approach to land use planning at the metropolitan scale should be "organic"; that is, areawide land use plans should seek to adjust land use development to natural patterns in the landscape rather than seek the imposition of an artificial design for development upon the landscape. Such organic planning, however, requires the collection and analysis of a great deal of information about the natural resource base and its ability to sustain development. Such information must include definitive data on the climate, physiography, geology, soils, mineral resources, surface water resources and associated shorelands and floodlands, ground water resources and associated recharge and discharge areas, woodlands, wetlands, fish and wildlife habitat areas, and areas having scenic, historic, scientific, and recreational value. Such definitive data on the natural resource base must be in a form readily relatable to similar data on the cultural base of the planning area; that is, data on the demography and economy, on existing land use patterns, on existing travel patterns, and on the transportation and utility networks which interconnect and serve the various land use activities.

Space limitations preclude discussion here of the application of all of the various types of natural resource related data required for sound metropolitan development planning. The application of soils data to metropolitan land use planning, however, provides a particularly good example of the approach required and will, therefore, be utilized herein as such an example. It is important to note, however, that soils are only one of the factors to be considered in metropolitan land use planning and that the selection of soils data as an example herein is not intended to imply that the other kinds of natural resource base related data—or, for that matter, cultural data—are not important. Indeed, such data must be given the same careful consideration as the soils data in the areawide land use planning process.

II. IMPORTANCE OF SOILS IN METROPOLITAN LAND USE PLANNING

The soils of an area are one of the most important elements of the natural resource base, influencing both urban and rural development. The soil resource has been subject to grave abuse and misuse through improper land use development. Serious health, safety, and pollution problems have been created by failure to properly consider the capabilities and limitations of soils during the planning and design stages of both rural and urban development projects. Such problems are usually very costly to correct and may create personal hardships out of all proportion to the relatively simple steps required to avoid them. Such problems include malfunctioning septic tank sewage disposal systems, surface and ground water pollution, flood damages, footing and foundation failures, soil erosion, and stream and lake sedimentation.

Knowledge of the soil resource and its ability to sustain development can not only help to avoid such problems but can also contribute to reducing development costs. Such practices as the placement of streets and highways on unstable soils, excavation of basements and utility trenches in shallow bedrock areas, the development of industrial and commercial sites on steep slopes, and the construction of underground utilities in high ground water areas all result in additional site preparation and construction costs in order to overcome the limitations of the soils for the desired uses. Such increased costs may include the cost attendant to the removal of poor soils and their replacement with stable materials, blasting of rock, extensive grading and terracing, and the use of tight sheathing and dewatering systems to control ground water seepage. Failure to recognize soil limitations in the planning and design stages of development projects may also result in greatly increased maintenance and operating costs and the creation of slum and blighted areas.

To help avoid further abuse and misuse of this important element of the natural resource base, a need exists in any metropolitan land use planning program to examine not only how land and soils are presently used but how they can best be used and managed. This requires definitive data about the geographic location of the various kinds of soils; about the physical, chemical, and biological properties of these soils; and about the capability of these soils to support various kinds of rural and urban land uses.

For land use planning application, the inventory required to provide the necessary soils data should be designed to permit preliminary assessment on a uniform areawide basis of:

1) The engineering properties of soils as an aid in the consideration of desirable spatial distribution patterns for residential, commercial, industrial, agricultural, and recreational land use development. This

requires knowledge of the suitability and limitations of soils for specific applications, such as private on-site sewage disposal facilities, agricultural and urban drainage systems, foundations for buildings and structures, and water storage reservoirs and embankments as an aid in the planning and design of specific development proposals and in the application of such land use plan implementation devices as zoning, subdivision control, and official mapping ordinances.

2) The biological properties of soils, including both agricultural and nonagricultural soil-plant relationships and natural wildlife relationships, as an aid in the consideration of desirable spatial distribution patterns for permanent agricultural and recreational greenbelts and open spaces.

3) The location of potential sources of sand, gravel, and other soil-related mineral resources.

Such a uniform areawide assessment of soil capabilities is intended to provide the means of predicting the suitability of land areas for various kinds of land use and supporting public works facilities development and thereby to permit the preparation of plans which seek to adjust the metropolitan land use pattern broadly considered to one important element of the natural resource base.

III. DETAILED SOIL SURVEYS

Standard soil surveys, such as those conducted by the U.S. Soil Conservation Service, if accompanied by appropriate interpretations, can be adapted to meet the basic soils data needs of a metropolitan land use planning program. These surveys are made by carefully examining the soil in its natural state and delineating areas of similar soils on aerial photographs. The areas so mapped are keyed to a national classification system and thereby identified as belonging to a given series of, within defined limits, similar physical, chemical, and biological properties, these properties being determined by field and laboratory tests. The use of a national classification system makes it possible to predict the behavior of the mapped soils, based upon actual past experience with similar soils, under any various land uses.

The standard soil surveys have certain limitations, particularly with respect to depth surveyed and with respect to the possible inclusion of soils with slightly different properties within mapped areas because of map scale and field survey technique limitations. Nevertheless, these surveys represent the best available source of soils information for areawide planning. These surveys are carried out by experienced soil scientists and constitute a valuable basic scientific inventory which, if accompanied by the necessary interpretations, has multiple planning and engineering applications.

Ideally, the soils should be mapped on ratioed and rectified vertical aerial photographs at a scale which matches the scale of the basic planning base maps to be utilized in the areawide planning work. The finished photos should show the areas covered by the various soil type as delineated in the field surveys, together with an appropriate identification symbol. Key planimetric features, such as highways, railroads, streams, lakes, cemeteries, and major structures, should be identified on the finished photos as should the location of the U.S. Public Land Survey township range and section lines. Such a finished soils photo map is shown on Fig. 1. It should be noted that these suggested mapping procedures represent some departure from standard U.S. Soil Conservation Service practices. The U.S. Soil Conservation Service, however, has been willing to adapt its standard procedures in order to provide soils data in a form more readily usable in comprehensive areawide planning.

IV. SOILS DATA INTERPRETATIONS

The soil photomaps must be accompanied by the information necessary to utilize the soil survey data in plan preparation and implementation. This information should include not only definitive data on the properties of each soil type mapped but interpretations of these properties for planning and engineering purposes. Thus, each soil type mapped within the planning area should be rated in terms of the inherent limitations for specific land use planning and engineering applications. The information should identify pertinent properties of each soil relating to:

1) Potential agricultural use, including soil capabilities for common cultivated crops, crop yield estimates, woodland suitability groups, and crop adaptation.
2) Wildlife-soil relationships, including capability of the different kinds of soil to sustain various food plants and cover for birds and animals common to the planning area.
3) Nonfarm plant material-soil relationships, including suitability of different kinds of soil for lawns, golf courses, playgrounds, parks, and open space reservations.
4) Soil-water relationships by kinds of soil, including identification of areas subject to flooding, stream overflow, ponding, seasonally high water table, and concentrated runoff.
5) Soil properties influencing engineering uses, including depth to major soil horizons important in construction of engineering works, liquid limit, plastic limit, plasticity index, maximum dry density, optimum moisture content, mechanical analysis, American Association of State Highway Officials and the Unified System classifications, percolation rate, bearing strength, shrink-swell ratio, pH, depth to water table, and estimated depth to bedrock if within approximately 6 m (20 feet) of the ground surface.

An example of the type of information about pertinent soil properties required is shown in Table 1.

The information on pertinent soil properties must be identified by interpretations of these properties as exhibited by each soil type mapped for

Table 1—Selected measured and estimated chemical and physical properties of soils of southeastern Wisconsin.

Soil type† and number	Soil horizon Symbol Symbol	Depth (inch)	Classification USDA texture	Unified	AASHO	Mechanical analysis, percent passing sieve‡ No. 10, 2.0 mm	No. 200, 0.07 mm	Maximum dry density (pound/cubic feet)	Optimum moisture content	Permeability (inch/hour)
Bono silty clay loam 217										
	A	0–12	Silty clay loam	MH	A-7	100	100	107	18	0.2 –0.8
	B	12–36	Silty clay	CH	A-7	95	95			0.2 –0.8
	C	36+	Silty clay	CH	A-7	95	95	109	18	0.05–0.2
Morley silt loam 297										
	A	0–12	Silt loam	ML	A-4	100	85	98	25	0.8 –2.5
	B	12–36	Silty clay	CH	A-7	100	95			0.2 –0.8
	C	36+	Silty clay loam	CL	A-6	100	90	120	14	0.2 –0.8
Blount silt loam 299										
	A	0–10	Silt loam	ML	A-4	100	85	98	25	0.8 –2.5
	B	10–36	Silty clay	CH	A-7	100	100			0.2 –0.8
	C	36+	Silty clay loam	CL	A-6	100	95	120	14	0.2 –0.8

Soil type† and number	Soil horizon Symbol	Depth (inch)	Percolation rate (minute/inch)	Liquid limit	Plasticity index	Shrink-swell potential	Bearing strength	Reaction (pH)	Depth to water table (feet)	Susceptibility to erosion
Bono silty clay loam 217										
	A	0–12	120–300	55	30	High	Poor-low bearing capacity	6.6–7.3	Seasonal	A-Slight
	B	12–36	120–300			High		6.6–8.5		
	C	36+	300+	38	22	High		7.4–8.5	0–1	
Morley silt loam 297										
	A	0–12	31– 60	56	32	Low-moderate	Poor-low bearing capacity when wet	5.6–7.0	3–5	A-Slight
	B	12–36	61–120			High		5.6–7.0	5	BMCN-Moderate
	C	36+	61–120	27	12	Moderate		7.4–8.5		DKEF-Severe
Blount silt loam 299										
	A	0–10	31– 60	56	32	Low-moderate	Poor-low bearing capacity when wet	5.6–7.3	0–2	A-Slight
	B	10–36	61–120			High		5.6–7.3		B-Moderate
	C	36+	61–120	27	12	Moderate		7.4–8.5	3–5	

† All three soils are moderately susceptible to frost action, have low bearing strength, and a depth of more than 5 feet to bedrock. Variations in these properties would be shown in additional columns of the table.
‡ 100% of all samples passed no. 4 sieve (4.70 mm).

planning purposes. These interpretations should include:

1) Suitability ratings for potential intensive residential, extensive residential, commercial, industrial, transportational, natural and developed recreational, and agricultural land uses.
2) Suitability ratings for septic tank disposal field, low building foundations, trafficability, surface stabilization, and road and railway subgrade and earthwork uses.
3) Suitability ratings for use as a source material for road base, backfill, sand or gravel, topsoil, and water reservoir embankments and linings.
4) Rating with respect to flooding potential, watershed characteristics, susceptibility to erosion, and susceptibility to frost action.
5) Suitability for wildlife habitat and habitat improvement, lawns, golf courses, playgrounds, and parks and related open areas requiring the maintenance of vegetation.

An example of the kinds of interpretive ratings required are set forth in Tables 2, 3, 4, and 5. The interpretive data, as shown in the tables, should be accompanied by a text clearly identifying the basis for the suitability ratings, including the pertinent properties and design and development considerations involved.

V. GRAPHIC DATA REDUCTION AND DISPLAY

In the application of soil data, or other natural resource base-related data, the planner is concerned not only with the properties of the various soils, and the interpretation of these properties in terms of suitability for various land use and supporting public works facility applications, but also with the spatial distribution of the various soils, the areal extent covered by those soils, and their location with respect to other factors influencing regional development, such as existing land uses, transportation service areas and related accessibility patterns, and public utility service areas. Moreover, the necessary soils information may be used either graphically as, for example, to show how soils having various properties are distributed relative to one another, to other elements of the natural resource base, and to elements of the cultural base; or quantitatively as, for example, to determine the total area covered by soils having certain selected properties. Therefore, the soils data resulting from the soil surveys must be further adapted for use in comprehensive areawide planning. This requires the appropriate transformation of the soil maps and attendant interpretive data into the two forms in which it is actually used in the planning operations: graphic and numeric.

In order to permit the efficient application of the soils data in graphic form, a series of interpretive soils maps should be prepared at a scale which matches the scale of the planning base maps to be used. For metropolitan

Table 2—Suitability rating† of soils of southeastern Wisconsin for rural and urban land use development.

| Soil type and number | For agricultural use | Residential development | | | Commercial and industrial development | Transportation systems |
| | | With public sewer | Without public sewer | | | |
			Less than 1 acre	1 acre or more		
76 Will loam	Fair Good when drained (poor for trees)	Poor	Very poor	Very poor	Good when drained	Poor
217 Bono silty clay loam	Good when drained (poor for trees)	Very poor	Very poor	Very poor	Poor	Poor
297 Morley silt loam	Good on 0–6% slope Fair on 7–12% slope (fair for trees)	Good	Questionable	Poor	Fair on 0–6% slopes Poor on slopes over 6%	Poor
298 Ashkum silty clay loam	Good for crops when drained Good for pasture (poor for trees)	Very poor	Very poor	Very poor	Poor	Poor
299 Blount silt loam	Good for crops when drained Good for pasture (fair for trees)	Fair	Very poor	Questionable	Poor	Poor
398 Ashkum silt loam	Good for crops when drained Good for pasture (poor for trees)	Poor	Very poor	Very poor	Poor	Poor

† Suitability rates apply to entire soil profile and its position in the landscape.

Table 3—Suitability ratings and limitations of soils of southeastern Wisconsin for specific engineering purposes.

Soil type and number	Limitations for		Suitability as a source of		Corrosion potential	
	Road subgrade	Foundation for low buildings	Topsoil	Sand and gravel	Metal	Concrete
217 Bono silty clay	Very poor	Very poor	Good-surface Very poor-subsoil	Very poor	Very high	Low
297 Morley silt loam	Poor	Fair	Good-surface Poor-subsoil	Very poor	Moderate	Low
299 Blount silt loam	Very poor	Poor	Good-surface Poor-subsoil	Very poor	Very high	Low

land use planning purposes, this scale should not be smaller than 1:24,000. Interpretive maps should be prepared for at least seven kinds of potential land uses: i) agricultural; ii) large lot residential without public sanitary sewer service; iii) small lot residential without public sanitary sewer service; iv) residential with public sanitary sewer service; v) industrial; vi) transportation route location; and vii) intensely developed recreational. Each interpretive map should show the soil limitation ratings developed as an integral part of the detailed soil survey; namely, very slight, slight, moderate, severe, severe to very severe, and very severe. These terms are defined as follows:

1) Very slight: little or no soil limitations, very good suitability for use.
2) Slight: slight soil limitations, easy to overcome during development, good suitability.
3) Moderate: moderate soil limitations can be overcome with careful design and good management, fair suitability.
4) Severe: severe soil limitations, difficult to overcome during development, poor suitability.
5) Severe to very severe: very severe soil limitations, very difficult to overcome, require detailed on-site investigations, questionable suitability.
6) Very severe: very severe soil limitations that lead to serious construction and maintenance problems, very poor suitability for use.

Desirably, the interpretive maps are color coded using a "stop-go" legend. Figures 2 through 5 illustrate such color coded interpretive maps prepared for the soil photo map shown in Fig. 1.

Additional interpretive maps may be prepared as required and permitted by the interpretive data accompanying the soil photo maps. For example, slope maps may be readily prepared from the soils data using the following slope ranges significant for planning and engineering purposes: 0 through 1%, over 1 through 5%, over 5 through 8%, over 8 through 11%, over 11 through 14%, over 14 through 19%, over 19 through 29%, and over 29%. Other types of additional interpretive maps will suggest themselves as the areawide planning work progresses to more and more definitive phases and may extend to include special interpretive maps for the location of such

Table 4— Suitability rating† of soils of southeastern Wisconsin for recreational development.

Soil type and number	Playgrounds, parks, and picnic areas	Bridle paths and nature and hiking trails	Golf courses	Cottages and utility buildings	Camp sites	Remarks
76 Will loam	Poor	Poor	Poor	Very poor	Very poor	Suited to wildlife and ponds; High water table
217 Bono silt clay loam	Poor	Poor	Poor	Very poor	Very poor	Suited to wildlife and ponds
297 Morley silt loam	Good on 0–2% slopes; Fair on 3–6% slopes	Good on 0–12% slopes; Fair on slopes over 12%	Good on 0–6% slopes; Fair on 7–12% slopes	Poor	Good on 0–6% slopes; Fair on 7–12% slopes; Poor on slopes greater than 12%	
298 Ashkum silty clay loam	Poor	Poor	Very poor	Very poor	Very poor	Suited to wildlife and ponds
299 Blount silt loam	Fair	Fair	Fair	Poor	Poor	Seasonally high water table; Subject to ponding
398 Ashkum silt loam	Poor	Poor	Poor	Very poor	Very poor	High water table; Suited to wildlife and ponds

† Suitability rating applies to entire profile including subsoil and substratum; suitability rating for all other use considers entire soil profile.

Table 5—Suitability ratings, limitations, and selected properties of the soils of southeastern Wisconsin for watershed management purposes.

Available water capacity (inch/inch)	Flooding potential	Irrigation potential	Suitability for reservoir embankments and linings
0–10 −0.2	Subject to ponding	Poor	Good to fair impervious
10–36 −0.18			Medium to low stability
36+ −0.16			High volume change
0–10 −0.02	None	Fair-A,B, and M slope	Good to fair impervious
10–36 −0.18		Poor-C and N slope	Low stability
36+ −0.16		Very poor-D,E, and F slope	Large volume change
0–10 −0.2	Subject to occasional ponding or flooding	Fair at A and B slope	Good to fair impervious
10–36 −0.18			Low stability
36+ −0.16			Large volume change

special land uses as solid waste disposal facilities and sewage sludge disposal areas.

VI. QUANTIFICATION OF MAPPED DATA

In order to permit the efficient application of the soils data in numeric form, the soil mapping units should be measured within appropriate data reduction cells. In areas of the United States covered by the U.S. Public Land Survey system, the one-quarter section (65 ha, more or less) makes a particularly good cell for this purpose. The percentage and total areas of each of the various soil types within each quarter section should be measured, coded, and transferred to magnetic tape for machine processing, tabulation, and use in planning analyses and model application. The soil mapping units may be measured either by using random sampling techniques or preferably through the use of an interactive digitizer system. Once the basic data are on magnetic tape, the percentage and total areas of each of the various soil suitability groupings within the planning area and any subareas of the planning area, such as watersheds, planning analysis districts, or traffic analysis zones, can be readily determined by machine methods. Even more importantly, however, once the soils data are on magnetic tape, they can be readily correlated with other factors influencing areawide development, the data for which can also be stored on magnetic tape. This ability to correlate soils data with other essential planning data by machine methods is an extremely important and useful advantage.

VII. USE OF SOILS DATA IN METROPOLITAN LAND USE PLANNING

The process of plan design is essentially one of finding the least costly way to meet stated objectives. In any land use planning effort it is, therefore, necessary to link geographic location with development costs. In this way, alternative land use patterns can be explored, and the least costly alternative which meets the agreed-upon objectives adopted.

A. Formulation of Objectives and Standards

Detail soil surveys not only provide the means for relating development costs to geographic location, since development costs vary with soil type and since the soil types can be geographically mapped, but also provide an important basis for the formulation of sound regional land use development objectives and supporting standards. An example of the application of detail soils data to the formulation of regional land use development objectives and supporting standards and to the design of regional land use plans can be found in the work of the Southeastern Wisconsin Regional Planning Commission. The Commission defines objectives as ends toward the attainment of which plans and policies are directed. Each objective is supported by a set of standards which are defined as criteria used as a basis of comparison to determine the adequacy of plan proposals to attain the stated objectives.

One basic land use development objective and several supporting standards formulated and adopted by the Commission in its regional land use planning program relate directly to the application of soil surveys and attendant interpretive analyses. The basic objective calls for the protection, wise use, and sound development of the natural resource base of the Region. In addition to standards relating to that objective for inland lakes and streams, wetlands, woodlands, and wildlife, the following specific standards were developed based upon soil survey data and interpretive analyses:

1) Urban development, particularly for residential use, shall be located only in those areas which do not contain significant concentrations of soils rated in the regional detailed operational soil survey as having severe or very severe limitations for such development. Significant concentrations are defined as follows:

   a) In areas to be developed for low-density residential use, no more than 2.5% of the gross area should be covered by soils rated in the regional soil survey as having severe or very severe limitations for such development.

   b) In areas to be developed for medium-density residential use, no more than 3.5% of the gross area should be covered by soils rated in the regional soil survey as having severe or very severe limitations for such development.

   c) In areas to be developed for high-density residential use, no more than 5.0% of the gross area should be covered by soils rated in the regional soil survey as having severe or very severe limitations for such development.

   These standards are based upon development of neighborhood units utilizing conventional land subdivision design layouts, with lot sizes throughout the neighborhood unit uniformly approximating the average lot size required to meet the desired neighborhood population level and gross population density. If larger areas of a potential neighborhood unit than those specified above are covered by poor soils and are placed in open space use without varying the lot size and subdivision layout, the population level and gross population density of the neighborhood unit may be adversely affected, as may the quality of the urban services provided. If variations in the subdivision layout design and lot size are permitted, such as cluster subdivision, minimum population levels necessary to sustain a desirable level of urban services may be achieved in areas covered by much higher percentages of poor soils than recommended in the standards, up to 75% of low-density neighborhoods, up to 50% of medium-density neighborhoods, and up to 44% of high-density neighborhoods.

2) Land developed or proposed to be developed for urban uses without public sanitary sewer service should be located only in areas covered by soils rated in the regional soil survey as having moderate, slight, or very slight limitations for such development.

3) New industrial development should be concentrated in planned industrial districts in areas which contain soils rated in the regional soil survey as having only moderate, slight, or very slight limitations for such development.

4) New regional commercial development should be concentrated in planned regional commercial centers in areas which contain soils rated in the regional soil survey as having only moderate, slight, or very slight limitations for such development.

5) All prime agricultural areas, defined as those areas which contain soils rated in the regional soil survey as having only slight or very slight limitations for agricultural uses and which occur in concentrated areas over 13 km^2 (5 mile^2) in extent that have been designated as exceptionally good for agricultural production by agricultural specialists, should be preserved.

6) All agricultural lands surrounding adjacent high-value scientific, educational, or recreational resources and covered by soils rated in the regional soil survey as having moderate, slight, or very slight limitations for agricultural use should be preserved.

7) All agricultural areas which are covered by soils having moderate limitations for agricultural uses should be preserved in agricultural uses if these soils occur in concentrations greater than 13 km^2 (5 mile^2) and surround, or lie adjacent to, areas which qualify as prime agricultural areas or occur in areas which may be designated as desirable open spaces for shaping urban development.

8) A minimum of 50% of the area of all watersheds in agricultural use should be under conservation treatment which recognizes the soil limitations.

9) All urban residential development, except single-family residences

on lots of 2 ha (5 acres) or more in area and located on soils rated in the regional soil survey as suitable for the soil absorption method of sewage disposal, should be served by centralized public sanitary sewerage facilities conveying liquid wastes to a sewage treatment plant.

The foregoing examples demonstrate the incorporation of soils data and interpretations directly into statements of regional land use development objectives and standards. Once stated, these objectives and standards become guidelines for land use plan design, test, and evaluation.

B. Regional Land Use Plan Design

Detail soil survey data provided a particularly important input to land use plan preparation by the Commission. The use of detail soils data in a large-scale regional land use planning effort was unprecedented at the time such use was initiated by the Commission. Four alternative regional land use plans were prepared—a controlled existing trend plan, a satellite city plan, a corridor plan, and an uncontrolled existing trend plan. All four plan designs were organically derived from graphic analyses of natural resource and cultural base data.

For the preparation of the alternative regional land use plans, interpretive soil maps at a scale of 1:24,000 were prepared using the "stop-go" color coding system illustrated herein. These interpretive soil maps were based on the interpretive ratings accompanying the detailed soil survey maps. The particular interpretations chosen for this application included the interpretations for residential development served by public sanitary sewer systems, for residential development without public sanitary sewer on lots less than 0.4 ha (1 acre) in area, for residential development without public sanitary sewer on lots 0.4 ha (1 acre) or more in area, for commercial and industrial development, for agricultural use, and for transportation system development.

Once the interpretive soil maps were prepared, it was possible to measure and thus quantify the amount of land in each U.S. Public Land Survey section that had severe and very severe limitations for urban development even if served by public sanitary sewer. By subtracting this poorly suited area from the gross area of the section and by further subtracting areas committed to existing urban development, primary environmental corridor (less any poor soils in such corridor), and water, it was possible to arrive at a "net" land area for each section. This "net" land area was termed *developable land* and was assumed to be potentially available for future urban development. Once this process was completed, the alternative regional land use plans were prepared using well-developed land use planning techniques for balancing the forecast demand for, and supply of, land for the various uses and for spatially distributing the various needed land uses within the planning area.

The regional soils data provided an important input to the delineation of what the Commission has termed primary environmental corridors. Although these environmental corridors occupy only about 17% of the region, they contain almost all of the remaining high value wildlife habitat areas, about one-half of all the remaining woodlands, about two-thirds of all the remaining wetlands, and about 85% of the remaining undeveloped lake and stream shoreline and associated floodlands. The corridors also contain the significant ground water recharge and discharge areas of the region, areas covered by organic soils, and certain significant physiographic and cultural features, such as scenic areas and vistas and historic sites and structures. The environmental corridors are thus a composite of the best remaining individual elements of the natural resource base of the region. The preservation of these corridors in essentially natural open uses, including park and parkway, limited agricultural, and country estate type uses is essential to maintain a high level of the environmental quality in the region, to protect the natural beauty and cultural heritage of the region, and to avoid serious environmental and developmental problems, such as flooding and water pollution. The plan recommends that these corridors be refined as urban development continues in the region and that they be preserved and protected from encroachment by incompatible types of urban development. These corridors will also serve to provide the communities within the region with additional park and outdoor recreation areas.

The regional land use plan finally selected for adoption from among the alternatives available is shown on Map 1. It represents a conscious continuation of historic development trends within the region. Urban development would, in general, continue to occur in roughly concentric rings along the full periphery of, and outward from, existing urban centers. The plan proposes, however, to regulate, in the public interest, the urban land market in order to provide for a more orderly and economical regional development pattern, thus avoiding the intensification of areawide developmental and environmental problems. In this respect, the regional land use plan embodies three relatively simple but important ideas. First, the plan recommends that urban development be encouraged to occur only in those areas of the region that are covered by soils suitable for urban development, that can be readily served by extensions of the existing public water supply and gravity drainage sanitary sewerage systems, and that can be readily and efficiently provided with other essential urban facilities and services, such as mass transit. These areas are represented by the yellow, orange, and brown colors on Map 1. Second, the plan recommends the preservation in essentially open natural uses of the primary environmental corridors of the region, the dark green areas on Map 1. Finally, the plan recommends the maintenance in agricultural use of the remaining prime agricultural lands of the region, shown in light green on Map 1.

The adopted regional land use plan provides for the conversion of almost 15,594 ha (38,600 acres) of vacant and agricultural lands to urban residential use in the 30-year period from 1970 to 2000. This new urban residential development would take place primarily in four density categories.

1) *Suburban* (0.5 to 1.5 dwelling units per net residential hectare; 0.2–

0.6 D.U./acre),

2) *Low* (1.7 to 5.4 dwelling units per net residential hectare; 0.7–2.2 D.U./acre),

3) *Medium* (5.7 to 17 dwelling units net residential hectare; 2.3–6.9 D.U./acre), and

4) *High* (17.3 to 44.3 dwelling units per net residential hectare; 7.0–17.9 D.U./acre).

Because so much of the urbanizing portion of the region is covered by soils that have severe and very severe limitations for the use of on-site soil absorption sewage disposal systems, the adopted plan proposed to serve all of the new medium- and high-density residential development with public sanitary sewerage facilities. This would mean that by the year 2000 over 92% of the total urban area within the region would be served by public sanitary sewerage facilities. All new low and suburban density urban residential development which could not be economically and feasibly served by public sanitary sewerage facilities was placed in the plan design on soils which have only very slight, slight, or moderate limitations for development utilizing on-site soil absorption sewage disposal facilities. Within the areas shown for residential development by 2000, there are numerous small pockets of soils unsuited for development even with public sanitary sewers. These small areas can be avoided in most cases through proper subdivision design and placed in minor drainageways and local parks and open spaces.

Of the more than 1,040,100 acres of land used for agriculture within the region in 1970, almost 40%, or about 163,985 ha (404,900 acres), was classified as prime agricultural land. The delineation of prime agricultural land, as noted above, was based, in part, on the regional soil survey. Urban expansion by 2000 within the region is expected to require the conversion of about 32,319 ha (79,800 acres) of agricultural land to urban use. The adopted regional land use plan recommends the preservation of all remaining agricultural lands. In accordance with the regional development objectives and standards set forth above, nearly 160,583 ha (396,500 acres), or about 98%, of the net prime agricultural lands are recommended for retention in agricultural use at least through 2000.

VIII. SOILS DATA AND REGIONAL LAND USE PLAN IMPLEMENTATION

Each Commission planning report that recommends for adoption a regional or subregional plan element contains specific plan implementation recommendations to those federal, state, areawide, and local units of government that have the legal powers and financial means to implement most effectively the particular plan element under consideration. Certain of these plan implementation recommendations relate directly to, and often incorporate, the regional soil survey and its accompanying interpretive analyses. Important among such implementation recommendations are those relating to the incorporation of soils data in local zoning regulations, land subdivision regulations, and health and sanitary regulations.

The soil survey and accompanying interpretations have, to date, been directly incorporated into local zoning ordinances in accordance with regional plan implementation recommendations in the following ways:

1) Through the creation of special zoning districts related to certain kinds of soils, with particular emphasis in this respect on exclusive agricultural, conservancy, and certain types of residential zoning districts.
2) Through the incorporation of special use regulations relating to certain kinds of soils.
3) Through the delineation of zoning district boundaries and in the determination of special hazard areas, such as floodland areas.

Soils data have similarly been incorporated into local subdivision control ordinances, both in the form of general suitability clauses and in the form of special provisions relating to the control of grading operations, the design of drainage facilities, the removal of natural ground cover, and control of erosion and sedimentation.

Perhaps most importantly with respect to implementation of the adopted land use plan has been the incorporation of soils data into local health and sanitary regulations. Such regulations serve in effect to prohibit the installation of septic tank sewage disposal systems on soils having high water tables, low permeability, or excessively high permeability, and on excessively steep slopes.

To date, the detailed soil survey data and accompanying interpretations have been incorporated by specific reference into eight local zoning ordinances covering 2,720 km² (1,050 mile²) of area, or approximately 50% of the total land area of the region; into four local land subdivision control ordinances covering 2,266 km² (875 mile²) of area, or about 33% of the total area of the region; into five local sanitary ordinances covering 5,154 ha (1,990 mile²), or approximately 75% of the total land area of the region. Together these local land use control ordinances, being based upon the same soils data as was the regional land use plan, contribute significantly to the implementation of the regional land use plan.

In addition, many miscellaneous uses of the soils data have contributed to regional land use plan implementation, including the use of such data in land appraisal and assessment; in the development of cost estimates for rural and urban development proposals, street and highway location and design, storm water drainage design, and specific site selection; and in the preparation of neighborhood unit development plans.

IX. SUMMARY AND CONCLUSION

Metropolitan planning is becoming increasingly accepted as a necessary governmental function in most of the large urban regions of the United States. Such planning must recognize the existence of a limited natural resource base to which both rural and urban development must be properly adjusted in order to ensure a pleasant and habitable environment for life. In metropolitan planning, then, the selection of the best areawide development plans from among the practical alternatives available must be based, in part, upon a careful assessment of the effects of each particular alternative on the underlying and sustaining natural resource base.

Although metropolitan planning should be comprehensive, addressing many functional areas, including transportation, sewerage, and water supply, its most basic concern must be with land use. The approach to land use planning at the metropolitan scale should be "organic"; that is, areawide land use plans should seek to adjust land use development to natural patterns in the landscape rather than seek the imposition of artificial designs upon the landscape. Such organic planning, however, requires the collection and analysis of a great deal of information about the natural resource base and its ability to sustain development. Such information must include definitive data on the climate, physiography, soils, mineral resources, surface water resources and associated shorelands and floodlands, ground water resources and associated recharge areas, woodlands, wetlands, fish and wildlife habitat areas, and areas having scenic, historic, scientific, and recreational value. Such definitive data on the natural resource base must be in a form readily relatable to similar data on the cultural base of the planning area and amenable to application in both graphic and numeric analyses to seek out and define patterns in the natural and cultural base which should be reflected in the adopted land use plans.

Because space limitations precluded discussion of the application of all of the various types of natural resource related data required for sound metropolitan development planning, this chapter emphasized the application of soils data to such planning. In this respect, the chapter was intended to provide an example of the scope and depth of the natural resource base inventory required and the means by which such data can be applied to metropolitan level land use plan preparation and implementation. Because of the relatively advanced state-of-the-art and the attendant availability of detailed soils surveys and mapping, and importantly attendant interpretations of the mapped data for planning and engineering purposes, the application of soils information in planning makes a particularly good example of the manner in which all pertinent resource base-related information should be used in such planning. It should be stressed, however, that soils are only one of the factors that must be considered in metropolitan land use planning and that the selection of soils data as an example in this paper is not intended to imply that the other kinds of natural resource base-related data—or for that matter, cultural data—are not important. Indeed, such data must be given the same careful consideration in the areawide land use planning process as the soils data illustrated herein.

PLANNING THE USES AND MANAGEMENT OF LAND

Chapter 19—Planning Metropolitan Land Uses in Relation to Natural Landscape Features

KURT W. BAUER

Figures 1, 2, 3, 4, 5, and Map 1

Fig. 1—Soils photo map.

Map 1

RECOMMENDED LAND USE PLAN FOR THE REGION: 2000

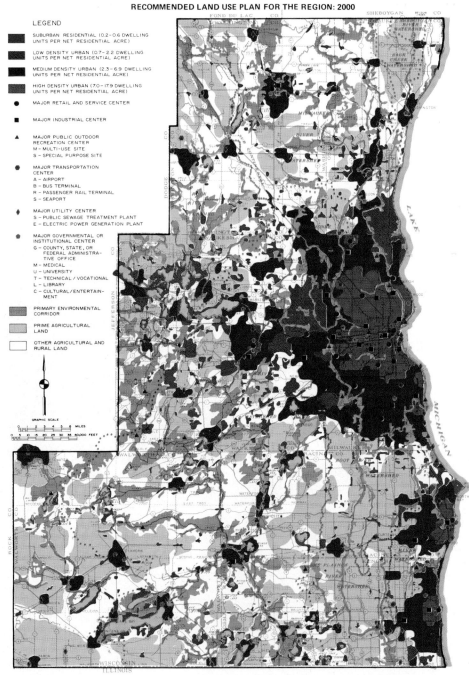

Source: SEWRPC.

Map 1—Recommended land use plan for the region in the year 2000.

20 Residential, Commercial, and Light Industrial Land Uses

CHRIS J. JOHANNSEN, TERRY W. BARNEY, AND
ALBERT A. KLINGEBIEL

*University of Missouri, Columbia, Missouri, and
Soils and Land Use Technology, Inc.,
Silver Spring, Maryland, respectively*

I. INTRODUCTION

Planning commissions, health departments, highway departments, local governments, builders, developers, and others are increasingly aware of the value of soil data and interpretations in making decisions involving the location of residences, commercial businesses, and light industries. During the late 1950's and early 1960's, there was growing recognition of urban clientele as potential users of soil surveys (Hockensmith, 1960; Bartelli, 1962; Robinson et al., 1955). The data needs of these users have become more sophisticated. In addition to general soil maps for broad land use planning, they want specific soils data for on-site planning and evaluation. It is important to know what kind of information can be obtained for urban uses from the standard soil survey and what additional information needs to be obtained by a soil scientist at a specific building site. It should also be recognized that for more detailed evaluation of soils for foundations of larger buildings, more sophisticated tests and evaluations are needed beyond those commonly provided by a soil surveyor.

Most of the detailed soil maps that are available to planners, developers, and other urban users are made and published in the United States by the cooperators of the National Cooperative Soil Survey, which includes the USDA Soil Conservation Service, USDA Forest Service, and Agricultural Experiment Stations of the Land Grant Universities. The soil maps are made at scales of 1:15,840, 1:20,000, and 1:24,000. Even the maps made at the larger scale (1:15,840) commonly contain delineations 4 to 5 acres (1.6 to 2.0 ha) in size, and no smaller than 3 acres (1.2 ha). This is due partly to the limitations of the map scale—the inability, for example, to locate very small areas precisely—and to the labor cost involved in making a map with a large amount of detail. Thus, for an evaluation of a building site, it is usually necessary to verify the soil map by making additional soil borings.

The map user must recognize that the soil scientists who make these maps normally examine the soils to a depth of 6 feet (1.8 m) or less. However, there are many soils where they can predict with reasonable accuracy the nature of the soil properties to much greater depths. Some examples are deep loess and volcanic soils, alluvial and lacustrine deposits, deep glacial deposits, deep sands, some coastal plain soils, and numerous others. Soils that are shallow to bed rock can be predicted as to the depths until rock is encountered. There are many other soil features equally important to soil use that are adequately shown by the soil survey, such as texture, slope, stones, wetness, flooding, permeability, erosivity, and other properties. More detailed soil borings should be made for specific building sites because of the variability of the soils and the properties.

As the users make more specific requests, soil scientists need to closely evaluate their mapping procedures, data collection techniques, and the reporting of the data. For the user, they can provide the basic data for determining the costs and benefits of reducing or removing soil limitations for specific uses. Except for special, highly detailed soil maps that could be made for specific building sites, it is not likely that the standard published soil surveys will ever contain all of the detail requested by builders and developers. It would be a waste of effort to make highly detailed soil maps of broad areas when only a very limited acreage will ever be used as a construction site.

II. IMPORTANT SOIL CONDITIONS

By interpreting soil maps, one can determine soil conditions such as slope, susceptibility to flooding, seasonal wetness, and other hydrologic conditions that are important considerations in locating foundations. Properties influencing foundation support are those affecting bearing capacity and settlement under load (Soil Conserv. Serv., 1971). The properties affecting bearing strength and settlement of a natural soil are density, wetness, flooding, plasticity, texture, and shrink-swell potential. The amount and ease of excavation are important considerations in placing foundation footings and basements. Properties influencing excavation are wetness, slope, soil texture, type of clays, depth to bedrock, stoniness, and rockiness. Detailed engineering tests for bearing qualities are not generally made for individual home sites; thus, the soil survey with on-site evaluation of the soil properties by a soil scientist serve as an important function to the builder.

When a basement is planned for a structure, conditions that will influence its construction are a high water table (either temporary or permanent), depth to rock, drainage, and shrink-swell potential (Baumann & Dries, 1972). Drainage conditions include surface drainage, such as ponding or excessive runoff, and internal drainage influenced by impervious layers that hinder downward movement of water.

Olson (1964) listed soil conditions when considering an estate-type residence. In addition to factors mentioned for foundations, the suitability for septic tanks, and conditions affecting aesthetic value such as topography and the difficulty of establishing or maintaining grass, shrubs, and trees, should be considered.

For large buildings such as those required for industry, many soil conditions are overcome by the engineering design. Cost becomes an obvious factor but information from soil surveys can be used in the preliminary site evaluation to help determine the kind and degree of soil condition that needs to be overcome. Tests are conducted before, during, and after construction progresses. Designs are tested, and load and compression tests, as well as tests on the building materials themselves, are performed. For many industrial sites, aesthetics and landscaping become strong architectural and engineering considerations (Olson, 1973).

All of these are normal operating procedures for the construction of large buildings but they prove to be too costly for the construction of an average house or small building. Soil surveys are especially helpful in the site selection for larger buildings in that they can show soils that will present problems in construction. As a result, alternate sites can be studied and costs to overcome undesirable conditions compared, thus resulting in a savings in construction costs.

The Town of Norfolk in Massachusetts had such an experience in selecting a site for a school. A school site was selected but when the soil map showed the soil to have a severe soil limitation for a building site, the authorities withdrew the site from consideration. It was estimated that the additional cost of construction at this site was $80,000 more than for a more favorable site that was available for use.

III. SITE SELECTION

A. Important Soil Characteristics

Site evaluation is an extremely important process. Problems like wet basements, septic tile filter field failures, cracked walls in foundations, flood damages, road failures, and expensive construction costs can be avoided by carefully examining the site before construction begins. Ritchie and Swanson (1957) observed that "built-up" communities in Hartford County, Connecticut, were found on terrace soils. It was also noted that terrace soils are relatively level, are free of boulders, usually offer good drainage, and permit easy excavation. Developers prefer these types of locations because of the ease of construction and the relatively low cost of site preparation.

Many soils have unique conditions that are recognizable by the layperson. Klingebiel (1967a) noted that most anyone can learn to read the clues written on the landscape that influence site quality, such as evidence of wetness, flooding, steep slopes, and rocks. Vegetation also reflects differences due to soil conditions.

Porter and Mitchell (1965) identified specific soils that caused land slides, were located in the flood plains, had high shrinking and swelling, had drainage problems, or were affected by underlying rock. Specific soil characteristics involved in each condition could be identified more easily when relating to the problem.

Miller (1967) emphasized the complexity of soil patterns and the complexity of individual soils. Soils with poor drainage characteristics were pointed out as having black or gray surfaces and gray subsoils. Persons selecting homesites were encouraged to drive past the site during or immediately after a rain to evaluate surface drainage. Soils with high clay content, and especially those with expanding clays such as montmorillonite, will cause special construction problems. Designs for basement foundations, walls, horizontal slabs, and roads should consider the expansion-contraction phenomenon due to the clays.

Soils that have a high shrink-swell potential are not common to all areas of the country, but they differ enough from other kinds of soil so that even small areas where they do occur are delineated on maps. There are large areas of these kinds of soil in the Dallas, Waco, and San Antonio areas of Texas. These soils expand when wet and shrink when dry. Tests on Bell clay have shown volumetric changes as high as 55% between wet and dry conditions. Structures that are placed in or on these soils without the benefit of special design or reinforcement will crack and commonly become unusable in a short time.

Evidences of the destruction of homes, foundations, walls, roads and streets, sidewalks, and other structures are visable in all areas where these expansive soils occur. Charles Tipps (1963), corrosion engineer, points out that in the San Antonio, Texas, area, even where special foundations are used, some damage to structures takes place. It is essential that the very best-known designs be used to withstand the tremendous forces exerted by these soils.

Specific factors affecting the suitability of an area for a home site are texture, permeability, soil depth, slopes, erosion, surface runoff, shrink-swell, water table, and flooding (Baumann & Dries, 1972). The site is usually evaluated in terms of the greatest influence from one or more of these factors. Scrivner et al. (1971) listed similar factors but also included amount of course fragments frost heave potential, and depth to contrasting layers.

Depth to rock is an important item in determining the cost of excavation for pipe lines, roads, basements, etc. Numerous examples can be cited about how the use of a soil survey can help people determine the presence of rock and to show alternative sites or routes that may be more favorable for excavation.

An article published in the *Ithaca, New York Journal* (10 Sept. 1968, p. 9) pointed out that an unanticipated amount of rock along a pipeline under construction would increase the cost of excavation by $235,000. This problem could have been avoided by studying the published soil survey of the area. With this existing information, engineers during the planning stages could have estimated where and how much rock would be encountered. In addition, it would have been possible to evaluate alternative routes that were relatively free of rock.

Yahner (1968) emphasized the factors that would affect septic systems since most suburban and rural homes use this method for sewage disposal. The effects of soil permeability and water table are obvious on the performance of a septic system but are many times ignored. The location of bedrock materials and sand and gravel layers provide the possibility of ground water contamination and, therefore, should be avoided. Many dream homes have turned into nightmares because of sewage problems. William H. Bender (1971) provided information on how soil surveys could be utilized in selecting the site of an absorption field of a residential septic system.

Other accompanying concerns would be the suitability of the soils for road construction, the stability of embankments, and landscape design (Olson & Warner, 1974). Engineers utilize specific soil information in their design. Engineering soils classifications (Asphalt Inst., 1964; PCA, 1962) emphasized that grain size, mineralogy, density, porosity, bearing capacity, expansion and shrinkage, cohesion, shearing, and compression are all important soil characteristics that may need to be tested for engineering purposes. Engineering analyses also indicate soil behavior under varying moisture and temperature conditions.

Soil maps can be especially helpful to developers in planning for streets and roads in a subdivision or for major highways. Numerous examples can be cited where soils shallow to rock or those with poor bearing qualities (wet, clay, organic soils) could be avoided by adjusting the alignment slightly. If realignment is not a reasonable solution, the map will provide information about the kind of soil problem so that cost estimates can be made for overcoming the problem.

Certain geologic features have soils with unique properties. One excellent example is glacial lake beds which have soils that are topographically low and clay contents that are high (Gray, 1971). Runoff is high because of the low permeability of these soils. These conditions combine to make frequent flooding a severe limitation on land use in old lakebed areas. Terrace soils and loess soils have an identified hazard of slumping of slopes. Slumping may result when natural and artificial slopes are cut into saturated material, excess load is added too close to the edge of the slope, lawns are watered frequently, or natural saturation is increased due to the operation of septic tank filter fields. A further problem is that the fractured upper surface of slumping material allows the rapid infiltration of rain water, which in turn contributes to additional slumping (Gray, 1971).

Hillside slip is common in many areas of the country where soil and geologic slumping conditions exist. The probability of these conditions existing in your area can be predicted by a soil scientist or geologist from a soil survey and from field observations. An example of how this situation was overlooked involved a family living in Fairfax County, Virginia, who awoke one morning to find that about one-half of their backyard had sunk 3 feet, leaving a jagged, earthquake-like scar. Not only was the house in jeopardy from further slippage but the neighbor below was in line to receive the unwanted soil. There are ways of preventing or retarding hillside slip, but they are costly. The best solution is to avoid these sites in the first place.

The first soil surveys were designed to provide information to farmers emphasizing limitations as a concept of farming patterned to fit the capability of the soil. An eight-class system was outlined for farmers by Hockensmith and Steele (1943). Although the interpretations were designed primarily for farm uses, it is possible to draw some general conclusions even for nonfarm uses due to the nature of the capability classification (Klingebiel, 1967b).

With the availability of basic soils data by soils shown on a soils map, it is possible to develop numerous kinds of interpretations for various uses. The more detailed soil maps at scales of 1:15,840 to 1:24,000 are especially useful to planners, developers, and others. Single-purpose soil groupings on maps, such as soil depth, slope, wetness, flooding, soil texture, soil permeability, and soil reaction, are commonly developed for these users. Soil potential or soil limitation for "on site" waste disposal suitability for home sites, sanitary land fills, and road locations are examples of interpretations based on a set of soil properties using specific parameters as criteria.

In the late 1950's and early 1960's, when demands for soil surveys for nonfarm uses were increasing rapidly, it seemed especially important to stress the kind and degree of soil limitations each kind of soil had for a particular use. In this way it was possible to emphasize to the decision makers and to the public that there were soil problems that needed to be considered if the soil were to be used successfully for nonfarm uses. There was plenty of evidence to show the problems resulting from improper use. Thus, these kinds of interpretive maps served a very useful purpose. The ratings were designed to point out the kind and degree of soil limitations. They *do not* imply that the soil cannot or should not be used for a particular use. That is a planning decision that must be made after economic and other factors are considered (Mausel et al., 1976). McCormack (1974) points out that if the soil limitation ratings are not evaluated further in determining the feasibility of overcoming the limitations, then the soils data have not been fully utilized.

Some kinds of soil limitations can be overcome more easily than others. In some areas, soils with severe limitations must be used and their limitations modified to make the area acceptable for a specific use. In some instances people are willing to live with the limitations such as occasional flooding, high water tables, or expanding clays. Others spend the necessary money to correct or reduce the hazard through soil drainage, adequate flood control, use of reinforced foundations, and similar construction techniques (Johnson & Bartelli, 1974). At a price, most soil problems can be overcome. How much one is willing to do to overcome soil problems is a decision that must be made by the builder based on his desire to overcome the limitation, live with it, or seek a better site.

To arrive at the soil potential for a particular use, it is essential that the practices that might be used to overcome the limitations be identified and their costs determined. An estimate of any continuing limitations after corrective measures have been installed should also be made.

B. Planning and Development

Emphasis needs to be placed on the planning phase of site selection and the fact that soil surveys are made at different intensities based upon the specific need for the soil data. They can provide a broad overview of a large area and allow one to pinpoint those areas that are most likely to have favorable or unfavorable properties for a particular use. General soil maps that broadly show the general landscape and soil features often satisfy the needs of general planning. This provides pertinent information to assist regional or county planning commissions in making decisions on the locations of subdivisions, commercial businesses, and industrial tracts. Information on transportation routes, utility installations, schools, and recreation sites will also supplement the soils information needed in the decision-making process. The general maps are not a substitute for the detailed maps, which are ideally suited for operational planning (Marshall, 1971).

The detailed soil survey is needed to guide land use decisions in the development of the single tract of land or in the development of the operational plan for a town or community. Most planners find that a study of the soils will usually indicate a need for more specialized studies and testing before specific decision can be made.

Soils surveys have been used in establishing zoning criteria by assisting in: (i) setting minimum lot size, which is especially important for homes served by septic systems; (ii) regulating problem soils such as those with high water tables, shallow bedrock, unstable structural bearing characteristics, and other factors affecting structures; (iii) protecting flood plains by delineating its location and the susceptibility or possibility of flooding; (iv) providing an educational device since properties of soils can be demonstrated; and (v) serving as a zoning map since basic land use information can be superimposed over the soil map (Yanggen et al., 1966).

Quay (1966), a planner, noted that if the soil properties are studied, evaluated, and interpreted for subdivision design, the development would conform to the capabilities of the land. This facilitates the establishment of subdivision units that are more harmonious with the natural physical environment. This approach was further supported and developed by White and Kresse (1972), who performed a complete site analysis using information on roads, bedrock, soils, slope, surface drainage, vegetation, and scenery. By recognizing and incorporating each of these site characteristics, it was possible to develop an ecological plan that included the retention of all possible existing vegetation, use of the best-suited areas for building, and use of aesthetic qualities. In addition, stream flow was regulated and homes were clustered to enlarge the community space.

Phillips (1969), an engineer, suggested that one should develop a site plan compatable with existing topography and soil conditions. To minimize hydrology and drainage problems, one should protect exposed areas such as roads and reservoirs as soon as construction is complete, install and maintain sediment traps during construction, and establish all permanent vegetation as rapidly as possible. Water behavior from watershed areas can be interpreted from the soil characteristics, and suggested by Obenshain et al. (1962). Engineers are able to use the soils information in designs that minimize erosion conditions as well as in estimating the runoff due to normal rains and high-intensity storms.

The flooding of homes and business establishments is an experience that thousands of people in the United States experience every year. Many homes are totally destroyed and the damages run into the millions of dollars annually. It would be safe to assume that some flood damage occurs annually to houses and other buildings in three-fourths of all the counties in the country. Hundreds of case histories could be cited but numerous local experiences can be obtained to illustrate adequately the point. Again, soil surveys show areas that are subject to flooding. Many communities have developed ordinances based on soil surveys preventing people from building houses and other buildings on flood-prone soils.

Flood plains can be delineated by soil surveys (Yanggen et al., 1966), but urban development usually causes higher peak discharges of runoff water through these areas (Leopold, 1968). This is the result of the increased area which is impervious to water due to construction and the decreased lag time due to rapid runoff by streets, storm sewers, and lined waterways. The stream becomes flashier in that flood peaks are higher and flows during nonstorm periods are lower. There is also concern about the decreased quantities of water that are available for ground water recharge.

The demand for land has put pressure on the use of flood plains for residential and industrial areas. Proposed flood controls and drainage in many areas become extremely expensive. To realize a tax benefit from areas that have been protected, a very intensive land use is needed (Montgomery & Wenner, 1965).

Flood plain areas and other geologic features such as glacial lake beds (Gray, 1971) should be avoided whenever possible. The cost of development in these areas can be extremely high. Most cost savings can be made through proper site selection (Klingebiel, 1966); however, future cost savings will likely be from the recognition of the soil hazards at a given site. The application of new technology is helping to overcome many problems that have always been great hazards to development.

Improvement of septic tank design (Bouma, 1975) is one example where soils which were previously not suited for septics may now be considered. This author further points out a concern for quality of construction and construction materials which may result in failures previously attributed to the soils.

The application of sludge and waste waters from municipalities and industries to the land as an alternative to costly treatment plants has many recycling and energy-saving opportunities (Pound & Crites, 1973). Johannsen

(1977) stressed the important role of soil surveys in selecting sites for applying these wastes to agricultural lands.

The future requires that we recognize the need for more and better planning (Galloway, 1963). Continued urbanization and the accompanying pressures that it brings to bear on land use has accelerated the need for retrieval of information from soil surveys. Recreation or second homes located farther into rural areas are on the increase (Silliman, 1974). This factor alone has highlighted the need for increased applications of soils data in the planning scheme.

Computers are assuming a larger role in data retrieval from soil surveys. Nichols and Bartelli (1974) showed how interpretive maps can be made from soil surveys using a computer. The Maryland State Planning Division requested interpretive maps that located prime farmland, flood plains, steep slopes, areas of instability, permeability, depth to bedrock, and depth to seasonal water tables, plus had the ability to retrieve the data by computer for specific locations (Shields, 1976). Kling and Olson (1975) demonstrated how soils information would be just a part of the total resource data that can be utilized by the computer in land use planning.

IV. CONTROLLING EROSION

The causes of urban soil erosion differ considerably from the causes of agricultural erosion. In agricultural areas soil erosion will occur during specific times of the year when land is prepared for food and fiber production. In urban construction, land development activities can occur at any time of the year and cause complete exposure of the disturbed soils to precipitation and storm runoff water for extended periods of time (Powell et al., 1970).

The energy responsible for erosion is provided by falling rain and flowing runoff water. One inch of precipitation falling on 1 acre of exposed soil weighs 110 tons. Therefore, an average rainfall of 40 inches at a specific location would have 4,500 tons of rain falling on each acre during the year (Thronson, 1971). The intensity of the rainfall and the amount of cover are very important factors to consider in evaluating the erosion and sediment yields from a specific location (Wischmeier, 1959).

A positive correlation between urban development and sediment yield was reported by Anderson and McCall (1968). Wolman and Schick (1967) measured sediment yields from urbanizing areas ranging from 1,000 to 100,000 tons/mi² per year. This compares to 200 to 500 tons/mi² per year in an urbanized drainage basin (Leopold, 1968). The conclusion is that sedimentation increases with the activity of the construction process of an urban area. For example, Anderson and McCall (1968) reported the following sediment yields for several watersheds in the Washington, D.C., area:

1) Undeveloped watershed—146 tons/mi² per year.
2) Watershed with construction starting—280 tons/mi² per year.

3) Watershed with construction well underway—690 tons/mi^2 per year.

4) Watershed with advanced construction—2,300 tons/mi^2 per year.

Cost of correcting erosion and sedimentation deposition problems resulting from land development activities often are unjustifiably transfered to the taxpayer (Thronson, 1971). The consequences of the erosion from a construction operation affect areas farther downstream and the total costs are difficult to establish. The cost of measures to rectify the damage incurred are usually borne by those not directly benefiting from the construction development. In a study of the Seneca Creek watershed located near Washington, D.C., Brandt et al. (1972) reported erosion control costs of $1,125/acre with 91% control of the potential erosion. The damages from uncontrolled erosion from urban construction could reach $1,500/acre.

Another type of sediment from urban areas is street litter or sanitation debris. This material consists of dirt and dust, leaves, twigs, grass clippings, tin cans, tree branches, material eroded from buildings and sidewalks, fallout of air pollution particles, household refuse, and other street wash (Powell, 1976). Construction debris mixed with these sediments is also considered to be a major portion of pollution, but varies greatly according to the management practices of the construction firm.

Bryan (1970) studied the runoff from a 1,067-acre (432-ha) urban drainage basin in North Carolina and found that the pesticide concentrations in the sediment increased after the urban area had been completely developed. He found that a total concentration of 1.16 ppm was the average concentration of the runoff water. Kelling and Peterson (1975) showed that textural and compaction discontinuities within the soil profile formed during the building and lawn construction were the greatest factors affecting water infiltration. Water intake was reduced about 35% on disturbed over undisturbed profiles and therefore fertilizer runoff losses can be significant from residential sites.

Practices considered suitable for erosion and sedimentation control during construction vary with topography, soil erodability, rainfall intensity, surrounding cover, degree of recontouring required, and general construction practice. One must be concerned with the surface protection of the exposed soils and entrapment of runoff and sedimentation. Establishing a good vegetative cover is a primary objective on all areas exposed during the construction phases (Brandt et al., 1972). Annual species serve to provide excellent cover on a temporary basis, while perennial cover crops and sods should be established for more permanent control. Brandt et al. (1972) also reviewed studies showing the effectiveness of mulch covers and methods of applications. Mulches are used to enhance vegetative growth by conserving soil moisture, moderating soil temperatures, reducing the soil erosion, improving soil properties, and usually improving stands and plant populations. Mannering and Meyer (1963) reported excellent results with the use of wheat straw mulch for water infiltration and erosion control. Untreated areas lost 12 tons/acre, while 1, 2, and 4 tons of straw/acre resulted in essentially no erosion. To achieve the best performance from straw mulch, it must be treated or anchored to prevent movement by wind and water. Spraying the mulch with asphalt or using a mulch-anchoring tool are the most common methods employed (Dudeck et al., 1970).

Control methods for reducing runoff include such standard practices as terraces and diversions. These practices should be developed along with the design plans of the construction project. Bond (1975) illustrates an erosion and sedimentation control plan for a specific site in the Neshaneny Creek watershed in Bucks County, Pennsylvania. This plan called for stream-crossing installations; sediment and settlement basins, installed prior to any clearing or earth-moving operations; diversions for control of surface water; and borrow areas divided, cleared, and grubbed or stripped only as needed. It also called for trees within 10 feet (3 m) of stream cut or grubbed; idle, disturbed areas mulched or temporarily revegetated; areas stripped of vegetation reseeded as rapidly as possible; and areas not planned for revegetation left in a rough, graded condition to increase infiltration and decrease runoff. It is important to emphasize that specific measures need to be developed for each site due to the factors that cause every site to be different.

LITERATURE CITED

Anderson, P. W., and J. E. McCall. 1968. Urbanization effect on sediment yield in New Jersey. J. Soil Water Conserv. 23:142–144.

Asphalt Institute. 1964. Soils manual for design of asphalt pavement structures. Manual Ser. no. 10. The Asphalt Inst., Asphalt Inst. Build., College Park, Md. 261 p.

Bartelli, L. J. 1962. Use of soils information in urban-fringe areas. J. Soil Water Conserv. 17: 99–103.

Baumann, W. E., and F. Dries. 1972. Soil considerations in home site selections. Circ. 9406. Coop. Ext. Serv., Oklahoma State Univ., Stillwater, Okla.

Bender, W. H. 1971. Soils and septic tanks. USDA Agric. Inf. Bull. 349. 12 p.

Bond, R. L. 1975. Erosion control at construction sites: A case history. Soil Conserv. 40(8):18–19.

Bouma, J. 1975. Septic tanks now possible on nearly all soil types. Crops and Soils 27(5):8–10.

Brandt, G. H., E. S. Conyers, M. P. Ettinger, F. J. Lowes, J. W. Mighton, and J. W. Pollack. 1972. An economic analysis of erosion and sediment control methods for watersheds undergoing urbanization. The Dow Chem. Co., Midland, Mich. 181 p.

Bryan, E. H. 1970. Quality of storm water drainage from urban land areas in North Carolina. Rep. no. 37. Water Resour. Inst., North Carolina State Univ., Raleigh, N.C. 44 p.

Dudeck, E. A., N. P. Swanson, L. N. Mielke, and A. R. Decrick. 1970. Mulches for grass establishment on a fill slope. Agron. J. 62:810–812.

Galloway, H. M. 1963. We need more land use planning. Crops Soils 15(4):7–10.

Gray, H. H. 1971. Glacial lake deposits in southern Indiana—Engineering problems and land use. Geolog. Land Surv. Prog. Rep. 30, Dep. of Nat. Resour., State of Indiana.

Hockensmith, R. D. 1960. Soil surveys furnish basic data for all land uses. Soil Conserv. 26(5): 100–102.

Hockensmith, R. D., and J. G. Steele. 1943. Classifying land for conservation farming. USDA Farmers Bull. 1853.

Johannsen, C. J. 1977. Site selection and land-use considerations. p. 30–41 (Chapt. 3). In L. W. Jacobs (ed.) Utilizing municipal sewage wastewaters and sludges on land for agricultural production. North Central Reg. Ext. Publ. 52. Michigan State Univ., East Lansing, Mich.

Johnson, W. M., and L. J. Bartelli. 1974. Rural development: Natural Resource Dimension. J. Soil Water Conserv. 29:18–19.

Kelling, K. A., and A. E. Peterson. 1975. Urban lawn infiltration rates and fertilizer runoff losses under simulated rainfall. Soil Sci. Soc. Am. Proc. 39:348–352.

Kling, G. F., and G. W. Olson. 1975. Role of computers in land use planning. Inf. Bull. 88. Coop. Ext. Serv., Cornell Univ., Ithaca, N.Y. 12 p.

Klingebiel, A. A. 1966. Cost and returns of soil surveys. Soil Conserv. 32(1):3–6.

Klingebiel, A. A. 1967a. Know the soil you build on. USDA Agric. Inf. Bull. 320. 13 p.

Klingebiel, A. A. 1967b. Land resources available to people in the United States. p. 23–57. *In* Proc. 16th Annu. Meet. Agric. Res. Inst., Nat. Res. Counc., Washington, D.C.

Leopold, L. B. 1968. Hydrology for urban land planning—a guide book for hydrologic effects of urban land use. U.S. Geolog. Surv. Circ. 554. 18 p.

Mannering, J. V., and L. D. Meyer. 1963. The effects of various rates of surface mulch on infiltration and erosion. Soil Sci. Soc. Am. Proc. 27:84–86.

Marshall, R. M. 1971. Soil resources, their use and limitations. *In* Planning and zoning for better resource use publication. Soil Conserv. Soc. of Am., Ankeny, Iowa. 34 p.

Mausel, P. W., C. L. Scrivner, J. C. Baker, and C. J. Johannsen. 1976. A soil guide for the Kansas City Region. Mid-America Reg. Counc., Kansas City, Mo. 98 p.

McCormack, D. E. 1974. Soil potentials: A positive approach to urban planning. J. Soil Water Conserv. 29:258–262.

Miller, F. P. 1967. Selecting soils for building sites. Dep. of Agron. Fact Sheet 190. Ext. Serv., Univ. of Maryland, College Park, Md. 4 p.

Montgomery, R., and K. A. Wenner. 1965. Soil survey saves Lake County taxpayers' money. Ind. Acad. Sci. Proc. 74:325–327.

Nichols, J. D., and L. J. Bartelli. 1974. Computer-generated interpretive maps. J. Soil Water Conserv. 29:232–235.

Obenshain, S. S., H. C. Porter, and R. E. Devereux. 1962. Soil survey for urban planning and other uses. Bull. 538. Virginia Agric. Exp. Stn., Virginia Polytech. Inst., Blacksburg, Va. 26 p.

Olson, G. W. 1964. Application of soil survey to problems of health, sanitation and engineering. Memoir 387. Agric. Exp. Stn., Cornell Univ., Ithaca, N.Y. 77 p.

Olson, G. W. 1973. Engineering uses of soils. N.Y. Food Life Sci. Q. 6(4):8–15.

Olson, G. W., and J. W. Warner. 1974. Engineering soil survey interpretations. Inf. Bull. 77. Coop. Ext. Serv., Cornell Univ., Ithaca, N.Y.

Phillips, R. R. 1969. Solutions to urban-fringe hydrology and drainage problems. p. 41–46. *In* Proc. Am. Soc. Agric. Eng., 3–6 Dec. 1969, Chicago, Ill. ASAE, St. Joseph, Mo.

Porter, H. C., and W. G. Mitchell. 1965. Soils for home sites. Bull. 295, Agric. Ext. Serv., Virginia Polytechnic Inst., Blacksburg, Va.

Portland Cement Association. 1962. PCA soil primer. Portland Cement Assoc., Skokie, Ill. 52 p.

Pound, C. E., and R. W. Crites. 1973. Wastewater treatment and reuse by land application. Vol. I and II. EPA-660/2-73-006a and EPA-660/2-73-006b, USEPA, Washington, D.C.

Powell, M. D., W. C. Winter, and W. P. Bodwitch. 1970. Community action guide for soil erosion and sedimentation control. Natl. Assoc. of Counties Res. Found., Washington, D.C. 64 p.

Quay, J. R. 1966. Use of soil surveys in subdivision design. p. 76–86. *In* Soil surveys and land use planning. Soil Sci. Soc. of Am., Madison, Wis.

Richie, A., and C. L. W. Swanson. 1957. Soils and land use, Hartford County, Connecticut, an area of specialized agriculture and rapid urbanization. Bull. 606. The Connecticut Agric. Exp. Stn. 36 p.

Robinson, G. H., H. C. Porter, and S. S. Obenshain. 1955. The use of soil survey information in an area of rapid urban development. Soil Sci. Soc. Am. Proc. 19:502–504.

Scrivner, C. L., J. H. Lee, A. J. Preston, and H. E. Grogger. 1971. Soil data use in community planning. Community Decision Making Guide 7775. Ext. Div., Univ. of Missouri, Columbia.

Shields, R. L. 1976. New generalized soil maps guide land use planning in Maryland. J. Soil Water Conserv. 31:276–280.

Silliman, M., Jr. 1974. What is happening to our soil resources: losses to urbanization and recreational development. p. 22–26. *In* 29th Soil Conserv. Soc. of Am. Proc., 11–14 Aug. 1974, Syracuse, N.Y. SCSA, Ankeny, Iowa.

Soil Conservation Service. 1971. Guide for interpreting engineering uses of soils. U.S. Government Printing Office, Washington, D.C. 86 p.

Thronson, R. E. 1971. Control of sediments resulting from highway construction and land development. USEPA, Off. of Water Programs. 50 p.

Tipps, C. W. 1963. The soil survey offers help to builders. The Broadcaster, San Antonio, Tex. 40(8):146–153.

White, D. J., and Kresse, E. J. 1972. Planning to save natural resources in residential development. J. Soil Water Conserv. 27:152–155.

Wischmeier, W. H. 1959. A rainfall erosion index for a universal soil-loss equation. Soil Sci. Soc. Am. Proc. 23:246–249.

Wolman, M. G., and P. A. Schick. 1967. Effects of construction on fluvial sediment, urban and suburban areas of Maryland. Water Resour. Res. 3:451–462.

Yahner, J. E. 1968. Houses, septic systems and soils. Crops and Soils Notes no. 96. Dep. of Agron., Purdue Univ., West Lafayette, Ind.

Yanggen, D. A., M. T. Beatty, and A. J. Brovold. 1966. Use of detailed soil surveys for zoning. J. Soil Water Conserv. 21:123–126.

21 Vegetation Types, Functions, and Constraints in Metropolitan Environments

JAMES A. SCHMID

Jack McCormick & Associates, Inc.
Berwyn, Pennsylvania

I. INTRODUCTION

Urban landscapes by definition are dominated by the works of man. Natural objects, such as the plants which collectively make up urban vegetation, survive in cities because people want, or tolerate, or ignore, them. City plants are affected by people's ideas, customs, and activities, as well as by natural environmental factors such as climate and soil. Thus both human behavior and environmental constraints must be considered when the planning of metropolitan vegetation is discussed.

The vegetation of every metropolitan area differs sharply in quantity, pattern, and species composition from that which would exist locally in the absence of human activity. In contrast to farm or forest areas, vegetation does not receive first priority as an urban land use. Townspeople bulldoze forests, replant trees, mow lawns, cultivate flowers. Hence the vegetation of each human settlement comes to reflect the felt needs, cultural practices, and landscape traditions of its occupants. Vegetation is affected also by the inadvertent consequences of urban-industrial activity, such as air pollution. People can rearrange environmental factors to encourage or to exclude vegetation, but the economic cost of departing drastically from natural conditions seldom is defrayed for long by any social group. More common, and more enduring, are efforts to shape vegetation to human purposes within the constraints offered by local combinations of rock, climate, topography, soil, and water supply.

The vegetation of one city resembles or differs from that of the next, in part because of common or contrasting environmental constraints, and in part because of shared or antithetical human ideas and ideals. The same is true of the vegetational patterns within a single city. In few cities has the counterpoint of variation among environmental patterns and cultural patterns been studied as it creates the distinctive urban landscape. Yet city dwellers cannot escape noticing such patterns casually, even subliminally, in the course of their everyday lives. Because a potentially vast flora is influenced by so many disparate environmental and cultural forces acting at different rates and intensities in the urban places of the earth, urban vegetation is a living artifact of great complexity that is beginning to attract widespread attention from investigators trained in a variety of disciplines (e.g., Andresen, 1975, 1976; Santamour et al., 1976; Detwyler, 1972; NE For. Exp. Stn., 1977).

This chapter will describe the basic types of vegetation that are found in American cities and the roles they play in the human environment. It will outline the effects that urban soils and other environmental constraints have on the plant communities shaped by Americans. Finally, it will comment on factors that should be considered during revegetation efforts by metropolitan land managers, including the protection of remnant natural vegetation in urban areas.

II. TYPES OF URBAN VEGETATION

Vegetation types in North America range from virtually untouched wilderness to intensively managed farmlands, forest plantations, and cityscapes. Urban activity shares with mining the tendency to remove the indigenous, wild vegetation from sizeable tracts of land; like agriculture, silviculture, and ranching, urbanization results in new patterns of plant cover that reflect both man and nature. American urban landscapes are not devoid of green plants. In general the intensity of vegetation disturbance decreases outward from urban centers, and the percentage of the land surface occupied by green plants increases toward the outer fringes of the metropolitan area. American cities seldom display distinct edges except along waterways. Beyond the typical "shatter belt" of little-used peripheral land reverting to forest or scrub while its owners await urban purchasers, vegetation management may be either intensive again (in farmland) or virtually nonexistent.

1. REMNANT NATIVE VEGETATION

Where periurban land is unfavorable for human use as building sites, as a result of steepness of slope, aridity, or susceptibility to floods, it may retain relatively little-disturbed plant communities. Examples are the chapparal-covered slopes above Los Angeles, the desert outside Phoenix, riparian forests on the river floodplains of Dallas or Fort Worth, and tidal marshes around New York. Legal restrictions and public ownership may help enforce the preservation of wild vegetation in these sites, as in the forest preserves around Chicago or on the reservoir margins of public water supplies tributary to Boston. If access to such places is sufficiently difficult, and people live far enough away, the effects of humans on the contemporary wild vegetation may be difficult to detect. Data on the value of forests in protecting watersheds and preserving water quality are readily available (e.g., Anderson et al., 1976; Karr & Schlosser, 1978). The discussion will return to such areas in the final section of the chapter.

More genuinely urban vegetation types, however, coexist with people inside the inhabited sections of the city proper. The following four distinctively urban types are usually recognizable in any American city.

2. CONTAINER VEGETATION

In the central city where land values peak as a result of industry and commerce, container vegetation is a minor landscape feature. The physiological tolerance of its constituent plants frequently may be taxed. Street trees, tiny parks, and green churchyards are treasured ornaments, and substantial effort may be expended by wealthy individual urbanites, by businessmen, or by public administrators to sustain the precarious existence of the outdoor greenery. The vegetation never dominates the landscape, and it reflects the human effort expended on its containers and cultivation to compensate for generally adverse environmental factors. The prime opportunity for most apartment dwellers and office workers to interact with plants occurs indoors. Sometimes the indoor plants spill over into the outdoor landscape in summer window boxes.

3. LAWNSCAPE

Where the social and economic need to pave the entire land surface is less, Americans favor grass lawns as the principal component of urban vegetation, bounded sometimes by shrubs and shaded by scattered trees. The lawnscape is basically a two-dimensional feature, and does not hide buildings, automobiles, or roadways. The trees seldom form a continuous canopy. Individuals have a greater opportunity for outdoor vegetation management in residential districts with low-rise buildings than in central cities, and the quantity of green open space increases to a maximum in suburban parks and neighborhoods with single-family detached houses.

Lawns require continuous maintenance. The image of the lawnscape is derived from the European pasture, but cattle and sheep today are not readily kept on urban plots. Thus their role is played by gasoline-powered lawnmowers, and the pasture has been refined to manicured turf whose tending is governed by social convention. Local ordinances may permit the municipality to cut grass on private property if it is judged to be a fire hazard, and then send the negligent owner the bill. The neighbors usually have complained loudly about appearances, however, long before the fire department is called in.

4. SCRUB-WOODLAND

In large parks and in a few residential districts, shrubby undergrowth may be allowed to displace lawns, and the trees may be massed in forest-like clusters. In such areas the vegetation takes on greatly increased visual significance, and may overshadow the structures of man. Of central importance, there is enough vegetation in the first 3 m above the ground that the sight lines of ground-level pedestrians are obscured. Trees typically form a closed canopy. Grass lawn is insignificant or absent. People may need to undertake little maintenance, because the vegetation essentially sustains itself.

5. WEEDPATCHES

Finally, there are the unmanaged communities of ruderal plants on scraps of waste ground. Symbols of dereliction, they are not conspicuous in the more prosperous sections of well-run cities. But their herbs and grasses thrive without human help in the railroad rights-of-way, in back alleys, and in the urban core wastelands spawned by the demolition that long precedes "urban renewal." When left alone for several years, they may support a few hardy trees and shrubs, as well as herbs that elsewhere at least are considered to be weeds. By far the most prominent volunteer tree in American metropolitan areas is the exotic ailanthus.

Five types, then, of outdoor urban vegetation can be established as the basis for discussion in the context of American cities (Table 1). Usually it is not difficult to recognize which type prevails in any given place, although intergradation may occur. The types differ not only in quantity of plant material and, hence, in their gross appearance, but also in floristic composition, extent of land occupied, and geographical location within the metropolis. Above all, they differ in the amount of human intervention necessary to establish and maintain them and in the social connotations which they convey to local inhabitants. Subtypes within each category can be developed for specific metropolitan areas to accommodate distinctive local features. The types also differ in the actually and potentially beneficial roles they can play for the people who live near them.

III. ROLES OF URBAN VEGETATION

That vegetation occupies as much of the modern urban landscape as it does is a fact worthy of comment. Contemporary Americans, after all, do not depend on city plants for food or fiber, firewood or oxygen. The understanding of how vegetation benefits urbanites, or potentially can benefit them, requires knowledge gathered by scholars in many disciplines. From the natural sciences must come the measurements and theory of how the urban ecosystem functions with respect to climatic phenomena, the movement of air masses, the growth requirements of cultivated plants, and a host of related information needed by landscape design professionals. Equally important, from the social sciences must come the appreciation of what urbanites want from urban vegetation and why, what social constraints must be satisfied by the vegetation that could be cultivated in urban areas to yield increased benefits to people, and how great are the relative costs of creating and maintaining alternative vegetation types such as those previously described. Most of the environmental roles played by vegetation are accomplished simply because the vegetation, the biomass, is there. Others,

Table 1—Characteristics of principal American urban outdoor vegetation types.

Type	Physiognomy	Flora	Location and extent	Human input	Actual and potential benefits	Examples
Container vegetation	Individual street trees, isolated shrubs, flowering herbs in pots or geometric beds	Exotics; popular, showy flowers; rugged hybrids	Central cities; small, scattered patches	Intensive preparation of containers; frequent replanting	Ornament, some shade; small potential for environmental modification	Container-grown trees in commercial areas; street trees in cramped sidewalk wells; window boxes and pots
Lawnscapes	Mowed grassland 10 cm tall or less with scattered shade trees, occasional shrub borders	Exotic grasses, chiefly exotic woody species; a few native trees in forested regions	Small residential plots outside commercial districts; newer public parks; suburbia generally	Intensive maintenance: frequent mowing, fertilizing, weeding, irrigating; relatively simple to install	Ornament, shade, recreational space, wastewater disposal; modest potential for environmental modification	Broad age and income spectrum of urban districts; new suburban office complexes; some old, landscaped parks; newer parks generally
Scrub-woodland	Moderately dense to dense tree canopy with undergrowth of shrubs and nongrass herbs	Typically, exotic shrubs and herbs; some native trees in forest regions; uncommonly, native shrubs and herbs	Low-density suburbia; old, landscaped parks	Little maintenance; costly to create rapidly from bare ground; care necessary to preserve native trees during construction	Ornament, shade, full range of environmental benefits	Relatively high income residential neighborhoods; major nineteenth-century parks
Weed patches	Herbaceous plants 30 cm to 2 m tall; uncommonly, with shrubs and trees	Cosmopolitan herbaceous weeds, native weeds, exotic and native oldfield trees and shrubs	Blighted districts with derelict land; rail and road rights-of-way	Little and erratic or no input after major disturbances such as clearing, cutting, or herbicide spraying	Some erosion control; domestic pet exercise grounds; wildlife habitat; limited potential environmental benefits	Lands awaiting urban renewal; disused industrial sites; railroad rights-of-way
Native remnants	Diverse	Native species; exotics chiefly along trails and other sites of disturbance	Large preserves on urban fringes, relatively isolated and inaccessible, at least when first established; buffer zones costly or undesirable to develop for intensive use	Little or no input, except protection against exploitation, encroachment, or overuse	Erosion and flood protection, wildlife habitat, numerous environmental benefits if large biomass	Hard to develop lands such as steep slopes, floodplains, marshes, railroad rights-of-way in the midwestern U.S.

such as ornament and historic artifact, actively must be appreciated by people because they are quintessentially social.

A. Ornament

The prime reason why nonweedy plants persist in cities, and even are cultivated there at great expense, is because green plants are needed for ornament. By ornament here is meant not simply optional outdoor decoration easily to be dispensed with, but rather a feature of the urban environment which the inhabitants actually consider essential to their individual and collective well being (Schmid, 1975). Vegetation is a visual and aesthetic necessity that provides both delight to its beholders and nonverbal information concerning the urban socioeconomic system.

Were green plants suddenly to vanish, urbanites would find their environment greatly impoverished. Hence it is widely recognized that large, old trees give an air of long-settled attractiveness to residential landscapes, as well as the amenity of summertime shade. Thus forested tracts zoned for residential use are priced higher than otherwise similar but treeless land, and tax assessors take trees into account when computing property values (Payne, 1973).

Urban vegetation, unlike that of working farms, ranches, and forests or natural wildernesses, is first of all a social phenomenon, an expression of social-class behavior and an object of fashion. The front yards of suburban neighborhoods show these aspects most clearly, but they can be found just as surely in the handful of plants which are grown around central city apartment house entrances or as the embellishments of commercial establishments. Where income levels or corporate profits are high, the expanse of vegetated land, the floristic diversity, and (within limits) the biomass of vegetation are greater than in contemporaneous districts where income levels are low or where profit margins are slim. Over time as measured in units of 30 to 50 years, the popular plants installed in new neighborhoods of equivalent social standing change, but this process has received little analysis.

The fascinating interplay between vegetation patterns and patterns of social behavior has been illustrated in detail for few cities. In Chicago, for example, expensive neighborhoods with large lots tend to have more trees per lot, but not necessarily more diverse kinds of trees, than less expensive blocks (Schmid, 1975). Nineteenth-century homes have deciduous shrubs and hedges; newer homes, evergreen foundation plantings. Hedges along property lines are not common in post-1945 Chicago suburbs. Where incomes are high enough for homeowners to purchase much nursery stock, the diversity of shrubs is greatest in new suburbia. Food plants are almost never cultivated in front yards. Dense scrub-woodland vegetation is a minority style in the residential landscape, and is found only around some houses in the upper range of incomes. As Thorstein Veblen (1899) reported from Chicago four generations ago, species and arrangements of plants are vested with social-class connotations, and provide information about the people associated with them.

Furthermore, ideas about urban vegetation types and the landscapes they create are potent social forces, fostered and reinforced by symbolism in language and literature. No small part of the post-1945 boom in sprawling suburbs was due to the widely held belief that the green lawns of single-family houses are ideal settings for family life for those who can afford them. Whether myth or reality, the belief is strong enough to have supported the investment of many billions of dollars by American society, and it requires the services of millions of people in keeping up the proper appearances by mowing, fertilizing, watering, and weeding the lawns.

Plants and vegetation types play an important, if ironic, role in the symbolism of suburb, street, and subdivision names. Major urban streets and suburban parkways may be embellished with abundant plantings of trees, shrubs, or flowers to distinguish them from ordinary streets. For the most part, however, American city streets are not differentiated by separate species of trees. It is common for streets to bear the names of trees, but rarely do the plantings correspond to the street names. Few prospective homebuyers actually may expect to find oaks in Oak Park or elms in Elmwood, but there is no question that the mental image of tree-lined streets helps sell real estate. Names like Cornfield Acres or Dandelion Meadows would be less likely to convey the proper impression to potential purchasers.

Like the appearance and furnishings of the houses themselves, vegetation is an object of concern and enjoyment for the inhabitants of single-family residential neighborhoods. The landscaping makes a public statement to passersby who may never enter, a statement more likely to be made through the automobile at curbside in a central-city neighborhood. Apartment dwellers may be less directly concerned with everyday vegetation management, although the landscaping of apartment entrances also conveys its social meaning. Apartment dwellers also frequently may use the vegetation of public parks and generally pay extra rent if attractive roof gardens, lakes, parks, or golf courses are nearby. Some homeowners find gardening a delightful hobby; others, an onerous but virtually inescapable chore.

Ornament is the foremost role that vegetation currently plays in American cities, but it is not the only role. To the extent that vegetation has only visual ornamental utility, it can be replaced by artificial imitations, such as plastic trees and synthetic grass (Krieger, 1973). So long as the artificial greenery is viewed from a distance, it may satisfy people's formal expectations, particularly in biologically inhospitable sites. As viewed by the spectators, artificial turf in a football stadium may look better than real grass, especially during games on rainy days.

But living organisms can provide other environmental benefits to urbanites, and at lower cost. These roles include the local amelioration of climate, air quality improvement and monitoring, noise reduction, waste water disposal, economic products, features of historic interest, and habitat for wildlife. The list is not exhaustive. Such benefits probably contribute as much or more to the total experience of aesthetic attractiveness of vegetation as its visual patterns of form and color.

As these other actual and potential environmental effects of urban vegetation are described, it will become evident that they are more likely to be brought about when they accompany than when they are in opposition to what here is broadly termed *vegetation's ornamental role.* To the extent that a large biomass of vegetation is necessary to accomplish environmental amelioration that is perceptible by people, it is necessary that ideas about style and design accommodate the appropriate quantity and placement of green plants in the urban landscape.

B. Climatic Amelioration

Local microclimates are influenced greatly by the quantity, species composition, and siting of vegetation. The shelterbelt value of evergreen and deciduous trees and shrubs long has been recognized by farmers, ranchers, and orchardists (van Eimern et al., 1964; Van Haverbeke, 1977). For more than a century, popular garden books have been reminding homeowners that significant benefits can be achieved by strategic placement of trees and shrubs to give summer shade, not block winter sun, and break winter winds (Federer, 1971). But there is little evidence that microclimatic benefits have been achieved by most urban vegetation managers, other than the amenity of summer shade. Where lots are small, street trees may be the only trees present. Typically they are widely spaced as a result of preferences or ordinances; seldom are they massed. There rarely is a sufficient number of large, dense shrubs to affect the climate that pedestrians experience wherever container plants, lawnscapes, or weedpatches are found, except perhaps around the foundations of buildings. Only in proximity to planted shrub-woodland or remnant forest is there likely to be a perceptible vegetation-related difference in winter microclimate in residential neighborhoods. Commercial and industrial districts typically have too little vegetation for significant local climatic effects, although notable exceptions may be corporate headquarters recently established in suburban estates or the vast buffer zones around various energy facilities.

Lawnscapes and the shade provided by even a relatively few large street . trees, however, can enhance summer amenity substantially, as virtually every urbanite knows. There is a great opportunity for using vegetation to help conserve the energy needed to heat and cool houses through the strategic placement of vines, shrubs, and trees (Robinette, 1972). As the use of solar energy becomes more widespread, yet another social constraint on the placement of trees and other vegetation will be the desire not to block the flow of sunshine to low-level collectors. Little information is available on the costs and benefits to individual homeowners of microclimatic amelioration by urban and suburban vegetation.

On a broader geographical scale, the tree-form vegetation of large parks measurably can influence mesoclimate some blocks distant. In the absence of midsummer surface winds, the cooler air that results from shade and evapotranspiration flows outward along the ground surface from areas with trees, and is replaced by the heated air formed over pavements. Maximum advantage could be taken of this phenomenon if abundant moisture for evapotranspiration could be assured when most needed both directly by the plants themselves and indirectly by human beneficiaries. For street trees with restricted root volume, however, evapotranspiration may be limited when its benefits could be greatest. Even the conscientiously irrigated vegetation of residential areas may be denied water during extended periods of drought. The entire ground surface does not need to be forested in order to affect air temperatures and moisture content significantly. Numerical estimates are few, but one theoretical calculation showed that, if one-third of the land surface of an area were vegetated, two thirds of the potential effect of a complete plant cover on daily maximum air temperatures could be expected (Oke, 1972).

C. Air Quality Enhancement and Monitoring

The quality of the air in urban areas can be affected favorably, if sufficient vegetation is present (Warren, 1973). Where there are large expanses of vegetation, as in major parks, combustion generally is insignificant, and the air is not contaminated by discharges of pollutants. Hence such spaces dilute the dirtier air from surrounding districts. They also are places where dust (particulate matter) can settle. The more extensive the leaf surfaces, the more effective the filtration. Conifers generally are more effective filters than broadleaf deciduous trees, even when the deciduous leaves are present, although air pollutants may affect the health of the conifers more severely.

Plants also have been shown to take up gaseous pollutants into their leaves. Where concentrations of pollutants are too great, damage to leaf tissue can result, and the plants may be weakened or killed (Hindawi, 1970). Unfortunately, the toxic effects of urban pollution now extend far downwind from most American urban areas. Plant breeders are working to develop varieties of urban ornamentals resistant to air pollution as well as varieties capable of absorbing pollutants efficiently (see, for example, Gerhold, 1977).

Vegetation is no substitute for technological means to reduce emissions of polluting substances. But vegetation is an important sink for such pollutants as ozone, sulfur dioxide, nitrogen dioxide, and heavy metals. The millions of trees that can be grown on a few hundred hectares of land can absorb thousands of tons of pollutants annually (Murphy et al., 1977).

The value of vegetation in absorbing atmospheric pollutants generated by urban and industrial activity has seldom been calculated. A hypothetical analysis of the value of densely forested public open space in scavenging airborne pollutants recently was developed for the St. Louis, Missouri, Air Quality Control Region (AQCR) by DeSanto et al. (1977). Reductions were known to be needed in the anticipated 1985 emissions of total suspended particulates (TSP) and sulfur dioxide (SO_2) in order to maintain ambient air quality within national standards. Comparisons were developed for attaining the needed air quality improvement both by technological means (stack-gas scrubbers) at major sources and by dense afforestation of presently vacant or agricultural land in the region using coniferous and deciduous trees (Table 2). The technical vegetation uptake data were based on a monumental review of the available literature (DeSanto et al., 1976a).

It was found to be technically possible to accommodate the anticipated increase in TSP by planting forests on about 7.3% of the land area of the AQCR, primarily steeply sloping and floodprone areas devoid of trees. Sufficient available land was found to exist within those parts of the region surrounding major TSP sources to accommodate the new forests within that area centered on the Mississippi River projected to have the region's highest ambient TSP concentrations. The capital costs of the afforestation including land purchase, however, were expected to exceed $6 billion, as opposed to slightly more than $3 million for stack controls at power plants. No incidental social or environmental benefits from the public open space or its proposed 130 million trees were quantified in the report, although a substantial need for additional public open space currently exists in the region. Presumably, a significant proportion of the $1.5 billion in land costs could be attributed to public open space needs unrelated to air quality maintenance. Even then, however, the stack precipitators probably would show strong monetary cost advantages.

By comparison, if some 440 thousand deciduous street trees were established alongside the 2,300 km of roadways in St. Louis (costs not estimated), they would be expected to remove less than 1% of the required amount of particulate matter when they attained full size. The street trees would not be located only in the most polluted areas, but throughout the region.

The results of the analysis for SO_2 were strikingly different from those for particulate matter, because forest vegetation is far more efficient at scavenging SO_2 than TSP. To achieve the needed air quality improvement, only 250 ha would suffice after afforestation. The capital cost would be about $13 million as compared with $21 million for technological processes. Annual maintenance of the vegetation plus taxes forgone would total about 6% of the annual operating cost of the technological processes to decrease sulfur emissions. A cost effectiveness analysis showed the open space vegetation method to cost less than one-third as much as the technological alternative, with even greater direct cost advantage over the years beyond 1985. If the "TSP forest" were established by 1985, of course, the SO_2 benefit would be obtained at no additional cost.

On the basis of their literature review, DeSanto et al. (1977) described a 4-ha unit of forest for maximum pollutant uptake. An outer perimeter band 20 m wide of deciduous trees surrounds a 160-m-square block of conifers. The forest is interrupted by a 20-m-wide open swath through its center, oriented normal to the prevailing wind direction. All of the trees are spaced on 3-m centers, for a total of 2,800 conifers and 1,376 deciduous trees per 4-

Table 2—Hypothetical costs of achieving ambient air quality standards for sulfur dioxide (SO_2) and total suspended particulates (TSP) in the St. Louis Air Quality Control Region, Missouri-Illinois, by 1985 (DeSanto et al., 1977).

Pollutant	A	B	C	D	E	F	G	H	I	J
O_3			87,400.0							
SO_2	1,042	169	678.0	20,875	9,482	250	3,088	9,551	478	56
CO	252	0	2.0							
TSP	132	40	0.33	3,086	381	122,517 (7.3% of total AQCR)	1,519,211	4,594,388	229,719	27,443
NO_x			0.32							
PAN			0.17							
NMHC	121		?							

A — Total 1985 anticipated emissions (000 metric tons/year).
B — Control needed to meet standards (000 metric tons/year).
C — Estimated uptake rate by planted forest hectare (metric tons/year).
D — Technological reduction—capital cost ($000, 1977 dollars) to achieve standards, 1985.
E — Technological reduction—annual operation cost ($000, 1977 dollars) to achieve standards, 1985.
F — Land needed (ha) for vegetation sink to achieve standards, 1985.
G — Vegetation sink—land cost ($000, 1977 dollars) @ $12.4/ha to achieve standards, 1985 (if private land is purchased by the public).
H — Vegetation sink—planting capital cost ($000, 1977 dollars) @ $37.5/ha to achieve standards, 1985.
I — Vegetation sink—annual operation ($000, 1977 dollars) @ $1.865/ha.
J — Vegetation sink—annual taxes lost ($000, 1977 dollars) @ $0.224/ha (if private land is purchased by the public).

ha block. How close the 4-ha blocks should be spaced with respect to one another was not indicated. A low diversity of cultivated trees was envisioned: eastern white pine as the only conifer; English oak, Norway maple, European small-leaved linden, European aspen, and European white birch as the deciduous trees. The probability that a forest of the proposed composition would survive on the substantial expanse of Mississippi River floodplain recommended for afforestation was not estimated by the authors. Native floodplain species of trees might offer better prospects on such sites, if replanting and maintenance are to be minimized.

The SO_2 analysis rests on the crucial assumption that locally produced sulfur compounds are present near the surface locally, where they can be affected by vegetation. Because major sources such as power plants typically have stacks hundreds of meters tall, however, the assumption of complete local fallout may not be justified. It is becoming increasingly apparent that high-level emissions typically travel hundreds or thousands of kilometers downwind from their sources and contribute to acidic rainfall over a vast region depending on meteorological conditions (Husar et al., 1978). The major conclusion of DeSanto et al. (1977)—that vegetation is a cost-effective means to enhance air quality as compared with available sulfur emissions control technology—therefore, is not fully substantiated.

Several other pollutants were touched upon in the report, although they were not expected to exceed ambient standards in St. Louis and hence were not studied in detail. Carbon monoxide is expected to be absorbed by the plants and soil in each model forest hectare at the rate of 2 metric tons/year. The authors opined that roadside vegetation in particular could be useful in reducing the elevated concentrations of carbon monoxide that typically are found along highways, and they sketched the arrangement of plantings that they believe would maximize the effect. Plants also affect concentrations of pollutants linked in the atmospheric oxidant cycle. Nitrogen oxides uptake was reported as 0.32 metric tons/ha per year; ozone, as 87,400 metric tons/ha per year; and peroxyacyl nitrates, as 0.17 metric tons/ha per year. Because some green plants also contribute hydrocarbons to the atmosphere, however, their overall contribution to atmospheric oxidant problems is uncertain.

The U.S. Environmental Protection Agency since 1976 has maintained a formal hydrocarbon emissions offset policy which allows the construction of new hydrocarbon emissions sources in regions that exceed national standards only when the sponsors of the new source can demonstrate that the net effect of the new source will be a reduction of total regional emissions. Ordinarily the offset is accomplished by discontinuing operations at some existing source that emits more hydrocarbons than the proposed new source. During 1977 Louisiana State officials seeking to attract a major automobile assembly plant near Shreveport proposed that pine forests in the region be cut to offset the anticipated emissions of paint hydrocarbons by terminating the existing emissions of terpenes by the pine trees. The proposal was not favorably received by federal officials (Anon., 1977). People perceive the terpenes released by conifers as characteristic and valuable constituents of "fresh" air (Turk & D'Angio, 1962).

Because plants are affected by very low concentrations of air pollutants, they have been used as biological indicators to monitor ambient air pollutant concentrations. They are less expensive and easier to maintain than mechanical monitoring devices. Selected varieties of a number of cultivated species show special susceptibility to particular gases: for example, gladiolus to fluorine, "pinto" beans to ozone and nitrogen compounds, "Bel-W3" tobacco to ozone, alfalfa to sulfur dioxide. The damage during air pollution episodes even to ordinary, common weeds can be interpreted by plant pathologists skilled in diagnosing the effects of air pollutants (Leone et al., 1964). Nettle-leaf goosefoot, for example, is even more sensitive to hydrogen fluoride than gladiolus (Benedict & Breen, 1955).

Both the severity of damage and the rate of pollutant uptake are complicated by factors such as the age of individual plants, their state of nutrition and moisture when exposed, and their previous life history. The joint presence of several pollutants may cause greater damage than any one contaminant alone, and the varied genetic constitution of individual plants within a single species may give rise to great variation in sensitivity.

Possibly the most studied indicators of urban pollutants are lichens, very few of which can tolerate contaminated urban atmospheres. Urban "lichen deserts" have been mapped in more than 100 cities around the world, particularly in northern Europe (LeBlanc & Rao, 1973). Such maps can identify areas where chronic, long-term air pollution is likely to be most detrimental for human health.

The interpretation of plants as pollution indicators is complicated by the fact that widespread, relatively low concentrations of pollutants are replacing the highly destructive, identifiable plumes once generated by smelters and other industrial sources. The landscape effects of generalized chlorosis, early senescence, and reduced growth are difficult to identify and detect (Brandt, 1972). But the adverse effects on the vegetation of farmlands and forests downwind from urban and industrial centers is real, not to mention the effects on vegetation within the cities themselves. Development of commercial tree and crop varieties that can withstand air pollution is a major task of plant breeders working to maintain economic productivity.

There is little specific guidance yet available for the detailed placement of vegetation in proximity to people to maximize air quality benefits (see DeSanto et al., 1976b). The air quality improvement that can be obtained from urban vegetation presumably will require action primarily by public vegetation managers. The combined effect of numerous small plantings by individual homeowners also may be significant. Homeowners no doubt will continue to enjoy the fragrances of home-grown ornamentals, both flowers and conifers, which are their most tangible air quality benefits from vegetation.

D. Noise Reduction

Just as plants recently have been demonstrated to affect air quality beneficially, their effects on noise levels have been measured to be significant. Like air quality effects, noise effects of vegetation are complex and controversial. The intensity of any sound diminishes as the sound energy radiates outward from its source. Vegetation and soil between listener and source provide an excess reduction of sound energy over the decrease attributable to ordinary distance decay. In contrast, hard pavements increase the transmission of sound, as do single lines of trees strategically placed atop berms (Cann & Manning, 1974). Soft, permeable soil attenuates relatively low-frequency sound; field corn effectively muffles high-pitched sound (Aylor, 1972). Suburban plantings of trees and shrubs about 6 m wide and 10 m or less tall can reduce the perceived loudness of passing automobile traffic by half within a distance of less than 30 m from roadways (Cook & Van Haverbeke, 1977). This may be sufficient to allow normal conversation outdoors where it would not be possible otherwise. Grass lawns add to the noise attenuation. Such dimensions are within the spatial constraints of a great deal of single-family house suburbia.

The empirical and theoretical investigation of kinds and arrangements of vegetation for noise control is underway in several centers. Results in the literature are contradictory, and quantitative guidelines are few. Plantings can complement and enhance solid barriers such as walls and embankments. Noise barriers are most effective when sited close to the noise source. A site near the listener is next best; least effective is a barrier halfway between source and listener. Visual screening of intrusive objects psychologically reinforces the effect of sound reduction. Vegetation density as scored visually, however, is not necessarily a reliable measure of its noise-attenuating ability. Neither vegetation nor solid noise barriers are effective when the noise source is at a higher elevation than the listener.

More than a century ago Frederick Law Olmsted and Calvert Vaux demonstrated that traffic on through streets could be rendered unobtrusive when they depressed the roadways behind plant-covered embankments in New York's Central Park. Their example has been followed occasionally by subsequent highway planners. But it is surprising how seldom individual urbanites wall their homes and yards off from traffic arteries on their own initiative. Indeed, dense scrub-woodland plantings that could be effective in reducing noise are the exception rather than the rule in the urban landscape, and are more common along quiet back streets than along noisy thoroughfares. One can speculate on possible explanations for this behavior in the absence of definitive research. Perhaps urbanites grow oblivious to or fond of traffic noise, and thus take no steps to screen it out. More likely, perhaps homeowners may not recognize the potential for vegetation to reduce noise levels significantly. Or perhaps widely held notions about appropriate American landscaping style preclude installation of vegetation dense enough to cut noise levels.

Here is an opportunity for research in human behavior linked to parallel research in acoustics and atmospheric physics such as that of Blair (Christopher Blair, 1975. Effect of trees on noise barrier performance. M.S. Thesis, Massachusetts Inst. of Technol., Cambridge, Mass. 131 p.). The economic cost of creating dense vegetation seems unlikely to be a factor, because the necessary outlay is small, as compared with walls or other solid barriers, if a householder is not in too great a hurry. "Instant" transplanting of large shrubs and trees, of course, can be costly.

E. Economic Products

Few Americans look upon urban vegetation as a source of economically significant products. In contrast, many European cities continue to find timber production within their limits a profitable enterprise (Holscher, 1971). Scientific forest management long has been practiced in such centers as Frankfurt-am-Main (Ruppert, 1960) and Zurich. Wood is more abundant and less expensive in North America, and urban trees are more likely to be regarded as urban solid waste than as a source of municipal revenue, except insofar as they add value to the local tax base. Philadelphia generates half a million board feet of sawlogs and 3,000 cords of pulpwood annually—a quantity of wood large enough to supply a small sawmill in continuous operation (Thornton, 1971).

Urban tree harvesting is complex, and high-value timber rarely is produced on American streets. Most city trees are of species with low commercial value, and harvestable trees are widely scattered and expensive to remove. Because of the ravages of Dutch elm disease, some midwestern towns have sold their parkway elms for timber, to forestall probable loss of even the salvage value (Professor Forest Stearns, Univ. of Wisconsin-Milwaukee, personal communication, 1973).

Individuals can grow foodstuffs, but the significance of home vegetable production in American towns and cities is not readily apparent. Urban land costs and air pollution do not encourage city dwellers to garden for profit. Nearly half of American households, some 31 million of them, grew vegetables during 1973, but kitchen gardens are relegated to back yards. Very seldom are food plants placed in front yards. Fruit and nut trees are uncommon on city streets, possibly because urban foresters perceive them to create litter and liability problems. Vegetable gardening gains and loses popularity from time to time in suburbia. Some writers of garden books stress the quality of home-grown produce and its exercise and amusement value rather than its low cost (Burrage, 1954). Many municipalities have made garden plots available on public lands for a nominal fee, and numerous Americans currently are enthusiastic about this venerable European practice (Drake & Lawrence, 1976; Bur. of Outdoor Recreation, 1975; Menninger, 1977). Public garden plots have been widely reported to improve social relations among the residents of blocks where they have been established.

F. Waste Water Disposal

Land disposal of treated waste water effluent has become the subject of renewed attention during the past two decades as an alternative to disposal of effluent to streams or the ocean. Vegetation enhances the quality of effluent recharged to ground water and complements the filtering action of soil. Effluent, in turn, stimulates plant growth when properly applied.

The Federal Water Pollution Control Act Amendments of 1972 (Public Law 92-500) established the elimination of pollutant discharge to waterways as a part of the National goal to restore water quality. In arid sections of the nation the recycling of waste water long has been recognized as necessary, and irrigation water is a valuable commodity even if the water previously was used for urban purposes. The potential for irrigation using treated effluent in the humid east, however, long was neglected. Only for widely spaced private households have septic tanks been used for wastes distributed locally where soils are suitable. These systems incidentally provide water and nutrients to the grasses of their leaching plots, and may contribute to ground water supplies.

A system to maximize plant growth and ground water recharge was designed at University Park, Pennsylvania, during the 1960's using treated waste water effluent (Sopper & Kardos, 1973; see Chap. 26 "Surface Applications of Sewage Effluent and Sludge" by W. E. Sopper). Here optimal rates of effluent application were determined empirically for several types of vegetation. As a result the growth rates of irrigated trees increased, hay yields were higher than on unirrigated control plots, and irrigated fields gave bumper crops of field corn (equalled by local farmers using commercial fertilizers only in years when rainfall was abundant). Nutrients that remain in the effluent after secondary sewage treatment are beneficial to the growing plants.

Under the central Pennsylvania conditions, effluent to a depth of 5 cm is applied rapidly by sprinklers; the soil is allowed to dry between such weekly applications. At this rate about 525 ha (1,300 acres) of land would be required to accommodate the effluent generated by 100,000 people, and some additional land would be necessary for storage of the effluent prior to its distribution. Because every system must be shut down occasionally for maintenance, the effective annual irrigation rate may be less than 250 cm (100 inches) above normal rainfall. Effluent can be applied to land used for park purposes and to golf courses. It probably could be used to advantage by street trees, if an efficient and economic distribution system were available.

Some constituents of waste water are not readily filtered by a spray-irrigation system. Heavy metals from industrial discharges may be concentrated in biological food chains, so industrial wastes may not be suitable for land disposal. Road deicing salts pass through the soil matrix to ground water, because chloride ions are not readily captured by roots or soil particles. Nitrates are taken up by actively growing plant roots and are converted to gaseous nitrogen by bacteria, but are not stored efficiently in the soil matrix.

As research on land disposal systems is conducted in various locations, the adaptability of the spray irrigation concept for waste water disposal under various conditions is being demonstrated. Useful recent keys to the enormous literature are those of Carlile and Stewart (1977) and Kardos et al. (1974). On Cape Cod, for example, experimental irrigation rates are being used as great as 10 cm/week. The upper limit of irrigation rates that benefit forage crop yields and preserve ground water quality has not yet been determined on Cape Cod. Within the range of rates examined so far on Cape Cod, the yield of crops is linearly proportional to the total amount of treated waste water applied. Harvesting of hay removes about half of the nitrogen and potassium and 15% of the phosphorus applied in the effluent (Deese et al., 1978). Because of the advantages in increased crop yields, as well as enhancement of water quality, the U.S. Environmental Protection Agency is sponsoring extensive research on vegetation and soil as waste water filters, and the future of such systems appears bright as a means of disposal for treated domestic waste water effluent in many urban regions.

G. Historic Artifacts

Vegetation can serve as an object of historic interest in a metropolitan area. Individual trees may live for several centuries, and they can preserve living associations with historic persons and events. Large, old trees are not easily replaced, and frequently inspire widespread respect and concern. They may serve as reminders of land uses that antedate current urban activities and of human generations long past. Long-established and well-maintained gardens can become objects of general appreciation.

Historic vegetation patterns, too, can enhance historic architectural remains. Historic styles of planting have been recreated in many restorations of historic districts, as in the numerous eighteenth-century herb gardens in the northeastern states.

One special kind of historic interest is an interest in cultivating the plant species and even the vegetation types native to a given region. Botanical gardens and arboreta in the midwest have sponsored efforts to recreate stands of prairie. On the Atlantic coast there is scattered interest in "cultivating" goldenrods and other wild plants of oldfields to form a low-maintenance meadow vegetation. Some homeowners transplant and encourage forest undergrowth around their homes. Such efforts appear to spring from several sources. In part there is a widespread desire to escape the routine maintenance of lawnscapes. Some people derive from scientific botanical training a knowledge and appreciation of native plants, which they then seek to propagate. Many native species present a horticultural challenge, because their requirements are not well known; others are easily established and require virtually no effort to maintain. Some people have a keen interest in local history which extends to the wild vegetation of pre-settlement times. It is reasonable to expect a wider role for cultivated native species and recreated native vegetation types, if fossil fuel shortages give support to native plant fashions in urban landscapes. If there is no gasoline to run the lawnmower, people may replace the lawn. But the conservative practices of nurserymen who offer only the reliable "best seller" cultigens provide an impediment to the more widespread propagation of native plants by urbanites generally.

H. Wildlife Habitat

Finally, vegetation is necessary if populations of wildlife are to survive in urban areas, where the living creatures not under human control have the most frequent opportunities to be seen and to give delight to people. Vegetation undoubtedly is responsible to a great extent for the characteristic differences in urban fauna observed in the several parts of metropolitan areas. Central cities support an impoverished fauna of pigeons, house sparrows, nighthawks, rats, mice, and cockroaches; suburban wildlife typically includes native songbirds, squirrels, rabbits, raccoons, opossums, skunks, and deer. Large parks and other green areas, especially when linked by corridors along which animals can travel, can increase the urban fauna substantially. Habitat requirements of various classes of urban fauna have been receiving scholarly attention during recent years (guides to the scattered literature are Schmid, 1974; Gill & Bonnett, 1973). Vegetation rich in native plant species is capable of supporting more kinds of desirable wildlife than uniform plantings of exotic species. Where disturbance by domestic pets (or former pets that have run wild) is not too intense, urban weedpatches can provide habitat attractive to wildlife. Seedeating birds may be benefited especially by the prolific fruiting of many common weeds such as foxtail grasses and pigweeds. There is still a need for additional research to inform planning efforts to maximize the wildlife habitat value of urban plantings. At present both the U.S. Fish and Wildlife Service and the U.S. Forest Service are supporting ongoing research on urban wildlife (Thomas & DeGraaf, 1973; Noyes & Progulske, 1974), and wildlife biologists no longer are constrained to study only pest control and the propagation of game species (Larson, 1972). The literature on urban insects recently was reviewed by Frankie and Ehler (1978).

IV. CONSTRAINTS THAT AFFECT URBAN VEGETATION

In the wild landscape where human activity is little evident, vegetation patterns are closely related to the array of habitat factors which are present at any given site. Many urbanites use the techniques of horticulture to overcome soil, exposure, temperature, and water conditions unfavorable to the plants they want to grow, and actively discourage those weedy plants which they dislike. When a region with diverse habitat conditions and patterns of vegetation is urbanized, the old patterns may be nearly obliterated, and a new set of constraints on plant growth become operative. Cultivated ornamentals in general tolerate the conditions found around houses or structures: open sites, ample sunshine, little competition, disturbed soil tailored to their nutritional requirements, and water as necessary to supplement precipitation. Fast-growing floodplain trees such as silver maple and ash may be planted widely on uplands, so that native and cultivated patterns of vegetation increasingly diverge.

In the vicinity of Chicago, for example, the originally distinct patterns of vegetation which marked the sandy beach ridges, the poorly drained flats of the glacial lake plain, and the steep morainal slopes are not apparent in the patterns of ornamentals in residential districts. Yews and junipers around foundations, bluegrass lawns, plantain-lilies, daylilies, and (in summer) garden geraniums are found in every neighborhood on all kinds of substrates (Schmid, 1975).

Natural habitat factors always affect urban vegetation. Climate imposes basic limitations on what can be grown outdoors. Thus southern Florida, Texas, and California spas are distinguished by their citrus and palm trees. Arizona towns have cacti; Mobile, Alabama, has liveoaks and magnolias with festoons of Spanish-moss. Northeastern suburbs support countless azaleas and rhododendrons, but the less acid soils and water supplies of the midwest mean that these ericaceous shrubs cannot be maintained there without special care. Habitat factors unique to urban areas, however, derive from human activity.

Natural soils usually are disturbed severely when a tract of land is developed for urban use. Slopes may be graded, and drainage may be accelerated by soil compaction and storm sewers. Irrigation water may become available in arid landscapes. And people may be willing to nurture cultigens through unfavorable seasons indoors or in greenhouses. The increased temperatures of the urban "heat island" produced by combustion may affect delicately regulated plant behavior, such as the flowering date of ornamental shrubs and bulbs. Urban heat also produces a longer frost-free season in the central city than in the suburbs. It is not possible to generalize the many natural habitat changes across the nation as a whole, so attention will be focused here on the human rather than the natural environmental influences on urban vegetation.

A. Basic Urban Design

Vegetation in urban areas occupies the space left after buildings and roadways have been constructed. Ordinarily there is more such space in residential than in commercial or industrial districts. The trees that exist on a tract of land before development seldom are preserved during the construction period; it is rare to find a street or sidewalk that has been curved to avoid a predevelopment tree. Typically trees are uprooted that might interfere with the proposed buildings or might get in the way of construction activities. Shrubs and wild herbaceous vegetation generally are cleared, so that the new owner of the house or commercial building can or must begin his landscaping de novo, possibly with soil material completely different from that present before development.

The extent and shape of spaces devoted to greenery may be dictated by zoning ordinances and setback regulations. In consequence, they may be homogeneous over extensive districts, but may differ between areas developed at different times. Where streets are curved or offset, scrub-woodland may attain greater visual prominence than where there is a regular grid pattern design. In some cities areas that are best left in native vegetation, rather than developed, wisely have been preserved; in others, floodplains, steep slopes, and wetlands may long have been unprotected against development. During recent years environmentally protective laws and regulations have begun to increase the area preserved as open space, and typically vegetated, in growing metropolitan regions. In a few areas environmental inventories are being integrated as part of the information base used for basic planning decisions, and new techniques are being devised to accommodate such data (e.g., Fabos & Caswell, 1977). Rarely have environmental data been incorporated into the local zoning maps and ordinances that form the basic land use controls under the American political system, despite promising steps at the federal level and by many state governments since the National Environmental Policy Act (Public Law 91-190) became law in 1970.

Lot sizes and street trees may limit the amount of sunshine available, and consequently the kinds of plants that can be grown. Vegetables in particular require full sun. Shrubs, flowers, and some grasses can be grown where there is considerable shade.

B. Socioeconomic Characteristics of Neighborhoods and Their Inhabitants

People organize themselves into groups whose members share ideas and tastes in many things, including landscape design. Such groups are differentiated not only by the amount of time and money they have available to speed on landscaping, but in the way that they choose to spend their resources. Garden clubs may provide a formal means of disseminating shared tastes. In some, but not all, metropolitan areas, garden clubs are among the most exclusive of social institutions. In American cities, single-family house neighborhoods tend to be occupied by people of homogeneous tastes and life styles. Therefore, one would expect relative uniformity of public, front-yard vegetation within neighborhoods and greater variation between neighborhoods. In fact this is generally the case.

Uniformity of landscaping reaches its peak in new suburbs or tracts where dozens and hundreds of blocks are constructed almost simultaneously. Here developers may install stereotyped plantings which persist for years by sheer inertia. Sociologists report widely shared attitudes toward vegetation maintenance, which is a significant activity for suburban homeowners (Riesman, 1968, p. 392). Conversational humor is the means for supporting neighborhood norms and curbing deviations toward either the shabbiness which might lower property values or the elaborateness of plantings which might push up the general standard of effort required (Gans, 1967). Old neighborhoods tend to exhibit a greater variety of front-yard landscape styles, and their residents feel less pressure for conformity to shared ideals (Meyersohn & Jackson, 1958). Homeowners whose motivation for keeping up their own lawns is based primarily on a sense of community responsibility take strongest exception to unkempt lawns in their neighborhood (Robert Reynolds. 1972. Differences in perception and function of the lawn in Ann Arbor, Michigan. M.A. Thesis. Univ. of Michigan, Ann Arbor, Mich. 52 p.).

The social rules which apply to front yards are weakened or relaxed with respect to back yards, where a much greater degree of privacy is customary. It is rare that homeowners wall off their front yards from public view by masonry or dense hedges. Indeed, some suburbs enact ordinances prohibiting such measures. Yet front lawns seldom appear to receive the use for recreational or other purposes that would justify the land traditionally devoted to them. Veblen's "reputable futility," the display of useless items chiefly to show one's ability to afford them, still is a potent social force that affects American front yards (Veblen, 1899, p. 132–137).

Several alternative arrangements have begun to appear in American residential landscapes. Clustered groupings of townhouses permit a reduction in build-over land, and enable the preservation of a larger extent of open, vegetated land at a gross density equivalent to traditional single-family house layouts. In the northeastern states grass lawns are being replaced by pachysandra, and ivy is a popular ground cover in coastal California. Neither requires mowing, but neither can be walked upon. In some areas inhabited by residents of at least upper middle class status, the desire to preserve remnant forest or reestablish low-maintenance scrub-woodland can be observed. Such is distinctly a minority preference at the present time; the author is aware of no instances where native prairie has been reestablished as front-yard vegetation, although prairie is being grown experimentally at several institutions in the mid-continent.

Particular species or genera of plants become fashionable and then lose favor in accordance with the whims of taste. This process has received relatively little study, like the rest of the social actions which create urban vegetation patterns (a few brief comments were offered by Wright, 1934). The "high tradition" of garden design is the province of landscape architects employed in the public service or by the wealthy few who are conversant with the historic styles of Europe or other cultures (Newton, 1971). But for most urbanites who shape the vegetation of their own small plots, garden design is created in a vernacular tradition. What is planted depends on what the nurseries sell or what the neighbors are willing to share. Imitations of gardening practice may spread up, as well as down, the socioeconomic hierarchy from the "elite" of skilled horticulturists in any urban neighborhood.

People plant not only what seems fashionable, however, but also what they know and enjoy. Midwestern homeowners, given a choice of street trees to be planted in their parkways, overwhelmingly request maples. It is not surprising, then, that highway departments and municipal foresters in the northeastern and north central states also plant great numbers of maples

(Long et al., 1973). The popularity of maples has endured for a century. Other street trees are prominent in other sections of the nation.

Little attention has been given to ethnic differences in the vegetation patterns of American urban areas. By the time the children of immigrants move into the suburban neighborhoods, they are likely to have assimilated mainstream cultural practices. The opportunity to affect vegetation may be sharply limited for new immigrants in densely settled urban neighborhoods unless public garden plots are available.

C. Neighborhood Stability

Gardens cannot be constructed so rapidly as buildings or houses. Thus a period of years is required before the vegetation of a neighborhood, public park, or corporate headquarters can reach maturity. Young street trees may require one or more human generations to attain full stature. Hence some landscape architects have advocated the planting of large trees rather than small nursery stock (Baer & Gordon, 1972). Neighborhood inhabitants or land use zoning may change, bringing new owners or residents with contrasting ideas concerning vegetation before the plantings in a district can mature.

When a residential neighborhood maintains its social standing over many decades, the change of its inhabitants may be gradual, and overall goals in landscaping may be preserved. Vegetation is most likely to be altered shortly after a property changes ownership. It is always easier, quicker, and less costly for a new owner to add incrementally to the vegetation which already exists on his lot, than to root it all out and begin anew. Homebuyers consider existing vegetation as one of the factors influencing their choice of homes. As time passes they are likely to become accustomed to this vegetation and to grow satisfied with it. Trees, and even beds of shrubs and perennial herbs, may outlast the houses themselves in socially stable neighborhoods where rebuilding takes place.

In neighborhoods where population shifts bring drastic changes of the social class of occupants, however, the repercussions on vegetation may be severe. Examples can be found where single-family residences are converted to boarding houses or replaced by commercial uses, or where land is earmarked for "urban renewal." Limited observations of population change in residential neighborhoods support the inference that social class dominates race or ethnic group in affecting the maintenance and patterns of vegetation (Schmid, 1975).

D. Epidemic Diseases and Insects

Despite the efforts of nurserymen, botanical gardens, and arboreta to find and demonstrate promising new plants for use in urban areas, the number of species of trees, shrubs, and herbs that become common is far smaller than the number of species that are known to be growable in any urban area. The actual diversity of urban plants is substantially less than the potential diversity. Consequently the vegetation of cities is almost as vulnerable to outbreaks of pests and diseases as the monocrop plantings of commercial farms and forests.

The most spectacular example from the northeastern section of the United States during the past 40 years has been the Dutch elm disease, to which the American elm is especially susceptible (Laut & Schomaker, 1976). The disease is caused by an exotic, Eurasian fungus which blocks the vascular system of the host tree. The fungus was introduced into New York and the Ohio Valley during the 1930's with imported elm logs from which the bark had not been removed. Already the disease was ravaging elms in Western Europe. The fungus is spread by introduced and by native species of bark beetles, and can travel between adjacent trees through root grafts. The disease has been recorded from Nova Scotia to eastern Texas, and from the Dakotas, Wyoming, and Colorado to Georgia. It now is known even in populations of introduced American elms in California and the intermontane west. The U.S. Forest Service (1977) estimated that the 77 million elms in incorporated areas in 1930 were reduced by more than half nationwide to 34 million by 1976. For municipalities in the northeastern states in which elm was the predominant street tree, Dutch elm disease caused an extraordinary loss in amenity. Millions of dollars continue to be spent annually on Dutch elm disease research and on control programs in areas where the elms have not yet been eliminated.

Dutch elm disease was not the first major introduced disease of trees in North America this century, and there is no reason to think it will be the last. Numerous examples could be cited. Prior to World War I another fungal blight eliminated the American chestnut as a principal forest tree (Shear & Stevens, 1917). A virus disease of elms, phloem necrosis, took a heavy toll in the southern midwest during the 1940's and 1950's, before it was overshadowed in importance by Dutch elm disease (Baker, 1949). Yet another disease, oak wilt, resembles Dutch elm disease in that it, too, is produced by a fungus, is spread by insect and by squirrel vectors, and can be transmitted underground through root grafts. All the organisms involved, however, are native to North America. Oaks are found in urban areas, but are substantially less abundant than elms formerly were. Oak wilt could have widespread adverse effects in forests (Himelick & Fox, 1961).

Because urban trees and other plants may be under stress from the circumscribed rooting space, limited water supply, air pollution, and trampling associated with urban areas, they may be affected greatly by insect attack even when no diseases are involved. Urbanites may respond by applying insecticides which kill valuable insects and other wildlife as well as the target species. Regulations concerning insecticides have become increasingly stringent during recent years, and specialists in urban entomology actively are pursuing research on alternative means for insect control in urban environments (Frankie & Koehler, 1978).

V. PLANNING URBAN REVEGETATION

This discussion of the planning of urban vegetation will address first several general considerations. Then it will conclude with comments on the survival of remnant native vegetation in the urban landscape.

A. General Considerations

There are many managers and planners of urban vegetation. Some are homeowners; others, apartment superintendents. Yet others are commercial gardeners and nurserymen. A few are professional planners and landscape architects employed by private or public clients. Collectively they produce the vegetation of American urban landscapes.

Their efforts are expended chiefly on two of the types of vegetation previously described, container vegetation and lawnscapes. They all ignore weedscapes, and they rarely affect remnant native plant communities. All are guided by their understanding of appropriate forms of vegetation as ornament, and by their knowledge of the environmental conditions needed to grow their chosen plants.

The effective performance of the majority of roles previously described for urban vegetation would necessitate a substantial quantity of vegetation in close proximity to urbanites. To the degree that such roles become understood more widely and that they harmonize with the formal requirements of vegetation as ornament, they may be more widely achieved than at present. But many urbanites may prefer the noise of automobile traffic to dense shrubbery enclosing their lawns, and there is much that needs to be discovered concerning the optimum use of plants to counter air pollution.

As research continues on the quantification of benefits to be gained from vegetation, urban planners and landscape architects will gain new goals to implement in new and rebuilt neighborhoods. These can be expected to parallel the current interests in linking building design to climatic parameters and energy efficiency. Some of the roles can be played simultaneously in multiple use of green open space; others may prove better adapted to single-purpose compartmentalization of the landscape. Few American cities will emulate Zurich, with one quarter of its land occupied by municipal forest; the price of wood is just too low in North America.

Managers of public vegetation must give heed to the lessons of Dutch elm disease and chestnut blight. Data on trees ordered for municipalities and for highways still show a strong tendency for urban foresters to rely on relatively few species of trees known to be reliable. Block after block on Manhattan Island and in Philadelphia have been planted to London plane, or ginkgo, or honey locust. Should a major disease attack any of these, great swaths could be laid as bare as were the elm-clad streets of Chicago during the 1960's. The disease potential is enhanced further by the vegetative (nonsexual) propagation of clones of common trees by nurserymen. Not only may all the London planes on the street be the same species; they may all be genetically identical cuttings from the same parent.

Native species could become more prominent as cultivated plants, both because of their intrinsic attractiveness and because they are supportive of wildlife. Consider for example a shrub or small tree of the eastern deciduous forest known as fringe-tree. It is not surprising to find a handsome fringe-tree in the splendidly maintained Longwood Gardens west of Philadelphia, but a fringe-tree atop the subway in the neglected median strip between the traffic lanes on Upper Broadway in New York has flowered every year for decades in conditions as severely urban as can be found anywhere. Another example is the witch-hazel, whose yellow flowers appear in late autumn when little else is blooming. Witch-hazels flourish in New York's Central Park, but are rare in nurseries or planted suburbia. Government agencies long have subsidized the propagation of many kinds of trees and shrubs for commercial forestry or for wildlife benefit in rural areas. Making little-known native ornamentals available to urbanites might be an increasingly beneficial future activity. Common wildlife can be encouraged by planting a number of introduced and native plant species (Sharp, 1977). Native plants, however, can be expected to have the greatest value to native animals in general.

There is a great opportunity to maximize the human benefits to be derived from urban vegetation, and the challenge cuts across disciplines and professions. The process of vegetation management can be viewed as a productive enterprise to the extent that people enhance environmental quality and property values by their actions. At the same time, gardening can be viewed as a consumptive activity and a socially constructive use of leisure time. It need not require large inputs of fossil energy, nor need it generate substantial wastes, particularly if people turn away from the current practice of maintaining lawnscapes with substantial inputs of fossil-fuel derived energy. Woodland needs far less human and fossil-fuel input than grass lawn.

Whether public policy should subsidize greater expanses of vegetated land in urban areas, and how the greater quantities of green space might be accomplished if warranted, are interesting questions beyond the scope of this chapter. Central cities have relatively small quantities of vegetation, yet they have relatively high levels of noise and air pollution. How much space should be devoted to vegetation to affect the public welfare optimally, however, is not evident. Too much green space conceivably could lead to excessive commuter travel; unwanted and unused open spaces can become unsafe social vacuums (Jacobs, 1961). How vegetation can best be brought into contact with urbanites also will require careful attention from those who would maximize its benefits to humans.

B. The Protection of Remnant Natural Vegetation

One of the goals which urban vegetation managers may consider is the preservation of remnant natural vegetation. As indicated early in this chapter, native vegetation is most likely to survive in the urban landscape on sites that are not favorable for construction purposes. On such sites, provided that human interference is not too severe, natural plant communities can be expected to survive and reproduce. It may be that a minimum critical size is necessary for the long-term survival of a remnant stand of native vegetation. Within an area smaller than the minimum critical size, local populations of native species eventually can be expected to become extinct, without natural or artificial recolonization. At present there is little understanding of what the critical size of a plot should be to insure the long-term persistence of representative vegetation types. Forests may be damaged by wide-ranging air pollution, as in the watershed above Los Angeles (Miller & Elderman, 1977), but little is known generally of the effects of air pollution on remnant stands of native vegetation in urban areas. Current research concerning the effects of air pollution on vegetation centers on cropland and commercial forests.

Under certain circumstances native plants that antedate American cities survive as part of ornamental urban vegetation. Prairie does not persist in the urban landscape because it is not valued. Wetland vegetation types (marshes, bogs, swamps) are destroyed when standing water is eliminated through filling or accelerating drainage. Individual trees are the most likely plants to remain when an area is converted to urban residential uses. Ordinarily, no vegetation is preserved in commercial or industrial districts.

Even when a forested tract is converted to low-density residential use, however, the survival of its trees is not assured. Where single-family lots are large, say 1 ha (2.5 acres) or more per house, forest may be retained to give privacy and reduce the effort needed to maintain the appearance of the property. There is sufficient space on such a lot for house, outbuildings, and lawn, with room to accommodate the forest as well. In such areas the forest may persist for decades or centuries.

Where average lot size is smaller, say 0.1 to 0.4 ha (0.25 to 1 acre), there is greater disruption, unless the homes are clustered adjacent to the forest rather than within it. Even if care is taken not to remove the trees outright during construction, they nevertheless are exposed to many risks. Tree trunks in new subdivisions seldom are protected during construction with sheaths or barricades. Equipment may be parked or driven across the shallow rooting zones; or excavations, sidewalks, or roadways may damage part of the root system. Soil may be piled up temporarily or cut away to form a final grade, again with adverse effects on the roots. In consequence, dead or dying trees can be observed in most new subdivisions in forested tracts for 5 or 10 years (Schmid, 1975).

Other factors, too, are changed by urban growth. As a forest stand is opened for homesites, lawns, and roadways, the penetration of wind and sun to ground level is increased. Wind-throw increases, and the soil dries more quickly after rains. Runoff is expedited by storm sewers. Undergrowth, at least near the house, usually is replaced by lawn, and leaves are removed to insure the survival of grass. Lawn fertilizer may be applied, and the lawn may be watered. Herbicides may be used to suppress weedy forbs. At the edges of the lawn, aggressive exotic escapes such as myrtle or honeysuckle may invade the remaining undergrowth.

Ordinarily in small plots, regeneration of the surviving canopy trees is suppressed. Volunteer saplings usually do not grow where the owner's formal requirements dictate. Thus replacement trees are sought from commercial nurseries and are the commonly cultivated kinds, seldom the once predominant native species. As the decades pass, forested lots come increasingly to resemble the lots of contemporary houses which initially lacked trees. Forest remnants become scrub-woodland or lawnscapes.

There are many opportunities to increase the persistence of native vegetation when a forested tract is subdivided. All agents in the process—developer, construction workers, new residents—must recognize that the native vegetation is both valuable and fragile. Otherwise it simply is brushed away as of little consequence.

Because native vegetation remnants that do survive in urban landscapes are more likely to be accidental than planned, they may be unfamiliar to most urban residents. Yet they can be recreated by transplanting or other means, given the motivation on the part of land managers to do so. Once reestablished, they can be preserved indefinitely, given knowledgeable management that includes protection from excessive trampling. Their plant communities tend to be complex arrangements rich in species, as compared with the simple linear or area patterns of species-poor ornamental vegetation. They are thus objects of inherent scientific interest, as well as habitats that support attractive populations of wildlife.

Unless they are located so as to harmonize with, contrast with, or otherwise complement, ornamental vegetation, however, remnant stands of vegetation may be viewed as weedy growth that renders the landscape untidy or that conceals surreptitious human behavior. Public education may be needed to counteract these ideas. The preservation of remnant stands of vegetation is a part of the general preservation of our cultural and natural heritage, and their management must be entrusted to knowledgeable professionals who understand their requirements. If natural plant communities should vanish entirely from urban areas, there still would be a great deal of cultivated vegetation. But the quality of our environment would be diminished.

ACKNOWLEDGMENTS

For helpful comments on an earlier draft of this chapter the author is indebted to Dr. William Overlease of West Chester State College and two anonymous reviewers. Advice offered was not always accepted, and the full responsibility for any errors that remain is that of the author.

LITERATURE CITED

Anderson, H. W., M. D. Hoover, and K. G. Reinhart. 1976. Forests and water: effects of forest management on floods, sedimentation, and water supply. USDA-FS, Pacific Southwest Forest and Range Exp. Stn., Gen. Tech. Rep. PSW-18/1976, Berkeley, Calif. 115 p.

Andresen, J. W. 1975. Community and urban forestry, a selected and annotated bibliography. USFS, Southeast Area, State and Private Forestry, Atlanta, Ga. 195 p.

Andresen, J. W. (ed.). 1976. Trees and forests for human settlements. Univ. of Toronto, Centre for Urban Forestry Studies, Toronto, Ontario, Canada. 417 p.

Anonymous. 1977. Louisiana officials study tree-chopping to comply with emissions offset policy. Air/Water Pollut. Rep. 15(41):408.

Aylor, D. E. 1972. Noise reduction by vegetation and ground. J. Acoust. Soc. Am. 51:197–205.

Baer, W. C., and G. Gordon. 1972. Tree planting reconsidered—an argument for big transplants. Landscape Archit. 62:236–239.

Baker, W. L. 1949. Studies on the transmission of the virus causing phloem necrosis of American elm, with notes on the biology of its insect vector. J. Econ. Entomol. 42:729–732.

Benedict, H. M., and W. H. Breen. 1955. The use of weeds as a means of evaluating vegetation damage caused by air pollution. p. 177–190. In Proc. 3rd Natl. Air Pollut. Symp., 18–20 Apr. 1955, Pasadena, Calif. Stanford Res. Inst., Los Angeles, Calif.

Brandt, C. S. 1972. Plants as indicators of air quality. p. 101–107. In W. A. Thomas (ed). Indicators of environmental quality. Plenum Press, New York, N.Y.

Bureau of Outdoor Recreation, Pacific Southwest Regional Office. 1975. Profiles of California community garden projects. USDI, San Francisco, Calif., not paged (32 p.).

Burrage, A. C. 1954. Burrage on vegetables. Van Nostrand, New York, N.Y. 208 p.

Cann, R. G., and J. E. Manning. 1974. Barriers to reduce aircraft noise: a scale model study of two Los Angeles communities. Cambridge Collabor. Rep. 74-4, Cambridge, Mass.

Carlile, B. L., and J. M. Stewart (ed.). 1977. Land application of wastewater, a bibliography. USDI, Off. of Water Res. and Technol., Water Resour. Sci. Inf. Center, OWRT/WRSIC 77-204, Washington, D.C. 406 p.

Cook, D. I., and D. F. Van Haverbeke. 1977. Suburban noise control with plant materials and solid barriers. USDA-FS Rocky Mt. For. and Range Exp. Stn., Res. Bull. EM100. 74 p.

Deese, P. L., R. F. Vaccaro, B. H. Ketchum, P. C. Bowker, and M. R. Dennett. 1978. Ionic distribution in a spray irrigation system. p. 39–66. In R. C. Loehr (ed.) Food, fertilizer, and agricultural residues, Proc. of 9th Cornell Agric. Waste Manage. Conf., April 1977, Cornell Univ., Syracuse, N.Y. Ann Arbor Science Publishers, Inc., Ann Arbor, Mich.

DeSanto, R. S., W. H. Smith, J. A. Miller, W. P. McMillen, and K. A. MacGregor. 1976a. Open space as an air resource management measure. Vol. I, Sink factors. Prepared by COMSIS Corp. for USEPA, Research Triangle Park, N.C. variously paged (298 p.). EPA-450/3-76-028a; PB 261 758.

DeSanto, R. S., R. A. Glaser, W. P. McMillen, K. A. MacGregor, and J. A. Miller. 1976b. Open space as an air resource management measure. Vol. II: Design criteria. Prepared by COMSIS Corp. for USEPA, Research Triangle Park, N.C. variously paged (178 p.). EPA-450/3-76-028b.

DeSanto, R. S., K. A. MacGregor, W. P. McMillen, and R. A. Glaser. 1977. Open space as an air resource management measure. Vol. III: Demonstration plan (St. Louis, Mo.). Prepared by COMSIS Corp. for USEPA, Research Triangle Park, N.C. variously paged (136 p.). EPA-450/3-76-028c; PB 266 450.

Detwyler, T. R. 1972. Vegetation of the city. p. 230–259. In T. R. Detwyler and M. G. Marcus (ed.) Urbanization and environment. Duxbury Press, Belmont, Calif.

Drake, S. Y., and R. L. Lawrence. 1976. Recreational community gardening, a guide to organization and development. USDI, Bur. of Outdoor Recreat., Washington, D.C. 70 p.

Fabos, J. G., and S. J. Caswell. 1977. Composite landscape assessment: assessment procedures for special resources, hazards, and development suitability. Part II of the Metropolitan Landscape Planning Model (METLAND). Univ. of Massachusetts Agric. Exp. Stn., Res. Bull. 637, Amherst, Mass. 323 p.

Federer, C. A. 1971. Effects of trees in modifying urban microclimates. p. 23–28. In Trees and forests in an urbanizing environment. Univ. of Massachusetts Coop. Ext. Serv., Planning and Resour. Dev. Ser. 17, Amherst, Mass.

Frankie, G. W., and L. E. Ehler. 1978. Ecology of insects in urban environments. Annu. Rev. Entomol. 23:367–387.

Frankie, G. W., and C. S. Koehler (ed.). 1978. Perspectives in urban entomology. Academic Press, New York.

Gans, H. J. 1967. The Levittowners. Pantheon Books, New York. 474 p.

Gerhold, H. D. 1977. Effect of air pollution on Pinus strobus L. and genetic resistance: a literature review. Corvallis Environ. Res. Lab., Office of Res. and Dev., USEPA, Corvallis, Oreg. EPA-600/3-77-002.

Gill, Don, and P. A. Bonnett. 1973. Nature in the urban landscape: a study of city ecosystems. York Press, Baltimore, Md. 209 p.

Himelick, E. B., and H. W. Fox. 1961. Experimental studies on the control of oak wilt disease. Univ. of Illinois Agric. Exp. Stn. Bull. 680, Urbana, Ill. 48 p.

Hindawi, I. J. 1970. Air pollution injury to vegetation. Natl. Air Pollut. Control Admin. Pub. no. AP-71. U.S. Government Printing Office, Washington, D.C. 44 p.

Holscher, C. E. 1971. European experience in integrated management of urban and suburban woodlands. p. 133–138. *In* Silas Little and J. H. Noyes (ed.) Trees and forests in an urbanizing environment. Univ. of Massachusetts Coop. Ext., Planning and Resour. Dev. Ser. Pub. 17, Amherst, Mass.

Husar, R. B., W. E. Wilson, Jr., M. C. MacCracken, and R. M. Perhac. 1978. Rep. on the Int. Symp. on Sulfur in the Atmosphere. [7–14 Sept. 1977, Dubrovnik, Yugoslavia.] p. 3–5. *In* Abstr. of 3rd Natl. Conf. on the Interagency Energy/Environment R & D Progr., 1–2 June 1978, Washington, D.C. USEPA and U.S. Office of Energy, Minerals & Industry, Washington, D.C.

Jacobs, Jane. 1961. The death and life of great American cities. Vintage Books, New York. 458 p.

Kardos, L. T., W. E. Sopper, E. A. Myers, R. R. Parizek, and J. B. Nesbitt (ed.). 1974. Renovation of secondary effluent for reuse as a water resource. EPA-660/2-74-016. USEPA, Office of Res. and Dev., Washington, D.C. 495 p.

Karr, J. R., and I. J. Schlosser. 1978. Water resources and the land-water interface. Science 201:229–234.

Krieger, M. H. 1973. What's wrong with plastic trees? Science 179:446–455.

Larson, J. S. 1972. Man and wildlife in the modern northeastern landscape. Agric. Sci. Rev. 10(1):1–6.

Laut, J. G., and M. E. Schomaker. 1976. Dutch elm disease: a bibliography. Colorado State For. Serv., Fort Collins, Colo. 135 p.

LeBlanc, Fabius, and D. N. Rao. 1973. Evaluation of the pollution and drought hypotheses in relation to lichens and bryophytes in urban environments. Bryologist 76:1–19.

Leone, I. A., E. Brennan, and R. H. Daines. 1964. Plant life as air pollution indicators. Proc. Northeast. Weed Control Conf. 18:451–457.

Long, A. J., H. D. Gerhold, and M. E. Demeritt, Jr. 1973. Metropolitan tree planters survey, initial results. Pennsylvania State Univ., College of Agric. Res. Pap. 41, University Park, Pa. 14 p.

Menninger, Rosemary. 1977. Community gardens in California. State of California, Off. of Planning and Res., Sacramento, Calif. 39 p.

Meyersohn, Rolf, and R. Jackson. 1958. Gardening in suburbia. p. 271–286. *In* William Dobriner (ed.). The suburban community. Putnam, New York.

Miller, P. R., and M. J. Elderman (ed.). 1977. Photochemical oxidant air pollutant effects on a mixed conifer forest ecosystem, a progress report [for] 1976. Prepared by the Univ. of California at Riverside Statewide Air Pollut. Res. Center for USEPA, Corvallis, Oreg. 362 p. EPA-600/3-77-104.

Murphy, C. E., Jr., T. R. Sinclair, and K. R. Knoerr. 1977. An assessment of the use of forests as sinks for the removal of atmospheric sulfur dioxide. J. Environ. Qual. 6:388–396.

Newton, N. T. 1971. Design on the land: the development of landscape architecture. Belknap Press of Harvard Univ. Press, Cambridge, Mass. 714 p.

Northeastern Forest Experiment Station. 1977. Use of vegetation, space and structure to improve amenities for people. Proc. of Conf. on the Metropolitan Physical Environment, 25–29 Aug. 1975, Syracuse, N.Y. USDA-FS General Tech. Rep. NE-25, Upper Darby, Pa. 447 p.

Noyes, J. H., and D. R. Progulske (ed.). 1974. Wildlife in an urbanizing environment. Univ. of Massachusetts Coop. Ext. Serv., Planning and Resour. Dev. Ser. 28, Amherst, Mass. 184 p.

Oke, T. R. 1972. Evapotranspiration in urban areas and its implications for urban climate planning. Vol. III, p. 57.1–57.9. *In* Teaching the teachers on building climatology. Swedish Natl. Inst. for Building Res., Stockholm, Sweden.

Payne, B. R. 1973. The twenty-nine tree home improvement plan. Nat. Hist. 82(9):74–75.

Riesman, David. 1958. The suburban sadness. p. 374–409. *In* William Dobriner (ed.) The suburban community. Putnam, New York.

Robinette, G. O. 1972. Plants, people, and environmental quality: a study of plants and their environmental functions. U.S. Government Printing Office, Washington, D.C. 132 p.

Ruppert, Kurt. 1960. Der Stadtwald als Wirtschafts- und Erholungswald. BLV Verlags-Gesellschaft, Munich, Germany. 174 p.

Santamour, F. S., Jr., H. D. Gerhold, and S. Little. 1976. Better trees for metropolitan land-scapes. *In* Proc. Symp., 4–6 Nov. 1975, Washington, D.C. USDA-FS Gen. Tech. Rep. NE-22, Upper Darby, Pa. 256 p.

Schmid, J. A. 1974. The environmental impact of urbanization. p. 213–251. *In* I. R. Manners and M. W. Mikesell (ed.) Perspectives on environment. Assoc. of Am. Geograph., Washington, D.C.

Schmid, J. A. 1975. Urban vegetation: a review and Chicago case study. Univ. of Chicago, Dep. of Geography, Res. Pap. 161, Chicago, Ill. 266 p.

Sharp, W. C. 1977. Conservation plants for the northeast. USDA-SCS Program Aid 1134. U.S. Government Printing Office, Washington, D.C. 40 p.

Shear, C. L., and N. E. Stevens. 1917. *Endothia parasitica* and related species. USDA Bull. 380. U.S. Government Printing Office, Washington, D.C.

Sopper, W. E., and L. T. Kardos (ed.). 1973. Recycling treated municipal wastewater and sludge through forest and cropland: proceedings of a symposium. Pennsylvania State Univ. Inst. for Res. on Land and Water Resour., University Park, Pa. 463 p.

Thomas, J. W., and R. M. DeGraaf. 1973. Non-game wildlife research in megalopolis: the Forest Service program. USDA-FS Gen. Tech. Rep. NE-4, Upper Darby, Pa. 12 p.

Thornton, P. L. 1971. Managing urban and suburban trees and woodlands for timber prod-ucts. p. 129–132. *In* Silas Little and J. H. Noyes (ed.) Trees and forests in an urbanizing environment. Univ. of Massachusetts Coop. Ext., Planning and Resource Dev. Ser. Pub. 17, Amherst, Mass.

Turk, Amos, and C. J. D'Angio. 1962. Composition of natural fresh air. Air Pollut. Control Assoc. J. 12:29–33.

U.S. Forest Service. 1977. Dutch elm disease: status of the disease, research, and control, 1977. U.S. Government Printing Office, Washington, D.C. 49 p.

van Eimern, L. J., R. Karschon, L. A. Razumova, and G. W. Robertson. 1964. Windbreaks and shelter belts. World Meteorol. Organ. Pub. 147, Tech. Note 59, Tech. Pub. 70, Geneva, Switzerland. 188 p.

Van Haverbeke, D. F. 1977. Conifers for single-row field windbreaks. USDA-FS, Rocky Mountain For. and Range Exp. Stn. Res. Pap. RM-196, Fort Collins, Colo. 10 p.

Veblen, Thorstein. 1899. The theory of the leisure class. Macmillan, New York. 400 p.

Warren, J. L. 1973. Green space for air pollution control. North Carolina State Univ. School of Forest. Resour. Tech. Rep. 50, Raleigh, N.C. 118 p.

Wright, R. L. 1934. The story of gardening. Dodd Mead, New York. 475 p.

section VII

Planning for Transportation Systems and Utility Corridors

USDA Soil Conservation Service

VII

22 Soil Considerations in Siting Highways, Airports, and Utility Corridors

DONALD E. MC CORMACK AND DONALD G. FOHS

Soil Conservation Service, USDA,
and Federal Highway Administration,
Washington, D.C.

I. INTRODUCTION

Highways and transportation facilities have an obvious primary function—to transport people or objects from one point to another. The ideal path is a straight line. It is shorter and quicker. Being shorter, it is less expensive. Or is it?

Even in primitive footpaths this ideal is illustrated. However, such primitive routes also illustrate another basic principle in route selection: certain situations may present obstacles to the straight line. The footpaths avoid the boulder, the tree, and the swamp. One wonders if we have learned so much more today. Well-worn Indian trails that were used by early settlers are in many places the routes for major highways. Examples are I-81 in the Shenandoah Valley of western Virginia and U.S. 20 in northern Ohio.

Our purpose in this chapter is to review sources of soils data, to identify soil properties that influence the location, design, and performance of transportation systems and utility corridors, and to discuss the use and value of soil surveys and other sources of soils data in planning these systems and corridors. First, broad aspects of their planning are discussed.

Although the get-out-of-the-mud philosophy prevailed prior to the 1920's and the shorter-and-quicker-is-cheaper philosophy prevailed in the 1950's, today the role of highway transportation is quite different. Recent policies of the Federal Highway Administration (FHWA) that deal with transportation planning illustrate the direction of the current approach:

> Transportation exists to meet an interconnected set of broad national, state, and community, social, economic, and environmental goals, and its profound effects on development must be consistent with these goals. To achieve this consistency, the FHWA encourages the coordination of transportation planning at all levels of Government with land-use planning and other social, economic, and environmental planning (Trans. Res. Bd., 1977).

> Effective planning must include a mechanism for maintaining cooperation between state transportation agencies, local governments, and local transportation agencies. In order to achieve this cooperation and effective planning process, the FHWA requires State and metropolitan planning agencies to provide for input from appropriate local officials, to allow for public participation, and

to improve the linkage between the planning and programming of projects. Furthermore, the planning process must be comprehensive and coordinated, incorporating all modes of transport, community development, and land use.

If the Nation's overall transportation system is to work efficiently and provide adequate mobility for all, several modes of transport are required, all operating within a well-coordinated, interconnected, and cooperative framework. Thus FHWA policy is that transportation planning at all levels of Government should be multimodal, and special attention should be given to the need for improved intermodal transfer facilities and access to terminals (Fed. Highw. Admin., 1976).

Transportation planning is a complex process: land use and the concentration of people and activities influence transportation systems, and transportation systems influence land use and activities. The soil has a basic influence on both land use and transportation. For a thorough discussion of these interrelationships, see Bauer (1969).

Among the objectives of land use planning, conserving land resources and maximizing the productive capacity of land are receiving increasing attention (McCormack, 1974). Recognizing limitations in soils and other natural resources before commitments are made for building subdivisions or other nonfarm developments is a vital early step in planning. Some natural resources have unique suitability for a given use that justifies extreme efforts to preserve them for that use. For example, some soils are prime farmland, producing high yields with a minimum of production costs. Some of these soils are poorly suited for urban uses. Examples are the organic muck and peat soils and the naturally poorly drained, level soils of the Cornbelt. It is a serious error to use these soils for urban development when well-suited soils are nearby.

More common is the situation where the soils are well suited for both farming and urban development. With the increasing concern for maintaining our capacity to produce food and fiber, we must find ways to build on nearby soils that are not so well suited for farming. This will require that practices be identified to overcome the limitations for building. The kinds of practices needed will depend on the nature of the soil. In general, we need to determine, among soils that are not prime farmland, those that have the highest potential for urban development.

Jagged mountains are not good places for cities or highways, but neither are fertile plains. The form of a city—its outline or periphery—must fit the landscape in a rational fashion. Compromises between the often conflicting objectives of resource conservation and inexpensive construction and maintenance are likely as growth pressures mount. However, the planning of transportation systems must take into account where the people and their activities *should be*, because these systems are among the main determinants of where they *will be*.

Major highways and their interchanges can be located in those areas around the periphery of a city where urban expansion will be encouraged. Comprehensive land use plans should identify these areas so that the overall plan for future growth makes the best use of the natural resources. The land use plan should precede the planning of new transportation systems, although it is apparent that existing transportation systems will have an important bearing on it. If interchanges or major highways must be located in areas where urban expansion is to be discouraged, and obviously they must in some situations, then rigid controls of land use in the area must be sought or the land use plan will not be effective.

Changing the location of transportation facilities a few miles one way or another may have little influence on their cost or utility. As we will see later in this chapter, it may even reduce costs substantially. It may also contribute to the urban form sought by the community in their comprehensive plan. From this perspective, the transportation system is actually one of the vehicles that helps to implement the comprehensive plan.

Information about soils and their limitations and potentials is one of the major data inputs required to develop comprehensive land use plans that make the best use, for the community and the nation, of our limited natural resources (Bauer, 1969). In addition to soils data, a wide range of social and economic data is required for planning transportation systems. Refer to the publication *Statewide Transportation Planning Needs and Requirements* (Natl. Coop. Highw. Res. Progr., 1972) for discussions of the importance and use of social and economic data.

II. SOURCES OF SOILS DATA

In this section the kinds of data available from soil surveys, geologic surveys, remote sensing, and engineering soil surveys is discussed. A summary of the kinds of soil data commonly provided by these sources is presented in Table 1.

Table 1—Summary of sources of data about soil properties.†

Kind of soil information	Soil surveys‡	Geological surveys	Engineering soil surveys	Remote sensing
Soil texture	+	*	+	*
Clay mineralogy	+	−	*	−
Depth to bedrock	+	+	+	*
Kind of surficial bedrock	+	+	+	*
Soil density	+	*	+	−
Content of rock fragments	+	*	+	−
Erodibility	+	*	−	*
Surface geology	*	+	*	*
Soil pH	+	−	−	−
Salinity	+	−	−	−
Corrosivity	+	−	−	−
Depth to seasonal water table	+	*	−	*
Atterberg limits	*	−	+	−

† + A primary source; * general data; − little or no information or data not normally provided.
‡ Information for upper 2 m of soil.

1. SOIL SURVEYS

Because they are available for about 60% of our land and 75% of our rapidly developing urban areas, soil surveys represent by far the largest source of data for planning transportation systems and utility corridors (See also Chapt. 4 in this book).

Soil surveys and geologic surveys supplement one another and together provide extensive data for planning transportation systems. In both kinds of surveys, the reliability of data is higher relatively close to the surface, simply because here the material is easier to observe and thus is observed at closer intervals than deeper strata. Soil surveys provide a much more detailed description of the upper 2 m than geologic surveys provide for the deeper strata. Type of parent material is identified in soil surveys, for example, loamy glacial till. Numerous observations in road cuts, gullies, and other exposures are made during the conduct of soil surveys, and it is common that sufficient data are assembled to conclude that "the C horizon as described generally extends to a depth of at least 20 feet." Of course the occurrence of anomalies is greater at depths of >2 m than at shallower depths. Geologic surveys normally provide little information on the upper 1 to 2 m of weathered soil, emphasizing instead the unweathered strata considered to be the C horizon or parent material by the pedologist.

In soil surveys, soil texture is described in 12 basic classes: sand, loamy sand, sandy loam, loam, silt, silt loam, silty clay loam, sandy clay loam, clay loam, sandy clay, silty clay, and clay. In addition, content of coarse fragments is indicated through modifiers such as gravelly and very gravelly. Soil chemistry is also described, including pH, cation exchange capacity, salt content, and percent base saturation. Soil density is also described. More qualitative data on some of these properties for the deeper geologic strata may be provided by geologic surveys. Soil surveys also provide information about seasonal soil moisture regimes, normally not included in geologic surveys.

Soil Taxonomy (Soil Surv. Staff, 1975) is the soil classification system used by pedologists as a base for organizing knowledge about soils in all soil surveys in the United States. *Soil Taxonomy* recognizes soils as natural bodies whose properties are derived from natural processes amenable to our understanding and description, and focuses on the in situ soil. The system and its application in highway engineering was the subject of a symposium of the Transportation Research Board in January 1977: the publication of this symposium provides a valuable reference (Transp. Res. Bd., 1977).

The use of *Soil Taxonomy* as a base for organizing soil data for the highway engineers is no less logical than its use in farming or forestry. Selection of criteria is not based on a particular use or method of manipulation of soil, but on the natural properties of soils. Soil surveys using this comprehensive classification system provide an understanding of the order in the natural landscape and can be a useful tool in making transportation systems function effectively. Use must be made of soil surveys, geologic surveys, remote sensing, and other tools in such a way that information from one source supplements that available from the others.

Where soil surveys are not already available, it is possible to prepare a soil survey of a strip a few hundred yards wide along the proposed highway. For many years, this has been the standard procedure of the Michigan Department of State Highways (1970). Also, the Soil Conservation Service has prepared strip maps in some states through special agreements with state departments of transportation. A strip map is less useful than a complete soil survey of a broad area because there may be especially favorable soil conditions just outside the strip mapped.

The scale of most soil surveys is 1:15,840, 1:20,000, or 1:24,000; most geological surveys have a scale of 1:24,000. On soil surveys with a scale of 1:15,840, contrasting soils as small as 1 ha in extent can be delineated. However, it should be noted that neither soil nor geologic surveys delineate all small areas of contrasting soil conditions; onsite investigations are needed for designing engineering structures to determine the nature of the soil. Such specific data are usually not required for planning decisions, however.

2. GEOLOGIC SURVEYS

Geologic surveys of various kinds are available for about 20% of the nation in publications by the U.S. Geological Survey or by state geological surveys. Where surveys of the surficial geology are available, they provide soil information of considerable value in planning transportation systems. In general, highway engineers rely on soil surveys for information about properties of soil horizons in the upper 2 m, and on geologic surveys for information about the strata below that depth. The term *soil* in common geologic and engineering usage refers to the unconsolidated earthy material above bedrock, and thus differs from the pedologic definition (Soil Surv. Staff, 1975) which refers to soil as ". . .the collection of natural bodies on the earth's surface, in places modified or even made by man of earthy materials, containing living matter and supporting or capable of supporting plants out-of-doors. . . Soil includes the horizons near the surface that differ from the underlying rock material as a result of interactions, through time, of climate, living organisms, parent materials, and relief. . .. The lower limit of soil. . .is normally the lower limit of biologic activity, which generally coincides with the common rooting depth of native perennial plants."

Data furnished by surveys of surficial geology include the kind of surficial bedrock and the kind of unconsolidated formation, for example, alluvium, loess, glacial till, outwash, and marine deposits. In some surveys broad categories of the texture of the various strata are identified, for example, marine clays and the depth to bedrock, especially where deposits of glacial drift, loess, or other sediments overlie the bedrock. In many geologic surveys, the texture of the strata is not identified.

3. REMOTE SENSING

Interpretations of aerial photographs have been extensively used to identify surface features, including soil properties of importance in planning transportation systems. With a minimum of ground-truth, that is, on-the-ground study of distinctive images and patterns, it has been shown to be possible to develop useful maps of soil conditions (Highw. Res. Bd., 1972). However, such maps are not as reliable as soil surveys developed through the use of complete ground transects, because ground-truth is much less.

Where soil surveys have been completed, remote sensing projects to identify soil conditions for planning transportation systems should be initiated only after careful consideration of the additional information that would be gained. In areas where data on fault zones, the strike of rock formations, or similar data are needed, remote sensing projects may be required. Where geologic surveys are available but soil surveys are not, remote sensing projects with ground truth can provide valuable additional information about the nature and occurrence of the surface soils. It is especially important that these projects be considered where soil surveys cannot be prepared for a strip of land along the proposed route.

4. ENGINEERING SOIL SURVEYS

Engineering soil surveys are generally conducted only after a corridor or preliminary location for a route has been established (Spangler, 1966). The scale and detail of these surveys are highly variable depending on the purpose of the survey and the complexity of the terrain and soils. Soils are commonly classified according to the Unified (U.S. Army Corps of Eng., 1960) or AASHTO (1972) classification of the subsoils. Engineering soil surveys are conducted by consulting various sources such as soil surveys, geologic surveys, and well logs, and by supplementary field exploration. For roadway design these surveys are verified by test pits or auger borings. For bridges deep borings are made and undisturbed samples acquired for engineering tests.

5. HIGHWAY TEST DATA

It is standard procedure in designing highways and other transportation facilities to sample and test soils at intervals along the route. Sampling patterns include a standard spacing, such as 100 m, or selected points no more than a specified distance apart, representing unique landforms. Through this testing a vast amount of soil data has been obtained. But in only a few states have these data been organized to aid in *planning* transportation systems.

One state making use of these data is South Dakota, where personnel of the Department of Transportation have evaluated the range in soil test results for soils identified in soil surveys (Thomas, 1971). Statistical study of the data proved that each soil did in fact have a distinctive range in test results. For example, for the C horizons in Houdek soil mapping units, about

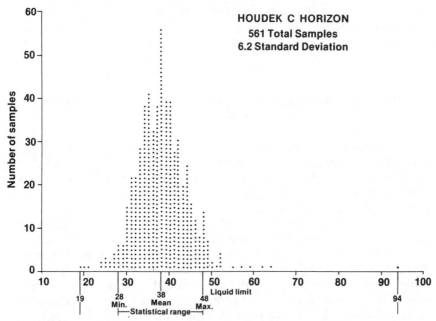

Fig. 1—Frequency distribution of liquid limit of 561 samples of C horizons of Houdek soil mapping units.

68% of the test results for liquid limit were in the range 32 to 44 (Fig. 1). When analysis was sufficient to prove the validity of this approach, work was initiated to identify the kind of soil at all sites sampled. Data can be assembled only for those areas where soil surveys have been completed, but widescale use of soil surveys in planning transportation systems can permit a substantial reduction in the testing required for designing highways.

Another noteworthy effort is the development of a soil data system for Kentucky (Spradling, 1976). Much of the soil data gathered for the design of highway projects were being discarded after each project was completed. Recognizing the value of these data, the Kentucky Department of Transportation devised a computer system which organized them according to kind of soil as identified by soil surveys and according to geologic formation as identified by geologic surveys. Each kind of soil was characterized as fully as possible through analysis of available data, and the value of the resulting information for the planning of transportation systems, and for land use planning in general, has been clearly demonstrated. In addition, the data have proved to be useful as a guide for planning subsurface exploration programs to obtain data needed for design.

In every state, test data obtained for immediate use in design can be organized so that they are useful in planning, not only for transportation systems but also for other land use systems. Organization of the data according to discrete land units, such as the map units of soil surveys and geological surveys, is essential so that the data can be extended to areas where no test data exists. Analysis of the data by land units will help to identify those soil or geologic areas where soil conditions are relatively uniform and those where they are complex.

III. SOIL PROPERTIES AFFECTING TRANSPORTATION SYSTEMS

Soil information, regardless of the kind of survey that obtains it, is an important requirement for planning transportation systems. The kinds of soil information of most value are discussed in this section. They are: composition, erodibility, chemistry, moisture regime, depth, density, slope, and kinds of geologic formation.

Soil depth, moisture regime, and slope are not considered soil properties by engineers. Instead, they consider them to be site conditions. This does not mean that the engineers attach less significance to these parameters than the soil scientists, or that they attach insufficient significance to them. Among these site conditions, or soil properties, the in situ soil moisture regime is the most subtle and difficult for specialists other than pedologists to identify. Perhaps for this reason, it is responsible for a high proportion of the difficulties or failures experienced in planning and designing transportation systems.

1. SOIL COMPOSITION

Soil composition refers to the basic constituents of the soil mass. The principal components of any soil mass are the solid particles, water, and air. We arbitrarily set aside consideration of soil, water, and air for separate chapters and consider here the particulate solids in soils.

The amount and type of clay in a soil have the most influence on the properties of interest to the engineer. In addition to the mineralogy of the clay fraction, other factors such as particle-size distribution, nonclay mineral composition, organic matter content, and geologic history control the engineering properties of soils (Grim, 1962).

The compressibility of clayey soils must be considered in designing engineering structures. Strength, stability, and bearing capacity of clay soils are generally much lower than that of sandy or gravelly soils. The imposition of a load on a clay soil mass by an earth embankment or structure in excess of the load that this mass had experienced before (geologic time) will cause the clay to consolidate. Compression of the soil results in cracking of embankments and settlement of foundations with resulting distress and possible failure of the structures. Consolidation tests are conducted to determine the maximum past or preconsolidation load and the rate of magnitude of consolidation of the soil foundation.

All clay soils shrink and swell with changes in moisture content. However, swell potential is much greater in clayey soils dominated by 2:1 expanding clay minerals, such as montmorillonite, than in the nonexpanding clays such as kaolinite.

In general, the stability of slopes is less in clayey soils than in soils of coarser texture. In one aspect clayey soils are more favorable than silty soils; they tend to be less susceptible to frost-heaving. The formation of ice lenses, as moisture migrates upward in soils due to capillary action, is a common cause of heaving and weakening of soils upon thawing. This results in the failure of pavements in cold climates. Because clayey soils have slower compacted permeability than silt loam, loam, and sandy loam soils, water moves more slowly to the ice lenses in the clayey soils and thus less frost-heaving occurs.

The location of sandy and gravelly soils is of value in planning transportation systems. Locating highways and other facilities in areas of granular soils can result in large cost savings compared to construction in finer textured soils, where it is generally necessary to bring in granular material for the subbase, at considerable expense (Thornburn, 1966).

It is common practice in highway construction to waste the A1 horizon of mineral soils because its generally higher content of organic matter makes it compressible in its natural state and difficult to compact. The thickness and organic matter content of A1 horizons are indicated by soil surveys. This information is useful for identifying not only those areas where the A1 horizon is favorable as a construction material, but also those areas where it is especially suited as a source of topsoil.

The location of organic soils, that is, mucks or peats, is also shown by soil surveys. Where such materials are <2 m thick, the depth to and properties of the underlying soil horizon are also indicated.

The content of gravel, cobbles, channers, boulders, and other coarse fragments in soil horizons are indicated by soil surveys. Classes of particle sizes and sizes and shapes of various coarse fragments are defined in the *Soil Survey Manual* (Soil Surv. Staff, 1951).

Soil surveys identify the mineralogy of the clay-size particles in soils with >35% clay. Because silt and sand grains are largely quartz, soil descriptions commonly refer to the mineralogy of these particles only if a considerable proportion is minerals other than quartz. Examples of importance to highway engineering are soils with a high proportion of mica grains, which make the soils difficult to compact and compress, and which impart a slippery, spongey quality, and soils high in the amorphous glass typical of volcanic ash. The latter have unusually high liquid limits and tend to have thixotropic qualities.

The composition of each soil horizon in the upper 2 m of the soil profile is identified. This information permits the selective use of specific horizons in engineering construction. The identification of thin deposits of loess or sandy glacial outwash that overlie contrasting deposits, such as clayey glacial till, can be highly useful in planning transportation systems. Also useful is the identification of a thin, clayey argillic horizon (Soil Surv. Staff, 1975) between horizons of coarser texture. This kind of information is indicated by soil surveys.

2. SOIL ERODIBILITY

One aspect of the description of specific soil horizons that highway engineers have recently begun to use is information on their erodibility. This information is used in planning for revegetation of exposed subsoils.

A recent report by the National Cooperative Highway Research Program (1975) summarizes information on design procedures and construction practices to minimize erosion, beneficial landscaping procedures, and maintenance practices for erosion control installations. In this report the Universal Soil Loss Equation (Wischmeier & Smith, 1965) and maps and reports prepared by the Soil Conservation Service are cited as primary tools for the highway designer. Soil surveys identify the erodibility of each soil horizon, which may vary widely among the horizons exposed in a road cut.

3. SOIL CHEMISTRY

The pH and other chemical properties of each soil horizon may influence transportation systems. These properties are described in soil surveys. Low pH or high salt content in horizons exposed in roadcuts or in the materials exposed in roadfills may explain the inability to establish a protective vegetative cover that results in chronic soil erosion problems. Extremely acid soils or soils high in sulfates may cause the concrete used for culvert pipes and foundations for structures to deteriorate rapidly. Salts in soils indicate a hazard of corrosion of metals and may also influence the type of material used for drainage structures.

4. SOIL MOISTURE REGIMES

Pedologists make many observations of seasonal water tables as they make soil surveys. They also infer patterns of seasonal soil saturation with water from the presence and extent of low-chroma, grayish colors. These colors are in many cases the only evidence noted during a dry late summer period that the soil is usually saturated in the winter and spring.

The engineering properties of a given soil, such as density, strength, and plasticity, vary significantly with changes in moisture content. The magnitude of the changes in engineering properties with changes in soil moisture content depends on the nature of the soil. Engineers express the plastic properties of soil materials in terms of plastic limit, liquid limit, and plasticity index. This was first proposed by Atterberg (1911). Although the limit values are based on empirical tests, they have been found to be very useful as index properties that correlate with more fundamental properties such as shear strength and compressibility (Grim, 1962).

Index values and particle-size distribution are used to organize soils into discrete groups or classes displaying similar engineering behavior. The engineer relies on these values as a measure of the quality of the soil material; if it is of low plasticity it generally will perform satisfactorily regardless of the moisture content. In addition, he generally bases his designs on the results of tests conducted when the soil is in the worst possible condition, that is, at saturation. The bearing capacity is frequently evaluated by the California Bearing Ratio test performed on specimens that have been immersed in water for 4 days. The quality and durability of soils stabilized with cement or hydrated lime and used for pavement base or subbase construction are evaluated by measuring the unconfined compressive strength of compacted specimens that have been immersed or vacuum saturated.

Soil surveys describe the depth to seasonal high water table for each soil series. This soil quality is important in determining the location of the planned grade relative to the natural soil surface (McCormack, 1974). The most widely applied technique to minimize frost heaving is to place base or subbase material not susceptible to frost action to a depth 25% greater than that of the anticipated frost penetration. To determine the depth of soil to be replaced, the thickness of the capillary fringe and the average depth of frost penetration should be determined.

Soil wetness is especially serious in the secondary roads where less grading is done than on larger highways. Low bearing capacity and high frost action due to wetness are responsible for many failures in secondary roads.

5. SOIL DEPTH

Where bedrock is within the depth of cuts required for highway construction, it commonly presents difficulties in excavation. The degree of difficulty must be known to estimate construction requirements. Some kinds of bedrock create environmental problems when they are exposed. Some geological surveys indicate the kind of surficial bedrock and the depth of unconsolidated soil material that overlies it.

Soil surveys indicate the depth to and kind of underlying bedrock where it is within a depth of 2 m. The depth to indurated soil horizons, such as petrocalcic (caliche) horizons and duripans (Soil Surv. Staff, 1975), and the depth to dense compact fragipans and glacial till are also identified. Descriptions of soil series commonly indicate the typical depth and the range in depth to such horizons.

6. SOIL DENSITY

The strength and bearing capacity of a soil vary directly with its density, that is, the higher a given soil's density the greater its bearing capacity. The compaction of regraded soils placed in the highway fill or subbase is important in highway construction. To measure the compaction characteristics of soils, Proctor tests are commonly carried out in the soil laboratories of state highway departments. Two index properties, the optimum moisture content and maximum dry density, are determined; the former is the moisture content at which maximum density is achieved with a standard compactive effort, and the latter is the density achieved. A recent study shows a high correlation between these parameters and clay content and soil texture as indicated by soil surveys (McCormack & Flach, 1977).

Low in situ density of uncompacted natural soils below the highway fill may indicate low bearing capacity and high compressibility; data on this soil property can be of value in planning transportation systems. Until very recently, few data on the in situ density of soils have been published in soil surveys. However, a large amount of data on this important soil property has been gathered by soil horizon. In the future, published soil surveys will include these data.

The structure of each soil horizon is described in all published soil surveys. Soil structure is related to soil density. In general, horizons with granular or crumb structure or with fine or medium, moderate to strong blocky structure have lower density than horizons that are massive or have weak or coarse blocky, prismatic, or columnar structure (Soil Surv. Staff, 1951).

7. SOIL SLOPE

Pedologists consider slope to be a soil property because they define soil as a three-dimensional body of which the configuration of the surface is an important attribute. The degree of slope controls the configuration of the boundaries between subsurface soil horizons. The permeability of subjacent soil horizons is generally different. As a result, as water percolates in the soil profile, it tends to accumulate at the upper boundary of the less permeable horizons. When these boundaries are sloping, seep lines develop and can cause problems in stabilizing cut slopes.

Soil surveys give the dominant slope of soil mapping units as a percentage that indicates the number of meters of change in vertical elevation per 100 m of horizontal distance. Topographic maps have contour lines that mark specific vertical intervals in elevation.

8. KINDS OF GEOLOGIC FORMATION

Knowledge of the kind of geologic formation in an area of highway construction is helpful in highway planning, and through past experience the performance of many formations is well known. Although detailed geologic surveys are available only for scattered areas, generalized geology maps indicating the surficial formation are available for many areas.

Most soil series have formed in a particular kind of parent geologic material. This information is included with the description of each soil series in published soil surveys. For example, some soil series formed in loess, some in compact glacial till of loam texture, some in marine clay, and so on. In many areas, soil surveys contain the only published information that characterizes the surface geologic formations. In some areas where geologic surveys are available, soil surveys provide more detail, and indicate small areas of contrasting geology not shown on the geologic survey (Fig. 2).

IV. USE OF SOIL SURVEYS IN PLANNING
TRANSPORTATION SYSTEMS

The value of soil surveys for planning transportation systems has long been recognized. In the 1920's, when the Bureau of Public Roads was an agency of the U.S. Department of Agriculture, there was close communica-

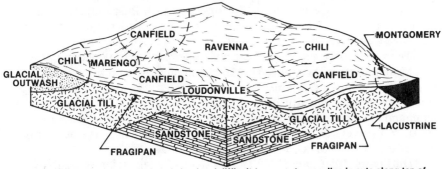

Canfield—Mostly A-4; fragipan is hard and difficult to excavate; seepline in cuts along top of fragipan; erodible.
Chili—Mostly A-4 above 3 feet, A-1 and A-2 below, probable source of granular material; suitable for winter grading; stable.
Loudonville—Hard sandstone bedrock at 2 to 3 feet; mostly A-4; erodible.
Marengo—High water table much of year; mostly A-6; high potential frost action; fill needed.
Montgomery—High water table much of year; high shrink-swell; compressible clay; fill needed; mostly A-7.
Ravenna—Seasonal high water table; mostly A-4; high potential frost action; fragipan is hard and difficult to excavate; seepline in cuts along top of fragipan.

Fig. 2—A soil landscape in northeastern Ohio and pertinent engineering information for each soil series.

tion between pedologists and highway engineers. In 1925, Rose stated that the first step in a subgrade study is to establish the location of the various soil types. He added that "only when the soil types (pedologic) are identified and the points at which the soil changes from one type to another are determined, it is possible to select samples such that the test results may be considered as applying to all parts of the road in which the sampled types of soil are located." This conclusion was reached at a time when soil surveys were much more general and less precise than they are now.

Since the 1920's, the Michigan Department of State Highways has used soil surveys as an integral part of its route selection and design programs (Michigan Dep. of State Highw., 1970). Extensive use is made of soil survey information, such as particle-size distribution, depth to seasonal high water table, depth to bedrock, and several other properties. For each soil series in Michigan, the following information is provided: adaptation to winter grading; normal depth to water table; wind erosion characteristics; recommended location of plan grade with respect to natural ground; kind of slope protection required; estimated percent of boulder excavation; nature of subgrade and shoulder stabilization required; recommendations for special subbase under pavements; and estimates of the required excavation materials susceptible to frost heaving.

During the period between 1948 and 1953, the Highway Research Board published numerous papers on the usefulness of pedologic principles of soil classification and mapping to highway engineers (Highw. Res. Bd., 1948-1953). Belcher (1948) argued that the pedologic classification filled a need for a classification of soils based on their fundamental properties. Olmstead (1948) pointed out the advantages of the pedologic system, which considers the characteristics of soils associated with their natural environment. He emphasized the importance of soil properties that are related to soil moisture and ground water that are identified in soil surveys. As a result of these early efforts, soil surveys are widely used in highway planning.

More recently, Thornburn (1966) thoroughly reviewed the applications of pedology in highway engineering. He illustrated the values of soil surveys and the pedologic classification system. Also, correlations between soil series and engineering soil test results in South Dakota have led to extensive use of soil surveys in planning transportation systems in that state (Crawford et al., 1973; Thomas, 1971).

During the 1950's and 1960's, the extent of engineering soil data published in soil surveys has gradually increased, largely because of greatly increased engineering testing of horizons of soil series. Early in the 1950's, the Bureau of Public Roads initiated a testing program to determine the particle size distribution and Atterberg limits of representative soil series. Several of the dominant soil series in each soil survey area were selected for testing. For each soil series, the two to four major soil horizons were sampled at two or three sites in the soil survey area. The sites were chosen to represent the modal or typical member of the soil series and members that are finer and coarser textured than the typical member. Thus the range in properties of each soil series was tested.

In the mid-1960's the Federal Highway Administration discontinued this testing program at the national level but encouraged the state highway departments to continue it. Most states are doing so, and a large volume of data has been developed. It is estimated that these efforts have made available test data for more than 10,000 soil profiles representing at least 25,000 tested samples.

The kind of soil engineering data published in soil surveys in the mid-1970's is illustrated in Tables 2 and 3. These data are available for about 35% of the counties in the nation in published form and are available in unpublished form for another 25% of the counties.

Numerous specific applications of soil survey information in planning transportation systems are discussed below.

1. ROUTE SELECTION

The fact that certain conditions represent obstacles to the location of footpaths, and even to highways, has already been noted. The choice between removing the obstacle or going around it may be difficult but it must always be made. Soil maps of strips may not provide a broad enough picture of the alternatives. For example, if a strip 400 m wide is surveyed, and organic soils extend all the way across it, the question "How far would we need to go to get around it?" is very pertinent. Thus, soil surveys of broad areas are helpful in route selection.

Deep organic soils present difficult problems to highway construction. Because of the extra expense of building highways on these soils, they are avoided where possible. Soil surveys show areas with organic soils >2 m in

Table 2—Estimated soil properties significant in engineering.

Soil series and map symbols	Depth from surface (inches)	USDA texture	Classification Unified	Classification AASHTO	Coarse fraction >3 inches (%)	No. 4 (4.7 mm)	No. 10 (2.0 mm)	No. 40 (0.42 mm)	No. 200 (0.074 mm)	Liquid limit (%)	Plasticity index
Bogart: BgA, BgB, BhB	0-7	Silt loam	ML	A-4	0-2	90-100	80-100	70-90	60-80	25-35	2-10
For properties of Haskins part of BhB, see Haskins series.	7-46	Loam, gravelly sandy loam.	ML, SM, SC	A-2, A-4, A-6	0-5	60-95	50-90	30-70	25-60	15-30	4-13
	46-60	Very gravelly sandy loam to gravel and sand.	SW-SM, SM, GW-GM, GM	A-1, A-2	0-5	40-75	35-60	20-40	5-20	<25	NP-4
Canadice: Ca	0-8	Silt loam	ML, CL	A-6	0	100	95-100	90-100	80-95	30-40	11-15
	8-53	Silty clay loam, silty clay.	CL, CH	A-7, A-6	0	100	95-100	90-100	80-100	38-55	17-32
	53-60	Silty clay, clay	CL, CH	A-7	0	100	95-100	90-100	90-100	40-55	20-32
Caneadea: CcA, CcB	0-7	Silt loam	ML, CL	A-6	0	100	95-100	90-100	70-95	30-40	11-15
	7-48	Silty clay, clay	CH, CL	A-7	0	100	90-100	90-100	90-100	42-60	19-35
	48-68	Silty clay	CH, CL, MH	A-7	0	100	95-100	80-100	90-100	40-55	19-32
Canfield: CdA, CdB, CdC, CdC2, CfB, CfC. Properties not estimated for Urban land part of CfB and CfC.	0-8	Silt loam	ML	A-4	0	90-100	85-100	80-100	70-90	25-40	4-10
	8-22	Silt loam or loam	ML, CL	A-4, A-6	0	90-100	80-95	70-90	55-80	25-40	6-15
	22-59	Loam, fine sandy loam.	ML, CL, SM, SM-SC	A-4, A-6	0	90-100	75-95	70-85	45-70	19-35	4-12
	59-82	Fine sandy loam	ML, SM, CL	A-4	0-5	80-95	75-95	70-85	45-65	15-30	4-12
Carlisle: Cg	0-60	Muck	Pt	--	--	--	--	--	--	--	--
Chili: CnA, CnB, CnC, CoC2, CpA, CpB, CpC, CtD, CtE, CtF, CuB, CuC, CwC2, CwD2, CwE. For properties of Oshtemo part of CtD, CtE and CtF, see Oshtemo series. For Wooster part of CwC2, CwD2, and CwE, see Wooster series. Properties not estimated for Urban land part of CuB and CuC.	0-9	Loam, gravelly loam, silt loam.	ML, SM	A-4, A-2	0	70-100	60-95	50-85	40-75	<40	NP-10
	9-35	Loam, gravelly clay loam.	ML, SM, SC	A-4, A-6	0	70-95	60-90	50-80	35-70	<30	NP-12
	35-54	Very gravelly sandy loam.	SM, GM	A-1, A-2	0-5	45-80	40-75	25-55	15-35	--	NP
	54-70	Gravelly sand	SW-SM, GW, GM	A-1	0-10	30-60	25-55	10-30	2-15	--	NP
Damascus: Da	0-9	Loam	ML	A-4	0-2	90-100	80-100	70-90	60-85	25-35	4-10
	9-39	Sandy loam, gravelly sandy clay loam.	SM, CL, SC	A-4, A-6	0-5	70-100	60-90	50-80	35-70	20-40	4-15
	39-60	Loamy sand, very gravelly sand.	GW-GM, GM	A-1, A-2	0-5	35-80	25-70	20-60	10-35	<30	NP-6

Table 3—Estimated degree and kind of limitation of soils for land use planning.

Soil series and map symbols	Septic tank absorption fields	Sewage lagoons	Dwellings with basements	Dwellings without basements	Roads and streets	Shallow excavations	Sanitary landfill (trench)
Caneadea:							
CcA	Severe: very slow permeability; seasonal high water table.	Slight	Severe: seasonal high water table; low strength.	Severe: seasonal high water table; low strength.	Severe: low strength.	Severe: seasonal high water table.	Severe: seasonal high water table; clayey.
CcB	Severe: very slow permeability; seasonal high water table.	Moderate: slope.	Severe: seasonal high water table; low strength.	Severe: seasonal high water table; low strength.	Severe: low strength.	Sever: sonal high water table.	Severe: seasonal high water table.
Canfield:							
CdA	Severe: slow permeability; seasonal high water table.	Slight	Moderate: seasonal high water table.	Slight	Moderate: frost action.	Moderate: seasonal high water table.	Moderate: seasonal high water table.
CdB, CfB Urban land part of CfB not rated.	Severe: slow permeability; seasonal high water table.	Moderate: slope.	Moderate: seasonal high water table.	Slight	Moderate: frost action.	Moderate: seasonal high water table.	Moderate: seasonal high water table.
CdC, CdC2, CfC Urban land part of CfC not rated.	Severe: slow permeability.	Severe: slope	Moderate: seasonal high water table; slope.	Moderate: slope.	Moderate: slope; frost action.	Moderate: seasonal high water table; slope.	Moderate: seasonal high water table.

(continued on next page)

Table 3—Continued.

Soil series and map symbols	Septic tank absorption fields	Sewage lagoons	Dwellings with basements	Dwellings without basements	Roads and streets	Shallow excavations	Sanitary landfill (trench)
Carlisle: Cg	Severe: high water table.	Severe: organic soil.	Severe: organic soil; unstable; high water table.	Severe: organic soil; high water table; soft and compressible.	Severe: organic soil; high water table.	Severe: organic soil; high water table.	Severe: organic soil; high water table.
Chili: CnA, CpA	Slight	Severe: rapid permeability.	Slight	Slight	Slight	Moderate: gravelly layers.	Severe: pervious substratum.
CnB, CpB, CuB Urban land part of CuB not rated.	Slight	Severe: rapid permeability.	Slight	Slight	Slight	Moderate: gravelly layers	Severe: pervious substratum.
CnC, CoC2, CpC, CuC, CwC2 Urban land part of CuC not rated. For Wooster part of CwC2 see WuC2 in that series.	Moderate: slope.	Severe: rapid permeability; slope.	Moderate: slope.	Moderate: slope.	Moderate: slope.	Moderate: slope; gravelly layers.	Severe: pervious substratum.
CtD, CtE, CwD2, CwE For Wooster part of CwD2 and CwE see WuD2 and WuE2 in that series.	Severe: slope	Severe: rapid permeability;	Severe: slope	Severe: slope	Severe: slope.	Severe: slope.	Severe: pervious substratum.

thickness, as well as areas where they are thinner. For the latter soils, the kind of underlying material is also identified. They also identify the nature of the organic material in three categories—fibric, hemic, and sapric—based on degree of decomposition of the organic residues (Soil Surv. Staff, 1975). Fibric soils, the least decomposed, are likely to be the least suitable for hydraulic consolidation (Michigan Dep. of Highw., 1970).

Clayey soils, because of their compressibility and low permeability, generally require a thick pavement section. Deep foundations (piles, caissons, drilled shaft, and so on) are commonly required rather than cheaper spread footings. The slopes of both cuts and fills tend to be unstable in clayey soils, and generally need to be less sloping than on other soils. This may increase the width required for the right-of-way. Swelling clays present severe problems to construction, maintenance, and operation of highways and other transportation facilities. It has been estimated that >$1 billion is spent annually to repair damages to roads and streets due to swelling soils (Jones & Holtz, 1973). These problems are discussed in companion papers by Bartelli and McCormack (1976) and Lytton et al. (1976).

Thus, for numerous reasons, clay soils are avoided where possible in route selection. Also, soils that are highly susceptible to frost action or shallow to bedrock and a seasonal high water table are avoided if possible. In addition to showing the location of unfavorable soils, soil surveys also show the location of granular soils on which little or no subbase is needed.

2. PLANNING FOR MORE DETAILED STUDIES

Soil surveys identify areas with very uniform soils, such as broad areas of soils formed in thick loess, and areas where contrasting soils occur in complex patterns, such as the soils common to terminal moraines. Assembling highway test data by soil mapping units, as done in South Dakota (Crawford et al., 1973) and in Kentucky (Spradling, 1976), helps to verify the nature of soil patterns described by soil surveys. With this information a sampling and testing program can be planned to make most effective use of available funds and manpower.

3. PLANNING DRAINAGE REQUIREMENTS

Identifying those areas where seasonal high soil water tables are near the surface is important in planning transportation systems. This information is especially important in planning the elevation of the pavement relative to the natural ground surface (Michigan Dep. of State Highw., 1970). Keeping the pavement well above the zone of saturation safeguards against frost-heaving and problems of compressibility associated with wet soils.

In Michigan, the estimated lineal feet of bank drains needed per 1,000 feet of cut below natural ground elevation are based on the soil series (Michigan Dep. of State Highw., 1970). These estimates, by soil series, are made both for subgrade undercutting and for edge drains to intercept seepage or lower the water table. Soil surveys are the only reliable source of information about seasonal high water tables in most areas and are widely used to supply this information.

4. PLANNING FOR EROSION CONTROL

Erosion from poorly designed and maintained highways is in many areas a major source of sediment that pollutes streams and lakes. If highly erodible soil horizons are in a road cut, special designs or practices can be used to minimize erosion. For example, a lower slope angle of the cut, mulching, or additional fertilization may be planned. The diversion of run-off from sloping soils above the road cuts, a suggested practice in most kinds of soil, may be critically important on highly erodible soils.

In establishing vegetation to control erosion on cut slopes, difficulty caused by very low pH, salinity, very dense soil horizons, seeplines, or low soil fertility is indicated by soil surveys.

5. RECOGNIZING EXCAVATION AND GRADING PROBLEMS

Saturated zones that make excavation difficult or impossible, bedrock that requires blasting, dense and compact soil horizons that have unusually high energy requirements for excavation, common boulders that make excavation difficult, and sandy or gravelly horizons that can be graded in the winter are among the properties of soils identified by soil surveys.

Not only is this information of value to the transportation agency, it is excellent information for contractors. It gives them a valuable insight into likely difficulties in excavation and earth-moving and thus permits more accurate bids. In more level areas, most highway excavations are <2 m deep; in all areas, the nature of soil in the upper 2 m is important.

6. LOCATING SOURCES OF SAND AND GRAVEL FOR SUBBASE

Soil surveys show the location of soils with sandy and gravelly horizons in the upper 2 m. Although this information may not be adequate for finding suitable sources of these materials (the horizons may be too thin), it certainly provides an important clue as to the best places to start looking. In many soils with sandy or gravelly lower horizons, granular materials extend to a depth of many feet and are a valuable source. Finding a source near the construction area can reduce costs substantially, and contractors and transportation agencies use soil surveys for this purpose.

7. SELECTING POSSIBLE CHEMICAL STABILIZERS FOR FINE-GRAINED SOILS

Frequently, sand and gravel for base and subbase are not available within an economical distance for hauling to highway construction projects. Consequently, local fine-grained soils are treated with cement, hydrated lime, or bituminous materials to increase their strength and stability so that they will be suitable for subbase or base course construction.

Criteria for selection of the type and amount of stabilizing chemical for

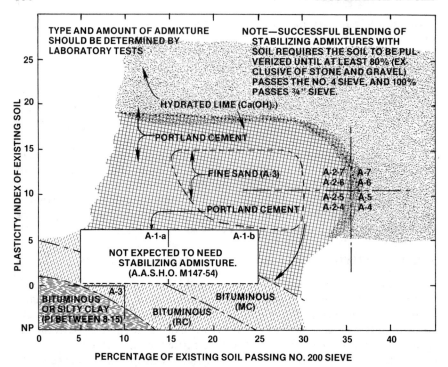

Fig. 3—Suggested stabilizing admixtures suitable for use with soils as indicated by plasticity index and amount passing a no. 200 sieve.

laboratory trials are based on the AASHTO or Unified Soil Classification System class for the soils in question. The reader is referred to *Soil Stabilization: A Mission Oriented Approach* (Epps et al., 1971). Figure 3 presents suggested amounts of cement as a stabilizer according to classes of soils in the AASHTO system.

Miles D. Catton, in his 1962 resume of soil-cement technology (Catton, 1962), indicated that "soils identified by the pedological system used in the United States are identical soils, possessing identical physicochemical properties with identical soil-cement relations." The Portland Cement Association provides guidelines for selecting the quantity of cement for various soils based on the soil series and horizon (Catton, 1962). Quality criteria for soil-cement mixtures used in base courses depend on the soil type. Examples of the use of the AASHTO and Unified soil class to determine cement requirements are presented in Table 4.

8. LOCATING SOURCES OF TOPSOIL

To ensure that areas affected by highway construction are properly vegetated to prevent erosion, it is usually necessary to import topsoil and distribute it over the surface of cuts and fills. If a good topsoil layer is provided, successful first seedings are much more likely and the vigor of estab-

Table 4—Cement requirements for various soils.

AASHO soil classification	Unified soil classification	Usual range in cement requirement†		Estimated cement content used in moisture-density test	Cement content for wet-dry and freeze-thaw tests
		% by vol		% by wt.	
A-1-a	GW, GP, GM, SW, SP, SM	5 to 7	3 to 5	5	3 to 5 to 7
A-1-b	GM, BP, SM, SP	7 to 9	5 to 8	6	4 to 6 to 8
A-2	GM, GC, SM, SC	7 to 10	5 to 9	7	5 to 7 to 9
A-3	SP	8 to 12	7 to 11	9	7 to 9 to 11
A-4	CL, ML	8 to 12	7 to 12	10	8 to 10 to 12
A-5	ML, MH, OH	8 to 12	8 to 13	10	8 to 10 to 12
A-6	CL, CH	10 to 14	9 to 15	12	10 to 12 to 14
A-7	OH, MH, CH	10 to 14	10 to 16	13	11 to 13 to 15

† For most A horizon soils, the cement content should be increased 4 percentage points if the soil is dark gray to gray and 6 percentage points if the soil is black.

lished vegetation is easier to maintain. Soil surveys are used to locate soil horizons that are good sources of topsoil.

It is usually most practical to make full use of the A horizons of the soils of the construction area, as less earth moving is required than if all topsoil is imported. Along a linear right-of-way it would be reasonable to move the A horizon to both edges of the right-of-way so that a ridge of stockpiled topsoil would be on each edge. Some soils have no horizons suitable for topsoil, whereas other soils have suitable B as well as A horizons. Finding a topsoil source as close as possible to the construction area can result in substantial cost savings.

9. LOCATING REST AREAS

The nature of the soil in rest areas cannot be determined by testing along the centerline of the highway. Soil surveys provide valuable information for the selection of sites for rest areas (McCormack, 1972). For example, soils that are soggy and waterlogged during several months of the year are not desirable. Where soil absorption systems are to be used for sewage disposal, it is important that deep, well-drained soils with sufficient permeability and filtration capacity be used. Criteria for rating soils for intensive recreation uses are appropriate for judging their suitability for rest areas (SCS, 1971).

10. PLANNING SECONDARY ROADS, STREETS, AND PARKING LOTS

For less intensively used transportation facilities, less care is generally exercised in design and construction. The design of these facilities is often based on subdivision regulations or building codes applicable, without testing, to all areas of a municipality. For several reasons, this practice is discouraged by both the pedologist and the engineer. Testing is encouraged. However, where for any reason testing is not done, it is better to base the design on soil survey information than to use no soil information at all.

V. USES OF SOIL SURVEYS IN PLANNING
UTILITY CORRIDORS

Most soil properties important in planning transportation systems are also important in planning utility corridors. Depth to bedrock, the presence of a seasonal high water table, deep organic soils, swelling clays, boulders, and corrosivity to concrete and steel are important soil properties. Soil properties related to potential frost action and compressibility are generally less important to utility corridors than to transportation systems because utility lines commonly have some flexibility.

Susceptibility of trench walls to sloughing is important in locating utility corridors. The soil quality is closely related to soil properties identified by soil surveys. It is usually mentioned in descriptions of the most susceptible soils, that is, loose granular soils and silty or loamy soils with zones of saturation.

To enhance the appearance of utility corridors, vegetation should be established or maintained. Often overlooked is the need to replace the topsoil where excavations are made for pipelines or other construction. Commonly, the areas affected are small and the added cost of excavating the A horizon, stockpiling it, and spreading it over the regraded surface is not great. This practice improves the prospect for obtaining vigorous vegetation required to minimize erosion.

VI. COST AND OTHER SAVINGS RESULTING FROM THE
USE OF SOIL SURVEYS

An extensive evaluation of the benefits accruing through the use of soil surveys was developed by Klingebiel in the mid-1960's (Klingebiel, 1966). He found that the cost-benefit ratio ranged from 1:45 for areas of low-intensity land use, such as range and woodland, to 1:120 for areas of high-intensity land use, such as the fringes of rapidly growing urban areas. During the first year after a soil survey is completed, benefits total $2 for each dollar spent in preparing the survey. Included as benefits were those derived in planning highways and airports.

To emphasize the value of general soil maps in evaluating alternative highway alignments, Thornburn (1966) analyzed the differences in costs of earth work in various kinds of soils and terrain. He superimposed on a soil map two possible alignments for a 10-mile segment of an interstate highway in Ford County, Illinois. These alignments were only 3 miles apart and thus could be considered potential route locations. Choice of the route having the more favorable soil was shown to result in a savings of $810,000 in construction costs.

Methods of determining the economic value of soil surveys with a mathematical model were discussed by Bie and Ulph (1972). Although the model was used to evaluate agricultural development, it could be adapted to evaluate nonagricultural applications, including the planning of highways and utility corridors.

There is extensive opportunity to increase the use soil surveys for planning and designing secondary highways (Thornburg, 1966). For such lighter construction, annual maintenance costs may be needlessly high. The proper use of existing soil survey data for secondary highways could save millions of dollars annually in maintenance costs.

LITERATURE CITED

American Society for Testing and Materials. 1972. ASTM Standards, Part 4. Philadelphia, Pa.

Atterberg, A. 1911. On the investigation of the physical properties of soils and on the plasticity of clays. Int. Mitt. Bodenkd. 1:10–43.

Bartelli, L. J., and D. E. McCormack. 1976. Morphology and pedologic classification of swelling soils. Trans. Res. Rec. no. 568. Transp. Res. Bd., Washington, D.C.

Bauer, K. W. 1969. Resource conservation and the urban transportation planning process. *In* Highw. Res. Rec. no. 271, Transp. Res. Bd., Washington, D.C.

Belcher, D. J. 1948. On soils classification. Trans. Am. Soc. Civil Eng. 113:937–940.

Bie, S. W., and A. Ulph. 1972. The economic value of soil survey information. J. Agric. Econ. 23:285–297.

Catton, M. D. 1962. Soil cement technology—a resume. J. Portland Cem. Assoc. Res. Dev. Lab. 4(1):13–21.

Crawford, R. A., J. B. Thomas, and M. Stout, Jr. 1973. Computerized soil test data for highway design. Proc. 52nd Annu. Meet. of the Highway Res. Bd., Jan. 1973, Highway Res. Board, Washington, D.C.

Epps, J. A., W. A. Dunlap, B. M. Gallaway, and D. D. Currin. 1971. Soil stabilization: a mission oriented approach. Highw. Res. Rec. no. 351. Washington, D.C.

Federal Highway Administration. 1976. A statement of national highway transportation policy. FHWA, Washington, D.C.

Grim, R. E. 1962. Applied clay mineralogy. McGraw Hill Book Co., Inc., New York.

Highway Research Board. 1948–1953. HRB Bull. 13, 22, 28, 46, 62, 83, and 22R. Highw. Res. Bd., Washington, D.C.

Highway Research Board. 1972. Remote sensing for highway engineering. Highw. Res. Rec. no. 421, Washington, D.C.

Jones, E. D., Jr., and W. G. Holtz. 1973. Expansive soils—the hidden disaster. Am. Soc. Civil Eng., Civil Eng. PP49-51.

Klingebiel, A. A. 1966. Cost and returns of soil surveys. Soil Conserv. 32(1):3–6. U.S. Soil Conserv. Serv., Washington, D.C.

Lytton, R. L., R. L. Bogges, and J. W. Spotts. 1976. Characteristics of expansive clay-roughness of pavements. Transp. Res. Rec. no. 568. Transp. Res. Bd., Washington, D.C.

McCormack, D. E. 1974. Soil potential: a positive approach to urban planning. J. Soil Water Conserv. 29:258–262.

McCormack, D. E. 1972. Use of soil surveys in roadside development. Roadside Dev. Conf., Nov. 1972, Ohio Dep. of Transp., Columbus, Ohio.

McCormack, D. E., and K. W. Flach. 1977. Soil series and soil taxonomy. *In* Soil taxonomy-soil properties. Transp. Res. Rec. no. 642. Trans. Res. Bd., Washington, D.C.

Michigan Department of State Highways. 1970. Field manual of soil engineering. Lansing, Mich.

National Cooperative Highway Research Program. 1972. Statewide transportation planning needs and requirements Synthesis no. 15. Transp. Res. Bd., Natl. Res. Counc., Washington, D.C.

National Cooperative Highway Research Program. 1975. Erosion control on highway construction. Synthesis no. 18. Transp. Res. Bd., Natl. Res. Counc., Washington, D.C.

Olmstead, F. R. 1948. The appraisal of terrain conditions for highway engineering purposes. HRB Bull. 13. Highw. Res. Bd., Washington, D.C.

Rose, A. C. 1925. Field methods used in subgrade surveys. Public Roads 6:93–101.

Soil Conservation Service. 1971. Guide for interpreting engineering uses of soils. Mimeo. Washington, D.C.

Soil Survey Staff. 1951. Soil survey manual. USDA Handbook no. 18. U.S. Government Printing Office, Washington, D.C.

Soil Survey Staff. 1975. Soil taxonomy: a basic system of soil classification for making and interpreting soil surveys. Agric. Handbook no. 436. Soil Conserv. Serv., Washington, D.C.

Spangler, M. G. 1966. Soil engineering. 3rd printing. International Textbook Co., Scranton, Pa. p. 70-84.

Spradling, D. 1976. A soil data system for Kentucky. Res. Rep. 441. Bur. of Highw., Dep. of Transp., Lexington, Ky.

Thomas, J. B. 1971. Soil engineering test data—proposed highway routes. Special Rep. USDA-SCS and South Dakota Dep. of Highw., Pierre, S. Dak.

Thornburn, T. H. 1966. The use of agricultural soil surveys in the planning and construction of highways. p. 87-103. *In* L. J. Bartelli, J. V. Baird, M. R. Heddleson, and A. A. Klingebiel (ed.) Soil surveys and land use planning. Am. Soc. of Agron., Madison, Wis.

Transportation Research Board. 1977. Soil taxonomy-soil properties. Trans. Res. Record no. 642. Transp. Res. Bd., Washington, D.C.

Transportation Research Board. 1977. Transportation research needs related to social, economic and environmental issues. Transp. Res. Circ. no. 187. Trans. Res. Bd., Washington, D.C.

U.S. Army Corps of Engineers. 1960. The unified soil classification system. Tech. Memo. no. 3-357, Vol. 1. U.S. Army Eng. Waterways Exp. Stn., Vicksburg, Miss.

Wischmeier, W. H., and D. C. Smith. 1965. Predicting rainfall-erosion losses from cropland east of the Rocky Mountains. Agric. Handbook no. 282. USDA-SEA, Washington, D.C.

23 Soil Considerations in Highway Design and Construction

J. ALLAN TICE

Law Engineering Testing Company
Raleigh, North Carolina

I. INTRODUCTION

Within any developed area, the general location of new transportation facilities is frequently governed by considerations unrelated to the suitability of the soils. Only when high costs and construction delays begin to be noted is the impact of soil conditions appreciated. For planning development of new areas, it seems reasonable to gather information about the soil characteristics as part of the basic data upon which the plan is predicated. Then, the effects of soil problems on proposed routes can be evaluated during the overall planning.

In an excellent book written for a nontechnical audience, *Cities and Geology,* Leggett (1973) has discussed and illustrated the important role of geology in land use planning. Geology, in the sense used by Dr. Leggett, encompasses all aspects of the crust of the earth—soil, rock, and water. Transportation facilities frequently have to consider all three materials in planning, thus combining elements of geology, hydrology, and soil mechanics. The term *geotechnical engineering* is often used to describe the overlapping disciplines involved in the study of using earth materials for engineered construction.

This chapter will be devoted primarily to soil problems but will also touch briefly upon problems associated with rock and ground water. It is aimed at providing the land use planner with a general understanding and knowledge of the importance of various soil properties affecting land use for transportation facilities. The role of geotechnical information in site evaluation is first discussed followed by a discussion of engineering characteristics of soil. Means of obtaining geotechnical information are reviewed to complement material presented in earlier chapters. Finally, techniques used to deal with geotechnical problems are discussed.

II. ROLE OF GEOTECHNICAL INFORMATION
IN SITE EVALUATION

A. Importance

The construction of a transportation facility involves much work with the earth; in 1973, for example, a study found that the greatest proportion of highway construction cost, 34%, was for earthwork and subbase construction. By 1976, the percentage had reached an estimated 40%. Not only is earthwork important from a technical standpoint, it obviously plays a major role in economic considerations. Proper use of geotechnical information in the site and route selection stages does not necessarily mean that costs will be decreased; rather, a better definition of potential problems will be obtained so that economic comparisons of different routes can be more reliable.

As one example of how geotechnical information is important in the planning process, consider the following history. Three routes for a section of interstate highway were being evaluated. Two followed a valley route for most of the length, ascending a mountainside to a plateau by way of a natural gap. The third route gently climbed up the mountainside to the plateau. At the time of route selection, little geotechnical information was available to the planners. As the mountain route was significantly shorter, did not require urban disruption and was apparently cheaper, it was selected. During construction, approximately 50 landslides occurred along the route, most after initial grading had been completed. Investigations found the cause to be related to the presence of a weak colluvial, or gravity-transported, soil overlying an equally weak clay derived from weathering of a shale formation. The ultimate cost for completing the road exceeded the original estimates many times, the opening of this important segment was delayed 3 years, and the route will always have a relatively high maintenance cost. Had the planners obtained even qualitative geotechnical information in the beginning, the landslide potential of the mountain route could have been included as part of the data on which the decision was to be made. In retrospect, the highway planners believe their decision would have been the same due to the high right-of-way costs for the other two routes. But, with a foreknowledge of the landslide potential, better design plans would have been used, and the public alerted that this construction would be costly and slow.

B. Geotechnical Factors

Because geotechnical information is only a part of the overall planning process, it is important that the land use planner learn to identify those factors that are likely to have the greatest impact on cost or performance and those that will provide the most information. This is particularly important in a preliminary route selection when many corridors are under consideration and time for study may be limited by available funds. Listed below are factors that should be considered in a preliminary route comparison. Further discussion about most of these factors and how to evaluate them is provided in subsequent sections.

1) Topography—The shape of the ground surface will indicate the amount of cutting and filling needed to reach a planned grade. The topography also provides a clue as to the nature of the soil and rock below the surface. The configuration of natural slopes gives some guidance as to possible cut slope configuration. Drainage patterns and streams which will require structures can be located.

2) Geology—Knowledge of the types of rock present along a proposed route, the amount of soil cover, the structure of the rock, and the location of any faults provides information on ease of excavation, need for rock cuts (which are costly), possible sources of rock for aggregates, possible areas of landslide potential in cut slopes, and possible areas of ground water problems.

3) Soil Characteristics—The types of soil present and their origin, the depth of the soil and changes in type with depth, the consistency (hard or soft, loose or dense), and the engineering classification of the soils will provide the planner enough information for a very qualitative assessment about the stability of cuts and the suitability of the soils for use as pavement subgrades, foundations for structures, and embankment fills.

4) Minimum Data for Planning—For the purpose of comparing routes or site locations, qualitative assessments can usually be made by trained geotechnical engineers using only the information available from published topographic maps, aerial photography, geologic maps, soil survey reports, and local experience. For any more detailed planning, some form of direct exploration should be included.

III. ENGINEERING CHARACTERISTICS OF SOIL IMPORTANT TO TRANSPORTATION FACILITY DESIGN

A. Introduction

Any transportation system relies upon soil to provide both foundation support and materials for construction. Figure 1 illustrates a typical section for a highway or railroad traversing rolling terrain. Soil slopes in the cuts must not be so steep that soil material will move out of the cut down into the roadway, the soil underneath the embankment must be capable of providing satisfactory support for the embankments, the soils which form the base for the pavement (subgrade) must be capable of providing adequate support for the thickness of pavement selected, and the fill materials

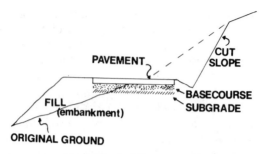

Fig. 1—Typical highway section.

must be placed in a fashion such that they will not undergo severe movement due to their own weight.

In studying soils for the design of transportation facilities, many properties are determined by laboratory tests and used in the design of the various parts of the facility. For general planning purposes, however, it is obviously impractical to perform laboratory tests on all types of soil that might be encountered over several different routes. Engineering soil classification systems have been developed which group soils according to similar engineering characteristics to make the general assessment of soil conditions on a particular route easier. Most USDA soil survey reports now give engineering classifications for the soils mapped and often give ranges of particular soil properties. The engineering classification systems and their relation to the USDA soil survey classifications will be discussed in this chapter.

The soil properties discussed in this chapter may be divided into two general groups: those which describe the soil material itself—moisture content, unit weight, and distribution of particle sizes—and those which describe the response of the soil to an external action such as application of a load. The properties in the first group are frequently called *classification and identification properties,* while those in the second group are often referred to as *engineering properties.* Through much research and experience, correlations have been evolved which allow qualitative estimates of engineering properties to be made when various classification and identification properties are known or when the engineering soil classification is known.

It is important to note here that many soils have a certain particle arrangement resulting from their formational process. When this structure is destroyed, as by excavating the soil and placing it in a fill, properties which were measured before the disturbance will often be significantly different than those same properties measured after the disturbance. Therefore, a land use planner should not consider all soil properties as constants but should attempt to estimate the properties of a particular soil that are appropriate to its intended use.

The remainder of this chapter will first discuss classification and identification properties of soils then describe various engineering soil classification systems. The engineering properties important for transportation facilities will then be described.

More detailed information on the tests to measure the properties described and on classification systems can be found in standard texts on soil mechanics, such as Sowers and Sowers (1970), Lambe and Whitman (1969), and Terzaghi and Peck (1967).

B. Classification and Identification Properties

1. PARTICLE SIZE DISTRIBUTION

Soils are a mixture of many different sizes of particles. By using appropriate testing procedures, a reasonably accurate determination can be made of the distribution of the various particle sizes within a given soil sample. Although soil particles may range in shape from nearly spherical to extremely elongated rectangles, the "size" of a particle is usually taken as the smallest square sieve opening through which the particle passes. Numerous organizations have proposed naming criteria for various ranges of particle sizes as illustrated in Fig. 2. Although there is disagreement about some of the precise dividing points on the size scale, all naming systems divide soils into the same general classes—clay, silt, sand, gravel, and coarser materials. Often, the clay and silt size particles are termed *fines* as they are too small to be seen with the unaided eye. Soils referred to as *fine-grained* soils are those which have >50% of their particles finer than the dividing line between sand and silt. For the fine-grained soils, the actual distribution of particles

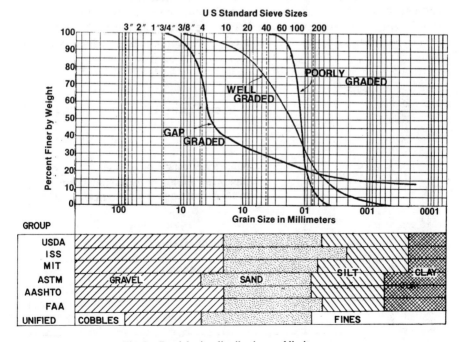

Fig. 2—Particle size distribution and limits.

has less effect on the soil behavior than does the distribution for coarse-grained soils. Also, behavior of soils containing a significant portion of clay particles is affected by chemical and electrolytic reactions between the clay minerals themselves as well as by mechanical interaction between the particles. For all other particle sizes, mechanical interaction governs the soil behavior.

The grain size distribution is important for coarse-grained soils, is needed in design of drainage and filter systems, and is useful for evaluating frost susceptability. Most engineering classification systems also use the grain size distribution as the basic part of the system.

2. ATTERBERG LIMITS

The *Atterberg limits,* named for the Swedish soil scientist, A. Atterberg, are moisture contents representing the boundaries between different states of behavior of a mixture of soil particles smaller than 0.42 mm (no. 40 sieve) and water. They are based on the concept that a soil-water mixture can exist in any of four states, depending upon the water content. When the soil is totally dry, it behaves as a true solid. With increasing amount of water, the behavior of the soil changes through a semisolid state to a plastic state and finally to a liquid state. Figure 3 illustrates the state concept and the relation of the various limits which are defined below.

The *liquid limit* is the highest moisture content at which the soil still behaves as a plastic solid. The *plastic limit* is the lowest moisture content at which the soil behaves as a plastic solid. The *shrinkage limit* is the moisture content dividing semisolid behavior and solid behavior. No further reduction in volume of the soil occurs below the shrinkage limit. The *plasticity index,* which is taken as the difference between the liquid limit and the

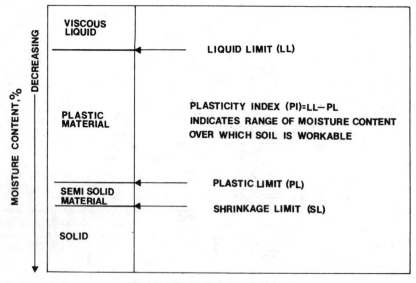

Fig. 3—Atterberg limits definitions.

plastic limit, indicates the range of moisture content over which the soil can be easily worked.

The Atterberg limits, especially the liquid limit and the plasticity index, can be used to provide qualitative estimates of such engineering characteristics as strength and compressibility. Most engineering soil classification systems also rely upon the Atterberg limits to distinguish various groups of fine-grained soil within the classification system.

3. UNIT WEIGHT

Often erroneously called "*density*", the *unit weight* is the weight per unit volume of a soil. Knowledge of the unit weight of the soil in place is important in estimating settlement and in analyzing cut slopes for stability.

4. MOISTURE CONTENT

The *moisture content* of a soil is expressed as the weight of water divided by the weight of dry soil. The moisture content, when compared with the Atterberg limits for fine-grained soil, gives an indication of whether the material will be easily workable or will present problems during construction. Also, the relationship of the existing moisture content to the liquid limit is an indication of the past stress history that the soil has undergone.

C. Engineering Classification Systems

1. INTRODUCTION

Most soil pedological descriptions provide little information about the engineering characteristics of a particular soil, although with experience rough correlations can be drawn. For engineering use, classification systems have been developed which group soils having similar engineering characteristics. The two most widely used classification systems—the Unified Classification System and the AASHTO (American Association of State Highway and Transportation Officials) System will be described below. Both systems rely upon only the Atterberg limits and the particle size distribution to classify a soil. Generalized statements about the engineering properties of a soil can be made once the classification is known.

2. UNIFIED CLASSIFICATION SYSTEM

The Unified Classification System was initially developed by Dr. Arthur Casagrande of Harvard University and has been adopted by the Corps of Engineers and the Bureau of Reclamation, among others. The system has two major groups—coarse grained soils ($>50\%$ by weight is retained on a no. 200 sieve) and fine-grained soils ($>50\%$ passes a no. 200 sieve). Coarse-grained soils are further subdivided on the basis of particle size distribution and type of fines present. Table 1 briefly lists the coarse-grained soil subdivisions and their descriptions. The fine-grained soils are

Table 1—Unified Classification System—coarse-grained soils (more than half is larger than no. 200 sieve).

Group symbol†	Name	General suitability for roads and airfields
GW GP	Well-graded gravel Poorly graded gravel	Excellent to good for embankments, subgrades, and base base courses. Very slight potential frost damage. Essentially incompressible. Excellent drainage.
GM GC	Silty gravel Clayey gravel	Good for embankment, fair to good for subgrades. Slightly compressible. Poor drainage.
SW SP	Well-graded sand Poorly graded sand	Good to fair for embankments, subgrades, poor for bases. None to very slight potential frost damage. Essentially incompressible. Excellent drainage.
SM SC	Silty sand Clayey sand	Good for embankments, fair to poor for subgrades, not suitable for bases. Slight to high potential frost damage. Slight to medium compressibility. Poor drainage.

† Soils with G prefix have at least 50% of coarse fraction larger than no. 4 sieve size. Soils with S prefix have more than 50% of coarse fraction smaller than no. 4 sieve size.

grouped on the basis of their Atterberg limits as shown in Fig. 4a. Table 2 briefly describes the fine-grained subgroups. More detailed information on the group descriptions and techniques for classifying a given soil may be found in any soil mechanics text. Laboratory tests are necessary to verify a classification, but a reasonably accurate classification can easily be made using simple field procedures.

Table 2—Unified Classification System—fine-grained soils (more than half is smaller than no. 200 sieve).

Group symbol†	Name	General suitability for roads and airfields
ML	Inorganic silt, silty fine sand or clayey silt	Fair to good for embankments, poor to fair for subgrades, unsuited for bases. Medium to very high potential frost damage. Slight to medium compressibility. Fair to poor drainage.
CL	Inorganic clay of low plasticity, sandy clay, silty clay, lean clay	Poor to fair for embankments, subgrades, unsuited for bases. Medium potential for frost damage. Medium compressibility. Practically impervious.
OL	Organic silt of low plasticity	Poor for embankments, subgrades, unsuited for bases. Medium to high potential frost damage. Medium to high compressibility. Poor drainage.
MH	Inorganic silt of high plasticity	Poor for embankments, subgrades, unsuitable for bases. Medium to very high potential frost damage. High compressibility. Fair to poor drainage.
CH	Inorganic clay of high	Poor to fair for embankments or subgrades, unsuited for other use. High potential for frost action, shrink-swell. High compressibility. Practically impervious.
OH	Organic clay of high plasticity	Very poor for subgrades, unsuited for other uses. High compressibility. Practically impervious.
Pt	Peat	Unsuited for any use. Very high compressibility.

† Distinction of groups based on Atterberg limits, See Fig. 4a.

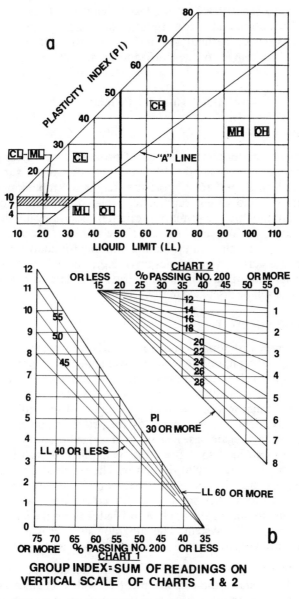

Fig. 4—*(a)* plasticity chart for Unified Classification System; *(b)* charts for determining AASHTO group index.

3. AASHTO CLASSIFICATION SYSTEM

The AASHTO Classification System is aimed at classifying soils on the basis of performance as a subgrade material and as such is more often associated with highway planning than is the Unified System. The charts shown in Fig. 4b and Table 3 are used to assign the soil classification. Both grain size distribution and Atterberg limits are required before a classification can be assigned. Techniques for field classification are not as easily applied for this system as for the Unified System.

D. Engineering Properties

1. INTRODUCTION

The engineering properties of soil of primary concern for transportation facilities are those related to the ability of the soil to support traffic load, to stand on slopes, to support the weight of embankments, and to satisfactorily respond to environmentally related stresses. Shear strength and compressibility are the primary properties used in evaluating embankment foundation performance and cut slope stability. These same properties are also very important in evaluating building foundations and they are discussed in standard soil mechanics texts, e.g., Sowers and Sowers (1970). The properties important for resisting traffic loads and environmentally related stresses will be discussed in this section.

2. SUBGRADE SUPPORT

The subgrade is that portion of soil immediately beneath the pavement structure. Depending upon the type of pavement, the subgrade may play a major or a minor role in the thickness design and ultimate performance of the pavement. An asphaltic concrete pavement system relies upon the soil subgrade for the major proportion of the support of the traffic. The design of this type pavement system is based on the principle that each succeeding layer of asphalt, aggregate base coarse, then soil subgrade, spreads and distributes the applied load so that a stress is applied to each layer which is within the support capability of that layer. The required thickness of pavement structure is based upon a measurement of the support value of the subgrade soil. On the other hand, a reinforced concrete pavement is structurally designed to absorb the applied traffic load and the soil plays a relatively minor role in the system. The subgrade support is measured differently for the two types of pavement and will be discussed separately.

a. **Subgrade Support: Flexible Pavement**—Because the design of pavements actually predates the establishment of soil mechanics as a science, many pavement design techniques evolved based upon past experience with soils in a given area or on the use of empirical tests related to past experience. Thus, there is no one method of evaluating subgrade support which is universally accepted by the highway community today. There are some areas where pavements are still designed based upon either the soil classification or simply upon the designer's past experience with the soils in his area. These pavements, while they may be conservatively designed, generally function adequately. Empirical tests related to past experience have been

Table 3—AASHTO Classification System.

| Parameter | Granular materials† (35% or less passing no. 200 sieve) | | | | | | | Silt-clay materials† (35% passing no. 200 sieve) | | | |
| | A-1‡ | | A-3 | A-2 | | | | A-4 | A-5 | A-6 | A-7-5, A-7-6 |
	A-1-a	A-1-b		A-2-4	A-2-5	A-2-6	A-2-7				
Sieve analysis, percentage passing:											
no. 10	50 max.										
no. 40	30 max.	50 max.	51 min.								
no. 200	15 max.	25 max.	10 max.	35 max.	35 max.	35 max.	35 max.	36 min.	36 min.	36 min.	36 min.
Characteristics of fraction passing no. 40:											
Liquid limit				40 max.	41 min.	40 max.	41 min.	40 max.	41 min.	40 max.	41 min.
Plasticity index	6 max.		NP	10 max.	10 max.	11 min.	11 min.	10 max.	10 max.	11 min.	11 min.
Group index	0		0	0	0	4 max.	4 max.	8 max.	12 max.	16 max.	20 max.
Usual types of significant constituent materials	Stone fragments, gravel, and sand		Fine sand	Silty or clayey gravel and sand				Silty soils		Clayey soils	
General rating as subgrade	Excellent to good							Fair to poor			

† General classification.
‡ Group classification.

winnowed down until only two are currently widely used, both of which will be discussed later. Attempts to place the pavement design on a more rational basis related strictly to material characteristics has led to wider use of tests to measure the shear strength and the deformation characteristics of the soils and relate these to a consistent pavement design methodology. This approach will not be discussed in this chapter.

The two most commonly used empirical means of evaluating subgrade support are the California bearing ratio (CBR) and the stabilometer (R-value) method. Both of these tests measure the soil deformation under a system of applied loading. Samples of soil are prepared in the laboratory to conditions which are expected to approximate those existing after construction in the field. Samples may be subjected to innundation to represent complete saturation, presumably the worst condition to be encountered during the life of the highway. Figures 5 and 6 illustrate the general characteristics of both tests. Both tests can be performed upon undisturbed samples of soil obtained from an area where the pavement will be placed in a cut but they are more commonly performed on samples prepared to specified laboratory conditions.

The results of the tests are used to establish a range of subgrade support existing over a design section and a design value for establishing the pavement thickness. It would not be practical either economically or from a

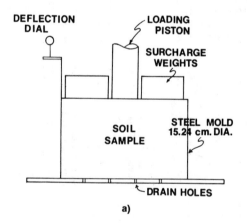

a)

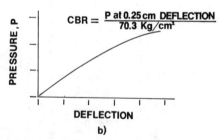

$$CBR = \frac{P \text{ at } 0.25 \text{ cm DEFLECTION}}{70.3 \text{ Kg/cm}^2}$$

b)

Fig. 5—Schematic of California bearing ratio test: *(a)* Test set up; *(b)* Typical results.

Table 4—Different ranges for subgrade support values as related to soil classification.

Unified classification	Range of CBR	Range of R value	Range of modulus of subgrade reaction, kg/cm³
GW	40–80	70–85	5.5–8.3
GP	30–60	65–80	5.5–8.3
GM	20–60	55–80	2.8–8.3
GC	20–40	55–70	2.8–8.3
SW	20–40	55–70	5.5–8.3
SP	10–40	40–70	5.5–8.3
SM	10–40	40–70	2.8–8.3
SC	5–20	30–55	2.8–8.3
ML	1–15	0–50	2.8–5.5
CL	1–15	0–50	1.4–5.5
MH	1–10	0–40	1.4–2.8
CH	1–15	0–50	1.4–5.5

construction standpoint to design a separate thickness of pavement for each type of soil. Therefore, the roadway is divided into convenient sections based upon topography, soil conditions, or other suitable criteria, and a constant thickness pavement design based upon the lower range of subgrade support values is selected. Different ranges for subgrade support values as related to soil classification are shown on Table 4. These values should not

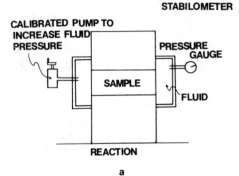

STABILOMETER

CALIBRATED PUMP TO
INCREASE FLUID
PRESSURE

PRESSURE
GAUGE

SAMPLE

FLUID

REACTION

a

$$R= \dfrac{100}{100 - (2.5/D_2)\,[(P_v/P_h)-1]+1}$$

R = STABILOMETER VALUE

P_v = APPLIED VERTICAL PRESSURE 11.25 Kg./cm.²

P_h = MEASURED HORIZONTAL PRESSURE
AT P_v = 11.25 Kg./cm.²

D_2 = DISPLACEMENT OF FLUID NEEDED TO
RAISE P_h FROM .35 to 7.03 Kg./cm.²
MEASURED USING CALIBRATED PUMP

b

Fig. 6—Schematic of stabilometer test: *(a)* Test set up; *(b)* Typical results.

be used for actual design but do give an indication of the range of values for various types of soil.

b. Subgrade Support: Rigid Pavement—A rigid concrete pavement is designed based upon an elastic analysis method which requires that the soil be evaluated in terms of an elastic response. The soil is assumed to behave essentially as a spring which will undergo a known deformation with applied load. The constant relating deformation to applied load is known as the *modulus of subgrade reaction*. The modulus of subgrade reaction, or k, is normally evaluated using a plate-load-bearing test. In this test, plates of various diameters are pressed into the soil by jacking against a loading frame as illustrated in Fig. 7. The amount of plate deflection vs. applied load is plotted and the modulus of subgrade reaction determined either at a specified plate pressure or as the slope of the line at a plate pressure corresponding to the expected traffic loadings.

Because the plate load test must be conducted on soil in-place in the field, it should either be conducted at times when the soil moisture is highest or the results should be corrected for possible soil saturation sometime in the life of the pavement. A suitable correction can be established by performing laboratory consolidation tests, one test performed on the soil at the same moisture as the plate load test is performed and a second test performed with the sample saturated.

The modulus of subgrade reaction can be estimated from knowledge of the soil's classification as shown on Table 4. Such estimates are often adequate because the actual thickness of the concrete pavement is relatively insensitive to rather large fluctuations in the modulus of subgrade reaction

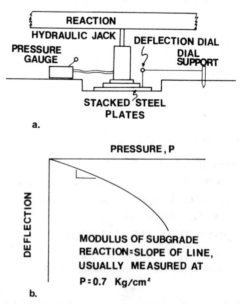

Fig. 7—Schematic of plate load test: *(a)* Test set up; *(b)* Typical results.

used in design. The required concrete thickness is often governed by factors other than the strength of the soil subgrade.

c. **Maximum Dry Density**—If a sample of relatively dry soil is mixed with a small amount of water, then packed into a mold of known volume using a given compaction energy, and the process repeated at progressively higher moisture contents, it will be found that the weight of the compacted samples first increases with increasing moisture content then begins to decrease. The highest unit weight reached is called the *maximum dry density* and the moisture content at which it is attained is termed the *optimum moisture content.* The laboratory test to determine the maximum dry density is often called the *Proctor compaction test,* after R. R. Proctor who first presented the concepts of compaction. Figure 8 illustrates the results of typical compaction tests on several types of soil.

The purpose of the compaction test is to provide a standard against which the effectiveness of field compaction is judged. (Field compaction will be discussed in the next section.) The energy used in the laboratory tests

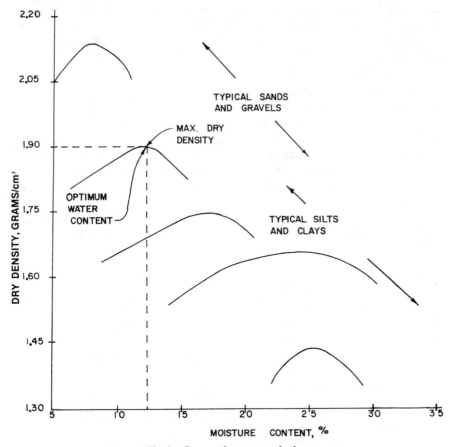

Fig. 8—Compaction test terminology.

has been set as a result of large-scale field rolling tests with different types and weights of equipment. One of two energy levels can be selected for the laboratory test depending upon the weight of field equipment expected for the field work. The standard Proctor test uses an energy comparable to small- and medium-sized equipment. The modified Proctor test uses a higher energy and should be used when heavy equipment is anticipated.

3. ENVIRONMENTAL STRESSES

a. Frost—Certain soils when exposed to freezing temperatures and availability of water form lenses of ice in the soil. These ice lenses tend to attract more water and grow in size as long as the freezing temperatures remain. The increasing thickness of the ice lenses causes heave of the ground surface. This phenomenon is well known in the northern states and causes many problems with pavement performance. The major difficulty occurs during the spring—the soil thaws near the surface but deeper ice lenses remain frozen, trapping water which causes softening of the soil. Heavy loads applied when the soil is in this softened condition can cause pavement breakup in extreme cases. It is generally agreed that all soils having 3% or more particles finer than 0.02 mm are considered susceptible to frost heaving. Further subdivision of soils susceptible to frost has been made by the Corps of Engineers as shown in Table 5. The higher the F number, the higher the frost susceptibility.

b. Shrink-Swell Behavior—Many of the fine-grained soils which contain appreciable amounts of clay minerals exhibit a tendency to change volume with change in moisture content, i.e., shrink on drying and swell on wetting. Pavement construction often results in a change in the moisture regime of natural soils underneath. Prevention of evaporation can cause increases in moisture leading to pavement cracking as the soil swells. Also, soils with a high swell potential, if placed in fills at relatively low moisture contents, can produce damaging swelling if later flooded by rain water or rising ground water. Shrinkage is not as often a problem but can worsen later swelling due to large cracks which provide water access to more of the soil.

Table 5—Corps of Engineers classification of soils for frost.

F-1	Gravely soils containing between 3 and 20% finer than 0.02 mm by wt
F-2	Sands containing between 3 and 15% finer than 0.02 mm by wt
F-3	a. Gravely soils containing > 20% finer than 0.02 mm by wt
	b. Sands, except very fine silty sands, containing > 15% finer than 0.02 mm by wt
	c. Clays with plasticity indexes of > 12
	d. Varved clays existing with uniform subgrade conditions
F-4	a. All silts including sandy silts
	b. Very fine silty sands containing > 15% finer than 0.02 mm by wt
	c. Clays with plasticity indexes < 12
	d. Varved clays existing with nonuniform subgrade conditions

The swell potential of a soil can be measured by several types of laboratory tests. The Federal Housing Administration uses a specially designed test apparatus, the PVC meter, to evaluate a soil's swell potential. The test procedure and equipment are described in detail by Henry and Dragoo (1965). Briefly, a soil sample is compacted into a ring, sandwiched between porous stones, and wetted. The pressure resulting from the swell of the soil is measured and converted to a PVC value from 0 to 10 by means of a correlation chart. The higher the PVC value the higher the potential for swelling.

A soil's potential for volume change can be qualitatively assessed using either Atterberg limits or by measuring the coefficient of linear extensibility (COLE) as described by Grossman et al. (1968). Sowers and Sowers (1970) suggest that clayey soils having a plasticity index (PI) between 15 and 30 should be considered as having a moderate volume change potential, while soils with a PI greater than 30 should be considered as having a high volume change potential. Franzmeier and Ross (1968) report that COLE can be related to swelling potential as measured by the PVC test as follows:

PVC Value	*COLE*
0 to 2, noncritical	0 to 0.03
2 to 4, marginal	0.03 to 0.06
4 to 6, critical	0.06 to 0.10
over 6, very critical	over 0.10

4. QUALITATIVE ASSESSMENT OF ENGINEERING PROPERTIES

In evaluating soils for land use planning it is not usually necessary to know the actual value of engineering properties of the soils; rather, qualitative assessments are generally sufficient to allow comparative judgments or to identify possible problem zones. Familiarity with the Unified or AASHTO Classification Systems described earlier and the general characteristics of the various classification groups will greatly help a land use planner gain a broad picture of soil characteristics. Tables 1 and 2 illustrate the kind of general information available. Many publications of the USDA Soil Survey contain both Unified and AASHTO classifications for the various soil series as well as quantitative laboratory testing in some cases.

IV. OBTAINING SOIL AND ROCK INFORMATION

A. Qualitative

1. LITERATURE

Previous chapters have indicated that information can be obtained from soil surveys published through the U.S. Department of Agriculture. Aerial photography as a tool for obtaining qualitative information has also been mentioned. The information obtained from soil survey maps and from air photo study can provide much of the needed qualitative information about potential transportation facility sites. Because rock and ground water often have an important effect on siting, information on these factors should be gathered also. The best sources of information on rock and ground water are the publications and maps of the State Geological Surveys or the U.S. Geological Survey. In many places the soil overburden has been formed by chemical and climatic weathering processes, thus a knowledge of the geology can be a guide to the types of soil. Of particular assistance to land use planners are the U.S. Geological Survey maps showing geologic hazards which are now available for some areas. Such hazards as landslide-prone materials, faults, and expansive soils or rocks are illustrated.

In many states the State Geological Survey has prepared maps with explanatory tests for each county within the state. The texts discuss such items as ground water, soil types, and sources of sand and gravel—all items of interest to the planner.

Another useful source of information about area soil conditions is the series of flood plain maps prepared for cities or other governing units under the National Flood Insurance Program. These maps generally show the predicted flood limit from a 100-year storm for all major streams in the area. Soils found in flood plain areas are very often weak and compressible, and can present numerous problems for a transportation facility. Conversely, many flood plains are good sources of sands and gravels. So, location of the flood plain is a useful piece of planning information.

As more and more governmental units enter into land use planning, land use capability maps are being prepared for some planning areas. Such maps attempt to show, usually by a series of overlays or a set of maps of the same area, information on a scale of desirability. Thus, areas with slopes between 8 and 15% may be shown as unsuited for heavy industry but suitable for residential development. Similarly, other ground and cultural features are coded at various levels of suitability. In using information obtained from such maps, the land use planner is cautioned to remember that an engineering solution may be available to permit economical use of land which is mapped as unsuitable. The land use capability maps indicate problem areas; information later in this chapter will discuss how the engineer copes with problem areas.

2. OBTAINING QUALITATIVE INFORMATION

Often the planner must develop plans for areas where soil and geologic literature is not available. In these circumstances the approach likely to produce the most useful results economically is aerial photographic study supplemented by field reconnaissance by a trained geologist, engineering geologist, or soils engineer. The interpretation of aerial photographs to reveal information about soil and geology is discussed in numerous texts, among them Lueder (1959) and Way (1973). Mintzer and Strubler (1967) discuss how aerial photographic interpretation can be supplemented by selective exploration to develop preliminary engineering reports on proposed highway locations.

B. Quantitative

1. DIRECT EXPLORATION

While qualitative information may be all that is necessary to determine general locations of soil, rock, or ground water problem areas, more definitive information is essential for design purposes. Such information can only be obtained by direct exploration of the areas in question. Such direct exploration includes subsurface investigation and laboratory testing.

2. SUBSURFACE INVESTIGATION

In a typical subsurface investigation, borings are advanced into the soil and rock strata and samples are obtained of the various layers. Tests can be conducted in the borehole (Standard Penetration Test, vane shear, pressuremeter, etc.) and high quality, relatively undisturbed samples can be obtained for testing in the laboratory. Piezometers or observation wells can be sealed into the completed borehole to provide information on ground water levels.

The planning of a subsurface investigation must be done by a person trained in soil mechanics or engineering geology if the full benefits of the investigation are to be obtained. Sowers and Sowers (1970) and Hvorslev (1949) describe factors to consider in planning the investigation. One of the primary considerations in executing a subsurface investigation is that the plan made beforehand must not be viewed as rigid but must be constantly compared to the data being obtained and revised as needed to meet the objectives of adequate information for least cost.

3. LABORATORY TESTING

During the borings, visual descriptions and classifications of soil and rock samples can be made. To obtain exact information on the engineering properties described earlier, laboratory testing is required. Laboratory test procedures are generally standardized to reduce the effects of varying sample treatment and test procedure. Organizations such as the American Society for Testing Materials (ASTM) and the American Association of State Highway and Transportation Officials (AASHTO) publish books of standard test methods. Texts on laboratory testing by Lambe (1951) and Bowles (1970) also describe routine test procedures, as do several chapters in the book *Methods of Soil Analysis,* Part 1 (Black, 1965).

V. COPING WITH GEOTECHNICAL LIMITATIONS

A. Improvements of Available Soils for Subgrades

1. GENERAL

When soils existing at the site of a proposed facility have undesirable properties, three approaches are possible—remove the undesirable soil and bring in better soil from off-site, design the facility to cope with the poor properties, or attempt to improve the properties of the on-site soil. The most economical approach can be any one of these or a combination, and all should be given consideration before a final decision is made. This section discusses the more common techniques used to improve the properties of the existing soils. For more discussion on the techniques discussed below, the reader should consult the references cited in each subsection.

2. COMPACTION

The most common and simplest means for improving the engineering properties of a soil is to increase its density or unit weight by rolling it with heavy equipment. Such a process is called *compaction* or *densification*. While compaction can be effective to shallow depths for in-place soils, it is normally associated with soil used to construct fills. Soil obtained from an excavated area is transported to the placement site, spread in relatively thin layers, the moisture content adjusted up or down as necessary, and the layers are rolled with equipment appropriate for the soil type. For sands, heavy vibratory rollers or rubber-tired rollers are most effective. For fine-grained soils, rubber-tired or sheepsfoot rollers provide the most efficient compaction. The rolling process is continued until a desired level of compaction is achieved. Field measurements are made of the density of the soil being compacted and the results are compared to the results of the laboratory compaction test. Usually it is required that the field density be 95 to 100% of the laboratory maximum dry density.

Any material which is to be placed by construction should be compacted as a matter of good engineering practice. Soils which have poor subgrade strength in their natural condition can often be used if they are removed, dried or wetted as needed, and replaced with proper compaction. Compaction under controlled moisture content conditions can also be beneficial in reducing the swell potential of clayey soils.

One further point should be noted about compaction. In evaluating the effectiveness of compaction it is normal to express the actual compacted density as a percentage of the laboratory test, i.e., 95% of standard Proctor. Such comparisons are too frequently extended to natural undisturbed soils. The engineering properties of an undisturbed soil cannot be reasonably assessed by comparing the in-place density with the density obtained in a laboratory compaction test; such comparisons are meaningless and should be avoided.

Costs associated with soil compaction are generally related to equipment time and are included by contractors in their cost for overall earthwork, normally using cubic yards as the unit of measure. Depending upon the distance soil is moved, the existing moisture content compared to the range specified for compaction, the time of year, and the degree of compaction specified, costs can be extremely variable. Assuming nominal haul distances and "average" conditions, prices for placement and compaction of fill soil should be between $0.50 and $3.50 per cubic yard in place. A better idea of prices in a particular area can be obtained from highway departments or by examining results of recent bids on construction projects in the area.

Further general information about the effects of compaction on soil properties can be obtained from a standard soil mechanics text such as Sowers and Sowers (1970), Leonards (1962), or Lambe and Whitman (1969).

3. CEMENT TREATMENT

Most inorganic soils can be improved by adding small quantities of portland cement. Organic soils or soils with a high sulfate content are not suitable. Also, because of difficulties with mixing, soils with a high clay content are usually avoided. Cement stabilization is accomplished by breaking up the soil, adding generally small percentages (2 to 10%) of cement, mixing the soil and cement, adding water as needed, then spreading and compacting the mixture. Dramatic increases in soil strength, reductions in compressibility, and resistance to water action can be achieved. Where good rock to make aggregate for road bases is scarce, sands and sandy soils can often be improved sufficiently to serve as a road base material. In many areas with low traffic volumes, excellent roads can be constructed using cement-stabilized soils as the entire pavement.

Because cement is relatively expensive compared to soil, a laboratory test program is required to establish the minimum cement content necessary to produce an acceptable improvement in the soil property under consideration. Strength tests and tests employing alternate freezing and thawing or alternate wetting and drying are used to judge the effectiveness of the content. Typical cement contents needed vary from 2 to 4% for well-graded sands to 8 to 12% for a fat clay. Based on treating a 15-cm-thick (6-inch) layer with 6% cement, typical costs for cement treatment range from $1.00 to $2.25 per 0.01 m² (yd²). Cement cost and transportation are the biggest cost variables. Additional information on cement stabilization can be found in books by Woods (1960), Ingles and Metcalf (1973), the Portland Cement Association, and publications of the Transportation Research Board.

4. LIME TREATMENT

Lime is used both as a means of making soil more workable in preparation for addition of cement and as a means of increasing the strength of clayey soils. Organic soils and soils containing little clay show little response to lime treatment. Only hydrated lime (calcium hydroxide) or quicklime (calcium oxide) are suitable for stabilization use; agricultural lime (calcium carbonate) is not effective. The addition of lime to a clayey soil results in an immediately apparent decrease in the plasticity and an increase in the workability of the soil. The swell potential of clayey soils is greatly reduced by lime treatment. Compaction and curing of the mixture also results in a long-term strength gain as the lime reacts with the clay minerals to form cementitious compounds. Quicklime, although difficult to use safely, is an effective drying agent for wet soils.

Between 1 and 3% lime is normally adequate to make clayey soils more workable while between 3 and 8% is needed to effect a strength gain. Normal treatment depth for subgrade improvement is 15 to 30 cm (6 to 12 inches), although recent techniques developed have made depths up to 61 cm (24 inches) feasible for in-place soils. Costs for a 15-cm-thick (6-inch) lime treatment typically range between \$1.00 and \$2.00 per 0.01 m^2 (yd^2) depending on the area involved and the ease of mixing. Further information about lime stabilization can be obtained from Ingles and Metcalf (1973) or the National Lime Association.

5. OTHER STABILIZATION TECHNIQUES

Stabilization of subgrade soils can be accomplished by other means not as common as the ones discussed above. Mixing a well-graded aggregate into a weak soil will often provide a stable platform to speed construction or form a usable subgrade. Liquid asphalts can be used with clean sands to improve their strength. Certain chemicals have also been found effective with clayey soils but the cost is usually relatively high.

B. Frost-Susceptible Soils

Where frost-susceptible soils exist, the design of functional pavement systems must include provisions to minimize damage due to frost heave. Where suitable quantities of non-frost-susceptible soils are available, undercutting to below the depth of frost penetration and constructing the road bed of better soil can be done. The depth of undercutting is selected based on historical temperature data and charts relating the air temperatures to the depth of frost penetration in granular materials.

An alternative approach is to design the pavement for the reduced subgrade strength that occurs during the spring thaw. The pavement is thus overdesigned for other periods of the year. Also, this approach does nothing to reduce the surface irregularities and cracking from frost heave during the winter.

In recent years some states have experimented with using insulation materials such as styrofoam in subgrades to prevent frost penetration. Good information on design for frost susceptible soils can be obtained from the Cold Regions Research Engineering Laboratory of the U.S. Army Corps of Engineers.

C. Handling Swelling Soils

Where soils susceptible to swelling are present, special construction and design precautions must be taken to prevent damage. Use of lime to reduce the swell potential is a common remedy. Using relatively high moisture contents during compaction can be effective. In many soils, swelling can be controlled by applying sufficient vertical pressure from overlying materials to counteract the swell pressures. Undercutting the potentially swelling soils to depths of 30 to 61 cm (1 to 2 feet) and replacing them with nonswelling material often provides sufficient confining pressure so that minimum swell will occur even if the soils are unnundated.

D. Foundation Problems

The presence of weak or compressible soils presents problems for support of structures such as bridges and for proper performance of earth fills. In the case of structures, few options are available—a deep foundation extending through the soft soils to better material is usually chosen. Earth fills present a somewhat different problem as a foundation structure is usually not feasible. Where soft soils must be crossed by a highway fill, the techniques briefly described below are usually considered.

1) Structural Replacement—Long pile-supported trestles can be more economical where the soft soil is relatively thin, fill is costly, or where water seasonally floods the area.

2) Remove and Replace the Soft Soil—If the soft soil is not too thick, and good quality fill is available at low cost, the soft soil can be taken out and replaced with better material. The state of Louisiana has built many miles of road through the bayou swamps by dredging out soft soil and replacing it with sand fill obtained from the bottom of the Mississippi River. Environmental problems associated with disposal of the dredge spoil are making this approach less and less feasible.

A means of removing the soft soil without dredging is to place the better fill so high as to intentionally cause a shear failure in the soft soil. The material which fails moves up and out and is replaced by the fill. This technique, known as *mud waving,* or a *moving surcharge,* requires close control and usually some excavation ahead of the fill to prevent entrapment of soft soil by the fill.

3) Reduce Weight—The weight of the accumulated earth in the fill is the cause of excessive shear stress and settlement of the soft soil. By building the fill of lightweight materials, the desired height can sometimes be obtained without the undesirable results. Materials such as styrofoam, sawdust, and lightweight aggregate have been successfully used. Using such an approach requires careful analysis of the properties of the substitute material to determine its suitability as a fill.

4) Accelerate the Settlement—Earth fills can withstand substantial settlement with no ill effects, but the pavement on the fill or structures adjacent to the fill may well be rendered unusable before the settlement stops. The common bump where a road supported on fill meets a bridge structure founded on deep piles is an illustration of settlement distress. Settlements in clay soils may take 1 to 2 years or more to occur. If as much settlement as possible is allowed to occur before the road is paved, resulting distress can be often reduced to manageable proportions.

The simplest approach is to build the fill several years in advance of the paving and structures and allow it to sit. Although lawsuits have been known to induce sufficient delays, there is not usually enough time for this approach. To speed up the settlement process, numerous holes can be bored into the clay layer and filled with sand. Such sand drains allow water to escape from the clay more quickly and settlement to occur more rapidly. Waiting time can be reduced as much as 50%. To further increase the rate of settlement, fill can be placed higher than the planned grade, thus applying more pressure to the soil. Such an approach is called *surcharging*.

E. Ground Water

The location of the ground water level and its range of seasonal fluctuation is an important geotechnical factor to consider in planning. It is obviously desirable to avoid situations requiring construction below the ground water level, but often grade requirements will place some sections of a route below or near the ground water level. When a cut is made that intersects a ground water level, slope stability must be carefully studied. Some form of permanent drainage system is usually necessary to prevent future problems.

The design of any pavement system is not complete until drainage has been considered both for ground water and for surface infiltration. If the aggregate base course of a pavement becomes saturated; it loses its ability to reduce stresses transmitted to the soil subgrade and pavement failures are the inevitable result. Underdrains and drain trenches are common methods for controlling water levels near pavements. Cedargren (1967) provides an excellent discussion of drainage techniques.

F. Excavation Problems

One of the most important cost aspects of the grading for a highway is the cost of removing, hauling, and placing the materials used in the construction. Any evaluation of conditions along a proposed route is incomplete without considering the potential excavation problems. Excavation is most cheaply and quickly accomplished by use of scrapers and self-loading pans. These types of equipment can handle most soils but experience difficulty where large and numerous boulders occur, where the soils are clayey and wet, and in hard soils. Hard soils often occur as a transition in the weathering profile from soil to rock. Such terms as *disintegrated rock, partially weathered rock, saprolite,* and *hard pan* are used to indicate materials that conventional equipment cannot easily, if at all, excavate. Most of these transitional materials can be loosened by ripping, a process in which a large bulldozer drags one or more large steel teeth through the material, breaking it up so a pan or front end loader can load it. Rock usually requires drilling and blasting for removal.

LITERATURE CITED

Black, C. A. (editor-in-chief). 1965. Methods of soil analysis, Part 1. Agronomy no. 9. American Society of Agronomy, Madison, Wis.

Bowles, J. E. 1970. Engineering properties of soils and their measurement. McGraw Hill Book co., New York.

Cedargren, H. R. 1967. Seepage, drainage, and flow nets. John Wiley & Sons, Inc., New York.

Franzmeier, D. P., and S. J. Ross, Jr. 1968. Soil swelling: laboratory measurement and relation to other soil properties. Soil Sci. Soc. Am. Proc. 32:573–577.

Grossman, R. B., B. R. Brasher, D. P. Franzmeier, and J. L. Walker. 1968. Linear extensibility as calculated from natural-clod bulk density measurements. Soil Sci. Soc. Am. Proc. 32:570–573.

Henry, E. F., and M. C. Dragoo. 1965. Guide to use of the FHA soil PVC meter. FHA-595, Fed. Housing Admin., Washington, D.C.

Hvorslev, M. J. 1949. Subsurface exploration and sampling of soils for civil engineering purposes. The Eng. Found., New York.

Ingles, O. B., and J. B. Metcalf. 1973. Soil stabilization, principles, and practice. John Wiley & Sons, Inc., New York.

Lambe, T. W. 1951. Soil testing for engineers. John Wiley & Sons, Inc., New York.

Lambe, T. W., and R. V. Whitman. 1969. Soil mechanics. John Wiley & Sons, Inc., New York.

Leggett, R. F. 1973. Cities and geology. McGraw Hill Book Co., New York.

Leonards, G. A. (ed.). 1962. Foundation engineering. McGraw Hill Book Co., New York.

Lueder, Donald. 1959. Aerial photographic interpretation, principles and applications. McGraw Hill Book Co., New York.

Mintzer, O. W., and R. A. Struble. 1967. Combined techniques for terrain investigation. Highway Res. Rec. 156, Transport. Res. Bd., Washington, D.C.

Sowers, G. B., and G. F. Sowers. 1970. Introductory soil mechanics and foundations. 3rd ed. The MacMillan Co., London.

Terzaghi, Karl, and R. B. Peck. 1967. Soil mechanics in engineering practice. John Wiley and Sons, Inc., New York.

Way, D. S. 1973. Terrain analysis. Dowden, Hutchinson and Ross, Inc., Stroudsburg, Pa.

Woods, K. B. 1960. Highway engineering handbook. McGraw Hill Book Co., New York.

24 Vegetation for Transportation Systems and Utility Corridors

ROBERT W. DUELL

Rutgers University
New Brunswick, New Jersey

I. INTRODUCTION

Critical attention has been directed to vegetation for transportation systems utility corridors in increasing measures recently, largely because of two major concerns of our society, namely, "environmental quality," and the "energy crisis."

Concern for our environment has been building at an unprecedented rate in recent years. This may be a normal reaction to an equally unprecedented rate of technological development, which some fear could be getting out of control, and whose future disadvantages might outweigh present advantages. The deep dependence on fossil fuels, including that for transportation, by society as we currently know it in the United States, was brought into sharper focus by the recent "energy crisis." Reordering priorities, therefore, affected many aspects of our lives, and we will continue to live with restrictions for the forseeable future.

These concerns have roots in the past that are relevant to our attitudes and policies regarding needs for particular vegetative cover. An earlier crisis, the "dust bowl" that developed in our south-central wheatlands in the early 1930's, brought about the formation of the U.S. Soil Conservation Service in 1935. Joselyn (1969) traced the evolution of the philosophy of roadside design and justifications for mowing, and Hottenstein (1969) related roadside practices to the evolution of erosion control concepts. Soil and water conservation practices were oriented toward production agriculture initially, but experiences with such practices, soils, plants, and other materials have evolved to form the basis for many of our roadside establishment and maintenance operations today.

A. The Complete Highway

The concept of "the complete highway" originally related to the roadway proper, rather than the associated vegetation, and entailed the objectives of utility, safety, economy, and beauty. The last aspect was highlighted during President Lyndon Johnson's administration (1963-1969), particularly in connection with the construction of the interstate highway system, when roadside beautification was given unprecedented financial support. Properly executed, roadside beautification, in opening scenic vistas, screening less desirable views, removing billboards, and establishing aesthetically attractive vegetation, certainly contributed to the theme of environmental improvement. Another stimulus to encourage and demonstrate the compatibility of highways with the environment in an aesthetically pleasing manner was the initiation, in 1967, of awards for photographs and descriptions of roadside development projects. These awards are given by the U.S. Department of Transportation, Federal Highway Administration, Office of Engineering Highway Design Division, in 11 catagories. These include: new and reconstructed rural and urban highways, special structural features, special facilities, sympathetic treatment of environmental features, and landscaping.

Nearly all states are represented in the 11 categories of this annual contest: really beautiful results from all areas of the nation are shown annually.

B. Importance of Building in Minimum Maintenance

While the vast interstate highway system was frequently financed at the rate of 90% federal funds for construction, no money was allocated to states for their maintenance. The addition of more than 1 million acres of roadsides of this sytem to the state roadside maintenance budgets was a large factor that caused many states to reduce the areas and frequencies of roadside mowing. This policy of reduced mowing by many states (Joselyn, 1969) began before the energy crisis of the mid-1970's, but was certainly carried further by the need to save more fuel and reduce maintenance costs. The realization that there must be justification for every acre mowed was developing. An awareness was growing that we must build into roadside design and specifications, factors that would assure minimum maintenance. By so doing we maximize the "economy" aspect of the complete highway concept.

The economical maintenance of vegetation for transportation systems and utility corridors now appears to command top priority, as long as it does not vitiate the other facets of the complete highway, namely, utility, safety, and beauty.

By way of economizing on energy expenditures, it has been suggested that mass transport systems development be accelerated, and highway system building be curtailed. While the youth of today generally favor the concept of more mass transport systems, a recent survey (Anon., 1976) indicated their strong desire to own and operate their own cars.

1. VEGETATION FOR AIRFIELDS

Far fewer reports on airfield, railroad, powerline, and pipeline vegetation are to be found than exist for roadside vegetation. Although the topography of airfields is uniform in comparison with roadsides, special problems do exist. Peters et al. (1973) state that erosion on airfields is more severe than might be expected for, in addition to the natural forces of wind and water, there are other disrupting forces, including downdraft and jet blasts of aircraft, vehicular traffic, and accidental fuel spillage.

Cationic oil-in-water emulsions containing a high-strength elastomer, or resins, or both, appear promising for stabilizing soils composed of a range of materials, including rock, gravel, sand, or finer particles. Such stabilization is particularly appropriate where jet blasts can be anticipated to be severe enough to eliminate any form of vegetation.

Horonjeff (1962) recommends that for erosion control, shoulders of "dense turf," 25 feet in width, be provided on both sides of paved surfaces for taxiways serving jet transports. Dense turf will serve but, he allows, a thin bituminous asphalt surface may substitute. The Federal Aviation Agency specifies that "dense turf," usually in "3 inches of topsoil," be used after a bituminous asphalt surface at the end of the runway, and, for "a distance thereafter," a "half density turf is adequate." No specifications as to species, cultivar, or management of this turf were found.

Minimum maintenance vegetative cover surrounding landing strips at airports has an importance that exceeds the conventional cost and hazard factors associated with the management of roadside vegetation.

Mowing equipment could interfere with airplane guidance systems, and, according to B. Schaedler (Landscape Architect, Port of New York Authority, personal communication, 1977), jet aircraft noise and heat could exceed Occupational Safety and Health Act (OSHA) standards for persons operating the mowers even when they wear protective devices. For these reasons, when grassed areas have to be mowed, landing strips must be closed to air traffic. Airport managers are, therefore, understandably interested in minimizing mowing.

In spite of frequent jet aircraft passage, and the noise and pollution associated with such activity, the large areas of grass attract birds, including sea gulls, (near coastal areas) that, in large numbers, could be a hazard to aircraft. Seeds of grasses and weeds, as well as associated turf-inhabiting insects, are undoubtedly attractive to such wildlife.

Where jet aircraft turn, wait, and accelerate their engines prior to take-off, the heat and blast may exceed the tolerance of any soil-stabilizing vegetation. Asphalt surfaces have been melted under such conditions.

2. RAILROAD RIGHTS-OF-WAY

A long-standing policy of subjugation of vegetation is the standard practice for railroad rights-of-way and rail yards. Railroads tend to follow more level terrain then highways, but their facilities are safeguarded against erosion mainly by stone ballast rather than vegetative cover, and aesthetics of the right-of-way appear to be of little concern to the rail industry. In an article entitled "Who's responsible for what in weed control?" railroad vegetation control specialists, herbicide manufacturers, and control applicators all argued that there was need for more research with regard to vegetation on railroads (Anon., 1975). Contemporary herbicide research is involved primarily with agricultural rather than industrial problems. The non-selective chemicals used by railroads are researched less than the selective herbicides used in agriculture. The specialists deplore the fact that many of the chemicals in use on railroad rights-of-way were developed 20–30 years ago, and that too few new and superior products were available for their needs.

Large, powerful brush cutters mounted on tracks are advertised as being capable of cutting a 17.1-m swath, or 8.5 m from the center of the line of track. With two operators, each controlling 2.1-m diameter cutting heads, mowing can proceed at up to 6.4 km/hour (4 mph), and trees up to 61 cm in diameter can be cut. Other track-mounted machines have booms extending 18.3 m. Off-track and on/off-track vehicles, with a variety of mower attachments, are available to railroad vegetation managers, in addition to more conventional mowing equipment.

A hypothetical evaluation is presented by Brooks (1975) indicating the logic of investing $28 to $37 per km ($45 to $60 per mi) of railroad track annually for chemical vegetation control to protect an annual investment of $1,145 per km ($1,855 per mi) in tie and ballast cost. The life expectancy of rail ties and track fasteners would be decreased by the vegetation and the moisture held by the soil and plant debris that such vegetation would entrap on the ballast. Ballast fouled with moisture-retaining debris leads to instability of the roadbed and costly maintenance. Lightly used branch lines may be sprayed only 4 m, while single-track main lines may be sprayed 8 m.

Soil sterilization is particularly appropriate, Crafts (1975) points out, when used to create a firebreak around objects such as electrically operated switches on railroad rights-of-way.

3. POWERLINE AND PIPELINE CORRIDORS

Like highways, powerlines and pipelines traverse a great variety of geographic features and encounter diverse ecosystems. Land disturbance through these corridors is much less than with highways, but vegetation must be controlled to protect the utilities, and to permit access for inspection and repair. Generally much of the original vegetation recovers and persists in these corridors, and is relied upon for erosion control. For many years mechanical control, the chopping of woody species, was the only practical recourse for maintaining such vegetation. With the advent of 2,4-D (2,4-dichlorophenoxyacetic acid) and 2,4,5-T (2,4,5-trichlorophenoxy-acetic acid), most broadleaf weeds, shrubs, and tree stump sprouts could be controlled more economically by spraying than by cutting. Certain resistant species proved troublesome, but the development of additional herbicides largely solved these problems. Drift-control agents aided in assuring against off-target kill of vegetation. Prior to the National Environmental Policy Act of 1970, according to Gross (1976), many rights-of-way were sprayed by broadcast application from the ground or from the air which usually resulted in vast "brown outs" that were aesthetically objectionable and potential sources of erosion. More discriminating treatment of specific vegeta-

tive cover may involve i) foliar application, ii) basal spraying with oil-herbi-
cide mixtures, iii) stem girdling and application thereon of herbicides to prevent sprouting, iv) application of solid forms of herbicides to plant bases,
and v) chemical treatment of stumps to control regrowth. Conceivably, the
corridor could develop a pleasing assortment of selectively saved vegetative
forms. Niering and Goodwin (1974) also deplored indiscriminate broadcast
spraying of right-of-way as being ecologically unsound. The selective
approach of herbicidal control should minimize undesirable effects such as
the "swath" appearance that frequently resulted from past efforts to control vegetation, and, instead, maximize environmental quality at lower
costs. Architectural effects, such as illustrated in Fig. 1, are aesthetically
pleasing, and provide diversified habitats favoring a variety of wildlife.

The shrub communities saved by the selective use of herbicides prove to
be relatively stable in adapted ecosites of rights-of-way. Niering and Goodwin stressed the point that, in contrast to the conventional American viewpoint, more than one relatively stable vegetative type can persist concomi-
tantly on a given type of site. The maintenance of dense shrubs under
powerlines excludes the seedlings of trees that eventually would have to be

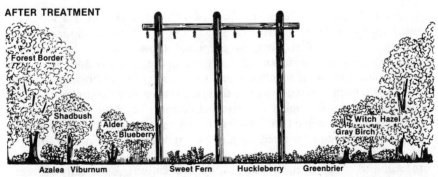

Fig. 1—Diagrammatic bisect of an electric transmission right-of-way showing tree and shrub
vegetation prior to and after selective herbicide treatment. Shrubs and low-growing trees
have been preserved where they do not interfere with the utility operations (permission of
Niering & Goodwin, 1974).

removed. Trees present a hazard to power lines: i) when they are tall enough and close enough to break the line should they fall on it, or short out the conductor, ii) when they constitute sufficient combustible material that they would jeopardize the line in case of fire, or iii) when they impede access to and through the right-of-way. Near intersects of roadways and power lines, trees may be cut off high enough so passing motorists may be unaware of the existence of the right-of-way, but low enough so as not to endanger the lines. Some tall trees may be left standing in deep valleys if lines are strung high enough.

Gross (1976) found that multiple use could be made of transmission rights-of-way. With proper agreements between the utility representative and the user, and considering topography, location, and vegetative cover, the following might be appropriate:

1) *Recreation*—parks, trails, playing fields, and other activities involving pedestrians.
2) *Forestry and Range*—grazing, sawmills, and lumber yards.
3) *Industrial*—gravel pits, land fills, and parking lots.
4) *Residential*—gardens, yards, and small buildings.
5) *Agricultural*—pasture, grain and seed crops, and orchards.
6) *Miscellaneous*—utilities underground and aboveground, streets, and storage.

On occasion, vegetation may be introduced to powerline and pipeline rights-of-way. Woody species are selected to screen facilities, and grasses or grass-legume mixtures should be established where land has been disturbed, particularly where pipeline trenches were dug. Turfgrasses compete with woody species to the extent of retarding the development of young specimens (Nielsen & Wakefield, 1978). While this may be disadvantageous in the establishment of woody specimens, it could contribute to their stabilization and a decreased management requirement.

II. ROLES OF VEGETATION

Erosion control is the prime function of right-of-way vegetation. The contributions of various forms of vegetation are being scrutinized more carefully to best utilize them in perpetual protection of the soil and appurtenances of our transportation systems and utility corridors. Planning for the establishment of vegetation and the construction of engineering features should be integrated to assure that these two aspects complement each other. During establishment in critical situations, vegetation often cannot cope with severe erosive forces by itself, and its success is enhanced by the mechanical protection offered by mulches, terraces, diversions, spillways, and such fixtures. Eventually, vegetative cover should provide continuing protection to maintain these man-made modifications. Essentially all vegetation of higher taxonomic orders protects soil by providing a canopy to intercept raindrops and neutralize their kinetic energy, thus reducing dispersal of soil aggregates that could cause soil pore plugging and increased run-off with the resultant accelerated erosion. Accumulated leaf litter also provides a mulch that protects soil and becomes part of the soil organic matter that enhances soil aggregation, aeration, infiltration, nutrient recycling, and better potential productivity of the site.

A. Grasses Generally Serve Best

Since grass seed is relatively inexpensive, and various species and cultivars can be sown quickly and inexpensively to establish a protective cover for soils of most environments in a relatively short time, it is not surprising that grass covers most of our roadsides and nonforested utility corridors.

Grass is diverse, and the roughly 5,000 species of the family *Gramineae* occupy vast portions of every continent except Antarctica. Species adapted to temperature regimes ranging from arctic to tropical and moisture regimes ranging from marshes to near desert are recognized. Numerous cultivars of many grass species are available. While these add to the complexity of choice, their proper selection can assure a better fit of vegetation to the site and intended use. The grass root is unique in that its dense fine system is particularly efficient at binding soil particles together to resist erosion. Sod-forming types are particularly efficient in humid areas where water erosion problems can be anticipated. Channels left by the approximately one-third of the roots that die annually provide for water infiltration. Rhizomes, stolons, and roots interweave and can form sods of appreciable tensile strength. Such grasses are particularly serviceable where traffic is a factor. They are often superior in wear tolerance and tend to support traffic when soils are soft because of high moisture content or loose sand. Recovery of control of vehicles accidently leaving the paved surface is facilitated by a strong roadside turf. Should the wheels of vehicles cut up a sod-forming turfgrass, self-repair by vegetative spread is possible. Many bunch type grasses, especially those evolved in arid areas where wind erosion is prevalent, are deep rooted and withstand dessicating winds. If their population is reasonably dense they will "still," or stabilize the soil between plants.

Vegetation selection is usually based on many parameters. A multitude of options is available, and combinations are innumerable. An example of a simplified systematic approach to selection of some of the more common species is given in Table 1. Only a few grasses are cited as examples that are typically considered as being near either extreme of a parameter. Many intermediates could be cited. Occasionally species with broad adaptability to one or more factors may be listed in both ends of a classification. Bermudagrass, for example, is tolerant of extremely high rates of fertilization, but will survive under very infertile conditions. It will also tolerate very humid conditions and moist soils, but is very drought resistant.

More specific selections should be made on the basis of cultivars (commercially available varieties of a species), and in many instances the outcome may be markedly affected. The common-type varieties of Kentucky bluegrass such as 'Kenblue' or 'South Dakota certified' may survive on sites

Table 1—Utilitarian classification of erosion control grasses.

Parameter	Classification	Examples
Fertility	High	Bermudagrass, Kentucky bluegrass (turf types), ryegrass, orchardgrass
	Low	Bermudagrass, fine fescues, bluestems, centipede, zoysia, bahiagrass
Moisture	High	Bermudagrass, reed canarygrass, ryegrass Kentucky bluegrass, timothy
	Low	Bermudagrass, buffalograss, fine fescues, bahiagrass
Season	Warm	Buffalograss, bermudagrass, bahiagrass, centipede, zoysia, St. Augustine
	Cool	Kentucky bluegrass, fine fescues, quackgrass, bromegrass
Form	Bunch	Timothy, orchardgrass, bluestem, crested wheatgrass, Chewings fescue
	Sod	Kentucky bluegrass, quackgrass, bermudagrass, spreading fescues, zoysia, centipede, bahiagrass
Height	Short	Buffalograss, bermudagrass (some), Kentucky bluegrass, fine fescues, bahiagrass
	Tall	Bromegrass, switchgrass, reed canarygrass, bluestem
Texture	Fine	Kentucky bluegrasses, fine fescues (Chewings, spreading, creeping, hard, sheep's)
	Coarse	Tall fescue, orchardgrass, bromegrass, reed canarygrass, switchgrass
Longevity	Annual	Ryegrass, rye, sudangrass
	Perennial	Ryegrass, Kentucky bluegrass, fescues

of low productivity, while turf types such as 'Merion' would fail in 1 or 2 years.

While cultivar differences may be critical, they are often overlooked in specifications for highway seedings. Hottenstein (1969) listed components of seed mixtures used on roadsides throughout the United States, and very few cultivars are specified; the most frequently mentioned was 'Kentucky 31' tall fescue. When only species are indicated in specifications, contractors interested in maximizing profits often use "common," which in reality may be a cultivar that failed to meet certification standards and may well be unsuited for the site and/or intended use.

B. Legumes Sown With Grasses

Most temperate zone legumes fix atmospheric nitrogen (in symbiotic relationship with appropriate rhizobia) in root nodules to the extent that associated grasses, as well as the legumes themselves, also benefit from this nitrogen. Vigorous plant development is thus fostered by these associations as long as other essentials for plant growth are also adequate.

Some legumes commonly sown along roadsides or other rights-of-way are short lived under these conditions, and their disappearance may leave spaces that are later occupied by weeds. Red, white, and alsike clovers are usually short lived, and reseeding of these species is not reliable. Crimson clover and Korean lespedeza are reseeding annuals that are more dependable particularly in association with warm season grasses such as bermudagrass in the southeastern U.S.

Perennial lespedezas, such as serecia and the lower growing virgata are long-lived legumes in their area of adaptation in the southeastern U.S., but they are slow starting. Sown with weeping lovegrass that is vigorous in the seedling stage during warm seasons, the lespedezas gradually begin to appear as the grass population declines after several seasons, and thereafter often dominate even steep, dry slopes. These lespedezas defoliate completely in winter leaving brown stems standing, but their leaflets provide a good protective mulch on the soil surface.

Crownvetch has gained recognition primarily as a roadside ground cover. This legume is also slow developing as a seedling and must be sown with a grass where an erosion potential exists. The seedcoat of crownvetch is so hard that scarification is essential in order to obtain reasonable germination.

Woodruff and Blaser (1970) pointed out the desirability of having some hard seed of crownvetch in mixtures with grass. Readily germinating crownvetch would likely succumb to competition from the grass in the mixture that must be vigorous enough to allay erosion. With the decline of the original grass cover in subsequent seasons, the later germinating crownvetch seedlings might establish satisfactorily. Crownvetch, once established, spreads by decumbent stems and creeping rootstocks that give rise to new shoots. Typically, this pink flowering legume dominates grass associates as well as weeds and most volunteering species in areas where it is well adapted.

While crownvetch prefers well-drained sites, birdsfoot trefoil tolerates imperfectly drained soils. It is also a weak seedling, but will not dominate roadsides to the extent of excluding weeds and associated grasses, as crownvetch commonly does. Maintenance of stand of the yellow-flowered birdsfoot trefoil is assured if mowing is limited so that ripe seed is shed annually.

The perennial pea and flat pea are also found along roadsides. The former is often an escape from gardens, and has showy clusters or white, pink, or red flowers. The latter species is more vigorous vegetatively, but has less conspicuous pink flowers. Both may have potential in the northeastern U.S. for roadside cover, particularly where variation in vegetative form is needed.

Most legumes are tap rooted. As such they may gain access to deep soil moisture and be drought resistant. Hardpans may be penetrated by tap roots to the extent that with the demise of the legume, subsequent growth of grasses may be enhanced by improved soil moisture relationships, as well as by residual leguminous nitrogen.

Most legumes are high in protein, calcium, and moisture content. These species, therefore, provide forage that is attractive to grazing wildlife. Grasses closely associated with them tend to be succulent and nutritious also. Deer attracted by this vegetation on roadsides constitute a hazard to motorists. Lespedezas and crownvetch are not as attractive to deer as are most legumes.

C. Woody Vegetation—Variety in the Landscape

Selective cutting and thinning of existing woody vegetation along the sides and medians should be done so as to save and expose attractive specimens. Major trees, 15 cm or more in diameter, should be kept back 9.1 m or more where speed limits are 88.5 km/hour (55 mph). Smaller trees may be located closer to traveled lanes, but their growth potential and future maintenance needs should be considered. Even small shrubs must be kept back a minimum of 2.4 m to allow vehicles to leave the roadway in emergency situations.

Size at maturity is a major factor determining the location and selection (species and cultivar) of woody specimens to be planted. Either native-type woody species or those that appear compatible with surrounding native vegetation generally are preferred. These types should not require a high degree of maintenance, constitute a hazard to right-of-way users, or harbor plant diseases or insects that might trouble other vegetation.

Grimm (1976) points out the particular advantage of deciduous plant materials along roadways in industrial areas. The combination of airborne particulates and oily auto exhaust materials develops a coating on the foliage of plants that can significantly impede photosynthesis. The longer term build up on the foliage of evergreen species retards their growth. Deciduous plants avoid this long-term accumulation, and fare better along heavily trafficked roadways, such as the New Jersey Turnpike.

A handbook was developed by Zak et al. (1972) to assist in the selection of woody and herbaceous plants, particularly for establishment under various situations found along Massachusetts roadsides. They selected 22 woody and 3 herbaceous (legumes) species on the basis of roadside tests; a table gives their adaptability to specific roadside environments. A four-step sequential procedure is suggested: i) consideration of soil texture, drainage, slope aspect, steepness, fertility, and pH, as well as plant characteristics and plant use; ii) selection of preliminary plants; iii) study of the specifics of plant establishment techniques; and, finally, iv) implementation. While this guide is specific for Massachusetts, it may be applicable to similar environments, and could also serve as a guide for other environments and other plant materials. This handbook describes several woody species reportedly capable of fixing atmospheric nitrogen.

Woody vegetation may serve several purposes including screening of headlight glare, traffic guidance, noise abatement, erosion control, wildlife feed and/or shelter, snow drift control, beautification, and adding diversity to the landscape. Selected shrubs and trees may be planted as delineators, suggests Korns (1968), that arouse the consciousness of the motorist to a greater awareness of curves, structures, or traffic alterations. Increasing lateral enclosures by vegetation or land forms has been shown to cause drivers to reduce driving speed (Anon., 1969).

Plantings should not reduce sight distance on the roadway, be distractive to the motorist, or occur with rhythmic uniformity that would constitute a form of highway hypnosis.

D. Flowers Added to Seed Mixtures

Although species such as bluebonnets in Texas and goldenrod in New York may volunteer in profusion along rights-of-way, they usually develop only after some years have elapsed. The first obstacle to establishing wild flowers may be finding an adequate source of seed.

Recently more and larger seed producers have offered commercial quantities of wild flower seeds. Butcher (1976) announced the release of the midwest's first certified varieties of native wild flowers, the culmination of a 10-year joint effort by the Soil Conservation Service (SCS), the Kansas and Nebraska Experiment Stations, and the Nebraska Department of Roads. Limited quantities of these seeds are expected to be available from the SCS Plant Materials Center in Manhattan, Kansas, in the fall of 1978. Plants for increase were selected on the basis that they were neither noxious nor poisonous, that they have an erosion-resistant root system, and that they associate readily with vegetation characteristics of rights-of-way.

The associated vegetation and management imposed are critical in the maintenance of wild flowers. A dense sod-forming grass would exclude many types of wild flowers, while a very open bunch grass would permit the ingress of more competitive weeds and eventually shrubs. The use of herbicides along rights-of-way usually precludes the maintenance of wild flowers unless exceptional care in selective application is exercised.

E. Combinations of Vegetative Forms

Judiciously used, combinations of all of the above forms, grasses, legumes, shrubs, trees, and wild flowers should add interest to the corridor and balance to the environment in the best sense of "the complete highway." No single cultivar, species, seed mixture, or type of vegetation can be expected to best cover and protect the variable soils encountered along any appreciable length of transportation or utility system. Fitting the best available and practical vegetative covers to particular portions of these systems requires appreciable discretion.

III. FITTING VEGETATION TO THE ENVIRONMENT

Several screening processes are functional in determining appropriateness of vegetation to be used for our transportation systems or utility corridors. The broadest factor is the macroclimate of the area, which is a product of thermal and moisture components. The macroclimate is modified in many instances by meaningful influences of microclimatic effects impinging on plant lite. Finally we must consider the use we plan to make of this vegetative cover.

A. Factors Limiting Species Adaptation on a Gross Scale

Minimum temperatures have long been used as a basis for mapping hardiness zones on a large scale. Weather stations average their minimum value for each year over many years to approximate an 18°C range that might be expected at particular locations. These data are accumulated to construct isotherms on maps, such as Fig. 2, which was made available by the cooperation of several agencies with the USDA. Hardiness zone limits have proven useful in planning selections of woody fruit and ornamental species in particular. Survival of some such plant materials is so critically affected by minimum temperatures that 9°C zones are sometimes essential. Directions for use and interpretations usually accompany the better hardiness zone maps. Nursery catalogs frequently reproduce and refer to hardiness zone maps, such as Fig. 2, to indicate adaptability of species or differential adaptability of cultivars within species. Frequently exceptions with regard to modifying factors of location or management for specific plant materials will be noted in catalogs as being important to their adaptability.

Grasses and legumes used for erosion control have generally not been mapped as precisely to hardiness zones as have woody plants. This may be because their reproductive buds are in close proximity to the ground and benefit from the thermal buffering of the earth plus the insulation of thatch and leaf litter. Such vegetation is commonly classified as either cool or warm season. Some warm season perennial grasses will survive very low winter temperatures, but will not be active long enough to be practical out of their region of adaptation. Conversely, cool season grasses may survive, but not prosper, in warmer climates.

The negative effect of increasing altitude on plant hardiness zones because of lower temperature is best shown in Fig. 2 in the area of the Rocky Mountains. Similarly, it can be seen that there is an appreciable positive effect on temperature, and hence hardiness zone, because of proximity to large bodies of water, notably the oceans, Gulf of Mexico, and Great Lakes.

Moisture availability also frequently limits plant adaptability on a large

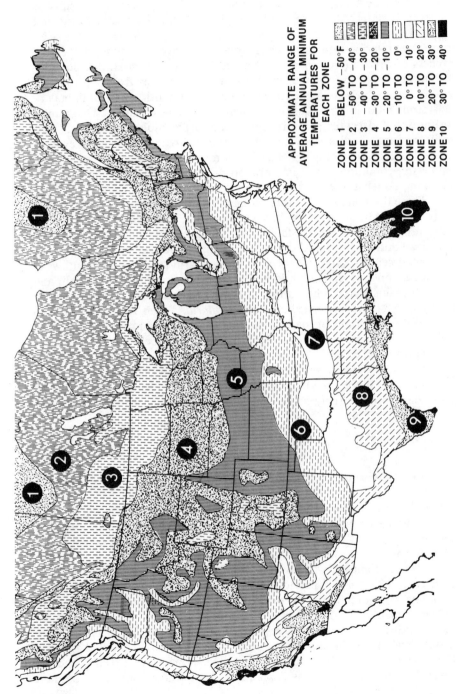

APPROXIMATE RANGE OF
AVERAGE ANNUAL MINIMUM
TEMPERATURES FOR
EACH ZONE

ZONE 1   BELOW −50°F
ZONE 2   −50° TO −40°
ZONE 3   −40° TO −30°
ZONE 4   −30° TO −20°
ZONE 5   −20° TO −10°
ZONE 6   −10° TO   0°
ZONE 7   0° TO 10°
ZONE 8   10° TO 20°
ZONE 9   20° TO 30°
ZONE 10   30° TO 40°

Fig. 2 —The zones of plant hardiness.

scale. Moisture availability is a much more difficult factor to quantify and illustrate precisely on a map relating to plant adaptability. Nonetheless, it is often critical to plant performance, and must be considered in plant selection. Precipitation rates for a given area may prove misleading, for effectiveness of precipitation may be modified by several factors. Seasonal distribution of precipitation may be skewed toward or away from the season of plant needs, which are higher in warm seasons. Intensity of rainfall may be uniformly mild, in which case effectiveness would be enhanced. Geographic features that affect temperature regimes also affect moisture regimes. Proximity to large bodies of water, particularly those crossed by prevailing westerly winds, generally indicates better moisture regimes. The same wind and water conditions result in more moisture on the western side of mountain ranges such as the Rockies than on the eastern side.

These thermal and humidity factors that combine to constitute climate were specified by Ward (1969) in delineating four major regions of turfgrass adaptations in the United States, namely, i) a cool humid region of the northeast and north-central states; ii) a warm humid region of the southeast and south-central states; iii) the arid and semiarid region of the southwestern states; and iv) the cool arid and semiarid region of the mountain and western plains states. The northwest coast is designated *cool humid* while the southwest coast is called *arid* and *semiarid*. When Hottenstein (1969) compiled descriptions of roadside seeding mixtures and related seeding data from each state, he categorized them into six charts including: i) northeast, ii) southeast, iii) central, iv) north-central, v) northwest, and vi) southwest. Subdivisions, sometimes within a state, are given on the basis of precipitation received. Ward (1969) developed a comprehensive study on the climate and adaptation of turfgrasses. The reader is referred to that article for further edification.

B. Local Environmental Alterations by Construction of Rights-of-Way

Innumerable island climates are encountered enroute, especially in hilly or mountainous terrain, where land clearing, combined with cutting through highs and filling low areas, results in drainage changes, thus increasing the diversity of the habitat markedly.

Clearing rights-of-way through wooded areas causes a sudden, marked increase in exposure of previously shaded and wind-sheltered vegetation. Thinning vegetation along the periphery of the cleared path so as to reveal specimen plants too often gives rise to unnecessarily early exposure, resulting in further loss of existing vegetation and the need for increased later maintenance trimming to remove dead wood. Increased thermal fluctuations affecting recently exposed and, hence, nonacclimated bark and increased dessication of exposed plants on well-drained sites are common causes for such losses.

1. CUT AND FILL DAMAGE

"Saved" specimen trees and shrubs may sustain additional injury when lateral roots are severed by excavation operations, such as making bank cuts. Loss of such roots decreases not only the plant's ability to obtain nutrients and moisture, but may also jeopardize its resistance to high winds. The latter is, of course, particularly pertinent to tall trees singled out of dense stands.

Existing vegetation is also endangered by fill situations that directly or indirectly affect root aeration. The allowable depth of fill over the roots of perennials varies appreciably and depends upon numerous factors including the species (recognizing genetic variation within species also), the condition and age of the particular plant, the porosity of the fill material, and the moisture status of the immediate area subsequent to filling. The judicious placement of tile and gravel over the root system (usually extending from the trunk to the drip line of trees) prior to the addition of fill is expensive, but is sometimes resorted to in an effort to save large trees. Vegetation beyond the toe of fill slopes may be lost because of root burial by material subsequently eroded from the bank. Losses of native vegetation because of excessive changes in drainage, either flooding or draining, are often extensive along roadways. Such drastic changes should be avoided where possible to prevent the destruction of plant cover. Otherwise additional expenses in revegetating with adapted species may be required.

2. DAMAGE FROM DEICING SALT

The movement of deicing materials from road surfaces as drainage or spray has resulted in injury to vegetation that has been well documented (Button & Peaslee, 1967; Thomas, 1967; Foote et al., 1970; Butler, 1972). The roadside shoulders and shoulder slopes are in immediate jeopardy from salty runoff, according to Foote et al. (1970). Thomas (1967) recorded dieback of Kentucky bluegrass in strips averaging 1.1 m, but extending as much as 4.6 m wide.

Deicing salts are often not applied uniformly, but as experience indicates the need, and drainage is not uniform, but follows natural or established flow patterns. Depressed medians of dualized roads usually receive runoff from both sides, and vegetation therein may be particularly subject to salt injury. Salts may be concentrated in certain pockets where flushing may be insufficient, or diluted by other relatively salt-free watersheds. Dilution is most critical in regions that receive heavy snowfall, requiring more frequent deicing, but little warm season precipitation.

Salt spray sent up by the wheels of traffic tends to move in the direction of prevailing winter winds, and its effects may be seen as patterns particularly on evergreen trees and shrubs. These patterns do not appear on associated grasses, which suggests they may be more salt-tolerant than the trees.

Button and Peaslee (1967) noted that maples, birch, and pine appear to be more sensitive to salt damage than white and black oaks. They noted slow degeneration of mature sugar maple trees exposed to runoff containing applications of salt and continued good growth of originally similar trees on the uphill side. Symptoms of salt-injured trees were smaller leaves with leaf burn (necrotic spots) and an overall unhealthy appearance. Injured trees had a higher concentration of sodium and chlorine and a decreased content of calcium, magnesium, and potassium in plant tissue.

Salt used for deicing roads increased eightfold in 12 years, according to Butler (1972), and many states were following similar trends. Northeastern and north-central states (Anon., 1971) have applied as much as 20 metric tons of salt per lane-km, or about 5 kg/m^2 of pavement per year. Public safety demands the use of deicing salts during winter storms, but recent public awareness of environmental damage from road salts dictates the need to use them more judiciously. Butler (1972) points out the need for plants that are tolerant of the type of drastic environmental changes that salt drainage and spray bring about. Among the more salt-tolerant grasses he cites salt grass and bermudagrass. These are strongly rhizomatous, however, and break up asphalt pavement. Nuttall alkaligrass and weeping alkaligrass are moderate and low-growing grasses, respectively. Although not rhizomatous, they are described as similar to Kentucky bluegrass, and they will form a dense turf when mowed at 4 cm or less. Several other alkaligrasses may have promise along roadsides, and selections within species are being made in Colorado.

It behooves us then to plan for salt-tolerant grasses adjacent to pavements and other areas where excess salt might be expected to be troublesome, and to keep sensitive woody species at safe distances.

C. Considerations of Slope Aspects

That south-facing slopes are warmer than north-facing is a well-accepted fact. The sun's rays strike south-facing slopes more directly, thereby warming them more, evaporating more moisture from them, and drying their soils and vegetation. Many ecological studies have involved comparisons of north- and south-facing slopes. Geiger (1965) points out, however, that although sunshine is equally distributed in morning and afternoon, the solar energy of the forenoon is used mainly to dry surfaces on which it impinges, while in the afternoon most of the energy is effective in raising the temperature, and, if moisture exists, drying further. In the northern hemisphere it is the southwest-facing slopes that are the warmest, and not the south-facing slopes, as is generally assumed.

Prevailing winds in New Jersey are from the northwest from October to April inclusive, according to Dunlap (1967), but are from the southwest for the remainder of the year. These, of course, further dry out soil and vegetation on the southwest-facing slopes.

In a study involving 13 cool season grasses over a three-year period on 4:1 slopes in eastern Nebraska, Dudeck and Young (1970) found that north vs. south exposure did not greatly influence their performance. Crownvetch however, showed severe symptoms of moisture stress on south-facing slopes in midsummer. Kentucky bluegrass and western wheatgrass annually rated somewhat better on north-facing slopes than on the south-facing slopes.

Diseker and Richardson (1962) reported that, during winter months, south-facing slopes, subject to more freezing and thawing, lost three times as much surface soil as north-facing slopes. This, of course, can further aggravate the already difficult problem of plant establishment and maintenance on such slopes.

It is frequently observed that the tops of slopes are more sparsely vegetated than the central and lower portions. Less moisture flows over this upper portion (reducing opportunities for infiltration), and more air flows over the edge of the bank, tending to dry this strip more. Airflow is up the bank during the heating process of a normal sunny day, and down the bank during evening cooling.

Brooks and Blaser (1964) reported that in their trials plant establishment was better on north-facing slopes that were also cooler and moister. McKee et al. (1965) reported further that it was near the top of south-facing slopes where the greatest difficulty in plant establishment was encountered. The upper portions of these south-facing slopes was 9–18°C warmer than the lower portions. The toe of a slope usually accumulates the nutrients, moisture, and fine soil particles that retain them, after they erode from the higher portions. The retention of moisture would have a direct moderating effect on temperature fluctuations, and, coupled with nutrient enrichment, would lend additional temperature moderation because of improved vegetation production.

Huffine et al. (1974) reported greater summer injury to roadside vegetation from heat and drought on west-facing slopes than on east-facing slopes. Solar effects, as detailed by Geiger (1965) above, may combine with effects of prevailing winds to the detriment of plant cover on exposed slopes.

D. Location and Use Constraints on Vegetation

While climate and site affect adaptation of vegetation on rights-of-way, planners may discriminate among vegetative materials on additional bases. Matching the vegetative cover to that of the surrounding area makes the utility corridor seem somewhat less intrusive. While minimum maintenance vegetation is the goal, we must accept the fact that the location influences the type of vegetation needed and the management required.

Rural areas are extensive, and are, therefore, appropriately planted with materials that require the least intensive management. Coarser grasses that are mowed less may appear more like fields outside the right-of-way. Wherever traffic would not be interfered with, agricultural use may be considered. Several western and midwestern states are currently letting contracts for haymaking along roadsides. Properly managed arrangements present mutual advantages for many interests.

Bunch type grasses and short-lived legumes may be sowed to provide quick erosion protection for disturbed soils, but they would soon provide openings that seeds of woody vegetation from adjacent land might exploit to initiate naturalization that would in time really blend the right-of-way with the countryside. In areas of deciduous forests, evergreens are not considered appropriate for roadside planting except where their distinctiveness may serve to alert motorists to a needed change in traffic conditions ahead, such as an interchange or pavement narrowing under a bridge.

According to Korns (1968), screen plantings of tall, dense evergreens serve effectively in many instances to hide unsightly scenes from the highway user, or to protect nearby residents from the intrusion of headlight glare. Perhaps more functional psychologically than physically is the planting of trees and shrubs along highways for noise abatement. Tests have shown that only dense stands of trees, on the order of 100 m wide, are effective in materially reducing highway noise.

Urban areas are dense and intensely active; hence, these aspects are often carried over to right-of-way planting and maintenance. Residential properties may be landscaped with a profusion of well-groomed ornamental vegetation. Increased planting of woody materials in a setting of finer grass that receives more frequent mowing and occasional weed control spraying is often required on roadsides through urban areas. In areas of very heavy traffic the accumulation of combinations of dust and automotive emissions coats foliage to the extent of impairing photosynthesis. Under these conditions Grimm (1976) found that deciduous trees fare better than evergreens, for the former present new clean surfaces that are exposed for less than one full year.

Roadside rest stops are subjected to more use and closer public attention than other rights-of-way areas. Hence, they are most intensely planted, groomed, and managed. The presence of appropriate native vegetation, and shade trees in particular, is often a prime consideration in selecting a site for a roadside rest stop. Deciduous trees provide shade that is 3 to 6°C cooler than pine trees, which would certainly be appreciated by picnickers or resting motorists during hot weather. Where such established trees are available they should be used to advantage, rather than planting trees that would take many years to provide adequate shade, or relying on constructed shade shelters. The proper thinning and pruning of existing trees to permit establishing durable and attractive turfgrass in the area requires additional skill and planning. Roadside rest areas receive heavy pedestrian traffic, and, although paved paths and picnic table bases are provided, adjacent lawns are usually subjected to appreciable wear.

Lawns for rest stops should be established with shade-tolerant and wear-resistant grasses of the best cultivars available. This is a difficult planning decision. Gibeault et al. (1972) have ranked turfgrass species as to shade tolerance, and also wear resistance. Sherman and Beard (1976) have studied wear resistance of cool season grasses intensively. The problems encountered are additive; shading makes foliage more succulent and, therefore, more susceptible to wear. Traffic that generates wear also tends to compact soils and impair the rooting environment to the further detriment of turfgrass survival by way of decreasing water entry and O_2–CO_2 exchange in the soil. Foliage of trees intercepts moisture as well as light, and roots of trees also compete with grass roots for nutrients and moisture. In addition, studies by Whitcomb and Roberts (1973) indicate allelopathic incompatibilities between certain shade trees and turfgrasses.

Of the warm season grasses, bermudagrass is generally recognized as being very wear resistant but not shade tolerant. St. Augustine grass is more shade tolerant but not as wear resistant as bermudagrass. Bahiagrass is both shade tolerant and wear resistant.

Among cool-season grasses the fine fescues have the reputation for shade tolerance in dry sites, and rough-stalked bluegrasses have fared well in moister sites. Neither tolerates much wear, however. The common-type Kentucky bluegrasses are not found in shaded areas, and Merion is known to succumb to powdery mildew in shaded locations. Recent testing of improved turf-type Kentucky bluegrasses indicates that certain cultivars have superior shade tolerance. Because of their dense rhizome system they would likely tolerate appreciable wear as well.

IV. MODIFICATION OF SOILS

Modifying soils to establish and maintain vegetation involves economics and engineering, as well as architectural and agronomic considerations.

Turelle (1973) points out the economy of a maintenance program in comparison with making repairs after an extended period of neglect. This practice, however, requires competent decision-making to assure the best allocations of limited resources. A good preventive maintenance program anticipates requirements to allocate resources (labor, equipment, and materials) at the most expedient time to maximize plant response while minimizing stress on other management factors.

Following a statewide inventory of roadside erosion in Wisconsin, Briggs (1973) reported that 73% of sediment-producing sites were found along town roads, as compared with 24% along county roads, and only 3% along state roads. Better design of state roadsides favored superior vegetative cover, which reduced sediment production. Existing vegetation provided erosion control for 95.5 km out of every 100 km of highway. An estimated 54% of sediment-producing areas could be corrected by fertilizing, seeding, and mulching; 37% would require, in addition, reshaping of the slope, and another 9% of the sites would require that structures also be added to alleviate special problems so as to insure the establishment and permanence of vegetative cover.

A. Primary Grade Considerations

The primary grade that essentially determines the topographic features of the roadway and roadside is developed as an engineering phase. The height and steepness of cuts and fills determine, in part, water loss and erosion potential. Watersheds above these disturbed banks must be diverted. Steeper banks, both cuts and fills, would be less consumptive of real estate and also more economical to construct because less earth moving is involved. With most soils, banks steeper than 2:1 are not constructed because their stability, per se, and maintenance of erosion-controlling vegetation becomes impractical. Banks may be divided by terraces, or serrated steps (Rodie, 1971). Blaser (1976) pointed out that serrations may be made on cut banks in the excavation process. It is important to have the rises smaller than the nearly horizontal treads, and that the treads be graded inward slightly. Soil slumping from the individual 45-cm rises is essentially all caught on the 60-cm (or more) tread, and serves to cover sown seed. Infiltration is enhanced and runoff is reduced, thereby conserving soil, nutrients, and seed to ameliorate establishment of vegetative cover.

Concern for erosion and water pollution from highway construction sites prompted the Federal Highway Administration to establish 70,000 m² as the limit of erodible earth that may be exposed at any one time (Connor, 1970). This is at the discretion of the supervising engineer, however, and typically far greater areas are found in various stages of construction before roadbeds are paved and roadsides are seeded and mulched for erosion control.

The materials used in fill areas serve not only as the base for the roadbed, but also as the anchorage and growing medium for roadside vegetation. Some consideration for the latter should be shown, but evidence thereof is essentially nil. Where topsoiling is practiced, soil testing of the primary grade generally is not.

Compaction of fill material is essential for roadbed stability. Compaction of fine soils when wet, often unintentionally by construction traffic, particularly in the median or on road shoulders, leads to excessively hard soil that is more conducive to runoff than infiltration and plant establishment. Recognition and correction of this condition by tillage and gypsum treatment would contribute to better roadside vegetation and less corrective maintenance later.

In current design, drainage systems seldom conserve moisture for roadside vegetation. Sediment-control basins are more likely to be constructed on a temporary basis primarily to reduce sedimentation off-site. Barnes (1973) points out, however, that basins may also be constructed for prolonged use with provisions for periodic clean-out. They may also serve as water-recharge basins. Ground water recharge is becoming increasingly important in areas where well water usage has increased and water tables are receding. Coastal communities concerned with salt water intrusion are also appreciative of ground water recharge from such basins.

B. Topsoil and Its Use

Topsoiling may be considered, particularly if agronomically superior material can be saved from the excavated site. The higher organic matter in topsoil is valued for its greater cation exchange capacity, moisture-holding ability, and its slow N release characteristics, Dark-colored, wet excavations that appear high in organic matter may have high free sulfur contents and become extremely acid upon oxidation. Excessively high salt contents have also been encountered in such saved "topsoil." Soil testing in advance of excavation might preclude stockpiling surface soils that may not be better than lower horizons.

If the physical condition of the surface fill soil is satisfactory, consideration should be given to correcting pH and fertility as an alternative to topsoiling. Blaser and Woodruff (1968) point out that most topsoils are relatively poor in quality and contain many weed seeds. Weeds in the topsoil initially may proliferate during the year or more that topsoil piles await redistribution, having a negative impact that may outweigh any positive effects of the topsoil on establishing proper vegetative cover. They concluded that judicious liming and either two or three applications of conventional fertilizers, or inclusion of a slow release nitrogenous fertilizer, might give better results than topsoiling. Beavers et al. (1968) concur that a nitrogenous fertilizer be reapplied approximately 6 weeks after seeding, and again a year after seeding. Young (1968) asserts that establishment may best be bolstered by adding increments of fertilizer during the critical seedling stage. If perennial seedlings can be sufficiently well established so their root systems tap a large volume of soil, then obtaining sufficient moisture and nutrients is assured, and success in vegetating the area is enhanced. With the development of a good root system, and accumulation of its own organic matter, which will recycle nutrients and improve moisture efficiency, a better vegetative cover may be expected to develop and persist.

C. Secondary Grading

Secondary grading and final finishing are essentially smoothing operations. The bigger and better equipment used to build today's super-highways is often used to create more and deeper cuts and fills that are greater challenges to successful vegetation. While these surfaces can be and often are, smooth-shaped, Andrews and Jacobs (1966) point out that it is particularly desirable, when topsoiling is intended, that the primary grade be left rough in order to obtain greater cohesion between topsoil and subsoil.

Hottenstein (1969) recognizes the need for tillage to loosen the seedbed, and also advises the fine preparation and reduction of surface clods. Steep slopes that cannot be traversed by conventional vehicles may be tilled by dragging a heavy chain with spikes welded across the links to dig into the soil as the chain turns while it is pulled over the face of the bank. Smoothing and breaking clods may be accomplished under these conditions by dragging heavy anchor chains with links 15–20 cm long over the slope. Smaller-linked chains are sometimes then substituted for more smoothing. Stones and other objects larger than 5 cm are often removed by hand raking.

Excessive pulverizing of fine-textured soils destroys aggregation, and predisposes the soil to crusting that may impede seedling emergence and accelerate runoff. Similarly, reducing microrelief promotes runoff. Links of heavy anchor chains create significant mini terraces that can be constructed on the contour to retain precipitation, promote seedling establishment, and retard erosion.

Blaser (1976) recognized that intense preparation of the surface of fill slopes may be undesirable, and suggested they be left rough with clods intact and stones in place. These will not erode, and crevices between them will accept lime, fertilizer, and seed. Numerous favored microclimates, he found, gave rise to seedlings that eventually covered and protected the clods and finally the entire bank. Energy savings are realized in reduced seedbed preparation and because the rough surface discourages mowing that might be a hazard to, and on, these steep banks.

To establish vegetation on steep, hard cut banks, Woodruff et al. (1972) cut furrows on the contour approximately 7.5 cm deep and 45 cm apart. They successfully established weeping lovegrass on 1:1 banks under these conditions.

V. SEEDLING ESTABLISHMENT

Proper preparation of the seedbed is particularly important in seedling establishment under difficult conditions, such as are frequently encountered along roadsides and rights-of-way where land disturbance has occurred. Young (1968) points out that most disturbed sites are relatively unproductive. The more fertile topsoil is often lost, and the subsoil that remains may have been compacted. If the disturbed site is made fertile by replacing the topsoil and even liming and fertilizing, it may still be relatively unproductive if it lies at a steep angle such as a roadside cut, fill, or bridge abutment, for water availability may become limiting to plant production.

A. Fertilization and Liming

The need for fertilizer (rate and ratio) and lime should be determined in part by soil testing. Because of extreme variability often encountered along rights-of-way, particularly where cuts and fills are involved, practicality dictates that generalized recommendations be accepted for large areas.

To enhance the efficiency of applied lime and fertilizer they should be incorporated into the soil. This decreases opportunities for loss by surface erosion and increases their availability to plants sown on the site. Incorporation may be by conventional tillage to a depth of 5 to 10 cm, or, as described above, to a rough, cloddy surface on less accessible roadside banks. This is more important for less soluble materials such as limestone and most phosphate forms than for N and K forms that in time might leach deeper into the root zone. Faix et al. (1970) showed better growth and nodulation of crownvetch in an acid soil where lime was incorporated than where lime was added to the surface 0.5 cm.

It is widely recognized that seedling responses to available P in the seedbed are often significant (Duell, 1974). Fertilizers for establishment, even on agricultural soils, are usually high in P. Grades such as 10–8.7–8.3 are commonly used. Rates applied should be limited by the effects of the soluble constituents on germination and emergence of sown species. Ward and Blaser (1961) noted reductions in emergence of several forage plants as increments of nitrogen applied at seeding were increased from 0–22–45–90 kg/ha. Differences were quite marked in 2 dry years, but somewhat less in a wet year.

Nitrates tend to remain in solution in the soil and exert an osmotic effect limiting water availability to seeds and seedlings. Phosphates are slowly soluble in water, and the dissolution products are rapidly rendered insoluble, while K tends to be adsorbed by colloids in the soil.

Quantities of fertilizers applied in roadside seeding operations often range from 672.5 to 1,681.3 kg/ha of the equivalent of 10–8.7–8.3. Blaser and Woodruff (1968) report that the best turf cover in roadside studies four or more years old resulted where an application of 448.3 kg/ha of urea-form was included with 448.3 kg/ha of 10–8.7–8.3 at seeding. Without a slow release fertilizer or follow up fertilization, sod degeneration on a poor soil may begin 6 months after seeding.

B. Seed Placement

Proper depth of placement and good seed-to-soil contact enhance establishment. Normally only a small fraction of the seeds sown emerge and fewer still become established. This is particularly true with small seeded grasses sown extensively. Sund et al. (1966) estimate this at 5 to 62% when commercial machines are used in agricultural operations. Depth of seed placement is greater for larger seeds, and sandy soils, but should range from 0.7 to 1.3 cm. Deeper placement was advantageous under dryer conditions, according to Nelson et al. (1970), and, in contrast with surface seeding, there was no loss by rodent and bird feeding. Surface or shallow placement increases the risk of dessication shortly after germination.

Compaction of the entire seedbed surface, especially with corrugated rollers, is often advantageous, particularly under dry conditions. Seedlings emerge in furrows left by the last set of rollers, where moisture is adequate and coverage is not excessive. Equipment that dispenses metered quantities of seed and fertilizer at controlled depths with compaction only over the seed rows may have particular merit. Such "band seeding" and other establishment techniques were reviewed by Duell (1974).

Hydroseeders are used today to apply seed, fertilizer, lime, and short fiber mulch, separately or in combination, in slurry form, particularly on steep slopes where conventional distributing equipment should not venture. Hydroseeders are frequently used to vegetate roadsides where terrain is variable. Their use on land that can be traversed by conventional equipment is questioned, for seeds and fertilizer are left on the soil surface. Coverage is usually provided by mulching, but there is a large potential for dessication of seedlings. Also, fertilizer P is more vulnerable to loss through surface erosion, and is less accessible to seedlings. High winds may interfere with proper dispersal of the liquid slurry, and hydroseeding is more expensive than drill or broadcast establishment as Rodie (1971) pointed out. Establishment of grass by hydroseeding was inferior to that obtained by incorporation and rolling in studies by Beard et al. (1971).

If soil moisture at the depth the seed is placed is maintained adequately there is no need for soil compaction over the seed. This condition often prevails in the late winter or early spring to the extent that successful establishment of many grasses and legumes by surface or "frost-crack" seeding, particularly on fine-textured soils, can be relied upon. Otherwise, without irrigation or perhaps ample mulch, surface drying is a real possibility.

C. Mulching

Proper mulching ameliorates soil surface conditions by conserving moisture and erodible fine soil particles, and minimizing surface temperature fluctuations that could prove lethal to seedlings. Mulch serves best where these factors are apt to be limiting. Many forms of mulch and modes of application have been researched (Duell, 1969). Short fiber mulches, such as wood cellulose and paper fiber, can be applied at about 1,500 kg/ha by hydroseeding; adherence is good when "plastered" on to slopes steeper than 1:1. Long fiber mulch, such as hay and straw, is often applied at 1 to 2 metric tons/ha by special chopper blowers that accept conventional bales. Anchorage is important. A mulching coulter may be used to press some of the mulch stems into the soil in rows 20 to 30 cm apart on the contour. This resulted in superior erosion control according to Barnett et al. (1967), but "tacking" surface-applied hay or straw with asphalt as an adhesive was also very effective, and is a popular practice.

Hay and straw generally provide better insulation than short fiber mulches, and may persist on the soil surface for two years or more (Richardson et al., 1963). They do frequently contain seeds, and Huffine et al. (1974) have attributed failures of roadside seeding to weedy mulches. Most broadleaf weeds can be removed from grass stands with selective herbicides. Forage grasses introduced to roadsides by seed in hay mulches cannot be selectively removed and constitute a particular weed problem where superior fine grasses are desired (Duell & Schmit, 1975). Most mulch specifications stipulate weed-seed-free materials, but grass seed in hay is often overlooked. Small grain straw should be properly threshed. It is not likely to contain seed of perennial grasses, and, therefore, is preferred over hay mulch, particularly where a neat appearance and less mowing are important.

A 5-cm depth of wood chip mulch was found to provide good erosion control, and Zak et al. (1971) report that seedlings of medium- and large-seeded woody species were able to penetrate this cover and establish well. Greater depths of wood chips are commonly placed around transplanted woody specimens for prolonged protection and better weed control.

When woody specimens are planned for roadsides, detailed specifications are generally provided as to species, cultivar, height, caliper, root ball size, and whether a burlap cover is required. Hole size, specific location, quantity and quality of fertilizer per hole, and nutrient release characteristics are stated. Quality of back-fill soil, shape of the saucer around the plant, mulching, staking for support, and irrigation policy to follow planting are also commonly included. Arrangements for replacement of specimens lost on the project are written into the agreement between the contractor and the agency.

Studies by Nielsen and Wakefield (1977) indicate that the competition offered by turfgrass around several species of woody ornamentals could not be overcome by fertilization, irrigation, or the combination. Such competition could seriously limit establishment of ornamentals on poor sites. Planned deterioration of protective mulch with the subsequent ingress of grass might advantageously limit rate of growth after establishment.

VI. DEVELOPING FINAL PLANS

Ideally, these vegetative systems should ensure the most attractive (green) landscape for the most months of the year with the least cost of maintenance. Proper specifications for better establishment or conservation of superior vegetation, and rational management of it, should reduce costs and enhance the environment.

While grasses generally serve best in stabilizing disturbed sites of transportation systems and utility corridors, there are instances where eventual domination by legumes or woody species is warranted. Discretion as to proper species and cultivar selection and establishment must be exercised on a local basis considering site and use factors.

Environmental concerns must be accommodated. To this end, many state and municipal governments have enacted legislation to enforce standards relating to soil erosion and sediment control. Guidelines for attaining such control have been developed cooperatively by personnel of such institutions as Agricultural Experiment Stations, Soil Conservation Services, and Departments of Transportation.

Available methods and materials are already voluminous and improvements appear continuously. Particular rewards should accrue to those who put it all together in planning better vegetation to provide utility, safety, economy, and beauty for our transportation systems and utility corridors.

LITERATURE CITED

Anonymous. 1969. Highway aesthetics—functional criteria for planning and design. Highw. Res. Rec. 275:25–38.

Anonymous. 1971. Environmental pollution by de-icing salts. Public Works 102:1–44.

Anonymous. 1975. Who's responsible for what in weed control? Railw. Track Struct. 71:19–24.

Anonymous. 1976. Automobiles choice of today's teenagers. Public Works 107:3:104

Andrews, O. N., Jr., and J. A. Jacobs. 1966. Roadside soil fertility. Public Works 97:4:90.

Barnes, R. C., Jr. 1973. Erosion control structures. In Soil erosion: causes and mechanisms; prevention and control. Highw. Res. Bd. Spec. Rep. 135:94–98.

Barnett, A. P., E. G. Diseker, and E. C. Richardson. 1967. Evaluation of mulching methods for erosion control on newly prepared and seeded highway backslopes. Agron. J. 59:83–84.

Beard, J. B., J. A. Fischer, J. E. Kaufmann, and D. P. Martin. 1971. Improved establishment and maintenance of roadside vegetation in Michigan. Res. Proj. 144. Michigan Agric. Exp. Stn., East Lansing. 66 p.

Beavers, J., A. L. Cox, M. D. Swanner, H. T. Barr, and C. L. Mondart, Jr. 1968. Erosion control study. State Proj. no. 736-00-35-Fed. Aid Proj. no. HPR-1 (6). Louisiana State Univ., Agric. Expt. Stn., Baton Rouge, La.

Blaser, R. E., and J. M. Woodruff. 1968. The need for specifying two or three step seeding and fertilization practices for establishing sod on highways. Highw. Res. Rec. 246:44–49.

Blaser, R. E. 1976. Personal communication. Agron. Dep. Virginia Polytech. Inst. and State Univ., Blacksburg, Va.

Briggs, W. M. 1973. Inventory of roadside erosion in Wisconsin. In Soil erosion: causes and mechanisms; prevention control. Highw. Res. Bd. Spec. Rep. 135:77–81.

Brooks, C. R., and R. E. Blaser. 1964. Effect of fertilizer slurries used with hydro-seeding on seed viability. Highw. Res. Rec. 53. Nat. Res. Counc. 30–34.

Brooks, M. R. 1975. Chemical vegetation control and economic track maintenance. Railw. Track Struct. 71:21.

Butcher, J. K. 1976. Prairie wildflowers on the horizon. Soil Conserv. 42(2):16–17.

Butler, J. D. 1972. Salt-tolerant grasses for roadsides. Highw. Res. Rec. 411:1–6.

Button, E. F., and D. E. Peaslee. 1967. The effect of rock salt upon roadside sugar maples in Connecticut. Highw. Res. Rec. 116. Nat. Res. Counc. 121–131.

Crafts, A. S. 1975. Modern weed control. Univ. of California Press, Berkeley.

Conner, S. H. (assoc. ed.). 1970. Highway construction and soil erosion. Public Works 101:8:92.

Diseker, E. G., and E. C. Richardson. 1962. Roadside sediment production and control. Am. Soc. Agric. Eng. 4:62–68.

Dudeck, A. E., and J. O. Young. 1970. Performance of crownvetch and selected cool season grasses on roadside backslopes as affected by slope exposure and nitrogen fertilization. Agron. J. 62:397–399.

Duell, R. W. 1969. Highway vegetation: for utility, safety, economy, and beauty. N. J. Agric. Exp. Stn. Bull. 882. 30 p.

Duell, R. W. 1974. Fertilizing forage for establishment. p. 67–93. In D. A. Mays (ed.) Forage fertilization. Am. Soc. of Agron., Madison, Wis.

Duell, R. W., and R. M. Schmit. 1975. Better grasses for roadsides. Transp. Res. Rec. 551:30–41.

Dunlap, D. V. 1967. Climates of the states: New Jersey. U.S. Dep. of Commerc. U.S. Government Printing Office, Washington, D.C.

Faix, J. J., D. M. Elkins, and J. H. Jones. 1970. Crownvetch seedling growth on an acid soil as influenced by soil preparation and lime placement. Agron. J. 62:485–487.

Foote, L. E., D. L. Kill, and A. H. Bolland. 1970. Erosion prevention and turf establishment manual. Minnesota Dep. of Highw. 44 p.

Geiger, R. 1965. The climate near the ground. Harvard Univ. Press, Cambridge. p. 420.

Gibeault, V. A., V. B. Youngner, R. Baldwin, and J. Breece. 1972. Perennial ryegrass in California. Calif. Turfg. Cult. 22(2):9.

Grimm, D. G. 1976. Turnpike goal: harmony with environment. Public Works 107:10:88.

Gross, F. H. 1976. Environmental concerns and multiple use of transmission rights-of-way. Proc. West. Soc. Weed Sci. 29:208-221.

Horonjeff, R. 1962. The planning and design of airports. McGraw-Hill Book Co., New York. p. 420-421.

Hottenstein, W. L. 1969. Highway roadsides. *In* A. A. Hanson and F. V. Juska (ed.) Turfgrass science agronomy, 14:603-637. Am. Soc. of Agron., Madison, Wis.

Huffine, W. W., L. W. Reed, and G. W. Roach. 1974 Roadside development and erosion control. Misc. Pub. MP-93, Agric. Expt. Stn., Oklahoma State Univ., Stillwater. 110 p.

Joselyn, G. B. 1969. Wildlife—an essential consideration determining future highway roadside maintenance policy. Highw. Res. Rec. no. 280:1-14.

Korns, C. H. 1968. Establishment of vegetation. Final Rep. conducted for the Mississippi State Highw. Dep., and the U.S. Dep. of Trans. Fed. Highw. Admin. Bur. of Pub. Roads. Mississippi Agric. Exp. Stn., State College, Miss.

McKee, W. H., Jr., A. J. Powell, Jr., R. B. Cooper, and R. E. Blaser. 1965. Microclimatic conditions found on highway slopes. Highw. Res. Rec., Natl. Res. Counc. 93:38-43.

Nelson, J. R., A. M. Wilson, and C. J. Goebel. 1970. Factors influencing broadcast seeding in bunchgrass range. J. Range Manage. 23:163-170.

Nielsen, A. P., and R. C. Wakefield. 1978. Competitive effects of turfgrass on the growth of ornamental shrubs. Agron. J. 70:39-42.

Niering, W. A., and R. H. Goodwin. 1974. Creation of relatively stable shrublands with herbicides: arresting "succession" on rights-of-way and pastureland. Ecology 55:784-795.

Peters, J. D., F. S. Rostler, and B. A. Vallerga. 1973. Promising materials and methods for erosion control. *In* Soil erosion: causes and mechanisms; prevention and control. Highw. Res. Bd. Spec. Rep. 135:105-117.

Richardson, E. C., E. G. Diseker, and B. H. Hendrickson. 1963. Crownvetch for highway bank stabilization in the Piedmont Uplands of Georgia. Agron. J. 55:213-215.

Rodie, E. B. 1971. Beautification as well as building is highway department goal. Wyoming Highway Dep. Public Works 102:6:66-69.

Sherman, R. C., and J. B. Beard. 1976. Turfgrass wear tolerance mechanisms I, II, III. Agron. J. 67:208-218.

Sund, J. M., G. P. Barrington, and J. M. School. 1966. Methods and depths of sowing forage grasses and legumes. p. 319-323. *In* Proc. 10th Int. Grassl. Congr., 7-16 July 1966, Helsinky, Finland. Valtioneuvonston Kirpapaino.

Thomas, L. K. 1967. Rock salt (sodium chloride) injury to Kentucky bluegrass. Highw. Res. Rec. 161. Natl. Res. Counc. p. 116-120.

Turelle, J. W. 1973. Factors involved in the use of herbaceous plants for erosion control on roadways. *In* Soil erosion: causes and mechanisms; prevention and control. Highw. Res. Bd. Spec. Rep. 135:99-104.

Ward, C. Y. 1969. Climate and adaptation. *In* A. A. Hanson and F. V. Juska (ed.) Turfgrass Science. Agronomy 14:27-79. Am. Soc. of Agron., Madison, Wis.

Ward, C. Y., and R. E. Blaser. 1961. Effect of ntrogen fertilizer on emergence and seedling growth of forage plants and subsequent production. Agron. J. 53:115-121.

Whitcomb, C. E., and E. C. Roberts. 1973. Competition between established tree roots and newly seeded Kentucky bluegrass. Agron. J. 65:126-129.

Woodruff, J. M., and R. E. Blaser. 1970. Establishing crownvetch on steep acid slopes in Virginia. Highw. Res. Rec. 335:19-28.

Woodruff, J. M., J. T. Green, and R. E. Blaser. 1972. Weeping lovegrass for highway slopes in the Virginias. Highw. Res. Rec. 411:7-14.

Young, W. C. 1968. Ecology of roadside treatment. J. Soil Water Conserv. 23:47-50.

Zak, J. M., J. Troll, J. R. Havis, L. C. Hyde, P. A. Kaskeshi, and W. W. Hamilton. 1972. A handbook for the selection of some adaptable plant species for Massachusetts roadsides. Rep. 25-R5-2656, Roadside Dev., Univ. of Massachusetts, Amherst. 44 p.

Zak, J. M., J. Troll, and L. C. Hyde. 1971. Direct seeding along highways of woody plant species under wood-chip mulch. Highw. Res. Bd. Abstr. 41:(12)3.

section VIII

Planning for Waste Disposal and Utilization on Land

USDA Soil Conservation Service

VIII

25 Principles and Processes Involved in Waste Disposal and Management[1]

V. VAN VOLK AND EDWARD R. LANDA

Oregon State University
Corvallis, Oregon

I. INTRODUCTION

Waste products from agricultural and forestry operations, municipalities, and industry have long been applied to land. In many cases, the material was applied to the land merely to dispose of a waste product with little concern for agricultural production. These areas often were managed as sanitary landfills, but simple open dumps also existed. In some cases, however, waste products do have value and may be applied to agricultural land to enhance crop production. The value is most easily measured in terms of nutrient availability and improved soil physical conditions. Agricultural waste products such as food processing wastes, crop residues, and animal waste products have been applied to agricultural land and provide nutrients and additional organic matter to improve soil physical and chemical properties.

Sewage sludges from municipalities have also been applied to agricultural land and, although in most cases application rates have not been controlled except by common judgment, increased crop production has generally resulted from the application of these materials. Lime is often a constituent in the waste products from industrial operations, and has been added to agricultural land with good results.

In the past, disposal of waste products from a particular enterprise has caused less concern within the managing organization than transportation, energy, labor, and proximity to natural resources. These factors often determined location of a particular industry or treatment facility, as opposed to a location which facilitated disposal or utilization of the waste product. With increased emphasis on environmental quality and recycling of materials, industries and municipalities, as well as agricultural and forestry operations, now direct considerable attention to the wise management of their waste resource. Planning for the efficient and economical utilization or disposal of waste products is now essential for successful farm, community, and production management.

[1] Contribution from the Oregon Agricultural Experiment Station Technical Report Series no. 4944. Supported by the Oregon Agricultural Experiment Station and the U.S. Environmental Protection Agency.

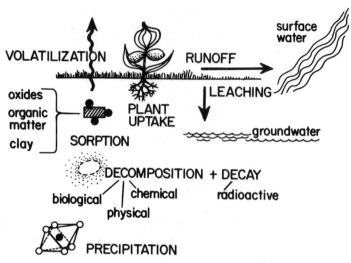

Fig. 1—Fate of waste materials in soils.

The purpose of this chapter will be to direct attention towards an overview of planning processes and considerations of soil-water-air-waste interactions (Fig. 1) which must be made to develop good disposal/utilization options for waste materials. Examples are presented to give the reader an appreciation of some potential environmental and social problems that may arise, and how these problems may be predicted and resolved.

II. WASTE PRODUCTS AND CURRENT DISPOSAL/UTILIZATION PRACTICES

Waste products may be characterized by their source: agricultural, forestry, municipal, and industrial. Waste products from these four sources may vary widely and each material must be characterized prior to the development of a disposal or utilization procedure.

Agricultural wastes are largely organic materials and are almost exclusively returned to agricultural land. Crop residues and animal wastes have almost always been incorporated into a crop production program, with the exception of some grass seed and rice residue disposal by field burning. Crop residues which are added to soils generally require higher nitrogen fertilizer application for good crop production because of the high C/N ratio of the crop residue (see Sect. IV-A.).

Waste from dairy, beef, swine, and poultry operations are largely carbonaceous, and also have been added to soils to improve crop productivity. Nitrogen, phosphorus, and potassium, as well as some micronutrients in animal manures, crop residues, and industrial/municipal wastes have been recognized as an economic benefit in recent years with the increase in fertilizer costs (Table 1). Wastes from animal operations have sometimes

Table 1—Chemical composition of selected waste materials.

Material	N	P	K	Reference
		%		
Dairy cow manure	2.7	0.5	2.4	Benne et al. (1961)
Hog manure	2.0	0.6	1.5	Benne et al. (1961)
Wheat straw	0.7	0.06	0.9	Fenster (1976)
Cannery waste	0.97	0.14	0.13	Reed et al. (1973)
Paper mill sludge	2.33	0.50	0.74	Dolar et al. (1972)
Paper mill sludge	0.15	0.29	0.85	Dolar et al. (1972)
Sewage sludge	13.72	2.99	1.40	Sommers et al. (1976)
Sewage sludge	1.50	1.84	0.20	Sommers et al. (1976)

presented a problem with respect to odor and large accumulations in areas where insufficient adjacent land has been available for the waste disposal. Labor and aesthetic considerations have sometimes reduced the use of animal manure as fertilizers.

Similar to agricultural waste, forest waste products are also largely carbonaceous. Slash produced during tree harvest is either burned or left to decompose, generally with minimal efforts to incorporate the residue into the surface soils. Bark and sawdust produced during milling operations have been used as mulches in horticultural operations, and are potentially valuable soil conditioners when the problems associated with wide C/N ratios (see Sect. IV-A) are recognized (Bollen & Glennie, 1961). Sawdust is currently used extensively in the manufacture of paper products.

Effluents from municipal sewage treatment plants have generally been disposed on land and into waterways. Effluents from secondary sewage treatment plants should be of sufficiently good quality so that disposal into waterways will not impair water quality. Increasing efforts by federal, state, and local agencies are being made to insure adequate sewage treatment prior to discharge into waterways. In areas where effluent (mainly in the southwestern U.S.) has been used for land application, increased crop production and ground water recharge have been observed (Wells et al., 1976).

Sewage sludges from municipal sewage treatment plants have been disposed at sea, in sanitary landfills, on agricultural and waste lands, and by incineration. With increased concerns regarding environmental pollution, dwindling resources, and costs of equipment and energy required for incineration, application of sewage sludge to agricultural and other disturbed lands is becoming more popular.

Considerable research is now under way to investigate the effect of sewage sludge constituents on soil, water, and crop quality. Special emphasis has been placed on the efficient plant utilization of nitrogen and phosphorus present in the waste product, and on the effects of trace elements such as cadmium, nickel, copper, zinc, and lead on plant growth. Availability indexes for nitrogen in sewage sludge have been proposed (Pratt et al., 1973). Similarly, guidelines have been proposed for the maximum application of cadmium, nickel, copper, zinc, and lead to soils of given chemical properties (Dowdy & Larson, 1975).

Solid wastes from municipalities have generally been disposed in sanitary landfills, and, with correct operation, many of these sanitary landfills have been successful. Successful landfill operation includes odor and pest control by frequent and complete covering of the waste with soil, and compaction if possible. Refuse can generally be compacted from a loose volume of about 119–178 kg/m³ (200–300 lb/yd³) to 593 kg/m³ (1,000 lb/yd³). However, many industrial solid wastes are either dense or densely packing materials, or, as in the case of most dewatered sludges, are incapable of supporting compaction equipment (Oliver & Drehwing, 1972). Well-managed sanitary landfill sites are generally covered with sufficient topsoil so that recreational areas or other useful land options can be established when the filling is completed.

Industrial wastes vary widely, from highly carbonaceous materials such as food processing wastes to materials which are almost totally inorganic. Calcium sulfate is a common industrial waste constituent. For example, wet-process phosphoric acid production yields about 3–4 tons of by-product gypsum for every ton of acid (Behmer, 1976). This gypsum can be used for a soil amendment as a source of calcium and sulfur, and the large quantities available may be particularly valuable in the reclamation of sodic soils. With the wide variability in industrial waste composition, quantification of chemical and physical properties of the waste is especially important.

When planning any disposal or utilization program, an accurate physical and chemical characterization of the waste material must be made so that possible interactions between waste constituents and the soil, air, water and organisms can be evaluated. Long- and short-term variations in the composition of the wastes must be known and considered in developing the management plan. The volume and seasonal distribution of the waste must also be established. At many locations, the waste is produced on a seasonal basis such as in food processing industries, whereas in other situations the waste stream is constant throughout the year.

III. LAND, WATER, AND AIR RESOURCE INFORMATION

Land, water, and air resource information must be collected so that the impact of the waste application on them may be assessed. Superimposed upon the impact of the waste application on land, water, and air resources is the impact of the waste application on the aesthetic or human values associated with the resources.

A. Land

A complete inventory of the soil resource in the possible application areas must be made. The variability, distribution of each soil series, and current use of soils in the area must be determined. Chemical and physical properties of the soils under consideration for waste disposal must be either measured or data assembled from published information. Soil physical properties of importance would include texture, structure, hydraulic conductivity, infiltration rate, drainage, and slope. Chemical properties of importance would include cation exchange capacity, organic matter content, exchangeable bases, trace element content, electrical conductivity, and soil pH.

Information on the soil resource can be generally obtained from sources such as the Soil Conservation Service, Bureau of Land Management, county extension offices, U.S. Forest Service, and state soil mapping programs. After identification of soils which possibly could be used in a waste management program, on-site investigations of the resource must be made.

Hall et al. (1976) have outlined some of the site selection criteria needed in selecting a location for sewage sludge and waste water application on agricultural lands. Suitable soils should:

1) Be at least 3 feet thick without restrictive layers such as fragipans, and underlying substrata should be free of coarse water-conducting channels;
2) Have high surface infiltration capacity and moderate subsoil permeability;
3) Be well- to moderately well-drained;
4) Have moderate to high moisture-holding capacity;
5) Be slightly acid to moderately alkaline in reaction (pH 6.5–8.2);
6) Have medium to high organic matter levels in the surface horizon;
7) Have slopes of <4% and occur on landscape positions where the movement of surface and subsurface water in the form of runoff and seeps does not present a hazard to the overall water quality in the drainage basin.

Soil variability within a given site, particularly in soils developed from interstratified bedrock materials or from glacial till or outwash deposits, may be extensive and should be evaluated during the on-site inspection.

B. Water

The water resources in areas under consideration for waste utilization must also be inventoried. The quality, quantity, seasonal flow rates, and current usage of underground aquifers, surface lakes, and streams should be determined by measurement, or by reference to historical records. Information on water quality and flow rates may be available through previous testing programs conducted by the U.S. Geological Survey, the U.S. Army Corps of Engineers, and state monitoring programs.

Water quality standards for lakes and streams have already been established in many locations in conjunction with federal guidelines. The feasibility of wate disposal or utilization on land would have to be assessed within the limits of water quality suggested in state and federal guidelines. In most instances, land application for waste disposal and utilization will not be approved if impairment to water quality occurs.

The extent or distribution of the influence of the waste application on water quality is often a difficult question to answer. In a small area water quality may be reduced, however, in a large area such as a watershed, the overall effect of the waste application may not be observed. In this sense, the planning operation must look at the overall usage of land in a given area in relation to the waste disposal and utilization operation on a portion of that land.

C. Air

At many locations, the air resource has been of vital concern. In most states, air quality standards now exist such that, prior to the use of land for waste disposal, permits must be obtained with information indicating the effect of the waste disposal/utilization operation on air quality. Again, it becomes important that the characteristics of the waste be known, such that problems which may be associated with volatilization of particular components in the waste can be ascertained. Information on air quality standards are available from the U.S. Environmental Protection Agency and from state agencies concerned with air monitoring programs.

Climatological data for any proposed location for the land disposal or utilization of waste materials should be carefully evaluated. If agricultural utilization is planned, the length of the growing season and other climatic factors will be of importance in the selection of the crop management program to be used. Precipitation and potential evapotranspiration data should be examined to determine periods of the year when the soils may not be able to assimilate waste materials. For example, snow cover and frozen ground may severely limit waste applications. As soil temperature will greatly affect the rate of microbial and chemical degradation of waste components, monthly temperature records for the site should be examined. A knowledge of the above factors is essential in the design of adequate waste storage facilities to handle materials during periods when land application is not possible or advisable. Wind direction and velocity data will aid in assessing potentially detrimental effects associated with volatilization of noxious or odorous waste components. The National Weather Service of the U.S. Department of Commerce should be consulted for desired climatological data.

IV. INTERACTIONS BETWEEN WASTE AND SOIL, WATER AND AIR

After the waste product has been produced, it commonly is collected at a given location and processed further before ultimate utilization or disposal. Useful constituents such as nitrogen are often stripped from the waste stream prior to its collection and formal designation as the waste product. Waste processing commonly involves drying, compaction, or aeration to either consolidate or render the material more suitable for future use. In land application programs, the waste may either be applied directly to the land without intermediate storage, or it may be stored prior to use. Storage becomes a critical problem in areas where rainfall or agricultural considerations of crop management may preclude immediate application to the land surface.

The application rate of the waste material will depend on the dedicated use of the land, and the chemical and physical properties of the soil and waste material. If the land is to be used for agricultural purposes, the waste application rates would generally be less than if the land is dedicated to a long-term waste disposal site. With long-term waste disposal sites, generally little concern is expressed for vegetation except for the need for aesthetic appearances. With some waste products (e.g., radioactive materials, pesticides), waste characteristics will preclude maintenance of an agricultural farming program, and the land must be dedicated to disposal of the waste materials.

In other locations, agricultural operations will be maintained, and under these conditions waste should be applied such that no impairment to crop production would be observed. In calculating the amount of a waste material such as sewage sludge that may be safely and productively applied to crop land, an appreciation of the beneficial effects associated with the addition of nitrogen, phosphorus, and potassium must be balanced by an awareness of potential problems. Heavy metal uptake from the sludge-amended soil by the plants and their subsequent transfer into the food chain, ground water contamination by nitrates associated with applications in excess of crop nitrogen requirements, and crop trace element (e.g., Zn, Fe) deficiencies associated with soils high in available phosphorus must all be considered as potential problems. Sommers and Nelson (1976) have presented guidelines for application rates of sewage sludge to agricultural land which are based on:

1) The nitrogen requirement of the crop;
2) The readily available (i.e., ammonium and nitrate-nitrogen) nitrogen in the sludge;
3) The mineralization rate of the organic nitrogen in the sludge;
4) The expected nitrogen-loss from ammonia volatilization and denitrification;
5) The residual sludge nitrogen in the soil;
6) The available phosphorus in the soil;
7) The trace element (Pb, Zn, Cu, Ni, Cd) content of the sludge in relation to the cation exchange capacity of the soil.

For most waste applications, incorporation into the soil surface or injection below the soil surface is recommended. By incorporating the waste material with the soil, the processes which will serve to release plant nutrients and degrade the waste can proceed most rapidly. With rapid incorporation, any problem of odors can be diminished.

After application of the waste material to the soil, a series of interactions between the soil and waste will occur. These processes include degradation, sorption, leaching and surface runoff, and volatilization.

A. Degradation

Microbial degradation of waste materials is a very important process which affects many carbonaceous wastes applied to soils. The soil abounds with microorganisms, some of which proliferate under anaerobic conditions, while others respond more favorably to aerobic conditions. Aerobic microorganisms produce carbon dioxide and water as principal reaction products while anaerobic organisms produce methane and reduced nitrogen and sulfur compounds (Alexander, 1977). Both anaerobic and aerobic microbial degradation occurs in soils, with anaerobic degradation dominating with increased soil water content. With anaerobic microbial degradation, odorous intermediary products such as sulfides or mercaptans may be produced.

Temperature plays a major role in the rate of microbial degradation of waste products added to soils. Most soil microorganisms are mesophiles, with a temperature optimum of 25–37°C. Maximum respiratory activity in soils, as judged by the breakdown of carbonaceous materials, generally occurs in the 30–40°C range (Alexander, 1977). The rate at which the organic carbon of anaerobically digested sewage sludge was evolved as CO_2 by microbial activity was found to be largely independent of differences in soil texture or chemical composition, with soil temperature as the major factor influencing the production rate (Miller, 1974). Using a modified degree-day concept as a measure of the total heat input to the soil-sludge system, a highly significant correlation between CO_2-evolved and degree days was obtained. Relationships of this type should make it possible to predict the rate of decomposition of carbonaceous wastes in different climatic zones using available temperature data.

Soil moisture status will also affect the rate of degradation of waste products in soils. Waste pesticides and pesticide manufacturing residues have been disposed by soil burial (Davidson et al., 1976). The major degradation product of the insecticide DDT (1,1,1-trichloro-2,2-bis [ǫ-chlorophenyl] ethane) in aerobic soils is DDE (1,1-dichloro-2,2-bis [ǫ-chlorophenyl] ethylene). In a study of the Raber silty clay loam, sterile and nonsterile soil treatments showed the DDT to DDE conversion to be predominantly a chemical process with some microbial contribution. While air-dry sterile soils at 30°C showed <0.5% conversion of the applied DDT to DDE after 140 days, their field-moist (1/3-bar) and flooded counterparts showed almost 6% conversion (Guenzi & Beard, 1976).

The carbon/nitrogen ratio of most soils is about 12:1. If waste material which has a higher C/N ratio is added to soils, additional nitrogen must be supplied to allow maximal microbial activity. The nitrogen in the soil will be utilized by the microorganisms such that nitrogen will become unavailable for plant growth. After equilibrium has again been established following the addition of the waste material, the C/N ratio will again return to 12:1. The amount of nitrogen which must be applied to maintain good crop growth will be a function of the rate at which microbial activity occurs, and the time lapse between waste application and plant growth.

Paper mill sludges represent the case of a waste product which typically has a high C/N ratio. The incorporation of large quantities of such sludges having organic carbon/total nitrogen ratios of 140–150:1 into soils has been shown to generally result in severely depressed yields of oats due primarily to the immobilization of available soil nitrogen by microorganisms degrading the sludge (Dolar et al., 1972). The addition of readily available mineral nitrogen (supplied as ammonium nitrate) at a rate of 168 kg nitrogen/ha (equivalent to 2.5% sludge by weight of surface soil) to such paper mill sludge would reduce the C/N ratio of the added material to about 50:1, and was shown to result in oat yields equivalent to those obtained on similarly fertilized soils without sludge additions.

As Dolar et al. (1972) point out, the cost of any additional nitrogen fertilizer, above that normally applied for a given crop yield, that might have to be added to correct a C/N imbalance in a waste product-amended soil must be considered in the cost of this type of disposal. Alternatives to the use of increasingly costly commercial nitrogen fertilizers, however, do exist in the case of land utilization of such high carbon wastes, and include:

1) Allowing the treated land to lie fallow for a year while decomposition proceeds;
2) Planting the land to a legume crop such as alfalfa which can fix atmospheric nitrogen; or
3) Utilizing sewage sludge or effluent to supply the required nitrogen.

B. Sorption

With addition of water to the soil waste mixture, some waste constituents will be solubilized. Salts such as sodium, potassium, calcium, and magnesium chloride will dissociate readily into cations and anions. Most sodium and potassium salts are soluble, however, calcium and magnesium salt solubility is generally not as high.

The cations added to the soil may be sorbed to exchangeable or nonexchangeable sites in the soil. Ions sorbed on exchange sites will displace ions already on those sites. The strength of cation bonding to exchange sites generally increases with valency and decreasing ion size (i.e., increases with increasing surface charge density of cation). For this reason, sodium and potassium ions in soils are generally more mobile than calcium and magnesium, so that sodium is seldom found in soils which receive sufficient leaching rainfall.

Most soils possess a net negative charge on the clay minerals and organic matter such that positively charged ions are sorbed. While phosphate anions represent a special case to be discussed later, negatively charged anions such as sulfate, chloride, and nitrate are mobile in the soils and will generally follow the water front. Thus, such anions released during the initial solubilization process are generally mobile. Some soils, however, have a considerable anion exchange capacity. These soils are generally found in tropical conditions, have a high iron and aluminum oxide content, and are often quite acid. In such soils, anions may be retained rather than leached. In addition to the simple cation and anion exchange reactions, soil water containing soluble ions can be trapped in dead-end pores. With drying of the soil, the salts crystalize and are deposited on the walls of the pore.

Soil pH plays an important role in the precipitation of elements added with waste products. Trace elements such as cadmium, chromium, zinc, copper, lead, and iron form insoluble oxide, hydroxide, and carbonate products with increased soil pH. Lime should be added to acid soils to adjust the pH to 6.5–7.0 to precipitate the trace elements when waste products which contain possible toxic trace elements are added to soils. With precipitation, the rate of movement of these trace elements through the soil and to water tables, and the uptake of trace elements by plants are generally reduced. For example, a recent Georgia study (Touchton et al., 1976) showed the application of 6.7 metric tons/ha of dolomitic limestone to significantly reduce the zinc content of coastal bermudagrass grown on a sewage sludge-amended Cecil sandy clay loam.

Soil moisture content and the resultant oxidative state of the soil may also affect the bioavailability of elements added to soils in waste materials. Bingham et al. (1976) found less cadmium uptake by rice in sewage sludge-amended soil under flooded as compared to nonflooded conditions, presumably due to the precipitation of highly insoluble cadmium sulfide under the reducing conditions accompanying soil saturation.

Phosphate compounds in the soil are also relatively insoluble. If a waste product contains soluble phosphates, such as sodium or potassium dihydrogen phosphate, the phosphorus solubilized upon wetting will readily react with iron and aluminum oxides, and with calcium compounds (Dean, 1949). Iron and aluminum phosphate compounds would predominate in more acid soils, and calcium compounds would predominate in more alkaline soils. Because of the precipitation reactions, phosphate ions are not particularly mobile in the soil. Maximum phosphate availability to plants occurs between the pH of 6.5 and 7. Reduced phosphate availability occurs below 6.5 due to the precipitation of the iron-aluminum phosphate, and above pH 7 due to precipitation of calcium and magnesium phosphate compounds.

As phosphate-containing detergents and other chemicals are commonly used in both industry and the home, it is conceivable that the phosphate sorption capacity of a soil receiving effluents from a septic tank or a sewage treatment plant may be exceeded, and that the phosphate may "breakthrough" and enter the ground water. Sawhney and Hill (1975) determined the phosphate sorption capacities of B-horizon material from six Connecticut soils in the laboratory. The soils showed sorption capacities of from 9 to 29 mg P/100 g soil. However, in field studies of soils which received prolonged phosphate applications, considerable phosphate sorption capacities were demonstrated in spite of the predicted saturation of the phosphorus sorption sites. It appears that the alternate wetting and drying that occurs in field soils may expose fresh mineral surfaces, thus continually creating new sites for phosphate sorption, and thereby regenerating the soil.

Ion chelation or complexation reactions also occur in the soil after the addition of waste products. Many trace elements chelate or complex readily with organic materials. The waste product may serve as the source of the trace element which interacts with soil organic matter, or conversely, trace elements in the soil may interact with organic matter added as a waste product. Water and alkali extracts of poultry litter and sewage sludge, respectively (Tan et al., 1971a, b), contain polysaccharide-like soluble organic matter which can combine with a variety of metals including zinc, copper, iron, and aluminum. Such chelating agents can transform solid-phase forms of metals, occurring in either the waste material or the soil, into soluble metal complexes, thereby increasing the transport and bioavailability of these elements in the soil (Elgawhary et al., 1970a, b). However, chelation of metals by insoluble humic components of either the waste or soil organic matter may have the opposite effect, and render the metals less available for movement and plant uptake (Kirkham, 1977).

The transformations of nitrogenous compounds have received considerable attention with respect to waste application to soils. Organic nitrogen compounds added to soils undergo microbial transformation. Initially, a fraction of the organic nitrogen compounds are converted to ammonium-nitrogen. The ammonium cation may then be oxidized to nitrite, and eventually to nitrate. The positively charged ammonium ions can be retained in the soil on ion exchange sites. The nitrate anions are not sorbed in most soils and can move with the wetting front. After the formation of the nitrate anion, the process of denitrification can occur. During denitrification, the nitrate nitrogen is reduced to nitrogen gases under anaerobic conditions. The process of denitrification occurs readily in soils which contain periodic high water tables.

Ammonium- and nitrate-nitrogen are readily available to plants. Some waste products contain significant amounts of these forms of nitrogen. In many wastes, however, organic nitrogen is the predominant form, and such nitrogen is not available until mineralization has occurred. It has been estimated for sewage sludge that approximately 15–20% of the organic nitrogen applied to the soil becomes available to the plant during the first year of decomposition, and that about 3% of the remaining organic nitroen is released annually for at least three subsequent years (Sommers & Nelson, 1976).

C. Leaching and Overland Flow

Ions which are readily water soluble and not sorbed by the soil, namely chloride, nitrate, and, to a lesser extent, sulfate, follow the wetting front. Endelman et al. (1974) found that 2.5 cm of irrigation water leached nitrate and chloride anions, applied as the water soluble potassium salts to the surface of a loamy sand soil, about 15–20 cm in the profile. Such high rates of movement under irrigation or rainfall conditions can rapidly remove these anions from the rooting zone, and create the potential for ground water contamination. Nitrates in the ground water are of particular concern as consumption of such contaminated water by infants can produce methemoglobinemia, a condition which results in oxygen deficiency due to impairment of the ability of hemoglobin to transport oxygen in the bloodstream (Straub et al., 1977).

While sewage effluent may be initially low in nitrate-nitrogen, nitrification of the predominant organic- and ammonium-nitrogen following soil application will yield the highly mobile nitrate anion. For example, of the average total nitrogen concentration of 47 mg/liter measured during 1973 in the sewage effluent at Fort Devens, Massachusetts, 23.4, 21.4, 1.3, and 0.1 mg N/liter occurred as organic-, ammonium-, nitrate- and nitrite-nitrogen, respectively. Yet nitrate-nitrogen comprised the major nitrogen species in ground waters sampled in the vicinity of effluent application fields. These waters showed nitrate-nitrogen levels of 10–20 mg/liter throughout the year (Satterwhite & Stewart, 1976). The permissible nitrate-nitrogen concentration promulgated in the federal drinking water standard is 10 mg/liter (Straub et al., 1977). These ground water contamination problems can be minimized by using application procedures, such as alternate flooding and drying, which promote denitrification (Lance & Whisler, 1972).

Factors which affect the movement of water in the soil will affect the depth to which the ion will penetrate in the soil. Soil texture has often been used to assess the rate of ion movement in soils. Water generally moves more slowly through fine- as compared to coarse-textured soils. Often times, however, a soil may have a relatively fine texture, and it would appear that water movement would be quite slow. However, due to soil macropores resulting from earthworm, mole, and other soil animal activity, as well as root channels and cracks between soil aggregates, water may move faster than would be predicted simply by soil texture (D. Hammermeister. 1978. Water and anion movement in selected soils of western Oregon. Ph.D. Thesis, Oregon State Univ., Corvallis). The time required for ion appearance or "breakthrough" from a soil column will depend on soil moisture content, ion diffusion and convection rates, adsorption, and ion exchange (Nielsen & Biggar, 1961).

To estimate the extent to which an ion may move vertically through the soil, one may measure the amount of rainfall added to the soil, subtract evapotranspiration losses, and distribute the resultant water through the pore volume of the soil. In arid regions where potential evapotranspiration exceeds rainfall, there will be very little recharge of deep ground water. In other locations, because of higher rainfall, cooler temperatures, and less evapotranspiration, water will move much deeper into the soil profile. Similarly with waste water applications to soils, the loading rate will determine the depth to which the water and its soluble, nonsorbed constituents will move in the soil profile. As microbial degradation of organic molecules contained in the waste water will be greatest in the aerobic, microbe-rich topsoil, application rates of waste water should be selected such that these constituents will remain in the upper soil zone for an adequate length of time to allow for a high degree of breakdown (Kardos, 1967).

As the relative biodegradability of organic molecules varies tremendously, the nature of the constituent organics will dictate required degradation times. For example, while Thomas and Bendixen (1969) showed the waste organics in septic tank effluents to be readily biodegradable in soil, with about 60% of the applied carbon evolved as CO_2 over a period of 5 mo, Miller (1974) showed anaerobically digested sewage sludge to be rather resistant to further decomposition in soils, with a maximum of 20% of the added carbon oxidized to CO_2 during a 6-mo incubation period. Pesticides also vary widely in their biodegradability in soils. While the chlorinated hydrocarbon insecticide DDT shows a persistence (time required to lose 75–100% of the pesticide) of about 4 years in soils, the phosphate insecticide malathion shows a persistence of only about 1 week (Hiltbold, 1974). If application rates are excessive with respect to the optimum described above, these materials will move rapidly below the depth of active microbial activity without undergoing extensive degradation, thereby creating the potential for long-term ground water contamination.

In essence, the soil acts as a chromatographic column. The soil may stop or reduce the rate of movement of given elements in the soil. Just as the nature of the eluting solvent can influence the rate of movement of a material in a chromatographic column, the leaching solution moving through a soil may also influence the movement through the soil profile of waste components (Fig. 2). The quantity of strontium-90 (^{90}Sr) initially applied to the

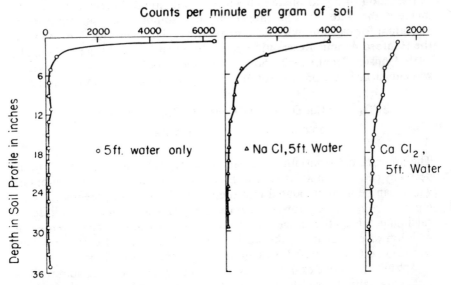

Fig. 2—Distribution of ^{90}Sr in soil profile after leaching with water or aqueous salt solutions. Reproduced from *Health Physics*, vol. 11, no. 12, p. 1317–1324, 1965, by permission of the Health Physics Society.

surface of each soil column was equal, and equivalent concentrations of NaCl and CaCl₂ were used to leach the columns (Schulz, 1965). The divalent cation (i.e., Ca^{2+}) displaced the ^{90}Sr most effectively and caused it to move with the leaching water. This behavior is due to an ion-exchange reaction of the type:

Enhanced ^{90}Sr movement seen with calcium chloride as compared to sodium chloride as the eluent reflects the ion exchange selectivity favoring replacement of the divalent strontium ion by the divalent calcium cation as compared to the monovalent sodium cation. Thus, in the case of a soil detention basin used for low-level radioactive effluents containing ^{90}Sr, the introduction of a waste stream high in a divalent or trivalent cation salt may increase the downward movement of the ^{90}Sr over that observed when the waste stream was dilute or dominated by monovalent cations, and thereby increase the potential for ground water contamination with the radionuclide.

As discussed earlier, phosphates may be immobilized in nonacid soils as calcium phosphates. Thus, if the soil in question were calcareous, the introduction of a phosphate-rich waste stream could decrease, rather than increase the rate of ^{90}Sr movement by isomorphous substitution of strontium for calcium in a calcite to apatite replacement reaction. Work at the Hanford Atomic Reservation in southeastern Washington (Ames et al., 1958; Honstead et al., 1962) showed the retention of ^{90}Sr by calcareous soils was enhanced in the presence of phosphate ion due to a reaction of the type:

$$3PO_4^{3-} + 5CaCO_3 + OH^- \longrightarrow Ca_5(PO_4)_3(OH) + 5CO_3^{2-}$$
$$\text{calcite} \qquad\qquad\qquad \text{apatite}$$

The presence of strontium is incidental to the replacement process and indeed any cation such as strontium, magnesium, barium, zinc, or plutonium which can be accommodated into the apatite lattice can potentially be removed by this process. Ions such as cesium (Cs) which cannot substitute for calcium in the apatite lattice will not be removed by this process. Hence, the addition of phosphate to the waste stream of such a soil disposal system would not effect the mobility of another important fission product, ^{137}Cs.

While the above examples have related to nuclear wastes, admittedly a rather specialized case, the principles are equally applicable to nonradioactive materials in more typical industrial wastes and municipal sewage sludges. In all cases of land application, it should be recognized that changes in the composition of the waste material applied to soils (e.g., ionic strength, ionic composition, pH) can produce interactions which may alter the movement of potentially harmful waste constituents in the soil profile.

Placement of waste materials on the soil surface without incorporation may render materials susceptible to mass transport and leaching from the site of application in association with runoff water, and may create the potential for surface water contamination. In the upper midwest region of the United States, animal manure has long been spread onto frozen fields. A recent Minnesota study (Young & Mutchler, 1976) of the spring snowmelt runoff from plots on which dairy manure had been applied to frozen ground showed nutrient losses to be dependent upon the receiving land surface. Up to 20% of the total nitrogen and 17% of the orthophosphate-phosphorus applied in the manure were washed off alfalfa plots with the spring runoff. Nutrient concentrations in the spring runoff (i.e., mg/liter) from manured, fall-plowed corn plots were higher than from check plots receiving no manure. But the surface-applied manure cover also serves as a mulch which results in higher temperatures in the underlying soil, and thus more rapid thawing and resumption of infiltration capability, and in a retardation of runoff water. On fall-plowed, frozen fields, the manure mulch reduced the total volume of spring runoff by about 80–100%, and because of this, total nitrogen and phosphorus losses, expressed on a kg/ha basis, were similar to those observed from the check plots. Thus while manure spreading on a frozen alfalfa field may represent a potential hazard to surface water quality, its application to a fall-plowed, frozen field may be a wise resource management practice which both recharges the soil with moisture for crop use and reduces soil erosion by the snowmelt waters. Similar studies in New York (Klausner et al., 1976) suggest that manure disposal on snow-covered land should be avoided during periods of active thawing if excessive nitrogen and phosphorus losses in the runoff waters are to be avoided. Where land application is considered inadvisable during periods of frozen soil, adequate waste storage facilities must be included in the management plan.

D. Volatilization

Volatilization problems associated with waste application to soils may occur during storage, application, and while the waste remains on the soil surface.

During the process of storage and/or land application, it is important to assess the changes in the waste product which may occur due to the release of volatile compounds. For example, ammonia volatilization and, to a lesser extent, denitrification, over the course of 3 summer months resulted in a loss of over 50% of the initially present nitrogen from feedlot runoff stored in a holding pond in Illinois (Dickey & Vanderholm, 1977).

Also, during land application of sewage sludge or nitrogen-rich animal wastes, ammonia gas may be released such that some nitrogen, a beneficial plant nutrient, may be lost to the atmosphere prior to interaction with the soil. A series of studies (Lauer et al., 1976) carried out over a period of 2 years in the spring, summer, and winter in New York dealing with the volatile loss of ammonia from dairy manure spread on the soil surface at rates of from 34 to 200 metric tons/ha showed total losses of ammonia over periods of 5 to 25 days ranging from 61 to 99% of the total ammoniacal nitrogen (ammoniacal nitrogen content of manure is about 24% of the total nitrogen content). These studies indicate that volatile losses of ammonia from manure spread on the soil surface will be rapid and occur over a wide range of weather conditions, and suggest that if the goal of a waste management program is to preserve the ammoniacal nitrogen from crop utilization, then surface spreading should be accompanied by simultaneous incorporation into the soil.

The rate of ammonia loss was also affected by the application rate. The volatilization of ammonia from manure appears to be optimal under drying conditions. Higher rates of volatile loss of ammonia were observed from the thinner, faster-drying manure covers associated with low application rates than from the thicker, slower-drying manure covers associated with high applications. For example, the initial (first 5–7 days after spreading) ammonia loss rate from the 34 metric tons/ha application, typical of that used by farmers on crop land, exhibited a mean half-life of 1.9 days (i.e., 50% of total ammoniacal nitrogen lost in first 1.9 days, a total of 75% lost after 3.8 days, etc.), while at an application rate of 200 metric tons/ha the mean half-life of the ammonia loss was 3.4 days.

Even after application to the soil, especially under high pH conditions, ammonia may be lost to the atmosphere. Ammonia volatilization can become a problem when prevailing winds and land application are such that other resources are affected. For example, a study in northeastern Colorado (Hutchinson & Viets, 1969) demonstrated the nitrogen enrichment of surface waters by sorption of ammonia volatilized from cattle feedlots, and thus the potential for increasing the rate of eutrophication of neighboring downwind lakes.

After waste has been incorporated into the soil, volatilization is generally of less concern. Soils have the ability to sorb gases such as hydrogen sulfide, mercaptans (Bohn, 1972), ammonia (Mortland, 1970), and elemental mercury vapor (Landa, 1978) which might evolve from waste-amended soils, and thus soil incorporation will decrease volatile loss of these materials to the atmosphere. Also, air exchange within the soil profile to the surface is relatively slow, such that if volatilization is occurring, the concentration which occurs at the surface is minimal and generally not recognizable. The Metropolitan Sewerage District of Chicago has changed from surface to subsurface applications of sewage sludge to agricultural land because of complaints registered on odors. While soil incorporation is usually the key to successful reduction of odor problems, the landfill disposal of particular odorous sludges from the manufacture of animal glue has required, in addition to soil cover, the use of chemicals which mask or counteract the odors (Oliver & Drehwing, 1972).

V. TRANSPORTATION OF WASTE PRODUCTS

As part of the planning procedure to handle land application of waste materials, one must consider the different systems by which the waste is transported from the source to the land application site. Systems which should be considered include pipeline, train, rail, barge, and truck. Properties of the waste materials again are factors in the kind of transport system which can be selected. In some situations, it may be necessary to either dewater material to reduce volume and weight for handling, or to add water to produce conditions suitable for pumping through pipeline systems.

In most cases, pipeline and barge or river transport of waste materials is most economical. However, barge transport is often not feasible because of the location of waste sources. Waste application to land has generally involved property adjacent or close to the waste source. Under these conditions trucks are generally used to haul the waste. A very convenient arrangement is to couple natural resource transportation to a facility with waste transport from the industrial site. An excellent review article on the transportation of waste products and the problems associated with different styles and processes has been prepared (Miner & Hazen, 1977).

VI. COMMUNITY INVOLVEMENT IN PLANNING FOR WASTE DISPOSAL

Planning for waste disposal or utilization in land is best accomplished prior to the development of the waste problem. By acquainting the community with natural resources required, including energy and labor, and the waste disposal problems associated with a given industry, one can alleviate potential public relations problems.

Purdue University agricultural economist John O. Dunbar has discussed tactics that may be of value in gaining public acceptance for projects involving the recycling of waste materials to the land (Dunbar, 1973). Among his recommendations are:

1) Involve the people in the decision-making process.
2) Provide the people with the information needed to make wise decisions.
3) Keep the people informed of latest developments.

In formulating the educational and informational programs required to gain public acceptance, Dunbar (1973) suggests that the various target audiences, e.g., the uninterested general public, the decision makers and others already concerned about environmental problems, the people with vested interests, and the professionals from government agencies and institutions who work directly with the people who will be most affected by this decision, be presented with individually tailored programs aimed at their specific concerns, interest levels, and prior knowledge.

Many environmental pollution problems associated with waste disposal now recognized were not given much consideration at the time when particular cities or industries were developed and located. It is these situations which create serious problems with respect to planning. Often waste materials from these industries, prior to environmental considerations, were disposed by dumping into rivers or landfills. Under current practices, these alternatives are often no longer acceptable and new efforts must be made to accommodate the waste materials in the most economical and acceptable fashion.

VII. LOCAL, STATE, FEDERAL AGENCY COOPERATION

To successfully initiate a waste disposal utilization program on land involves the combined efforts of the waste producer as well as the local, state, and federal agencies. Requirements for conservation of the air, water, and soil resources will be examined by officials at the local, state, and federal agency levels. It is important that state agencies be informed of plans and proposals for waste management such that county extension agents, pollution control agency specialists, and other personnel have sufficient time to digest the proposal and acquaint their constituencies with any associated problems. If problems do exist with the proposal, then the waste producer must be receptive to suggested changes or alternatives.

It is recognized that oftentimes all will not be happy with procedures adopted to handle waste, either through disposal or utilization methods. It is in these mixed situations where the entire good of the community and area must be considered. Under these conditions, every reasonable effort should be made to appease the limited group of irate citizens.

As a key to the successful waste disposal or utilization on land, it has often been recognized that research or demonstration programs are quite useful. With the successful operation of such programs, the community can see effects of waste application on the land and how it may affect their living conditions. In addition, the effect of the waste product on the soil, water, and air can be evaluated. These studies should be conducted by qualified research personnel through universities or impartial agencies, and generally require at least 1 year lead time to accomplish. With the development of appropriate backup research and demonstration programs, the public is generally much more receptive to the adoption of a land disposal/utilization operation.

VIII. SUMMARY

The key to planning for successful waste disposal utilization involves an initial assessment of air, water, and land resources in a given area, accurate information on the chemical and physical properties of the waste product, and its production rate. Changes in the waste product and its composition variability with time, and potential changes in manufacturing processes, must also be known. With the above information, interactions between the resources and the waste material can be ascertained. Acceptability for agricultural land application should mean that the land to be used for agricultural production is not so contaminated that the crops grown will be unsatisfactory for animal or human consumption. If a site is to be dedicated for waste disposal without attempts for agricultural management, the effects on air and water resources must still be ascertained.

Monitoring for changes in soil, plant, air, and water quality may also be required for a successful waste disposal or utilization program. Design of monitoring programs relates closely to specific sites and waste materials. Appropriate monitoring programs should be established in conjunction with state and federal environmental quality control personnel.

To accomplish a successful land waste or disposal utilization system, one must have active involvement of officials on the local, state, and federal levels. The extent of activity on the different levels depends on the magnitude of the waste disposal operation and the types of problems associated with the waste material. Often times waste products may be handled through local agencies where a farmer or city manages a waste problem without involvement from federal agencies. However, in some cases with noxious chemicals and larger programs, federal agencies will be involved, especially if financial support is required.

In association with proposals to land-cultivate waste materials, it is important that research demonstration grants be established to develop appropriate background information on the waste interactions with the soil, water, and air. Education of the public as to the problems and the benefits of the waste material is important for the success of a waste disposal/utilization operation on land.

LITERATURE CITED

Alexander, M. 1977. Soil microbiology. John Wiley and Sons Inc., New York.

Ames, L. L., Jr., J. R. McHenry, and J. F. Honstead. 1958. The removal of strontium from wastes by a calcite-phosphate mechanism. *In* Proc. 2nd U.N. Int. Conf. Peaceful Uses Atomic Energy, 1–13 Sept. 1958, Geneva 18:76–81.

Behmer, D. E. 1976. Management of chemical wastes. p. 216–225. *In* Land application of waste materials. Soil Conserv. Soc. Am., Ankeny, Iowa.

Benne, E. J., C. R. Hoglund, E. D. Longnecker, and R. L. Cook. 1961. Animal manures—What are they worth today? Michigan State Univ. Agric. Exp. Stn. Circ. Bull. 231. 15 p.

Bingham, F. T., A. L. Page, R. J. Mahler, and T. L. Ganje. 1976. Cadmium availability to rice in sludge-amended soil under flooded and nonflooded culture. Soil Sci. Soc. Am. J. 40:715–719.

Bohn, H. L. 1972. Soil absorption of air pollutants. J. Environ. Qual. 1:372–377.

Bollen, W. B., and D. W. Glennie. 1961. Sawdust, bark and other wood wastes for soil conditioning and mulching. For. Prod. J. 11:38–46.

Davidson, J. M., L. T. Ou, and P. S. C. Rao. 1976. Behavior of high pesticide concentrations in soil water systems. p. 206–212. *In* W. H. Fuller (ed.) Residual management by land disposal, Proc. Hazardous Waste Res. Symp., 2–4 Feb. 1976, Tucson, Ariz. EPA-600/9-76-015. USEPA, Cincinnati, Ohio.

Dean, L. A. 1949. Fixation of soil phosphorus. Adv. Agron. 1:391–411.

Dickey, E. C., and D. H. Vanderholm. 1977. Feedlot runoff holding ponds—nutrient levels and related management aspects. J. Environ. Qual. 6:307–312.

Dolar, S. G., J. R. Boyle, and D. R. Keeney. 1972. Paper mill sludge disposal on soils: effects on the yield and mineral nutrition of oats (*Avena sativa* L.). J. Environ. Qual. 1:405–409.

Dowdy, R. H., and W. E. Larson. 1975. The availability of sludge-born metals to various vegetable crops. J. Environ. Qual. 4:278–282.

Dunbar, J. O. 1973. Public acceptance—educational and informational needs. p. 207–211. *In* Proc. Joint Conf. Recycling Municipal Sludges and Effluents on Land, 9–13 July 1973, Champaign, Ill. Natl. Assoc. State Univ. and Land Grant Colleges, Washington, D.C.

Elgawhary, S. M., W. L. Lindsay, and W. D. Kemper. 1970a. Effect of EDTA on the self-diffusion of zinc in aqueous solution and in soil. Soil Sci. Soc. Am. Proc. 34:66–70.

Elgawhary, S. M., W. L. Lindsay, and W. D. Kemper. 1970b. Effect of complexing agents and acids on the diffusion of zinc to a simulated root. Soil Sci. Soc. Am. Proc. 34:211–214.

Endelman, F. J., D. R. Keeney, J. T. Gilmour, and P. G. Saffigna. 1974. Nitrate and chloride movement in the Plainfield loamy sand under intensive irrigation. J. Environ. Qual. 3: 295–298.

Fenster, C. R. 1976. Use of plant residues. p. 91–97. *In* Land application of waste materials. Soil Conserv. Soc. Am., Ankeny, Iowa.

Guenzi, W. D., and W. E. Beard. 1976. The effects of temperature and soil water on the conversion of DDT to DDE in soil. J. Environ. Qual. 5:243–246.

Hall, G. F., L. P. Wilding, and A. E. Erickson. 1976. Site selection considerations for sludge and wastewater applications on agricultural land. p. 2.1–2.8. *In* B. D. Knezek and R. H. Miller (ed.) Application of sludges and wastewaters on agricultural land: a planning and educational guide. Ohio Agric. Res. and Dev. Center Res. Bull. 1090. North Central Res. Publ. 235.

Hiltbold, A. E. 1974. Persistence of pesticides in soil. p. 203–222. *In* W. D. Guenzi (ed.) Pesticides in soil and water. Soil Sci. Soc. Am., Madison, Wis.

Honstead, J. F., L. L. Ames, Jr., and J. L. Nelson. 1962. Mineral reactions—a new waste decontamination process. Health Phys. 8:191–196.

Hutchinson, G. L., and F. G. Viets, Jr. 1969. Nitrogen enrichment of surface water by absorption of ammonia volatilized from cattle feedlots. Science 166:514–515.

Kardos, L. T. 1967. Waste water renovation by the land—a living filter. p. 241–250. *In* N. C. Brady (ed.) Agriculture and the quality of our environment. Am. Assoc. Adv. Sci. Pub. 85, Washington, D.C.

Kirkham, M. B. 1977. Organic matter and heavy metal uptake. Compost Sci. 18:18–21.

Klausner, S. D., P. J. Zwerman, and D. F. Ellis. 1976. Nitrogen and phosphorus losses from winter disposal of dairy manure. J. Environ. Qual. 5:47–49.

Lance, J. C., and F. D. Whisler. 1972. Nitrogen balance in soil columns intermittently flooded with secondary sewage effluent. J. Environ. Qual. 1:180–186.

Landa, E. R. 1978. Soil water content and temperature as factors in the volatile loss of applied mercury (II) from soils. Soil Sci. 126:44–48.

Lauer, D. A., D. R. Bouldin, and S. D. Klausner. 1976. Ammonia volatilization from dairy manure spread on the soil surface. J. Environ. Qual. 5:134–139.

Miller, R. H. 1974. Factors affecting the decomposition of an anaerobically digested sewage sludge in soil. J. Environ. Qual. 3:376–380.

Miner, J. R., and T. E. Hazen. 1977. Transportation and application of organic wastes to land. p. 378–425. *In* L. F. Elliott and F. J. Stevenson (ed.) Soils for management of organic wastes and waste waters. Am. Soc. of Agron., Madison, Wis.

Mortland, M. M. 1970. Clay-organic complexes and interactions. Adv. Agron. 22:75–117.

Nielsen, D. R., and J. W. Biggar. 1961. Miscible displacement in soils: I. Experimental information. Soil Sci. Soc. Am. Proc. 25:1–5.

Oliver, A. J., and F. J. Drehwing. 1972. Land disposal of residues from the animal glue industry. p. 317–330. *In* Proc. 1972 Cornell Agric. Waste Manage. Conf., College of Agric. and Life Sci., Cornell Univ. Graphics Manage. Corp., Washington, D.C.

Pratt, P. F., F. E. Broadbent, and J. P. Martin. 1973. Using organic wates as nitrogen fertilizers. Calif. Agric. 27(6):10–13.

Reed, A. D., W. E. Wildman, W. S. Seyman, R. S. Ayers, J. D. Prato, and R. S. Rauschkolb. 1973. Soil recycling of cannery wastes. Calif. Agric. 27(3):6–9.

Satterwhite, M. B., and G. L. Stewart. 1976. Evaluation of an infiltration-percolation system for final treatment of primary sewage effluent in a New England environment. p. 435–449. *In* R. C. Loehr (ed.) Land as a waste management alternative, Proc. 1976 Cornell Agric. Waste Manage. Conf., College of Agric. and Life Sci., Cornell Univ. Ann Arbor Science Publ. Inc., Ann Arbor, Mich.

Sawhney, B. L., and D. E. Hill. 1975. Phosphate sorption characteristics of soils treated with domestic waste water. J. Environ. Qual. 4:342–346.

Schulz, R. K. 1965. Soil chemistry of radionuclides. Health Phys. 11:1317–1324.

Sommers, L. E., and D. W. Nelson. 1976. Analyses and their interpretation for sludge application to agricultural land. p. 3.1–3.7. *In* B. D. Knezek and R. H. Miller (ed.) Application of sludges and wastewaters on agricultural land: a planning and educational guide. Ohio Agric. Res. and Dev. Center Res. Bull. 1090, North Central Res. Publ. 235.

Sommers, L. E., D. W. Nelson, and K. J. Yost. 1976. Variable nature of chemical composition of sewage sludges. J. Environ. Qual. 5:303–306.

Straub, C. P., V. M. Goppers, and A. DuChene. 1977. Water quality and status trends in Minnesota. Univ. of Minnesota Water Resour. Res. Center Bull. 95, Minneapolis, Minn.

Tan, K. H., R. A. Leonard, A. R. Bertrand, and S. R. Wilkinson. 1971a. The metal complexing capacity and the nature of the chelating ligands of water extract of poultry litter. Soil Sci. Soc. Am. Proc. 35:265–269.

Tan, K. H., L. D. King, and H. D. Morris. 1971b. Complex reactions of zinc with organic matter extracted from sewage sludge. Soil Sci. Soc. Am. Proc. 35:748–752.

Thomas, R. E., and T. W. Bendixen. 1969. Degradation of wastewater organics in soil. J. Water Pollut. Control Fed. 41:808–813.

Touchton, J. T., L. D. King, H. Bell, and H. D. Morris. 1976. Residual effect of liquid sewage sludge on coastal bermudagrass and soil chemical properties. J. Environ. Qual. 5:161–164.

Wells, D. M., R. M. Sweazy, F. Gray, C. C. Jaynes, and W. F. Bennett. 1976. Effluent reuse in Lubbock. p. 451–466. *In* R. C. Loehr (ed.) Land as a waste management alternative, Proc. 1976 Cornell Agric. Waste Manage. Conf., College of Agric. and Life Sci., Cornell Univ. Ann Arbor Science Publ. Inc., Ann Arbor, Mich.

Young, R. A., and C. K. Mutchler. 1976. Pollution potential of manure spread on frozen ground. J. Environ. Qual. 5:174–179.

26

Surface Application of Sewage Effluent and Sludge

WILLIAM E. SOPPER

The Pennsylvania State University, University Park, Pennsylvania

I. INTRODUCTION

The current interest in recycling municipal waste water and sludge on the land is the result of the general public awareness of the nation's growing water pollution problems. This public awareness peaked during the 1960's and environmentalists demanded action that would stop the trend toward total pollution of our environment. The first major step in the fight against water pollution was taken in 1970 with the passage of the Water Pollution Control Act. This Act was later amended in October 1972 with the passage of Public Law 92-500 (Federal Water Pollution Control Act Amendment of 1972). The objective of this legislation milestone was to restore and maintain the chemical, physical, and biological integrity of the nation's waters.

One of the major contributors to the pollution of our lakes and streams is the discharge of raw wastes or partially treated wastes from municipal waste water treatment plants. Over 150 million Americans use public sewage today and more than 26 billion gallons of waste water are discharged daily into water courses throughout the United States.

One of the initial steps taken by Congress after passage of the Act was to provide federal funds for cost-sharing to upgrade and improve the degree of treatment in publicly owned waste water treatment plants. The Act also encourages waste treatment management that provides for the recycling of potential sewage pollutants through the production of agriculture, silviculture, or aquaculture products.

II. HISTORICAL BACKGROUND

Man has been disposing of human waste on the land for centuries. One of the earliest systems was an irrigation project designed to treat waste from Bunslau, Prussia, in 1559 and operated for over 300 years (Buswell, 1928). During the latter part of the nineteenth century pollution of many rivers in Europe reached unacceptable levels and land disposal of sewage increased. Many "sewage farms" were developed during this period. Land disposal in the United States also dates back to before the turn of the century. According to Rafter (1899) the first attempt at large-scale sewage irrigation was at Augusta, Maine, in 1872. Untreated sewage was used to irrigate a hay field and a vegetable garden. He also reported that in 1881 a land disposal system was developed at Amherst, Connecticut, where sewage was used to irrigate a hay crop. By 1935, there were 113 systems in 15 western states using waste water for crop irrigation. The number of systems has been continually increasing. Thomas (1973) reported that as of 1972 there were 571 municipalities using land application. At the present time, land application systems tend to predominate in the water-short areas of the western U.S.

III. WASTE WATER TREATMENT

The characteristics of sewage effluent and sludge depend upon the degree of treatment. The three levels of treatment—primary, secondary, and tertiary—are classified on the basis of removal of constituents, usually biological oxygen demand (BOD) and suspended solids. Primary treatment consists of physical processes that remove solids in the waste water by screening and sedimentation. Primary treatment will remove approximately 35% of the BOD and 60% of the suspended solids present in the raw waste water.

Secondary treatment consists of various biological processes to remove most of the remaining suspended solids and organic matter left in the waste water primary treatment. The two basic treatment processes are activated sludge and trickling filter. In the trickling filter installation, the waste water flows over a coarse bed of rocks on which bacteria are growing. As the waste water trickles down through the bed of rocks, the bacteria consume most of the organic matter. In an activated sludge system the activity of the microorganisms is increased by bringing air and sludge heavily laden with microorganisms into close contact with the waste water in an aeration tank for several hours. Secondary treatment will remove from 80 to 95% of the BOD and suspended solids.

Tertiary treatment, or advanced waste water treatment (AWT), is the term usually applied to additional processes used after conventional biological treatment to achieve greater removal of BOD, suspended solids, phosphorus, nitrogen, and other constituents that might pollute the receiving stream. Some of the processes being used are chemical coagulation, electrodialysis, activated carbon adsorption, lagooning, filtration, reverse osmosis, distillation, ion exchange, and foam separation. Many of these processes are similar to those used to treat potable water supplies.

Land application of waste water, after secondary treatment, is also an advanced treatment method. This approach, more commonly referred to as the "living filter" method, considers the waste water and the nutrients it contains as a resource rather than as a product for treatment and disposal. Treatment of the waste water is provided by natural biological and chemical processes as it moves through the living filter provided by the soil, plants, microorganisms, and related ecosystems. The renovated water then percolates to recharge the ground water reservoir (Fig. 1).

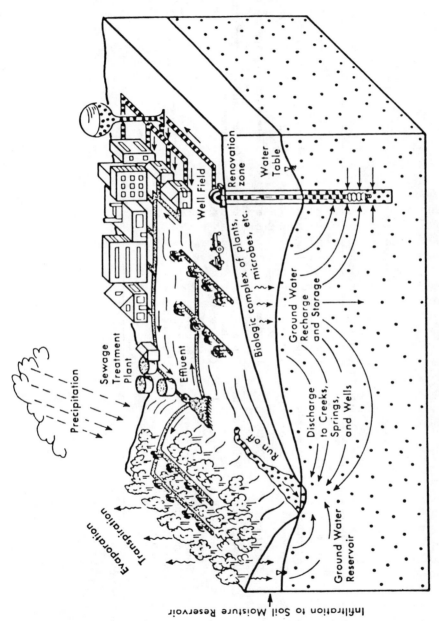

Fig. 1—The waste water renovation and conservation cycle.

Table 1—General design considerations.†

Waste water characteristics	Climate	Geology	Soils	Plant cover	Topography	Application
Flow volume	Precipitation	Ground water	Type	Indigenous to region	Slope	Method
Constituent load	Evapotranspiration	Seasonal depth	Texture	Nutrient removal capability	Aspect of slope	Type of equipment
	Temperature	Quality	Infiltration/permeability	Toxicity levels	Erosion hazard	Application rate
	Growing season	Points of discharge	Type and quantity of clay	Moisture and shade tolerance	Crop and farm management	Types of drainage
	Occurrence and depth of frozen	Bedrock	Cation exchange capacity	Marketability		
	Storage requirements	Type	P adsorption potential			
	Wind velocity and direction	Depth	Heavy metal adsorption potential			
		Permeability	pH			
			Organic matter			

† From USEPA (1977).

IV. APPLICATION TECHNIQUES

Waste water can be applied to the land by a variety of methods. Because land application inherently is site specific, and because a wide range of design possibilities are available, the designer must rely on a comprehensive understanding of the principle involved as well as detailed site evaluations by specialists. A representative list of factors that should be considered in the design of land application system is presented in Table 1. The three most commonly used methods are slow-rate irrigation, overland flow, and rapid infiltration-percolation (Fig. 2). The success of a land treat-

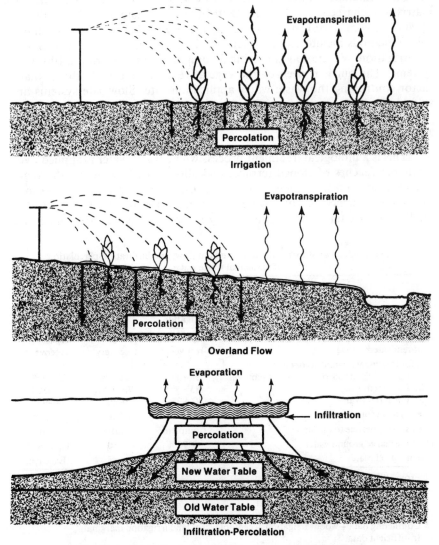

Fig. 2—Methods used for land application of municipal waste water.

ment system will depend upon the capability of the selected method of application, project objectives, and site characteristics. A comparison of the three alternative methods in respect to use objectives is presented in Table 2. General site characteristics related to slope, soil permeability, depth to ground water, and climate for each method are given in Table 3 and general design features are given in Table 4.

1. SLOW-RATE INFILTRATION

Irrigation is probably the most common method in use. It involves the application of effluent to the land for treatment and for meeting the nutrient needs of vegetation. Some water is lost by evaporation and transpiration while the remainder of the renovated waste water percolates through the soil matrix to recharge ground water. Distribution of waste water is usually by fixed or moving sprinkler systems or by surface application. Surface application methods include ridge and furrow irrigation and border strip flooding irrigation. Vegetation is a critical component of slow-rate infiltration systems. The nutrient need of the vegetative cover is usually the primary factor controlling the waste water application rate. Slow-rate systems are suitable for both cropland and forestland.

2. OVERLAND FLOW

This is a biological treatment process where waste water is applied over the upper reaches of sloped terraces and allowed to flow across the vegetated surface to runoff collection ditches. Little waste water infiltrates into the soil and, hence, ground water recharge is not an objective with this method. A vegetative cover is necessary to obtain adequate treatment and

Table 2—Comparison of irrigation, overland flow, and infiltration-percolation of municipal waste water.†

| | | Type of approach | |
| | Irrigation | Overland flow | Infiltration-percolation |
Objective			
Use as a treatment process with a recovery of renovated water‡	0–70% recovery	50–80% recovery	Up to 97% recovery
Use for treatment beyond secondary:			
1. For BOD§ and suspended solids removal	98 + %	92 + %	85–99%
2. For N removal	85 + %¶	70–90%	0–50%
3. For P removal	80–99%	40–80%	60–95%
Use to grow crops for sale	Excellent	Fair	Poor
Use as direct recycle to the land	Complete	Partial	Complete
Use to recharge ground water	0–70%	0–10%	Up to 97%
Use in cold climates	Fair#	--††	Excellent

† From USEPA (1977).
‡ Percentage of applied water recovered depends upon recovery technique and the climate.
§ BOD = Biochemical oxygen demand.
¶ Dependent upon crop uptake.
# Conflicting data—woods irrigation acceptable, cropland irrigation marginal.
†† Insufficient data.

Table 3—Comparison of site characteristics for land treatment processes.†

Characteristics	Principal processes			Other processes	
	Slow rate	Rapid infiltration	Overland flow	Wetlands	Subsurface
Slope	<20% on cultivated land; <40% on non-cultivated land	Not critical; excessive slopes require much earthwork	Finish slopes 2 to 8%	Usually <5%	Not critical
Soil permeability	Moderately slow to moderately rapid	Rapid (sands, loamy sands)	Slow (clays, silts, and soils with impermeable barriers)	Slow to moderate	Slow to rapid
Depth to ground water	60 to 90 cm (minimum)	3 m (10 feet) (lesser depths are acceptable where underdrainage is provided)	Not critical	Not critical	Not critical
Climatic restrictions	Storage often needed for cold weather and precipitation	None (possibly modify operation in cold weather)	Storage often needed for cold weather	Storage may be needed for cold weather	None

† From USEPA (1977).

Table 4—Comparison of design features for land treatment processes.

Feature	Principal processes			Other processes	
	Slow rate	Rapid infiltration	Overland flow	Wetlands	Subsurface
Application techniques	Sprinkler or surface‡	Usually surface	Sprinkler or surface	Sprinkler or surface	Subsurface piping
Annual application rate, m	0.6 to 6	6 to 170	3 to 21	1.2 to 30	2.4 to 26
Field area required, ha§	23 to 224	0.8 to 22	6.4 to 44	4.4 to 112	5.2 to 56
Typical weekly application rate, cm	1.3 to 10	10 to 305	6.3 to 7.5¶ 7.5 to 40.6#	2.5 to 63	5 to 50
Minimum preapplication treatment provided in U.S.	Primary sedimentation††	Primary sedimentation	Screening and grit removal	Primary sedimentation	Primary sedimentation
Disposition of applied applied waste water	Evapotranspiration and percolation	Mainly percolation	Surface runoff and evapotranspiration with some percolation	Evapotranspiration, percolation, and runoff	Percolation with some evapotranspiration
Need for vegetation	Required	Optional	Required	Required	Optional

† From USEPA (1977).
‡ Includes ridge-and-furrow and border strip.
§ Field area in ha not including buffer area, roads, or ditches for 1 Mgal/d (43.8 L/s) flow.
¶ Range for application of screened waste water.
# Range for application of lagoon and secondary effluent.
†† Depends on the use of the effluent and the type of crop.

for protection against erosion, although crop production is not a major objective. Renovated water collected at the bottom of overland flow slopes may be reused or discharged directly to surface water.

3. RAPID INFILTRATION-PERCOLATION

Waste water is applied to highly permeable soils in basins by flooding or sprinkling. The basins may or may not be vegetated. Vegetation is not required and is not part of the treatment process. Treatment is accomplished by natural physical, chemical, and biological processes as the waste water percolates through the soil matrix. The primary objective of this method is ground water recharge. This method requires the least amount of land area to treat a given volume of waste water. Ground water wells or underdrains may be used to intercept the renovated water and return it to the surface for reuse.

V. EXPECTED TREATMENT PERFORMANCE

The expected quality of treated water from each of the three land treatment processes is given in Tables 2 and 5. The highest quality treated water is obtained with the slow-rate infiltration method. With this method organics are reduced primarily by biological oxidation within the surface soil layer. Suspended solids are removed by filtration. Nitrogen is removed primarily by crop uptake and harvest. Although most slow-rate infiltration systems are designed to maintain aerobic soil conditions, some nitrogen may be lost by denitrification. The frequency of waste water application can be varied to create temporary anaerobic conditions that would favor denitrification. Phosphorus is removed from solution by adsorption and chemical precipitation. Removal efficiency is mostly dependent on soil properties.

With the overland flow system, organics and suspended solids are removed primarily by biological oxidation, sedimentation, and grass filtration. Removal of nitrogen is mostly by denitrification, although plant up-

Table 5—Expected quality of treated water from land treatment processes.†

Constituent	Slow rate‡		Rapid infiltration§		Overland flow¶	
	Average	Maximum	Average	Maximum	Average	Maximum
			mg/liter			
BOD	<2	<5	2	<5	10	<15
Suspended solids	<1	<5	2	<5	10	<20
Ammonia nitrogen as N	<0.5	<2	0.5	<2	0.8	<2
Total nitrogen as N	3	<8	10	<20	3	<5
Total phosphorus as P	<0.1	<0.3	1	<5	4	<6

† From USEPA (1977).
‡ Percolation of primary or secondary effluent through 1.5 m (5 feet) of soil.
§ Percolation of primary or secondary effluent through 4.5 m (15 feet) of soil.
¶ Runoff of comminuted municipal waste water over about 45 m (150 feet) of slope.

take may also contribute if the plant is harvested. Some nitrogen may also be lost by ammonia volatilization. Phosphorus is again removed by adsorption and chemical precipitation. However, because of the limited contact with the soil matrix, phosphorus removal is usually the lowest of the three methods.

In the rapid infiltration-percolation system the only significant mechanism for nitrogen removal is denitrification. Hydraulic loading and organic loading must be carefully controlled to alternately create anaerobic and aerobic conditions. As in all of the other systems, the phosphorus is removed by adsorption and chemical precipitation as the waste water percolates through the soil.

VI. CROP SELECTION AND MANAGEMENT

The selection of the vegetative cover to be utilized or established and maintained on a waste water land application site will depend upon many factors. The following are some of the criteria which should be considered:

1) Water requirements and tolerance,
2) Nutrient requirements and tolerance,
3) Optimum soil conditions for growth,
4) Season of growth and dormancy requirements,
5) Sensitivity to toxic heavy metals and salts,
6) Nutrient utilization and renovation efficiency,
7) Ecosystem stability,
8) Length of harvesting rotation,
9) Insect and disease problems,
10) Natural range, and
11) Demand or market for the product.

The primary choices include annual and perennial agricultural crops and forest vegetation. Each vegetation type has distinct advantages and disadvantages. Perennial groups are more suitable than legumes or annual row crops and grains. In general, they have fiberous root systems; are sod forming, which aids in erosion control and provides for high infiltration rates; are tolerant of a wide range of ecological conditions; have a long period of growth; and have a high uptake of nutrients, particularly nitrogen. On the other hand, legumes can fix all the nitrogen they need from the air.

Under the "living filter" concept of land application of waste water, the vegetative cover is an integral part of the renovation system in that it provides for the uptake and removal of nutrients in the waste water.

A. Crop Yields

As one might expect crop yields are usually increased as a result of land application of waste water. Secondary treated domestic waste water has considerable fertilizer value. For instance, the application of waste water at 5 cm/week during the growing season at the Penn State Project provides the

Table 6—Crop yields at various levels of application of waste water.

Crop	Waste water application rates, cm/week		
	0†	2.5	5.0
	bu/ha		
Wheat	118.0	111.0	133.0
Corn	180.0	254.0	259.0
Oats	202.0	278.0	217.0
	metric tons/ha		
Alfalfa	4.9	8.3	11.5
Red clover	5.5	11.0	10.3
Corn stover	8.0	16.3	19.0
Corn silage	9.7	14.4	13.5
Reed canarygrass	3.2	--	11.3

† Control areas received commercial fertilizer ranging from 224 kg of 0-20-20 for oats to 900 kg/ha of 10-10-10 for corn.

equivalent of 232 kg of nitrogen (N), 245 kg of phosphate (P_2O_5), and 254 kg of potash (K_2O) per hectare. This would be equal to applying 2.2 metric tons/ha of a 10-10-11 fertilizer annually. Some examples of crop yields at various levels of application of waste water are given in Table 6. Yield increases will vary according to the waste water application rate, period of application, and rainfall. While the yields shown in Table 6 are typical, over a 10-year period the 5-cm/week application of waste water resulted in annual yield increases ranging from −8 to 346% for corn grain, 5 to 130% for corn silage, 85 to 191% for red clover, and 79 to 139% for alfalfa.

B. Nutrients Removed by Crops

The contribution of the vegetative cover to the waste water renovation process is readily evident when one considers the quantities of nutrients, expressed in kg/ha, removed in crop harvest. Such data indicate that the effective life of a land application system can be extended considerably where a suitable crop is utilized and harvested.

The amounts of nutrients removed annually vary with the type of crop, amount of waste water applied, amount of rainfall, length of growing season, and the number of harvests. Average nutrient contents of crops irrigated with waste water are usually higher than control crops, even though control crops receive normal applications of commercial fertilizer. Average nutrient contents for corn silage and reed canarygrass are given in Table 7. The efficiency of the perennial grass for nutrient removal is quite obvious.

A measure of the contribution of crops as a renovating agent can be assessed by computing a "removal efficiency" expressed as the ratio of the weight of the nutrient removed in the harvested crop to the weight of the same nutrient applied in the waste water.

Average renovation efficiencies for silage corn and reed canarygrass crops are given in Table 8. At the 5-cm/week level of application of waste water, the corn silage removed 179 kg of N, 48 kg of P, and 145 kg of K per

Table 7—Average nutrient content of vegetation.

Crop	Waste water application rate	Nutrient content		
		N	P	K
	cm/week		%	
Corn silage	0	1.63	0.23	1.13
	2.5	2.16	0.26	1.27
	5.0	1.80	0.32	1.16
Reed canarygrass	5.0	3.69	0.50	2.23

hectare. Reed canarygrass, which is a perennial grass, was even more efficient in that it removed 457 kg of N, 63 kg of P, and 277 kg of K per hectare. The difference was primarily due to the fact that the grass is already established and actively growing in early spring even before the corn is planted. From the values in Table 8 it might appear that the renovation efficiency of the perennial grass is lower than the silage corn. This is not true, since it should be remembered that the annual period of irrigation is longer for the perennial grass (30 to 52 weeks) and shorter for the corn (16 to 20 weeks). Thus, more waste water and greater amounts of nutrients are applied on the reed canarygrass area. Nevertheless, both crops removed over 100% of the N and K applied in the waste water. Silage corn also removed over 100% of the P applied, whereas the reed canarygrass crop only removed 63%.

C. Waste Water Renovation by Crops

The fate of nitrogen is one of the most critical parameters in the design of land application systems and the principal parameter monitored to determine if the waste water is satisfactorily renovated. The major goal of most land application systems employing the "living filter" concept is to produce potable water for recharge to the ground water reservoir. In terms of nitrogen, this means that the nitrate-N concentration of soil percolate water leaving the root zone should not exceed 10 mg/liter (USPHS potable water standard). The second most important constituent is phosphorus. Like nitrogen, it is a major plant nutrient found in waste water and must be removed by the "living filter" system. Although the vegetative cover will utilize available phosphorus, most of the phosphorus in waste water is removed and fixed by the soil matrix.

Table 8—Average renovation efficiency of silage corn and reed canarygrass crops receiving waste water at the application rate of 5 cm/week.

Nutrient	Corn silage	Reed canarygrass
		%
Nitrogen	145	122
Phosphorus	143	63
Potassium	130	117

Table 9—Mean annual concentration of P in soil water at the 120-cm depth in the agronomic ecosystems.

Year	Corn, Hublersburg soil, cm/week		Reed canarygrass, Hublersburg soil, cm/week	
	0	5	0	5
	mg/liter			
1965	0.032	0.022	--	--
1966	0.045	0.036	--	0.055
1967	0.039	0.054	--	0.053
1968	0.041	0.060	--	0.052
1969	0.066	0.070	--	0.035
1970	0.034	0.075	--	0.038
1971	0.048	0.061	--	0.061
1972	0.022	0.035†	0.067	0.054†‡
1973	0.013	0.020†	0.036	0.052†‡
1974	--	--	0.044	0.066‡
1975	0.054	0.043	0.083	0.048‡
1976	0.015	0.011	0.016	0.033‡
1977	0.021	0.017	0.036	0.033‡

† Application rate increased to 7.5 cm/week.
‡ Anaerobic digested sludge was injected into the sewage effluent at a ratio of approximately 1 part liquid sludge to 13 parts sewage effluent.

At the Penn State Project, percolate water samples are collected at the 120-cm soil depth after each weekly application of waste water for chemical analyses to determine the degree of waste water treatment and renovation. Mean annual concentrations of phosphorus and nitrate-nitrogen for the agronomic areas during the period 1965 to 1977 are given in Tables 9 and 10. Mean annual phosphorus concentrations in the sewage effluent have

Table 10—Mean annual concentration of NO_3-N in soil water at the 120-cm depth in the agronomic ecosystems.

Year	Corn, Hublersburg soil, cm/week		Reed canarygrass, Hublersburg soil, cm/week	
	0	5	0	5
	mg/liter			
1965	5.2	9.7	--	--
1966	4.7	7.0	--	3.7
1967	3.4	7.1	--	3.3
1968	4.5	9.5	--	3.1
1969	9.4	13.5	--	2.5
1970	10.3	10.9	--	2.4
1971	6.2	9.6	--	3.3
1972	9.4	10.6†	1.7	7.7†‡
1973	7.4	7.4†	1.5	9.2†‡
1974	24.9	8.4	1.6	8.7‡
1975	13.8	6.8	11.0	15.8‡
1976	14.2	11.5	0.5	16.2‡
1977	11.9	10.4	2.8	9.7‡

† Application rate increased to 7.5 cm/week.
‡ Anaerobic digested sludge was injected into the sewage effluent at a ratio of approximately 1 part liquid sludge to 13 parts sewage effluent.

varied from 2.5 to 10 mg P/liter. Phosphorus concentrations in the percolating water at the 120-cm soil depth have been consistently decreased by more than 98% since the initiation of the project in 1963. Even when water application rates were increased from 5 to 7.5 cm/week in 1972–1973 the degree of renovation was essentially unchanged. The differences between the mean annual concentrations of phosphorus on the control and irrigated areas are quite small and insignificant considering that more than 21 m of sewage effluent have been applied over the 15 years. It should also be noted that starting in the year 1971 the reed canarygrass area has been irrigated with a mixture of sewage effluent and liquid digested sludge (approximately 1 part of sludge slurry to 13 parts of effluent). This effluent-sludge mixture had a total P concentration of 20 to 25 mg/liter and an orthophosphate level of 10 to 15 mg/liter. These data indicate that phosphorus is not leaching out of the soil profile into the ground water at significantly higher concentrations from the waste water-treated areas than from the control areas and that there appears to be no decreasing trend evident in terms of satisfactory phosphorus removal.

Nitrate-nitrogen renovation was not as efficient on the agronomic areas. Nitrate-nitrogen concentrations were decreased below the 10-mg/liter level recommended by the Public Health Service (PHS) for drinking water on the corn rotation area that received the 2.5-cm/week treatment but not at the 5-cm/week level. At the higher application rate (5 cm) the mean annual concentration remained below the PHS limit only when grass-legume hays occupied 28 to 68% of the site during the period 1965 to 1968. Starting with 1969 the entire site has been planted with corn. Increases in the application rate from 5 to 7.5 cm during 1972 and 1973 did not significantly affect the degree of renovation on the corn area.

On the other hand, the 5-cm/week reed canarygrass area has been exceptionally efficient in nitrogen removal and has consistently maintained the mean annual concentration of nitrate-nitrogen in percolating water below the 10 mg/liter limit except for 1975 and 1976. This area is irrigated year-round and, therefore, received twice as much nitrogen as the corn area. Even when water application rates were increased to 7.5 cm/week during 1972 and 1973, mean annual concentrations were increased somewhat but still remained within acceptable levels.

VII. APPLICATIONS IN FOREST ECOSYSTEMS

Forest land is the largest single land use type in the United States. Except for the Great Plains and the arid southwestern U.S., forests are abundant and well distributed; they can be found near most metropolitan areas where wastes are generated. Forests and brushland occupy 33% of the total land area of the United States (Table 11). In the highly populated northeastern U.S., forest land represents 68% of the total land area, outranking cropland by a ratio of 5:1. Even in New Jersey, the most densely populated state, nearly half of the land area is in forest. Most forest lands are located

Table 11—Land area of the United States by land use.†

Land use	Area	Proportion
	million ha	%
Forest land		
Commercial timberland	202.4	22.0
Unproductive	94.7	10.3
Reserved	7.0	0.8
Deferred	1.1	0.1
Total forest land	305.2	33.2
Cropland	172.9	18.8
All other land	441.2	48.0
Total all land	919.3	100.0

† From U.S. Forest Service (1973).

in rural areas, usually readily accessible, and have lower land values than agricultural lands. In addition, forest land represents a great potential for recycling municipal waste water, due partly to the high infiltration and permeability of the soil generally found in established forests.

To adequately realize the forest potential, it has to be recognized that forest ecosystems behave differently than agricultural systems in a number of ways. Forests have a long-term potential for nutrient storage in comparison to short-term potential and annual harvesting for agricultural systems. Unlike agricultural systems, forests are in a continual flux of equilibrium and nutrients added accumulate and are recycled within the system. Because the forest is a stable ecosystem, it has the capacity to receive periodic overloads of waste water without adverse effects to the ecosystem or to soil percolate water quality. In addition, waste water usually can be applied over a longer period of time, annually, to forests than to row crops. In fact, in many parts of the country waste water can be applied year-round in forest ecosystems. By incorporating forests in a land application system, a municipality may be able to reduce storage requirements and operating costs since less intensive management is required.

The wider buffer zones usually required in open agricultural systems are not necessary in most forest systems. The need for these buffer zones is to reduce the transmission of viruses and bacteria via aerosols produced by spray irrigation. In forest systems the production of aerosols is greatly reduced because of lower sprinkler pressures, reduced wind velocities, and the physical barrier provided by the trees.

The potential for introduction of trace elements into the human food chain is greatly reduced in forest systems. Consequently, the public health aspects and social acceptability of waste water application to such lands may be more easily managed. The only exception is via free-ranging wildlife such as deer that might forage on forest vegetation and be harvested and consumed by humans. Results of studies on health considerations have shown that some heavy metal concentrations increased slightly in cottontail rabbits' tissues captured on waste water-irrigated forests (Wood et al., 1975). The data indicated that while copper concentrations in the kidney increased by less than 10%, kidney cadmium concentrations decreased by more than 25%; however, the increased levels found were still within the normal range in nature.

The infiltration capacity of most forest soils greatly exceeds the combined rates of precipitation and waste water irrigation and usually is not a limiting factor in the design of forest systems. The well-developed surface organic layer found in most forest soils maintains the high infiltration rate, protects the surface soil from raindrop impact, insulates and protects the soil from freezing, and provides a favorable environment for microbial and invertebrate activity that contribute to the biological renovation process.

The permeability of most forest soils generally is greater than most agricultural soils because of minimum tillage, low vehicular traffic, and decomposition of deep-penetrating root systems. Research also has shown that forest systems can be installed on slopes greater (15 to 40%) than those recommended for agricultural systems. Forest land treatment systems are presently operating on slopes up to 40%.

A. Waste Water Renovation

The long-term capacity of a forest ecosystem to adequately renovate waste water is dependent upon vegetative uptake of nutrients, soil sorption properties, rate of loading, chemical characteristics of the waste water, climate of the area, and leachate water quality standards. Vegetative uptake is dependent on the species type, stand structure, and age. In addition to the forest stand, nutrient uptake by the understory and ground herbaceous vegetation can also be important. This is particularly true during the establishment period of a new forest. Nitrogen uptake by vegetative cover and the transformation of nitrogen to the nitrate form are the primary factors one must consider in determining waste water loading rates. One must also consider the chemical forms of nitrogen in the waste water; for instance, a highly nitrified waste water will be more difficult to renovate than a waste water that contains nitrogen primarily in the ammonium and organic form. As in the case of agricultural soils, the sorption capacity of forest soils is the principal factor in the renovation of phosphorus and trace metals.

During the past 16 years waste water has been irrigated in several forest ecosystems at The Pennsylvania State University. Application rates and the fate of nitrogen for these forest ecosystems are given in Table 12. Results from these studies provide some insight into the long-term efficiency of forest ecosystems to renovate waste water. Satisfactory renovation was obtained in all forest ecosystems (eastern mixed hardwoods and red pine) where waste water was applied during the growing season at the rate of 2.5 cm/week, with total annual nitrogen loadings of approximately 150 kg N/ha.

The data in Table 12 also indicates that forest ecosystems may be quite sensitive to waste water application rates and may have a low threshold of collapse in terms of renovation, *Ecosystem collapse* being defined as that

Table 12—Mean annual concentration of NO_3-N in soil water at the 120-cm depth in the forest ecosystems.

Year	Red pine I, Hublersburg soil, cm/week		Red pine II, Hublersburg soil, cm/week		Hardwood, Hublersburg soil, cm/week		White Spruce— old field, Hublersburg soil, cm/week		Hardwood, Morrison soil, cm/week	
	0	2.5	0	5	0	2.5	0	5	0	5
					mg/liter					
1965	0.9	2.2	0.9	3.9	--	0.0	0.3	8.0	--	--
1966	0.1	2.1	0.1	9.3	0.1	0.2	0.1	5.0	0.1	10.6
1967	0.9	1.7	1.8	13.8	0.3	1.4	0.3	6.1	1.4	19.2
1968	0.9	2.7	1.6	20.0	0.1	8.0	0.2	3.7	0.1	25.9
1969	0.2	4.2	0.5	24.2	0.1	7.2	0.2	2.3	0.3	23.7
1970	<1	5.3	<1	8.1	<1	5.0	<1	3.5	1.0	42.8
1971	2.6	8.3	2.6	2.1	0.5	5.8	0.5	3.8	0.8	17.6
1972	6.0	21.8†	6.0	14.5‡	4.7	23.9†	3.2	11.8‡	4.7	22.9
1973	0.5	13.7†	0.5	8.7‡	3.0	14.7†	0.5	13.5‡	1.3	17.3
1974	0.7	16.1	0.7	7.8	1.5	14.5	0.5	10.9	0.5	14.3
1975	1.3	11.9	1.3	5.1	1.7	11.6	0.8	12.9	0.8	9.0
1976	0.7	9.8	0.7	4.3	1.2	12.5	0.8	8.4	0.6	4.8
1977	0.7	5.0	0.7	3.7	1.4	9.4	0.9	6.9	1.1	5.1

† Application rate increased to 3.8 cm/week.
‡ Application rate increased to 7.5 cm/week.

point in time when the ecosystem is no longer able to remove nitrogen and the concentration of nitrate-N in soil water at the 120-cm depth exceeds 10 mg/liter. In 1972, when the water application rate was increased from 2.5 to 3.8 cm/week, the forest ecosystem renovation system collapsed and the soil water mean annual nitrate-N concentration increased significantly to 23.9 mg/liter in the mixed hardwood stand and to 21.8 mg/liter in the red pine plantation. However, it should also be noted that some of this increase in nitrate-N leaching was due to tropical storm "Agnes." During the period 21–25 June 1972 there was a total of 24.05 cm of rain. This large amount of rainfall also significantly increased the mean annual concentration of nitrate-N in the soil water of the control forest (0.1 to 4.7 mg/liter). The increased application rate was applied again in 1973 and the results obtained are more indicative of what might happen under normal climatic conditions. Waste water renovation was still unsatisfactory, however, the mean annual nitrate-N concentration in soil water was only 14.7 and 13.7 mg/liter in the hardwood forest and red pine plantation, respectively. During the period 1974 to 1977 the application rate was reduced to 2.5 cm/week. It is quite obvious that ecosystem recovery after chronic applications of waste water is extremely slow. Mean annual nitrate-N concentration remained above 10 mg/liter until 1976 when it decreased to 9.8 mg/liter in the red pine plantation and until 1977 when it decreased to 9.4 mg/liter in the mixed hardwood forest.

Renovation to drinking water quality of nitrate-N was unsatisfactory when waste water was applied in a similar red pine plantation at a higher rate (5 cm/week with a total annual nitrogen loading of appoximately 310 kg N/ha). Results given in Table 12 indicate that this forest ecosystem was only able to satisfactorily renovate waste water during the first 4 years of operation (1963 to 1966). Mean annual concentration of nitrate-N in soil water gradually increased from 3.9 to a peak of 24.2 mg/liter in 1969. In November of 1968, a snow storm accompanied by high winds results in a complete blowdown of the plantation. In 1969 the area was clearcut and all trees were removed. Sewage effluent irrigation was continued and immediately a dense cover of herbaceous and shrub vegetation developed. With the development and growth of this perennial herbaceous vegetative cover, the mean annual concentration of nitrate-N in the soil water decreased from 24.2 mg/liter in 1969 to 8.3 mg/liter in 1970 and to 2.9 mg/liter in 1971. Increasing the application rate from 5.0 to 7.4 cm/week in 1972 increased the nitrate-N concentration in the soil water to 14.5 mg/liter. Even though this concentration exceeds 10 mg/liter, it is obvious that the new developing ecosystem composed of invading pioneer species of herbaceous and tree vegetation was very efficient in renovating waste water. In 1972, tropical storm "Agnes" increased the mean annual concentration of nitrate-N in the soil on the control area from 2.6 to 6.0 mg/liter. On the irrigated area, in 1973, with the increased application rate under normal climatic conditions, the nitrate-N concentration in soil water was only 8.7 mg/liter. It is obvious that the pioneer vegetation ecosystem was able to recover quickly from the chronic applications of waste water and that the renovation efficiency of the new ecosystem is much greater than the original red pine ecosystem. Even though the red pine ecosystem was very inefficient in renovating the waste water during the period of 1963 to 1969, reaching a peak concentration of 24.2 mg/liter of nitrate-N in soil water, the new developing pioneer vegetation ecosystem was extremely efficient, as indicated by the fact that mean annual nitrate-N concentration in the soil water was only 3.7 mg/liter in 1977. This is quite significant when one considers that almost 21 m of sewage effluent had been applied on this area as of 1977. The results obtained from this area dramatically illustrate the interrelationship between the application rate, the type of vegetation, and the system of management.

The white spruce-old field forest ecosystem has been somewhat exceptional in terms of nitrogen renovation in comparison to the other forest ecosystems. Waste water has been applied in this area during the growing season at the rate of 5 cm/week with excellent renovation. Average annual nitrogen loading was 310 kg N/ha during the 16 years except from 1972 and 1973 when nitrogen loading was increased to 430 kg N/ha. It received the highest application rate on the Hublersburg soil and yet has consistently maintained nitrate-N concentration in soil water below 10 mg/liter throughout the period of 1963 to 1971. Increasing the application rate in 1972 resulted in a slight increase in concentrations of nitrate-N in the soil water. However, the ecosystem quickly recovered. Average leaching losses of N at the 5.0-cm/week irrigation rate was 109 kg N/ha per year or 35%. At the increased irrigation rate (7.5 cm/week) the leaching loss of N was 323 kg/ha per year or 75%. In 1963 at the start of the project the area was primarily an open field with a few scattered white spruce saplings (1 or 2 m in height).

Although the trees are now more than 9 m in height, the spruce stand is still sparse with fairly large open areas occupied by perennial herbaceous vegetation and shrubs. Much of the renovation efficiency of this forest ecosystem must be attributed to the dense herbaceous vegetative cover. Average annual dry matter production of this herbaceous cover is approximately 6,000 kg/ha, with an average annual nitrogen uptake of 120 kg N/ha. It appears that the annual and perennial vegetation that occupy these open areas during the growing season (irrigation period) provide temporary storage for nitrogen and hence reduce the nitrate-N leaching losses. In the fall, vegetation growth ceases and nitrate-N is again available for leaching. However, since irrigation has ceased by this time, the concentration of nitrate-N in soil water remains at an acceptable level. The desynchronization effect of nitrate-N application, vegetation utilization, and soil water leaching is one of the primary factors contributing to the renovation efficiency of this ecosystem.

Satisfactory renovation was not achieved with year-round application of waste water in a mixed hardwood forest on a sand loam soil at an application rate of 5 cm/week. Results indicate that irrigation throughout the entire year of forest ecosystems on sandy soils with sewage effluent is not feasible. Mean annual concentration of nitrate-N in soil water continually increased, reaching a peak within 5 years (1970) of 42.8 mg/liter. During the study period unknown amounts of liquid digested sludge were periodically injected into the sewage effluent and spray irrigated on the area. These sludge applications probably account for the unexplained fluctuations in the mean annual nitrate-N cncentrations in the soil water during the period 1968 to 1971. The increase in nitrate-N concentration in soil water in 1972 was partially the result of tropical storm "Agnes." At the end of the growing season in 1974 it was decided to cease sewage effluent irrigation in this forest ecosystem and to evaluate the rate of ecosystem recovery in terms of nitrate-N renovation efficiency. Within 1 year the mean annual concentration of nitrate-N in soil water decreased from 14.3 to 9.0 mg/liter. In 1976 and 1977 sewage effluent was again applied during the growing season at the rate of 5.0 cm/week. Results indicate that the forest ecosystem is again providing satisfactory renovation of the waste water. Nitrate-N concentrations of percolating water at the 120-cm soil depth were below 10 mg/liter (4.8 mg/liter in 1976 and 5.1 mg/liter in 1977).

All of the forest ecosystems at the Penn State project in Pennsylvania have shown a sustained capacity to remove phosphorus as the waste water percolates through the soil. The concentration of phosphorus in the waste water applied varied from 2.5 to 10.5 mg P/liter with an average annual application of 95 kg P/ha. Foliar uptake in the mixed hardwood forest was 9 kg P/ha (9.5%). Soils analyses indicated a significant increase in phosphorus concentrations to a depth of 60 cm on a silt loam soil and to a depth of 150 cm on a sandy loam soil (Richenderfer et al., 1975). In general, the concentrations of soluble P in soil leachate at the 120-cm depth remained near background control levels of 0.05 mg P/liter (Sopper & Kerr, 1978a). In the white spruce-old field ecosystem less than 2% of the phosphorus added by growing season waste water irrigation at 5.0 cm/week during 10 years was leached. In a mixed hardwood forest with a sandy loam soil which was irrigated year-round with waste water at 5.0 cm/week, the phosphorus concentrations in leachate water were somewhat higher. After 8 years of irrigation, average annual concentrations in soil leachate at the 120-cm depth peaked at 0.39 mg P/liter. However, over the same period of time total phosphorus leaching loss was less than 1.2% of the total amount added by waste water irrigation (Sopper & Kerr. 1979).

B. Tree Growth

Tree growth and wood fiber production may be increased by waste water applications. The response, as with agricultural crops, is primarily due to the nutrients supplied by the waste water. Tree growth responses in forest ecosystems at the Penn State project are given in Table 13. Waste water irrigation significantly increased diameter growth of all species except red pine at the high application rate (5 cm/week). The greatest growth response was exhibited by white spruce. After 16 years of waste water irrigation, the average diameter of the white spruce trees was 20.3 cm, in comparison to 10.1 cm in the unirrigated forest; the average height of the control trees was 4.5 m, whereas the trees irrigated with waste water had an average height of 9.2 m.

Eight tree species were also evaluated to determine which species might be best suited for sites to be used as disposal areas for waste water. One- and two-year-old seedlings of European larch, Japanese larch, white pine, red pine, white spruce, pitch pine, Austrian pine, and Norway spruce were planted with some plots irrigated with 5 cm of effluent per week and some plots maintained as a control. First-year survival on the irrigated plot was 88% and on the control plot, 52%. The total height growth of surviving

Table 13—Average annual diameter and terminal height growth in Penn State forest ecosystems irrigated with waste water.

Species	Weekly irrigation amount	Average annual diameter growth	Average annual terminal height growth
	cm	mm	cm
Red pine	0	1.5	42
	2.5	4.3	58
	5.0	1.5	49
White spruce	0	4.5	25
	5.0	10.0	60
Red maple	0	2.6	--
	2.5	13.0	--
Sugar maple	0	2.6	--
	2.5	13.0	--
Oaks	0	4.1	--
	2.5	4.8	--
	5.0	6.0	--

Table 14—Five-year total height growth of tree seedlings irrigated with waste water
at 5 cm/week.

| Species | Total height | |
	Irrigated	Control
	cm	
European larch	207	†
Japanese larch	195	†
White pine	155	64
Red pine	91	49
White spruce	83	67
Pitch pine	83	30
Austrian pine	82	57
Norway spruce	73	43

† No trees of these species survived on the control plots.

seedlings at the end of 5 years is shown in Table 14. Results indicate that European and Japanese larch and white pine had the greatest growth response to waste water irrigation.

Coupled with increased growth, irrigation of trees with municipal waste water also affects the anatomical and physical properties of wood fibers. Studies have been conducted which report that alterations of wood fibers of red pine, red oak, and aspen resulting from waste water irrigation enhanced the value of the fiber as a raw material for pulp and paper (Murphey et al., 1973a, 1973b; Murphey & Bowier, 1975). Although the accelerated growth generally results in reduced specific gravity and wood density, lumber cut from irrigated trees can still be used for most general structural purposes.

C. Trace Metals

One of the major factors limiting the long-range use of sewage effluent and sludge on land has proved to be the potential hazard associated with the presence of certain heavy metals. These metals remain bound in the soil, and thus any problems they may create could be difficult to correct. The inadequate understanding of the potential long-range effects of these metals on animals and humans consuming plants grown on waste water-treated soils has led to a very conservative position on the part of regulatory groups.

The elements of most concern are zinc, copper, nickel, and cadmium. These elements, particularly cadmium, are toxic to animals and man when ingested in sufficient amounts, and their entry into the food chain accordingly should be kept to acceptable levels. The concern about the presence of these elements in waste water is that, after years of repeated application of sludge to soils in quantities sufficient to supply the plant nutrients needed, the heavy metals added in the sludge could build up to levels that would be toxic to crops and, in turn, to animals and man. The heavy metals are strongly bound to the organic matter, particularly in sludges, and the concentrations of the metals usually are too low to result in immediate detrimental effects on crops if the sludges are added in amounts sufficient to meet the nutrient requirements. The fear is that, as the organic matter added in the sludges decomposes over a period of years, the metals will be released in the soil, and they will become toxic unless the properties of the soil are such that the soil binds the metals.

Injury to plants can arise from high concentrations of zinc, copper, and nickel. A number of factors, many of which are only poorly understood, are involved in this toxicity. These include the total amounts of each metal added, the degree of soil acidity of pH, interactions among these metals, the ability of the soil to bind these elements in an unavailable form, and the plant species grown. Since the availability of these metals when present in excess is much lower in approximately neutral soils (pH 7.5 to 7) than in acid soils, the extent of accumulation of the metals in plants can be limited to some degree by liming. Organic matter and clay are the soil constituents that are most important in binding the heavy metals. Accordingly, soils well supplied with organic matter and clay can receive the greatest amounts of sludge high in heavy metals without eventually developing toxicities; sandy soils which contain little clay and which usually are low in organic matter can receive the smallest amounts.

The vegetable crops are the most sensitive to excesses of heavy metals. Most field crops are more tolerant. The grasses are the most tolerant. It seems possible, therefore, that long-continued use of heavy metal-bearing sewage sludges on a given land area might limit the types of crops that could be grown.

Even less is known of the significance to animals and man of the heavy metals in sewage sludges used as fertilizer. Zinc, cadmium, copper, and nickel are all toxic to animals in sufficient concentrations, although experiments with swine have shown that concentrations of copper far higher than those normally found in plants are beneficial to the swine. Evidence now available indicates that crop plants, especially the grains, are injured before they accumulate dangerous amounts of these metals. Experiments with citrus trees indicate that excess copper in the soil is toxic to the trees. The copper is mostly confined to the absorbing roots and it is there that the primary damage is done.

The principal concern is about cadmium. Cadmium is a cumulative trace metal, and its toxicity to animals and humans has been documented, although not as a consequence of application of sewage sludge to soil. Permissible levels of daily intake for humans, however, have not been established. It is known that the cadmium content of most foods is less than 0.05 ppm and that plants will accumulate cadmium from soil treated with sewage sludge even when the soil has been limed to neutrality. More cadmium goes into plant leaves than into the grain, and some leafy vegetables such as spinach can accumulate considerable cadmium.

It seems evident that concern over possible toxicities from application of sewage sludge to agricultural land in certain instances is entirely legitimate and proper. If sewage sludge is proposed for application to agricultural land, it is important that the content of heavy metals be known. If the metal concentrations are medium to high and the sludge is applied repeatedly to the same land, there is reason to monitor the composition of the crop and perhaps of the soil. Alternatively, sludges high in heavy metals might be applied to nonagricultural land. Sludges exceptionally high in cadmium should probably always be used on nonagricultural land to provide an ample safety factor.

Sewage effluent and sludges contain inorganic salts of potassium, sodium, magnesium, and calcium. When a large quantity of waste is applied to supply plant nutrients, more salts may be added to the soil then are leached out by water from irrigation and natural precipitation. Except for isolated locations, this salt buildup is most likely in drier regions. In areas where soils are naturally high in inorganic salts, even relatively small applications of waste water can increase salt concentrations enough to reduce yields.

The salt content of organic wastes is extremely variable and is dependent on the salt put into the process as well as the management of the waste after it is produced. The salinity hazard of using organic wastes as fertilizers can be reduced by: (i) analyses of each waste for salt as well as nutrients so that proper rates of application can be determined, (ii) conjunctive use of wastes and inorganic fertilizers where the salt effect limits the amount of waste that can safely be applied, (iii) management of wastes to preserve the nitrogen content so that the weight of waste and of salt per unit of nutrients added can be kept to a minimum, (iv) continuing education of farm managers concerning salt management, and (v) reduction of the salt in the rations for farm animals to reduce the salt content of manures.

The sewage effluent from municipal waste water treatment plants receiving primarily domestic wastes generally do not contain high levels of trace metals. In addition trees usually are not as sensitive to trace metal toxicity as are agricultural crops.

During the past 16 years secondary treated municipal sewage effluent has been spray irrigated on forestland at various application rates at The Pennsylvania State University. In 1975 and 1976, soil and vegetation samples were collected from all control and irrigated plots for trace metal analysis. The highest application of waste water applied was at a rate of 5 cm/week. At this rate approximately 21.3 m of sewage effluent were applied during the period 1963 to 1976. Soil samples were collected at the 0- to 5-, 5- to 10-, 10- to 15-, and 15- to 30-cm depths. In the old field-white spruce area, results of the analyses indicated that there was a statistically significant increase in zinc and nickel concentrations at all depths in the waste water-irrigated plot. No significant change was found for concentrations of copper, chromium, lead, cobalt, or cadmium. It should be noted that the increases in zinc and nickel concentrations were still within the normal range found in Pennsylvania soils. Analyses of soil samples collected periodically from 1963 to 1976 indicated that there was no increasing trend in the concentrations of chromium, lead, cobalt, cadmium, and nickel

Table 15—Extractable trace metal concentrations in the surface 30 cm of soil in the Penn State white spruce—old field forest ecosystem irrigated for 14 years with municipal waste water.

Year	Cu	Zn	Cr	Pb	Co	Cd	Ni
				μg/g			
			Irrigated†				
1963	0.65 C*	3.23 B	0.09 A	4.61 A	1.80 C	0.04 A	0.56 B
1965	0.95 BC	3.78 B	0.06 A	4.21 A	2.75 B	0.04 A	0.67 AB
1967	1.43 A	6.15 AB	0.04 A	4.45 A	3.21 AB	0.07 A	0.89 A
1971	1.23 AB	6.01 AB	0.07 A	4.19 A	3.73 A	0.05 A	0.54 B
1976	1.92 D	7.48 A	0.01 A	3.29 A	1.87 C	0.03 A	0.73 AB
			Control				
1963	0.93 AB	2.45 A	0.07 A	2.99 A	1.23 A	0.05 A	0.31 A
1965	0.66 B	2.63 A	0.08 A	3.76 A	2.12 A	0.05 A	0.28 A
1967	1.16 A	1.93 A	0.08 A	3.66 A	1.81 A	0.03 A	0.30 A
1971	0.92 AB	3.91 A	0.10 A	3.69 A	1.43 A	0.06 A	0.35 A
1976	2.49 C	2.85 A	0.10 A	3.75 A	0.70 A	0.07 A	0.88 A

* Means followed by same letter are not significantly different from each other at the 0.05 level of significance.
† Application rate was 5 cm/week during the growing season.

(Table 15). There was a slight increase in copper and zinc concentrations in the surface 0- to 30 cm of soil; however, as stated before they were within the normal range found in Pennsylvania soils. Results of foliar analyses of predominate herbaceous vegetation indicated a slight increase in copper concentrations on the irrigated plot (Table 16). Concentrations of zinc, chromium, lead, cobalt, cadmium, and nickel remained the same or decreased on the irrigated plot. Cadmium concentrations in the foliage of wild strawberry was 0.08 ppm in the waste water-irrigated plot in comparison to 0.21 ppm on the unirrigated plot. This decrease in concentration is at-

Table 16—Foliar trace metal concentrations in selected species in the white spruce-old field forest ecosystem irrigated during the growing season with municipal waste water for a period of 13 years.

Weekly irrigation amount	Cu	Zn	Cr	Pb	Co	Cd	Ni
cm				μg/g			
			White spruce				
0	3.31 A*	70.66 A	0.91 A	4.10 A	2.82 A	0.172 A	6.89 A
5	3.39 A	22.40 B	0.85 A	3.11 A	2.50 A	0.089 A	2.91 B
			Goldenrod				
0	9.71 A	85.96 A	1.33 A	6.16 A	2.68 A	0.676 A	4.70 A
5	12.98 B	35.24 B	1.04 B	7.25 A	2.17 B	0.148 B	3.00 B
			Wild strawberry				
0	5.30 A	41.36 A	0.95 A	7.89 A	3.67 A	0.212 A	5.70 A
5	7.39 B	35.66 A	1.12 A	7.64 A	3.20 A	0.076 B	3.68 B

* Means followed by same letter are not significantly different from each other at the 0.05 level of significance.

tributed to biological dilution due to the greater biomass production resulting from the waste water irrigation.

In general, it was concluded that spray irrigation of treated waste water from the University sewage treatment plant did not significantly increase the heavy metal concentrations in the soil or vegetation when applied over a 14-year period. However, it should be noted that the raw waste treated at the plant came primarily from domestic sources. If waste water from sources other than domestic are to be applied on the land, proper management and careful monitoring are essential to avoid soil toxicity problems and hazards to the food chain.

VIII. LAND APPLICATION OF SLUDGE

There has been considerable interest in the use of municipal sludge for the production of agricultural crops. Factors that have contributed to this increased interest are primarily economic. Commercial fertilizer costs have increased, stabilized sludge availability at low costs have increased, and the costs of alternative methods of sludge disposal have increased. In many areas sludge has been suggested as a source of plant nutrients to enhance the production of agricultural crops.

However, sludge contains almost every conceivable element or compound found in wastes from human, domestic, commercial, and industrial sources. It may contain substantial quantities of organic matter, plant nutrients, trace metals, and some potentially hazardous compounds. Some concern has been raised concerning the potential health hazard of using sludges on agricultural land and the potential introduction of trace metals into the human food chain.

A possible alternative is to utilize stabilized municipal sludges to reclaim and revegetate marginal lands or barren lands disturbed by mining activities.

With the renewed interest in coal as a prime energy source, expanded production is forecast for both underground and surface mining in order to meet the increasing demand for affordable energy. By 1 Jan. 1974, surface mining of coal had disturbed over 1,620,000 ha of land in the United States, with less than 607,500 ha properly reclaimed. Strip mining of bituminous coal has affected 31 states. At current production rates, the U.S. Geological Survey has estimated that approximately 2,590 km^2 of land are disturbed annually and that the removal of the remaining recoverable coal resources could result in a disturbed land area covering 183,890 km^2. In Pennsylvania alone, it has been estimated that strip mining of coal has adversely affected 4,827 km of streams and 810 ha of impoundments as a result of erosion and acid mine drainage, besides causing the loss of productive cropland and forestland, wildlife habitat, and recreational hunting areas.

Strip mine spoil banks are highly variable in nature, consisting of soil, subsoil, and unweathered rock. They often provide a harsh environment for seed germination and subsequent plant growth. Usually they are highly acid, devoid of organic matter and plant nutrients, have a low water-holding capacity, and contain toxic levels of such elements as iron, aluminum, and manganese. In order to alleviate these conditions, large applications of lime and fertilizer are required. Often organic soil amendments and mulches are necessary to obtain a satisfactory vegetation establishment. Without a proper vegetative cover, many spoil banks contribute directly to water pollution due to acid drainage production and soil erosion.

During the past 10 years various studies and demonstrations have been conducted to determine the feasibility of using treated municipal sewage sludge for the reclamation and reforestation of mined lands. The results provide insight on rates, techniques, and methods of application and environmental impacts.

One such study reported by Kerr et al. (1979) was initiated in May 1974 in the city of Scranton, Pennsylvania. Heat-dried sludge was obtained from the Scranton-Dunmore waste treatment plant and transported by truck to a burned anthracite refuse bank where it was spread and later incorporated with a farm tractor and cultivator. Sludge application rates were 0, 40, 75, and 150 dry metric tons per hectare. The area was subsequently planted with 10 species of tree seedlings and broadcast-seeded with 5 species of grasses and 5 species of legumes.

Results of the analyses of the sludge indicated that the highest sludge application rate was equivalent to applying 20 metric tons/ha of a 15-4-0 commercial fertilizer. This represents 3,015 kg/ha of N, 831 kg/ha of P, and 38 kg/ha of K. In terms of economics, this would cost $68.00 per metric ton if purchased commercially, which is equivalent to $1,360/ha at the highest sludge application rate.

The sludge applications significantly improved the harsh site conditions. By September 1974 the entire sludge-treated area had a lush vegetative cover. Even after the fifth growing season there was no apparent deterioration of the vegetation cover; in fact, the dry matter production of the herbaceous vegetation more than doubled. This in part is due to the fact that sludge acts as a slow-release fertilizer. Since most of the nutrients supplied by the sludge are in the form of organic compounds, only a certain percentage of such compounds are mineralized and released for plant uptake each year. The single application of sludge provided plant nutrients to sustain vegetation growth for a period of 3 to 5 years. By the end of this period, a permanent vegetative cover was established. The natural process of nutrient recycling is now sufficient to sustain such vegetation.

Average height and diameter growth measurements of the hybrid poplar cuttings at the end of five growing seasons are given in Table 17. The addition of 150 metric tons/ha of sludge nearly doubled the height growth of the hybrid poplar. The average stump diameter of the hybrid poplar in the 0-ton/ha plot was 2.5 cm. In the 150-tons/ha plot the average was 6.1 cm. This indicates that after 5 years the production of biomass more than quadrupled with the addition of sludge. The total domestic production of pulpwood in the United States was approximately 73 million cords in 1972. Based on moderate projections, the demand for domestic production of

Table 17—Average height and diameter growth of hybrid poplar at the end of the fifth growing season.

Sludge treatment	Height	Diameter
metric tons/ha	m	cm
0	2.46	2.5
40	3.41	4.2
75	3.80	4.7
150	4.53	6.1

pulpwood is expected to increase to 160 million cords by the year 2000 (U.S. For. Serv., 1973). The use of sludge on disturbed lands may provide an economical method of establishing and growing wood fiber, thereby returning the land to productive use.

While the benefits of using sludge to reclaim land seems obvious, there is still some reluctance on the part of land owners and local government officials to undertake such projects. In 1977, a cooperative effort was initiated to bridge the gap between available technical information and public understanding. Plans were developed to establish demonstration sites in the bituminous and anthracite coal mining regions of Pennsylvania. The first site was established in May 1977 in Venango County. As reported by Sopper and Kerr (1978b), the site was selected because it was representative of bituminous strip mine spoil banks that have been recontoured after mining without topsoil replacement. Hence, the surface soil material was extremely acid. Several previous attempts to revegetate the area with applications of lime, fertilizer, and seed were unsuccessful and the demonstration site was essentially barren. Four of the approximately 40 ha of disturbed land were selected for sludge application.

To maximize the value of the demonstration project, both liquid digested sludge and stabilized dewatered sludge were used. The liquid digested sludge was obtained from Farrell and Oil City, and the dewatered sludge from Franklin and Oil City. At the Franklin waste treatment plant, the sludge is dewatered by centrifuging, and at the Oil City plant, the sludge is dewatered by spreading on sand drying beds.

In May 1977 liquid-digested sludge was hauled to the site, transferred to a vacuum tank liquid manure spreader, and applied. One ha received 10.5 dry metric tons/ha and 1 ha received 6.9 dry metric tons/ha of solids. During the same period, dewatered sludge was transported by coal trucks to the site and spread with manure spreaders. One ha received 183.7 dry metric tons/ha and 1 ha received 89.6 dry metric tons/ha of solids. Immediately after spreading, the sludge was incorporated into the surface spoil material with a disc. All sludge-treated areas were then broadcast seeded with a mixture of two grasses and two legumes. A straw mulch was applied at the rate of 3.8 metric tons/ha.

A monitoring program was established for 3 years following sludge application. This program included annual sampling of vegetation and spoil, monthly sampling of water from ground water wells and adjacent lakes, and monthly sampling of leachate water at the 0.9-m depth. Results indicated that there was no detrimental effect to the ground water, vegetation, or spoil due to the sludge application. Four months after the sludge applications, a complete lush vegetative cover existed on all sludge-treated areas. The surrounding spoil bank areas, which previously had been treated with lime and commercial fertilizer, essentially remained barren with only sparse vegetation present.

The results of these studies indicate that properly treated municipal sludge is a valuable resource. This waste product can be used beneficially to revegetate bituminous strip mine spoil and anthracite refuse banks throughout the Appalachian region. This ultimately restores them to an aesthetically acceptable and productive state without adverse environmental impact.

IX. WATER QUALITY MONITORING

As with any waste water treatment facility, a comprehensive monitoring program will be required to ensure that environmental degradation is not occurring. Some monitoring requirements are similar to those required for conventional systems. One example of this is the monitoring of water quality at various stages in the process prior to application. Other monitoring requirements are generally unique to land application systems and these are the only ones mentioned here.

a. Renovated Water—The monitoring of renovated water may be required for either ground water or recovered water, or both. Recovered water may include runoff from overland flow or water from recovery wells or under drains.

b. Ground Water—Water quality parameters that should be analyzed in the ground water include: (i) those normally required for drinking water supplies, (ii) those that may be required by regulatory agencies, and/or (iii) those necessary for system control.

c. Recovered Water—Monitoring requirements for recovered water will depend on the disposition of the water. If the water is to be discharged, the parameters to be analyzed must include those required by regulatory agencies. If the water is to be reused, analysis of additional parameters may be required by cognizant public health agencies. Monitoring of the flow rate of recovered water may be important for system control and also may be required as a result of water rights considerations.

d. Vegetation—When vegetation is grown as a part of the treatment system, monitoring may be required for the purpose of optimizing growth and yield. Conventional farm management techniques would generally apply; however, in many cases special factors must be considered because of the normally higher hydraulic loading rates.

For some systems a more detailed vegetation monitoring program may be required in which the uptake of certain elements is analyzed. This analysis would generally be required only in cases where potentially toxic constituents are present in the waste water in abnormally high concentrations.

e. Soils—In almost all cases, the application of waste water to the land will result in some changes in the characteristics of the soil. Consequently, some type of soil monitoring program will be necessary for most systems with at least annual sampling recommended. Characteristics that are commonly monitored are salinity, pH, and potential toxic metal concentrations.

X. PLANNING

A community interested in recycling sewage effluent and/or sludge on the land is faced with a multitude of considerations which must be evaluated before a well-managed program can be established. The process of planning a land application system begins with the collection of basic data on the chemical and physical qualities of the waste water and sludge. This is usually followed by site selection and evaluation of potential sites in relation to soils, geology, hydrology, topography, and land use. Site accessibility and proximity to the treatment plant must also be considered.

The general climate of the area must also be considered, particularly in relation to the design and operation of the system. Information on precipitation, evapotranspiration, temperature, and wind must be evaluated to determine (i) length of growing season, (ii) waste water hydraulic loading rate, (iii) number of days waste water and sludge can be applied, and (iv) storage requirements. If year-round operations are planned, winter temperature conditions and incidence of frozen soil must be considered.

The design and operation of a specific land application system will depend upon management goals. Although basic design goals are the same for all systems (waste water and sludge utilization and renovation with minimum environmental damage), design procedures will differ for systems being developed for agricultural land, forestland, or for the reclamation of barren disturbed land.

Planners should also be familiar with all local, state, and federal regulations and guidelines related to land application of waste water and sludge. Most state regulatory agencies have issued either specific regulations, guidelines, or informational bulletins.

Throughout the planning stages, an effort should be made to obtain the support of local officials, land owners, and the general public. Securing and maintaining local support is essential to the successful implementation of a project. Programs should be developed which will encourage public participation and promote a public awareness of the land treatment technology. Public resistance to land application projects usually results from lack of information or misinformation. Open communication and exchange of information between the public, local officials, planners, and design engineers is one of the best ways to assure acceptance and approval of a potential land treatment system.

XI. SUMMARY

Land application of municipal waste water and sludge can result in multiple benefits. Waste water and sludge can provide the necessary moisture and plant nutrients for maximum crop production. Simultaneously the plant-soil-microorganism ecosystem can adequately accept these waste products and alter them to an environmentally acceptable state. In general, no problems should be encountered if current state and federal guidelines are followed in the design of all land application systems.

ACKNOWLEDGMENT

Research reported here is part of the program of the Waste Water Renovation and Conservation Project of the Institute for Research on Land and Water Resources, and Hatch project no. 2214 of the Agricultural Experiment Station, The Pennsylvania State University, University Park, Pennsylvania. Partial support was also provided by the Office of Water Research and Technology, USDI, as authorized under the Water Resources Research Act of 1964, Public Law 88-379, and by the Pinchot Institute for Environmental Forestry Research, Forest Service, USDA. Portions of this research were also supported by the Bureau of Mines, USDI, under Grant no. G0133133 and the USEPA under Grant no. S-804511-01.

LITERATURE CITED

Buswell, A. M. 1928. The depth of sewage filters and the degree of purification. Bull. no. 26, Div. of State Water Surv., State of Illinois.

Kerr, S. N., W. E. Sopper, and B. R. Edgerton. 1979. Reclaiming anthracite refuse banks with heat-dried sewage sludge. *In* W. E. Sopper and S. N. Kerr (ed.) Utilization of municipal sewage effluent and sludge on forest and disturbed land. Pennsylvania State Univ. Press, University Park, Pa.

Murphey, W. K., and J. J. Bowier. 1975. The response of aspen to irrigation by municipal wastewater. Tappi 58(5):10–11.

Murphey, W. K., R. L. Brisbin, and A. P. Binotto. 1973a. Tracheial properties of red pine stem and crown wood from trees irrigated with sewage effluent. Bull. 789. Pennsylvania Agric. Expt. Stn., University Park, Pa.

Murphey, W. K., R. L. Brisbin, W. J. Young, and B. E. Cutter. 1973b. Anatomical and physical properties of red oak and red pine irrigated with municipal wastewater. p. 295–310. *In* Recycling treated municipal wastewater and sludge through forest and cropland. The Pennsylvania State Univ., University Park, Pa.

Rafter, G. W. 1899. Sewage irrigation, Part II. U.S. Geolog. Surv. Water Supply and Irrig. Pap. no. 22.

Richenderfer, J. L., W. E. Sopper, and L. T. Kardos. 1975. Spray irrigation of treated municipal sewage effluent and its effect on chemical properties of forest soils. USDA For. Serv. General Tech. Rep. NE-17. Northeast. Forest Exp. Stn., Upper Darby, Pa. 24 p.

Sopper, W. E., and S. N. Kerr. 1978a. Utilization of domestic wastewater in forest ecosystems —The Pennsylvania State University Living Filter Project. p. 333–340. *In* Land treatment of wastewater, Vol. 1. U.S. Army Corps of Eng., Cold Regions Res. and Eng. Lab., Hanover, N.H.

Sopper, W. E., and S. N. Kerr. 1978b. Utilization of municipal sludge for strip-mined land reclamation. p. 230–239. *In* Acceptable sludge disposal techniques. Inf. Transfer, Inc., Rockville, Md.

Sopper, W. E., and S. N. Kerr. 1979. Renovation of municipal wastewater in eastern forest ecosystems. *In* W. E. Sopper and S. N. Kerr (ed.) Utilization of municipal sewage effluent and sludge on forest and disturbed land. The Pennsylvania State Univ. Press, University Park, Pa.

Thomas, R. W. 1973. Land disposal II: An overview of treatment methods. J. Water Pollut. Control Fed. 45:1476–1484.

U.S. Environmental Protection Agency. 1977. Process design manual for land treatment of municipal wastewater. EPA 625/1-77-008. Washington, D.C. 502 p.

U.S. Forest Service. 1973. The outlook for timber in the United States. For. Resour. Rep. no. 20. USFS, Washington, D.C. 367 p.

Wood, G. W., P. J. Glantz, H. Rothenbacher, and D. C. Kradel. 1975. Faunal response to spray irrigation of chlorinated sewage effluent. Res. Pub. no. 87. Inst. for Res. on Land and Water Resour., The Pennsylvania State Univ., University Park, Pa. 89 p.

27   Subsurface Applications of Sewage Effluent

JOHANNES BOUMA

Soil Survey Institute
Wageningen, The Netherlands

I. INTRODUCTION

On-site subsurface soil disposal of septic tank effluent is the most common means of domestic liquid waste treatment in unsewered areas. As of 1970, there were more than 16 million private septic systems in use in the United States. The use of these systems has been increasing at a rate of about 500,000 new systems per year. But a large number of people still do not have satisfactory waste systems. About 3 million households use privies or directly discharge their untreated sewage. Besides, many existing septic systems are malfunctioning because they contaminate ground or surface waters.

Increased emphasis on environmental quality and public health calls for satisfactory treatment and disposal of domestic liquid wastes for *all* homes in unsewered areas. This need is reflected in regulatory codes which vary widely among different states and often go only so far as to limit the use of the traditional on-site disposal system to soils which are more or less arbitrarily defined as being suitable (USDHEW, 1967). Recent advances in soil physics, soil chemistry, microbiology, and engineering allow a more specific definition of practical problems and of technical solutions.

The discussion in this chapter will emphasize the comprehensive nature of the problem which not only involves technical aspects relating to many different disciplines, but also economic, social, and regulatory considerations. Technical aspects of infiltration and disposal to be discussed are summarized in flow sheets (presented later as Fig. 5a and 5b).

II. SOIL LIMITATIONS USING CURRENT CRITERIA FOR THE CONVENTIONAL SYSTEM

The conventional system for on-site disposal and treatment of domestic liquid waste consists of a septic tank followed by a subsurface seepage bed or trench (Fig. 1).

The septic tanks' primary purpose is to keep the soil absorption field from becoming clogged by solids suspended in the raw waste water. Waste water is discharged from the home directly into the tank where it is retained

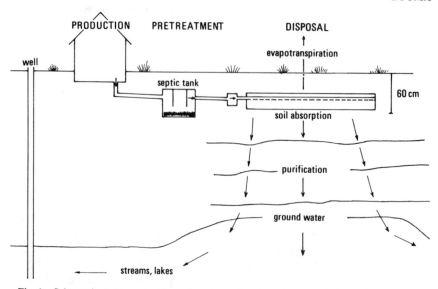

Fig. 1—Schematic cross-section through a conventional septic-tank soil disposal system for on-site disposal and treatment of domestic liquid waste.

for 1 day or more. During this time, the larger solids settle to the bottom and a sludge blanket develops. The greases, oils, and other floating particles rise to the top to form a scum layer (Fig. 1).

In addition to acting as a settling chamber and providing storage for the sludge and scum, the septic tank also digests or breaks down the waste solids. Anaerobic bacteria (organisms that live without oxygen) feed on the sludge, reducing its volume. In the process soluble organic matter is released from the sludge into the effluent. Methane and carbon dioxide gases are also produced and vented from the tank through the house vent. Only about 40% of the sludge volume is reduced in this manner, however, and the accumulated solids must be pumped from the tank once every 2 to 3 years. If the solids are not pumped out, the tank will fill, resuspend the accumulated solids, and wash them into absorption fields where they quickly clog the soil pores.

Effluent coming from the septic tank is not of a high quality nor is it consistent, but this is not necessary if suitable soil is used for final subsurface disposal. The tank does remove up to 60% of the BOD (biochemical oxygen demand) and 70% of the suspended solids. Indicator microorganisms, which are microorganisms that indicate the possible presence of disease bacteria, are not reduced to low levels.

The size of the septic tank system is critical in terms of its performance. Therefore, health codes often require certain minimum sizes as a function of loading. The septic tank effluent is released by gravity flow to a subsurface gravel-filled seepage bed or trench (USDHEW, 1967). Successful functioning of the system is only achieved if the surrounding soil absorbs the volume of effluent produced and if it is purified by processes of filtration, adsorption, and oxidation which occur as effluent moves through the soil pores. Some regulatory codes require that a minimum of 90 cm (3 ft) of permeable, unsaturated soil be available for percolation below the bottom of the seepage area to achieve adequate purification (USDHEW, 1967). In practice, this implies that ground water and bedrock levels should not occur at shallower depth. The determination of bedrock depth may offer problems because large transition zones may exist between what is undisputably "soil" and "rock." More important is the determination of the most relevant level of the ground water. A liquid waste disposal system will have to function during the entire year. The requirement that ground water should not occur within 90 cm below the bottom of the system implies that the highest level of the ground water during the year should be considered. This may offer problems because observations are often made at times when the water level is lower. Soil mottling patterns can be used to estimate the highest ground water level (Soil Surv. Staff, 1951, 1975), but some problems, to be discussed later in this chapter, remain.

In addition to soil requirements, there are also site limitations. Construction on strongly sloping land and on land which is subject to flooding is not allowed, as these conditions may interfere with proper functioning. These soil and site requirements are also used in soil survey interpretations to define soil limitations for on-site liquid waste disposal (USDA, SCS, 1971). "Slight," "moderate," "severe," and "very severe" limitations describe a sequence of increasing difficulties to be encountered when existing septic tank technology is applied to construct on-site disposal systems. Construction in soils having slight or moderate limitations is considered feasible, but soils with severe or very severe limitations generally cannot be used. More specifically, the severe limitation implies that major soil reclamation, special design, or intensive maintenance would be required to construct a satisfactory system. The soil survey approach follows some attractive and realistic assumptions. First, satisfactory on-site disposal and treatment of septic tank effluent is possible by means of soil absorption in soils with slight limitations. However, problems may occur even in these soils due to construction practices or other causes not directly related to the soil. Limitations are therefore always present, although they generally can be overcome with present technology. Second, satisfactory on-site disposal is not necessarily impossible on soils with severe or very severe limitations, but even a professional application of available technology will generally not result in a satisfactory system. The absolute impossibility of on-site disposal is thus never implied, but a practical limit is suggested at least for the present time, because of technology limitations. More recently, the concept of "soil potential" has been introduced (McCormack, 1974), describing the feasibility to overcome limitations by using innovative technology.

Of particular interest, and most subject to criticism and revision, is the determination of soil permeability with the percolation test (USDHEW, 1967; Bouma, 1971; Bouma et al., 1972). This test is useful as a device to rank different soils in their relative capacity to accept clean water from a small cylindrical hole in the soil. But percolation rates are physically poorly defined and cannot be used to predict flow phenomena around seepage areas where the soil is often unsaturated due to clogging or to intermittent application of limited volumes of effluent. However, prediction of such flow phenomena is essential to allow a rational design of soil disposal systems. Hydraulic conductivity and hydrodynamic dispersion data to be discussed in the following sections can be used to physically characterize these flow phenomena.

III. BASIC PRINCIPLES OF SOIL ABSORPTION AND PURIFICATION OF SEWAGE EFFLUENTS

A. Liquid Movement

1. INTRODUCTION

Movement of liquid waste into and through the soil is essential for achieving adequate on-site disposal and treatment. Modern soil physical theory can be used to describe and predict rates of liquid movement, but there are two problems which unfortunately limit the practical usefulness of this approach: (i) soil physical theory describing liquid movement and dispersion in soils is complex and involves considerable mathematical input, and (ii) the theory has been largely derived for and applied to isotropic, homogeneous porous media which often do not resemble natural soils as found in the field. However, a good definition of flow processes in soils must be obtained, because modern systems can only be developed if these data are available. The current level of soil physical knowledge has been well summarized (Baver et al., 1972; Hillel, 1971; Klute, 1973; ISSS, 1976). Attempts have also been made to simplify flow theory allowing use by pedologists (Nielsen et al., 1973; Bouma et al., 1972, 1974a; Bouma, 1975, 1977a). The reader is referred to these publications; only a summary will be presented here.

2. THEORY

Steady flow of liquid through saturated and unsaturated soil can be described by the well-known Darcy flow equation:

$$q = K \cdot (dH/dz) \qquad [1]$$

where q = flux (cm/day); dH/dz = gradient of the hydraulic head (cm/cm), the latter composed of the pressure potential h, due to capillary forces (cm), and the gravitational potential z, due to gravity (cm) ($H = h + z$); and K = hydraulic conductivity (cm/day), which is equal to the flux when the hydraulic gradient is one.

Saturated soil, in which all pores are filled with water, has the highest K value (K_{sat}). A high K_{sat} value as such does, of course, not imply that water moves rapidly through the soil, because this will depend on the hydraulic gradient. Moisture contents below saturation are associated with lower K values because the available water is contained in the smaller pores due to the relatively high capillary forces they can exercise as compared with the large pores, and because smaller pores can conduct much less water than larger ones at a given hydraulic gradient. Soils may be unsaturated as a result of either barriers at the infiltrative surface or an application rate which is lower than K_{sat}. The decrease of K upon decreasing moisture content is characteristic for each soil material, because it is a function of the pore size distribution. K can be presented as a function of the pressure potential (h) or of the moisture content.

Emphasis on this aspect of soil physics is necessary because real flow rates of effluent into and through the soil must be known to allow rational sizing of systems. Unfortunately, a simple flow meter for direct measurement of flow rates in unsaturated soil does not exist. The *indirect* procedure to be followed involves the in situ measurement of pressure potentials with tensiometers (which yields dH/dx). By reading the appropriate K values from a K-h curve, a flux q can be calculated according to Eq. [1]. This approach has been followed to characterize the effects of clogged layers and crusts on infiltration in operating waste disposal systems and to calculate their resistance (Bouma, 1975) as follows:

$$q = K_b \cdot [(H_o + M + Z_b)/Z_b] = (1/R_b) \cdot (H_o + M + Z_b) \qquad [2]$$

where K_b = hydraulic conductivity of the barrier (cm/day); H_o = the positive hydraulic head on top of the barrier (cm); M = pressure potential in soil below the barrier (cm); Z_b = thickness barrier (cm); and $R_b = Z_b/K_b$ = hydraulic resistance (days) of the barrier, which can be calculated if the other terms are known. Knowing R_b, a functional relationship between M and q (the latter is usually equal to K during steady flow) can be found for given values of H_o and Z_b. This allows a *prediction* of the hydraulic effect of barriers on different soils (Bouma, 1975).

These calculations apply only to steady flows in relatively deep and homogeneous deposits. Occurrence of soil horizons with very different K curves at shallow depth below the surface of infiltration may influence the infiltration process considerably, as can be shown by calculating steady flow profiles (Bouma, 1973, 1977a).

Hydraulic conductivity curves are thus essential to predict flow rates. Many methods do exist to measure K (Klute, 1972) but they are laborious and costly. Good experience has been obtained in Wisconsin with the crust test (Bouma et al., 1971; Bouma & Denning, 1972; Bouma, 1977a). Fluxes, as discussed, refer to the velocity of a free water surface moving into the soil and are therefore not a good measure for the *real* velocity of the liquid inside the soil pores, since at least 40% of the soil is composed of the solid phase. An "average" velocity (q^1) within the soil pores can be calculated as: $q^1 = 100\, q/\epsilon$, where ϵ = waterfilled porosity (%). This *real* velocity, is of great interest when discussing purification of liquid waste during soil percolation, because this value can be used to calculate travel times (T) as follows: $T = L/q^1$, where L = length of sample (assuming "piston-type flow"). Slow movement through fine pores implies better contact during a longer time, as compared with fast movement through large pores, and can be expected to result in better purification. This aspect will be further-illustrated in section III-B.

The calculation of the "average" real veloctiy (q^1) and travel time (T), as discussed, is meaningful only in homogeneous soils without root and worm channels and planar voids. But most soils do have these larger pores and then travel times may be much shorter than estimated following this calculation procedure, due to "short circuiting" along larger voids. The following example will illustrate this phenomenon. Assume a 30-cm-high soil core with a diameter of 10 cm, filled with a very slowly permeable clay and one continuous vertical channel with a diameter of 0.5 mm. Total porosity is 50 vol % (consisting mainly of the very fine pores in the clay, since the channel has a volume of 0.01 vol %). K_{sat} of the core was 15 cm/day and was entirely due to the channel (Bouma & Anderson, 1973). Following the standard calculation of q^1, we find: $q^1 = 1500/50 = 30$ cm/day. Calculated travel time = $30/30 = 1$ day. But flow only follows the one channel, so the real $q^1 = 1500/0.01 = 150.000$ cm/day (no movement assumed through the clay). It follows that travel time = 17 sec. The standard calculation leads thus to erroneous results which may highly overestimate the filtrative capacity of the soil, because it overestimates travel time.

These processes can sometimes physically be characterized by applying the theory of hydrodynamic dispersion which determines and analyses breakthrough curves (e.g., Brenner, 1962; Cassel et al., 1974; Anderson & Bouma, 1977a, b; and many others). A detailed discussion of these phenomena is beyond the scope of this text. However, short circuiting of liquid waste through structured soil, either to ground water or to drains which discharge to surface water, can form a serious practical problem which is often not recognized because the effluent continues to be absorbed into the soil to give the appearance that the system is functioning properly.

The following examples may serve to further illustrate these phenomena for natural soils in which large pores follow irregular unknown patterns, in contrast to the previous, hypothetical example (Anderson & Bouma, 1977a, 1977b). Five undisturbed large soil columns with a height of 55 cm and a diameter of 10 cm were sampled in situ in silt loam soils with well-developed subangular-blocky structures in four Wisconsin soil series (average K_{sat} = 9 cm/day). Chloride breakthrough was determined for four different flow regimes by applying a chloride solution to columns filled with untraced water: (i) saturated flow, starting in a saturated soil; (ii) saturated flow starting in a drained soil; (iii) a once a day application of 1 cm; and (iv) flow through a surface crust at a rate of 1 cm/day. Results presented in Table 1 also indicate calculated travel times assuming lack of dispersion, discussed earlier ($T = L/q^1$). Clearly, ignoring dispersion phenomena may result in unrealistic estimates of travel times and in unreliable interpretations of monitoring data. The time which is needed for liquid to flow through a certain volume of soil can be manipulated by chosing a suitable loading regime. Liquid follows the larger pores during saturated flow (at

Table 1—Measured travel times for four flow regimes through large, undisturbed silt loam soil columns with a subangular blocky structure, as derived from chloride breakthrough data. Calculated travel times were based on assumed piston-type flow (no dispersion). Each value is the average of five independent measurements (after Anderson & Bouma, 1977a, b).

Flow regime	Appearance of first trace	
	Measured	Calculated
	hours	
Continuous saturation	18	66
Drained, then continuous saturation	1	--
Daily application of 1 cm	72	594
Infiltration through crust (1 cm/day)	206	594

least if they are vertically continuous), thereby bypassing fine porous, slowly permeable peds through which movement occurs very slowly. Even faster penetration was observed when a large quantity of liquid was applied to a drained soil column in which the larger pores were filled with air (Table 1). Apparently, liquid flowed very rapidly into these air-filled voids, strongly increasing the "short-circuiting" effect. This condition is common in disposal systems when a large volume of effluent is applied by pumping as a once-a-day dose.

Two solutions can be suggested to reduce the effect of "short-circuiting": The loading rate can be reduced to a level where liquid will flow through the fine, rather than through the large, pores. *Flow through the latter occurs only when the fine pores cannot conduct the amount of liquid applied.* Reducing the loading rate to 1 cm/day resulted in a much increased travel time (Table 1). Secondly liquid can be applied through a crust, which allows a steady infiltration with no participation of the larger pores, which remain filled with air all the time. Even though total daily infiltration was identical, travel times through the crusted columns were almost three times longer than those receiving a once-a-day dose when movement into the large pores was still possible (Table 1).

3. INTERPRETATION OF MEASUREMENTS

a. **Measurement of Hydraulic Conductivity Curves**—In situ measurements of hydraulic conductivity curves were made in many Wisconsin soils. Curves in Fig. 2 illustrate some major types of curves that could be distinguished. Coarse porous sands have the highest K values at saturation, but values drop very strongly as pressure potentials decrease at decreasing moisture contents, due to lack of many fine pores. Fine porous clays, on the contrary, have low K values at saturation, but a much slower decrease as the soil becomes increasingly unsaturated. Of particular interest is the curve for silt loam, which shows a high K_{sat} value due to larger structural pores such as worm and root channels and planar voids, but a very sharp drop after these pores have emptied and waterflow has to occur through the fine-porous natural aggregates (peds).

Presentation of one curve for a large group of soils represents a strong

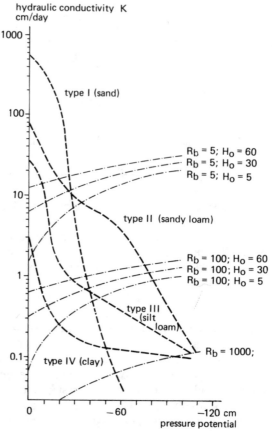

Fig. 2—Four types of hydraulic conductivity curves and a graphical representation of the hydraulic effects of different crusts with varying resistance (R_b in days) and height of ponded liquid on top (H_o in cm).

simplification because no expression is provided for natural variability. Research is in progress to allow expression of K data as a "band" rather than as a curve (Baker & Bouma, 1976). This will allow an expression of the statistical probability that a K value will be higher or lower than any given flow rate, which is most realistic considering field variability. The reported K curves were used to estimate infiltration rates into clogged seepage areas, as discussed in section III-A-2. Perhaps more importantly, K data can also be used to calculate and predict steady and unsteady flow regimes in different unclogged soils as a function of the application rate (see, for example, Magdoff & Bouma, 1974).

   b.   Soil Clogging—Tensiometric measurements were made in situ around operating seepage areas in many soils. Results, which were summarized by Bouma (1975), showed that effluent was ponded in many of the studied seepage systems, whereas the surrounding soil was unsaturated. This indicates the presence of a barrier to flow at the infiltrative surface (section III-A-2) which can be due to biological clogging or to compaction and puddling. Biological clogging is due to the accumulation of suspended solids and associated biological growth under anaerobic conditions. The genesis of the clogging mat, which occurs partly on top of and inside the soil and which has a total thickness of a few centimeters, is a biochemical process which does not occur if sterile water is applied to sterile soil (Allison, 1947). Thomas et al. (1966) studied biological clogging of sand. A sharp decline in infiltration rate coincided with the onset of anaerobic conditions as indicated by cessation of nitrification. Black sulfide accumulation resulted from the anaerobic environment and was not considered to be a primary cause for clogging. The recovery of the infiltration rate after aeration results from destruction of the clogging compounds (e.g., McGauhey & Krone, 1967; Popkin & Bendixen, 1968). Rapid oxidation of the clogging mat can be achieved by applying perioxide (Harkin et al., 1975). The beneficial effect of many commercially available enzymes, etc., has never been scientifically established. Clogging of the bottom area of seepage systems appears to start at the point of inlet and to progress thence, because these systems are fed by gravity flow. The more or less continuous trickle of effluent entering the pipe that leads into the gravel-bed will locally overload the underlying soil, causing anaerobic conditions and formation of a clogged layer. Effluent will then move farther into the system where the infiltration rate into unclogged soil is higher, until, of course, the entire bottom area is clogged (Bouma et al., 1972). The effects of clogging are evident well before complete ponding, as is shown by gradually decreasing infiltration rates (Magdoff & Bouma, 1974). Hydraulic resistances (R_b) were calculated for clogged layers in different soils. Systems in coarse sand, varying in age between 2 and 12 years, had clogged layers with almost identical R_b values of 6 days for the bottom of trenches or beds and 13 days for sidewalls (Bouma, 1975).

This result indicates that the clogging layer in these soils approaches some equilibrium resistance, which supports the results of Kropf et al.[1] All these systems had effluent shallowly ponded in the trench. Results for non-aggregated fine porous sandy loam soil were different. Resistances varied between 34 and 9,000 days for bottom areas (flow rates 1.9 and 0.03 cm/day, respectively) and between 80 and 4,000 days for sidewalls (flow rates 0.6 and 0.04 cm/day, respectively) (Bouma, 1975). Very strong clogging was probably enhanced by the pore size distribution of these soils and by the mechanical instability of larger pores such as channels, but also by the high hydraulic head in one of the systems which may have forced suspended solids deep into the infiltrative surface.

This effect of a high hydraulic head was also observed in other systems. Increasing the head will increase the infiltration through the barrier (Kropf et al.)[1], *but only if the resistance of the barrier remains the same.* This appears not to be so, as discussed. Besides, the increase of infiltration through

[1] F. W. Kropf, K. A. Healy, and R. Laak. 1974. Soil clogging in subsurface seepage systems for liquid domestic wastes. Presented at the 7 Sept. 7th Congr., Int. Assoc. of Water Pollut. Res., Paris.

an unchanged barrier would be relatively minor, as is illustrated in Fig. 2, where the effect of increasing the head from 5 to 60 cm is shown for two crust resistances of 5 and 100 days (see section III-A-2). For example, a barrier with $R_b = 100$ days induces a flow rate of 0.5 cm/day ($H_O = 5$ cm), 0.7 cm/day ($H_O = 30$ cm), and 1 cm/day ($H_O = 60$ cm) in a sand. Corresponding pressure potentials were -42, -40, and -38 cm, respectively. Clayey soils with well-developed natural aggregates ("peds") had only clogging when K_{sat} values were below approximately 10 cm/day, with R_b values of about 20 days (flow rate, 0.7 cm/day). The latter value was also obtained for a series of laboratory experiments using large, undisturbed cores (Daniel & Bouma, 1974). Kropf et al.[1] assumed that the clogging mat would reach some equilibrium resistance which would determine the infiltrative capacity of any soil, independent of its physical properties. This conclusion, is physically incorrect, as can be illustrated in Fig. 2. The effect of a clogged layer is *also* determined by the physical properties of the underlying soil. For example, a clogged layer with a resistance of 5 days ($H_O = 5$ cm: shallow ponding) induces a flow rate of 7 cm/day in a sand, but only of 1.8 cm/day in the clay. Data obtained in the Wisconsin studies show that the conclusion of Kropf et al.[1] is correct for (shallowly ponded) medium and coarse sands where a minimum equilibrium flow rate of 5 cm/day (including a safety margin) appears to be associated with clogging independent of system age (Walker et al., 1973a). But the apparent unpredictability of clogging resistance in many soils makes the clogging phenomenon less attractive from a management point of view. Most preferable is a condition where effluent is intermittently applied to an open, well-aerated soil surface. Such a regime may result in an increase of biological activity, essentially promising eternal life for the infiltration system (Bouma et al., 1975b). Our measurements allow questioning of serial distribution systems, which are sometimes used on sloping sites and consist of a series of trenches in which the first is completely filled before liquid moves into the second, etc. This could give rise to strongly developed clogging due to the high hydraulic heads in the trenches. Unfortunately, no monitoring data are available.

The measurements also allow a judgement as to the effectiveness of sidewall and bottom areas in seepage systems. Neither the exclusive emphasis on bottom areas by many health codes (USDHEW, 1967) nor that on sidewall areas (Winneburger, 1975) appears justified since *both* contribute to flow. This has consequences for system design as will be further discussed in Section IV.

c. Soil Puddling and Compaction—Compaction and puddling of clayey soils was another major reason for ponding of effluent in seepage systems in soils containing appreciable amounts of clay. Compaction is a result of driving on or working in wet soil with a plastic consistancy (Soil Survey Staff, 1951; Bouma, 1969). The individual clay plates will move relative to one another and will absorb water and expand. The mechanism destroys larger pores, such as channels and planar voids which are essential for good infiltration (Anderson & Bouma, 1973). Excavation of seepage trenches and beds in wet clayey soil may form barriers with resistances of about 60 days in silt loams and of 500 days in clays (Bouma, 1975). The problem of compaction was particularly evident in broad seepage beds where construction often involved driving with excavation equipment over the infiltrative surface (Bouma et al., 1975b). Construction of narrow trenches allows no opportunity for such compaction. Compacted soil generally does not allow adequate infiltration rates (Fig. 2) and systems thus affected may fail instantly by releasing effluent to the surface. Slight compaction could theoretically result in only a small and still acceptable drop in infiltration rate. However, even then removal of the slightly compacted layer should be recommended to allow the system to start with a well-exposed, open, soil surface. Only strong drying of compacted soil, which results in cracking, may restore the infiltrative capacity, but this is not practical. Otherwise, the compacted soil must be removed to restore the often adequate infiltrative capacity of particularly many silt loam or silty clay loam soils.

B. Biological Transformations

1. PATHOGENS IN SEPTIC TANK EFFLUENT

Counts of coliform bacteria, fecal streptococci, and pathogens (*Pseudomonas aeruginosa,* staphylococci, salmonellae, and enteric viruses) are high in septic tank effluent but viruses are high only if infections have occurred (McCoy in Bouma et al., 1972; Ziebell et al., 1975a). Salmonellae were detected in 59% of 17 different septic tank pumpout sludges, which shows clearly that septic effluents need to be purified before release to either ground water or surface water (Ziebell et al., 1975a).

It must be assumed that the fecal bacteria in the septic effluent are the survivors of the intestinal flora, and that counts of total coliform (TC), fecal coliform (FC), and fecal streptococci (FS) can be used here, as in standard water analysis, to reflect the possible presence of human pathogens, that is, *Salmonella* spp., *Shigella* spp., etc. Detection of the actual pathogens in a sewage-soil system would be even more difficult than in a sewage-water system. The overwhelming numbers of soil bacteria, as well as their known potential for antogonism, have made it very difficult to detect either the pollution indicators or actual human pathogens in nature. Also the natural presence of fecal bacteria from wild animals and insects and from green plants for at least some of the "total coliform" flora makes the interpretation of counts difficult (Geldreich, 1966).

The picture is complicated by the presence of both coliforms and streptococci on green plants, especially their buds and flowers. Much research has been done to account for this and to devise tests to separate this background pollution from the human fecal pollution which concerns public health. By using counts of fecal coliform (FC) some clarification is possible. Combining such FC counts with fecal streptococcus (FS) counts still further differentiates the true fecal pollution. Geldreich (1966) reports the ratio of FC/FS to be different for human vs. animal pollution. For the fresh feces of man the FC/FS ratio is in the range of 4.4 and for lower animals including poultry the range is 0.1 to 0.6. These ratios are sufficiently different that they may be used as partial evidence of the source of pollution in soils and waters (McCoy in Bouma et al., 1972).

2. REMOVAL OF PATHOGENS BY SOIL PERCOLATION

Removal of pathogens in the soil may be due to various mechanisms, which can be illustrated by analyzing monitoring data and results of column experiments. Clogging zones are very effective in removing indicator organisms. Complete removal within 4 cm below the infiltrative surface was observed in a clogged system in coarse sand (Bouma et al., 1972). The high bacterial population in the crust zone may be due to both trapping by adsorption and to growth. High populations of actinomycetes, *Pseudomonas,* and *Bacilles* were found in the aerated zone below the clogged layer. All three groups are active producers of antibiotics and thus may play an important role in the rapid die-off of the fecal coliforms and streptococci (McCoy in Bouma et al., 1972). *The removal of fecal bacteria from percolating effluent is very strongly a function of the flow regime.* Rapid movement results in short travel times, little contact between soil and effluent, and poor purification. For example, significantly better purification was achieved when effluent was applied at a rate of 5 cm/day to a sand, as compared with a 10 cm/day rate (Ziebell et al., 1975b). Identical results were found when polio-virus type 1 (strain CHAT) was added to septic tank effluent and applied to 60-cm-long sand columns (Fig. 3) (Green & Cliver, 1974). In these experiments 60 cm of sand was completely effective in removing very high concentrations of virus from percolating effluent, if loading rates did not exceed the recommended rate of 5 cm/day. Removal of pathogens involves biological processes and is therefore sensitive to the temperature level. Ziebell et al. (1975a, b) reported decreased removal rates at lower temperatures (5°C vs. the normal 20°C) but also rapid build-up of the clogging layer which changed the flow regime from intermittent to steady, thus improving travel time and removal. Green and Cliver (1974) added virus to some small sand columns. Then one set was placed at 8°C, the other at 20°C while a small daily application of effluent without virus was continued. After 4 weeks at room temperature the sand contained 2.5% of the initially applied virus, whereas the sand at 8°C still retained 57% of the original virus, indicating a much lower inactivation at lower temperature. Inactivitation of virus (loss of ability to replicate in tissue culture) is only one mechanism of removal which must be considered. Also, detention (reduced rate of passage related to the flow regime) and retention (immobilization) play a role. Green and Cliver (1974) and Ziebell et al. (1975b) also demonstrated the high retention power of fresh sand vs. sand which had already been used for percolation during some time. The difference, which is of no great practical significance because seepage systems will have to oper-

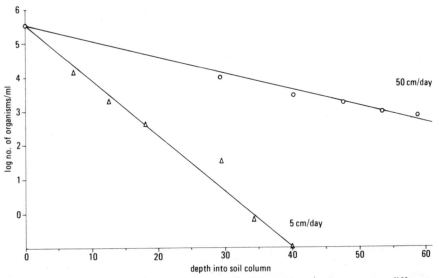

Fig. 3—Removal of poliovirus (added to septic tank effluent) in sand-columns at two different flow regimes (after Green & Cliver, 1974).

ate continuously for a long time, is probably due to the formation of bacterial slimes in "conditioned" sands, shielding part of the mineral fraction and its adsorptive capacity. The results discussed clearly demonstrate that perhaps 60 but certainly 90 cm of sand can be effective in removing pathogenic bacteria and viruses from septic tank effluent if the loading rate does not exceed 5 cm/day and if temperatures do not become too low. The effect of the latter should receive due attention in continuing research by monitoring of ground and drainage water also in cold periods. The process of purification is more complicated in aggregated clayey soils with large pores such as root and wormchannels and planar voids. Intermittent application of effluent, in particular, may result in rapid vertical movement of pathogens along air-filled voids in the drained soil (see section III-A-2). Ziebell et al. (1975b) demonstrated poor purification of effluent following a once-a-day dosing regime of 1 cm of septic tank effluent (spiked with fecal coliform, fecal streptococci, and pathogens (*Staphylococcus aureus* and *Pseudomonas aeruginosa*) into large 55-cm-long undisturbed, uncrusted columns of an Almena silt loam. Complete removal of fecal indicators and pathogens could be achieved by reducing the dosing rate to 3 mm/day (Fig. 4). The difference, as discussed in section III-A-2, is due to relatively slow movement *through* the peds at the low flow rate as compared with relatively fast movement *around* the peds at the high flow rate. Little data are as yet available to estimate flow processes and travel times in natural, heterogeneous soils and systems should be monitored closely to document the possible occurrence of "short-circuiting." This applies particularly to shallow-trench systems (with or without tile drains, to be discussed in sections IV-B-2 and IV-C-2-b).

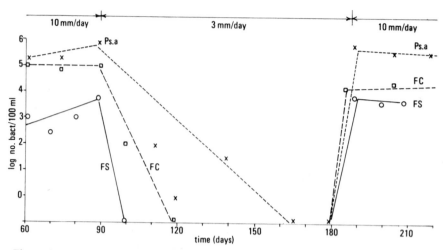

Fig. 4—Removal of fecal indicators and pathogens (as indicated by counts in column effluents) in 55-cm-long undisturbed, unclogged columns of Almena silt loam soil. The microorganisms were added to septic tank effluent (after Ziebell et al., 1975b). *FC* = Fecal Coliform; *FS* = Fecal Streptococcus; *Ps.a* = *Pseudomonas aeroginosa*.

As a general rule, individual applications should be low and should be well distributed over the entire seepage area. Several smaller applications are better than a single large one from a purification point of view. However, this regime can result in early clogging (section III-A-3-b). Some compromise between the conflicting demands of purification and disposal must always be found when designing systems. The compromise will be different in different soils.

C. Chemical Transformations

1. NITROGEN

   a.   Nitrogen Transformation—Nitrogen (N) and phosphorus (P) are the nutrients arising from home waste disposal that are of most concern to authorities. In most cases soil disposal systems are incapable in removing the major portion of the N from the percolating septic tank effluent but are reasonably efficient in removing P. However, where systems are located in sandy soils or in shallow soils over creviced bedrock, removal of both N and P may be grossly inadequate leading to obvious ground water pollution and possible public health problems (Walker et al., 1973a, b). Nitrogen transformations are mainly governed by the aeration status of the soil, which, in turn, is determined by the hydraulic conditions.

   The predominant forms of N in home wastes are ammonium-N (NH_4^+-N) and organic N. The N concentration ranges from 40–80 mg/liter and an average family of 4 contributes about 30 kg N/year (Siegrist et al., 1976; Walker et al., 1973b). Anaerobic conditions prevail in the septic tank and microbial enzymes such as proteases, ureases, and deaminases begin the treatment. The resulting N product contains predominately soluble ammonium (about 75%) and organic N (25%) (Otis et al., 1975). Ammonium in solution undergoes sorption to soil particles almost immediately by cation exchange and can also be immobilized in small amounts by incorporation in microbial or plant biomass.

Under anaerobic soil conditions the NH_4^+ could be leached to the ground water. Eventually, the cation exchange sites in the soil beneath a seepage bed would become equilibrated with the cations in the effluent. The effluent would then move to the ground water with its cation composition essentially unchanged (Magdoff et al., 1974a, 1974b).

Nitrification ($NH_4^+ \rightarrow NO_2^- \rightarrow NO_3^-$) is an aerobic reaction performed primarily by obligate autotrophic organisms and NO_3^- is the predominant end product (Alexander, 1961). It is extremely important in septic systems since NO_3^- easily passes through soils with percolating effluents and, if allowed to accumulate in ground water, both pollution and public health problems can result (Sikora & Keeney, 1975). Immobilization of NO_3^- by plants in the immediate vicinity of disposal fields can occur as indicated by the characteristic lush growth often seen near septic systems. But this amount is minor inasmuch as the amount of N in septic systems greatly exceeds that which can be utilized by nearby plants.

Denitrification is another important N transformation in septic systems. It is the only mechanism by which the NO_3^- concentration in the percolating (and oxidized) effluent can be decreased. Dentrification or the reduction of NO_3^- to N_2O or N_2 is a biological process performed primarily by ubiquitous facultative heterotrophs. In the absence of O_2, NO_3^- acts as an acceptor of electrons generated in the microbial decomposition of an energy source (Sikora & Keeney, 1975). However, in order for the denitrification to occur in soils beneath a home waste disposal system, the N must usually be in the NO_3^- form and an energy source must be available. Therefore nitrification, an aerobic reaction, must occur before denitrification. For these two reactions with opposite aeration requirements to occur in the same proximity require special circumstances (Lance, 1972). Therefore, knowing the aeration conditions beneath a seepage bed will give us information as to the probable N forms present.

Effluent from septic systems located in sands will be undergoing predominantly aerobic reactions with NO_3^- as the N end product. At the observed 25-cm tension below the crust (Bouma et al., 1972), there are significant numbers of pores filled with air and gas exchange with the environment is adequate. Mineralization and nitrification are rapid and complete. Walker et al. (1973a), Magdoff et al. (1974a, 1974b), and Bouma et al. (1974b) have demonstrated this to be the case in field systems located in sands and laboratory column studies employing sands. However, incomplete nitrification may occur in more clayey soils, such as silt loams and clays (Sikora & Corey, 1976).

b. Nitrogen Pollution—Although N is a major element in eutrophication, consideration of the many nonpoint sources of N to waters have resulted in the conclusion that lake protection strategies should emphasize control of phosphorus inputs.

Nitrogen, on the other hand, poses more of a threat to health than to surface water quality. Nitrate (NO_3), the end product of aerobic nitrogen metabolism in soils, and nitrate (NO_2), the intermediate in nitrification, are toxic to humans. This toxicity arises from the hypoxia associated with nitrite reaction with hemoglobin to reduce the oxygen-carrying capacity of the blood. With adults, lethal toxicity is virtually nonexistent. Clinical recognition of NO_3 (NO_2) toxicity in infants has resulted in essentially complete elimination of this problem. However, much less is known of the chronic toxicity (i.e., subclinical effects) of NO_3, and the U.S. Public Health Service recommendation of an upper limit of 10 mg/liter of NO_3-N in potable water is certain to be retained for the foreseeable future (Natl. Acad. Sci., 1972). Toxicity to livestock may also occur, but this appears to be of limited occurrence and primarily associated with feed rather than water (Hazard. Mater. Adv. Comm., 1973).

Recently a number of nitroso compounds have been found to be carcinogenic to laboratory animals, and man is probably also susceptible (S. R. Tannenbaum. 1976. Nitrates, nitrites, and N-Nitroso compounds as environmental hazards: a personal perspective. Am. Can. Soc. Sci. Writers Sem., 26 Mar. 1976. mimeo; Magee, 1971). Significant pollution of ground water below seepage systems was reported by Woodward et al. (1961), Walker et al., (1973b), and Ellis and Childs (1973), among many others.

Dilution by uncontaminated ground water is the only significant mechanism of lowering NO_3-N concentration in the ground water below seepage beds overlying aerobic soils (Walker et al., 1973b, and many others).

2. PHOSPHORUS

a. **Phosphorus Transformations**—Phosphorus in septic tank effluent originates from two main sources, detergents with phosphate builders and human excreta. Siegrest et al. (1976) have estimated that clotheswashers contribute about 55% of all P, and human excreta about 15%. They estimate total P per capita to be about 1.3 kg/year.

The anaerobic digestion occurring in the septic tank converts most of the P, both organic and condensed phosphate forms, to soluble orthophosphate. Magdoff et al. (1974b) and Otis et al. (1975) found more than 85% of the total P in most septic tank effluents studied to be in this form. The relatively small amounts of organic P and also the condensed phosphates present in many septic tank effluents will be converted to the orthophosphate form over a period of time. The condensed phosphates such as meta-, pyro-, and tripolyphosphate will react with soils in a manner similar to orthophosphate (Black, 1970). Median total P concentrations in septic tank effluent were approximately 16 mg/liter (Magdoff et al., 1974b; Otis et al., 1975; Siegrist et al., 1976). At low P concentration (<5 mg P/ml) in the equilibrium solution, the phosphate ion becomes *chemisorbed* on the surfaces of Fe and Al minerals in strongly acid to neutral systems and on Ca minerals in neutral to alkaline systems. As the concentration in the soil solution is raised, there comes a point above which one or more phosphate *precipitates* may form. This can be predicted from a knowledge of the ion activity products (solubility products) if all of the relevant ion activities are known (Beek & DeHaan, 1974). Ion activity products of some of the more important compounds are given by Lindsay and Moreno (1960).

In the pH range encountered in septic tank seepage fields, hydroxyapatite is the stable calcium phosphate precipitate. However, at relatively high P concentrations similar to those found in septic tank effluents, dicalcium phosphate or octacalcium phosphate are formed initially, followed by a slow conversion to hydroxyapatite (Lindsay & Moreno, 1960, Magdoff et al., 1974b). Subjecting a previously well-aerated noncalcareous soil to reducing conditions will almost invariably result in an increase in dissolved inorganic P. This is to be expected as much of the P in soils is bound to ferric iron which is converted to soluble ferrous form under reducing conditions.

The rate at which P is sorbed from solution onto the surfaces of soil constituents has been shown to consist of a rapid initial reaction followed by an important, much slower, reaction which appears to follow first order kinetics (see, for example, Kuo & Lotse, 1973). A detailed discussion of this topic is beyond the scope of this text.

Walker et al. (1973b) determined that P extracted from sandy soils beneath septic tank seepage fields in central Wisconsin which had operated for several years ranged from about 100 to about 300 $\mu g/g$. Madoff and Keeney (1976) reported an immobilization of 121 μg P/g by a sandy soil in a column study which ran for less than a year. Other data of Magdoff and Keeney (1975) show P immobilization to be higher in finer textured soils (307 μg P/g immobilized in silt loam soils).

b. Phosphorus Pollution—There is no evidence that P in drinking water constitutes a threat to human health. Rather, P is of chief concern in relation to surface water quality as it is the nutrient limiting productivity (eutrophication) of lakes and impoundments.

Several cases of significant P contamination in ground water below seepage beds have been reported (e.g., Ellis & Childs, 1973).

3. EVALUATION

Nitrate is formed in nearly all but the heavier textured soils. Phosphorus contamination of ground water would be expected primarily in sandy soils low in organic matter, soils with high water tables, or shallow soils over creviced bedrock. Since some P sorption occurs in all these cases, contamination would not become apparent until the soil absorption field had been in operation for a number of years.

The crucial decision as to whether or not unacceptable ground water pollution with N and P occurs will be determined by (i) local soil and site conditions, (ii) local geohydrological conditions, (iii) the density of systems, (iv) the quality of system construction and maintenance, and (v) the degree of ground water contamination which is considered acceptable. No specific limits can be defined which apply to all soils and sites. But there will be a number of situations where ground and surface water pollution with N and

P form a realistic problem, for example when many systems exist in sandy soils with shallow watertables around small lakes. Then, alternative procedures must be developed to reduce the input of N and/or P, by improving removal or by limiting the number of homesites in a given area. Laboratory experiments to remove nitrates by denitrification and excess P by precipitation have been made (Sikora & Keeney, 1975; Sikora et al., 1976). Results do indicate the technical feasibility of the system, but practical use cannot as yet be anticipated due to the required high maintenance. A field system, which was, however, only operated during the summer, was used successfully in Michigan (Erickson et al., 1971).

IV. ALTERNATIVE SYSTEMS

A. Introduction

The separation between "suitable" and "unsuitable" soils, as made by many health codes (for example, USDHEW, 1967) has a somewhat arbitrary character, if only because of the wide variety of soil and site factors considered and their different relative significance. Also, some factors such as nutrient removal are not considered at all at the present time. The factors of high ground water or bedrock, for example, create different problems and call for a different analysis than the factor of slow permeability or steep slope. A series of separate definitions of critical values for each individual factor, as provided now, may result in a rather inflexible system and may divert attention from the major area of concern, which is to provide adequate on-site treatment and disposal of liquid waste.

An alternative procedure is to define general criteria for adequate on-site soil disposal and treatment to be followed by the description of system designs considered suitable for particular groups of soil and site conditions, each one presenting a unique combination of important factors. *In this concept, every soil is a problem soil.* This is realistic, since many systems in "suitable" soils fail because of poor construction or management. As stated, research is to develop systems which provide good treatment of liquid waste. But this can only practically be realized by not only judging potential soil and site suitability, but by also somehow including an evaluation of the crucial factors of construction and management. The following broad definition for acceptable performance of any one-site soil system is proposed: "Acceptable on-site disposal and treatment of domestic liquid waste implies complete infiltration into the seepage system at all times, followed by transformations during soil percolation to the effect that neither the ground water aquifer nor surface waters are contaminated at any time to a degree that is unacceptable in terms of human health or environmental quality." Limited cost of any system in terms of construction and maintenance must be added as a practical requirement since, in fact, "anything can be done anywhere" if cost forms no limitation.

The general requirements of the definition will be specified in discussing the different systems that were designed for particular soil and site conditions (Fig. 5b shows a schematic representation in terms of a flowsheet). A separation will be made between those systems that can be considered as modified conventional systems and those that are essentially different. Defining disposal systems for particular soil and site conditions, as discussed, could result in regulatory codes in which such systems, defined in detail as a package (Bouma, 1974), would be rigidly required for certain soils and sites. This could leave inadequate room for relevant modifications to be made by qualified engineers and soil scientists. A code should always remain a means, not a purpose in itself. Presentation of modified and new designs in this publication reflects a well-tested state of knowledge. But continued development, modification, and testing is essential! Descriptions of systems will be presented in general terms in this publication. The reader will be referred for more details to other articles.

B. Modified Conventional Designs

1. GENERAL ASPECTS

Conventional designs are currently limited to permeable soils with relatively deep ground water and bedrock levels, on sites with limited slopes. Modified designs apply to such soil and site conditions. The capacity of a soil to accept liquid for an extended period of time can only be judged by using well-defined physical theory, rather than percolation rates (Section III), and a scheme, based on recent research results, will be used to judge this important factor (Fig. 5a). The infiltration rate at saturation, when there is no barrier of any type at the infiltrative surface, is always highest for all soils because all pores contribute to flow. This rate is equal to the hydraulic conductivity at saturation (K_{sat}) if free flow can proceed downwards without obstructions in a relatively deep soil. However, the infiltration rate at equilibrium may be lower than K_{sat} due to decreased hydraulic gradients, if slowly permeable soil occurs at shallow depth below the infiltrative surface. This problem is often eliminated due to the point-source character of on-site disposal, which allows lateral movement away from the system through the subsoil. The maximum infiltration rate in any soil will therefore be assumed to be equal to K_{sat} of the soil horizon in which infiltration occurs. But, soil conditions should always be checked to see if this assumption is reasonable. If not, a modified rate should be defined.

On-site disposal of effluent is obviously feasible only if soils can accept liquid and some minimum infiltration rate is required to allow economical absorption of effluent within a reasonably small area. For example, a large area of 100 m² (1,111 ft²) is needed to absorb 800 liters of effluent per day at an infiltration rate of 8 mm/day, and even larger areas are needed at lower rates. Obviously, economical and technical considerations dictate some minimum flow rate below which construction of a seepage area is not practical. This value, which will be called i_{min} (Fig. 5), and which may be com-

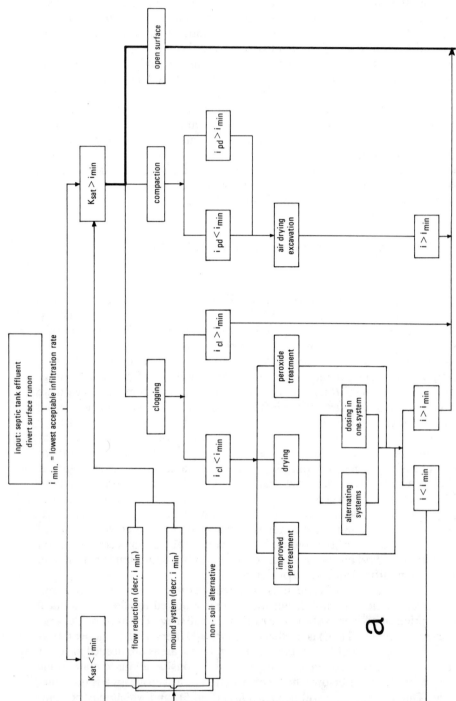

Fig. 5a—Flow sheet illustrating aspects of soil infiltration of septic tank effluent, as discussed in text.

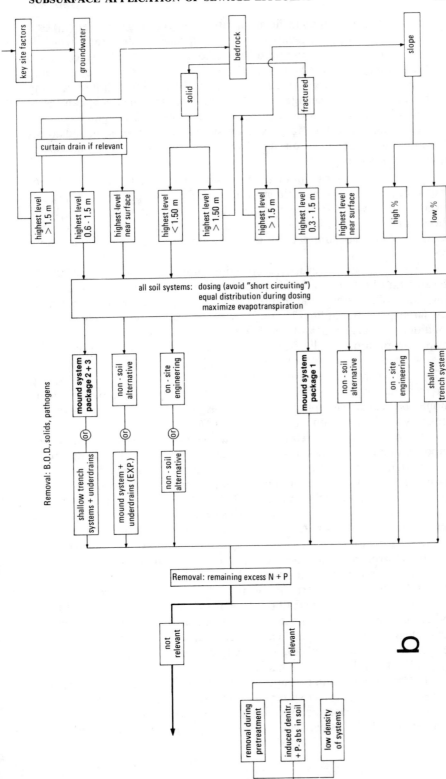

Fig. 5b—Flow sheet illustrating the choice of on-site disposal and treatment systems for different limiting site conditions, as discussed in text.

pared with K_{sat} or with an infiltration rate through a clogged layer (i_{cl}) or a compacted layer (i_{pd}), depends on: (i) the expected loading rate, which is supposed to have been minimized by excluding addition of surface water, (ii) the available suitable land, and (iii) technical considerations regarding construction of very large systems in terms of distribution of liquid, leveling of the bottom of the seepage area, etc. One constant single i_{min} can therefore not be defined, but a value of 1 cm/day may be used as a guide.

The diagram in Fig. 5a presents a summary of aspects related to infiltration, some of which discussed in Section III. The following aspects apply to *all* systems:

1) The amount of liquid to be absorbed by the infiltration system should be restricted to the effluent produced. For example, landscaping can divert surface water from the seepage area and water runoff from roofs should never be piped into the septic tank. Sometimes, curtain drains may be used to intercept (unpolluted) ground water moving towards the system (see Section IV-C).

2) Conditions for evapotranspiration should be optimized to reduce the amount of effluent to be absorbed by the soil. This requires use of shallow absorption systems and planting of grasses or shrubs which can evaporate large quantities of liquid in the growing season. Unfortunately, climatic conditions in large parts of the United States do not allow year-around evapotranspiration of all effluent produced by an average family, as can clearly be demonstrated with physical calculations (Tanner & Bouma, 1975). Statements to the effect that evapotranspiration rates are adequate for total disposal, as reflected by the requirement that seepage systems should be sealed with plastic sheets so as to prevent "pollution of the ground water", are erroneous (Bernhard, 1975).

3) The system by which effluent is applied to the disposal field is very important and determines to a large extent the degree of success of operation, both in terms of extended infiltration and of effluent purification. The traditional system of effluent application uses gravity flow into highly perforated large pipe (USDHEW, 1967). This system results in local overloading and associated poor purification (Section III-B) and progressive clogging (Section III-A-3-b). A new pressure distribution system, using small diameter pipe with few holes was developed which allows equal distribution of effluent over the entire seepage area during each application. The reader is referred to other publications for details (Otis et al., 1974; Converse et al., 1974). Use of these systems, or any other system which realizes equal distributions of relatively small dosages of effluent, is recommended in all soil disposal systems, because local overloading with associated problems of rapid clogging and poor purification are avoided, whereas relatively long periods of aeration are introduced for all parts of the seepage area (see also section IV-B-2, following).

4) Construction and management practices of disposal systems should be well controlled. Perfect system designs can be ruined by poor construction practices, for example by working in wet clayey soils (Section III-A-3-c). Even well-built systems can malfunction if the septic tank is not peri-

odically pumped out or if the loading rate is drastically increased, for example after enlarging a house, without also increasing the size of the system.

2. THE SHALLOW-TRENCH SYSTEM

The shallow-trench system is ideal in "permeable" soils ($K_{sat} > i_{min}$, see Fig. 5a) with "deep" ground water and bedrock (see section IV-C). The infiltrative surface should preferably be shallow, for example between 45 and 60 cm below the soil surface for the following reasons:

1) K_{sat} values are generally highest in the upper, most porous, part of the soil.

2) Organic matter contents and the associated adsorptive capacity decrease sharply with depth, but may still be significant near the surface.

3) The activity of earthworms and other soil fauna, which may be crucial to maintain an open infiltrative surface (Section III-A-2) is usually highest in the upper part of the profile where nutrients are to be found.

4) Plant roots of vegetation surrounding the seepage area can still remove significant quantities of effluent from shallow systems, whereas this is more difficult at greater depth where rooting intensity is lower.

5) Soils start to dry in spring at the soil surface and drying proceeds gradually downwards. Construction practices at shallow depth where the soil tends to be drier will result in less puddling than construction at greater depth where moisture contents will remain higher for a longer time.

6) The distance from a shallow system to the soil surface and the atmosphere is relatively small, offering better opportunities for diffusion of air to soil surrounding the seepage system, as compared with deep systems.

7) Freezing of the seepage area in winter does not seem to occur when the 20-cm-high gravel-filled trench is covered with at least 30 cm of soil (Bouma et al., 1974b). This may be partly due to the relatively high temperature (10°C) of the effluent applied.

Shallow trenches, with a width not exceeding about 90 cm, are preferred over beds which are often much wider. Beds may offer more opportunities for bottom-compaction (Section III-A-3-c) and less sidewall area for lateral liquid absorption. The sidewall area is active in absorbing effluent (Winneburger, 1975), but so are bottom areas (Section III-A-3-b). Exclusive emphasis on sidewalls results in systems with narrow deep trenches, thereby losing many advantages of the shallow systems, as discussed. This conclusion is particularly relevant for humid climates, where lateral hydraulic gradients in wet periods may become inadequate to allow lateral movement from trenches (Bouma, 1975). Sizing on bottom area is therefore appropriate in these areas, thereby considering sidewalls_as extra capacity, useful when needed.

Equilibrium flow rates of 5 cm/day in coarse and medium sands allow sizing of bottom areas according to this rate. This implies that systems may be expected to have adequate size even if clogging would occur following dosing of effluent. Unfortunately, such equilibrium flow rates are not as well defined for other soils (Bouma, 1975; Section III-A-3-b); and then ponding of effluent often indicated failure ($i_{cl} \leq i_{min}$ in Fig. 5a). The main goal must then be to avoid ponding conditions while maintaining the attractive relatively low, constant, flow rates, associated with clogged systems. Intermittent application of effluent may avoid ponding conditions (section IV-B-1, point 3).

The optimum daily loading rate for shallow-trench systems in soils other than sands is still subject to experimentation. Rates of 3 cm/day have been applied successfully in sandy loam and silt loam soils (conductivity types II and III in Fig. 2). Higher rates should be avoided because flow along ped faces may result in short-circuiting of effluent and poor purification (section III-B).

Effluent may periodically be applied to one system (dosing, Fig. 5a) or two systems may be built, periodically shifting use between the two. Indications are that the former procedure is often satisfactory and most economic. However, it is advisable to leave room for the possible construction of a second system, if the need ever arises. Treatment of a clogged system with peroxide (Harkin et al., 1975), or any other substance which decomposes the clogging mat, may cure the "symptoms" but not the "disease." For example, the effect of such measures are bound to be short-lived in overloaded or poorly maintained systems.

C. New Designs

1. INTRODUCTION

Four broad types of soil and site conditions have traditionally been considered inadequate to allow satisfactory on-site disposal of septic tank effluent. As discussed, these are: (i) the occurrence of high ground water or (ii) bedrock, (iii) low permeability of the soil, and (iv) steep slopes (USDHEW, 1967). New designs, which often represent a further development of established concepts, will be discussed for each of the four types. Sometimes, soils or sites are inadequate due to more than one type of condition, for example in slowly permeable soils with seasonally high ground water levels. Then, the most limiting condition must be selected on which a new design is to be based. Several of the new designs have been described in detail in "packages" of the Small Scale Waste Management Project (Converse et al., 1975a, 1975b, 1975c). The reader is referred to these publications for details.

2. GROUND WATER NEAR THE SOIL SURFACE

a. The Determination of the Highest Level of Ground or Perched Water Tables—The ground water level or ground water table can be defined as a generally planar surface in the soil, often approximately parallel to the soil surface, where all pores are filled with water at atmospheric pressure. These pressures become positive at greater depth and negative at depths closer to the soil surface. Some soils with fine pores may still be completely saturated at low negative pressures, because of a high air-entry value, indicating that water cannot easily be displaced by air. However, technically such soil is considered to occur *above* the ground water level. Most often, all pores below the ground water level are filled with water, forming the ground water aquifer.

However, different soil types are found with shallow, slowly permeable soil horizons overlying permeable deposits with a deep ground water level. Saturated conditions may occur in wet periods on top of and in the slowly permeable soil horizon which, in turn, still rests on unsaturated soil with deep ground water. Such a shallow water table is often referred to as a *perched* water table. It often occurs only seasonally and differs from the real ground water table in that saturated conditions do not extend all the way downward. In fact, the perched water table only exists because of the inadequate vertical conductivity at saturation of the slowly permeable horizon. The saturated condition is then dynamic in that water moves downward through the slowly permeable horizon at gradients which are often close to 1 cm/cm (gravity flow). Lateral movement over the horizon may complicate this picture, but the condition remains essentially different from the one existing in one continuous ground water aquifer, in which movement in the saturated zone depends on varying lateral and vertical gradients which often are relatively small, thus presenting a more static and stagnant condition. The latter offers less opportunity for contact between soil and effluent, and thus for associated purification by adsorption and filtration, than constant downward gravity-flow of effluent from a perched water table. Ziebell et al. (1975b) demonstrated good removal of fecal indicators from effluent during such flow through a 55-cm-long vertical soil core (K_{sat} = 5 cm/day).

Research results largely support the general assumption that saturated soil is unsuitable as a medium for waste disposal and treatment. Inadequate removal of fecal indicators and pollution of ground water was reported in a sand-system in which the seepage trench was located in the ground water aquifer (Walker et al., 1973b). However, others report adequate removal under such conditions (Ingham, 1976; Bouma, 1977b). Still, adding raw septic tank effluent to relatively static ground water aquifers will result in the presence of a strongly polluted volume of liquid near the soil surface, subject to surfacing under adverse conditions. Besides, patterns of ground water movement are often very difficult to predict due to the heterogenity of natural soils, and the fact that pathogens are not found in some wells placed around the system does not necessarily mean that they are not present elsewhere (Walker et al., 1973b). Use of ground water aquifers close to the soil surface as a principle medium for waste absorption and purification would therefore seem to include too many risks to be generally acceptable. The current requirement that at least 90 cm of unsaturated soil should occur between the seepage area and the ground water level (USDHEW, 1967) is more acceptable as a general rule because then unsaturated flow results in significant purification *before* liquid enters the ground water aquifer (section III-B). Saturated conditions associated with seasonally perched water tables may present a different picture, because of much better defined vertical movement of effluent to the unsaturated subsoil. But also here effluent will accumulate in the shallow perched water table subject to surfacing under adverse conditions which may be enhanced by lateral flow over the slowly permeable soil horizon. However, in that case curtain drains may be very appropriate to collect unpolluted perched water moving towards the disposal system from adjacent higher areas. The required distance of unsaturated flow can be relaxed to less than the normally required 90 cm under well-studied soil conditions where seasonally perched water occurs and where surfacing is unlikely.

The previous discussion resulted in the definition of a maximum allowable level of the water table in a soil during the entire year, but water tables fluctuate widely and direct measurement of the highest levels, which generally occur in the wet season, is technically not possible in all soils because of obvious economic limitations. Moreover, what may be observed as the highest level in a dry year is not representative for the required level in a very wet year. Indirect criteria such as soil mottling features have therefore been widely and successfully used to *estimate* the highest water levels. Saturation of soil in presence of an energy source for microorganisms may result in reduction of iron compounds. When these soluble compounds are removed by flowing water, the remaining soil has a gray color, whereas the reduced iron may oxidize elsewhere as a red "mottle". Occurrence of gray *and* red spots ("mottling") is considered an indicator for periodic saturation with water, and can be used to estimate highest ground or perched water levels. Some problems may remain in interpreting mottling or lack of it. A few unmottled soils *are* periodically saturated, and occurrence of gray mottles (defined specifically in terms of having chroma's of two or less by Soil Survey Staff, 1975) may not always indicate saturation but negative moisture potentials near saturation (Vepraskas et al., 1974; Vepraskas & Bouma, 1976; Veneman et al., 1976). Despite these problems use of mottling criteria has generally been quite successful to estimate the highest level of naturally occurring ground or perched water.

However, one final complication remains. A relatively large volume of effluent is added to the soil by a disposal system. Natural ground water levels are, of course, established only by natural processes such as rainfall and evapotranspiration. A large rise of natural ground water levels may therefore result from additions of effluent, particularly in soils which have a low lateral permeability and a low air-filled porosity. Calculations can be made to estimate the expected rise of the ground water as a function of system dimensions and loading rate and such calculations are recommended (see, for example, Bouma et al., 1975a). Generally, however, the point-source character of these systems allows good lateral movement of the applied effluent, and consideration of naturally occurring ground water levels, as discussed, in judging soil suitability seems justified in view of the magnitude of all parameters involved.

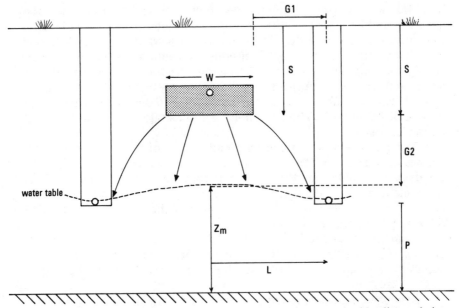

Fig. 6—Schematic cross section of a subsurface shallow seepage trench with adjacent drains, used to illustrate the calculation of required dimensions of the system.

b. Systems: Lowering the Water Table or Raising the System—Two basic approaches can be followed when ground or perched water tables are too high. Either the water level is lowered by tile-drainage for a subsurface system or the system is built above the ground as a mound when water levels remain unchanged.

A schematic cross section of a tile-drained subsurface system is presented in Fig. 6. The bottom of a seepage system with width, W, occurs at depth, S, below the soil surface. Effluent is assumed to flow from the system to the lowered ground water level as indicated. The distance between the drains is $2L$. The height from the drains to some impermeable layer is assumed to be P, and the ground water rises to a height of Z_m below the system, which is separated from the drains by a minimal lateral distance of $G1$ and from the highest level of the ground water by a minimum distance of $G2$ (G dimensions to be selected by purification criteria). Assuming a loading rate of q cm/day and a known K_{sat} of the soil below the system, it follows:

$$\frac{(Z_m^2 - P^2)}{L^2} = \frac{q}{K_{sat}} \text{(Childs, 1969, p. 240).}$$

This approximate equation, based on the Dupuit-Forchheimer assumption, can be used to develop general solutions to the defined problem as to how wide a trench should be built and how deep and how far apart the drains should be placed to allow disposal of effluent at a selected loading rate to a soil with a given K_{sat}. The shallow-trench system (section IV-B-2) is considered optimal in terms of dimensions and depth of the trench ($W = 90$ cm; $S = 45$ cm). The G values which characterize the minimal distances of lateral and vertical unsaturated flow can arbitrarily be defined as 90 cm, so: $L = 135$ cm. A value of 100 cm is assumed for P in the examples but P will vary in different soils. Three examples will illustrate some aspects of this particular design.

Example 1 relates to a constant loading rate of 5 cm/day in a highly permeable soil ($K_{sat} = 500$ cm/day) and a slowly permeable soil ($K_{sat} = 10$ cm/day). Required drain depth (which is equal to $S + G2 + (Z_m - P)$ is the minimal depth of 135 cm in the former case *(S + G2)* and 173 cm in the latter. The lower the K_{sat} of the soil, the deeper the drains should be, and this may present technical problems.

Example 2 relates to loading rates of 5 and 1 cm/day in a slowly permeable soil ($K_{sat} = 10$ cm/day). Required drain depths are 173 and 144 cm, respectively. At a given K_{sat} of the soil, drains can be shallower as the loading rate is decreased.

Example 3 relates to loading rates of 5 cm/day in a slowly permeable soil ($K_{sat} = 10$ cm/day) comparing $G2 = 90$ cm (standard) with values of 60 and 30 cm. Corresponding drain depths are then 173, 143, and 113 cm, which illustrates the obvious fact that reducing the required distance of unsaturated flow results in attractive shallower drain depths.

These systems are attractive from a viewpoint of disposal, but to be "out-of-site" should not imply "to be out of mind." Liquid is discharged at some point from a tile drain and the entire system malfunctions if the quality of that liquid is not satisfactory *at all times.* The analysis of just an occasional sample is inadequate. However, satisfactory purification is much more difficult and costly to document than all too obvious surfacing of effluent on lawns and in basements. Human nature being what it is, one instance was observed by the author where the septic tank was directly connected with the drains, forming a "perfect" disposal system. A schematic cross section of a mound system is shown in Fig. 7. Very detailed descriptions of these systems and discussions of their capacity to purify effluent were presented by Magdoff et al. (1974a, 1974b), Bouma et al. (1975a), and Converse et al. (1975a, 1975b, 1975c). Effluent is periodically pumped into a seepage system inside a mound, preferably composed of a medium-sized sand which acts as a (covered) sandfilter. The height of the sand between the seepage area and the original soil surface can be 60 or 30 cm, depending on the level of the highest ground water. There is no clear discharge point, as in tile-drained systems, because the underlying soil absorbs the effluent which flows laterally away into the ground water. Small elongated trenches are required in mounds over slowly permeable soils to allow this lateral movement without causing too high a rise of the water table (Bouma et al., 1975a). Mound systems are often preferable to subsurface trenches with tile drains due to a number of considerations: (i) the topsoil, with relatively high

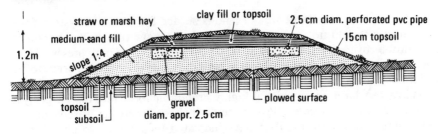

CROSS SECTION A – A

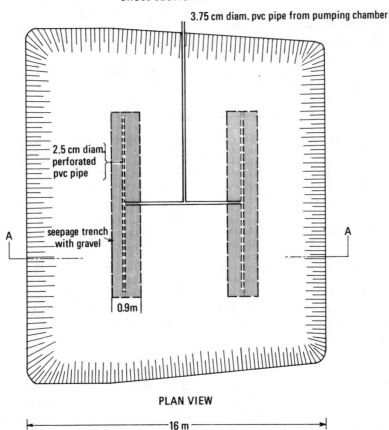

PLAN VIEW

Fig. 7—Cross section and plan view of a mound system for on-site disposal and treatment of septic tank effluent in slowly permeable soils with seasonally high ground water tables (after Converse et al., 1975b).

organic matter contents, is used rather than bypassed for treatment of the liquid waste; (ii) digging in the soil, with all possible associated problems of compaction, etc., is unnecessary; (iii) infiltration occurs in the sand of the fill which allows adequate sizing and this avoids surfacing of effluent if clogging would occur at some future time (section III-A-2-b); (iv) the requirement to have 30 to 60 cm of sand below the seepage trench in the mound implies that a large area of land is needed for the entire system since side slopes should not be too steep, and the seepage trench in the mound should be covered with at least 30 to 45 cm of soil. This may present practical problems if not enough land is available, but these would seem to be minor as compared with the increased potential for absorption and purification in a very large area, which is highly preferable to surface discharge by a drain pipe. Mound systems have successfully been applied in Wisconsin and elsewhere and monitoring data have indicated their ability to absorb and treat domestic liquid wastes. The possibility to construct a mound system with underdrains for very poor site condition can be considered (Fig. 5b). No experimental data on such a system is as yet available. All these systems, including the tile-drained subsurface trench systems, are expensive, at a cost varying between $2,800 and $5,500 (average cost, $3,600). However, when constructed properly, these systems may function for a very long time and then cost figures per year are relatively low.

3. BEDROCK NEAR THE SOIL SURFACE: MOUNDS

A distinction must be made between creviced, permeable bedrock such as many limestones, and massive impermeable types such as shales. Criteria for new systems for both conditions are entirely different. The problem of shallow soil over permeable bedrock is one of inadequate purification due to the occurrence of only a thin layer of soil on top of the bedrock. The obvious solution is to add sand to the existing soil by building a mound system, to the effect that the vertical distance of unsaturated flow is adequate for purification (excluding nitrate removal). Column studies and experimental field systems have indicated successful operation of systems consisting of 45 cm natural soil and 60 cm of sand below the seepage field in the mound (Magdoff et al., 1974a, 1974b; Bouma et al., 1974b). Due to the high conductivity of the bedrock, seepage beds rather than trenches can be built inside these types of mounds (Converse et al., 1974a). Dosing and equal distribution of effluent are effective as in all systems to optimize the purification potential of the sandfill and the in situ soil (section IV-B-1). The occurrence of impermeable, uncreviced, bedrock is often associated with ground water tables. Then, alternatives discussed for these conditions in Section IV-B-2 apply. However, there are some obvious differences. Occurrence of impermeable bedrock introduces a clear "impermeable layer" (Section IV-B-1), but to predict lateral flow patterns in generally hilly country is very difficult. No general guidelines can be provided because local soil conditions, depth of bedrock, and topography will have to determine the features of the design. However, the shallow depth of natural soil will require some type of mound system, rather than a drainage system.

4. LOW SOIL PERMEABILITY: REDUCE LOADING RATE

If the capacity of a soil is inadequate to accept a certain volume of liquid within a certain area, two solutions can be proposed. Either the area is increased when the applied volume remains the same, or the applied volume (the loading rate if expressed as a volume per unit area) is reduced if the area remains the same. Both have the effect of reducing the loading rate. This reduction can only proceed to a certain point, in view of the average volume of effluent produced by a family and the feasible size of a disposal system (Section IV-B-1). The diagram of Fig. 5a will further illustrate this discussion. Definition of some minimum infiltration rate i_{min} served to exclude all soils with a $K_{sat} < i_{min}$, and all soils where $i_{cl} < i_{min}$ (Fig. 5a). Four alternative procedures are suggested:

1) A decrease of i_{min} could result in adequate K_{sat} or i_{cl}. Flow reduction would allow smaller flow rates in the same large seepage area. These smaller rates could be achieved by using special toilets with low water consumption or perhaps composting toilets, showers with special nozzles, and low-flow washing machines. A discussion of these features is beyond the scope of this text, but strong emphasis on use of at least some of these devices seems quite justified. However, use of flow reduction could change the physical and chemical characteristics of the liquid waste which could, in turn, affect soil infiltration and clogging phenomena. Very little data are available on the latter aspect.

2) Improving the quality of the liquid waste before application to the soil could possibly enhance infiltration. This aspect would apply only to the case of $i_{cl} < i_{min}$. Mechanical aeration of septic tank effluent strongly reduces the BOD, but the content of suspended solids is not reduced (Otis et al., 1975; Otis & Boyle, 1976). Infiltration into sands was improved after aeration, but the effect for slowly permeable, clayey soils was not significant as demonstrated by a large series of column experiments (Daniel & Bouma, 1974). This alternative appears therefore not to be a realistic one for this important type of soil.

3) Use of a mound system (Sections IV-C-2-b and IV-C-3) implies the creation of a very large bottom area, to be used for infiltration in the natural soil, while the seepage trench inside the mound (in which the distribution system occurs) is small because it was sized for the sandfill. Objections to very large seepage areas expressed in the definition of i_{min} were derived from expected problems with leveling and liquid distribution. But these do not apply, of course, to the bottom area of a mound, which may well be larger than 360 m² (4,000 ft²). An added advantage is the improved quality of the septic tank effluent as it reaches the original soil surface after percolation through 60 or 30 cm of unsaturated sand in the fill.

4) Use of nonsoil alternatives are recommended if the soil system can not be manipulated to provide adequate disposal and treatment. A discussion of these systems is beyond the scope of this text which is soils-oriented. But use of intermittent sandfilters, loaded with septic tank or aerobically treated effluent, followed by disinfection, is being studied (Sauer et al., 1976). These systems may be complicated and in need of much supervision, which can perhaps be best provided in the context of a sanitary district (Stewart, 1975).

Confining attention to soil-aspects, mound systems appear most attractive for conditions where $K_{sat} < i_{min}$. However, in many cases these soils have also high water tables in humid climates. Then, criteria apply developed in Section IV-C-2-b and described by Bouma et al. (1974a).

5. EXCESSIVE SLOPES

Limiting slope classes have been defined as a function of soil permeability (USDHEW, 1967). The lower the permeability, the lower the allowed slope. The major concern limiting use of strongly sloping land centers on possible surfacing of unpurified effluent downslope from the system. Whether or not this is likely to occur will be very much a function of soil profile characteristics and of the loading regime. Flow from a well-operating seepage system is generally vertically oriented, possibly somewhat cone-shaped. But this occurs only if no slowly permeable layers, such as fragipans, occur in the flow systems. Lateral flow over such horizons, followed by surfacing, could indeed be unacceptable. However, if such horizons do not occur, there is no valid reason to not accept the practical guide that construction of seepage systems on sloping land can be allowed as long as excavation equipment can be operated. But effluent should be equally distributed during dosing in small trenches which are to be constructed perpendicular to the slope. Application of serial distribution systems needs further research (Section III-A-2).

V. USE OF SOIL SURVEY TO EXTRAPOLATION EXPERIMENTAL DATA

A. Three Extrapolation Procedures

Different innovative on site disposal and treatment systems have been described that can be used to overcome limitations of different soils for the conventional system consisting of septic tank and subsurface seepage bed. These innovative systems are currently tested under field conditions and data obtained will only be relevant if extrapolations can be made to other soils that are somehow characterized as being identical. Three procedures can be followed here (Fig. 8).

1) The soil at experimental site A is characterized in the field at some observation points by emphasizing key properties that have been defined as critical for achieving satisfactory movement and purification of liquid waste, as discussed. The same characterization will have to be made at any future location (B) where a new system is to be built to determine whether the soils are identical. If so, within limits, technology used at Site A is extrapolated to Site B.

2) The soil at experimental Site A is observed and classified in the field at some observation points following taxonomic schemes of the Cooperative Soil Survey. If the taxonomic classification of a soil at any new location B is identical to the one at Site A, technology is extrapolated from A to B.

3) The soil at experimental Site A is observed and classified in the field

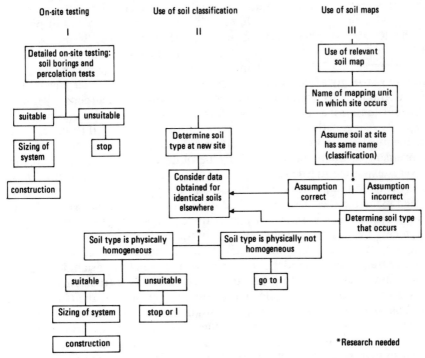

Fig. 8—Flow sheet illustrating three procedures for evaluating site and soil conditions relevant for construction of an on-site disposal and treatment system.

as in (2) and it is assumed that sites occurring elsewhere in mapping units named for the same soil series have identical key properties. Technology is extrapolated if Site B occurs in a mapping unit named for the soil series observed at Site A.

Key properties, discussed in the previous sections, were: (i) hydraulic conductivity characteristics, which are a function of soil texture and structure; (ii) occurrence of ground water; (iii) occurrence of bedrock; and (iv) site characteristics, such as slope and landscape location. These data are available for all our experimental sites. Application of the first extrapolation procedure would require measurement of K curves at any new site and several soil borings to study key soil properties and variability in an area of perhaps 90 m² in which a seepage system is to be built. These auger holes would serve for observation of ground water or bedrock levels, if present, or of indicative soil morphological features such as mottling. This procedure is currently required in Wisconsin by state law except that percolation rates are measured rather than K curves. The procedure is effective but time-consuming, and extrapolations are confined to isolated, single sites. Application of the second extrapolation procedure assumes that taxonomic classifications, based on pedological criteria, adequately reflect key soil properties for liquid waste disposal. This is realistic, within limits, for ground water or bedrock levels, since soil series descriptions list a range of observed diagnostic features. However, hydraulic conductivities of pedons within a series, or phases thereof, may vary (Bouma, 1969; Bouma & Hole, 1971). Moreover, textural differences may occur in the same soil series at depths exceeding 1.50 m which may not be reflected in separate phases, and this may strongly affect liquid movement from a subsurface seepage trench. For example, soils in glaciated areas may have formed in a relatively homogeneous loess cover of 1.50 m over heterogeneous sandy and clayey glacial deposits. Diagnostic surface and subsurface horizons may then be identical in identical taxonomic units at different locations, even though rates of movement through the subsoil may be quite different, so much so that several experimental designs for seepage systems may be required. However, a routine application of the second extrapolation procedure would make available increasingly detailed data on magnitude and variability of key properties in soil series, or phases thereof, assuming that on site measurements needed for extrapolation procedure (1) are made as well. This could mean that on site measurements would not be needed anymore for well-characterized taxonomic soil series with proven low variability at some future time. The required procedure would then be to: (i) classify a soil at any prospective new site following taxonomic schemes of the Cooperative Soil Survey; (ii) check the variability of key properties measured elsewhere in this series; and (iii) determine whether this variability is sufficiently low to allow direct interpretation of site suitability or whether variability has been so high that on site determination of key properties is still necessary. Soil series with proven low variability of key properties could be directly associated with certain types of innovative systems as discussed in section IV.

The third extrapolation procedure is more difficult to accept from a conceptual point of view. Soil mapping units are cartographic units which delineate areas within landscapes and which are normally named for the dominant series within the mapping unit. This unit would contain the named series, other series that do not significantly differ from the named series with respect to "use and management," and some percentage of contrasting inclusions (15–20% is often cited). Use of this procedure can only be satisfactory if mapping units named for a soil series have few inclusions and if the soil series itself has a low variability of key properties, as discussed in the context of the second extrapolation procedure. Another problem is one of scale posed by use of detailed soil maps which do not allow showing separate areas if smaller than approximately 1 ha (2 acres). However, a seepage area of 90 m² (approx. 0.01 ha) is considered large and this difference shows that this third procedure of extrapolation is not acceptable except when applied to very homogeneous soil mapping units. However, few data are available on the variability of soil mapping units and the third extrapolation procedure can only become viable if more data of this type are generated. Besides, the relative cost of on site testing is very low as compared with the construction of a home. The discussion of the third extrapolation procedure is included here because it is being applied already to test

site suitability for conventional systems and to show the effect of introduc-
ing innovative technology on land-use patterns (Beatty & Bouma, 1973).
For example, the current Wisconsin administrative code allows denial of a
permit for a conventional septic tank on the basis of a "severe" or "very
severe" interpretive rating of a soil shown to occur on a specific site on a
soil map. However, the property owner is permitted to present evidence to
overrule any denial made on the basis of the soil map interpretation.

Limitations of extrapolation procedures (2) and (3) should not lead to
the conclusion that the first procedure of extrapolation is the only viable
one because the other procedures have some specific and attractive advantages:

1) On-site K measurements and observations have less meaning when
they are obtained by a routine case-by-case procedure which does not aim
for the gradual development of correlative relationships with taxonomy,
which would allow extrapolation, as discussed, thus saving time and money
and making use of soil survey data more attractive.

2) Soil maps can be used, assuming that soil mapping units are reasonably homogeneous, to show the potential future impact of innovative technology on land use patterns *before any development has taken place*
(Beatty & Bouma, 1973). Many soils not suitable for on site disposal now
may be used in the future and this has implications which depend on how
large an area will potentially be affected and where such areas occur. If this
analysis indicates the potential for major change in large areas, attempts
may be initiated early to create new zoning laws if such developments are
considered undesirable. If, on the other hand, this analysis indicates that future effects will be minimal, concern can be channeled in time to more
worthy causes.

Variability of key properties in taxonomic soil series or soil mapping
units is a critical factor because advantages of their use diminish strongly as
they become more heterogeneous. Obtaining key soil properties, as defined,
by on-site inspections and by applying K measurements in situ and measuring ground water (or perched water) levels during the year will take time and
current soil characterization procedures will have to be used as long as more
detailed data are not available.

B. Conclusions

A future soil characterization program for on site liquid waste disposal
should allow the definition of certain soil series that are relatively homogeneous in terms of their key properties. This requires a routine application
of the taxonomic soil classification system at any site where a disposal system is to be built and where detailed tests are made. The purpose is to allow
extrapolation procedure (2), as discussed, for relatively homogeneous soil
series. In addition, more data should be generated on the variability of soil
mapping units named for specific series because use of soil maps for regulatory purposes and for purposes of demonstrating the impact of certain new

technologies on land-use patterns is based on the inadequately tested assumption that mapping units are reasonably homogeneous. Definition of certain "homogeneous" mapping units could allow extrapolation procedure (3), as discussed, but this largely untested procedure is as yet not very attractive.

The feasibility of using soil survey interpretations based on "potential" rather than "limitations" will depend on the degree of variability of key soil properties in specific taxonomic soil series or in mapping units. Too much variability would not allow general use of either soil taxonomy or soil maps for extrapolations of rather elaborate innovative "construction and management packages" (section IV) developed at specific sites to overcome limitations encountered when using present technology.

ACKNOWLEDGMENT

The author acknowledges helpful comments by R. J. Otis, F. G. Baker, and D. R. Keeney (Univ. of Wisconsin).

LITERATURE CITED

Alexander, M. 1961. Introduction of soil microbiology. John Wiley and Sons, Inc., New York.

Allison, L. E. 1947. Effect of microorganisms on permeability of soil under prolonged submergence. Soil Sci. 63:439-450.

Anderson, J. L., and J. Bouma. 1973. Relationships between hydraulic conductivity and morphometric data of an argillic horizon. Soil Sci. Soc. Am. Proc. 37:408-413.

Anderson, J. L., and J. Bouma. 1977a. Water movement through pedal soils. I. Saturated flow. Soil Sci. Soc. Am. J. 41:413-418.

Anderson, J. L., and J. Bouma. 1977b. Water movement through pedal soils. II. Unsaturated flow. Soil Sci. Soc. Am. J. 41:419-423.

Baker, F. G., and J. Bouma. 1976. Variability of hydraulic conductivity in two subsurface horizons of two silt loam soils. Soil Sci. Soc. Am. J. 40:219-222.

Baver, L. D., W. H. Gardner, and W. R. Gardner. 1972. Soil physics. John Wiley and Sons, New York. 498 p.

Beatty, M. T., and J. Bouma. 1973. Application of soil surveys to selection of sites for on-site disposal of liquid household wastes. Geoderma 10:113-122.

Beek, J., F. A. M. de Haan. 1974. Phosphate removal by soil in relation to waste disposal. p. 77-86. In Proc. Int. Conf. on Land for Waste Manage., 1-3 Oct. 1973, Ottawa Canada, Agric. Inst. of Canada. Dep. of Environ. and Natl. Res. Counc. of Canada, Ottawa.

Bernhard, A. P. 1975. Return of effluent nutrients to the natural cycle through evapotranspiration and subsoil-infiltration of domestic wastewater. p. 175-181. In Proc. Symp. Home Sewage Disposal. Pub. 1975. Am. Soc. Agric. Eng., St. Joseph, Mich. 242 p.

Black, C. A. 1970. Behavior of soil and fertilizer phosphorus in relation to water pollution. Chapt. 6. In T. L. Willrich and G. E. Smith (ed.) Agriculture practices and water quality. Iowa State Univ. Press, Ames.

Bouma, J. 1969. Microstructure and stability of two sandy loam soils with different soil management. Agric. Res. Rep. no. 724, Pudoc, Wageningen. p. 109.

Bouma, J. 1971. Evaluation of the field percolation test and an alternative procedure to test soil potential for disposal of septic tank effluent. Soil Sci. Soc. Am. Proc. 35:871-875.

Bouma, J. 1973. Use of physical methods to expand soil survey interpretations of soil drainage conditions. Soil Sci. Soc. Am. Proc. 37:413-421.

Bouma, J. 1974. New concepts in soil survey interpretations for on-site disposal of septic tank effluent. Soil Sci. Soc. Am. Proc. 39:941–946.

Bouma, J. 1975. Unsaturated flow phenomena during subsurface disposal of septic tank effluent. J. Am. Environ. Eng. Div. Am. Soc. Civil Eng. Vol. 101. no. EE6, Proc. Pap. 11783. p. 967–983.

Bouma, J. 1977a. Soil survey and the study of water movement in unsaturated soil. Soil Surv. Pap. 13. Soil Surv. Inst., Wageningen, Netherlands. 107 p.

Bouma, J. 1977b. Unsaturated flow during soil treatment of septic tank effluent. Closure Discussion. J. Environ. Eng. Div. Proc. Am. Soc. Civ. Eng. 103(EE3):509–510.

Bouma, J., D. I. Hillel, F. D. Hole, and C. R. Amerman. 1971. Field measurement of unsaturated hydraulic conductivity by infiltration through artificial crusts. Soil Sci. Soc. Am. Proc. 35:362–364.

Bouma, J., and F. D. Hole. 1971. Soil structure and hydraulic conductivity of adjacent virgin and cultivated pedons at two sites: a typic argiudoll (silt loam) and a typic eutrochept (clay). Soil Sci. Soc. Am. Proc. 35:316–319.

Bouma, J., and J. L. Denning. 1972. Field measurement of unsaturated hydraulic conductivity by infiltration through gypsum crusts. Soil Sci. Soc. Am. Proc. 36:846–847.

Bouma, J., W. A. Ziebell, W. G. Walker, P. G. Olcott, E. McCoy, and F. D. Hole. 1972. Soil disposal of septic tank effluent: a field study of some major soils in Wisconsin. Inf. Circ. no. 20, Geol. Nat. Hist. Surv., Madison, Wis. 240 p.

Bouma, J., and J. L. Anderson. 1973. Relationships between soil structure characteristics and hydraulic conductivity. Chapt. 5. p. 77–105. In R. R. Bruce (ed.) Field soil moisture regime. SSSA Spec. Pub. no. 5.

Bouma, J., F. G. Baker, and P. L. M. Veneman. 1974a. Measurement of water movement in soil pedons above the watertable. Inf. Circ. no. 27, Wis. Geol. Nat. Hist. Surv. 166 p.

Bouma, J., J. C. Converse, W. A. Ziebell, and F. R. Magdoff. 1974b. An experimental mound system for disposal of septic tank effluent in shallow soils over creviced bedrock. p. 367–378. In Proc. Int. Conf. on Land for Waste Manage., 1–3 Oct. 1973, Ottawa, Canada, Agric. Inst. of Canada. Dep. of Environ. and Natl. Res. Counc. of Canada, Ottawa.

Bouma, J., J. C. Converse, R. J. Otis, W. G. Walker, and W. A. Ziebell. 1975a. A mound system for on-site disposal of septic tank effluent in slowly permeable soils with seasonally perched water tables. J. Environ. Qual. 4:382–388.

Bouma, J., J. C. Converse, J. Carlson, and F. G. Baker. 1975b. Soil absorption of septic tank effluent in moderately permeable fine silty soils. Proc. ASAE. 18(6):1094–1099.

Brenner, H. 1962. The diffusion model of longitudinal mixing in beds of finite length. Numerical Values. Chem. Eng. Sci. 17:295–298.

Cassel, D. K., T. H. Krueger, F. W. Schroer, and E. B. Norum. 1974. Solute movement through disturbed and undisturbed soil cores. Soil Sci. Soc. Am. Proc. 37:36–38.

Childs, E. C. 1969. The physical basis of soil water phenomena. John Wiley and Sons, New York. 491 p.

Converse, J. C., J. L. Anderson, W. A. Ziebell, and J. Bouma. 1974. Pressure distribution to improve soil absorption systems. p. 104–116. In Proc. Symp. Home Sewage Disposal. Pub. 175. Am. Soc. Agric. Eng., St. Joseph, Mich. 242 p.

Converse, J. C., R. J. Otis, and J. Bouma. 1975a. Design and construction procedures for fill systems in permeable soils with shallow creviced or porous bedrock. Rep. Small Scale Waste Manage. Proj. College Agric. Life Sci., Madison, Wis.

Converse, J. C., R. J. Otis, J. Bouma et al. 1975b. Design and construction procedures for mounds in slowly permeable soils with seasonally high water tables. Rep. Small Scale Waste Manage. Proj. College Agric. Life Sci., Madison, Wis.

Converse, J. C., R. J. Otis, and J. Bouma. 1975c. Design and construction procedures for fill systems in permeable soils with high water tables. Rep. Small Scale Waste Manage. Proj. College Agric. Life Sci., Madison, Wis.

Daniel, T. C., and J. Bouma. 1974. Column studies of soil clogging in slowly permeable soils as a function of effluent quality. J. Environ. Qual. 3:321–327.

Ellis, B., and K. E. Childs. 1973. Nutrient movement from septic tanks and lawn fertilization. Tech. Bull. 73-5. Mich. Dep. Nat. Res., Lansing, Mich.

Erickson, A. E., J. M. Tiedje, B. G. Ellis, and C. M. Hansen. 1971. A barriered landscape water renovation system for removing phosphate and nitrogen from liquid feedlot waste. p. 232–234. In Proc. Int. Symp. on Livestock Wastes. Am. Soc. Agric. Eng., St. Joseph, Mich.

Geldreich, E. E. 1966. Sanitary significance of fecal coliforms in the environment. Cincinnati Water Res. Lab., Water Pollut. Control Res. Ser. Pub. no. WP-20-3. 122 p.

Green, K. M., and D. O. Cliver. 1974. Removal of virus from septic tank effluent. p. 137–144. *In* Proc. Symp. Home Sewage Disposal. Pub. 175. Am. Soc. Agric. Eng., St. Joseph, Mich. 242 p.

Harkin, J. M., M. D. Jawson, and E. G. Baker. 1975. "Causes and Remedy of Failure of Septic Tank Seepage Systems". Proceedings 2nd Natl. Conf. on Individual on-site Wastewater Systems. Ann Arbor, Mich.

Hillel, D. 1971. Soil and water. Academic Press, New York. 288 p.

Hazardous Materials Advisory Committee. 1973. Nitrogenous compounds in the environment. EPA-SAB-75-001. U.S. Environ. Prot. Agency, Washington, D.C.

Ingham, A. T. 1976. Unsaturated flow during soil treatment of septic tank effluent. Discussion J. Environ. Eng. Div. Proc. Am. Soc. Civ. Eng. 102(EE5):1128–1130.

International Society of Soil Science (ISSS). 1976. Final report soil physics terminology. Bull. no. 49. p. 26–36.

Klute, A. 1972. The determination of hydraulic conductivity and diffusivity of unsaturated soils. Soil Sci. 113:264–277.

Klute, A. 1973. Soil water flow theory and its application in field situation. p. 9–37. *In* Bruce et al. (ed.) Field soil water regime. SSSA Spec. Pub. no. 5.

Kuo, S., and E. G. Lotse. 1973. The kinetics of phosphate adsorption and desorption by hematite and gibbsite. Soil Sci. 116(b):406.

Lance, J. C. 1972. Nitrogen removal by soil mechanisms. J. Water Pollut. Control. Fed. 44:1352–1361.

Lindsay, W. L., and E. C. Moreno. 1960. Phosphate phase equilibria in soils. Soil Sci. Soc. Am. Proc. 24:177–182.

Magdoff, F. R., and J. Bouma. 1974. The development of soil clogging in sands leached with septic tank effluent. p. 37–48. *In* Proc. Symp. Home Sewage Disposal. Pub. 175. Am. Soc. Agric. Eng., St. Joseph, Mich.

Magdoff, F. R., J. Bouma, and D. R. Keeney. 1974a. Columns representing mound-type disposal systems for septic tank effluent. I. Soil-water and gas relations. J. Environ. Qual. 3:223–228.

Magdoff, F. R., D. R. Keeney, J. Bouma, and W. A. Ziebell. 1974b. Columns representing mound-type disposal systems for septic tank effluent. II. Nutrient transformations and bacterial populations. J. Environ. Qual. 3:228–234.

Magdoff, F. R., and D. R. Keeney. 1975. Nutrient mass balance in columns representing fill systems for disposal of septic tank effluents. Environ. Lett. 10(4):285–294.

Magee, P. N. 1971. Toxicity of nitrosamines: their possible human health hazards. Food Cosmet. Toxicol. 9:207–218.

McCormack, D. 1974. Soil potentials: a positive approach to urban planning. J. Soil Water Conserv. 29:258–262.

McGauhey, P. H., and R. B. Krone. 1967. Soil mantle as a wastewater treatment system. SERL Rep. no. 67-11. Univ. of California, Davis. 200 p.

National Academy of Sciences. 1972. Accumulation of nitrate. Comm. on Nitrate Accumulation, Natl. Res. Council, Washington, D.C.

Nielsen, D. R., J. W. Biggar, and K. T. Erh. 1973. Spatial variability of field-measured soil-water properties. Hilgardia. 42(7):215–260.

Otis, R. J., J. Bouma, and W. G. Walker. 1974. Uniform distribution in soil absorption fields. Proc. of 2nd Northwest Water Assoc.-EPA Nat. Ground Water Qual. Symp. J. Tech. Div. NWWA. Nov.–Dec. 1974. p. 409–417. Reprinted in: Ground Water. Vol. 12 no. 6.

Otis, R. J., W. C. Boyle, and D. R. Sauer. 1975. The performance of household wastewater treatment units under field conditions. p. 191–201. *In* Proc. Symp. Home Sewage Disposal. Pub. 175. Am. Soc. Agric. Eng., St. Joseph, Mich. 242 p.

Otis, R. J., and W. C. Boyle. 1976. Performance of single household treatment units. J. Environ. Eng. Div. ASCE Vol. 102:533–548. (Proc. Pap. 11895).

Popkin, R. A., and Th. W. Bendixen. 1968. Improved subsurface disposal. J. Water Pollut. Control Fed.:1499–1514.

Sauer, D. K., W. C. Boyle, and R. J. Otis. 1976. Intermittent sand filtration of household wastewater. J. Env. Eng. Div. ASCE Vol. 102:789–803. (Proc. Pap. 12295).

Siegrist, R., M. Witt, and W. C. Boyle. 1976. Characteristics of rural household wastewater. J. Env. Eng. Div. ASCE Vol. 102:533–548. (Proc. paper 12200).

Sikora, L. J., and D. R. Keeney. 1975. Laboratory studies on stimulation of biological denitrification. p. 64–74. *In* Proc. Symp. Home Sewage Disposal. Pub. 175. Am. Soc. Agric. Eng., St. Joseph, Mich. 242 p.

Sikora, L. J., and R. B. Corey. 1976. Fate of nitrogen and phosphorus in soils under septic tank waste disposal fields. Am. Soc. Agric. Eng. Proc. 5:866–870.

Sikora, L. J., M. G. Bent, R. B. Corey, and D. R. Keeney. 1976. Septic nitrogen and phosphorus removal test system. Ground Water 14:309–314.

Soil Survey Staff. 1951. Soil survey manual. USDA Handbk. 18. 503 p.

Soil Survey Staff. 1975. Soil taxonomy. A basic system of soil classification for making and interpreting soil surveys. Agric. Handbk. 436, USDA-SCS. 754 p.

Stewart, D. E. 1975. Legal planning and economic considerations of on-site sewerage systems. p. 222–231. *In* Proc. Symp. Home Sewage Disposal. Pub. 175. Am. Soc. Agric. Eng., St. Joseph, Mich. 242 p.

Tanner, C. B., and J. Bouma. 1975. Influence of climate on subsurface disposal of sewage effluents. p. 111–117. *In* Proc. 2nd Natl. Conf. on Individual On-site Waste Water Systems, Ann Arbor Mich.

Thomas, R. E., W. A. Schwartz, and T. W. Bendixen. 1966. Soil chemical changes and infiltration rate reduction under sewage spreading. Soil Sci. Soc. Am. Proc. 30:641–646.

U.S. Department of Agriculture, Soil Conservation Service. 1971. Guide for interpreting engineering uses of soils. U.S. Government Printing Office no. 0107-0332. 77 p.

U.S. Public Health Service (USDHEW). 1967. Manual of septic tank practice. Publ. 526, 93 p.

Veneman, P. L. M., M. J. Vepraskas, and J. Bouma. 1976. The physical significance of soil mottling in a Wisconsin toposequence. Geoderma 15:103–118.

Vepraskas, M. J., F. G. Baker, and J. Bouma. 1974. Soil mottling and drainage in a mollic hapludalf as related to suitability for septic tank construction. Soil Sci. Soc. Am. Proc. 38:497–501.

Vepraskas, M. L., and J. Bouma. 1976. Model studies on mottle formation simulating field conditions. Geoderma 15:217–230.

Walker, W. G., J. Bouma, D. R. Keeney, and F. R. Magdoff. 1973a. Nitrogen transformations during subsurface disposal of septic tank effluent in sands. I. Soil transformations. J. Environ. Qual. 2:475–479.

Walker, W. G., J. Bouma, D. R. Keeney, and P. G. Olcott. 1973b. Nitrogen transformations during subsurface disposal of septic tank effluent in sands. II. Ground water quality. J. Environ. Qual. 2:521–525.

Winneberger, J. H. T. 1975. Ryon's septic tank practices corrected. p. 215–222. *In* Proc. Symp. Home Sewage Disposal. Pub. 175. Am. Soc. Agric. Eng., St. Joseph, Mich. 242 p.

Woodward, F. L., F. J. Kilpatrick, and P. B. Johnson. 1961. Experience with ground water contamination in unsewered areas in Minnesota. Am. J. Public Health 51:1130–1136.

Ziebell, W. A., J. L. Anderson, J. Bouma, and E. McCoy. 1975b. Fecal bacteria: removal from sewage by soils. Pap. no. 75-2579. Am. Soc. Agric. Eng., St. Joseph, Mich. 24 p.

Ziebell, W. A., D. H. Nero, J. F. Deininger, and E. McCoy. 1975a. Use of bacteria in assessing waste treatment and soil disposal systems. p. 58–64. *In* Proc. Symp. Home Sewage Disposal, Am. Soc. Agric. Eng., St. Joseph, Mich. 242 p.

28   Application of Thermal Effluent

LARRY L. BOERSMA

Oregon State University
Corvallis, Oregon

I. INTRODUCTION

Water power, wood, coal, petroleum products, and natural gas have provided the energy needed to fuel our industrial society. Now the fuels which
were used to support activities are running low. The accumulation rate of
natural energy resources is so slow that they must be considered finite when
viewed in relation to the present rate of consumption. More importantly,
energy use is increasing at an accelerating rate. There is thus a strong incentive to consider alternative sources of energy while at the same time learning
to use available energy resources more efficiently.

One concept which merits serious study is the possible use of energy
currently being "wasted". The term *waste heat* refers to all forms of energy
being discharged to the environment without having been used to the fullest
possible extent. The term *thermal effluent* is generally understood to denote
the low-grade energy appearing in the form of warm water such as the condenser cooling water from power plants based on the steam cycle. Although
the steam power plants generate most of the thermal effluents, it must be
recognized that warm water is discharged in many industrial applications.

This chapter examines methods for the use of waste energy. The need
to base solutions for efficient energy use on the design of integrated systems
is emphasized. An integrated system is an assembly of components each
chosen for its contribution to the efficiency of energy use, food production,
and manufacturing. Such assemblies could include greenhouses, facilities
for converting organic wastes from livestock operations into protein, facilities for extracting protein from plant leaves, aquaculture, food processing,
and waste treatment. Although attention is given to several of these possible
applications, soil warming is discussed in detail.

II. CHARACTERIZATION OF THE RESOURCE

1. SOURCES OF WASTE HEAT

Figure 1 shows the sources from which energy is derived and the uses of
this energy projected for the United States during the year 1980. The rates
of energy use are shown in millions of barrels of oil equivalents per day (10^6

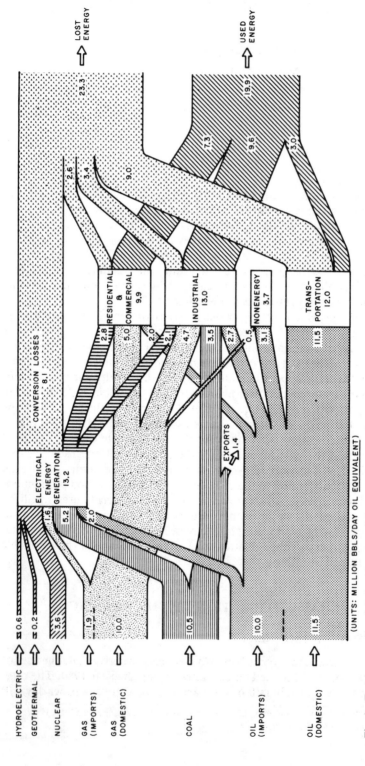

(UNITS: MILLION BBLS/DAY OIL EQUIVALENT)

Fig. 1—Energy sources and their use projected for the year 1980 in million barrels of oil/day equivalents. The total energy use is expected to be 48.3×10^6 barrels oil equivalents of which 19.9 will be used productively and 23.3 will be lost as waste heat. The conversion losses in the power generation process are 8.1 units or 17% of all energy used and 35% of the energy wasted from all sources.

Table 1—Conversion factors for physical quantities frequently used to express energy or work, heat, and power.

To convert from	Multiply by	To obtain	Units
Energy or Work			
Btu	× 1,055.000	= joule	J
Cal	× 4.187	= joule	J
Kilowatt-hour	× 3.600 E + 6	= joule	J
Heat			
Btu/ft^2	× 1.136 E + 4	= joule/m^2	J/m^2
Btu/hour-ft^2-°F	× 5.678	= watt/m^2-kelvin	W/m^2-K
Cal/cm^2	× 4.184 E + 4	= joule/m^2	J/m^2
Cal/g	× 4,187.00	= joule/kg	J/kg
Cal/g-°C	× 4,187.00	= joule/kg-kelvin	J/kg K
Power			
Btu/sec	× 1,054.00	= watt	W
Btu/min	× 17.57	= watt	W
cal/sec	× 4.184	= watt	W
cal/min	× 0.069	= watt	W
General conversions			
1 barrel of oil	=	42 gallons	
1 barrel crude oil	=	5,800,000 Btu	
1 kWh	=	3,412 Btu	
1 ft^3 natural gas (CH$_4$)	=	1,000 Btu	
1 ton coal	=	26,000,000 Btu	

barrels/day-oil equivalents). One barrel of oil equals 42 gallons and 1 barrel of crude oil contains 5.8×10^6 Btu. Factors for conversion to other units are in Table 1.

Hydro, geothermal, and nuclear sources are not expected to contribute much to the total energy supply in 1980. The three main sources of energy will be gas, coal, and oil. Although total rate of energy use continues to increase, the relative contribution from each source is expected to remain more or less the same during this century (Center for Strat. and Int. Studies, 1973).

Energy is utilized in five major categories. These are: generation of electricity, heating and cooling of residential and commercial buildings, industrial processing, nonenergy applications, which include all categories where organic materials are used as a raw material, and transportation. The final disposition of the energy is in the form of useful work or in the form of rejected energy. This discussion is concerned with the energy which is rejected.

The waste heat rejected from each of the five major industrial categories is not equally suitable for recovery and further use. A large portion of the waste heat occurs in the transportation sector. Most of this is dissipated to the atmosphere through car radiators. No beneficial recovery of this energy can be contemplated because of its dispersed nature. Waste heat produced in the residential and commercial sectors offers little opportunity for further utilization. The energy wasted in residential applications is also too dispersed for consideration of further use. These losses must be minimized through conservation and in-house uses of waste heat. Large commercial installations may produce waste heat in the form of warm water or heated air of sufficient quantity to merit development for beneficial use. However, the wasted energy is usually dissipated to the atmosphere and not available in a form which allows its transportation to other locations for further use. Waste heat generated in industrial processes is being increasingly considered for further use at the plant itself. As the cost of energy increases, companies are rapidly developing methods for utilizing the waste heat resulting from manufacturing processes.

Only the waste heat resulting from the generation of electrical energy in thermal power plants is readily available for further use. The waste heat resulting from power generation merits serious consideration for productive uses. Land application would be an important part of a plan for the use of this waste heat.

2. BENEFICIAL USE VS. DISPOSAL

The loss of waste heat is costly in terms of monetary losses as well as in terms of the accelerated depletion of a finite resource. Beneficial and productive uses of the waste heat should be developed where possible. This report deals specifically with land applications of the waste heat. The purpose may be the enhancement of crop growth or the use of the soil as a heat sink. In the latter application, the merits of land application of waste heat are judged on the basis of the ability of the soil to provide the desired degree of cooling. Both uses of land for the disposal of waste heat must be evaluated in terms of the contributions made to the total land use plan.

3. RATES OF WASTE HEAT GENERATION

The efficiency of the power-generating process based on the steam cycle is about 33%, that is, for every three units of energy used, one unit of electricity is obtained and two units of waste heat must be disposed of. The amount of waste heat produced in the United States in the process of generating electricity each year is very large. In 1970, the rate of waste heat production from thermal power plants was equivalent to 4.6 million barrels of oil per day. At that time, total oil imports were equivalent to 3.5 million barrels of oil per day. It is estimated that in 1980 (Fig. 1), the rate of waste heat production from thermal power plants will be equivalent to 8.1 million barrels of oil per day, while the total rate of oil importation will be equivalent to 10 million barrels of oil per day.

The comparison of the rate at which energy is lost in thermal power plants with the rate at which oil is imported into the United States is given for several reasons. It demonstrates the need to seriously consider the development of beneficial uses for waste heat. The effects of the high cost of imported oil on the economies of the western world are well recognized and understood. The ability to utilize waste heat in a productive manner would be attractive.

Table 2—Projected generating capacity and rates of waste heat production in MW obtained by assuming the indicated operating efficiencies.

Year	Projected generating capacity	Projected operating efficiency	Rate of waste heat production
	1,000 MWe	%	1,000 MW
1970	147	34	286
1980	301	37	512
1990	562	41	809
2000	955	46	1,121
2010	1,458	53	1,341
2020	2,160	61	1,382

4. FUTURE RATES OF WASTE HEAT GENERATION

When making decisions about the use of waste heat produced by power-generating plants, it is desirable to know the future availability of this resource in terms of amount and location. The rate at which waste heat from thermal power plants will be available in the future can be obtained by estimating the rate of power production in the future and estimating the efficiency with which electricity can be generated. The efficiency of power generation is expected to increase in the future. At the same time, the demand for electric energy is expected to increase. Table 2 was developed by making certain assumptions about the development of these two variables. This table indicates that the rate at which waste heat will be available in the future may be expected to increase.

The present trend toward the construction of large power plants, those generating 1,000 MW-electric (MWe) or more, is expected to continue. Furthermore, there will be increasing interest in siting several of these large plants in one location. Thus, one may expect to have large quantities of waste heat available at a few central locations.

5. QUALITY OF THE WASTE HEAT

The quality of the resource is determined by the temperature at which it is available, the form in which it is available, and the reliability with which it is available.

Figure 2 shows how water is used to dispose of the reject heat resulting from the process of generating electricity. Energy, in the form of fossil fuel or nuclear fuel, is used to produce heat which turns water to steam. As the temperature of the steam rises, it expands and is thereby able to drive the turbine which in turn drives the generator. When most of the useful work has been extracted from the steam, it reaches the condenser where it is cooled to the point of condensation. Cooling the steam is accomplished by pumping the cooling water through copper tubes in the condenser.

In order to extract the most useful work from the steam, it is advantageous to maintain the temperatures in the condenser as low as possible. In general, the power company manager will try to obtain cooling water with the lowest possible temperature at the point of entry into the condenser

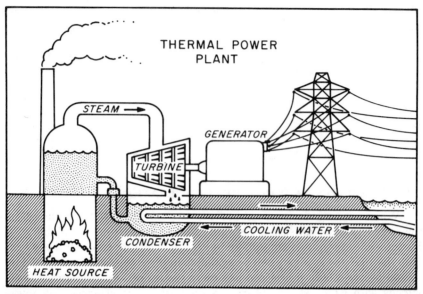

Fig. 2—Schematic diagram of a thermal power plant. The adjective *thermal* describes the power-generating process based on the steam cycle. Steam is produced by heating water with a heat source which may consist of fossil fuel such as coal, oil, or gas, a nuclear fuel, or solar energy. Following its passage through the turbines, the steam must be cooled to condensation in the condenser. This is accomplished by pumping cold water through copper pipes in the condenser. The cooling water absorbs the heat which is termed *waste heat*.

and limit the temperature rise of the water as it passes through the condenser. The temperature of the cooling water leaving the condenser is therefore dictated by the inflow temperature and the temperature rise which the plant manager is willing to accept.

Three cooling systems are used (Fig. 3, 4, and 5). Each of these provides a characteristic temperature regime of the condenser cooling water. Until recently, most thermal generating plants were sited near rivers, lakes, or other bodies of water sufficiently large to allow the use of a once-through cooling system (Fig. 3). The cooling water is taken from a river or lake, passed through the plant, and discharged at a higher temperature. Once-through cooling systems produce many different temperature regimes of the outflow water. For example, where the plant uses a river as the source of its cooling water, the annual temperature cycle is determined by the annual temperature cycle of the water in the river. The temperature of the water in the river may vary dramatically when a small stream is used. It may range from near freezing during the winter to 20 to 25°C during the warmest part of the summer.

Where a river is not available, a cooling pond may be used. A reservoir is constructed (Fig. 4) for the specific purpose of providing a sink for the reject energy. Since the coldest water will be at the deepest part of the lake, the water intake will be positioned at that point. The warm water will be returned to the surface of the lake where it cools due to radiative heat loss and

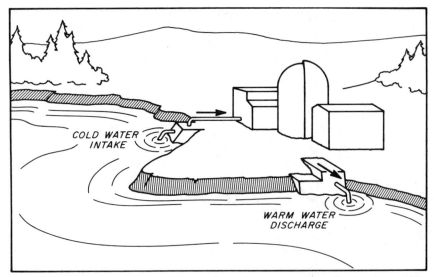

Fig. 3—Schematic diagram of a once-through cooling system. Water is taken from a large body of water, passed through the condenser, and returned to the source at a higher temperature.

evaporation. As the water cools, it will move to deeper parts of the lake by convective currents and eventually be reused. It is generally assumed that about 1 ha of lake surface is necessary to provide adequate cooling capacity for each MWe of generating capacity. An example of the temperature regime of the cooling water in a system using a cooling pond is shown in Fig. 5.

With the increased concern about the possibility of environmental

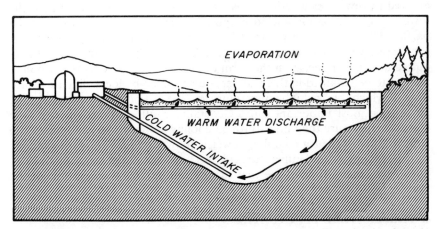

Fig. 4—Schematic diagram of a cooling system using a large pond. Water is taken from the pond, passed through the condenser, and returned to the pond. Since cold water will be at the bottom, the intake is located there. The heated water is discharged near the surface. The water in the pond loses heat due to evaporation and radiation.

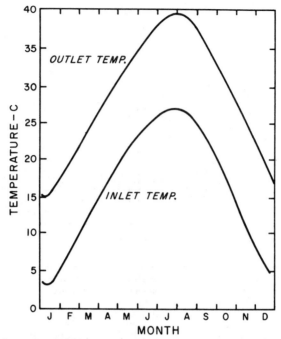

Fig. 5—Expected temperatures of the condenser cooling water at the outlet of the condenser for a 1,100 MWe power plant using a cooling pond. Climatic conditions are those of Pendleton, Oreg. The temperature rise of the cooling water is 12.4°C (Boersma et al., 1974).

changes caused by increased water temperatures, closed cycle cooling systems have been developed. These make use of cooling towers (Fig. 6). The condenser cooling water is discharged in the lower part of the tower and allowed to flow over a series of baffles to collect in a reservoir below the tower. The water cools due to evaporative heat loss as it flows over the baffles. The cold water is pumped from the reservoir below the tower to the condenser. The rate of evaporation must be sufficient to carry away the required amount of energy in the form of latent heat. The degree of cooling which can be obtained in this manner is determined by local climatic conditions of which the dry bulb temperature and the wet bulb temperature of the air are the most important ones. Generally, cooling towers operate at a higher temperature than once-through cooling systems. An example of the temperature profile for a cooling tower is shown in Fig. 7. For the example shown, cooling water temperatures at the condenser outlet range from 15°C during the coldest time of the year to 40°C during the warmest time of the year.

6. TEMPERATURE FLUCTUATIONS

The large changes in the temperature of the cooling water during an annual cycle (Fig. 5 and 7) pose one of the greatest difficulties to the engineer trying to design beneficial uses for this water. The temperature of the

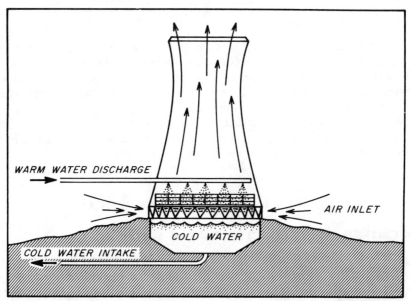

Fig. 6—Schematic diagram of a cooling tower. Condenser cooling water is discharged in the lower part of the tower and flows down in thin layers over a series of baffles to a pond below the tower. Heat is lost by evaporation. The cold water is returned to the condenser.

resource is lowest during the winter when heat for applications such as space heating is most needed. The temperature is highest during the summer when little heat is needed.

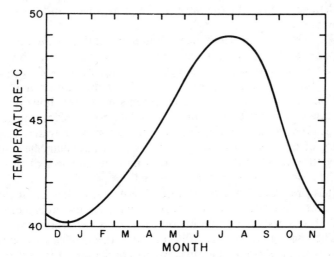

Fig. 7—Expected temperatures of the condenser cooling water at the outlet of the condenser for a 1,100-MWe power plant using a natural draft cooling tower. Climatic conditions are those of Portland, Oreg. The temperature rise of the cooling water is 20.8°C (Boersma et al., 1974).

7. STEAM BLEED-OFF

The potential use of reject heat can be enhanced by increasing the temperature of the condenser cooling water using a technique called *steam bleed-off*. This technique involves using part of the steam normally passed through the condenser to increase the temperature of the cooling water after it has passed the condenser. By doing so, less energy will be available for the generator and therefore the efficiency of the power plant is decreased. Obviously, this technique, though desirable from the standpoint of waste heat utilization, is not attractive for the operator of the plant.

III. PLAN FOR USE OF WASTE HEAT

1. CRITERIA FOR PRODUCTIVE USES OF WASTE HEAT

The discussion about amount and quality of waste heat leads to a set of criteria for the use of this resource. The potential for utilization of warm water at a given location must be considered in terms of the following general criteria.

1) The use of waste heat should not interfere with normal operation of the power plant. Some methods, such as the use of steam bleed-off to increase the temperature of the condenser cooling water, require close cooperation between the user of warm water and the power plant operator. Although such methods are possible, the first choice should be the one which requires no modification to the routine operation of the power plant. This allows the greatest degree of independence for the operator of the power plant and the user of the waste heat.

2) The user of the waste heat should be able to operate for short periods of time without the supply of warm water. This is a correlary to the first criterion again stressing the desired independence of the two systems. Some degree of communication and cooperation between the two systems remains necessary, however. For instance, it might be possible to schedule power plant outages to coincide with periods of minimal demand for warm water. The operator of the waste heat complex may need an auxiliary heat source to be utilized when the warm water supply is unexpectedly lost during the time when it is absolutely needed.

3) It is preferable to use a "closed" system for the use of the warm water. This means that the warm water is circulated in a closed conduit and does not come in contact with water from other sources. The cooling water is usually treated with chemicals to prevent the growth of algae in the pipes of the condenser. It is undesirable to mix this water with the water of the system to be heated. The closed system does have the disadvantage that it requires a heat exchanger to transfer the heat to the medium where it is to be used. Heat exchangers are usually very expensive.

4) The temperature of the cooling water is low when uses for industrial processing are considered. Few industrial processes are available where water in the temperature range of 40 to 50°C is useful. However, a promising application of the waste heat is the stimulation of life cycle processes. Several biological uses for waste heat have been proposed. These include: aquaculture, the heating and cooling of greenhouses, enhancement of biological decomposition processes, warming of waste treatment facilities to enhance the rate of growth of algae and bacteria, frost protection, and soil warming.

5) Water is a finite resource and therefore systems should be considered in which the water is recycled.

6) In the evaluation of the economic feasibility of the use of warm water, no credit should be allowed for the cooling of the water. It is important to recognize that each system for waste heat utilization must be an economically feasible enterprise on its own merits. No credit should be given to the heat removal capacity of the system utilizing the waste heat.

7) The power plant must always have a primary heat sink capable of handling the entire heat load. This arrangement is necessary in order to obtain a license for the operation of a nuclear power plant. It again stresses the necessary independence between the power plant operator and the user of the waste heat.

8) Pollution problems such as those arising from disposal of agricultural and domestic waste should be solved in concert rather than as individual problems. Therefore, integrated systems, the components of which enhance each other, should be considered.

2. INTEGRATED SYSTEMS OF PRODUCTION

The most challenging and interesting of the criteria for the use of waste heat is the last one indicating the need for the development of integrated systems of production. In present methods of operation, food is harvested, processed, packaged, delivered, consumed, and eventually excreted. The energy required to go through this cycle is very large in industrialized nations. Table 3 indicates that energy is used in industrialized societies at a much higher rate than in countries which do not have a highly developed industrial capacity. The rate of energy use in the United States is more than twice that of west European countries, and nearly 20 times that of China and Brazil.

The waste of garbage, sewage, packaging, and the energy of disposal are unproductive expenses. We must consider design options which allow us to change this open-ended system of management into a closed cycle of regeneration going from solar heat to human energy without the great losses that are currently incurred. This may be done by designs in which the waste product of one industry becomes the raw material of a second industry. We have called such systems *integrated systems* (Boersma & Rykbost, 1973).

An example of an integrated system is shown in Fig. 8. It is an assembly of components each chosen for its contribution to the efficiency of energy use and food production. Such assemblies could include greenhouses, facili-

Table 3—Comparison of energy consumption rates in different countries (Source: U.N., 1972).

Country	Kg per capita (coal equivalent)	Energy use as multiple of Nigerian use
USA	11,244	191
United Kingdom	5,507	93
West Germany	5,223	89
USSR	4,535	77
France	3,928	67
Japan	3,267	55
Italy	2,682	45
Mexico	1,270	22
China	561	10
Brazil	500	8
Philippines	298	5
India	186	3
Indonesia	123	2
Pakistan and Bangladesh	96	2
Nigeria	59	1
World average	1,927	33

ties for converting organic wastes from livestock operations into protein, facilities for extracting protein from plant leaves, aquacultural operations to produce livestock feed, waste treatment facilities, and food processing plants. Interactions and feedback between components should be considered and the assembly of components should be designed and operated to maximize productivity and profit while minimizing pollution problems.

The use of waste heat from various sources, but in particular that discharged in the power-generating process, could be an important consideration in the design of integrated systems. These allow the use of waste heat on a large scale. Whereas, for example, soil warming would only use an insignificant fraction of the total amount of waste heat available, it would be an important component in a total system. The concept is based on the observation that energy problems, pollution problems, and food production problems must be solved in concert rather than as individual problems. In such systems, the energy use efficiency would be greatly increased by arranging energy consuming processes in an orderly cascade of decreasing input/output temperatures. These systems would allow recycling of raw materials for more efficient use of available resources.

Integrated systems should not only include industrial uses. The utility components of local communities should be considered as well. For example, management of waste water should be part of the total project.

3. PLANNING FOR THE USE OF WASTE HEAT

Components which could become part of an integrated system of food production and processing units were shown in Fig. 8. The diagram was not produced to show the most desirable arrangement or mix of components. That can only be established upon completion of a detailed engineering and economic analysis. Rather, the diagram is to be used for discussion of the opportunities for efficient use of waste heat, product recycling, and pollu-

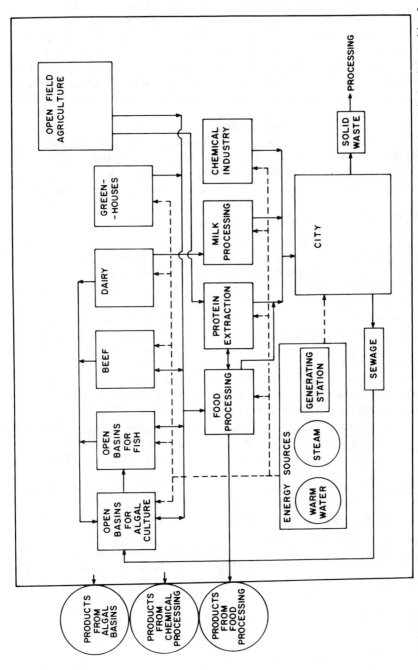

Fig. 8—Schematic diagram of components of an integrated system for the use of waste heat from several sources, but in particular that resulting from the power-generating process.

tion abatement. Waste heat should be used to satisfy existing and future energy needs in the region where the power plant is to be constructed.

A conceptual design should start with a characterization of the area in terms of questions about its ultimate development potential: what is the climate, how suitable is the climate for various agricultural enterprises, what is the potential for industrial development, where should people live, what are the recreational opportunities, what markets could be served by the region, should agriculture be emphasized, should industry be emphasized. The accumulation of this information would provide guidelines for design.

Each specific application of waste heat must be carefully described in terms of energy requirements and production rates: what temperatures are required for the growth of certain crops, how are these temperatures best maintained, what type of heat exchanger should be used, what are the energy requirements for the specific climatic conditions encountered.

4. SCHEDULE OF PLANNING TASKS

An early step in the development of a plan for use for warm water should be the determination of the best mix of components for the region. For example, it might well be that the region should emphasize the growing of crops to serve food processing and bioconversion industries. Thus one would choose applications for the enhancement of biomass production and processing. The current uncertainty about future energy supplies and food supplies has increased man's search for new sources of energy which are economically feasible. Thus one may expect to see many of these alternatives incorporated in future designs.

The accomplishment of the design tasks must progress from a conceptual design to the construction and operation of pilot plants. Several steps involving data accumulation and use are indicated below.

1) Conceptual design: size of warm water resource; climate; soils; size of population; markets; and possible future market growth.
2) Description of components: energy requirements; products; and rate of production.
3) Selection of component mix: energy needs; energy flows; product flows; and determination of size of components.
4) Engineering design: complete engineering design, based on the information accumulated.
·5) Economic analysis: an economic analysis must be performed to determine the economic feasibility of the chosen arrangements. Comparisons with other methods of production must be made.

IV. PROBLEMS

1. SIZE OF POWER PLANTS

The temperature of the condenser cooling water is generally low. The amount of heat which can be extracted from this water per unit volume is therefore small. This means that large volumes of water have to be moved to obtain the desired degree of cooling. A power plant generating 1,000 MWe with an operating efficiency of 33.3% discharges 2,000 MW of waste heat or 8.37×10^9 cal/sec. The rate of flow of cooling water required to remove heat at this rate, allowing a 10°C temperature rise of the water, is 837 m^2/sec. Flowing at the high velocity of 10 m/sec, this flow rate requires a conduit with a cross section of 83.7 m^2 or a pipe with a diameter of 10.3 m. The complexity of the problems involved in moving water at this rate through a utilization complex is obvious.

2. NUMBER OF SITES

Planning for waste heat use must include a consideration of the number of power plant sites and the amount of waste heat to be dissipated at each site. Table 1 shows projected rates of power production. Since this rate is given in units of 1,000 MWe each it suggests that 301, 955, and 2,160 such units are required in 1980, 2000, and 2020, respectively. Several projections for the installed capacity needed during each of these points in time have been prepared (Cornell Univ., 1973; Center for Strat. and Int. studies, 1973; Ford Found., 1974). The number of sites would increase by decreasing the installed capacity per site. However, the trend in power plant design is to increase the number of plants per site. The number of sites may therefore be smaller than indicated.

3. RATE OF ENERGY DISSIPATION

All reject heat must ultimately be dissipated to the atmosphere. The proposed uses depend on heat loss by radiation, convection, and latent heat lost in the process of evaporation. All these processes occur at the water to air, or land to air, interface. This rate is highest at the water to air interface. Lightly loaded cooling ponds where the increase in temperature above equilibrium conditions is small require about 2 ha/MWe. The corresponding ratio for heavily loaded ponds is 1 ha/MWe. Applications which involve the use of such ponds, for example for aquaculture, would require from 1,000 to 2,000 ha of pond surface for a 1,000 MWe station. The required surface area can be decreased by using techniques which increase the rate of heat loss such as mixing and spraying. The uses of these ponds should be compatable with the techniques used to enhance rate of heat loss (Brown, 1975).

The rate of heat loss at the land-air interface is very low. Experimental data indicate a ratio of about 10 ha/MWe (Boersma et al., 1972; Rykbost et al., 1976) so that 10,000 ha would be required for a 1,000 MWe power plant. Enhancement of rate of heat loss is possible. The indicated ratio depends on soil properties and atmospheric conditions and varies widely!

V. SOIL WARMING

1. OBJECTIVES OF SOIL WARMING

Two quite different objectives of soil warming are recognized. In one application, the objective is the warming of the soil for optimum plant growth. The design of the soil warming system is this case is guided by the comparison of the value of the increased yield with the cost of owning and operating the system. The goal is to achieve an optimum soil temperature with the lowest possible cost of the soil warming system.

It is also possible to use the soil as a heat sink. Research workers at the Pennsylvania State University (de Walle, 1974) proposed a system in which waste heat from power generation is dissipated by pumping the cooling water through a network of pipes buried in agricultural land. Concurrently, municipal waste water is distributed over the heated soil surface through an overhead sprinkler system. Thus, two purposes are served. The waste water sprayed over the heated land serves to maintain a high soil water content and high soil thermal conductivity. The waste water percolating through the heated soil is rapidly renovated. Development of this specific application was prompted by the desire to develop an alternative to the use of either dry or wet cooling towers.

2. METHODS OF APPLICATION OF WARM WATER TO THE SOIL

Waste heat available from the condenser cooling water can be used to increase the temperature of the soil in the open field. Crop production in many regions of the world is limited by low air and soil temperatures during part of the growing season. Heating the soil with condenser cooling water could lengthen the growing season as well as stimulate the rate of growth of plants. One would expect to obtain higher yields due to the more rapid growth and the longer growing season. It might also be possible to grow crops not well suited to specific climatic regions.

It is difficult to impart the heat in the condenser cooling water to the soil by distributing the warm water by means of sprinkler irrigation or flood irrigation. Cline et al. (1969) demonstrated that warm water discharged through a sprinkler was cooled below the air temperature by the time the droplets reached the ground surface under a variety of water temperature and nozzle pressure conditions. Only the larger droplets remained at temperatures above the ambient air temperature. This is so because the droplets lose heat rapidly due to evaporative and radiative cooling as they travel through the air.

Surface irrigation with warm water is also an unsatisfactory means of imparting the heat to the soil. Wierenga et al. (1970) found that the application of 14.4 cm of water at 21.6°C initially warmed the surface of the soil but that the effects were of short duration. The soil cooled rapidly because of the increased evaporation. The temperature rise due to radiation from the sun was small because of the increased heat capacity. There was little difference in the temperature of the soil between plots flooded with warm water and plots flooded with water at 4.1°C except for a short initial period. A nonirrigated plot had higher temperatures than either of the irrigated plots.

In addition to the difficulties encountered with imparting heat to the soil by flood irrigation, there is a possibility of heat damage to crops when shallow roots or above ground plant parts are exposed to hot water. When plants come in contact with water at 35°C or warmer, death generally results.

These conditions led to the proposal to warm the soil by pumping the warm water through a network of underground pipes. The degree of soil warming which can be achieved in this manner depends on the thermal properties of the soil, the temperature of the water in the pipes, and the radiation received at the soil surface.

3. THERMAL CONDUCTIVITY OF THE SOIL

Heat is transported through soils mainly by conduction. The rate of heat flow in a homogeneous medium is proportional to the temperature gradient and to the thermal conductivity. This can be seen by considering two parallel planes in the soil kept at constant temperatures T_1 and T_2. Heat flows from the plane with the highest temperature to the plane with the lower temperature according to

$$H = \lambda (T_1 - T_2)/d, \tag{1}$$

where H is the heat flux density (cal/cm² sec), λ is the thermal conductivity of the soil (cal/cm sec °C), T_1 and T_2 are the soil temperatures at the two planes (°C), and d is the distance between the two planes (cm).

Equation [1] indicates that one of the most important considerations in the design of a subsurface soil warming system is the thermal conductivity of the soil. Figure 9 shows the thermal conductivity of two soil materials as a function of water content. In a dry soil, heat is transfered by conduction through the soil particles or through the air in the pore spaces. The soil matrix consists of particles touching each other at several points. Heat passing through the soil must move from particle to particle by conduction at

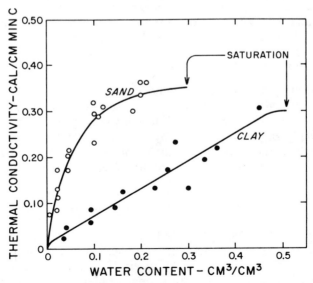

Fig. 9—The thermal conductivity of a sandy soil and a clayey soil plotted according to DeVries (1966), Tables 7.5 and 7.6.

the points of contact. The conductivity of this dry material is low because the cross-sectional area available for heat flow is extremely small.

The conductivity of the solid particles depends on the nature of the material and ranges from about 1.2 cal/cm min°C for sand grains to 0.42 cal/cm min °C for clay particles. The indicated thermal conductivities pertain to the solid materials. The thermal conductivity of the soil made up of these materials is much smaller because the heat can only be conducted at the points of contact. Heat can also pass by conduction through the air in the pores. The conductivity of the dry air between the soil particles is extremely low. Thus, dry soil does not conduct heat well. Dry soil is in fact an excellent insulating material.

The addition of water to the soil greatly increases its thermal conductivity. As water is added, the first increment forms rings around the points of contact between the soil particles. This results in a large increase in the surface area available for heat flow to occur from particle to particle. As a result, the thermal conductivity of the soil increases rapidly as small increments of water are added. The functional relationship between thermal conductivity of a soil and its water content depends on the mineralogical composition of the material and its pore size distribution. The thermal conductivity of a sandy soil increases more rapidly than that of a clayey soil with an increase in water content.

Heat is also transferred through the soil by the diffusion of water vapor from warm regions to cold regions. This process contributes substantially to a rate of heat transfer in soils which are only partially saturated with water.

The dependency of the thermal conductivity of the soil on its water content as well as the water movement resulting from temperature gradients have important consequences with respect to the design of systems for warming the soil with condenser cooling water or the use of the soil as a heat sink. When the soil is dry, the conductivity is very low and little heat transfer can occur. When the soil is wet, however, the thermal conductivity is high and the rate of heat transfer can be substantial.

4. HEAT CAPACITY OF THE SOIL

The heat capacity per unit volume of soil, C_v, is the amount of heat required to raise the temperature of 1 cm^3 of soil by 1 degree (cal/cm^3°C). A related unit is the specific heat C_d, which is the amount of heat required to raise the temperature of 1 g of soil by 1 degree (cal/g°C), where $C_v = \varrho C_d$ and ϱ is bulk density of the soil (g/cm^3). The heat capacity C_v of a soil is obtained by adding the heat capacities of the soil constituents according to

$$C_v = x_s C_{vs} + x_w C_{vw} + x_a C_{va}, \qquad [2]$$

where x_s x_w, and x_a denote volume fractions of solids, water, and air, respectively, and C_{vs}, C_{vw}, and C_{va} denote heat capacities of solids, water, and air. The values of $C_{vw} = 1.00$ cal/cm^3°C and $C_{vs} = 0.46$ cal/cm^3°C apply for soils over the temperature range of about 5 to 30°C. Some soils contain a large amount of organic matter for which $C_{vo} = 0.60$ cal/cm^3°C so that

$$C_v = 0.46\,x_m + 0.60\,x_o + 1.00\,x_w \text{ cal/cm}^3\text{°C}, \qquad [3]$$

where x_m, x_o, and x_w are the volume fractions of mineral solids, organic matter, and water, respectively (de Vries, 1966). This equation omits the contribution of the air, assuming its heat capacity to be insignificant.

5. WATER MOVEMENT DUE TO TEMPERATURE DIFFERENCES

The movement of water vapor molecules through pores spaces in the soil contributes to the transfer of heat. The diffusion of water vapor molecules from warm regions to colder regions in the soil is due to the differences in water vapor pressures corresponding to differences in temperature. As a result of the migration of water in the vapor phase as well as in the liquid phase, the soil adjacent to a heated pipe may gradually dry out. The drying can be substantial when the temperature at the surface of the pipe is high and the heat flow density is high. The drying can be minimized by maintaining the surface temperature of the pipe low and by utilizing a pipe with a large diameter to reduce the heat flux density.

The water lost from the soil near the pipe can be restored by water movement through the soil due to water potential gradients. Rewetting of the soil near the pipe is aided by placing the pipe close to the soil surface. Rewetting is easier in a coarse-textured soil than in a fine-textured soil.

VI. ENGINEERING CONSIDERATIONS

1. INCREASE IN SOIL TEMPERATURE

The prediction of soil temperature in a soil with line heat sources is a complex problem. Soil temperatures fluctuate on a daily basis due to the daily course of the radiation cycle. The daily temperature cycles are superimposed on annual temperature cycles. The increase in soil temperature due to line heat sources is superimposed on these dynamic conditions. Results for a given set of climatic conditions are shown in Fig. 10 (Boersma et al., 1972).

Temperature profiles show the degree of soil warming resulting from line heat sources at a depth of 92 cm spaced 185 cm apart, with a temperature of 34.5°C (Boersma et al., 1972). The diagrams indicate the changes in temperature in a horizontal as well as in a vertical direction. Temperatures of control plots, not heated, but subject to natural temperature variations, are shown also.

The temperature increase achieved in the root zone depends on the time of the year. The discussion may be focused on the 24°C isotherm. It was chosen because 24°C is an optimum root temperature for many crops. In February only a small area of the soil had a temperature of 24°C or higher

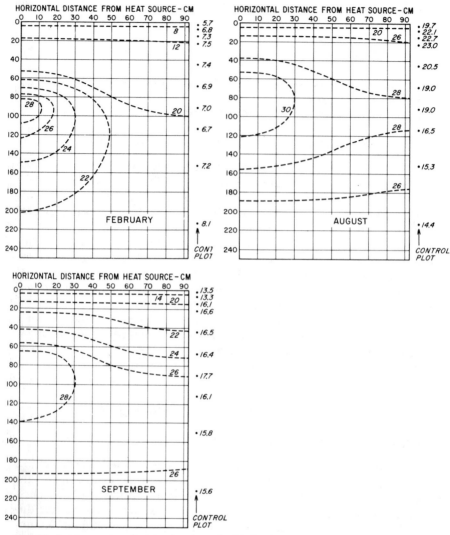

Fig. 10—Isotherms measured in plots heated with line heat sources with a temperature of 34.5°C, located 92 cm below the soil surface with a spacing of 185 cm. The soil surface was maintained free of vegetation. Soil temperatures in plots subject to the prevailing climatic conditions, termed *control plots,* are also shown. The solid dots mark depths at which temperatures were measured (Boersma et al., 1972).

and the isotherm was well below the root zone. The remainder of the profile was much colder although warmer than the control plots. The soil surface was at the same temperature as the control plots. In August the entire profile was warmer than 24°C except for the upper 10 cm. This was in contrast to the control plot which was much colder throughout. The temperature distribution in September shows the onset of the annual cooling cycle. The 24°C isotherm has already receded to lower depths.

Table 4—Average daily temperatures for several dates at depths from 0 to 125 cm and the temperature increase due to soil warming. The average temperatures shown in the last column are for the total profile from 0 to 220 cm (Rykbost et al., 1976).

Dates	Depth below soil surface (cm)							Avg.
	5	15	25	65	95	155	215	
	°C							
Control (not heated)								
1 Nov. 1970	9.5	8.8	8.9	10.2	11.6	13.1	13.6	--
24 Dec. 1970	3.2	3.7	3.8	5.6	6.8	9.2	10.9	7.4
19 Feb. 1971	4.9	5.7	6.0	6.9	6.9	7.3	8.1	7.0
2 Apr. 1971	9.7	9.1	9.2	7.5	7.3	7.4	8.1	7.8
10 May 1971	--	--	--	--	--	--	--	--
20 June 1971	17.9	17.7	17.4	15.1	14.3	12.1	11.5	13.9
14 July 1971	--	--	--	--	--	--	--	--
11 Aug. 1971	22.5	22.3	22.4	19.3	17.7	15.3	14.4	17.6
16 Sept. 1971	15.6	16.2	16.4	16.3	16.1	15.8	15.6	16.0
25 Jan. 1972	3.7	4.9	5.2	6.8	7.0	8.0	9.6	7.2
5 Mar. 1972	8.5	8.9	8.8	7.5	7.3	8.0	9.2	8.1
No cover (heated)								
1 Nov. 1970	9.9	11.9	13.1	18.4	22.1	21.8	21.5	19.3
24 Dec. 1970	4.5	7.2	8.8	15.6	20.0	20.6	20.4	18.9
19 Feb. 1971	6.4	9.5	11.5	19.1	23.2	22.5	21.5	19.5
2 Apr. 1971	12.0	13.4	14.3	19.5	23.0	22.1	21.4	20.0
10 May 1971	16.6	18.1	18.6	21.4	25.8	23.8	21.9	23.2
20 June 1971	18.4	20.8	21.8	25.4	27.6	25.5	23.1	24.6
14 July 1971	18.4	22.1	22.9	26.3	28.0	26.2	23.8	25.4
11 Aug. 1971	24.0	25.6	26.3	29.3	29.9	27.6	25.0	27.5
16 Sept. 1971	18.1	20.4	22.0	25.7	27.9	26.9	25.0	25.4
25 Jan. 1972	4.4	8.1	10.2	19.1	23.8	22.8	22.5	19.4
5 Mar. 1972	11.4	12.8	13.5	20.1	24.5	24.2	23.5	21.2
Temperature increase								
1 Nov. 1970	0.4	3.1	4.2	8.2	10.5	8.7	7.9	--
24 Dec. 1970	1.3	3.5	5.0	10.0	13.2	11.4	9.5	11.5
19 Feb. 1971	1.5	3.8	5.5	12.2	16.3	15.2	13.4	12.5
2 Apr. 1971	2.3	4.2	5.1	12.0	15.7	14.7	13.3	12.2
10 May 1971	--	--	--	--	--	--	--	--
20 June 1971	0.5	3.1	4.4	10.3	13.3	13.4	11.6	10.7
11 Aug. 1971	1.5	3.3	3.9	10.0	12.2	12.3	10.6	9.9
16 Sept. 1971	2.5	4.2	5.6	9.4	11.8	11.1	9.4	9.4
25 Jan. 1972	0.7	3.2	5.0	12.3	16.8	14.8	12.9	12.4
5 Mar. 1972	2.9	3.9	4.7	12.6	17.2	16.2	14.3	13.1

More complete data are shown in Table 4. The influence of soil warming on temperatures near the soil surface is small. The temperature increases were less than 3°C at 5 cm and ranged from 3 to 4°C at 15 cm. The increases at any depth remained nearly constant throughout the year even though the actual temperatures changed by as much as 15°C.

The actual temperature depends on the local climatic conditions as the heat field is imposed on an annual temperature cycle. It is of interest to have the capability to predict temperature distributions in soils heated by pipes carrying warm water. This is needed for extrapolation of the results to different temperatures of the heat sources and various combinations of depth and spacing. Kendrick and Havens (1973) presented an equation which allows the computation of the temperature distributions.

$$
\begin{aligned}
&T_{(x,y)} - T_S = \\
&\frac{(T_W - T_S)\ln\left(\dfrac{x^2+(h-y)^2}{x^2+(h+y)^2}\right)^{1/2} + \displaystyle\sum_{n=1}^{N}\ln\left(\dfrac{(nS-s)^2+(h-y)^2}{(n-Sx)^2+(h+y)^2}\right)^{1/2}}{\ln\left[\dfrac{2h-R}{R}\right] + \displaystyle\sum_{n=1}^{N}\ln\left(\dfrac{nS^2+(2h-R)^2}{(nS)^2+R^2}\right)^{1/2}} \\
&+ \frac{\displaystyle\sum_{n=1}^{N}\ln\left(\dfrac{(nS+x)^2+(h-y)^2}{(nS+x)^2+(h+y)^2}\right)^{1/2}}{\ln\left[\dfrac{2h-R}{R}\right] + \displaystyle\sum_{n=1}^{N}\ln\left(\dfrac{nS^2+(2h-R)^2}{(nS)^2+R^2}\right)^{1/2}}, \qquad [4]
\end{aligned}
$$

where $T_{x,y}$ is the soil temperature at the point (x,y), T_S is the temperature of the soil surface, T_W is the temperature of the heat source, R is the radius of the heat source (cm), S is the lateral spacing between heat sources (cm), and N is the number of heat sources on either side of the center heat source. The solution of this equation requires decisions about depth and spacing and knowledge of the thermal conductivity of the soil as a function of water content and of the surface temperature of the soil.

This equation was tested (de Walle, 1974; Rykbost et al., 1976) and found to make acceptable predictions of the average soil temperature. However, the equation does have limitations. Discrepancies observed between predictions made with Eq. [4] and experimental results can be attributed to two assumptions made in the analysis on which the equation is based. The theoretical model assumes steady state conditions which in fact do not exist. The derivation furthermore assumes that the temperature field of the heat sources is imposed on a medium initially at the temperature of the soil surface. The last assumption is a serious limitation. During the winter, soils at depths below the heat source are much warmer than the soil surface. Thus calculated values are much lower than actual temperatures.

2. RECOMMENDED SOLUTION OF THE SOIL HEAT FLOW PROBLEM

The best approach to describing the heat flow problem associated with line heat sources appears to be a numerical solution. The engineer faced with the problem of predicting these temperature fields is advised to consult with scientists who have addressed this problem. Experimental data on this problem are available for several climatic conditions and for many combinations of depth and spacing (Knudsen & Boersma, 1975).

3. RATE OF HEAT LOSS FROM THE SOIL

Kendrick and Havens (1973) also presented an equation which relates rate of heat loss from buried pipes to depth and spacing of the pipes and the thermal conductivity of the soil,

$$Q = \frac{2\pi\lambda(T_w - T_s)}{\ln\left[\dfrac{2h-r}{R}\right] + \sum\limits_{n=1}^{N} \ln\left(\dfrac{((ns)^2 + 2h - R)^2)}{(ns)^2 + R^2}\right)^{1/2}} \qquad [5]$$

where Q is the rate of heat loss (cal/cm² min), λ is the thermal conductivity (cal/cm min °C), T_w is the heat source temperature, T_s is the temperature of the soil surface, h is the depth of the heat source (cm), R is the radius of the heat source (cm), S is the lateral spacing between heat sources (cm), and N is the number of heat sources on either side of the center source.

Equation [5] shows the rate of heat loss to be proportional to be thermal conductivity of the soil and proportional to the temperature difference between the warm water pipe and the soil surface. Thus, the rate of energy dissipation will be high when the soil is wet and cold at the surface. This condition prevails in most moderate climates. The rate of heat loss will be low when the soil surface is warm and/or the soil is dry. This condition exists during the summer. Thus the rate of heat loss varies during the year in a cycle which corresponds to the annual cycle of climatic changes (Table 5). Rykbost et al. (1976) obtained the regression equation.

$$Q = 0.00375 + 0.00742\,(T_w - T_a)\ \text{cal/cm}^2\ \text{min}, \qquad [6]$$

Table 5—Rates of energy dissipation, heat source temperatures, mean air temperatures, and total precipitation for monthly periods. Heat sources were 92 cm deep and 185 cm apart. Plots were heated continuously for 2 years prior to making measurements (Rykbost, 1973).

Month and year	Energy dissipation rate	Heat source temperature	Mean monthly air temperature	Total monthly precipitation
	cal/cm² min	——— °C ———		cm
1971				
January	0.0303	32	4.1	27.2
February	0.0267	33	5.0	13.6
March	0.0262	33	5.8	15.7
April	0.0225	33	8.8	11.1
May	0.0192	33	12.7	5.9
June	0.0186	35	13.9	6.3
July	0.0165	35	18.8	0.1
August	0.0145	35	19.7	1.2
September	0.0161	35	13.9	7.9
October	0.0177	(36)	10.3	7.1
December	0.0251	(37)	3.9	25.7
1972				
January	0.0294	38	3.6	25.7
February	0.0279	36	6.1	13.0
March	0.0258	36	9.4	16.4
April	0.0229	36	7.9	10.8
May	0.0221	(36)	13.7	6.0
June	0.0121	37	16.4	2.6
July	0.0133	37	20.5	0.2
August	0.0108	37	23.2	0.6

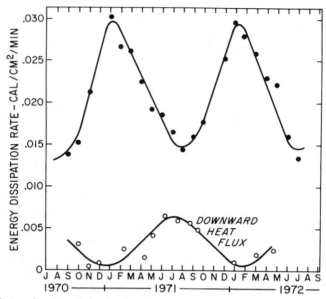

Fig. 11—Rates of energy dissipation in cal/cm² day. The total energy dissipation rate was measured and the downward flux was calculated. These fluxes apply to the experimental conditions only (Rykbost et al., 1976).

where T_w is the temperature of the pipe and T_a is the temperature of the air. Equation [5] predicts a zero rate of energy dissipation, when $(T_w - T_a) = 0$, while the regression equation predicts a small heat loss. The coefficients in the regression equation depend on system design and thermal conductivity of the soil. Results suggest that the rate of heat loss can be predicted for a given system design when the air temperature is known.

The total energy flow consists of a downward flux and an upward flux (Fig. 11). For the conditions shown, the downward flux accounted for less than 5% of the total flux during the winter, but for over 40% of the total flux during the summer.

4. LAND AREA NEEDED FOR ENERGY DISSIPATION

Approximate estimates of the land area required to dissipate the waste heat from a 1,000 MWe power-generating station can be obtained using measured or calculated rates of energy dissipation. The range in rates of heat loss in one experiment (Rykbost et al., 1976) were from 0.012 cal/cm² in the summer to about 0.030 cal/cm² in the winter. Assuming a power generating efficiency of 34%, an area of approximately 9,200 ha would be required to dissipate the waste heat during the winter and 23,000 ha during the summer. These results assume a pipe diameter of 0.5 cm, a depth of 100 cm, and a constant heat source temperature of 35°C. Allowing for a temperature drop of 10 along the heat source length would increase the area requirements by about 50%. This system would require between 15,000 and 30,000 ha to reduce cooling water temperatures by 10°C.

Soil is not an efficient primary heat sink. However, soil warming holds promise as a method to increase the growth rate of certain high value crops. Furthermore, the rate of heat loss can be increased according to Eq. [5] by making certain that λ has the highest possible value, by maintaining a high pipe temperature, and by placing the pipes at a shallow depth with a narrow spacing.

The application in which the soil is used as the primary heat sink (de Walle, 1974) uses several of these management techniques. The soil is maintained at a high water content by continued watering with sewage effluent so that λ remains high. The pipes are placed at shallow depth and close together.

VII. THE SOIL AS A HEAT SINK

Experiments conducted at the Pennsylvania State University (de Walle, 1975) indicate that 2,000 ha of land with 2-inch diameter pipe installed at a depth of 1 ft with a spacing of 2 ft in a sandy soil would be required to dissipate the waste heat from a 1,500 MWe thermal power plant using a nuclear energy source. This corresponds to a ratio of 1.33 ha/MWe. This ratio indicates a rate of heat loss equivalent to a lightly loaded cooling pond. The research workers state that preliminary cost analysis indicated the system to be the economically competitive method of waste heat dissipation. Some nonquantified costs and benefits included the fertilizer value of the waste water and water savings. In the method of waste heat dissipation, water is not lost due to evaporation as it is with wet cooling towers. This benefit would favor soil warming over wet cooling towers, particularly when the cost of water becomes high.

VIII. CROP GROWTH

The effect of soil temperature on the rate of plant growth and development is qualitatively well established. Most plants grow best at an optimum temperature which is often higher than the temperature of the soil in the spring.

Since the introduction of the concept of soil warming with power plant waste heat, many experiments have been initiated for the purpose of quantifying the effect of soil warming on the growth of crops (Knudsen & Boersma, 1975). The results have been highly variable. Yield increases varied widely from year to year for the same crop in the same field, from crop to crop in a given region, and from region to region. The most complete summary of these experiments was published by Mays (1977)

Growth patterns of peppers and strawberries on heated and control plots are compared in Fig. 12. Both crops accumulated a higher percentage of their final yield early in the growing season. This advantage was small, however, and disappeared later in the season. The yield increase which may

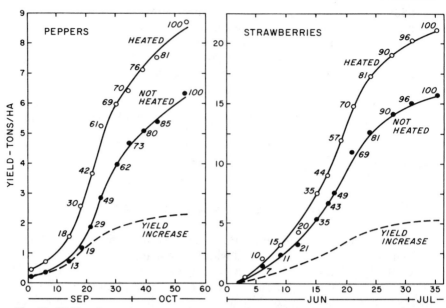

Fig. 12—Yield and growth response of peppers and strawberries in heated and control plots (Rykbost et al., 1975a).

be expected in a given year seems to depend on a combination of factors which determine how favorable the year is for crop growth. Soil warming seems to be most effective when climatic conditions and management factors are limiting (Fig. 13).

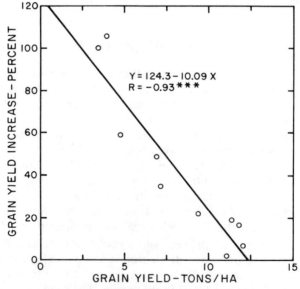

Fig. 13—Yield increase due to soil warming expressed in percent of unheated yield as a function of unheated yield. The high yield increases due to soil warming occurred when unheated yields were low (Rykbost et al., 1975b).

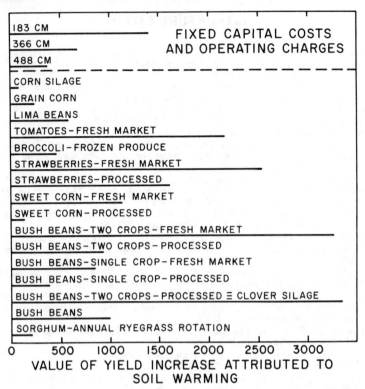

Fig. 14—Comparison of soil warming costs with values of yield increases attributable to soil warming in $/ha. Costs are shown for heat source spacings of 185, 366, and 488 cm. The values of yield increases shown were based on experimental results obtained on plots with heat source spacing of 185 cm (Schmisseur et al., 1975).

Results of an economic feasibility analysis for several crops are summarized in Fig. 14 by showing the value of increased yields attributable to soil warming in relation to soil warming cost.

Some crops are identified which have the potential to be profitably produced with soil warming. These are high value crops such as tomatoes or strawberries, or crops which could be double cropped as a result of soil warming such as bush beans. Most low value crops do not offer, at least at this time, such development potential.

The economic feasibility of producing crops with soil warming methods is directly related to the annual cost attributable to soil warming methods and to the value of the additional product. The major components of annual costs are annual fixed capital charges directly related to the soil warming system investment and the grower opportunity costs.

Capital outlays, hence, annual fixed capital charges, can be reduced by using less expensive material and/or a less dense network of pipe. The annual fixed capital charges are nearly proportional to the spacing of the heating pipes. The potential for using wider spacing and thereby dramatically reducing the cost depends on the relationships between yield and spacing. This relationship has not been studied satisfactorily in test plot experiments.

LITERATURE CITED

Boersma, L. L., E. W. R. Barlow, and K. A. Rykbost. 1972. Use of reactor cooling water from nuclear power plants for irrigation of agricultural crops. WRRI-12. Water Resour. Res. Inst., Oregon State Univ., Corvallis.

Boersma, L., L. R. Davis, G. M. Reistad, J. C. Ringle, and W. E. Schmisseur. 1974. A systems analysis of the economic utilization of warm water discharge from power generating stations. Bull. no. 48. Eng. Exp. Stn., Oregon State Univ., Corvallis.

Boersma, L., and K. A. Rykbost. 1973. Integrated systems for utilizing waste heat from steam electric plants. J. Environ. Qual. 2:179–188.

Brown, G. A. 1975. General problems in reject heat utilization. p. 20–24. In J. G. Knudsen and L. Boersma (ed.) Future developments in waste heat utilization. Circ. no. 49. Eng. Exp. Stn., Oregon State Univ., Corvallis.

Center for Strategic and International Studies. 1973. Understanding the "National Energy Dilemma": A report of the Joint Committee on atomic energy. The Center for Strat. and Int. Stud., Georgetown, Univ., Washington, D.C.

Cline, J. F., M. A. Wolfe, and F. P. Hungate. 1969. Evaporative cooling of heated irrigation water by sprinkler application. Water Resour. Res. 5:401–406.

Cornell University. 1973. Report of the Cornell workshops on the major issues of a National Energy Research and Development program. College of Engineering. Cornell Univ., Ithaca, N.Y.

De Vries, D. A. 1966. Thermal properties of soils. p. 210–235. In W. R. van Wijk (ed.) Physics of plant environment. North-Holland Publ. Co., Amsterdam, The Netherlands.

deWalle, D. R. 1974. An agro-power-waste water complex for land disposal of waste heat and waste water. Res. Publ. no. 86. Inst. for Res. on Land and Water Resour. The Pennsylvania State Univ., University Park, Pa.

Ford Foundation. 1974. A time to choose—America's energy future. Energy Policy Project. The Ford Found., New York, N.Y.

Kendrick, J. H., and J. A. Havens. 1973. Heat transfer models for a subsurface, water pipe, soil-warming system. J. Environ. Qual. 2:188–197.

Knudsen, J. G., and L. Boersma. 1975. Future developments in waste heat utilization. Circ. no. 49. Eng. Exp. Stn., Oregon State Univ., Corvallis.

Mays, D. A. 1977. Special problems and opportunities in use of waste heat for soil warming. p. 511–527. In Land application of waste material. Soil Conserv. Soc. of Am., Ankeny, Iowa.

Rykbost, K. A. 1973. An evaluation of soil warming for increased crop production. Ph.D. Thesis, Oregon State Univ., Corvallis. (Diss. Abstr. Sec. B, 34:1826B–1827B[1973]). (Diss. Abstr. Sec. B, 34:1826B–1827B [1973]).

Rykbost, K. A., L. Boersma, and G. D. Jarman. 1976. Soil temperature increases induced by subsurface line heat sources. Agron. J. 68:94–99.

Rykbost, K. A., L. Boersma, H. J. Mack, and W. E. Schmisseur. 1975a. Yield response to soil warming: vegetable crops. Agron. J. 67:738–743.

Rykbost, K. A., L. Boersma, H. J. Mack, and W. E. Schmisseur. 1975b. Yield response to soil warming: agronomic crops. Agron. J. 67:733–738.

Schmisseur, W. E., L. Boersma, and K. A. Rykbost. 1975. Yield response to soil warming: economic feasibility. Agron. J. 67:794–799.

United Nations. 1972. Statistical yearbook. U.N., New York, N.Y.

Wierenga, P. J., R. M. Hagan, and D. R. Nielsen. 1970. Soil temperature profiles during infiltration and redistribution of cool and warm irrigation water. Water Resour. Res. 6:230–238.

29

Locating Animal Feedlots and Managing Animal Wastes Applied to Land[1]

FRED A. NORSTADT

Science and Education Administration
Agricultural Research, USDA
Fort Collins, Colorado

I. INTRODUCTION

Decisions and efforts by legislators, agency personnel, and planning groups on zoning, land use, and priorities must be compatible with maintaining animal production as a significant enterprise. Informed, concerned citizens can create a climate leading to environmental decisions based on fact. Pollution must be curbed, but without hampering the worldwide effort to grow more food for more people. Potential environmental problems in animal production arise from: (i) the animal confinement, (ii) runoff control and storage facilities, and (iii) cropped land receiving manure and runoff. Enough research information is now available to solve these problems.

The Council of Agricultural Science and Technology summarized some of the factors leading to problems with animal manures (CAST Rep., 1975). Not many decades ago, animals were produced in many small units scattered over the countryside. Animal feed was grown nearby, and the animal manures were applied to the same cropland for fertilizer. Today, the agricultural producer, no matter what his product—plant or animal—must specialize for economic reasons. Animal production units vary in size, but it is common for tens of thousands of beef animals or hundreds of thousands of poultry to be confined in a single production unit.

Concentrating the animals concentrates the manure. Thereby, effective utilization of manure as a fertilizer is a problem, generally because of insufficient suitable cropland nearby. Other economic constraints, including relatively low-cost and easily managed chemical fertilizers, transportation, and labor costs, confound the problem.

Land-use competition and problems of waste disposal from animal production are an outgrowth of specialization in agricultural enterprises; human population increases, shifts, and concentrations; and accompanying demands for food, goods, and services. The various uses of land must be re-

[1] Contribution of Science and Education Administration, USDA, Ft. Collins, CO 80522, in cooperation with Colorado State Univ. Agric. Exp. Stn.

conciled among the demands of agriculture, industry, transportation, housing, trade, and recreation (Talmadge, 1975, p. 22). Perhaps the critical point of goals and land-use policies is that agricultural land can be converted into nonagricultural uses much more readily, and often with nearly irreversible changes, than is the case for the reverse.

One estimate of the quantities of animal manures in the United States is about 1.5 billion metric tons (1.7 billion tons) per year on the wet basis or (assuming 20% solids) about 308 million metric tons (340 million tons) per year on the dry basis (CAST Rep., 1975). Fortunately, about 50% of these wastes are deposited on croplands, pastures, and rangelands in a diffuse and essentially innocuous manner. Animals confined for intensive production produce the other 50% of manures (Table 1).

All animal manures contain about the same chemical elements that serve as plant nutrients, yet in different combinations and proportions, depending on the kind of animal, its diet, and the management of the manure (Table 2). However, one estimate is that the nitrogen (N), phosphorus (P), and potassium (K) amount to about 19, 38, and 61% of those elements used annually in chemical fertilizers in the United States (CAST Rep., 1975). Therefore, manures can contribute significantly to conservation of chemical fertilizers. That animal manures can increase crop yields has been demonstrated repeatedly, mainly because of N, P, and K contents.

In selecting a site for animal production or utilization of the animal manures, we must subscribe to three rigid conditions: (i) the particular manure must be beneficial or at least innocuous when applied to soil; (ii) it must not be detrimental to public health; and (iii) it must not cause air or drainage-water pollution (Menzies & Chaney, 1974). Environmental concerns stemming from the animal manure production and utilization center

Table 1—Estimated quantities of manure and the N, P, and K distributed or available for application to land from dry livestock and poultry manures in a recent year.[†]
(Source: USEPA, USDA, 1979).

Source	Manures dry weight	% recoverable[‡]	N	P	K
	million metric tons		— thousand metric tons —		
Dairy cows	21.4	86	506	125	641
Beef cows[§]	36.9	4	807	336	732
Beef feeders	9.4	100	238	83	117
Swine	7.9	64	473	200	325
Sheep[§]	3.1	50	93	34	148
Layers	3.0	100	83	62	62
Broilers	3.4	100	122	48	159
Turkeys	1.3	69	43	18	24
Total	86.4	--	2,365	906	2,208

[†] Based on unpublished data developed by D. L. Van Dyne, Econ. Res. Serv., and C. B. Gilbertson, ARS-USDA. 1977. The United States Agricultural census for 1974 and estimates of element losses in current management systems were used to compute the values.

[‡] Includes any areas of production where manure may be collected for use elsewhere—collectible manure.

[§] Beef cows and many sheep are on rangeland, and their manure is not collected and applied to cropland.

Table 2—Some properties of animal manures (adapted from Loehr, 1968; Perkins & Parker, 1971).

Animal	Moisture†	Element composition					
		N	P	K	S	Ca	Fe
	%	kg/metric ton					
Dairy	79	5.6	1.0	5.0	0.5	2.8	0.04
Beef feeders	80	7.0	2.0	4.5	0.9	1.2	0.04
Swine	75	5.0	1.4	3.8	1.4	5.7	0.28
Sheep	65	14.0	2.1	10.0	0.9	5.8	0.16
Layer hens	37	20.0	19.1	18.8	4.9	34.2	1.34
Broilers	25	22.7	10.7	17.0	3.5	19.7	1.22

† Percent moisture, wet basis.

around odors, human health, surface and ground water contamination, and soil and crop problems (Loehr, 1968).

Odors result from the natural decomposition processes that start as soon as the manure is excreted and continue as long as any utilizable material remains as food for microorganisms living everywhere in soil, water, and the manure. Odor strength depends on the kind of manure and the conditions under which it decomposes (Alexander, 1961). Although occasionally unpleasant, the odors are not dangerous to health in the quantities customarily noticed about animal production units and fields where the manures are spread for fertilizer.

Most disease-causing organisms—bacterial, rickettsial, viral—are incapable of prolonged growth or multiplication outside the living body (Diesch, 1970). In the soil environment, most of them soon die and are degraded into harmless substances (Waksman, 1966). However, human population shifts and concentrations, increasing numbers of animals raised in confinement, changing animal waste disposal practices, and changing occupational and recreational methods may so disturb ecological systems that the potential for zoonosis becomes significant in the future. Therefore, each animal production unit and its associated manure utilization system will have to be considered and evaluated by experts as to its potential for disease transmission.

Soil can effectively degrade the organics from animal manures, but the soluble salts, including nitrate, may leach into tile drainage lines or ground water (CAST Rep., 1975). Ground water degradation can be limited by judicious use of animal manures and proper design and management of animal confinements.

Surface waters can be contaminated by runoff from fields fertilized with animal manures if the wastes are improperly managed, for example, by surface application followed by heavy rains or irrigation before incorporating them. It is now a law that runoff from feedyards or other animal production units must be controlled.

In the soil-plant system utilizing animal manures, both the salt content and the fertilizer value must be considered. All animal wastes contain sodium (Na), potassium (K), calcium (Ca), and magnesium (Mg) salts. Sodium in excessive amounts can degrade the soil structure, particularly in irrigated areas. Essentially all soils and crops can utilize nutrients derived from animal manures, but the amounts must be carefully regulated to be compatible with the particular soil and crop (Mathers & Stewart, 1970). A particular site can be used indefinitely if wastes are applied at rates to supply the crop need for the major fertilizer element of least content and deficiencies are offset with chemical fertilizer (Norstadt et al., 1977).

II. LOCATING ANIMAL FEEDLOTS

A. Site Selection

Figure 1 is a schematic of an animal production system showing the production inputs, climatic and physical environmental factors, pollution potentials, and the marketable output. A production facility is best planned in its entirety and in relation to the surrounding geographical area. Although originally intended for waste water systems, the U.S. Environmental Protection Agency (USEPA, 1975) bulletin, *Evaluation of Land Application Systems,* has an excellent section titled "Site Characteristics," which covers topography, soils, and geohydrology. Some publications give discus-

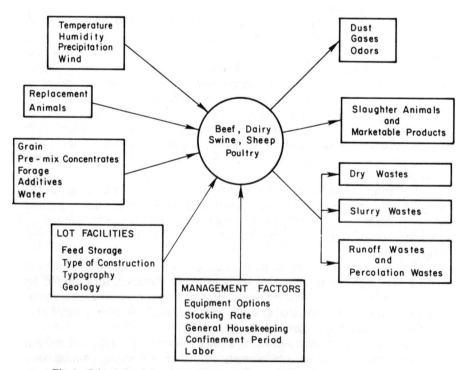

Fig. 1—Schematic of an animal production system (adapted from Shuyler, 1973).

sions of site selection (USEPA, 1972; Flack & Carlisle, 1974; Midwest Plan Serv., 1974, 1975a, 1975b; Olson, 1974; Witty & Flach, 1977).

Planners should prepare a map to enable them to visualize factors affecting the animal production site as well as the proposed area receiving the manures. The map should show distances to neighboring farms, streams, lakes, cities, and other facilities within a 5- to 20-km radius. Perimeter land use, land-use plans, climate, topography, geology, prevailing wind direction, and cropping systems all influence the use of a site for animal production or waste disposal. Poor planning and management can lead to impaired ability of the soil to produce crops, degrade the quality of surface and ground water, and cause nuisance complaints by neighbors.

1. TOPOGRAPHY

Animal production facilities and feedlots are readily adaptable to sites that, for topographic or other reasons, are marginal for intensive crop production. Because of the marginal classification, these lands may have a much lower dollar value than prime farmland. However, problems resulting from rugged topography, shallow underlying rock strata, a high water table, or poor drainage must be balanced against a low initial cost. Some earthmoving will likely be required in the construction of any animal production facility. Most state regulations require location of pens away from streams and irrigation canals and outside of the 10-year flood plain of river systems (USEPA, 1972).

Topographical quadrangle maps, available from the U.S. Geological Survey, show land contour and the locations of watercourses, access routes, residential areas, and recreational areas. Considerable detail concerning soil types, rock strata, and water tables may be obtained from soil surveys available from the Soil Conservation Service (SCS) of the U.S. Department of Agriculture. The nearest SCS office is listed under the "United States Government" in the telephone directory. Farmers, ranchers, construction engineers, land use planners, or anyone dealing with land use can obtain expert help and advice from the SCS.

Inasmuch as biological activity in manure degradation (and odor production) is promoted by water, animal pens should be sloped (2 to 8%) to make them self-draining. Feed efficiency and disease control also are better in a dry environment or one that soon dries after a storm. Detail on recommended slopes of animal pens can be found in Witty and Flach (1977).

2. SOILS

The functions of soils in locating animal production facilities are covered comprehensively in the publications: *Environment Protecting Concepts of Beef Cattle Feedlot Wastes Management* (Shuyler et al., 1973), *Livestock Waste Facilities Handbook* (Midwest Plan Serv., 1975a), and *Agricultural Waste Management Field Manual* (SCS, 1975). Each local state university and extension offices, as well, will have relevant publications and personnel who can help.

Several soil properties affecting construction and location of animal facilities, with which the local SCS experts are familiar, follow:

1) Natural soil drainage	8) Erodibility
2) Permeability	9) Load-bearing capacity
3) Infiltration rate	10) Slope
4) Flood hazard	11) Contents of sand, silt, and clay
5) Depth to water table	12) Shrink-swell potential
6) Seasonal wetness	13) Corrosivity
7) Depth to bedrock, stoniness	14) Soil structure

Several factors can be briefly summarized to characterize an acceptable soil and site for animal facilities as follows:

1) Not subject to flooding (no loss of pollutants from the site);
2) Well-drained;
3) Available water capacity greater than 20 cm in the upper 150 cm of the soil profile;
4) At least 150 cm of soil above consolidated rock;
5) No jointed bedrock with channels at shallow depths;
6) No infiltration for animal confinement, runoff control, or manure storage facilities.

The soil is a strong buffer and inactivator of what would otherwise be many serious environmental pollutants. All soils act as sponges to some degree, retaining water and gasses in their pores. Thereby, pollutants are delayed in their passage through the soil profile whether they be suspended in solution or vaporized. This property is dependent upon the relative proportions of sand, silt, and clay; the amount of organic matter; and the actual arrangement and physical structure of the soil particles and particle aggregates. In addition, aeration, rate of gas diffusion, and leaching are dependent upon pore sizes, pore distribution, and water retention of a particular soil.

The general requirements of soil organisms are energy, nutrients, water, favorable temperatures, and lack of harmful conditions such as extreme acidity or alkalinity, or water-logging (Russell, 1961). All animal manures added to soil are part of the energy and nutrient sources for soil inhabitants. "The soil organisms are living right up to their income in the matter of nutrients and energy supply" (Russell, 1961, p. 202). They are not overfed and are capable of utilizing any amount of animal manures compatible with crop fertilizer requirements in normal agricultural soils (Martin & Focht, 1977; Gilmour et al., 1977).

Chemical elements in animal manures are excreted as ions or they may be part of organic compouns. The cations Na^+, K^+, magnesium (Mg^{2+}), and calcium (Ca^{2+}) can react immediately with the ion exchange complex of the soil. In these reactions, the cations replace or attain chemical equilibrium with other cations already held on the negative charge sites of the complex. The elements N, sulfur (S), and P are excreted in the manure as parts of organic compounds which undergo biological degradation and oxidation in the soil to yield the anions nitrate (NO_3^-), sulfate (SO_4^{2-}), and phosphate

(PO_4^{3-}). Negatively charged ions are attracted to and held on the soil anion exchange complex.

3. HYDROGEOLOGY

The environment below ground surface is complex and generally not easily determined. If attenuation is minimal, potential pollutants will pass in sequence through: (i) the land surface; (ii) the zone of aeration (the zone between the land surface and the water table); (iii) the zone of saturation (the ground water reservoir) to a stream; (iv) the stream course; and (v) the sea (LeGrand, 1970).

Each potential construction site should be examined to ensure maximum protection from ground water pollution. Highly permeable, loose soils, shallow soils over fractured bedrock, and shallow soils should be avoided as pen areas or runoff and solid manure storage pits. Water with its waste content will take preferred paths, flowing readily through permeable zones and shunning or flowing with difficulty through relatively impermeable materials. If the water table is deep, percolation through overlying zones of sands, silts, and clays leads to marked attenuation of pollutants.

Contamination of ground water with bacteria or NO_3-N is a potential hazard. Excessive NO_3-N in drinking water (above 45 ppm NO_3 or 10 ppm NO_3-N) can lead to nitrate poisoning or methemoglobinemia (an oxygen-deprived condition in infants sometimes referred to as blue babies). Nitrate poisoning affects both livestock and humans (especially children and pregnant females).

Present efforts are directed toward regulating the amount of infiltration from pen surfaces and impoundments. Heavy soils (high clay content, expanding, or tight soils) generally have a low infiltration or seepage rate and are ideal for construction of pens and waste retention and storage structures. If the soils prove unsuitable, soil sealing or concrete or asphalt liners can be very expensive corrective measures. Thus, the advantage of careful site selection is apparent.

A shallow aquifer (high water table) is vulnerable to contamination and should be avoided. Widely fluctuating water tables may lead to shifts of concrete manure storage pits and damage to those structures, with subsequent contamination of the aquifer.

4. NUISANCE POTENTIAL

Existing federal and state laws indicate the need to keep feedlot runoff out of streams to prevent degradation of water quality. As yet, most states do not have air quality regulations for livestock and poultry operations, but they likely will in the future. While some odor from an animal operation is inevitable, regulations when adapted will probably not permit unusual or particularly pungent odors.

Manure packs in lamb finishing pens, beef cattle feedlots, or other animal confinements provide abundant energy and nutrients for soil organisms. Animal manures have a high biochemical oxygen (BOD) demand and create anaerobic environments in the manure pack and in the soil (Norstadt & Porter, 1976; Parr, 1974).Consequently, the microbial end products include such toxic and offensive substances as organic acids, amines, alcohols, methane, hydrogen sulfide, mercaptans, and reduced Fe and Mn. These substances preclude growth of a wide-ranged, mixed population of organisms otherwise found in aerobic, cultivated soils. For these reasons, animal confinements are malodorous unless dept clean and dry (Mosier et al., 1977).

Animal production units seldom directly benefit the people who complain about disagreeable odors around their residences, places of work, or recreational areas. In some cases, odors may become such a nuisance to individuals that life patterns and established transportation routes are changed to avoid them.

Use of privacy fences, vegetative shelterbelts, and/or land formations suitable for visual concealment, or a site located far from highways, may prevent problems. Proximity to residential areas should be avoided. Although wind direction is sufficiently variable that in most areas it is not a factor, if possible a site should be selected so that prevailing winds mix and disperse malodors away from inhabited areas and air drainage patterns caused by day and night temperature changes do not trap odor-laden air. For example, on the west side of Fort Collins, Colorado, there is no detectable cattle feedlot odor; on the east side of the city the odors are always noticeable. In this instance, a distance of 3.2 km (2 miles) and prevailing westerly winds combine to make the difference. With proper site selection, construction and operating costs may often be reduced and public acceptance assured even though certain pollution control facilities and practices are not used.

Attitudes of immediate neighbors have to be considered. Agreements for free manure application and/or a steady market for neighbors' grain or hay in return for freedom from nuisance complaints may have merit. Zoning may be used in some areas to prevent encroachment of residential, shopping, and recreational development. An expensive, but positive, approach to zoning is the purchase of buffer land.

B. Confinement Facilities

For guidelines on locating and arranging confinement facilities, good sources are: *Farmstead Planning Handbook, Livestock Waste Facilities Handbook,* and *Livestock Waste Management with Pollution Control* (Midwest Plan Serv., 1974, 1975a, 1975b). Especially helpful is the technical help provided by the SCS, the State Experiment Stations and Extension Services, and the departments related to environmental protection within each state.

Concentration of animal manures and their decomposition products is greatest at the points of manure elimination and collection of the wastes. Shelters and lots can be on bare soil or paved surfaces, depending on the animal and geographic location (Table 3).

Table 3—Estimated percentage distribution† of livestock and poultry management systems in the continental U.S. (Source: USEPA, USDA, 1979).

Management systems	Areas of the United States			
	%			
	Northeast & Lake States	Southwest, Delta, & Southern Plains	Mountains & Pacific	Corn Belt, Northern Plains, & Appalachian
Dairy‡				
Stanchion	63	7	4	22
Loose housing	6	38	14	34
Free stall	26	22	35	41
Unpaved lot, limited housing	5	33	47	3
		West of 98th meridian		East of 98th meridian
Beef				
Breeding stock				
Pasture		90		90
Other		10		10
Feeders				
Outdoor, unpaved lot without shelter§		85		56
Outdoor, unpaved lot with shelters§		4		31
Outdoor, paved lot with/without shelter§		11		13
		Major producing states#		All other states
Swine				
Pasture		25		50
Paved lot¶		17		5
Unpaved lot¶		41		40
Confined housing		17		5
				All regions
Sheep				
Breeding stock				
Pasture				70
Confinement				30
Feeder lambs				
Pasture				35
Outdoor, unpaved lot with shelter††				35
Outdoor, unpaved lot without shelter††				20
Outdoor, paved lot with/without shelter††				10
Layers				
Caged with dry manure-holding system				70
Caged with flush, slurry, pit slurry				10
Loose housing with bedded floors				20
Broilers				
Loose housing				100
Turkeys				
Outdoor or range (some with housing)				50
Loose housing				50

† Based on unpublished data developed by D. L. Van Dyne, Econ. Res. Serv., and C. B. Gilbertson, ARS-USDA, 1977. The U.S. Agricultural Census for 1974 was used to compute the values.

‡ 70% use stack or bunker storage; 20% use manure-holding pond or lagoons; 10% use other methods of manure management.

§ About 40% of the units require runoff-control facilities.

¶ About 30% of the units require runoff-control facilities.

Includes the Corn Belt and Lake States, South Dakota, Nebraska, Kansas, Texas, Kentucky, Tennessee, North Carolina, and Georgia.

†† About 20% of the units require runoff-control facilities.

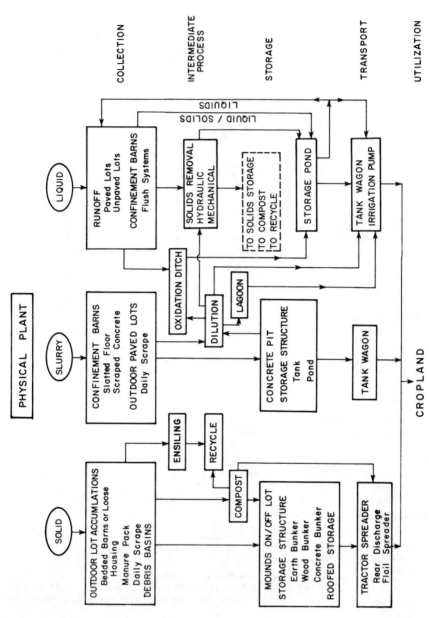

Fig. 2—Manure management systems for animal production units (Source: USEPA, USDA, 1979).

Figure 2 shows the several manure management systems used in animal production. For each physical state of the manure—solid, slurry, or liquid—the several origins and subsequent managements show the potential points of pollution. Obviously paved surfaces and waterproofed, lined containments offer the best protection against loss and movement of pollutants. However, they are expensive. In land use planning, one must consider all segments of animal production to reasonably balance what is desired against what can be afforded or tolerated.

1. TYPE OF CONSTRUCTION

Some of the factors affecting the type of construction are as follows (Midwest Plan Serv., 1975a):

1) Operation
   a) Size and type
   b) Capital
   c) Mechanization level
   d) Owner preferences
2) Farm
   a) Size
   b) Soil type
   c) Topography
   d) Crops
3) Regulations controlling air, water, and noise pollution
4) Proximity of Neighbors
5) Climate
   a) Precipitation: (i) amount, (ii) distribution, and (iii) evaporation
   b) Temperature norms
   c) Prevailing winds
6) Animal
   a) Type
   b) Ration
   c) Housing
   d) Management
   e) Manure characteristics

The importance of each of the six foregoing major factors is illustrated by considering no. 3, Regulations. Federal regulations apply in all states. Each cattle feedlot with more than 1,000 animal units is required to have a permit if it discharges off-premises. Regulations are subject to change, but feedlots of *all new* construction must prevent discharge of polluted runoff from a 25-year, 24-hour storm. In addition, the runoff control facility must contain the maximum volumes of runoff expected or treated manure generated during normal operation of the system. By 1 July 1983, existing feedlots that require a permit must meet the same criteria as new systems.

Judicious design of a solids settling unit, which is part of a runoff control facility, illustrates why a production facility is best planned in its entirety and in relation to the surrounding climatic and geographical area. The solids settling unit is designed for a 1-hour storm, because 1 hour of detection is enough for settling out most solids. It can be designed for the 10-year, or even 1-year frequency, if it discharges to a facility designed for the required 25-year, 24-hour storm. Failure of the settling unit to retain all liquids for 1 hour, as would occur with a storm greater than the one used for design, would not cause failure of the entire runoff pollution control system.

States can impose additional or more stringent requirements, such as facilities with greater runoff-holding capacity, specific times for emptying the holding ponds, zoning laws, and public health measures relating to milk, meat, or egg production. Any of these requirements affect the design, construction, and operation of a facility. Hence, it is imperative to be informed by consulting personnel at one or more of several state offices: extension agricultural engineering (agricultural college), pollution or water quality control agency, board of health, and agencies responsible for specific animal products such as meat, milk, or eggs.

2. STOCKING RATE

The areas recommended per animal depend on the type of animal; whether it is confined in a building, pen, or cage, or loose in a feedlot or exercise yard; and the climate, season, and weather conditions. Some typical area requirements for paved and unpaved feedlots are given in Table 4, according to climatic regions (Fig. 3). Bulletins published by the State Experiment Stations and available from their extension service offices contain space requirements for closely confined animals.

Table 4—Areas per animal for paved and unpaved feedlots by climatic area of the continental U.S.† (Source: USEPA, USDA, 1979).

	Climatic area							
	Cold		Cool		Warm		Hot	
Livestock type	Arid	Humid	Arid	Humid	Arid	Humid	Arid	Humid
	m²/animal							
Dairy								
Paved	9.3	9.3	7.0	9.3	9.3	9.3	9.3	9.3
Unpaved	92.9	92.9	55.7	92.9	55.7	92.9	55.7	92.9
Beef								
Paved	9.3	9.3	5.6	9.3	4.6	5.6	4.6	5.6
Unpaved	41.8	41.8	27.9	41.8	13.9	27.9	13.9	27.9
Swine								
Paved	1.9	1.9	1.9	1.9	1.4	1.9	1.4	1.9
Unpaved	11.6	11.6	9.3	11.6	7.0	9.3	7.0	9.3
Sheep								
Paved	1.9	1.9	1.9	1.9	1.4	1.9	1.4	1.9
Unpaved	9.3	9.3	7.0	9.3	4.6	9.3	4.6	7.0

† Unpaved lot areas for turkeys are 1.4 m²/bird for all climatic regions. Pasture areas for turkeys are 16.3 m²/bird for all climatic regions. Paved lots are not recommended for turkeys.

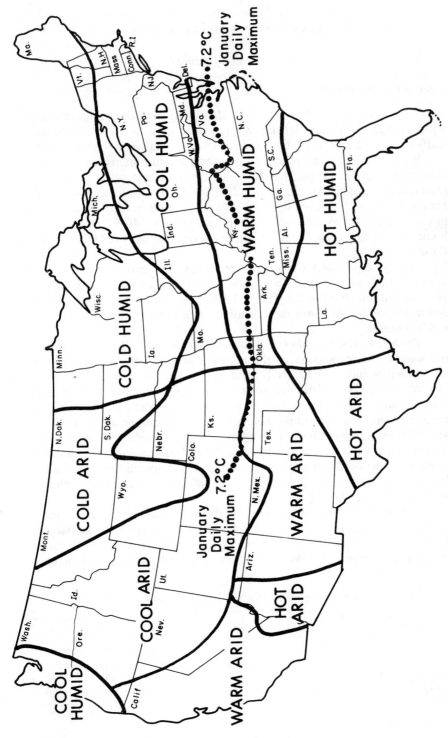

Fig. 3—Climatic regions of the continental United States. (Source: USEPA, USDA, 1979).

III. MANAGING ANIMAL WASTES

A. Controlling Runoff

1. RUNOFF PROPERTIES

Water has little buffering quality, that is, its pH can be shifted easily. Small amounts of certain substances in solution or suspension can dramatically alter its properties with no apparent visible change in the water itself.

Runoff waters from an animal pen carry manure materials in suspension and in solution (Table 5). Solids—undigested fragments of grain, bran, fibers, and colloidal materials (including the excreted microbes)—are fine enough to be easily moved by water. Materials used in compounding feed mixtures are often pulverized or ground to improve digestion efficiency. Some 30% of the solids in cattle manure are of colloidal size ($<2~\mu$m) (McCalla et al., 1970).

The amount of solids removed from a feed pen in runoff will increase greatly with rainfall intensity and with slope of the lot surface. McCalla et al. (1970) found about 11.5 kg/m³ (1.3 tons/acre-inch) were removed under Nebraska conditions. Snowmelt runoff is more viscous and has a higher solids content.

The Na, K, Ca, and Mg salts in animal manures readily dissolve in runoff waters. Decomposition of the manures after excretion releases more salts with ions such as SO_4^{2-}, NO_3^-, and NH_4^+ (McCalla et al., 1970).

Wadleigh (1968) lists a number of waterborne diseases transmissible with animals, including anthrax, brucellosis, coccidiosis, encephalitis, erysipelas, mastitis, ornithosis, gastroenteritis, and salmonellosis. Diesch et al. (1975) found that salmonella and leptospires survived for a long time in a manure slurry, but that leptospires lost their virulence and were unable to infect when exposed to a manure environment. Salmonella were transmitted by aerosols, but leptospires were not. Over 100 diseases can infect both man and animals (Diesch, 1970).

The pathogen content of manures from animal confinements today probably is less than in the past, because the modern operator maintains the health of the animals better than his predecessor (Menzies, 1977). Stockpiling and storage help to reduce pathogen concentrations in the manure.

Table 5—Pollution characteristics of untreated animal wastes, summary of values (Miner & Willrich, 1970).

Animal	Animal weight	Solids	BOD†	N	P
	kg		kg/day		
Beef cow	454	4.5	4.5	0.14	0.2
Dairy cow	454	4.5	0.5	0.18	0.02
Swine	100	0.41	0.1	0.03	0.003
Poultry	5	0.03	0.01	0.001	0.001

† Biochemical oxygen demand.

Besides, the modern farm animal operation is oriented toward good animal nutrition, health, and disease control. It is reasonable that the standard practice of spreading solid manure on land presents no serious disease hazard. The risk inherent in spray irrigation of liquid manure or runoff effluents is essentially eliminated by restricting animals from sprayed pastures for a week to 10 days of sunny weather (Elliott & Ellis, 1977). Exposure to heat, ultraviolet radiation, and drying is lethal to *Salmonella,* fecal coliforms, and probably viruses (Menzies, 1977).

2. RUNOFF VOLUME

The SCS method can be used to estimate the amount of direct runoff from rainfall events on animal pens. The procedure is summarized concisely in manuals by Shuyler et al. (1973) and by Azevedo and Stout (1974). Factors affecting the volume include: (i) drainage area, (ii) storm rainfall, (iii) lot management, (iv) slope, and (v) moisture conditions of the manure on the lot. Data from the SCS method closely match experimental results from Nebraska, Kansas, and Colorado. For rains exceeding 1.3 cm (0.5 inch) a good estimate is 0.7 times the precipitation.

3. EFFECTS ON RECEIVING WATERS

Animal feedlot runoff varies widely in its characteristics, depending on rainfall intensity, temperature, feedlot surface moisture content, and manure accumulation (Armstrong & Rohlich, 1970; Miner & Willrich, 1970). Research data indicate the concentration of pollutants in runoff is relatively independent of ration fed (Shuyler et al., 1973). Concentration is highest during initial runoff (Table 6).

If the runoff reaches a stream, the material moves as a slug of contaminated water which is slow to disperse and mix with the receiving water. High BOD of pen runoff depletes the dissolved oxygen (DO) in the stream. Oxygen-using life dies or is seriously affected as the slug passes by (Table 7). Eventually, enough mixing and decomposition brings the DO to a sufficient life-supporting level. Recovery of still bodies of water, such as reservoirs and lakes is longer than for flowing water and depends on the biological breakdown time, dilution, mixing by wave action and currents, and other factors (Campbell & Whitley, 1970).

Table 6—Concentration change of pollutants in runoff with time from a concrete-surfaced cattle feedlot (adapted from Shuyler et al., 1973).

Hour	BOD†	NO₃-N	NH₄-N	Organic N
	mg/liter			
11:35 p.m.	16,800	625	525	532
11:58 p.m.	6,120	975	526	315
12:25 a.m.	7,400	1,000	485	36
2:25 a.m.	9,950	900	543	285

† Biochemical oxygen demand.

Table 7—Water quality changes as a slug of feedlot runoff passes a sampling point in a stream (adapted from Shuyler et al., 1973).

Time elapsed after storm	DO†	BOD‡	Cl⁻	NH₄-N
		mg/liter		
Before rainstorm	8.4	2	11	0.06
13 hours	7.2	8	19	12.00
20 hours	0.8	90	50	5.30
46 hours	6.8	5	31	0.44
117 hours	6.2	3	25	0.08

† Dissolved oxygen.
‡ Biochemical oxygen demand.

4. REGULATIONS

All of us have responsibility for environmental quality and the use of both renewable and depletable resources. Regulations governing animal feeding facilities directly affect the people designing, developing, or managing a facility (Shuyler et al., 1973). State and local regulations will affect feeding site selection. There are restrictions on the minimum distance that a lot can be located from surface waters, residential dwellings, municipalities, recreational areas, and highways.

Other requirements affect runoff control facilities and management, including solid and runoff-carried waste storage and the disposal of the liquids and solids. Each state has specific agencies to be contacted, a list of which is included in the manual by Shuyler et al. (1973). Zoning and other local restrictions can be determined by consulting the appropriate county agency.

5. LAND MODIFICATION

Because of land costs, availability of suitable land, vagaries of climate and weather, and manure characteristics, the *ideal* combinations of factors to control runoff are seldom realized. Modifications can control wind movement and snow distribution, divert overland flows from offsite and control runoff and transport of manure from the site (Norstadt et al., 1977).

Good landscaping can provide noise abatement, reduce wind movement and, where applicable, control snow distribution in addition to improving aesthetic considerations. Windblown manure materials will accumulate in depressions and be subject to overland movement and leaching with rains. The SCS can provide recommendations for species and management for natural, living windbreaks. It is a common practice to use board windbreaks (about 2.5 m high) as a solid fence about cattle feedlots. Barriers must be properly placed to control snow distribution and unwanted drifts to avoid excessive volumes of melt water. Well-distributed snowmelt will minimize transport of manure materials.

Runoff originating offsite creates the same problems as that originating onsite. Diversions can be utilized to protect an area or a structure from runoff or shorten the length of slope to control erosion (USEPA, 1972; Midwest Plan Serv., 1975a). So-called *clean* runoff diverted away reduces the amount of waste volume, or it can be diverted into a waste system if needed for dilution. Failure of a diversion on some locations could create more damage than no structure. Engineering standards and specifications can be obtained from local SCS offices.

Runoff, erosion, and transport of manure materials on sloping lots can be controlled with terraces, which restrict slope length and provide orderly disposal of runoff (Jacobson, 1961). Many states have legal requirements for the diversion or impoundment of runoff. Publications are available in many states outlining both regulations for runoff control and suggested methods of compliance (Melvin, 1971).

6. CONTROL STRUCTURES

Terraces can be designed for specific needs. The broadbasin terrace to control runoff and collect transported solids has been widely accepted for use in cattle feedlots in Nebraska (Swanson et al., 1973). Solids are detached by raindrop impact and moved by runoff flow. Bedloads and part of the suspended solids settle out when flow velocity decreases or runoff is impounded. Solids accumulating in impoundments reduce the storage capacity. Decomposition of organic materials of the manure causes odors. If such materials accumulate to a depth of 30 cm or more, they may dry too slowly to permit ready removal after draining the effluent.

Improved drainage from slopes will likely cause increased solids transport. Solids removal from an unpaved lot should not disturb the contiguous manure pack, because an intact manure layer reduces mixing of manure and soil by animal traffic. Several researchers have studied the transport and settling characteristics of manure solids (Gilbertson et al., 1972; Swanson et al., 1971). It is not always feasible or necessarily desirable to fully minimize transport. Installations can provide satisfactory separation of solids for temporary storage or for immediate disposal on soil. Terrace basins equipped with riser inlets suffice for onsite separation (Swanson et al., 1973; Linderman et al., 1976). Swanson and Mielke (1973) described a flow-through solids trap for feedlot runoff. Low slope channels and baffles were used to settle solids from runoff.

Separation by settling of solids is a common farm application (see Midwest Planning Serv., 1975a, for discussion of a design and dimensions). Odors are markedly reduced in holding ponds if the settlable solids are removed from the runoff. Both fractions, solids and liquids, are easier to handle and use. The solids-separation feature is particularly desirable if an animal production unit is near an urban area, even though additional land area and particular topography are needed for the system operation.

The storage for runoff must meet the established safety margins for storms. A minimum design volume provides sufficient space for bacterial populations to assist in waste degradation (Midwest Planning Serv., 1975a). Several designs and space requirements are discussed in the publications by

Midwest Planning Service (1975a, 1975b). Design and systems vary with the particular production unit and climate.

Impoundments are required for runoff storage before final disposal. Soil considerations and construction specifications are comparable to those for farmponds (Matson, 1961). The SCS technicians can help, particularly if both soil problems and a potential for ground water pollution exist. Runoff control structures should not be constructed without a competent consultant.

B. Preventing Ground Water Contamination

Two major potential sources of ground water contamination are the animal confinement and runoff control and storage facilities. Enough research information is now available for effective control of these sources.

1. THE ANIMAL CONFINEMENT AND RUNOFF CONTROL AND STORAGE FACILITIES

Contamination of soil profiles with large amounts of NO_3-N from unpaved feedlots is most likely (Viets, 1974):

1) When the feedlot is first established and before an impermeable manure pack develops;
2) On abandoned lots with weed growth breaking up the manure pack;
3) On lots stocked with too few animals (< 100 cattle/ha or equivalent);
4) On lots frequently scraped to the soil surface; and
5) On seasonally used lots, as with small farms.

It is well documented that well-managed animal confinements and the structures used for runoff confinement on soil are largely self-sealing (Lehman et al., 1970; Mielke & Mazurak, 1976; Oliver et al., 1974; Sewell et al., 1975). Salts, manure organics, and animal traffic combine to form a manure-soil combination essentially impenetrable to water. So long as a lot is used continuously and a manure layer near to the manure-soil interface is undisturbed, little infiltration will occur (Mielke & Mazurak, 1976; Norstadt & Porter, 1976; Viets, 1974). Infiltration is so slow that the decomposition processes can dispose of any NO_3-N formed in the soil profile (Norstadt & Porter, 1976).

2. GROUND WATER STUDIES

Ground water contamination is doubly troublesome. The rates of turnover or replacement of the waters are slow compared to those of surface waters and the mantle strata are not easily examined or sampled.

The problems of stratification and slow or incomplete mixing that are characteristic of waters in aquifers were reviewed by Viets and Hageman (1971). Movement and replenishment of the underground waters are more rapid in humid than in arid climates. It is estimated that some western

Table 8—Water table concentrations of nitrate N according to degree of use of the feedlot (data calculated from Stewart et al., 1967b).

Feedlot			
Length of use yearly	Animals	No. of samples	NO$_3$-N, ppm
Continuous	Beef cattle	18	11.5
6–9 mo	Beef cattle	6	15.0
3–6 mo	Beef cattle	3	23.3
0–3 mo	Beef cattle	1	11.0
Continuous	Dairy	4	14.3

aquifers contain waters at least 186 years old on the average, whereas eastern basins may have a comparable age of only 30 days.

Fluctuations in well water depths and composition are common and often erratic. Determining trends in composition is thereby difficult unless closely spaced samples are studied over a long time. Stability of NO$_3$-N in deep water tables is not known. Vertical and horizontal movement of nitrate is slow through the aeration zone. Therefore, changes in ground water quality may reflect changes in surface N levels many tens or hundreds of years ago (Adriano et al., 1973). Careful management and monitoring are desirable to prevent initial pollution, since "die-away" or attentuation is likely to be very slow.

Core-drilling studies in Colorado (Stewart et al., 1967a) did not show a higher NO$_3$-N concentration in the surface of the water table under corrals than under grassland, irrigated cropland, and dryland. The area has an average annual precipitation of 35–40 cm. In some cases the water beneath the lots contained organics and had a bad odor. Other, later studies showed very little NO$_3$-N percolated (Lorimer et al., 1972; Elliott et al., 1972; Norstadt & Porter, 1976).

On the other hand, ground water samples collected near old feedlots showed elevated nitrate-nitrogen concentrations (Goldberg, 1970; Smith, 1967). In the data of Stewart et al. (1967b), water table concentrations of NO$_3$-N were higher in those samples drawn from feedlots of low concentrations of cattle (dairy) or low frequency of use (Table 8). These data show the importance of points three and five listed previously concerning reasons for soil profile contamination with NO$_3$-N.

C. Applying Manures on Cropland

Efficient collection, storage, and use of manure has long been a goal for crop production, particularly when available soil nitrogen was low and fertilizer nitrogen unavailable or costly (Viets, 1974). Animal manure is a resource that should be recycled, and Viets says its *disposal* without beneficial use is an indication of something seriously wrong with the food production system. It is with this sort of philosophy that land use planners need to approach animal production units and utilization of their major by-product, manure.

1. BENEFITS

Soil tilth refers to the physical conditions of the soil and is used to describe factors such as aggregate formation and stability, moisture content, aeration, infiltration rate, drainage, and waterholding capacity. These factors all influence the ease of tillage, fitness of a seedbed, and impedance to seedling emergence and root penetration. Livestock and poultry manures improve soil tilth and are compatible with most soils (McCalla, 1942, 1946; Robinson, 1964; Russell, 1961; Zook, 1936). The poorer the soil, the greater will be the benefit of manure on soil tilth.

Livestock and poultry manures supply many of the chemical elements essential to plant growth (Barnett et al., 1973; Carreker et al., 1973; Gardner & Robertson, 1946; Stucker & Erickson, 1975). When enough N is supplied by animal wastes, P and K are usually adequate for crop production. The P and K may exceed crop needs, and in the interest of conservation of these fertilizer elements, it is suggested that approximately one-half of the N be supplied by manure with the balance coming from commercial mineral fertilizers (Olsen & Barber, 1977).

The P in soils is so strongly held by adsorption and precipitation reactions that solution concentrations seldom exceed 1 ppm (Keeney & Wildung, 1977; Black, 1970). Phosphorus added to soils coprecipitates with Ca, Mg, iron (Fe), or aluminum (Al). These forms then dissolve or revert to less available occluded or precipitated forms. Dissolved P is believed to be strongly held in the soil by adsorption reactions.

Animal manures contain from 1 to 2% K (dry wt basis), or about the same as the ration fed the animals. The soil has a large capacity to adsorb K. While the manures may be applied as either solids or liquids, most of the K is water soluble, and readily reacts with the soil or is "tied-up," not moving in either runoff or percolating water (Olsen & Barber, 1977).

There are reactions with organic substances classified as complexation, chelation, and biological transformation (Keeney & Wildung, 1977). Although these reactions are important in soil fertility, particularly in regard to plant availability of the essential minor elements zinc (Zn) and Fe, they are not completely understood. Fortunately, animal manures improve the soil's behavior governing all the plant nutrients and their availability for crop production.

Detailed discussions of the effects of animal manures on soils and plant growth can be found in the book, *Soils for Management of Organic Wastes and Waste Waters* (Elliott & Stevenson, 1977).

2. METHODS OF LAND APPLICATION

The method of application depends on whether the material is in solid, slurry, or liquid form. Solids are usually spread with rear-discharge spreaders, uniformly, and in a single operation before land preparation for cropping. Volatilization loss of ammonia N from surface-applied manure is reduced by prompt soil incorporation.

Up to 85% of the settlable solids in runoff from a lot can be expected to accumulate in a solids separation system. Solids are utilized by field spreading immediately or after storage, drying and using as bedding, or even processing further for refeeding. The solids decompose slowly compared to whole lot manure and are relatively innocuous. Their salt content is low, since they have been leached by the runoff water.

Liquids can be handled by any type of sprinkler or through gated pipes into furrows or borders (SCS, 1975). If the liquid has high concentrations of salts and N, it can be diluted with water and used for crop fertilization. If disposal alone is the objective, the amount applied to a given field area has to be carefully regulated to avoid soil and crop damage. Procedures for calculation of application rates are discussed in the SCS publication, *Agricultural Waste Management Field Manual* (1975). Extension service personnel and the SCS technicians can give help and guidance in system design, site location, and management for disposal of both solid and liquid components of runoff.

3. ACCEPTABLE RATES

a. Agronomic Rates—An agronomic rate is beneficial use compatible with maximum crop utilization. All animal manures contain essentially the same fertilizer elements, only in different amounts and combinations, depending on the animal type, its ration, and the management of the manure after excretion. Since N is both the most used element for production of optimal yields and the most mobile element (thus creating potential for surface and ground water pollution), it is the most logical component on which to base manure rates. In irrigated areas, however, salt buildup in the soil may limit application rates. Also, in nonirrigated, humid, and dryland regions, manure rates must be reduced if salt accumulations reduce yields. *Because of these factors, the most useful criteria for determining land application rates of livestock and poultry manures are N and salt.*

When manure is applied year after year to the same field, the availability of N in the manure for crop use is important in determining land application rates. The rate at which N mineralizes can be determined by using a series of decay constants described by Pratt et al. (1973). Mineralization is rapid the first year after application and decreases in subsequent years. For example, decay constants of 0.35, 0.15, 0.10, and 0.05 mean that 35% of the N in residue becomes available the first year, 15% of the residual N becomes available the second year, 10% the third year, and 5% the fourth year and each following year. Poultry manures have a very high mineralization rate because they are high in uric acid and urea, substances that readily release NH_4^+-N. Manure on outdoor lots or in storage exposed to weathering have low decay constants since N may have been lost through runoff or volatilization of ammonia N (NH_3-N). Mathers and Goss (A. C. Mathers and D. W. Goss. 1976. Estimating animal waste applications to supply nitrogen requirements. Agron. Abstr., Am. Soc. Agron., Madison, Wis. p. 150) derived an equation, using decay constants of Pratt et al. (1973) and

Willrich et al. (1974) to account for the N release from all animal manures. Using the equation, they developed values to indicate the amount of manure (prior to adjustment for N losses) required to supply 100 kg (220 lb.) of N annually as well as the reduced rates for succeeding years for repeated application to the same land for 20 years (USEPA, USDA, 1979).

If values for soil-available N and potential N losses are known, the following equation can be used to adjust the values to calculate the total N required for crop fertilization:

$$N_T = N_c - N_s + N_v + N_d + N_l + N_r,$$

where

N_T = total N required,
N_c = N content of crop,
N_s = N available in soil,
N_v = N volatilization loss,
N_d = N denitrification loss,
N_l = N leaching loss, and
N_r = N runoff loss.

These components and management of the manure, soil, crop, and water are modeled in Fig. 4 and discussed in detail in the forthcoming Section 208 Planning Manual (USEPA, USDA, 1979). Suffice it to say here that, with proper management, animal manures can supply at least a portion of the N needs for cropping, providing there is no salt problem. The above-cited USEPA, USDA-SEA manual, and the bulletins by Powers et al. (1973, 1974) help determine whether a potential salt problem will develop with utilization of animal manures.

b. Utilization Potential with Different Crops—Even when manures are applied at agronomic rates, a good soil test program is recommended to determine if element concentrations approach toxic levels or if an excessive level of one element has reduced availability of another to the crops.

Experiments across the United States have demonstrated compatibility of animal manures with nearly every soil and crop. Of course, animal manures are not concentrated N sources. They are bulky, often odorous, and require adjustments in machinery for spreading and incorporation. Most state experiment stations have done recent research in use of animal manures and have developed guidelines and bulletins describing modern practices (Meek et al., 1975; Powers et al., 1973, 1974; Peele et al., 1973).

4. POTENTIAL PROBLEMS WITH ANIMAL MANURES

a. Nitrate and Salt—Potential soil problems center about NO_3-N concentrations, its movement into ground waters, and salt. Pertinent publications discussing those problems include those by Powers et al. (1973, 1974) and Adriano et al. (1971). Sugarbeet crop quality is particularly sensitive to soil NO_3-N content, especially late in the growing season, and manure rate must be carefully regulated (Halvorson & Hartman, 1975).

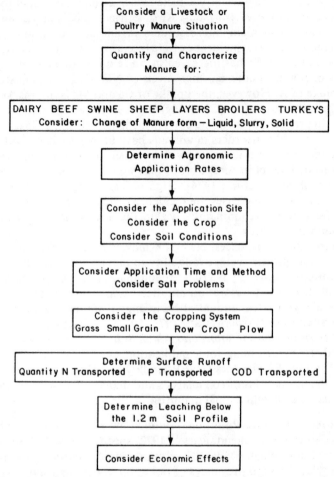

Fig. 4—Flow chart for modeling cropland utilization of animal manures (adapted from USEPA, USDA, 1979).

Ground water contamination at a manure utilization site is a result of poor use and management of the manure, soil, crops, and water. These factors and their bearing on control are discussed in detail in "Site Design and Management for Utilization and Disposal of Organic Wastes" (Norstadt et al., 1977), the publication by Stewart et al. (1975), and the above-cited joint publication of USEPA and the USDA-SEA for Section 208 planners (1979).

In most soils the anion exchange capacity is much weaker or less tenacious than the cation exchange capacity. This is why N, in the form of NO_3^-, can be a serious ground water pollutant. For, as soon as the N compounds added to the soil or contained in soil organic matter are biologically converted and oxidized to NO_3^-, the NO_3^- is free to move with percolating water. If the quantity of NO_3^--N is not excessive when crop growth is vigorous, the released NO_3^--N will be absorbed by plant roots and not leach into the ground water (Viets, 1971).

Crop yields can be adversely affected when elements essential for plant growth reach excessive levels in soils. Also, nutrient imbalances in soils have been associated with metabolic disorders in animals consuming forages grown on these soils. The incidence of grass tetany, a disorder characterized by low blood Mg levels, has increased in cattle on pastures receiving large quantities of poultry manures. High levels of NO_3^--N in the soil stimulate forage uptake of K. However, the uptake of Ca and Mg is not markedly affected. Thus, the ratio of $K/(Ca + Mg)$ is increased, which may induce Mg deficiency in pregnant or lactating cows (Stuedemann et al., 1975).

Other metabolic disorders in animals have been associated with excessive N accumulation in soils treated with livestock and poultry manures. Accumulations of NO_3-N in forage crops may approach toxic levels (Pratt et al., 1973; Wallingford et al., 1974). High N fertilization of tall fescue, regardless of N source, increases the incidence of fat necrosis, the formation of hard, fat lesions predominantly within the abdominal cavity of cattle (Stuedemann et al., 1975).

Manures containing excess Na and K may adversely affect soil physical properties, among them water availability to plants, water infiltration, and soil structure. It is generally Na that predominates in animal wastes and can lead to soil structure deterioration and decreased infiltration. In the semiarid and arid regions, the amount of Na in animal manures and in irrigation water are of concern (Powers et al., 1973, 1974). Those two reports, *Diagnosis and Improvement of Saline and Alkali Soils* (U.S. Salinity Lab. Staff, 1954), and the forthcoming joint publication of USEPA and the USDA-SEA for Section 208 planners (USEPA, USDA, 1979) describe the procedures and determinations of soil analysis and management to cope with salt problems associated with animal manures.

b. Nonpoint Source Pollution—Public Law 92-500, the Federal Water Pollution Control Act Amendments of 1972, specifies as part of Section 208 that local planning shall: (i) identify, if appropriate, agriculturally and silviculturally related nonpoint sources of pollution, including runoff from manure disposal areas, and from land used for livestock and crop production; and (ii) set forth procedures and methods (including land use requirements) to control to the extent feasible such sources and control the disposal of pollutants on land or in subsurface excavations within such areas to protect ground and surface water quality (U.S. House of Represent., 1972).

The law clearly states that both avenues of water pollution—surface and ground water—are to be controlled. Land use planners and producers must take into account the factors affecting all water pollution. Economic effects have also been studied to determine how shifts in animal waste management will affect the producers. Pertinent publications include those by Coote et al. (1975), the University of Maine (1972), Peele et al. (1973), and Michigan State University (1976). Local Section 208 planning is under way. Guidance and publications are available from state and federal agency personnel concerned with nonpoint source pollution.

Runoff control also applies to the cropped areas receiving the animal wastes. In view of the shortages of energy and fertilizer, the animal manures are best utilized at agronomic rates to promote good crop yields and partially replace mineral fertilizers. Proper rates and methods of application, and other management factors, are summarized in a forthcoming joint publication of USEPA and the USDA, SEA for Section 208 planners. When available in 1979, the publication can be obtained from the USDA Office of Information, Washington, D.C., and the USEPA Robert S. Kerr Environmental Research Laboratory, Ada, Oklahoma.

IV. SUMMARY

The objectives implied in corrective measures for control. of ground and surface water pollution will be achieved when the evaluation and planning procedures are used by groups of specialists. All interested and qualified people need to be represented by planning commissions composed of farmers, engineers, agronomists, hydrologists, soil scientists, and economists, working together to integrate land use variables into what seems to be the best management system.

There are land use practices for animal production and utilization of manures that minimize risks to the environment, but it is not conceivable that one could plan well enough to eliminate all risks or to anticipate all contingencies. Because animal and manure management practices vary throughout the United States, no single group of control measures can be applied everywhere.

LITERATURE CITED

Adriano, D. C., R. S. Ayers, F. T. Bingham, R. L. Branson, A. C. Chang, et al. 1973. Nitrates in the upper Santa Anna river basin in relation to groundwater pollution. California Agric. Exp. Stn. Bull. 861. 59 p.

Adriano, D. C., P. F. Pratt, and S. E. Bishop. 1971. Nitrate and salt in soils and ground waters from land disposal of dairy manure. Soil Sci. Soc. Am. Proc. 35:759–762.

Alexander, M. 1961. Organic matter decomposition. p. 154–161. *In* Introduction to soil microbiology. John Wiley & Sons, Inc., New York, N.Y.

Armstrong, D. E., and G. A. Rohlich. 1970. Effects of agricultural pollution on eutrophication. p. 314–330. *In* T. L. Willrich and G. E. Smith (ed.) Agricultural practices and water quality. The Iowa State Univ. Press, Ames.

Azevedo, J., and P. R. Stout. 1974. Farm animal manures: An overview of their role in the agricultural environment. California Agric. Exp. Stn. Manual 44. 109 p.

Barnett, A. P., S. R. Wilkinson, J. A. Stuedemann, and W. A. Jackson. 1973. The value of poultry manure on cropland. p. 29–37. *In* 17th Annu. Poultry Health and Manage. Short Course Proc., 6–7 Mar. 1973, Poultry Sci. Dep., Clemson Univ., and Clemson House South Carolina Poultry Improvement Assoc., Clemson, S.C.

Black, C. A. 1970. Behavior of soil and fertilizer phosphorus in relation to water pollution. p. 72–93. *In* T. L. Willrich and G. E. Smith (ed.) Agricultural practices and water quality. The Iowa State Univ. Press, Ames.

Campbell, R. S., and J. R. Whitley. 1970. Effects of agricultural pollutants on recreational uses of surface waters. p. 331–343. *In* T. L. Willrich and G. E. Smith (ed.) Agricultural practices and water quality. The Iowa State Univ. Press, Ames.

Carreker, J. R., S. R. Wilkinson, J. E. Box, Jr., et al. 1973. Using poultry litter, irrigation, and tall fescue for no-till corn production. J. Environ. Qual. 2:497-500.

CAST Report. 1975. Utilization of animal manures and sewage sludges in food and fiber production. Rep. no. 41. Counc. for Agric. Sci. and Technol., Dep. of Agron., Iowa State Univ., Ames. 22 p.

Coote, D. R., D. A. Haith, and P. J. Zwerman. 1975. Environmental and economic impact of nutrient management on the New York dairy farm. Agric. Eng. Dep., Cornell Univ. Ithaca, N.Y. Search Agric. Vol. 5, no. 5. 28 p.

Diesch, S. L. 1970. Disease transmission of water-borne organisms of animal origin. p. 265-285. In T. L. Willrich and G. T. Smith (ed.) Agricultural practices and water quality. The Iowa State Univ. Press, Ames.

Diesch, S. L., P. R. Goodrich, B. S. Pomeroy, and L. A. Will. 1975. Survival of pathogens in animal manure disposal. USEPA, EPA-660/2-75-012. Corvallis, Oreg. 129 p.

Elliott, L. F., and J. R. Ellis. 1977. Bacterial and viral pathogens associated with land application or organic wastes. J. Environ. Qual. 6:245-251.

Elliott, L. F., T. M. McCalla, L. N. Mielke, and T. A. Travis. 1972. Ammonium, nitrate, and total nitrogen in the soil water of feedlot and field soil profiles. Appl. Microbiol. 28:810-813.

Elliott, L. R., and F. J. Stevenson (ed.). 1977. Soils for management of organic wastes and waste waters. Am. Soc. of Agron., Madison, Wis. 650 p.

Flack, K. W., and F.J. carlisle. 1974. Soils and site selection. p. 1-17. In Factors involved in land application of agricultural and municipal wastes. A preliminary document of the USDA-ARS, Washington, D.C.

Gardner, R., and D. W. Robertson. 1946. Comparison of the effects of manures and commercial fertilizers on the yield of sugar beets. p. 27-32. In Am. Soc. Sugar Beet Technol. 4th General Meet. Proc., 12-14 Feb. 1946, Denver, Colo. Am. Soc. of Sugar Beet Technol., Fort Collins, Colo.

Gilbertson, C. B., J. A. Nienaber, T. M. McCalla, J. R. Ellis, and W. R. Woods. 1972. Beef cattle runoff, solids transport, and settling characteristics. Trans. ASAE 15:1132-1134.

Gilmour, C. M., F. E. Broadbent, and S. M. Beck. 1977. Recycling of carbon and nitrogen through land disposal of various wastes. p. 173-194. In Lloyd R. Elliott and F. J. Stevenson (ed.) Soils for management of organic wastes and waste waters. Am. Soc. of Agron., Madison, Wis.

Goldberg, M. c. 1970. Sources of nitrogen in water supplies. p. 94-124. In T. L. Willrich and G. E. Smith (ed.) Agricultural practices and water quality. The Iowa State Univ. Press, Ames.

Halvorson, A. D., and G. P. Hartman. 1975. Long-term nitrogen rates and sources affect sugarbeet yield and quality. Agron. J. 67:389-393.

Jacobson, P. 1961. Mechanics of water erosion. p. 401-413. In Agricultural engineers handbook. McGraw-Hill Book Co., Inc., New York.

Keeney, D. R., and R. E. Wildung. 1977. Chemical properties of soils. p. 75-97. In Lloyd R. Elliott and F. J. Stevenson (ed.) Soils for management of organic wastes and waste waters. Am. Soc. of Agron., Madison, Wis.

LeGrand, H. E. 1970. Movement of agricultural pollutants with ground water. p. 303-313. In T. L. Willrich and G. E. Smith (ed.) Agricultural practices and water quality. The Iowa State Univ. Press, Ames.

Lehman, O. R., B. A. Stewart, and A. C. Mathers. 1970. Seepage of feedyard runoff water impounded in playas. Texas Agric. Exp. Stn. Bull. MP-944. College Station, Tex. 7 p.

Linderman, C. L., N. P. Swanson, and L. N. Mielke. 1976. Riser intake designs for feedlot solids collection basins. Trans. ASAE 19:894-896.

Loehr, R. C. 1968. Pollution implications of animal wastes—a forward-oriented review. USEPA, EPA-660/2-74-042. Robert S. Kerr Water Res. Center, Ada, Okla. 148 p.

Lorimer, J. C., L. N. Mielke, L. F. Elliott, and J. R. Ellis. 1972. Nitrate concentrations in groundwater beneath a beef cattle feedlot. Water Res. Bull. 8:999-1005.

McCalla, T. M. 1942. Influence of biological products on soil structure and infiltration. Soil Sci. Soc. Am. Proc. 7:209-214.

McCalla, T. M. 1946-47. Value of organic matter in soil. p. 22-31. In Nebr. Crop Improve. Assoc. 37th and 38th Ann. Rep.

McCalla, T. M., L. R. Frederick, and G. L. Palmer. 1970. Manure decomposition and fate of breakdown products in soil. p. 241-255. In T. L. Willrich and G. E. Smith (ed.) Agricultural practices and water quality. The Iowa State Univ. Press, Ames.

Martin, J. P., and D. D. Focht. 1977. Biological properties of soils. p. 115–169. *In* Lloyd R. Elliott and F. J. Stevenson (ed.) Soils for management of organic wastes and waste waters. Am. Soc. of Agron., Madison, Wis.

Mathers, A. C., and B. A. Stewart. 1970. Nitrogen transformations and plant growth as affected by applying large amounts of cattle feedlot wastes to soil. p. 207–214. *In* Proc. Cornell Univ. Conf. on Agric. Waste Manage., Rochester, N.Y. 19–20 Jan. 1970. Cornell Univ., Ithaca, N.Y.

Matson, H. W. 1961. Water management, conservation use, and legal aspects. p. 492–503. *In* Agricultural engineering handbook. McGraw-Hill Book Co., Inc., New York.

Meek, B., L. Chesnin, W. Fuller, R. Miller, and D. Turner. 1975. Guidelines for manure use and disposal in the Western Region, USA. Bull. 814. Washington State Univ., Pullman. 18 p.

Melvin, S. W. 1971. How to comply with Iowa's feedlot runoff control regulations. Iowa State Univ. Coop. Ext. Serv. Pm-511. 4 p.

Menzies, J. D. 1977. Pathogen considerations for land application of human and domestic animal wastes. p. 575–585. *In* Lloyd R. Elliott and F. J. Stevenson (ed.) Soils for management of organic wastes and waste waters. Am. Soc. Agron., Madison, Wis.

Menzies, J. D., and R. L. Chaney. 1974. Waste characteristics. p. 18–36. *In* Factors involved in land application of agricultural and municipal wastes. A preliminary document of the USDA, SEA, Washington, D.C.

Michigan State University. 1976. Beef feedlot design and management in Michigan. Michigan State University, East Lansing. Res. Rep. no. 292. 32 p.

Midwest Plan Service. 1974. Farmstead planning handbook. Midwest Plan Service MWPS-2. Iowa State Univ., Ames. 44 p.

Midwest Plan Service. 1975a. Livestock waste facilities handbook. Midwest Plan Service MWPS-18. Iowa State Univ., Ames. 94 p.

Midwest Plan Service. 1975b. Livestock waste management with pollution control. Midwest Plan Service MWPS-19. Iowa State Univ., Ames. 89 p.

Mielke, L. N., and A. P. Mazurak. 1976. Infiltration of water on a cattle feedlot. Trans. ASAE 19:341–344.

Miner, J. R., and T. L. Willrich. 1970. Livestock operations and field-spread manure as sources of pollutants. p. 231–240. *In* T. L. Willrich and G. E. Smith (ed.) Agricultural practices and water quality. The Iowa State Univ. Press, Ames.

Mosier, A. R., S. M. Morrison, and G. K. Elmund. 1977. Odors and emissions from organic wastes. p. 531–571. *In* Lloyd R. Elliott and F. J. Stevenson (ed.) Soils for management of organic wastes and waste waters. Am. Soc. Agron., Madison, Wis.

Norstadt, F. A., and L. K. Porter. 1976. Interactions of beef cattle wastes with soil. p. 763–775. *In* Jerome O. Nriagu (ed.) Environmental biogeochemistry. Ann Arbor Science Publ., Inc., Ann Arbor, Mich.

Norstadt, F. A., N. P. Swanson, and B. R. Sabey. 1977. Site design and management for utilization and disposal of organic wastes. p. 349–376. *In* Lloyd R. Elliott and F. J. Stevenson (ed.) Soils for management of organic wastes and waste waters. Am. Soc. Agron., Madison, Wis.

Oliver, J. C., W. C. Fairbank, J. L. Meyer, and J. M. Rible. 1974. Subfloor monitoring of shady grove dairy liquid manure holding pond. Calif. Agric. 28:6–7.

Olsen, S. R., and S. A. Barber. 1977. Effect of waste application on soil phosphorus and potassium. p. 197–215. *In* Lloyd R. Elliott and F. J. Stevenson (ed.) Soils for management of organic wastes and waste waters. Am. Soc. Agron., Madison, Wis.

Olson, E. A. 1974. Locating a new feedlot. Coop. Ext. Serv. Rep. G73-65. Univ. of Nebraska, Lincoln. 3 p.

Parr, J. F. 1974. Organic matter decomposition and oxygen relationships. p. 121–139. *In* Factors involved in land application of agricultural and municipal wastes. A preliminary document of the USDA, ARS, Washington, D.C.

Peele, T. C., H. P. Lynn, C. L. Barth, and J. N. Williams. 1973. Land application of animal waste. Bull. 570. Clemson Univ., Clemson, S.C. 18 p.

Perkins, H. F., and M. B. Parker. 1971. Chemical composition of broiler and hen manures. Res. Bull. 90. Univ. of Georgia, Athens. 17 p.

Powers, W. L., R. L. Herpich, L. S. Murphy, D. A. Whitney, H. L. Manges, G. W. Wallingford, et al. 1973. Guidelines for land disposal of feedlot lagoon water. Coop. Ext. Serv. Bull. C-485, Kansas State Univ., Manhattan. 7 p.

Powers, W. L., G. W. Wallingford, L. S. Murphy, D. A.Whitney, H. C. Manges, and H. E. Jones. 1974. Guidelines for applying beef feedlot manure to fields. Coop. Ext. Serv. Bull. C-502. Kansas State Univ., Manhattan. 11 p.

Pratt, P. F., F. E. Broadbent, and J. P. Martin. 1973. Using organic wastes as nitrogen fertilizers. Calif. Agric. 27:10–13.

Robinson, R. R. 1964. Earth worms in relation to soil productivity. CA-14-1. SEA and Soil and Water Conserv. Res. Div., USDA, Beltsville, Md. 4 p.

Russell, E. W. 1961. Soil conditions and plant growth. Longmans Green and Co., Ltd., London, England. 688 p.

Sewell, J. I., J. A. Mullins, and H. O. Vaigneur. 1975. Dairy lagoon system and groundwater quality. p. 286–288. In Managing livestock wastes. 3rd Int. Symp. on Livestock Wastes. Proc., 21–24 Apr. 1975, Univ. of Illinois, Urbana-Champaign, Ill. Am. Soc. Agric. Eng., St. Joseph, Mich.

Shuyler, L. R. 1973. National animal feedlot wastes research program. USEPA, EPA-R2-73-157. Robert S. Kerr Water Res. Center, Ada, Okla. 33 p.

Shuyler, L. R., D. M. Farmer, R. D. Kreis, and M. E. Hula. 1973. Environment protecting concepts of beef cattle feedlot wastes management. USEPA Project no. 21 AOY-05. Robert S. Kerr Water Res. Center, ada, Okla. 8 Chap. (no consecutive paging).

Smith, G. E. 1967. Fertilizer nutrients as contaminates in water supplies. p. 173–186. In N. C. Brady (ed.) Agriculture and the quality of our environment. Plimpton Press, Norwood, Mass.

Soil Conservation Service. 1975. Agricultural waste management field manual. Soil Conserv. Serv., USDA, Washington, D.C. 16 chap. (no consecutive paging).

Stewart, B. A., F. G. Viets, Jr., G. L. Hutchinson, and W. K. Kemper. 1967a. Nitrate and other water pollutants under fields and feedlots. Environ. Sci. Technol. 1:736–739.

Stewart, B. A., F. G. Viets, Jr., G. L. Hutchinson, W. D. Kemper, F. E. Clark, M. L. Fairbourn, and F. Strauch. 1967b. Distribution of nitrates and other water pollutants under fields and corrals in the middle south Platte Valley of Colorado. USDA ARS 41-134. USDA, Washington, D.C. 206 p.

Stewart, B. A., D. A. Woolhiser, W. H. Wischmeier, J. H. Caro, and M. H. Frere. 1975. Control of water pollution from cropland. Vol. I. USDA, ARS, and USEPA, Office of Res. and Dev. U.S. Government Printing Office, Washington, D.C. 111 p.

Stucker, T., and S. Erickson. 1975. Livestock wastes as a substitute for commercial nitrogen fertilizer. Ill. Res. 17(3):10–11.

Stuedemann, J. A., S. r. Wilkinson, D. J. Williams, H. Ciordia, J. V. Ernst, W. A. Jackson, and J. B. Jones, Jr. 1975. Longterm broiler litter fertilization of tall fescue pastures and health performance of beef cows. p. 264–268. In Managing livestock wastes. 3rd Intl. Symp. on Livestock Wastes. Proc. Am. Soc. agric. Eng., St. Joseph, Mich.

Swanson, N. P., J. C. Lorimor, and L. N. Mielke. 1973. Broad basin terraces for sloping cattle feedlots. Trans. ASAE 16:746–749.

Swanson, N. P., L. N. Mielke, J. C. Lorimor, T. M. McCalla, and J. R. Ellis. 1971. Transport of pollutants from sloping cattle feedlots as affected by rainfall intensity, duration, and recurrent. p. 51–55. In Livestock waste management and pollution abatement. Int. Symp. on Livestock Wastes Proc., 19–22 Apr. 1971, ASAE Pub. PROC-271. Am. Soc. Agric. Eng., St. Joseph, Mich.

Swanson, N. P., and L. N. Mielke. 1973. Solids trap for beef cattle feedlot runoff. Trans. ASAE 16:743–745.

Talmadge, H. E. 1975. Conservation of the land, and the use of waste materials for man's benefit. Comm. Print, Comm. on Agric. and For., U.S. Senate, 94th Congress, 1st session, 25 Mar. U.S. Government Printing Office, Washington, D.C. 69 p.

U.S. Environmental Protection Agency. 1972. Cattle feedlots and the environment. USEPA, Seattle, Wash. 64 p.

U.S. Environmental Protection Agency. 1975. Evaluation of land application systems. EPA-430/9-75-001. USEPA, Washington, D.C. 182 p.

U.S. Environmental Protection Agency, U.S. Department of Agriculture. 1979. Animal waste utilization on crop and pastureland. USDA Utilization Res. Rep. no. 6. Natl. Tech. Inf. Serv., Springfield, Va. (in press).

U.S. House of Representatives. 1972. Federal Water Pollution Control Act Amendments. PL 92-500. 18 Oct. 1972. Libr. of Congr., Washington, D.C.

U.S. Salinity Laboratory Staff. 1954. Diagnosis and improvement of saline and alkali soils. L. A. Richards (ed.) USDA Agric. Handbk. no. 60. U.S. Government Printing Office, Washington, D.C. 160 p.

University of Maine. 1972. Maine guidelines for manure and manure sludge disposal on land. Misc. Rep. 142. Univ. of Maine, Orono. 21 p.

Viets, F. G., Jr. 1971. Water quality in relation to farm use of fertilizer. Bio. Sci. 2:460–467.

Viets, F. G., Jr. 1974. Animal wastes and fertilizers as potential sources of nitrate pollution of water. p. 63–76. *In* Effects of agricultural production on nitrate in food and water with reference to isotope studies. Int. Atomic Energy Assoc., Vienna, Austria.

Viets, F. G., Jr., and R. H. Hageman. 1971. Factors affecting the accumulation of nitrate in soil, water, and plants. USDA Agric. Handbk. no. 413. U.S. Government Printing Office, Washington, D.C. 63 p.

Wadleigh, C. H. 1968. Wastes in relation to agriculture and forestry. USDA Misc. Pub. 1065. U.S. Government Printing Office, Washington, D.C. 112 p.

Waksman, S. A. 1966. Microbes and the survival of man on earth. Agric. Sci. Rev. 4:1–14.

Wallingford, G. W., L. S. Murphy, W. L. Powers, and H. L. Manges. 1974. Effect of beef-feedlot-lagoon water on soil chemical properties and growth and composition of corn forage. J. Environ. Qual. 3:74–78.

Willrich, T. L., D. O. Turner, and V. V. Volk. 1974. Manure guidelines for the Pacific Northwest. ASAE Pap. no. 74-4061. ASAE, St. Joseph, Mich. 12 p.

Witty, J. E., and K. W. Flach. 1977. Site selection as related to land and soil properties for utilization and disposal of organic wastes. p. 327–345. *In* L. R. Elliott and F. J. stevenson (ed.) Soils for management of organic wastes and waste waters. Am. Soc. Agron., Madison, Wis.

Zook, L. L. 1936. Maintenance of organic matter in dry-land soils. 17th Annu. Rep. Nebr. Potato Improve. Assoc., Lincoln, Nebr. p. 61–67.

30   Sanitary Landfill Site Selection and Management

F. GLADE LOUGHRY AND WILLIAM D. LACOUR

Department of Environmental Resources
Commonwealth of Pennsylvania
Harrisburg, Pennsylvania

I. INTRODUCTION

A. Magnitude of Disposal Problem and Necessity for Planning

Solid waste is a product of society which increases with advancing technology and affluence, corresponding as well to population growth. Primitive cultures and subsistence economies historically have had little to throw away. The relic artifacts that do remain exist because they were lost accidentally or as a result of some disaster. Prior to the shift to modern machinery and power farming, most agricultural cultures found ways to recycle wastes and repair simple equipment. When something was thrown away it was so dispersed in the rural setting that the waste did not become a community problem. As population became concentrated in cities and towns, waste accumulations assumed menacing proportions. Technology added gadgets and materials which complicated disposal and presented new hazards. A shift of some agricultural production from traditional farms to feed lots, large dairies, broiler plants, and egg factories concentrated waste at points remote from the farms. Affluence and so-called "planned obsolescence" add to the volume of waste generated by communities. The tonnage of municipal waste has been noted to fluctuate directly with the economic cycle. Community waste management has become a fact of municipal life which must be planned for just as are problems and responsibilities related to transportation, fire protection, police protection, and provision of a safe, plentiful water supply or a progressive school system. Because of the nuisances and hazards of accumulation of trash and garbage, the demands made on municipal officials are directed toward getting rid of it as soon as possible. The foremost concern is to provide for prompt and efficient collection with a minimum of associated littering, odors, noise, flies, or rats. Usually the appropriateness of the ultimate destination is given little consideration compared with concern shown for these factors. The initial responsibility for removal having been accomplished, the next task is to provide for disposal.

B. Options

There are several broad options available to the planner considering community solid waste disposal. Each method has advantages and its own set of limitations. All involve widely varying and ever present costs. Since any system selected involves major committment of time, money, and physical resources, they deserve careful study and evaluation for both immediate and long-time effects. A comprehensive community plan for solid waste management which is responsive to factors such as community growth, industrial changes, and disposal site suitability has become essential. Once a disposal system is selected it is difficult to change abruptly without experiencing financial loss. Generally the categories of waste management can be grouped under the following four categories.

1. REUSE OR RECYCLING

The conservation approach to managing solid waste focuses on the potential to reutilize them and convert them to commodities. Much metallic "waste" is now disposed of in this manner. After all, such discarded material is only a waste to the primary manufacturing process and it retains its inherent value which can be given up to another suitable manufacturing process. Glass and old newspapers are other materials that are frequently salvaged for reprocessing to useable materials. Markets for scrap metals and waste paper are very sensitive to economic conditions and sometimes are not available, thus forcing the materials into other disposal channels.

More sophisticated recycling is provided by processing a waste to a new useable product. An example of this is composting putrescible municipal solid wastes, sometimes in combination with sewage sludge, to make a stabilized compost that has potential usefulness as a soil amendment or mulch and is freed of its hazardous and objectionable characteristics. Not everything that becomes solid waste currently has a recognizable potential for recycling so there are some materials that have to be placed in other channels.

2. BURNING

Since much of the material collected as municipal solid waste is combustible, burning is an effective way of reducing the volume. Much of the criticism deserved by the old style "dump" stemmed from the practice of setting them on fire to get rid of bulky paper and wood. Such open burning caused air pollution and conveniently cooked the garbage for the rodents and flies. Incineration in suitable furnaces may avoid air pollution and reduce the volume of waste. Some incinerators utilize the heat produced for steam or power generation. Metallic wastes are mostly retained in the ash which remains to be disposed of by some other means. Pyrolysis or burning in the absence of oxygen is beginning to be used as a means of obtaining useful products from carbonaceous wastes.

3. DUMPING IN WATER

Much municipal solid waste including sewage sludge has been disposed of by dumping it in water. Ocean dumping is being reduced because of recognition of the vulnerability of coastal environments and international relations. Dumping into water areas such as marshes, swamps, flooded quarries, and pits was considered a desirable way of land reclamation as recently as 15 years ago. Since then the effect of leachate on water quality has been recognized and this practice is condemned. Waste disposal into water appears to be a declining alternative as water use becomes more critical and environmental concern grows.

4. LAND DISPOSAL

Most waste materials have had their origin on land and in nature would have returned to the land. But when waste becomes concentrated, its disposal on the land becomes complicated. Soil in a broad sense is nature's renovating and recycling agent. But selection of sites and organization for delivery of large quantities of waste becomes involved in many conflicting interests. Planning based on consideration of many variables is required. Some attempts have been made to apply municipal wastes to the surface of the ground as a mulch and soil amendment. Usually the material is composted, but sometimes it is merely shredded or milled before placement. Dumping has already been mentioned as disposal with very minor regard for the pollution which occurs in the local environment. The more enlightened approach to disposal on land is the sanitary landfill which is the topic of this chapter. Sanitary landfill will likely remain with us as the only total disposal technique which will be utilized far into the foreseeable future if not as the sole system serving a group of municipalities, certainly as a back up to advancing technology development.

C. Definitions

A few terms need to be defined in the specific sense of their use in this chapter.

1. WASTE

Waste is defined as useless, unwanted, or discarded materials resulting from normal activities. Solid wastes are refuse in the solid state including semiliquid or wet wastes with insufficient moisture and other liquid contents to be free-flowing. Containerized liquids are included when they are disposed of without removal.

2. SANITARY LANDFILLING

Sanitary landfilling is defined as the disposal of solid waste by burial within 24 hours of deposit without creating nuisances or hazards to public health or safety, and utilizing the principles of engineering to apply a compacted earth cover sufficiently thick to prevent combustion, blowing litter, or problems from insect or rodent infestation (Pa. Dep. of Environ. Res. Rules and Reg., Chap. 75).

3. SOIL

Soil is the collection of natural bodies on the earth's surface, in places modified or even made by man of earthy materials, containing living matter and supporting or capable of supporting plants out-of-doors. Its upper limit is air or shallow water. At its margins, it grades to deep water or to barren areas of rock or ice. The lower limit of soil is normally the lower limit of biologic activity, which generally coincides with the common rooting depth of native perennial plants (Soil Survey Staff, 1975).

4. LEACHATE

Leachate, as used here, is the effluent of a sanitary landfill during the degradation of the organic and reactive inorganic contents. It consists of water that has entered the fill plus intermediate and final decomposition products, metal salts, and any soluble material disposed of at the site.

II. SITE SELECTION

A. General Factors

1. QUANTITY OF WASTE

Total solid waste generation that can be considered as community disposal problems was estimated as 0.80 metric tons per capita in 1970 and projected as increasing at a rate of 0.015 tons per capita per year. This includes domestic trash and garbage, commercial and institutional wastes, demolition and construction wastes, and some industrial wastes. It excludes such bulky wastes as mining wastes, and crop residues and animal manures that remain on farms where the crops were grown. In the United States about 170,000,000 metric tons of waste are disposed of in sanitary landfills. Planning has to take into consideration the projected rate of growth in total production of waste and also the effect of changes in method. Recycling programs, waste processing facilities, or new incinerators proposed for a given community will draw off a portion of the landfill demand for that area.

2. TRANSPORTATION

In planning a landfill operation and selecting a site, it is necessary to consider its accessability. Distance and road conditions affect efficiency of use of equipment and labor. These must be weighed against the cost of site development and operation. Economical hauling distance is partly dependent on size of planned operation, and with larger operations transfer stations and large tractor trailers can be used to haul wastes to more remote landfill sites.

3. COMPETING LAND USE

Sites that have the physical characteristics of soils, geology, slope, and drainage that make them most desirable for sanitary landfills providing natural renovating are in high demand for many other uses. They are also among the best sites for agricultural production, housing, roads, airports, productive forestry, golf courses, and the disposal of sewage effluent.

4. AESTHETICS

The appearance of the site during operation and after completion are important considerations. Some of the physical site characteristics can help in achieving these conditions. If soil is good for reestablishing vegetation and if slopes are gentle to moderate, the task of achieving a pleasing landscape is made easier. Selection of vegetative materials can be done with aesthetic effects in mind.

5. SOILS

The nature of the soil at a proposed sanitary landfill site is a key to much of the design and performance of the site. The use of the soil itself as a construction material and the information about other site conditions that can be gained from interpretation of soil data are basic to sound planning.

6. GEOLOGY

Certain bedrock conditions contribute to operational problems and hazards of sanitary landfills. Chief among these are the solution caverns of carbonate rocks and open joints in many kinds of rocks especially where they occur as anticlines and in faulted areas. A special hazard is involved in areas with coal or lignite where accidental fire in a landfill can spread into a coal vein. Mining laws may impose restrictions or prohibitions on waste disposal where coal is mined.

7. WATER QUALITY

Hazards of water pollution is a legitimate concern in sanitary landfill planning and development. Protection of water quality involves separation of the waste from ground water, flooding, and discharge to either streams or lakes without renovation. Both the regional water table and seasonally perched water tables are potential carriers of the pollutants from a landfill.

8. PUBLIC ACCEPTANCE

Often there is strong local objection to the location of a sanitary landfill when plans are announced. Planners must take this into consideration or a plan based on only physical and economic site selection will not be available for development until after lengthy litigation and may never be realized. Planning should include provisions for clean operation and for vegetative screens. Hours of operation can be selected to minimize the impact of equipment noise. A public relations program to keep the neighbors informed of what is planned and how it will work can help to minimize concern and win acceptance. A prompt and effective job of placing final cover and revegetating completed sections will allay fears.

B. Factors to be Considered in Planning Phases

In anticipation of the establishment of a solid waste processing or disposal site, consideration must be given to the best use of the land that is available. Among the more important planning considerations not to be ignored are such factors as future planned use of the land, access to the facility, roadway conditions in the vicinity of the site, bridge sizes and capacities, zoning requirements, and adjacent land uses.

1. LAND USE

Economic factors achieve high significance in planning for land disposal of solid wastes since the criteria for suitable soils, as described in this chapter, are such that sites meeting and exceeding the minimums may be at the same time highly desirable for farming, housing sites, schools, industries, golf courses, and many other uses. Since there is always much competition for the best land, previously established uses, anticipated land uses, and owner constraints tend to increase the value of the land often to the point that exorbitant investment demands are placed on municipalities seeking to set aside potential backup sites for their present solid waste management system.

2. INTERMUNICIPAL AGREEMENTS

To avoid proposing only interim solutions to long-lasting solid waste problems, municipal officials must apply tried planning approaches. The advantages to be gained by entering into intermunicipal agreements with those neighboring communities most likely to have similar waste disposal needs should be recognized. Many times these municipalities are seeking lasting solutions to similar problems yet are restricted by budget or manpower from achieving success. Community sites must be designed to accommodate the industries located in and adjacent to them. The lack of disposal capability has quite often deterred the expansion of industry and stifled the economic outlook of the community.

3. AESTHETICS

The interpretation of the aesthetics of a proposed landfill site is an aspect of vital concern which can only be adequately considered by astute individuals with perception. Only during the planning stages can the greatest benefits be achieved here. Trained observation and comparison with standards such as are outlined in "Aesthetics in Environmental Planning" will bolster the planning at any proposed site. Visual ugliness, adverse olfactory nuances, and maligned land uses must be recognized in advance and dealt with through deft moderation of design elements.

4. ADEQUACY

A further consideration which must occur in the planning stages of land disposal site development is the adequacy of the site selected to serve as the community's solid waste disposal site for the period of time required. At times, small sites anticipated to be rapidly filled are chosen as sanitary landfills, particularly when there is a need to fill small canyons, pits, or stripped lands. Such sites can offer close-in disposal capability for winter months or may serve as interim sites at times when major new sites are in the design phases. Generally, however, most new site development will be on a larger scale than previously used due to the increasing trends toward provision of long-range facilities and to compensate for ever-increasing volumes of solid waste generated. Obviously miscalculation of the rate of utilization of site will result in losses of efficiency or too excessive costs for the location of a replacement site. Careful planning will minimize such unfavorable occurrences.

5. PLANNING ADVANTAGES

The rising costs evident today, the ever-closing distances between domestic and industrial demands, and the increased interrelationships between urban, suburban, and rural activities warrants the minimal time, energy, and talent invested in planning. The application of planning approaches to solid waste management site selection will serve to minimize health hazards and the potentials for pollution. The net gain will be a much better facility to serve the public and the development of increased respect for the decision-makers responsible for the solid waste management system.

C. Soil Survey Data in Landfill Planning

Information on soils for sanitary landfill planning is needed at two levels; first, for preliminary screening of sites, and then for specific site evaluation and detailed planning. Completed soil surveys, mostly made by the Soil Conservation Service, are available on some scale for most of the United States and partial soils information is available for most of the other land included in Soil Conservation Districts or Grazing Districts. Some of the more populous states have completed surveys. Where the soil surveys are published or interim data are available to planners, they furnish a source of information about location of suitable soils and slopes in relation to existing land use patterns, roads, streams, and lakes. Because of publication scale, limitations on time for investigations, and the complexity of the soil pattern in the landscape, the standard soil survey does not furnish all the precision of delineations that is required for construction at a site where even a small area of an unexpected soil can create a great hazard. Possible landfill site limitations are usually included among the engineering or urban use interpretations in published soil surveys. These interpretations do not constitute suitability determinations as accompanying texts or notices make clear, but indicate the probability that within a delineated area conditions prevail which help determine the hazards involved and the difficulty of overcoming them. Loughry (1967) used Soil Survey data to make state-wide estimates of suitable soils in Pennsylvania; and Warman et al. (1974) used soil and geology for an inventory of sanitary landfill possibilities in Alabama.

When a specific site is seriously considered for development, a detailed on-site investigation should be made by a professional soil scientist. Pits for examination and description of the soil should be a routine part of the study and some chemical and physical testing may be required for adequate evaluation.

III. SITES FOR MUNICIPAL WASTES WITH NATURAL RENOVATION

A. Municipal Wastes—Characteristics and Hazards

The solid waste disposal problems which most frequently and persistently comes to land planners are those associated with municipal wastes. This mixture of household garbage and trash with similar wastes from commercial establishments, institutions, and offices also frequently includes . wastes from small industrial plants. Lawn and garden wastes are often included and street sweepings add seasonal quantities of leaves. Ashes from coal-fired furnaces and cinders from the streets add inert bulk. Where a municipal system accepts waste from light industry plants, chemicals and metals properly classified as industrial wastes are mingled with the municipal trash.

A quantitative estimate of municipal solid waste disposed of in 1971 places the total amount at 113 million metric tons, according to the Solid Waste Staff (1974). The amounts and percentage distribution of major types of materials are given in Table 1. This table shows almost two-fifths

Table 1—Material in municipal solid waste as disposed in 1971.

Type of material	As disposed†	
	10^6 metric tons	%
Paper	43.0	37.8
Glass	11.3	10.0
Metal	11.4	10.1
Plastic	4.2	3.8
Rubber and leather	3.1	2.7
Textiles	1.8	1.6
Wood	4.2	3.7
Food	16.1	14.2
Subtotal	95.1	83.9
Yard waste	16.5	14.6
Miscellaneous inorganics	1.7	1.5
Total	113.3	100.0

† Weight adjusted to moisture content of mixed waste usually delivered to disposal sites.

Table 2—Projected total solid waste quantities for disposal.

Assumed annual compound growth	Projected waste for disposal		
	1980	1985	1990
%	10^6 metric tons		
2.5 (low)	141	159	181
3.5 (medium)	154	181	209
4.5 (high)	169	209	263

of the total to be paper and about one-seventh to be food wastes. These, along with wood and textiles, make up more than half of the total weight, and are rapidly putrescible. Some of this waste goes to incinerators and relatively small amounts, particularly metals, glass, and paper, are salvaged. Historically, most of the remainder plus the residue from incineration went to dumps or remained scattered as litter.

As civic improvements have been made there has been a shift from open dumps to sanitary landfills. This movement is still under way and the need for landfill sites is expected to increase even though greater emphasis is being placed on salvage and recycling. This is due to projected growth rates of solid waste generation as suggested in Table 2 from Solid Waste Staff (1974), outstripping the technology for feasible salvage operations.

The high proportion of putrefactive material in the collected waste contributes to hazards and nuisances of odors, insect breeding, and water pollution. Food and yard wastes attract and provide harborage problems with rodents. Combustible materials are a fire hazard. Blowing paper and plastic are a nuisance. Various inclusions of chemicals and metals have the potential of water pollution. All of these may be hazardous, however, production of leachate and its discharge without renovation is the greatest potential hazard of landfill operation.

B. Functions of Soil in Sanitary Landfill

For small- and medium-sized landfills dependent on in-situ assimilation of the waste, soil is the major factor in prevention of hazards and nuisances (Herriman, 1972). Choice of a site with soil that can accomplish the key functions becomes a prime consideration in planning for this kind of sanitary landfill.

1. CONTAINMENT

The soil forms the foundation, sidewalls, and cover of a landfill using natural materials. Substitutions for soil are hazardous. Rock which is often proposed and sometimes tried as a base and walls for landfills in quarries and strip mines usually has enough open joints or fissures to permit escape of leachate and gas. Gravel beds also fail in the requirements for containment and purification. Neither rock nor gravel has significant renovative capacity, unless combined with controlled aeration, recycling, and chemical treatment of leachate.

2. FIRE SAFETY

Over three-fourths of the material reaching municipal landfills is combustible to varying degrees and fire prevention is necessary to avoid air pollution and safety hazards. Earthen barriers are effective firewalls and waste is separated into cells which should be completed on a daily basis. When sanitary landfill is placed in coal strip pits, a thick buffer of compacted soil is needed between the waste and exposed coal seams to prevent fire originating in the fill spreading into the coal. Soil cover placed daily retards flow of air into a cell and also reduces chances of the fill being ignited accidentally or by incendiary act.

3. COVER

Soil is ordinarily used as cover for a sanitary landfill. This is the most distinctive difference between a sanitary landfill and an open dump. Placement of soil over compacted waste helps to maintain the compaction and prevents blowing of paper and other light trash. Fire prevention as discussed in the preceding paragraph is facilitated by soil cover. Soil for covering the landfill is often scarce because of the amount needed. Various substitutes have been proposed. Materials such as crushed stone, fly ash, mine waste, and cinders have been proposed for cover. Each meets some of the requirements but fails in others.

In planning a landfill it is important to inventory potential cover material on the site or available nearby. Plans should provide for efficient use.

4. VECTOR CONTROL

Quantities of foodstuff and decaying vegetation in municipal waste are attractive to insect and rodent vectors of disease such as flies, mosquitos, rats, and ground squirrels. Daily cover of at least 15 cm (6 inches) of soil and cover of at least 30 cm (1 foot) for areas to remain undisturbed for longer periods excludes these pests if the waste and soil are properly compacted. This practice also reduces such nuisances as flocks of gulls, crows, and starlings.

5. RENOVATION

The ideal soil contributes to the renovation of the waste by allowing some penetration of air and water into the fill to promote oxidation and allow the escape of gas. Soil in the bottom of the landfill and in cell walls provides slow filtration. During slow passage of leachate there is some opportunity for the modification of the metal content of the waste by ion exchange with the soil. This is limited by the capacity of the soil. For large deep landfills there is the probability that the leachate will overwhelm the exchange capacity of the available soil and be discharged with little change.

6. RESTORATION

Sanitary landfill should not be considered as an ultimate land use. Rather it should be planned as an interim use pending conversion to a more permanent use. Recently completed areas of sanitary landfill are not suitable for all land uses. Gas production and settling as organic wastes decompose make such sites hazardous for housing for many years. Use areas such as parking lots and light traffic roadways need to be designed with loose surface material or permeable, flexible paving to permit escape of gas and adjust to differential settling.

The remaining land uses including public parks, golf courses, shooting preserves, farming, forestry, and range land are all able to utilize former sanitary landfill sites to advantages. Good planning and operations which follow the plan are needed to facilitate such uses. For all of these applications there is dependence on vegetation for erosion control, beautification, and production. So it is important that the final cover on completed sections of a sanitary landfill be soil that provides a good medium for establishing vegetation. This can be described in general terms as having medium texture, free of large stones, and with satisfactory fertility status. Also, the final cover should be at least 61 cm (2 feet) thick to provide for available moisture storage and a satisfactory root zone. For immediate conversion to cropland a deeper cover should be planned. For forestry, extensive farming, parks, and golf courses, it is expected that deep-rooted plants will be able to utilize moisture and nutrients in the upper part of the decomposing waste after becoming established in the soil cover.

An example of planning for interim use of an area for waste disposal is the Hanover, Pennsylvania, Sanitary Landfill which was located on a farm purchased for the purpose. After a plan was developed and approved, most of the land was continued in crop production with only the area scheduled for immediate landfilling excavated for trench-type operation. Also, some land needed for an operations building and for screen planting was immediately landscaped and trees and shrubs started. Trenches are laid out across the slope. As a trench is completed and covered, it is fertilized and seeded as a strip of small grain. The block of trenches filled from 1968 to 1972 has been completed and has reappeared as a field of mixed grass and legume hay with about the same boundaries and contours as the former farm field.

C. Soil Characteristics Involved

1. DEPTH

The depth or thickness of soil mantle over rock is a measure of the useable cover material as well as of the filtering and renovating potential of the loose material. It is an important consideration in deciding between trench type construction and area type. The filtering and renovating effects of soil are limited and directly related to the quantity of soil available. Many other factors keep it from being a simple proportionality. Guidelines and regulations for sanitary landfills usually disregard these and establish parameters consisting of a minimum thickness of soil under the base of the landfill and a ratio between total thickness of compacted waste and the thickness of the soil base. Table 3 based on Pennsylvania regulations illustrates this (Loughry, 1967, 1973). This in turn establishes the area required for a given amount of waste and sets the lifetime of a landfill serving a municipality. Additional soil is required for daily, intermediate, and final cover.

Table 3—Soil characteristics used in determining site suitability for sanitary landfills.

Soil site characteristics	Suitable range	Range of limited suitability	Unsuitable range
Depth:			
of developed solum	Over 0.9 m	0.4–0.9 m	<0.4 m
to hard rock	Over 3.7 m	1.2–3.7 m	<1.2 m
to fissured rock		Over 1.8 m	<1.8 m
to gravel or coarse sand		Over 1.8 m	<1.8 m
Drainage	Well-drained		All with restricted drainage
Depth to seasonal high water	1.8 m from bottom of planned trench for each 1.8 m lift of refuse	1.8 m minimum	<1.8 m
Soil texture	Sandy loam, fine sandy loam, loam, silt loam, silty clay loam, sandy clay loam		Sand, loamy sand, silt, clay, sandy clay, silty clay, clay loam, fly ash, incinerator residue, organic soils
Slope	0–8%	8–15%	>15%
Stoniness	Nonstony, slightly stony	Very stony	Extremely stony, stony land
Flooding hazard	None	Flooded less frequently than once in 50 years	Flooded more frequently than once in 50 years

2. TEXTURE

Proper operation of a municipal waste landfill requires that waste be covered with earth the same day that it is deposited in the fill. This means 5 or 6 days a week, every week of the year, regardless of weather. So cover material needs to be workable even when it is raining. This bars highly sticky and plastic soils. Table 3 lists clay, sandy clay, silty clay, and clay loam textures as unsuitable.

Very silty and very sandy soils that lack enough clay to serve as binder and provide some structural stability erode very readily when either wet or dry. The newly covered waste can be exposed by sheet and rill erosion during a storm if these materials are used. On the same site when it is dry the same kind of material will be removed by wind erosion. It should be kept in mind that daily cover is only six inches thick and that the most popular operating method uses compaction in sloping cells by equipment moving up the slope. It is only when the cell reaches the upper limit of a lift that a level surface is provided.

In northern regions freezing of the cover material is an operational problem during cold weather. It is countered in various ways. Stockpiling sufficient cover material is common. However, if the soil holds enough capillary water, the stockpile may freeze. This hazard is reduced if soil is a loam with moderately stable aggregation and if the stockpiling operation does not destroy the natural structure. Covering a stockpile to keep out rain and snow is occasionally tried. Another approach to the freezing problems is the use of heavy equipment able to break through the frozen layer in a new trench and dig out unfrozen soil for immediate placement. Still another way is to substitute some industrial waste such as incinerator ash or power plant ash as daily cover material during the winter period when biological activity is low and the immediate objective is to prevent blowing trash and fire. If additional soil cover is not added when weather becomes warmer other soil functions are missing. The two materials mentioned often add some pollutants which make the leachate stronger and more difficult to renovate. Figure 1 illustrates construction of a sanitary landfill in a trench with cover material being dug from the extension of the cut.

3. DRAINAGE

The natural internal drainage or aeration status of the soil at a site is important in several ways. The water table in the soil and its fluctuations, including duration at various levels, are components of the aeration status of a soil. The regional watertable and any perched watertable present at a site are significant. This includes watertables perched above fragipans. The distance from the bottom of a landfill to the highest level reached by the watertable is a measure of the distance leachate from the waste will have to travel through renovating soil before it mingles with ground water and processes of oxidation virtually cease. Once it is in the regional ground water

Fig. 1—Progressive construction of trench-type sanitary landfill with one lift. Soil excavated from extension of the trench to the right is used for daily cover on the sloping ramp and final cover on completed section at left (Pennsylvania Dep. Environ. Res. photo).

aquifer, leachate is very hard to remove and will remain as a pollutant until dilution lessens its hazards or it is discharged at a spring or stream.

During the early years of a landfill, the abundant supply of biodegradable material produces anaerobic conditions within the fill itself. The breakdown of organic wastes is hastened by air penetrating the landfill to renew the oxygen supply. The aerobic process is much more rapid and complete than the anaerobic. Soil surrounding the fill and covering the waste that has larger voids filled with air allows more oxygen diffusion than a saturated soil (Merz & Stone, 1962).

4. CATION EXCHANGE CAPACITY

Leachate usually includes significant quantities of heavy metal ions. The amount varies with the source of the waste and the stage of weathering of the fill, but often hazardous amounts of one or more metals will be present in the fill. Very little has been done on actual measurement of the quantitative efficiency of the soil in stabilizing these metals by ion exchange. By analogy with soil physical chemistry and with solution chemistry it is tempting to assume that passage through the soil holds back heavy metal ions until the di- and mono-valent ions have been displaced. In a complex reaction between a variable solution of organic decomposition products and metals with the soil, such a conclusion is far from safe. Parameters that have been proposed for standards for ion exchange capacity for soil used at a landfill (Noble, 1976) appear to be in this category. As a generality leachate that has contact with soil loses some of its heavy metals as compared with leachate that flows directly from the decomposing waste.

5. pH

The soil reaction is an additional variable in the renovating of leachate. As it relates to the solubility of metals in compounds, it determines the mobility of these elements through the soil. It is common for anaerobic leachate to be slightly alkaline. Organic acids produced by partial decomposition are weak and ineffective in dissolving metals. On the other hand, the ferrous form of iron is more soluble than the ferric, and the organic matter is very effective in reducing the iron to the less stable form. Also, intermediate products of organic matter form chelates with various metals decreasing their reaction with the cation exchange minerals.

When leachate reaches aerobic zones of soil and oxidation can proceed rapidly, mineral acids are formed and the pH shifts to the acid range, unless an excess of basic elements were a part of the waste. When the leachate becomes acid a moderately alkaline soil is effective in delaying passage of pollutants.

D. Use of Site

1. EXPECTATIONS

When a location is found for a sanitary landfill economics dictate that maximum use be made of the area available. When the landfill is planned with full dependence on the soil for renovation, the soil characteristics already described determine the safe capacity. Furthermore, the proposed use of the land after completion of the landfill influences the planning, operation, and management.

Usually it is good practice to stockpile surface soil separate from other soil stripped from the site, and reserve it for final cover if revegetation is planned. An adequate sanitary landfill plan includes the final elevations and contours to leave the area useable, aesthetically pleasing, and protected from erosion.

2. DURATION

The longevity of a sanitary landfill operation at a site can be estimated from the population of its service area and the area and thickness of the planned fill. Generally, for a landfill dependent on natural renovation by the soil, one 1.8- or 2.4-m lift or two 1.8-m lifts of compacted refuse is all that can be renovated. With a decision on the thickness of the fill and the area of the site which is useable, it is easy to calculate the volume capacity. Average values for per capita production of waste are used in the next step to calculate the annual volume to be disposed of in the service area. With this information it is possible to plan a comprehensive waste disposal program utilizing landfills. The need for new locations can be anticipated early and developed without crisis. Also, the completion of a fill at a specific site can be approximately scheduled and future land use plans made a part of a municipal or regional development plan.

3. MANAGEMENT

The capacity and useful life of a landfill site can be extended by a number of management practices which permit more efficient use of the available volume. The most obvious measure is to secure greater compaction of the trash in place. Waste usually arrives at the sanitary landfill in a semi-compacted condition in compactor trucks or trailers. At small landfills much of the waste still arrives without any precompaction. The use of proper equipment can greatly increase the density in the cells. On large landfills this is done by special rollers or vibrating compactors. Small landfill operations use crawler tractors with a front end blade or bucket and construct the cells on a slope with the tractor climbing the slope and pushing waste up from the bottom. The same equipment is used to spread and compact a 15-cm (6-inch) layer of soil as daily cover to enclose and isolate the cell (Fig. 1). Greater compaction reduces aeration and favors fully anaerobic decomposition, thus altering leachate characteristics and gas production. Compaction reduces the settling during decomposition of the waste and makes it easier to reach a stable settled grade for the finished landfill.

Very good compaction can be attained if the waste material is shredded before it is placed in the fill because large angular pieces are avoided. Also materials are mingled so that hard and soft fragments pack together with fewer and smaller voids. Other advantages have been claimed for this process including the potential for salvaging metals by magnetic or ballistic separation.

Exclusion of bulky waste which will not compact and which resists decomposition is another way of conserving space, and serves as well to make the site more stable and useful after completion. Prime examples of this kind of waste are large appliances such as refrigerators, stoves, washing machines, and dryers. Automobile and truck tires, and bed springs are especially difficult to handle in landfills. Their flexibility allows them to be compressed by compacting equipment and immediately spring back when pressure is released. If this is repeated several times tires can work their way up through the soil cover that is being placed. Tires and the metal appliances have some salvage value, but in some places lack a ready market. This particularly affects small landfills where haulers and individuals often abandon such objects.

Paper and paper products constitute much of the bulk of a sanitary landfill and over half of the readily biodegradable proportion. Paper is frequently salvaged from the waste stream. This is effective in decreasing the bulk of the landfill contents, reducing the amount of settling of the final grade, and lightening the renovation load on soils at the site. Salvage of metals, glass, and plastics aids in quicker restoration of the site and adds more flexibility in choice of future use of the land.

4. GAS PRODUCTION

Gas is a natural product of the decomposition of biodegradable municipal waste. If the decomposition takes place in an aerobic medium with an excess of oxygen, the final products of carbon compounds are carbon dioxide (CO_2) and water (H_2O). Under anaerobic conditions, which are common in sanitary landfills, there is little oxygen available other than present in organic and inorganic compounds in the waste. Under these conditions methane (CH_4) is the principal gas produced from municipal waste. Some carbon monoxide (CO) is commonly produced. Sulfur in the waste often shows up as hydrogen sulfide (H_2S). Some denitrification takes place with release of gaseous nitrogen (N_2). Some intermediate products of the decay of waste are complex organic gases with offensive odors which are characteristic of anaerobic landfills that do not have adequate provision for ventilation.

The methane presents a hazard of explosion if confined. Both methane and carbon monoxide are poisonous and lighter than air. Permeable soil or rock strata allow diffusion of these gasses. Where the gas is confined by a less permeable upper layer, it can travel considerable distances and reach buildings. The diffusion of gas from landfills has been extensively studied in California (Calif. State Water Qual. Bd., 1965, 1967; Merz & Stone, 1964). Scattered incidents of gas hazard from landfills and dumps in other parts of the country have been reported in newspapers and in records of official investigations. Sites where landfills extend down into gravelly substrata under river terraces with finer textured soils on the surface, or into fractured rock under soil with perched watertables, are specially prone to this migration of gas. The same effect is produced by paving over a recently completed fill.

5. MONITORING

Sanitary landfills as a source of large quantities of pollutants need certain precautions against failure. Monitoring is the common method of detecting when the renovating capacity of the site has been overcome or bypassed (Apgar & Langmuir, 1971). A well up-gradient of the ground water flow system and one or more wells down-gradient are the usual monitoring pattern. Tests are made for the various heavy metals that are frequently in landfills, plus specific conductance, chemical oxygen demand, dissolved solids, sulphates, and chlorides. In some cases tests are also made for fluorides, phenols, pesticides, and arsenic.

IV. SITES FOR SANITARY LANDFILL WITH COLLECTION AND TREATMENT OF LEACHATE

A. Situations Where Used

There are several sets of conditions where natural renovation by soil is not an adequate method of solid waste disposal. It is important to recognize these situations and plan for them. When a determination is made that special facilities are required for collection and treatment of the waste products, there are many changes in priorities. Size of area usually is less. Initial construction costs are usually higher, and operating costs include treatment of leachate. While soil is not the primary renovating agent it is still used in several ways. Soil requirements at the site are different and in some ways less stringent than for the natural renovation landfills. Soil still serves as the supporting base for the liner which contains the fill and for cover. It is important that there be adequate stability to prevent mass movement which could rupture the liner. Angular coarse fragments in the base and border need to be removed or covered to protect against punctures. Some factors in choice of this method follow.

1. LARGE VOLUME

Where it is desired to dispose of a large volume of waste in a limited site, the renovative powers of the soils can be overwhelmed by the sheer quantities of decomposition products. Prolonged use indicates a need for rapid decomposition and shrinkage of volume. In such a situation the use of soil is limited to daily cover and to a reserve for final cover which is usually many years in the future, and often undetermined.

2. SPECIAL HAZARDOUS WASTES

Some wastes contain significant amounts of substances that cannot be adequately biodegraded or chemically reacted with soil. Phenolic compounds, many pesticides, and toxic industrial wastes are examples of hazardous materials that need to be specifically treated after collection.

3. LACK OF SUITABLE SOIL

In planning for a sanitary landfill it is sometimes found that there is no area of soil available for this use that can meet the standards for a natural renovation site. Distance of haul from the source and cost of a suitable soil area then have to be balanced against the greater construction costs of a lined sanitary landfill and treatment facilities. Since a system with collection and treatment of leachate is not dependent on the renovating capacity of a limited thickness of soil, the fill can be started deeper and piled higher to increase the quantity or waste disposed of on a given area. Volume of the waste in place decreases as decomposition advances, and compaction occurs from the weight of new material above. This helps to increase the capacity of a site. Investment in treatment facilities encourages careful management to get the most use of a site.

B. Construction Features

1. FABRIC LINERS

Artificial liners of heavy sheet plastic or rubber have been installed under some landfills to provide an impermeable barrier to liquids and gases. Such liners have a moderate amount of flexibility to accommodate to slight changes in surface of the compacted base. The complete liner is assembled by joining large strips of the fabric with carefully cemented or welded seams. Unless very uniform soil that is free of coarse fragments is in the site, a sand base, at least 25 cm thick is needed under the fabric. Twenty-five cm or more of sand is also placed on top of the liner to protect it from sharp objects in the waste and to provide a permeable medium for flow of leachate.

Distance from the watertable is not so critical because there is no flow of pollutants from the interior of the landfill to the soil. If the watertable is shallow, drains should be placed underneath the liner to prevent stability problems with saturated soil.

A lining extending up the sides of a pit prevents escape of gases into the soil or rock formations. If the soil placed as final cover is fine and densely packed there is concentration of dangerous gases in the fill. Venting through perforated pipes placed vertically in the fill is sometimes used to draw off methane and other hazardous gases.

2. PAVED LINERS

Some use has been made of asphalt liners similar to canal and lagoon liners instead of plastic liners. Several techniques of placement have been demonstrated, including repeated spraying with hot asphalt, hot mix asphalt rolled and sealed, slabs of asphalt-impregnated fibers joined and sealed, and asphalt-coated fabrics. These liners need the same protection by adjacent layers of sand that is provided to plastic liners.

3. CLAY LINERS

In some instances it is possible to produce an extremely slowly permeable base for a landfill using soil materials. Hydraulic conductivities of the magnitude of 10^{-6} cm/sec or less are sought. It is possible to accomplish this for only a few sites using natural soils present at the site. For more sites the natural soil needs to be supplemented with a swelling clay of the bentonite family. In nearly all instances the clay liner requires thorough mixing and compacting to assure uniformity and adequate thickness. Only in rare cases are natural soil layers such as fragipans or claypans so slowly permeable and sloping toward a collecting point where they can serve as the impermeable

liner without reworking. There are conflicting opinions about the effectiveness of clay liners for containing diversified wastes. Research on ponds for
agricultural waste indicate that the organic components under anaerobic
conditions help seal even a permeable soil with organic slime. On the other
hand many leaking lagoons allow the escape of toxic industrial chemicals.
Specific application of clay liners to mixed landfills is still too new for conclusions to be drawn as to the range of their effectiveness for solid waste.

4. COLLECTION SYSTEMS

Where it is found necessary to collect and treat leachate each site presents its special conditions. Systems range from a simple trench or low dam
across a natural drainageway where leachate is discharging, to elaborate tile
fields laid in gravel between the sand cover of the liner and the base of the
waste. Artificial liners are laid with a slight gradient toward a collection
point. For large landfills more than one collecting area may be used. If
coarse sand is used as the protective cover for the liner, it provides natural
permeability but it is subject to clogging by slime and by redeposited metals.
Much of the basal flow is through the lower layer of waste and over the
compacted soil used to cover cells within the fill.

5. TREATMENT SYSTEMS

The simplest and quickest method for meeting the problem of leachate
discharging from a landfill where it is a menace or nuisance is to pump it
back and spread it on the surface of the fill. This recycling can only be considered a temporary measure. The aeration afforded by pumping and spraying has some renovating effect on organic components. But in humid areas
the return of water to the site just increases future leachate discharge. In
arid areas there is an even more rapid buildup of metals in the leachate.

Aeration in waste lagoons is commonly used to reduce the organic
matter content of leachate and oxidize elements of the waste which are
present in reduced forms. Thorough aeration precipitates much of the iron
as ferric compounds and converts sulfides to sulfates.

Maintaining moderately alkaline conditions by addition of lime precipitates most of the heavy metals. Flocculation and separation of the precipitate after chemical treatment and aeration usually produces a relatively
clean liquid except for dissolved chlorides, sulfates, and nitrates.

Surface application of leachate on the soil for renovation by air, sunlight, and biological action is often tried. It usually results in damage to the
soil and vegetation because of the high concentration of pollutants in leachate.

At least one attempt has been made to dispose of leachate in a subsurface seepage field similar to those used for septic tank effluent. According to unpublished records of the Pennsylvania Department of
Environmental Resources, such a system was installed by the York City
Landfill in an attempt to prevent a discharge to a stream. Subsequent investigation showed that even where initial soil permeability was satisfac-

tory, the addition of the concentrated leachate very quickly clogged the seepage field.

C. Management

1. SPEEDING DECOMPOSITION

When it is desired that maximum utilization be made of a lined site and the control of leachate is provided by collection and treatment, measures may be taken to speed decomposition. Waste when it is placed is not ordinarily saturated and it takes some time to reach the point where excess water becomes the vehicle of leachate. In humid areas of the eastern U.S. it has been estimated that from 1 to 2 years is required to start leaching due to natural rainfall on a 1.8-m (6-foot) layer of municipal trash deposited in dry weather (Remsen, 1968). In arid and semiarid areas a thick landfill may never become saturated and decomposition is slow. Addition of water to provide optimum conditions for decay hastens the breakdown of the waste. After leaching starts, leachate is sometimes pumped back on the fill. The disadvantages of returning raw leachate have been described in an earlier section. Leachate that has been aerated and chemically treated can be effectively recycled through the landfill. Nitrates in the treatment effluent can help the biodegradation of the carbonaceous wastes, and sulfates can speed the solution of metals.

2. SALVAGE OF LEACHATE PRODUCTS

The treatment of leachate results in a concentration of metals. The sludge produced is itself a hazardous waste. It has a potential for reclamation of metals, but no instances of its use have been reported. Ordinarily, it is stored in place or given some further treatment to stabilize it.

3. COLLECTING GAS

Large lined landfills accumulate gases including a high proportion of methane. This poses an explosion and fire hazard. A system of flues and stacks can be used to carry off methane from the body of waste. Some proposals have been made for collecting and using the gas. At present all systems known to the authors are simply vent stacks above the surface of the fills.

V. STORAGE OF NONDEGRADABLE WASTES

Some industrial wastes are hazardous if spread on the land or discharged to water. Profitable salvage methods have not been found or markets are not available where the wastes are located. Various storage devices are used for holding such hazardous wastes in immobile form.

Patented processes are proposed for transferring the wastes to silicate or aluminate complexes which resist leaching. The senior author, several years ago, recommended encapsulation of heavy metal sludges in lime or limestone dust as a means of storing them in natural conditions at several sites (Loughry, 1972). Some of the sludges buried have metal contents similar to currently mined ores and will eventually be reprocessed and used.

VI. DEMOLITION WASTES, SITE CLEARANCE WASTES, AND EXCAVATION SPOILS—RANGE IN CHARACTERISTICS

There are many bulky wastes that constitute urban or public disposal problems that are marginal to the usual concept of sanitary landfills yet must be disposed of in a sanitary manner. These materials range from soil and rock which have no putrescible materials, to wood and fresh vegetation, which are completely biodegradable. Their proper disposal becomes a major planning concern because they often require more volume than the total household trash and garbage collection of the municipality that is concerned. The principal categories need different handling because of their diversity.

1. WOOD, PLASTER, AND METAL BUILDINGS

Waste from demolition of deteriorated residential and small commercial structures has a high proportion of slowly biodegradable material in the form of lumber, wall paper, and fiber-board. Metals from plumbing and lighting installations and paint constitute a hazard to ground water unless isolation is maintained. Salvage of metals and some lumber reduces the amount of pollutants produced from these wastes so that isolation distances can usually be made less than for the standard landfill. Some soil usually needs to be used with lumber to fill voids and to serve as a barrier to fire. Soil is needed for final cover in order to establish vegetation.

2. BRICK, STONE, AND CONCRETE

The waste from tearing up pavements and demolishing fireproof buildings is nonputrescible and largely insoluble. These materials can be used as simple landfill to fill low areas. If structural metal has been salvaged, the remaining material is inert. Where the fill is to be used as a base for other landfilling, enough soil should be used to fill voids. Final soil cover is required to permit revegetation and to allow tillage if that is required.

3. TREES, STUMPS, AND BRUSH

In areas where air pollution controls are strict it is often necessary that debris from clearing rights-of-way for highways, pipe lines, and power lines be landfilled. The same requirements apply to areas being cleared for a different land use. These materials are almost entirely biodegradible except for adhering soil. They are bulky and difficult to compact. If allowed to dry, they are highly combustible. The same precautions for protection of ground water are needed as for municipal trash and garbage. However, there is a much narrower range of pollutants because metals and industrial chemicals are lacking. Natural renovation can be expected to be fully effective if the site meets the soil requirements for a standard municipal landfill.

4. EARTH

Soil and soil material from excavations in natural soil sometimes becomes a disposal problem in an urban setting. If it is within a feasable haul distance from a municipal landfill it can be an asset. It usually makes satisfactory cover material unless it contains a high proportion of large rocks.

VII. EMERGENCY SITES FOR QUICK DISASTER RESPONSE

A. Need and Nature of Materials

When disasters strike, suddenly producing large quantities of waste, there is very little time for planning and site procurement. The cleanup operation has great urgency for the elimination of public health hazards and the restoration of services. Such wastes include materials not normally sent to municipal landfills. Some characteristics of the waste can be pointed out for general categories of waste.

1. MAJOR DISASTERS: FLOODS, TORNADOS, EARTHQUAKES, ETC.

Major disasters are indiscriminate in their impact and usually affect relatively large areas. An entire municipality may receive damage and the destruction may be almost total within some areas, such as a floodplain, the path of a tornado, or along an active fault. The waste produced includes a high proportion of demolition waste from wrecked buildings but also includes furnishings of the wrecked buildings and, in case of floods, much of the furnishings of buildings which survived the flood. Large quantities of putrescible material similar to garbage comes from grocery stores and food handling establishments. A wide variety of hazardous wastes comes from drug stores, pesticide dealers, paint stores, and many kinds of industrial establishments. All of the waste from flood areas is wet and frequently it is coated with mud.

2. INDUSTRIAL OR TRANSPORTATION ACCIDENTS

This category of disaster is usually smaller and localized but may require quick response and often results in exotic wastes with unusual hazards. Volume of waste from a transportation accident may be only one truck load or a few railroad cars. If it is a load of industrial chemicals which saturates the soil it may involve finding a place to safely dispose of the contaminated soil before leaching moves the chemical to the ground water, or erosion carries it into a stream. A damaged load of pharmaceuticals may have to be buried while Food and Drug inspectors stand by to guard against pilfering. What these accidents lack in volume of waste is overshadowed by the complexity of hazards that are involved.

B. Sites

The preceding discussion indicates that at best the special wastes generated by disasters present as serious a pollution problem as common municipal waste and in some instances include materials which should not be entrusted to the soil for renovation. Large quantities arrive at a site in a very short time. Often there is inadequate provision for site preparation and soil is lacking for cover material. When daily placement of waste is many times the volume of a recommended landfill cell, the placing of soil barriers is neglected. After fills constructed in this manner partially dry, there is a hazard of fire which is very hard to control.

The volume of waste involved and the suddenness of the need make it imperative that advance planning be done and disaster response agencies informed of the plan. The alternative is costly mistakes in case of disaster.

1. SPECIAL PERMITS FOR EXISTING LANDFILLS

The bulk of waste from major disasters is so great that they can shorten the useable life of a conventional municipal landfill by several years. The use of emergency vehicles can overtax the access roads and the operating routine of the conventional landfill. Municipalities which depend on incinerators or partial salvage operations do not have facilities for the added load and have to turn to landfilling during the peak of the cleanup.

Smaller disasters that produce limited amounts of waste may be in the range where the cleanup can be directed to existing landfills. The limits on such use should be set as part of an over-all plan and should be thoroughly understood by both the landfill management and the disaster response agencies. For some exotic wastes, only the landfills with treatment facilities should be used.

2. NEW SITES

For orderly procedure in disaster cleanup, suitable sites should be predetermined and tentative plans prepared. Often this would include conditional contracts for use if needed. Such provisions are needed to avoid requisitioning sites under emergency powers and then settling costs by lengthy negotiations or litigation while a hastily constructed landfill smolders or leaches. Such sites should meet the site requirements for conventional sanitary landfills.

C. Case Histories

The floods in the Susquehanna Basin of Pennsylvania associated with Tropical Storm Agnes, 20–22 June 1972, illustrate a widespread disaster with acute solid waste disposal problems. In Harrisburg and neighboring communities along the main stem of the river, record high water flooded many homes, businesses, and industries with very muddy water. Oil spills added to the property damage. There was relatively little structural damage, so demolition waste was not excessive. Damaged paneling and flooring did make some wood waste. This damage was not confined to the floodplains but included contents of many flooded basements in upland sections. Several emergency landfill sites were put into use very quickly but with varying results. One, which was started in a parking lot on state-owned land but soon transferred to an abandoned shale pit, received a general mixture of the debris. It came under management before it was completed and was finished with approved soil cover and then revegetated. It produced a small amount of leachate but soon stabilized. Two were started on state-owned farmland. These sites had soil and geology clearance as satisfactory for landfilling. Trench type landfills were used and the depth of waste was limited. These received much putrescible material including merchandise, groceries, ice cream, and the stock of a flooded liquor store. No pollution problems have been noted.

Another temporary dumping place was at the edge of a major airport. This fill soon caught fire and smoldered until it could be quenched and moved.

In one suburban area a large fill was packed in a ravine. It buried the natural surface drain and seasonal ground water discharge points. So it has continued to leach. The waste was not provided with soil barriers. When it caught fire it continued to smolder until a trench was dug through it and filled with earth.

VIII. USE OF SOIL IN CONTAINING AND RENOVATING WASTE

Soil has been discussed in its relationships with specific types of landfill operations and from the standpoint of soil characteristics involved in effective landfill operation. Its limitations have been pointed out. But in spite of definitely limited capacities, it remains clear that soil has properties that make it adaptable to a range of conditions in landfill operation. The interaction of soil clays with ions in solution provide a buffer for concentrations of pollutant cations. Filtration through the soil stops particulate matter. The retention in the soil allows time for biodegradation of some dissolved organic matter.

Physical properties based on individual soil particles with a wide range in size, aggregated into larger particles make soil a good construction material. Within a range that includes intermediate textures and avoids extremes, natural soil provides good bearing strength and stability for supporting and confining landfills. Soil and site characteristics that provide optimum conditions for a landfill in humid temperate areas are listed in the second column of Table 3. The third column of this table lists some marginal or limited conditions and the final column lists the parameters which are considered as excluding landfilling of municipal waste with natural renovation. This table is based on Pennsylvania Solid Waste Management Regulations arranged in the format developed by the Soil Conservation Service for soil interpretive tables.

Sites which are to be provided with collection and treatment facilities have less stringent soil requirements. The physical factors that provide stability still have to be considered for support of the liner and the weight of waste to be placed. Design is dependent on the construction of slopes where soil cover can be placed and stabilized.

IX. FUTURE LAND USE OF SANITARY LANDFILL SITES

Sanitary landfilling with natural renovation is usually not considered as permanent land use. The capability of the soil to receive and purify waste is eventually reached or more cover material is not available. The mark of a real sanitary landfill, as contrasted with a dump, is the appearance of the site after filling is completed.

A. Uses Not Involving Vegetation

In areas of urban growth a site used for landfill is often destined for industrial or commercial use. Fill with earth, or stones, brick, and concrete, is preferred. These materials can be compacted to a desired level. They will not be so vulnerable to uneven settling and to gas production as mixed municipal and industrial wastes. Where waste contains putrescible materials, the presence of methane and the prospect that the area will continue to settle for many years until the organic part is consumed make construction hazardous. The use of columns for building support and an open space ground level used for parking are ways of reducing these hazards. The most common use not involving vegetation is as parking lots. When an area which has recently been used as a landfill for municipal solid waste is converted to a parking lot some soil or similar material is required as the first cover to serve the functions of containing loose refuse, excluding vectors, and preventing accidental fires. Standards of this material are not as high as for soil that also has to support vegetation. For several years on such sites it is generally recommended that surfacing be with loose gravel or crushed stone. These permit the escape of gas and allow for regrading where differential settling takes place.

B. Revegetation of Landfills

Uses to follow sanitary landfill most frequently involve revegetation. Sites in municipal ownership may be destined to be parks, golf courses, playgrounds, forests, arboretums, or athletic fields. In nonpublic operations they may be planned for golf courses, recreation areas (Fig. 2), eventual development for housing, or simply for resale without planned use.Some sites are leased from landowners with the expectation that the former use will be restored. This is often as farmland (Fig. 3). Where cropland is involved, it is possible to plan the operation so that final contours are convenient for field layout that favors easy tillage and erosion control.

A wide range of vegetative types can be adapted to landfill sites. Objectives of using vegetation are erosion control, aesthetics, and productivity. These usually come in the order named, at least initially in the site restoration. With a large area of fill graded to final slopes and covered with 61 cm (2 feet) of compacted soil, runoff is initially very high and the cover can be broken by gullies that quickly penetrate to the waste. It is important to seed as soon as grading is completed, and to use quick-starting plants. Mulching may be required in dry areas, during colder seasons, and on steep slopes in humid areas. In areas with wind erosion hazard and with cover material subject to blowing, mulch will require stabilizing.

Public reaction to "dumps" carries over to sanitary landfills. It is de-

Fig. 2—A camping site and picnic area on a covered and landscaped sanitary landfill area in the foreground (Pennsylvania Dep. Environ. Res. photo).

Fig. 3—Restored farmland on former sanitary landfill site (Pennsylvania Dep. Environ. Res. photo).

sirable that as rapidly as possible the completed sections of a large operation be converted to an aesthetically pleasing landscape. The vegetation to be used must vary with the climate. For steeper side slopes that border a fill, shrubs, vines, and grasses that do not require much maintenance are desirable. When possible they should also look good.

On moderate slopes the revegetation plan should be part of the eventual plan for the new use. For parks, golf courses, playgrounds, and grazing lands suitable grasses should be selected. For woodland use the trees should be those that are adaptable and desired, with a temporary cover of grasses or other vegetation during the establishment period if this is acceptable forestry practice for the area. Cropland in humid areas can frequently go into a regular rotation or cropping plan. In this case, immediate performance may be disappointing unless good soil is used for final cover and care is taken to prepare a good seedbed. Soil cover is usually compacted during placement for the sake of reducing infiltration. This is directly opposed to developing an ideal rootzone for plants. Soil should be tested for plant nutrients and fertilizer used as needed for the crop.

There has been a lot of speculation about the effect of gas on the growth of vegetation on a landfill but there is very little documentation to back the claim that the waste must be stabilized before vegetation can survive. The authors have seen healthy tree plantations, field crops, pastures, and extensive grasslands on sites which were revegetated as soon as covered and graded. Some restrictions on growth can be traced to shallowness of total soil cover. With only 61 cm (2 feet) of soil there is insufficient available moisture capacity for higher production of many crops. The provision of more soil cover may be warranted in some cases where high productivity is of prime importance. As stabilization of the waste progresses, deep-rooted plants will begin to draw on the moisture in the fill material.

LITERATURE CITED

Apgar, M. A., and Donald Langmuir. 1971. Groundwater pollution potential of a landfill above the water table. J. Nat. Water Well Assoc. 9:6:76–96.

California State Water Quality Control Board. 1965. In-situ investigation of movements of gases produced from decomposing refuse. California State Water Qual. Bd., Pub. no. 31.

California State Water Quality Control Board. 1967. Final report. In-situ investigation of movement of gases produced from decomposing refuse. California State Water Qual. Bd. Pub. no. 35.

Herriman, R. C. 1972. Soil and landscape factors in siting sanitary landfills. J. Soil Water Conserv. 27(2):78–80.

Loughry, F. G. 1967. The soil factor in sanitary landfill. Proc. Pa. Acad. Sci. 41:156–160.

Loughry, F. G. 1972. Soil science and geologic principles applied to disposal of metallic wastes. p. 31–33. In Proc. 1st Tech. Conf. Environ. Conf., 7 Apr. 1972. The Pennsylvania State Univ. Chapter and Keystone Chapter SCSA.

Loughry, F. G. 1973. The use of soil science in sanitary landfill selection and management. Geoderma 10:131–139.

Merz, R. C. 1954. Final report on the investigation of leaching of a sanitary landfill. California State Water Pollut. Control Bd. Pub. no. 10.

Merz, R. C., and Ralph Stone. 1962. Landfill settlement rates. Public Works 93(9):103.

Merz, R. C., and Ralph Stone. 1964. Gas production in a sanitary landfill. Public Works 95(2):84.

Noble, George. 1976. Sanitary landfill design handbook, the science and art of site selection, investigation, and design. Technomics Publ. Co., Inc., Westport, Conn. p. 62–69.

Pennsylvania Department of Environmental Resources. 1971. Solid waste management. Pa. Dep. of Environ. Res. Title 25, Rules and Reg. Chap. 75.

Redding, M. J. 1973. Aesthetics in environmental planning. USEPA Rep. no. EPA-600/5-73-009.

Remson, Irwin, A. A. Fungaroli, and A. W. Lawrence. 1968. Water movement in an unsaturated sanitary landfill. J. Sanit. Eng. Div. Proc. of Am. Soc. of Civil Eng. 94(SA2):307–317.

Soil Survey Staff, Soil Conservation Service. 1975. Soil taxonomy. USDA Agric. Handbk. no. 436.

Solid Waste Staff. 1974. 2nd Rep. to Congr., resource recovery and source reduction. USEPA Pub. SW-122.

Warman, J. C., R. K. Rainer, and A. S. Chipley. 1974. Will current research answer today's problems at the sanitary landfill? Ground Water J. 12(6):378–387.

section IX

Planning Diverse Land Uses and Management Programs

USDA Soil Conservation Service

IX

31 Watershed Planning and Management

W. D. STRIFFLER

Colorado State University
Fort Collins, Colorado

I. INTRODUCTION

Throughout the ages, man has primarily been an exploiter of the land and its resources. History contains many examples of civilization which flourished as long as the land and its resources supplied their needs, but which fell into decline and eventually disappeared as forest cover and water supplies declined and as erosion and sedimentation proceeded unchecked. Even the history of the United States has been a history of exploitation. As timber supplies were depleted new sources were sought to the west. "Worn out" farms were abandoned and new lands developed. It has taken several hundred years of development in this country for man to learn that the land and its resources are not inexhaustible. It has taken equal time to learn that a close relationship exists between land use and the quantity and the quality of water originating from that land, and that the water resource may be controlled or "managed" by planning and controlling land use activities within a drainage basin.

Awareness of this relationship first became evident in the late 19th Century when the Division of Forestry published a bulletin entitled *Forest Influences.* This stimulated much scientific debate concerning the role of forests, culminating in the publication of a review by Raphael Zon entitled, *Forests and Water in the Light of Scientific Investigation* (Zon, 1927). The establishment of the U.S. Forest Service and the National Forest System during this period also recognized the importance of preserving and protecting streams and waters, and investigating the relationship between forests and water.

Management of public lands proceeded with some awareness of the effects of land use upon the water resource. The establishment of the Soil Erosion Service (later the Soil Conservation Service) in 1933 began a program to promote better land use practices on private land (Bennett, 1939).

However, it was not until the passing of the National Environmental Policy Act of 1969 (NEPA) that all federal agencies and federally controlled industries were required to evaluate or predict the impact upon the environment of all land use activities (PL 91-190). The passage of this act has stimulated a great interest in defining relationships, evaluating potential impacts, and developing land use planning methods. This chapter reviews the important watershed characteristics and hydrologic processes which must be considered in land use planning.

II. WATERSHED MANAGEMENT OBJECTIVES

Watershed management has been defined by Frank (1969) as "the analysis, protection, repair, utilization and maintenance of drainage basins for optimum control and conservation of water with due regard to other resources." This definition basically defines the primary functions or objectives of the watershed manager, namely, analysis, protection, restoration, and water yield management. The definition is significant in that it suggests some optimum level of control and recognizes that water is only one of the resources being managed on the watershed.

A. Watershed Analysis

All land use management activities require an initial evaluation of the land and its resources. Such evaluations may consist of simple inventories of a particular resource or may expand into an analysis of all resources and probable consequences of management. The primary function of the resource analysis is to serve as a tool for planning and implementing a management plan with a minimum disturbance to the other resources.

Watershed management depends upon the management of the other resources. Any land use activity within the watershed will have an impact on the water resource and, in fact, management of the water resource is frequently accomplished by managing or manipulating other resources. The watershed analysis, therefore, traditionally considers all resources present in the watershed with particular emphasis on the water resource. In addition to inventorying water and related resources, basin characteristics important to planning should also be evaluated. This would include climatic characteristics of the watershed, soil characteristics, topography, and the kinds and condition of vegetation present. Of particular importance to the planner is the recognition or identification of existing or potential problem areas within the basin. Identification of flood plains, geologic hazard areas, avalanche paths, wet soil areas, etc., prior to the planning phase may save the planner considerable time and effort.

In contrast to the watershed analysis covering an entire watershed are the more detailed analyses of specific sites within the watershed which are being considered for specific development. Analyses of this type might include site feasibility studies, disturbed area studies, and Environmental Impact Statements (EIS). Of these, the latter (EIS) are now required as part of the land use planning process on all federal lands or by agencies and industries subject to federal regulation. Environmental impact statements include basic inventories of resources on the site as well as detailed analysis of probable consequences of a proposed action, methods of mitigating the impacts, and alternatives to the proposed action. The primary purpose of the EIS is regulatory, that is, to help determine whether a proposed action will be permitted. Although the preparation of an EIS requires that planning be completed to the point that the impact of the plan can be evaluated, it also serves as a watershed management planning tool since it identifies watershed impacts and prescribes protective measures to minimize the impact.

B. Watershed Protection

As previously mentioned, any land use activity has an impact on the water resource. The role of the manager in watershed protection is to be familiar with land use-water resource relationships and help in the land use planning process so as to minimize any detrimental effects. Land use activities which entail a disturbance to the surface of the watershed require careful preplanning to minimize the effects.

Protection is probably the most important function of the watershed manager. By thoroughly understanding land use-water relationships and identifying potential problem areas before undertaking an activity, much damage may be prevented. Protection measures are generally much less costly than rehabilitation measures.

A number of guidelines are now available for planning protective measures for specific cases such as residential construction (USEPA, 1973a), crop lands (USEPA, USDA, 1975), forest practices (USEPA, 1973b), road construction (Utah State Univ., 1976), and mining (USEPA, 1973c). In addition, many states now have regulations specifying kinds of protective measures to be applied during specific land uses.

C. Watershed Rehabilitation

Watershed rehabilitation refers to the repair or restoration of the water resource after damage has occurred. Damage may be either to the water resource or to the land surface. Direct damage might include the discharge of pollutants directly into the water resource or mechanical damage to a water course. Indirect damage or damge to the land surface might include reduction of the vegetation cover due to fire, over-grazing by domestic or wild animals, or uncontrolled recreational use, or it might include physical disturbance to the land surface such as surface mining or road or other construction activities. Damages of either type may result in accelerated erosion, land slides, flooding, and water quality damage.

Watershed restoration measures include both revegetation measures and structural measures. Revegetation measures refer to practices designed to revegetate a disturbed area such as seeding, tree planting, and application of fertilizer and mulches. Successful revegetation depends on many factors, including species selection, climatic regime, and soil characteristics. Species should be selected with specific objectives in mind such as vegetative form, rooting characteristics, method of regeneration, drought resistance, etc. Since revegetation depends on the vagaries of the weather, even the best planned revegetation project may fail. An extended dry period, an intense storm, or unseasonably high or low temperatures may cause a failure in a revegetation project, requiring it to be repeated. Many guidelines are available to aid in revegetating specific regions or activities (USEPA, 1975).

In some restoration projects, vegetation by itself may not be sufficient to achieve a stable site. Steep slopes, highly erodible soils, or areas subject to concentrated flow of water may require structural measures in addition to vegetation measures. Structural measures are usually designed to reduce the erosive energy of flowing water. Since erosivity is a function of volume and velocity of flow, measures designed to reduce either are effective in reducing surface erosion. Measures which reduce surface gradients and length of flow are effective in reducing velocities and include regrading, diversions, contour furrows, and terraces. Structures designed to temporarily store some of the runoff help to reduce the volume of flow. These include contour trenches, check dams, debris basins, etc. Measures designed to protect a bare soil bank would include rock riprap and a large variety of channel structures (Hudson, 1976).

Structural measures are highly effective if properly designed and constructed, yet are also very costly and should be considered as a supplement to revegetation methods.

D. Water Yield Management

A management objective of increasing concern is management for water yield. Particularly in water-short states such as Arizona, methods of increasing useable water supplies by land management are of considerable interest.

Methods of increasing yield generally are concerned with either increasing precipitation or decreasing losses on the watershed. Weather modification to increase precipitation has demonstrated a good potential for augmenting winter snowpack accumulation in high mountain regions. However, effectiveness in other regions and situations is still questionable. Regardless of its effectiveness, weather modification is a highly specialized science and is not generally considered an important factor in land use planning.

Water yield management by land management activities is an important consideration in many areas. Ever since the early watershed studies at Wagon Wheel Gap, Colorado, (Bates & Henry, 1928) demonstrated an increased streamflow after removing the forest cover, much research has been directed towards the relationship between forest and water and methods of increasing yields. Studies in Colorado, North Carolina, West Virginia, and many other experimental watersheds in this country and around the world (Hibbert, 1967) indicate that removal of forest cover (i.e., reducing transpiration losses) will effectively increase streamflow. Other techniques which have been tested and demonstrated effectively are (i) conversion of deep-rooted brush species to shallow-rooted grasses and shrubs, and (ii) removal of phreatophytes and other high water users from along water courses and flood plains (Ffolliott & Thorud, 1974).

All of the methods discussed above have relied upon decreasing water use by vegetation as a means of increasing streamflow. Another approach which has also been tested and applied are methods of reducing water intake by soils. Water falling as rain cannot enter the soil, and therefore runs off as surface runoff to the stream channel or storage reservoir. These techniques of "water harvesting" have been most widely applied in semiarid regions where small water-harvesting areas have been used to fill stock tanks or supply water for local needs. Methods of sealing the soil surface range from paving the watershed with asphalt, to lining catchment areas with plastic or neoprene covers, to chemical sprays and soil sealants (Medina, 1976).

Although all of these techniques have been demonstrated to increase water yields, widespread application has not developed due to other limitations. Clear-cutting of forests has been criticized as causing long-term ecological degradation. Although still practiced in some forest types, it has been effectively banned in many national forests. Similarly, conversion of brush and chaparral areas is damaging to wildlife habitat and the large-scale phreatophyte removal projects of the southwestern U.S. are being challenged both from the wildlife habitat standpoint and because of potential water quality problems resulting from use of herbicides along water courses (Maddox, 1972).

In spite of these limitations, water yield management will continue to be of concern to land use planners. For example, several questions are currently being tested in the courts. If a landowner removed a row of cottonwood trees from along an irrigation ditch, can he claim rights to the water saved? Similarly, can a mountain home developer claim rights to water "salvaged" by his activities in developing a subdivision. These cases point out one of the unanswered questions in water yield management. That is, if streamflow can be increased by land management activities, who owns the "new" water, and can rights be established for that water?

III. WATERSHED CHARACTERISTICS TO BE CONSIDERED IN PLANNING AND MANAGEMENT

Watershed considerations in land use planning are primarily related to protection activities. First of all, protecting the water resource or conducting management activities so as to minimize the resulting impact upon the quantity or quality of the adjacent stream or reservoirs, and secondly, to protect the land use activity from damage by hydrologic elements. Both types of protection require a knowledge of the hydrologic behavior of the watershed which in turn depends upon the physical characteristics of the watershed. Physical characteristics to be considered include climatic characteristics, soils, topography, and vegetation.

A. Climatic Characteristics

Climatic characteristics affecting the hydrologic behavior of the watershed are primarily related to precipitation characteristics, the driving input in the hydrologic system, and those climatic elements that determine the rate of evaporation and transpiration losses from the watershed.

The amount of precipitation received in a watershed and the manner in which it is received are always important considerations in most land use planning activities. The amount received annually, the seasonal distribution, the form of precipitation (rain or snow), and the magnitude of storms to be expected will all have an effect upon the hydrology of the basin.

Generalized information adequate for planning purposes is available for most states in the *Monthly Climatic Data and Annual Summaries* published by the National Weather Service. Although a precipitation gage may not be located in a particular watershed, estimates of annual and seasonal precipitation can be obtained from the climatic atlases available.

Similarly, information for design purposes on the expected frequency-intensity-duration of storms can be determined for the United States from the National Weather Service Publication, TP-40, or the newer state atlases now available.

The atlases and publications available are most reliable where the density of the gage network and length of record are greatest. In remote mountain areas where gage density is minimum and topographic influences are maximum, published atlases may not be sufficiently accurate for planning purposes, and the planner may be forced to base design on "best guess" estimates.

The evaporation potential for a watershed may or may not be an important consideration in land use planning depending upon the intended use of a watershed. Certainly, uses related to plant growth would be concerned with evaporation potential as a means of determining periods of stress during a growing season.

The evaporation potential or potential evapotranspiration (PET) can be estimated using any of the many empirical or rational formulae available (Tanner, 1967). The simpler formulae are based on empirical relationships between air temperature and evaporation losses. More sophisticated formulae combine energy terms (solar radiation) and aerodynamic terms (wind movement) to approximate the energy and transport functions in the evaporation process.

Data for estimating potential evapotranspiration are less common and more difficult to extrapolate than precipitation data. Temperature stations are usually found in the larger communities but are only occasionally found in agricultural or forested areas. Because of the strong variations in temperature with elevation and aspect, it is difficult to extrapolate for long distances from a temperature station to a specific watershed area. However, the common procedure is to do just that. By collecting data from the existing stations around the area of interest, a temperature vs. elevation relationship is determined, which is then used to estimate a temperature value for the mean elevation of the watershed being studied. This procedure is satisfactory for mean monthly or even weekly temperatures but it is less reliable for shorter time periods.

Similarly, solar radiation, wind, and other climatic data are rarely found for specific watershed areas. Again, knowing how these elements vary with topography, it is possible to derive useable estimates for specific situations. Tables of potential solar radiation, for example, are published for various latitudes, slopes, and aspects (Frank & Lee, 1966). If a reasonable estimate of cloud cover can be determined, a radiation value suitable for planning purposes can be obtained.

By using both precipitation and potential evapotranspiration data, an annual water budget can be determined for the watershed which identifies periods of water excess and water deficit. For uses such as irrigation planning, water budgets are highly useful since they indicate periods requiring irrigation scheduling and the general amount required.

B. Soils

In land use planning, the soils present must be considered from several aspects. Probably the most important consideration is the suitability of the soil for the proposed use. Another related consideration is the role of the soil in the hydrology of the basin. It is well known that the rainfall/runoff process is strongly influenced by the nature of the soil present in the watershed (Musgrave, 1955).

1. HYDROLOGIC CHARACTERISTICS OF SOIL

Although many soil physical properties can be measured, the characteristics most important to the hydrology of a watershed are those which affect the intake and transmission of water through the soil mantle, and the storage of water within the soil profile. The intake of water or infiltration of water into the soil is considered a surface process and subject to many influences in addition to the physical characteristics of the soil. The infiltration process will be discussed later in this chapter.

Permeability, the ability of a soil to pass water and air through the soil matrix, is largely determined by the ratio of pore space to solid material and the size distribution of the pores. If the pore spaces are filled with water, the rate of water movement is called the *saturated hydraulic conductivity* and is primarily the result of water draining through the profile under the influence of gravity. If the pore spaces contain air as well as water, the *unsaturated hydraulic conductivity,* in addition to gravity, is subject to energy and temperature gradients. Permeability is therefore primarily determined by the texture of the soil. Permeabilities range from very slow (15 mm/hour) to the very rapid (500 mm/hour) (SCS, 1971).

As water drains from the soil profile, a certain proportion is held in the profile against the force of gravity. The upper or maximum amount of water held defines the *field capacity* or the water-holding capacity of the soil. This is generally considered to be the storage volume which needs to be filled before water can pass on to the ground water reservoir. It is also considered the primary source of water for plant use. As water is removed from the profiles by plant roots, the energy with which the water is held tends to increase until a point is reached at which the plant can no longer take in sufficient water to survive. This point, termed the *permanent wilting point,* defines the lower limit of the available water capacity (AWC) of the soil. Although the concepts of field capacity ($-1/3$ bar) and wilting point (-15 bars) have been defined rather arbitrarily, they serve a useful purpose in planning.

Both the permeability and the water-holding capacity of a soil are subject to limitation by the thickness of the soil mantle. A soil may have physical characteristics indicating a highly permeable soil, but, if the soil mantle is shallow, or if an impeding layer occurs in the profile, the pores will soon become saturated and the rate of movement will be greatly reduced. Similarly, a soil may have a high water-holding capacity based on texture analysis of the surface layers, but if the soil is shallow, the total amount of water stored may not be enough to supply a crop during a dry period and a dry site will result.

2. HYDROLOGIC SOIL GROUPINGS

In an effort to simplify the interpretation of soil hydrologic characteristics, the Soil Conservation service has developed the concept of Hydrologic Soil Groupings in which all soils may be assigned to one of four categories. Hydrologic soil groupings are based on minimum infiltration rates and soil depths for the range of soil types (Musgrave, 1955). The four infiltration groups are defined as follows:

Group A—very permeable deep sands and deep aggregated silt of loessal origin; they have little clay and colloid, and the silts have enough organic matter to provide good aggregation; infiltration rates greater than 7.6 mm/hour (0.3 in/hour).

Group B—Sandy soils and silt loams of moderate depth and above average infiltration; minimum infiltration rates from 7.6 to 3.8 mm/hour (0.30 to 0.15 in/hour).

Group C—Shallow soils in all texture classes; minimum infiltration rates from 3.8 to 1.3 mm/hour &0.15 to 0.05 in/hour).

Group D—Soils with high-swelling rates in the surface or subsurface because of high clay or colloid content; minimum infiltration rates less than 1.3 mm/hour (0.05 in/hour).

These categories are based on a large number of infiltration measurements under different soil textures and cover conditions. Although originated by the SCS for agricultural soils, the concept has been adopted by other land management agencies and applied to forest and rangelands as well (BLM, 1974; USBR, 1973).

Although the system tends to greatly over-simplify the hydrologic properties of soils, it is a useful concept for planning purposes, particularly for watersheds where soil surveys are available.

C. Watershed Characteristics

The hydrologic response of a watershed is also strongly influenced by the physical characteristics or physiography of the watershed. Since watershed physiography is largely the result of erosional processes in the evolution of the basin, an examination of the watershed characteristics will reveal much about the hydrologic behavior of the watershed. Characteristics of interest include general surface characteristics such as channel gradients, density, and branching characteristics.

In general, physiographic characteristics reveal the drainage efficiency of the basin, that is, how efficient the basin is in delivering water received as rainfall to the basin outlet. A basin with steep slopes, a high drainage density (km of channel/km² of basin area), a short overland flow distance, and a compact shape would be a highly efficient hydrologic system. In contrast, a basin with gentle relief, a low drainage density with little channel branching, and elongated shape would be a less efficient drainage system.

The more efficient a drainage system, the faster the response to storm events. Thus, efficient drainage systems would tend to respond to storm rainfall faster and have higher peak flows than a less efficient system. Similarly, the more efficient system would tend to have lower base flows.

Much work has been done to develop numerical quantification of physiographic parameters and to relate numerical expressions to basin hydrology (Gray, 1962). However, the primary value of such quantitative geomorphic measurements is to compare one basin to another.

Geomorphic characteristics of particular interest in land use planning would include any factors which would tend to limit land use activities. This would include slope steepness, area of the drainage basin, channel gradient and meander width, and the width of the flood plain.

D. Vegetation

The density and vigor of the vegetation covering a watershed serves as an index to the hydrologic condition of the watershed. A dense vigorous vegetation cover, whether a forest cover or agricultural crop, indicates that the watershed is in a stable condition. The presence of a forest cover indicates that the watershed has been stabilized for an extended period and, from the protection aspect, has reached an optimum with respect to hydrologic functions. In other words, the watershed surface is stable, erosion is reduced to a minimum, sediment input into the channel system is nil, and the channel has stabilized over a period of time to the point that bank erosion and channel shifts are infrequent and sediment loads are very small.

In a forested watershed, the condition of the forest cover also serves as an index to potential problem areas. Areas with a sparse or no tree cover should be examined for potential problems. A sparse or poor tree cover may simply be the result of marginal site conditions such as shallow soils, low water availability, or poor fertility, or it may indicate a prior disturbance such as fire or blow downs. Active landslide areas and avalanche paths are also readily detected by lack of tree cover.

Methods of determining the effectiveness of the vegetation cover vary considerably among the various agencies and vegetation types. Hydrologic condition surveys as conducted by the U.S. Forest Service and Bureau of Land Management basically look at the ground cover. If the vegetation cover is a ground vegetation, the completeness of the ground cover serves as the vegetation part of the hydrologic condition index. If a forest cover occurs, in addition to the density of the crown canopy, the depth and extent of surface organic layers (litter and humus) are considered. Ground cover densities greater than 70% are classified as good condition cover while densities less than 30% are classified as poor. Similarly, deep friable humus types are considered good ground cover while thin compact organic layers are considered poor (BLM, 1969).

For mapping broad areas, aerial photographic and remote sensing techniques now permit rapid mapping and evaluation over broad areas. For planning purposes, aerial photo maps are probably one of the most useful tools the planner can obtain.

IV. HYDROLOGIC PROCESSES TO BE CONSIDERED IN PLANNING AND MANAGEMENT

In addition to a consideration of the watershed characteristics, it is also necessary to understand the hydrologic processes and how they may be affected by land use changes. Processes of primary interest in planning are the surface, subsurface, and channel flow processes.

A. Surface and Subsurface Flows

Water falling as rain on the land surface is disposed of in several ways. Some of the water is intercepted on the surface of the vegetation and evaporated back into the atmosphere. Some of the water is absorbed by the soil surface and redistributed within the soil mantle. When precipitation rates exceed infiltration rates, excess water accumulates on the surface and flows off as surface runoff or overland flow. The streamflow hydrograph resulting from the rainfall event is thus the result of rainfall falling directly into the stream channel plus overland flow, plus a subsurface flow component in certain situations.

The process as just described is basically the classical or Hortonian concept of the rainfall-runoff process (Horton, 1933). This concept has served as the fundamental principle upon which most hydrologic design and prediction methods have developed. Using this concept, the storm hydrograph resulting at some downstream point on a small watershed can be subdivided into base flow and storm flow or overland flow components. A great deal of research has been done to develop hydrograph analysis techniques. Similarly a great deal of research has been done on developing prediction methods for hydrologic design purposes. Methods such as the Rational Method and the SCS Curve Number Method are based on an assumed infiltration capacity for the watershed (SCS, 1957). Although many of the methods developed work well for prediction purposes at a downstream point, it has been more difficult to verify the assumed hydrologic functioning of the upland areas of the watershed. Attempts at directly measuring infiltration rates have had little relationship to infiltration rates calculated from hydrographs. In addition, foresters have commented for many years on the obvious absence of surface runoff during intense storms on upland forested watersheds (Zon, 1927).

This apparent inconsistency between theorized and observed processes in upland watersheds has led to the development of the variable source concept of streamflow generation by Hewlett (1961) and others (Hewlett & Nutter, 1970; Hewlett & Troendle, 1975; Hewlett & Hibbert, 1963). The basic concept of streamflow generation process is that infiltration is seldom a limiting factor in forested and other well-vegetated watersheds. As water enters the soil mantle it recharges soil mantle storage and, under the influence of hydraulic gradients, commences to flow downslope in a path roughly parallel to the slope. Flow may occur along an impeding layer, a bed rock interface, or other favorable flow paths as a lateral or *translatory* flow. As flow approaches the channel, it recharges a soil storage zone adjacent to the channel which serves as the *source area* for channel flow. This source area expands rapidly as water is received during a storm event and contracts more slowly as water drains to the channel following the storm. Hence the expression *variable source area.*

The variable source area concept satisfies many of the criticisms of the infiltration concept. However, it has been more difficult to apply the concept for prediction purposes. Approaches such as that of Dickenson and Whitely (1970), who developed a relationship between minimum contributing area and a basic moisture index based on soil water content and storm rainfall, should prove valuable for future applications.

It should be emphasized that, in spite of the evidence supporting the variable source concept on well-vegetated basins, the infiltration concept does apply in many situations. Urbanizing watersheds, disturbed watersheds, and poorly vegetated watersheds all experience overland flow. However, even here the subsurface component may be much more important than previously thought.

As suggested by Hewlett and Troendle (1975), one of the stimuli for investigating the variable source area concept has been the recent interest in defining nonpoint source pollution processes. Conventional infiltration theory has been unable to explain nonpoint source processes whereas the dissolution of salts in the soil profile and subsequent transport within the soil mantle to the stream is compatible with variable source area processes.

An example of pollution by subsurface flow processes is the growing problem of saline seeps in the northern Great Plains (Doering & Sandoval, 1976). The most commonly accepted theory of saline seep development requires an upslope recharge area. Rain falling on this upslope recharge area infiltrates the soil and percolates downward, dissolving accumulated salts enroute until it encounters a highly permeable zone. Water accumulates and flows along this zone until the accumulation becomes great enough or the permeable zone sufficiently close to the surface to wet the soil. At this point continued wetting and drying causes an accumulation of salts at the surface and eventual elimination of the desired plant cover. Repeated wetting and drying cycles in the recharge area tend to concentrate additional salts into the leach zone where they, in turn, are dissolved and transported downslope.

Although the saline seep problem is probably a special case of subsurface flow, it does serve as a good example of the interactions between geologic, climatic, and cultural influence in creating a serious land use problem. Major efforts are now underway to learn to control the problem (Krall & Brown, 1976).

B. Channel Processes

Channel processes of primary interest to the planner would be the processes which would affect land use planning. Processes of concern would thus include those relating to streamflow volume and stream quality. Stream volume problems might include situations with either too much flow (flooding) or too little flow. Quality problems would include physical quality parameters such as sediment concentration, temperature, color, odor, and biological and chemical parameters such as dissolved oxygen content, dissolved solids, salinity, coliform bacteria content, and many more.

Potential flooding is probably one of the most important processes of concern in planning. Methods for estimating flood peaks for certain size storms, and methods for delineating flood plains have received considerable attention by hydrologists. As a result many techniques are available for estimating flood peaks (USWRC, 1977). The suitability of the various methods depend to a great extent upon the watershed characteristics, especially the watershed size or area. Perhaps the best method of determining flood size and frequency is to use available streamflow data. If a long-term record of discharge exists for a particular watershed, it is a relatively simple procedure to determine the magnitude and frequency of flood events. Unfortunately, the developing watershed rarely has discharge data available and other methods must be used. Alternative methods range from relatively simple equations such as the Rational Formula to highly complex procedures based on basin geometry and cover condition. Regardless of the method selected, successful application usually involves a great deal of "art" and experience by the user.

Peak flow estimations are necessary for design of channel structures such as bridges, culverts, and dams and also for determining the flood plain. Flood plain estimation involves estimating the peak flow for a particular return period, that is, the maximum flow recurring on the average once in 100 years, and then determining the water surface profile in the particular geometry of the watershed. Flood plain determinations are now required for federal flood insurance programs and a strong effort is underway to zone flood plains for activities which would not be damaged by periodic flooding.

One of the major difficulties in flood peak estimation and flood plain determination is that values determined for one set of conditions will not apply as the watershed undergoes change. Urbanizing watersheds, for example, will have higher flood peaks as development proceeds. It may be necessary in these situations for periodic reevaluation.

In contrast to flood problems are problems of insufficient flow for certain uses. Problems of instream flows or minimum flows have only recently received major consideration as water management problems. Problems currently being addressed include minimum flows to support cold water fisheries in mountain streams. This is a particular problem in western states where storage reservoirs or irrigation diversions may reduce flow volumes below acceptable levels for certain uses.

C. Soil Vegetation Interaction

As has been evident throughout this chapter, the relationship between rainfall and runoff for any watershed is primarily determined by the magnitude of the intermediate processes which in turn are strongly influenced by the soils and vegetation present in the watershed. Since manipulation of surface vegetation is one of the few tools available to the manager, it is necessary to understand how vegetation affects the hydrologic process, and conversely, how the hydrology of the basin may be modified or managed through the vegetation.

Since vegetation occupies the surface of the watershed, the most direct influence is upon the surface processes. However, surface processes are also strongly influenced by the soils present in the watershed. Together the soils and vegetation exert a dominant influence on surface processes and, as a result, on channel processes also.

Much research has been directed toward defining the relationship between soils, vegetation, and processes such as infiltration, surface runoff, and erosion. Many studies have been published which present qualitative relationships. It is more difficult to define quantitative relationships which may be used for prediction purposes. Because of the growing demand for predictive tools in environmental assessment, attempts at defining useable relationships have intensified.

Attempts at developing infiltration equations have largely concentrated on defining soil hydraulic properties. Many studies have shown, however, that initial infiltration rates are strongly influenced by the condition of the surface, including vegetation and litter. Holton (1971) presents an infiltration capacity storage term which is directly related to vegetation density. Although vegetation is important in determining the initial infiltration rate, the ultimate or final infiltration rate is a function of soil transmission properties.

Overland flow is also directly influenced by vegetation. Studies of overland flow processes indicate that as the vegetation density increases, the resistance to flow increases. Emmett (1970) observed that resistance to flow by a grass cover in Wyoming caused decreased velocity and increased depth of overland flow. Decreasing velocities allows the surface water more time to infiltrate the soil and also reduces the erosive energies.

Although quantitative relationships between vegetation and surface infiltration and runoff processes have been difficult to define, the relationship between vegetation and surface erosion has advanced to a more practical state. Vegetation assists in protecting the soil surface from erosion in two ways. First, it shields the surface from raindrop impact, and, secondly, it helps to protect the soil from the erosive energy of flowing water, both by reducing the overland flow velocity, and by helping to physically bind the soil into a resistant root mat. Because of its effectiveness in controlling surface erosion, design criteria for vegetative protection are included in most protection criteria. Examples of vegetation applications are grassed waterways, vegetation buffer strips along streams, contour strip-cropping systems, and wind breaks, to name a few. Similarly the popular methods of estimating erosion losses from disturbed areas such as the Universal Soil Loss Equation (Wischmeier & Smith, 1965) and the Musgrave Equation (Musgrave, 1947) include crop or vegetation factors. Although originally designed for agricultural lands, recent modification to the vegetation factors have been incorporated for undisturbed areas (Wischmeier, 1975). Soil loss equations not only predict soil loss from disturbed sites, but tell the manager how much vegetation is required to stabilize the site.

V. HYDROLOGIC MODELS

As the demand for predictive tools in hydrology and watershed management has grown, so has the variety and sophistication of the tools available. Early reliance on empirical formulae has given way to new, more deterministic techniques. This has been partly the result of limitations in empirical methods and partly the desire of the scientist to understand and simulate the complex workings of the entire hydrologic process, now made possible by the development of high speed computers. The result has been the development of a large number of hydrologic system models ranging from simple subprocess models to highly complex total basin or watershed models. As used in this chapter, the term *model* will refer to a mathematical representation of a process or group of connected processes, although other types of models can also be defined (Amorocho & Hart, 1964; Snyder & Stall, 1965). Even within the limitations imposed, a great deal of variety occurs. Deterministic vs. stochastic, lumped vs. distributed, and component part models vs. integrated system models are examples of the variety within the general family of mathematical models (Dawdy, 1969).

The concept of hydrologic modeling is not new. Hydrologists have long been attempting to describe hydrologic processes in mathematical equations. One of the earliest watershed models developed was the Stanford Watershed Model (Linsley & Crawford, 1960). This model went through a period of development culminating in the Stanford Watershed Model IV, probably one of the most widely known and applied models around the world. The Stanford IV has subsequently been modified and adapted for many uses by many investigators. Many other watershed models have also been developed, some for special limited applications and others more general in nature.

Early development of integrated system (watershed) models was largely from a scientific framework. A major objective was to try to understand the interaction between processes and to simulate the hydrologic functioning of the watershed so that response to changes in parameters could be evaluated. As models developed further, and as hydrologists became more confident that process simulation was giving correct results, practical applications of models also increased. Today, hydrologic models offer the planner a powerful tool. For the first time, proposed land use changes or treatments can be evaluated with respect to hydrologic changes, before the treatment is applied (Onstad & Jamieson, 1970). What will happen, for example, if we remove the forest cover from a watershed; or half the forest cover, or one third the forest cover, in small patch cuts? How will water yield and flood frequency change if a home site development and shopping center are constructed in a natural watershed? This is not to say that all land use impacts can be accurately predicted. The success of model applications still depends upon the expertise and experience of the modeler. The universal model suitable for all situations has not yet been and may never be developed. However, special purpose models perform well for their intended uses. Hydrograph simulations for parking lots, stream runoff from melting snow packs, and effects of vegetation modifications can be simulated with acceptable accuracy.

Much of the past development of hydrologic models has been concerned with rainfall/runoff processes. A new level of complexity is added when we attempt to couple runoff models with sediment yield or water quality models. However, efforts are now well under way to develop such models and it is inevitable that practical water quality models will soon be available.

LITERATURE CITED

Amorocho, J., and W. E. Hart. 1964. A critique of current methods in hydrologic system investigations. Trans. Am. Geophys. Union 45(2):307–327.

Bates, C. G., and A. J. Henry. 1928. Forest and streamflow experiments at Wagon Wheel Gap, Colorado. U.S. Weather Bur., Monthly Weather Rev. Suppl. 30. 79 p.

Bennett, H. H. 1939. Soil conservation. McGraw-Hill Book Co., Inc. 993 p.

Bureau of Land Management. 1969. Cover. Sec. 7313 of Bur. of Land Manage. Manual. U.S. Government Printing Office, Washington, D.C.

Bureau of Land Management. 1974. Surface water hydrology. Sec. 7315 of Bur. of Land Manage. Manual. U.S. Government Printing Office, Washington, D.C.

Dawdy, D. R. 1969. Mathematical modeling in hydrology. p. 346–361. *In* The Progress of Hydrology. Proc. 1st Int. Sem. for Hydrology Professors, 13–25 July 1969, Natl. Sci. Found., Univ. of Illinois, Urbana, Ill.

Dickinson, W. T., and H. Whitely. 1970. Watershed areas contributing to runoff. Int. Assoc. Sci. Hydrol. Publ. no. 96. p. 1.12–1.28.

Doering, E. J., and F. M. Sandoval. 1976. Hydrologic aspects of saline seeps in southwestern North Dakota. p. 303–311. *In* Saline Seep Control Symp. Proc. Montana Coop. Ext. Serv. Bull. 1132.

Emmett, W. W. 1970. The hydraulics of overland flow on hillslopes. U.S. Geol. Surv. Prof. Pap. 662A.

Ffolliott, P. F., and D. B. Thorud. 1974. Vegetation management for increased water yield in Arizona. Univ. of Arizona. Agric. Exp. Stn. Tech. Bull. 215. 38 p.

Frank, B. 1969. New concepts in watershed management. Am. Soc. Agron. Spec. Pub. Ser. no. 4. Soil Sci. Soc. of Am., Madison, Wis. p. 55–65.

Frank, E. C., and R. Lee. 1966. Potential solar beam irradiation on slopes. Tables for 30° to 50° latitudes. U.S. For. Serv. Res. Pap. RM-18. Rocky Mountain For. and Range Exp. Stn. 116 p.

Gray, D. M. 1962. Derivation of hydrographs for small watersheds from measurable physical characteristics. Iowa State Univ. Agric. and Home Econ. Exp. Stn. Res. Bull. no. 506.

Hewlett, J. D. 1961. Soil moisture as a source of base flow from steep mountain watersheds. Southeast. For. Exp. Stn., Stn. Pap. 132. 11 p.

Hewlett, J. D., and A. R. Hibbert. 1963. Moisture and energy conditions within a sloping soil mass during drainage. J. Geophys. Res. 68:1081–1087.

Hewlett, J. D., and W. L. Nutter. 1970. The varying source area of streamflow from upland basins. p. 65–83. *In* Proc. of Symp. on Interdisciplinary Aspects of watershed Manage., 3–6 Aug. 1970, Montana State Univ., Bozeman, Mont. Am. Soc. Chem. Eng., New York.

Hewlett, J. D., and C. A. Troendle. 1975. Non-point and diffused water sources. A variable source area problem. p. 21–46. *In* Watershed Management. Proc. of Symp., 11–13 Aug. 1975, Utah State Univ., Logan, Utah. Am. Soc. Chem. Eng., New York.

Hibbert, A. R. 1967. Forest treatment effects on water yield. p. 527–543. *In* Proc. Int. Symp. on Forest Hydrology, 29 Aug.–10 Sept. 1965, Natl. Sci. Found., Pennsylvania State Univ., University Park. Permagon Press, New York.

Holton, H. N. 1971. A formulation for quantifying the influence of soil porosity and vegetation on infiltration. p. 228–247. *In* Biological Effects in the Hydrologic Cycle. Proc. of the 3rd Int. Sem. for Hydrology Professors. 18–30 July 1971, Natl. Sci. Found., Purdue Univ., West Lafayette, Ind.

Horton, R. E. 1933. The role of infiltration in the hydrologic cycle. Trans. Am. Geophys. Union 14:446–460.

Hudson, N. 1976. Soil conservation. Cornell Univ. Press, Ithaca, N.Y. 320 p.

Krall, J. L., and P. L. Brown. 1977. Cultural practices for the control of saline seep in the Northern Plains. p. 64–77. *In* Conservation Tillage. Proc. of Great Plains Workshop. 10–12 Aug. 1976, Great Plains Agric. Counc. and GPE-2 Conserv. Tillage Task Force, Fort Collins, Colo. Great Plains Agric. Counc. Publ. no. 77.

Linsley, R. K., and N. H. Crawford. 1960. Computations of a synthetic streamflow record on a digital computer. Int. Assoc. of Sci. Hydrol. Publ. no. 51. p. 526–538.

Maddox, G. E. 1972. Ecologic-economic values in phreatophyte control. p. 257–259. *In* Am. Water Resour. Assoc. Symp., Watershed in Transition, 19–22 June 1972, Fort Collins, Colo. AWRA Proc. Ser. no. 14, Urbana, Ill.

Medina, J. 1976. Harvesting surface runoff and ephemeral streamflow in arid zones. p. 61–72. *In* Conservation in arid and semi-arid zones. FAO Conserv. Guide no. 3.

Musgrave, G. W. 1947. The quantitative evaluation of factors in water erosion—a first approximation. J. Soil Water Conserv. 2:133–138.

Musgrave, G. W. 1955. How much of the rain enters the soil? *In* Water. USDA Yearbook. p. 151–159.

Onstad, C. A., and D. G. Jamieson. 1970. Modeling the effect of land use modifications on runoff. Water Resour. Res. 6(5):1287–1295.

Snyder, W. G., and S. B. Stall. 1965. Men, models, methods and machines in hydrologic analysis. J. Hydraulics Div. ASCE 9(HY2):85–100.

Soil Conservation Service. 1957. National engineering handbook. Sect. 4, Suppl. A. The hydrology guide for use in watershed planning. U.S. Government Printing Office, Washington, D.C.

Soil Conservation Service. 1971. Guide for interpreting engineering uses of soils. U.S. Government Printing Office, Washington, D.C. 87 p.

Tanner, C. B. 1967. Measurement of evapotranspiration. *In* Irrigation of agricultural lands. Agronomy 11:534–574. Am. Soc. of Agron., Madison, Wis.

U.S. Bureau of Reclamation. 1973. Design of small dams. 2nd Ed. U.S. Government Printing Office, Washington, D.C. 816 p.

U.S. Environmental Protection Agency. 1973a. Processes, procedures, and methods to control pollution resulting from all construction activity. EPA 430/9-73-007. 234 p.

U.S. Environmental Protection Agency. 1973b. Processes, procedures and methods to control pollution resulting from silvicultural activities. EPA 430/9-73-010. 91 p.

U.S. Environmental Protection Agency. 1973c. Processes, procedures and methods to control pollution from mining activities. EPA 430/9-73-011. 390 p.

U.S. Environmental Protection Agency. 1975. Methods of quickly vegetating soils of low productivity, construction activities. EPA 440/9-75-006.

U.S. Environmental Protection Agency, U.S. Department of agriculture. 1975. Control of water pollution from croplands. Vol. I. A manual for guideline development. ARS-H-5-1. 111 p.

U.S. Water Resources Council. 1977. Guidelines for determining flood flow frequency.

Utah State University. 1976. Erosion control during highway construction. Vol. I, II, III. Prepared for Natl. Coop. Res. Progr., Transport. Res. Bd., Natl. res. Counc. Utah State Univ., Logan, Utah.

Wischmeir, W. H. 1975. Estimating the soil loss equations cover and management factor for undisturbed areas. p. 118–124. *In* Present and prospective technology for predicting sediment yields and sources. ARS-5-40.

Wischmeir, W. H., and D. D. Smith. 1965. Predicting rainfall-erosion losses from cropland east of the Rocky Mountains. USDA Agric. Handbk. no. 282. 47 p.

Zon, R. 1927. Forests and water in the light of scientific investigation. U.S. For. Serv. Bull. U.S. Government Printing Office, Washington, D.C. 126 p.

32 Land Uses on Shorelands, Flood Plains, Wetlands, and Coastal Zones

VICTOR W. CARLISLE

University of Florida, Gainesville, Florida

FRANK G. CALHOUN, JR.

Texas A&M University, College Station, Texas

I. INTRODUCTION

Unless there is a compelling reason not to, such as agriculture or commercial mineral deposits to be exploited, people tend to live near bodies of water. Man appreciates both the beauty and economic advantages of the land-water interface. However, he often pays a heavy price for such advantages in the form of disastrous storms, floods, pollution, and unanticipated high costs of construction and maintenance.

Beaches, barrier islands, and tidal marshes are evolutionary land forms and ecosystems that have traditionally served as vanguards of coastal stabilization. They are spatial buffers in temporal equilibrium with oceanic forces and the lithosphere. Intrusion of modern man and his attendant structures threaten both the stability of this equilibrium and the quality of life at this interface.

Floodplains are periodic escape valves for rivers. Development decisions involving this landform are too often made out of ignorance of natural overflow cycles and the downstream effects of such development.

Interior wetlands are fragile ecosystems that were often considered as nuisances following mans' initial encounter with them. More recently, among other potential benefits, they have been recognized as an important habitat for wildlife meriting greater care in decisions concerning their use.

The wetter of these ecosystems to varying degrees have been poorly studied by soil scientists in the past. Tidal marshes and wetlands were especially inhospitable environments in which to attempt to delineate soil boundaries with any accuracy. We yet know too little about the genesis, morphology, and properties of submerged and periodically submerged soils to either classify them well or predict their behavior. In older soil surveys such areas were cartographically and categorically generalized to the point that the mapping unit descriptions were of little value in planning and development decisions. Land use pressures on wet areas have now forced scientists to investigate them much more closely.

The nature and soils of shorelands, coastal zones, floodplains, and wetlands must be more thoroughly understood before rational decisions can be made concerning their management and preservation.

II. DEFINITIONS

a. Shorelands—According to Clark (1974), *shorelands* are defined as the terrain of the coastal watershed down to the upper margin of the wetlands (Lower margin of coastal floodplain). Both in scientific and popular usage, *shoreline* and *shore* are commonly interchangeable terms and sometimes *shoreline* may mean *shoreland*. Most frequently the term *shoreland* is used in conjunction with inland bodies of water and, in addition to points of contact between water and land, it includes all land areas occurring in close proximity to the shoreline.

b. Floodplains—Floodplains (Schwartz et al., 1976) consist of nearly level land situated on either side of a channel which is subject to overflow flooding. These natural overflow channels of rivers, streams, lakes, oceans, and other bodies of water are usually delineated in terms of some specific flood size, such as the area that would be inundated by the highest expected storm water level that will, on the average, occur once within a 50-year period.

c. Wetlands—Wetlands (Veatch & Humphrys, 1966) are areas that are permanently wet, or intermittently water covered, such as swamps, marshes, bogs, muskegs, potholes, swales, glades, and overflow land of river valleys. Large open lakes are excluded but areas that are more or less regularly wet or flooded or areas where the water table stands at or above the land surface for at least part of the year are included. For coastal usage Durrenberger (1973) defined wetlands as land types such as salt marshes and brackish marshes subject to saline and/or tidal influences.

d. Coastal Zones—Coastal zones are defined with difficulty, since the Magnuson Coastal Zone Management Act of 1972 leaves the precise definition of the landward coastal zone boundary to state discretion; however, it provides the following guidance for landward boundaries: "The coastal zone must include within it those lands which have an existing, projected or potential uses which have direct and significant impact on the coastal waters."

As defined by the Louisiana Advisory Commission on Coastal and Marine Resources (1973) the *coastal zone* includes waters and shorelands, strongly influenced by the coastal waters and in proximity to the shoreline, including transitional and intertidal areas, marshes, swamps, natural levees, and beaches. Many states are still in the process of precisely defining their coastal zone.

III. SHORELANDS AND COASTAL ZONES

Due to similarity in problems of management and preservation, shorelands and coastal zones are discussed under common headings in this Chapter. Figures for the extensiveness of shorelands and coastal zones are not readily available but, according to the U.S. Department of Commerce (1976), there are 135,540 km of shoreline in the United States with the following approximate regional distribution: Alaska, 56.1%; South Atlantic-Gulf, 17.4%; North Atlantic, 10.2%; Great Lakes, 4.4%; North Pacific, 3.4% Texas Gulf, 3.0%; Lower Mississippi, 2.3%; California, 2.1%; and Hawaii, 1.1%.

Shorelands and coastal zones are very appealing to a wide variety of resource users. Their proximity to lands with energy and minerals, developed markets, and transportation systems, together with a large population base, have made these areas desirable for residential, industrial, and recreational purposes. According to Schaefer (1972), 30% of the total U.S. population lives within an 80-km belt along out coastlines, representing only about 8% of the total land area. Lauf (1975) points out that all of Wisconsin's lake areas are now an easy day's travel time of major urban centers and so are subject to extreme development use and abuse. Coastal marsh environments provide valuable services in addition to fisheries production. These areas provide recreational opportunities, buffering from coastal storms, fur-bearing animal production, and treatment of municipal and industrial waste effluents. Gosselink et al. (1974) estimated the value of these services at several thousand dollars per acre.

A frequently repeated cross section of a coastal zone perpendicular from the ocean (Fig. 1) includes a beach, barrier island or dune, marsh, and upland, respectively. The entire coastal zone is usually interspersed with estuaries which are extremely productive ecosystems resulting from the mixing of fresh and salt waters, creating a nutrient trap where nutrients cycle between organisms, water, and sediments (Odum, 1961). Phytoplankton, benthic plants, mud algae, and salt marsh grasses are the primary producers in this nutrient-rich system which forms the base of a food web supporting a variety of organisms including most fin- and shellfish.

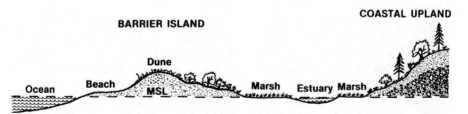

Fig. 1—Cross section of hypothetical coastal zone showing various land-water relationships.

A. Nature and Soils of Beaches and Barrier Islands

Beaches and barrier islands are constantly changing though the rate of change varies considerably. Changes in the coastline result from changes in sea level, wave action, nearshore currents, and sediment supply. According to Tanner (1977), three main groups of processes which provide that the coastline will not be fixed in space and time are (i) sea level changes, (ii) land level changes, and (iii) coastal erosion and deposition. Although total sea level change during Pleistocene time has been roughly 200 m, mean sea level for the past 5,000 years has been almost stable. Future changes are certain; however, it would not be wise to base land use plans on changes in mean sea level. Land level changes result from constant movement of rock masses that are the foundation of our continents. Such movements are usually very slow—measured in a few centimeters per year—but spectacular movements occur at time of major earthquakes. Every uplift must be countered by a downwarp of some kind, perhaps under the ocean surface, thereby changing the slope of the ocean basin, and thereby changing sea level. These relatively small movements, usually a fraction of 1 mm annually, should not be made a basis for short-range planning. Tanner (1977) considers erosion and deposition, the two end-effects of sediment transport, as the most important processes changing present-day coast lines. Movement of particles along the beach is continuous in response to wind and waves. The beach can be thought of as a giant conveyor belt, which runs primarily in one direction and never runs empty. This means that, as the system continues to operate, either new material must be dumped on the conveyor belt in the same area, or material will be obtained from the beach itself to keep the belt fully loaded. When the latter happens, we say that the beach is eroding. Most sand, lost by erosion, is carried to deeper water, from which it is not being returned. In a study of 135 km of open Gulf beaches in the Florida Panhandle (Tanner, 1977), 34% of the total was judged stable, 14% aggrading, and 52% eroding. The ratio between eroding and aggrading beaches was roughly 4:1 (km vs. km). The U.S. Department of Commerce (1976) classified the total U.S. shoreline (including Hawaii and Alaska) of 135,540 km as follows: 76% noneroding; 21% noncritically eroded; and 3% critically eroded.

Soils of shorelands and coastal zones are extremely varied (Godfrey, 1976). Soils of the barrier islands and beaches along the coastlines are mostly sands. In general, sands along the northeastern U.S. coast are nearly all siliceous; therefore, Typic Quartzipsamments are frequently first to develop. As the vegetative cover increases, organic materials added to the surface produce organic acids that are leached downward. Over a period of time this results in the development of a leached layer below the surface soil and an accumulation of darkened organic materials in the lower part of the profile. Thus, Spodic Quartzipsamments or even Spodosols may be found where migrating dunes have buried former woodlands. Development of Spodosols depends on the relative stability of the dunes; frequently changes are too rapid for soil development. Farther south the carbonate fraction increases, adding more available calcium to the nutrient reservoir. Along the Florida coast carbonate sands are dominant. Frequently, Typic Udipsamments belonging to the carbonatic family are dominant soils. In terms of nutrients, sands are notably poor and the carbonate sands are only somewhat better. Dominant features of these soils are high permeability, low water-holding capacity, and low cation exchange capacity. Nutrients are vigorously recycled and at any given time most cations are complexed in plants or organic humus.

B. Management and Preservation of Beaches and Barrier Islands

Barrier islands and beaches begin in New Hampshire and with the exception of a few breaks continue south to Florida and west to the Mexican border. The Pacific shore has few barrier islands but numerous barrier beaches. We frequently overlook the great importance of barrier islands in creating and maintaining extensive networks of highly productive estuaries and wetlands along the coastal zone. While fragile, they provide physical barriers that protect the estuaries and mainland from high energy forces. This protection allows the development of tidal wetlands and marshes. These estuaries and wetlands are among the most important benefits of barrier islands.

In their natural state the undeveloped barriers are uniquely beautiful landscape features. They also provide a habitat for numerous species of birds, fish, shellfish, reptiles, and mammals. Barriers are most effective as storm buffers when their dunes are well-formed and protected from wind erosion by beachgrass. Not only does beachgrass help prevent wind from eroding dunes but it helps build dunes by trapping sand. Unfortunately, beachgrass does not tolerate excessive foot or vehicular traffic. When the stabilizing cover of beachgrass is destroyed, sand particles are no longer protected from wind and cuts are eroded into the dune. Under natural conditions these erosion cuts are recolonized by beachgrass. The greatest damage to vegetation has recently occurred with the development of summer residences and cities on barrier islands. Extreme urbanization from New Jersey to Florida with high rise buildings built on foredunes often completely destroys the natural vegetation. This destruction is proceeding at an accelerating pace.

Natural values of barriers and public access are rapidly lost due to intensified development. According to Clark (1976), more than half of the major barrier islands and beaches are already committed to private housing and commercial enterprise. Man is attracted to barrier islands mostly for recreational and aesthetic pursuits and for real estate development. The barrier islands dynamic nature, which allows them to yield and reform under wave and wind stress, is hostile to man's objectives. Through bulkheads, seawalls, groins, and dune stabilization efforts, man has tried with little success to impose an artificial stability on barrier islands and beaches.

With increasing human activity along barrier islands, beaches, and the entire coastal zone, it is not possible to preserve the pre-existing ecological regime. The real problem is to decide what ecological revisions and adjustments are desirable and, from the standpoint of long-range welfare of mankind, how they can be attained.

Although similar environmental forces are at work along the coasts, basic differences must be recognized in management programs for barrier islands and beaches. No simple management program can be applied to all barrier island environments. Like other natural ecosystems, barrier islands and beaches will take care of themselves if left alone. In areas where development is to be allowed, it appears best that initial regulatory responsibility be administered by communities through local zoning, building, and other ordinances.

C. Nature and Soils of Coastal Marshes

Marshes provide essential habitat for many forms of life and supply basic nutrients to coastal ecosystems. They remove contaminants from water, help stabilize the shore, and absorb flood waters.

Net primary productivity of a Georgia salt marsh was reported by Odum to be 22 metric tons/ha per year. This is 25% greater than the highest yields of wheat and corn obtained in northern Europe and nearly 10 times greater than the average world wheat yield (E. P. Odum. 1960. The role of tidal marshes and streams in estuarine production. Presented at the 19th Annu. Meet., Atlantic States Marine Fisheries Comm.).

The major soils of the marshes are Histosols. These organic soils form in intertidal salt marshes and associated brackish or fresh water wetlands without regard to the underlying silts, sands, gravel, or even rock. Organic layers thicken over a period of time since decay rates are very slow in the anaerobic intertidal areas.

In a detailed investigation of Louisiana Coastal Marshlands by Brupbacher et al. (1973), soil materials were sampled at 366 sites along 39 north-south transect lines that were 3.2 km apart, sampling at 0.4-km intervals along each transect. Organic soils were identified in 64% of the samples and 36% were classified as mineral. Mineral soils in this area usually contain enhanced amounts of clays. Mineral soil textures included sandy clays, silty clays, clays, mucky clays, and peaty clays. Organic soil materials were classified as clayey mucks, clayey peats, mucks, and peats. Clay-textured materials contained from 1.5 to 10% organic matter; mucky clays and peaty clays 10 to 16%; and organic soils contained more than 16% organic matter. Predictably, organic N increased with organic matter content. The C/N ratios in fresh water marsh were lower than in brackish or salt water marsh, suggesting that organic matter in the fresh water marsh was at a more advanced stage of decomposition. Total water-soluble salts increased with increases in organic matter content. Concentrations of Na^+, Mg^{2+}, and K^+, both water-soluble and dilute acid-extractable, increased from fresh to brackish to salt water areas of the Coastal Marshlands. Acid-extractable Ca^{2+} was highest in soil material from the fresh marsh. The highest amounts of acid-extractable P occurred in clay-textured soils from the salt water marsh. Large variations were found in the amounts of all extractable cations, indicating that generalizations would be too broad to be of much value and determinations must be made on representative samples from specific sites to be of interpretable value.

D. Management and Preservation of Coastal Marshes

Human influence on the salt marsh environment is increasing. Perhaps the most destructive forces wrought by man are vehicle traffic, dredging and filling, and pollution. Recreational vehicle traffic is a problem of increasing concern in salt marshes. Vehicles disrupt the surface soil and create depressions which accumulate saline waters. With evaporation, the salinity can become too high for the survival of marsh vegetation. Access to marshes should be restricted to stabilized paths or roadways. Damage by foot traffic can be greatly reduced by providing wooden walkways in heavily visited areas.

One of the greatest threats to salt marshes, particularly smaller areas, is dredging and filling. Filling completely destroys the marsh vegetation. Cain (*in* Marshall, 1967) estimated that, of 322,400 ha of estuarine habitat in Florida less than 2 m deep, some 24,300 ha or 7.5% has been lost to dredging and filling. The significance of this loss is disproportionate to the percentage figure because this represents a loss of the most productive estuarine communities. Typical real estate fills are approximately 2 m above mean sea level, usually accompanied by a seawall along the water edge.

Pollution consisting of detritus and chemical compounds from agricultural operations, industry, and sewage frequently jeopardizes the marsh ecosystem. Additional research, as pointed out by Ranwell (1972), is needed to definitely establish the nutritive or toxic effects that varying amounts of these substances have on marsh vegetation. Conventional sewage disposal techniques function poorly or not at all due to the naturally high water table.

The salt marsh environment is not suitable for development of any kind. This productive and essential system should remain unexploited by activities of man that would permanently alter its basic structure.

E. Nature and Soils of Coastal Uplands

Soils of the adjacent uplands within coastal zones are equally as, if not more, variable than those of beaches, dunes, and marshes. Ultisols, Spodosols, Entisols, Alfisols, Mollisols, Histosols, and Vertisols occur within the coastal zone from Maine to Texas. Along the northeastern U.S. these soils are frequently silt loams and fine sandy loams in areas affected by glaciation. Farther to the south there is a gradual but pronounced increase in sands with maximum amount occurring in the Entisols, Spodosols, and Ultisols along the coastal areas of South Carolina, Georgia, Florida, and Alabama. The Ultisols, Mollisols, Vertisols, and Inceptisols that are dominant in the coastal zones of Mississippi, Louisiana, and Texas have enhanced amounts of silts and clays. Alfisols, Entisols, and Inceptisols are the dominant soils occurring in the coastal zones of California, Oregon, and Washington. Steep escarpments with less than 1 m loamy or gravelly soil over sandstone or shale frequently occur adjacent to beaches along the west coast. Sands and loamy sands of the Spodosol and Entisol soil orders most frequently occur adjacent to shoreland beaches.

F. Management and Preservation of Coastal Uplands

Coastal resources have always been in high demand and it is safe to predict that all of these resources will be utilized even more intensively in the future. Esthetic appeal of the coastal zone has resulted in rapid population increases that are becoming more urban and affluent. Recreation, retirement, and second homes are in great demand. Industries, particularly those requiring large amounts of water, have long favored coastal sites. Additional industries locate nearby to service the labor force. As population increases, conflicts develop over competing resources. For example, municipalities and industries use water for waste disposal which pollutes estuaries and prevents the growth and harvesting of seafood.

The adjacent uplands are better suited for development than other areas within the coastal zone. Soil properties greatly influence the use of land by man. Soil maps and soil resources must be considered in land-use plans since the nature and properties of soils determine their potential for residential, industrial, recreational, and agricultural uses.

The problem is how to allocate an essentially fixed supply of coastal zone resources among the growing public and private demands for coastal areas. Large portions of our coastal zone can be defined as critical areas. Nehman et al. (1975) consider these areas critical because of declining biological productivity in the wake of increasing urban and industrial development. Historically, coastal zone developments have been guided by the principle of "highest and best" economic use of the land. Standards and regulations to control development have been based principally on economic criteria. Clearly research, planning, and management are necessary components for the preservation and proper utilization of our coastal zones.

IV. FLOODPLAINS

According to Schneider and Goddard (1974), one-sixth of the urban lands in the United States lie within the natural 100-year floodplains. The Mississippi River valley contains the largest contiguous floodplain in the

U.S.. This area, below its confluence with the Ohio River, has an occasional width of 130 km with a total area estimated at 129,500 km². Over one-half of such floodplains has already been developed.

The general and predictable pattern of urban growth has been one of settlement on the floodplain, followed by expansion to higher areas. Most major cities of the United States and of the world have followed this pattern. A study of 26 urbanized areas of the United States by Schneider and Goddard (1974) indicated that about 16.2% of the urbanized area is in floodplains. The amount of development on these floodplains averaged 52.8%.

A. Nature and Soils

Natural levees are frequently formed near channels of mainstreams and their tributaries. During flood stage streams move rapidly with increased sediment loads. These sediments remain in suspension until the stream overflows its banks and with this accompanying decreased stream velocity sediments are deposited. Sand and coarse materials are deposited soon after overflow which results in coarse-textured materials being deposited along the natural levees. A slightly higher elevation from the surrounding areas is characteristic of natural levees. Velocity of water decreases as distance from the channel increases, resulting in the deposition of finer textured materials with a large percentage of clay-size sediments. Subsequent dissection of natural levees and back swamps by migrating river channels, abandonment of old channels, and rechannelling greatly complicate the somewhat simple original depositional patterns.

Carter (1970) presented a rather comprehensive review regarding the genesis of floodplain soils occurring in the Mississippi River Valley. Depth and duration of the water table affect soil genesis since soluble products of plant decomposition in the presence of free water cause reduction and solution of iron oxides. Plants add organic matter and nitrogen to soils. The darkening and development of an A horizon due to increased organic matter content is one of the earliest indications of horizon development in young sediments. Animals in the soil convert raw plant residues into humus and mix the humus with mineral portions of the soil. Tunneling by animals helps break down the original structure of soil and facilitates movement of water, particularly in sediments with high clay contents. Character of the parent material determines, to a large extent, the texture and mineralogy of soils. Individual particle size is little changed after deposition in floodplains. Soil drainage and color are also influenced by parent materials.

Typic Udifluvents have developed in areas of young deposition where natural levees are still being formed. Vertic Haplaquepts are in the back swamps of young and intermediate age and Aquic Udifluvents, Fluvaquentic Eutrochrepts, Aeric Fluvaquents, and Typic Fluvaquents occur in areas between the levee and back swamp. It is readily appreciated that the patterns of soils and soil development have been greatly influenced by the kinds of parent material deposited. The sequence of sandy soils along the channels, loamy soils on top and back sides of levees, and clayey soils in the back swamps is common along many large streams. Local differences in topography are largely due to the low ridges of natural levees and depressional areas of the back swamps. Dissection by migrating river channels has added to the complexity of original depositional patterns. Influence of topography on soil genesis in floodplains is largely that of soil drainage and of water table height and duration. Time, of course, is required for the soil-forming processes to express themselves as soil characteristics. Time is essential for the accumulation of organic matter, leaching of bases, translocation of silicate clays, and reduction and transfer of iron in floodplain soil materials.

Floodplain soils exhibit extreme differences in physical properties largely due to the great variation in particle size distribution. The older or better developed soils of the Mississippi floodplains according to Brown (1970) are Alfisols, intermediate-aged or soils with weakly differentiated horizons are Inceptisols, and soils with no clearcut pedogenic horizon development are Entisols. Most floodplain soils have relatively low organic matter contents that decrease rapidly with depth; however, soils on younger natural levees often contain an erratic distribution of organic and inorganic materials due to stratification. Floodplain soils are frequently severely limited in their use for residential and industrial purposes because of wetness, flood hazards, and high contents of expanding-type clays. These clays result in extreme volume changes upon wetting and drying, low shear strength, and high compressibility. They are severely limited for use as septic tank filter fields. Cation exchange capacity of floodplain soils is usually closely related to clay content. Due mainly to the high proportion of montmorillonitic clays, the cation exchange capacity frequently approaches 1 meq/100 g for each percent of clay present. The clay fraction of these soils is usually high in montmorillonite and illite with much lower amounts of chlorite, vermiculite, and kaolinite. Often clay mineralogy of floodplain soils is remarkably uniform over rather large areas. The high shrink-swell potential of these soils is clearly related to montmorillonitic clays. Floodplains contain some of the most fertile and productive soils in the United States.

B. Management and Preservation

Floodplains are very attractive for settlement by man. Rivers associated with floodplains provide a means of transportation, source of water, and facilitate the disposal of waste materials. The relatively flat topography usually results in less expensive costs of such transportation facilities as roads, railroads, and airports. Areas in close proximity to streams are aesthetically attractive for building sites.

High water table, poor permeability in soils that have a high clay content, and excessive shrinkage upon drying and swelling upon wetting are common undesirable soil characteristics of many floodplain soils. Obviously, any use of floodplains should recognize flood hazards. In recent years many floodplain areas have been subdivided and homes have frequently been purchased on these lands by individuals that wee not knowledgeable regarding flood frequency. This can be prevented if local governments practice proper planning and reasonable control over floodplain use.

Traditional methods for dealing with floods include the construction of dams, levees, and floodwalls to control stream flow. Despite the tremendous engineering success of these structures, flood damage continues to increase due to the accelerated encroachment of development into the floodplain. With continued intensification of floodplain use this trend is projected to accelerate.

In areas subject to development pressures, every effort should be made to obtain engineering data necessary for a floodplain ordinance consisting of a text with regulations which apply to use of land subject to flooding and a zoning map delineating areas subject to flooding. Yanggen (1972) suggested that a detailed soil survey map can be used to delineate floodplains for regulatory purposes in areas where regulation is needed but there is a lack of time and money necessary to generate detailed engineering data. The rationale for using soil maps is that floodplain soils occur on distinct geomorphic surfaces, usually in areas of active deposition. These distinctive soils are identified in the field and delineated by soil surveyors. Soil survey maps record past flooding events as evidenced by the presence of flood deposited soils. Additional details regarding the use of soils, information for delineating riverine floodplain zoning districts, and incorporating such information into land use regulations are presented in this publication (see Chapter 39, "Incorporating Soils Information into Land Use Controls," by Douglas A. Yanggen).

As pointed out by Goddard (1976), comprehensive floodplain management includes all planning and action needed to determine, implement, and revise plans for the best use of a region's water and floodable land resources. Corrective measures to control floods include dams, reservoirs, levees, channel improvements, floodproofing, flood forecasting, and evacuation. Preventive measures are tools available for controlling man's activities. Floodplain regulations represent an effective measure. They guide the use and development in flood-prone areas through the application of zoning, subdivision regulations, building codes, and health regulations. Flood insurance is a major tool since it relates to the costs of safe development with regard to flood hazards. Extension of utilities and construction of streets into flood hazard areas can be controlled through development policies. Tax adjustments for land dedicated to open space can be effective but has been rarely used. Open space reserved for recreational uses reduces flood damage in an incidental way. Warning signs may inform prospective buyers of flood hazards. Sound floodplain regulations include two basic requirements pertaining to flooding. Adequate open area is needed for passage of floodwaters and structures in the floodplain must be constructed at a reasonably safe elevation. Probably due to loss of life, property, health, and safety hazards, public regulation of floodplains has been more readily accepted than the regulation of prime agricultural lands for development purposes. Residential, commercial, and light industrial land use in floodplains are discussed in this publication (see Chapter 20, "Residential, Commercial, and Light Industrial Land Uses," by C. J. Johannsen, T. W. Barney, and A. A. Klingebiel).

V. WETLANDS

Shaw and Fredine (1971) reported 30.1 million ha of wetlands in the contiguous U.S. Wetlands are a classic case of conflict in resource utilization. They provide a vital part of the ecology of migrating waterfowl which is the principal wildlife resource associated with wetlands. To farmers, wetlands are often a costly nuisance which encourages their drainage and conversion to cropland. Goldstein (1971) described wetlands in a variety of depths, areas, and seasonal life spans. Some have surface water only after rain storms or the spring thaw and are usually dry during the remainder of the season. Others form shallow lakes, ponds, potholes, sloughs, and marshes that constitute the major breeding and resting areas in the U.S. for waterfowl along the Mississippi Flyway. Benefits of waterfowl population maintenance accrue primarily to hunters but the burden of maintenance is borne largely by farmers. Estimates by Wootan and Purcell (1949) show the location, by states, of nearly 8.5 million ha of undeveloped wet soils that were considered physically feasible to drain and convert to cultivation.

A. Nature and Soils

Swamps, marshes, bogs, and associated wetlands that are not directly related to floodplains are scattered throughout much of the United States. Histosols and mineral soils high in organic matter content commonly occur in wetlands. The largest contiguous body of organic soils in the continental U.S. occurs in the freshwater wetlands of the Florida Everglades. This sawgrass marsh lies in a trough approximately 65 km wide and 160 km long with both sides bounded by low, sandy ridges. Elevations are approximately 5 m above sea level at the south shore of Lake Okeechobee (Cooke, 1945) with a slope from north to south of about 5 cm/km (Clayton et al., 1942). Histosols formed in these wetlands from remains of vegetative growth under conditions of greater addition than decomposition of organic matter over a period of time. Depth of organic materials over a large part of the area is now < 1 m and probably < 200,000 ha has a depth of > 1.5 m (Zelazny & Carlisle, 1974). By far the most extensive Histosols of the Florida Everglades consist of almost completely decomposed plant remains or Medisaprists. These soils are important in the production of sugarcane, winter vegetables, forages, and sod.

Another large area of organic soils, dominantly Medihemists and Medisaprists, occurs in southern Louisiana. Radiocarbon dates by Mc-

Farlen (1961) indicated that these soils began to develop approximately 3,000 years ago. The rate of accumulation averaged 10 cm per 100 years in areas relatively undisturbed by levee sedimentation. In addition to subsidence upon drainage, many of these soils dry irreversibly forming hard massive layers that do not readily absorb water. Undrained Histosols in this area are used primarily for wildlife but drained areas are utilized for tilled crop and pasture production.

Most organic soils have a relatively low bulk density. Subsidence begins immediately after drainage. Extreme volume changes upon wetting and drying, low shear strength, subsidence, and high compressibility contribute to severe limitations of these soils for residential and industrial uses. With water control and proper soil management practices, Histosols are among the most productive agricultural soils of the world.

Typic Borohemists, Cumulic Haplaquolls, and Typic Haplaquolls commonly occur in saucer-shaped depressions, sloughs, potholes, and drainage ways of north central states. Many wetland areas occur throughout the northeastern U.S. in the level depressions of old glacial lake beds that receive runoff from surrounding uplands and have somewhat restricted drainage outlets. Lacustrine deposits remained at the bottoms of glacial lakes when ice dams melted and the lakes drained. Mollic Haplaquepts, Typic Medisaprists, Aeric Haplaquepts, and Udollic Ochraqualfs are representative soils in these areas. Soils that are permanently saturated (Typic Hydraquents) occur in Mississippi and Louisiana. Bearing strength of these clayey soils is sometimes too low to support grazing animals.

B. Management and Preservation

Inland wetlands are important parts of the land and natural water regime. They provide an essential habitat for many species of wildlife. In many areas, the vegetation produced in wetlands rivals the most intensive land-based agriculture in terms of organic matter produced. When properly drained and managed, wetlands frequently are used for agricultural production. Drained and filled wetlands, particularly near heavily populated areas, have been used for urban development.

Use of wetland soils for agricultural and urban development is frequently further restricted by their physical, chemical, and mineralogical properties. Subsidence of Histosols upon drainage at rates up to 3 cm/year (Stephens, 1969) creates many foundation problems related to building and maintenance of housing, streets, sewers, and other services. Special foundations with pilings are needed to stabilize houses and other construction. Even with adequate foundations, houses built on former wetlands become increasingly separated from the ground level with time (Fig. 2). Subsidence of wetlands drained for agricultural production results in increased chances of inundation and therefore increased pumping costs. Maintenance costs for drainage, streets, sidewalks, sewers, and other utilities are much higher than corresponding costs on stable soils. These costs must ultimately be

Fig. 2—Dwelling constructed on Histosol (Typic Medisaprist) at Belle Glade, Fla., originally with two-step entrance, shows amount of subsidence over 35-year period. Pilings are in limestone approximately 1.7 m below present surface.

borne by the taxpayer. Subsidence problems usually occur to a much lesser extent in Mollisols, Inceptisols, Alfisols, and Entisols that are associated with the inland wetlands. Subsidence of the land surface due to excessive water withdrawal by municipalities and heavy industries has also been noted in a few areas.

Wetland soils with appreciable amounts of montmorillonitic clays are subject to extreme volume changes upon wetting and drying. These soils, even when adequately drained, are severely limited for residential, industrial, and transportational uses. Additional discussions regarding the development of inland wetland regulations through application of soils information are presented in this publication (see Chapter 39). Most inland wetlands are privately owned and influencing the use of these areas to protect the public interest is a difficult task. Unfortunately, as pointed out by Smith and Badenhop (1975), potential income from the use of many wetlands for agricultural production, foregone through maintaining the wetlands as a native environment, is a cost borne by the landowner while the major benefits accrue to other members of society. Few individual landowners are willing to sacrifice potential income for the public welfare. Workable judgments regarding use of wetlands can be made by local people if they are provided with sufficient data describing the location, amount, importance, and local, regional, and national interrelationship of wetlands in their area.

VI. CONCLUDING REMARKS

McHarg (1969) suggested that elaborate inventories of all ecosystems be used to identify environments as to their suitability for various land uses, particularly urbanization. The more intrinsically an environment is suitable for any specified use, the less adaptation is necessary, resulting in maximum-benefit/minimum-cost solutions. Obviously, additional scientific insights and creative designs are needed to help establish a balanced and self-renewing environment.

Soils of land-water interfaces seldom possess many desirable qualities for construction but historically man has been attracted to these regions. Realistically, it is not possible to stop all development on shorelands, coastal zones, floodplains, and wetlands. In significant areas, preservation can be assured only through public acquisition. Development needs to be regulated in other areas so that these fragile ecosystems are altered only within tolerances which do not weaken or destroy them. Where development is allowed it appears best for these regulations to be administered by communities through local zoning, building, and other ordinances. We must learn more about the capacities of these areas to absorb increases in population and the activities of man.

LITERATURE CITED

Brown, D. A. 1970. Characterization of representative soil series. Physical properties. p. 23–26. In D. A. Brown (ed.) A monograph of the soils of the Southern Mississippi River Valley alluvium. Southern Coop. Ser. Bull. 178. Arkansas Agric. Exp. Stn., Fayetteville, Ark.

Brupbacher, R. H., J. E. Sedberg, Jr., and W. H. Willis. 1973. The coastal marshlands of Louisiana, chemical properties of the soil materials. Louisiana Agric. Exp. Stn. Bull. 672.

Carter, O. R. 1970. Genesis of the soils of the valley. p. 10–18. In D. A. Brown (ed.) A monograph of the soils of the Southern Mississippi River Valley alluvium. Southern Coop. Ser. Bull. 178. Arkansas Agric. Exp. Stn., Fayetteville, Ark.

Clark, John. 1974. Coastal ecosytems, ecological considerations for management of the coastal zone. The Conservation Found., Washington, D.C.

Clark, John. 1976. Preface. p. iii–v. In J. Clark (ed.) Barrier islands and beaches. Tech. Proc. of 1976 Barrier Islands Workshop, Off. of Coastal Zone Manage., Natl. Oceanic and Atmos. Admin., 17–18 May 1976, Annapolis, Md. The Conservation Found., Washington, D.C.

Clayton, B. S., J. R. Neller, and R. V. Allison. 1942. Water control in the peat and muck soils of the Florida Everglades. Florida Agric. exp. Stn. Bull. 378.

Cooke, C. W. 1945. Geology of Florida. Florida Geol. Surv. Bull. 29.

Durrenberger, R. W. 1973. Dictionary of the environmental sciences. Natl. Press Books, Palo Alto, Calif.

Goddard, J. E. 1976. The nation's increasing vulnerability to flood catastrophe. J. Soil Water Conserv. 31:48–52.

Godfrey, P. G. 1976. Comparative ecology of East Coast barrier islands: Hydrology, soils, and vegetation. p. 5–31. In J. Clark (ed.) Barrier islands and beaches. Technical Proc. of the 1976 Barrier Islands Workshop, Off. of Coastal Zone Manage., Natl. Oceanic and Atmos. Admin., 17–18 May 1976, Annapolis, Md. The Conservation Foundation, Washington, D.C.

Goldstein, J. H. 1971. Competition for wetlands in the Midwest: An economic analysis. The Johns Hopkins Press, Baltimore, Md.

Gosselink, J. G., E. P. Odum, and R. M. Pope. 1974. The value of the tidal marsh. Pub. no. LSU-SG-74-03. Center for Wetland Resour., Louisiana State Univ., Baton Rouge, La.

Lauf, Ted. 1975. Shoreland regulations in Wisconsin. Coastal Zone Manage. J. 2:47–58.

Louisiana Advisory Commission on Coastal and Marine Resources. 1973. Louisiana wetlands prospectus. Baton Rouge, La.

Marshall, A. R. 1967. Dredging and filling. p. 107–113. In J. D. Newsom (ed.) Proc. of Marsh and Estuary Manage. Symp., 19–20 July 1967, School of Forest, and Wildl. Manage., U.S. Fish and Wildl. Serv., Louisiana Wildl. and Fisher. Comm., and Wildl. Manage. Inst. Louisiana State Univ., Baton Rouge, La.

McFarlen, E., Jr. 1961. Radiocarbon dating of late Quarternary deposits, South Louisiana. Geol. Soc. Am. Bull. 72:129–158.

McHarg, I. L. 1969. design with nature. The Natural History Press, Garden City, N.Y.

Nehman, G., G. Boles, N. Dee, and J. Griffin. 1975. Land use and environmental planning: An application in the South carolina coastal zone. Water Resour. Bull. 11:759–769.

Odum, E. P. 1961. The role of tidal marshes in estuarine production. Conservationist 15(6): 12–15.

Ranwell, D. S. 1972. Ecology of salt marshes and sand dunes. Chapman and Hall, London.

Schaefer, M. B. 1972. Conservation of biological resources of the coastal zone. p. 35–79. In J. F. Peel Brahtz (ed.) Coastal zone management, multiple use with conservation. John Wiley & Sons, Inc., New York.

Schneider, W. J., and J. E. Goddard. 1974. Extent and development of urban floodplains. Geol. Survey Circ. 601-J. Washington, D.C.

Schwartz, C. F., E. C. Thor, and G. H. Hloner. 1976. Wildlife planning glossary. Pacific Southwest Forest and Range Exp. Stn., USDA For. Serv., Berkeley, Calif.

Shaw, S. P., and C. G. Fredine. 1971. Wetlands of the United States: Their extent and value to waterfowl and other wildlife. U.S. Dep. of Interior. Fish and Wildl. Serv. Circ. 39. Washington, D.C.

Smith, G. F., and M. B. Badenhop. 1975. An evaluation of environmental quality: Opportunith costs of channelization and land use change in the floodplain of the Obion-Forked Deer River Basin of West Tennessee. Tennessee Agric. Exp. Stn. Bull. 552.

Stephens, J. C. 1969. Peat and muck drainage problems. J. Irrig. Drainage Div., Am. Soc. Chem. Eng. 95:285–305.

Tanner, W. F. 1977. Our mobile coast. p. 2–22. In L. W. Skelton (ed.) Symp. on Coastal Zone Manage., 8–9 Aug. 1976, Univ. of West Florida, Pensacola Beach, Fla. Univ. of West Florida, Pensacola, Fla.

U.S. Department of Commerce. 1976. Natural hazard management in coastal areas. Natl. Oceanic and Atmos. Admin., Off. of Coastal Zone Manage., Washington, D.C.

Veatch, J. O., and C. R. Humphrys. 1966. Water and water use terminology. Thomas Printing and Publ. Co., Kaukauna, Wis.

Wooten, H. H., and M. R. Purcell. 1949. Farm land development, present and future by clearing, drainage, and irrigation. USDA Circ. 825.

Yanggen, D. A. 1972. The use of detailed soils information for delineating and regulating floodplains: Legal and administrative considerations. Water Resour. Center, Univ. of Wisconsin, Madison, Wis.

Zelazny, L. W., and V. W. Carlisle. 1974. Physical, chemical, elemental, and oxygen-containing functional group analysis of selected Florida Histosols. p. 63–78. In A. R. Aandahl (ed.) Histosols: Their characteristics, use, and classification. Soil Sci. Soc. Am., Madison, Wis.

33

Nonpoint Pollution: Problem Assessment and Remedial Measures; Economic and Planning Considerations for Designing Control Methods

T. C. DANIEL AND ROBERT R. SCHNEIDER

University of Wisconsin
Madison, Wisconsin

I. INTRODUCTION

Public Law 92-500, the latest in a series of amendments to the Federal Water Pollution Control Act of 1948, reemphasized and strengthened the nation's water quality program. As the program proceeded, it became clear that pollutants contributed from nonpoint sources can equal or exceed those from point sources. Thus, to achieve the nation's water quality goals, management of nonpoint as well as point sources is essential. The purpose of this paper is to define nonpoint pollution, identify the major nonpoint pollutants and their sources, describe alternative remedial measures, and discuss planning factors which must be considered prior to effective program design.

A. Definition of Nonpoint Pollution

The following criteria serve to characterize nonpoint pollution:
1) It occurs over an extensive area and is primarily transported over land before entering navigable waters;
2) It enters the receiving waters in a diffuse manner and is usually intermittent in flow;
3) It is not easily monitored at the point of origin and the contaminants are not traceable to their exact source; and
4) Its magnitude is related to certain uncontrollable climatic events.
Although the bulk of nonpoint pollution is associated with surface runoff, under specific circumstances nonpoint pollution of ground water can result from water percolation through the unsaturated zone.

B. Land Use and Water Quality

The rate of pollutant encroachment into the aquatic system is extreme-ly variable, depending on geology, land use, climate, topography, and type of vegetation. As land is changed from its original state to intensive use, the associated water quality deteriorates. In general, the more intensive the land use, the poorer the water quality, with transition periods between different uses being especially critical. For example, stable forest systems are general-ly associated with high-quality waters while urban areas tend toward poorer water quality. Construction sites (transitional areas) are subject to excessive runoff and tend to contribute to reduced water quality.

C. Transport Mechanism

The major transport mechanism for nonpoint pollution is surface runoff water. Generally, the greater the runoff volume—either total annual or individual event—the greater the nonpoint pollution load. Hence, one or two major events during a year might account for the major portion of non-point pollution (Alberts et al., 1978).

The contaminants that are transported during runoff events may be in an available form or as component parts of the suspended solids, especially sediment. Although the bulk of the contaminant load is associated with sus-pended solids, the dissolved portion can be significant and, in some cases, the most important contributor to the total load. The presence of soluble nutrients is critical because of their availability and potential impact on the growth of aquatic plants.

II. NONPOINT POLLUTANTS OF MAJOR ENVIRONMENTAL CONCERN

A. Nutrients

The entry of nutrients—principally N and P—into surface water will accelerate lake eutrophication, causing the rapid growth of rooted aquatic weeds and noxious algae blooms. This excessive growth may at times lower the dissolved oxygen content of the water, alter the fish population, inter-fere with recreational uses of the water, and in general impair water quality. Case examples of accelerated nutrient input to the nation's waters as a result of nonpoint runoff are well documented (Loehr, 1974; Uttormark et al., 1974; Randall et al., 1977; Alberts et al., 1978).

Nitrogen in the form of nitrate (NO_3^-) and nitrite (NO_2^-) when present in excessive concentrations in ground water supplies (>10 mg/liter N as NO_3^-) causes methemoglobinemia in infants (Winton et al., 1971). Nitrate ingestion by livestock also has been associated with reduced weight gain, lowered general resistance, and disrupted metabolism (Wood et al., 1967; Jones et al., 1966; Marrett & Sunde, 1968; Case, 1970).

B. Potential Toxins

The misuse of organochlorine insecticides—most notably DDT—exemplifies the reasons for concern over pesticides. Evidence clearly shows that the organochlorine insecticides persist in the environment for >20 years (Edwards, 1972).

The impact of pesticide use on water quality depends on the persistence and formulation of the chemical used, rate and method of application, and the mobility of the chemical. Pesticides may enter surface waters solubilized in runoff water or adsorbed by suspended eroded soil particles (Bovey et al., 1974). After entering the aquatic environment, the pesticide may decompose to nontoxic metabolites or may persist and undergo biomagnification by the aquatic food chain.

Bacterial contamination of surface waters is a potential threat to the health of livestock and humans. Many infectious diseases originate in animal manure and may be transmitted through water, including anthrax, encephalitis, tetanus, histoplasmosis, leptospirosis, bronchitis, and salmonellosis (Diesch, 1970).

Urban runoff is also a significant source of bacterial pollution (Geldreich et al., 1968; Vaughn & Harlow, 1965). While combined sewer overflow is the greatest concern, unsewered urban runoff and separate storm sewer discharges can be significant sources of intermittent pollution to recreational beaches.

While toxic metal concentrations in nonpoint runoff are low, the total loading and potential for biomagnification are reasons for concern. Examples of toxic metals are Cd, Cu, Cr, Pb, Ni, and Zn. The effects of high levels of intake of these metals on aquatic and human life have received considerable study. However, the sources and long-term effects of low dosages from nonpoint pollution are less well defined.

It has been found that Pb and Zn are the major metal contaminants in urban storm water, but Hg is of major toxicologal concern even though present in small amounts (Vitale & Sprey, 1974). Researchers have estimated that a city of the size of San Francisco could discharge through storm sewers approximately 113 metric tons of Pb and 14 metric tons of Hg per year. These values are comparable to or greater than industrial discharge. In addition to creating a potential health hazard, the discharge of these metals can impair the efficient operation of sewage treatment plants.

C. Organic Carbon

Primary sources of organic carbon (C) are concentrated animal areas, urban sites, and livestock bedding. In water, bacteria use the C as an energy source, consuming O_2 in the process. When the C load exceeds the assimilative capacity of the water, the dissolved O_2 level may be severely depressed to a point below that required for fish survival. In extreme cases, anaerobic conditions may develop resulting in the release of foul-smelling gases and floating masses of decaying solids. See Miner et al. (1966), Vitale and Sprey (1974), Colston and Tafuri (1975), and Randall et al. (1977) for quantification of the C entry from various sources into receiving waters.

D. Sediment

Sediment has been said to be the nation's largest single water pollutant (by weight) exceeding the entire sewage load by a factor of 500 to 700 times (Glymph & Carlson, 1966). Sediment increases the turbidity of water, thereby reducing light penetration, impairing photosynthesis, altering oxygen relationships, and reducing the available food supply for certain aquatic organisms. In addition, sediment carries with it nutrients, organic matter, and potentially hazardous pesticides and metals. Indeed, the major portion of nonpoint contaminants entering surface water is associated with particulate matter, especially sediment (Loehr, 1974; Uttormark et al., 1974; Schuman et al., 1973).

E. Priority Pollutants

The design of control strategies for nonpoint pollution reduction requires ranking of those pollutants having highest priority for control. Pollutants having potential public health hazards are of prime significance. While pathogens and pesticides are health hazards, they are localized in magnitude and their impact on the environment can be minimized by the wise use of management techniques. In addition, federal and state safeguards are in operation which require extensive pesticide screening so that new pesticides are safer to use.

Increases in population, recent changes in life styles, and industrialization have increased the potential for toxic metal contamination in urban areas and comprehensive control programs appear to be warranted. However, the exact sources of specific problem metals are often not known, and the design of control programs will be delayed until more information on the sources of the metals and their impact on the environment is available.

Eutrophication of water as a result of runoff from nonpoint sources is a problem of national scope. Most research to date reveals that noxious aquatic weed growth results from the addition of excessive amounts of nitrogen (N) and phosphorus (P). Nitrogen usually is not the limiting nutrient because of the natural background levels and the ability of most filamentous bluegreen algae to fix atmospheric N. Phosphorus is the most limiting nutrient in fresh waters and this is the nutrient that man can have the greatest success in controlling (Lee, 1973). Thus, programs for minimizing the rate of eutrophication resulting from nonpoint pollution should center on limiting the P input to surface water.

Without question, sediment is the nation's single largest water quality contaminant. Not only does it physically impair water quality, but it also is a major carrier of P, pesticides, and toxic metals to the nation's surface water. Programs that reduce the sediment load to surface waters will go a long way toward alleviating many of the problems of nonpoint pollution.

III. MAJOR SOURCE AREAS OF NONPOINT POLLUTION

Many potential source areas exist for nonpoint pollution, including atmospheric fallout, mining, silvicultural activities, and irrigated agriculture. However, such sources are site specific and therefore limited in national scope. For review articles concerning these topics the reader is referred to Loehr (1974), Uttormark et al. (1974), and USEPA (1973).

Because of the land area involved, the single largest contributor of nonpoint pollution to surface waters is agricultural land use. Urban centers are priority sources because of the amounts and types of pollution involved and the high demand in these areas for quality water for consumptive and recreational use.

A. Sediment and Phosphorus from Agricultural Land

Sediment and P movement in a watershed is quantified in two ways: loss and yield. The former refers to the amount of contaminant that is displaced in the upland portion of a watershed. In broad terms, soil and P loss data represent the potential load available to enter surface water. The actual amount of sediment and P entering the water is expressed in terms of yield and is considerably less than predicted loss values.

1. SEDIMENT FROM AGRICULTURE

Natural background levels of soil loss for the United States have been estimated to range from 0.7 to 1.6 metric tons/ha per year (Wischmeier, 1976). Reported annual soil loss from agricultural activities ranges upward to 200 metric tons/ha per year depending on site conditions and degree of management. It was estimated for 1970 that soil loss for 50% of the nation's cropland averages 7 to 18 metric tons/ha per year, 30% averages < 7 metric tons/ha per year, and 20% averages > 18 metric tons/ha per year (USDA, 1970).

Sediment yield from agricultural land is variable and ranges from 1 to 40 metric tons/ha per year (Olness et al., 1975; Alberts et al., 1978). Generally, the data indicate that well-managed rangeland approximates natural background levels and that cultivated cropland produces sediment yields somewhat higher than comparably located land having crop cover most of the year.

The degree of ground cover, tillage method used, and degree of conservation practices implemented all affect the amount of soil loss and eventual sediment yield in a watershed (Romkens et al., 1973; Olness et al., 1975; Dragoon & Miller, 1966; Burwell et al., 1975; Schuman et al., 1973).

2. PHOSPHORUS FROM AGRICULTURE

Agricultural use of fertilizer has been consistently pointed to as one of the major sources of nutrients leading to eutrophication of the nation's waters. However, most research indicates that eutrophication as a result of fertilizer use is minimal. Several studies have shown that not more than 2% of added fertilizer was lost as a result of surface runoff (Gburek & Heald, 1974; Johnson et al., 1976).

While fertilizer usage is not a major cause for concern, sound management techniques must be incorporated into farming operations to prevent local problems of water quality deterioration. Little P is lost when fertilizer is incorporated into the soil rather than applied broadcast. Increasing evidence indicates that the type of crop cover and residue management system used influence the content of P in runoff water (Burwell et al., 1975; Timmons & Holt, 1970).

Disposal of animal waste on land is a potential source of pollution to surface waters. When properly carried out, land disposal of manure is a sound management practice that returns nutrients to the soil and improves tilth. However, improper rates, methods, and timing of applications may lead to significant water quality problems (Powers et al., 1975). Manure applied to frozen land has the potential for substantial loss of soluble nutrients, especially if applied immediately prior to an active melt or an early spring rain. Similarly, manure applied to land and not properly incorporated leads to substantial losses of nutrients when heavy rains occur.

Agricultural activities permit higher P yields than forest activities. Yield values for total P range from 0.1 to a high of 4.31 kg/ha per year and variability is attributed to the interaction of climatic, geological, and edaphic factors (Schuman et al., 1973; Olness et al., 1975; Taylor et al., 1971). Average values for total P yield are approximately 0.5 kg/ha per year. Thus, when compared to those values received from streams draining forested areas, agricultural land use results in an approximately twofold increase in P yield.

Transport of P is greatest during periods of high runoff and subsequent erosion because P is associated primarily with sediment. Investigations have determined that up to 85% of the P yield from an agricultural watershed can be associated with sediment (Taylor et al., 1971; Burwell et al., 1975).

For temperate regions having snow cover, greatest potential for P yield occurs in late winter or early spring during times of highest flow. Areas outside the snow belt show greatest yield of P during crop planting as this is frequently the period of greatest rainfall and minimum crop cover (Alberts et al., 1978).

3. REMEDIAL MEASURES

Numerous watershed studies have demonstrated that soil and water conservation practices are very effective in reducing surface water runoff, sediment, and nutrient yield from agricultural land. In an 8-year study of four watersheds, those watersheds receiving sound conservation practices suffered minimal sediment loss; yield values were <1 metric ton/ha per year (Spomer et al., 1973). On watersheds where less intensive conservation practices were applied, sediment yield values approached 40 metric tons/ha per year.

Watershed studies in Iowa demonstrated that runoff volume, sediment, and nutrient yields from terraced watersheds were dramatically lower than from watersheds not using conservation practices (Schuman et al., 1973). In another study, sediment yield, surface runoff, and suspended sediment concentrations were reduced 46, 24, and 30%, respectively, in a watershed receiving conservation practices over another watershed where no conservation practices were used (Dragoon & Miller, 1966). It was concluded that conservation practices resulted in an approximately 50% reduction in sediment yield and that this reduction was due primarily to a decrease in surface water yield. Sediment yields of approximately 14 metric tons/ha per year were determined for the area conventionally farmed as compared to 9 metric tons/ha per year for the watershed where conservation practices were employed.

In a similar study in Iowa, sediment yield from a level terrace treated watershed was approximately 2 metric tons/ha per year, a 20-fold reduction when compared to values for untreated areas (Burwell et al., 1974). Similar values in nutrient yield reduction were obtained when the two watersheds were compared. Total P yields of 0.45 and 0.97 kg/ha per year were obtained for the treated and untreated watersheds, respectively.

B. Nonpoint Pollution from Urban Storm Water

Precipitation in an urban area generates considerable runoff due to the high percentage of impervious surfaces and resultant low infiltration capacity. The runoff is transported to discharge points either through separate storm sewers or sanitary sewers. In the latter case, design criteria are built into the system so that when certain flow volumes are reached, the excess water bypasses the sewage treatment facility and enters the receiving waters directly. Urban runoff in the form of storm sewer discharge or combined sewer overflow is a significant source of nonpoint pollution (Kluesener & Lee, 1974).

Due to the immense volume of storm water, shock loadings may be generated that are 100 to 1,000 times greater than for treated effluent (Bradford, 1977). Perhaps more importantly, storm water runoff can be responsible for a large portion of the total annual waste loads generated from urban areas. In one watershed study, the annual urban runoff of COD was equal to 91% of the raw sewage yield, the BOD yield was equal to 67%, and the suspended solids yields were 20 times those contained in municipal waste (Colston & Tafuri, 1975). It was further estimated that if complete removal of organics and suspended solids was provided by upgrading existing treatment plants, the total reduction in pollutant discharge would be only 52% of the COD, 59% of the BOD, and 5% of the suspended solids.

Thus, it becomes increasingly clear, as pointed out by Randall et al. (1977), that sound water quality planning must take into consideration the contaminants arising from urban runoff and that simply addressing the existing water quality objectives by a program of advanced waste treatment is at best unwise.

1. YIELD OF SUSPENDED SOLIDS

Suspended solids provide the largest contribution of contaminants from urban land use activity. Solids generated from established urban areas (commonly <1 metric ton/ha per year) vary with land use, population density, amount of traffic, drainage characteristics, and frequency of maintenance practices (street cleaning). The main source of suspended solids is street runoff containing litter, chemicals, dead vegetation, eroded materials, traffic residuals, and animal droppings. Streets in industrial areas contribute more solids than residential areas. Commercial areas tend to produce the lowest amount of solids, probably due to the high frequency of street cleaning.

Suspended solids from areas undergoing urban development are predominantly sediment. Approximately 1,600 ha are developed daily to accommodate the requirements of the expanding population of the United States. During construction, surface cover is removed, producing maximum erosivity. Rates of erosion under these circumstances can be 75 times greater than that of comparable rural lands. Sediment yields from 4 to 550 metric tons/ha per year have been measured depending on the size of the drainage area and the portion of land undergoing construction (Wolman & Schick, 1967). Sediment concentration in runoff water from these areas ranges from 3,000 to 150,000 mg/liter as compared to 2,000 mg/liter in waters draining natural or agricultural land.

Although usually small in area, construction sites over a short period of time can be responsible for contributing more sediment to streams than was previously deposited in several decades (Thomas, 1970).

2. PHOSPHORUS YIELD

The nonpoint load of P in streams draining urban watersheds generally will be dominated by that carried in surface runoff. A comprehensive investigation involving 15 watersheds reported average yield values of 2.8 kg/ha per year (Avco Corp., 1970). The highest value reported was 8.8

kg/ha per year resulting from runoff from a light industrial area. The proportion of unused land, arterial streets, and industrial land use was found to be an important factor determining P loadings.

A comparison of P yield values from urban watershed investigations in different geographic locations shows a range of values from 0.4 to 3.4 kg/ha per year with a mean value of 1.5 kg/ha per year (Sawyer, 1947; Bryan, 1970). Urban land use, when compared to other sources of nonpoint runoff, results in the highest yields of P per unit area, i.e., three times higher than runoff from agricultural land use.

The sources of P in urban drainage remain unclear. Several studies suggest that leaf litter is an important source and that the bulk of the P is associated with the silt and clay fractions of urban runoff (Kluesener & Lee, 1974; Sartor & Boyd, 1972).

3. TOXIC METALS

Although additional data are needed, it is clear that potential health hazards exist to humans and other animals from heavy metals found in urban runoff. The metals of most concern in urban runoff are Pb, Zn, Cu, Cr, Cd, Ni, and Hg. Lead, Zn, and Cu comprise the bulk of the loadings although the remainder which are found in lesser amounts are potentially more toxic (Wilber & Hunter, 1975). Usually these materials are associated with the particulate fractions contained in runoff.

The exact magnitude of metals loadings to receiving waters is presently under evaluation. However, it seems clear that the quantity arising from nonpoint sources is comparable to that from industrial point sources. It has been estimated that a typical city—such as Atlanta—discharges 45 to 113 metric tons/year of Pb and 3 to 14 metric tons/year of Hg (Vitale & Sprey, 1974). Researchers report that metals found in street runoff can be 100 to 1,000 times greater than sewage-associated metals on a slug load basis (kg/hour) and from 10 to 100 times greater on a concentration basis (mg/liter) (Pit & Amy, 1973).

Identification of the exact sources of metal contamination is just beginning. However, some general trends with respect to land use are clear. Most investigations have found that street material from commercial areas contains a higher concentration of toxic metals (mg/kg) than material found in residential or industrial areas. However, industrial areas are the highest in terms of total loading (kg/curb km) and commercial areas the lowest (Pitt & Amy, 1973).

4. REMEDIAL MEASURES

As more complete information on the specific sources of urban contaminants becomes available, new, more effective, site-specific remedial measures will be developed. At present, however, there are several methods that will reduce or treat urban runoff, including source control, collection systems, storage, and treatment.

Source control measures minimize contaminant loads by either controlling the volume of water available for runoff (e.g., roof storage, porous pavement, intentional ponding) or limiting the entry of the pollutant (e.g., air pollution standards, construction site erosion control, increased street sweeping, use of unleaded gasoline, improved methods for deicing pavements).

Collection systems are designed to intercept and transport storm water runoff. Examples include control of infiltration and inflow, flushing pipelines to remove accumulated pollutants, injection of polymers to increase pipe-carrying capacity, improved use of regulators for increased sewer storage capacity, and preliminary quality and quantity control.

Storage, because of its simplicity, relatively low cost, and good response to intermittent flow and changes in quality, is often viewed as the most desirable method of improving storm water management. However, it must be combined with other facilities for treating the retained water and settled solids. Storage may be in-line produced by restricting flow downstream from the regulator diversions causing water to back up and utilize excess volume in the upstream sewers, or off-line produced by lagoons, tanks, underground silos, and tunnels.

Treatment processes may be physical such as sedimentation, dissolved air flotation, screening, filtration, and swirl concentration or biological such as high rate trickling filtration and various types of oxidation lagoons. Biological processes produce a high-quality effluent for a relatively low cost but the organisms must be maintained or produced for each storm event and are subject to eradication by hydraulic or organic overload. Physical treatment followed by the addition of chemicals requires a high initial investment and generates increased sludge but is adaptable to automated systems, is resistant to changes in quality and quantity of flow, and is efficient in removing P.

The best approach to storm water management would probably utilize a combination of two or more of the methods described to provide an optimal program. See Lager and Smith (1974), Vitale and Sprey (1974), USDA (1977), USEPA (1975), and Oberts (1977) for more details on urban storm water management.

IV. PLANNING NONPOINT POLLUTION CONTROL

Having given the background concerning the nature and magnitude of pollutants from nonpoint sources, we now turn to a different perspective—that of the planner charged with preparation of areawide waste treatment management plans as required by Section 208 of P.L. 92-500. In addition to a plan for point source pollution control, these plans are to include the development of a regulatory program for controlling or treating all nonpoint sources of pollution. Although the USEPA will allow substantial flexibility in the contents required, it suggests the following as desirable attributes of the state water quality management plan: i) identification of water quality problems; ii) establishment of goals and standards for water quality protection; iii) delineation of organizational and program responsibilities and interrelationships; iv) establishment of priorities and resource commitments for water program activities; and v) establishment of the relationship between water quality management and other state programs and policies.

Planning activities are to be related to water quality through stream standards established by use categories, e.g., natural, recreational, industrial. The state is responsible for assuring that pollutant loading from all point and nonpoint sources does not exceed the applicable standards.

For nonpoint sources the state is to identify and evaluate "all measures necessary to produce the desired level of control through the application of 'best management practices'" [40 CRF 131.11(j)(2)]. *Best management practices* (BMPs) are defined by the USEPA as "a practice or combination of practices that is determined by a state after problem assessment, examination of alternatives practices, and appropriate public participation to be the most effective, practicable (including technological, economic, and institutional considerations) method of preventing or reducing the amount of pollution generated by nonpoint sources to a level compatible with water quality goals" [CFR 130.2(q)].

A. The Planners' Problem

The single most striking characteristic of the nonpoint pollution problem is the impossibility of fitting it neatly into either academic disciplines or agency responsibilities as they have been traditionally defined. This can be seen clearly in Fig. 1 in which the evaluation of a candidate BMP is decomposed into separate subproblems; cost estimation, site effectiveness, pollutant transport (delivery), water quality impacts, and valuation. Each of these subproblems has traditionally been dealt with, if at all, independent of the others. We will look at each with the objectives of investigating some of the technical issues which are of concern to planners as well as, where appropriate, the relationship of existing agencies and/or institutions to each problem level.

1. THE COST ESTIMATION-ALLOCATION PROBLEM

The planner faces a number of issues concerning the costs of nonpoint pollution control. Costs may be tangible dollar expenses or intangible costs involving everything from matters of deep principle to the nuisance cost of preparing forms establishing compliance with land use restrictions. They may be borne by the public as administrative costs, as enforcement costs, or as incentive payments to landowners. They may be incurred privately in the form of direct costs for pollution-control practices or as a reduction in income resulting from changing land management practices (e.g., reducing the intensity of row crops in a crop rotation). In addition the planner must consider how present costs are to be compared with future costs and, finally, he should have some knowledge concerning the agencies involved in re-

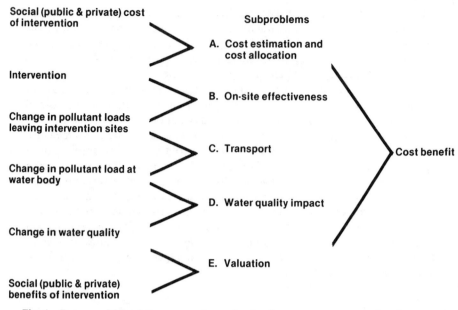

Fig. 1—Decomposition of the process for evaluating best management practices into component subproblems.

lated (cost-sharing) programs. These are the issues that we touch upon, albeit all too briefly, in this section.

On theoretical grounds, economists generally prefer a system in which polluters bear the costs of pollution control through effluent charges levied at a rate equal to the damages imposed by the (marginal unit of) pollutant. The impracticality of such a system for nonpoint pollution control combined with the political power of the agricultural establishment has led to a proliferation of cost-sharing programs using public funds to achieve landowner cooperation.

Within the context of a voluntary cost-sharing program there are major unresolved issues concerning the relative merit of "hard" versus "soft" control techniques. "Hard" techniques are those involving relatively high current capital costs with little, if any, subsequent operating or administrative costs required. In an agricultural context "hard" control techniques include such structures as check dams and parallel tile outlet terraces for sediment control purposes, and manure storage and barnyard diversions for the control of manure runoff. In an urban context "hard" techniques might include the use of sediment catch basins and the construction of infiltration areas in parking lots. "Soft" agricultural pollution control techniques are typically land management techniques such as reduced tillage, less intense rotations, construction and maintenance of grassed water-ways, contour strip cropping, and restricted manure spreading. Increasing the frequency of street sweeping and restricting lawn fertilization would be examples of "soft" urban techniques. These so-called "soft" technology techniques tend to be characterized by low initial capital costs and recurrent operating and/or administrative and enforcement costs. It should be noted that this distinction between "soft" and "hard" techniques, while useful, is not exhaustive. Urban storm water treatment for example, involved *both* high capital costs and recurrent (operating) costs.

In general, society's preference for present versus future welfare constitutes an economic argument favoring "soft" techniques as opposed to "hard." In concrete terms, this preference can be viewed in terms of the amount of money required in the future to compensate for a sacrifice of $X today. If, for example, we must repay $X(1 + r)$ in 1 year to induce a sacrifice of $X at present, the annual rate of time preference is r. It follows that, were repayment to be forthcoming in 2 years, it would require $X(1 + r)$ $(1 + r)$ or $X(1 + r)^2$ and, in general, a sum of $X(1 + r)^t$ paid in year t would be necessary to induce a payment of $X today. The discounting or present value formula imbodies this same concept, but rather than looking at the future value of a present expenditure it looks at the present value of a series of future costs and benefits. The formula relating present value to future costs and benefits is given by:

$$PV = \sum_{t=0}^{T} (B_t - C_t)/(1 + r)^t$$

where PV is present value and C_t and B_t are the costs and benefits accruing in any year t. The effect of discounting on the choice of techniques is illustrated in Table 1. Note that, in undiscounted dollars, the "hard" technique yields $500 net benefits over the 15-year period while the "soft" technique costs $500 more than it contributes in benefits. When discounted at 8%, however, the "soft" technique produces a positive $3 in benefits, while the "hard" technique now costs $410 more than it contributes. Obviously, this

Table 1—Effect of discounting on choice of techniques.

Costs and benefits	Discounting year				Total
	0	5	10	15	
			$		
		Hard			
Costs	1,000	0	0	0	1,000
Benefits	0	200	300	1,000	1,500
$B_t - C_t$	−1,000	200	300	1,000	500
$\dfrac{B_t - C_t}{(1 + 0.08)^t}$	−1,000	+136	+139	+315	−410
		Soft			
Costs	250	250	500	500	1,500
Benefits	550	250	200	0	1,000
$B_t - C_t$	300	0	−300	−500	−500
$\dfrac{B_t - C_t}{(1 + 0.08)^t}$	300	0	−139	−158	+3

example was "cooked" to emphasize the importance of the timing of costs and benefits when comparing techniques.

Although engineering techniques demanding large initial expenses tend to have relatively low present value, they generally possess the advantage of being relatively inexpensive from an administrative point of view. A further advantage of engineering solutions is their relative ease of cost-sharing. Determining a cost-sharing formula for a project involving only an initial investment cost is much simpler than attempting to cost-share land-management techniques for which the actual cost to the farmer is determined by a complex range of climatological and economic factors; factors which often change unexpectedly from one year to the next.

In general, planners have been reluctant to go beyond voluntarism in agricultural nonpoint pollution control and have tended to rely on the established local, state, and federal soil and water conservation agencies to expand their mission to include water quality concerns. As a local unit of government having the mandate and statutory authority to coordinate soil and water conservation programs at the local level, the Soil and Water Conservation Districts (SWCD) is a logical focus for planners' attention. Much can be learned also from the 40-year record that the Agricultural Stabilization and Conservation Service (USDA-ASCS) has established for cost-sharing through its Agricultural Conservation Program (USDA-ACP).

The link between this ACP program and cost sharing under the Rural Clean Water Program (RCWP) has been institutionalized through the ASC committee (composed of three local farmers responsibility for dispensing ACP funds) which, together with the SWCD, determines the priority for assistance among individual land owners. Technical expertise in land management for soil erosion control is provided by the Soil Conservation Service (USDA-SCS) and coordinated by the SWCD. The historical weakness of this local SWCD-SCS-ACS structure has been its inability to resist pressure to cost-share practices most popular among its rural constituency rather than those most clearly consistent with its publicly articulated goals; and its inability to ensure that those lands most in need of treatment get priority assistance (GAO, 1977; Held & Clawson, 1965). The Rural Clean Water Program (RCWP) contains language which appears to demand the establishment of a tighter relationship between the program's goals and the disposition of funds. However, the technical uncertainties to be discussed in the following sections will inevitably leave scope for some continued politicization of cost-sharing programs. Establishing and maintaining cost-sharing priorities will undoubtedly be the major challenge to good planning in the future.

Other incentive programs also have been established to promote the adoption of nonpoint pollution control practices. Various states offer tax-relief incentives as does the federal government in the form of (i) the Soil and Water Deduction, (ii) the Investment Credit, and (iii) a provision allowing rapid depreciation of pollution control facilities. Low-cost loans are also available from the Small Business Association to finance certified pollution control practices. With the exception of the conservation deduction, however, these programs have developed little interest and are unlikely to become relevant in a voluntary program (Moore et al., 1978).

2. SITE EFFECTIVENESS

From a social point of view, the relevant measure of site effectiveness is the change in value of water per unit change in cost of intervention. Prior to any estimation of water quality benefits, however, the on-site effectiveness of the intervention technique must be predicted. For most erosion-sedimentation control techniques, the predictor of choice has become the Universal Soil Loss Equation (Wischmeier & Smith, 1965). With over 20 years of development it has become institutionalized in the SCS through the widespread dissemination of relevant charts, coefficients, example usages, and related apparatus including pocket circular slide-rules. This equation predicts soil loss (in metric tons/ha) as a function of slope and length of field, soil type (erodibility), region (rainfall intensity), crop or rotation (including woodlands), and management technique (terracing, cultivation method, strip cropping, contouring, etc.). Thus, for example, the soil equation allows a technician to predict that a given slope is losing 20 metric tons of soil per ha as presently managed, but would have losses reduced to 10 metric tons per ha if contour strip cropped or to 2 metric tons per ha if terraced.

To the extent that sediment *is* the nonpoint problem, the Universal Soil Loss equation and the accumulated experience of SCS and SWCD technicians with its application are invaluable in assessing the problem and determining the least-cost control techniques. Despite the well-documented affinity of most pollutants for soil particles, however, too narrow a focus on sediment can lead to serious misallocation of pollution-control resources. For example, although reduced tillage studies show dramatic decreases in sediment runoff, they also indicate potential increases in dissolved phosphorus loading (Romkens et al., 1973). If dissolved phosphorus is considered a more serious pollutant than sediment, a point we consider below, the effectiveness of some minimum tillage techniques becomes doubtful from the standpoint of water quality.

Unlike pollutant control techniques corresponding to traditional soil erosion control practices, those relating to the prevention of pollution from animal wastes are characterized by neither as extensive a scientific basis nor the same degree of agency support. Animal waste research has been conducted in three broad areas: (i) the design of structures to store manure or divert water from areas of animal waste accumulation, (ii) the biochemical properties of animal waste, and (iii) the mobility of animal waste over the land surface. The first two of these areas are reviewed in the excellent SCS compilation *Agricultural Waste Management Field Manual* (USDA-SCS, 1975). The third research area is discussed in the context of the pollutant transport problem considered below.

The high cost of animal waste control structures combined with the natural desire of SWCDs to spread cost-sharing funds over as many landowners as possible has led to relative neglect of the animal waste problem.

This is further exacerbated by the fact that in many districts technicians consider their mission to be that of erosion control and are reluctant to expand their role to include the control of animal waste.

3. THE TRANSPORT PROBLEM

The transport problem refers to the problem of estimating or predicting the change in the quantity and quality of a pollutant that is associated with its movement from the intervention site to the water body. Where unchannelized flow distances are extremely short, as in most urban conditions, the problem can generally be safely ignored. In agricultural conditions, however, the judicious use of transport distances to immobilize or process potential pollutants can result in major cost savings.

For sediment, the most commonly employed estimating technique is to use a "delivery ratio" to translate soil loss (as predicted by the Universal Soil Loss Equation) into yield. This "delivery ratio" is often determined as a function of watershed size (Roehl, 1962). Major limitations of this method from a policy standpoint are that it yields no information concerning: (i) the relative delivery rates for farms at various locations within a watershed, (ii) the manner in which delivery rates may change with changes in soil conserving practices, and (iii) the manner in which nutrient concentrations in the sediment change with changes in delivery.

Several attempts are presently being made to route the transport of sediment and associated complexes with hydrological models (Crawford & Linsley, 1966; Patterson et al., 1974; Hydrocomp Int., 1969; Frere et al., 1975). Evaluation of these models is difficult, however, due to the propensity of their designers to use all available data in their "calibration" leaving none for validation. In view of the tremendous computational costs of continuous simulation models, there remains serious doubt as to whether the questionable improvement in their predictive capability over the more simple, steady state, long-run models of the Kling and Olson (1975) genre is justified. (Such models are based on establishing a grid network over the land and estimating delivery ratios between adjacent cells.)

Research concerning the transport of animal wastes in runoff water has concentrated on determining the effectiveness of buffer strips as biological filters. Much of this work has been carried out as part of the effort of the International Reference Group on Great Lakes Pollution from Land Use Activities (PLUARG) (Draper et al., 1978; Moore et al., 1978) and has focused on estimating the quantities of animal wastes available for runoff at various distances from water bodies and then applying to these estimated quantities empirically derived delivery ratios. Their estimates indicate that between one-half and two-thirds of all manure phosphorus (total) entering a water body could be controlled by applying remedial measures to feedlots and beef and dairy barnlots located within 100 feet of surface channels. Clean water diversion techniques (often referred to as the *Environmental Eye*) appear to be the most cost-effective technique for reducing nutrient and sediment outflow from these animal concentration areas. This management technique consists of diverting clean water from the feedlot area by means of upslope berms and diversion ditches, removing roof water with properly sized gutters and downspouts, and treating water falling directly on the barnyard area by means of settling ponds, serpentine ditches, or low-slope, low-gradient ditches. Approximately 250 of these management structures have been installed in Lafayette County, Wisconsin, at costs ranging from $1,500 to $3,500 per farm.

4. THE WATER QUALITY IMPACT PROBLEM

The state of knowledge concerning water quality response to nonpoint pollutants does not yet allow firm predictions of the timing, magnitude, or, in some cases, direction of impact. To assess the impact of sediment, for example, it is necessary to consider its constituent properties and analyze their interaction with other constituents of the waterbody.

The work of Vollenweider (1975) and Dillon (1975) shows considerable promise for predicting the eutrophic status of a lake from knowledge of its phosphorous loading. Sakomoto (1966) and Dillon (1975) have shown the concentration of total phosphorous to be a very good predictor of summer chlorophyll concentrations. Although this technique shows promise for predicting the impact due to phosphorus loading from soluble phosphorous leached from manure or decaying vegetative matter, the light-inhibiting effect of sediment-produced turbidity combined with the relative biological inactivity of sediment-bound phosphorus suggests that the Vollenweider-Dillon-Sakomoto method is likely to lead to an overestimate of the contribution of sediment to eutrophication problems. In some cases sediment reduction has actually been blamed for an increase in the incidence of algal blooms (Carpenter & Geyer, 1965; Hartung, 1965). In general, the role of sediment-borne nutrients is determined by the ambient nutrient concentrations in the water body.

The association of sediment with pesticides and heavy metals has received considerable attention (Lichtenstein et al., 1970; Chesters & Konrad, 1971; Hutchinson, 1975; Browman & Chesters, 1977). As in the case with phosphorus, considerable controversy exists concerning their eventual fate under these conditions. Some experts feel that sediment acts as a "sink" and that the contaminant is biologically unavailable. Others believe that reactions with the sediment may enhance availability and in some cases increase the toxicity.

5. THE VALUATION/STANDARDS PROBLEM

The planning of nonpoint pollution control is complicated by serious technical and conceptual problems regarding the estimation of the benefits of water quality improvement. In general, empirical estimates of the value of a water body have been extremely weak and fraught with methodological problems (Peskins & Seskin, 1973). Furthermore, there are serious if not insurmountable problems relating to both the nature and value of benefits accruing to future generations; values typically ignored in benefit measurement. An accounting of short-run benefits should include improvements in public health, improved recreation and aesthetics, and improved fisheries.

Long-run benefits include those relating to health and to the avoidance of irreversible environmental damage.

Predicting pollution control benefits requires first predicting the environmental changes to result from pollutant reduction and then imputing to those changes an economic value. Combining the weaknesses of the prediction and the valuation methods often results in a value more appropriately considered conjecture than estimate. This is especially true with respect to estimating benefits to be expected far in the future. Early concern was expressed by Pigou (1932) and Ramsey (1928) over intertemporal welfare distribution and the appropriate rate at which the benefits of future generations may be discounted in the formation of policy in the present. Krutilla and Fisher (1975) note that, although uncertainty of future generations' preferences and technology may argue for some discounting of their benefits (rather, our conception of their benefits), the argument cuts both ways where environmental policy is considered. Many ecosystems, they argue, are unique and irreproducible, providing our reservoir of genetic information to future generations. One cannot anticipate such genetic information being supplanted by technology; rather, it is the raw material of technological advance. Technological advance may, however, supplant the need to destroy ecosystems. It is this asymmetry that is the most compelling argument for preservation.

Faced with insufficient technical knowledge and the difficulty if not impossibility of ethical choice concerning intertemporal welfare; faced in short with the temporal myopia of mortals, policy-makers have tended to abandon the search for benefit/cost maximization. The compromise has become a policy of minimizing the cost of meeting water quality standards. The standards are established using much less esoteric and, it's probably fair to say, more politically defensible criteria. They are to be developed by the states and reviewed at least every 3 years in public hearing after which, if modified, they are sent to the USEPA for approval (40CFR 130.17). The standards are to protect the public health or welfare and serve the goals of PL 92-500 (elimination of the discharge of pollutants into navigable waters by 1985, and the "protection and propagation of fish, shellfish, and wildlife and (the provision) for recreation in and on the water by 1983"). At a minimum the standards are not to allow the water quality to degrade to a point where it interferes with or becomes injurious to existing instream water uses. No degradation will be permitted in "high quality waters which constitute an outstanding national source such as waters of national and state parks and wildlife refuges and waters of exceptional recreational or ecological significance" (CFR 130.17e).

B. Public Participation: The Essential Ingredient

In light of the preceding review of the technology and the institutions of nonpoint pollution control it should come as no surprise that, more than any other factor, public participation has been the key to successful programs. For, despite the existing expertise, despite the very real strengths of existing organizations, despite the best intentioned planners, the nonpoint pollution problem is simply not solvable through a mechanical application of existing technology by existing institutions. It is evident from experience in Wisconsin, as well as elsewhere, that where local people are convinced of the nonpoint pollution problem they are willing to act, but where they have not been convinced they will adopt a posture of passive resistance.

Clearly, the threat of federal government intervention and regulation is not, in the absence of local recognition of the problem, a sufficiently stable or desirable cornerstone upon which to build a nonpoint pollution control program. Local suspicion of program motives combined with the difficulties of communicating the scientific basis of program priorities, especially with respect to agricultural impacts, makes the role of local participation and involvement assume a critical importance. Where appeals couched in terms of best management practices, tons per acre, or parts per million often fail, a documentation of long-term degradation of local water resources has a surprising effect upon the local water quality consciousness. Local identification of the nonpoint pollution control program with outside intervention inevitably creates an environment of hostility and resentment. Local participation, involvement, and initiative, on the other hand, leads to identification of local problems and an assumption of responsibility for their solution. The importance of the example set by local government through, for example, controlling roadside erosion and exercising discretion in road salting, cannot be overestimated.

The willingness of local government to play an active role in nonpoint pollution control has been evidenced in Wisconsin, where at least six counties have developed their own cost-sharing programs to promote nonpoint pollution control practices. The funds available have been in the range of $10,000 to $50,000 per county annually and have generally been restricted to promoting specific practices not considered by county officials to be receiving high enough priorities under the ACP program. One county, for example, applied all of its cost-sharing funds to promote minimum tillage; others emphasized streambank protection and barnyard runoff controls. Furthermore, at least one county and one town have restricted agricultural practices on steep slopes. Other counties and municipalities have amended subdivision ordinances and building permit procedures to include considerations of soil loss and runoff.

As experience with local initiative accumulates, it is becoming increasingly evident that the responsiveness of local institutions to water quality issues is directly proportional to their involvement in the problem identification stage of the water quality program. A particularly useful technique has been to encourage local units of government (SWCD's are an obvious choice) to participate in drafting a "state-of-the waters" document. This document, if it is identified with local institutions and prepared with maximum citizen participation can become the focal point for the local water quality effort. It should contain, if possible, a comparison between aquatic populations in the past and in the present, as well as an inventory of any rare and/or endangered species. A comparison of the accomplishments in planning areas that have used this type of a problem identification technique with those that have relied on simulation models seems to suggest that serious problems lie ahead for those who attempt to solve nonpoint pollution problems technocratically.

V. SUMMARY AND CONCLUSIONS

Some estimate that at least half of the pollutants which find their way into our waters come from nonpoint sources. These contaminants arise from various land use activities, the most significant on a nationwide basis being agricultural and urban land runoff.

Each watershed is different in predominant land use, geology, soils, and topography and, hence, it is impossible to develop a list of nonpoint source areas and corresponding BMPs common to all watersheds. Funding limitations make it essential that the nonpoint pollution program be based upon the selection of priority watershed selection. The available evidence indicates that the criteria for choosing among watersheds as well as for choosing problem areas within a watershed should list pollutants in the order of priority: (i) contaminants having potential health hazard, especially toxic metals; (ii) pollutants emanating from concentrated animal areas, particularly those in close proximity to a stream; and (iii) sediment from highly erosive areas.

Due to the impossibility of treating an entire watershed and the fact that in most watersheds only a small percentage of the land area is responsible for the bulk of the nonpoint pollution problem, it is necessary to identify critical areas that, if managed, would provide the greatest pollution reduction for the least cost. This is perhaps best accomplished by relying on local citizens and agencies (SWCDs) best acquainted with the area and, where adequate resources exist, supplementing their information with modeling techniques being developed for this purpose. Early local involvement in the identification of problems is essential to the success of program implementation.

While additional time in which to develop a broader data base may be desireable, the problem is too far advanced to wait—the public, the law, and the courts say we must act now. One cannot delay pollution control until research reveals the best possible allocation of pollution-control dollars. Rather, we must learn from our experience, carefully measuring and analyzing the effectiveness of techniques as they are tried, always showing a willingness to suspend judgement until the results are in. This is essentially the USEPA's answer to the need for planning and decision-making in an environment of uncertainty. "The development of the (water quality) plans," writes Russel Train, "will involve an *iterative process* of establishing attainable water quality goals, identifying necessary controls and regulatory programs, and determining the resulting environmental, social, and economic impact" (Preamble to CFR 131, emphasis added).

The USEPA has recognized the necessity to continually update plans as the state-of-the-art improves and the planning environment changes. A major challenge confronting planners is that of incorporating this flexibility into the complex of institutional arrangements necessary for plan implementation.

While it is true that gaps in our knowledge of the problem remain and much research needs to be done, effective BMPs have been developed, particularly for minimizing urban runoff, managing concentrated animal areas, and reducing erosion. Commencing now with what we do know, recognizing that refinements can and will be made as new information becomes available, will go a long way toward solving the nonpoint pollution problem.

LITERATURE CITED

Alberts, E. E., G. E. Schuman, and R. E. Burwell. 1978. Seasonal runoff losses of nitrogen and phosphorus from Missouri Valley loess watersheds. J. Environ. Qual. 7:203–208.

Avco Corporation. 1970. Storm water pollution from urban land activity. Rep. no. 11034FKL. USDI, Water Qual. Admin., Washington, D.C. 325 p.

Bovey, R. W., E. Burnett, C. Richardson, M. G. Merkle, J. R. Baur, and W. G. Knisel. 1974. Occurrence of 2,4,5-T and picloram in surface runoff waters in the blacklands of Texas. J. Environ. Qual. 3:61–64.

Bradford, W. L. 1977. Urban stormwater pollutant loading: A statistical summary through 1972. J. Water Pollut. Control Fed. 49:613–622.

Browman, M. G., and G. Chesters. 1977. The solid-water interface: Transfer of organic pollutants across the solid-water interface. p. 49–105. In I. H. Soffet (ed.) Fate of pollutants in the air and water environments, Part I, Vol. 8. John Wiley & Sons, Inc., New York.

Bryan, E. H. 1970. Quality of stormwater drainage from urban land areas in North Carolina. Rep. 37. Water Resour. Res. Inst., Univ. of North Carolina, Chapel Hill, N.C. 44 p.

Burwell, R. E., G. E. Schuman, R. F. Piest, R. G. Spomer, and T. M. McCalla. 1974. Quality of water discharged from two agricultural watersheds in southwestern Iowa. Water Resour. Res. 10:359–365.

Burwell, R. E., D. R. Timmons, and R. F. Holt. 1975. Nutrient transport in surface runoff as influenced by soil cover and seasonal periods. Soil Sci. Soc. Am. Proc. 39:523–528.

Carpenter, J. H., and J. C. Geyer. 1965. A research program for the Potomac River. Rep. for the Dep. of Sanitary Eng., District of Columbia, and Bureau of Environ. Hygiene, State of Maryland.

Case, A. A. 1970. The health effects of nitrates in water. p. 195–198. In Proc. nitrate and water supply: source and control. Univ. of Illinois, Urbana, Ill.

Chesters, G., and J. G. Konrad. 1971. Effects of pesticide usage on water quality. BioScience 21:565–569.

Colston, N. V., and A. N. Tafuri. 1975. Urban land runoff characteristics. p. 120–128. In William Whipple, Jr. (ed.) Urbanization and water quality control. Am. Water Res. Assoc., Minneapolis, Minn.

Crawford, N. H., and R. K. Linsley. 1966. Digital simulation in hydrology: Stanford watershed model IV. Stanford Univ. Tech. Rep. no. 39.

Diesch, S. L. 1970. Disease transmission of water borne organisms of animal origin. p. 265–285. In T. L. Willrich and G. E. Smith (ed.) Agricultural practices and water quality. Iowa State Univ. Press, Ames, Iowa.

Dillon, P. J. 1975. The application of the phosphorus-loading concept to eutrophication research. Sci. Ser. no. 46. Inland Water Directorate, Canada Center for Inland Waters, Burlington, Ontario.

Dragoon, F. J., and C. R. Miller. 1966. Sediment characteristics for two small agricultural watersheds. Trans. Am. Soc. Agric. Eng. 9:66–70.

Draper, D. W., J. B. Robbins, and D. R. Coote. 1978. Estimation and management of the contribution by manure by livestock in the Ontario Great Lakes Basin to the phosphorus loading of the Great Lakes. Proc. 1978 Cornell Conf. on Best Management Practices for Agriculture and Silviculture, Apr. 1978, Rochester, N.Y. Ann Arbor Sci. Publ., Inc., Ann Arbor, Mich.

Edwards, C. A. 1972. Insecticides. p. 304–315. *In* C. A. I. Goring and T. W. Hamaker (ed.) Organic chemicals in the soil environment. Marcel Dekker, New York.

Frere, M. H., C. A. Onstad, and N. H. Holtan. 1975. ACTMO, an agricultural chemical transport model. USDA-ARS.

Gburek, W. J., and W. R. Heald. 1974. Soluble phosphate output of an agricultural watershed in Pennsylvania. Water Resour. Res. 10:113–118.

Geldreich, E. E., L. C. Best, B. A. Kenner, and D. J. VanDonsel. 1968. The bacteriological aspects of stormwater pollution. J. Water Pollut. Control Fed. 40:1861–1864.

General Accounting Office. 1977. To protect tomorrow's food supply, soil conservation needs priority attention. Comptroller General, Washington, D.C. 59 p.

Glymph, L. M., and C. W. Carlson. 1966. Cleaning up our rivers and lakes. Pap. no. 66-711. Am. Soc. Agric. Eng., St. Joseph, Mich. p. 43.

Hartung, O. H. 1965. Comprehensive planning as viewed by Missouri River public water supplies associations. Am. Soc. Civil Eng., Environ. Eng. Conf., Kansas City, Kans.

Held, R. B., and M. Clawson. 1965. Soil conservation in perspective. Published for Resources for the Future, Inc. by John Hopkins Press, Baltimore, Md. 344 p.

Hutchinson, T. C. (ed.). 1975. International conference on heavy metals in the environment, Vol. 1–3. Toronto, Ontario, Canada.

Hydrocomp International. 1969. HSP operations manual. Palo Alto, Calif.

Johnson, A. H., D. R. Boulden, E. A. Goyette, and A. M. Hedge. 1976. Phosphorus loss by stream transport from a rural watershed: Quantities, processes, and sources. J. Environ. Qual. 5:148–157.

Jones, I. R., P. H. Weswig, J. F. Bone, M. A. Peters, and S. O. Alpan. 1966. Effect of high nitrate consumption and lactation and vitamin A nutrition of dairy cows. J. Dairy Sci. 49:491–499.

Kling, G. F., and G. W. Olson. 1975. Role of computers in land use planning. Inf. Bull. no. 88. Plant Sci. Agron. 3, Cornell Univ., Ithaca, N.Y.

Kluesener, J. W., and G. F. Lee. 1974. Nutrient loading from a separate storm sewer in Madison, Wisconsin. J. Water Pollut. Control Fed. 46:920–936.

Krutilla, J. V., and A. C. Fisher. 1975. The economics of natural environments. John Hopkins Univ. Press, Baltimore, Md.

Lager, J. A., and W. G. Smith. 1974. Urban stormwater management and technology: An assessment. USEPA Rep. no. 670/2-74-040. U.S. Government Printing Office, Washington, D.C.

Lee, G. F. 1973. Role of phosphorus in eutrophication and diffuse source control. Water Res. 7:111–128.

Lichtenstein, E. P., K. R. Schulz, R. F. Skrentry, and Y. Tsukano. 1970. Toxicity and fate of insecticide residues in water. Arch. Environ. Health 12:199–212.

Loehr, R. C. 1974. Characteristics and comparative magnitude of nonpoint sources. J. Water Pollut. Control Fed. 46:1849–1870.

Marrett, L. E., and M. L. Sunde. 1968. The use of turkey poults and chickens as test animals for nitrate and nitrite toxicity. Poult. Sci. 47:511–519.

Miner, J. R., R. I. Lipper, L. R. Fina, and J. W. Funk. 1966. Cattle feedlot runoff—its nature and variation. J. Water Pollut. Control Fed. 38:1582–1591.

Moore, I. C., F. W. Madison, and R. R. Schneider. 1978. Estimating phosphorus loading from livestock wastes: some Wisconsin results. Proc. 1978 Cornell Conf. on Best Management Practices for agriculture and Silviculture, April 1978, Rochester, N.Y. Ann Arbor Sci. Publ., Inc., Ann Arbor, Mich.

Moore, I. C., R. R. Schneider, and F. W. Madison. 1978. Role of tax relief in agricultural nonpoint source pollution control. Mimeo Rep. Univ. of Wisconsin, Water Resour. Center, Madison, Wis.

Oberts, G. L. 1977. Water quality effects of potential urban best management practices: A literature review. Technol. bull. no. 97. Dep. of Nat. Resour., Madison, Wis. 25 p.

Olness, Alan, S. J. Smith, E. D. Rhoades, and R. G. Menzel. 1975. Nutrient and sediment discharge from agricultural watersheds in Oklahoma. J. Environ. Qual. 4:331–336.

Patterson, M. R., J. K. Munro, D. E. Rields, R. D. Ellison, A. A. Brooks, and D. D. Huff. 1974. A user's manual for the Fortran IV version of the Wisconsin Hydrologic Transport Model. Oak Ridge Natl. Lab., Oak Ridge, Tenn.

Peskins, H. M., and E. P. Seskin (ed.). 1973. Cost benefit analysis in water pollution policy. Urban Inst., Washington, D.C.

Pigou, A. C. 1932. The economics of welfare. MacMillan, Inc., New York.

Pitt, R. E., and Gary Amy. 1973. Toxic materials analysis of street surface contaminants. Environ. Prot. Technol. Ser. EPA-R-2-73-283. USEPA, Washington, D.C. 133 p.

Powers, W. L., G. W. Wallingford, and L. S. Murphy. 1975. Research status on effects of land application of animal wastes. USEPA Res. Rep. Ser., U.S. Government Printing Office, Washington, D.C. 96 p.

Ramsey, F. P. 1928. A mathematical theory of saving. Econ. J. 38:543–559.

Randall, C. W., J. A. Garland, T. J. Grizzard, and R. C. Hoehn. 1977. The significance of stormwater runoff in an urbanizing watershed. Prog. Water Tech. 9:547–562.

Roehl, J. W. 1962. Sediment source areas, delivery ratios and influencing morphological factors. Int. Assoc. Sci. Hydrol. 59:202–213.

Romkens, M. J. M., D. W. Nelson, and J. V. Mannering. 1973. Nitrogen and phosphorus composition of surface runoff as affected by tillage method. J. Environ. Qual. 2:292–295.

Sakomoto, M. 1966. Primary production by phytoplankton communities in some Japanese lakes and its dependence on lake depth. Arch. Hydrobiol. 62:1–28.

Sartor, J. D., and G. B. Boyd. 1972. Water pollution aspects of street surface contaminants. U.S. Government Printing Office, Washington, D.C. 236 p.

Sawyer, C. N. 1947. Fertilization of lakes by agricultural and urban drainage. N. Eng. Water Works Assoc. J. 61(2):109–127.

Schuman, G. E., R. G. Spomer, and R. F. Piest. 1973. Phosphorus losses from four agricultural watersheds on Missouri Valley loess. Soil Sci. Soc. Am. Proc. 37:424–427.

Spomer, R. G., K. E. Saxton, and H. G. Heinemann. 1973. Water yield and erosion response to land management. J. Soil Water Conserv. 28:168–170.

Taylor, A. W., W. M. Edwards, and E. C. Simpson. 1971. Nutrients in streams draining woodland and farmland near Coshocton, Ohio. Water Resour. Res. 7:81–87.

Thomas, J. R. 1970. Soil erosion in the Detroit metropolitan area. J. Soil Water Conserv. 25:8–10.

Timmons, D. R., and R. F. Holt. 1970. Leaching of crop residue as a source of nutrients in surface runoff waters. Water Resour. Res. 6:1367–1375.

U.S. Department of Agriculture. 1970. Basic statistics—national inventory of soil and water conservation needs. USDA Stat. Bull. no. 461, USDA, Washington, D.C. 122 p.

U.S. Department of Agriculture. 1975. Agricultural waste management field manual. USDA-Soil Conserv. Serv., Washington, D.C.

U.S. Department of Agriculture. 1977. Standards and specifications for soil erosion and sediment control in developing areas. USDA, Washington, D.C.

U.S. Environmental Protection Agency. 1973. Methods for identifying and evaluating the nature and extent of nonpoint sources of pollutants. EPA Rep. no. 430/9-73-014. U.S. Government Printing Office, Washington, D.C. 168 p.

U.S. Environmental Protection Agency. 1975. Processes, procedures and methods to control pollution resulting from all construction activity. EPA Rep. no. 430/9-73-007. U.S. Government Printing Office, Washington, D.C. 234 p.

Uttormark, P. D., J. D. Chapin, and K. M. Green. 1974. Estimating nutrient loadings of lakes from nonpoint sources. EPA Rep. no. 660/3-74-020. USEPA, U.S. Government Printing Office, Washington, D.C.

Vaughn, R. D., and G. L. Harlow. 1965. Report on pollution of the Detroit River, Michigan waters of Lake Erie, and their tributaries. U.S. Dep. of Health, Education, and Welfare, Public Health Serv., Div. of Water Supply and Pollut. Control, Washington, D.C.

Vitale, A. M., and P. M. Sprey. 1974. Total urban water pollution loads: The impact of storm water. Natl. Tech. Inf. Serv., USDC, Springfield, Va. 183 p.

Vollenweider, R. A. 1975. Input-output models. Schweiz. Z. Hydrol. 37(1):53–84.

Wilber, W. G., and J. V. Hunter. 1975. Contributions of metals resulting from stormwater runoff and precipitation in Lodi, New Jersey. p. 45–54. In William Whipple, Jr. (ed.) Urbanization and water quality control. Am. Water Resour. Assoc., Minneapolis, Minn.

Winton, E. F., R. G. Tardiff, and L. J. McCabe. 1971. Nitrate in drinking waters. J. Am. Water Works Assoc. 63:95–98.

Wischmeier, W. H. 1976. Cropland erosion and sedimentation. p. 31–57. *In* Control of water pollution from cropland, Vol. 2—An overview. U.S. Government Printing Office, Washington, D.C.

Wischmeier, W. H., and D. D. Smith. 1965. Predicting rainfall-erosion losses from cropland east of the Rocky Mountains. Agric. Handb. no. 282, USDA-ARS.

Wolman, M. G., and A. P. Schick. 1967. Effects of construction on fluvial sediment in urban and suburban areas of Maryland. Water Resour. Res. 3:451–464.

Wood, R. D., C. H. Chaney, D. W. Waddill, and G. W. Garrison. 1967. Effect of adding nitrate or nitrite to drinking water on the utilization of carotene by growing swine. J. Anim. Sci. 26:510–513.

34 Reclamation Alternatives for Disturbed Lands and Their Application in Humid Regions

PAUL SUTTON

Ohio Agricultural Research and Development Center, Wooster, Ohio

I. INTRODUCTION

Land disturbances can be broadly classified as those resulting from natural causes and those caused by man's activities. Disturbances resulting from natural causes such as landslides or deposition of sediments by water or wind are in many cases influenced by man's activities. In hilly topography where landslides are already present, earth movement associated with mining or construction will increase the chances that other landslides will occur unless measures are taken to prevent them. Removal of vegetation from land can increase the runoff of rainfall which may increase flooding and erosion. This contributes to the deposition of sediments in areas such as bottom lands, stream channels, lakes, and harbors. The removal of vegetation can also contribute to wind erosion which would be more prevalent in the drier climates.

Some of man's activities that have resulted in relatively large areas of land being disturbed are surface mining and construction. These activities usually require relatively large quantities of earth materials to be moved. Large areas of land are disturbed each year by stripmining of coal. Other surface-mined minerals supply raw materials for manufacturing. Land disturbances also result from the construction of highways, electrical power lines, pipelines, water reservoirs, preparation of building sites, landfills, and disposal of dredging materials.

The environmental problems caused by land disturbance are widespread and can be serious without proper reclamation. Many of these problems have been associated with the failure to establish a vegetative cover to control erosion on the disturbed areas. In areas surface mined for coal, the failure to establish vegetation on many of these lands is caused by highly acid conditions resulting from the oxidization of sulfur. By sound planning and the use of proper reclamation practices, many of the environmental damages associated with land disturbances can be eliminated.

A general definition for reclamation is the process of reconverting disturbed land to its former or other productive uses. In cases such as roadbanks, earth dams, and construction sites, reclamation will usually consist of establishing a vegetative cover to minimize erosion and to improve the appearance of the area. Reclamation of surface-mined lands usually requires grading to some specified topography and, if required, replacement of soil material to the surface and establishment of a vegetative cover.

The federal "Surface Mining Control and Reclamation Act of 1977," enacted in August 1977, will regulate coal surface mining and reclamation. Prior to this law, most states in which coal has been mined had surface mine laws regulating mining and reclamation. Abandoned surface mines that were mined prior to the enactment of comprehensive reclamation laws and that require additional reclamation are referred to as *orphan spoil banks* or *orphan lands*.

II. SURVEY CLASSIFICATION AND CHARACTERIZATION OF DISTURBED LANDS

A. Types of Land Disturbance

Surface mining, construction, and landfills result in land disturbances which cause environmental problems and concerns. Over 12 million ha of land have been disturbed by surface mining in the eastern U.S. (Table 1). More than half of this has been disturbed by mining for coal. Abandoned and unreclaimed surface-mined coal lands are situated predominantly in Illinois, Indiana, Ohio, Pennsylvania, West Virginia, and Kentucky. Stone, clay, and sand-gravel have been mined throughout the United States and are generally associated with population centers and consumer demands.

Approximately one-fourth of the coal reserves in the United States lie in the midwestern U.S., and one-fourth are in Appalachia. Surface mining of coal has expanded steadily in recent years and is expected to continue to grow due to increased energy needs and greater dependence on coal to meet these needs. In the United States, about 40,000 ha of land are disturbed each year by surface mining for coal. By the year 2000, it is estimated this will increase to 68,000 ha (USDA, 1974).

Urban development removes 300,000 ha of land yearly from the rural environment of the United States (USDA, 1974). In rural areas, transportation utilizes approximately 52,000 ha a year for highways and airports. During construction of roads and site preparation for construction of buildings, water courses are sometimes disturbed and the delivery of sediments to drainage ways and streams is accelerated. Cuts and fills also create barren areas that need to be stabilized.

Residential, commercial, and institutional solid waste totals some 250 million metric tons a year. Three-fourths of this waste goes into 14,000 open dumps (USDA, 1974), which average 14 ha in size and occupy a total land

Table 1—Land disturbed by surface mining in eastern U.S. as of 1 Jan. 1974, by states and principal minerals mined (Grim & Hill, 1974; USDI, 1974).

State	Hectares	Minerals
Alabama	72,965	Coal and stone
Arkansas	19,426	Stone
Connecticut	6,205	Stone, sand and gravel, feldspar
Delaware	1,865	Sand and gravel, clays
Florida	100,917	Phosphate rock and stone
Georgia	15,535	Clays, stone, sand and gravel
Illinois	74,324	Coal, stone, sand and gravel
Indiana	60,149	Coal, stone, sand and gravel
Iowa	19,587	Stone, sand and gravel, gypsum
Kentucky	117,424	Coal, stone
Louisiana	9,195	Sulfur
Maine	5,381	Sand and gravel, stone, zinc
Maryland	6,757	Stone, sand and gravel, coal
Massachusetts	9,376	Sand and gravel, stone, clays
Michigan	9,153	Iron ore, copper, sand and gravel
Minnesota	27,974	Iron ore, sand and gravel, stone
Mississippi	354	Sand and gravel
Missouri	8,341	Stone, iron ore
New Hampshire	1,782	Sand and gravel, stone, clays
New Jersey	4,941	Stone, sand and gravel, zinc
New York	33,187	Stone, sand and gravel
North Carolina	13,203	Stone, sand and gravel, phosphate rock
Ohio	133,750	Coal, stone
Pennsylvania	193,590	Coal, stone, sand and gravel, coal†
Rhode Island	1,620	Sand and gravel, stone
South Carolina	14,378	Stone, sand and gravel, clays
Tennessee	50,908	Coal, stone, zinc
Vermont	1,762	Stone, sand and gravel
Virginia	29,202	Coal, stone, sand and gravel
West Virginia	111,865	Coal, stone
Wisconsin	31,721	Sand and gravel, stone, iron ore

† Bituminous and anthracite coal.

area of approximately 190,400 ha. At the present rate of filling, 500 new dumping sites will be needed each year.

B. Chemical and Physical Characteristics

The chemical and physical characteristics of disturbed lands are determined by the type of geologic materials present and the rearrangement of these materials during the earth-moving process. The chemical and physical properties of soils have been studied quite extensively. However, the different strata underlying the soil may have properties quite different from the soil. Unless the different strata are segregated during earth-moving operations, the disturbed lands become a mixture of the different strata. By obtaining information on the chemical and physical properties of the materials, the more desirable materials can be placed so the land will be more suitable for the intended use. This approach is usually more satisfactory than amelioriation of the more undesirable materials.

1. CHEMICAL CHARACTERISTICS

Detailed studies have been conducted to determine the chemical characteristics of coal surface mine overburden. The properties that have received attention are: i) percentage and type of iron disulfide; ii) pH and potential acidity from pyritic sulfur; iii) soluble salts and plant nutrient status; and iv) acid-neutralizing capacity from carbonates, clay exchange, and weathered silicates (Smith, 1971).

In areas where iron disulfide minerals are exposed, extremely acid conditions are often encountered. Iron disulfide occurs either as marcasite or pyrite in unmined coal and in the undisturbed strata associated with coal (Caruccio, 1968). Upon exposure to the atmosphere, it is readily decomposed and compounds are formed by a complex series of chemical reactions to produce acid and associated hydrous iron complexes. The general equations for the reaction are (Hill, 1978):

$$2FeS_2 + 2H_2O + 7O_2 \rightarrow 2FeSO_4 + 2H_2SO_4$$

$$FeS_2 + 14Fe^{3+} + 8H_2O \rightarrow 15Fe^{2+} + 2SO_4^{2-} + 16H^+$$

$$4FeSO_4 + O_2 + 2H_2SO_4 \rightarrow 2Fe_2(SO_4)_3 + 2H_2O$$

$$Fe_2(SO_4)_3 + 6H_2O \rightarrow 2Fe(OH)_3 + 3H_2SO_4$$

The rate of reaction is a function of the oxygen concentration, temperature, degree of surface saturation by water, and pH of the solution in contact with the pyrite (Smith, 1971).

In studies conducted with coal mine spoils, Smith et al. (1976) concluded that, in the humid region of the United States above the permanent water tables, pyritic minerals capable of forming sulfuric acid have been oxidized and largely destroyed to depths of approximately 6 m. The oxidation penetrates deeper in rocks that have been fractured by geologic processes. Materials with a Munsell color chroma greater than two indicated that the pyrite had been destroyed. Insignificant exceptions were noted where the pyrite was encased in a ground mass of tough cemented sandstone, hard mudrock, or limestone (Smith et al., 1976).

If sufficient bases are present, the acid produced by pyrite oxidation will be neutralized. Grube et al. (1973) developed an acid-base accounting method to determine if disturbed material would result in a potentially acid-toxic soil. The exposure of highly acid-producing materials results in the formation of acid which is discharged into nearby streams. As shown in the equation, acid production can be reduced or eliminated by controlling the supply of oxygen.

Since the pyrite is originally concentrated in certain beds, the best treatment in reclamation is to return these materials to their former environment to minimize the amount of acid resulting from weathering. Also, this procedure should be followed for any land disturbance where other undesirable strata are encountered. These materials should be segregated and placed so as to create the most favorable situation for reclamation of the area and for the intended use. To do this, the physical and chemical properties of the strata that will be affected must be known prior to the disturbance. Core samples can be taken ahead of the earth-moving operations and the different strata analyzed to identify the materials that should be covered.

Coal mine spoil banks are generally toxic to plants if the pH of the surface material is less than 4.0 on more than 75% of the area. In West Virginia, very little plant invasion occurred on old sandstone spoils with a pH below 4.0 (Smith et al., 1974). In southern Indiana, surface-mined lands with a pH below 3.5 and specific conductance above 2 mmhos/cm were apparently toxic and limited plant establishment (Byrnes & Miller, 1973).

Struthers (1964) and Vimmerstedt and Struthers (1968) reported the results of different coal mine spoils that were placed in lysimeters and the leachate collected and analyzed for pH, total salts, Ca, Mg, Na, K, Al, Mn, and Fe. Quantities of salts produced in 1 year varied from 102 kg to more than 205 metric tons/ha. The high soluble salt associated with some surface mine spoils and other disturbed areas in the humid areas prevents successful establishment of vegetation.

Tyner and Smith (1945) reported that hydrogen-ion concentration appeared to be the chief factor determining the success of vegetation of coal mine spoils in West Virginia. They found that with 0.48 to 0.75% total sulfur in the spoil the pH ranged from 2.45 to 2.68. Low pH is detrimental to plant growth in extreme situations but pH per se may not be the main problem associated with revegetation of highly acid soils. Elements such as Fe, Al, and Mn become more available to plants as the soil pH decreases. Under very acid conditions, such as those found on some mine spoils, these elements become toxic to plants (Bennett, 1971; Berg & Vogel, 1968).

In early reclamation efforts, one treatment was to let the extremely acid spoils (pH 4.0) weather, thus permitting the oxidation of acid-producing pyritic materials and leaching of the acid (Kohnke, 1950). This may require many years for some areas (Knabe, 1964). In areas with lower quantities of pyritic materials, the leaching treatment has proven successful (Riley, 1973). When dealing with barren areas that have weathered for several years, the potential of the acid-producing materials may be greatly reduced and relatively small amounts of soil amendments may be required for establishing vegetation. This can be estimated by the quantity of unoxidized sulfur remaining and a lime requirement determined. Theoretically, for each 1.0 kg of sulfur available to produce sulfuric acid, it takes 3.125 kg of calcium carbonate to neutralize the acidity (Smith et al., 1974).

In field studies large quantities of limestone have been applied based on lime requirements, and revegetation of these areas has been a failure (James & Morst, 1965; Sutton, 1970). James and Morst (1965) attributed the failure to revegetate to the movement of acid into the surface layer by capillary action. This problem could be overcome by using irrigation to prevent capillary movement of acid into the surface or by adding additional amounts of limestone.

Several of the available plant nutrients may be deficient in disturbed lands. Results of studies have indicated that nitrogen is deficient on disturbed areas (Berg, 1973; Bennett et al., 1976). This is more likely to occur where areas have been disturbed and the topsoil not returned to the surface. Other elements such as P, K, Ca, and Mg may be deficient (Bennett et al., 1976). In the areas with limestone formations, P is most frequently deficient, whereas with sandstone formations P, K, Ca, and Mg may be deficient (Bennett et al., 1976; Barnhisel, 1977; Mays & Bengtson, 1974).

2. PHYSICAL CHARACTERISTICS

The texture of the new soil in disturbed areas will be related to the type of materials present, the placement of these materials, and degree of weathering. Spoil derived primarily from sandstone strata usually is initially coarser than spoil derived from shale (Van Lear, 1971). In surface mining, the texture may range from rock fragments to the soil-size particles of sand, silt, and clay. Rock or shale fragments increase drainage and reduce water-holding capacity, but the coarse fragments and texture will increase rooting depth (Smith, 1971). Where fine-textured spoils have been excessively packed by heavy machinery, restricted rooting and wilting of some plant species has been noted (Smith et al., 1971). In Appalachia, approximately two-thirds of the coal mine spoil material is finer textured than sandy loam and one-third is of coarse-textured material and large rock fragments (Armiger et al., 1976).

In Florida, phosphate mining produces sand tailings that are nearly sterile and almost without plant nutrients (Hortenstine & Rothwell, 1972). Iron mine tailings from iron mines on Michigan's Upper Peninsula are finely crushed bedrock lacking organic matter and have a low plant nutrient status (Sherton & Duffek, 1970).

Overburden above mineable layers of kaolin in Georgia consists of relatively uniform layers of sands, sandy loams, sandy clays, and clays (May et al., 1973). The spoil material is a mixture of all strata, including nonmerchantable kaolin and viscous clays. Textural classes of the spoil banks range from sand to clay.

Color will influence surface temperature. A study conducted in Pennsylvania on coal stripmine spoils with air temperatures 30 to 35°C showed that level spoil surfaces reached maximum temperatures of 50 to 55°C on the lightest colored materials and 65 to 70°C on the darkest materials (Deely & Borden, 1973). The average temperature difference observed between the lightest and the darkest spoil was approximately 15°C.

Weak soil structure is a deficiency of mined lands as compared to undisturbed soils. This deficiency would be more serious when clay-textured soils are used for cultivated crops. If these lands are to be used for cultivated crops, sandy loam surface textures would be preferred because of the ease of tillage (Grube et al., 1974).

C. Environmental Problems Associated with Disturbed Areas

Unless managed properly during and after disturbance, there are a number of environmental problems that can occur with disturbed areas. Some of these are: i) stream pollution; ii) floods; iii) landslides; iv) loss of fish and wildlife habitats; v) unreclaimed land; vi) erosion; and vii) impairment of natural beauty (Grim & Hill, 1974).

Stream pollution will result from the drainage of water containing acid and salts into the streams where oxidizable pyrites are exposed. It was estimated by the U.S. Public Health Service in 1962 that approximately 2.9 million metric tons of acid are discharged annually into streams from active and abandoned underground mines and stripmines in the Appalachian Region (Udall, 1966). It was thought that not more than 25% of the acid problem can be attributed directly to strip mining.

Floods can result from increased rainfall runoff and from sediments occupying space and restricting flow in rivers, reservoirs, lakes, and ponds. Erosion is closely associated with the sedimentation problem, resulting in the loss of valuable soil or the removal of materials that could be improved by weathering. This continually keeps exposing unweathered toxic materials on some of the coal mine spoils.

In a 1965 Department of Interior study, it was estimated that almost 3,726 km of streams and 6,070 ha of impoundments in 20 states could provide suitable fish and wildlife habitat if acid pollution were sufficiently reduced. Many of the unreclaimed disturbed areas do not cover sufficient areas to create a problem of food for wildlife.

Landslides can be a problem both in surface mining of hilly areas and in the construction of highways. Water contributes to slides by adding weight to the soil, reducing the shear strength of soil, and lubricating the sliding plane. The factors about which information is needed to analyze a landslide for corrective measures are the geology and geological structure of the area and the location of seepage strata (Baker, 1953). If the source of water is wet-weather springs or surface runoff, diversion ditches can be used. If the water source is water-bearing strata, the source must be located and the water removed by ditching or tiling. Measures should be taken to avoid landslides during earth movement. These include proper compaction of fills and the removal of surface and subsurface water through proper drainage. In the mountains of eastern Kentucky, relatively stable spoilbanks are possible when the fill bench widths are controlled (Weigle, 1966). The steeper the slope, the narrower the fill bench must be. Also, the block-cut method of mining eliminates the placement of spoil on the outer slopes (Grim & Hill, 1974).

Unreclaimed land that is completely barren shows little or no improvement with time because without vegetation organic matter is not being added to aid in the soil-forming processes. Once stabilized with a good vegetative cover, the erosion and sedimentation can be controlled.

III. EFFECTS ON WATER TABLE

A. Quantity

Land disturbances may affect the water table by changing the infiltration rate and by fracturing the water table into discontinuous units. Fracturing would be encountered with deeper disturbances such as mining and deep excavations. The infiltration of rainfall into areas may be changed by slope changes, type of vegetation established, and compaction of the area by grading with machinery.

There are a number of interrelated factors that influence ground water reestablishment after land has been disturbed (Herring, 1977). These are: i) climate; ii) overburden characteristics; iii) aquifer coefficients; iv) topography; v) recharge and discharge; and vi) water use. Climate affects the amount of precipitation and temperature. The intensity of rainfall will influence the infiltration of water into the soil. Also, when the surface of the soil is frozen, the infiltration is zero. Temperature will influence evapotranspiration and thereby influence the amount of water available for recharge.

In mining and other land disturbances, the disturbed materials have different properties than the undisturbed. There will generally be a layered sequence which is changed during mining operations. Originally unconsolidated materials are often mixed with broken rock material. However, due to state and federal legislation, there is increased interest in replacing the unconsolidated materials, including topsoil, back in their original sequence in the spoil.

In open pit mining where aquifers are disrupted, the water drains into the pits and has to be pumped out. The spoil that is placed where the minerals have been removed in certain cases becomes an aquifer. The levels of water in the open pits will correspond to the water table in the spoil materials. Land disturbance by surface mining will adjust to a new steady-state condition that will be dependent upon the hydrological character of the mine spoils (Van Voast et al., 1976). Available information indicates that coal mine spoils will transmit as much or more water than the coal beds they replace, and that water in them will be confined against strata of less conductive materials (Van Voast et al., 1976; Herring, 1977).

Studies with a coal mine refuse pile 16 ha in size composed largely of low-grade coal, shales, and clay indicated that approximately 25% of the applied water infiltrated into the pile and later emerged as a base flow (Good et al., 1970). The refuse pile maintained a steady outflow from an internal storage capacity which was replenished by rainfall.

The changes in topography by land disturbances such as area surface mining are well known. In the past, typical changes were the formation of a series of ridges of cast overburden and valleys and final-cut pits. The depressions filled with water after mining was completed. State and federal reclamation laws require extensive grading, and in some states the land must be returned to the approximate original contour. As a result, the extensive grading of the spoils is more compacted and slopes on the reclaimed areas are more gentle, but are also much longer. This eliminates the depressions that allow water to accumulate and percolate into the spoil. Also, the final-cut areas are filled with overburden from mining and materials from the highwalls. The net result of this mining and reclamation practice is to cause more surface runoff from reclaimed areas following precipitation than would have occurred under some of the older practices. Recharge to the water table is essentially derived from local precipitation which percolates through the soil and overburden materials.

The transformation of impermeable layers such as rock into broken, unconsolidated, very permeable spoil will probably result in a greater ground water recharge and stream runoff. In Indiana, it was found that mining one-half of a watershed had apparently increased ground water recharge and runoff approximately four times (Harza Eng. Co., 1975). However, if disturbance increases the surface flow of water from large watersheds and reduces water infiltration through compaction of high-clay content materials on the surface, ground water recharge may be decreased and the water tables lowered.

B. Quality

When land disturbances fracture rock formations, the water percolating through these materials may become highly mineralized. In Appalachia, mining has drained water from rocks and the pyrite associated with the coal beds are exposed to air (Emrich & Merritt, 1969). Oxidation of the pyrite produces high iron and sulfate concentration and a low pH in the water. Some of this water may enter the ground water. If the acid water moves through reactive basic materials such as beds of limestone, the acid will be neutralized but the iron and sulfate concentration will be increased.

The movement of polluted water into the ground-water system will depend on the hydrology of the area and the extent of the disturbance. In Pennsylvania, oil and gas wells have been reported to act as a conduit system, permitting acid mine drainage to move downward from the stripmines to underlying aquifers (Emrich & Merritt, 1969).

Surface mining will result in changes in water quality of the aquifers in the spoil (Pietz et al., 1974; Herring, 1977). Chemical qualities of mined-land ground water will be influenced by climate, type of overburden material, topography, mining and reclamation practices, and time. In Kentucky, the total dissolved solids changed from approximately 325 mg/liter before mining to 2,600 mg/liter in the spoil aquifer (Herring, 1977). Significantly higher electrical conductivity, and concentrations of Cl^-, SO_4^{2-} Kjeldahl N, K, Na, Ca, Mg, Zn, Cd, Cr, Ni, Mn, Pb, and Fe, were found in mine-land ground waters in Illinois (Pietz et al., 1974). In Pennsylvania, the ground waters in and about a coal stripmine were found to have a higher dissolved solids content than the ground waters from the unmined areas (Caruccio, 1968).

A study in progress in Ohio will evaluate the effect of surface mining for coal on the hydrology and water quality of watersheds (Hamon et al., 1977). To evaluate water quality and quantity before, during, and after mining, a series of wells at different depths was established in the watersheds.

IV. PURPOSE OF RECLAMATION AND ALTERNATIVES

A. Reclamation

The term *reclaimed* is not clearly defined, and variation occurs in its definition from state to state (Arminger et al., 1976). Reclamation standards frequently change with the advent of new knowledge and techniques. What is satisfactorily reclaimed by a given set of standards may be entirely unsatisfactory by another or revised set of standards.

In cases where disturbed areas are to have a vegetative cover established, reclamation consists of grading the area to conform to some specified topography, and then seeding or planting. In many of the surface-mined areas, the surface configuration would be the approximate original contour, or a flatter topography in the hilly and mountainous areas.

Probably the most damage from unreclaimed lands in humid areas results from erosion and sedimentation. This damage is reflected in reduced carrying capacity of streams and drainage ditches, filled reservoirs and navigation channels, destroyed habitat for fish and other aquatic life, increased flood crest, degradation of water recreation facilities, increased industrial and domestic water treatment costs, destruction of crops, premature aging of lakes by enrichment of the water with silt-carried plant nutrients that promote algae growth, and reduced productivity of flood plain soils.

The barren lands resulting from stripmining for coal are often referred to as *orphan lands* because no person or organization has the responsibility for restoring the vegetation on these lands. The first law controlling stripmining of coal was enacted by West Virginia in 1939. Indiana followed in 1943, Pennsylvania in 1945, Ohio in 1947, Kentucky in 1954, and Maryland in 1955 (Barrows, 1974). By 1977, 40 states had reclamation laws. In 1977, federal legislation entitled "Surface Mining Control and Reclamation Act of 1977" was enacted to apply rules and regulations to the reclamation of coal surface mined lands. It is expected that state governments will assume responsibility for administering this law.

B. Alternatives for Reclamation

The chemical and physical properties of disturbed areas will influence their use. However, in many instances properties of areas are such that more than one land use can be realized by manipulation of the materials during earth-moving operations. In cases where the properties indicate one land use, these areas can usually be ameliorated for another use.

Through the use of preplanning and an orderly placement of materials in the disturbed profile, these lands can be made to best suit the intended use. For surface mining where large quantities of overburden are moved, some of the improvements that can be made are: i) level land in hill areas; ii) water impoundments; iii) obtain higher concentrations of weatherable minerals in the new soils; iv) increase levels of plant-available P, Ca, Mg, and K; v) obtain deeper profile for plant roots; and vi) obtain boulder-free surfaces (Grube et al., 1974).

Where proper planning and reclamation have been accomplished, a number of uses can be made of disturbed lands. Due to the rather large number of hectares of these areas, interest is increasing in using lands for agricultural purposes. Topography and soil characteristics will have a large influence on the types of land use. The land must be suitable for the operation of machinery if row crops, forages, and improved pastures are to be produced. Where steeper topography is encountered, these areas would largely be limited to forestry, wildlife habitat, and recreational purposes.

For agricultural uses, Kohnke (1950) listed land with a 70% maximum slope as suitable for forestry, 25% maximum slope as suitable for improved pasture, and 10% maximum slope as suitable for rotation crops. With the use of no-tillage, slopes greater than 10% could be used for row crops.

Unless proper preplanning is done, the soils are likely to have a lower fertility status and moisture-holding capacity than undisturbed soils. However, the lower moisture-holding capacity may be compensated for by a deeper rooting zone. If these shortcomings exist, proper management practices such as applying fertilizers, light grazing, and using soil conservation practices will be needed to keep the land productive.

V. STABILIZATION AND EROSION CONTROL

A. Stabilization of Areas

Unstable areas are subject to wind or water erosion and landslides in the steeper areas. Unless stability is established at the start, poor conditions for the establishment of plants will result and high erosion rates will result in sustained off-site damages.

In hilly terrain where conditions already exist for landslides, surface grading, the removal of earth from the base of a hill, improper compaction of fill materials on slopes, and failure to provide adequate drainage can cause slides. The potential for slides is great where mining is conducted on steep slopes and the spoil placed on the outslopes of the hill. The loose spoil absorbs large quantities of water, which acts as a lubricant between the spoil and the original vegetated surface and also adds an increased load on unstable bearing surfaces. In West Virginia, it was found the maximum stable outer slope for surface mining was approximately 66% in a predominantly sandstone bedrock and 50% in a predominantly shale area (W. Va. Div. of Reclam., 1975). By proper drainage and controlled spoil placement, landslides can largely be prevented.

B. Erosion Control Measures

In drastically disturbed lands where large quantities of earth are moved, the vegetation, and, to some extent, the type of materials and the degree and length of slope, can be controlled. Where large areas are to be disturbed over long periods of time, such as in surface mining, one good rule for erosion and sediment control is to plan earth-moving activities in such a manner as to minimize the amount of disturbed area to be exposed for a minimum amount of time before reclamation is completed.

Sediment yield from active mining and construction sites yield approximately 200 times more sediment than grassland (USEPA, 1973). Sediment yield from disturbed areas is the result of erosion and the movement of this eroded material from the area. Since sediment causes considerable off-site damages, it is essential that steps be taken for its control.

The objective of an erosion control plan should be to control or eliminate sediment pollution during the earth-moving operations and until the area has been reclaimed. This is particularly important in the mining industry where large areas are affected and also where topsoil or other materials are stockpiled for later use as a top-dressing.

Erosion control measures available for use are: (i) sediment basins and holding ponds; (ii) terraces and diversions; (iii) mulches; (iv) vegetation; (v) chemical stabilizers; and (vi) changing the contour. The type of control used will largely depend upon the operation and the area.

Sediment retention basins and holding ponds can be effectively utilized for collection and holding of eroded material before it reaches the main streams, thus preventing damage to areas downstream. Sediment basins should be located on all drainageways carrying concentrated flows from the disturbed areas. They should be located as close to the sediment source as possible and before the drainageways reach the main streams. These structures must be properly designed to prevent failures. A discussion on types of sediment control basins can be found in the reference by Grim and Hill (1974).

Terraces break steep long slopes with benches that will decrease runoff velocities and help trap sediment. Terrace design involves the proper spacing and location of the terraces and the design of a channel with adequate capacity (Frevert et al., 1955). The runoff must be removed at nonerosive velocities in both the channel and the outlet. Diversions can be used to divert water away from an area or as a waterway. They should be stabilized with a vegetative cover and, if large concentrated flows are encountered, they can be stabilized with rip-rap. Tillage operations or roughing the surface along the contour will help reduce erosion.

Mulching with organic materials such as straw, hay, woodchips, wood fiber, and other natural and manufactured products can be used to provide short-term soil stabilization. Mulch is also used in the establishment of a vegetative ground cover to protect the seedbed from excessive erosion prior to germination of the seed and until the vegetation becomes established. Mulch lowers the surface temperatures, which can be critical for dark materials, and helps conserve soil moisture during seedling establishment. Mulches can be produced in-situ by the seeding of small grains in the fall, and summer annuals in the spring and summer (Bennett et al., 1976). Herbicides can be used to kill the spring and summer annuals. These residues make a satisfactory mulch for broadcast seedings of grasses and legumes in the fall or spring without additional seedbed preparation (Armiger et al., 1976).

A good vegetative cover will reduce erosion by: (i) reducing the raindrop impact; (ii) decreasing runoff velocity; (iii) binding soil particles by the plant roots; (iv) increasing water infiltration; and (v) reducing soil moisture, which increases storage capacity (Frevert et al., 1955). A quick establishment of thick stands of grasses and legumes will largely prevent erosion on long slopes. Tree plantings require several years before a vegetative canopy is established and the surface has sufficient litter cover to prevent erosion. Under these conditions, other erosion control measures, such as mixed plantings of grasses and legumes with trees, mulches, or chemical stabilizers, can be used.

Generally a 2:1 (50%) slope is the maximum slope upon which vegetation can be established and maintained satisfactorily (USEPA, 1976). Maximum vegetative stability cannot be attained on slopes steeper than 3:1 (33%).

Chemical soil stabilizers are designed to coat and penetrate the soil surface and bind the soil particles together. They are used to provide erosion control and soil stabilization during seedling establishment. They are used both in place of a temporary mulch material and in conjunction with organic materials to act as a mulch tack and soil binder. Chemical stabilizers generally work best on dry and highly permeable soil that is not subject to concentrated flows. When used alone, many of these chemicals do not meet the three functions of a mulch: to conserve moisture, moderate soil temperature, and provide soil stability (Arminger et al., 1976).

Since the degree and length of slope has an influence on erosion, a change in the shape of the area to a more level topography will help reduce erosion. In the mountain-top removal method of mining, the entire top of the mountain is removed to the mineral seam. This leaves relatively large, flat areas in the mountainous regions where the mineral seams are shallow enough for the entire hilltop to be removed. Also, in mining operations where entire hilltops are removed and the land restored to approximate original contour, as required by some state laws, the steeper slopes in many cases can be reduced.

VI. VEGETATION ADAPTABILITY AND REVEGETATION TECHNIQUES

The revegetation of disturbed areas is one of the most important means of preventing accelerated soil erosion. However, the effectiveness of vegetation in stabilizing the soil will be limited unless existing and future site conditions are adequately assessed in the selection of plant materials and proper establishment and management practices are followed.

A. Plant Species

Each plant species has its own growth characteristic that determines its value in stabilizing soil. Grasses and legumes are the most effective plant materials for controlling erosion in the early stages of reclamation. However, trees and shrubs have an advantage of providing a permanent or semipermanent cover on disturbed areas with little or no additional care and maintenance. The selection of the proper species for planting should be based on chemical and physical properties of the soil material, topographic influences, climate, use, and management planned. Many studies have been conducted to determine adaptation of various plant species for revegetation and stabilization of stripmined lands in the eastern U.S. (Bennett, 1971; Brown, 1971; Vogel & Berg, 1968; Ruffner, 1973; Tyner & Smith, 1945; Grandt & Lang, 1958). Recommended plant species to use in a given area can be obtained from the Soil Conservation Service or the state Cooperative Extension Service.

1. GRASSES

Grasses are especially well suited for stabilizing mine spoil and other disturbed areas. They are relatively easy to establish on various site conditions and provide a quick and dense ground cover. Many of the grass species are economically important and can be used for forage production.

Among grass species, a degree of adaptability to various site conditions exist. Species are available for different exposure conditions and for planting during the spring, summer, and fall. Some species are highly tolerant of wet soils, while others do well on dry, droughty soils. Certain species are better adapted to acid soils than others (Vogel & Berg, 1968). In large, surface-mined areas, it will usually be desirable to seed a mixture of grasses because of the variability in the soils. Grass species commonly used in seeding disturbed areas are listed in Table 2.

2. LEGUMES

Several legume species have been used successfully to revegetate disturbed lands in the eastern U.S. (Table 3). Some legumes are grown alone and others do better in combination with grasses and other legumes. The use of legumes on disturbed areas is extremely important since they supply an available source of N for nonleguminous plants, increase the N content of soils, serve as soil builders, and aid in protecting soil surfaces from erosion. Before legumes are planted, the seed should be treated with the proper inoculant to insure the presence of nitrogen-fixing bacteria needed to carry out N fixation. It is important that an effective and efficient strain of rhizobium be used with a particular legume.

Table 2—Commonly used grasses for revegetation of disturbed lands.†

Name	pH range‡	Remarks
Bahiagrass	4.5–7.5	Tall extensive root system. Maintained at low cost once established.
Barley	5.5–7.8	Cool season annual. Provides winter cover.
Bermudagrass	4.5–7.5	Does best at pH of 5.5 and above. Grows best on well-drained soils.
Bluegrass, Canada	4.5–7.5	Does well on acid or droughty soils, or soils too low in nutrients to support good stands of Kentucky bluegrass.
Bluegrass, Kentucky	5.5–7.0	Shallow root; best adapted to well-drained soils of limestone origin.
Bluestem, big	5.0–7.5	Strong, deep rooted, and short underground stems.
Bluestem, little	6.0–8.0	Dense root system; grows in a clump and more drought tolerant than big bluestem.
Bromegrass, smooth	5.5–8.0	Tall, sod forming, drought and heat tolerant.
Canarygrass, reed	5.0–7.5	Excellent for wet areas, ditches, waterways, gullies. Can emerge through 6 to 8 inches of sediment.
Deertongue	3.8–5.0	Very acid tolerant; drought resistant. Adapted to low fertility soils.
Fescue, creeping red	5.0–7.5	Grows in cold weather. Wide adaptation. Slow to establish.
Fescue, tall	5.0–8.0	Does well on acid and wet soils of sandstone and shale origin. Drought resistant. Ideal for lining drainage channels.
Lovegrass, weeping	4.5–8.0	Grows well on infertile soils. Short-lived in northeastern U.S.
Millet, foxtail	4.5–7.0	Requires warm weather during the growing season. Cannot tolerate drought.
Oats	5.5–7.0	Bunch forming. Winter cover. Requires nitrogen for good growth.
Oatgrass, tall	5.0–7.5	Short-lived perennial bunchgrass, matures early in the spring. Good on sandy and shallow shale sites.
Orchardgrass	5.0–7.5	Tall-growing bunchgrass. Good fertilizer response. More summer growth than timothy or bromegrass.
Redtop	4.0–7.5	Tolerant of wide range of soil fertility, pH, and moisture conditions.
Rye, winter	5.5–7.5	Winter hardy. Survives on coarse, sandy spoil. Temporary cover.
Ryegrass, annual	5.5–7.5	Excellent for temporary cover. Can be established under dry and unfavorable conditions. Quick germination; rapid seedling growth.
Ryegrass, perennial	5.5–7.5	Short-lived perennial bunchgrass. Longer lived than weeping lovegrass or tall oatgrass.
Sudangrass	5.5–7.5	Summer annual for temporary cover. Drought tolerant. Cannot withstand cool, wet soils.
Switchgrass	5.0–7.5	Withstands eroded, acid, and low-fertility soils. Kanlow and Blackwell varieties most often used. Drainageways and terrace outlets.
Timothy	4.5–8.0	Stands are maintained perennially by vegetative reproduction. Shallow, fibrous root system. Usually sown in a mixture with alfalfa and clover.
Wheat, winter	5.0–7.0	Requires nutrients. Poor growth in sandy and poorly drained soils. Use for temporary cover.

† Source: USEPA, 1976.
‡ Optimum growth occurs within these ranges.

Table 3—Commonly used legumes for revegetation of disturbed lands.†

Name	pH range‡	Remarks
Alfalfa	6.5–7.5	Requires high fertility and good drainage.
Clover, Alsike	5.0–7.5	Good for seeps and other wet areas. Dies after 2 years.
Clover, red	6.0–7.0	Should be seeded in early spring.
Clover, white	6.0–7.0	Stand thickness decreases after several years.
Flatpea	5.0–6.0	Seed is toxic to grazing animals. Good cover.
Lespedeza, common	5.0–6.0	Low-growing wildlife feed. Acid tolerant.
Lespedeza, Korean	5.0–7.0	Less tolerant of acid soils than common lespedeza.
Lespedeza, Sericea	5.0–7.0	Woody, drought tolerant, seed should be scarified.
Sweetclover, white	6.0–8.0	Tall growing. Produces high yields.
Sweetclover, yellow	6.0–8.0	Tall growing. Can be established better than white sweetclover in dry conditions.
Trefoil, birdsfoot	5.0–7.5	Survives at low pH. Plant with a grass.
Vetch, crown	5.5–7.5	Excellent for erosion control. Drought tolerant. Winter hardy.
Vetch, hairy	5.0–7.5	Adapted to light sandy soils as well as heavier ones. Used most often as a winter cover crop.

† Source: USEPA, 1976.
‡ Optimum growth occurs within these ranges.

3. TREES AND SHRUBS

Several tree species are available for planting on disturbed areas (Table 4). Trees have limited use as soil stabilizers during early periods of growth. Erosion control with trees only may take up to 10 years before the canopies close and an effective cover is established. Their shallow, nonextensive root system, as well as their slow and upright growth, severely limits their effectiveness in stabilizing soil. Trees should be used in combinations with grasses and legumes to provide a long-term protective cover. On large tracts of land not suited for forage or row crop production, trees may be the only logical choice of vegetation where a future income is anticipated from the land.

Various shrubs are available for planting on disturbed areas. Although they are primarily useful as wildlife habitats and for esthetic purposes, some species have been developed that can help stabilize the soil. Due to its spreading characteristic, bristly locust will develop a complete canopy in 2 to 3 years under good growing conditions. Other commonly used shrubs on disturbed areas are listed in Table 4.

B. Climate and Soil Requirements for Various Species

Precipitation and temperature are two major factors in determining the climate of any region. Climate factors such as temperature, sunlight exposure, wind exposure, and rainfall have to be considered when selecting plant species. Some of the herbaceous species are adapted to cool growing seasons, whereas others are better suited to warm seasons and will not survive the winters in the north. These characteristics have been pointed out in Tables 2, 3, and 4. Species that are not tolerant of droughty conditions should not be selected for use in such areas.

Table 4—Commonly used trees and shrubs for revegetation of disturbed lands.†

Name	Remarks
Trees, conifers	
Virginia pine	Tolerant of acid spoil and low moisture supply. Slow development. Good for wildlife.
Pitch pine	Deep rooted and very acid tolerant. Deer like small seedlings. Plant in bands or blocks.
Loblolly pine	Rapid early growth. Marketable timber products. Susceptible to ice and snow damage.
Scotch pine	Good for Christmas trees if managed properly. Can be planted on all slopes.
Shortleaf pine	Some insect problems. Will sprout freely if cut or fire killed when young. Good marketable timber.
Austrian pine	Can be planted on all slopes. Plant in bands or blocks.
Japanese larch	Should be planted on unleveled and noncompacted spoil. Provides good litter.
Red pine	Sawfly damage in some areas. Plant on all slopes.
Eastern red cedar	Tall, narrow growth. Best on dry, sandy soils.
Mugho pine	Survives on acid spoil. Develops slowly. Low growing. Good cover for wildlife.
Trees, hardwoods	
Black, locust	Can be direct seeded. Wide range of adaptation. Rapid growth; good leaf litter. Use mixed plantings.
Bur oak	Better survival with seedling transplants than acorns.
Cottonwood	A desirable specie for large-scale planting. Good cover and rapid growth.
European black alder	Rapid growing. Wide adaptation. Nitrogen fixing, nonlegume. Can survive pH 3.5 to 7.5.
Green ash	Use on all slopes and graded banks with compact loams and clays. Plant in hardwood mixture.
Hybrid poplar	Rapid growth. Good survival at low pH. Marketable timber after 20 years. Cannot withstand grass competition.
Red oak	Makes slow initial growth. Good survival, plant on upper and lower slopes only.
European white birch	Makes rapid growth on mine spoil. Poor leaf litter and surface coverage.
Sycamore	One of the most desirable species for planting. Poor ground cover.
Shrubs	
Amur honeysuckle	Good for wildlife. Shows more vigor and adaptability as plants mature.
Bristly locust	Extreme vigor. Thicket former. Good erosion control. Rizomatous, 1.5–2.1 M.
Autumn olive	Nitrogen-fixing nonlegume. Good for wildlife. Can survive pH 3.5. Wide adaptation. Up to 15 feet tall.
Bicolor lespedeza	Can be established from planting and direct seeding. Ineffective as a ground cover for erosion control.
Indigo bush	Has high survival on acid spoil. Leguminous. Not palatable to livestock. Thicket former. Slow spreader.
Japanese fleeceflower	Grows well on many sites, especially moist areas. Excellent leaf litter and canopy protection.
Silky dogwood	Grows best on neutral spoil pH. Can withstand pH range of 4.5 to 7.0. Poor surface protection.
Tatarian honeysuckle	Upright shrub, forms clumps. Does well on well-drained soils. Takes 2 years for good cover.

† Source: USEPA, 1976.

C. Soil Amendments

Detailed analyses of the soil material from a disturbed area are essential to the planning of a revegetation program (Bennett, 1971). These analyses can be used to determine the presence or absence of elements essential for plant growth and to determine the presence or absence of soluble elements that may be toxic to plants. In most cases, limestone and a complete fertilizer (N, P, and K) are needed for plant establishment and growth on most acid spoils in the eastern U.S. (Bennett et al., 1976).

Sewage sludge and power plant fly ash are materials that have been tested for use on acid mine spoils (Peterson & Gschwind, 1973; Capp & Gillmore, 1973). These materials can contribute significantly to plant nutrition on disturbed lands for vegetative cover and crop production.

Studies have been conducted to evaluate the use of sewage sludge in the reclamation of acidic coal mine spoils (McCormick & Borden, 1973; Sutton, 1973; Montague & Hill, 1976; Hill et al., 1977). Generally, large quantities of sewage sludge are required to establish vegetation on toxic spoils. Bennett et al. (1976) reported tall fescue yields on an acidic spoil (pH 3.2) with conventional fertilizer were approximately 1,233 kg/ha as compared to over 11,362 kg/ha where 224 metric tons/ha of sewage sludge were applied.

Lejcher (1972) reported 303.7 metric tons/ha increased the pH on an acidic coal mine spoil from 2.31 to 6.39. Sewage sludges contain considerable N and P but are low in K. Besides the addition of plant nutrients, considerable amounts of organic matter are added which will increase water-holding capacity and improve soil tilth.

Because of the wide range of soil materials and landscapes, recommendations for application of sludges on drastically disturbed lands must be considered on a site-by-site basis.

Fly ash is a by-product of coal-burning, power-generating plants, and has a potential use as a soil amendment for disturbed lands. Some advantages attributed to the use of fly ash are neutralization of acidity, added plant-available P, lowered spoil density, and increased subsurface moisture when applied at the rate of 136 metric tons/ha (Plass & Capp, 1974). As is the case with many of the so-called waste materials, caution must be exercised in the use of fly ash because, in some cases, the material may decrease plant growth due to (i) boron toxicity, (ii) injury from a high concentration of soluble salt, (iii) phosphorus deficiency induced by reaction of soil phosphorus with hydroxides and oxides of aluminum and iron in fly ash, or (iv) nutrient deficiencies resulting from high soil pH (Bennett et al., 1976).

D. Equipment

With suitable topography, disturbed lands can be seeded with farm equipment that is used for making forage seedings, such as cultipacker seeders, band seeders, and grain drills. Also, tree planters are available for transplanting young tree seedlings. On rough terrain, heavier equipment will be needed than that normally used on undisturbed lands. In the rough terrain, other types of equipment, such as hydroseeders and aerial equipment, can be used. In any seeding, a good seed-to-soil contact should be made for good seed germination.

In areas where there is freezing and thawing of the soil, a broadcast seeding can be made on the surface and the seeds covered by the freezing and thawing action. In some of the steep areas the seed may be broadcast on rough surfaces and seed coverage can be accomplished by mechanical manipulation or rainfall.

E. Time of Seeding

Seedings on disturbed lands should be made as soon as possible after the site has been graded to control erosion. Where large tracts of land are continually being graded, as is the case in stripmining, it is desirable to extend planting seasons. By selection of plant species, it is possible to establish a plant cover throughout the growing season. However, biennial and perennial species should be seeded in time to become well established before winter. The recommended seeding dates should be followed as closely as possible in order to obtain successful stands.

In a study conducted in eastern Kentucky, Vogel (1974) found herbaceous vegetation could be seeded on spoilbanks any time between 1 March and 1 November to provide a protective ground cover to control erosion. Davis (1973) evaluated fall versus spring planting of 10 coniferous tree species and 5 hardwood shrub species on strip-mine spoils in western Pennsylvania and found that spring planting is better than fall planting, especially on acid spoils.

LITERATURE CITED

Armiger, W. H., J. N. Jones, and O. L. Bennett. 1976. Revegetation of land disturbed by strip mining of coal in Appalachia. ARS-USDA, ARS-NE-71.

Baker, R. F. 1953. Analysis of corrective action for highway landslides. Proc. Am. Soc. of Civil Eng. May, Vol. 79, Separate Pap. no. 190.

Barnhisel, R. I. 1977. Reclamation of surface mined coal spoils. Kentucky Agric. Exp. Stn. CSRS I AG no. D-E 762.

Barrows, H. L. 1974. ARS research on strip mine reclamation. p. 98. In Proc. 28th Annu. Meet., 10–14 Feb. 1974, Natl. Assoc. of Conserv. Dist., Houston, Tex. Natl. Assoc. of Conserv. Dist., League City, Tex.

Bennett, O. L. 1971. Grasses and legumes for revegetation of strip-mined areas. p. 23–25. In D. M. Bondurant (ed.) Proc. Revegetation and Economic Use of Surface-mined Land and Mine Refuse Symp., 2–4 Dec. 1971, School of Mines, West Virginia Univ., Pipestem State Park, W. Va. West Virginia Univ., Morgantown, W. Va.

Bennett, O. L., W. H. Armiger, and J. N. Jones, Jr. 1976. Revegetation and use of eastern surface mine spoils. p. 195–215. In Land application of waste materials. Soil Conserv. Soc. of Am., Ankeny, Iowa.

Berg, W. A. 1973. Evaluation of P and K soil fertility tests on coal-mine spoils. p. 93–104. In R. J. Hutnik and G. Davis (ed.) Ecology and reclamation of devastated land. Vol. I. Gordon and Breach Sci. Publ., Inc., New York.

Berg, W. A., and W. G. Vogel. 1968. Manganese toxicity of legumes. Res. Pap. NE 1119. U.S. Forest Serv., Washington, D.C.

Brown, J. H. 1971. Use of trees for revegetation of surface mined areas. p. 26–28. *In* D. M. Bondurant (ed.) Proc. Revegetation and Economic Use of Surface-mined Land and Mine Refuse Symp., 2–4 Dec. 1971, School of Mines, West Virginia Univ., Pipestem State Park, W. Va. West Virginia Univ., Morgantown, W. Va.

Byrnes, W. R., and J. H. Miller. 1973. Natural revegetation and cast overburden properties of surface-mined coal lands in southern Indiana. p. 285–306. *In* R. J. Hutnik and G. Davis (ed.) Ecology and reclamation of devastated land. Vol. I. Gordon and Breach Sci. Publ., Inc., New York.

Capp, J. P., and D. W. Gillmore. 1973. Soil-making potential of powerplant fly ash in mined-land reclamation. p. 178–186. *In* Research and Applied Technol. Symp. on Mined-Land Reclamation, 7–8 Mar. 1973, Natl. Coal Assoc., Pittsburgh, Pa. Bituminous Coal Res., Inc., Monroeville, Pa.

Carruccio, F. T. 1968. An evaluation of factors affecting acid mine drainage production and the ground water interactions in selected areas of western Pennsylvania. p. 107–151. *In* 2nd Symp. on Coal-Mine Drainage Res., 14–15 May 1968, Coal Ind. Advis. Comm., Pittsburgh, Pa. Bituminous Coal Res., Inc., Monroeville, Pa.

Davis, Grant. 1973. Comparison of fall and spring planting on strip-mine spoils in the bituminous region of Pennsylvania. p. 525–538. *In* R. J. Hutnik and G. Davis (ed.) Ecology and reclamation of devasted land. Vol. I. Gordon and Breach Sci. Publ., Inc., New York.

Deely, D. J., and F. Y. Borden. 1973. High surface temperatures on strip-mine spoils. p. 69–79. *In* R. J. Hutnik and G. Davis (ed.) Ecology and reclamation of devastated land. Vol. I. Gordon and Breach Sci. Publ., Inc., New York.

Emrich, G. H., and G. L. Merritt. 1969. Effects of mine drainage on groundwater. Ground Water 7(3):27–32.

Frevert, R. K., G. O. Schwab. T. W. Edminister, and K. K. Barnes. 1955. Soil and water conservation engineering. John Wiley and Sons, Inc., New York.

Good, D. M., V. T. Ricca, and K. S. Shumate. 1970. The relation of refuse pile hydrology to acid production. p. 145–151. *In* 3rd Symp. on Coal Mine Drainage Res., 19–20 May 1970, Coal Ind. Advis. Comm., Pittsburgh, Pa. Bituminous Coal Res., Inc., Monroeville, Pa.

Grandt, A. F., and A. L. Lang. 1958. Reclaiming Illinois strip coal land with grasses and legumes. Univ. of Illinois Agric. Exp. Stn. Bull. 628.

Grim, E. C., and R. D. Hill. 1974. Environmental protection in surface mining of coal. Environ. Prot. Technol. Ser. EPA-670/2-74-093.

Grube, W. E., Jr., R. M. Smith, J. C. Sencindiver, and A. A. Sobek. 1974. Overburden properties and young soils in mined lands. p. 145–149. *In* 2nd Res. and Applied Technol. Symp. on Mined-Land Reclamation, 22–24 Oct. 1974, Natl. Coal Assoc., Louisville, Ky. Natl. Coal Assoc., Washington, D.C.

Grube, W. E., Jr., R. M. Smith, R. M. Singh, and A. A. Sobek. 1973. Characterization of coal overburden materials and minesoils in advance of surface mining. p. 134–152. *In* Research and Applied Technol. Symp. on Mined-Land Reclamation, 7–8 Mar. 1973, Natl. Coal Assoc., Pittsburgh, Pa. Bituminous Coal Res., Inc., Monroeville, Pa.

Hamon, W. R., Faz Haghiri, and Darwin Knochenmus. 1977. Research on the hydrology and water quality of watersheds subjected to surface mining. p. 37–39. *In* 5th Symp. on Surface Mining and Reclamation, 18–20 Oct. 1977, Natl. Coal Assoc. and Bituminous Coal Res., Inc., Louisville, Ky. Natl. Coal Assoc., Washington, D.C.

Harza Engineering Company. 1975. Hydrologic effects on strip mining—Busseron watershed, Indiana. Soil Conserv. Serv., USDA, AG-103-00160.

Herring, W. C. 1977. Groundwater re-establishment in cast overburden. p. 71–87. *In* 7th Symp. on Coal Mine Drainage Res., 18–20 Oct. 1977, Natl. Coal Assoc. and Bituminous Coal Res., Inc., Louisville, Ky. Natl. Coal Assoc., Washington, D.C.

Hill, R. D. 1978. Methods for controlling pollutants. p. 687–704. *In* F. W. Schaller and Paul Sutton (ed.) Reclamation of drastically disturbed lands. Am. Soc. of Agron., Madison, Wis.

Hill, R. D., K. R. Hinkle, and R. S. Klingensmith. 1977. Reclamation of orphan mined lands with municipal sludges—case studies. Mining Pollut. Control Rep. Indus. Environ. Res. Lab., Cincinnati, Ohio.

Hortenstine, C. C., and D. F. Rothwell. 1972. Use of municipal compost in reclamation of phosphate-mining sand tailings. J. Environ. Qual. 1:415–418.

James, A. L., and M. Morst. 1965. Control of acidity of tailings dams and dumps as precursor to stabilization by vegetation. J. S. Afr. Inst. Min. Metall. 65:489–495.

Kohnke, Helmut. 1950. The reclamation of coal mine spoils. Adv. Agron. 2:317–349.

Knabe, Wilhelm. 1964. Methods and results of strip-mine reclamation in Germany. Ohio J. Sci. 64(2):75–105.

Lejcher, F. R. 1972. Strip mine reclamation utilizing treated municipal wastes. p. 371–376. *In* Proc. Natl. Symp. of Watersheds in Transition, 19–22 June 1972, Am. Water Resour. Assoc. and Colorado State Univ. Am. Water Resour. Assoc., Urbana, Ill. Ft. Collins, Colo.

May, J. T., H. E. Johnson, H. F. Perkins, and R. A. McCreey. 1973. Some characteristics of spoil material from kaolin clay strip mining. p. 3–14. *In* R. J. Hutnik and G. Davis (ed.) Ecology and reclamation of devasted land. Vol. I. Gordon and Breach Sci. Publ., Inc., New York.

Mays, D. H., and G. W. Bengston. 1974. Fertilizer effects on forage crops on strip-mined land in northeast Alabama. TVA, Natl. Fertilizer Dev. Center Bull. Y-74.

McCormick, L. H., and F. Y. Borden. 1973. Percolate from spoils treated with sewage effluent and sludge. p. 239–250. *In* R. J. Hutnik and G. Davis (ed.) Ecology and reclamation of devastated land. Vol. I. Gordon and Breach Sci. Publ., Inc., New York.

Montague, A., and R. D. Hill. 1976. The potential for using sewage sludge and compost in mine reclamation. Mining Pollut. Control Rep. Indus. Environ. Res. Lab., Cincinnati, Ohio.

Peterson, J. R., and J. Gschwind. 1973. Amelioration of coal mine spoils with digested sewage sludge. p. 187–196. *In* Research and Applied Technol. Symp. on Mined-Land Reclamation, 7–8 Mar. 1973, Natl. Coal Assoc., Pittsburgh, Pa. Bituminous Coal Res., Inc., Monroeville, Pa.

Pietz, R. I., Cecil Lue-Hing, and J. R. Peterson. 1974. Groundwater quality at a strip-mine reclamation area in west central Illinois. p. 124–144. *In* 2nd Res. and Applied Technol. Symp. on Mined-Land Reclamation, 22–24 Oct. 1974, Natl. Coal Assoc., Louisville, Ky. Natl. Coal Assoc., Washington, D.C.

Plass, W. T., and J. P. Capp. 1974. Physical and chemical characteristics of surface mine spoil treated with fly ash. J. Soil Water Conserv. 23:119–121.

Riley, C. V. 1973. Chemical alterations of strip-mine spoil by furrow grading-revegetation success. p. 315–331. *In* R. J. Hutnik and G. Davis (ed.) Ecology and reclamation of devastated land. Vol. II. Gordon and Breach Sci. Publ., Inc., New York.

Ruffner, J. D. 1973. Projecting the use of new plant materials for special reclamation problems. p. 233–242. *In* Res. and Applied Technol. Symp. on Mined-Land Reclamation, 7–8 Mar. 1973, Natl. Coal Assoc., Pittsburgh, Pa. Bituminous Coal Res., Inc., Monroeville, Pa.

Sherton, S. G., and Ralph Duffek. 1970. Establishing vegetation on iron mine tailings. J. Soil Water Conserv. 25:227–230.

Smith, R. M. 1971. Properties of coal overburden that influence revegetation and economic use of mine soils. p. 5–6. *In* D. M. Bondurant (ed.) Revegetation and economic use of surface-mined land and mine refuse. West Virginia Univ., Morgantown.

Smith, R. M., W. E. Grube, Jr., Thomas Arkle, Jr., and A. A. Sobek. 1974. Mine spoil potentials for soil and water quality. Environ. Prot. Technol. Ser. EPA-670/2-74-070.

Smith, R. M., A. A. Sobek, Thomas Arkle, Jr., J. C. Sencindiver, and J. R. Freeman. 1976. Extensive overburden potentials for soil and water quality. Environ. Prot. Technol. Ser., EPA-600/2-76-184.

Smith, R. M., E. H. Tyron, and E. H. Tyner. 1971. Soil development on mine spoil. West Virginia Univ. Agric. Exp. Stn., Bull. 604T.

Struthers, P. H. 1964. Chemical weathering of strip-mine spoils. Ohio J. Sci. 64(2):125–131.

Sutton, P. 1970. Reclamation of toxic coal mine spoilbanks. Ohio Rep. 55(5):99–101.

Sutton, P. 1973. Establishment of vegetation on toxic coal mine spoils. p. 153–158. *In* Res. and Applied Technol. Symp. on Mined-Land Reclamation, 7–8 Mar. 1973, Natl. Coal Assoc., Pittsburgh, Pa. Bituminous Coal Res. Inc., Monroeville, Pa.

Tyner, E. H., and R. M. Smith. 1945. The reclamation of the strip-mined coal lands of West Virginia with forage species. Soil Sci. Soc. Am. Proc. 10:429–436.

Udall, S. J. 1966. Study of strip and surface mining in Appalachia. U.S. Dep. of Interior, Washington, D.C.

U.S. Department of Agriculture. 1974. Our land and water resources current and prospective supplies and uses. Econ. Res. Serv., Washington, D.C.

U.S. Department of Interior. 1974. Mineral yearbook. 1972. Vol. 1, Bur. of Mines House Doc. 93-22.

U.S. Environmental Protection Agency. 1973. Methods for identifying and evaluating the nature and extent of nonpoint sources of pollutants. EPA-4030/9-73-014, Washington, D.C.

U.S. Environmental Protection Agency. 1976. Erosion and sediment control, surface mining in the eastern U.S., EPA Technol. Transf. Sem. Publ., Vol. 1, EPA-625/3-76-006.

Van Lear, D. H. 1971. Effects of spoil texture on growth of K-31 tall fescue. USDA For. Serv. Res. Note NE-141. 7 p.

Van Voast, W. A., R. B. Hedges, and J. J. McCermott. 1976. Hydrologic aspects of strip mining in subbituminous coal fields of Montana. p. 160–172. *In* 4th Symp. on Surface Mining and Reclamation, 19–21 Oct. 1976, Natl. Coal Assoc. and Bituminous Coal Res., Inc., Louisiville, Ky. Natl. Coal Assoc., Washington, D.C.

Vimmerstedt, J. P., and P. H. Struthers. 1968. Influence of time and precipitation on chemical composition of spoil drainage. p. 152–163. *In* 2nd Symp. on Coal Mine Drainage Res., 14–15 May 1968, Coal Ind. Advis. Comm., Pittsburgh, Pa. Bituminous Coal Res., Inc., Monroeville, Pa.

Vogel, W. G. 1974. All-season seeding of herbaceous vegetation for cover on Appalachian strip mine spoils. p. 175–188. *In* 2nd Res. and Applied Technol. Symp. on Mined-land Reclamation, 22–24 Oct. 1974, Natl. Coal Assoc., Louisville, Ky. Natl. Coal Assoc., Washington, D.C.

Vogel, W. G., and W. A. Berg. 1968. Grasses and legumes for cover on acid strip mine spoils. J. Soil Water Conserv. 23:89–91.

Weigle, W. K. 1966. Spoil bank stability in eastern Kentucky. Min. Congr. J. 52(4):67–75.

West Virginia Division of Reclamation. 1975. Drainage handbook for surface mining. West Virginia Dep. of Nat. Resour., Charleston, W. Va.

35 Reclaiming Disturbed Lands in Arid Regions[1]

A. D. DAY

University of Arizona
Tucson, Arizona

K. L. LUDEKE

Cyprus Pima Mining Company
Tucson, Arizona

I. INTRODUCTION

Large areas of land are disturbed throughout the semiarid and arid regions of the world. The removal of earth, rock, and overburden materials in the recovery of underground minerals disturbs millions of hectares annually. The abandonment and/or relocation of agricultural farm lands and livestock feeding operations leaves vast areas in need of reclamation. Interstate, intrastate, and local highway networks occupy large geographical areas that must be rehabilitated.

II. CLASSIFICATION AND CHARACTERIZATION

Disturbed lands in semiarid and arid regions may be classified into three principal categories: (i) mineral wastes, (ii) agricultural areas, and (iii) highway slopes and medians.

The United States Bureau of Solid Waste Management estimated that by 1980 the United States mineral industries will be generating between 2 and 4 billion metric tons of solid wastes annually (Frey, 1970). Mineral wastes consist of barren overburden, submarginal grade ore, milling wastes, and strip-mine spoils. The total accumulated mineral solid wastes in the United States has been reported to be about 22.7 billion metric tons covering 800,000 ha of land (Donovan et al., 1976).

In the dry regions of the world poorly managed agricultural land has created pollution problems (Love, 1970). Large acreages of crop land adjacent to cities in the irrigated areas of the southwestern U.S. have been taken out of cultivation because of the increased demand for water for

[1] Contribution from the Arizona Agric. Exp. Stn., University of Arizona, Tucson, Arizona; and Cyprus Pima Mining Co., P. O. Box 7187, Tucson, Arizona. Approved for publication as Arizona Agric. Exp. Stn. J. Article no. 2679.

domestic purposes. Overgrazed rangelands in dry climates are subject to wind and water erosion. The most serious impact of mineral wastes on air quality occurs in semiarid and arid regions, such as the southwestern U.S. (Donovan et al., 1976). The relocation of cattle feeding operations in low-rainfall areas creates odor and dust pollution problems for nearby population centers.

The development of federal, state, and local highway systems disturb many acres of land throughout both arid and humid regions in the United States (Howlett, 1967). In dry climates, dust pollution from barren road cuts, medians, and highway slopes is associated with many multicar accidents each year.

III. RECLAMATION PURPOSES AND ALTERNATIVES

The primary purpose for reclaiming disturbed lands in semiarid and arid regions is to stabilize the spoil material and prevent it from being moved by winds and flash floods, the common transporting agents in dry climates (Fig. 1). After disturbed areas have been stabilized, a second objective for reclamation is to revegetate the barren soil materials, so that they will blend into the surrounding landscape and minimize visual pollution. Donovan et al. (1976) reported that disturbed soil materials have a serious impact on air quality, especially in arid regions.

The principal methods used to stabilize disturbed land areas in dry climates are physical, chemical, and vegetative. Physical stabilization, with the use of topsoil and/or overburden soil materials, has been used successfully to control air pollution along highways and adjacent to mining operations (Janbu, 1954). Chemical stabilization has been effective in reducing wind and water erosion of mineral wastes (Struthers, 1964). Vegetative

Fig. 1—Tailing pond slopes illustrating erosion. Unstabilized tailing pond slopes are subjected to severe wind and water erosion that can reduce the success of vegetative stabilization.

stabilization has been successfully used along highways (Richardson, 1967), in vacant urban areas (Wyman, 1972), on over-grazed rangelands (Bridges, 1942), and around mining operations (LeRoy & Keller, 1972).

Federal laws are being developed to regulate disturbed land pollution throughout the United States (King, 1974). Federal agencies have been cooperating with mining industries, throughout the United States, in the organization of legal requirements dealing with the reclamation of mineral wastes (Carter, 1974). A number of states in the continental U.S. have formulated strict state regulations governing the exploration of potential mineral deposits, current mining operations, and the disposal of mineral wastes (Colorado House of Rep., 1976). Local restrictions are frequently imposed upon mineral industries that constantly monitor potential sources of land, air, and water disturbance (King, 1974).

Disturbed land pollution has stimualted a variety of aesthetic concerns and objections throughout the semiarid and arid regions of the world (Epler, 1974). Various professional organizations outside and within the mining and metalurgical industries have expressed specific aesthetic concerns (Ludeke, 1973a). Public servants in local communities have worked in cooperation with professional organizations in the development of local guidelines regulating the environment.

IV. SPOIL REPLACEMENT AND REVEGETATION TECHNIQUES

Spoil replacement in semiarid and arid regions has been accomplished on a number of disturbed lands by capping with topsoil and/or overburden soil material. Ludeke (1973a) found that it was possible to cap copper tailing pond berms with a layer of desert topsoil to control wind erosion of the tailing soil material. This physical means of stabilization did not, however, control water erosion in southern Arizona, where flash floods frequently occur. Capping tailing ponds with desert soil did allow indigenous plant species to reestablish themselves on the area, at least partially, over a period of years.

Janbu (1954) illustrated that unstable waste materials may be effectively contained by using physical techniques. In some instances, a layer of overburden, which was the surface soil material, was placed over loose soil materials to prevent their movement by wind and water erosion. Since the surface of many overburden soil materials is extremely rough and rocky, it may be difficult for native plant species to establish themselves on unstable soil materials that have been contained in this manner.

Struthers (1964) observed that petroleum biproducts (bitumen emulsions) have been used to partially stabilize fine soil materials; however, this form of chemical stabilization provided only temporary control and it was a very expensive way to contain waste materials. Chemical stabilization involves the reaction of a chemical reagent with the waste material to form an air- and water-resistant crust or surface layer (Dean et al., 1974). Chemicals may be effective stabilization agents in areas where physical and vegetative techniques are impractical due to poor accessability and rough and rocky terrain.

LeRoy and Keller (1972) noted that various plant species have been used to stabilize a variety of disturbed land areas throughout the world for many years. Astrup (1951) stated that the following characteristics should be considered in choosing plants for erosion control and uniform ground cover on disturbed soils: (i) plants must have the ability to thrive under the existing conditions of soil, moisture, and exposure; (ii) rapid growing species should be chosen since they provide earlier protection; (iii) plants producing the most mulch are most effective in controlling erosion; (iv) plants should be resistant to insects and diseases; and (v) plants that are poisonous to man or animals should not be used. Augustine (1966) noted that stabilizing critical areas where fine sand is the primary soil material is best accomplished with grasses and mulches. Knabe (1964) observed that, when shrubs and trees were transplanted in critical areas without grasses, small rodents invaded the areas and destroyed the newly transplanted species. Hafenrichter (1967) stated that grasses, which have fibrous root systems, were more effective in improving soil aggregation than were legumes. Coupland (1958) reported that great variation occurs between the water requirement of different plant species in relation to the amount of dry matter produced. Generally, in areas where erosion has exposed subsoils which have a low level of plant nutrients, a high rate of fertilization is required for successful plant establishment. A thick, vigorous vegetative cover is better able to prevent water erosion, resist the ravages of diseases, and stand abuse from wild life traffic than is a shallow-rooted sod of non-vigorous plants (Friday, 1961). Vigorous grass covers are more attractive and offer more competition to weed growth than do sparse stands of grass (Salfer, 1948). Plants require many essential elements for growth, which are absorbed from the soil by the root system and then transported into the upper parts of plants. Nitrogen (N) is found to be the most frequent limiting fertilizer element for the establishment of vegetative cover on disturbed soil sites (Curry et al., 1964).

The Arizona Agricultural Experiment Station (AES) has considerable experience in the reclamation of copper mining wastes. Four different soil materials (tailing, tailing-overburden, overburden, and local desert soil) were identified in copper mining wastes (Ludeke, 1973b). The physical and chemical properties of these four soil materials were studied and described by Ludeke et al. (1974). Day and Ludeke (1973) proposed the use of vegetative stabilization of copper mining wastes. They also noted that straw from cereal grains planted on copper tailing with a "Hydroseeder" and incorporated into the top 15 cm of tailing with a "Sheepfoot Roller" resulted in the most desirable soil material for plant growth. Copper mining wastes were successfully rehabilitated in Arizona by establishing a number of different plant species on their surfaces. Day et al. (1975) reported that perennial grasses were more easily established and maintained than most other plants in tailing soil material from copper mines, due to their drought tolerance and low water requirements. Day and Ludeke (1973) found that giant

Fig. 2—A tailing pond berm stabilized with barley. After the tailing pond is constructed, barley may be planted to stabilize the slope and provide organic matter, which may be incorporated into the surface soil material to provide a suitable soil medium for the establishment of perennial grass species. The barley plant has a fibrous root system that is capable of holding the fine tailing soil material in place.

bermudagrass can be used effectively to stabilize copper mine tailing disposal-berms in southern Arizona. Day et al. (1976) suggested that forage for livestock can be produced by growing barley on copper mining wastes if the crop is heavily fertilized with commercial, inorganic fertilizers, and supplied with irrigation water throughout the growing season (Fig. 2).

Edgerton et al. (1975) used municipal sewage effluent and sewage sludge to provide plant nutrients in the revegetation of coal mine spoils in Pennsylvania. Jones et al. (1975) used a two-step seeding system, successfully, to revegetate surface coal mine spoils in West Virginia. Small grain species were seeded the first year to give a quick ground cover and to produce a straw mulch into which perennial legume and grass species were interseeded the second year. Gould et al. (1972) inventoried the soil characteristics and vegetation production of areas leased by Western Coal Company for strip mining in New Mexico. They observed that Indian ricegrass, fourwing saltbush, and winterfat grew best on coal spoils in New Mexico. Thames and Crompton (1974) discovered that the texture of coal mine spoils in northern Arizona was similar to the texture of a clay loam soil with little structure.

The Arizona AES has current experiments to identify and evaluate plant species adapted for the revegetation and stabilization of coal strip mine spoils on the Black Mesa of northern Arizona. There is an urgent need to develop effective cultural practices for growing plant species for protection against wind and water erosion and to provide food and cover for wild-life on all disturbed land areas (Thames & Verma, 1975).

When revegetation is utilized in the reclamation of disturbed lands in low-rainfall areas, planting dates are determined by rainfall and temperature. In the southwestern U.S., winter-grown plant species used to revegetate copper mining wastes are usually planted in December because temperature and rainfall conditions are ideal during that period. Over-grazed rangelands and agricultural areas that have been taken out of commercial production are usually reseeded during periods when moisture and temperature conditions are ideal for the particular plant species being used to revegetate these areas (Wright, 1975). Ground covers for highway slopes also are usually seeded when moisture and temperature conditions are optimum.

The preparation of the surface of most mineral wastes for revegetation usually includes some form of cultivation and leveling to break up surface crusts and clods, fill in depressions, and produce a firm seedbed suitable for planting. Barren rangelands and other agricultural areas must be cleared of objectionable debris and cultivated to a depth of 5 to 10 cm to provide a suitable soil medium for seeding. Highway slopes and medians are usually prepared for planting by breaking up the compacted surface area to provide a suitable seedbed for seed germination and seedling emergence (Wakefield et al., 1976).

Since most mineral wastes are very low in plant nutrients, careful attention must be given to their correct fertilization prior to planting. It is usually necessary to apply both macro- and micronutrients to mining wastes prior to planting and throughout the growing season. Under natural rainfall conditions, nitrogen (N), phosphorus (P), and potassium (K) are usually applied in granular form, using a fertilizer spreader. Under irrigated conditions, N, P, and K are normally injected into the irrigation water at each irrigation. Livestock manures and municipal wastes are frequently used in the revegetation of mineral wastes to provide sufficient micronutrients for plant growth. Nitrogen, phosphorous, and potassium are the principal plant nutrients applied to agricultural areas and highway slopes prior to re-seeding. The foregoing fertilizers are normally applied in granular form with a fertilizer spreader.

In most semiarid and arid regions of the world supplemental irrigation water is required to establish effective plant vegetation on mineral wastes, abandoned agricultural areas, barren overgrazed rangelands, and highway slopes. The irrigation water used in the revegetation of the foregoing areas is often obtained from wells located adjacent to the disturbed sites. Sprinkler irrigation is essential when complete vegetative cover is required over the entire surface of the exposed site. In instances when random vegetation may be sufficient, drip irrigation is frequently employed.

Hydroseeding is a relatively new technique that has been used effectively in the reseeding of disturbed areas in dry climates. In hydroseeding, the fertilizer, seed, soil conditioners, mulching materials, wood fiber, and irrigation water are all applied in a single operation. The principal advantages of hydroseeding are: (i) it can be used to seed successfully unaccessible sites, (ii) it is a rapid method of planting disturbed areas, (iii) it provides a more uniform coverage than most conventional reseeding methods, and (iv) since the fertilizer, seed, mulch, and soil amendments are all applied simultaneously, the overall cost of reseeding is reduced.

V. VEGETATION ADAPTABILITY

Vegetation adaptability is essential in the successful reclamation of all disturbed lands in semiarid and arid regions. Since indigenous plant species are adapted to the area in question, they are frequently used in the initial stages of a revegetation program; however, their extremely slow growing characteristics require many years to obtain satisfactory ground cover. Although indigenous plants and cacti may be used to stabilize disturbed areas in the southwestern U.S., the sparse vegetation that they provide is inadequate to effectively control wind and water erosion (Fig. 3). The Arizona Interagency Range Technical Sub-Committee (1969) reported that introduced species are frequently preferred to indigenous species in disturbed land reclamation because of their higher adaptability, greater availability of seed, and lower cost. Most introduced perennial species are difficult to establish on barren waste soil materials. When sprinkler irrigation was

Fig. 3—Tailing pond berms stabilized with indigenous plants and cacti. Although indigenous plants and cacti may be used to stabilize tailing ponds, the uneven vegetation that they provide is inadequate to effectively control wind and water erosion. The high density plant cover that grasses provide is more desirable and successful in stabilizing fine tailing soil material than indigenous plants and cacti.

Fig. 4—A tailing pond berm stabilized with perennial plant species. When perennial grasses, shrubs, and trees are grown together on tailing ponds, they provide an appealing and permanent form of vegetation that effectively stabilizes tailing soil material.

available, a number of annual, agronomic plant species have been used effectively during the initial stages of revegetation of disturbed soil materials in dry climates. Important advantages of planting annual agronomic species, such as barley, on a newly disturbed soil material is that these species germinate quickly, produce impressive vegetative growth, and add large amounts of organic matter for incorporation into the surface. Ludeke et al. (1974) reported that mulching with organic matter improved the germination and seedling establishment of most perennial grass species because the addition of organic matter to disturbed soil materials improved the soil moisture conditions around germinating seeds, insulated the soil surface against excessive heat and cold, and bound the soil particles together around established seedlings (Fig. 4).

Ludeke (1976) developed barley composite crosses by selecting parents from a diverse group of genotypes collected from throughout the world. These materials comprised a wide genetic base from which he selected specific genotypes for use in solving unusual environmental problems on disturbed land areas and which could be useful in semiarid and arid regions of the world.

VI. ENVIRONMENTAL CONSIDERATIONS

National, state, and local agencies are promoting the beautification of all disturbed land areas throughout the semiarid and arid regions of the world. Careful selection of adapted plant species has enabled the mineral in-

Fig. 5—A landscaped service road. Carefully selected plant material provides attractive land-scaping for essential service roads in disturbed land areas.

dustries in the southwestern U.S. to revegetate their waste materials with a variety of plants that maintain the natural desert beauty (Ludeke, 1973a). Howard (1972) reported that a variety of plants have been used effectively in the beautification of a number of problem areas along interstate, intra-state, and local highway systems in the low-rainfall areas in the western U.S. (Fig. 5). Robinette (1972) pointed out that carefully selected plants have been used to reduce visual pollution on disturbed lands in metropoli-tan areas. For example, strategically located plants have enhanced the appearance of parks, parking lots, and city streets.

When a variety of adapted grass, shrub, and tree species are used in the revegetation and stabilization of disturbed soil materials in semiarid areas, they provide an optimum sanctuary for wildlife. Since a symbiotic relation-ship usually exists between plants and animals on reclaimed soil materials; the presence of animal life often introduces new plant species. Since effec-tive revegetation encourages the encroachment of wildlife, the reclamation of barren and overgrazed agricultural areas has created a sportsman's para-dise in a number of western states.

All disturbed soil materials must be carefully prepared to support plant life. Initial vegetation usually consists of annual species that germinate quickly, produce rapid vegetative growth, and add large amounts of organic

Fig. 6—A vegetatively stabilized tailing pond. The effective stabilization of tailing soil material using a variety of carefully selected plant species converts unsightly copper wastes into attractive man-made structures that blend into the surrounding landscape. These tailing pond slopes are vegetatively stabilized and are no longer susceptible to wind and/or water erosion.

matter to the soil surface. The incorporation of organic matter into the surface soil material provides a loose soil medium that has adequate soil moisture-holding capacity to permit the establishment of slow-germinating and slow-growing perennial grass species. Following the establishment of perennial grasses, adapted shrubs and trees may be included to add variety and create vegetation that blends nicely into the surrounding landscape (Fig. 6). If the foregoing procedures are followed carefully they result in an attractive, nearly maintenance-free climax vegetation on the disturbed land areas throughout the semiarid and arid regions of the world.

ACKNOWLEDGMENTS

The authors express their appreciation to Mr. Eric H. Sorensen for his assistance with the literature review. To all others who contributed in any way and are not mentioned here, the authors are deeply grateful.

LITERATURE CITED

Arizona Interagency Range Technical Sub-Committee. 1969. Guide to improvement of Arizona rangeland. Arizona Agric. Exp. Stn. Bull. A-58.

Astrup, M. H. 1951. Ground cover plants and planting. Highw. Res. Bd. Roadside Dev. 11: 34–38.

Augustine, M. T. 1966. Using vegetation to stabilize critical areas in building sites. Soil Conserv. 32(4):78–80.

Bridges, J. O. 1942. Reseeding practices for New Mexico ranges. New Mexico Agric. Exp. Stn. Bull. 291. 48 p.

Carter, L. J. 1974. Strip mining: a practical test for President Ford. Science 186:1190.

Colorado House of Representatives. 1976. Colorado mined land reclamation act HB-1065. State of Colorado, Act 32, Title 34. 29 p.

Coupland, R. T. 1958. The effect of fluctuations in water upon the grasslands of the Great Plains. Bot. Rev. 24:274-339.

Curry, R. L., L. E. Foote, O. N. Andrews, and S. A. Jackobs. 1964. Lime and fertilizer requirements as related to turf establishments along the roadside. Highway Res. Rec. 53: 1-25.

Day, A. D., and K. L. Ludeke. 1973. Stabilizing copper mine tailing disposal berms with giant bermudagrass (*Cynadon doctylon* L.). J. Environ. Qual. 2:314-315.

Day, A. D., K. L. Ludeke, G. O. Amaugo, and T. C. Tucker. 1976. Copper mine wastes: good potential as medium for growing livestock forage. Engin. Min. J. 177(2):90-92.

Day, A. D., T. C. Tucker, and K. L. Ludeke. Sept.-Oct. 1975. Vegetation and mine wastes. Agric. College Counc. for Environ. Studies, ACCES 1(1):2-3.

Dean, K. C., R. Havens, and M. W. Glantz. 1974. Methods and costs for stabilizing fine-sized mineral wastes. U.S. Dep. of Interior, Bur. of Mines Rep. RI-7896. 26 p.

Donovan, R. P., R. M. Felder, and H. H. Rogers. 1976. Vegetative stabilization of mineral waste heaps. USEPA. Environ. Prot. Technol. Ser. EPA-600/2-76-087.

Edgerton, B. R., W. E. Sopper, and L. T. Kardos. 1975. Revegetating bituminous strip-mine spoils with municipal wastewater. Compost Sci. 16(4):20-25.

Epler, W. C. (ed.). 1974. Cyprus Pima Mining Company wins top Arizona environmental award. Pay Dirt 422:1, 3.

Frey, D. N. 1970. Policies for solid waste management. U.S. Dept. of Health Educ. and Welfare. Bur. of Solid Waste Manage. Bull. 75. 65 p.

Friday, D. T. 1961. Advancement in erosion control protection by fertilizer. 20th Short Course on Roadside Dev., Ohio State Univ. and Ohio Dep. of Highways 1:106-115.

Gould, W. L., V. W. Howard, and K. A. Valentine. 1972. Soil characteristics, biotic composition, and vegetative production of areas leased by Western Coal Company for strip mining near Fruitland, New Mexico. New Mexico Agric. Exp. Stn., Spec. Rep. no. 20. 49 p.

Hafenrichter, A. L. 1967. Lassoing the west's rampaging dunes. p. 317-321. *In* J. Hayes (ed.) USDA, Yearbook of Agric.

Howlett, M. R. 1967. Roads that fit our environment. p. 222-225. *In* J. Hayes (ed.) USDA, Yearbook of Agric.

Howard, G. S. 1972. Plants for problem areas of the western states. p. 154-167. *In* J. Hayes (ed.) USDA, Yearbook of Agric.

Janbu, H. 1954. Stability analysis of slopes with dimensionless parameters. Harvard Soil Mechanics Ser. 46:29-54.

Jones, J. N., Jr., W. H. Armiger, and O. L. Bennett. 1975. A two-step system for revegetation of surface mine spoils. J. Environ. Qual. 4:233-235.

Knabe, W. 1964. Strip-mine reclamation in Germany. Ohio J. Sci. 64(2):75-105.

King, T. (ed.). 1974. Executive summary legislative government task force. 2nd Arizona Symp. Energy-Environment-Growth, 13 Dec. 1974, Carefree, Ariz. Off. of the Governor, Arizona State Fuel and Energy Office, Phoenix, Ariz. 111 p.

LeRoy, J. C., and H. Keller. 1972. How to reclaim mined areas, tailing ponds, and dumps into valuable lands. World Min. 8:34-41.

Love, R. M. 1970. The rangelands of the western U.S. Sci. Am. 222:88-96.

Ludeke, K. L. 1973a. Vegetative stabilization of tailing disposal berms. Min. Congr. J. 59(1): 33-38.

Ludeke, K. L. 1973b. Soil properties of materials in copper mine tailing dikes. Min. Congr. J. 59(8):30-37.

Ludeke, K. L. 1976. Evaluation and selection of spring barley (*Hordeum vulgare* L.) for the revegetation and stabilization of copper mine tailing disposal berms. Ph.D. Diss. Univ. of Arizona, Tucson. (Libr. Congr. Card no. Mic. 76-28222).

Ludeke, K. L., A. D. Day, L. S. Stith, and J. L. Stroehlein. 1974. Pima studies tailings soil makeup as prelude to successful revegetation. Eng. Min. J. 175:72-74.

Richardson, E. C. 1967. Let's keep our backroads beautiful. p. 237-239. *In* J. Hayes (ed.) USDA, Yearbook of Agric.

Robinette, G. 1972. Plants for easing visual pollution or ways to overcome ugliness. p. 22-27. *In* J. Hayes (ed.) USDA, Yearbook of Agric.

Salfer, F. J. 1948. Fertilizers, lime-mulches—their part in establishing roadside vegetation. 7th Short Course on Roadside Dev., Ohio State Univ. and Ohio Dep. of Highways 1(2): 10–25.

Struthers, P. H. 1964. Chemical weathering of strip-mine spoils. Ohio Sci. J. 64(2):125–131.

Thames, J. L., and E. J. Crompton. 1974. Reclamation studies on the Black Mesa. Prog. Agric. Agriz. 26(1):14–16.

Thames, J. L., and T. R. Verma. 1975. Coal mine reclamation on the Black Mesa and the four corners area of northeastern Arizona. p. 48–64. *In* M. K. Wali (ed.) Practices and problems of land reclamation in North America. Univ. of North Dakota Press, Fargo.

Wakefield, R. C., R. S. Bell, J. A. Jagschitz, A. J. Chapham, A. T. Dore, A. P. Nielsen, and B. C. Laskey. 1976. Establishment of roadside vegetation in Rhode Island. Rhode Island Agric. Exp. Stn. Bull. no. 416.

Wright, L. N. 1975. Improving range grasses for germination and seedling establishment under stress environments. p. 3–22. *In* R. S. Campbell and C. H. Herbel (ed.) Improved range plants. Soc. Range Manage., Range Symp. Ser. no. 1. Am. Soc. of Agron., Madison, Wis.

Wyman, D. 1972. Parks, malls, roadsides: public area plantings. p. 76–80. *In* J. Hayes (ed.) USDA, Yearbook of Agric.

section X

Integrated Land Use Planning and Plan Implementation

USDA Soil Conservation Service

X

36   Information Systems for Land Use Planning

CHARLES R. MEYERS, MICHAEL KENNEDY, AND R. NEIL SAMPSON

Office of Surface Mining and Reclamation, Washington, D.C.;
University of Kentucky, Lexington, Kentucky; and
Soil Conservation Service, USDA, Washington, D.C.,
respectively.

I. INTRODUCTION

Because of the finite nature of resources, it has become imperative that resource conservation and allocation decisions be made in a broader land use planning and management context. Ever-increasing competitive demands for resources now require a greater understanding of the effects of our resource-related decisions in the natural, social, and economic environment. Data, which will yield the types of information required for rational decisionmaking, are the foundation of this understanding. Determining data needs and developing data handling methodologies are required to support sophisticated analysis so that these management needs can be met (USDI, 1976).

To cope with the myriad of causes and effects encountered in the management, conversion, and use of land, the data that support planning will be at least partially processed by automated, information-handling equipment. The development and characteristics of such a computer-based tool—we call it a *Spatial Information System*—are discussed.

II. LAND USE PLANNING AND THE NEED FOR INFORMATION

A. Land Use Planning Defined

Throughout the literature and debates on land use, there is little consistency in the way people define the term *land use planning*. We enter the debate only long enough to define terms for this section of the monograph. We suggest that there are several processes commonly called *land use planning*. All affect the way in which land resources are used, but real differences exist. Confusion rises from lumping them all under one general heading.

One type of land use planning deals with lands that an individual, corporation, or agency manages, controls, or owns. An example is a farmer. Another is a federal land management agency, such as the U.S. Forest Service, the Bureau of Land Management, or the Tennessee Valley Authority. For reasons that seem appropriate (and/or for lack of a better term), we call this type of planning *land management planning.*

Another type of planning that commonly involves land resources is planning aimed at construction of a project: a building, a subdivision, or a new town. It may also be a flood control, irrigation, or highway project. The distinguishing feature of this planning is that the decisionmaker can envision the end product he seeks. Planning identifies the logical steps in building the project most efficiently. We term this type of planning *project planning.*

Finally, there is planning where governments make plans that guide the use of land resources owned by individuals, corporations, or functional agencies of government. Decisions are made through the political process instead of by an owner, a company, or a management agency. The end product sought is usually defined in such broad terms (a high quality environment, for example) that little actual guidance results. This type of planning involves public policies, rules, and regulations that guide how other people can manage or use their land. It is this process that we call *land use planning.*

B. Differences Between Types of Planning

The distinction between these three types of planning is not whether the planning is done in the private or public sector. In the public sector, at the state level, for example, land management planning may be done by an agency administering state lands, project planning by the highway department, and land use planning by a state planning agency. There is a similar separation of tasks at the local level among the park department, street department, and planning commission. In the private sector, we commonly find the first two types but not the third. Thus, land use planning, as we have defined it, is the governmental process that directly regulates or influences the use of land not owned or directly controlled by the planning government.

The differences between the types of planning do not make one type of planning any more important, relevant, or significant in developing strategies for improving the effectiveness of land use planning programs. Because goals must be developed differently and used differently throughout the process, because data needs are vastly different, and because the decision-making processes are totally different, proposals to transfer project planning techniques directly to land use planning are likely to be unsuccessful.

The key difference between land management planning and land use planning is embodied in the notion that land use planning regulates or influences land not owned or controlled by the planning government. Nearly every unit of government owns land of some sort. There obviously is a great deal of planning that goes into the management of these lands, but this planning seeks management options within an established and fairly stable framework of goals and objectives. For example, the dedication of an area as a park is accompanied by a commitment to certain management goals. Obviously, there is more than one way to manage a park, so a great deal of planning is needed, but this planning need not consider whether or not park land is the proper land use. That decision, already made, was a land use decision. Thereafter, planning is a management task.

Another difference is the degree to which policies and programs can be argued on idealogical grounds. Nearly every major issue in land use control can be argued on the basis that it represents governmental intervention in a traditionally private domain. This brings out fervent constitutional, libertarian, and pseudoreligious arguments that are both loud and influential. "Under these conditions," Richard Bolan noted, "simulation models, cost-benefit analyses, and the planner's traditional use studies are introduced to no avail" (Bolan, 1967). A land use decision, even in a small town, may involve several departments, as well as a broad range of private interests. Some of these may see threats to their well-being in the decision. Full cooperation among several groups may be essential to successful arrival at a decision, and such cooperation may be difficult to obtain.

Land use decisions often have secondary effects—difficult, if not impossible, to predict—that overshadow primary effects. An ordinance designed to bring about a desired growth pattern may alter complex economic relationships and cause different private decisions to be made, undermining the desired pattern.

In contrast, carrying out a land management plan is often within the ability of the single person or agency that made the plan. Following approval of the plan and appropriation of needed budgets, the plan can often be implemented with a minimum of help or coordination from other people or agencies. Accomplishment of the plan depends greatly on the quality of the plan, the availability of funds, the quality and accessibility of the data, and the ability of the land user or land management agency. The prospects of carrying out a substantial part of a land management plan are good—vastly better than for most land use plans—for reasons already discussed.

The major difference between project planning and land use planning is one of dealing with capital improvement projects as differentiated from living, changing communities. Project planning can and must identify a definite end-state. Whether the goal is a flood control dam, a highway, a new building, or an irrigation project, it must be carefully and expertly rendered into drawings and plans before construction begins. Good planning depends on being able to visualize successfully what is to be built, then planning a workable way of producing it in the appropriate time span.

Project planning deals best with inanimate, structural end products. Variables and uncertainties are few in relation to the known parameters. (Traffic counts may turn out differently than forecast; but the bearing strength of concrete, the proper slope of shoulders, and the amount of right-of-way needed are liable to remain constant.) Miscalculation of variables, therefore, is not likely to render the final project worthless.

Land use planning, on the other hand, deals with a community that must be thought of as a living system. A town (or county or state) is more than streets, buildings, pipes, and wires. It is the habitat of a dynamic human population in a changing environment, affected not only by physical elements but also by strong and constantly shifting economic and social forces. It does not reach a static end-state, then freeze in time and space. It remains a living, evolving, learning social structure. To forecast even a momentary end-state at some point in the future is to deal with few known "laws" and many variables, most of which are poorly understood. For a description of one land use planning technique, see Chapter 38, "A Case Study in Ecological Planning: The Woodlands, Texas."

From project planning comes the dictum "first plan, then implement." A good builder doesn't begin cutting boards and pounding nails until his house plans are complete. Transferring this idea to land use planning, however, doesn't work. Land use plans change the moment the first major decision is made on a development proposal.

In a fast-changing community the combination of private actions and public decisions, coupled with changing public concerns for environmental quality, economic activity, or social welfare, makes land use policies and goals very fluid. Planning and implementation comprise an interrelated, ongoing process. Day-to-day implementation decisions become a continuation of the planning process, a constant updating. Written plans serve as reminders of where the community was and where it wanted to go at one time. Such plans diminish in value unless they are revised regularly.

Project planning, however, is an integral part of land use planning. Highway networks, sewer systems, and power transmission networks are strong determinants of the land use patterns that emerge in any area. Land use planning is an effort to coordinate these networks so that a rational community pattern emerges. The coordination effort introduces the complexity of evaluating projects versus goals, needs, and opportunities. Again, the constant reevaluation of community goals sets land use planning apart. Land use planning decides whether or not a sewer system should be built. Project planning designs the system. There are many similarities that lead to confusion among the three types of planning. Land management planning is similar to land use planning in that neither can rely too heavily on the end-state concept appropriate to project planning. A pristine, primitive parkland evolves at a slow pace set by geological and biological processes, but it evolves nonetheless. A farm caught up in man's technical tinkering as well as changing social, cultural, political, and economic conditions changes more rapidly. Both the park and the farm are like the community in that they do not stop changing at some specific time, place, or condition. Planning methodologies based entirely on an accurate prediction of the end-state, therefore, are of dubious value.

Land management planning and project planning are similar in that both vest a great deal of control in a single decisionmaker. Resources are under ownership or management control in both, and decisions reached or designs made have an excellent chance of success. A rational planning process that evaluates alternatives within a given set of objectives is both possible and preferable. To a practitioner experienced in either land management or project planning, the continual political goal-testing that dominates land use planning seems to be a wasteful, inefficient effort that detracts from the resolution of issues or the creation of plans.

Presuming that there are indeed three separate planning processes and that they exhibit similarities that confuse people, the next question is "so what?". Is this merely quibling to define academic points that have little practical relevance? Or does it make a significant difference how you define the problem before you propose strategies, techniques, data collection, and solutions? Our belief is: There is a tremendous difference in the way each process is implemented and the tools needed for each. One of the most easily overlooked differences is the application of analysis and data handling technology to the three types of planning. Possibly part of the problem lies in the fact that, in addition to having differences, there are also some very fundamental similarities. For example, all three processes require spatial or geographic data, although each requires different formats, scales, and use of what may be in some cases the same data.

Past history has shown that, during implementation, all three of these processes have spent a large percent of resources, both dollars and man power, on the task of data collection and preparation of the data to be used for analysis and decisionmaking. The amounts spent, in many cases, have been so great that the actual use of the data—analysis and interpretation—has suffered because of time and budget limitations remaining after the data are ready for use. This points up to a growing need for a clear understanding of the type of planning and the techniques to be used for analysis before the process of data collection begins. In addition, a point that should never be forgotten—"There is more than one way to skin a cat"—almost always holds true when designing or selecting a data handling technique to be used.

III. THE PRIMARY NEED: A SYSTEM FOR THE ORGANIZATION OF DATA

The ability of a living system to sense change in its environment is one of the requisites for the survival of the system. People have many and varied ways of sensing their environments and either modifying them or changing location. A *group* will generally sense its environment through the observations of its members who pool information. Groups generally have the same options as individuals when the environment begins to turn sour: modify it or move. At the level of the *organization,* the problem becomes more difficult. This is particularly true if the organization is large and has responsibility for considerable territory. (An example of such a system is a region, state, or commonwealth.) Moving is out of the question; further, a number of difficulties arise in the system's determination of what its environment is, when changes occur to it, and what the effects of the changes are.

Perhaps only recently has it been necessary, due to the modifications of the environment by human endeavors, for states to develop more than a rudimentary sensing system. In any event, most states do not, today, have adequate mechanisms for comprehending their environments, either for making intelligent decisions about how they might be changed constructively or for dealing with changes that occur as a result of natural or human activity over time (Counc. State Gov., 1974).

The effect of man's activities on the natural environment has changed our mental model of the world from (A) to (B), as shown in Fig. 1. This change—the realization of "spaceship earth"—has occurred during the past decade and has had many profound and far-reaching effects.

A state has no eyes, ears, etc., at the system level. It must rely, basically, on the sensory powers of humans or the outputs of artifacts that humans construct. Then individuals or groups code the information for the governmental decider "subsystem." Such coding takes considerable time to prepare and deliver. Further, the number of types of coding is quite small; usually the coding is confined to written memoranda. In rare instances, the coding is oral ("Fern Creek's out of its banks."), and sometimes the coding is done with maps or photographs; however, such coding usually requires expert decoding before the decider subsystem can process it, and the form of the decoded information is simply recoded written memoranda.

Now we have reached a time when the speed at which humans can and do change a state's environment is threatening the well-being (or even survival) of both the humans and the state itself. Manifestations of this fact are the concern about environmental quality, resources, pollution, and land use planning. Many federal and state agencies are involved with these matters, which are generally seen, or at least legislated upon, as independent problems. If one views these problems in the context of a system, he finds that a prime cause of government's inability to deal with the problems is the lack

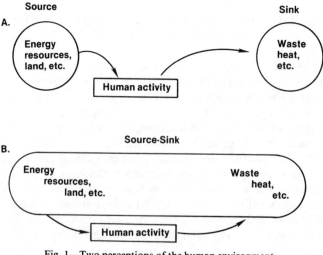

Fig. 1—Two perceptions of the human environment.

of ability to collate and comprehensively understand the great amount of environmental data already in existence (Larsen et al., 1978).

A. Spatial Data

An approach to solving this problem is to store environment data, based on its spatial location, in digital form in a computer's data base. Such a data base should be able to store any qualitative or quantitative information which can be related to a point, line, or area on the earth's surface (USDI, 1975b). A few examples of such data variables are: elevation, soil type, incidence of human illness, average pollution levels, and so on.

For purposes of this chapter the following definition, amplified by the discussion below, is issued. *Spatial data* are many symbols, graphics, or information, residing on some physical medium or device, that are associated with geographic or position locator. Spatial data, then, are any data which are referenced by their location in space. Some important classes of spatial data are:

1) Maps, which usually depict conditions, either of the environment or of a human population, on a physical analogue of the earth's surface.
2) Some photographic materails which can be related to specific geographic areas.
3) Files of information that contain spatial locators. Such files might be handwritten, printed, computer written, or computer readable.

In identifying any set of spatial data, three elements are essential: (i) the *data*, (ii) the physical *medium* on which they are recorded, and (iii) the spatial *locator* (USDI, 1975a). Some examples of each of these are shown in Table 1.

Table 1—Examples of data, spatial locators, and physical media.

Data

Slope of the earth's surface	Incidence of crimes	Location of state office
Average household income	Point of employment	facilities, historic markers
Flood plains	Average pollution levels	Natural gas usage
Land use and land cover	disappearances of persons	Electrical transmission line
Traffic flow averages	Employee work stations	corridors
Property values	Student enrollments	Core drillings
Wells	Broadcasting stations	Soil types
Slide-prone areas		

Spatial locators

Names (of towns, counties,	Geographic coordinates	Street addresses
schools, any entity of	(latitude-longitude, state	Mile stations (highway,
physical location)	plane coordinates, Carter	river)
Districts (census, school	coordinates, etc.)	
voting, fire, etc.)		

Physical media

Paper (maps, charts, tables,	Photographic film (aerial	Computer-readable tapes,
card files)	photography)	cards, or disks
Cathode ray display tubes		

B. Components of an Information System to Process Spatial Data

The problem of providing adequate environmental sensing and information storage is not an unsolvable one. In fact, many of the components of the solution mechanism already exist. Present now or available to many planning offices are:

1) Facilities, presently in use, for remote sensing of the entire surface area of the state at a useful resolution (e.g.), satellite sensing).
2) Techniques for high-resolution remote sensing (aircraft).
3) A large quantity of natural science data about the nature of the land surface and subsurface. Many of these data are in the form of maps.
4) More than adequate computing power or capacity to obtain it.
5) Devices capable of storing massive amounts of data.
6) Some expertise in storage of environmental and demographic data based on attempts at spatially oriented data bases for specific purposes (e.g., census work, areas of critical environmental concern, energy resource location, and so on).

There are, however, some components of an effective, overall environmental sensing mechanism lacking:

1) A comprehensive understanding by state governments of the relationship of the system's environment to the system itself. (A gross example: the failure to recognize that the "energy problem" and the "pollution problem" are simply instances of a single larger problem relating to resource allocation.) There is little comprehension of how a state can make use of the information it does possess in a systematic, rather than an ad hoc, way. This stems from a lack of perception of the state as a system in an environment. It is correctable by a more comprehensive set of information sources which present issues as systemic rather than individual problems.
2) A paragigm for the storage of data—data which may be considered as spatially distributed. More examples of variables whose data fit in this category are locations of energy sources, public facilities, soil types, crime and accident occurrences, census districts, labor and employment resources, historical landmarks, water usage, wildlife habitats, and geographic features. No adequate, common format exists for storing spatially distributed data such as these and hence, the state's capability for comparing such data is small and erratic. The problems of obtaining a common format relate to several subproblems:
   a) A large number of data are involved in even one variable. (A data base which deals with two- or three-dimensional, spatially distributed data will either (i) not cover much area, (ii) not have very high resolution, or (iii) be very large.)
   b) These data, if collected at all, are gathered by many agencies, each with a specific mission.

c) The data vary widely in the resolution with which they are available and required. This variability exists between types of data and within types, depending on spatial location (e.g., incidence of differing land use would be greater in urban than rural areas).

d) The data in a spatial-data base change over time; updating or replacing data becomes a major problem, as does estimating the accuracies of incorrect or out-of-date data.

e) Many of the data which do exist are in graphic form—photos and maps—which defy rigorous and intensive analysis and comparison. Interpreting graphic data is an art—and not a very well-developed one at that—if the objective is predicting the effects certain changes to the environment will produce.

3) Models that can analyze or simulate our complex environment. The models which deal with even a single variable such as water pollution and its effects are not yet adequate. Models which simulate more than a few variables in more than a superficial way are non-existent.

4) A political commitment to begin comprehensive energy, environmental, land use, and natural resource planning. For many reasons, a state tends not to deal with matters affecting its welfare until they reach semicrisis proportions (e.g., an estimated 60 to 80% of the incidence of human cancer is attributable to environmental conditions created by humans. But, after all, how many people contract cancer—now?).

C. Spatial Data Bases

We turn our attention now to elements and concerns related to a data base that consists of spatial data. Spatial data, most generally, are numbers and/or symbols depicting a characteristic or fact about something in the three-dimensional world for which location is of primary importance.

But all material objects and living systems have spatial location. So first we eliminate three general classes of conditions, facts, or objects that are *not* the focus of attention.

1) Conditions that change quickly in time—in a matter of hours, days, or even weeks. Pollution levels, weather, tides, will not be included, although average pollution at a point, climate, and ranges of tides could be included.

2) Objects that move about in space—like automobiles, wildlife, or people. However, data about flows of these objects past a certain point at a certain time might well be included.

3) Data in which the difference in spatial coordinates is small. *Small* is defined to be less than 1 m. The data discussed here would not, for example, reflect two changes of soil condition that occurred within 30 cm of each other. That is, the minimum resolution of the data is

1 m; the working resolution of the best systems presently operating is larger by two orders of magnitude (Oak Ridge Natl. Lab., 1971).

D. Spatial Data Bases—Inherent Difficulties

There are not many spatial data bases around compared to the large number of nonspatial data bases in existence in government and the private sector. Despite their clear applicability to the resource management field, they have not successfully materialized very often (USDI, 1975d). There are several reasons for their scarcity.

1) The simplest reference that can be made in spatial data base is to a point. But no material object is ever at just one point. Many of the things we deal with are either lines, areas, or volumes, so the referencing system becomes more complicated.

2) The spatial data base stores information about the continuum of two- or three-dimensional space. There are no neat methods, similar to methods used for associating discrete items like cars with license plate numbers, that can provide one-for-one correspondence between conditions on the earth and data points that are spatially distributed.

   For practical purposes, there are an infinite number of data which could be collected about the real world, yet we store only a finite number of these. In one sense, we are "screening out" an infinite amount of potential information. Clearly, it takes considerable forethought to select a finite set of discrete symbols (letters and numbers) representing the contemporary real world that also can become part of a data base which will be used in solving the problems of the future.

3) In addition to the difficulty of referencing a continuum of three-dimensional space, there also are problems with the continuous nature of the data themselves. Soil type is a good example. Just as no two snowflakes are exactly alike, no two soils are alike. Soils must be categorized into groups. A judgment about which group a particular soil belongs to is then made. In variables like elevation, the somewhat parallel issue of precision becomes a factor. Are distances most appropriately measured (vertically) to the nearest meter or the nearest centimeter?

4) The data in a spatial data base won't develop as a natural consequence of some already ongoing process. Other data bases often benefit from data derived by other processes. For example, a clerk processing applications for auto license tags may type the pertinent information about the car, owner, and tag onto a multipart carbon form. One of the copies becomes part of a data base. Thus, the data base develops as a result of the tag-selling process which must occur anyway; all that's needed in an extra copy of the data. Spatial data bases about the environment have not evolved as consequences of

other processes, however. Generally, the work starts almost from scratch.

5) One cannot get an entire spatial data base of any size developed before part of it is incorrect, since some of the values in the real world will have changed over time. Land use is an example of a variable having data values that change rapidly—sometimes even on a daily basis. Even "stable" characteristics like topography change over time.

6) While general discussion of spatial coordinates is easy, decisions about which ones to use are more difficult. For example, a natural tendency to let flat surfaces represent curved ones has led to difficulty more than once. It happens again when attempts are made to build spatial data bases that cover large land areas. Several methods presently are used to represent the curved surface of the earth in two-dimensional data bases.

7) While it is true that considerable data of the types important to this discussion have been collected, many of them are not directly usable in a spatial data base. This happens because these data, collected by groups or agencies with specific missions to serve, have been assembled in nonuniform categories or have been interpreted in a specific manner for a particular purpose. For example, early soils data may not contain the necessary information that will enable measurement of some environmental effects of land use activities.

E. Spatial Information System Defined

To make a definition, a spatial information system has, as its primary source of input, a base composed of data referenced by spatial (or land, or geographic) coordinates. The system accepts parameters, examines its data base, and provides information in forms for human understanding, decisionmaking, and action (Kennedy & Meyers, 1977). In an automated spatial data information system, a major part of the "device" which does the processing is an electronic digital computer. Much of the data base it uses is stored on electronic or magnetic tapes or disks.

How such data are stored is a matter of great concern; Because a decision here will affect everything that will follow—data collection, product accuracy, system efficiency, etc.—we devote some attention to it.

F. The Storage Paradigm

This discussion pertains primarily to an automated spatial information system but applies to any system in which information about the environment is expressed in discrete symbols (numbers, letters, symbols). Despite the various outputs of which they are capable—graphs, drawings, pictures—digital computers deal only with discrete symbols and their com-

binations. They take in discrete symbols, combine them according to pres-
set rules (for one example, the rules of arithmetic), and write out discrete
symbols. The discrete symbols of output may be only a point of light on a
cathode ray tube but it is an individual entity nonetheless, How, then, does
one represent the continuum of the environment in the discrete storage
"brain" of a computer. There are three answers: idealization, aggregation,
and probabilization.

In *idealization* we pretend that we can substitute easily manipulated
symbols for actual three-dimensional, real world objects. For example, we
might pretend that an oil well can be represented by a point, or that a gas
transmission system can be represented by a sequence of straight lines. We
may further idealize by only identifying two of the three dimensions.

In *aggregation* we put together entities of somewhat similar characteristics. For example, saying that a county has X acres on which cotton is
grown and Y acres where tobacco is grown is a statement of aggregation;
the information about where these acres are is not in the statement.

In *probabilization* or *assumption* we use data of which we are (more or
less) certain and interpolate or extrapolate to get information which we can
(more or less) assume to be correct. A point on a topographic map midway
between the 1,250- and 1,260-foot contours might be estimated to be at
about 1,255-foot elevation. (To get a better estimate one might also
consider the relationships of the 1,240 and 1,270-foot contours). In any
event, in the absence of a blunder, the elevation of such a point is not less
than 1250 feet nor more than 1260 feet; thus, in some cases, there are
bounds on the error introduced by probabilization.

With these three approaches to using symbols to represent the environment, we describe some schemes that have been used or proposed for storage of data on areas.

1. CELL

In this scheme a (usually) square grid, resembling a checkerboard, is
imagined to lie over the earth area of interest. Data within each square are
then aggregated for each variable type. For example, if the variable were
land use, the data recorded might be 35% type A, 20% type B, and 45%
type C. If the variable were population by age, the data might be 1 to 5 years
(52 people), 6 to 8 years (24 people), etc. The LUNAR (Land Use and
Natural Resource) System of New York State is an example of a cell system.

An advantage of a cell system is that, since the same geographical unit
is being used for each variable, the data may be easily compared (Meyers
et al., 1973). Suppose the Spatial Information System contained data about
population density and land value as two different variables. The system
could be asked to combine the data from these two variables, cell by cell, to
suggest sites which would be inexpensive and disturb few people. One procedure for doing this would be to make a transparent map with the cell in
shades of gray of each variable; the darker shade would indicate the less desirable (greater population or higher land value) condition of the cell. An at-

tempt to shine light through the two maps, laid one on the other, would highlight the more desirable cells. Such a technique is called *overlaying.*

Overlaying might also be done arithmetically if, instead of using shades of gray, two numbers between 1 and 10, one for each variable, were assigned for each cell. A computer could be asked to add the numbers and produce a composite value for each cell; the lower the composite value, the more desirable the cell.

The disadvantages of the cell system are several. One is that it implies a level of aggregation which must be a compromise among all the variables stored. A cell size must be chosen—for example, a square kilometer— which might be too large for some applications or some data and too small for others. Another disadvantage is the loss of geographic specificity. You might know, for example, that 10% of a cell is soil type A and 10% is in slope category S; what you don't know, and what might be vital, is whether it is the soil A that is at slope X.

Once the data are collected at one cell size it is not easy to disaggregate them. Also, a real commitment is made when the checkerboard is laid down, since data are collected within cells and not across cells; thus, attempts to look at areas which cross cell boundaries are difficult.

2. POLYGON

A polygon system is one that depicts areas on the earth's surface as irregular geometric figures composed of three or more straight lines. For example, a map of vegetation could be depicted as a set of polygons with lines enclosing similar vegetation types. Such representations can be stored in the memory of a computer, as well as on a map, by storing the coordinates of each point and indicating that there are lines between points. An example of a polygon system is CGIS (Canadian Geographic Information System). See Chapter 37, "The Canadian Land Inventory System," for a description of the data and their use which this system was designed to handle.

An advantage of a polygon system is its geographic specificity. Although some precision is surrendered by limiting oneself to straight lines— when nature throws curves—this loss is minimal and can be offset by using more and shorter straight-line segments.

A major disadvantage of the polygon system is that the data dictate the size, number, and configuration of the polygons. This has several implications. For one, if the question is asked of a polygon-based Spatial Information System, "Here is a location, what's the soil type?", the system must go through some real gymnastics to give an answer. (A cell system, on the other hand, can't answer at all, but it can say what percentage of each soil is close by.) A more serious disadvantage comes when a polygon system is asked to compare or overlay two or more variables—and the ability to do this is a major reason to have a Spatial Information System. Overlaying several polygon maps or several polygon computer files is quite a feat. Taking the simple case of three variables with a triangle polygon in each, a small sketch will show that the result of an overlay process can yield 17 polygons. The practicality of searching several overlaid polygon files for a suitable site for, say, an airport, is limited, even with high-speed computing equipment.

3. DOT

Dot systems are relatively new. In a dot system a regular pattern of dots is imagined to lie over the geographic area. Then, for each variable, such as soil type or land use, a single data value is recorded. This value might be the most predominant soil type or land use within the area *surrounding* the dot or it might simply be the condition *at* the dot.

The dot system resembles a cell system with two major differences: (i) the spacing between the dots is much smaller than the distances between centers of adjacent cells, and (ii) only a single datum is recorded for each area surrounding the dot. An example of a dot system is the LANDSAT information developed on a routine basis by satellite. In this system, information based on electromagnetic radiation at several wave lengths is available for dots which have an implied area, called a *picture element* or *pixle,* of about 1 acre.

Another type of dot system is the Dot Probability System developed at the University of Kentucky. In this system, the datum stored at a dot is the condition that is precisely at that dot. There is the implication that the condition at the dot is representative of the condition of the area surrounding the dot but there are no guarantees. Dot systems have the easy referencing and overlay capabilities of cell systems, the geographic specificity of polygon systems, and a rather profound internal storage advantage over either cell or polygon systems. The disadvantage is that they are based on the idea of homogeneity of the area surrounding the dot, as with the LANDSAT system, or on probabilistic measures, as with the dot probability technique.

IV. PRODUCTS OF A SPATIAL INFORMATION SYSTEM

We now turn our attention to the output of a Spatial Information System. To have a chance to be useful in decisionmaking, a product of a spatial information system must meet several criteria:

1. The decisionmaker must know it is available.
2) He must be able to understand it.
3. He must have some reason to believe that it is worth his time to determine how to use it.
4) The assistance to aid the decisionmaker's understanding of the product must be available.
5) The product must be available at the time it is needed.
6) It must be relevant to his area of concern.
7) It must have considerable accuracy and integrity; if the product lets the decisionmaker down, a long time will elapse before he again depends on such information.

Products from a spatial information system can be classified in several ways. We use the terms *origin, media, format, purpose,* and *audience.*

1. ORIGIN

A product can come from a manual process or an automated device. Combinations of the two are possible, as when color markers are used to enhance computer output.

2. MEDIA

We use the term *media* to denote the carriers for the information presented to the decisionmaker. Common media are paper, photographic materials (opaque ones like photographs and translucent ones like slides and films), and electronic visual devices like cathode ray tubes. Three-dimensional electronic displays activated by laser beams—called *holograms*—may be available in the future, but more conventional products are now available that can meet more important, if less exotic, criteria. Almost all products of existing spatial information systems are designed to respond to the sense of vision in some manner.

3. FORMAT

While the number of visual media that carry information are limited, the number of forms or formats that information can assume are without limit. An infinite variety can be obtained with characters—the 26 letters of the alphabet, 10 arabic number symbols, and some special symbols. This type of information is called *character-based* information. Character-based information can appear in the form of text, tables, lists, formulae, etc. The way in which information is organized has a tremendous impact on whether or not it will be useful. Character information can be processed by an individual in serial fashion (like a reader "processing" this line of text) or in search mode—a procedure in which a person scans organized groups of characters in order to find desired information. Looking up a number in a telephone directory exemplifies use of the search mode—followed, of course, by serial mode. The best products allow a user of character-based information to quickly grasp two things: the overall scheme of organization of the information (revealed by tables of contents, sections on "how to use this information," etc.) and the subject of the information itself (illustrated by introductions, table titles, lists of parameters relating to the information, etc.). Development of products which can meet these criteria is an art and a science.

Graphic information—pictures, photographs, drawings, maps, displays, graphs, diagrams, etc.—is as versatile as character-based information. In manual systems, graphic products are produced by photographic techniques, drafting, drawing, and cartographic techniques. With automated systems (USDI, 1975c), graphic products are usually made

1) by pen on paper with a device called a *plotter*;
2) with electrical charges or magnetic flux on a specially treated glass surface. (The most common form of device is the cathode ray tube [CRT]. Mention of the TV tube—although an obvious example of a

CRT—is misleading because most graphic products displayed do not resemble the "photographic" image seen on television);

3) with "hardcopy" machines which can reproduce, on paper, the images appearing on CRT-like surfaces; and

4) with characters (letters, numbers, and symbols) printed on paper— not for their traditional meaning, but for their visual density.

In any of these instances, the information product usually is a diagram or drawing without real limits on its diversity. This type of display may be composed of points, lines, and shadings of areas. If a graphic product is on an electronic display, it may be possible to quickly change some of its elements to allow an examination of alternatives or to create an animation effect.

Simplistically, character-based information is read, while graphic information is viewed. Both can help a decisionmaker form a more complete mental model of an issue, but they provide information in different ways.

It is seldom that any information is either totally character based or graphic. Combinations of the two are the most effective (graphs have descriptive headings and designations, reports have diagrams and illustrations), although the process of "marrying" the two is not always straightforward, particularly when using automated equipment.

4. PURPOSE

Another classification which might be considered during design of a product from a spatial information system is the general purpose or purposes of that product or information. Some of the possible purposes include inventorying, analyzing, explaining, documenting, defending, managing, forecasting, and monitoring.

The design of the product is frequently more effective if the purpose is kept well in mind. For example, if the major purpose is monitoring, the most appropriate product is one which reflects a change over time rather than the production of two documents, each of which shows the situation at a given point in time. This sounds elementary, but the amount of effort that has been spent in trying to compare two similar documents, side by side, to ascertain the differences between them is staggering. If the spatial information system has the capability to produce two documents, it can be adapted to compare the information found in each and generate precisely the information required. Other purposes will be most appropriately met by differing formats. The important point to consider, for each product, is how that product will be used.

5. AUDIENCE

A good spatial information system will be capable of producing many sorts of information products at varying levels of detail and sophistication. An additional classification for these products might be the audience for whom the product is intended. Attempts to develop a "super product" should be avoided, however. As various products evolve, this becomes a strong temptation. Those responsible for system and product design and evolution keep adding more "bells and whistles" which the designers, of course, understand completely. But a person charged with making a decision, who is looking at the product for the first time, may find that an elaborate demonstration interfers with his understanding of—and use of—the information.

One approach designed to avoid this problem is the development of an information product series—several forms of information of similar origin, media, format, and purpose—showing different levels of detail. As a product series is used, the first priority should be development of a product appropriate for the needs of the decisionmaker. That product should be supplemented by others of the same general form which provide more detail or additional information. For example, if information on the limits of the 100-year floodplain for a river is needed, the information product should not show the 20-year plain, the 50-year plain, and 200-year plain, the normal yearly range of bodies of waer, or the expected annual rainfall, etc. Instead it should clearly show the 100-year floodplain, with a notation that more detailed or sophisticated information is available for other floodplain limits in roughly the same format. If the system can product a complicated map, it should also have the ability of producing less complicated ones.

V. CONCLUSION

There are major differences between land management planning, project planning, and land use planning. There does, however, exist a similarity among these three types of planning—the need for good geographic or spatial information. One must be careful about the data collected for decisionmaking, depending on which sort of planning is involved as well as many other factors, such as time, financial resources, and the sorts of decisions which must be made. To have the flexibility to cope with planning of all three sorts and to be able to assess in advance the effects our land conversion processes will have, it is our thesis that a new tool is needed—the general purpose spatial information system.

We are simply beyond the time when the intuitive correlation of information which comes from maps can tell us of the myrid effects of our land conversion changes. There are too many variables and the processes for integrating the data from several maps are too weak. Thus, as preposterous as it may seem, it is now necessary to take spatial data from the satisfying, two-dimensional map format and break them up into digital pieces (numbers, letters, symbols) so that a computer can accept and process them. Three factors make this a workable possibility: (i) computers are now very fast (say 20 million operations per second or more) and can store amounts of information which are hard even to comprehend; (ii) a great deal of data about land use and land cover is being sensed by satelite and the format of that information is compatible with the ways in which computers store information; (iii) great strides have been made in both computer graphics, allowing visual display of integrated, two-dimensional information, and in the digitization of graphic information for input to computers.

The development of a general purpose spatial information system is a large undertaking. It may strain the resources of an organization even as large as a state; it will certainly strain the creative ability of such an organization if the system is to be general enough to serve all of its users well and for the time frame, say 25 years, necessary to justify its construction. But to fail to develop a spatial information system will result in the emergence of many *ad hoc* automated geographic information projects and data files. Already the same data are recollected for different projects and functions. And already the excessive costs of developing separate, incompatible systems to process them has begun. For example, the citizen of Wisconsin spends more than $17 *per capita* for its widely diverse methods of collecting, analyzing, and storing land information. This is only direct cost, of course. The other costs, such as decisionmakers not having access to the available or potentially available information, may be greater (Larsen et al., 1978).

In the coming decade, probably two sorts of automated information systems will be most useful on the state level. First will be those that provide information about *people* (drivers, employees, taxpayers, etc.). Many states already have sophisticated computer systems, programs, and data bases to deal with information related to persons. Second, states will have to develop information systems, as we have discussed, in which the data are identified by *place.* These spatial information systems may well turn out to be the more important.

The decision about whether to allow the undisciplined development of separate systems to serve specific needs and functions and to take precedence over the construction of a general purpose, centralized system is at hand. Unfortunately, most states do not seem to be aware that they face this decision. Thus, the inevitable development of spatial information systems for land and resource planning provide less utility, arrive later, and cost more than necessary.

LITERATURE CITED

Bolan, R. S. 1967. Emerging views of planning. J. Am. Inst. Planners. p. 236.

Council of State Governments. 1974. A legislator's guide to land management. Counc. of State Gov., Washington, D.C.

Kennedy, Michael, and C. R. Meyers. 1977. Spatial information systems: An introduction. Urban Studies Center, Univ. of Louisville, Louisville, KY.

Larsen, B., et al. 1978. Land records: The cost to the citizen, a Wisconsin case study. Univ. of Wisconsin, Madison, Wis.

Meyers, C. R., R. C. Durfee, and T. C. Tucker. 1973. Computer augmentation of soil survey interpretation for regional planning applications. *In* Plants, Animal and Man, Proc. 28th Annu. Meet. of Soil Conserv. Soc. of Am., Oct. 1973, Little Rock, Ark. SCSA, Ankeny, Iowa.

Oak Ridge National Laboratory Science Foundation Environmental Program. 1971. Regional modeling. Chap. II-E. *In* Environ. and Technol. Assess. Progress. Rep., June–Dec. 1970. ORNL-NSF-EP-3. Oak Ridge Natl. Lab., Oak Ridge, Tenn.

U.S. Department of the Interior. 1975a. Information/data handling: A guidebook for development of state programs. USDI, Washington, D.C.

U.S. Department of the Interior. 1975b. Information/data handling requirements for selected state resource management programs. Tech. Supp. Rep. C. USDI, Washington, D.C.

U.S. Department of the Interior. 1975c. Information systems: Technical description of software and hardware. Tech. Supp. Rep. D. USDI, Washington, D.C.

U.S. Department of the Interior. 1975d. Issue papers. Tech. Sup. Rep. E. USDI, Washington, D.C.

U.S. Department of the Interior. 1976. State resource management programs primer: Critical areas and information/data handling. USDI, Washington, D.C.

37 The Canadian Land Inventory System

DONALD B. COOMBS AND J. THIE

Lands Directorate, Environment Canada
Ottawa, Canada

I. INTRODUCTION

When the world's human population was smaller than it is now, it was possible for nations, particularly those of the New World, to place no restraints on land development on the assumption that land and resources were inexhaustible. This approach to resources was indicative of the thinking in Canada well into the 1950s and early 1960s.

It became apparent in recent years that Canada's agricultural community was in serious trouble both economically and socially because the land base could not support all the demands made upon it. The situation warranted a reappraisal of agricultural land-use practices and the application of modern scientific technology to produce satisfactory economic and social benefits.

To develop good land management practices, an understanding of the physical nature of the land resource's capability to sustain and support the agricultural industry was required. An inventory of Canada's lands suitable for agricultural use and the identification of possible alternative land use opportunities was the first step; thus, the Canada Land Inventory (CLI) program—a comprehensive survey of land capability and use designed to provide a basis for resource and land use planning—evolved. The CLI included assessment of land capability for agriculture, forestry, recreation, and wildlife. An inventory of present land use and pilot land use planning projects in each of Canada's ten provinces were essential parts of the program.

To place the Canada Land Inventory in perspective, the first part of the chapter provides a sketch of Canadian land settlement and, as a prerequisite to integrated land use planning, the factors which led to the development of a land resource information base.

The chapter proceeds to describe the objectives, organization, and content of the CLI program. A brief outline of the classification methodology is developed for each sector. The chapter concludes with examples of how the Canada Land Inventory information is applied to integrated land use planning situations.

II. THE CANADA LAND INVENTORY PROGRAM: A NATIONAL SYSTEM FOR COLLECTING RESOURCE DATA

A. Historical Background

Although Canada's total area is estimated at slightly over 9.8 million km², the population and associated land use activities are concentrated largely in the southern one-third of the country; the people are historically linked to an agrarian way of life and the exploitation of renewable resources.

Physical constraints such as climate have imposed limitations to further northward extension of particular land use options such as agriculture; however, major land use problems emerging today arise from intense sociological and technical changes taking place in the settled areas of Canada (Maxwell, 1972).

During the period of initial land settlement, which started in eastern Canada, very little technical information existed to guide the settlers. A wide range of soils and land types were occupied and, if settlement occurred on good agricultural land, it was more often by accident rather than design. The first cycle of farm abandonment began when pioneers found themselves located on unproductive land. Once established, however, farming communities tended to perpetuate and enlarge mainly through family association or through the arrival of new immigrants of the same ethnic stock as the original settlers.

Toward the end of the nineteenth century, certain agricultural areas in eastern Canada had developed to the point where significant surpluses of grain and forage products were being produced. These surpluses provided an important export trade in agricultural products. In the early 1900s particularly this trade began to assume a position of prime importance in the national economy as the farm commodities from the newly settled areas of western Canada entered the flow of agricultural exports. Unlike the slower settlement processes experienced in eastern Canada, the agricultural settlement of the prairie lands and mountain valleys of western Canada was large scale, swift, and dramatic. It occurred primarily in the first decade of the century and was commercially oriented and dependent upon the products of technology—above all the railroad.

By the 1920s, the contemporary land settlement pattern of the country had emerged. At this time, the status of the agricultural industry was marked by comparative stability and modest prosperity in eastern Canada, and by growth, considerable prosperity, and optimism in western Canada.

The 1930s brought a series of events that were to produce revolutionary changes in the agricultural industry and in land management practices generally. These events unleashed forces which were to generate social problems of national significance that have continued to the present time.

The Great Depression of the 1930s coincided with an unprecedented dry spell on the Canadian Prairies and on the central plains of the neighbour to the south. Drought and associated wind erosion converted much of the short-grass prairie country, which had been placed in cereal production, into a vast dust bowl. Only later was it recognized that the precipitation regime of the semiarid territory made it unsuited for cereal-crop production.

In response to this crisis, the Canadian Government passed the Prairie Farm Rehabilitation Act of 1935. This Act and later amendments to it enabled the conversion of cultivated semiarid lands to permanent grassland, the establishment of community pastures, the resettlement of the affected populations, the provision of agricultural land management services, and the development of large irrigation systems and water control projects.

A land capability survey formed part of this program. Although limited to the assessment of the land's physical capability for sustaining cereal crop production, this survey represented the first large-scale attempt in Canada to apply a scientific approach to assessing land use capability; it was an important predecessor of the Canada Land Inventory.

B. Prelude to Inventory

The decades of the 1940s and 1950s were momentous ones for Canadian agriculture. Science-based technology was applied by the industry on a grand scale. A scarcity of labor and spiralling costs made mechanization mandatory for viable farm operations. Changes in market patterns and conditions contributed to increased crop specialization.

Although these forces presented opportunities for increasing the efficiency, productivity, and income of farms, certain prerequisites were necessary before advantage could be taken of the new opportunities; the farm must be located on reasonably productive land suitable for mechanized operation; it must have access to sufficient capital for underwriting investments in machinery and other necessary farm inputs; it must contain sufficient acreage to spread the costs of labor and machinery and thereby keep these unit costs at competitive levels. Finally, farm operators must be skilled in farm-management business practices and in the application of new products of science and technology such as inorganic fertilizers, pesticides, and herbicides.

Unfortunately, many Canadian farm operations could not meet these exacting conditions. As a result, large numbers of farms located on poor soils and even small farms on good soils were unable to adjust to the new economic climate. This situation initiated a new round of farm abandonment which is still continuing. In the 1960s, it is estimated that the number of farms in Canada declined at the rate of 10,000 a year. Although many people who gave up farming were able to find alternative employment in the industries of the growing urban centers, thousands of farm people could not find viable employment opportunities, and poverty conditions emerged in many of the country's rural areas.

The Canadian Government responded to this situation by passing the

Agricultural Rehabilitation and Development Act of 1961 (later renamed the Agriculture and Rural Development Act). This Act, known by the acronym ARDA, enabled the federal government to undertake farm enlargement and consolidation programs, land improvement schemes, and land use adjustment projects in cooperation with provincial governments.

As the ARDA programs were being formulated, it became evident that a rational approach to land use adjustment and planning could not be undertaken without knowledge of the land's capability to support agriculture and other feasible alternative uses. To provide this knowledge the Canada Land Inventory project was launched in October 1963.

C. Objective and Organization

The Canada Land Inventory is a comprehensive survey of land capability and land use designed to provide a partial data base for broad-scale resource and land use planning. It includes assessment of land capability for agriculture, forestry, recreation, wildlife, present land use, and pilot land use planning projects. It was established as a cooperative federal/provincial program administered under the Agricultural Rehabilitation and Development Act (ARDA) of June 1961 (Environ. Canada, 1970a).

Under the aegis of ARDA, comprehensive resource management and social planning programs took shape along with provincial government ventures in the sphere of regional development planning. It became increasingly apparent, however, that without a land capability inventory any programs of land adjustment and regional economic development would be based on subjective judgements made in the absence of essential resource information. The Canada Land Inventory was designed to respond to this information need, with the underlying objective to provide a basis for land use planning.

The project, started in 1963, was essentially completed in 1975-76. It covered the settled parts of Canada and the adjacent forest fringe—an area of approximately 2.6 million km^2 (Fig. 1). Data are provided on maps at three scales for each sector. Field maps are prepared at the 1:50,00 scale and published maps at the 1:250,000 and 1:1,000,000 scales. In addition, because of the volume of data produced (20,000 maps at the 1:50,000 scale and 1,200 at the 1:250,000 and 1:1,000,000 scales), a computerized data bank known as the Canada Geographic Information System (CGIS) was developed to facilitate storage, retrieval, and analysis of information.

The CLI is designed primarily for planning rather than for management. It is of a reconnaissance type; it provides information essential to land development planning at the municipal, provincial, and federal levels of government. It does not provide the detailed information required for individual parcels of land or for land planning in small watersheds, local government units, etc.

The broad objectives of the Canada Land Inventory are to classify lands according to their present use and capabilities, to obtain a firm estimate of the extent and location of each land class, and to encourage use

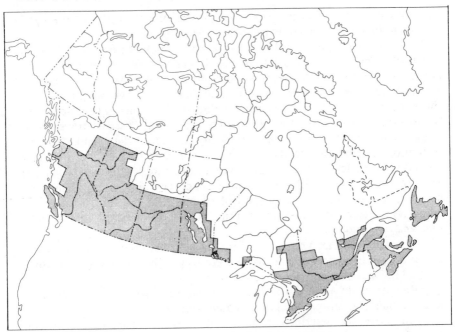

Fig. 1—Areas covered by the Canada Land Inventory.

of the CLI data in land use planning and decision-making. These objectives can be refined further in the following three program activities:

1) *Activity Number 1*—To classify and map lands according to their capabilities and present land use. The CLI establishes a common base for data description and presentation; it provides for the physical generation of maps and related data covering present land use, and land capability for agriculture, forestry, recreation, and wildife—ungulates and waterfowl. In addition, supplemental programs in Sport Fish Capability and Agroclimatology were implemented in some provinces.

The role of the federal government was primarily one of enabling and coordination. Thus, the Government of Canada financed all incremental costs incurred by the provinces in the conduct of the Inventory. It also directed the development of national capability classification systems and provided coordination services to ensure their consistent application.

The provinces carried out the work within their own jurisdictions and they were, therefore, responsible for the planning of provincial programs and the preparation of capability maps. Inventory committees, chaired by a provincial CLI coordinator, were established in each province to direct this work which was carried out by federal and provincial resource agencies, university groups, and private consultants.

2) *Activity Number 2*—To obtain a firm estimate of the extent and location of each land class. The CGIS (Environ. Canada, 1976a; Tomlinson et al., 1976) was established to apply the processing and data handling capabilities of large-scale computers to the difficult task of reducing, tabulating, manipulating, and analzying the volumes of data collected by CLI. Because

of the great mass of data to be generated it was obvious that an automated system of data handling would be an indispensable tool.

The CGIS is operational and has a scale capability of 1:500 through 1:1,000,000 for input of map data. Presently, the bulk of the data in the data base is at a scale of 1:250,000. In addition to CLI data, maps showing present land use, census enumeration areas, and administrative, watershed, and shoreline boundaries serve as source documents. This cartographic information, along with the associated classifications, is traced and prepared for input into the geographically organized data bank. The information, coded and placed on magnetic tape, permits economic and easy retrieval of detailed or general information. For each separately designated area (map face) on a CLI map, the data bank contains: (i) an identifying number; (ii) the shape and location of boundaries; (iii) the classification data; (iv) the calculated area; and (v) the location of a central point by latitude and longitude.

Maps of a similar type (e.g., all present land-use maps or all recreation maps) are grouped together to form a coverage. Each coverage will comprise all the mapped land in Canada.

Raw or analzyed data for selected geographic areas may be retreived either in map format (graphic) or in tabular format.

Any coverage described in area units may be added to the system. Special coverages, other than those contained in the data bank, may be entered after consideration of such factors as applicability, resources available, time, and cost.

3) *Activity Number 3*—To encourage use of CLI data in land use planning. In November 1967, the CLI program was extended to cover pilot projects in land-use planning.

It was realized that the maximum usefulness of the Inventory could be achieved only by developing and evaluating applications of the data in the planning process. The objectives were twofold: to provide opportunities for the assessment of the adequacy of data in development planning and to familiarize those engaged in land resource planning and management with the data.

It is anticipated that the pilot projects could promote greater cooperation and coordination among resource sector specialists in developing multidisciplinary approaches to land planning. Under this program the federal government underwrote the costs of a provincially proposed and sponsored pilot-scale, land use planning study.

As few restraints were imposed by the federal government, maximum flexibility was achieved in the use of the data and in the design and organization of studies to meet the variety of needs across the country.

III. THE CLI LAND CAPABILITY CLASSIFICATION SYSTEMS

One of the major challenges of the CLI Program was the development of national land capability classification systems. Initially, the task appeared formidable because of the geographical diversity of Canada and the number and complexity of factors which determine a viability of a particular land use at a given time and location.

It quickly became apparent that, if a data base having a viability over a reasonably long period of time was to be produced, the more dynamic socioeconomic determinants of land use could not be considered. For this reason, such factors as present land use, vegetative cover, accessibility, tenure, and market conditions were excluded from the assessment process. Although these factors are critical in determining the highest and best use of land at any given time and location, it was decided that consideration of them should take place only at the time when land use plans are being prepared and implemented. The elimination of these factors permited lands to be evaluated strictly on the ability of their inherent physical characteristics to support specified uses under current technological conditions and good management practices.

The five land capability classification systems developed for the CLI project, although dealing with different land uses, are similar in the following respects:

1) All are interpretive classification systems in which soils or land types are grouped into one of seven classes on the basis of their capability for production. The systems, therefore, are comparable in a relative but not necessarily in an absolute sense.

2) With the exception of the recreation sector, which presents details of the positive features of the landscape, all systems list the limiting factors which downgrade land units from the highest capability.

3) All systems are national in character; thus, a class assigned to an area in eastern Canada has the same meaning as a similar class either in central or western Canada.

4) All site factors are incorporated into the capability rating.

5) Only physical factors are assessed—not locational, economic, or accessibility factors.

6) The systems are meant to serve as a basis for land use planning, but not for land management.

A. Soil Capability for Agriculture

The capability classification for agriculture (Environ. Canada, 1969a) was the first system to be developed; it is based on a system originally designed by the Soil Conservation Society of America. The classification work conducted by the federal and provincial soil survey organizations is based on the interpretations of the data provided by soil survey maps and reports prepared by the National Soil Survey. Since the Survey was established in 1921, soil reports cover most of the settled areas of Canada. Through interpretation, the soils are mapped by land units having homogenous characteristics according to their general ability for the production of common field crops; it takes into account the effects of climatic and soil limitations in a system of mechanized farming.

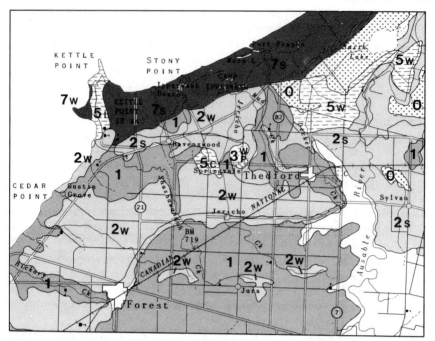

Fig. 2—Agriculture. Symbol 3_P^W indicates Class 3 land unit with wetness (W) and stoniness (P) as limitations.

1. CAPABILITY CLASSES FOR AGRICULTURE (FIG. 2)

In this classification the mineral soils are grouped into seven classes depending on the degree of limitation and into thirteen subclasses according to the kinds of limitation. Class 1 soils have no significant limitations and, together with Classes 2 and 3, are considered capable of sustaining production of common field crops. Class 4 soils are physically marginal for sustained arable agriculture. Soils in Class 5 are unsuitable for annual field crops but suitable for forage production and improved pasture. Those in Class 6 are restricted in their use of native grazing. Class 7 is unsuitable for agricultural use. Organic soils are not included in the classification but are shown separately on the maps.

The classification system is based on the following criteria:

1) Soils will be well managed and cropped using a largely mechanized system.

2) Land requiring improvements (including clearing) that can be made economically by the owner is classified according to its limitations or hazards in use as if the improvements have been made. Land requiring improvements deemed beyond the means of the individual owner is classed according to its present conditions.

3) These factors are not considered: distance to market, type of roads, location, size of farm, type of ownership, cultural patterns, skill or

resources of individual operators and hazard of crop damage by storms.

The classification does not include capability of soils for trees, fruit trees, small fruits, ornamental plants, recreation, or wildlife.

The classes are based on intensity rather than on the type of agricultural limitations which they display. Each class includes many kinds of soils; many soils in a class require different treatment and management.

2. SUBCLASSES

Subclasses are divisions within classes that have the same kind of limitations for agricultural use. Thirteen different kinds of limitations are recognized at the subclass level such as (C) denoting adverse climate for crop production as compared to the 'median' climate or (E) denoting soils where damage from erosion is a limitation to agricultural use.

3. ORGANIC SOILS

The interpretative capability classification is not applied to organic soils since usually there is insufficient information on organic soil areas to make an interpretive judgement. Organic soils are designated by the letter O.

B. Land Capability for Forestry

The national land capability classification for forestry (Environ. Canada, 1970b) was developed on the basis of completed pilot projects conducted in each province, and a subsequent regional and national meeting of provincial, federal, and university specialists. Basic data for classification were available in most provinces in the form of soil survey and forest inventory maps and reports. Interpretation of these data, together with new field survey data, permitted the system to be developed.

Fully compatible with the other sectors, the forestry capability classification system serves to indicate those lands on which intensive management practices might be justified. In this classification all mineral and organic soils are grouped into one of seven capability classes according to their ability to grow commercial timber. Capability is in terms of mean annual increment per hectare, expressed in cubic meters for indigenous tree species growing as full-stocked stands and assuming good management practices.

1. CAPABILITY CLASSES FOR FORESTRY (FIG. 3)

Classes 1 to 3 lands range from those having no important limitations to the growth of commercial forests with productivity over 7.8 m³/ha per annum to lands having moderate limitations with productivity down to 4.9 m³/ha. Classes 4 and 5 lands have moderately severe to severe limitations;

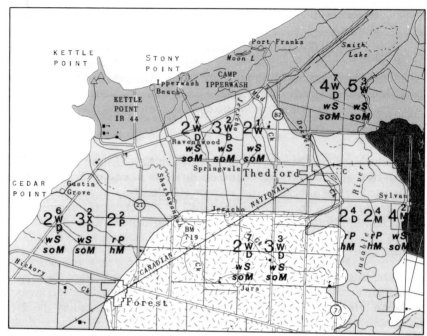

Fig. 3—Forestry. Symbol   4W   5W
                7   3
                     D
                 wS   wS
                soM   soM

This complex unit indicates 70% Class 4 land with moisture (W) and compactness (D) limiting soil factors, white spruce (wS) and soft maple (soM) dominant species; 30% Class 5 with moisture (W) limiting factor and same species.

productivity ranges from 4.8 down to 2.2 m³/ha. Class 6 have very severe limitations; whereas, Class 7 have limitations so severe as to preclude growth of commercial forests. Productivity is usually less than 0.7 m³/ha per annum.

Associated with each capability class is a productivity range based on the mean annual increment of the best species or group of species adapted to the site at, or near, rotation age. Productivity ranges are expressed in gross mechanical cubic meter volume and for tree diameters to a minimum of 10.16 cm. The productivity ranges are for 'normal' or fully stocked stands. Since only well-stocked stands are measured to indicate the capability class, the implication is that only good management produces such stands.

In a capability class, factors such as location, access, distance to market, size of units, ownership, or present state are not considered. Classification is based on the natural state of the land without improvements such as fertilization, drainage, or other ameliorations. Improved forest management may change the productivity range.

2. CAPABILITY SUBCLASSES

Subclasses, when shown, always represent a limitation to growth and are used only when the limitations affect the class level. Such factors as climate, soil moisture, permeability and depth of rooting zone, and soil factors which individually or in combination adversely affect growth are identified. These factors in the classification of a land unit are related to the indigeneous species which can be expected to yield the volume associated with each class.

C. Land Capability for Wildlife

The Wildlife Sector of the Canada Land Inventory has some unique aspects, particularly the great diversity of wildlife species, their different environmental requirements, their mobility, and other behavioral attributes. One national series of maps cannot effectively represent the capability of land to produce or support all species of wildlife. For this reason, the current capability inventory is restricted to two main groups of species which occur across Canada: ungulates, which are the responsibility of the provincial governments, and waterfowl, which by treaty are the responsibility of the federal government. The classification system (Environ. Canada, 1969c) is the same for both groups, with slight modifications due to their different environmental requirements.

Criteria for capability mapping were developed by officials of the Canadian Wildlife Service and the Provincial Game Agencies. The mapping program for waterfowl capability was implemented by Canadian Wildlife Service officials, while ungulate capability mapping was carried on by Provincial officials. Categories used in the classification system are: the capability class, the capability subclass, and, for ungulates, the indicator species.

All environmental factors are taken into consideration when assigning a capability class to a unit of land. The class boundary is determined by physical characteristics of the land which are significant to ungulates and waterfowl. Thus the capability class is an expression of the environmental factors that control the numbers of ungulates or waterfowl produced and supported on a unit of land.

In general, the needs of all wildlife are much alike: each individual and species must be provided with a sufficient quality and quantity of food, protective cover, and space to meet its needs for survival, growth, and reproduction. The ability of the land to meet these needs is determined by the individual requirements of each species or group of species under consideration, the physical characteristics of the land, and those factors that affect the plant and animal communities.

In an interpretative land classification system for wildlife, criteria and procedures must be the same for the system to be uniform. All wildlife capability maps were prepared as follows:

1) The separation of the land surface into homogeneous units for classification is on the basis of physical characteristics that are significant from a wildlife standpoint.

2) The assignment of a class to each unit of land is on the basis of all known or inferred relevant information about the unit, including parent material, soil profile, depth, moisture, fertility, landform, climatic factors, and vegetation which reflect the quality and quantity of food and cover available to wildlife.

3) Classifications are based on the natural state of the land under good wildlife management practices. Management practices which are practical and feasible are assumed.

4) Factors such as location, access, ownership, distance from cities or roads, or present condition of a land unit are not considered in assigning a capability class. Present cover and production in an area are used only for additional information. Excessive or insufficient hunting pressures do not limit the capability of the land and are not used in assigning classification values.

5) The degree of limitation determines the class designation. The subclass is the factor which causes the limitation. The limitations and the class may be changed by the advent of new and improved management techniques; it is unlikely that significant changes can be made except by costly and continuing practices.

1. CAPABILITY CLASSES FOR WATERFOWL (FIG. 4)

The basic unit of the classification system is the capability class which denotes the ability of land or water to support or produce waterfowl. The capability class level is determined by the degree of limitation which affects either the quality or quantity of habitat for waterfowl. Classes 1 to 3 range from lands having no significant limitations to the production of waterfowl (where soils are fertile with good water-holding characteristics and good wetlands) to areas having slight limitations due to occasional droughts, climatic conditions, or the physical conditions of the land that affect the quality and quantity of the habitat. Classes 4 and 5 lands have moderate to moderately severe limitations to the production of waterfowl. These areas are dominated by temporary ponds and other limitation factors such as climate, soil moisture, salinity, flooding, or poor interspersion of water areas. Classes 6 and 7 have severe limitations degrading downward to a capability that is negligible or nonexistant.

2. CAPABILITY SUBCLASS

In general the classes are divided into subclasses according to the nature of limitations that determine the class level. These denote significant limiting factors that may affect either waterfowl or the ability of the land to produce suitable habitat conditions. Examples are: *Aridity* (A)—land

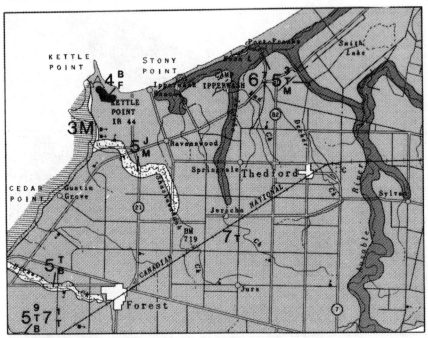

Fig. 4—Wildlife waterfowl. Symbol 3M indicates area of Class 3 with limitations due to poor water-holding capacity of soils (M).

Symbol 6T $\begin{smallmatrix}7 & 3 \\ 3T \\ M\end{smallmatrix}$

This complex unit indicates 70% Class 6 adverse topography (T); 30% Class 5 adverse topography (T) and poor waterholding capacity of soils (M).

susceptible to periodic drought, *Climate* (C)—where adverse climatic factors inhibit development of favorable habitat and restrict waterfowl production, or *Soil Moisture* (M)—where soils have a poor water-holding capacity adversely affecting the formation of permanent water areas.

3. CAPABILITY CLASSES FOR UNGULATES (FIG. 5)

The basic unit of the classification system is the capability class, which denotes the ability of land to support or produce wild ungulates. The capability class level is determined by the degree of limitations which affect either the quality or quantity of habitat for the animals. Classes 1 to 3 lands generally have no significant limitations for the production of ungulates. The classes range from lands which provide a wide variety of food plants and other habitat elements, to lands which have slight limitations due to factors that affect the quality and quantity of habitat, such as the availability of food and cover. Classes 4 and 5 lands have moderate to moderately severe limitations usually arising from a combination of two or more factors such as shallow soils, topography, flooding, and climate. Classes 6 and

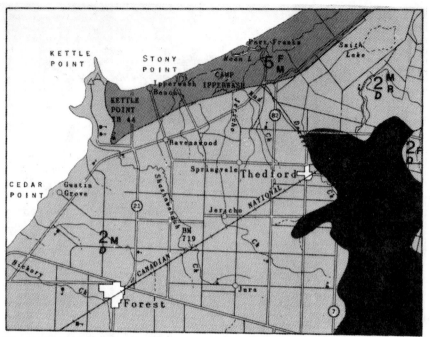

Fig. 5—Wildlife ungulates. Symbol 2M indicates Class 2 land having moderate limitations
                                      DR
due to deficient soil moisture (M) and soil depth (R); ungulate specie is deer (D).

7 have severe limitations to limitations so severe that there is little or no ungulate production.

4. CAPABILITY SUBCLASSES

With the exception of Class 1, the classes are divided into subclasses according to the nature of limitations that determine the class level. Usually, the limitations do not have a direct effect on the animals but they do affect the ability of the land to produce suitable food and cover plants. For convenience the subclasses are placed in two main groups: those relating to climate and those relating to inherent characteristics of the land.

Significant climatic factors, for example, would be Aridity (A) restricting the development and growth of suitable food and cover plants or Snow Depth (Q) resulting in limitations caused by prolonged periods of snow conditions reducing the mobility of animals and the availability of food plants. For land, Fertility (F) indicates a limitation due to lack of available nutrients in the soil for optimum growth of food and cover plants, whereas Landform (G) indicates the limitation is a poor distribution or interspersion of landforms to provide optimum ungulate habitat.

An additional factor is provided in the ungulate subclass information to identify the species for which capability ratings are assigned, for example, Antelope (A), Caribou (C), and Elk (E).

D. Land Capability for Outdoor Recreation

The objectives of the recreation-land classification program (Environ. Canada, 1969a) are twofold: to provide a reliable estimate of the quality, quantity, type, and distribution of outdoor recreation resources within settled parts of Canada and to supply basic information for the formulation of policy and plans by the levels of government involved. Compatibility with other sectors of CLI is mandatory to facilitate intersector comparisons in integrated resource management planning.

The recreation sector's initial task was to develop a national classification system acceptable to all provinces and, in conjunction with the provinces, to apply the classification to all lands within the inventory area. A seven-class classification system was developed to rank land according to its capability for outdoor recreation and to recognize present popular preferences.

The recreation-land classification, though consisting of classes like the other systems, differs from them in that lands are classified according to their limitations for use. The basis of the classification is the quantity of recreation (measured in visitor days or hours) that may be sustained per unit area per year under perfect market conditions. Thus, lands with a capability to sustain intensive use, such as sandy beaches and slopes suitable for skiing, are rated higher than lands which support less intensive uses, such as pastoral landscapes offering interesting viewing experiences. For purposes of uniformity, class ranking does not take into consideration present use or accessibility.

1. CAPABILITY CLASSES FOR RECREATION (FIG. 6)

Classes 1 to 3 lands have a very high to moderately high capability for outdoor recreation; capability ranges from a natural capability to engender and sustain an extremely high total annual use based on intensive activities to a moderately high total annual use. Classes 4 and 5 lands have a moderate to moderately low capability based on dispersed activities. Class 6 lands have a low capability lacking natural attractiveness or presenting severe limitations to recreational use, whereas Class 7 lands have very low capability.

2. CAPABILITY SUBCLASSES

There are 25 recreational features which represent the primary uses of land for recreation as indicated by present popular preferences. The opportunities for recreation provided by a feature or combination of features and assessed in terms of quantity of use determine the class of the land unit. Recreation features are considered as aspects of land units providing opportunities for recreation.

Examples of recreational features indicated by subclass are Angling (A), denoting land which provides access to water with natural capability

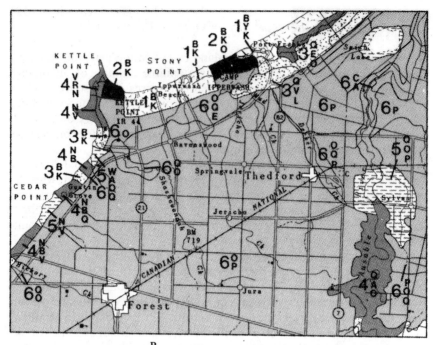

B
Fig. 6—Recreation. Symbol 1 K indicates Class 1 land suitable for beach activities (B), com-
J
fortable water temperatures, wet beach gradient 2 to 5% with 3.3 m minimum length of fine-
grained sand or pebbles. (K) indicates shoreland suited for organized tent or trailer camping
and (J) indicates areas offering opportunities for gathering or collecting rocks, fossils, etc.

for production, harvesting, or viewing sportfish; Beach (B), shoreland
capable of supporting beach activities; Deep Inshore Water (D), shoreland
with deeper water inshore suitable for swimming, boating, mooring, or
launching; Glacier (G), area offering a glacier view or experience; and
Lodgings (N), land suited for family cottage or other recreation lodging use.

E. Classification of Land Use

In addition to the mapping of the land resource capability sectors
within the CLI boundary, present land use was considered essential in the
program for determining the extent and nature of existing uses, particularly
agricultural lands. A classification for mapping land use (McClellan et al.,
1968) was devised and a program initiated to cover the areas of Canada lying within the CLI boundary (Fig. 7).
Mapping was done on 1:50,000 National Topographical System map
sheets or, if they were not available, at the most suitable alternative scale, and
adjusted by photographic reproduction. The 1:50,000 map sheets were later
generalized to 1:250,000 for input into the Canada Geographic Information

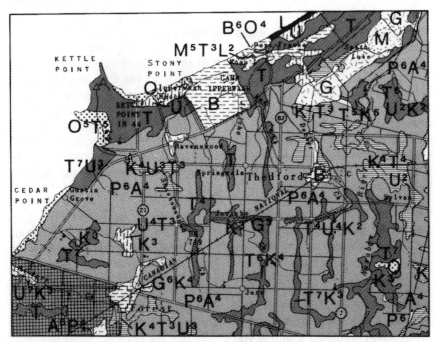

Fig. 7—Land use. Symbol T⁷ U³ indicates a complex unit consisting of 70% of productive woodland (T) and 30% of nonproductive woodland (U).

System for reference and overlay analysis with other CLI data and related information.

Land-use information was mapped with the aid of aerial photographs and frequent ground checks. Symbols based on the classification developed for this purpose were used to identify the nature of land use. The minimum land unit identified and classified represented an area on the 1:50,000 map by a square of 0.32 by 0.32 cm, which corresponds to an area of 2.6 ha on the ground.

IV. USE OF CLI INFORMATION

As already outlined, the CLI sector maps are based upon national interpretative classification systems which have been designed for specific objectives.

Because these interpretative classification systems identify only that biophysical information from the landscape that is required in accordance with predetermined objectives, the resulting data provide only one of several important inputs required in an environmental data bank.

When combined with other environmental, social, and economic factors, these interpretations provide the basis for the derivation of environmental management policies and land use planning programs which are consistent with desired social values and goals (Dean & Romaine, 1972).

A. Land Use Planning

In three studies conducted in each of the Maritime provinces of Nova Scotia, New Brunswick, and Prince Edward Island, the CLI data have been applied to regional planning concerned with the rationalization of the agricultural industry, associated land use adjustments, and the economic improvement of the rural resource base. In each of the three studies, the CLI data provide the basis for the initial physical analysis of available renewable resources. Detailed socioeconomic data, gathered concurrently, are utilized to influence decisions that were made during the capability analysis phase.

In 1966, the Government of Ontario launched a program called Design for Development aimed at regional development through comprehensive planning. Under this program, regional land use planning was undertaken so that the regions of the province could be developed according to an orderly plan based on environmental, social, and economic considerations. The CLI data formed an important input for the analysis of the physical capabilities of the land base. The analysis identified resource growth zones in addition to and complementary to urban growth areas. Predominant resource use was designated in areas where there was little or no overlap between land potentials. Multiple and competing resource use areas were designated along with zones of conflict between urban and resource use. Furthermore, zones of damage-prone environments or physical hazards were indicated.

The primary purpose of the pilot land use study undertaken in the Rocky Mountain Foothills of Alberta was to provide the province with a design for the most beneficial allocation of the conflicting resource demands in the area. Opposing interests in the study area included: coal, oil, and natural gas extraction, range and forest management, recreation and hydroelectric development, and wilderness and wildlife habitat preservation and protection. An overriding factor was that the area is the headwaters of the South Saskatchewan River, which flows across the semiarid region of the Prairie Provinces.

The study had two additional purposes, namely to develop a coordinated planning process that could be extended to other regions of the province and, to develop an analytical computer-based procedure for efficiently processing the large volume of data necessary for the physical, economic, and social analysis. The CLI capability data which formed a major input into the initial phase of the study included an assessment of the renewable and nonrenewable resource potential, a compilation of current land use, and a review of basic legislation.

As an alternative to the above studies, the Province of British Columbia elected to carry out Land Capability Analysis studies in conjunction with their ongoing Canada Land Inventory Program. A similar approach was taken by Newfoundland. The Land Capability Analysis map was compiled by a group of specialists representing the following professions: biology, agrology, ecology, pedology, forest economics, sociology, geography, education, forestry, climatology, and landscape architecture. Usually, the specialists who had prepared the CLI sector maps were present; moreover, each had thorough knowledge of the area under discussion. The analysis is restricted to the physical capabilities identified in the CLI data because no social or economic inputs are considered at this time since data in these files are incomplete.

Land capability analysis maps were compiled using an overlay technique involving 'prime use areas' (generally the first three classes of each sector) for the five capability sectors (Rees, 1977). Prime use areas were identified on the map except where two or more were coincident. In areas where no single high 'prime use' capability was evident from the first overlay, conflict was resolved in committee by reverting to class ratings and making trade-off comparisons between sectors. While only a single use is shown on the finished map, it is recognized that other uses are possible.

The resulting British Columbia land capability analysis maps are thus basically an evaluation of physical land capabilities and show the 'best' prime use of land from an ecological viewpoint within the narrow range of choice provided by the original CLI resource sector information. Social and economic factors are explicitly excluded from the analysis; thus, there is no pretence that this system comprises an overall land use planning process. It serves rather as a reference point for land managers and planners when considering the allocation or alienation of 'best' prime use land in land use or development programs.

Perhaps the single most dramatic and significant example of the application of CLI data in Canada, arising out of the British Columbia land capability analysis map studies, is that province's designation of Agricultural Land Reserves. These were established by the British Columbia Land Commission in the 1970's with the principle objective of preserving agricultural land for farm use.

Rapid growth and urbanization in British Columbia had consumed nearly 4,050 ha (10,000 acres) of prime agriculture lands per annum. CLI agricultural data for British Columbia indicated that less than 5% of the province's lands were suitable for agriculture. Based on the availability of CLI data, which recorded the location and paucity of the supply of good agricultural land, the British Columbia Land Commission was able to react to the need to help future agricultural land use options open. Most significantly the identification of all land with agricultural potential within the short time constraints of the Land Commission Act, necessitated as it was by the quickening pace of alienation of farm land for urban purposes, would have proved an unsurmountable problem had it not been for the existence of the Canada/BC Land Inventory (CLI) (McCormack, 1970; British Columbia Land Comm., 1974).

While the identification of potential Agricultural Land Reserves was perhaps the most important use of CLI data, several other aspects of the British Columbia Land Commissions operations are worth mentioning in the context of CLI. Small farm, orchard, and ranch holdings were acquired to facilitate consolidation of farm lands and to encourage younger farm families through career farm leases. Other special projects of the Commission, such as assistance in routing rail and road right-of-way, land assembly for experimental spray irrigation, and identification and acquisition of greenbelt, land bank, and park lands, were also facilitated by the availability of CLI data (Rees, 1977).

Similarly, the other provinces in Canada have used the CLI data in selecting areas for zoning on the basis of land capability and for the formulation of guidelines to assist in resolving land allocation problems and as a follow-up to regional planning and development programs.

At the national scale, CLI data provide the basis for an assessment of the nature of land use and land use changes in Canada particularly in terms of the encroachment of urban sprawl into agricultural and other 'prime' resource lands (Environ. Canada, 1976b). Although Canada has the second largest land area of any nation, through CLI it has been established that only 10% of that area is, in practical terms, suitable for agriculture. From this 10% the nation obtains a variety of produce including large quantities of food for the world market. Owing to the dependence of Canada on the produce of land, it is essential to understand the limits of the land resource, the location of prime lands, and the forces that may effect the capability of the land resource to continue to serve Canada's needs (Environ. Canada, 1976b; Gierman, 1977; Manning & McCuaig, 1977).

CLI provides base data for an ongoing program of monitoring land use change in Canada, enabling an examination and measurement of the manner in which 'prime' lands are converted to uses other than what their natural capabilities may indicate are the best. Studies examining the rate of rural or urban land conversion in major metropolitan areas in Canada with over 25,000 population have been undertaken and will be continued at regular intervals (Gierman, 1976; 1977).

B. Management and Development Programs

In areas committed to land use planning studies, or where the studies were not completed in time, single sector resource capability information serves as a basis for the specific follow-up surveys and research, for the identification of areas for certain kinds of preferred activities or use, and for guidelines as follow-up management plans and programs (McCormack, 1970). More specifically, the CLI data are used in:

1) Land use zoning programs either to preserve prime significant or sensitive areas from being converted to nonreversible or incompatible land uses or, conversely, to restrict the types of land use commitments on those areas which inherently pose a hazard to development.

2) The acquisition of lands for subsequent consolidation into agricultural management units, for the development of new parks or for the acquisition of wetlands for waterfowl. As such, the CLI data are

used not only as the basis for land banking programs, but as a means for determining the subsequent use and disposition of these lands.

3) Compensation programs designed for the relocation of resource use activities, and individuals that are affected by encroaching resource developments such as hydro-electric reservoirs.

4) Environmental studies designed for selecting transportation and transmission corridors, and for assessing environmental impacts associated with site-specific development projects such as airports, pulpmills, and deep seaport facilities.

The use of CLI data was the subject of a questionnaire circulated at random in 1976 to some 500 individuals involved in a variety of occupations having relativity to the practices of land use management or planning, or the provision of information relating to the same. There were 365 replies, most indicating a familiarity with and use of CLI data in a wide variety of ways.

A selection of specific uses of CLI data noted in the questionnaires is as follows:

1) Land use studies in an area proposed for grassland National Park, Saskatchewan.

2) Preparation of a report for a local government district on drainage priorities for the area.

3) Advice to local farmers from their agricultural representative on farm land utilization.

4) Studies on the promotion of forage and grassland management on Class 4 and 5 agricultural soils.

5) Use in university studies for examination of relationship between soils, land-use, and land capability.

6) Identification of areas with intensive forest management potential.

7) Reassessment of farm lands for tax purposes based on CLI Agriculture soils capability.

8) The identification and introduction of zoning controls on hazard lands.

9) CLI data used as a teaching tool in climatological studies related to agricultural land use.

10) The determination of best use of noncommitted lands in regional land use planning studies.

11) The development of land capability classification for fruit trees.

12) Location of power line rights-of-way in relation to preservation of high value agricultural lands and associated environmental impact studies.

13) Reference data for considering farm loans related to productivity and soil ratings.

14) Study of recreational capabilities of cottage sites in regional outdoor recreation planning.

15) Examination of municipal boundary proposals in terms of conversion of rural to urban lands.

16) Waterfowl breeding surveys.
17) Used in the supervision of field service activities in the identification and management of grazing lands.
18) Economic studies in the establishing of rural estate values.
19) Teaching a course in integrated land use in forestry.
20) Site selection for industrial parks in regional land use planning studies.
21) Environmental impact studies: oil and gas pipeline locations; trans Canada pipelines.
22) The monitoring of land use change over a period of time and related loss of agricultural lands.
23) Cost/benefit studies for the implementation of drainage and land development schemes.
24) The inventory of land-based resources in urban commutershed for land use planning.
25) Evaluation of forest sites for intensive management—stand improvement, thinning, and fertilization.
26) Research studies into provincial land use policy.
27) Examination of land capability of hobby farms to study relation of land use to capability.
28) The assessment of areas identified for potential hydro development.
29) Evaluation of areas for future additional provincial park sites and determining the suitability of adjoining lands for extension of provincial parks.
30) Assessing areas for future highway locations across the province to minimize impact in 'prime-use' agriculture and other resource lands.
31) Examination of recreation potential of proposed reservoir and dam sites in a major river basin water supply study.

V. IMPACT OF CLI ON RESOURCE MANAGEMENT IN CANADA

The CLI program produced about 20,000 1:50,000 scale maps, 1,200 1:250,000 and 1:1,000,000 scale maps, and reports covering about 2.5 million km^2 of Canada's land at a cost of about $37 million. Use and misuse has been extensive. Though no comprehensive cost/benefit studies have been carried out yet, results of user surveys indicate that much of the total cost has already been recovered through the reduction of incremental cost related to new activities and environmental impact assessment, prior knowledge and quantification of problem areas, and more effective planning, implementation, management, and use of land.

The success achieved in gaining general acceptance and application of the CLI program was due largely to the manner in which the cooperative program was implemented. The classification work for a resource sector was undertaken by or through the government agency responsible for the planning and management of that sector. Thus the chief potential user of the data frequently is the same agency that was responsible for preparing the capability maps for a particular sector. By placing the land capability classification function close to the resource planning and management function, knowledge of the Inventory's potential use for planning was readily available to the personnel who could make most use of it.

Also, well over 1,500 professional, research, technical, and student staff were involved on a full- or part-time basis. Many of these have moved on to resource management and planning positions. Their multidisciplinary experience filled a vacuum that was created by the shift from single to comprehensive resource management.

In most provinces, the organization set up to carry out the CLI program was absorbed in the government structure. In British Columbia, the CLI team evolved into the Resource Analysis Branch with multidisciplinary staff of about 120, representing a unique integrated and concentrated effort towards environmentally sound use of the land resource, unequalled elsewhere in Canada. At the federal level, the CLI program became the nucleus of the Lands Directorate in the Department of Environment. This directorate, with headquarters in Ottawa and regional offices in Vancouver, Edmonton, Burlington, Quebec City, and Halifax, is responsible for continued federal-provincial cooperation in land inventories, land use monitoring, land use policies, and the promotion of environmentally sound land use planning.

Under auspices of the now virtually completed CLI program, other initiatives were taken that are continuing. The Subcommittee on Bio-Physical Land Classification started in 1966 the development of an ecologically based land inventory system for the more than 5 million km² that lie outside the CLI area. This system, presently developed further through the Canada Committee on Ecological (Biophysical) Land Classification (Canada Comm. Ecolog. Land Class, 1977a), is designed for rapid reconnaissance as well as detailed surveys (Canada Comm. Ecolog. Land Class., 1977b) and avoids limitations of the CLI systems. Rather than creating several interpretative maps, it provides one ecological base map from which a multitude of interpretations are possible (Jurdant et al., 1977). The CLI computer data bank has evolved into the Canada Land Data System. National significant and consistent data are continuously added to the CLI base to provide support for national land use policies and national perspective studies. A Canada Land Use Monitoring Program is being developed, building on the CLI land use base to provide material for and measure impact of policies, regulations, and plans. In his look at CLI in retrospect, W. E. Rees (1977) observes:

> In spite of many valid reservations concerning the structure and quality of CLI data, the program has contributed immensely to a revolution in land and resource planning in Canada.
>
> Apart from a basic planning framework and large quantities of data, the CLI has provided a number of indirect benefits to environmental management;

a medium for improved communication (and perhaps reorganization) of administrative and management agencies in the resource field; a stimulus for the development of improved approaches both to resource inventory itself and to land-use through integrated management; and an impetus for revision of land-use legislation, regulation and procedures. Clearly the CLI has served well to underscore the inadequacy of former approaches.

In a time when public participation is considered an integral part of planning and management, the Canada Land Inventory has allowed a rational public and political involvement in land use planning, policy design, and regulation. In recent national, provincial, and regional elections, environmental impact hearings, and regional planning exercises, Canada Land Inventory classes and statistics consistently provided the framework for debate and opinion-forming, especially related to the urban-agriculture land use conflict.

The CLI classification has become very much a part of public vocabulary.

LITERATURE CITED

British Columbia Land Commission. 1974. Annual report. Burnaby, British Columbia, Canada.

Canada Committee on Ecological Land Classification. 1977a. Ecological (biophysical) land classification in Canada. J. Thie and G. R. Ironside (ed.) Proc. 1st Meet. CCELC, 25–28 May 1976, Petawawa, Ontario. 269 p. Ecolog. Land Classif. Ser., no. 1. Lands Directorate, Ottawa, Ontario, Canada.

Canada Committee on Ecological Land Classification. 1977b. Ecological (biophysical) land classification in urban areas. E. B. Wiken and G. R. Iron (compil. and ed.) Proc. of a Workshop, 23–24 Nov. 1976, Toronto, Ontario. Ecolog. Land Classif. Ser. no. 3. Lands Directorate, Environ. Canada, Ottawa, Ontario, Canada.

Dean, P. B., and M. J. Romaine. 1972. Application of the Canada Land Inventory in land-use planning in Canada. In 7th World Forestry Congr., Oct. 1972, Buenos Aires, Argentina. Lands Directorate, Environ. Canada, Ottawa, Ontario, Canada.

Environment Canada, Lands Directorate. 1969a. Soil capability classification for agriculture. The Canada Land Inventory Rep. Ser. no. 2. Environ. Canada, Ottawa, Ontario, Canada.

Environment Canada, Lands Directorate. 1969b. Land capability classification for outdoor recreation. The Canada Land Inventory Rep. Ser. no. 6. Environ. Canada, Ottawa, Ontario, Canada.

Environment Canada, Lands Directorate. 1969c. Land capability classification for wildlife. The Canada Land Inventory Rep. Ser. no. 7. Environ. Canada, Ottawa, Ontario, Canada.

Environment Canada, Lands Directorate. 1970a. Scope, organization and objectives. The Canada Land Inventory Rep. Ser. no. 1. Environ. Canada, Ottawa, Ontario, Canada.

Environment Canada, Lands Directorate. 1970b. Land capability for forestry. The Canada Land Inventory Rep. Ser. no. 4. Environ. Canada, Ottawa, Ontario, Canada.

Environment Canada, Lands Directorate. 1976a. Canada Geographic Information System overview. Environ. Canada, Ottawa, Ontario, Canada.

Environment Canada. 1976b. Land capability for agriculture. Lands Directorate, Environ. Canada, Ottawa, Ontario, Canada.

Gierman, D. M. 1976. Rural land use changes in the Ottawa-Hull urban region. Occas. Pap. no. 9. Lands Directorate, Environ. Canada, Ottawa, Ontario, Canada.

Gierman, D. M. 1977. Rural to urban land conversion. Occas. Pap. no. 16. Lands Directorate, Environ. Canada, Ottawa, Ontario, Canada.

Jurdant, M., J. Bélair, V. Gerardin, and J. Ducruc. 1977. L'inventaire du Capitale—Nature: Méthode de classification et de cartographie écologique du territoire. 202 p. Série de la classification écologique du territoire, no. 2. Lands Directorate, Ottawa, Canada.

McClellan, J. B., L. Jersak, and C. L. A. Hutton. 1968. A guide to the classification of land use for the Canada Land Inventory. Lands Directorate, Environ. Canada, Ottawa, Ontario, Canada.

McCormack, R. J. 1970. Interim report on progress and use—Canada Land Inventory. Lands Directorate, Environ. Canada, Ottawa, Ontario, Canada.

Manning, E. W., and J. D. McCuaig. 1977. Agricultural land and urban centres. Lands Directorate, Environ. Canada, Ottawa, Ontario, Canada.

Maxwell, J. W. 1972. The Canada Land Inventory. Notes for the Sem. Surveys and Assessment of Nat. Resour. as a Basis for Sci. Planning, 7th Commonwealth Comm. Meet., Canberra, Australia, 23 Oct.–5 Nov. 1972. Lands Directorate, Environ. Canada, Ottawa, Ontario, Canada.

Rees, W. E. 1977. The Canada Land Inventory in perspective. Lands Directorate, Environ. Canada, Ottawa, Ontario, Canada.

Tomlinson, R. F., H. W. Calkings, and D. F. Marble. 1976. Computer handling of geographical data: an examination of selection of geographic information systems. Nat. Resour. Res. Ser. Vol. 13, UNESCO, Paris, France.

38 A Case Study in Ecological Planning: The Woodlands, Texas

ARTHUR H. JOHNSON, JONATHAN BERGER, AND
IAN L. MC HARG

University of Pennsylvania
Philadelphia, Pennsylvania

I. INTRODUCTION

In reviewing the publications and reports in the regional and landscape planning literature and project reports from the profession, one finds a lack of uniformity in methodology, with ad hoc procedures "suited to the particular problem" a common approach. A method is presented in this chapter for determining the inherent suitability of a landscape for assimilating human activities and their artifacts. The approach is suggested in the writings of McHarg (1969) and exemplified by Juneja (1974), and has been applied professionally to a wide array of sites and locations. The method of landscape analysis described here is one part of a more comprehensive planning process which includes the social, legal, and economic factors which must be melded into a comprehensive plan that responds to the needs, desires, and perceptions of the people for whom the planning is being done. In developing an area, one would like to achieve the best fit between each human activity and the portion of the landscape to which that activity is assigned. As a starting point, a landscape may be thought of as being comprised of elements or components which may be labeled *geology, physiography, soils, hydrology, vegetation, wildlife,* and *climate.* Each landscape element may provide opportunities for certain land uses, and likewise, there may be constraints to each kind of desired land use imposed by components of the landscape. Areas which are most suitable for a specific use will have the greatest number of opportunities provided by the landscape and the least number of, or least severe, constraints imposed by the landscape on that particular use.

By using the approach of combining analyses of opportunities and constraints, the environmental impacts of the planned uses can be minimized, and the energy required to implement and maintain the proposed uses and artifacts can likewise be minimized. For example, areas where the water table is near the surface frequently or for extended periods provide an obvious constraint to subdivision housing in unsewered areas. This property of the landscape lowers the inherent suitability of such areas for that use. The situation can be ameliorated by the addition of sewers or by other engineering solutions, but costs, either economic or ecological, will be incurred, and additional energy will be required for installation and maintenance. This same area may provide little constraint to a golf course or park. Areas which are on the lee side of vegetative or physiographic barriers to winter winds provide a slight advantage for housing as energy costs for winter heating will be somewhat reduced. This same property of a site produces little opportunity for a park or golf course if the use is confined to the warm seasons. Thus the pattern of land uses assigned to the landscape could be controlled to a large degree by the characteristics and properties of the landscape. To this end, a careful analysis of the physiography, geology, soils, hydrology, plants, animals, and climate-microclimate of an area should be carried out and the implications for specified land uses determined by trained scientists.

The approach outlined here is designed to be flexible. It has been applied to areas ranging in size from a few hectares to a few hundred square kilometers and to urban, suburban, and rural areas.

There are also mechanisms to incorporate new data which may be generated after an initial plan has been formulated. Although flexible, the method is designed to be as objective as possible. The solutions are replicable and the methods of analysis overt and explicit.

Additionally, the method may be used to derive performance requirements (i.e., conditions which must be met by the developers) for the development of areas of less than prime suitability. The impact of any use on the landscape (or the impact of the landscape on the land use) can be mitigated by engineering to have the same result as the same development in the most suitable areas. The areas of prime suitability thus may become a "meter stick" for specifying what additional measures should be taken to minimize impacts on the land-use by the landscape, and on the landscape by the land use.

II. OUTLINE OF THE METHODS

A flow chart of the planning process of which this method of landscape analysis is a part is given in Fig. 1. The stream of landscape analysis identified by the box in Fig. 1 is the subject of this chapter and this part of the process is dependent upon the input of natural scientists. Clearly, the assembly of scientific data and its interpretation requires the perceptions and expertise of soil scientists, geologists, meteorologists, hydrologists, and ecologists. For a plan to be sound, the interpretations for opportunities and constraints must be suitable for the level of information obtained. The judgment and experience of trained scientists is necessary in collecting and interpreting data from the landscape. It should be the planners' charge to combine the natural scientists' perceptions with those of social scientists and engineers to cast these into a comprehensive plan within a sound legal and economic framework.

The first step in this holistic approach to analyzing a particular land-

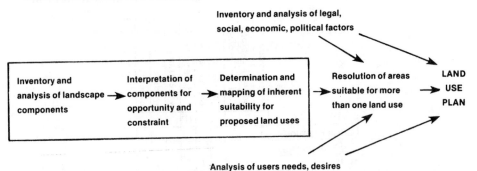

Fig. 1—Flow chart of the ecological planning process. Box indicates the part of the process treated in this chapter.

scape is to collect information and map the components of the landscape. Some representative inventory maps which have generally been proven useful are listed in Table 1. The level of detail of the data will be determined by the available information, time, and available resources which are related to the size of the area.

An inventory of the landscape in a parcel of, say, 10 ha can be carried out in considerable detail, whereas for a 1,000-km² site published reports may constitute the bulk of the useable information. In general, as the size of the area to be planned increases, the level of detail decreases and the uniformity of information across the various categories listed in Table 1 decreases.

The next step is to determine how the landscape functions as an interacting system of related components. For this purpose, a two-dimensional array like that shown in Fig. 2 may be used as a guide. Each element in the matrix identifies the possible interaction or relationship of two of the landscape components, and the sum of the bivariate relationships includes all of the major interactions and processes important in the landscape. Knowledge of how the various components of the landscape affect and are affected by one another leads to an understanding of how the whole system

Table 1—Some useful inventory maps.

1. Physiography	Elevation, slope
2. Geology	Bedrock or subsurface geology, surficial deposits, geologic cross-sections.
3. Soils	Series or phases, drainage classes, hydrologic groups, capability group, depth to seasonal high water table, etc., as applicable.
4. Hydrology	Depth to water table, aquifer yields, direction of ground water movement recharge areas, water quality, surface waters (lakes, streams, wetlands), flood zones, drainage basins, etc.
5. Vegetation	Distribution of associations, communities, and habitats as identifiable, areas important as noise buffers, food supplies for wildlife, nesting areas, etc.
6. Wildlife	Identification of species and their habitats and ranges, movement corridors, etc.
7. Climate	Macro- and microclimate parameters (temperature, moisture, wind). Ventilation and insolation may be determined in conjunction with physiography.
8. Resources	Mineral or other valuable natural resources.

	physiography	bedrock geology	surficial geology	soils	ground water	surface water	vegetation	wildlife	climate
physiography						11			
bedrock geology									
surficial geology									
soils					1	2	3	4	5
ground water							6	7	
surface water							8	9	
vegetation								10	
wildlife									
climate									

Fig. 2—Simple version of a matrix arraying landscape components. The interactions or relationships identified by each element in the matrix are organized into this format which facilitates systematic evaluation of disruptions of natural processes which may accompany specific human activities. Numbers refer to an example given in the text.

works. This should indicate chains of events which might occur due to some proposed land uses. The completeness of understanding will, of course, depend upon the level of information used and the perceptions and abilities of the scientists who contribute to the understanding of the natural system. It is safe to assume that a complete understanding of a landscape and its processes is never achieved—the planner must deal with incomplete information, and care must be taken that the inferences drawn from the data are justifiable given the detail and completeness of the data base from which they are made.

The categories shown in Fig. 2 may be varied to suit the nature of the landscape and level of information used in the analysis. In a small area with detailed information, one can subdivide the categories to a more detailed level, producing a larger matrix. Increasing the detail of information used allows a better understanding of the processes which may be affected by development or other changes in land use.

To understand the links between landscape elements and proposed land uses the set of matrices shown in Fig. 3 may be useful if there are a number of land uses which need to be considered. Matrix I describes the relationship between land uses and development activities. Matrix II describes the relationship between development activities and the landscape. Matrix III is the same as Fig. 2. These arrays are one way of organizing the information which is brought to bear on the final land use plan, helping to make the assimilation of a large amount of information orderly and explicit.

As an example of how this process may be used, consider the development of an area which requires a substantial amount of paving and impermeable surfaces such as roofs and roads with attendant drainage improvements. Consider high density housing; one of the major impacts is on

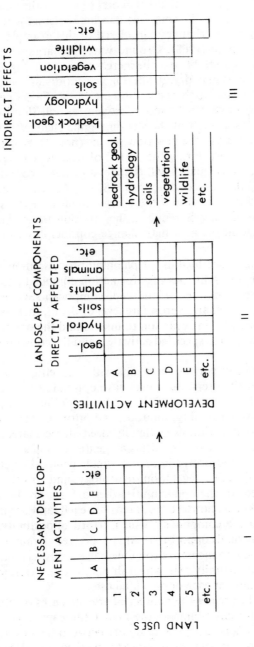

Fig. 3—Organization of information for assessing the relationship between a set of desired land uses and the impacts they will have on the landscape.

the hydrologic regime. Portions of the landscape are rendered impermeable and other landscape components will also change in response to the new conditions. By using Fig. 2, the changes in other parts of the landscape may be evaluated by considering the components which interact with the hydrologic system. Many of the changes considered in this example are defined quantitatively by Leopold (1968). Ground water recharge will be reduced and the depth to the water table may be increased (no. 1 in Fig. 2), marshes and seasonally wet areas may dry up altering vegetation and wildlife (no. 6, 7, 10), and surface water discharge will be increased. Flood peaks will be higher and bankfull stage will be more frequent as will floods of a given magnitude (no. 2). As a result of the stream regime changes, stream channels will enlarge to adjust to the new flow regime (no. 11), suspended solids loads will increase at least during the period of channel enlargement, low flows will decrease, water quality will change, and steam communities will necessarily adjust to the new conditions (no. 8, 9). The vegetation and wildlife will be changed (no. 3, 4) and the energy balance of the site may be altered as transpiration may be reduced, the soil moisture balance altered, and the microclimate in the area may change considerably as observed in large conurbations.

The information assembled in the planning process amounts to someone's interpretation and synthesis of information compiled and arrayed in map and matrix form to define the landscape components. Given sufficient information of this type at an appropriate level of detail, there is a basis for interpreting the assembled information to understand the opportunities afforded by the landscape for specified activities, and the constraints imposed by the landscape.

Determination of opportunities begins with a specific set of land uses which are desired by the users. Such uses have optimal or prerequisite conditions for their implementation and these must be defined, i.e., swimming areas require good water quality, appropriate bottom material and topography, and accessibility. Houses optimally need stable material beneath, well-drained soils for onsite sewage disposal, gentle to moderate slopes, and perhaps a good view and protection from winter winds. For each desired land use, the geology, soils, vegetation, hydrology, and/or other inventory maps are interpreted for the opportunities they afford, producing a set of opportunity maps which show the best areas for each land use individually based on the landscape components which afford opportunity. For each land use, the individual opportunity maps derived from each of the pertinent landscape components are combined by overlay techniques to produce a composite opportunity map which shows the opportunities afforded by the whole landscape for each desired land use.

In most cases the greater the number of concurrences of opportunities found in a particular environment, the higher the capability of that environment for the defined use. The trade off between the environments of higher and lower capability will be increased capital costs of design and construction as well as increased energy costs for construction and maintenance if performance requirements are met. Users can decide between the possible

Table 2—Types of constraints.

Legally defined constraint	Rules of combination with other uses
Inherently hazardous to life and health	Preempts nearly all development
Hazardous to life and health through specific human action	Allows some land uses but not others
Unique, scarce, or rare } Vulnerable resource }	Requires regulation through performance requirements

trade-offs. Using the method outlined in Fig. 3, the consultant scientists can demonstrate the attendant environmental costs and benefits of any desired scheme.

Constraints, defined here as adverse impacts of the land upon the land use and adverse impacts of the land use upon the land, are best expressed using the vocabulary of the National Environmental Policy Act and the health and welfare provisions of the states' and federal constitutions (Table 2). Some land forms because of the natural processes are "inherently hazardous to life and health." Examples would be flood-prone areas, areas subject to landslides, areas subject to collapse, and areas of fire-prone vegetation.

Other natural factors present "hazards to life and health through specific human action." Examples are the pollution of ground and surface waters from septic tanks in soils with a seasonally high water table, or the pollution of domestic ground water supplies through construction or waste disposal on an aquifer recharge area. Certain land forms with associated vegetation and land use can be classified as "unique, scarce, or rare." Alteration of these areas through development would mean the loss to society of irreplaceable features. Social scientists (historians, ethnographers, archaeologists, folklorists, and art historians) and natural scientists value such areas. Finally, particular landforms may be "vulnerable resources" which need regulation to "avoid social costs." Depending on the environment under study, these would include prime agricultural soils, high quality gravel deposits, and scenic features, among others.

Planners and their consultant scientists can evaluate every inventory map and determine from the categories of data the relevant set of constraints. These constraints are mapped. Unlike opportunities, the concurrence of numerous constraints may not be as significant as the existence of one constraint which represents a "hazard to life and health."

The next step in the procedure is a synthesis of opportunities and constraints for a selected land use to produce a suitability map which identifies a gradient of suitabilities for that prospective use. The areas with the greatest number of opportunities and least constraints are the most suitable for the specified land use. The method of combining the opportunities and constraints and ranking the suitability may be arbitrary but is explicit if an array is used to show how decisions of suitability were made. The matrix in Fig. 4 shows the determination of most suitable land and land of secondary suitability for housing with septic tanks. The example is oversimplified, but

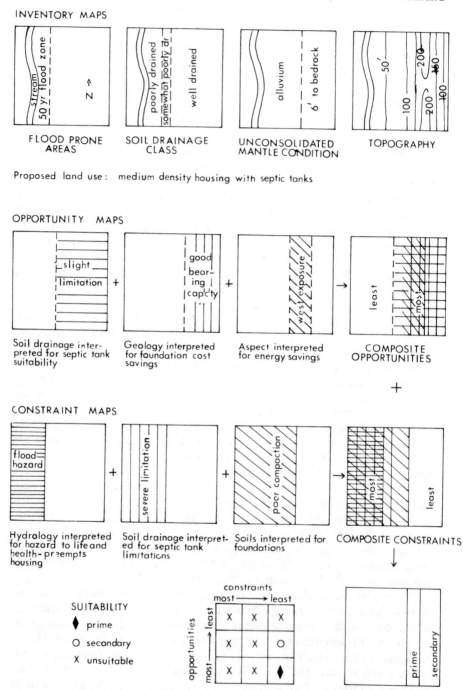

Fig. 4—Overlay method for determining suitability for a specific land use by combination of opportunities and constraints.

the method has been applied successfully to complex landscapes. The reliability and accuracy of the map overlay techniques this method employs are discussed by McDougal (1975).

The suitability maps for the land uses that the landscape must accommodate are then assessed. Where there are areas which are of primary suitability for only a single use, that use should be allocated to the suitable areas if the other relevant social, economic, and legal factors are favorable. In many instances, multiple suitabilities will arise. That is, some areas will be highly suitable for more than one use. Clearly, prime agricultural lands will be suitable for housing, recreation, and other uses. In these cases, land uses are assigned based on the needs and desires of the users which can be determined by surveys and interviews (Berger, 1978) or reflected in local officials or spokespersons for the users. Such allocations are also subject to legal and economic considerations which should also be incorporated into a land use plan.

III. APPLICATION

A simplified example is given below which is a summary of a portion of the plan for the new city called *The Woodlands,*[1] now being developed just north of Houston, Texas. A site map is shown in Fig. 5. The site presented many problems for such a development. It was entirely forest—a pleasant place to live, but a difficult environment to build in. It is extremely flat with few slopes greater than 5%. As a result of the topographic and rainfall characteristics, nearly a third of the site is in the 100-year flood plain of Panther, Bear, and Spring Creeks. Drainage of storm runoff was poor. Many depressions exist on the flat terrain which is dominated by impermeable soils, and standing water was common. The determination of housing sites and housing densities in the Woodlands is used as an example of the method of landscape analysis outlined above.

A. Nature of the Site

The Woodlands is located in the Gulf Coastal Plain and is underlain by unconsolidated formations comprised of Quaternary and Tertiary age gravels, sand, silt, and clay, in various combinations and proportions. The formations strike northeast, roughly parallel to the coast, and dip southeast at 1 to 2 m/km. Several of the units are good aquifers and are sources of high-quality water. The bearing strength of the geologic units underlying the site is adequate for most development purposes. There are subsidence problems in the Houston area, but subsidence should not affect the Wood-

---

[1] Wallace, McHarg, Roberts, and Todd. 1974. Project Reports for Woodlands New Community: (I) An Ecological Inventory, (II) An Ecological Plan, (III) Phase I: Land Planning and Design Principles, (IV) Guidelines for site planning. Wallace, McHarg, Roberts, and Todd, Philadelphia, Pa.

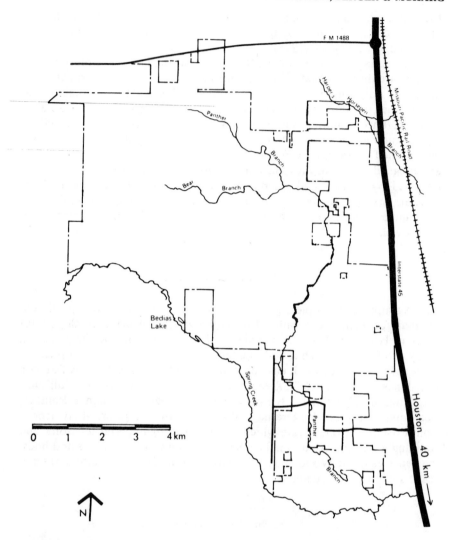

Woodlands New Community

Fig. 5—Regional location and site map of Woodlands New Community.

lands; ground water withdrawals and recharge have been carefully determined in the planning for the area, as described in more detail below.

The hydrologic regime was an extremely important consideration in designing the plan for the Woodlands community. There were flooding and storm drainage problems to be dealt with and a water supply to be developed.

Recharge of water was of primary importance to diminish the risk of subsidence on the site as well as down dip in Houston, which pumps from the same aquifers. Additionally, ground water was planned as a means of augmenting baseflow in the creeks to enhance the amenity value of artificial lakes to be constructed on the site.

Spring Creek and lower Panther Creek are the only perennial streams within the site. The others are intermittent, flowing during periods of storm runoff. During low flow periods, discharge is low since baseflow is limited, but storm periods produce large peak flows due to the heavy precipitation events and predominance of impermeable soils.

The soils on the site are mostly paleudults. Surface horizons are generally sandy or loamy with well-developed argillic horizons below. The Woodlands soils were grouped according to permeability and storage capacity in inches of water the soil will store beyond field capacity above the slowly permeable layers or the seasonal high water table. Figure 6 shows the profiles rated according to the permeability of the horizons, and Table 3 summarizes the pertinent properties.

The site is a mixed woodland dominated by loblolly pine. In mature stands, the pines are associated with oaks, sweet gum, hickories, tupelo, magnolia, and sycamore. The woodlands provide an amenity for development as well as limiting runoff and erosion. Additionally, the forest provides habitats for wildlife. Eight major vegetation associations were recognized: (i) shortleaf pine—hardwood; (ii) loblolly pine—hardwood; (iii) loblolly pine—oak—gum; (iv) pine—oak; (v) mixed mesic woodland; (vi) pine—hardwood; (vii) floodplain vegetation; and (viii) wet weather pond. Much of the forest has been logged at one time or another.

There are a multitude of types of wildlife present on the site. Those types which are abundant include songbirds, rabbits, raccoon, squirrels, oppossum, armadillo, white-tailed deer, and wild turkey. The persistence of most of these types can be promoted by careful management and by maintaining suitable habitats and territories and movement corridors which are large enough to suit the species. Floodplain areas in the Woodlands provide a diversity of habitats suitable for several desirable forms of wildlife, so that type of vegetation association has a high value for wildlife preservation. Forest edge conditions provide a diversity of habitats and also encourage a diversity of wildlife. These edge conditions occur around wet weather ponds, which increases their value for wildlife protection. The ponds also serve as sediment traps and temporary shortage basins during storm periods, amounting to a significant value for the ponds.

The climate of the area is subtropical with warm, moist summers and mild winters. The climate factors were used in site planning but were not of overriding importance in determining suitability for development and so will not be discussed here.

B. Planning for Development

An overall plan for locating best areas for development including high- and low-density residential, commercial, recreational, municipal, industrial and open space land uses was derived from the inventory of the landscape. Economic consultants produced a housing market analysis for the Houston

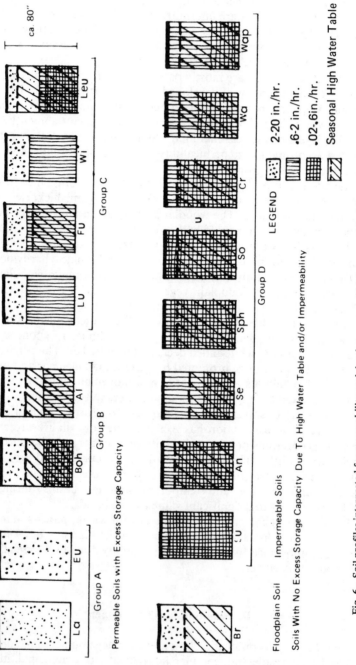

Fig. 6—Soil profiles interpreted for permeability and depth to seasonal high water table. Map unit designations refer to Table 3.

Table 3—Some properties of the soil series present on the Woodlands sites.

Map designation	Soil series	Drainage	Depth of permeable soil (>5 cm/hour)	Depth to seasonal high water table
			cm	
La, Eu	Lakeland, Eustis	Well	200	300
Br	Bruno	Well	200	75
Boh	Boy	Moderately well	125	75
Al	Albany	Poorly	120	75
Lu, Fu	Lucy,	Well	53	200
	Furquay	Well	58	75
Leh, Wi	Wicksburg,	Poorly	68	75
	Leefield	Poorly	86	38
Co, COG, Se,	Conroe, Segno,	Poorly to	0	Variable
Seg, Su, An,	Susquehanna,	Moderately well		
SS	Angie, Sunsweet			
Sph	Splendora	Poorly	0	38
So-Bo, TK				
So	Sorter	Poorly	0	38
Cr	Crowley	Poorly	0	38
Wa	Waller	Poorly	0	38
Wap	Waller Ponded	Very poorly	0	38

Region which showed seven feasible housing types for the Woodlands New Town. Engineers and landscape architects described the attributes of each development type in terms of space occupied by buildings, space covered by other impervious surfaces, and vegetation cleared (Table 4).

C. Relationship of Development Activities to Landscape Processes

The desired land uses and their attendant development activities would affect soils, vegetation, ground water levels, stream flow, and stream channel form. Modification of these landscape elements would affect the following processes: the balance between infiltration and overland flow, channel deposition and erosion, storage and movement of ground water, and the

Table 4—Development types with clearance and coverage requirements determined by a housing market analysis.

Housing type	Clearing required	Coverage by impermeable surfaces
	%	
Single family, 2.5 DU†/ha (1 DU/acre)	37	24
Single family, 6.9 DU/ha (2.75 DU/acre)	70	36
Single family, 10 DU/ha (4.0 DU/acre)	50	43
Patio houses, 15 DU/ha (6.0 DU/acre)	90	51
Garden apartments, 37.5 DU/ha (15 DU/acre)	85	45
Townhouses, 25 DU/ha (10 DU/acre)	95	55
Elevator apartments, 100 DU/ha (40 DU/acre)	70	50

† DU = dwelling unit.

regenerative capacity of the forest and wildlife communities. The effects on the hydrology of the site are essentially the same as identified in Fig. 2.

Given these forecasted impacts of urbanization, several interest groups wished to mitigate potential adverse environmental impacts. The regional water management commission wanted to maintain the recharge of the city of Houston's ground water supply. The new town developers wanted to maintain a healthy forest as the prime marketing element of the new town. The Department of Housing and Urban Development had environmental guidelines for the processing of guaranteed loans. In response to these different interests the five guidelines listed below for the plan and design of the new town were established:

1) Minimize disruption of the hydrologic regime by creation of a natural drainage system which allowed removal of the low-frequency event runoff and recharged as much precipitation as possible from high- and low-frequency storms to maintain ground water reserves.

2) Preservation of the woodland environment.

3) Preservation of vegetation providing wildlife habitats and movement corridors.

4) Minimization of development costs.

5) Avoidance of hazards to life and health.

1. REQUIREMENTS TO MINIMIZE DISRUPTION OF THE HYDROLOGIC REGIME

Since the Woodlands site is a flat landscape with large areas of impermeable soils and streams of low gradient, conventional means of storm water management called for site drainage through a large and expensive network of concrete drainage channels. These would decrease recharge to the ground water reservoir, and call for the removal of vegetation. To avoid these environmentally and economically expensive problems a "natural" drainage system was devised.

Calculations of cleared area and impervious area for typical Woodland's residential clusters indicated the magnitude of development impacts on surface runoff, soil storage capacity, and forest cover. The design aim was to promote infiltration of high-frequency, low-volume storm water (up to 25 mm of precipitation in 6 hours) in order to reduce the period of standing water and increase movement into the ground water reservoir. For purposes of this design storm (25 mm in 6 hours), the soils were assumed to be at field capacity and flood plains were assumed to be left in their naturally forested state.

As a design tool to promote percolation, the most abundant soils were grouped according to their capacity to accommodate water from the high-frequency storm. Available storage capacity was calculated from the depth of the permeable soil layer, the depth to the seasonal high water table, and the air-filled pore space at field capacity. The proportion of each soil map unit which needed to be left undisturbed to absorb runoff from the cleared portion was calculated (Table 5).

Table 5—Tolerance of soils to coverage by impermeable surfaces based on ability to store storm runoff from a 6-hour 25-mm storm.

Group†	Soil series	Available storage capacity	% of area that can be made impermeable
A	Lakeland, Eutis	High	90
B	Boy, Albany	Medium	75
C	Furquay, Lucy, Leefield, Bruno, Wicksburg	Low	50
D	Angie, Crowley, Segno, Sorter, Spendora, Susquehanna, Waller	None	100 (effectively impermeable under present conditions)

† The designation of A, B, C, and D is not related to slope or hydrologic group as defined by the Soil Conservation Service.

With the onsite recharge capacity of the soils known, the capability of any soil environment to handle any development type could be determined. In some cases higher densities on lower recharge capacity soils were possible if adjacent land had a moderate to high storage capacity to handle the storm runoff not recharged by the lower capacity soil. Housing densities could be increased in this case, since all of an area of high recharge capacity soil could be used as a sump for the runoff from adjacent areas developed on soils not suitable for storage of storm runoff.

Given the need to "borrow" recharge capacity from adjacent soils the juxtaposition of soil types on the landscape became important in addition to the on-site recharge capability of a soil in determining housing suitability. Soil patterns based on drainage relationships were identified for their suitability for the different development types. Figure 7 shows one example. For each drainage relationship, management guidelines, housing suitabilities, and siting considerations were specified.

2. REQUIREMENTS TO PRESERVE THE WOODLAND ENVIRONMENT

Different vegetation types gave rise to different levels of clearing. Based on their desirability to the projected residents, their tolerance to disturbance, the soils on which they grow, and their regenerative requirements, the forest types were rated somewhat subjectively on a scale of allowable clearing. For example, large pure hardwood or nearly pure hardwood stands are relatively scarce in the region, attractive to the residents, intolerant of soil compaction and change in ground water levels, better landscape shade trees, and slower to regenerate than pure pine stands which abound in the area. Clearing of hardwood stands was considered less desirable than clearing of pine stands. Figure 8 is a summary of the recommended clearance percentages based on the amenity value of the various forest types.

The gradient of tolerance from pure hardwood to pure pine is a gradient of opportunity and constraint for the development types. The more tolerant the vegetation to clearing the greater the opportunity for higher density housing. The lower the tolerance to clearing the greater the opportunity for lower housing densities.

D Soils with slope greater than 1% are impermeable and
therefore have minimal recharge capacity. When runoff
from these soils cannot be recharged on A, B, or C Soils,
it should be directed to a swale, water storage area, or area
of uncleared D Soil with slope less than 1% which can be
temporarily flooded. .

Management Guidelines

The extent of clearing and the amount of impervious
surface are not restricted except for limitations established
by existing vegetation. (See vegetation guidelines.)

Housing Suitability

Since D Soils are already impervious they are especially
suited to high density development.

Siting Considerations

Situate and design buildings, roads, and paths so as not
to impound runoff.

Major pedestrian traffic should be on fill parallel to the
line of slope, or raised on posts if traffic is perpendicular
to the line of slope.

Fig. 7—Management guidelines, housing suitability, and siting considerations for group D
soils (no ability to store 6-hour 25-mm storm).

3. MOVEMENT CORRIDORS

Wildlife needs cover, food, and water. The design objective was to provide for wildlife needs so that a maximum number of species present on the
site could remain after development. Large areas offering diverse vegetation
and water would make suitable wildlife refuges. These refuges would be
connected by corridors of vegetation. Vegetation in refuges and corridors
would be preempted from development. The corridors were provided by the
design of a natural drainage system as described below.

4. REQUIREMENTS TO AVOID HAZARDS TO LIFE AND HEALTH AND COST SAVINGS FOR CONSTRUCTION

The ecological inventory of the Woodlands showed that flood hazard
was the only natural hazard to life and health. Development in the area
along major streams inundated by the projected 100-year flood (under development conditions) was preempted. In addition to the use of some soils
as sinks for high-frequency storm drainage, a system of naturally occurring

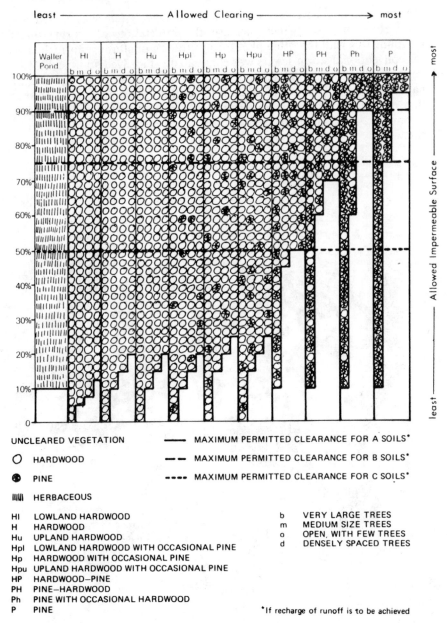

Fig. 8—Suggested clearance percentages based on vegetation types.

swales and stream corridors supplemented with man-made swales was designed to carry storm runoff from the low-frequency events. Development in the 25-year flood zone of the smaller drainage ways was also preempted. The swales and stream corridors were left in a vegetated condition which helped preserve the woodland environment and maintain corridors for wildlife movement. Wherever possible, the drainage system was routed over permeable soils to further increase the infiltration of storm runoff. Coupling this with the siting plan for infiltration of storm runoff, the need for conventional storm sewers was eliminated. This saved an incredible $14 million dollars in development costs and raised land values due to the elimination of unsightly concrete ditches, in addition to minimizing the disruption of runoff-recharge relationships, helping preserve the woodland environment, and helping to provide for the maintenance of wildlife on the site.

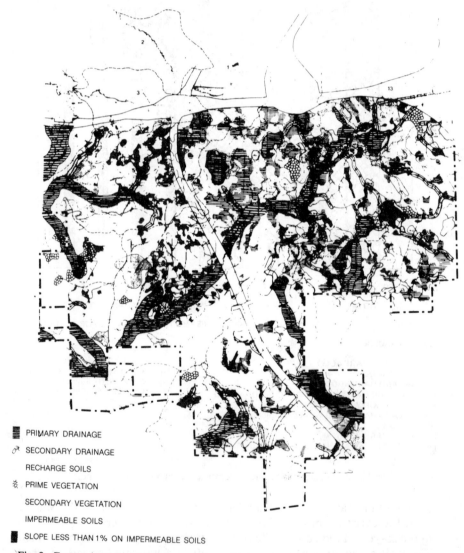

PRIMARY DRAINAGE

SECONDARY DRAINAGE

RECHARGE SOILS

PRIME VEGETATION

SECONDARY VEGETATION

IMPERMEABLE SOILS

SLOPE LESS THAN 1% ON IMPERMEABLE SOILS

Fig. 9—Factors interpreted for opportunity and constraint for a portion of the Woodlands site.

D. Opportunities and Constraints

The constraints to housing were the flood zones and restrictions placed on clearance by the vegetation analysis. This meant that areas prone to flooding, wetland areas, and hardwood areas were considered restrictions to development. These factors are shown in Fig. 9 for one portion of the site. Opportunities for various housing types were determined from the allowed clearance of vegetation and the impermeable surface allowed by the soil groups so as to allow infiltration of the high-frequency storm. Figure 10 shows the distribution of soil groups and the vegetation types mapped with constraint factors for a subarea of Fig. 9. The different soil groups of Fig. 9 are most suited to different types of housing, since the storage capacity of the soils for the 6-hour 25-mm event must not be rendered inadequate by too much impermeable surface. The suitabilities are identified in Table 6.

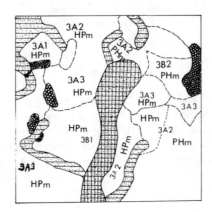

OPPORTUNITIES

CONSTRAINTS

3A1   A or B soils which receive no run-
      off from adjacent soils

3A2   A or B soils which receive runoff
      from C, D soils

3A3   C soils which receive no runoff

3B1   D soils, >1% slope, does not
      drain to A or B soils

3B2   D soils, <1% slope

HPm   medium size hardwood – pine
      45% clearance

PHm   medium size pine – hardwood
      60% clearance

100 yr flood zone

drainage easement

wet weather pond
(prime vegetation)

Fig. 10—Mapped opportunities (as determined by soils and vegetation) and constraints for a subarea of Fig. 9. Suitability for the housing types is given in Table 6.

Table 6—Housing suitabilities related to runoff holding capacity of soil groups A, B, C, and D.

Map code	Housing suitability
3A1	All types and densities suitable.
3A2	A or B soils used for recharge of runoff from C or D soils should not be developed or cleared. C and D soils for which A or B soils have been provided to accomplish recharge have no development restrictions.
3A3	Low-density housing
3B1	Suited to high-density housing with runoff carried by natural drainage system.
3B2	All types suitable, but drainage will be required.

For those areas that are not restricted by the defined constraints, a certain percentage of clearance was allowed, based on the vegetation present, a maximum amount of coverage by impermeable surfaces was set by the water-holding capacity of soils, and a certain type of housing with its characteristic density could be accommodated. Figure 11 shows the clearance, coverage, and allowed density for the area in Fig. 9.

E. Summary

The development will surely have impacts on the landscape and the natural processes occurring within it, but the development scheme allows for minimum disruption of the hydrologic cycle—recharge is maximized, exacerbation of flooding by development minimized, the ground water and baseflow to streams augmented vis a vis conventional drainage, and erosion

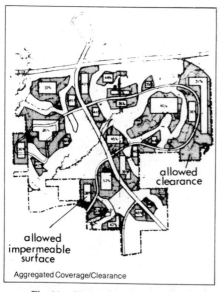

Aggregated Coverage/Clearance

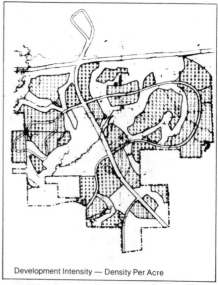

Development Intensity — Density Per Acre

Fig. 11—Clearance-coverage and housing densities determined for the area shown in Fig. 9.

hazard reduced due to vegetated drainage ways. Desirable wildlife and vegetation are also preserved. Planning for the Woodlands encompassed far more. Site planning and phasing were considered in detail, as were the location of roads and industrial, commercial, and recreational areas. Engineering and economic considerations were incorporated into the overall development plan. Wildlife and the other components of the landscape were treated in much more detail than described here. The scope of the example is limited, as the inclusion of larger areas and more land uses greatly increases the complexity, and would require a great deal more space to describe.

An understanding of the features of a landscape, i.e., the soils geology, hydrology, vegetation, and wildlife, as well as how they interact or are linked by natural processes, allows some understanding of the effects specified types of development will have on the whole ecosystem. Certain elements of the landscape may therefore become determinants of the pattern of planned land uses so as to minimize the adverse affects on the landscape. In the Woodlands example, vegetation, soils, and the nature of the hydrologic conditions of the site were the most important determinants in the siting of residences. In other areas, certain other natural features may be more important determinants of planned land use patterns. For instance, areas underlain by cavernous limestone bedrock, fault zones, or areas of vertisols may preclude building, or the ameliorative design strategies necessary to protect lives, property, or natural resources will be costly. Ecological planning as it is described here is sound in practice as well as in concept. In the case of the Woodlands, this type of planning saved the development corporation money in construction costs.

Presently there are 2,500 residents in the Woodlands, and the first phase of development is underway. The ecological plan was submitted to HUD in 1972 and led to a $50,000,000 loan guarantee, the largest under Title VII provisions.

LITERATURE CITED

Berger, J. 1978. Towards an applied human ecology for landscape architecture and regional planning. Hum. Ecol. 6(2):179–199.

Juneja, N. 1974. Medford—performance requirements for the maintenance of social values represented by the natural environment of Medford Township, New Jersey. Center for Ecol. Res. in Planning and Design, Univ. of Pennsylvania, Philadelphia, Pa. 63 p.

Leopold, L. B. 1968. Hydrology for urban land planning—a guidebook on the hydrologic effects of urban land use. U.S. Geology Surv. Circ. 554. 18 p.

McDougal, E. B. 1975. The accuracy of map overlays. Landscape Planning 2(1):23–31.

McHarg, I. L. 1969. Design with nature. Doubleday Natural History Press, Garden City, N.Y. 197 p.

39 Incorporating Soils Information into Land Use Controls

D. A. YANGGEN

University of Wisconsin
Madison, Wisconsin

I. INTRODUCTION

The traditional urban focus of land use planning and land use controls has broadened to include rural areas within recent decades. The 1950's and 1960's saw a growing population with increased mobility, rising standards of living, and changing consumer preferences. These factors resulted in population movement from relatively high-density central cities to relatively low-density suburbs and beyond. These same factors, along with increased leisure time and earlier retirement, also led more people to purchase recreational property, particularly waterfront lands. Problems that all too often characterized this sprawled development, such as failing septic tanks and damage to houses built upon flood plains, brought about a growing interest in land use planning and land use controls in rural areas. In addition to these problems, the 1970's have seen a growing public awareness of the limited and fixed nature of our natural resource base. Among the important resource issues on the public agenda are protection of wetlands and preservation of essential agricultural lands.

Ideally, these issues are addressed on a local level within the context of a comprehensive local or regional land use plan. These plans should be based upon inventory and analysis of population factors, economic activities, and the natural resource base including soils information. A typical plan may include the following land use policies: a pattern of cohesive urban growth; appropriate location of various uses on suitable soils; preservation of productive agricultural lands; and protection of wetlands, flood plains, and other important natural resource areas. Land use controls that use soils information, such as zoning ordinances, subdivision regulations, sanitary codes, and certain special purpose regulations, can be important tools to achieve these objectives.

This chapter discusses the role that detailed soils information can play in preparing and administering land use control measures. Four regulatory programs using soils information are described: (i) state and local control of unsewered subdivisions and septic tank installation; (ii) zoning designed to protect agricultural lands; (iii) wetland regulations; and (iv) floodplain zoning. The physical and/or conceptual basis for using soils information is addressed in several other chapters. (see, for example, Bartelli, Chap. 5, "Interpreting Soils Data" Miller, Chap. 12, "Defining, Delineating, and Designating Uses for Prime and Unique Lands;" and Bouma, Chap. 27, "Subsurface Applications of Sewage Effluent." The focus in this chapter is how soils information can be used in a regulatory framework to define the resource to be regulated, classify and inventory soils in relation to the selected definition, and identify the physical location of the defined resource. The physical and legal basis for using soils information in land use controls and techniques to strengthen soil-based regulations are also discussed.

II. THE PHYSICAL AND LEGAL BASIS FOR USE OF SOILS INFORMATION IN LAND USE CONTROLS

A. Physical Basis

Soils are classified to facilitate an understanding of the features and properties of the soil in order to better predict its behavior for many uses. Soil surveys are detailed, scientific inventories of the major physical and chemical characteristics of soil. The soil characteristics studied include size and arrangement of soil particles, kinds and amounts of periodic wetness, and kinds and arrangement of horizons (layers). Published soil surveys include a text and maps which describe and show the locations of defined units with unique combinations of soil characteristics. Interpretative sections of the text for the use and management of the soils are included for cropland, woodland, wildlife, recreation, and engineering (Beatty & Yanggen, 1966) (see Chap. 5, "Interpreting Soils Data").

B. Legal Basis

Land use controls represent an exercise of governmental police power which allows restrictions on the use of private property necessary to protect the public health, safety, and general welfare. These regulations must comply with certain basic requirements designed to ensure protection of constitutionally guaranteed private property rights.

Land use controls adopted and administered in accordance with proper enabling legislation will generally be found constitutionally valid if challenged in court if (i) the regulations serve valid public objectives; (ii) the regulatory means are a reasonable method of accomplishing a valid objective; (iii) the regulations do not unfairly discriminate against parcels of land that are similarly situated, i.e., are based upon a reasonable system of classification; (iv) there are sufficient standards to prevent the arbitrary exercise of discretionary power, if the regulations vest discretionary power in a local administrative agency; and (v) the regulations do not constitute a "taking," i.e., the property owner must be left with some reasonable use (usually framed in economic terms) of his property (U.S. Water Resour. Counc., 1971).

It is not possible to make blanket generalizations concerning the validity of various land use regulations since the determination may vary with the circumstances of particular cases. It is clear, however, that the factual basis of land use controls is very important. "The absence of clear theoretical guidelines makes the *facts* become much more important than the law. What goes into the balance is more important than the balancing. Both in drafting and defending land use regulations, careful factual preparation is called for." (Bosselman et al., 1973, p. 293).

Using soils information can give regulations a sounder factual basis and thus strengthen them in terms of some of the basic tests of legal validity discussed above. Soil-based land use controls can help ensure that the regulations are reasonably related to achieving a valid public objective. An example is septic tank system regulations which protect public health (an objective which receives strong judicial support) by restricting private waste disposal in areas found unsuitable on the basis of scientific interpretation of soil properties. Soils information can also support a finding that a classification system is reasonable, e.g., where soils information is used to identify productive agricultural lands to be included in exclusive agricultural zoning districts. This would also help to ensure that the regulated lands are capable of producing a reasonable economic return and thus the regulations did not constitute a "taking" which deprived the property owner of all reasonable use.

III. EXAMPLES OF SOIL-BASED LAND USE REGULATIONS

A. Soils Information and Regulation of Unsewered Subdivisions and Septic Tank Systems

1. SUBDIVISION REGULATIONS

Subdivision regulations control the conversion of undeveloped land into building sites by requiring prior local and/or state agency approval before plats (scale drawings of monumented lots) can be recorded and lots can be sold. One of the purposes of subdivision regulations is to ensure adequate provision for public improvements such as streets, sewer and water facilities, and drainage ways. The subdivider can be required to install these necessary improvements or pay the municipality for the cost of installation (Freilich & Levi, 1975).

In areas outside the range of public sewerage systems, it is important to determine the suitability of soils within the subdivision for septic tank soil absorption systems. For example, Wisconsin statutes condition approval of plats, among other things, upon compliance with "The rules of the department of health and social services relating to lot size and lot elevations necessary for proper sanitary conditions in a subdivision not served by public sewer. . . ." (s. 236.13(1)(d) Wis. Stats. 1975). Other states may have similar provisions but the Wisconsin regulations will be used as an example. The physical features which affect the operation of a traditional soil absorption system are permeability, slope, ground water, bedrock, and flooding. Whether the soils within the subdivision are suitable for soil absorption systems and the minimum lot area required are determined primarily on the basis of soil boring and percolation tests. These tests must follow a procedure specified by state administrative rules and tests must be made by a soil tester certified by the department. The rules also contain standards which require that a specific percentage of each lot have a minimum elevation above high ground water (5 feet or 1.5 m), bedrock (5 feet or 1.5 m), and flood water (2 feet or 0.61 m). Additional requirements set maximum ground slopes (10 to 20% depending on the measured percolation rate) and require soil having a percolation rate of 60 min per inch or faster at least 3 feet (or 0.91 m) below the proposed bottom of the soil absorption system (H65, Wis. Adm. Code). Flooding data is usually evaluated on the basis of the highest flood of record unless a state or federal agency has established the 100-year flood level. Ground slopes are evaluated on the basis of slope information delineated on the subdivision plat by a registered land surveyor. Soil percolation tests need not be conducted if the department waives the requirement and bases minimum lot area on detailed soil map information. The department also uses detailed soil maps to cross-check data submitted on high ground water, depth to bedrock, slopes, and permeability of soils and may undertake its own field investigation in cases of uncertainty.

These state administrative rules, which apply when five or more lots of 1.5 acres (0.6 ha) or less in size are created within a 5-year period, are frequently supplemented by local subdivision ordinances which regulate divisions of less than the five lots or division of lots over 1½ acres (0.6 ha) in size. Detailed soils information is also used in the administration of local subdivision regulations. Subdividers are encouraged to use detailed soil information in the initial layout of subdivisions prior to plat preparation and many do so.

2. SEPTIC TANK REGULATIONS

In Wisconsin, state and local regulations for on-site waste disposal systems (sanitary regulations) supplement the soil boring and percolation tests required for unsewered subdivisions. Other states may have similar regulations, but the Wisconsin provisions will be used for illustration of the use of soils information in land use regulations. The state regulations contain, in addition to standards for septic tanks, specifications for the design, location, and minimum soil absorption area for septic tank systems on each lot.

There may be considerable variability in the ability of soil to absorb sewage effluent on the individual lots in a subdivision approved for on-site waste disposal since the maximum number of soil boring and percolation tests required is two tests per acre (0.4 ha). The subdivider may choose to make the initial soil and percolation tests of sufficient specificity to comply with the individual septic tank systems requirements by specifying the building area, well area, and two shallow soil absorption areas on the lot, but most subdividers do not choose to do so.

The individual septic tank system regulations specify soil boring and percolation tests, construction, location, and size requirements for septic tanks and soil absorption systems (H. 62.20 Wis. Adm. Code). A suitable alternate soil absorption area must be identified on each lot to reduce problems if the original site eventually fails to function properly. The size and design of each proposed soil absorption system is determined from the results of soil boring and percolation tests. At least three percolation tests and three soil borings must be conducted by a certified soil tester in the location of a proposed soil absorption system in the manner specified by the rules. Percolation tests, but not soil boring tests, may be waived by the department where a detailed soils map shows suitable soils and this fact is confirmed by soil bore test data. The department may also deny permission to install an on-site liquid waste disposal system where a detailed soils map and interpretative data show a lot consists entirely of soils having severe or very severe limitations for on-site liquid waste disposal. The property owner, however, may present soil percolation and bore test data to prove that a suitable site does exist.

Minimum separating distances between soil absorption systems and lot lines (5 feet, or 1.5 m), habitable buildings (25 feet, or 7.5 m), water wells (50 feet, or 15 m), and the high water mark of any lake, stream, or other water-course (50 feet) are also required. Soil absorption systems are not permitted in floodways but may be installed in floodplain areas outside the floodway with the written approval of the department and local government. The department rules are incorporated in county sanitary codes and are administered primarily on the county level by county sanitarians or county zoning administrators. Each county has zoning, subdivision regulations, and sanitary (individual septic tank) codes which apply within their unincorporated shoreland areas. Shorelands are defined by statutes as the lands "within the following distances from the normal high water elevation of navigable waters. .1,000 feet [305 m] from a lake, pond or flowage; 300 [91.5 m] feet from a river or stream or to the landward side of the floodplain, whichever distance is greater" (s. 59.971(1) Wis. Stats. 1975). Counties are required to adopt shoreland regulations consisting of zoning, subdivision regulations, and sanitary codes for shoreland areas. The majority have chosen to adopt county-wide subdivision regulations and sanitary codes.

3. COUNTY ADMINISTRATION OF SUBDIVISION REGULATIONS AND SEPTIC TANK REGULATIONS

Subdivision regulations for nonstate plats (lots over 1½ acres (0.6 ha) in size or fewer than five in number) are reviewed by the County Zoning Administrator and approved by the County Planning and Zoning Committee. Soils information in the form of detailed soils maps, soil borings, and percolations tests is used extensively in the administration of county subdivision regulations. Technical assistance with soils-related problems is available to counties from the Soil Conservation Service personnel, University of Wisconsin Extension Specialists, and the Department of Health and Social Services engineers and soil scientists.

Sanitary regulations are administered on the county level by county zoning administrators or sanitarians. Two permits are required. The first is a state septic tank permit which is required before a septic tank dealer may deliver a septic tank. State septic tank permits are issued by the county sanitarian or zoning administrator who sends a copy to the department. The second required permit is a local sanitary permit also issued by the county sanitarian or zoning administrator. Most Counties require a sanitary permit before issuing a building permit. The sanitary permit is issued only after a determination that soils are adequate for on-site waste disposal. This assures that there will be an area for an acceptable system prior to constructing a dwelling. The sanitary permit is not issued until soil borings and percolation tests are made by a certified soil tester. Certified soil testers are licensed by the department and are required to pass a written examination to test their ability to evaluate site and soil conditions (s. 145.045, Wis. Stats., 1975). They perform the required tests including percolation tests and soil borings to determine soil type and depth. The test results are reported on a standard form giving the soil type, percolation rate, slope, depth to ground water and bedrock, and the recommended location for the soil absorption system. The design and layout of the disposal system is based upon these test results and the number of bedrooms and plumbing fixtures in the home. The system must be installed by a plumber or septic tank installer licensed by the department.

Soil maps are very useful to screen areas for subdivisions and other land uses that require on-site liquid waste disposal. Using soil maps can help eliminate tracts of land that have severe limitations and can help in locating areas suitable for the intended use. Soil maps should not be the only source of information used to evaluate site conditions for a particular lot or soil absorption area. This is due primarily to limitations posed by the scale at which soil survey maps are published, i.e., 1:15,840 or 1:20,000. At this scale, areas of about 2 acres (0.8 ha) are usually the smallest shown on the map. In addition, scale limitations result in inclusions of other soils within the defined soil mapping units. These inclusions may differ in drainage, slope, and other characteristics. For these reasons, decisions concerning the suitability of a small area of land for liquid waste disposal should usually be supplemented by soil boring and percolation test information.

B. Soils Information and Exclusive Agricultural Zoning

1. EXCLUSIVE AGRICULTURAL ZONING—IN GENERAL

The continuing loss of good farm land through conversion to other uses is becoming a matter of public concern. A need to ensure adequate world food supplies and reasonable domestic food prices and recognition of the economic importance of maintaining local farms and related agricultural businesses are part of this concern. So, too, are an increasing recognition of the economic, environmental, and energy costs of urban sprawl. Farmers have a direct interest in protecting their operations from interference from urban land uses. Conflicts between agricultural and urban uses can arise over such issues as farm noise and odor, fence maintenance, and trespass. Separating farm and urban uses can also help reduce the cost of public services and help keep farm property assessments from rising as rapidly as they would if nearby farmland were being developed.

Exclusive agricultural zoning based on detailed soils information can delineate productive farmlands and limit their use to agriculture and necessary related activities. What follows is a brief description of several somewhat different approaches to exclusive agricultural zoning using soils information. These approaches vary in terms of the regulatory provisions, the way in which soils information is used, and the degree of land use planning undertaken prior to adopting the zoning.

2. EXCLUSIVE AGRICULTURAL ZONING—IN COLUMBIA COUNTY

Columbia County, located in south central Wisconsin, was the first county in the state to adopt exclusive agricultural zoning. Approximately 70% of the county's 510,700 acres (206,833 ha) are in agricultural use. The county contains some very fertile and productive prairie soils. Columbia County was experiencing significant development pressures in rural areas. These pressures came in large part from the Madison metropolitan area located within easy commuting distance on the Interstate Highway. The County Extension Agent estimated that the county had been losing about 3,000 acres (1,215 ha) of agricultural land over the past several years. Residential development in rural areas increased taxes on agricultural land. This, in turn, led farmers to sell more lots to pay the increased taxes. There were also complaints from nonfarm residents who felt annoyed by the noise and odors of farming operations. In March 1973, the County Board amended the general agricultural zoning district which had served as a catch-all for a mixture of agricultural and nonagricultural land uses. In its place they substituted provisions to limit residential development in agricultural districts to farm residences and one additional structure per farm for farm labor.

The following statement was adopted by the county to explain the new zoning policy:

> In areas having prime agricultural soils, all types of residential development should be discouraged, unless the housing unit will be for farm labor. In areas having marginal agricultural soils, housing units could be permitted where they are not in conflict with existing agricultural uses, and where these future housing units would be located in such a fashion as to minimize their impact on the agricultural tax base.

The policy also states that:

> Future residential developments should be encouraged to locate in areas where they could be adequately served with central sewer and water, be conveniently

located close to schools and shopping facilities and have adequate police and fire protection.

When Columbia County amended the text of the zoning ordinance to establish an exclusive agricultural zone, it did not change its zoning district maps which had placed most rural lands in the agricultural district, including productive and marginal agricultural soils as well as nontillable lands (Deknatel & Harris, 1974). County officials recognized that, because of this fact, not all lands in the agricultural district could be protected against non-farm residences. Instead, they use the written policy statements described above to evaluate applications to rezone agricultural land to permit residential development. The Zoning Committee inspects most parcels of land proposed to be rezoned from agricultural use. A form which accompanies zoning petitions notes, among other things, the soil classification for agricultural use and suitability of soils for residential use based upon the detailed soil survey. Additional standards applied in considering rezoning requests include potential for land use conflicts between agricultural and urban uses and costs of providing necessary public services for nonagricultural uses. Few petitions for rezoning have been approved for Class I, II, or III agricultural land.

3. EXCLUSIVE AGRICULTURAL ZONING—IN WALWORTH COUNTY

Walworth County, Wisconsin, which lies in the southeast corner of the state between Milwaukee and Chicago, has also adopted exclusive agricultural zoning. The county covers an area of 576 mi^2 (1,492 km^2) with small cities and villages throughout the area. Recreation (there are 37 lakes in the county) and agriculture (there are more than 1,300 farms) are important mainstays of the local economy. More than two-thirds of the land area is rated as prime farmland. The attractive physical setting of the county and its proximity to large urban metropolitan areas brought about development pressure. Farmland was being consumed at an alarming rate. Approximately 300 scattered building sites were located in a several-year period with 70% of them occurring on prime agricultural land. To counteract the loss of productive agricultural soils and reduce the urban sprawl characteristic of metropolitan regions, the County embarked on a revision of its zoning (Ihlenfeldt et al., 1975).

Walworth County's approach to agricultural zoning, which also uses detailed soils information, differs from the approach used by Columbia County. The more complex Walworth County ordinance has 26 separate use districts including 5 agricultural zones (A-1 Prime Agricultural Land District; A-2 Agricultural Land District; A-3 Agricultural Land Holding District; A-4 Agricultural Related Manufacturing, Warehousing, and Marketing District; and A-5 Agricultural-Rural Residential District). These use districts are delineated on large-scale zoning base maps. As a result, the permitted use of each parcel of agricultural land is predesignated rather than requiring a case-by-case determination at the time development permission is sought. A brief description of the five agricultural districts follows.

The stated purpose of A-1 Prime Agricultural Land District is to "maintain, preserve and enhance agricultural lands historically exhibiting high crop yields. Such lands are generally covered by Class I, II, & III soils as rated by the U.S. Department of Agriculture, Soil Conservation Service. As a matter of policy, it is hereby determined that the highest and best use of these lands is agriculture." Uses not associated with agricultural operations are not permitted in this district which has a 35-acre (14.2-ha) minimum lot size. The A-2 Agricultural Land District has as its purpose "to maintain, preserve and enhance lands historically utilized for crop production but which are not included within the A-1 Prime Agricultural Land District and which are generally best suited for smaller farm units, including truck farming, horse farming, hobby farming, orchards, and other similar agricultural-related farming activity." Minimum lot size in the A-2 district is 5 acres (2 ha) which permits the same general activities as the A-1 district along with hobby farming and nonfarm residences. The A-2 zoning thus applies to lands with a wide range of uses from general farming to nonfarm residences. The A-2 district with a 5-acre minimum lot size also serves as a buffer between prime agricultural areas and higher density residential areas. The A-3 Agricultural Land Holding District generally is located adjacent to cities and villages where urban expansion is planned to take place. It permits only agricultural and open space uses on a minimum size 35-acre tract. These areas are expected to be rezoned when the affected municipality determines it is economically and financially feasible to provide public services and facilities for nonagricultural use. The status of the A-3 district is required to be reviewed at least every 5 years. The A-4 Agricultural Related Manufacturing, Warehousing, and Marketing District is designed to provide for the location of manufacturing, warehousing, storage, and related industrial and marketing activities such as canning plants, feed and grain mills, and livestock sales facilities which are dependent upon agriculture. Other industrial uses not so closely allied to agriculture would be located in a traditional industrial district. The A-5 Agricultural-Rural Residential District permits single family dwellings and limited agricultural activities on small parcels with a minimum lot size of 40,000 feet^2 (3,720 m^2) on lands which may be productive soils but are not readily useable for agricultural production, e.g., remnant parcels severed from farms by road construction (Southeast. Wisconsin Reg. Planning Comm. Newsl., 1976).

4. EXCLUSIVE AGRICULTURAL ZONING—IN MICHIGAN

A Michigan publication, "The Use of Zoning to Retain Essential Agricultural Lands," outlines an approach to agricultural land retention with other features (Michigan Farm Bur. et al., 1976). It suggests the preparation of an agricultural plan to provide a factual base to support agricultural zoning. The three basic purposes of the agricultural plan are to: (i) document the importance of the agricultural industry; (ii) locate essential agricultural land areas; and (iii) explain how zoning will be applied to preserve agricultural land. The importance of the agricultural industry is established by data substantiating its economic, agricultural production, and environmental contributions. The criteria for identification of essential agricultural lands is based upon the classification system developed by the U.S. Soil Conservation Service (SCS) for inventorying prime and unique farmland. (This system is discussed in a following section.) The lands contained within the soil mapping units indicated by this classification are included within an Agricultural Production District (exclusive agricultural) unless they fall within certain exceptions. The exceptions, designed to insure legal validity of the zoning, include land areas: (i) served by public sewer and water; (ii) immediately adjacent to intense urban development; (iii) within an approved subdivision plat; and (iv) with no history of economic agricultural production. Permited uses in the Agricultural Production District are limited to agricultural production and residences for the farm owner and employees. Other uses clearly related to or compatible with agricultural production would be permitted by special approval. One or more buffer zoning districts permitting agricultural production as well as single family homes on large lots are suggested to reduce land use conflicts between commercial agriculture and incompatible intensive land uses.

5. USE OF SOILS INFORMATION TO DELINEATE EXCLUSIVE AGRICULTURAL ZONING DISTRICTS

The previously discussed systems of exclusive agricultural zoning employed by Wisconsin Counties define prime farmland in terms of SCS land capability classes. This interpretive classification groups various soil mapping units into eight classes, i.e., Class I–VIII, primarily on the basis of their capability to produce common cultivated crops and pasture plants without deterioration of the soil over a long period of time.

a. The Soil Conservation Service Land Inventory and Monitoring Memorandum Method—The suggested Michigan approach is adapted from a more comprehensive attempt to develop a quantitative national classification system to define the most productive agricultural land. This system is contained in a Land Inventory and Monitoring (LIM) Memorandum developed by the SCS (Soil Conserv. Serv., 1975). The memorandum sets forth four possible categories of land needed for present and future food and fiber production, i.e., prime farmland, unique farmland, farmland of statewide importance, and farmland of local importance. Prime farmland is the land best suited for food, feed, forage, fiber, and oilseed crops (excluding land in urban use or under water). It could be presently in crops or pasture, range or forest. Prime farmland has characteristics that assure sustained high yields of adapted crops and returns a profit when managed according to modern farming methods. The criteria are based upon the following soil, climate, and topographic features: soil moisture, soil temperature, growing season, soil acidity, soil salinity, soil permeability, contents of coarse fragments, soil depth, and soil erodibility. In terms of land capability classes, prime farmland is about equal to Class I and II and also includes some Class III land.

Unique farmland is land other than prime farmland that is used to produce specific high-value food and fiber crops. It has a special combination of soil quality, location, climate, growing season, and moisture supply that favor the growth of a specific crop when treated and managed according to modern farming methods. Examples of such specialty crops are citrus, olives, cranberries, mint, avocados, and other fruit and vegetables.

Farmland of statewide importance is land in addition to prime and unique lands which is determined by a state agency to possess certain important characteristics. This could include Class III and Class IV lands not included within the prime and unique categories as well as land which could be potentially productive, e.g., by irrigation. These state-identified criteria will vary widely depending upon not only the type, but amounts of productive soil available (e.g., some states have little prime land) and its importance to the state's agricultural economy.

Farmlands of local importance are additional lands identified on the basis of criteria developed by local officials. SCS has begun a program of preparing interpretive mapping of one or more of the four categories of agricultural land starting with counties with available soil survey data where rapid land use changes are present or likely. Plans are to do 250 county-mapped farmland inventories (at a scale of 1:100,000 or 1:50,000 for small counties) in fiscal year 1977 and 300 a year from 1978 until all 3,068 counties are inventoried (Dideriksen & Sampson, 1976). These farmland maps will be very useful in showing broad patterns of important farmland on a local basis. Large-scale maps, however, would be required for delineating zoning districts maps. For agricultural zoning purposes the detailed soil survey maps at a scale of 1:20,000 or 1:15,840 could be used as a zoning base map for rural counties if maps of a larger scale are not available. Chapter 12 "Defining, Delineating, and Designing Uses for Prime and Unique Lands" gives additional details of these concepts.

b. Procedures Used in Walworth County—The criteria used to define land for inclusion in the Prime Agricultural District were that the lands have the following characteristics: (i) be classified as Class I, II, or III soils according to SCS land capability classification; (ii) be part of a large contiguous block of land not having experienced significant urban encroachment; and (iii) consist of relatively large farm units (average 200 acres [81 ha]) where division of lands into small farm and residential parcels had not occurred. Where a significant portion of the soils are unsuitable for on-site waste disposal, this influenced the decision to include the area in the exclusive agricultural zoning district.

The procedure began with a refinement of the regional land use plan on a county-wide basis. Overlaid on this map were two broad categories of lands—prime soils (Class I-III) and secondary soils (Class IV-VIII) to show general soil patterns on a county-wide basis. More detailed maps were then prepared for each town using a series of 1 inch = 1,000 feet transparent milar overlays showing (i) existing land use including urban uses; (ii) suitability of soils for on-site waste disposal; and (iii) prime and secondary agricultural soils. In addition, areas of high environmental quality such as prime park sites and areas of high forestry and wildlife value were delineated. By following this procedure, a preliminary pattern of prime agricultural soils on a town basis emerged. In order to refine town land use maps into zoning base maps at a scale showing a parcel by parcel designation, this information was transferred on a 1 inch = 400 feet scale aerial photo base map covering four sections (2,560 acres [1,037 ha]). Agricultural Stabilization and Conservation Service records were also used to ensure the parcel had a record of crop production.

c. Wisconsin's Farmland Preservation Law—In the summer of 1977 a new law was passed to help agricultural landowners and local governments in Wisconsin preserve farmland (Barrows, 1978). The Farmland Preservation Program provides property tax relief to eligible farmers who participate in local programs to preserve farmlands. The amount of potential tax credit received is based upon a statutory formula which provides the most tax credit to farmers with high property taxes and low net household income. The law also contains incentives to local governments to adopt agricultural preservation plans and/or exclusive agricultural zoning ordinances. Continuing eligibility of landowners past 1982 requires county adoption of at least one of these measures. The maximum potential credit is available to eligible landowners where there is both exclusive agricultural zoning and an agricultural preservation plan. State financial assistance is available to counties to map agricultural lands and prepare agricultural preservation plans. Both Columbia and Walworth counties have adopted agricultural preservation plans and exclusive agricultural zoning ordinances which were certified by the state, thus making their landowners eligible for the maximum credit.

C. Soils Information and Inland Wetland Regulations

1. INLAND WETLAND REGULATIONS—IN GENERAL

It is estimated that our nation's wetlands have been reduced by almost one half in the last 100 years (from 127 million acres (51.4 million ha] to 70 million acres [28.3 million ha]) (Thurow et al., 1975). In earlier times, many people considered wetlands to be worthless areas which should be converted to more productive agricultural or urban uses. Most of the loss in wetlands was due to agricultural drainage, but filling for residential, commercial, and industrial development, highway construction, and solid waste disposal have also had a major impact in urban areas. Today, public sentiment is changing as people are becoming aware of the many valuable functions wetlands perform. Wetlands can furnish habitat for a wide variety of plants and animals, store floodwaters, improve the quality of water entering lakes and streams by trapping sediment and nutrients, and provide outdoor class-rooms and open space in urban areas. In addition, wetland soils often pose construction problems such as unsuitability for on-site waste disposal and poor structural bearing capacity.

One way to maintain the natural functions of wetlands is to protect them from unwarranted conversion through regulations. These regulations can take the form of either wetland conservancy zoning or special wetland laws which require a permit prior to undertaking regulated activities. Wet-land regulations restrict dredging and filling and also generally attempt to limit permitted activities to nonintensive uses to minimize the impact of de-velopment. Different wetland regulations vary in terms of the stringency of their provisions, the specificity of the wetland definition, and the method used to delineate the wetlands. In order to adopt and administer reasonable wetland regulations, it is important to describe the wetland functions de-signed to be protected, define wetlands to specify the areas to be regulated, and delineate these areas on a map.

2. DEFINING INLAND WETLANDS

The definition of a wetland should encompass its key parameters in order to specify the areas that will be subject to land use controls. Wetlands are complex natural systems which can be defined in terms of their water re-gime, plants, and soils. Water in wetlands may be ponded, at-the-surface, or subsurface. A wide variety of water-tolerant species of plants are found in wetlands. Like other natural plant communities they are dynamic and their composition changes over time. However, since wetlands are a transi-tion area between dry land and open water, it may be particularly difficult to locate them and delineate their boundaries on the basis of water level or plant types. Water-logged areas in the spring may be dry during much of the rest of the year and the wetland plant community may shrink in times of drought and expand in years with heavy rainfalls. The distinctive soils of wetlands are influenced by hydrologic and biologic processes. Wetland soils may be composed mainly of mineral materials (sand, silt, and clay) or or-ganic materials (peat and muck). Wet mineral soils form where the water table is slightly below the land surface for much of each year. Organic soils form where the water table is at or above the surface most of the time and dead plants remain saturated and decay very slowly. The morphology of wetland soils thus integrates over time the interactions of the climate, plants, water regime, and parent material (Yanggen et al., 1976).

3. DELINEATING INLAND WETLANDS

An important next step, closely related to the problem of defining a wetland is locating the wetland boundaries. Some wetland control programs do not map the wetlands as a part of the regulations. Instead they rely on the regulatory definition to determine whether a proposed activity will take place in a wetland. The imprecision and administrative confusion associated with this approach make it at best a stop-gap measure until wetland maps can be obtained (Thurow et al., 1975).

The U.S. Geological Survey (USGS) Topographic Map is the best known and most widely available source showing the location of wetlands. These maps identify wetlands by a cartographic swamp symbol. The boundaries of the wetland are not delineated by a line but must be interpreted from the location of the outer edge of the swamp symbol. Topographic maps are generally available at a scale of 1:24,000. These maps comply with National Map Accuracy Standards which means that 90% of all features must be within 1/40 of an inch of their true horizontal position. At this scale the location of a point may be off by at least 50 feet (15.25 m). Since an ordinary number 2 pencil line placed on this map is 50 feet wide an error of 100 feet is easily possible (Greulich, 1975). The location of wetlands on USGS maps is based primarily upon steroscopic interpretation of air photos indicating vegetative cover at the time the photo was flown.

Detailed soil survey maps published at a scale of 1:20,000 or at a scale of 1:15,840 can also be used to identify wetland areas. The same problems attendent on scale limitations also exist for soil maps.

Aerial photo maps at a larger scale, if they comply with National Map Accuracy Standards, can be correspondingly more accurate (the scale and accuracy of maps prepared photogrametrically depend upon ground control, i.e., ground measurements made prior to flight). At a scale of 1:4,800, for example, features would be within 10 feet (3 m) of their true horizontal position. While highly desirable, the cost of accurate maps at this scale may preclude their use by some local units of government.

Another approach is to shift the burden for accurate mapping to the developer. Some wetland ordinances require an application for a wetland permit to be accompanied by an accurate plan at a more detailed scale (e.g., 1:600 or 1:1,200). These plans prepared by a registered land surveyor based on an actual field survey can be "tied into" a more generalized map by being plotted on a USGS map or soils map.

Under any of the above approaches, it is desirable to provide that, in cases of doubt, field inspection may be made by qualified persons to determine wetland soils and plant types to more accurately locate wetland boundaries.

4. THE CONNECTICUT INLAND WETLAND ACT

The Connecticut Inland Wetland Act passed in 1972 is designed to protect that state's wetlands by charging municipalities (or the state if municipalities fail to act) with the responsibility of regulating the use of wetlands. Municipal wetland regulatory agencies which review permits for regulated activities must decide whether the proposed activity will be injurious to the wetland under the terms of the act. One of the distinctive features of this law is its definition of inland wetlands by soil classification. Inland wetlands are defined as ". . .land . . .which consists of any of the soil types designated as poorly-drained, very poorly drained, alluvial, and floodplain by the National Cooperative Soils Survey." The alternative of a vegetative definition for inland wetlands was considered in Connecticut, but would have required a new map of the entire state. On the other hand, detailed soil survey maps were completed for over two-thirds of the state (McCluskey, 1973).

The morphology of the soils classified as wetlands by the Inland Wetlands Act can be divided into three categories: (i) poorly drained and very poorly drained mineral soils; (ii) very poorly drained peat and muck; and (iii) well-drained and moderately well-drained alluvial soils. Poorly drained and very poorly drained mineral soils are saturated with water within 3 feet (0.914 m) of the surface for at least 2 months of the year. Very poorly drained soils can be identified in many instances by a predominantly gray or bluish gray subsoil or by distinct mottles just below the surface. (Mottles are streaks and spots of yellow, brown, red, or gray.) Soils with distinct mottles within 6–10 inches (15 to 25 cm) of the surface are commonly mapped as poorly drained (Hill, 1973).

Very poorly drained peat and muck are organic soils which form in water-filled depressions from dead plants and algae. Peat soils are fibrous and often contain layered or matted plants such as reeds, sedges, or mosses. As peat decomposes due to a fluctuating water table, it changes to a darker material called *muck*. Muck is less fibrous than peat and has a blocky or granular structure. Well-drained and moderately well-drained alluvial soils are young geographically and lack profile development. They may also contain buried organic rich soil horizons which represent former flood plain surfaces (Yanggen et al., 1976).

In Connecticut, a field exercise was conducted to determine the variability of placement in soil boundaries by soil surveyors. Six SCS soil surveyors were instructed to segregate only poorly drained, very poorly drained, and alluvial soils. The soil boundaries of all six surveyors were superimposed to produce a composite map that delineated areas of undisputed wetlands, areas of undisputed upland, and a disputed zone between the two. There was a considerable variability in the wetland mapping due largely to the surveyor's difficulty in accurately locating his points of observation on the map even at larger scales of 1:1200 and 1:2400. It was concluded that the use of the soil survey may be limited if high degrees of accuracy are required in the location of boundaries on the map. Another problem involves classification of soil in glaciated areas with considerable variances. Of the 15 poorly drained mineral soils mapped in Connecticut, 12 have ranges that extend them into somewhat poorly drained soils (not defined as wetlands under the act). To extend the definition of wetlands to include the somewhat poorly drained soils would include some areas not associated with prolonged wetness, i.e., not wetlands. Thus soil series and types which include somewhat poorly drained classes may require on-site inspection by a soil scientist in cases of dispute where precise identification is required (Hill, 1973).

D. Soils Information and Riverine Flood Plain Regulations

1. RIVERINE FLOOD PLAIN REGULATIONS—IN GENERAL

Periodic inundation of the flood plains of rivers and streams is a natural event which occurs when they perform their function of carrying flood flows from heavy rainfall or snowmelt. As man develops the flood plain, houses, businesses, and industries suffer flood damage, and so, too, do streets, utilities, and other public facilities serving these flood-prone areas.

Land use controls such as zoning and subdivision regulations can be used to adjust man's activity to the flood threat. Regulations can help keep development with a high flood damage susceptibility away from floods as an alternative to protective works which attempt to keep floods away from development. The basic purpose of flood plain zoning is to guide and control the future development of flood hazard areas so as to limit potential flood damage.

The flood plain is the area adjoining a stream which has been or may be covered by flood water. The areal extent of the flood plain varies with the magnitude of the flood, i.e., the flood plain limits depend upon the size of the flood discharge. For regulatory purposes, a flood discharge of a 100-year frequency is commonly used to delineate the limits of flood plain areas. The riverine flood plain for any given size flood can be divided into a floodway and a floodway fringe.

The floodway is the channel of a stream and those portions of the flood plain adjoining the channel which are needed to carry and discharge flood flows. In times of flooding, a sufficient portion of the adjoining overbank must be preserved to convey flood flows. Encroachment by structures or fill in these high velocity areas adjacent to the stream channel obstructs flood flows and has a partial damming effect. For regulatory purposes a floodway is delineated as an area to be kept free of obstructions so as not to increase natural flood levels more than a selected amount.

The floodway fringe is the portion of the flood plain which lies landward of the floodway. Although this area may be inundated, flood velocities will be relatively low and flood depths shallow. Flood plain zoning ordinances usually permit development in the floodway fringe such as buildings, storage, and fill provided development is protected from floods to the regulatory flood elevation.

Location of the boundaries of the flood plain, floodway, and floodway fringe is necessary for complete regulation of flood hazard areas. Flood data collection and interpretation, and mapping of the regulatory boundaries are usually the most time-consuming and expensive elements in developing flood plain regulations. In urban areas or other areas subject to substantial development pressure, this engineering analysis should be performed and the regulatory boundaries mapped prior to adoption of regulations.

To develop accurately delineated maps for flood plain regulations three basic steps are necessary:

1) determine the magnitude of the discharge of the regulatory (e.g., 100-year recurrence interval) flood;
2) determine the elevation of the selected flood discharge (flood profile) based upon a hydraulic engineering analysis of the stream channel and overbank areas. Unless obstructed, floodwaters follow the general slope of the stream channel and thus flood heights vary for each point along the stream. The flood profile shows the elevation of the flood along the course of a stream. The elevations shown on the flood profile when indicated on topographic maps show the flood limits. When a flood susceptible use is to be located in the floodway fringe the profile of the regulatory flood determines the height to which the use must be elevated or otherwise protected; and
3) delineate the floodway through hydrologic studies which route flood flows from upstream to downstream areas without increasing flood heights and velocities beyond selected amounts (Yanggen, 1972).

A two-district flood plain zoning ordinance can be used in areas where detailed engineering analysis of the type described previously has determined the flood plain, floodway, and profile of the regulatory flood. Although the details of two-district flood plain ordinances may vary, the general approach is to divide the flood hazard area into a Floodway District and a Floodway Fringe District.

Within the Floodway District, permitted uses are limited to those which have a relatively low flood damage potential and which will not obstruct flood flows. Prohibited uses involve structures, fill, or storage of materials which would be hazardous in times of flood or would materially obstruct flood flows.

The boundaries of the Floodway Fringe District, like those of Floodway District, are shown on the zoning map which accompanies the written text of the zoning ordinance. Since the floodway fringe does not contribute appreciably to the passage of flood flows and has relatively low depths and velocities, the ordinance permits almost all uses in the Floodway Fringe Districts. However, structures which would be substantially damaged by inundation are required to be elevated by fill or other methods to a point above the regulatory flood elevation, or are required to be flood proofed. Open-space uses, storage, and certain structures are permitted to be located below the regulatory flood elevation if they have limited flood damage potential and will not damage other lands during flooding because of their buoyancy or toxic nature.

In cities or other areas of high value land, every effort should be made to obtain the engineering data necessary for a two-district flood plain zoning ordinance. However, there may be circumstances where regulation is needed but there is a lack of time and money necessary to develop this detailed engineering data. An example of this type of situation would be the need to regulate scattered rural flood plain development in agricultural or recreational areas. Rather than leave such areas unregulated, detailed soil survey information can be used, in some cases, to delineate flood plains for regulatory purposes.

2. USE OF SOILS INFORMATION TO DELINEATE RIVERINE FLOOD PLAIN ZONING DISTRICTS

The rationale for using soils information to delineate riverine flood plains is that flood plain soils are often found on distinct geomorphic surfaces, usually in areas of active deposition. Detailed soil survey maps can be interpreted to provide a record of past flooding events as evidenced by the presence of these flood-deposited soils. Alluvial soils on contemporary flood plains are young and do not show the normal sequence of horizons which are present in older soils on adjacent upland slopes. Most soils formed in alluvium along streams, together with peat and muck deposits that are a part of stream bottomland, are flooded at frequent intervals. Rarer floods, e.g., the 100-year flood, will inundate additional areas. Non-alluvial soils most apt to be flooded or ponded include somewhat poorly to very poorly drained mineral soils associated with the alluvial soils or connected to the alluvial bottomlands by waterways of low gradient. In some places, deposition can reduce the carrying capacity of the physiographic flood plain to a point where well-drained soils on low terraces or gently sloping uplands near the stream also flood. A soil scientist familiar with soil patterns in the particular reach of the stream can use ancillary data such as floods of record and high water marks to identify additional areas likely to be inundated by rarer events (Lee et al., 1972).

Studies which have compared flood plain boundaries delineated by engineering methods with flood plains delineated by detailed soil survey interpretations show relatively good agreement between the two methods in the case of mature landscapes which have streams well incised into deep valleys. Detailed soil survey interpretation of flood plain areas is less accurate in glaciated areas with low gradient slopes and a poorly defined drainage pattern or where recent man-made obstructions have raised flood heights beyond that recorded by the soil characteristics (Parker et al., 1970).

3. ADMINISTERING SOIL-DELINEATED FLOOD PLAIN ZONING

Soils information can thus be used in some cases to delineate the boundaries of the regulatory flood plain to an acceptable degree of accuracy. This area is designated as the *General Flood Plain District* on the zoning map. However, additional information is necessary to reasonably regulate flood plain development. The two other essential elements which must be determined are: (i) the location of the area within which encroachment is prohibited, i.e., the floodway; and (ii) the height of the regulatory flood elevation. These determinations can be made on a case-by-case basis at the time development permission is sought.

Within the General Flood Plain District most open-space uses are permitted as a matter of right. (These uses are similar to those permitted in the

Floodway District of a two-district zoning ordinance.) All other uses, i.e., fill and structures, are Special Exceptions. An applicant for a Special Exception use is required to submit certain information about the site, i.e., valley cross-section, stream slope, and other data needed to evaluate the flood hazard. Through an engineering procedure called *normal depth analysis,* approximations are made of the flood heights and the effects of encroachment. Such case-by-case analysis can be made, of course, only where such expert engineering review is available.

4. SOIL-DELINEATED FLOOD PLAIN ZONING IN WISCONSIN

Wisconsin law requires counties, cities, and villages to adopt reasonable and effective flood plain zoning ordinances within their respective jurisdictions where serious damage from floods may occur. The law further provides that if local governmental units fail to adopt adequate regulations the state is to adopt them for the noncomplying locality. If the state adopts the ordinance, the community must pay the cost of the adoption process and administer the ordinance as if it had been locally enacted (s. 87.30 Wis. Stats., 1975).

Engineering studies serve as the basis for delineation of the regulatory flood plain in urban and urbanizing areas in Wisconsin. However, since counties are also required to adopt flood plain zoning where serious damage from floods may occur, other methods for delineation are also recognized. The relevant portion of the Wisconsin administrative code (N.R. 116, Wis. Adm. Code) recognizing the use of detailed soil surveys as an alternative method is as follows:

NR 116.09 DATA REQUIRED TO BE SHOWN ON FLOOD PLAIN ZONING MAPS. . . . .
(2) WHERE ADEQUATE ENGINEERING DATA DOES NOT EXIST.
Where adequate engineering data does not exist, experience flood maps, flood prone area maps, flood hazard boundary maps, aerial photos or *detailed soils maps may initially serve as a basis for flood plain,* [emphasis added] provided that:
(a) The associated text of the zoning ordinance provides for a special exception procedure similar to Sections NR 116.20(2) and NR 116.21(3) to ascertain the effects of the proposed construction of every project upon flood flows and the flood protection elevation; and
(b) The local unit of government has initiated a program to ultimately obtain an engineering study for regional flood data in problem areas.

Of the counties adopting flood plain zoning ordinances in compliance with the state standards, 13 counties have used the detailed soil survey as the predominant method of flood plain delineation in rural areas. Most are located in the southwestern portion of Wisconsin, in the so-called "Driftless Area"—a mature landscape with streams incised into deep valleys. The rate of building developing in this largely rural area of the state is relatively low. As a result, requests for state-level engineering review to determine the floodway and regulatory flood protection elevation as a part of the special exception administration procedure have been few in number.

Table 1—General ranking of potential for using detailed soil survey information for selected land use controls.

Factors affecting utility	Regulation of unsewered subdivisions	Septic tank regulations	Exclusive agricultural zoning	Wetland regulations	Flood plain zoning
1. Relationship of regulatory issue to soil properties and features	High	High	High-medium	High-medium	Medium
2. Specificity of soil mapping unit	High-medium	High-medium	High	Medium	Medium-low
3. Scale and accuracy of soil map	Medium-low	Low	High-medium	Medium-low	Medium-low

IV. SUMMARY AND CONCLUSIONS

A. Evaluation of Use of Soils Information in Selected Land Use Controls

An evaluation of the utility of basing land use controls upon soils information depends upon the type of information used and the specific regulatory context within which it is applied. Basic considerations are: (i) the extent to which the regulatory issue addressed is related to soil properties and related landscape features; (ii) the specificity with which these properties and features are reflected in the soil mapping unit; and (iii) the scale and accuracy of the soil map (Table 1). The following discussion relates these factors to the four regulatory programs previously discussed, i.e., subdivision and septic tank regulations, exclusive agricultural zoning, wetland regulations, and flood plain zoning.

1. SUBDIVISION AND SEPTIC TANK REGULATIONS

On-site liquid waste disposal through use of soil absorption systems is clearly a regulatory issue directly related to soil properties. The accuracy of soil taxonomic classifications for ground water and bedrock is generally considered adequate for regulatory purposes, but permeability (hydraulic conductivity) may vary and thus on-site tests are required in many cases. Related landscape features such as slope and flooding are also generally not disclosed with sufficient specificity to obviate the need for on-site inspection. Soil mapping units which are homogeneous, i.e., do not contain dissimilar inclusions and which have a low variability of key soil properties, may be sufficiently accurate to determine soil conditions. The biggest drawback, however, is the scale of detailed soil maps which precludes delineating areas smaller than 2 acres (0.8 ha). This does not permit identifying the specific location of soil absorption sites which may range from 2,500 to 5,000 feet^2 (232.3 to 464.5 m^2) in area. Detailed soils maps are thus most useful for determining the general suitability of soils within areas proposed for development where on-site investigations is used to more precisely determine specific conditions.

2. EXCLUSIVE AGRICULTURAL ZONING

Soils information should be a major consideration in deciding which lands should be zoned for exclusive agricultural use. Detailed soil mapping units can be interpreted to establish suitability for a variety of agricultural uses including potential yields for common field crops, hay, and pasture. The relative rate of erosion for each soil mapping unit and management practices to keep soil losses within allowable limits can also be determined. Since exclusive agricultural zoning ordinances will typically provide for a minimum parcel size of 35 acres (14.2 ha) or more, the scale of detailed soil survey maps should generally not pose a limitation.

The determination of which areas should be kept in agricultural use will vary among different regulatory jurisdictions depending upon the type of soils present, the farming methods practiced, and the specific land use objectives to be implemented. Among the questions which must be addressed to define the specific regulatory objectives are the following: (i) Is the intent to preserve the most productive farm land or land in productive farms? In the latter case, for example, lands in permanent pasture which were an integral part of a farm operation might be included even though not Class I–III soils. (ii) Are lands which are productive under selected management practices such as conservation tillage on steep slopes, irrigation of droughty soils, or drainage of wet soils to be included? (iii) Are lands devoted to specialized agricultural production such as cranberries and other fruits and vegetables to be regulated? (iv) Must the land selected have a history of productive agricultural use or merely potential for such use? Is potential for agricultural use to be determined purely on physical grounds (i.e., a wooded area with Class II soils) or economic grounds (e.g., irrigable sandy soils in an area in transition to irrigated agriculture)?

There are other factors which may preclude designation of productive agricultural land for exclusive agricultural zoning. Among these nonsoil related factors are: (i) whether substantial urbanization has already occurred; (ii) present investment in public sewer, water, and other facilities to serve urban development; and (ii) existing or planned land use which is incompatible with agriculture.

3. WETLANDS REGULATIONS

Soils are an important indicator of wetland conditions along with vegetative types and the water regimen. Soil conditions can integrate the latter two factors over time and thus provide a more permanent record less subject to periodic fluctuation. Not all wetlands can be distinguished by soil types. Restricting the definition of a wetland to poorly drained mineral soils would exclude areas considered wetlands by other criteria, but including all somewhat poorly drained soils would include areas which are not wetlands. In addition, the accuracy and scale of detailed soil survey maps may be insufficient when regulating relatively small areas with high land values. On-site investigation and use of other information such as ground water conditions and vegetative types can be used to supplement soils information to often produce a reasonable degree of accuracy in such cases.

4. FLOOD PLAIN REGULATIONS

Soils information is a useful indicator of lands subject to frequent flooding in mature riverine flood plains. Lands in these areas likely to be inundated by rarer events (e.g., the 100-year flood) can also be identified by experienced personnel considering physiographic elements and other data such as flood records. This soil-based delineation can be used to establish initial regulatory jurisdiction. Applicants seeking development permission within these areas can be required to submit additional information in the form of valley cross-sections, stream slope, etc. Engineers can use this information to perform normal depth analysis or other engineering calculations and make the necessary estimate of flood heights and determine areas which must remain unobstructed to pass flood flows. Soils maps are generally not definitive of regulatory flood plain boundaries in young landscapes with low gradient slopes and a poorly defined drainage pattern. In addition, the scale of soils maps may be insufficient when regulating small tracts with relatively high land values.

B. Conclusions

1. GENERAL ADVANTAGES

There are a number of advantages to using soils information in the drafting and administration of appropriate land use controls. Detailed soil surveys may be readily available in many areas which lack other resource inventories. Soils information can be interpreted for multiple purposes in land use planning and regulations. Soil mapping units and their interpretations which are part of a national system provide objective standards and a common basis of classification. In some instances, e.g., wetland delineation, soils integrate other key parameters and reflect a stable measurement of ephemeral phenomena. People may be better able to understand regulations using soil information than those using other concepts, e.g., identification of flood-prone areas on the basis of flood-deposited soils rather than engineering calculations of the limits of inundation of a hypothetical flood. The detailed soil survey map at a scale of 1:15,840 (4 inches to the mile or 6.3 cm to the kilometer) may be the best available base map in some rural areas. In short, knowledge of the location and responses of soils to various land uses allows land use to better fit the natural landscape and gives regulations a stronger basis in fact than may otherwise be possible.

2. LIMITATIONS AND TECHNIQUES TO MINIMIZE THEM

Reasonable regulatory use of soils information must be based upon a recognition of both its potentials and limitations. Not all land use issues are directly related to soils and most regulatory concerns involve other factors.

The mapping unit may include too broad a range of soil properties to accurately reflect the particular physical features sought to be regulated. The presence of inclusions may preclude complete reliance on soil information for site specific determinations. Map scale and accuracy may be insufficiently precise for regulating small areas of high value land. Soil maps reflect past physical conditions which may have been changed by human intervention after the inventory was completed.

Appropriate drafting techniques and administrative provisions can be used to minimize many of these limitations. A statement of regulatory purpose and intent can specify the objectives designed to be achieved and can identify the role that soils information plays. Where administrative flexibility in the form of conditional permits is relied upon, explicit standards, including nonsoil related factors, should be stated. A hearing procedure can be specified to permit applicants to show that soils are different from those mapped by submitting expert testimony to establish this fact. The regulations can require the applicant to provide additional information about the site, prepare an accurate large-scale map, and plot the location of the proposed development and other features on the map. The results of on-site investigation and advice from soil scientists and other technicians can be stated as additional factors upon which the regulatory authority may base its decisions. Soils information may be transposed to more accurate maps of larger scale and may be combined with other appropriate resource information. Involving soil scientists, planners, lawyers, and other persons with needed expertise in the drafting and administration of land use controls based upon soils information can improve the factual and legal basis needed to develop sound and workable regulations.

LITERATURE CITED

Barrows, R. L. 1978. Wisconsin's farmland preservation program. Univ. of Wisconsin-Ext. G 2890. Madison, Wis.

Beatty, M. T., and D. A. Yanggen. 1966. Role of detailed soil surveys in preparation and explanation of zoning ordinances. p. 160–174. In L. J. Bartelli, A. A. Klingebiel, J. V. Baird, and M. R. Heddleson (ed.) Soil survey and land use planning. Soil Sci. Soc. Am., Madison, Wis.

Bosselman, R., D. Callies, and J. Banta. 1973. The taking issue. U.S. Government Printing Office, Washington, D.C. p. 293.

Deknatel, C., and S. Harris. 1974. Zoning to preserve agriculture: Columbia county. Dep. of Admin., Madison, Wis. p. 3.

Dideriksen, R. I., and R. N. Sampson. 1976. Important farmlands: A national view. J. Soil Water Conserv. 28(4):195–197.

Freilich, R. H., and P. S. Levi. 1975. Model subdivision regulations. Am. Soc. of Planning Off., Chicago, Ill.

Greulich, G. 1975. Problems in delineating wetland boundaries. In Proc. 2nd Wetlands Conf., 9 Jan. 1974. Rep. no. 24. Inst. of Water Resour., Univ. of Connecticut, Storrs.

Hill, D. E. 1973. Inland wetland soils. In Proc. Wetlands Conf., 20 June 1973. Rep. no. 21. Inst. of Water Resour., Univ. of Connecticut, Storrs.

Ihlenfeldt, S. W., J. Johnson, and J. W. Clark. 1975. People-planned land uses. Univ. of Wisconsin-Ext. G 2729. Madison, Wis.

Lee, G. B., D. E. Parker, and D. A. Yanggen. 1972. Development of new techniques for delineation of flood plain hazard zones—Part I. Water Resour. Center, The Univ. of Wisconsin, Madison.

McClusky, D. S. 1973. Editorial commentary on the Connecticut tidal wetlands survey. *In* Proc. Wetlands Conf., 20 June 1973. Rep. no. 21. Inst. of Water Resour., Univ. of Connecticut, Storrs.

Michigan Farm Bureau, Cooperative Extension-Michigan State University Center for Rural Manpower and Public Affairs-Michigan State University, Division of Land Resource Programs-Michigan Department of Natural Resources. 1976. The use of zoning to retain essential agricultural lands. East Lansing, Mich.

Parker, D. E., G. B. Lee, and D. A. Yanggen. 1970. Using soil maps to delineate flood plains in a glaciated low-relief landscape. J. Soil Water Conserv. 25(3):96–99.

Soil Conservation Service, U.S. Department of Agriculture. 1975. Land inventory and monitoring memorandum—3 regarding prime and unique farmlands. USDA, Washington, D.C.

Southeastern Wisconsin Regional Planning Commission Newsletter. 1976. Walworth County rezoning nears completion. 16(2):1–13. Waukesha, Wis.

Thurow, C., W. Toner, and D. Erley. 1975. Wetlands. p. 37–51. *In* Performance controls for sensitive lands. Planning Advisory Serv. Rep. no. 307, 308. Am. Soc. of Planning Off., Chicago, Ill.

U.S. Water Resources Council. 1971. Regulation of flood hazard areas. Vol. 1. U.S. Government Printing Office, Washington, D.C. p. 514–515.

Wisconsin Administrative Code—H 62.20, H 65, and NR 116, 1977.

Wisconsin Statutes—sections 59,971(1), 87.30, 145.045, and 236.13(1)(d), 1975.

Yanggen, D. A. 1972. The use of detailed soils information for delineating and regulating flood plains. Water Resour. Center, Univ. of Wisconsin, Madison. p. 5.

Yanggen, D. A., C. D. Johnson, G. B. Lee, L. R. Massie, R. L. Ruff, and J. A. Schoenemann. 1976. Wisconsin wetlands. Univ. of Wisconsin-Extension, G 2818, Madison. p. 4–5.

40 Institutional Mechanisms for Land Use Planning and Land Use Controls

RAYMOND D. VLASIN AND DANIEL A. BRONSTEIN
Michigan State University, East Lansing, Michigan

I. INTRODUCTION

Few things could have had a more profound influence on our heritage, our culture, our values, and our standard of living than our land resources. They have influenced our songs, poetry, art, and literature and our political and group attitudes and actions. Few things have been more involved in shaping our individual and community plans for production, consumption, and living than our land resources. Because of the importance of land to the well-being of our people, many private and public actions have been taken—attempts to plan, guide, and control its use and to help prevent its misuse (Rohman, 1976).

This chapter focuses on one of the arrays of actions concerning land— the institutional aspects of land use planning and land use controls. It treats in order: (i) important considerations and relationships for land use planning and control processes; (ii) the institutional setting of land use planning; (iii) means for directing land use and the coordination of action, policy goals, and operational targets for planning and guidance of land use; and (iv) some challenges ahead. The first of these provides a backdrop against which the others are developed and discussed.

II. IMPORTANT CONSIDERATIONS AND RELATIONSHIPS FOR LAND USE PLANNING AND CONTROL

Land resources, including their associated waters and climates, have both facilitated and bounded nearly all the location, production, distribution, consumption, recreation, and living processes of man. The land resources enjoyed by residents of the United States have been both abundant and varied in nature. By any standard, the goods and services produced from these land resources have been bountiful. For example, with some few exceptions, there is sufficient land in the U.S. for meeting all our *current* domestic needs for food and feed and for making major contributions to world trade and world food security (USDA, 1973, 1974; Lee, 1978).

If one concentrates only on these aggregate perspectives, however, one may fall victim to an unwarranted sense of security. Aggregate data on land supplies and uses in the United States mask important regional differences. Further, current aggregate data do not report adequately some important national trends such as changes in ownership and increases in land parcelization and sale (Vlasin, 1975).

A. Old Considerations and Trends

Several basic, if not old and familiar, considerations should not be overlooked in approaching the land use planning and land use control processes. First, and possibly foremost, is the finite nature of our land resources. We have the basic fund of land resources we settled as pioneers, that we enjoy today, and that will carry us into the next century. We have added capital improvements, modified soil, slope, and fertility, changed land cover, shifted land uses, brought land under irrigation, and let other lands return to permanent cover. Still, the fund of land is basically constant.

Second, the demands placed on that land resource base, through both private and public actions and transactions, are sizeable, varied, and increasing in number and variety. These countless actions and transactions are operating against a fixed land resource base. They are also operating through market arrangements and through administrative and governmental processes designed in earlier times and under less complex conditions.

Third, through inheritance, sale, land development, and land speculation, we have increased parcelization of many lands. With increased parcelization comes scattering of ownerships to both different residents and absentee owners. This scattering of ownerships magnifies the difficulties of achieving compatible land uses and decreases the efficiency and effectiveness of each land manager.

Fourth, the incidence of demands for land and changes in ownership and use do not occur uniformly across the United States. They concentrate in such places as expanding metropolitan regions, cities, and countries experiencing major population changes, areas with burgeoning recreation demands, and in jurisdictions accommodating intensive speculation, land parcelization, and land development.

Fifth, reliance solely on market forces to allocate land uses has been found wanting from the local, regional, state, and national perspectives. Public intervention in or constraints on the market processes have been instituted in a host of ways. Likewise, willingness to rely on the efforts of a public agency or governmental or quasi-governmental unit to protect the "public interest" as it acquires and manages land resources has been wanting in some instances. Public intervention in government and quasi-government land acquisitions and uses has occurred and continues to occur, with a new array of administrative requirements and procedures in recent years (Barlowe, 1972; Cutler & Bronstein, 1974).

Sixth, government intervention in private market transactions, and the acquisition and use decisions of individual public agencies and governmental units, has been a mixed blessing. There have been benefits in the public interest, but these have been accompanied by such costs as added administrative overhead to both the private and public sectors, lengthy delays resulting from imposed requirements such as multiple permits, and consequent frustration of otherwise viable economic development or land development ventures.

Seventh, since early times decisions about allocation of lands among major competing uses have been difficult. The difficulties seem to be intensifying. Today, major allocative decisions may be surrounded by vocal competing groups, calls for environmental and economic impact statements, requests for surveys of and open hearings on public opinions and preferences, analyses by planning commissions, requirements for multiple permits, elongated development periods, and increased capital costs of projects due to the resulting time delays.

Together, the above considerations and trends are a somber reminder of the difficult tasks before us. We have a finite fund of land resources. The number of uses and demands against that fund is large, varied, and growing in number and complexity. Allocative decisions among competing uses have been difficult in the past. Now the allocative decisions are becoming increasingly more complex and considerably more difficult.

The conditions and trends noted above significantly complicate the land use planning and land use control processes. However, they do not encompass the full range of important considerations. Also crucial are a series of ecological realities that affect how we view our land resources and their uses.

B. Ecological Relationships

In a real sense, land resources are the ecological platforms on which man has advanced, maintained, and changed his well-being and that of families and communities over time. As resources, lands and their associated water, climate, and stores of energy and minerals have productive attributes, capacities, and tolerances. They have various limiting and constraining properties as well. We call the composite of these facilitating and limiting properties and their interactions the *ecological relationships.*

Key ecological relationships or realities are basic to our human well-being. Ecologists inform us that such relationships must be reflected in our land planning and land use. The scientific literature and, increasingly, the planning literature, provides a growing fund of insightful writings about key ecological concepts and relationships and how these might be reflected in the broad area of resources planning and the more limited area of land use planning (McAllister, 1973).

Discussions about ecological regions, natural constraints, materials flow, assimilation capabilities, fragile environments, and ecological irreversibility tell us that a new and vital set of concepts about ecological relationships are now challenging old approaches and processes of land use planning (Cooper & Vlasin, 1973). Likewise, concepts about diversity and heterogeneity, integrated landscapes, and energy and materials management imply new challenges for simultaneously handling in the planning process agriculture, recreation, ecological greenbelts, storm water impoundments, waste recycling, and other developments. The size, location, and attributes of these various land uses and developments, we now know, must reflect ecological limitations, in addition to traditional socioeconomic considerations for compatible land uses and efficient land parcel management (Koenig & Edens, 1976).

Regardless of our technological genius to date, human activities remain coupled with the natural environmental subsystem of the earth's surface in various ways. For example, the energy and material resources required to support man originated from, and are returned to, the environmental subsystem. Utilization of these energy and material resources generates thermal and chemical by-products that are primarily treated as wastes for disposal into the surface environment.

The ability of the environmental subsystem to assimilate these wastes in an acceptable fashion depends upon their nature and concentration and the physical and biological characteristics of the environmental subsystems receiving them. Assimilation capabilities resulting from biological characteristics differ from region to region and within regions from one local environment to another. Such differences have implications for both the nature and magnitude of the production and consumption activities that can be conducted, as well as for the manner in which they are planned, arranged, and managed on the landscape (Cooper & Vlasin, 1973).

These ecological relationships and others represent both opportunities for and constraints upon the production and consumption activities of communities, regions, the nation, and beyond. Ecological relationships imply the need for more deliberate attention to regional and local differences—both in the resource base and in the capacity and tolerances for assimilating wastes. They imply the need for much greater attention to the location and design of industrial, commercial, residential, and recreational activities to insure compatibility with ecological characteristics. The ecological relationships also imply a need for greater attention to changes in settlement patterns and to the design of new ones that help conserve our stocks of energy and material resources and that minimize the adverse effects of by-products or wastes.

Under currently known technologies, shortages are projected for fossil fuels and for various nonenergy minerals. Worldwide shortages are also projected for agricultural land and food production. There is little evidence that current technologies, many of which are energy intensive, can be used to remove these constraints in agricultural land and food production over time (Comm. Resour. Man, 1969).

We have limited experience in reflecting or accommodating ecological relationships in our land planning and land use. While the ecological principles may be well understood by some, if not many, how those principles can manifest themselves in local and regional actions and outcomes is far from obvious.

We must try, however, to develop a better understanding of these ecological relationships and their implications for planning actions and outcomes. We must be willing to look at the ecological relationships at different scales of aggregation, from local environments to regions and beyond. Many of these relationships are obscure and will require the technical insights of the trained ecologist and allied scientists. Again, the complexities are major and must be addressed through both market arrangements and administrative and governmental processes designed in earlier times when complex ecological relationships were of little concern.

Added to the ecological relationships are an array of production and consumption conditions and relationships. While they have the advantage of being more visible or apparent, they are no less challenging. It is to this third set of conditions and relationships that we now turn.

C. Production and Consumption Conditions and Relationships

Lands have been adapted in a myriad of ways by individuals, groups, communities, and governmental units to serve their production and consumption needs and wants. For agriculture, the lands have been cleared and cut over, plowed and seeded, grazed and harvested in a variety of ways. They have been drained and shaped, ditched and irrigated. They have been limed and fertilized, sprayed and enhanced for greater productive response.

These and other agriculturally related actions regarding land, however, have not been in isolation from other public and private uses of land resources. Rather, from earliest times agricultural decisions were part of the array of production and consumption decisions and relationships that transformed the land. This array of decisions extended well beyond the land being transformed for agriculture. From the earliest time there were linkages between farming improvements (agricultural developments), local town and community services improvements (community developments), and improvements in market roads, transportation, and market facilities and services (economic developments).

The production and consumption relationships today, involving land and other natural resources, are far more complex and varied than at earlier times. This growing complexity is seen in the changes in demands for land. It is seen in the growth of new land uses. It is also seen in resulting landscape patterns, far different from those of earlier times.

Residences, as one land use, provide a visible example of these increased complexities. With the changes in agriculture in the United States, the number of farmsteads and farm homes in rural areas increased and then declined. More than offsetting that decline have been the rural nonfarm residences, and more recently mobile homes. They have spread in ever-increasing numbers along roads and highways and out into all manner of fields and woods. Cottages and homes border or cluster near the shorelines of reservoirs, lakes, and streams.

All manner of residential sites are being demanded, from opportunities for compact or dense residential development to scattered development for occupancy on a full- or part-time basis. A wide and growing array of residential-recreation sites is being demanded, ranging from beautiful homes in scenic places to the most primative cottage or isolated plot for parking a camper.

In some places residences have clustered together to form new communities. In other places they seem detached and spread over the landscape in helter-skelter fashion. They occur in all manner of combinations with commercial and industrial and agricultural neighbors. This new reality, and the demands for residences that propel it, immensely complicate land use planning and land use guidance and control, affecting both the processes involved and the outcomes expected and achieved.

Unfortunately, residential use is not the only land use that manifests this troublesome complicating trait. An array of other nonfarm land uses has grown steadily because of increased service demands, and other general population-based demands such as recreation, education and heritage, military preparedness, flood protection, and interstate transportation. Some of these service-based demands are familiar and longstanding while others are new and exotic. Some of the demands are for the land site. Others are for the amenities that the land provides (Vlasin, 1971).

Also being demanded is land for all manner of business, commercial, industrial, and service facility sites, places for shopping centers, processing and manufacturing plants, parking areas, storage and distribution facilities and terminals, schools and playgrounds, police and fire stations, hospitals and clinics, and centers for other public and private services.

All manner of public and private recreation facilities and services are being demanded. They range from large multipurpose parks and forests to more specialized facilities such as playgrounds, beaches, lakes and streams, wildlife refuges, scenic highways and trails, scenic overlooks, campgrounds, picnic areas, and playing fields.

There are in fact many other demands on land not yet mentioned. Some of these can be strictly land oriented—such as for waste disposal sites, new airports and airport expansions, new utility corridors, mobile home parks, public buffer strips, various rights-of-way, and more. Some are water oriented and actually reflect themselves in demand for land because of the associated water. These include such examples as sites for electric power generation, navigation, waterfowl and fish habitat, water-based recreation, municipal water supplies, and industrial processing sites. The growing list goes on.

Now, more than ever before, we are being challenged to avoid isolating and treating separately one set of demands. We cannot focus on the land required for agricultural production, or the land required for urban expansion, while ignoring other uses. Neither should one land use be left to fend more or less for itself while other uses are given priority status both in planning processes and in land use changes. There is some evidence that agriculture, until recent times, has possessed this dubious status among professional planners. In many jurisdictions in the past, agricultural land was categorized simply as "open space" for any and all potential uses.

Increasingly, those involved in land use planning are struggling with the growing number and variability of competing demands on the land. They are attempting to reflect the interrelationships among uses, including the various related, and sometimes competing, economic and social objectives. In addition, they are increasingly attempting to reflect local ecological and broader environmental considerations.

But added attention to ecological opportunities and constraints and the multiple purposes and demands for land are of little consequence unless there is some application on the landscape. That application is both made possible by and constrained by the institutional setting within which land use planning and action occur.

III. INSTITUTIONAL SETTING OF LAND USE PLANNING PROCESSES

Institutions are the formal or informal means by which groups take action. They constitute the "rules of the game" by which individual or group actions are guided, facilitated, or constrained. They range from being formal, such as the black-letter law, to being informal, such as customs, habits, and attitudes. They also range from the general, such as a national goal or policy, to the specific, such as specific laws and local ordinances, and specific administrative regulations and procedures.

Collectively, our institutions determine what occurs—in this case, what occurs on the landscape. There are, in fact, a myriad of land-related institutions that directly or indirectly affect the landscape. They range from the federal to the local level. They serve groups from exclusively public to exclusively private. They span land resource situations that range from a single purpose to multiple purposes. Their problem focus may range from the narrowest of physical resource concerns to the broadest of socio-cultural concerns relevant to human settlement and human well-being.

Rarely does one institution operate in isolation of others. More often, several institutions operate together in a patchwork of influences. Some of these influences may be reinforcing, while others are competing or counter to one another.

No single book could enumerate all the institutions that have influenced or now influence land use outcomes. However, a few key ones are especially worthy of mention here (For additional perspectives on a threefold framework for resource policy, which includes institutions, see Chapter 1, "Soils, Plants, and Land Use in the United States" by Raleigh Barlowe).

A. Attitudes and Policies Toward Land Development and Growth

Land development and economic growth have long been accepted symbols of progress in American society. They have often been championed by private operators and public officials alike as appropriate individual, community, and national objectives (Barlowe, 1977).

From early times in America, public policies have supported the concept of continued growth and increased use and development of land resources in the process. Growing populations brought pressures for establishing new farms and communities and for opening new lands along the frontier. Millions of acres of the public domain acquired by the United States were surveyed and offered for sale for homesteads to new settlers, or granted to the railroads.

As settlers moved inland and west, demands for new roads, canals, railroads, and other public improvements were created. Federal, state, and local governmental actions were taken to meet these and other public needs. National programs were devised. They provided internal improvements, and also facilitated the rise of business and industry.

Much of the expansion and growth of America's business economy between 1820 and the present day has been characterized by Raleigh Barlowe, an eminent land economist, as tied to a "bigger, better, richer" ethic. The quest for profits, increased production, and the better life was accompanied by increased demands for raw materials, larger projects, and greater economic activity. Growth and development, including all manner of land development, were accepted as necessary characteristics of a healthy and active society. These attitudes and the public policies that reinforced them have influenced individual, community, state, and national actions in land use allocations down to the present (Barlowe, 1977).

B. Other Reinforcing Beliefs

Our U.S. attitudes and policies concerning growth and development have been strongly reinforced by our acceptance of three other concepts. According to Raleigh Barlowe, these were (i) acceptance of fee simple ownership, (ii) espousal of the laissez faire doctrine, and (iii) commitment to the concept of manifest destiny (Barlowe, 1977).

The evolving British concept of fee simple ownership found ready acceptance in our new nation. Our land resources were bountiful. Individual ownership was viewed as desirable. And widespread ownership of land was accepted as a goal in national land policy. The frontier society and bountiful land resources reinforced the idea that every landowner should possess all the private rights of ownership and be free to develop and use his land as he determined best. The term *absolute ownership*, sometimes used to describe the frontier attitude, conveys both the spirit and the emotion behind this belief.

Reinforcing the attitude toward ownership of rights, economic growth and land development was a prevalent laissez faire economic philosophy. Governments were expected to make internal improvements for the public, provide protection, and preserve law and order, but do little else. Governments were to provide a maximum of freedom to individual operators and businesses permitting them to operate as they saw fit and to maximize their personal profits.

Also reinforcing attitudes towards ownership of rights and growth and development was a belief in *manifest destiny*. This belief held that the American people had a divine responsibility for settling and filling the continent to the west. Espoused as a policy doctrine in the early 1800's, this belief had strong roots in the Puritan view that, as God's chosen people, they had been sent to this continent with a mission to perform.

The U.S. emphasis on growth and development has led to many economic and social benefits—new employment, rising real incomes, increased standards of living, national growth and prosperity, and international economic leadership. However, this same emphasis on growth and development has contributed to rapid use and misuse of our resource base. It has caused greater demands on our raw materials and more rapid exploitation of various stocks of fixed resources in short supply. It has served to intensify some problems of environmental degradation, while contributing to resource scarcities (Barlowe, 1977).

The combined attitudes and policies toward land development and growth and the reinforcing beliefs about land ownership and limited government are still very much alive today. They constitute one social force affecting land use and our attitudes toward it. Other social forces include population, equity movements, and environmental movements (Morrison, 1976).

C. Population, Related Food Concerns, and Trade

While U.S. population growth is slowing, world population continues to grow at an astounding pace. In recent years we have reassessed our attitudes and our policies concerning population growth, food needs, and food security. Attitudes and policies about population and food influence how we plan and guide the use of our U.S. land resources. Further, these attitudes and policies, when translated into levels of trade and assistance, influence the projections we make about the future adequacy of our land resource base.

Since 1973, there has been a growing conviction that the U.S. should provide more food, particularly in response to foreign needs. Increased food production has been viewed as essential—internationally to meet food deficits and domestically to help retard or counter inflation. Increased food production has also been viewed as an essential contribution to necessary foreign trade and a favorable balance of payments. Agricultural exports have recently shouldered the burden of retarding a negative balance of payments and they are increasingly viewed as crucial to trade, and trade strategies involving needed petroleum and other minerals.

The United States has moved toward a greater commitment to help with world food security. It has entered discussions about world food reserves and world food stockpiles. It is considering approaches to aid the "food gap" or "food deficit" countries and those facing food crises or natural disasters. Such deliberations are occurring in a climate where the pervasive belief is that world population will continue to increase rapidly.

The future impacts on land from emerging attitudes and policies concerning population, food, and trade are not clear. However, the emerging attitudes and policies collectively point to more land being needed for agricultural production. For example, a 1974 rule of thumb indicated that, for each $1 billion of farm exports or their equivalent, an additional 2.43 to 2.84 million ha (6 to 7 million acres) of cropland would be required (USDA, 1974). Attitudes and policies concerning population, food, and trade will surely constitute an important part of the institutional setting in the years ahead. Our guess is that their prominence will increase over time.

D. Equity Attitudes and Actions

Closely paralleling the previous attitudes and policies are the equity movements. These are social movements and actions that increasingly question past traditions and past institutionalized arrangements for the ownership, control, and distribution of economic assets, including land resources. Some of these movements occur within the confines of the United States. Others have an international scope (Morrison, 1976).

"Have-nots" or "under-dog" groups are organizing and creating pressures for outcomes they believe to be fair and right. Their pressure for change seeks new, more equitable (to them) conditions, regardless of prior traditions or prior institutionalized arrangements. Improved conditions sought include more employment, increased real income, new opportunities, increased access to and availability of services, and more access to and use of natural resources.

Achievement of these new outcomes may impact land directly or indirectly. For example, pressures for more jobs and disposable income create added pressures for economic growth, which in turn places added pressures on land. Or, pressures for added economic growth and improved consumer status place added pressures on our energy resources, in turn placing pressures on industrial enterprises for oil drilling, strip mining, and related energy development activities, which in turn impact land resources.

We see on the international horizon questions raised by "have-not" countries and questions raised by other countries exporting resources to us that we consume at a relatively high per capita rate. Most prominent recently have been questions pertaining to petroleum supplies, production, export rates, and price schedules and related fees. Those trading with the United

States are raising important questions regarding their views of equity—conserving their resources for their own future benefit, the benefit of their people and governments.

The equity issues on the international level, particularly over energy consumption, likely will increase in the future. These external conditions will have internal impacts on the United States. For example, if the United States should respond by attempting to curtail its consumption of petroleum or mineral resources, internal growth could be retarded. Curtailed growth would almost certainly raise or intensify equity issues among groups domestically. To drive our United States economy harder under conditions of scarcity in imported resources would be to place a new round of impacts on our land resources.

E. Environmental Attitudes, Movement, and Change

Our society has long been concerned with the adequacy of land and related environmental resources to fulfill our human needs. During the last decade, we have added a second broad concern—a concern about citizen, industry, and government actions that adversely impact the quality of our land and related environment (Sax, 1971).

Within the decade of the 1970's we have made remarkable strides in determining the causes and effects of environmental degradation. We have created and implemented environmental legislation at the federal and state levels and various companion ordinances at the county, metropolitan, and municipal levels. We have created and now operate a host of governmental agencies, commissions, and committees, and various citizen groups and associations, to deal with environmental problems and administer environmental programs.

Much of the public has become environmentally conscious. The earlier public forums, E-days and E-weeks, have been largely replaced by difficult or routine political, legal, and administrative deliberations and actions about specific problems. Environmental impact assessment procedures are now an integral part of the administrative processes of government agencies, public utilities, and quasi-governmental groups, as well as of private corporations. Planning commissions and committees at all levels of government embody some analysis and review procedures that focus on environmental attributes and impacts (Anderson, 1973; Catalano & DiMento, 1976).

The environmental movement has directly questioned uncontrolled economic growth (Morrison, 1976). Likewise, it has highlighted population increases likely in the United States and abroad, and possible resource and food impacts and environmental changes implied by the projected increases. It has raised questions about the long-term productivity of resources and about opportunities for sustained productivity over time. Questions of natural beauty, unique sites, and endangered species have been raised to new levels of consideration and institutionalized.

The most recent phase of the movement has been the greatly expanded attention to chemical and biological hazards. Earlier concerns about air and water pollution have been supplemented by major new legislative and administrative actions regarding toxic substances. Earlier concern for emissions into the air and into water courses has now expanded to every part of the production, materials handling, processing, marketing and consumption processes. Direct and indirect impacts on the land resources are also a part of this wide-ranging concern.

While there have been many discernable gains from the environmental movement, it has brought some highly questionable and unwanted side effects. Environmentally related regulations have increased costs and caused delays for public agency programs, private industry output, and consumer products and processes. The magnitude of the regulations and their pervasiveness have generated a counter movement for simplification or removal of regulations and calls for new justifications of regulating agencies.

F. The Dual Themes

A review of major attitudes, beliefs, and policies toward the land show many different themes. The two major themes are land as a *resource* and land as an *environment*. The former, emphasized in early times, treats land as a resource to be exploited, as private property to be owned; man is the owner, individually determining the fate of land solely for his own use and profit. The latter, increasingly emphasized today, treats land as an environment to be shared, not only with other humans, but with all living things; man is the steward, whose aims are sustained use and preservation of the land as both ecosphere and natural home for this and all future generations of living things (Rohman, 1976).

The conflicts that have occurred and are now occurring over the uses of land resources have their roots in many different causes. In earlier times conflicts usually occurred between owners of land resources as each attempted to use his land as he determined best. The conflicts often centered on incompatibility of adjoining uses—between two or more private owners, or between private owners and the public.

At present, conflicts over incompatible uses still occur. However, an increasing number of recent conflicts have been between owners of land attempting to use it for some private economic purpose and other citizens—the latter viewing the intended or actual uses as destructive to the environment of which the land resource is an integral part.

The kit of tools that our society has devised grew out of the need to handle these various conflicts and, as possible, to help avoid other similar ones. It is to an overview of that kit of tools and to the purposes and objectives behind their use that we now turn. (For a detailed treatment of various land use controls, see Chapters 24 and 39).

IV. MEANS FOR DIRECTING LAND USE

The ownership, control, and use of land resources always take place within a complex institutional framework of cultural, economic, governmental, religious, political, and social phenomena. The various key considerations identified in the previous section collectively involve all of these phenomena.

Supplementing the broader attitudes, policies, and social movements described earlier are some specific institutions, such as the family and education, that directly impact the land resources. There are, additionally, major impacts from the array of government powers and from the effects of laws, customs, and religion. And a very substantial list of public measures exists for guiding and controlling use of land resources. Together they constitute part of the large and growing array.

This large and growing array of means for affecting the ownership and control of land and its uses may appear most ample. It permits various techniques to be used on different land use problems, as one would select various tools from a kit to repair different parts of an engine. However, this array of necessary means for directing land use is far from sufficient. Also needed are clear policy goals and operational targets. Only these can provide the objectives toward which action can be directed.

A lack of clarity about policy goals and operational targets can lead to confusion and conflict over what the outcomes can or should be. These conditions can totally frustrate the orderly use of otherwise effective institutional means for directing land use. Various means for directing land use, and different goals and targets, are addressed in order.

A. Some Specific Institutions that Directly Impact Land Resources

The institutional factors that affect the ownership, control, and use of land resources are sometimes called *landed institutions* (Barlowe, 1972). Of these factors, the concept of property rights is by far the most important. Other institutions that have important impacts upon ownership, control, and use of land resources are the family system and education, as well as government, law, custom, and religion.

The *family system* and *education* are two basic institutions that underlie or affect many of the concepts and attitudes people have concerning land ownership, control, and use. These two institutions have changed over time, and the variations in each are numerous. Still, young couples marry, have children, and raise and educate them, considering education for themselves and their children necessary for life in a modern society. Likewise, the single adults in households, with or without children, also view education as important for participation in and enjoyment of modern life.

Families and households are planning and resource-using units. As they seek the benefits of modern life and prepare for their future security, they acquire, develop, and use land resources. They buy and rent living units—houses and homes, places to reside, places to farm, properties to call their own. They buy and build cabins near lakes and streams and in the woods. They purchase land parcels for future use, for retirement plans, to hedge against inflation, to speculate for profit. They take all of these directly land-related actions and more as they progress through their lives.

These families and households also demand and obtain products and services from beyond the land they own, occupy, or otherwise use. Families and households demand a wide range of products and services to support modern life. Demands for food supplies, water supplies, building supplies and materials, transportation systems, utility services, public buildings and related services, and recreation services and facilities all translate into demands for land. The role of the family or household is stressed here because of the power of the consumer behind the uses to which land is put.

When we speak of the *educational system* we must remember that formal schooling is only a part of it. Since consumer demand plays such a large role in land-related decisions, other (here called *informal*) educational-informational institutions—providing books, magazines, newspapers, movies, radio, and television, and particularly, conveying advertising and life style messages—are at least as important as formal schooling.

Both formal and informal educational systems have taught us how to make a living through new skills and technologies, how to "get ahead" in life, and how to enjoy and appreciate life. They have raised the aspirations of individuals and families. In short, the educational systems have helped us see new possibilities for an improved life and equip ourselves and others to achieve it.

The formal educational system has in recent decades instructed about conservation and wise use of our land, water, and other natural resources. It has fostered increased understanding of the role of natural resources in our past, present, and future. The Land Grant Colleges and Universities, in particular, have conducted research and extension education on problems of resource use and on potentials for improved resource development, management, and protection. In the last decade the formal educational system focused on environmental problems. In fact, student groups helped initiate and lead calls for environmental improvement. These students were products of our school systems.

We are stressing the importance of the formal and informal educational systems because of their potential as institutions for change. They can and do influence the attitudes, beliefs, and values of all, from the very youngest to the most elderly. If the informal educational institutions follow the lead of the formal institutions and teach the ideas of objective analysis, open inquiry, and impersonal evaluation, it may, in the future, be possible to greatly expand the range of choices in land use decisions.

From early colonial times, *government* and related political institutions have had direct impact upon ownership and use of our land resources. The very limited roles of government in early days were consistent with the high personal value placed on economic, political, and religious freedom. In recent decades, all levels of government have expanded the scope of their activities to provide new economic and social opportunities for various constituancies. Its influences now extend into every home, farm, business, and industry.

Government activities impact land ownership and land use in two major ways. One is through the overall effect of "government policies and restrictions" on public and private decisions regarding land resources. The other is through the "organization and framework of government" on the development and administration of land resource policies (Barlowe, 1972).

Underlying these two major ways in which government impacts land ownership and land use are the basic government powers—taxation, regulatory or police power, eminent domain, expenditure, and government ownership and management. Given these basic powers, government has, for example, instituted property and inheritance taxes; protected property rights; enforced zoning ordinances, health standards, and building codes; created environmental regulations; acquired private lands for highways, reservoirs, and wildlife preserves; established credit facilities for homeowners, farmers, and businessmen; and reserved and managed large tracts of forest, grazing, and wilderness lands. These examples are merely representative, and do not begin to catalog the many direct and indirect governmental impacts.

All three levels of government are involved in the development and administration of policies affecting land resources. The federal government is, constitutionally, a government of limited powers. However, because of its broad administrative roles and its expanding implied powers, it can and does own and operate huge land areas, acquire private land for public projects, influence directly and indirectly a wide range of urban and agricultural land uses, subsidize various land use practices, and regulate a variety of interstate matters regarding land, water, air, and minerals and the broader environment. However, the federal government lacks many of the public powers required for resolving the day-to-day land use problems and conflicts that are confined to states and localities. Most of these powers are vested in the states, examples being property taxation procedures, land sales and transfers, landlord-tenant relations, water rights, land developments, and police protection. Local units of government, as authorized by the state, are enabled to carry out a variety of these same responsibilities but at the local level—land use planning, land use restrictions, building codes, and various general-purpose and special-purpose districts, including those for soil and water conservation, irrigation, and drainage. Legislative inventiveness and willingness to attack problems involving land resources has yielded a remarkable array of powers and techniques at federal, state, and local levels. The kit of governmental tools is large and varied. But, once again, there is the question of clarity in policy goals and operational targets—all the essential objectives toward which action is to be directed.

Although *law, custom,* and *religion* are important institutions in their own right, we will treat them but briefly here. Each involves collective action that is binding upon, or otherwise influences, individual action. They set various boundaries which limit acceptable individual and group behavior. While the influence of each is major, law is probably most pervasive in guiding human action. As Jacob Beusher, renowned teacher and attorney, has observed, "law is an all-pervading part of our social structure" and "there is no moment in our lives when our actions or inactions are not in some way subject to legal valuation" (Beuscher, 1951).

Law, custom, and religion provide means for changing current attitudes, beliefs, and values. Each influences our relations to other persons in individual and group settings. Each treats our relationships to the resources around us, our control over them, and our responsibilities toward them. Each deals with equity considerations, both in use of resources and in other ways. And each, directly and indirectly, targets on our responsibility to others in the past, at the present, and into the future.

B. Public Measures for Guiding and Controlling Land Use

Much is written about land use planning processes. One common theme in the literature is the belief that planning—careful, competent, and socially responsible—should precede the application of public measures for guiding and controlling land use. A second, less common, theme is that planning, without deliberate attention to follow through, is at best unproductive and at worst wasteful of human, natural, and financial resources. Lack of follow through in the case of careful and responsible planning also results in loss of potential economic and social benefits that may have resulted from the planned outcomes.

Earlier chapters discussed thoroughly the specifics of both the planning processes for land and the information required for technically competent and socially responsible planning. (See especially chapters 3, 5, 6, 9, 10, 14, 18, 19, 31, 33, 36, 38, and 39.) Our comments are intended to serve as supplements to those contributions.

One characterization of the powers of government states that, "The Federal Government has immense power to tax and spend; the State governments have lesser powers to tax and spend, but they have broad regulatory power; and the local governments have more limited power to tax and regulate, but they have a unique opportunity to hear or express the views of individual citizens" (USDA, 1974, p. 32).

This characterization embodies one important idea and suggests a second. It clearly highlights the important role of local governments for bringing forward the views and preferences of individual citizens and groups. It also suggests that a deliberate coordination of action by different levels of government could achieve more than can one governmental entity acting alone. We will address each in order.

Many communities develop "plans" that are never implemented. A major reason is that the *cooperation of the public* necessary for their use and implementation is overlooked in a number of important ways from the beginning of the planning process. It is not uncommon to find citizens who feel that planning is something that others do *to* them. Some citizens feel that those responsible for planning work behind the scene, quietly develop their plans, in isolation, and then "sell" them to the community. Still others feel the situation is even worse; that those responsible for planning make the plans and then try to force them on the community. By contrast, some officials feel that citizens have primarily their own "personal interests" in mind. Such officials see their responsibility as serving the "public interest," and they minimize or bypass citizen involvement in an effort to minimize opposition. Fortunately there is a growing body of public officials, citizens, and professionals who feel that citizen participation is a vital element in all public or community planning (Vlasin, 1974).

There are many reasons why citizens should be involved in the development and implementation of plans regarding land resources. First, land resources plans or more comprehensive plans cannot effectively meet residents' needs unless they are involved. The community residents (whether crossroad towns, cities, townships, counties, or multicounty regions) must be involved from the beginning so that the plans address their problems, preferences, and priorities to the extent possible.

Second, citizens under our democratic system have a right to participate in and shape public decisions on land use and other matters that affect them. If this right is to be a reality, those in the communities to be affected must be involved from the time the plan is initiated, through clarification of problems and opportunities involved, to the time the particular plan is completed and implemented.

Third, citizen involvement may constitute a necessary precondition to involvement of public oficials and citizen leaders. Citizen involvement almost certainly is a precondition to political acceptance of the planning process and the ultimate plan. Unfortunately there are numerous examples of plans developed by professionals or by planning consultants in substantial isolation from the citizens. Upon disclosure, such plans are then viewed with suspicion and hostility; public officials and civic leaders saddled with the responsibility of implementing the plans (particularly in the land use area) and enforcing their provisions have found the task nearly impossible (Vlasin, 1974). Citizens should never be bypassed or brought in after the fact. They should never be used as a rubber stamp. Neither should their involvement be a "token."

Citizen involvement is a crucial addition to, not a substitute for, analytic ability and technical information. Citizens can provide precise information on (i) the nature, location, magnitude and severity of problems, (ii) how they actually feel about the problems and opportunities and their preferences concerning future uses of resources, (iii) the possible and likely consequences of development and resource use efforts. The professionals can provide technical assessments of feasibilities, such as engineering, economic, environmental, social, cultural, administrative, and legal matters.

There is no one thing that can be done to provide all the technical and analytical information that may be needed. The chapters in Sections II through IX describe many of the major kinds of such information and their uses in planning. Existing federal, state, regional, and local public agencies that have assistance programs can help. The Soil Conservation Service has technicians and local soil and water conservation districts have other personnel. Educational institutions such as the land grant universities, agricultural experiment stations, cooperative extension services, and other state universities, community colleges, and private colleges can assist. The many special-purpose and multipurpose districts and associations can be of assistance. The emerging multicommunity and multicounty development districts can also constitute an important source of technical assistance. We cannot emphasize too strongly that the participation of the public is vital. Probably no other single input contributes as much to the ultimate success of the plan and its implementation and sustained use.

As there are an array of possible actions by the different levels of government, there are likewise an array of ways to *coordinate the actions by the different entities.* One of the most important ways is through the development of clearer goals and operational targets—discussed in detail in the next section.

A second way is through the development and use of an improved land use data and information system. One of our current major problems is an unquestioned reliance on some rather limited data concerning land availability and need. An agricultural example will help to illustrate the problem.

Data projections concerning the adequacy of land available for future needs trace back to two agencies at the federal level. The agencies are the Economics, Statistics and Cooperatives Service (ESCS) and the Soil Conservation Service (SCS). The ESCS (previously the Economic Research Service) has concluded from its projections for 1980 and 2000 that we have an adequate supply of farmland for the future—meeting domestic food and fiber needs to the year 2000 and still allowing land for other purposes. It appears that ESCS has not had the opportunity or resources to deal fully with alternative food security strategies or alternative foreign trade and balance of payments strategies.

An adequate supply of farmland to meet domestic needs also is reflected in the Conservation Needs Inventory (CNI) of the Soil Conservation Service (SCS). The 1967 CNI showed that of the 255.6 million ha (631 million acres) suited for regular cultivation, only 147.8 million ha (365 million acres) were used as cropland. About half of the remaining 107.7 million ha (266 million acres) suited for regular cultivation was in forests and somewhat less than half was in pasture. Most of this 107.7 million ha (266 million acres) would require improvements including drainage or irrigation, some at great cost, to bring them into production. Further, some of the land has a short growing season, or would not justify the loss of forest land or grassland if developed (Vlasin, 1975, 1976).

Although the CNI findings imply that our supply of agricultural land is adequate to meet domestic needs for the future, that supply will require continued investments, if not accelerated investment in conservation treatment. Any major new commitment by the United States to help meet world food demands or world food security would necessitate an investment in conservation treatment far beyond past investment levels.

A recent study by SCS shows that we have only 45 million ha (111.1 million acres) of potential cropland remaining in other uses that have the quality and availability for conversion to farming in the entire United States. This total is considerably lower than recent estimates by others, and far below the estimate derived from the 1967 CNI (Johnson, 1977).

Many resource specialists are definitely uneasy about the land use projections available and being used. Clearly, improvements in the data base and information about land resources would yield benefits from increased accuracy of decisions within governmental levels and from improved coordination among them.

A third way to help coordinate the actions by different entities is to systematically explore alternative institutional forms and various factual and site-specific situations in which they have proved effective. There are excellent individual analyses that imply potential benefits from such a systematic approach. Here are but a few brief examples.

In a recent analysis Bronstein (1973) examined the question of whether there should be one-stop licensing of power plants, or should plants be required to obtain separate permits (and hold separate hearings) for land use, water, air, and other major resource matters. The article concluded that the separate permit procedure was superior in the case of power plants.

By contrast, Barlowe (1977) has conducted analyses of land resource use for development ventures, including land developments for second homes and recreation properties. He has observed financial hardships to conscientious developers from multiple permitting requirements and delays associated with the one-at-a-time permit processes. In these instances one-stop permitting processes appeared to be superior in potential benefits for the developer and the agencies involved.

Many questions arise over the adequacy of environmental impact assessment processes and outcomes. A recent analysis of local government responses to state environmental impact assessment requirements bears directly on the question. Catalano and DiMento (1976) found that institutionalizing environmental impact assessments does not necessarily produce better decisions.

New techniques in the construction permit processes have been instituted in recent years to deal with large-scale uncontrolled residential growth. The Ramapo Plan (Golden V. Ramapo, 1972) and the Petaluma Plan (Construction Ind. Assoc. v. Petaluma, 1975) deal with subdivisions, apartment complexes, condominiums, and trailer parks. Both the Ramapo Plan and Petaluma's Residential Development Control System (RDCS) are separate from the zoning ordinances, although both presuppose the existence of zoning. While there are similarities in the two schemes, there are considerable and significant differences as well (Bronstein, 1977; Seneker, 1974).

Attitudes about zoning have come in for analyses that bear directly on the effectiveness of implementation. For example, Bronstein and Erickson (1973) found that zoning as understood by the general public and *not* as understood by lawyers, does not exist anywhere in the State of Michigan, all of the statutes, ordinances, and cases to the contrary notwithstanding. They found that in rural areas, apparently, property is rezoned virtually at the request of the owner. In unincorporated metropolitan areas, four out of five rezonings requested are granted. In incorporated metropolitan areas they found one out of two rezonings requested is granted (see also Ordway, 1976).

Still other innovative institutional measures and procedures could contribute to a systematic analysis of institutions. Subdivision regulation, for example, has been approached differently in Florida, Arizona, New Mexico, Colorado, California, and New York (Simko, 1978). The contrasts provided by these states and the analyses of their performance in subdivision regulation provide major insights into the effectiveness of various regulatory schemes.

Likewise there are a variety of examples of actions being taken to preserve agricultural land. We cite here the recent work by Yannacone (1975) providing an interesting legal-rhetorical attempt to integrate many new doctrines to preserve agricultural lands. He attempts to treat simultaneously agricultural lands, fertile soils, popular sovereignty, the trust doctrine, environmental impact assessment, and the natural law.

We have not attempted a cataloging of the many different analyses that might be conducted. However, the examples presented suggest viable possibilities for systematically analyzing alternative institutional forms and their effectiveness in specific situations.

C. Policy Goals and Operational Targets

Planning for land use is not an end in itself. It is a means to achieve other goals and objectives. Crucial questions are who decides those goals and objectives, what are those goals and objectives, and who benefits from them. Also crucial are the procedures used to transform the goals and objectives into reality—the implementation process discussed above.

One of the complicating factors is that, in the economist's terms, land is an intermediate good. Demand for land is really a demand for the goods and services that it can provide and support. Ours is a world of limited choices, possibly more limited than we realize, given our past population growth and projections for the future, our limited land base, and our now diminished stock of fossil fuels and mineral resources. Choices must be made among the uses of land. Such actions simultaneously cause choices among those for whom alternative uses have value. This constitutes a fundamental character of land in our contemporary experience (Libby, 1976).

We do have an arsenal of mechanisms for guiding the uses of land resources. Included in this arsenal is an array of direct federal programs, federally assisted state and local programs, and self-financed state, substate, and local programs that affect natural resource development, use, and protection. The expenditures are massive. There are also charitable, civic, and association programs that have backed financial and service support. But, despite this arsenal of governmental rules, regulations, programs, and nongovernmental initiatives, we are truly short of clearly defined policy goals and operational targets for action.

We can, more or less, use our land resources for several different existing and emerging policy objectives—objectives that are layered over one another in our political and governmental processes. We could, as a society or as components of it (states, substate regions, counties, townships), move toward the following:

1) Greater commitment to helping with world food aid and world food security, in addition to expanded trade in food, feed, and fiber. Emphasis here would include retention and protection of agricultural lands and development of those services that would augment this expanded commitment.

2) Increased emphasis on rural development, expanded agribusiness, and other income-producing and employment producing uses of land, timber, mineral, and recreation resources. Such rural development actions could have both positive and negative effects on our agricultural land base and its preservation and retention.

3) Closely related to the previous goal could be the goal of improved rural-urban population balance. This policy objective is based on the belief that economic and social gains can be achieved by retarding the growth of our largest metropolitan areas and by providing new economic and social opportunities in nonmetropolitan areas to keep population there.

4) Economic dispersion for ecological and social reasons. Environmental scientists and social scientists tell use we must give greater attention to economic dispersion to diminish the ecological burdens of social concentration and the social pressures and individual stress of high population densities.

5) Improved settlement patterns for increased energy efficiency. Included would be new patterns to minimize costly transit and transport, and integrate ecologically compatible farm and nonfarm activities, consistent with the assimilative capacities and tolerances of local environments.

6) Increased management of rural resources for the benefit of our urbanized population. Included would be greater emphasis on recreation, wildlife habitat, and aesthetic amenities, as well as the infrastructure needed by a modern urbanized society (in addition to production of agricultural, mineral, and energy products and services).

These broad goals or objectives are merely illustrative of various single-purpose policy goals. The goals which are adopted should probably contain elements of all of the above, as well as others such as conservation and improved management practices not listed here.

Even a casual survey of community, regional, state, or federal actions regarding land resources will indicate the need for more clarity, visibility, understanding, and agreement about goals. Clearer "policy goals" encompassing land are required at the state, multistate, and federal levels. Clearer "operational goals and targets" are required at the substate regional level and at the local levels. The latter might include the preservation of various economic activities such as agricultural production, supporting agribusiness, location of other economic activities within substate areas, location of supporting facilities and services, and development of specific guidelines for related land use. (See Chapter 3 for more details.)

The need for such operational goals and targets is particularly acute at the multicounty and multicommunity levels. Specific goals and targets could provide a basis for meshing assistance available from public programs and nonpublic sources. And they could provide a basis for assessing the progress and effectiveness of action.

We judge development of clearer policy goals and operational targets to be an important area for analysis and public action. It will not be easy. Public officials and citizen leaders may be reluctant to discuss goals for action. Problems of local participation are real. Attempts to develop goals and targets may lead to controversy. However, the need exists for goals and targets to give unifying direction to the array of possible public and private actions.

V. SOME CHALLENGES FOR ACTION

A. View of the Arena

We have visited the *institutional arena* together in our travels through several chapters of this book (1, 2, 3, 39, and 40). It is a large and complex arena and the game played is called *land resources development, use and management.* While it is played on the floor of the arena, spectators beyond the arena floor call for various actions.

This game is very serious. The stakes are high, ranging from well-being and survival of nations over the long run to major public and personal losses and gains in the short run. The stakes are high not only for us, but for people we have never seen, some living in distant lands, and some not yet born.

At closer look we see it is not a game at all. It is work, very serious work. The persons and groups involved have adversaries or become adversaries, as in a real game. But unlike a game, those involved gain and lose real resources and property rights, real opportunities and real money. These gains and losses of real fortunes and personal benefits drive the actions of those directly involved, as well as the citizen spectators, far more than we are willing to admit.

We hear people shout from beyond the arena floor. Some of these citizen spectators call for "equity" in resource use and for a chance at the "opportunities" land resources can bring. Others, in a large and growing group, shout for "environmental quality" and for "sustained resource productivity." They sit next to another group of citizen spectators who call for the "right to help decide" who is to be involved in the decisions on the arena floor—those who gain and those who lose. Still other groups and pockets of citizen spectators, some very vocal and appearing to be very strong, cry out for "economic development," for "community and economic growth," and for "more freedom in using private property." It is clear these people want government to help make these possible, or otherwise to "keep hands off."

As we scan more broadly we can see that the institutional arena is a large and interesting place. It is open-ended, with connections to all manner of other physical, biological, and economic arenas with issues, problems, opportunities, and decisions of their own. We learn that these connections are not well used in much land use planning and decision making, even though their use is necessary for improved outcomes in this institutional arena and in the others. We also learn that to be effective over time, land use planning and decision making must be physically, engineeringly, and environmentally sound; economically feasible; socially acceptable; and legally and administratively possible.

The institutional arena seems firm and fixed at any point in time. It guides and constrains our movements and those of others. Yet we have heard that the parts of the arena, particularly the rules governing actions in the arena, shift over time. Some of these shifts are so major that they are given the special name "social movements."

One can easily see that this arena was not built at one time. It was built a piece at a time, without any overall architectural plan. Some of its foundation was brought from abroad by the early colonists, and significant parts of it were forged during early land settlement days. Additions have been made to it since. Clearly the additions have grown rapidly in the decade of the 1970's.

We see that a very large set of rules exists that influence or guide individual and group action, on the floor of the arena and beyond. These rules come from many sources—attitudes, values, government regulations, codes and ordinances, state and federal laws, court actions, social customs and habits, and religious and other beliefs. Some rules are old and long-standing; others are quite new. We notice that not all the rules function in the same direction; some point participants in opposite directions and some cause them to work against one another. Because these many rules come from divergent sources, have many varied applications, and cause different impacts, they do not lend themselves to easy classification as do soils and plants. We can see that no one person knows all the rules that apply to land resource development, use, and management, and that new rules are being added at a rapid rate. Complicating matters further, one rule can eliminate another or change it drastically. The effects of any one rule can vary widely depending on whether it is used alone or in various combinations with other rules. Someone suggested that rules work best when used in reinforcing combinations with other rules.

Some rules, particularly those called *federal,* apply to the entire arena. Other rules, particularly those called *state* and *multistate,* apply to large portions of the arena. Some rules, called *local,* apply to only small patches of the arena. Many of the rules were described in past writings, showing how a rule has operated in a particular place during a specified time. But we also have learned that we know little about how well these rules (particularly state and local rules) would work if applied to different areas or patches of the arena.

Those actively involved in "land resources development, use, and management" on the floor of the arena have been neither orderly nor systematic. They covered the arena floor in a moving patchwork of groups and individuals. Individuals moved into and out of groups with ease. Some individuals were identified as *public sector* while others were identified as *private sector*. Some individuals were both at different times, while for still others no clear distinctions could be made.

Those on the arena floor clustered in large groups described as *families and households, governments, market systems, educational systems,* and *cultural and religious groups*. When individuals moved into a group, they took part in the actions of that group. As they moved to a second and a third, again they took part in the actions of those groups. Groups also merged and separated. As we watched closely, we saw some strange and confusing things.

Groups joined forces with other groups or worked through them. For example, the group *families and households* worked through those called *market systems* and caused what seemed to be the greatest combined impact on land resources. The group *governments* also impacted land resources in major ways. It did so as owner and manager of large and varied holdings of public lands, and in its role as implementor of many rules—regulations, codes, ordinances, state and federal laws, and court actions.

Those clustered in the group called *educational systems,* and those in nearby *cultural* and *religious groups* caused many indirect impacts on land resources by the attitudes and beliefs they encouraged. Both groups looked potentially very strong. Both appeared capable of causing more major changes in the arena if they had gone about their work strategically and systematically.

The group called *families and households* took on roles called *interested citizens* and approached those in the *governments* group called *planners*. We observed that before those in *governments* could take actions on behalf of the *interested citizens* and protect *families and households,* a *plan* was required. The *plan* is to involve citizen participants and citizen observers, as well as technicians. The *plan* is to have public input about public preferences, as well as technical inputs and analyses about physical, engineering, environmental, economic, administrative, and legal considerations.

Sometimes plans were developed in a way that encouraged and solicited input from interested citizens. In those instances, interested citizens were welcomed warmly by planners. At other times plans were so poorly undertaken that, when completed, they were met with suspicion and hostility. In some instances planners went out of their way to avoid interested citizens. Thus no implementation was possible, since all was lost in the planning stage.

The group called governments also tried to guide and constrain those called *market systems* and those called families and households on behalf of something called *public interest.* Governments and some of the families and households called *interested citizens* in turn took occasional actions against members of the governments groups because they did not fulfill the public interest or public trust. Public interest and public trust are not self-evident concepts. We observed that neither is simply the addition of individual interests. Both concepts are difficult to implement in practice.

We saw much confusion, on the floor of the arena and beyond. Something very important was missing. While some individuals and groups were working shoulder to shoulder, others were working at cross purposes. Some were in heated debate—the words *court action, class action,* and *enjoin* could be heard. Someone suggested that clear objectives were required. Clearer policy goals and operating targets were needed for improved action and outcomes. The arsenal of mechanisms for bringing about changes in land resources development, use, and management was sizable, but there were few targets toward which the arsenal of mechanisms could be directed and coordinated.

Another spectator near us turns and says surely we can do something to make the actions in this institutional arena better. We turn and . . .

B. Specific Challenges for Action

Many challenges confront us as we seek to improve our land resources development, use, and management. Some confront the political and governmental leadership of our nation. Some confront the very groups we observed earlier—families and households, government agencies and groups, market systems, educational systems, and the cultural and religious groups. And some challenges confront our scientific and professional community. We will list a number of these challenges and make but brief comments on each.

1. CLEAR GOALS

There is no more basic challenge in land resources development, use, and management than to develop clearer policy goals and operational targets. We know that land, water, and broader resources planning are not ends in themselves, but rather means to other goals and ends. Time and time again we have seen the need for more clarity, visibility, agreement, and understanding of federal and state goals to provide a basis for complementary action. As a part of this effort, there is a need to develop clearer operational targets at the substate regional level and the local level. Such operational targets could help address the range of issues concerning local economic growth or limitation, location of economic activities, location of supporting facilities and services, and development of specific guidelines for land and water uses. It is a potentially fruitful area. The need for such operational goals and targets is particularly acute at the multicounty and multicommunity levels. Likewise, the potential benefit at these levels appears to be quite high.

2. INTEGRATION OF POLICIES

Closely associated with development of clearer policy goals and operational targets is the integration of different policy arenas that need to be related one to another. At the national and state levels we need to clarify our food production policies, our rural development policies, and our land use policies, and link them together. In the process we need to clarify food requirements domestically, for international trade, and for world food security. Careful estimates of food requirements are essential for any land requirements projections, and for plans concerning needed land conservation investment and agricultural land protection and preservation.

An even broader challenge is to link food production, rural development, and land policies to other crucial policies such as energy, transportation, economic development, economic dispersion, rural-urban balance, and human settlement. Each relates to land use. Each possesses opportunities for new complementarities in the achievement of clarified policies for land resources.

3. IMPROVED SYSTEMS OF PARTICIPATION

A third challenge for the future is improving the means for participation in land use choices. It stems from two questions increasingly heard— who should be involved in deciding about land uses and how will others have access to those who make the choices? These are very basic questions, ones that do not lend themselves to quick and easy solutions. They go beyond the matter of local participation to the broader matter of political representation and accountability.

We could address these questions better if we had available a systematic examination of existing and emerging rules for deciding choices in land use. Also needed are analyses of alternative procedures or processes for dealing with participation in such choices (DiMento, 1977). Studies of how the market, as modified by various governmental interventions, can function more effectively in guiding land use toward socially determined objectives are also needed (Samuels, 1972). There is an abundance of theoretical solutions to such problems, dating from Plato through Galbraith. What is currently needed are empirical studies to help us choose among these many possible systems.

4. LOCAL PARTICIPATION

A fourth key challenge is how to arrange and insure meaningful local participation in decisions concerning land resources planning and control. A community can do much to make sure that citizen participation is encouraged. That participation should be early enough to be creative and contributing, not merely reactive. Citizen input can be sought about possible alternative choices and, in fact, it can be used to help identify such choices.

Clarity about the difference between what is "technically possible" and what is "socially preferable" is essential. Planners and other professionals need to know what the citizens prefer. Citizens need to know what outcomes are technically possible. Public officials who must make decisions on behalf of their constituents need to be clear about both. Unfortunately, thorough analyses to determine what actions are both technically possible and socially preferable are often overlooked by communities and regions in their desire to forge ahead.

5. IMPROVED DATA BASE AND INFORMATION SYSTEM

Another major challenge for the immediate future is the improvement of our land resource data base and related information system. The differences that exist in the projection of cropland availability for the future were discussed earlier. These and other land uses and land use potentials need to be subjected to reexamination so that an improved data base and information system can be developed. While improvements at the national level are called for, similar improvements in data bases and information systems are necessary for states, substate regions, and local governmental units. Both technical analyses and citizen participation can be enhanced by such improved data bases and the related information systems. Where and how these improvements can be instituted and maintained to insure objectivity, accessibility, and permanence are in themselves challenges. Many earlier chapters in this book address this challenge.

6. INTEGRATING ECONOMIC AND ENVIRONMENTAL DECISIONS

A sixth challenge is to redefine the currently perceived conflict between economic development and environmental capabilities. Rather than targeting on the conflict, the focus should be on how to increase the integration between economic development and environmental improvement decisions. For a variety of historical reasons, much of our economic planning, decision making, and implementation has been quite separate from our more recent environmental planning, decision making, and action. This separation has existed at the federal and state levels, and at substate regional and local levels. Experience indicates that this separation of economic development decisions and environmental improvement decisions need not continue.

There are many opportunities for integration of these decisions at all levels of government, as well as in the private sector. Key gains can be achieved at both local and substate regional levels. Environmental scientists have found that environmental capabilities are regionally specific (Koenig & Cooper, 1972). Substate regions can and must be treated differently to take advantage of a region's ability to support human use and economic activity, and its capacity to assimilate wastes (D. E. Chappelle. 1972. The economics of environmental quality. Paper presented at the Midwest Forest Economists Assoc. Meet., Thessalon, Ontario). Adverse environmental effects of economic development projects can be minimized if environmental considerations are an integral part of the location and design decisions.

Additional research is essential to increase the integration of economic development and environmental improvement decisions. Needed is important physical research, such as for identifying and categorizing environmentally fragile areas and environmentally resilient areas. Required also are analyses of possible institutions for specifying environmental limits and tolerances permissible for such areas, environmental controls and incentives that could be instituted, and effective processes for integrated planning and decision making.

7. SYSTEMATIZING ANALYSES OF INSTITUTIONAL MECHANISMS

A systematic exploration of the effectiveness of alternative institutional forms and of the factual situations in which they have proved most effective is still another major challenge. Excellent individual analyses of specific institutional mechanisms have been, and are being, conducted. There is no apparent systematic approach, however, to this field of inquiry—one that would maximize the aggregation and complementarity of analyses and findings.

An initiating approach similar to that recently employed concerning research requirements for environmental/land use planning could be used. In that instance a national agency (the Environmental Systems and Resources Division of the National Science Foundation's RANN—Research Applied to National Needs) helped bring together a group of university researchers and planning practitioners. They met in an intensive 2-week session to "think through" how the research requirements for environmental/land use planning might be met, and to identify new knowledge needed by practitioners and society to do a better job in planning our physical environment (McAllister, 1973). To address our research challenge, such units as the American Bar Association, the National Science Foundation, and the National Academy of Sciences—National Research Council could be invited to explore, if not spearhead, this effort.

8. UNDERSTANDING NEW VALUES

The challenge of *education* may well be the greatest challenge of all. Growth, individualism, personal profit, and resource exploitation are still pursued in ways that adversely affect the sustained use of our land resources. We must show where and how these and related traditional values are making it difficult or impossible to restore harmony in the man-nature relationship.

With renewed dedication we must help the public explore and understand new values. Historian Douglas Miller (1976) points out several possibilities. We might teach that the various land-related crises—energy, food, raw materials, population—are not separable aberrations. We have been using up irreplaceable resources at a rate that cannot be sustained. We can show the global nature of these crises; U.S. conditions are better understood when viewed in the global context. We should help people look at land use questions in a very long time frame. What we have done in the

United States in the most recent time period should not blind us to other perspectives or possibilites; neither should we accept short-term benefits that will work to the detriment of future generations. We should stress the need for cooperative expertise; none of the major problems in land resource use can be fully analyzed by a single discipline, a single profession, or a single occupational group. Finally, educators must take the lead in suggesting how traditional values might be modified to better meet the problems of the present and future.

C. Final Brief Perspective

Many of you who read this book will come from the physical and biological sciences, from the professions of agronomy or crop and soil sciences, or from allied areas of land resources use and physical and biological management. There has been over the years a major commitment of funds and manpower to crop and soil productivity and to increased food and fiber yield.

It appears that less scientific attention has been given to the loss of land supply than is given to an equivalent gain in productivity. Or phrased another way, we have given more emphasis to increasing productivity on a diminishing land base than to retarding the loss of land that cancels out the benefits of such increased productivity for society as a whole.

From both scientific and governmental perspectives, we detect different attitudes about research and extension education on increasing productivity per unit and on improving ways to plan, protect, and guide use of our stock of land resources. From both scientific and governmental perspectives it appears morally appropriate to help improve yields from land. We postulate it is just as appropriate to help plan, protect, and guide use of land resources, and to invest in the research and extension education that makes them possible.

As a final note, quality of life is tied directly to the range of choice and the freedom we have in our work and in other parts of our lives. The greater the joint attention to sustained productivity and stewardship of our stock of land resources, the wider will be our range of ecological choices over time. The careful use and protection of our land resource base, as we strive to enhance production, will surely provide more choices and more individual freedom for our future.

LITERATURE CITED

Anderson, F. 1973. NEPA in the courts. Resources for the Future, Inc., John Hopkins Univ. Press, Baltimore.

Barlowe, R. 1972. Land resource economics. 2nd Ed. Prentice-Hall, Inc., Englewood Cliffs, N.J.

Barlowe, R. 1977. Planning for development: Long-run goals, short-run realities. p. 30–44. *In* Planning for land development. Dep. of Resour. Dev., Michigan State Univ., East Lansing.

Beuscher, J. H. 1951. Farm law in Wisconsin. C. C. Nelson Publ. Co., Appleton, Wis. p. 1.

Bronstein, D. A. 1973. State regulation of power plant siting. Environ. Law 3:273.

Bronstein, D. A. 1977. Land use regulation: Construction permits. Ext. Bull. E-1070, Michigan State Univ., East Lansing.

Bronstein, D. A., and D. E. Erickson. 1973. Zoning amendments in Michigan. J. Urban Law 50:729.

Catalano, R., and J. DiMento. 1976. Local government response to state environmental impact assessment requirements: An explanation and a typology. Environ. Law 7:25.

Cooper, W. E., and R. D. Vlasin. 1973. Ecological concepts and application to planning. Environment: A new focus for land-use planning. Natl. Sci. Found., Washington, D.C.

Committee on Resources and Man. 1969. Resources and man. Natl. Acad. of Sci.—Natl. Res. Counc. W. H. Freeman and Co., San francisco.

Construction Industry Association v. Petaluma, 522 F. 2d 897 (9th Cir. 1975).

Cutler, M. R., and D. A. Bronstein. 1974. Public involvement in government decisions. Alternatives. 4:11.

DiMento, J. F. 1977. Citizen environmental litigation and the administrative process: Empirical findings, remaining issues and a direction for future research. Duke Law J. 1977: 409.

Golden v. Ramapo. 30 N. Y. 2d 359, 285 N.E. 2d 291 (1972). See also Comment, N.Y.U. L. Rev. 47:723 (1972).

Johnson, W. M. 1977. What has been happening in land use in America and what are the projections. J. Anim. Sci. 45:1464-1475.

Koenig, H. E., and W. E. Cooper. 1972. Design and management of environmental systems. Vol. I and II, Michigan State Univ., East Lansing.

Koenig, H. E., and T. C. Edens. 1976. Resource management in a changing environment: With applications to the rural sector. Michigan Agric. Exp. Stn., Michigan State Univ., East Lansing.

Lee, L. K. 1978. A perspective on cropland availability. Agric. Econ. Rep. 406. USDA, Washington, D.C.

Libby, L. W. 1976. From the perspective of a political economist. p. 10–12. *In* Perspectives on the land. Michigan State Univ., East Lansing.

McAllister, D. M. 1973. Environment: A new focus for land-use planning. Natl. Sci. Found., Washington, D.C.

Miller, D. T. 1976. From the perspective of a historian. p. 3–5. *In* Perspectives on the land. Michigan State Univ., East Lansing.

Morrison, D. E. 1976. From the perspective of a sociologist. p. 6–9. *In* Perspectives on the land. Michigan State Univ., East Lansing.

Ordway, N. 1976. Attitudinal changes within a political context of zoning administration in Atlanta: Some policy implications. Dep. Real Estate and Urban Affairs, Georgia State Univ., Atlanta.

Rohman, D. G. 1976. Perspectives on the land. Michigan State Univ., East Lansing.

Samuels, W. 1972. Welfare economics, power and property. *In* G. Wunderlich and W. L. Gibson, Jr. (ed.) Perspectives of property. Inst. for Res. on Land and Water Resour., The Pennsylvania State Univ., University Park.

Sax, J. L. 1971. Defending the environment. Alfred A. Knopf, New York.

Seneker, C. J. 1974. Land use regulations for urban growth control. Inst. of Gov. Affairs, Davis, Calif.

Simko, P. A., L. Allen, B. Kuder, and J. Schreier. 1978. Promised lands: Subdivisions and the law. Vol. 3. Inform, Inc., New York.

U.S. Department of Agriculture. 1973. Our nation's land and water resources. ERS-530. Economic Research Service, USDA, Washington, D.C.

U.S. Department of Agriculture. 1974. Our land and water resources. Misc. Pub. 1290. Economic Research Service, USDA, Washington, D.C.

Vlasin, R. D. 1971. Some key issues and challenges posed by nonagricultural demands for rural environments. Am. J. Agric. Econ. 53(2):235–239.

Vlasin, R. D. 1974. Planning and implementing rural development. J. Soil Water Conserv. 29(1):28–33.

Vlasin, R. D. 1975. Conservation, use and retention of agricultural lands for all-out food production. All-out food production: Strategies and resource implications. ASA Spec. Pub. 23. Am. Soc. of Agron., Madison, Wis.

Vlasin, R. D. 1976. Protection and preservation problems and challenges. Protection of essential lands. Michigan State Univ., East Lansing.

Yannacone, V. J. 1975. Agricultural lands, fertile soils, popular sovereignty, the trust doctrine, environmental impact assessment and the natural law. N. Dak. L. Rev. 51:615–653.

GLOSSARY

Common and Scientific Names of Plants

Ailanthus	*Ailanthus altissima* Mill.
Alder, European black	*Alnus glutinosa*
Alfalfa	*Medicago sativa* L.
Alkaligrass, nuttal	*Puccinellia nuttalliana* Hitchc.
Alkaligrass, weeping	*Puccinellia distans* L.
Ash, green	*Fraxinus pennsylvanica* Marsh.
Ash, white	*Fraxinus americana* L.
Aspen, bigtooth	*Populus grandidentata* Michx.
Aspen, European	*Populus tremula* L.
Aspen, quaking	*Populus tremuloides* Michx.
Azaleas	*Rhododendron* L.
Bahiagrass	*Paspalum notatum* Flugge
Barley	*Hordeum vulgare* L.
Bean	*Phaseolus vulgaris* L.
Beech, American	*Fagus grandifolia* Ehrh.
Bermudagrass, giant	*Cynodon dactylon* L. Pers. var. *aridus* Harlan et de Wet.
Birch, European white	*Betula verrucosa* Ehrh. (= B. pendula Roth)
Birch, white	*Betula papyrifera* Marsh.
Birch, yellow	*Betula alleghaniensis* Britton
Birdsfoot trefoil	*Lotus corniculatus* L.
Bluebonnets	*Lupinus subcarnosus* Hook
Blue grama	*Bouteloua gracilis* (H.B.K.) Lag. x Steud.
Bluegrass, Canada	*Poa compressa* L.
Bluegrass, Kentucky	*Poa pratensis* L.
Bluegrass, rough stalk	*Poa trivialis* L.
Bluestem, big	*Andropogon geradi* L.
Bluestem, little	*Andropogon scoparis* L.
Bromegrass, smooth	*Bromus inermis* Leyss.
Canarygrass, reed	*Phalaris arundinacea* L.
Cedar, eastern red	*Juniperus virginiana* L.
Centipede	*Eremochloa ophiuroides* (Munro) Hack.
Chestnut, American	*Castanea dentata* (Marsh.) Borkh.
Clover, alsike	*Trifolium hybridium* L.
Clover, crimson	*Trifolium incarnatum* L.
Clover, red	*Trifolium pratense* L.
Clover, white	*Trifolium repens* L.
Corn	*Zea mays* L.
Cotton	*Gossypium hirsutum* L.
Cottonwood, eastern	*Populus deltoides* Bartr.
Cottonwood, poplar	*Populus* L.
Dandelion	*Taraxacum officinale* Weber
Daylily	*Hemerocallis* L.
Deertongue	*Panicum clandestinum* L.
Dogwood, silky	*Cornus amomum*
Elm, American	*Ulmus americana* L.
Elm, Siberian	*Ulmus pumila* L.
Fescue, creeping red	*Festuca rubra* L.
Fescue, spreading	*Festuca rubra* L. *rubra* Hack.
Fescue, tall	*Festuca arundinacea* Schreb.

Fir, Douglas (coast form)	*Pseudotsuga menziesii* var. *menziesii* (Mirb.) Franco
Fir, Douglas (Inland form)	*Pseudotsuga menziesii* var. *glauca* (Beissn,) Franco
Flat pea	*Lathyrus sylvestris* L.
Fleeceflower, Japanese	*Polygonum cuspidatum*
Fringe-tree	*Chionanthus virginica* L.
Geranium, garden	*Pelargonium* L. 'Her.
Ginkgo	*Ginkgo biloba* L.
Gladiolus	*Gladiolus* L.
Goldenrod	*Solidago nemoralis* L.
Goosefoot, nettle-leaf	*Chenopodium murale* L.
Hackberry	*Celtus occidentalis* L.
Hemlock, western	*Tsuga heterophylla* (Raf.) Sarg.
Honeysuckle, amur	*Lonicera maacki podocarpa* L.
Honeysuckle, tatarian	*Lonicera tatarica siberica*
Indigo bush	*Amorpha fruticosa*
Ivy	*Hedera* L.
Juniper	*Juniperus* L.
Larch, European	*Larix decidua* Mill.
Larch, Japanese	*Larix leptolepis* Murr.
Larch, western	*Larix occidentalis* Nutt.
Lespedeza, bicolor	*Lespedeza bicolor*
Lespedeza, common	*Lespedeza striata* L.
Lespedeza, Korean	*Lespedeza stipulacea* Maxim.
Lespedeza, serecia	*Lespedeza cuneata* Dumont
Lespedeza, virgata	*Lespedeza virgata* (Thumb.) DC
Linden, European small-leaved	*Tilia cordata* Mill.
Liveoak	*Quercus virginiana* Mill.
Locust, black	*Robinia pseudoacacia* L.
Locust, bristly	*Robinia fertilis*
Locust, honey	*Gleditsia triacanthos* L.
Lovegrass, weeping	*Eragrostis curvula* (Schrad.) Nees
Magnolia	*Magnolia grandiflora* L.
Maple, Norway	*Acerplatanoides* L.
Maple, red	*Acer rubrum* L.
Maple, silver	*Acer saccharinum* L.
Maple, sugar	*Acer saccharinum* L.
Millet, foxtail	*Setaria italica* (L.) Beauv.
Myrtle	*Vinca minor* L.
Oak, black	*Quercus velutina* Lam.
Oak, bur	*Quercus macrocarpa*
Oak, English	*Quercus robur* L.
Oak, red	*Quercus rubra*
Oak, scarlet	*Quercus coccinea* Muenchh.
Oak, white	*Quercus alba* L.
Oat	*Avena sativa* L.
Oatgrass, tall	*Arrhenatherum elatius* L.
Olive, autumn	*Elaeagnus umbellata*
Olive, Russian	*Elaeagnus angustifolia* L.
Orchardgrass	*Dactylis glomerata* L.
Pachysandra	*Pachysandra terminalis* Sieb. & Zucc.
Perennial pea	*L. latifolius* L.
Pigweed	*Chenopodium* L.
Pine, Austrian	*Pinus nigra*
Pine, eastern white	*Pinus strobus* L.
Pine, jack	*Pinus banksiana* Lamb.

GLOSSARY

Pine, loblolly	*Pinus taeda* L.
Pine, longleaf	*Pinus palustris* Mill.
Pine, pitch	*Pinus rigida* Mill.
Pine, ponderosa	*Pinus ponderosa* Laws.
Pine, radiata	*Pinus radiata* D. Don
Pine, red	*Pinus resinosa* Ait.
Pine, scotch	*Pinus sylvestris* L.
Pine, shortleaf	*Pinus echinata* Mill.
Pine, slash	*Pinus elliottii* Engelm
Pine, Virginia	*Pinus virginiana*
Pine, western white	*Pinus monticola* Dougl.
Pine, white	*Pinus strobus*
Pinyon	*Pinus edulis* L.
Plane, London	*Platanus acerifolia* Willd.
Plantain-lily	*Hosta* Tratt.
Poplar, hybrid	*Populus* spp.
Poplar, yellow	*Liriodendron tulipifera* L.
Potato	*Solanum tuberosum* L.
Powdery mildew	*Eresiphe graminis* DC
Quackgrass	*Agropyron repens* (L.) Beauv.
Redtop	*Agrostis alba* L.
Redwood	*Sequoia sempervirens* (D. Don) Endl.
Rhododendrons	*Rhododendron* L.
Ricegrass, Indian	*Oryzopsis hymenoides* L.
Rutabaga	*Brassica rapa* L.
Rye, winter	*Secale cereale* L.
Ryegrass, perennial	*Lolium perenne* L.
St. Augustinegrass	*Stenotaphrum secondatum* Kuntze
Salal	*Gaultheria shallon*
Salmonberry	*Rubus spectabilis*
Saltbush, fourwing	*Atriplex canescens* L.
Salt grass	*Distichlis* Raf. *stricta* (Torr.) Rydb.
Soybean	*Glycine max* (L.) Merr.
Spanish-moss	*Tillandsia usneoides* L.
Spruce, black	*Picea mariana* (Mill.) B.S.P.
Spruce, Norway	*Picea abies* (L.) Karst
Spruce, sitka	*Picea sitchensis* (Bong.) Carr.
Spruce, white	*Picea glauca* var. *glauca*
Sudangrass	*Sorghum sudanense* L.
Sweetclover, white	*Melilotus alba*
Sweetclover, yellow	*Melilotus officinalis*
Sweetgum	*Liquidambar styraciflua* L.
Switchgrass	*Panicum virgatum* L.
Sycamore	*Plantanus occidentalis*
Tamarack	*Larix laricina* (Du Roi) K. Koch
Timothy	*Phleum pratense* L.
Vetch, crown	*Coronilla varia* L.
Vetch, hairy	*Vicia villosa* L.
Walnut, black	*Juglans nigra* L.
Wheatgrass, western	*Agropyron smithii* Rydb.
Wheat, winter	*Triticum aestivum* L.
Wild strawberry	*Fragaria virginiana* Duchesne
Willow	*Salix* L.
Winterfat	*Eurotia lanata* L.
Zoysia	*Zoysia* spp.

SUBJECT INDEX

Aeration, 775, 783
Agricultural land,
  planning uses, 226
    climate, 245
    data requirements, 231
    irrigated agriculture, 244
    maxmize air quality, 260–262
    nonirrigated agriculture, 246–250
    preserve water quality, 252, 253, 255, 257, 259
    reduce environmental effects, 251
    soils, 246
    topography, 245
    water, 244
  preservation, 40–42
    approaches, 42
  use
    capability classifications, 233–243
    control through zoning, 262–264
    rates of removal, 227–229, 291
    trends in area, 227–229, 291
    preservation, 197, 222, 223, 225, 227, 228, 312–315
    values to domestic and foreign exchange, 292
Agricultural Stabilization and Conservation Service, 842
Agricultural system, large-scale integrated
  examples, 273
  institutions for operating, 287–289
Air pollution control, effect on agriculture, 266
Animal production (See also Feedlots; Manure)
  environmental problems
    at animal confinement, 733–735, 739, 740
    manure on cropped land, 733–735, 754–757
    runoff control, 733, 739, 747, 749
    runoff storage, 733, 744, 749
  factors affecting, 733, 736–745
    economic priorities, 733, 743
    land use competition, 733
    zoning, 740, 744
  maintenance of, 733, 734
  plant nutrient recycling, 733, 751
  specialization in, 733, 734
Animal wastes. See Manure

Beaches and barrier islands
  management, 817
  preservation, 817, 827
  soils, 816, 817

Chemical fertilizers
  conservation of, 734, 751
  replacement by manure, 734, 751, 752
Clay, affecting construction, 488
Coastal zones
  hypothetical cross section, 815
  management, 819
  marshes, soils, 818
  preservation, 819, 827
  uplands, 820, 827
    soils, 819
  uses, 813
Common resources
  Tragedy of the Commons, 274–276
Compaction equipment, 778
Conservation Needs Inventory, 143, 154
Crop growth
  benefits from manure
    plant nutrients N, P, K, 752
    root growth, 751
    soil water relations, 751
    tilth, 751, 752
  cropping systems
    crop quality, 754, 755
    effective use, 733, 751, 753, 754
    fat necrosis, 756
    grass tetany, 756
    manure rates in, 753, 754
    manure utilization in different crops, 752–754
    nitrate problems, 754, 756
    salt problems, 754, 756
  root growth, 751
  soil water relations, 751
  tilth, 751, 752
Crop Reporting Service, 149

Data (See also Remote sensing)
  bank
    Canadian Geographic Information System, 912–914
    environmental management, 925
  bases, 144, 898, 899
    applications, 144
    geographic representation, 144
    systems, 144
  classification systems
    ancillary data, 172
    hierarchical, 170
  communication, 188
  organization, 893, 894
  reduction and display
    graphic use, 473

numeric use, 477
quantification, 477
relation to other factors, 473
use in metropolitan planning, 477
remote sensing needs
grid size, 168
ground resolution, 168, 169
sources
infrared photograph, 199
Landsat, 145, 150, 155, 198, 199
remote sensing (*See also* Remote sensing), 197
satellite, 197, 198
Topocon, 201
storage methods, 899
cell, 900
dot, 902
polygon, 901
Venn diagram, 188, 189
Data analysis, 187
overlay
limitations, 197
reduction, 188, 198
simplification, 198
techniques, 189–196
spatial, 187, 188, 895
use of polygons, 188
weighted, 203
Data applications and examples
electric transmission, 203, 207
electrical generating station, 216
farmland preservation, 197
highways, 189
high-S coal utilization, 202
housing location, 189
interstate, 203, 207
natural change, 217
onsite waste disposal, 215
recreation planning, 189
rural land assessment, 199
stream flow, 220
visual quality, 203, 207
water quality detection, 199
Data handling and display, technology and
techniques
computer graphic, 203
digital and analog scanning, 197
digital computing, 213
dispersion program, 216
edge-enhanced map, 199
interactive, 215
interpolation, 216
line printer, 209, 215
lithography, 203
microdensotometer, 199
modeling, 215, 216
multispectral scanner, 199
optimization, 203, 207, 215
plotter, 202
simulation, 217, 218
T. V. monitor, 198, 199

weighted composites, 207
Decomposition
aerobic, 778
anaerobic, 778
Disturbed land
agricultural, 875
chemical characteristics, 855–858
acidity and neutralization, 856, 857
plant nutrients, 858, 863
toxic elements, 857
construction, 854
effects on ground water, 860–862
chemical composition, 861
ground water recharge, 861
infiltration, 860
environmental problems
barren land, 859
landslides, 859
pollution, 859
highways, 875
human activity, 853
mining, 854, 855, 875
in eastern U.S., 855
surface, 854
natural, 853
physical characteristics, soil texture, 858
plant species for revegetating, 866–869
reclamation alternatives, 862, 863
management, 863
unreclaimed damages, 862
uses, 862, 863
revegetation techniques, 865–870
species selection, 866
seeding equipment, 870, 871
soil amendments
fertilizer, 870
fly ash, 870
sewage sludge, 870
stabilization
chemical soil stabilizers, 865
erosion control, 863–865
landslide, 863
mulches, 864, 865
sedimentation, 864
slope, 863, 865
terraces and diversions, 864
vegetation, 865

Ecological planning, 935–955
comprehensive plan, 936
ground water recharge, 944
hazards to life and health, 941
landscape analysis, 936
natural drainage, 948
performance requirements, 936
process, 937
suitability, 935
vegetation clearance, 949
wildlife corridors, 937
Woodlands, Texas, 935–955

Ecological relationships, physical and biological, 5
Ecology (*See* Ecosystems)
Economic framework for policies, 5, 6
Ecosystems
  complexity, 447, 448
  components, 447
  methods for guiding decisions on, 316
  prime and unique lands, 316
  stability, 448
  value of, 316
  wildland, 447
Effluent
  septic tank
    Biological Oxygen Demand, 666
    clogging, 672
  thermal, 705
Energy conservation
  requirements for urban vegetation management, 501–503, 515, 523
  urban vegetation for fostering, 506, 507
Environmental
  analysis, 148
  constraints, 941
  hazards to life and health, 950
  impact statements, 796
  opportunities, 940, 941
Erosion
  urban
    control, 493, 494
    sediment yields, 493, 494
Evapotranspiration potential, 800

Feedlots
  buffer land, 740
  climatic factors, 736, 743–745, 748
    precipitation, 736, 748
    temperature, 736, 748
    wind direction, 736, 740, 748
  design, factors affecting, 736, 740–743, 748
  geology and soil, 736, 739, 748
  ground water (*See* Ground water)
  isolation of, 737, 740, 748
  land modification, 739, 748
  locating, 733–740
    distance from streams or lakes, 737
    flood plain, 737
    guidelines, 736–739
    mapping area, 737
    planning, 737, 740–744
  managing, 733, 735, 736, 740, 744–748
  marketable output, 736, 740
  nuisance potential
    air quality, 734, 739, 740
    neighbor attitude, 734, 740
    odors, 734, 739, 740
  overland flow control, 748
  physical environmental factors, 736–739
    flood hazard, 737, 738
    geohydrology, 736, 739

    land use, 737
    leaching, 738, 739
    slope, 737, 748, 749
    soil as a buffer, 738
    soil drainage, 737, 738
    soil infiltration, 738
    soil surveys, 737
    soil texture, 738
    topography, 736, 737, 748
    water percolation, 738, 739
    water table, 737–739
  pollution potential, 734–736, 745–747, 750, 754–757
  privacy fences, 740, 748
  production inputs, 736
  regulations, 743, 744, 748
  runoff (*See* Runoff)
  snow control, 748
  solids (*See* Manure)
  stocking rate, 744
  surface of lot, 739, 740, 743, 746, 750
    paved, 740, 741, 743, 744
    unpaved, 741, 743, 744
  vegetative shelterbelts, 740, 748
  zoning, 740, 744
Fertilizers, animal manures as, 733, 734, 736, 751–756
Flood plains, 814, 820, 972–976
  characteristics, 972
  management, 822, 824
  nature, 821
  preservation, 822, 823, 827
  resulation of land uses, 972–974
  soils, 492, 821, 822
Flood protection, 823
Flood wastes, 785, 787
Forest action plan
  existing forest, 380
  new plantations, 380
Forest climates
  general information needs, 372
  temperature, 372
  wind, 372
Forest management
  intensity planning
    decision-making, 411, 412
    location and accessibility, 408
    market situation, 408
    personal objectives, 410, 411
    potential productivity, 409
    tree crop inventory, 409
  objectives, 377, 378
    need for revision, 380, 381
Forest productivity
  commercial and noncommercial land, 369
  factors determining, 368
  importance, 369
  maintenance, 373–375
  nutrient drain, 373–375
  nutrient pools and pathways of movement, 374

range, 369
site quality, 368
Forest regulation
  allowable cut, 376, 377
  area and volume control, 376, 377
  forest growth stimulators, 377
  framework
    target forest, 379
    treatment classes, 379
  mean annual increment, 376, 377
  normal forest, 376
  optimizing techniques, 377
  rotation age, 376, 377
  rotation age, 376, 377
  soil rent, 376, 377
  sustained yield, 376
  technical rotation, 376, 377
Forest resource description
  classification
    land base, 379
    soil, 379
  inventory, 378
  legal, 378
  timber cruising, 378
  working circles, 378
Forest site preparation
  slash burning, 382
  tractor scarification, 382
Forest soils
  environmental problems
    public recreation, 370
    water quality, 370
    wildlife habitat, 371
  fertilizer practices, 370, 384
  forest type conversion, 371
  information
    conservation plans, 408
    equipment limitations, 400, 401
    erosion hazard, 401
    hardwood competition, 404, 405
    local technical guides, 407, 408
    ordination of suitability groups, 406, 407
    seedling mortality, 402
    site index, 398
    soil surveys, 407
    special reports, 408
    species choice, 399, 400
    for the user, 405, 406
    windthrow hazard, 402
    woodland suitability groups, 406
  nutritional status, 370
  productivity potential
    estimation, 389, 390
    northern states, 391, 392
    Pacific Coast states, 390
    regional patterns, 390–392
    Rocky Mountain states, 392
    southern states, 390, 391
  regeneration and rehabilitation, 371
Forest soil-site relationships, 392–398
  aspen, 395

Douglas-fir, 393
factorial and holistic, 392, 393
hardwoods, northern, 396
larch, European and Japanese, 394
locust, black, 395
mixed pine-hardwoods, 397
National Cooperative Soil Survey, 397
Norway spruce, 397
oaks, 395
pines
  eastern white, 397
  jack, 396
  lodgepole, 394
  ponderosa, 394
  southern, 396
review of literature, 393–397
sweetgum, 397
walnut, black, 395
yellow-poplar, 395

Gas migration, 779
Gas production, 779
  methane, 788
Geotechnical
  engineering, 555
  factors
    geology, 557
    soil, 557
    topography, 557
  information
    importance, 556
    sources, 557, 571–574
  limitations, methods of handling, 574–579
Grasses
  transportation systems, vegetation for
    with legume mixtures, 588, 589
    planning, 588
Ground water, 688
  animal production effect on
    design of facilities, 739, 740, 743, 749
    management of feedlot, 739, 740, 750
  aquifer, 738, 739, 750, 751
  core-drilling studies
    feedlot use, 751
    land-use effect, 751
    nitrate in water, 739, 750, 751, 754
  hydrogeology, 736, 739, 750, 751
    aeration zone, 739, 750
    monitoring, 750
    saturation zone, 739, 750, 751
    strata arrangement, 737
    stratification of water, 750
    water mixing, 750
  monitoring, 779
  organic substances in water, 751
  perched water table, 688
  protection from contamination, 739, 749–751, 756
    hydraulic pathways, 739, 750
    impermeable materials, 739, 743

Ground water, protection from contamination (*continued*)
  infiltration, 739, 750
  nitrate, 739, 750, 754
  salts, 739, 750
  soil sealing, 739, 750
  soil texture, 739
  sewage effluent, subsurface application, 688
  table, 739, 750, 751
Growth management
  examples, 38, 39
  techniques, 36–39

Hydraulic conductivity, 671
  measurement, 672
  steady flow systems, 668
Hydrodynamic dispersion
  measurement, 670
    compaction, 674
    puddling, 674
Hydrologic processes, 804–808
  infiltration, 805
  rainfall-runoff, 804
Hydrologic data bases
  Canada, 126–134, 136
    Atmospheric Environmental Service, 128, 129
    Canadian climatic data base, 128, 129
    Canadian hydrometric and sediment data bases, 130–132
    Inland Waters Directorate, 126–134
    National Water Quality Data System, 133, 134
    Representative and experimental watersheds, 136
    Water Resources Document Reference Centre, 126, 127
  United States, 122–138
    Columbia River Operational Hydromet Management System, 135
    Environmental Data Index, 126
    National Oceanic and Atmospheric Administration, 126–128
    National Stream Quality Accounting Network, 130
    National Water Data Exchange, 122–125
    National Water Data Storage and Retrieval System, 129, 130
    representative and experimental watersheds, 135–138
    Science and Education Administration, 136, 137
    Snow Telemetry, 135
    state, 136
    Storage and Retrieval System, 132
    Tennessee Valley Authority, 134, 136
    U.S. climatic data base, 127, 128
    U.S. Environmental Protection Agency, 132, 136

U.S. Forest Service, 136–138
U.S. Geological Survey, 122–125, 129, 130, 136
Hydrologic data indexes, 122–124, 126, 127
Hydrologic data sources, 123–125, 127, 128, 130, 135, 138
Hydrologic processes
  floods, 806, 807
  infiltration, 802–805, 808
  models, 808, 809
Hydrologic properties
  saline seeps, 806
  subsurface flow, 806
Hydrology, 117, 125, 130, 138, 141

Infiltration, 805
Information
  costs, 187
  data distribution, 198, 199
  defined, 187
  relationships
    indicator, 202, 203
    spatial, 202
Information systems
  remote sensing
    digital analysis in, 167, 180
    machine processing in, 167
    numerical analysis in, 164, 180
    pattern recognition, 167
    photointerpretation in, 167
    visual analysis in, 164, 167
  spatial data
    components, 896, 897
    format, 903
    media, 903
    products, 902–904
    purpose, 904
Institutional framework for policies, 5, 6
Irrigation suitability classification
  U.S. Bureau of Reclamation, 233, 234

Land
  classification, 96, 914, 915
    relation to soil classification, 97
  conversion to nonagricultural uses, 227–229, 291, 734
  definition, 293
  prime
    approaches for defining, 299
    concept, 294–296
    criteria for defining, 297
    definitions, 302–306
    delineations, 307–310
    preservation methods, 312–315
  properties affecting soil behavior, 103
  reclamation
    definition, 854
    environmental considerations, 882–884
    legislation, 854, 862, 877

orphaned land, 854, 862
revegetation, 877–881
species adaptability, 882–884
spoil replacement, 877
types, 97
unique, 306
concept and definition, 306, 307
delineation, 307–310
preservation methods, 307–310
Land banking, 39, 40
Land capability
analysis
maps, 927
studies, 927
classifications
agriculture, 96, 915–917
Canadian system, 241
FAO system, 243
forestry, 917–919
land use, 924, 925
recreation, 923
Storie Index, 234–238
USDA system, 239
ungulate, 921, 922
waterfowl, 920, 921
wildlife, 919, 920
Land control mechanisms, 311
assessment, differential, 313
development rights, transfer and purchase, 314, 315
fee-simple lease, 314
special agricultural districts, 313
zoning, agricultural, 312, 313
Land cover data, 145, 146, 790
aquisition, 143, 145
biomass, 145
categories, 146
designating conflict areas, 155
synoptic coverage, 145
systems, 147
uses, 146, 154, 155
Land development
attitude and beliefs, 988, 989, 992
environmental movements, 991, 992
equity movements, 990, 991
growth and development, 989
land environment, 992
land resources, 992
population impact on, 989, 990
Landfill sites
completed, 788, 789
cover material, 773, 774
covering
daily, 774
final, 773, 774
intermediate, 774
lift design, 772
liners, 781–783
clay, 781
fabric, 781
gradient, 782

paved, 781
oxygen diffusion, 777
revegetation, 788–791
uses, 788
Land institutions
collective action, 995, 996
educational system, 994
family system, 993
government, 994–996
Land inventories
benefit/cost, 930
biophysical, 926
Canada Land Inventory, 911, 930–932
activities, 913, 914
development, 911
objectives, 912
ecological, 926
land use, 925, 926
use of data
land management, 928–930
land use planning, 926–928
Land management
Minnesota Land Management Information System, 148
planning, types of, 890–893
Land use
challenges
developing goals and policies, 1005, 1006
improving participation, 1007
integrating economic and environmental decisions, 1007, 1008
moral issues, 1009
understanding values, 1008, 1009
using data and information, 998, 999, 1007
classification systems, 146, 147
commercial, 485
constitutional and legal systems
citizen involvement, 996, 997
coordinating actions, 998, 1000
ecological relationships, 983–985
government's roles, 996–1000
historical development in U.S., 30, 31
institutional arena, 1002–1005
institutional relationships, 981, 1002–1005
policy objectives, 1000–1002
controversies
role in process of social change, 27, 28
environmental corridors, 481
federal programs, 42, 43
interests
land developers, 29, 30
land owners, 29, 30
private, 29, 30
public, 29, 30
light industry, 485
nature of, 928
objectives and standards, 478, 479
patterns
effects of soils and plants, 23

Land use, patterns (*continued*)
  recent trends with cropland, 12–16
  residential, 485
  soil features affecting, 486
  suggested organic approach, 468
  trends and changes, 19–21, 928, 931
    forest land, 19, 20
    grazing land, 19, 20
    parks and wildlife areas, 21
    transportation, 21
    urban uses, 21

Land use controls and guidance, 966, 998, 999, 1001, 1002
  soil-based, 959–962, 965, 968
    agricultural zoning, 962, 963, 965, 967, 968
    evaluation of soils information, 976–978
    flood plains, 972–974
    septic tank regulations, 960, 961, 963, 965, 968
    subdivision regulations, 959, 960
    wetland regulations, 968, 969
  subdivision, 34–35

Land use planning
  basic considerations, 982
  definition, 889, 890
  ecological relationships, 983–985
  evaluating land use proposals, 55, 56
  general framework, 366
  hydrologic impact, 117–121, 138
  importance, 468
  institutional relationships, 981, 987, 988, 990–992
  modeling (*See* simulation)
  production/consumption relationships, 985–987
  public and private forestry organization, 367
  purposeful response, 47, 48
  purpose of study, 51–54
  recent trends, 60–62
  regional plans, 480–483
    design, 480–481
    implementation, 482, 483
  simulation, 117–121, 135–138
  trends, 982, 983
  waste disposal, 696

Landscape components, 935
  matrices of, 938, 939
  urban, vegetation in, 499

Leachate
  anaerobic, 777
  biodegradation, 783
  collection and treatment of, 780–783
  definition, 766
  in freezing weather, 775
  recycling, 782
  salvage of, 783
  treatment facilities, 788

Livestock grazing on rangeland
  control of species, 330, 331
  grazing systems, 331
  planning elements, strategy or goal, 329, 330
  range seeding, 331
Livestock wastes (*See* Manure)

Manure
  application on land
    benefits, 751
    ammonia volatilization, 753
    methods, 752, 753
    N availability, 753, 754
    rates for cropping, 736, 752–754
    salts, 735, 753
    soil losses, 753, 754
  composition of, 734, 739, 752
  environmental concerns
    animal disease, 735, 746, 756
    crop problems, 735, 754, 756
    ground water contamnation, 734, 735, 754
    ground water (*See* Ground water)
    human health, 734, 735, 746
    management, 734, 742, 743, 755
    nonpoint source pollution, 756, 757
    odors, 734, 735, 739, 740, 749
    plant nutrients in, 734, 752
    pollution by, 735, 743, 754
    quantities produced, 734
    safe utilization of, 743, 746, 748, 752–756
  soil nitrate, 738, 739, 754
  soil salts, 734, 735, 738, 752–754, 756
  surface water contamination, 735, 739, 743, 744, 757
  water quality, 745, 747–751, 754, 756
Mulch, 764

National Environmental Policy Act, effect on land use planning, 795
National Parks, 445, 449
National wild and scenic rivers, 445
Natural environments
  deterioration, 445
  recreation potential, 446
  resources, demand projections, 3
Neighborhoods
  urban
    landscape conformity, 518, 519
    planting styles, 519, 520
    socioeconomic characteristics, 518, 520
    stability, 520
Nitrates, 735, 739, 750, 751, 783
Nitrogen
  denitrification, 679
  nitrification, 678

Nonpoint pollution
  agricultural sources
    cropland, 833
    fertilizer, 834
    land disposal of manure, 834
  best management practices, 839–846
    agricultural conservation practices, 835
    economic considerations, 839–842, 845,
      846
    incentive programs, 842, 843
    urban stormwater management, 837
  control
    public participation, 846–848
    local government involvement, 847, 848
  definition and characteristics, 829, 830
  pollutants
    bacteria, 831
    metals, 831, 837
    nutrients, 830, 831, 834, 836, 837
    organic C (animal waste), 831, 832, 843–
      845
    pesticides, 831
    priority of, 832, 833
    sediment, 832–834, 843
    suspended solids, 836
  transport mechanism, 830, 844
  urban sources
    construction sites, 836
    stormwater, 835, 836
  water quality impact, 845, 848
    land use relationship, 830

Phosphorus adsorption, 680–681
Planning
  activities, general sequence, 49
  alternative definitions, means for future
    decisions, 48
  attributes of
    alternatives, 49, 54–56
    consideration of side effects, 49
    future orientation, 49
    goals and objectives, 49, 50
    process, 48
    rationality, 49
  implementation, general means, 57, 58
  metropolitan
    historical development, 467
    natural resource base considerations,
      469, 470
  multiple-use
    problems, 440, 441
    public input, 437–441
  mutual learning process between planner
    and client, 59, 60
  rangelands
    landscape aspects of public, 337
  roles
    of the client(s), 59, 60
    of the planner-technician, 59, 60
  rural, 34, 35

Population projection, 3
Predictions
  of alternatives, 215
  techniques for
    cluster, 202
    dendogram, 202
    deterministic-parametric, 217, 218
    statistical, 216
    stocastic/probalistic, 217
Prime land
  approaches for defining, 299
  concept, 294–296
  criteria for defining, 297
  definitions, 302–306
  delineation, 307–310
  preservation methods, 312–315
Primitive areas, 463
Productivity indexes
  soil
    for prime land determination, 155
    for rural land assessment, 154
Public policy, framework for development
  of, 4, 5
Putrefaction material, 771
Pyrolysis, 764, 765

Rangelands
  characteristics, 321
  management, definition, 321
  planning
    aesthetic values, 336
    determinants of goals, 322, 323
    feedback mechanisms, 333, 334
    levels, 322, 323
    operational plan components, 326–329
    private lands, 322
    processes for plan development, 324–
      326
    public lands, 323, 336
    technical, 323
  products, 321
Rangelands landscape
  monitoring procedures, 340, 341
  planning guidelines, 341
  quality, 338
    analysis, 338, 339
    visual components, 338
    visual effects of management, 339
    visual vulnerability, 339
Rangelands recreation planning
  archaeological, 351–353
  carrying capacity
    ecological, 349
    concepts, 347, 348
    psychological, 348, 349
  historical resource planning, 351, 352
  integrated planning
    framework, 354, 355
    planning and management requirements,
      354

Rangeland recreation planning, integrated (*continued*)
  type conversion example, 357, 358
  major issues, 349–351
    off-road vehicles, 350
    public access, 350
    vandalism and harassment, 351
  paleontological planning, 351–353
Rangelands wildlife planning, 342
  animal species and populations, 343
  ecosystems, 342
  issues
    competition with domestic species, 344
    endangered species, 345
    habitat requirements, 344
    population dynamics, 344
    predation, 345
    public policies and actions, 346
  value, 343
Reclamation of metals, 783
Recreation
  activity, environmental impact of, 461
  allocating resources, 436
  benefits, 435–438
  conflicts
    among recreationists, 437
    avoidance through planning, 437, 438
    between resource users, 437
  levels of development, 436
  quantification of values, 435, 436
Recycling markets, 764
Reforestation
  artificial seeding, 383
  bare-root, 382, 383
  container stock or plug seedlings, 382, 383
  natural seedfall, 383
Regulations. *See* Land use controls; Guidance
Remote sensors
  aerial photography, 160, 179
  aircraft, 169
  Apollo 9, 172
  Landsat, 179, 181
  multispectral scanner systems, 161
  radar, 161
  Skylab, 169, 179
  thematic mapper, 182
  TIROS 1, 180
Runoff
  from animal confinements
    composition, 745–747
    decomposition, 746, 747, 749
    diseases carried by, 734, 735, 746
    disposal, 739, 747–749
    diversions to control, 739, 743, 747, 749
    drainage improvement, 749
    erosion, 748, 749
    ground water contamination from, 739, 754
    holding ponds, 744, 749
    human health, 734, 743, 746

    irrigation with, 746, 752, 753
    odors, 749
    receiving waters, 745, 747
    regulations affecting, 739, 743, 744, 748, 749
    salts, 735, 746, 747
    solids, 743–746
    solids separation, 743, 744, 749
    solids transport, 743, 744, 746, 749
    storage, 744, 749
    terraces to control, 748, 749
    utilization of, 746, 752, 753
    volume, 743, 744, 746, 747
  from cropped land, 735, 756, 757
  rainfall-runoff, 804
Rural Clean Water Program, 842

Scenic amenities
  importance and recognition of, 429, 430
  planning timber harvests
    computer aids, 433
    distant scene, 432
    levels of landscape management, 432, 433
    onsite visual impacts, 430
    planning team and process, 434, 435
    viewer preferences and reactions, 431
Septic systems
  absorption field sites, 486
  soil conditions, 486, 489
Settlement
  as affected by soils and plants, 7–9
  land preferences, 8–11
  patterns in North America, 8
Shorelands, 814, 815
  preservation, 827
  uses, 813
Shoreline, extent in U.S., 814–815
Silvicultural systems
  clearcutting, 381
  even-and-all-aged, 381
  seed-tree, 382
  shelterwood, 381
  single tree or group selection, 382
Site selection
  aesthetics, 767–769
  animal feedlots, 736–739
  competing land use, 767
  criteria for subdivisions, 492
  for different intensity uses, 491
  factors affecting suitability, 488
  geologic considerations, 767
  for home sites, 488
  important soil characteristics, 487, 488
  planning and development, 491
  planning approaches, 766, 768, 786
  public acceptance, 768
  quantity of waste considerations, 766
  soils, 767
  transportation factors, 767

water quality, 767
Sludge
    land application, 657–660
        effects on vegetation, 658
        monetary value, 658
    monitoring effect on water quality, 660,
        661
    planning for disposal, 661
Soil
    animal production on, 737–739
        design of facilities for, 737–741, 748
        management of, 737, 748, 754
    benchmark soils, 83
    biological properties, 469
    classification, 69, 558, 560–565, 570
        AASHTO System, 563–565
        Unified System, 561–563
        uses (*See also* Land use), 564, 567, 570,
            571
    definition, 766
    engineering properties, 469, 470–472, 486
    geologic characteristics, 736–739
    heat capacity, 722, 723
    hydrologic characteristics, 801
    hydrologic groupings, 802, 803
    hydrologic models, uses and limitations,
        809
    importance in planning, 469
    improvement for engineering works
        cement treatment, 575
        densification, 574
        lime treatment, 575, 576
    inclusion, 73
    inventory needs for planning, 469
    ion exchange, 738, 739, 754, 756
    limitations, correcting, 490, 491
    locational values, 469
    microorganisms
        growth requirements, 738
        manure degradation, 735, 738, 753
    modifications for vegetation
        fertilization and liming, 602
        grading, 600–602
        mulching, 604
        topsoil, 601
    resources for agricultural productivity, 7
    salt reactions with, 738, 752, 753
        phosphorus, 738, 752
        potassium, 738, 752
    structure degradation, 736, 756
    structure improvement, 751
    suitability ratings, 148, 474
        commercial development, 474
        construction materials, 475
        industrial development, 474
        limitations, 475
        recreation, 476
        residential development, 474
        watershed management, 477
    thermal conductivity, 721, 722
    variability, 7, 71

Soil and Water Conservation Districts, 842,
    843
Soil Conservation Service, 842, 843
Soil data
    cost savings, 552
    engineering, 85, 536
    for transportation planning, 533
    geological surveys, 535, 542
    highway test data, 537
    laboratory, 84, 86
    point, 83
    remote sensing, 536
    unpublished, 87
    use of soil taxonomy, 534
Soil family
    as basis for survey interpretation, 110
    moisture regime, 112, 113
Soil information
    biotic complex, 113, 114
    data processing, 114
Soil interpretation, 91, 667, 696
    guides, 70
    limitations, 73
    mapping unit
        components in landscapes, 94
        landscape features, 95
    potentials, 73
    relation of taxonomic and mapping units,
        95
    taxonomic classification and units
        soil series, 92
Soil mapping
    process, 74
    transects, 74
    unit, 69
        associations, 70
        complexes, 70
        consociations, 70
        kinds, 70
        miscellaneous areas, 70
        undifferentiated group, 70
Soil maps, 485
    generalized, 77
    interpretations, 490
    interpretive, computer-generated, 81
    schematic, 77
    value in urban development, 486–488
Soil performance, predictions of
    nonfarm, 105
    plant yields, 104–106
    sanitary facilities, 107
    'site index', 105
Soil phase, 69
Soil potential, 108, 490
    determination, 108
    moisture, 112
    rating model, 108–111
    temperature, 112
Soil properties, 486, 558–573
    AASHTO classification of, 101
    affecting plant root systems, 98

Soil properties (*continued*)
affecting soil erodibility, 101, 540
K value, 101
Universal Soil Loss Equation, 101, 102, 843
affecting transportation, 538–542, 545
affecting waste treatment, 102
affecting water availability and flow, 98
chemical, 540
compaction, 569, 570
composition, 538, 545
density, 541, 561
depth, 541
drainage, 486–488
moisture, 540, 561
modulus of subgrade reaction, 567, 568
particle size distribution, 559, 560, 565, 570
R-value, 567
shrink-swell, 486, 488, 570, 571
slope, 542
depth, 541
estimation of, 562, 565, 567, 570, 571
and geological features, 489, 492
physical, 738, 751, 752, 756
tests of, 566–573
unified classification of, 101
Soil scientist, 770
Soil surveys, 67, 534, 535, 696
availability, 85
base maps for, 470
content, 68
coverage, 85
detailed, 470
interpretations, 471, 667, 696
kinds, 71
minimum size delineations, 73
planning and development, 491
purpose, 68
scale, 73
uses, 71, 73, 477
earliest use of, 490
liquid waste disposal, 492
predicting construction costs, 487
preliminary site evaluation, 487
site analysis, 492, 493
zoning criteria, 491
value, 470
variability, 71
Soil-vegetation interaction, infiltration, 808
Stocking control, forest management
commercial thinning, 383, 384
competition control, 384
precommercial thinning, 384
Surface water
animal production effects on, 735
design of facilities, 739, 743, 746–748
management of, 739, 743, 746–748
runoff from feedlots, 735, 739, 743, 747–749
runoff from fertilized fields, 735, 748

tilth improvement, 752

Timber cover
stand age, 373
timber type map, 372
tree size, 372
Timber production
commercial forest land, 388, 389
landowners, 388, 389
growth potential, 412
land potential, 413
mean annual increment, 413
market location, 373
need for wood, 412
recreation areas, 373
reforestation, 413
sustained yield, 413, 414
Transportation planning
use of soil surveys
cost savings, 552
drainage requirements, 548
erosion control, 549
examples of published data, 545–547
excavation and grading difficulty, 549
history, 542–544
planning for more detailed studies, 548
rest area locations, 551
route selection, 544
secondary road and parking lots, 551
soil stabilizers, 574–576
sources of topsoil, 550
subbase sources, 549

Utility corridors
effects, 532
and land planning, 532
objectives, 531, 533
use of soil surveys, 533, 552

Vegetation
airfields, 582
combinations for transmission corridors, 591
environmental considerations, 592–594
cut and fill effects, 595
location and use constraints, 597–599
salt damage, 595, 596
slope, 596, 597
flowers, 591
landfill sites, 789–791
pipeline corridors, 584–586
planning, 605
powerline corridors, 584–586
railroad rights-of-way, 583
roles in metropolitan areas, 502–505, 510–514, 516
air quality enhancement, 507–511
510, 511

air quality monitoring, 511
climatic amelioration, 506, 507
food and fiber production, 513
historic values, 515
noise reduction, 511–513
object of scientific study, 500, 502, 525
ornament, 504–506
waste water disposal, 513–515
watershed protection, 500, 524
wildlife habitat, 516, 523
roles in transmission corridors, 581, 582, 586
erosion control, 586
seedling establishment, 602
seed placement, 603, 604
urban
constraints shaping, 516, 517
container, 501–503
damage by air pollution, 499, 507, 511, 524
defined, 499
diseases and insects, 516, 520–522
lawnscapes, 501–503
management challenges, 505, 506, 511, 522, 523
native remnants, 501–503, 523, 525
patterns, 499
persistence of plantings, 520, 524, 525
planning and designing, 517, 522–525
524, 525
quantity needed, 522, 523
research needs, 507, 512, 516, 519–525
scrub woodland, 501–503
time to mature, 520
types, 500–503
uniformity of patterns, 518–522, 525
weed patches, 502, 503
who manages, 522
zoning and setback ordinances, 517–519
woody, for transportation systems, 590, 591

Waste(s)
demolition, 784
hazardous, 783, 784
encapsulation of, 784
household
composition, 655, 666, 675, 678, 680
disposal and treatment systems, 682, 685, 687
purification, 675, 676, 679, 680

Waste disposal
emergency sites, 785
land application, 633, 854
crop selection and management, 642–644
crop yields, 642, 643
forest ecosystems, 646–652
historical, 633, 634
nutrient removal, 643, 644
planning, 661, 765–769, 772
renovation expected, 641, 642, 644–646, 648–652
trace metals, 653–657
tree growth, 652, 653
planning
air, 616
community involvement, 627, 628
information needed, 614–617
land, 611, 614
water, 615
Waste heat
amount, 705–708
planning use in soil
criteria for productive uses, 714, 715
economic considerations, 731
for soil warming, 719, 720, 722, 723
integrated systems, 715, 716
land area needed, 728, 729
rate of energy dissipation, 719
size and number of sites, 718, 719
quality, 709–711, 713, 714
rates of generation, 708, 709
sources, 705–708
Waste interactions
degradation
C/N, 619
moisture, 618
temperature, 618
leaching
anions, 622
moisture, 622
radionuclides, 623, 624
overland flow, 621, 625
sorption
chelation, 621
exchange, 619, 620
moisture, 620
pH, 620
phosphorus, 620
transformation, 621
transportation, 627
volatilization, ammonia, 625, 626
waste-soil-air, 616
disposal vs. utilization, 617
sewage sludge utilization, 617
Waste products, 611, 771
sources
agricultural, 612
forestry, 612
industrial, 614
municipal, 613, 614
transportation, 612–614
types and characteristics, 612–614
Waste water
land application, 637
planning, 661
techniques, 637–641
treatment, 634
treatment performance, 641, 642
Water
harvesting, 799

Water (*continued*)
  pollution control
    effect on agriculture, 265
  quality (*See also* Hydrologic data), 117,
    120, 130, 139, 141
  warm
    application to soil, 720, 721
    effects on crop growth, 729–731
    engineering of application systems, 723–
      726
Water Pollution Control Act, Public Law 92-
    500, 265, 633, 829
Water resource
  management
    integrated systems, 275
    river regulation subsystems, 277
    waste water subsystems, 278
    water distribution subsystems, 277
    watershed subsystems, 276
  moisture availability index
    classifying climate, 282, 283
  planning and design
    agricultural water requirement, 280
    climatic data, 279
    crop requirements, 281
    hydrologic data, 279
  soil classification, 283
    irrigation suitability classification, 20
    U.S. Bureau of Reclamation, 284–287
Watershed
  analysis, 155, 796, 797
  characteristics
    climatic, 800, 801
    physiography, 803
    for planning and management, 799
    soils, 801, 802
    vegetation, 803, 804, 808
  planning and management
    channel processes, 806, 807
    hydrologic processes in, 804
    objectives, 796
    soil-vegetation interactions, 807, 808
    subsurface flows, 804–806
    surface flows, 804, 805
  protection, 797
  rehabilitation, 797
  revegetation, 797
  runoff, variable source concept, 805
  yield management, 798, 799
Wetlands
  inland
    Connecticut Inland Wetland Act, 970,
      971
    defining and regulating, 968, 969
    delineating, 969, 970
  management, 825, 826
  nature, 824
  protection, 825–827
  soils, 824–826

  subsidence of histosols, 825
Wildland resources
  planning
    climate, 459
    geomorphology, 457
    hydrology, 456, 457
    information needs, 449, 450, 452, 458,
      461
    landscapes, 459, 460
    soil, 451–454
    vegetation, 454–456
    wildlife, 458
Wildlife resources
  game habitat management
    current examples, 439
    historic deficiencies, 438
  nonconsumptive uses
    birdwatching expenses, 439
    urban wildlife research program, 439,
      440
Windbreaks and shelterbelts
  culture after planting, 422, 423
  design
    farmstead, 418, 419
    field, 418
    livestock, 419
  establishment and management, site prepa-
    ration, 420, 421
  growth and soils, 419, 420
  planting, 422
  protection, 423
  purposes
    erosion control, 416
    farmstead protection, 417
    livestock protection, 417
    wildlife habitat, 417, 418
  renovation, 423
  spacing, 422
  species suitability, 421
Woodlands New Town
  planning for development, 945
  site, 943–945
  soils, 947

Yield models
  with climate, 150–152
  for corn, 150, 151, 153
  with energy costs, 154
  nutrient relationships, 153
  simulation, 150, 152
  with soil factors, 153
  for wheat, 151

Zoning (*See also* Land use controls)
  rural, 35
  urban growth management, criticisms and
    limitations, 32–34